THE CAMBRIDGE HISTORY OF
IRELAND

This volume offers new perspectives on the political, military, religious, social, cultural, intellectual, economic, and environmental history of early modern Ireland and situates these discussions in global and comparative contexts. The opening chapters focus on 'Politics' and 'Religion and War' and offer a chronological narrative, informed by fresh research. The remaining chapters are more thematic, with chapters on 'Society', 'Culture' and 'Economy and Environment', and often respond to wider methodologies and historiographical debates. Interdisciplinary cross-pollination – between, on the one hand, history and, on the other, disciplines like anthropology, archaeology, geography, computer science, literature and gender and environmental studies – informs many of the chapters. The volume offers a range of new departures by a generation of scholars who explain, in a refreshing and accessible manner, how and why people acted as they did in the transformative and tumultuous years between 1550 and 1730.

JANE OHLMEYER is Erasmus Smith's Professor of Modern History at Trinity College Dublin and the Director of the Trinity Long Room Hub, Trinity's research institute for advanced study in the Arts and Humanities. Since September 2015 she has served as Chair of the Irish Research Council. She has also taught at the University of California Santa Barbara, Yale University and the University of Aberdeen, and has held several visiting international appointments. A passionate teacher and an internationally established scholar of early modern Irish history, Professor Ohlmeyer is the author/editor of eleven books, including *Making Ireland English: The Aristocracy in Seventeenth-Century Ireland* (2012). She is currently working on a study of Colonial Ireland, Colonial India and preparing an edition of Clarendon's *Shorte View of Ireland*. She is a member of the Royal Irish Academy and was the Founding Vice President for Global Relations at Trinity (2011–14).

THE CAMBRIDGE HISTORY OF
IRELAND

GENERAL EDITOR

THOMAS BARTLETT, professor emeritus of Irish history,
University of Aberdeen

This authoritative, accessible and engaging four-volume history vividly presents the Irish story – or stories – from c.600 to the present, within its broader Atlantic, European, imperial and global contexts. While the volumes benefit from a strong political narrative framework, they are distinctive also in including essays that address the full range of social, economic, religious, linguistic, military, cultural, artistic and gender history, and in challenging traditional chronological boundaries in a manner that offers new perspectives and insights. Each volume examines Ireland's development within a distinct period, and offers a complete and rounded picture of Irish life, while remaining sensitive to the unique Irish experience. Bringing together an international team of experts, this landmark history both reflects recent developments in the field and sets the agenda for future study.

VOLUMES IN THE SERIES

VOLUME I
600–1550
EDITED BY BRENDAN SMITH

VOLUME II
1550–1730
EDITED BY JANE OHLMEYER

VOLUME III
1730–1880
EDITED BY JAMES KELLY

VOLUME IV
1880 to the Present
EDITED BY THOMAS BARTLETT

THE CAMBRIDGE HISTORY OF
IRELAND

*

VOLUME II
1550–1730

*

Edited by

JANE OHLMEYER
Trinity College Dublin

CAMBRIDGE
UNIVERSITY PRESS

CAMBRIDGE
UNIVERSITY PRESS

University Printing House, Cambridge CB2 8BS, United Kingdom

One Liberty Plaza, 20th Floor, New York, NY 10006, USA

477 Williamstown Road, Port Melbourne, VIC 3207, Australia

314–321, 3rd Floor, Plot 3, Splendor Forum, Jasola District Centre, New Delhi – 110025, India

79 Anson Road, #06-04/06, Singapore 079906

Cambridge University Press is part of the University of Cambridge.

It furthers the University's mission by disseminating knowledge in the pursuit of
education, learning, and research at the highest international levels of excellence.

www.cambridge.org
Information on this title: www.cambridge.org/9781107117631
DOI: 10.1017/9781316338773

First published 2018
Reprinted 2018

Printed in the United Kingdom by TJ International, Padstow, Cornwall

A catalogue record for this publication is available from the British Library.

ISBN – 4-Volume Set 978-1-107-16729-2 Hardback
ISBN – Volume I 978-1-107-11067-0 Hardback
ISBN – Volume II 978-1-107-11763-1 Hardback
ISBN – Volume III 978-1-107-11520-0 Hardback
ISBN – Volume IV 978-1-107-11354-1 Hardback

Cambridge University Press has no responsibility for the persistence or accuracy of URLs
for external or third-party internet websites referred to in this publication and does not
guarantee that any content on such websites is, or will remain, accurate or appropriate.

Contents

Contents

Contents

Illustrations

Figures

Maps

Contributors

ROBERT ARMSTRONG, Associate Professor of History, Trinity College Dublin.

CIARAN BRADY, Professor of History, Trinity College Dublin.

DAVID BROWN, Postdoctoral Researcher, Trinity College Dublin.

MARC CABALL, Associate Professor in History, University College Dublin.

IAN CAMPBELL, Senior Lecturer in Early Modern Irish History, Queen's University Belfast.

NICHOLAS CANNY, Professor Emeritus of History, NUI Galway.

ARLENE CRAMPSIE, Teaching Fellow in Geography, University College Dublin.

JOHN JEREMIAH CRONIN, Independent Scholar.

BERNADETTE CUNNINGHAM, Deputy Librarian, Royal Irish Academy.

JOHN CUNNINGHAM, Lecturer in Early Modern Irish and British History, Queen's University Belfast.

DAVID EDWARDS, Senior Lecturer in History, University College Cork.

JANE FENLON, Independent Scholar.

SUSAN FLAVIN, Lecturer in Early Modern History, Anglia Ruskin University.

RAYMOND GILLESPIE, Professor of History, Maynooth University.

D. W. HAYTON, Professor Emeritus of Early Modern Irish and British History, Queen's University Belfast.

BRENDAN KANE, Associate Professor of History, University of Connecticut.

PÁDRAIG LENIHAN, Lecturer in History, NUI Galway.

COLM LENNON, Professor Emeritus of History, Maynooth University.

FRANCIS LUDLOW, Postdoctoral Associate in History, Trinity College Dublin.

ANNALEIGH MARGEY, Lecturer in History, Dundalk Institute of Technology.

TED MCCORMICK, Associate Professor of History, Concordia University.

CHARLES IVAR MCGRATH, Associate Professor in History, University College Dublin.

MARY O'DOWD, Professor of Gender History, Queen's University Belfast.

TADHG Ó HANNRACHÁIN, Associate Professor in History, University College Dublin.

JANE OHLMEYER, Erasmus Smith's Professor of Modern History, Trinity College Dublin, Director of the Trinity Long Room Hub, and Chair of the Irish Research Council.

WILLIAM O'REILLY, University Senior Lecturer, Fellow and Tutor, University of Cambridge.

MICHEÁL Ó SIOCHRÚ, Associate Professor of History, Trinity College Dublin.

DEANA RANKIN, Senior Lecturer in English and Drama, Royal Holloway, University of London.

CLODAGH TAIT, Senior Lecturer in History, Mary Immaculate College, Limerick.

General Acknowledgements

As General Editor of the Cambridge History of Ireland, I wish to express my gratitude to all those who assisted in bringing these four volumes to publication. My fellow editors, Brendan Smith, Jane Ohlmeyer and James Kelly have been unstinting with their time and unwavering in their determination to bring their respective volumes to completion as expeditiously as possible. John Cunningham offered vital editorial support at key points in this process. The team at Cambridge University Press, headed by Liz Friend-Smith, supported initially by Amanda George and latterly by Claire Sissen and Bethany Thomas, has been at all times enthusiastic about the project. It has been a great pleasure working with them. My thanks to the often unsung archivists whose documentary collections were freely drawn upon by the contributors in all volumes, to those who helped source images, and to those who drew the informative maps. Lastly, my warmest thanks to all the contributors who gave freely of their expertise in writing their chapters, and for their patience in awaiting publication of their efforts.

Thomas Bartlett, MRIA
General Editor, The Cambridge History of Ireland

Acknowledgements

In November 2014 we held a workshop in the Trinity Long Room Hub in Dublin where contributors to all four volumes of *The Cambridge History of Ireland* met and discussed our vision for what, we hoped, would be a flagship series that would form part of Ireland's 'decade of commemorations' (2012–2022). This is the fruit of those discussions.

I am deeply grateful to my fellow contributors to volume II for providing such fresh perspectives on the political, military, religious, social, cultural, intellectual, economic and environmental history of early modern Ireland. They have been a delight to work with and I have truly appreciated their patience and good humour. Working closely with my fellow editors, Tom Bartlett, Jimmy Kelly and Brendan Smith, has been a privilege. John Cunningham deserves special thanks for his editorial assistance.

I am also grateful to the archives, libraries, galleries and institutions that have given permission for the reproduction of images. I would like to thank the team at Cambridge University Press and especially Elizabeth Friend-Smith, for their professionalism.

My colleagues in the Trinity Long Room Hub, our institute for advanced research in the arts and humanities, have provided great cheer and administrative assistance. Finally, I owe a particular debt of gratitude to my family – Shirley, Richard, Jamie and Simon – for their unstinting support.

Jane Ohlmeyer
Cruit Island, County Donegal and
Trinity College, Dublin

Conventions

Unless indicated otherwise dates throughout are given according to the Old (Julian) Calendar, which was used in Scotland, Ireland and England but not in most of continental Europe. The beginning of the year is taken, however, as 1 January rather than 25 March.

Unless otherwise stated all monetary values are sterling.

General Introduction

The aims of this four-volume History of Ireland are quite straightforward. First, we seek to offer students, and the general reader, a detailed survey, based on the latest research, of the history of the island from early medieval times to the present. As with other Cambridge histories, a chronological approach, in the main, has been adopted, and there is a strong narrative spine to the four volumes. However, the periods covered in each volume are not the traditional ones and we hope that this may have the effect of forcing a re-evaluation of the familiar periodisation of Irish history and of the understanding it has tended to inspire. A single twist of the historical kaleidoscope can suggest — even reveal – new patterns, beginnings and endings. As well, among the one hundred or so chapters spread over the four volumes, there are many that adopt a reflective tone as well as strike a discursive note. There are also a number that tackle topics that have hitherto not found their way into the existing survey literature. Second, we have sought at all times to locate the history of Ireland in its broader context, whether European, Atlantic or, latterly, global. Ireland may be an island, but the people of the island for centuries have been dispersed throughout the world, with significant concentrations in certain countries, with the result that the history of Ireland and the history of the Irish people have never been coterminous. Lastly, the editors of the individual volumes – Brendan Smith, Jane Ohlmeyer, James Kelly and myself – have enlisted contributors who have, as well as a capacity for innovative historical research, demonstrated a talent for writing lucid prose. For history to have a social purpose – or indeed any point – it must be accessible, and in these volumes we have endeavoured to ensure that this is the case: readers will judge with what success.

Thomas Bartlett, MRIA
General Editor, The Cambridge History of Ireland

MAP 1. Map of Ireland.

Introduction: Ireland in the Early Modern World

JANE OHLMEYER

Ireland's place in the early modern world is well illustrated through an examination of the contents of a wash pit at Rathfarnham castle in Dublin. Archaeological excavations in 2014 unearthed a veritable treasure trove of 17,500 well-preserved artefacts, probably dating from the second half of the seventeenth century. This extraordinary discovery offers a unique window into *élite* material culture but also highlights Ireland's global convergences. Built in the 1580s by Archbishop Adam Loftus, first provost and founder of Trinity College Dublin, Rathfarnham castle, with its thick *trace italienne* flanker towers, gun loops and mullioned windows, was typical of the fortified mansions constructed across early modern Ireland.[1] Protestant, well connected, and on the make, members of the Loftus family were amongst thousands of 'New English' settlers who colonised Ireland from the 1530s and made their fortunes, often by dubious means.

The Rathfarnham hoard provides a glimpse into the cosmopolitan material world, both public and private, of the Loftus dynasty and their household.[2] Extant fashion items recovered included leather and wooden shoe parts (heels, uppers, soles and buckles). Worn down heels suggest that these shoes had multiple owners, with mistresses passing on once-precious pumps to their daughters and maids and fathers handing down their shoes to their sons and servants. Though no textiles survived in the damp wash pit, archaeologists recovered wooden and metal buttons, pins and clasps. These fastened undergarments, dresses and jackets, no doubt made from locally manufactured woollens and linens or exquisite silks and satins, tailored in London, or

I undertook much of the research for this chapter during a sabbatical year (2014–2015) during which I was the Parnell Fellow at Magdalene College in Cambridge and a Visiting Professor in the School of Historical Studies at Jawaharlal Nehru University. I am grateful to my colleagues in Cambridge and Delhi for their hospitality and conviviality. I am also very grateful to John Cunningham for his research assistance.
1 See Chapter 14 by J. Fenlon.
2 Also see Chapters 12 and 13 by M. O'Dowd and S. Flavin.

colourful Indian calicoes, which were the height of fashion across Western Europe in the later decades of the seventeenth century. The survival of lace bobbins and bodkins invokes images of intricate lace collars and cuffs, set off with a delicate tortoiseshell fan, the frame of which is also extant. Even more exotic is a stunning (probably from Colombia) emerald, which was excavated along with gold brooches, rings mounted with semi-precious gems, amber beads, and finely engraved sleeve buttons made from silver, gold and glass. More intimate still, is a grooming kit – toothbrush, hairbrush and ear wax spoon – together with a handle for a razor, a fragment of a sponge and a glass jar apparently containing the remains of red lip or cheek rouge, which was derived from cochineal insects (native to Mexico). More mundane were the chamber pots, which have also been recovered; most were tin glazed and others, from Staffordshire and North Devon, more ornate.

Unsurprisingly no bulky household furnishings found their way into the wash pit, while other highly prized possessions – elaborate wall hangings, damask drapes and bed covers, or 'Turkey carpets' (so common in the inventories of other grand houses) – presumably perished. More durable luxury items were recovered: miniature glass figurines, probably from Nevers in France and the Venetian island of Murano in Italy; and exquisite blue and white Chinese porcelain, along with cruder Dutch and English copies. These extant ceramics suggest that the Loftuses kept up with the latest trends, drinking tea (from Asia) from Chinese porcelain cups and saucers, together with coffee (from Yemen in the Middle East), from fine English-made coffee cups. Sugar, readily available from plantations in the West Indies, could have been used to sweeten both beverages and hot drinking chocolate, the beverage of choice for the very rich. Equally fashionable were the flint crystal glass goblets, manufactured from the 1670s probably in London using innovative glass making technology, which were used to drink spirits and wines (excavated bottles suggest that wine was produced especially for the castle).

Scientific analysis of the food remains in the wash pit – especially bones, shells, seeds, nuts and even a banana skin – provides fascinating insights into everyday diet. The inhabitants of the castle ate meat, fowl, game, fish and foods made from a variety of cereals (especially oats and wheat), along with delicacies like apricots, bananas and peaches, grown in glass houses, and marrows and courgettes, plants from the New World that spread to Europe during the early decades of the sixteenth century. Though there is no extant archaeological evidence in the wash pit, they presumably used a variety of Asian spices, ubiquitous in Ireland by this period, in cooking, preservation and for medicinal purposes and ate potatoes, indigenous to the Andes. Tobacco was

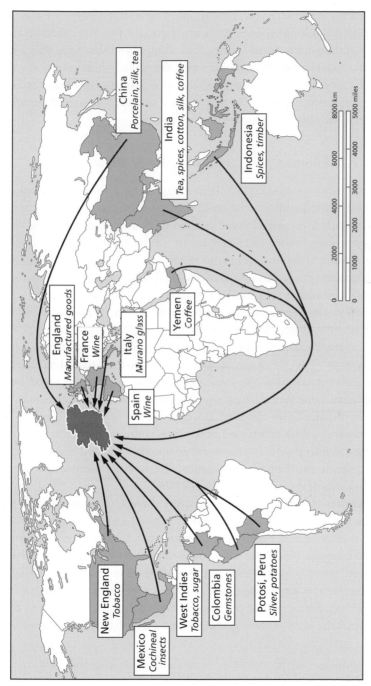

MAP 2. Ireland and the Early Modern World.

3

also native to the Americas and the recovery of a large number of clay pipes suggests that smoking proved a particularly popular pastime at Rathfarnham. The survival of coins, trade tokens, lead weights and wax seals tells a story of international commercial engagement. Particularly noteworthy is a silver 'piece of eight', mined and minted at Potosí in Spanish Peru and dated 1655, along with a jeton, struck at the end of the sixteenth century in Nuremberg, one of Europe's greatest centres of production.[3]

Global Convergences and Early Modernity

The Rathfarnham hoard reflects Irish interactions with and access to commodities and foodstuffs from all over the globe: Spanish America (modern-day Colombia, Mexico and Peru) and the Caribbean in the Atlantic World; to England, Italy, France and Germany in continental Europe; to China and India in Asia. It also illustrates some key features of early modernity. While relative localism characterised the medieval, the early modern period saw the swift and unprecedented global circulation of commodities, peoples, ideas and technologies. Processes like commercialisation, urbanisation and the growth of economies, determined by markets and money, were developments common across Europe, the Middle East and Asia, as was rapid population growth. The discovery of global sea passages established maritime connections between Europe, Asia and the Americas. This allowed for the circulation of New World silver, especially from the Potosí mines, which by the 1570s produced two-thirds of the total output of precious metals from the Americas, to Asia, often via Europe. It was this American silver, not the exchange of European manufactured goods, that allowed the Portuguese, Dutch, French and English to purchase the luxury commodities, initially spices and later textiles, so coveted in the West.

In addition to transforming commerce, these global interactions facilitated the rise of cosmopolitanism and of cultural and intellectual exchange, already revolutionised by Johannes Gutenberg's introduction of moveable type into printing. This made possible the unprecedented circulation of ideas. Over time, scientific discoveries and technological innovations, especially in ship construction, when four-masted galleons replaced galleys, underpinned European expansionism and by 1800 the West controlled 35 per cent of the globe. Thus the wars of the eighteenth century, unlike those of the sixteenth

---

3 A. Giacometti and A. MacGowan, *Rathfarnham Castle Excavations, 2014* (Dublin: Archaeology Plan, 2015), especially chapter 7.

and seventeenth, were truly global conflicts. The War of Jenkins' Ear (1739–1741), for instance, between Spain and Britain, involved naval action off Cartagena and Cuba and merged into the War of Austrian Succession (1740–1748), where French and British armies fought each other in North America and in India, as well as in Europe.

On land, military innovations facilitated the rise in the East of the 'gunpowder empires', the Mughals, Ottomans and Safavids; while in the West developments associated with the 'Military Revolution', especially *trace italienne* style fortifications (exemplified in the thick flankers of Rathfarnham castle), helped to drive state formation across Europe.[4] Confronted with the greatly increased costs of firearms, fortifications and armies, early modern states turned their attention to improving their land tax assessment and collection. In the East, the period saw the growth of large, stable states that attained size, efficiency and territorial reach not seen since antiquity. In South Asia, for instance, the Mughal Empire established its suzerainty over nearly the entire subcontinent of India and promoted religious and cultural pluralism. In terms of scale and wealth, the Mughal Empire compared favourably with the contemporary Ottoman and Safavid ones and with any state in Europe, where incessant warfare, triggered by dynastic jealousies and intense religious struggles, ensured that there was hardly a year of peace during the early modern period.

Ireland in 1550 and 1730

An important dimension of early modernity is that it is transitional, incorporating processes of change across time. A study of processes, structures and *mentalité* in such transitional moments is vital to understanding the problematic of continuity and transformation. This is one reason why this volume opens in 1550 and closes in 1730. Neither date is significant as the beginning or the end of anything; rather they represent 'transitional moments' marking Ireland's passage from medieval to early modernity and from early modernity to modernity.

During these years Ireland experienced, according to one scholar, 'the most rapid transformation in any European seventeenth century economy, society and culture'.[5] In some respects 1550s Ireland, with its patchwork of lordships,

---

4 See Chapter 10 by J. J. Cronin and P. Lenihan.
5 K. Whelan, 'Ireland in the World System 1600–1800', in H.-J. Nitz (ed.), *The Early Modern World-system in Geographical Perspective* (Stuttgart: Franz Steiner, 1993), 204.

its pastoral economy, limited urbanism, and its fighting and feasting culture, was very 'medieval', but this was also a period of transition as the Tudor state determined to increase its control over the island. In 1550, Edward VI, Henry VIII's sickly teenage son, oversaw attempts to make Ireland Protestant in the face of a Catholic Church, renewing itself under Jesuit guidance. The king launched an ambitious reform programme and instructed Humphrey Powell to publish *The boke of common praier after the use of the Churche of England* (1551), the first book to be printed in Ireland.[6] His lord deputy, Sir James Croft, launched aggressive military campaigns, first into Munster, where he secured the submission of the leading Gaelic chieftain, MacCarthy Mór, before turning to Ulster, where he captured Shane O'Neill, who, along with other Ulster warlords, had earlier in the year hoped to conclude treaties with envoys from France, England's great enemy.[7] In short, this was a period of political instability and religious uncertainty, exacerbated by dynastic insecurity as Catholic Mary succeeded Edward in 1553, only to be replaced five years later by her Protestant half-sister, Elizabeth I. Distractions at home meant that the Tudors did not get involved, at least until the later decades of the century, in the wars of religion that embroiled first Germany and central Europe, and, from the 1560s, France and the Netherlands.

One hundred and eighty years later, in 1730, wars were no longer fought over religion. Enlightenment thought, scientific advances and the writings of the French philosophers, questioned all accepted ideas and prepared the ground for political revolutions first in America and later in France.[8] This was the beginning of the 'Age of Revolutions' in other respects. Technological developments in cultivation, popularised in the 1730s in the writings of Jethro Tull, laid the foundations for the 'Agricultural Revolution'. Innovations in textile production, such as the flying shuttle (patented in 1733), marked an early step in Britain's 'Industrial Revolution'. During these years the Hanoverian king, George II, and his Whig 'prime minister', Sir Robert Walpole, did what they could to secure peace abroad, contain the Jacobite threat at home and restore prosperity after the disastrous consequences associated with the bursting of the South Sea Bubble (1720), the first financial crisis of modern times.

In early eighteenth-century Ireland the Protestant Ascendancy, shored up by a full raft of repressive penal legislation, was well established and the

6 See Chapter 18 by D. Rankin.
7 See Chapters 1, 7 and 8 by C. Brady, T. Ó hAnnracháin, and C. Lennon.
8 See Chapter 20 by I. Campbell.

majority Catholic population fully (and finally) reduced.[9] It is believed that between *c*.1550 and *c*.1730 the population of Ireland doubled (from roughly one million), which was the highest rate in contemporary Europe.[10] Society was ethnically diverse, with nearly one-third (*c*.27 per cent) of the population of immigrant stock, descendants of the 350,000 people – English, Scottish, Welsh and French Huguenots – who migrated to Ireland, mostly during the course of the seventeenth century.[11] Technological innovation and intensive proto-industrialisation characterised the development of the Irish linen indus-try and exports soared from 1.5 million yards in 1712 to 8 million in 1740. Earlier schemes for colonisation and commercialisation had transformed the economy into one that was money and market orientated and favoured landed estates with a rent-paying leasehold tenantry.[12] As a result the com-posite landed *élite* of the seventeenth century became increasingly Protestant and Catholics' landholding dropped from about 54 per cent in 1641, to 23 per cent in *c*.1670.[13] The building of villages and towns, with their 'big house', church, marketplace, school, court and jail, transformed the Irish landscape, as did the draining of wetlands and the fencing of open pastures. A sustained onslaught against the woodlands, largely due to iron smelting and the export of timber, resulted in massive environmental change.[14]

Chapters in this volume chart many aspects of the intense political, reli-gious, economic, environmental, intellectual and societal transformations between 1550 and 1730, along with the cultural trauma and dislocation that accompanied them.[15] No volume is ever comprehensive, so the contributors also identify areas that would benefit from fresh research.

Kingdom and Colony

Ireland formed an integral part of the English and, after 1707 and parliamen-tary union with Scotland, the British Empire. Yet Ireland was also colonial. Whether Catholic or Protestant, constitutional nationalists like Patrick Darcy, William Molyneux and Jonathan Swift fiercely resisted attempts to cast them as colonists, preferring to focus on Ireland's status as a kingdom first within a

9   See Chapters 5, 6 and 9 by C. I. McGrath, D. W. Hayton and R. Armstrong.
10 See Chapter 11 by C. Tait.
11 Nicholas Canny's foreword in K. Kenny (ed.), *Ireland and the British Empire* (Oxford University Press, 2004), xi.
12 See Chapters 21 and 22 by R. Gillespie and A. Margey.
13 See Chapter 23 by M. Ó Siochrú and D. Brown.
14 See Chapter 24 by F. Ludlow and A. Crampsie.
15 See Chapters 16 and 17 by M. Caball and B. Cunningham.

multiple monarchy and, with the Act of Union (1800/1), as an integral component of the British Empire.[16] Certainly, the Kingship Act of 1541, which declared Henry VIII king of Ireland and accorded those of Irish provenance the same rights as those of English origin, gave Ireland the constitutional status of a kingdom. Yet Poynings' Law (1494), which mandated that no parliament could meet in Ireland unless licensed to do so by the king and that the king and his English council approved all legislation to be submitted to an Irish parliament, remained on the statute books and restricted the legislative function of the Dublin parliament, which, as a result, met erratically during the early modern period. The Declaratory Act (1720) enshrined the subordinate position of the Dublin parliament to that of Westminster, which now had the authority to make laws for Ireland.

Baldly stated political, military, cultural, religious and economic concerns drove English rule in early modern Ireland. At a practical level, Ireland, with its very large Catholic population, represented a potential security threat to England. This meant that it had to be fully conquered, secured from internal insurrection and external invasion, colonised and 'civilised'. Central to this 'civilising' (or 'Anglicising') agenda was the promotion of the English language and the widespread use of English architecture, agricultural practices, culture, law, land tenures, systems of governance and religion (Protestantism).[17] Towns, especially corporate ones on the English model, were regarded as key features of the 'civilizing' process. During the early decades of the seventeenth century, Ulster's rate of incorporation (twenty-eight corporate towns were established) was second to that of England. One historian has suggested that Ulster served 'not so much a "laboratory" of empire [but] as a red hot crucible for precisely the kind of "civil society" that already characterised much of provincial England'.[18]

The military, political, economic, religious, social, legal and cultural initiatives that underpinned the interconnected processes that made Ireland English, which are discussed at length in this volume, began in the Middle Ages but gathered steam with the reform ('surrender and regrant') initiatives

---

16 K. Kenny, 'Ireland and the British Empire: An introduction', in Kenny (ed.), *Ireland and the British Empire*, 1–15, for a helpful overview of the current debate.

17 See Chapters 1, 2 and 3 by C. Brady, D. Edwards and J. Cunningham. Also see J. Ohlmeyer, 'Conquest, Civilization, Colonization: Ireland, 1540–1660', in R. Bourke and I. MacBride (eds.), *The Princeton Guide to Modern Irish History* (Princeton: Princeton University Press, 2015), 22–47.

18 P. Withington, 'Plantation and Civil Society', in É. Ó Ciardha and M. Ó Siochrú (eds.), *The Plantation of Ulster. Ideology and Practice* (Manchester University Press, 2012), 55–77, p. 69.

of the 1540s. Thanks to an aggressive policy of plantation, they gained further momentum during the early decades of the seventeenth century. With the completion of the Cromwellian reconquest and the mid-century revolution in landholding, a new order founded on English legal, administrative, political, landed and economic structures, the English language and English culture had been established. Out of this period of profound dislocation and transition emerged the Protestant Ascendancy of the eighteenth century. This was not a linear progression, nor was the outcome predestined. On the contrary, what is striking is the haphazard, messy and clumsy nature of the processes surrounding state formation and the very real limitations on central power.

Economic imperialism reinforced political dominance. From the 1660s (and the Navigation Acts), legislation consistently privileged the English economy over the Irish one and created a political economy of dependency centred on London, where trade was controlled, enterprise financed and joint stock companies established.[19] The novelty of the joint stock model of corporate enterprise and the advantage (and monopoly) it accorded to predominately English, often London, merchants and investors cannot be overstated and allowed them to acquire global portfolios of assets which often included Irish investments. Consider the example of the East India Company, the most successful of any joint stock trading network. Of the seventy-three men who served as directors of the East India Company during the 1660s and 1670s, over half had subscribed to the Adventurers' Act (March 1642), which offered Protestant speculators 2,500,000 Irish acres, and to subsequent schemes which, by the 1650s, represented the most ambitious attempt to plant Ireland at any point in the island's history. At least ten of these directors had close family members living on Irish estates acquired during these years or in the plantations of the early seventeenth century. Others were members of the Irish Society, itself modelled on the 1600 charter of the East India Company, which was the joint stock venture responsible for colonising, on behalf of the city of London, the entire county of *London*derry in an effort to bring capital and economic prosperity to a commercial backwater. The investment proved to be a long-term one; it was the later seventeenth century before the London companies began to see a meaningful return on an investment made generations before.

Many contributors to this volume carefully document the varied responses to these convulsive colonial processes. Some contemporaries embraced with enthusiasm the changes, while others espoused them in order to survive.

---

19 See Chapter 4 by T. McCormick.

Many clearly abhorred them. Some bards, reeling in the wake of political but not intellectual collapse, criticised the transformation in the landscape, 'the mountain all in fenced fields; fairs are held in places of the chase; the green is crossed by girdles of twisted fences'.[20] Some condemned the workings of the courts, or members of the Catholic *élite* who had converted to Protestantism. Others vented their spleen against the newcomers, whom they regarded as low-born thugs and as 'English-speaking bastards' who were drawn, according to John Lynch, 'from the barbers' shops, and highways, and taverns, and stables and hogsties of England'.[21] These writers, like the Ulster poet Fear Flatha Ó Gnímh who lamented that Ireland had become 'a new England in all but name', may have been appalled by the changes wrought by conquest, colonisation and commercialisation but they were powerless to stop, never mind to reverse, them.[22]

Given the political, cultural and economic emphasis on making Ireland English, what did 'Irishness' mean during these years? Strictly speaking only the Gaelic-speaking Catholic natives regarded themselves as being 'Irish'. Those of Anglo-Norman ancestry, such as the earls of Clanricard or the Butlers of Ormond, consistently stressed their 'Englishness' often at the expense of their 'Irishness', even if sixteenth-century commentators described them as 'Anglo-Irish' or 'English-Irish'. By the early seventeenth century, this community become known as the 'Old English' and represented themselves as the crown's loyal and devoted servants, arguing that their Catholicism in no way jeopardised their fealty to a Protestant prince nor their ability to serve him as their ancestors had done. Studies, largely by Gaelic literary scholars, suggest that after the defeat in the Nine Years' War (1594–1603) and the 'Flight of the Earls' in 1607, the native Irish, while acknowledging the centrality of Catholicism to their identity, increasingly adopted the same conciliatory, *politique* attitude towards the crown, which had traditionally characterised the Old English. Despite prohibitions against it, extensive intermarriage and cultural cross-assimilation had occurred between the two communities, with the result that many members of the former had become Anglicised and the latter Gaelicised. Predictably this further blurred boundaries between 'Irishness' and 'Englishness', as did the conversion to Protestantism of leading native

---

20 C. Maxwell (ed.), *Irish History from Contemporary Sources (1509–1610)* (London: Allen & Unwin, 1923), 291.

21 John Lynch, *Cambrensis Eversus*, trans. Mathew Kelly (3 vols., Dublin: Celtic Society, 1851–1852), iii, 75.

22 B. Cunningham and R. Gillespie, 'The East Ulster bardic family of Ó Gnímh', *Éigse*, 20 (1984), 108.

Irish and Old English figures. It also allowed ever-pragmatic contemporaries to juggle identities – often in order to secure an estate or dynasty – when it was politically expedient to do so.[23]

The 'New English' settlers, Catholic and Protestant alike, who colonised Ireland from the 1530s, flaunted their 'Englishness'. The onset of the First English Civil War after 1642 triggered an identity crisis for many, forcing Protestants living in Ireland to choose between king and parliament. Those who opted for Charles I continued to tout their 'Englishness', while those who sided with parliament and later Oliver Cromwell viewed themselves primarily as Protestants of Ireland. The other distinct ethnic group that settled in Ireland were the Scots. The first generation of migrants retained a strong sense of Scottish identity, but with the passage of time and presumably in a desire to become assimilated they became ever more 'Irish' (if Catholic) and 'English' (if Protestant). Other settlers, from both Scotland and England, described themselves as 'British'. For example, an analysis of over 500 widows, whose testimony is recorded in the 1641 Depositions, reveals that over one-fifth described themselves as 'British Protestants', with the vast majority residing in Munster and a few in Dublin and parts of the Pale. Interestingly, only a single widow from Ulster, the epicentre of migration from across the Stuart kingdoms, referred to herself as a 'British Protestant'. Instead, widows preferred using the label 'English Protestant', though one Wicklow widow hedged her bets by describing herself as a 'British, English Protestant'. A handful, possibly converts from Catholicism, opted for 'Irish Protestant' but the majority, nearly four-fifths of these widows, did not identify themselves at all. Despite this, the use of the descriptor 'British' by ordinary women is, nevertheless, significant since less than forty years had passed since the union of the crowns in 1603. The efforts of the Stuarts, especially James VI and I, to create a 'British' state clearly had some impact throughout Munster unless, of course, the commissioners who recorded their testimony put these words in the mouths of the women, which is also possible.[24]

Equally complex was how peoples from Ireland who operated on the world stage described themselves, or how their contemporaries, often oblivious to any national nuances around identity, perceived them. Usually, religious affiliation trumped ethnic provenance but concerns about divided loyalties complicated matters further. Ireland's closeness to England often compromised

---

23 For many noble examples, see J. Ohlmeyer, *Making Ireland English. The Irish Aristocracy in the Seventeenth Century* (New Haven and London: Yale University Press, 2012).

24 These conclusions are drawn from my ongoing research into widows in seventeenth century Ireland; also see http://1641.tcd.ie/.

the position of Irish Catholics eager to secure favour abroad or to serve Catholic princes, while Protestants from Ireland tended to be regarded with suspicion and preference was given to English Protestants.[25] Thus, whether at home or abroad, identity formation proved an ongoing and multi-layered process that was defined and redefined by prevailing political, religious and socio-economic developments.

Wider Contexts

Though subservient to London, 1730s Dublin was well on its way to becoming the second city of the British Empire and the sixth largest in Europe. Colonial and continental commerce, along with transatlantic trade, ensured that eight (out of ten) of the largest towns in Ireland were ports, with Cork trebling in size thanks in large part to the dominance it (and its hinterland) enjoyed over the provisioning trade. Thus early modern Dublin and Cork, like the rest of the country, operated in a number of interconnected and often overlapping geo-political contexts: that of the British Isles, continental Europe, the Atlantic World and global empires.

A deep appreciation of these wider contexts characterises each of the chapters in this volume. The obvious starting point is Britain, Ireland's closest neighbour. Whether as a kingdom and/or colony, Ireland formed part of the composite Tudor/Stuart/Hanoverian monarchy. Many of the country's institutions, structures and processes were modelled on those of England and the human interactions, with Wales and Scotland as well as England, were constant. Given its political and commercial dominance, London proved a popular destination for economic and other migrants from Ireland who quickly established well-networked, yet understudied, communities. Throughout the early modern period the histories of Britain and Ireland became inextricably intertwined. Events in one, especially during periods of plantation and the wars of the 1590s, 1640s and after 1688, influenced affairs in its neighbour. Debate over nomenclature and definitions of what constituted 'Britain' and 'Britishness' bedevils many (including the widows discussed above) as does the fact that, like it or not, events in England predominated. What is clear is that the (not so new) 'new British History' continues to provoke awkward questions that defy easy answers and provides a useful conceptual framework for the development of comparative history.[26]

25 K. Block and J. Shaw, 'Subjects without an Empire: The Irish in the Early Modern Caribbean', *Past & Present*, 210 (2011), 60. Also see Chapter 15 by W. O'Reilly.
26 See Chapter 25 by N. Canny.

While the focus on Anglo-Irish relations is understandable, it is also critical to remember that early modern Ireland formed part of continental Europe and enjoyed deep human, commercial, technological, cultural and intellectual interactions.[27] More Irish people migrated to the continent than to North America (an average of 500 men *per annum* migrated and if women and children are included, the figure probably stands at 700).[28] Of course migration was not a regular and ordered event; rather it occurred in waves, often in the wake of economic and political crisis at home. To some extent the geographic parameters within which these movements of peoples occurred were predictable. Irish Catholics tended to move to or enjoy particularly close relationships with the Catholic states of Italy, France, Spain, the Spanish Netherlands and the other Habsburg or pro-Habsburg states of eastern and central Europe. Irish Protestants orientated themselves towards Northern Europe, Scandinavia, the Baltic countries and the United Provinces. However, any sectarian analysis of these diasporas is too rigid. The economic and commercial considerations of many, and especially the Dutch, consistently overrode religious and political matters, particularly during the closing decades of the Thirty Years' War (1618–1648) and beyond. The levels of interaction, and the nature of the contact between Irish merchants, scholars, soldiers, and refugees and those of their host nations were also diverse, ranging from transient visits to permanent settlement, and often involved extensive internal mobility and migration throughout the continent. As the seventeenth century progressed, permanent settlements did emerge often around merchant communities, such as those in Spain (Cadiz, La Coruña, Malaga, Seville and Bilbao) and in France (Bordeaux, La Rochelle and Cognac). Detailed case studies of these communities collectively constitute innovative first steps towards recapturing the diverse and often complex nature of the Irish abroad, the processes of assimilation and appropriation that these migrants underwent and their varied senses of 'Irishness'.[29]

Recent scholarship has also highlighted the extent to which Irish people engaged in global expansionism and contributed to the imperial activities

27 See Chapters 19 and 20 by B. Kane and I. Campbell.
28 L. Cullen, 'The Irish Diaspora of the Seventeenth and Eighteenth Centuries', in N. Canny (ed.), *Europeans on the Move: Studies on European Migration, 1500–1800* (Oxford University Press, 1994), 124, 139.
29 N. Canny, 'Ireland and Continental Europe', in Alvin Jackson (ed.), *The Oxford Handbook of Modern Irish History* (Oxford University Press, 2014), 333–55 and J. Ohlmeyer, 'Seventeenth-century Ireland and Scotland and their Wider Worlds', in T. O'Connor and M. Lyons (eds.), *Irish Communities in Early Modern Europe* (Dublin: Four Courts Press, 2006), 457–84.

of the Portuguese, the Spanish, the French, the Dutch and, of course, the English. Irishmen, for example, participated in the voyages of discovery and of colonial enterprise. William Eris (or Ayres) from Galway sailed with Christopher Columbus on his historic voyage of 1492 to the Americas; three Galway sailors were with Ferdinand Magellan on his circumnavigation of the globe (1519–1522); others, for whom no record survives, could well have sailed with Vasco Da Gama, who after 1497, opened the direct sea route to Asia. By the turn of the seventeenth century, Irishmen were to be found in the French Caribbean, the Portuguese and later Dutch Amazon, and Spanish Mexico, where they joined colonial settlements, forged commercial networks and served as clergymen.[30]

Ireland – that 'famous island set in a Virginian sea' – also formed an integral part of the English Atlantic World.[31] Yet the overall numbers of Irish migrants crossing the Atlantic remained relatively small and probably averaged 200 *per annum* during the first half of the seventeenth century and 400 *per annum* during the second.[32] For the most part, these people travelled as indentured servants and labourers who settled in Virginia, Maryland, and the Carolinas and, by the later 1680s, New England. The harvest crises of the 1720s triggered further waves of emigration of Ulster Scots to America. These transatlantic settlers took with them direct experiences of colonisation and plantation in Ireland and, while the details might be a matter for debate, these undoubtedly shaped the development of the American colonies.[33] From the perspective of Ireland, the West Indies, the 'hub' of the Atlantic trading system, was more significant than the mainland colonies both as a destination for traders and transportees, and in economic terms. From the early decades of the seventeenth century, significant numbers of Irish people migrated (again, often as indentured servants and labourers) to this area and especially to Barbados and the Leeward Islands (Nevis, Antigua, St Christopher and Montserrat, known as the 'Irish island'). By the mid-seventeenth century, leading Irish merchant families had established themselves on Barbados and the Leeward Islands, where Irish capital funded the lucrative tobacco trade. A case study of the tiny island of Montserrat shows that the Irish, 'schooled in early English

---

30 See the Chapter 15 by W. O'Reilly.
31 T. Bartlett, ' "This famous island set in a Virginian sea": Ireland in the British Empire, 1690–1801', in P. J. Marshall (ed.), *The Oxford History of the British Empire*. Vol. II. *The Eighteenth Century* (Oxford University Press, 1998), 254. Also see Chapter 22 by A. Margey.
32 Cullen, 'The Irish Diaspora', 126–7, 139.
33 N. Canny, *The Elizabethan Conquest of Ireland: A Pattern Established 1565–1576* (Hassocks: Harvester Press, 1976) and A. Horning, *Ireland in the Virginian Sea* (Chapel Hill, NC: University of North Carolina Press, 2013).

imperialism (sometimes quite unpleasantly)', became aggressive and expert imperialists and slave masters themselves.[34]

The emphasis on Irish engagement with 'westward enterprises' is understandable given the scale of migration, but needs to be combined with research into Irish contributions to 'eastward enterprises' especially during the 'First British Empire' (*c*.1550–1770s) and as members of the East India Company, which enjoyed a monopoly over commerce with Asia. For example, during the 1670s Ireland served as a 'laboratory for empire' for seventeenth-century Bombay, much as it did for India in the nineteenth century.[35] Thanks to the agency of Gerald Aungier, the grandson of prominent early seventeenth-century planters, structures (especially corporate, legal and landed ones), and policies promoting Anglicisation, that were first implemented in Ireland, were later transferred to Bombay, often in a modified form that best suited local circumstances. Though primarily an 'English' colony, the extant censuses of 1670s Bombay reveal the presence of soldiers with Irish surnames: Butler, Barnewall, Kennedy, Talbot and O'Neill.[36] The ideology of 'improvement', popularised by Sir William Petty and his circle, quickly became a feature of the East India Company, with officials surveying and describing the environment, natural resources and peoples, just as Petty and others had done in Ireland from the 1650s. It is an interesting coincidence that Thomas Larcom, who worked on the Ordinance Survey of Ireland in the 1820s and 1830s and liaised closely with colleagues in Madras responsible for the Great Trigonometrical Survey of India, also prepared for publication an edition of the Petty's 'Down Survey'.[37]

In addition to examining how the Irish, people without an empire of their own, contributed to European expansionism, it is important to reflect on how the activities of these early modern empires impacted on Ireland. Thanks to the entrepreneurial activities of the Portuguese, and later the Dutch, spices from South Asia circulated widely. In his deposition of July 1645 William Bailie, a merchant from Hacketstown in County Carlow, lamented the loss of spices – cinnamon, cloves, mace and nutmeg – which he claimed the local

---

34 D. H. Akenson, *If the Irish Ran the World: Montserrat, 1630–1730* (Montreal and Kingston; London: McGill-Queen's University Press, 1997), 7, 174.

35 S. B. Cook, *Imperial Affinities: Nineteenth-Century Analogies and Exchanges Between India and Ireland* (New Delhi: Sage Publications, 1993); C. A. Bayly, 'Ireland, India and the Empire: 1780–1914', *Transactions of the Royal Historical Society*, sixth series, 10 (2000), 377–97.

36 These conclusions are drawn from my ongoing research on 'Eastward Enterprises: Colonial Ireland, Colonial India', *Past & Present*, (forthcoming, 2018).

37 B. Crosbie, *Irish Imperial Networks. Migration, Social Communication and Exchange in Nineteenth-century India* (Cambridge University Press, 2012), 110–11.

insurgents had stolen and then used to flavour their 'mornings draughts'.[38] The contents of the Rathfarnham wash pit, discussed above, highlight the interconnectedness of the early modern world and how the commercial activities of the English, Spanish, Chinese and Mughal empires extended to the periphery of Western Europe. Travel accounts, histories, plays and lavishly engraved maps, illustrated with representations of indigenous peoples and distant places, shaped mind-sets and fired imaginations about the exotic across Ireland.[39] Popular, racy novels, like Richard Head's *The English Rogue: Described in the life of Meriton Latroon*, first published in 1665 and in its fifth edition within two years, linked Ireland, Virginia and South Asia. The life story of the hero and narrator, Meriton Latroon, 'the English rouge', mimicked the childhood experiences of Head himself. Latroon was born in an 'Irish bog' in the mid-1630s, but fled to England in the wake of the 1641 rebellion having been rescued by his Irish servant ('the faithful infidel'), who pretended he was a Catholic 'and imploring their mercy with his howling *Chram a chrees* [possibly 'Grá mo chroí' or 'love of my heart'], and *St Patricks a gra* ['love of St Patrick'] procured my mothers, his own, and my safety'.[40] After a debauched career as a petty thief and highwayman in England, Latroon was deported to Virginia before travelling East to India, Ceylon, Siam and Java, where he married 'an Indian-black', settled in Bantam, became a prosperous trader and found God.[41]

Whatever the geo-political context, the fact that Ireland responded to similar sets of transformative processes as other states – globalisation, state formation, confessionalisation, the professionalisation of warfare, commercialisation and so on – facilitates comparative history across Ireland, Britain and more widely. For example, the relationships that the Austrian Habsburgs enjoyed with their nobles in Bohemia and Lower Austria offer some interesting points of comparison with Ireland. Throughout the Austro-Bohemian lands, a redistribution of estates to favoured individuals occurred, akin to the Irish land transfers, which resulted in the emergence of a new service nobility

---

38 Deposition of William Bailie, 16 July 1645, MS 812, f. 45r-v, Trinity College Dublin.

39 For a survey of some of the literature relating to the East available in Dublin libraries see, www.ucd.ie/readingeast/index.html, accessed 31 May 2017.

40 Richard Head, *The English Rogue: Described in the life of Meriton Latroon, a witty extravagant comprehending the most eminent cheats of both sexes* (London, 1666), chapter 1, p. 5 (the pagination is erratic). I am grateful to John Cunningham for this translation and for identifying another example of the use of '*Cramacrees*', www.earlystuartlibels.net/htdocs/misc_section/R8.html, accessed 27 July 2016.

41 Also see Carmen Nocentelli, 'Made in India. How Meriton Latroon became an Englishman', Jonathan Gil Harris (ed.), *Indography. Writing the 'Indian' in early modern England* (New York: Palgrave MacMillan, 2012), 223–48.

that owed its primary allegiance to the Habsburg monarchy.[42] Ireland's status as England's first 'colony' also allows for comparisons with the territories governed by other early modern expansionist states. Recent research suggests that the Spanish Habsburgs ruled their dominions in South America and interacted with their political *élite* there much as the Stuarts did in Ireland.[43]

Identifying differences is as important as examining the similarities. Prior to the 1690s the fact that many people in Ireland practised a religion different from that of their king would not have been tolerated elsewhere in contemporary Europe. Despite requiring office holders to take the Oath of Supremacy and securing conversions wherever possible, the crown effectively accepted religious pluralism and reached accommodations, especially with the Irish political *élite*. These arrangements were more akin to those made in the Ottoman, Safavid and Mughal empires than elsewhere in Europe.[44] For instance, from the mid-sixteenth century (the reign of Akbar) until the mid-seventeenth century (and the reign of Aurangzeb), *de facto* religious toleration characterised Mughal rule in India as the Muslim emperor did what he could to accommodate the majority Hindu faith. As in Ireland, the Mughal nobility was a composite body, comprising Muslims and Hindus and a variety of ethnic groups: Muslims from Central Asia who had come to India in the early sixteenth century, native Indian Muslims, the Rajput (Hindu rulers of Punjab) and other native lords. This service nobility was loyal to the *régime* and always ready to serve the emperor on the battlefield or as trusted officials, much as the Stuart peers were.[45] Of course, in other respects, especially their financial dependence on the emperor, the Mughal nobility was very different from its Irish counterpart and there was nothing in Ireland comparable to the land-revenue assignment system (*jagir*).[46] The fact that, in theory at least, the

---

42 J. Ohlmeyer, 'The Aristocracy in Seventeenth-century Ireland: Wider Contexts and Comparisons', *History Compass* (2014), 33–42.

43 N. Canny and P. Morgan (eds.), *The Oxford Handbook of the Atlantic World c.1450–c.1850* (Oxford University Press, 2011), especially chapter 9; C. Storrs, 'Empire and Bureaucracy in the Spanish Monarchy, *c.*1492–1825', a paper delivered at a colloquium on 'Empires and Bureaucracy' held in Trinity College Dublin in June 2011. This will appear with Cambridge University Press in a collection of essays edited by Peter Crooks; and J. H. Elliott, *Empires of the Atlantic World. Britain and Spain in America 1492-1830* (Yale University Press, New Haven, 2006), 16–28.

44 S. F. Dale, *The Muslim Empires of the Ottomans, Safavids, and Mughals* (Cambridge University Press, 2010).

45 M. Athar Ali, *Mughal India. Studies in Polity, Ideas, Society and Culture* (Oxford University Press, 2006).

46 J. F. Richards, 'Fiscal states in Mughal and British India', in B. Yun-Casalilla and P. O'Brien (eds.), *The Rise of Fiscal States: A Global History, 1500–1914* (Cambridge University Press, 2012), 410–41.

Mughal nobles held no hereditary titles or lands also allowed the emperor to exercise greater authority over them than the Tudor/Stuart crown could. But whether in India or Ireland, there is much to learn from looking at the operation of early modern empires, even if the scales of such empires might be very different, and how these empires accommodated *élites* and managed cultural, ethnic and religious difference.

New Departures

All of the essays in this volume offer fresh perspectives on the political, military, religious, social, cultural, intellectual, economic and environmental history of early modern Ireland. As in the *New History of Ireland*, this volume harvests 'the best contemporary scholarship' and highlights how scholarly research has flourished since volume 3 (*Early Modern Ireland, 1534–1691*) first appeared in 1976.[47] The chapters in Parts I and II, which focus on 'Politics' and 'Religion and War', offer a chronological narrative that is reasonably familiar but they bristle with perceptive insights, often informed by the availability of new archives or reinterpretation of familiar sources. The remaining essays are more thematic, with sections on 'Society' (III), on 'Culture' (IV), and on 'Economy and Environment' (V), all areas that received cursory treatment in the *New History of Ireland*, or none at all. A concluding afterword provides a broad overview of the historical writings on early modern Ireland from the sixteenth to the twenty-first centuries.

Where appropriate, contributors have responded to wider historiographical debates and adapted methodologies developed by scholars of early modern England or Europe, where the extant archival material is richer, and applied them to Ireland, often with great effect. Interdisciplinary cross-pollination – between, on the one hand, history and, on the other, disciplines like anthropology, archaeology, geography, literature and gender and environmental studies – informs many of the chapters. This is well illustrated by a particularly original contribution on the environment (Chapter 24), where the authors combine traditional historical sources, like the *Annals of the Four Masters* and the 1641 Depositions, with scientific data on tree-ring-based precipitation and volcanic activity, to enrich and complicate our understanding of the role extreme weather played in major historical events like the Nine Years' War and 1641 rebellion.

---

47 T. W. Moody, F. X. Martin and F. J. Byrne (eds.), *A New History of Ireland* III *Early Modern Ireland 1554-1691* (Oxford University Press, 1976 and reprinted 2001), quote at vi.

The possibilities that technology offers are also truly exciting. Scholars now enjoy unprecedented access to digital archives of state papers and contemporary pamphlets and publications; to more niche collections, like the records of the statute staple, the 1641 Depositions, military migration datasets and Sir William Petty's 'Down Survey'; and to 'big data', like the Books of Survey and Distribution, which record the names of landholders in 1641 and again in c.1670/5.[48] As emphasis shifts from the generation of digital data to how these resources can be interrogated and as technology becomes increasingly sophisticated and user-friendly, historians – together with literary scholars, historical geographers, linguists, computer scientists and other researchers – will be able to interrogate their sources and represent their findings in ways currently unimaginable.

As they stand, the essays in this volume offer a range of new departures. They represent the research of a generation of scholars who, to quote Nicholas Canny's Afterword in this volume, 'search ceaselessly after fresh knowledge, sophisticated methods and new perspectives that will aid the understanding of how and why people acted as they did' in the transformative and tumultuous years between 1550 and 1730.[49]

---

48 See Chapter 23 by M. Ó Siochrú and D. Brown.
49 See p. 663.

PART I

★

POLITICS

1

Politics, Policy and Power, 1550–1603

CIARAN BRADY

Fifteen-fifty – the starting date for this volume – is a singularly happy choice in regard both to the events which occurred in that year, and to those which did not. It is not like some other years in the sixteenth century, familiar because they have been conventionally agreed to signal the beginnings of some momentous historical process, such as 1534, traditionally recognised as the year marking the initiation of the Tudor (re)conquest, or 1547, the accession year of King Edward VI which in several interpretations both old and more recent has been seen to herald the abandonment of Henrician conciliation and a turn toward coercion in both political and religious matters. It is not, like 1558, the beginning of a long regnal period seen in retrospect to mark the beginnings of 'the Elizabethan conquest'; nor is it, like 1565, the commencement of a significant viceroyalty accredited with supplying the ideological motor behind that conquest.

Living with Contradiction

That anything so momentous did not begin in 1550 is not to say, however, that nothing significant took place at all. At least two events deserve notice. One was the reappointment to office of two of the men most closely identified with the great Henrician reform strategy heralded by the 'act for the kingly title' of 1541 and the policy known as 'surrender and regrant': Sir Anthony St Leger as viceroy and Sir Thomas Cusack as lord chancellor. The second was the launch of the first Tudor experiment in the plantation of areas under the rule of a Gaelic Irish dynasty in the midlands. Neither of these occurrences, admittedly, was to be of any lasting significance. The modest experiment in colonial enterprise, which was the brainchild of a small coterie of associates and creditors of St Leger, collapsed almost immediately to the loss of all those concerned. St Leger was recalled within ten months and though he was to regain office briefly between November 1553 and April 1556, he was never again to exert the power of initiative or control that he had enjoyed in the 1540s. Cusack also lost his post in 1556 and, despite his best efforts, never regained it.

Yet it is not in their relevance to subsequent developments in the sixteenth century that the real significance of these events lies. It is rather that, in their failure, their inconsequentiality and their apparently blatant contradictions, they not only defy the easy interpretative categories through which the later sixteenth century has been comprehended, but also emblematise the indeterminate character of so many events in the years that were to follow. For in the next half-century several other years might be selected to confirm the ambiguities of 1550. Fifteen sixty-two might be chosen as the year when the crown made an intense effort to reach an agreement with Shane O'Neill though a diplomatic visit and also the year of the forceful restructuring of the Laois–Offaly plantation as a military colony. Or 1570, when Sir Henry Sidney made war on the lordships of Desmond and Ormond, knighted the O'Connor Sligo and concluded a detailed and highly stable set of surrender and regrant arrangements with the O'Farrells of Annaly. Or 1574, when Walter Devereux, first earl of Essex callously assassinated the Gaelic lord, Sir Brian Mac Phelim O'Neill, but secured the reconciliation of the rebellious Gerald fitz James Fitzgerald, fifteenth earl of Desmond. Or 1584, when the most ambitious scheme for widespread plantation was instituted in Munster, and Sir John Perrot introduced his no less ambitious scheme for the granting of legal tenure to native landholders though the policy known as composition. Or, finally, 1603, when the great Ulster lords were at last defeated after a merciless war, and the vanquished rebel, Rory O'Donnell, became the first of his dynasty to be elevated to the peerage as earl of Tyrconnell.[1]

Such instances of the contradictions afflicting Tudor political actions in Ireland are a useful antidote to those overarching theses ranging from the once-dominant 'triumph of the centralising monarchy' to more sophisticated, but ultimately inconclusive, hypotheses concerning the influence of Renaissance ethnography and Reformation theology in the transformation of Tudor thinking about the government of Ireland. But as a means of explaining the nature of the Tudor presence in Ireland, and the corresponding indigenous response to that presence, they are not particularly helpful. And while detailed examinations of the complex character of decision-making processes

1 A full sense of the inconsistencies of Tudor actions in Ireland is readily obtained from a reading of that invaluable contribution to Irish historical scholarship, T. W. Moody, F. X. Martin and F. J. Byrne (eds.), *A New History of Ireland*, viii: *A Chronology of Irish History to 1976. A Companion to Irish History, Part I* (Oxford: Clarendon Press, 1982), 202–21.

in successive Tudor administrations in Dublin and in Whitehall have been based on a considerably more dependable body of evidence than any of the alternatives, structural-functional analyses of Tudor political and administrative processes have ignored two obvious questions.[2] First, why, in the face of so many repeated experiences of disappointment, failure and unintended consequences, were the Elizabethans (not especially known for their lack of imagination) incapable of devising answers to the obvious logistical and administrative problems confronting them in Ireland, and of adjusting their operations accordingly? And second, and more importantly, how, for all its promises of, and practical efforts towards, accommodation and assimilation, did the Elizabethan regime succeed in effecting a real form of conquest? An irreversible redistribution of land and wealth, and of political, legal and administrative office actually occurred. Why?

Any satisfactory answer to these questions must move beyond both the unsubstantiated 'ideological' interpretations and the alternative structural-functionalist explanations through which the period has most commonly been comprehended, and begin with the apparently more innocent question as to what the prime movers of historical change in Ireland – the senior figures in the English administration in Dublin and in Whitehall – themselves conceived to be their principal objectives, and what contemporary commentators regarded as their principal achievements. And when approached from this simple perspective, the answer is 'shiring'.[3]

Shiring: A Simple Policy and its Complex Contexts

In contrast to the imperfect and defective character of their efforts in relation to plantations, provincial presidencies, surrender and regrant and 'composition' settlements, the one major objective which English policy-makers

---

2 For further assessments of the strengths and limitations of these opposing approaches, see C. Brady, 'From Policy to Power: The Evolution of Tudor Reform Strategies in Sixteenth-century Ireland', in B. MacCuarta (ed.), *Reshaping Ireland, 1550–1700: Colonization and its Consequences. Essays Presented to Nicholas Canny* (Dublin: Four Courts Press [hereafter FCP], 2011), 21–42.

3 See amidst many contemporary examples, the 'Articles' sent by the Privy Council to the Irish Council insisting on the completion of shires and the appointment of genuine sheriffs, 31 May 1592, SP 63/164/49, enclosure (i), The National Archives, Kew [hereafter TNA]; this is of course, the central theme of Sir John Davies's *A Discovery of the True Causes why Ireland was never Entirely Subdued or brought under Obedience of the Crowne of England untill the Beginninge of His Maiesties Happie Reigne* (London, 1612); the centrality of shiring has for long been ignored by early modernists; thus C. L. Falkiner's 'The Counties of Ireland: An Historical Sketch of their Origin, Constitution and Gradual Delimitation', *Proceedings of the Royal Irish Academy*, 24:C (1903), 169–94, is especially relevant.

could claim to have seen through to completion was the effective division of the entire island into thirty-two shires or counties. Almost every major Tudor viceroy from Sir Edward Poynings on had made efforts to revive and extend those shires that had been abandoned and allowed to decay since the thirteenth century.[4] But it was only under the viceroyalty of Thomas Radcliffe, third earl of Sussex (1556–1565) that it truly got underway. In 1556 he not only organised the midland lordships of O'Moore and O'Connor, as the shires of Queen's County and King's County respectively, he did so by formal statute, and in the same parliament he secured the passage of a general statute committing the crown to the shiring of the entire country as its major priority.[5] Sussex was himself unable to advance the programmes of shiring beyond these beginnings, but, as in so many other areas, his ideas were developed in practice by his successor in office Sir Henry Sidney. In 1570, after a successful negotiation, Sidney converted Annaly, the country of the O'Farrells, into the county of Longford; and in the later 1570s, he began the re-shiring of Connacht, reviving the Anglo-Norman shires of Galway and Roscommon, and establishing new shires of Clare and Mayo. He also set about demarcating two shires of Ferns and Wicklow in the troublesome mountainous region separating Dublin from Wexford, an arrangement which was simplified by his immediate successor, Sir William Drury.[6] In the mid-1580s Sir John Perrot revived Sidney's unfullfilled plans to do the like in Ulster and laid the foundations for the shiring of all the lordships. The outbreak of rebellion in Ulster disrupted this.[7] But it was Perrot's demarcations that were revived and applied in the shiring of the whole of the province in the years immediately following 1603. So that, following Sir John Davies's boast, it might be said that it was through its shiring that Ireland had at last been conquered.[8]

Davies's claim may seem hollow. Shiring occurred mostly on paper. Such shires as were established remained unstable and fragmentary, their integrity sustained only by force. And it will be reasonably contended that any attention to the conventional structures of Tudor rule obscures the violent actions

4 S. G. Ellis, *Reform and Revival: English Government in Ireland, 1470–1534* (Woodbridge: Boydell Press, 1986).

5 3&4 Philip and Mary, Cap II, III, in *The Statutes at Large, Passed in the Parliaments held in Ireland: from the Third Year of Edward the Second, A.D. 1310, to the Twenty-sixth Year of George the Third, A.D. 1786 Inclusive* (20 vols., Dublin, 1786–1800), i, 241–46.

6 On Annaly, 'Indentures' with the O'Farrells, 11 February 1571, SP 63/31/9, 10, TNA; on Wicklow and Ferns, see the maps drawn up in March 1579, SP 66/1/2, TNA.

7 Perrot's 'Plat for the government of Ulster', October 1584, SP 63/112/23, TNA.

8 Davies, *Discovery*. I have used the modern edition printed in H. Morley (ed.), *Ireland under Elizabeth and James the First* (London: George Routledge and Sons, 1890), Davies's extensive discussion on shiring is presented at 326–42.

by which this rule was actually accomplished: dispossession, plantation, rule by coercive military officers; in short all the instruments of conquest. There is much in this. Yet the neglect of this exact measure of what the Tudors set out to do, persisted in doing and claimed to have completed has had the unfortunate effect of ignoring the degree to which this profound, and persistent, concern with shiring determined the character, development and final impact of all those other strategies and instruments of rule that have become so familiar. No less significantly, this dismissal of the obvious has led us to ignore a root source of the much sought for and persistently elusive ideological forces underlying the Tudor re-conquest which is to be found not in anthropological or theological innovations, but in far more ancient impulses.

The English concept of shiring – of the establishment of sovereignty over a territory through its division into sub-regions of clearly demarcated geographical boundaries with identical internal subdivisions and uniform legal, administrative and fiscal structures – can be traced back to the reign of Alfred the Great. The idea was adopted and expanded by the conquering Normans, whose departure from the fundamental concept appeared to be no more than a preference for the use of the term 'county' in place of shire. Effectively established over England by the close of the twelfth century, it was this framework of government, which the Angevin kings, notably King John, sought to erect in Ireland. In its early phases the process of shiring was remarkably successful, and recent meticulous research has attributed the progress of the policy to the accuracy with which the new shires were mapped over the existing Gaelic division of the *tricha cét*.[9] But all of this was halted and reversed from the mid-thirteenth century on, when the decline in royal power and the Gaelic revival accelerated the disappearance or internal decay of the shire until there was little surviving of the original system except the four shires of the English Pale.

In this period, an alternative system appeared throughout the island, both in areas that had and had not been shired. Supplanting or opposing the territorial division of the shire, there emerged a new mode of geopolitical demarcation: lordships defined by power relations rather than by property rights. Sustaining and confirming this unstable and shifting form of lordship was the politics of allegiance, clientage and faction within which greater warlords sought to assert their authority over lesser ones through the alternate

---

9 Originally, it was a term connoting a territory which could support the levying of 3,000 fighting men, the *tricha cét* had by the eleventh century it had become identified as a fixed measure of land. P. MacCotter, *Medieval Ireland: Territorial, Political and Economic Divisions* (Dublin: FCP, 2014).

application of protection and intimidation, favour and feud. Expansionist and inexorably hierarchical, this system, labelled in the early Tudor reform tracts as 'coign and livery', rapidly became pervasive throughout the island, as local warlords looked for alliance with regional powers and they in turn looked to figures of island-wide influence culminating in the great dynasties of the Fitzgeralds of Kildare and the Butlers of Ormond.[10] Yet while it gave an enormous amount of power to the dominant figures within it, 'coign and livery' was not only unstable; it was both violent and extraordinarily wasteful. It was this recognition that underlay the frequently demonstrated willingness on the part of the great figures – Kildare, Ormond, O'Neill, O'Brien, Desmond, etc. – to respond positively, if cautiously to proposals for reform. But it was the risks – more immediate and no less obvious than the advantages – that underlay a persistently guarded and conditional attitude towards such initiatives. Like nuclear disarmament negotiations, risks of an early and rapid response rendered the willing participant gravely vulnerable, at least in the short term, to violent exploitation by those less committed. And the greater the figure, the greater the risks involved. Such were the considerations underlying the rejection by the house of Kildare of the reform proposals put before it in 1534, with all its fateful consequences. Yet the fall of the house of Kildare (1536), and the temporary eclipse of the house of Ormond with the suspicious poisoning of James Butler, ninth earl, and his entourage in 1546 offered a rare opportunity for the reform of the system from the top down.

This was an opportunity that, as viceroy, the earl of Sussex was determined to seize by developing a remarkably detailed and nuanced strategy for the reform of Ireland.[11] On the surface there was little boldly original in Sussex's strategy. Like many before him, Sussex looked to the erection of provincial councils – the means by which the early Tudors had reasserted royal authority in Wales and in the north of England – as the key instrument for the recovery of English law in Ireland. But Sussex's approach was especially sensitive to variables of space and of time. Different areas required different treatments,

---

10 For a succinct summary, see the entry on 'Coyne' by David Edwards, in S. Duffy (ed.), *Medieval Ireland: An Encyclopedia* (London: Routledge, 2005), 184–6; also C. A. Empey and K. Simms, 'The Ordinances of the White Earl and the Problem of Coign in the Later Middle Ages', *Proceedings of the Royal Irish Academy*, 75:C (1975), 161–87.

11 Sussex's strategic thinking can be traced in his memorandum of 11 September 1560, Carew Papers, MS 614, ff. 271–80, Lambeth Palace Library; and more extensively in his 'Opinion', 1562, Carew Papers, MS 609, ff. 1–35, Lambeth Palace Library; the latter has been incompletely calendared in *Calendar of Carew Manuscripts, Preserved in the Archiepiscopal Library at Lambeth, 1515–1574*, ed. J. S. Brewer and W. Bullen (London: Longmans, Green, Reader & Dyer, 1867), 330–42.

depending on the rate of degeneration and on the degree to which they had fallen victim to the nefarious system of coign and livery.

Thus, for the shires of the Pale, no council was necessary, though the viceroy should act informally in that capacity, presiding over regular meetings of the sheriffs, magistrates and officers of the existing shires. For Munster, Sussex envisaged the establishment of a presidential council to be constituted of a president 'of English birth' and an English judge, but also of the earls of Ormond, Desmond and Thomond, together with the bishops of the province, eleven of the lesser lords and the mayors or 'sovereigns' of the six major towns. Though the president was to have authority to execute martial law, this was sanctioned only 'in times of necessity' and only then 'against persons that have no possessions'. For Connacht, Sussex proposed a similar structure, the president and justice of English birth being joined on the council by the earls of Clanricard and Thomond, the leading ecclesiastics, lesser lords and mayors.[12]

But for Ulster, Sussex had more forceful approaches in mind. In contrast to the other provinces, the president was explicitly described as 'martial' and allotted a far greater military force and stipend than was to be allowed for the other provinces. With a force of 800 men kept 'continually in pay', he was to assert his authority by such vigorous means as 'shall keep the love of the people toward him and shall keep all men in such fear of him as they will not be easily drawn into any conspiracy against him'.[13] By contrast, in south Leinster, where the O'Byrnes, O'Tooles and other Gaelic dynasties had 'of their own volition' begun to operate the procedures of shire government, Sussex recommended the maintenance of English captaincies, with the captain presiding over the Leinster dynasties being permitted to apply martial law only in certain prescribed circumstances. But certain Irish lords were to be exempted from the governance of the captains: Fitzpatrick, the lord of Upper-Ossory and his neighbour Mc Geoghegan, who had already agreed 'to have their countries made shire ground', were to be absorbed into the administrative and judicial structures of the new shires of Queen's County and King's County respectively. All of the remaining Gaelic lords were to be encouraged to follow their example.[14]

The gradualist and phased nature of Sussex's strategy implied in these proposals was made explicit in one of his memoranda, addressing the question

12 *Calendar of Carew Mss, 1515–1574*, 334–6.
13 *Calendar of Carew Mss, 1515–1574*, 331–4.
14 *Calendar of Carew Mss, 1515–1574*, 336–8.

of 'how the Irish may be induced to leave their Irish tenures' and to accept inheritance through primogeniture. In regard to this, Sussex proposed the introduction of 'constitutions' – a term which had a more interim and transitional connotation in the sixteenth century than the sense of a settled contractual agreement which it was later to acquire. Under these interim judicial arrangements certain fundamental principles were to be asserted. All forms of stealing, burning and 'wilful murder' were to be capital offences, as under English law. Accessories to theft and other petty crimes were to be punished accordingly, depending on the degree of their involvement. Trial by jury was to be established for disputes over land and chattels, empanelling freeholders for the former, and merely 'honest men' for the latter. But other provisions were more flexible: the invasion of a country by a neighbouring lord was to be punished by fine, not outlawry. No lord was to keep any strangers in his country without permission of the president and council, and no lord was to give 'byings' [payment] to anyone not resident in his country. Similarly, the practice of retaining was to be tolerated though regulated by 'booking' or registration with the regional governor and council. Irish lawyers – 'the Brehons' – would be admitted to plead under terms of English law in specified cases, and 'in all other matters after the order of the Brehon law or allowed customs, and to have fees to be appointed for their travail'.[15]

Sussex's programme was to become the blueprint for almost every further initiative in regard to the government of Ireland to be essayed by his viceregal successors over the next half-century. The establishment of regional presidential councils, the extension of surrender and regrant to all those lords willing to accept succession by primogeniture, the measured use of martial law, the construction of garrisons and forts, and, of course, the erection of shires were to continue to be the central concerns of Elizabethan government in Ireland down to the outbreak of rebellion in Ulster in 1594.

But three other closely related, though largely implicit, features of Sussex's Irish vision would not only exemplify the defining characteristics of all further Elizabethan initiatives in Ireland; they would also expose their underlying contradictions. One was the unquestioned assumption that the viceroy would retain total control of all policy initiatives launched throughout the island. A second was the relative unimportance of plantation or any similar colonial projects in this campaign for the establishment of English government in Ireland. And a third – the most fateful in its outcome – was a willingness to tolerate practices, such as retaining, the use of Brehon law and the

---

15 *Calendar of Carew Mss, 1515–1574*, 339–40.

collection of bonaght, which were fundamentally opposed to the principles of English law.

Politics: The Irish Viceroy in English and Irish Contexts

In principle, the Irish viceroy was a uniquely powerful and privileged figure within the Tudor political and administrative structure. Endowed with extensive prerogative powers delegated directly from the crown, the viceroy also enjoyed substantial judicial authority, especially after the establishment of the Court of Castle Chamber in 1560. Endowed with a handsome salary, the viceroy had the right of appointment to several profitable offices in the civil administration in Dublin and no less significantly to his own viceregal household, and was in addition the commander-in-chief of the only standing army within the Tudor state, the Irish garrison.[16]

The most peripheral of the Tudor dominions, Ireland was also potentially one of the most lucrative, holding out the prospect of speculation in land, both native and ecclesiastical, and more immediately in the perquisites of office, administrative, legal, and of course, military. All of these were worth striving for: and they were energetically sought after. This made the Irish viceroyalty singularly attractive, not only to those who would hold the office, but no less so to those who sought service under the viceroy, and even to those who were sufficiently influential with the monarch to determine who should actually get the job.

Two quite different forces intensified the inevitable susceptibility of the Irish viceroyalty to considerations of clientage. One was the tendency of successive viceroys to leave behind them a residue of office holders and dependants. Between 1550 and 1603, the average term of viceregal office was extremely short: an analysis of fifty commissions of appointment issued in the period reveals an average tour of duty of under two years. And while exceptional figures, such as Sir Henry Sidney and Sir William Fitzwilliam, held office for almost eight years each, their terms in office were interspersed with long periods when they had nothing to do with the country at all. But while some of their appointees departed with them, many more stayed on; and over time a body of servitors began to accrete which had increasingly less

---

16 For an extended discussion, see C. Brady, 'Viceroys? The Irish Chief Governors, 1541–1641', in P. Gray and O. Purdue (eds.), *The Irish Lord Lieutenancy: c. 1541–1922* (University College Dublin Press, 2012), 15–42.

interest in serving those who had been responsible for their appointment, and increasingly more interest in looking out for themselves in an environment rich with opportunity. This consequence was gradual and accumulative. The effects of the second force were, however, more immediate and more intensely destabilising, even though, at the time of his strategic formulations, Sussex might confidently have believed himself to be free from it.

Sussex took office under the most propitious circumstances. Appointed by Queen Mary with the express intention of rising above the sordid local deals which had disfigured the administration of St Leger, he could count on the solid backing of his sovereign in a manner which none of his predecessors had enjoyed. He was given a free hand in appointments to (and dismissals from) civil and military office. He was permitted to set his own priorities and devise his own detailed programme for the government of Ireland. Thus assured, he moved confidently to confront the hydra of Irish faction and its attendant system of 'coign' by frustrating the ambitions of the newly restored Gerald Fitzgerald, eleventh earl of Kildare, at every turn, refusing his claims and suits, and those of his allies, particularly among the Fitzgeralds of Desmond, while openly favouring those of the Geraldines' great rival, the house of Ormond. Unfair, such a strategy was also opportune. As long as he enjoyed the full backing of his sovereign, Sussex could use his independence to tame the house of Kildare while reminding Thomas Butler, tenth earl of Ormond, that all favour came only by grace of the crown. Yet such impunity as he enjoyed was fragile. His high-handed attitudes towards the collection of purveyance and no less significantly his reckless sack of the ecclesiastical seat of Armagh in 1557 lost him the support of the leading representatives of the loyal English-Irish community and left him dependent wholly on the confidence of Queen Mary. Thus on the accession of Elizabeth everything changed.

For Sussex was not only the Irish viceroy; he was also a highly prominent courtier (a close ally of the duke of Norfolk) whose principal achievement, before his appointment to Ireland, had been his leading role in the successful negotiation of the marriage alliance between Mary and King Philip. Inescapably, therefore, between 1559 and 1562 he again became embroiled in the immediate and urgent problem of the new regime: the question of the young queen's marriage options. A forceful proponent of an early marriage to a continental suitor, Sussex thus aligned himself strongly against those, most notably the rising favourite Lord Robert Dudley, who opposed it, and in doing so steadily compromised his peculiar strength as the non-partisan holder of the Irish viceroyalty.

This was an opportunity seized upon by Kildare, who rapidly made contact with Dudley. At first, Kildare sought to damage Sussex's Irish service through encouraging grievances against the viceroy's abuse of the prerogative power of purveyance, which had been complained of (so far without avail) since the last years of Queen Mary. In this he enjoyed limited success; but increasingly, and with Dudley's active support, Kildare moved to undermine Sussex through exploiting the viceroy's recurrent failure to defeat the figure he had identified as the principal opponent to the government's authority in Ulster, Shane O'Neill. The challenge posed by Shane to the authority of English government was complex, other dimensions of which will be discussed below. But most immediately, Sussex's resolute refusal to negotiate with Shane, coupled with repeated – and costly – failures to meet and defeat in him in the field offered a rich opportunity for the viceroy's opponents to do him damage. Shane's hugely embarrassing visit to Court in 1562 was followed (in the wake of yet another disastrous campaign against him) by a humiliating treaty combined to produce Sussex's reputational ruin – and personal collapse – by the end of 1563.[17]

The campaign against Sussex orchestrated by Kildare and Dudley did not succeed in rehabilitating Shane. But the lasting effect of the affair was to ensure that from henceforth the Irish viceroyalty would never again enjoy the independence and stability required to enable it to function effectively as an agent of policy, and would instead be bedevilled by the machinations of Court politics: suspicions of partisanship and the necessary correlative of calculated subversion. Sussex's successor as viceroy, Sidney, was to inherit the full consequences of this unhappy condition. Though he had served loyally under Sussex until his appointment as lord president of Wales in 1559, many at Court saw Sidney as a close political associate of his brother-in-law Dudley (since 1564, the earl of Leicester) who had undermined Sussex, and was therefore suspect. His opponents at Court – opponents of Leicester – thus sought to obstruct and subvert his administration in whatever way possible. In this they were supported (as Leicester had been by Kildare) by the invaluable backing of the now discomfited earl of Ormond, who in addition to being a figure of extensive sources of intelligence and connection in Ireland, had the further advantage of being a close confidant of Elizabeth herself.

17 On Sussex's career as a courtier, see S. M. Doran, 'The Political Career of Thomas Radcliffe, 3rd Earl of Sussex', unpublished PhD thesis, University of London (1977); on Kildare, see V. Carey, *Surviving the Tudors: The 'Wizard' Earl of Kildare and English Rule in Ireland, 1537–1586*. (Dublin: FCP, 2002).

From this all kinds of woes ensued for Sidney. At the very least he was unable to secure the kind of clearance of lesser offices that Sussex had achieved on the disgrace of St Leger, as so many of Sussex's appointments, including his brother and his brother-in-law, continued to hold senior positions within the Irish garrison. More seriously, Sidney's nominations for offices such as the lord chancellorship, and the archbishoprics of Armagh and Dublin, which were intended to serve as key agents in the implementation of his reform policies, were denied. But most serious of all was the rejection of his nominee for the post of president of the provincial council in Munster. Sidney's nominee, Warham St Leger, was perceived, like his father, Sir Anthony, to be sympathetic to the Geraldines, a quality that at once made him attractive to Sidney as a figure most likely to be acceptable to the unstable earl of Desmond, but also quite unacceptable to the favoured earl of Ormond. Elizabeth's refusal to sanction St Leger's appointment, even as he was actually in place, cancelled the plan to establish a council. But her further orders that Sidney should arrest both the earl of Desmond and his brother and despatch them to the Tower were even more fateful. Convinced that they had no friends at all among any of the contending parties within the Elizabethan Court, the surviving representatives of the house of Desmond, under the leadership of James Fitzmaurice Fitzgerald, burst into open rebellion (1568–1572), the first major revolt of the Elizabethan regime.[18]

Chastened by experience, Sidney's subsequent service in Ireland was characterised by attempts to escape from this disastrous association with partisan alliance. Thus on his return to office in 1568, he sought to reinvigorate his reform strategy not by means of viceregal initiative, but by the far more consensual processes of parliamentary statute. The proposed programme of Sidney's Irish parliament (1569–1571) is eloquent testimony to the endurance of the fundamental idea of the revival and extension of shiring as the core of the reform process. But while it was by no means a complete failure, the efficacy of Sidney's parliamentary programme, first depleted by the loss of several important bills, was vitiated by the rebellion of the brothers of the earl of Ormond, which, combined with the on-going rebellion in Desmond, consumed all his time, and ensured his recall. In his final term of service (1575–1578) Sidney continued his attempts to escape from the taint of partisanship by accepting appointments to senior office in his administration of figures known to be hostile to him such as Sir William Drury and Walter Devereux,

---

18 A. M. McCormack, *The Earldom of Desmond, 1463–1583: The Decline and Crisis of a Feudal Lordship* (Dublin: FCP, 2005).

first earl of Essex. But to little avail, his tenure being rescinded by Elizabeth under pressure of a slanderous Court campaign to the effect that he was attempting to make the Irish office his own private property.

Yet Sidney himself was not above playing at Court intrigue. He took a leading role in movements to unseat the viceroyalties of Fitzwilliam (1571–1574) and Lord Grey (1580–1582). And so the contagion of courtly intrigue continued: the viceroyalty of Sir John Perrot (1584–1588) was wrecked by sustained rumours generated in Ireland and spread at Court that he was venal, mentally disturbed and even traitorous. Sir William Russell's term of office (1594–1596) was dogged by his association with Robert Devereux, second earl of Essex. Essex's intrigues hindered the service of Russell's successor, Lord Burgh (1596–1597), and Essex's own viceroyalty (1599–1600) was, of course, fatally warped by the machinations of faction. Thus it was that one of the most powerful and most responsible offices in the Tudor political system – the one charged with bringing about the re-establishment of English law and government in Ireland – was from first to last distorted, impeded and subverted in its responsibilities by the chronic influence of partisanship, rivalry and intrigue operating within the regime itself; and one central assumption of Sussex's programme for the revival of English government in Ireland denied in practice.[19]

Policy: The Contradictions of Plantation

The occasional operations of opportunist Court politics were, however, only one of the ways in which interference from Whitehall fundamentally shaped the course of English government in Ireland. A second mode of intervention, though apparently more constructive, would prove no less subversive of the aims of Tudor government in Ireland. This concerned the strategy of plantation.

Despite a venerable historical tradition, hardly any of the major viceroys of the later sixteenth century were avid promoters of plantation as a means of re-establishing English rule in Ireland. His central role in the erection of

---

19 Evidence for the troubled service of each of the viceroys abounds in the sketches supplied in H. C. G. Matthew and B. H. Harrison (eds.), *Oxford Dictionary of National Biography* (60 vols., Oxford University Press, 2004); for an exemplary study of the intrigues surrounding one major viceroy, see H. Morgan, 'The Fall of Sir John Perrot', in J. Guy (ed.), *The Reign of Elizabeth I: Court and Culture in the Last Decade* (Cambridge University Press, 1995), 109–25.

the first Tudor plantation in Ireland notwithstanding, Sussex envisaged no further role for the strategy in his extensive and regionally discriminative policy memoranda. In the early 1570s Lord Deputy Fitzwilliam vigorously opposed colonial experiments in Ulster; and Sir John Perrot who assumed the viceroyalty in the year of the establishment of the Munster plantation immediately fell into conflict both with the speculative planters in Munster and with their supporters in Whitehall. To this general rule, Sidney seems a partial exception. In 1567 he lent approval to a number of small individual enterprises in south Ulster, and supported a scheme proposed by Warham St Leger, Sir John Fitzgerald and others in south-west Munster. But his accept-ance of the former was largely due to his concern to be seen to be above partisanship, while ironically, his support for the latter was suspected of being part of his sympathy for the house of Desmond. In any case, none of these proposals came to anything.[20]

In fact the real force behind those plantation projects which actually came into effect in Ireland – Sir Thomas Smith's experiment in the Ards peninsula (1571–1573), Essex's ambitious 'enterprise of Ulster' (1572–1575), and the grand scheme for plantation in Munster initiated in 1584 – lay in Whitehall where senior figures such as Lord Treasurer Burghley, Lord Chancellor Hatton or Secretary Sir Thomas Smith were either directly engaged in the projects or highly supportive of those who were.[21] Here arose another source of tension between the government at Whitehall and its chief agent in Ireland. The vice-roys' resistance to colonial enterprise was political rather than ethical. What they resented was any initiative that interfered with and diminished their authority and discretion in choosing the appropriate path towards realising the ultimate goal of establishing English government in Ireland. Dublin's attitude could be viewed as a simple managerial reflex; but behind Whitehall's enthusi-asm lay other impulses at once more complex, and more contradictory.

At one level of Whitehall's thinking, simple financial and strategic calcula-tions were at play. Essex's self-financing project promised to free Whitehall of the costs of expelling the Scots but also of establishing English government over a large part of Ulster, which had proven highly resistant to all previous efforts.[22] Similar considerations also conditioned Whitehall's attitude towards

20 N. Canny, *The Elizabethan Conquest of Ireland: A Pattern Established, 1565–76* (Hassocks: Harvester Press, 1976), chapter 4.
21 H. Morgan, 'The Colonial Venture of Sir Thomas Smith in Ulster, 1571–5', *Historical Journal*, 28 (1985), 261–78; M. MacCarthy-Morrogh, *The Munster Plantation: English Migration to Southern Ireland, 1585–1641* (Oxford University Press, 1986), chapters 1–2.
22 J. Sheridan, 'The Irish Hydra: English Policy and Plantations in Gaelic Ulster, 1567–79', unpublished PhD thesis, University of Dublin (2015), chapters 8–9.

Munster. The lands of the last earl of Desmond, from whose death in rebellion and attainder (1583/1584) the scheme had issued, were rich, highly cultivated and in need of little further development. Thus potential investors in this new, largely unexpected, increment of crown lands could be expected to pay competitive prices – both official and unofficial – in the initiation and development of their own private enterprise. But strategic and security considerations were also important. Desmond's lands encompassed, or were adjacent to, large stretches of the southern and south-western coastline. This territory was most vulnerable to intervention by foreign powers – notably Spain – and indeed had already been host to two small expeditions. Thus, as in the case of Essex, financial and strategic considerations converged: colonisation, rather than central viceregal action, seemed to be a cost-effective method of extending the English presence in Ireland.[23]

Yet there was also a third consideration, which, though muted, was ever-present in Whitehall's address to Ireland. This was the idea that colonisation was essentially good for the Irish. Rooted in the Renaissance revival of Roman ideas of cultural colonisation, it was inherent to a greater or lesser degree in all of Whitehall's legitimations of plantation. It appeared most obviously in Smith's highly articulate *apologias*, and it was also central to the justifications of Essex's claim to regain Ulster from the Scots. But it was no less present in the great scheme planned for Munster in the wake of the Desmond rebellion, where prospective grantees of attainted lands were to be required not only to develop their holdings in the best English manner and to encourage the neighbouring natives to follow their example, but to undertake responsibility for the revival and extension of English forms of local administration and justice.[24]

The contradictory tendencies of such impulses were multiple. Most obvious was the contrast between the crown's desire to save money by delegating responsibility to private enterprise, and its claim to be advancing a civilising mission. No less in contradiction was the acute concern about England's strategic security and the determination to economise; or the simple fear of invasion and the profession of the ideal of cultural reform. And finally, an even more profound tension affected the crown's relationship towards the Irish viceroys, formally the proxies of royal government in Ireland, but now in

---

23 MacCarthy-Morrogh, *The Munster Plantation*, chapter 2.
24 D. B. Quinn, 'Renaissance Influences in English Colonisation', *Transactions of the Royal Historical Society*, 26 (1976), 73–93; C. Brady, 'New English Ideology in Ireland and the two Sir William Herberts', in A. Piesse (ed.), *Sixteenth Century Identities* (Manchester University Press, 2000), 75–111.

practice to be overridden, on occasion, by Whitehall's assertion that it might disrupt such authority at its own discretion.

In so far as it was prompted by considerations of finance or England's security – priorities of English rather than Irish government – Whitehall's central role in the development of plantation schemes could be quite disruptive of the viceroys' strategic aims. Smith's and Essex's adventures in Ulster played a crucial role in the rise to provincial dominance of Turlough Luineach O'Neill, while Essex's failure did much to confirm the confidence of the MacDonells that they were irremovable from Ulster. But the conviction that plantation was a way of furthering the aim of extending English culture among the native population as a whole was even more damaging. Smith's fond contention that his project was exemplary in its aims may have been naïve, and Essex's professions that he had come to protect and cultivate the native Irish disingenuous; but, however self-deceiving, the belief that plantation was a supplement rather than an alternative to more conventional ways of 'making Ireland English' was a significant force in sustaining support for the policy at Court even when it ran into serious difficulties.

This was especially the case in Munster. The paper plantation worked out in elaborate detail, dividing the attainted Desmond lands into neat hierarchical allotments of between 4,000 and 12,000 acres, disintegrated almost immediately when mapped on to the fragmented and scattered realities of the Desmond estates. From this all kinds of confusions arose: between settlers and natives and between the settlers themselves. The natives posed several problems: there were those enjoying freehold status within these neat allotments whose complicity in the rebellion had not been proved; those who had been pardoned during the course of the rebellion; and those who denied they had ever been tenants of Desmond and whose lands were therefore not subject to the attainder. As these disputes proliferated, both natives and settlers appealed to English law, in the Dublin courts and in their petitions to the Privy Council in England. At first the Council stood firm: the settlers were supported, the claims of the inhabitants rejected. But steadily, as the pressure of litigation mounted, resolve softened. First it rejected the claims of its own chief surveyor (Valentine Browne) to the lands of MacCarthy-Mór, confirming the great Gaelic lord as an innocent in the rebellion. Next it conceded that the claims of the residents of lands over which Desmond had enforced demands for military service should be recognised as freeholders, not tenants, and decreed that they should remain without further molestation upon payment of a commuted service to the crown. Finally, a second commission of enquiry established in 1592 proved to be far more sympathetic to claims of innocence, allowing over 50 per cent of the claims submitted to it. In all these ways, the Council systematically shredded the neat blocs of the paper plantation, hugely delaying its development, and plunging its investors into despair. It did so for the best of reasons: the righteous conviction that it was demonstrating to all the inherent justice, fairness and consistency of English law. Yet while proudly asserting its principles, the Council did little to enforce them in practice; and, its repeated frustration of the viceroy's attempts to intervene in these intense local disputes simply allowed those settlers who decided to stay to take matters into their own hands, encouraging them to win through violence, intimidation and terror, what they could not secure by law.[25]

Power: The Contradictions of 'Composition'

The irony of a determination to affirm the principles of English law leading inevitably to violence and lawlessness did not, however, merely afflict the policy of plantation. It applied with greater, and ultimately more deadly, force to the policy which, far more than plantation, was central to the re-establishment of English rule in Ireland: the policy of surrender and regrant.

By 1550 most of the 'surrender and regrant' settlements negotiated by St Leger in the early 1540s had run into trouble. The disruption to the Irish vice-royalty during the Edwardian regencies, coupled with the emergence of other perceived priorities, most particularly defence against a fictional French – and a real Scottish – invasion, severely disrupted the process of assimilation in its crucial early stages. Complex issues in regard to disputed territorial boundaries, rights of over-lordship and even rights to succession that had been left deliberately undetermined in the haste to establish a basis for further negotiations were left to fester, and, in the absence of sustained viceregal attention, burst into open conflict. By the beginning of the 1550s, violent inter- and intra-dynastic disputes had erupted in Thomond, in Connacht, in Wicklow and in the midlands.[26] But nowhere was the conflict more violent than in *Tír Eoghain*. There, a bitter civil war waged within the family of Conn Bacach (the O'Neill and since 1542 earl of Tyrone) had resulted by 1553 in the emergence of the least likely figure within the feuding family as the principal power in the lordship, Conn's youngest son, Shane. In addition to sealing his claims to the O'Neillship, Shane sought to be recognised as the heir to the

25 A. J. Sheehan, 'Official Reaction to Native Land Claims in the Plantation of Munster', *Irish Historical Studies*, 23 (1983), 297–317.
26 C. Maginn, ' "Surrender and Regrant", in the Historiography of Sixteenth-Century Ireland', *Sixteenth Century Journal*, 38 (2007), 955–74.

earldom. Characteristically, St Leger had been willing to negotiate. But Sussex was not. Determined to enforce the authority of the crown and the settlements made under its law, Sussex insisted on sticking fast to the terms of the original treaty, and, regardless of his illegitimacy, to the succession of Conn's nominee, Matthew, the baron of Dungannon. This was an understandable position: an abandonment of Dungannon and his heirs would in practical terms indicate weakness, allowing similar challenges to be made across the island, encouraged of course by the factional politics of the Geraldines. But no less importantly, it constituted a challenge to the authority of English law, which regardless of his birth, had recognised Matthew as heir through the express will of the monarch.[27]

This persuasive position was, however, itself vulnerable on grounds both practical and principled. One was Sussex's manifest inability to defeat or suppress Shane in a series of costly campaigns between 1558 and 1561, which damaged his credibility as viceroy. But a second, far more damaging obstacle came in the form of the argument that Shane eventually presented when he had the opportunity to make his case at Court in 1562. The original agreement made twenty years before was, he argued, intrinsically and fatally flawed because in regranting to Conn all the rights and privileges that he had listed, the crown had, perhaps inadvertently but also conclusively, returned to him rights that he had derived from his assumption of the protective obligations as 'the officer' of the O'Neills. Thus whatever good faith was in place on both sides, a serious confusion had arisen which could only be resolved by starting again, by concluding a more satisfactory treaty with the current undisputed O'Neill, Shane.

This was clever: a move designed to enable the crown to save face while granting Shane the recognition he claimed. But it implicitly suggested that not only were all previous surrender and regrant settlements similarly flawed, but also that all future settlements with the great Gaelic lords would have to be preceded by complex and controversial negotiations to determine those rights as they claimed in their persons as would-be subjects and those which they were prepared to surrender totally as 'officers' of their people. These were implications the enormity of which the upholders of English law were not prepared to countenance. Thus in the short term it was decided to abandon negotiations with Shane, and to proceed by all means to his destruction. The practical removal of Shane by assassination in 1567 did not, however, resolve the problem in principle. And two years later it was Sidney who

---

27 C. Brady, *Shane O'Neill* (2nd edn., University College Dublin Press, 2015).

sought to address it by means, suitably enough, of a parliamentary bill of attainder against Shane.

As Shane's status as an outlaw with no legal rights had already been declared by proclamation, such a bill was legally redundant. But the significance of the act lay in its lengthy preamble, which in addition to listing all of Shane's manifold vices, offered a new and radical account of Irish history from its origins down to the present. Relying on the dubious authority of Geoffrey of Monmouth and Gildas, this new history claimed that the first people ever to settle in Ireland, Hiberus and Hermon who hailed from the Spanish region of Bayon, had been given prior permission to do so by their own lord Gurmundus, who happened also to be king of the Britons. Myth turned into truth by means of parliamentary statute; this discovery entailed that because all of the inhabitants of Ireland were directly subjects of the English crown since time immemorial, the claims of their so-called captains, the 'Os' and the 'Macs', were no more than unlawful usurpations made possible by long years of neglect when the English crown had failed to exert its right to rule. But such a right had never been renounced; rather it had been asserted on several historical occasions both before and after the coming of the Normans, had been reaffirmed by the Act of 1541 and finally re-iterated in the very statute attainting Shane.[28]

No empty piece of imperialist cant, the act attainting Shane was in fact another 'constitutional revolution' of the sixteenth century enabling the crown to transcend the difficulties associated with the earlier methods of surrender and regrant, to ignore the claims of the great lords and legitimately to open negotiations with its long lost subjects, the freeholding occupiers of the kingdom's land. Several of the statutes passed in the same parliament, such as those further outlawing coign and livery, regulating retainers, enforcing the registration of idle men, banning fosterage, and above all initiating the shiring of all un-shired territory and giving to the viceroy the right to regulate the boundaries of all shires, were intended to give statutory validation to the judicial and administrative framework to be introduced on the completion of the negotiations. The illegitimate regime of the overlords would at last be replaced by the shire and the sheriff.

Yet all of this was for the future. The key question remained as to how the great transformation was to be initiated in practice. And for this Sidney

---

28 C. Brady, 'The Attainder of Shane O'Neill, Sir Henry Sidney and the Problems of Tudor State-building in Ireland', in C. Brady and J. Ohlmeyer (eds.), *British Interventions in Early Modern Ireland* (Cambridge University Press, 2005), 28–48.

looked towards an instrument that was distinctly un-parliamentary. A product of his long experience of the malign operations of coign and of discussions with his close adviser Edmund Tremayne, the idea of 'composition' was founded on the recognition that this nefarious system could be destroyed neither through delicate diplomatic negotiation (Shane had proved that) nor through overt confrontation (Sussex had proved that); but only by transcending it. The crown, Sidney proposed, should beat the warlords at their own game by introducing into the system a military force whose exactions of coign would be so massive and so indefinite that not even the greatest figures in the system could oppose it. This demonstration of royal power was, however, to be immediately followed by a general offer to negotiate at all levels of landed society about a fixed, annual tax, to be rated exactly in relation to each individual family's claims to territorial possession, which would free those who agreed to it from all other forms of exaction, royal and seigneurial alike. Agreement to such a 'composition' (the term simply connoted 'a deal') would, in a far more finely gradated version of 'surrender and regrant', entail recognition of legal tenurial status at all levels of freeholding society. The fruits of the tax would be spent largely in its enforcement: thus sheriffs or, in places where shires had not been established, seneschals or captains would undertake the collection of the fixed payments and ensure that any attempts at other exactions would be firmly suppressed. There were some ancillary issues attendant on the individual deals, which Sidney had anticipated. Those lords who were cooperating with the process should be entitled to several concessions; seigneurial rights which they could show belonged to them as a matter of legal tenure would be allowed, and they would be granted a discount – and even an exemption – on their own tax liabilities to the crown. But most importantly of all, they would be allowed to keep whatever number of personal retainers they wished through a process of registration, 'booking', allowing the lords to decide between those they wished to protect and those they were content to abandon to the cruelties of martial law to be administered by the provincial president or his provost marshal.[29]

In principle, 'composition' was a powerful strategic instrument, penetrating deep beneath the effects of centuries of neglect, and seeking to revive the possibilities that had existed in the twelfth century, making the ideal of shiring again possible. In its immediate application, Sidney enjoyed some success,

---

29 C. Brady, *The Chief Governors: The Rise and Fall of Reform Government in Tudor Ireland, 1536–1588* (Cambridge University Press, 1994), 136–66; D. Heffernan (ed.), 'Six Tracts on "coign and livery", c.1568–78', *Analecta Hibernica*, 45 (2012), 6–45 and D. Heffernan (ed.), *Reform Treatises on Tudor Ireland, 1537–1599* (Dublin: Irish Manuscripts Commission, 2016).

especially in Munster where the earl of Desmond agreed to a general settlement. But further progress was frustrated on several counts: Sidney never got the great army he had sought for, his budget for the project was cut enormously, and as these restrictions indicate, he was subject, as ever, to subversion at court. But even deeper forces were at play. For the principal opposition to Sidney's project arose not at court but in Ireland, and not primarily within the lordships, but among the English of the Pale and the corporate towns who boycotted the administration, appealed directly to the queen and, after a sharp confrontation at Court, forced Sidney to back down and abandon his plans for composition altogether.

But the idea persisted, and was revived in 1584 by Sir John Perrot as the central part of his viceregal programme. Perrot made some crucial modifications. First, in regard to the Pale where Sidney had encountered so much trouble in his attempts to convert the costs of billeting into a composition rent, Perrot reached an interim settlement by summoning 'a grand council', which agreed a fixed sum for a period of three years. In Connacht, Perrot established a judicial commission to ratify the composition settlements made by the provincial president and so complete the process of legal recognition in the shortest possible time. But in Ulster, where Sidney had made no progress at all, Perrot, in three separate tours laid the foundations for an entirely new settlement of the province. A long sought for division of *Tír Eoghain* between Turlough Luineach and Hugh, whom Perrot had by statute created earl of Tyrone, was at last achieved. It was, moreover, supplemented by a treaty recognising one branch of the MacDonnells, headed by Sorley Boy MacDonnell, as subjects of the Irish crown. And Perrot completed these unprecedented agreements by a whole series of settlements with O'Donnell, O'Reilly, Maguire and other lesser lords, under which they undertook to have their territories redefined as shires and to pay a composition rent.[30]

Perrot's success in advancing the process of shiring in Ulster was unprecedented, but also short-lived. For while he encountered few obstacles in either Ulster or Connacht, real trouble presented itself in Munster and

---

30 B. Cunningham, 'The Composition of Connacht in the Lordships of Clanricard and Thomond, 1577–1641', *Irish Historical Studies*, 24 (1984), 1–14; H. Morgan, *Tyrone's Rebellion: The Outbreak of the Nine Years War in Tudor Ireland* (Woodbridge: Boydell Press, 1995), chapter 2; Perrot's record of journeys to Ulster and Connacht, September 1586; see among his several completed negotiations, those with Angus Mc Donnell, SP 63/124/29, TNA; with Turlough Luineach and Hugh O'Neill SP 63/124/38, TNA; with Sorley Boy MacDonnell and Rory McQuillan SP 63/124/83, 85, TNA; and with Hugh O'Donnell SP 63/125/14, TNA. Perrot's own summary of his achievements in Ulster is recorded in SP 63/139/7, TNA.

consequentially in Whitehall. Though he had been a servitor in Munster on more than one occasion, Perrot in company with his viceregal peers, had little enthusiasm for the plantation which was already being developed there at the time of his appointment. He could not, of course, oppose it. But neither could he ignore both the administrative and jurisdictional challenges that this independent English operation posed to his government. The issue arose in particular over 'composition'. Those lords who had previously agreed a composition rent and had survived the Desmond rebellion remained willing to yield a tax, and Ormond, now greatly disaffected through his exclusion from the plantation project and by attempts to dispossess some of those whom he had pardoned during his service against the rebels, concluded a complete composition settlement throughout his lordship. But for the freeborn Englishmen within the plantation such an idea was intolerable not only because they were unwilling to suffer its financial burden, but because it was constitutionally unacceptable. Munster, therefore, was rapidly evolving into two cultures: one which was willing for all kinds of historical reasons to accept the principle of annual taxation unmediated by the processes of parliamentary consent, and one for which such a regime was utterly inconceivable.[31]

What was emerging here, but in an exceptionally virulent form, was a recurrence of the most fundamental of all the contradictions afflicting the character of the English presence in Ireland. For while it was clear that the policy of composition was ideally suited to initiating the process of transforming the Irish lordships into shires, it was no less evident that it also entailed breaches of the fundamental principles of English constitutional law. The proposal to raise an annual tax on the country without parliamentary consent; the establishment of regional agencies to conduct the process which were in turn to be subvented by it, the exemption from all taxation of a complaisant privileged nobility all seemed to be driving the governance of Ireland in a direction which, while fast gaining ground elsewhere in Europe, was profoundly repugnant to conventional English modes of constitutional thinking. In short, by the middle of the 1580s, after some sixty years of sustained commitment to integrating Ireland into the Tudor realm, a painful paradox was beginning to emerge. Short of war and conquest, it was now becoming clear that the incorporation of Ireland into the English political, constitutional and legal system was likely to be attained only if the English were willing to contemplate the abandonment of some of the central principles underlying that system.

31 On Ormond's attitude, see especially D. Edwards, *The Ormond Lordship in County Kilkenny, 1515–1642: The Rise and Fall of Butler Feudal Power* (Dublin: FCP, 2003).

Resolving Contradiction: War

From an English perspective there were, therefore, deep constitutional and cultural grounds for rejecting composition and its methods. But in Ireland the consequences of its abandonment were deadly. When Sidney was recalled in 1578, Munster, the one area where composition had actually been introduced, rapidly became a theatre of civil war, as the Desmond kerne threatened with redundancy under the scheme came down from the hills, out of the woods and back from abroad to destroy it; and the province's lesser lords and free-holders, disappointed by the prospect of Desmond's survival, now watched on neutrally as the earldom crumpled. The consequences of Perrot's ruin were even more catastrophic. In 1589 a freeholders' revolt overthrew his settlement in Monaghan. In 1591 the return of Red Hugh O'Donnell plunged the lordship of Tír Conaill into internecine war and overt rebellion. Through the early 1590s in Breifne, in Fermanagh, in Iveagh, in Clandeboy, the lords who had subscribed to composition were either overthrown or forced to re-join with their old soldiers in rebellion. And in the middle of it all pressure mounted on that figure who more than anyone was crucial to the success of Perrot's Ulster scheme, Hugh O'Neill, second earl of Tyrone.[32]

As Desmond had shown, this was the inevitable consequence of aborted 'composition'. But in Ulster and North Connacht, a further force of dissolution – accelerating its pace and ensuring its violent consequences – was to be found among the very group who had been charged with bringing composition to completion. Variously described as sheriffs, seneschals or captains, depending on the stage at which it was understood the area over which they had governance had developed towards shiring, these officers had been intended since Sussex's time to function on an interim basis as supports for the development of the negotiations being undertaken between the viceroy and the local lords. As the recognition grew of the need for more local and intensive investigations and negotiations within the lordships, so did the importance of these officers, until they emerged under Sidney and Perrot as the key agents of government policy.[33]

As composition collapsed, however, the practical power and entrepreneurial opportunities enjoyed by such officials persisted, enhanced by the loss of

---

32 Mc Cormack, *Earldom of Desmond*; Morgan, *Tyrone's Rebellion*; D. McGettigan, *Red Hugh O'Donnell and the Nine Years War* (Dublin: FCP, 2005).

33 R. Rapple, *Martial Power and Elizabethan Political Culture: Military Men in England and Ireland, 1558–1594* (Cambridge University Press, 2012); D. Edwards, 'Beyond Reform: Martial Law and the Tudor Reconquest of Ireland', *History Ireland*, 5 (1997), 16–21.

control from the centre and by the internecine strife within the lordships precipitated by that collapse. Epitomised by the notorious conduct of Sir Richard
Bingham, the president of Connacht, and Humphrey Willis and Edward
Herbert, sheriffs of Fermanagh and Cavan respectively, the reckless, expro-
priative and violent actions of this military class once they had been released
from the authority of the viceroy were extensive throughout Connacht and
Ulster, intensifying immeasurably the political tensions both within and
between the lordships.

The direct consequence of this intense struggle for power, which occurred
within each of the Ulster lordships in the wake of the abandonment of composition, was the unprecedentedly powerful and prolonged rebellion of the
Ulster lords known retrospectively as 'the Nine Years war'. The label is not only
anachronistic; it is also misleading. The rebellion can only be said to have taken
on distinctive form when Tyrone openly committed to the cause of O'Donnell
and Maguire in the spring of 1595 and was proclaimed a traitor in June. But even
then, Tyrone continued to negotiate for an end to the rebellion and on submission secured a pardon in May 1596. Breaking the terms of the truce, Tyrone
was again in rebellion by the end of the year; but he had again submitted (to
Ormond) by the end of 1597. Two events in 1598 extended and intensified the
rebellion. The defeat of Sir Henry Bagenal, marshal of the royal army, at the
Yellow Ford precipitated widespread risings against the government throughout
the island, most especially in the plantation sites in Munster and the midlands.
And the accession of Philip III to the Spanish crown enormously increased the
chance of a serious Spanish intervention in aid of the rebels. But even as he now
sought to transform the rebellion into a full-scale war of independence, Tyrone
continued, as his secret negotiations with Essex indicated, to seek a permanent
peace with the crown. The *debâcle* at Kinsale in December 1601, itself a symptom of the uncertain and conditional nature of the Ulster lords' commitment
to all-out war, ended this critical phase and broke the strength of the rebels.[34]

The terms concluded with the defeated were the most generous ever negotiated by the Tudor regime, not only granting a general pardon, and restoring
them to all their lands, but even granting to Tyrone rights over lesser families
in the province, which would have been denied him under Perrot's composition.[35] All this was testimony to the continuing desire of the crown to secure

34 The most succinct account of the war is still to be found in C. Falls, *Elizabeth's Irish Wars*
(London: Methuen, 1950); but a more analytical study is J. McGurk, *The Elizabethan
Conquest of Ireland: The 1590s Crisis* (Manchester University Press, 1997) and J.O'Neill, *The
Nine Years' War, 1593–1603: O'Neill, Mountjoy and the Military Revolution* (Dublin: FCP, 2017).
35 N. Canny, 'The *Treaty of Mellifont* and the Re-organisation of Ulster, 1603', *Irish Sword*, 9
(1969–70), 249–62.

the allegiance of the native *élites* through assimilation rather than conquest. But no less enduring were the forces that had from the outset undermined that objective. Almost immediately after its conclusion Charles Blount, Lord Mountjoy, the viceroy who had negotiated the settlement, withdrew from Ireland to be only occasionally and decreasingly concerned with its maintenance. And in his absence the old tensions arose, as those within the lordships whose rebellion had been provoked by the social and cultural implications of reform remained unreconciled, while many of those who had originally supported it were either destroyed or totally disillusioned. In the meantime the martial men, emboldened by their experiences in the war, and embittered by their neglect in the settlement, continued as they had in the past to take matters into their own hands, their actions silently condoned by Mountjoy's proxy as viceroy, Sir Arthur Chichester, a figure who openly abandoned the grand viceregal ambitions envisioned by Sussex and identified himself wholly with the martial men. Thus within four years the artificiality of the treaty concluded at Mellifont was steadily revealed through the inability or unwillingness of all the parties to sustain it. The Ulster lords took flight. And the long-held aspiration of re-establishing English rule in Ireland was at last realised not in spite of, but because of its inherent contradictions.

2

Political Change and Social Transformation, 1603–1641

DAVID EDWARDS

When, in March 1603, the Stuart monarch James VI of Scotland became James I of England and Ireland following the death of Elizabeth Tudor, he inherited an Irish kingdom about to emerge from decades of military conflict. At length, Tudor forces had succeeded in breaking the resistance of autonomous Irish warlords opposed to the encroachment of central government; the country was conquered. James would waste little time capitalising on this. During his reign (1603–1625) and that of his son Charles I (1625–1649) Ireland would experience a series of sweeping changes, not the least of which would be the increased role of Scotland and Scottish people in everyday Irish life. For reasons of space the greater part of this chapter will focus on the English, who dominated the government, and their relations with both parts of the native population, the Gaelic Irish and the Anglo-Irish. The Scots will only be mentioned in passing, yet their growing presence symbolised both the extraordinary changes delivered by the Stuarts and the unforeseen consequences that it wrought.

At James's accession he and his ministers were beguiled by the prospect of forging a major new European state – a 'British' triple monarchy, no less – based on Anglo-Scottish political union and the Protestant religion. Ireland was but an afterthought; somewhere English and Scots might learn to interact, become partners and share a new 'British' identity. Towards this end, soon after his accession, James awarded wide areas of Counties Antrim and Down to Scottish supporters; in 1609, when the Ulster Plantation began, Scottish applicants received half of the land grants. Simultaneously, James advanced several Scotsmen to senior positions in the Irish government, and in the Irish established church. Yet the union James craved did not materialise. The Scottish advance enraged many English, who saw Ireland as a sister kingdom and subject territory of England, the control of which had been won with English treasure and blood. In Ulster, English and Scottish planters often lived separate lives; and regarding government positions, the Scots failed to build on their initial platform and were soon squeezed out by English obstruction. Resentments flourished, the full cost of which would become dramatically apparent in 1641, when Irish rebels in Ulster received assistance from Scottish settlers living among them. However, it is not necessary to venture so far ahead to appreciate the significance for Irish political affairs of the resurgence of Anglo-Scottish enmity.[1] Gradually the growing Scottish presence in Ireland weakened the state rather than strengthened it. The government was never as strong as it purported to be; the political union that underpinned it was fragile.

Completing Conquest: The Army and the Gaelic Lordships

To a large extent early Stuart Irish policy was about the completion of Tudor policy for the country, and was based on social and institutional 'reform' proposals traceable to treatises written in the reign of Henry VIII or in the reigns of his children.[2] This continuity in political thinking about Ireland was of course due to the continuity in crown personnel. Just as those English administrators and soldiers who had dominated the Irish government at King James's accession were retained by him long after 1603, so it was that the policy advocates, nearly all English, who had written tracts and treatises advising various solutions to the crown's Irish problem during the late Elizabethan period carried on articulating solutions well into the Jacobean era. As before, these policy-makers sought to achieve a broad Anglicisation of Ireland through a mixture of legal and administrative innovation in central and regional government, colonisation schemes and crude military compulsion. And as before, too, the pursuit of Anglicisation would mean a concerted effort to eliminate the aristocratic independence of the Gaelic and Gaelicized lordships, to be undertaken as part of England's historic 'civilising' mission in the country.[3] Unlike before, however, the implementation of policy progressed much further, affected all areas and did so remarkably quickly.

---

1 D. Edwards, 'Scottish Officials and Secular Government in Early Stuart Ireland', and J. Ohlmeyer, '"Scottish Peers" in Seventeenth-century Ireland', both in D. Edwards (ed.), *The Scots in Early Stuart Ireland: Union and Separation in Two Kingdoms* (Manchester University Press, 2016), 29–61, 62–94; N. Canny, *Making Ireland British, 1580–1650* (Oxford University Press, 2001), 477–84; M. Perceval-Maxwell, *The Outbreak of the Irish Rebellion of 1641* (Montreal and Kingston: McGill-Queen's University Press, 1994), 216–9.
2 See Chapter 1 by C. Brady, this volume.
3 D. Heffernan, 'Tudor Reform Treatises and Government Policy in Sixteenth-Century Ireland', unpublished PhD thesis, University College Cork (2012), 256–68.

The speed with which policy was turned into action was due partly to the fact that native resistance to English rule was crushed. When in March 1603 Hugh O'Neill, second earl of Tyrone capitulated to the viceroy and royal council at Mellifont Abbey, he was tricked into surrendering to Elizabeth I, pleading for her forgiveness 'on his knees', before being informed that the queen had been dead for nearly a week. Such treatment helped undermine the reverence Tyrone inspired among many Irish; by being deceived, made to surrender to a corpse, he was left humiliated. As an eyewitness recalled, 'the earl … could not contain himself from shedding of tears, in such quantity as it could not well be concealed', and no wonder: had he but held out a little longer, he would not have been so obviously a beaten man. The peace terms he was offered were in certain respects generous, but doubts remain over the sincerity of the government's negotiators; either way, he never recovered. Beneath the rebel leadership, among the general Irish population, sheer exhaustion played its part in bringing resistance to an end. After years of war the country was devastated, with famine widespread. At last it seemed that English power was dominant, and that the very great challenge Tyrone and his confederates had previously presented was utterly vanquished. Provided crown forces were maintained at a sufficient level it might be possible to impose the sort of alterations to Ireland and its social and political structures that English policy-makers had so long deliberated upon in their writings: which is to say, it was time to complete the conquest.[4]

To convince the new king that an ambitious programme was necessary to make Ireland, particularly its Gaelic parts, more controllable was not a difficult undertaking. As king of Scotland, James had been pursuing a political and military reduction of the Gaelic clans in the Western Isles and Highlands since the mid-1580s. The clans' constant evasion of state power antagonised him, an open challenge to his lofty assertion that his subjects must accept his divine right to rule. To some extent the fact that the Scottish Gaels seemed to draw strength from the Irish Gaels across the North Channel, making dynastic alliances with the lords of Ulster and Connacht, or generating large revenues through the unlicensed export of men and weapons into Ireland, predisposed James to adopt stern measures against Irish Gaeldom on succeeding to the throne in 1603. It was also, of course, a convenient means for him to reassure the English that he shared their

---

4 C. Maxwell, *Irish History from Contemporary Sources, 1509–1610* (London: Allen and Unwin, 1923), 197–8; N. Canny, 'The Treaty of Mellifont and the Reorganisation of Ulster, 1603', *Irish Sword*, 9 (1969–70), 380–99.

views about the incompatibility of a politically autonomous *Gaedhealtacht* continuing to operate largely intact within a wider 'British' state. It was important that he did. Previously, while fighting Irish rebels during the 1580s and 1590s, many English servitors had wondered why as king of the Scots he had done so little to stem the flow of military supplies into Ireland from western Scotland and the Isles. Following his succession, James set about burying such memories. He and his English and Scottish ministers agreed that left to their own devices the majority of the Gaels were typically 'wildmen', enemies of 'civility', naturally insubordinate. Scotland as well as Ireland would be much improved by their diminution. No less attractive, to the king at least, the English and Scots might strengthen their new bonds by pooling their efforts against the worst elements of this bothersome Gaelic world.[5]

The reduction of Irish Gaeldom faced one serious obstacle – the cost of the forces necessary to implement it. After James's Scottish agents had succeeded in decommissioning the greater part of the English army in Ireland in 1603–1604, paying off thousands of troops and despatching them homewards, the matter had arisen of how many soldiers were needed to control the country in a post-war era.[6] All discussion of the subject was linked to the wider question of crown finance. As James had discovered following his Westminster coronation, the kingdom of England was effectively bankrupt. Huge arrears remained from Elizabeth's near twenty-year war with Habsburg Spain, but probably the single largest debt had been accrued in Ireland, caused by the soaring cost of subduing the series of rebellions and foreign interventions that had occurred there.

English subventions and Irish Revenue

That a strong army was needed in Ireland was not seriously disputed. The country was only barely under royal control. The prospect of withdrawing troops from areas that might then revert to a form of independence once

---

5 M. Lynch, 'James VI and the "Highland Problem"', in J. Goodare and M. Lynch (ed.), *The Reign of James VI* (East Linton: Tuckwell, 2000), 208–27; M. MacGregor, 'Civilizing Gaelic Scotland: The Scottish Isles and the Stewart Empire', in É. Ó Ciardha and M. Ó Siochrú (eds.), *The Plantation of Ulster: Ideology and Practice* (Manchester University Press, 2012), 33–54; J. P. Summerville (ed.), *King James VI and I: Political Writings* (Cambridge University Press, 1994), 22.

6 D. Edwards, 'Securing the Jacobean Succession: The Secret Career of James Fullerton of Trinity College, Dublin', in Sean Duffy (ed.), *The World of the Galloglass: Kings, Warlords and Warriors in Ireland and Scotland, 1200–1600* (Dublin: Four Courts Press [hereafter FCP], 2007), 188–209.

native power recovered was a cause of concern. It was agreed that a strong garrison network would have to be maintained as a necessity to secure the gains of the war against Tyrone. However, because the Elizabethan wars had taken such a toll on the population and left whole regions desolate, it was obvious that the only way to pay for the garrison was via subventions from England. Accordingly, until such time as the kingdom of Ireland could generate sufficient revenues and taxes to pay for itself the size and cost of the Irish crown forces were subjected to constant review, with the king's ministers at Whitehall looking to curb Irish military expenditure year-on-year and the incumbents of Dublin Castle arguing against the proposed pace and scale of the cutbacks. Contrary to what was once thought, the castle held its own in these discussions. As shown in Figure 1, close examination of government financial records has revealed that the Irish administration continued to be heavily subsidised with English money throughout the entire first half of King James's reign (1603–1614). Three factors stand out: first, the army was by far the main consumer of government treasure in Jacobean Ireland, usually accounting for 75 per cent of annual expenditure; second, until 1615 the size of the subventions shipped in from England were sufficient to meet the costs of a significant peacetime force; and, third, after 1615, as English subventions dwindled, the army was sustained at the same level by Irish-generated tax revenues.

It is impossible to assemble precise figures of the annual size of the army, owing to a shortage of surviving annual lists of crown forces 'on the establishment', that is, financed directly by the crown. Yet a sufficient number of establishment lists have survived to recover at least an outline of the main fluctuations the army experienced. These documents show that after 1604 the size of the army stabilised for the remainder of the king's reign, ranging between 1,400 and 3,300 men (Figure 2), and that the average size of the army in the period 1605–1624 was 2,200 men. This was practically identical to the military establishment that had been retained in the country during most years of Elizabeth I's reign prior to 1588: in other words the Jacobean peacetime army was much the same size as the army which earlier had driven forward the Elizabethan conquest.

Compared with some of the armies on the continent, it is true, the English garrison stationed in Ireland under James VI and I was hardly huge, but then it was not meant for a continental war. Rather it was primarily a military police force, intended to impose order across the country after years of turmoil. That the 'order' it imposed was in many areas entirely new was highly significant. Indeed, it ensured that the army behaved – and was often perceived – as

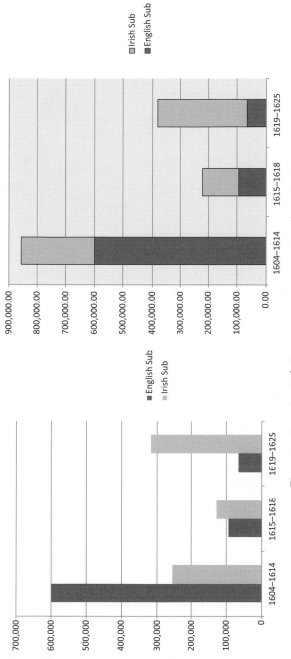

Figure 1. Financing Irish Government, 1603–1625 (pounds sterling).

Source: McLaughlin, 'The Making of the Irish Leviathan', i, chapter 6, appendix C.

Date of list	Officers	Soldiers	Warders	Constables	Total
Oct. 1604	49	4,274	236	12	4,571
Apr. 1606	25	1,014	355	21	1,415
Oct. 1607	33	1,984	492	35	2,544
Oct. 1608	39	2,414	775	67	3,295
Nov. 1611	39	1,612	425	28	2,104
Sept. 1616	84	1,907	190	18	2,199
April 1618	56	1,748	156	18	1,978
1622	66	1,910	153	19	2,148
Apr. 1623	37	1,566	171	16	1,790

Figure 2. The Irish Army on the Establishment, 1604–1624.
Sources: McLaughlin, 'The Making of the Irish Leviathan', 328, 339; TCD, Ms 672,
ff. 95r–101r, 116r–121v; Ibid., Ms 808, ff. 53r–58r.

a force of occupation, a physical expression of the conquest that it had helped to bring about and was intended to complete by preventing the reassertion of the old Gaelic and Gaelicised order. Besides which, the army's commanders, and very likely its rank and file, were nearly all veterans of the Elizabethan conflict. They were men who had fought the Irish rebels, suffered hardships at their hands, and lost friends and comrades; for many, their remaining on in crown military service during peacetime provided an opportunity to settle old scores with their former adversaries.

Confirmation that the army was intended to act aggressively in the Irish territories after peace was declared is provided by the wide recourse to martial law that its officers enjoyed. For almost two years after the Treaty of Mellifont, martial law commissions that had been issued in wartime were allowed to remain in force. Consequently, almost every officer in the army, and dozens of auxiliary commanders, continued to enjoy power of summary execution over the majority of the Irish population, authorised to hang or otherwise punish anyone below the rank of a lord or major landowner that opposed them or their men. Moreover, when the pre-Mellifont commissions were cancelled in 1605, rather than reduce its reliance on martial law, the Dublin government re-organised its use, the better to accommodate it to post-war conditions. Dozens of new commissioners were appointed by royal warrant signed by the viceroy in the following two decades, and still more by sub-commissions granted by the marshals of the army, the lords president of Munster and Connacht, and the commanders of the numerous garrisons, all of whom had power to devolve martial authority to officers of their own choosing. By this means, well into the 1620s the crown forces were able to ter-rorise the inhabitants of most parts of the country, and thereby demonstrate the increasing weakness of the Gaelic lords, who were unable to protect their followers (or subdue their adversaries) in anything like the robust manner they had managed before.

Through speedy deployment of the army and free-ranging application of martial law, the crown swiftly achieved something that had evaded the royal forces for much of the previous century: the demilitarisation of the native lordships. In the first ten years of James's reign there was a major culling of the traditional private forces of the lords and chieftains. Both hard and soft methods were deployed to achieve this. By insisting, as a sign of loyalty, that all local leaders 'book' or register their retainers and stand as guarantor for their future behaviour on pain of a hefty fine, the government succeeded in encouraging the native *élite* to shed excess military followers. Simultaneously, efforts to better control the import and sale of weapons helped ensure, over time, that the native soldiers who remained would find it increasingly dif-ficult to equip themselves. But it was the hard approach that brought the most dramatic results. With crown forces routinely out on patrol, scouring the countryside for ex-rebel swordsmen and 'wrongdoers', there were large numbers of executions by martial law. Additionally, a great many native sol-diers faced banishment from the country. Lacking a lord to offer them pro-tection, they were rounded up, brought to the coastal ports and transported overseas. How many were removed before 1608 is unclear. According to a report by the lord deputy, Arthur Chichester, between 1609 and 1614, his offic-ers and agents succeeded in implementing the removal of 6,000 'disaffected Irishmen' to Scandinavia, nearly all from Ulster, but his writings depict this as part of an ongoing process, and allude to other, earlier transports, encom-passing other parts of the country. That he described the victims of this pol-icy as 'disaffected' is highly suggestive. He also observed that the transportees from Ulster included Gaelic troops who had supported the crown 'in the last rebellion of Tyrone', as well as those of the province who were Tyrone's former adherents. Evidently, the clear out of Irish soldiers advanced indis-criminately, with a ready willingness to discard former allies along with the rest. The numbers of Irish military going into exile were further boosted by thousands of the so-called Wild Geese, who left of their own volition, bound mainly for Spain or Spanish Flanders, intending to earn a living abroad fighting for England's Habsburg enemies.[7]

The depletion of the native private forces during these years was only one part of the government's assault on Gaelic power. After Mellifont a policy emerged that was designed to deal a knockout blow to the Irish lords and chieftains. Abandoning concessions granted to ex-rebel lords on the cessation of hostilities, the administration began imposing a series of sweeping changes to Gaeldom early in 1605, the effects of which were nothing short of revolutionary. Some of these changes have attracted scholarly attention, while others have not; none have been scrutinised nearly enough.

Tanistry, the system of elective succession practised in the Gaelic territories for centuries, and which allowed the strongest man to become heir-apparent to a lord in preference to a weaker candidate or a child, was declared void by English judicial fiat in 1606, and replaced forthwith by primogeniture. Besides curtailing the rights of lords to nominate their successors and blocking the path to power of strong and assertive clansmen who were not the lord's first-born or nearest male heir, this decision had far-reaching consequences for landholding patterns and the broader political balance within each *tuatha*, or lordship. As had been intended: Sir John Davies, the official chiefly responsible for the policy, recognised that tanistry's disappearance would present an opportunity to bring Gaelic society generally into closer alignment with English social norms, and to place all Gaelic land tenures fully within the compass of English law and the crown courts. Hitherto, land in Gaelic Ireland had usually been held corporately by the ruling lineage (*derbfine*) and its affiliates; its distribution between the lord, his *tánaiste* and the rest had been determined by a mixture of sometimes fierce internal competition, bullying of lesser landholders, realignments and negotiation, the results being ratified by native judges (brehons) acting as arbiters. The abolition of tanistry swept this aside, and compelled the introduction of private property rights for all local landowners irrespective of their relations with the ruling lords and dynasties; such landowners were now to be known as freeholders, their rights protected by the government as tenants of the crown. To institutionalise this radical departure, the 'Commission for the Remedy of Defective Titles' followed, its members travelling through the country with military support to persuade native landowners to divide their lands into clearly designated freeholds and

---

7 G. Henry, *The Irish Military Community in Spanish Flanders, 1586–1621* (Dublin: Irish Academic Press, 1992), 28–9; D. Edwards, 'Legacy of Defeat: The Reduction of Gaelic Ireland after Kinsale', in H. Morgan (ed.), *The Battle of Kinsale* (Bray: Wordwell, 2004), 284–91.

tenancies and so secure clear title to what they held, under English common law. The sovereignty enjoyed by the lord time out of mind was gone. Likewise, his ability to increase at will his territorial share of the *tuatha* was greatly curbed; indeed the very notion of the *tuatha*, as a polity shared by people of ancient noble stock, was itself gravely diluted.[8]

Completing the rout, the traditional seigneurial right of the Gaelic lords to impose taxes on their subjects (and also the rights of their tanists to share in the proceeds) was abolished. A proclamation written by Davies and published by Chichester in March 1605 is best known for having declared all the people of Ireland as henceforth 'free, natural and immediate subjects of his Majesty', but it also spelled out what this would require in practice: the elimination of other versions of sovereignty. 'In his Majesty's name', it declared, all the Gaelic and Gaelicised lords must at once 'utterly forbear to use or usurp upon any of their tenants or dependents those odious and unlawful customs' that traditionally they had levied,

> which customs we will and command to be discontinued and abolished for ever in this Kingdom, as being barbarous, unreasonable and intolerable in any civil or Christian commonwealth.

Over the course of the next few years the abolition of the lords' private exactions was enforced by government commissioners at county level, at the newly extended sessions of assize. The chance survival of a document among the Castletown Papers permits a glimpse of the process as it would have occurred across the country. Having first invited, in autumn 1605, the landowners of the middling lordship of Upper Ossory to list the exactions demanded of them by Florence Fitzpatrick (MacGiollapadraig), third baron of Upper Ossory their overlord, Viceroy Chichester despatched two senior judges to Maryborough in Queen's County to deliver the crown's verdict in April 1606. Shorn of its context, the announcement reads like just another judgement of the court, but no-one who was present could have missed its momentousness. Though the baron had long been loyal to the crown, his hold over the community was seriously diminished. To ensure that everything went smoothly, Sir Henry Power, the English military governor of the region, looked on, supported by his force of 50 horse and 100 foot, and a commission of martial law to discourage opposition.[9]

---

8 H. S. Pawlisch, *Sir John Davies and the Conquest of Ireland: A Study in Legal Imperialism* (Cambridge University Press,1985), chapter 4.

9 Maxwell, *Irish History*, 208–10; D. Edwards, 'Lordship and Custom in Gaelic Leinster: Select Documents from Upper Ossory, 1559–1612', *Ossory, Laois & Leinster,*

The loss of private taxation rights brought instant economic decline. Though the Gaelic lords were offered a token compensatory sum to be collected from the inhabitants of each lordship, this in no way covered the scale of what they lost. For centuries they had been able to support themselves, their families and followers through a range of charges levied as 'hospitality' on their subject populations, charges encompassing everything from the cost of their children's marriages to the maintenance of their private bodyguards, scribes and musicians, even the upkeep of their hunting dogs. Henceforth they would have to pay for all this themselves, in hard cash generated from their personal estates – but with much of their land already set for customary services or payment-in-kind, they found themselves cash-poor and were forced to borrow. That their economic struggles created a crisis of patronage for the bards and rhymers who for centuries had commemorated their achievements is recorded in poems datable to 1605–1612, which lament the poets' sudden underemployment as the lords were forced to jettison servants and cut costs. Evidence of the lords' difficulties is also recorded in the burgeoning market in Gaelic land, with as much as 20 per cent of the territory of some lordships being placed in mortgage or sold to outsiders in the following decades; in other lordships it was higher still.[10]

It was, of course, in Ulster that the policy of reducing the mighty was pursued with greatest vigour. Even before Tyrone's rebellion Ulster had always seemed the most Gaelic province of the country, and the most resistant to English influence. Utilising the ring of forts extended during the recent war, the government maintained the garrison in the province at maximum levels even when trimming elsewhere. Hemmed in, Tyrone and his fellow magnates Rory O'Donnell, earl of Tyrconnell, and Cúchonnacht Maguire, lord of Fermanagh, hoped to weather the storm, but it was not to be. The pressure escalated. The officers and troops surrounding them were encouraged to keep pushing. Outlying lands were seized, fishing rights forfeited, livestock stolen, local women suffered 'many rapes', and besides numerous isolated killings and executions (particularly in O'Donnell's country), there was at least one massacre of civilians. Perpetrated by Sir Henry Folliott's troops on a food-gathering mission, the soldiers put to the sword Tyrone's herdsmen 'besides many other poor men, women and children' on encountering them with the earl's cattle in the west Tyrone borderlands. The introduction of the

4 (2010), 27–31; Catalogue of Fiants, Vol. ii: James I, no. 1048, Chancery Rolls Office, National Archives of Ireland.
10 R. Gillespie, *The Transformation of the Irish Economy, 1550–1700* (Dundalk: Dundalgan Press, 1991), 21–2; M. Caball, *Poets and Politics: Reaction and Continuity in Irish Poetry, 1558–1625* (Cork University Press, 1998), 93–107.

Commission for Defective Titles coincided with this, so that sub-lords like the O'Cahans in north Tyrone and the MacSweeneys and O'Boyles in Donegal were greatly encouraged to break free of traditional O'Neill and O'Donnell jurisdiction and to seek better terms, holding their lands from the crown. In 1606 Tyrconnell sent an envoy to Spain seeking aid; money was granted and a ship was hired. In the meantime, Tyrone renewed his efforts to win friends in high places by lobbying leading courtiers at Whitehall, and initiated negotiations to marry his son and heir to the daughter of the Scottish earl of Argyll. But, ever duplicitous, he was also contacted by a group of disaffected lords in the Pale who planned to attack Dublin Castle. When in summer 1607 this was disclosed to the authorities by one of the plotters, Tyrone was informed – and panicked. He could wriggle no more. Fearing arrest – or worse – he fled Dublin for Ulster, but he was no longer safe there, with the crown forces and his local enemies pressing from all sides. And so it was that he made the fateful decision to ride to Lough Swilly, where Tyrconnell and Maguire were waiting, ready to board a ship that was bound for Spain.[11]

Plantations and the New *Élite*

The invasion fears that were stoked by the Flight of the Earls revealed how the royal government continued to view Ireland as a country not yet properly subjugated, and the Irish lordships as an existential threat to the English and 'British' state. Historians often forget that the earls' departure took place just after the reduction of the Gaelic order had been introduced across the country. Should Tyrone, Tyrconnell and their fellow exiles have succeeded in attracting support for an invasion – for instance by recruiting the Irish regiment stationed in Spanish Flanders – few English officials doubted that many Irish lords would have rallied to join them. As such, it seemed an invasion force might target almost anywhere along Ireland's western coastline to secure a foothold. And yet the earls' departure overseas also had its positive side for the government. Their going left a large vacuum in the north of Ireland. It was primarily to plug that gap that the crown turned next to

---

11 M. Kerney Walsh, *Destruction by Peace: Hugh O'Neill after Kinsale* (Armagh: Cumann Seanchais Ard Mhacha 1986); J. McCavitt, *The Flight of the Earls* (Dublin: Gill and Macmillan, 2002), chapter 4; D. Edwards, 'The Plight of the Earls: Tyrone and Tyrconnell's Grievances and Crown Coercion in Ulster, 1603–7', in T. O'Connor and M. A. Lyons (ed.), *The Ulster Earls and Baroque Europe* (Dublin: FCP 2010), 53–76; D. Finnegan, 'Why Did the Earl of Tyrone Join the Flight?', in D. Finnegan, É. Ó Ciardha and M. Peters (ed.), *The Flight of the Earls: Imeacht na nIarlaí* (Derry: Guildhall Press, 2010), 2–12.

a policy of colonisation. A plantation, officials agreed, would shut the door on the exiles' hopes of returning, and render Ulster, finally, completely subdued. Moreover, once the threat that the exiles posed was nullified, Gaelic and Gaelicised lords in other provinces would be left with little choice but to accept the conquest as a *fait accompli*, and acquiesce in the government's re-ordering of their territories.

The planning and imposition of the plantation in Ulster is discussed at length in another chapter in this volume.[12] Comments on the northern scheme will therefore be confined to some of its political effects. Suffice to say, while the plantation enabled the seizure from the native population of over 3.6 million statute acres in Ulster,[13] and the creation of a major new colony of English and Scottish settlers who were granted most of the best land, nevertheless it fell short of achieving its primary object – full 'British' control of the province.

For the plantation to succeed as its planners had intended, it required four things: tight military security; growing Anglo-Scottish cooperation; the emergence of a permanent new colonial aristocracy committed to the plantation project; and a steady flow of large numbers of Protestant settlers from England, Scotland and Wales to develop a population large enough to occupy all the land that had been seized on its behalf. It failed to realise fully any of these requirements.

Despite the the presence of the most extensive garrison in Ireland and the continuous imposition of martial law on the native Irish, Ulster remained a threatening place for newcomers, and all through the 1610s and 1620s rumours persisted of an imminent invasion, to be led either by Tyrone or his sons. Meanwhile, on the forfeited lands, relations between the English and Scottish planters proved patchy at best. The English and Scots generally inhabited separate districts. Though theoretically under English law, many of the larger Scottish planters pursued *de facto* autonomy in the regions, possibly in reaction to the government's tendency to appoint mostly Englishmen to posts in local government. Whatever the case, the leading Scots kept their distance from their English counterparts, sought to make marital alliances mostly in Scotland, and rather than consider their estates part of a new 'British' political order in Ireland looked instead to a greater Scotland. Religion compounded the sense of division. Most of the Scottish Protestant settlers were Presbyterians, determined to escape the shackles of a state-controlled church, which, in contrast, most of the

---

12 See Chapter 22 by A. Margey, this volume.
13 P. Robinson, *The Plantation of Ulster* (Dublin: Gill and Macmillan 1984), xv, 86.

English appear to have accepted. Additionally, a large minority of the Scottish colonists were actually Catholics, and as such had nearly as much to fear from English Protestant rule as the native Irish of the province. Of course, had English settlement levels expanded as the government had optimistically projected, this would not have mattered. However, surviving evidence indicates that prospective English and Welsh immigrants found the Munster Plantation a far more appealing proposition than they did Ulster. In demographic terms, therefore, by 1630 the plantation had failed to make Ulster British. Though settler numbers had gradually crept upwards, especially among the Scots, the predominant population group remained the Gaelic Irish, dispossessed and brooding. It was a situation engendering much tension.

If Ulster was the largest colonial project undertaken by the Early Stuart government in Ireland, it was by no means the only one. Besides facilitating the re-planting of Munster, in which many thousands of English and Welsh participated, plantations were also imposed in the period 1612–24 in Gaelic and Gaelicised parts of Leinster and the midlands, and also in Connacht. Usually referred to as the 'minor plantations', in key respects these differed politically from the Ulster scheme.[14] As if to call time on King James's 'British' fantasy, they were mainly English projects, designed to reward three main interest groups: leading English courtiers at Whitehall; New English army captains whose Irish services were deemed to require extra compensation; and well-connected administrators in Dublin, mostly English, but also embracing a number of Anglo-Irish and Gaelic Irish help-meets. (There were very few Scottish beneficiaries.) Unlike Ulster in the wake of the Flight of the Earls, the minor plantations did not owe their origins to any particular state of emergency, but rather to the comparatively pedestrian matter of correcting perceived flaws in the legal title of native lords and gentry to their lands in the areas affected. In this regard they showed the extent to which Gaelic territories everywhere – and those that bordered them – were suddenly laid bare to outside interference as the conquest neared completion. With government authority unchallenged, it was time for the administrators to take the lead in shaping the new social order.

Capitalising on the appropriatory potential of the Commission for Defective Titles, officials in Dublin poured over medieval records to identify regions of the country that centuries earlier might have escheated to the crown. They also snooped into the private affairs of local ruling families to locate

---

14 B. Mac Cuarta, 'The Plantation of Leitrim, 1620–41', *Irish Historical Studies* 32:127 (2001), 297–320; J. Lyttleton, *The Jacobean Plantations in Seventeenth-Century Offaly* (Dublin: FCP, 2013).

further opportunities for forfeiture based, retrospectively, on English laws of succession. Having discovered territories suitably large for a plantation 'plat', and reached a favourable understanding with courtier-patrons at Whitehall, the officials could then instigate proceedings against the current occupants to have the area in question declared for the crown on various grounds, recent or historical. To help ensure compliance the native occupants were promised much of the targeted lands back, which henceforth they were to hold of the crown, paying an annual rent; the forfeited portions – often the better land – would be shared out among the scheme's initiators and various suitors who had inveigled their way into the project through patronage or investment.

By a distance the main losers in these plantations were the smaller Gaelic landowners, who lost practically everything, while the senior landowners lost between a quarter and a third of their holdings. The damage done cannot be counted in acres alone. As with the 'undeserving Irish' in Ulster, the dispossession of thousands of small landowners and their dependants added to the prevailing pressures in Leinster, the midlands and Connacht. Regarding the local lords affected by the schemes, their retention of age-old positions of social headship were jeopardised as they were compelled to sacrifice the small fry; nor should it be overlooked that soon after these plantations Gaelic leaders among such senior lineages as the Kavanaghs, O'Farrells, O'Carrolls and MacGiollapadraigs appear to have fallen deeper into debt, and to have mortgaged or sold land to survive.

Ultimately, though, the lesser plantations were of major significance because they confirmed the emergence of a major new power broker in the country – the entrepreneurial administrator, driving and manipulating events as much for private profit as public service. Originating in the late Elizabethan exchequer and the offices of the escheator and surveyor, and subsequently in the Court of Wards and Liveries, officials such Richard Boyle, John Bingley, Francis Blundell, William and Lawrence Parsons, Francis Annesley and Francis Edgeworth turned their expertise in uncovering 'concealed lands' for the crown into the creation of large personal fortunes for themselves and their high-status patrons. By 1641 Boyle was reputedly the wealthiest subject of the crown anywhere in the Three Kingdoms; he was certainly the richest man in Ireland. He had accumulated lands in seventeen counties, concentrated particularly in Munster, and was also a major industrialist.[15] But the gains made by his fellow administrators should not be overlooked; for instance, Annesley's

---

15 T. Ranger, 'Richard Boyle and the Making of an Irish Fortune, 1588–1614', *Irish Historical Studies* 10 (1957), 257–97.

surviving estate papers record properties across eight counties, while between them the Parsons brothers acquired estates in all four provinces.[16]

Overcoming early scandals, even criminal convictions and imprisonment, these wealthy men also went on to pursue major political careers. Boyle flew the highest, was made earl of Cork, a privy councillor, and lord treasurer and lord justice (acting governor) of Ireland, but the others also rose far. Three of them joined Boyle on the Irish Privy Council (Annesley, Blundell and William Parsons); two of them served both as government secretary and vice-treasurer (Annesley and Blundell); and one of them also served as lord justice (William Parsons). The point is, by taking control of the discovery of Irish land they took control of the government of the kingdom. Merging with the military servitors whose influence had also grown under Viceroys Chichester and Oliver St John, these administrator-servitors helped ensure that the Irish government was conducted primarily in the interests of colonial newcomers like themselves.[17]

The fate of the proposed settlement of Connacht in 1615 demonstrates how deeply embedded their power became. The king had appointed commissioners to implement surrender and regrant agreements with all the landowners of the western province, to regularise their position under English law and pardon past transgressions in matters of lost royal rights and revenues. This did not sit well with the servitors and their business associates. If everything in Connacht was regularised the potential for profiting from its landowners' legal and tenurial problems – for land-grabbing – would be greatly reduced. And so it was that procedures slowed down, documents went missing, new titles were not validated, patents remained un-enrolled. By 1621 nothing had changed and King James lost interest. The land question in Connacht would re-surface with a vengeance under Charles I.

The 'Old English', Religion, and the Failure of Compromise

The trouble in Connacht was all the more significant because it affected the other major element of the population, the Anglo-Irish lineages, as much as it did the Gaelic Irish. Descendants of medieval English colonists, the Anglo-Irish had adopted many native practices over the centuries, inter-marrying with

---

16 Francis Annesley, Baron Mountnorris (*c*.1585–1660), Sir Lawrence Parsons (d.1628), and Sir William Parsons (*c*.1570–1650): see entries in J. I. Maguire and J. Quinn (eds.), *Dictionary of Irish Biography* (9 vols., Cambridge University Press, 2009). For Annesley's estates, see Valentia Collection, MS E6/1,7, Oxfordshire History Centre.
17 V. Treadwell, *Buckingham and Ireland, 1616–1628: A Study in Anglo-Irish Relations* (Dublin: FCP, 1998).

Gaelic neighbours, forming alliances with them, speaking Gaelic, borrowing from brehon law and so on. Though this process of Gaelicisation was most pronounced in Connacht and along the western seaboard, the large Anglo-Irish population of the eastern and southern seaboards had often behaved similarly, while also maintaining strong ties with England. The hybridity that this engendered was a natural outcome of their situation, but since the revival of direct English rule under the Tudors and now the Stuarts it became a political problem. English policy-makers continuously railed against the Anglo-Irish as 'degenerate', accusing them of becoming as wild and rebellious as the Gaels, and of betraying superior English modes of civility. These modes included landholding practices. In places as far apart as the Dingle peninsula, County Kerry, the boggy hinterland of Athlone, County Westmeath or in the pastoral borderlands of south County Dublin, Anglo-Irish families possessed lands that they had acquired over the years from Gaelic families by purchase or other means. This risked being forfeited if surrender and regrant proved undeliverable and if the Commission for Defective Titles continued facilitating administrator-led land-grabbing.

Following James's succession the leaders of the Anglo-Irish had endeavoured, as before, to persuade the monarch and his ministers at Whitehall of their loyalty, and to emphasise their historical role as defenders of English power and influence in Ireland. Whether in petitions to his majesty or in major literary compositions such as the Latin epic *Ormonius* (published in London in 1615), Anglo-Irish representatives reiterated how their forebears had first conquered the country in the twelfth century and, more recently, how they themselves had played a major role in suppressing the rebellions against English royal dominion during the late sixteenth century. Their taxes, food and labour supplies had sustained the English army. Their towns and castles had withstood repeated rebel attacks. Until he went blind, their premier nobleman, Thomas Butler, tenth earl of Ormond, had been the crown's greatest soldier, and at the battle of Kinsale Richard Burke, later fourth earl of Clanricard, and Christopher St Lawrence, later ninth Baron Howth, had performed bravely against Tyrone. To underline their anglophile and loyalist credentials they began referring to themselves as 'Old English'. They insisted that whatever the 'New English' might say to the contrary, English power in Ireland was safe in their hands. They deserved a share in the governance of the country.[18]

18 A. Ford, ' "Force and fear of punishment": Protestants and Religious Coercion in Ireland, 1603–33', in E. Boran and C. Gribben (eds.), *Enforcing Reformation in Ireland and Scotland, 1550–1700* (Aldershot: Routledge, 2006), 91–130; J. McCavitt, *Sir Arthur Chichester, Lord*

Their arguments failed. Apart from the awkward fact that several Tudor-era rebellions had had Anglo-Irish leaders, King James and his ministers could not ignore the open Catholicism of the 'Old English'. In spring 1603 the news of James's succession had been greeted by huge popular demonstrations of Catholic defiance of Protestant rule in the southern Old English towns and cities of Kilkenny, Waterford, Clonmel, Cork and Limerick. Protestant clergy had been attacked (and, in Cork, killed); churches had been re-consecrated and masses held; bibles had been burned. As early as the 1604 Hampton Court conference the king had doubted Old English pledges of devotion, accusing them of having reduced him to 'but half a King, being Lord over their bodies, but their souls seduced by Popery'.[19] They had disregarded the warning, apparently mindless of James's need to reassure Protestants in England of his steadfastness in the cause of true religion. A proclamation banishing Jesuits and seminary-trained clergy as fomenters of discord went unheeded; the outlawed churchmen were offered sanctuary by leading Old English families, who hid them from the authorities and retained them as private chaplains.

Consequently, even before the Gunpowder Plot signalled the real danger posed to the state in England by Catholic extremists, James had been persuaded to take steps against Catholic leaders in Ireland. Their obvious wealth attracted government attention. The 'Mandates' policy of 1605–1607 was targeted largely at the richest citizens of Dublin and other towns, insisting on the attendance of aldermanic families at Protestant service on pain of punishment under the royal prerogative; unprecedentedly large fines were subsequently realised in the Court of Castle Chamber. Tellingly, instead of expressing disappointment at the aldermen's refusal to conform, or being concerned by the protest their treatment sparked among the lords and gentry of the wider Pale community, some senior administrators saw it as an opportunity for the state to expand future revenues by taxing 'popery'. For their own part, sections of the Old English leadership reckoned that eventually the king would relent and that a form of toleration might be negotiated, albeit in pounds, shillings and pence.

Deputy of Ireland, 1605–16 (Belfast: Institute of Irish Studies, 1998), chapters 7 and 10; C. Lennon, *The Lords of Dublin in the Age of Reformation* (Dublin: Irish Academic Press, 1989), chapter 6; M. P. Curtis, 'Provincial Government and Administration in Jacobean Munster', unpublished PhD thesis, 2 vols., University College Cork (2006) 68–84; D. Edwards, *The Ormond Lordship in County Kilkenny, 1515–1642: The Rise and Fall of Butler Feudal Power* (Dublin: FCP, 2003), chapter 5; N. J. Byrne, 'Jacobean Waterford: Religion and Politics, 1603–25', unpublished PhD thesis, University College Cork (2002).
19 W. Barlow, *The Summe and Substance of the Conference … at Hampton Court* (London, 1604), 95–6.

However, it was not until the last days of James's reign, in 1623–1624, that such negotiations could begin; even then it was only after the accession of his son Charles I in 1625 that progress was actually made. In the (many) intervening years the Dublin government, dominated by the New English servitor interest, was encouraged to penalise the Old English for their Catholicism. Possessing as they did considerable formal power in the regions, it was decided to loosen their grip by imposing Protestant officers in positions of local authority. Munster was a focal point. The recusancy disturbances of 1603 had been bitterest there, and it was felt that, if left unchecked, the sheer strength of Catholicism in the south might affect the recovery of the English plantation. Beginning in 1604 and continuing until 1620 those appointed sheriff of County Cork were all English Protestants; either they were army officers and adherents of the lord president, or known affiliates of Richard Boyle, earl of Cork, rapidly emerging as the province's greatest planter. A similar trend obtained in Counties Limerick and Kerry, where the lower number of available English Protestants was offset by reliance on a tiny group of native Protestants. Only Tipperary avoided the imposition of Protestant sheriffs, the county being a liberty jurisdiction under the earl of Ormond, but on the liberty's abolition in 1621, an English Protestant was immediately appointed (an army captain, bearing a martial law commission). All across local government the appointment of Protestants was facilitated by the requirement that office-holders swear an oath accepting James Stuart as king and denying the Pope's authority to depose him, something, of course, that no Catholic in conscience could do.

With Protestant sheriffs it became possible for the crown to take close charge of proceedings in the county courts, and in particular to police the conduct of juries. During Elizabeth's reign English commentators had often observed the difficulty of securing convictions of suspects due to the bias of jurors selected by the sheriffs, which they attributed to a mixture of local clannishness and mulish Catholicism. A determined effort was made to stamp it out. Surviving Castle Chamber documents record several high-profile cases of entire juries arrested for failing to convict indicted recusants or traitors that had been brought before the courts in Counties Dublin, Cork, Meath, Westmeath, Carlow and Tipperary, all Old English strongholds.[20] That the prosecution of juries occurred mainly during 1610–1613 should lay to rest the mistaken assumption that 'Mandates' and other anti-Catholic measures had

---

20 J. Crawford, *A Star Chamber Court in Ireland: The Court of Castle Chamber, 1571–1641* (Dublin: FCP, 2005), 480–1, 499–500, 501–2, 509–10, 510–11, 514–16.

somehow petered out in 1607 because of the Flight of the Earls. The policy had quickly re-emerged once the emergency passed and the Ulster Plantation was under way. Indeed, it had progressed right up to the opening of King James's long-delayed Irish parliament, in May 1613. Among other things, on the eve of elections, and in line with the king's express instructions 'for the suppression of papistry', Conor O'Devany, Catholic bishop of Down and Connor had been tried and publicly executed in Dublin on trumped-up charges of treason; a Protestant sheriff had ordered the destruction of Catholic religious images throughout County Kilkenny; and, conscious that senior Catholic churchmen were arriving from Europe to organise the population, the government had begun compiling detailed lists of the whereabouts of popish clergy to facilitate search-and-arrest operations.

The parliament revealed the lengths to which the crown was prepared to go to challenge Catholic power in Ireland. Determined to prevent the Old English demonstrating their customary hold over the bulk of the country's constituencies, Chichester authorised the creation of dozens of new parliamentary seats, to be filled with government nominees. In Ulster, despite the slow arrival of Protestant settlers, no fewer than thirty-six MPs were declared 'elected' from eighteen new boroughs. The Munster plantation returned sixteen pro-government MPs, and Connacht and Leinster both eight, giving the administration a working majority of thirty-two in the House of Commons. Despite legal challenges that reduced this figure, the damage was done. The majority Catholic population would never again securely control the Irish parliament, until modern times. The 'Protestant Ascendancy' was born.

The closing of the parliament in 1615 marked the end of the Chichester viceroyalty, the longest-running administration in over a century and by any measure the most momentous. Any hope among Irish Catholics that his departure would bring relief were soon dashed by his replacement, Sir Oliver St John (1616–1622), another soldier-governor committed to Protestantisation, expropriation, and military and legal repression. A version of 'Mandates' quickly re-emerged: more priests were hunted, more juries imprisoned; and the loyal city of Waterford had its charter forfeited when its civic leaders refused to disavow the Pope; other southern towns were forced to accept Protestant magistrates or suffer a similar fate. In 1618, with St John's collusion, the new earl of Ormond, Walter 'of the beads and rosary', saw the greater part of his vast Butler estate awarded to a Scottish courtier when the king intervened in an inheritance dispute, to 'arbitrate'. That Earl Walter had once been badly wounded fighting against rebels was disregarded. His role as a ringleader of the Catholic opposition in the Commons in 1613 was more pertinent; he and his admirers had to be taught a lesson. The king's arbitration set aside an entail dating back to Henry VIII, but when the earl protested he was imprisoned in London, where he remained for eight years. His lawyers were also imprisoned.

Relaxation, when finally it came, was the result of external factors. The better to attain a bride for Prince Charles in marriage negotiations held successively with Catholic Spain and France, King James was forced to recalibrate anti-Catholic policies in each of his three kingdoms. When these negotiations failed, and led to war, the government in Ireland had suddenly an even greater need of appeasing Catholic leaders, in order to raise adequate tax revenues to contribute to the war effort. It will be recalled that during the first decade of James's reign the Irish state had been funded by large monetary subventions from England. Since 1615 the scale of the subventions had dropped sharply as Ireland at length became self-financing (Figure 1). To meet the costs of war the government would need to tread carefully with the Old English; their wealth held the key to raising the huge amounts required.

Hence the 'Graces' of May 1628, which were the result of two years of talks between local community representatives and agents of Charles I. These offered a number of concessions long sought by Catholics, in return for war-subsidies amounting to a staggering £120,000 (sterling). What was conceded by the crown tells us much about the range of grievances that many Irish subjects felt after twenty-five years of Stuart rule. Predictably, several clauses addressed the antics of the army, imposing stricter controls on the troops and their officers; likewise, the growing numbers of provosts marshal, and their exercise of martial law, which was to be curbed. A revised oath of allegiance was to be introduced, the new wording of which would enable Catholics to serve as lawyers, and become office-holders again. Most importantly, however, the chronic uncertainty over land titles was addressed in detail. Several clauses sought to limit the capacity of administrators searching for 'concealments'; future investigations into old land tenures were 'not to extend above threescore years'; and in Connacht the abandoned patents of 1621 securing the natives' rights were to be enrolled and passed.[21]

Things, it seemed, augured well, and King Charles undertook to summon a fresh parliament in 1629 to pass the Graces into law. But, in the event, the wars ended and no parliament was held. Only a fraction of the Graces were ever put into effect (the lesser ones, involving technical

---

21 A. Clarke, *The Old English in Ireland, 1625–42* (London: Macgibbon and Kee, 1966), chapters 2–3, and appendix ii.

matters of administration), leaving Ireland's Catholics more insecure than before. As if designed to antagonise them further, the reins of government then passed temporarily to the earl of Cork and Adam, Viscount Loftus, men whose very careers exemplified the power and wealth that had accrued to the New English servitor interest through decades of land expropriation and religious and ethnic oppression. The prospect of compromise retreated.

Collapse

In 1633 the new viceroy, Sir Thomas Wentworth, later earl of Strafford, arrived in Dublin. He has continued to attract the admiration of many historians. Clever, energetic, supremely self-confident, Wentworth presented himself to his peers – and in his political papers to posterity – as a 'strong man' uniquely suited to the task of modernising the Irish state and freeing Charles I from the shackles of the various interest groups that strove to control parts of it for themselves. Certainly he made an impact. Identifying the New English servitors as the main obstacle to greater royal (and viceregal) authority, and disliking also the growing strength of the Scottish settlers in Ulster, he set about breaking the power of both. That he intended pursuing this goal without any favour to the Old English or Gaelic Catholics might ultimately have helped him succeed in forging the new era in Irish political life that he claimed he sought, in which service to an absolute monarchy would be exalted above all else – except that, by alienating all groups at once, he risked over-reaching himself while smashing apart the *status quo* on which government power actually rested. His policies proved perilously divisive. By alienating the New English servitors he prompted the earl of Cork to commence plotting against him in England; Cork's subsequent elevation to a seat on the English Privy Council should have persuaded him to change course. And by once more deceiving the Old English, extracting still further subsidies from them on another false promise of passing the Graces, he revealed himself to be every bit as unscrupulous as his predecessors. Maybe if the monarch he served had supported him more steadfastly when things went awry, Wentworth might eventually have prevailed, but Charles I was not so inclined: 'glacial, prudish, withdrawn, and shifty', the king was an unreliable friend, 'a runt', according to one estimate.[22] Accordingly, when the opportunity came knocking in 1640 to drive Wentworth from office the Old

22 J. Morrill, *Stuart Britain: A Very Short Introduction* (Oxford University Press, 2000), 31.

English Catholics soon found common ground with their former enemies the Protestant servitors.[23]

The chance to topple Wentworth owed its origins, of course, to the outbreak in 1639 of the Bishops' Wars between England and Scotland and the wider 'British' political crisis that this prompted. Wentworth's failure to defeat the rebellious Scots left him exposed to the machinations of his many enemies across the three kingdoms. While his subsequent impeachment and execution in England in 1641 created the conditions for the outbreak of a major Catholic rebellion in Ireland the following October, it is important to realise that the rebellion, when it came, did not arrive out of the blue.[24] The aura of unassailable government power that Wentworth projected was a brilliant contrivance, little else. A more realistic measure of prevailing conditions is that in 1639 he was forced to admit he was struggling to control the provinces with an army of more than 4,000 men, twice the force usually available to his Jacobean predecessors. He also conceded that trouble had been brewing for years, since before he assumed office.[25]

As far back as the beginning of the Ulster Plantation the history of early Stuart Ireland had been punctuated by a series of localised rebellions affecting many areas and necessitating the government's frequent recourse to emergency measures. In fact rebellions are recorded for at least twenty-three of the thirty-one years between 1610 and 1641. The years that appear to have been rebellion-free were 1612–1613, 1621–1623, 1630, 1633 and 1640. The picture that emerges from this chronological information suggests a markedly different narrative of the period than has often prevailed. The gaps between the rebellions were generally short, showing that native unrest was almost continuous. Considering the scale and aggression of the changes that were driven through by the government, dismantling the power of the Gaelic and Gaelicised lordships, and forfeiting millions of acres, this is not surprising. Inspection of the geographical spread of the rebellions leads to some important observations. All four provinces experienced rebellions, not just Ulster; the whole of Munster saw rebel actions, half of Connacht, and half of Leinster. Every

---

23 H. F. Kearney, *Strafford in Ireland: A Study in Absolutism, 1633–1641* (Manchester University Press, 1959); T. Ranger, 'Strafford in Ireland: A Re-evaluation', in T. Aston (ed.), *Crisis in Europe, 1560–1660* (London: Routledge and Kegan Paul, 1967), 271–93; J. P. Cooper, 'Strafford and the Byrnes' Country', *Irish Historical Studies* 15 (1966), 1–20; J. F. Merritt, 'The Historical Reputation of Thomas Wentworth', in J. F. Merritt (ed.), *The Political World of Thomas Wentworth, Earl of Strafford, 1621–1641* (Cambridge University Press, 1996), 1–23.

24 Perceval-Maxwell, *Outbreak of the Irish Rebellion.*

25 Historical Manuscripts Commission, *Report on the Manuscripts of Earl Cowper* (3 vols., London 1888–9), ii, 229–30.

coastal county was affected except Counties Dublin, Louth and Clare. While many of the rebellions were highly localised, with reports confining them to particular counties or districts, several were large-scale affairs and are best described as regional rebellions. Thus the years 1616–1619 saw widespread violence across the whole of central Ulster, while there was prolonged unrest in north-west Connacht during 1626–1629.[26] The regional rebellions all seem to have stemmed from areas affected by plantation. Government reports indicate that typically they involved lesser Gaelic or Anglo-Irish figures: the smaller fry, encountered earlier, who, having lost all they owned by government order, had taken to the woodlands, mountains and bogs to become outlaws and seek revenge.

Had these larger disturbances affected just one region at a time, the instability they fostered could have been managed by the government, but it seems that on several occasions rebellions spreading across one region coincided with rebellions spreading across another. Thus the Ulster troubles of 1616–1619 coincided with a serious outbreak in Wexford, Wicklow and Carlow in 1618–1619, and the Connacht unrest of the late 1620s was accompanied by rebellions in central Ulster, and also the midlands. All of which leads to perhaps the most interesting observation of all: the fact that multi-region rebellions appear to have grown in intensity heading into the 1630s, and that central Ulster was building up to a major outbreak, from 1627 to 1629 through 1634 to 1635, to 1638 to 1639. Viewed in this light the great Ulster rebellion of October 1641 (which of course went on to link with rebellions elsewhere in the country) was just the latest in an evolving series of rebellions provoked by the transformative policies of the early Stuarts.

---

26 D. Edwards, 'Out of the Blue? Provincial Unrest in Ireland before 1641', in M. Ó Siochrú and J. Ohlmeyer (eds.), *Ireland 1641: Contexts and Reactions* (Manchester University Press, 2013), 95–114.

Politics, 1641–1660

JOHN CUNNINGHAM

The fractured political landscape that resulted from the disaggregation of Irish society in 1641 cannot be adequately surveyed as a whole from any single viewing point. It is necessary to pursue instead a blend of differing perspectives, while grappling also with the increased multi-centring of *élite* politics that resulted from the outbreak of war across the three Stuart kingdoms. The recent and remarkable flourishing of scholarship on the history of Ireland in the mid-seventeenth century has gone some way towards meeting these considerable historiographical challenges, while the enhanced accessibility of key sources via digitisation seems set to underpin further worthwhile endeavour. The task of this chapter is necessarily more modest: to provide a coherent account of the key content and contexts of Irish politics between the 1641 rebellion and the Restoration.

Rebellion and Reaction

By 1641, recent political and military developments in the three Stuart kingdoms had served both to weaken the authority of the crown and to create a rich breeding ground for plotting and intrigue. Ireland's Catholic *élite* faced the challenges of exploiting the king's weakness so as to extract concessions, while also helping him to recover sufficient strength to make good on his promises. The first of these challenges could be pursued with some confidence via existing political means, but the second one presented enormous difficulties. In this context, the example of successful military action offered by the Scottish Covenanters after 1638 proved alluring to some. The plot that led eventually to rebellion can be traced to February 1641, when Rory O'More met Lord Maguire in Dublin and sought to persuade him that the Anglo-Scottish conflict had created a suitable opening for armed resistance in Ireland. Other leading men of the Ulster Irish became involved thereafter, and contact was maintained with Irish forces on the continent. O'More, his fellow MP Sir Phelim O'Neill and other future rebel leaders had lived through a period of rapid social and economic change and O'Neill himself was heavily in debt by 1641. They also feared the prospect of religious repression at the same time that a revitalised Irish Catholic church harboured ambitions for something more than mere and uncertain toleration.[1]

In October 1641 the failure of the Ulster-led plot to capture Dublin Castle gave rise to a complex and unplanned scenario. Unrest spread quickly across the country and Protestants were robbed and driven from their homes. As the social order crumbled, the rebels committed many murders and some large-scale massacres, such as at Portadown. Catholics likewise came under attack, both from state forces operating around Dublin and from those Protestants who were able to regroup and to mobilise themselves in Ulster and elsewhere. The rebels had intended to overthrow the government and to secure a strong position from which to negotiate with the king, while blocking any intervention by the English parliament or from Scotland. They hoped too that other Catholic *élites* across the island would lend their support in the aftermath of a successful coup. Instead the survival of the government allowed it to remain the crucial arbiter of political initiative in the short term. Led by Sir William Parsons and Sir John Borlase, it was well positioned to shape external perceptions of the rebellion and to obstruct various Catholic attempts to establish contact with the king. In the opening weeks of the conflict, Sir Phelim O'Neill in Tyrone and rebel groups in several other counties drew up sets of objectives and grievances, encompassing issues such as Catholic religious freedom, the protection of their estates and defence of the king's prerogative.[2] The rebels' capture of a large swathe of south Ulster and north Leinster did not, however, provide a sufficient basis for them either to cow the Dublin government into submission or to extract meaningful concessions from Charles I.

In the capital cities of the three Stuart kingdoms, the immediate focus was on organising an appropriate military response. With the king present in Edinburgh, the Scottish parliament professed itself willing to send forces to Ireland, but only in cooperation with the English parliament. The latter body showed little hesitation about assuming novel authority over Irish matters. Significantly, it also shared the Scottish assumption that military assistance was to be traded for possession of Irish land. The displaced Irish Protestants

---

1 M. Perceval-Maxwell, *The Outbreak of the Irish Rebellion of 1641* (Montreal and Kingston: McGill-Queen's University Press, 1994), 192–212.
2 Perceval-Maxwell, *Outbreak of the Irish Rebellion*, 213–84; N. Canny, *Making Ireland British, 1580–1650* (Oxford University Press, 2001), 461–550.

who flocked to London no doubt helped to foster an emphasis on revenge and on the prize of confiscated Catholic estates. Yet deep political divisions and uncertainties in Britain would ultimately help to retard the military response to rebellion in Ireland. The king's enemies refused to entrust him with control of newly raised forces, but the English parliament's authority in this matter was also open to question. The inevitable issue of finance also presented difficulties.[3]

Back in Ireland, fears and expectations of rapid and substantial military intervention from Britain exercised a key influence on political developments amidst widespread mistrust on all sides. The Dublin government's already strained relationship with the traditionally loyal Old English Catholics of the Pale was further undermined by its reluctance either to furnish them with arms against the Ulster rebels or to allow them to pursue a political solution to the crisis via the Irish parliament. Baulking at local Catholic offers of mediation and assistance, it prorogued the parliament on 17 November and instead looked hopefully across the Irish Sea. Cut off from the king and unwanted in Dublin, many influential Catholics now began to consider an accommodation with the advancing northern rebels. At a series of meetings in County Meath, Rory O'More took the lead in rehearsing rebel grievances and in asserting their continued loyalty to the king. By 7 December the lords of the Pale had decided to make common cause with the rebel movement.[4] At the same time, Catholics in many parts of the country were organising themselves at the county level to control and defend their regions. These developments provided a basis for the subsequent establishment of wider coordinated Catholic political structures.

The Catholic Confederation

In the first half of 1642, the impetus for such national structures came from several directions. From Connacht, Ulick Bourke, earl of Clanricard, dispatched an envoy, his chaplain Oliver Burke, to consult with the Palesmen. While Clanricard was anxious to quell the growing violence and to engineer a settlement between the Catholics and the king, the proposals carried by his chaplain included a plan for a provisional civil government in rebel-controlled areas. Shortly thereafter, in March 1642, a meeting of senior churchmen at

---

3 Perceval-Maxwell, *Outbreak of the Irish Rebellion*, 261–84.
4 Perceval-Maxwell, *Outbreak of the Irish Rebellion*, 240–60; A. Clarke, *The Old English in Ireland, 1625–1642* (London: Macgibbon and Kee, 1966), 171–92.

Kells, County Meath, declared the Catholic effort to be a just war and pronounced the excommunication of Catholics who declined to support it. The meeting also called for the establishment of a central authority. Further consultations took place in Kilkenny in May and June, where a group of clergy and laity endorsed an oath of association intended to bind Ireland's Catholics together in defence of 'God, king and country'. A provisional executive council was also set up, and preparations were made towards elections for a representative assembly.[5] The 'Confederate Catholics' were to govern much of the kingdom until 1649, while also conducting peace negotiations and maintaining a diplomatic presence at various European courts.

The Catholics made significant progress in relation to political structures by the summer of 1642, but other developments severely curtailed their grounds for optimism. Early in the year their professions of loyalty to the Stuart monarchy had been met with a proclamation in which the king called on the Catholics to surrender. By April the arrival of substantial military detachments from Scotland and England also threatened to overwhelm the various Catholic forces. The ruthless character of the conflict in its early stages, encompassing massacres of Protestant settlers and vicious reprisals by government forces, reduced the possibility of any speedy political compromise.[6] In London the proliferation of pamphlets that exaggerated the scale of Irish atrocities and linked them to alleged plots to root out Protestantism served to harden attitudes even further.[7] Such literature helped to inform the political context in which the Adventurers' Act was passed by the English parliament in March 1642. This legislation offered 2,500,000 acres of Irish Catholic land for sale to investors, with the resulting monies being earmarked to finance the suppression of the rebellion. The Adventurers' Act was a telling statement of intent, as the English parliament intruded further into Irish affairs and committed itself firmly to an aggressive policy of mass confiscation.[8]

The arrival of Dr Henry Jones in London around this time seemed likely to reinforce this legislative initiative. He carried the damning evidence of depositions recently collected from Protestant refugees by a team of commissioners in Dublin.[9] Despite the high hopes entertained by Jones and other Irish

---

5 M. Ó Siochrú, *Confederate Ireland, 1642–1649: a Political and Constitutional Analysis* (Dublin: Four Courts Press [hereafter FCP] 1999), 27–42.
6 Ó Siochrú, *Confederate Ireland* 27–9.
7 Perceval-Maxwell, *Outbreak of the Irish Rebellion*, 269–74; E. Darcy, *The Irish Rebellion of 1641 and the Wars of the Three Kingdoms* (Woodbridge: Boydell Press, 2013), 77–101.
8 K. Bottigheimer, *English Money and Irish Land: the 'Adventurers' in the Cromwellian Settlement of Ireland*, (Oxford: Clarendon Press, 1971), 30–114.
9 A. Clarke, 'The Commission for the Despoiled Subject, 1641–7', in Brian Mac Cuarta (ed.), *Reshaping Ireland, 1550–1700* (Dublin: FCP, 2011), 241–60; H. Jones, *A Remonstrance of*

Protestants, the outbreak of civil war in England from August 1642 meant that the resources intended for Ireland were instead diverted towards domestic conflict. For the Confederate Catholics, the king's decision to raise his standard against the English parliament lent greater credibility to their claims to be acting in defence of the royal prerogative. While the return home of Irish *émigrés* in the summer of 1642 boosted the Catholics' military capabilities, the first meeting of the Confederate general assembly in Kilkenny in October presented a key opportunity to progress their political agenda. With representation from all four provinces, the Confederates devised structures that Micheál Ó Siochrú has described as 'a fascinating mixture of conservatism and innovation'.[10] This 'model of government' included a supreme council, which combined executive, judicial and administrative functions. This body was also to be accountable to the legislative general assembly. The intended roles of provincial and county councils were also set out. Among the key objectives formulated at Kilkenny was the restoration of the privileges enjoyed by the Catholic Church before the Henrician Reformation. This issue would loom large in subsequent negotiations with Charles I, to whom the Confederates at Kilkenny reaffirmed their 'true allegiance'.[11] They would spend the following six years trying to negotiate a peace settlement that could surmount not only the tensions that existed around loyalty to church and crown, but also the conflicts that raged within and between various parties of clergy and laity.

Towards a Truce

As turmoil engulfed the three Stuart kingdoms, political division and factionalism were far from unique to Kilkenny. Key members of the Dublin administration quickly adopted differing positions on a range of issues, not least the terms on which a settlement should be reached in Ireland. From late 1642, efforts made by both the king and the English parliament to secure political and military support in Dublin caused further difficulties within the Irish council. Sir William Parsons and others who opposed any compromise with Irish Catholics tended towards sympathy with the English parliament, which was committed to a hard line against the Confederates.[12] The Royalist

---

Divers Remarkable Passages Concerning the Church and Kingdome of Ireland (London, 1642). The 1641 Depositions can be viewed at www.1641.tcd.ie.

10 Ó Siochrú, *Confederate Ireland*, 44–50.

11 Ó Siochrú, *Confederate Ireland*, 44–54.

12 R. Armstrong, *Protestant War: the 'British' of Ireland and the Wars of the Three Kingdoms* (Manchester University Press, 2005), 43–83.

position, personified in the Irish context by James Butler, earl of Ormond, was more pragmatic. As the three kingdoms continued in a state of flux throughout the mid-1640s, Ormond explored a range of political options, seeking an alliance that would best protect the interests both of Ireland's Protestants and of the crown. This complex process encompassed his negotiations with the Confederate Catholics. Ormond was closely related to many leading Confederates and his master was keen to strike a deal with the Catholics that would allow him to withdraw forces from Dublin to England. In January 1643 Charles authorised Ormond and Clanricard to meet with the Confederates and to hear their grievances. At this point, the king also set out his position on what were likely to be the key issues. While he showed some understanding of Catholic discontent at the English parliament presuming to legislate for Ireland, he was unwilling to make religious concessions or to make changes around Poynings' Law (1494), a statute that limited the independence of the Irish parliament. Charles was also determined to block any reversal of land transfers pre-dating 1625 and to retain his control over appointments to office in Ireland.[13] While the king's stance would prove unsatisfactory to many Confederates, a more conciliatory approach would have cost him much support both in Britain and among the Protestants of Ireland.

The confederates in turn set out their position in a remonstrance presented at Trim on 17 March 1643. In this document, they complained of the various legal disabilities under which Irish Catholics laboured and denounced the Adventurers' Act. In return for concessions from the king on Poyning's Law and other matters, they held out the prospect of substantial financial and military assistance. The Confederates also directed fierce criticism at the lords justice, and especially Parsons, accusing them of goading Catholics into rebellion.[14] Charles had already been preparing to remove Parsons from office and he issued the relevant order in early April. The Dublin government's ability to resist compromise was further curtailed a few months later when the king ordered that Parsons and three of his colleagues be removed from the Irish council altogether.[15] In the meantime, the collapse of English peace negotiations at Oxford had increased the king's need for support from Ireland. The Confederates' willingness to provide this support was further signalled in May 1643 when the general assembly appointed a delegation to negotiate a truce. Although a newly arrived papal envoy, Pier Francesco Scarampi, voiced

---

13 Ó Siochrú, *Confederate Ireland*, 61–2.
14 Ó Siochrú, *Confederate Ireland*, 62–3.
15 Armstrong, *Protestant War*, 83–5, 92–3.

objections, by 15 September a twelve-month armistice had been agreed. For the Confederates, this appeared to create the space needed for meaningful negotiations.[16]

For Ormond, the truce was a mixed blessing. While Charles promoted him to the office of lord lieutenant shortly afterwards, the English parliament threatened to impeach him as a traitor. In the short term, the truce created unrest among substantial sections of the Irish Protestant community, including Lord Inchiquin and his forces in Munster. Its political impact was also felt in London, where it reinforced the parliament's efforts to undermine the king by associating him with the Irish Catholic cause. Because the Irish truce created the prospect of strengthened Royalist armies in England, it encouraged the parliament to enter into an alliance with the Scots: the Solemn League and Covenant (1643). This pact included a commitment to the introduction of Presbyterian Church government across the three kingdoms. Subsequent efforts to persuade Protestants in Ireland to support the covenant tied its acceptance to the promise of increased material support from Westminster. These efforts proved most successful in the north, where the sizeable Scots and local Protestant forces were gradually detached from the Royalist cause.[17]

The Quest for Settlement

With sections of the Irish Protestant community agonising over the covenant, the Confederates turned their attention to negotiations with the king. In March 1644 a Confederate delegation reached the royal court at Oxford. It was led by Ormond's brother-in-law, Donough MacCarthy, Viscount Muskerry. They were followed shortly afterwards by a group of Dublin-based Protestants who were determined to block any settlement. As before, the Confederates offered military support to the king in exchange for a range of political, religious and legal concessions, including an act of oblivion for all offences committed since 1641. In response, the Irish Protestant agents sought reparation for their losses in the rebellion, the suppression of Catholicism and various other measures. The proceedings at Oxford highlighted some of the key obstacles that existed to a negotiated settlement, and led the king to refer the whole business back to Ormond in Ireland.[18]

---

16 Ó Siochrú, *Confederate Ireland*, pp 67–8.
17 Armstrong, *Protestant War*, 92–118.
18 Armstrong, *Protestant War*, 119–20; Ó Siochrú, *Confederate Ireland*, 70–3.

By the time that fresh negotiations got underway in the autumn, Ormond had lost the support of further sections of the Protestant community, most notably in Munster. His determination to avoid major concessions on religion and other vital matters helped to ensure that no breakthrough was achieved. Ormond was not helped by the lack of clear instructions from the king. This factor, along with his need to protect his narrowing Protestant support base placed Ormond in an extremely difficult position; Barry Robertson has suggested that his task 'probably bordered on the impossible'.[19] The differing expectations of the three main groupings within the Confederate movement, characterised by Ó Siochrú as the clerical, the moderate and the peace factions, were also set to have an increasingly disruptive effect on attempts at settlement.[20] By the spring of 1645, with no agreement in sight, the king was privately signalling his willingness to concede to Confederate demands. With his prospects in England looking increasingly bleak, he had also grown desperate enough to pursue avenues other than Ormond's peace talks.

Following defeat at the battle of Naseby in June 1645, the possibility of military assistance from Ireland appeared to offer Charles's best hope of continuing the fight. The potential value of such an intervention had recently been demonstrated on a smaller scale in Scotland by an Irish expeditionary force organised by Randall MacDonnell, earl of Antrim.[21] A few weeks after Naseby the Welsh Catholic Royalist Edward Somerset, earl of Glamorgan, arrived in Ireland. With the talks between Ormond and the Confederates floundering on the crucial issue of ecclesiastical property, Glamorgan moved to negotiate a separate and comprehensive religious settlement. Agreement was reached by the end of August; in return for an army of 10,000 men, Glamorgan conceded the public exercise of Catholicism and other key points. Controversy surrounded the question of whether or not Charles had authorised the earl to make such far-reaching concessions, and the extent to which Ormond was privy to Glamorgan's dealings remains unclear.[22] In any case, various issues not covered by Glamorgan's secret treaty remained as obstacles to the wider political settlement upon which depended the Confederates' speedy dispatch

19 B. Robertson, *Royalists at War in Scotland and Ireland, 1638–1650* (Farnham: Ashgate, 2014), 99–123; Armstrong, *Protestant War*, 121–3.

20 Ó Siochrú, *Confederate Ireland*, 73–5, 83–6.

21 J. Ohlmeyer, *Civil War and Restoration in the Three Stuart Kingdoms: The Political Career of Randal MacDonnell, Marquis of Antrim, 1608–1683* (Cambridge University Press, 1993), 129–51.

22 Ó Siochrú, *Confederate Ireland*, 87–8, 93–5; P. Corish, 'The Rising of 1641 and the Catholic Confederacy, 1641–5', in T. W. Moody, F. X. Martin and F. J. Byrne (eds.), *A New History of Ireland*, iii: *Early Modern Ireland, 1534–1691* (Oxford: Clarendon Press, 1976), 314–16; Armstrong, *Protestant War*, 139–42.

of military aid to the king. Another avenue pursued by the Royalists, via the exiled Queen Henrietta Maria and her Catholic courtier, Sir Kenelm Digby, was a direct treaty with Pope Innocent X. In Rome in November, Digby agreed to terms even more favourable than those granted by Glamorgan to the Irish Catholics.[23] By that point, however, a more meaningful papal intervention was already underway.

Rinuccini and the Ormond Peace

On 12 November 1645 Archbishop Giovanni Battista Rinuccini arrived in Kilkenny. As a papal nuncio, he became the most senior member of the *corps diplomatique* at the Confederate capital. Rinuccini is the best known and most controversial of the many diplomatic agents who moved between Ireland and the continent in the mid-seventeenth century. The Confederate representatives abroad, mostly clerics, sought official recognition and financial backing for their cause. Their main focus was on the major Catholic courts, where they could portray the Irish conflict as a religious war. Yet Ireland's established position as a minor dependent kingdom under the Stuart monarchy helped to ensure that France and Spain, mainly concerned with their own inter-rivalry, would refuse to engage fully with a Confederate movement whose legitimacy was very much open to question. While limited supplies and some agents were sent, these hesitant allies expected and received payback in the form of military manpower. The papacy was rather more enthusiastic about securing Ireland for Catholicism, but it could not offer the substantial financial or military supplies needed to bring this about.[24] Its main representative in Ireland, Rinuccini, would nonetheless exert a major influence on Confederate politics after 1645.

Tadhg Ó hAnnracháin has shown how Rinuccini's mission was intended as the culmination of the gradual process whereby a resident and pastorally active Catholic hierarchy was put in place in Ireland after 1618. This influential grouping had been educated on the continent, where they were imbued with the confidence of the Catholic Reformation. As a result, their objectives aligned with the main purpose of Rinuccini's mission: to establish the full and free practice of Catholicism in Ireland.[25] The nuncio's disruptive presence

---

23 Ó Siochrú, *Confederate Ireland*, 95–6, 99–100.

24 J. Ohlmeyer, 'Ireland Independent: Confederate Foreign Policy and International Relations during the mid-Seventeenth Century', in J. Ohlmeyer (ed.), *Ireland from Independence to Occupation, 1641–1660* (Cambridge University Press, 1995), 89–111.

25 T. Ó hAnnracháin, *Catholic Reformation in Ireland: the Mission of Rinuccini, 1645–1649* (Oxford University Press, 2002), 5–6, 39–81.

provided encouragement to those within the Confederate movement who had already begun to express their disquiet at the failure to extract firm religious concessions from Ormond. Rinuccini was thus able to exploit existing tensions in pursuit of his own ends. Before long he had extracted further concessions from Glamorgan, including the appointment of a Catholic lord lieutenant and the admittance of Catholic bishops into the Irish House of Lords.[26] The political fallout from the death of one of these bishops would soon disabuse Rinuccini of the notion that he had swiftly secured the future of Irish Catholicism.

In October 1645 Archbishop Malachy O'Queely of Tuam was killed in a skirmish near Sligo. His copy of the secret terms agreed in August between Glamorgan and the Confederates was duly discovered and swiftly dispatched to London, where it provided rich pickings for the parliament's propagandists.[27] By Christmas Ormond had become aware of the resulting publication. Realising its potential implications both for himself and the wider Royalist cause, he had Glamorgan arrested in Dublin and charged with treason. Under Rinuccini's influence, the Confederate supreme council reacted by demanding Glamorgan's release and by summoning a general assembly. When it convened early in February 1646, Rinuccini led the opposition to a final agreement with Ormond. Although Glamorgan had been released by this stage, the nuncio insisted that his earlier arrest had destroyed the credibility of his treaty with the Confederates. He instead persuaded his audience to await full confirmation of the generous terms agreed between the Pope and Sir Kenelm Digby, of which only a coded copy had reached Kilkenny. On this issue, the Confederate leadership agreed to wait until 1 May, while pressing ahead at the same time in the long-running negotiations with Ormond.[28]

The peace treaty that was eventually signed in secret at Dublin on 28 March was the result of a torturous process that had been stretched out over three years. Its terms included promise of a general pardon for all actions since 1641, confirmation that the plantation schemes pursued by Strafford in the 1630s would be abandoned, and abolition of the court of wards. Catholics were, moreover, to be allowed to occupy public office upon taking an oath of allegiance, as opposed to the Oath of Supremacy. Rather than providing a basis for settlement, however, the treaty would ultimately cause ructions within

---

26 Ó hAnnracháin, *Catholic Reformation*, 123–6; Ó Siochrú, *Confederate Ireland*, 83–5, 96–8.
27 *The Irish Cabinet, or, His Majesties Secret Papers, for Establishing the Papall Clergy in Ireland, with other Matters of High Concernment, taken in the Carriages of the Archbishop of Tuam, who was Slain in the Late Fight at Sliggo in that Kingdom* (London, 1645).
28 Ó Siochrú, *Confederate Ireland*, 98–101; Ó hAnnracháin, *Catholic Reformation*, 129–30.

the Confederate movement. A key point of disagreement, subsequently, was the extent to which the text of the treaty agreed in March differed from what had been discussed by the general assembly in the previous month. The further deterioration of the king's position around this time also shaped the political context in which the peace treaty was signed and disseminated. Before agreement was reached in Dublin, Charles had already publicly disowned Glamorgan and his religious treaty with the Confederates. Any remaining hope that Charles would instead endorse Digby's treaty with the Pope was dashed when the king surrendered himself to the Scots in April 1646. These developments meant that the vague promise in the Ormond peace treaty of 'further concessions' on religion appeared to carry little or no weight.[29]

The Confederate leadership, anxious for reconciliation with Ormond and the Royalists, now faced a major dilemma. Although Glamorgan had been discredited, the publication of the Ormond peace treaty unaccompanied by the Welsh earl's religious concessions was likely to alienate the clerical party and split the Confederate movement. Ormond was, however, opposed to the publication of Glamorgan's terms, while Clanricard advised that such a move would do nothing to assist the king, who was by now firmly in the grip of the Presbyterian Scots. These issues dominated a meeting of Confederate leaders that took place in Limerick early in June 1646. It was here that a furious Rinuccini at last learned that the terms of the Ormond peace treaty had already been finalised back in March. Pointing to the collapse of the king's cause in England, and emboldened by Owen Roe O'Neill's victory over a Scots army at Benburb, the nuncio now argued in favour of an outright Catholic conquest of Ireland. Having failed to win support for this stance, Rinuccini departed to attend a planned ecclesiastical congregation in Waterford. Meanwhile George Digby had arrived in Dublin, bringing word of the king's approval of the peace treaty that had been agreed with the Confederates in March.[30]

This news led Ormond to publish the peace treaty in Dublin on 30 July. The supreme council followed suit three days later and began its preparations to receive Ormond in Kilkenny. This caused the simmering tensions within the Confederate movement to erupt. Within days Rinuccini and the Catholic church leaders who were gathered at Waterford had rejected the peace. They proceeded to declare its acceptance a breach of the Confederate oath of association and threatened its main backers with excommunication. With support

29 Ó Siochrú, *Confederate Ireland*, 100–6, 109–11; Ó hAnnracháin, *Catholic Reformation*, 134–7.
30 Ó Siochrú, *Confederate Ireland*, 106–9; Ó hAnnracháin, *Catholic Reformation*, 136–8.

from the Catholic towns and key army commanders, Rinuccini and his allies quickly dismantled the peace treaty and, following a brief attempt at reconciliation, imprisoned some leading members of the peace faction. The nuncio was thereafter installed as president of a reconstituted supreme council, which was to rule in association with the ecclesiastical congregation. Determined to consolidate his political triumph, Rinuccini turned his thoughts to a military assault on the capital.[31] Having been forced by the unexpected turn of events to retreat in haste from Kilkenny to Dublin, Ormond had now to weigh other options, including surrender to the English parliament.

Protestant Alternatives

Ormond had invested considerable energy in the high-profile negotiations with the Confederates, but he had also proven willing to explore other means to secure his ends. The details of these complex initiatives have been reconstructed in the work of Robert Armstrong and others. For example, Armstrong has drawn attention to Ormond's efforts in the summer of 1645 to create 'a cross-religious third force' attractive to disillusioned sections of both the Confederate and Covenanter movements.[32] Kevin Forkan has stressed the significance of Ormond's secret dealings, via Humphrey Galbraith, with potential allies in Protestant Ulster in 1645–1646.[33] Ormond was clearly keen then to pursue alternatives that would enable him to avoid major concessions to, and dependence upon, the Confederate Catholics. An accommodation with the English parliament offered yet another possible means to avoid a treaty with the Confederates. Just as in Kilkenny, Ormond also had influential allies at Westminster. When English Parliamentarians became polarised into 'Presbyterian' and 'Independent' parties in the mid-1640s, most of Ormond's contacts gravitated to the former grouping. His good relations with influential Presbyterian politicians such as Denzil Holles helped to enable the prospect of an agreement to be explored in the second half of 1645. This endeavour was, however, extremely vulnerable to any change in the political landscape at Westminster.[34]

---

31 P. Corish, 'Ormond, Rinuccini and the Confederates, 1645–9', in Moody *et al.*, *A New History of Ireland*, iii, 320–1; Ó Siochrú, *Confederate Ireland*, 108–17.
32 Armstrong, *Protestant War*, 137–8.
33 K. Forkan, 'Ormond's Alternative: The Lord Lieutenant's Secret Contacts with Protestant Ulster, 1645–6', *Historical Research*, 81 (2008), 610–35.
34 P. Little, 'The Marquess of Ormond and the English Parliament, 1645–1647', in T. Barnard and J. Fenlon (eds.), *The Dukes of Ormonde, 1610–1745* (Woodbridge: Boydell Press, 2000), 83–99.

Such a change occurred in January 1646 when the English parliament appointed Philip Sidney, Viscount Lisle, as commander-in-chief of a projected Irish expeditionary force. Lisle was ultimately named as the parliament's lord lieutenant of Ireland for a twelve-month period, commencing in April 1646. He was closely identified with the anti-Scottish party at Westminster, the political Independents opposed to the policies of Ormond's Presbyterian friends. Lisle's appointment by parliament put him in direct competition with Ormond, whose authority was derived from the king. The Independents' determination to row back on the Solemn League and Covenant and to limit Scottish political influence in post-war England also coloured their approach to Ireland. The eventual result was a plan for a distinctly *English* reconquest of Ireland, led by Lisle.[35] The political momentum that developed behind this plan by the beginning of 1647 drew upon the enthusiasm and experience of a group labelled by Patrick Little as 'the Irish Independents'. With its roots in the pro-plantation Boyle circle of the pre-war period, its most notable member was Sir John Temple, one of those who had been dismissed from the Irish privy council along with Parsons in 1643.[36] Temple's opposition to any compromise with the Confederates was given full vent in his book *The Irish rebellion*, which was published in London in 1646. This influential work, which made extensive use of evidence from the 1641 Depositions, was designed to vindicate a harsh military solution to the Irish problem.[37] The middle ground from which Ormond sought to construct alliances with Confederates, Covenanters and others was to be rendered scorched earth.

Lisle eventually made his way to Munster in February 1647, where his political and religious outlook quickly alienated some powerful local interests. Before long Inchiquin, the parliament's lord president of Munster, began efforts to mobilise opposition to Lisle at Westminster. Lisle's fate was sealed shortly thereafter by a further shift in the balance of power within the English parliament. Amidst wider moves by the Presbyterians against both their Independent rivals and the increasingly powerful New Model Army, Lisle's Irish commission was allowed to lapse in April.[38] These alterations reopened the prospect of an agreement between the parliament and Ormond. At Kilkenny in February 1647 a new general assembly had reinforced the clergy's

35 J. Adamson, 'Strafford's Ghost: The British Context of Viscount Lisle's Lieutenancy of Ireland', in Ohlmeyer (ed.), *Ireland from Independence to Occupation*, 128–59.
36 P. Little, 'The "Irish Independents" and Viscount Lisle's Lieutenancy of Ireland', *Historical Journal*, 44 (2001), 941–61.
37 J. Temple, *The Irish Rebellion* (London, 1646).
38 Adamson, 'Strafford's Ghost', 144–54.

earlier rejection of the Ormond peace treaty, and fresh Confederate efforts at negotiation with Dublin made little headway.[39] Ormond was now increasingly inclined to surrender the capital to Parliamentarian forces, rather than pursue any further talks with the Confederates. The necessary treaty was signed on 19 June 1647, paving the way for Colonel Michael Jones to take command in Dublin.[40]

Royalism Revived

This development, and the series of disastrous military defeats suffered by the Confederates over the months following, set the scene for a tense meeting of the Confederate general assembly in November. Events in England also appeared to offer no respite, as the New Model Army had gained custody of the king and marched on London in August to secure its Independent allies in control of the parliament. By this point Rinuccini had stepped down from the supreme council and a number of the men overthrown by him in 1646 had returned to positions of influence.[41] Unsurprisingly, the Stuart monarchy remained central to Confederate political calculations. The public hangman at Kilkenny was duly ordered to burn a radical tract penned by a Lisbon-based Irish Jesuit, Conor O'Mahony, in which he advocated the election of a native king.[42] The Confederates instead weighed up the possibilities of negotiating with Queen Henrietta Maria and of seeking the protection of a foreign prince. After considerable wrangling, agents were appointed to travel to Paris, Madrid and Rome. The Confederates' main objective was to secure an agreement with the Stuart court in exile, which was to incorporate religious clauses approved by the Pope. The relevant agents eventually took ship on 10 February 1648.[43]

At the end of the previous year, Charles had signed an engagement with the Scots, with a view to building a new Royalist alliance. The king hoped to capitalise on divisions within and between the English parliament and its army, with Ormond once again designated to play a key role in Ireland. Ormond travelled to France in February 1648, where the Confederate envoys had arrived at the exiled Royalist court. Following advice from Ormond, Queen

---

39 Ó Siochrú, *Confederate Ireland*, 127–37.
40 Little, 'Ormond and the English Parliament', 93–7.
41 Ó Siochrú, *Confederate Ireland*, 151–61.
42 Corish, 'Ormond, Rinuccini and the Confederates', 324; Conor O'Mahony, *Disputatio Apologetica et Manifestativa de Iure Regni Hiberniae pro Catholicis Hibernicis contra Haereticos Anglos* (Lisbon, 1645).
43 Ohlmeyer, 'Ireland Independent', 105–6; Ó Siochrú, *Confederate Ireland*, 161–69.

Henrietta Maria determined that once again negotiations between the lord lieutenant and the Confederates offered the best way forward. The return to the Royalist fold of Inchiquin's Munster forces and the Scots in Ulster was also to be pursued. Back in Ireland, Ormond's envoy Colonel John Barry sought to engineer a truce between Inchiquin and Kilkenny. Rinuccini was opposed to this, in part because he feared that a truce would open the way for Ormond's return. After attempting to rally episcopal support, the nuncio fled from Kilkenny on foot of an alleged assassination plot against him.[44]

From this low point, the road to civil war among the Confederates was short. Having taken refuge with Owen Roe O'Neill in the midlands, Rinuccini learned of the truce with Inchiquin, signed on 20 May. He also received false intelligence that Thomas Preston's Leinster forces were on the march to attack O'Neill's camp. Determined to repeat the tactics that had proven effective in 1646, Rinuccini and some bishops pronounced the excommunication of all who supported the Inchiquin truce. This time, however, he met with opposition not only from the supreme council but also from a substantial part of the episcopate. The supreme council decided on an appeal to Rome and seized control of the Jesuit printing press in Kilkenny to prevent the easy circulation of the nuncio's decree of excommunication. Over the months following, the council continued to outmanoeuvre and progressively to isolate the nuncio, who had relocated to Galway. When a new general assembly met on 4 September 1648, Ormond's return was imminent and those who backed an agreement with him appeared to be in the ascendant at Kilkenny.[45] Unfortunately for them, the wider Royalist movement was again in turmoil after Oliver Cromwell's defeat of an invading Scottish army at Preston in August.

Despite the growing urgency for a settlement, the second Ormond peace treaty was not formally signed until 17 January 1649. Religious issues had again proved to be the main sticking point, in particular the question of ecclesiastical jurisdiction. News that Charles was to be put on trial for his life was one of the factors that helped to move matters towards a conclusion. But the executioner's axe ensured that the king would never have opportunity to accept, to reject or perhaps to fudge the terms that Ormond had agreed on his behalf. The Confederate government was promptly dissolved, with twelve commissioners of trust being appointed to manage Catholic-controlled areas. The Ulster Scots, horrified by the regicide, were also reconciled to the lord

---

44 Ó Siochrú, *Confederate Ireland*, 169–74.
45 Ó Siochrú, *Confederate Ireland*, 177–86; Ó hAnnracháin, *Catholic Reformation*, 201–6.

lieutenant, who now derived his authority from the new king, Charles II. Although O'Neill held back from joining this Royalist alliance, Rinuccini left Galway and sailed for home.[46]

The Politics of Conquest and Defeat

Having at last secured a peace treaty with the Catholics, Ormond was now determined to win full control of the kingdom. Unfortunately for him, Michael Jones in Dublin and a handful of other commanders remained loyal to the English parliament. To make matters worse, Antrim and other Catholics who opposed the peace had begun to explore the possibility of an alliance with the parliament. While the latter talks ultimately came to nothing, they encouraged the Irish involved to refrain from joining Ormond.[47] Meanwhile Oliver Cromwell was appointed in March 1649 to lead an expedition to Ireland. The leaders of the newly founded Commonwealth could point to a range of justifications for a conquest: the Royalist and Catholic threat from Ireland; revenge for 1641; the acquisition of Irish land to satisfy the adventurers; and the need for military success to boost the regime's popularity at home.[48] These motivations were underpinned by a wide domestic consensus on England's right to rule the neighbouring island, although there were some dissenting voices on this point.[49] In May, Sir William Parsons approached the council of state with a tract that he had penned to rehearse and to justify English dominion from earliest times to the present.[50] Against this background, Leveller-inspired unrest in the parliament's army was quickly crushed and Cromwell prepared to cross the Irish Sea.[51]

The massacres committed by Cromwell's troops at Drogheda and Wexford in the autumn of 1649 are among the most controversial episodes in Irish history. When the Catholic bishops gathered at Clonmacnoise towards the end of the year, they were able to point to those recent excesses as evidence that the English parliament was intent on 'the destruction of the lives of the inhabitants of this nation'.[52] From his winter quarters in Munster, Cromwell

---

46 Ó Siochrú, *Confederate Ireland*, 185–201.
47 Ohlmeyer, *Civil War and Restoration*, 217–9.
48 J. Wheeler, *Cromwell in Ireland* (Dublin: Gill and Macmillian, 1999), 64–7.
49 C. Durston, ' "Let Ireland be Quiet": Opposition in England to the Cromwellian Conquest of Ireland', *History Workshop*, 21 (1986), 105–12.
50 [William Parsons], 'Examen Hiberniae', MS 692, National Library of Ireland.
51 Wheeler, *Cromwell in Ireland*, 67–71.
52 *Certain Acts and Declarations made by the Ecclesiasticall Congregation of the Arch-Bishops, Bishops, and other Prelates: met at Clonmacnoise the Fourth Day of December 1649* (London, 1650), 3–6.

responded to the bishops by publishing a furious tirade against Catholicism, within which he included vague promises of favour to those who had not played prominent roles in the conflict. If his overtures made little impression on Ireland's Catholics, the same could not be said for the Protestants. Even before his arrival in Ireland, Cromwell had won over Lord Broghill, a figure of considerable influence in Munster. Late in 1649 Broghill helped to persuade Protestant garrisons in the south to defect from the faltering Royalist cause. By the end of April 1650 Cromwell had agreed terms with most of the remaining Protestant Royalist forces.[53] Under the pressure of war, Ormond's broad but fragile alliance had quickly fallen apart. Some respite was provided by O'Neill's belated decision to join forces with Ormond, but the general's death in November 1649 deprived his army of effective leadership. At Cromwell's departure from Ireland six months later, his army controlled a large swathe of territory. By contrast, Ormond had been reduced to threatening to leave the country unless the recalcitrant city authorities in Limerick and Galway agreed to admit Royalist garrisons.[54]

Faced with this bleak scenario, Charles II eschewed an expedition to Ireland and opted instead to travel to Scotland in June 1650, where he subscribed to the Covenant. By August the king had disowned the Ormond peace treaty, although he secretly informed Ormond that he had done so only out of political necessity. In any case the Catholic bishops, increasingly frustrated by successive military failures, had by this time run out of patience with the lord lieutenant. Recent meetings, including an assembly attended by Ormond at Loughrea in April, had failed to resolve Catholic grievances around issues such as military appointments and alleged financial corruption. At a gathering in Jamestown, County Leitrim, in August, the Catholic bishops agreed upon a public declaration outlining Ormond's alleged failure to uphold the 1649 peace treaty, his neglect of the Catholic interest and his ineffective management of the war effort. Having expressed their preference for a revival of Confederate power structures, the bishops urged Ormond to depart the kingdom. Ormond characteristically refused to bend to the will of the Catholic episcopate, but his position was becoming increasingly untenable. News of Cromwell's victory over the Scots at Dunbar on 3 September cast a further shadow over the Royalist cause. After a period of sustained bickering with the bishops, Ormond went into exile in December.[55]

53 J. Cunningham, *Conquest and Land in Ireland: The Transplantation to Connacht, 1649–1680* (Woodbridge: Boydell Press, 2011), 13–14.
54 M. Ó Siochrú, *God's Executioner: Oliver Cromwell and the Conquest of Ireland* (London: Faber & Faber, 2008), 129–32, 144–8.
55 Ó Siochrú, *God's Executioner*, 148–60.

Ormond's position at the head of the Royalists in Ireland was taken over by Clanricard. On the opposite side, Henry Ireton had succeeded Cromwell, his father-in-law, in mid-1650. With their military fortunes in decline, Clanricard and other Catholic leaders were increasingly attracted to the prospect of aid from the continent, this time from Charles, duke of Lorraine. Exiled from his patrimony by the French in the 1630s, Lorraine had pursued a successful career as a military contractor under the Habsburgs. By the 1650s he controlled substantial resources of men and money. Lorraine was gradually drawn into discussions around a series of disjointed proposals that emanated from different sections of the Irish political *élite*. He was most enthused by the notion of becoming 'protector' of the kingdom of Ireland, but in April 1651 Clanricard, anxious to prevent any diminution of Stuart sovereignty, blocked this scheme.[56] As the Royalist and Catholic leaders continued to strive desperately for a means to turn the tide of the war, Ireton led his forces across the River Shannon.

Such breakthroughs helped Ireton to contain emerging divisions within his regime. Although he had welcomed the arrival in January 1651 of four commissioners appointed by the Rump parliament to rebuild a civil government in Ireland, their presence had quickly generated tensions. The approach taken by one of the commissioners, John Weaver, was to become a particular source of grievance to English army officers in Ireland. Weaver did not hesitate to voice his displeasure at the extreme methods being employed by the officers in their attempts to pacify restless areas, including the widespread killing of civilians. As a religious Independent, he was also alarmed at the rapid spread of Baptist beliefs within the army. Following Ireton's death in November 1651, the Republican Weaver attempted to bring the army in Ireland to heel by imposing tighter civilian control, but he met with concerted opposition both from his fellow commissioners and from leading army officers. In April 1652 he retreated to Westminster, where his continued efforts to weaken the army's dominance of developing state structures in Ireland fed into the growing rift between the parliament and military interests in England.[57]

Weaver's return to London contributed to a long overdue increase in English political attention to Irish affairs. Over the previous two years the Royalist threat from Scotland and infighting over reform were among issues that had dominated the agenda at Westminster. Amongst the matters that

56 Ó Siochrú, *God's Executioner*, 162–78.
57 J. Cunningham, 'The Rump Parliament, Cromwell's Army and Ireland', *English Historical Review*, 129 (2014), 830–45.

had been neglected was a scheme drawn up by Ireton in March 1651 as he sought to bring an end to the conflict in Ireland. Borrowing from the approach employed by the English parliament as it endeavoured to reach a settlement with the king in the 1640s, Ireton proposed a sliding scale of punishments for his enemies in Ireland. There could be no mercy for any-one implicated in the 1641 rebellion, but the 'lower orders' and those who had not been heavily involved in the Confederate or Royalist movements were promised more lenient treatment. Landowners, apart from those who could demonstrate 'constant good affection' to the interest of the English Commonwealth, were faced with at least partial confiscation of their estates. Although Ireton's 'qualifications' were too harsh to bring about the speedy Catholic surrenders that he envisaged, the parliament's fail-ure either to endorse them formally or to propose an alternative approach deprived its representatives in Ireland of potential political alternatives to fire and sword.[58]

By the beginning of 1652 the collapse of Charles II's offensive in Britain and the inexorable advance of the parliament's forces in Ireland threatened to undermine any remaining Catholic resolve to continue in arms. Clerical efforts to bolster the war effort by resurrecting the Confederacy and by bran-dishing the threat of excommunication had proven ineffective. The divisions and desperation among the Catholics at home had also been reflected in the continued negotiations with the duke of Lorraine. In this process, the strength of individual agents' attachment to the Stuarts was one of the fac-tors that helped to determine the extent of the inducements that they offered to the duke. Clanricard rebuked the city of Galway for addressing Lorraine as 'Protector Royal', but the lord deputy could do nothing to break Sir Charles Coote's tightening siege of that town, the last major port in Catholic hands.[59] With even the boggy boltholes of Leinster coming under pressure from English military offensives, Colonel John Fitzpatrick moved to break the deadlock.

Fitzpatrick's surrender on terms in March 1652 provoked a decree of excom-munication and a wave of condemnation from his comrades. Nonetheless it was soon followed by other large-scale submissions, with most of the men concerned resigning themselves to exile. The only guarantee forthcom-ing on the practice of Catholicism was that it would not be permitted. The commissioners of parliament did promise, however, that nobody would be

---

58 Cunningham, *Conquest and land*, 17–22.
59 Ó Siochrú, *God's Executioner*, 181–6.

compelled to attend Protestant religious services or to pay recusancy fines.[60] This approach opened up the possibility that lay Catholics' consciences at least would remain intact, but the same could not be said for their estates. Most of the surrender terms agreed around this time followed Ireton's qualifications in providing for the whole or partial confiscation of almost all Catholic estates. Apart from effectively bringing the war to an end, the most significant consequence of the surrender negotiations was the emergence of a more moderate approach to the issue of prospective capital punishments. Ireton had proposed to exempt from pardon any Catholic involved in the first year of the conflict, every Catholic cleric and members of the first Confederate general assembly. By mid-1652 it had been agreed instead that in practice only persons proved guilty of murder should face the ultimate penalty.[61] It now fell to parliament to confirm the fate of a wasted population.

Land and Power

With the end of the Irish war in sight, Westminster turned its attention to the difficult questions of who precisely should govern Ireland and how exactly its vast tracts of confiscated land were to be divided up. The first of these questions quickly became bound up with Republican concerns about the extent of army power and the threat that it posed to civil government. It was in this context that John Weaver mobilised sufficient support in parliament to block the renewal of Cromwell's commission as lord lieutenant in April 1652. The abolition of the lord lieutenancy immediately undermined the position of Major-General John Lambert, who had been about to depart for Ireland to take up office as lord deputy. Weaver followed up this initial strike against military dominance of Ireland with a concerted campaign to limit the amount of land that would be granted to officers and soldiers in lieu of their substantial arrears of pay. At the same time the army's main competitors for Irish land, the civilian investors under the Adventurers' Act of 1642, were offered a range of inducements to encourage their plantation.[62]

This political struggle over authority and property in Ireland, which was part of the wider dispute between the parliament and army in England,

---

60 J. Cunningham, 'Lay Catholicism and Religious Policy in Cromwellian Ireland', *Journal of Ecclesiastical History*, 64 (2013), 769–86.

61 Cunningham, *Conquest and Land*, 24–6.

62 Cunningham, *Conquest and Land*, 27–8; Cunningham, 'Cromwell's Army, the Rump and Ireland', 845–8; Bottigheimer, *English Money and Irish Land*, 119–27. Also see Chapter 23 by M. Ó Siochrú and D. Brown, this volume.

was played out across the summer of 1652 and beyond.[63] The appointment of Cromwell's son-in-law Charles Fleetwood to a dual role in Ireland as commander-in-chief and as a commissioner of the civil government was just one indicator that the balance of power was tipping in favour of the army. In early August parliamentary debate on a bill relating to the Irish land settlement ground to a halt, most likely because the officers in Ireland had yet to be consulted about it. Meanwhile Ireton's qualifications had resurfaced. With some amendments and additions arising from the recent surrender negotiations, they were passed as the Act for the Settling of Ireland on 12 August.[64] Parliament's treatment of its Irish enemies had ultimately generated much less political controversy than its policy towards its servants and friends. Yet it remained clear that much work was required to clarify and to elaborate on the finer details of the post-war settlement.

Back in Ireland, a high court of justice was swiftly established to deal with those accused of murder. The rebel-leader Sir Phelim O'Neill was one of several hundred persons condemned to death.[65] In the absence of any major military threat, the English army officers found time to gather at Kilkenny in October to formulate their demands relating to the land settlement. They insisted on full satisfaction of their arrears before any land had been assigned to the adventurers. The officers entrusted the veteran officer Sir Hardress Waller with the task of representing their interests in London. He also continued their campaign against Weaver, who was still ensconced at Westminster and pushing for a substantial haircut on the debt owed to the Irish army. Weaver was eventually forced to resign from his Irish office in February 1653, after Waller had approached parliament with a lengthy petition of grievance signed by the officers in Ireland. Thereafter Waller secured some concessions relating to the army's share in the land settlement, but not without encountering further political resistance. This tense negotiation was still in progress when Cromwell expelled the parliament on 20 April.[66]

Before the Nominated parliament convened in July 1653, the main elements of the Irish land settlement had been finalised and announced by the interim army-dominated council of state. It seems that much of the detail was carried over from the bill previously under consideration by the Rump

---

63 On the English context, see B. Worden, *The Rump Parliament* (Cambridge University Press, 1974).

64 Cunningham, 'Cromwell's Army, the Rump and Ireland', 852–3; Cunningham, *Conquest and Land*, 29.

65 J. Wells, 'English Law, Irish Trials and Cromwellian State Building in the 1650s', *Past & Present*, 227 (2015), 77–119.

66 Cunningham, 'Cromwell's Army, the Rump and Ireland', 853–8.

parliament. The provinces of Ulster, Leinster and Munster were designated for plantation, with the backbone provided by a joint adventurer-army plantation stretching across ten counties. Catholic land entitlements were to be satisfied in the western province of Connacht under a scheme of transplantation.[67] The transplantation was central to the conquerors' vision of an anglicised and prosperous Ireland firmly attached to Protestantism. When the Nominated parliament rubber-stamped these arrangements, Fleetwood's government appeared well positioned to press ahead with the remaking of Ireland. He enjoyed strong support among the newcomers: the religious radicals and the army officers who served as governors of the administrative precincts into which the country was divided. Moreover, he felt no inclination, and saw little need, to reach out to Ireland's established communities, whose power and influence had been decimated by conquest.[68]

The Cromwellian Protectorate

This situation was short lived. The power structures put in place at the end of 1653 under the Instrument of Government rapidly altered the post-war political dynamic in Ireland. Cromwell's elevation to the position of lord protector proved especially disruptive. In the first place, it alarmed the radical interest in Ireland. Edmund Ludlow, one of Fleetwood's fellow commissioners, was just one of those who refused to accept the legitimacy of the Protectorate.[69] Second, the lord protector provided an alternative focus for Protestants and Catholics in Ireland who hoped to improve their position by winning concessions on landholding and other issues. Although Fleetwood was appointed to the revived office of lord deputy in 1654, he could do little to prevent Cromwell from showing favour to various petitioners. The Munster Protestants ultimately secured the indemnity promised them at their surrender in 1649. The Ulster Scots also resorted to articles granted by Cromwell during the conquest as they sought to avoid transplantation to Munster. The success of Catholic appeals to Cromwell was much more limited, but the very fact that they were free to make them caused Fleetwood great distress. Irish Catholic agents maintained a prominent presence in London for much of the decade. They lobbied against transplantation and from 1657 onwards they

---

67 *Acts and Ordinances of the English Interregnum, 1642–1660*, ed. C. Firth and R. Rait (London: Stationery Office, 1911), ii, 722–53.

68 T. Barnard, *Cromwellian Ireland: English Government and Reform in Ireland, 1649–1660* (Oxford University Press, 1975), 11–14, 98–106.

69 Barnard, *Cromwellian Ireland*, 101–9.

opposed efforts to enforce an anti-Catholic oath of abjuration in Ireland.[70] The Catholics' political efforts to obstruct the land settlement coincided with the appearance of a pamphlet published anonymously by the Munster Protestant Vincent Gookin at the beginning of 1655. This trenchant critique of the policy of transplantation was in essence an unprecedented attack on Fleetwood's administration.[71]

The growing weakness of Fleetwood's position was confirmed when Cromwell sent his son Henry to replace him at the head of the Irish government later in 1655. Henry Cromwell worked to reduce the power of the radicals favoured by Fleetwood and gradually came to depend on the 'Old Protestants', both at the local and national levels. This grouping of pre-1641 settlers also successfully demonstrated the political potential of another of the measures put in place in 1653: the admission of thirty MPs from Ireland to the protectoral parliaments. Their presence in parliament allowed the Old Protestants a formal input into debates on crucial issues such as trade, taxation and government. With leadership from Lord Broghill, they emerged as strong supporters of the Cromwellian regime and backed the proposal in 1657 to transform the Protectorate into a hereditary monarchy. Cromwell's refusal to assume the crown thus came as a blow to Old Protestant hopes for a stable bulwark against political and religious radicals. His death in September 1658 further heightened their anxiety. When army leaders forced Richard Cromwell to resign in May 1659, the progress made to date by the Old Protestants in recovering power and property appeared to be in jeopardy.[72]

The General Convention

With the Rump parliament back in power in England, Henry Cromwell was recalled from Ireland and efforts got underway to purge his supporters from the army and positions of influence. The political context was altered again in October when the Rump was once more shut down by the army. When George Monck decided to march from Scotland in support of the expelled

---

70 Cunningham, *Conquest and Land*, 48–70; Cunningham, 'Lay Catholicism and Religious Policy', 769–86.

71 V. Gookin, *The Great Case of Transplantation in Ireland Discussed* (London, 1655); J. Cunningham, 'The Gookin-Lawrence Pamphlet Debate and Transplantation in Cromwellian Ireland', in A. McElligott, L. Chambers, C. Breathnach and C. Lawless (eds.), *Power in History*. Historical Studies xxvii (Dublin: Irish Academic Press, 2011), 63–80.

72 T. Barnard, 'Planters and Policies in Cromwellian Ireland', *Past & Present*, 61 (1973), 31–69; P. Little, *Lord Broghill and the Cromwellian Union with Ireland and Scotland* (Woodbridge: Boydell Press, 2004), 124–69.

MPs, Broghill, Coote and other officers in Ireland moved successfully to seize control of garrisons across the country. Thereafter it became apparent that the Old Protestant leaders now in the ascendancy did not share the objectives of those who sought to restore a Republican government. Ludlow was prevented from landing at Dublin and the regicide Waller was arrested there in February 1660. By the end of that month a convention comprised of 138 members and dominated by the Old Protestants was in session in Dublin. Amongst its main priorities was the upholding of the recent massive transfer of Catholic lands into Protestant hands. The larger political issue of a return to Stuart monarchy was ultimately resolved elsewhere, when the English Convention parliament proclaimed Charles II king on 1 May 1660.[73]

Four decades have passed since Patrick Corish warned that historians investigating the mid-seventeenth century in Ireland risked disturbing ghosts.[74] Other scholars have echoed him in summing up the period by referring to Protestant winners and Catholic losers. Regardless of the particular approach taken, the ghosts, as Corish recognised, can hardly be avoided. Nor should the violence that birthed them be detached from the political processes explored in this chapter. In the 1640s Irish politics was dominated by failure. Settlements reached in desperation proved fragile. It is no surprise, however, that disputes of the sort that ripped apart early modern Europe evaded political resolution either in Kilkenny or elsewhere in the three kingdoms. The conflict in Ireland eventually became what hardliners on both the Catholic and Protestant sides had long wished it to be: a fight to the finish. In this, the winners were Protestant; Catholics were disenfranchised, transplanted and transported. *Élite* politics in post-war Ireland reflected the transformation set in train by conquest. It was now largely an intra-Protestant sphere of action, more closely dependent on England than heretofore. In the midst of all this change, some continuity was evident. Catholic agents travelled to London seeking concessions and the fulfilment of promises, just as they did before 1641 and were to do again after 1660. More significantly, the Old Protestants who had prospered prior to the rebellion gradually recovered influence in the 1650s. Their firm stance against any revival of Catholic political power would do much to shape the Ireland of Charles II.

---

73 The period leading up the Restoration is explored in detail in A. Clarke, *Prelude to Restoration in Ireland: The End of the Commonwealth, 1659–1660* (Cambridge University Press, 1999).

74 P. Corish, 'The Cromwellian Regime, 1650–1660', in Moody *et al.* (eds.), *A New History of Ireland, iii,* 385–6.

4

Restoration Politics, 1660–1691

TED MCCORMICK

The Restoration of the Stuart monarchy began and ended in Ireland. In December 1659, anti-radical officers led by Sir Theophilus Jones and supported by Roger Boyle, Lord Broghill and Sir Charles Coote (Old Protestant leaders in Munster and Connacht, respectively), seized Dublin Castle. This conservative coup paved the way for a General Convention in March 1660, which duly recognised the king in May.[1] Just over three decades later, William of Orange's victories over James II's armies at the Boyne and Aughrim, followed by the surrender of Limerick, marked the end of the line for the Stuart dynasty.[2] Yet the Restoration has a significance in Ireland's own history somewhat different from its place in the national histories of England and Scotland, or that the history of Britain writ large would suggest.[3] While the English Restoration, in particular, has often been seen as turning back the clock to before the Civil War, undoing any revolutionary achievement, in Ireland the Restoration witnessed the gradual consolidation of a certain kind of social and political revolution. This revolution centred on the Protestant expropriation of Catholic-owned land, and the concomitant transmutation of the social and political *élite*.[4] But it also went beyond the simple exchange of land, status and power. The Irish Restoration initiated,

---

1 S. J. Connolly, *Religion, Law and Power: The Making of Protestant Ireland 1660–1760* (Oxford University Press [hereafter OUP], 1992), 5–10. See A. Clarke, *Prelude to Restoration in Ireland: the End of the Commonwealth, 1659–1660* (Cambridge University Press, 1999).

2 R. Armstrong, 'The War of the Three Kings, 1688–91', in A. Jackson (ed.), *The Oxford Handbook of Modern Irish History* (OUP, 2014), 375–97. See J. G. Simms, *Jacobite Ireland, 1685–91* (London: Routledge and Kegan Paul, 1969).

3 T. Harris, 'Restoration Ireland – Themes and Problems', in C. Dennehy (ed.), *Restoration Ireland: Always Settling and Never Settled* (Aldershot: Ashgate, 2008), 1–17.

4 K. S. Bottigheimer, 'The Restoration Land Settlement in Ireland: A Structural View', *Irish Historical Studies* [hereafter *IHS*] 18:69 (1972), 1–21; L. J. Arnold, *The Restoration Land Settlement in County Dublin, 1660–1688: a History of the Administration of the Acts of Settlement and Explanation* (Dublin: Irish Academic Press, 1993); K. McKenny, 'The Restoration Land Settlement in Ireland: A Statistical Interpretation', in Dennehy (ed.), *Restoration Ireland, 35–52.*

accelerated, or completed a further series of transformations – in political interests and identities and in the mechanisms, modes and spaces of political participation – that can be seen as marking the beginnings of a distinctly modern Irish political culture.

Facets of the Irish Restoration

Since the professionalisation of Irish historical research, the dominant organising theme in the historiography of the later seventeenth century has been that of 'settlement': the contested and frustrated search for a sustainable socio-political order. For good reason: this was a dominant question in the politics of the period. An appeal to order in the wake of two decades of conflict, and a sense that the Cromwellian army, political radicals and sectarian 'fanatics' imperilled this order, justified the Old Protestant leaders and supporters of the December 1659 coup. Following a failed anti-monarchist coup led by the regicide Sir Hardress Waller the following February, many members of the Convention – like their counterparts in England – evinced a growing conviction that only monarchy could provide such an order.[5] The association of disorder with religious radicals or nonconformists of various kinds – Baptists, Quakers and others in the army, as well as Scottish Presbyterians in Ulster – helps to account for the conservative, episcopalian religious settlement that took shape through the Convention at the same time.[6] Despite differences of opinion over the degree of accommodation to be extended to dissenting groups, it was widely presumed that political stability depended on the pre-eminence of a particular confessional-*cum*-national community (either Protestant or Old English) and the subordination or exclusion of its untrustworthy rivals (whether papists or fanatics); the possibility of institutionalising toleration and a balance of interests was rarely advanced except by those on the margins or at the very top. Yet in practice such a neatly bifurcated order proved as impossible to realise after 1660 as before. This disparity between ideals and realities – embodied in the fact that the Restoration was made possible by the same men who benefited from Cromwellian expropriations – was a fertile breeding ground for what one historian has called 'the politics of resentment'. It ultimately doomed

---

5 See Charles Coote, *The Declaration of Sir Charls Coot, Lord President of Conaught, and the Officers and Soldiers under His Command* (London, 1660); Hardress Waller, *The Declaration of Sir Hardress Waller, Major-General of the Parliament's Forces in Ireland, and the Council of Officers There* (Dublin, 1660).
6 Connolly, *Religion, Law and Power*, 10.

the search for a universally acceptable settlement to failure absent another, more decisive, conquest.[7]

A related historiographical theme, prominent since the advent of the 'New British History', has been the politics of religion – or what the historical actors themselves thought of as the relationship between religious belief or church membership, on the one hand, and political allegiance, on the other. Given recent Irish experience and the wider tensions besetting Stuart Britain and Counter-Reformation Europe, anti-popery is a convenient rubric for Protestant opposition to substantive Catholic inclusion in any settlement. Yet this ignores significant and evolving political divisions on both sides of the confessional divide throughout the period 1660–1691, and – in the light of the ultimate triumph of the Protestant Ascendancy on the heels of the Williamite conquest – casts an air of inevitability over outcomes by no means preordained. In fact, the nuances of religious politics during the Restoration throughout the Three Kingdoms afforded unusual scope for experimentation with political alignments, criteria for inclusion and exclusion and technologies of rule. Even such failed projects as the Catholic 'Loyal Formulary and Remonstrance' of 1661 – a Gallican solution to the problem of Irish Catholic allegiance to an English Protestant king – point up the contingency of political developments from a contemporary perspective. The real significance of their eventual failure, moreover, lies not simply in the victory of one confession over another, but in the definitive crystallisation of politics around confessional identity – and the evaporation of alternative configurations – that that victory inaugurated.

Taking a broader perspective, both the search for settlement and the hardening of confessional boundaries were bound up with the longer-term process of 'making Ireland British' or 'English'.[8] This has often been described in terms of programmatic projects or strategies of rule, particularly during the Tudor and Stuart era of plantation, that the land settlement was intended by its framers – and has been taken by historians – to conclude. Yet beyond the land question, unplanned responses to changing circumstance sometimes altered Irish political structures from within and imposed new constraints from without, raising the question of Ireland's place not only in the expanding English empire (and commercial economy) but also in European

---

7 Bottigheimer, 'Restoration Land Settlement', 5–6; Clarke, *Prelude to Restoration*, 16–20, 316–18.
8 N. Canny, *Making Ireland British, 1580–1650* (OUP, 2001); J. Ohlmeyer, *Making Ireland English: The Irish Aristocracy in the Seventeenth Century* (New Haven: Yale University Press, 2012).

trends of administrative centralisation and bureaucratisation. Over the same period, Irish political culture changed markedly. In part this transformation ran along lines already familiar in England – including the advent of a political press and the appearance of new spaces for the exchange of opinion beyond the confines of the traditional political nation. In other respects, however, the manner in which these developments unfolded reflected Ireland's peculiar politico-religious makeup – as polemics printed in Dublin or London contended with critiques from Paris or Louvain – much as their substantive content revealed both an emergent sense of Ireland's distinctive present and future interests and an intensely local contest, in print and in the street, over the meaning of its past.

The Problem of Settlement

Settlement, as many contemporaries thought of it, implied the territorial and therefore political supremacy of one confessional group and the effective subordination if not total exclusion of others; this had long been part of the logic of plantation. Yet in practice the territorial question cut across politico-religious divisions. As soon as the king's restoration seemed assured, the fate of the Cromwellian land settlement, both as a programme for Ireland and as the bane or boon of individual fortunes, motivated innumerable appeals to the king either for confirmation or restitution. But Cromwell's legacy was complex. Originally designed to resettle a broad swathe of territory spanning Ulster, Leinster and Munster with a combination of London 'Adventurers', Cromwellian soldiers and other 'New Protestants' – while transplanting displaced Catholics to estates in Connacht – the settlement plan mutated into something much messier on the ground well before 1660.[9] While transplantation had dragged on, soldiers tired of waiting for their land and investors no longer interested in Irish plantation created a buyer's market for land debentures. Old Protestant families such as the Boyles, Cootes and Annesleys – the future makers of the Restoration, and by no means averse to retaining Catholic tenants – eagerly bought, as did some Catholics (the basis of a 'new interest') later. On the other side, dispossessed Catholics and Royalists returning from exile expected – and those with access to the king often secured – promises

---

9 See K. S. Bottigheimer, *English Money and Irish Land: the 'Adventurers' in the Cromwellian Settlement of Ireland* (OUP, 1971); T. C. Barnard, *Cromwellian Ireland: English Government and Reform in Ireland, 1649–1660* (2nd edn., OUP, 2000); J. Cunningham, *Conquest and Land in Ireland: The Transplantation into Connacht, 1649–1680* (Woodbridge: Boydell & Brewer, 2011).

of restitution. The result was a jumble of conflicting claims irreducible to the simple terms in which political arguments and identities were for the most part articulated.

The 'politics of resentment' in terms of which Tim Harris has characterised the Restoration in Ireland reflected this clash, and drew nourishment from the very different views of recent history, collective identity and justice held by the contending groups – loyal Catholics forced to defend themselves against fanatical regicides, from one perspective; Protestant English holding the fort against rebellious and massacring papists, from another.[10] The king maintained a self-consciously impartial stance that, like his grants of Irish land to friends and favourites, ignored territorial constraints and stakeholders' expectations. Aiming 'to reconcile these Jarring Interests', his Gracious Declaration of November 1660 promised something for everyone.[11] Adventurers and soldiers, regicides excepted, were confirmed in their holdings as of 7 May 1659, as were Old Protestants such as Broghill (now earl of Orrery), Coote (now earl of Mountrath) and Sir Theophilus Jones.[12] On the other hand, Protestants serving the king before the Royalist-Confederate ceasefire of 1643 – including James Butler, the Old English marquis, later duke, of Ormond, and the Gaelic Irish Murrough O'Brien, earl of Inchiquin – were to have their estates restored. So, too, were Catholics 'innocent' of rebellion (an oxymoron from the Cromwellian point of view) as well as 'ensign men' who had served in the king's forces abroad, and a slew of named individuals; officers owed arrears for service under Charles I were also to be paid in land.[13] Those displaced by these acts of restitution, finally, were to be assigned 'reprisals' elsewhere. Ormond feared that satisfying everyone would require 'a new Ireland', and so it proved.[14]

To give the Gracious Declaration and the acts of the General Convention statutory force, a parliament was called for May 1661.[15] Orrery and Mountrath, now joint Lords Justices, worried about the potential for a Catholic political

---

10 Harris, 'Restoration Ireland'.
11 *His Majesties Gracious Declaration for the Settlement of his Kingdome of Ireland, and Satisfaction of the Severall Interests of Adventurers, Souldiers, and Other His Subjects There* (London, 1660), 27.
12 Ibid., 5–8, 17–18.
13 Ibid., 9–10, 13–15, 20–9.
14 James Butler, duke of Ormond, quoted in Richard Bagwell, *Ireland under the Stuarts and during the Interregnum*, (3 vols., London: Longmans, Green and Co., 1916), iii, 23. See also [Nicholas French?], *A Narrative of the Earl of Clarendon's Settlement and Sale of Ireland* (1668), reprinted in *The Historical Works of the Right Reverend Nicholas French, D. D., Bishop of Ferns, &c., &c.*, ed. S. H. Bindon (Dublin: James Duffy, 1846), 71–126, at 83–4.
15 See Arnold, *Restoration in County Dublin*, 37–52; C. Dennehy, 'The Restoration Irish Parliament, 1661–6', in C. Dennehy (ed.), *Restoration Ireland*, 53–68.

resurgence, but in the event Protestant control of land and Catholic exclusion from corporations ensured that elections produced a predominantly New English House of Commons.[16] Indeed the lower house now became, for the first time, a Protestant preserve. Several Catholic lords did sit, but they now lacked their traditional influence over the Commons and formed a minority in the upper house, where Protestant laymen and Church of Ireland bishops outweighed 'Papists & such as are no enemie to their interests.'[17] Old and New Protestant defenders of the Cromwellian settlement thus came together to wield considerable institutional power at a moment when, as Lord Chancellor Maurice Eustace put it, the plan sketched in the Declaration was to be 'polished, squared, and fitted' as the legislative cornerstone of a new settlement.[18] Catholic lobbying, therefore, focused on Ormond (appointed lord lieutenant in late 1661, arriving in Dublin in mid-1662) and, even more, on patrons at the royal court. There, Sir Nicholas Plunkett's efforts were undercut by internal divisions – some inherited from the Confederacy, some reflecting the Interregnum split between Ormond and Richard Talbot and others reflecting the divergence between the dispossessed and the 'new interest'.[19] His mission was curtailed in April 1662, after Orrery revealed correspondence implicating Plunkett in Confederate offers of allegiance to continental monarchs and the Pope.[20]

The Act of Settlement was passed in late 1662. Its key practical provision, and ultimately its undoing, was the creation of a Court of Claims to assess the innocence of individual claimants, mostly Catholic, seeking the restitution of their lands.[21] Inasmuch as the rebellion was seen by many Protestants, and New Protestants in particular, as a matter of collective Irish Catholic guilt – and since mere habitation in rebel areas was seen as evidence of rebellion – few such judgments were anticipated when the court set to work in January 1663. In practice, however, the commissioners who served as judges were often divided, either by factional loyalties, corruption or genuine differences of opinion over the application of the criteria or the merits of a particular

16 Dennehy, 'Restoration Parliament', 55.
17 Ohlmeyer, *Making Ireland English*, 337–41; compare F. James, *Lords of the Ascendancy: the Irish House of Lords and Its Members, 1600–1800* (Washington, DC: Catholic University of America Press, 1995), 35–6.
18 Maurice Eustace, *The Speech of the Right Honourable the Lord Chancellor of Ireland made … the 8th. of May 1661* (London, 1661), 8; Bottigheimer, 'Restoration Land Settlement', 8; S. J. Connolly, *Divided Kingdom: Ireland 1630–1800* (OUP, 2008), 128–35.
19 Arnold, *Restoration in County Dublin*, 46; A. Creighton, 'The Remonstrance of December 1661 and Catholic Politics in Restoration Ireland', *IHS*, 34 (2004), 16–41, at 21–2.
20 Arnold, *Restoration in County Dublin*, 46–7.
21 Arnold, *Restoration in County Dublin*, 53–70.

case.[22] The court's proceedings thus disappointed both sides, and galvanised opposition among Old and New Protestants. The shock that greeted some verdicts shows in the counsel's response when the judges found the Catholic James Allen innocent despite the testimony of several witnesses, thus defeating the Presbyterian earl of Mount Alexander's claim to Allen's estate: 'Sirs, if you judge this man innocent, we must believe the English cut one another's throats and that there was no Irish rebellion or rebels.'[23] With the Commons in an uproar, the speaker, Sir Audley Mervyn, complained to Ormond – in person and, provocatively, in print – that 'the establisht religion is in danger to be undermined by casting the predominancy of temper upon a Popish interest'.[24] In this hysterical atmosphere, the very Protestant character of the settlement appeared to be under threat. Of more than 800 claims the court heard, only a small fraction of claimants were judged guilty of rebellion.[25] Many of those restored seemed to Protestants anything but innocent.

Alarm over such restorations – in parliament, among the large body of ex-Cromwellian soldiers still in the army, and in the overlapping communities of interested Protestants – generated the first full-blown political crisis of the Restoration. Ormond, having discovered a plot to seize Dublin Castle ('and me in it'), responded with resentment to Mervyn and all but blamed the Commons for fomenting rebellion, proroguing parliament.[26] Word of the Commons' inflammatory proceedings meanwhile reached the king, who angrily invited New Protestants to consider 'the insecurity of their position', not least in the light of the English parliament's attitude, and advised them to 'fall again into that temper which it becomes good subjects to have'.[27] A second, more serious plot against Dublin Castle, attributed to a Presbyterian conspiracy and directed by Thomas Blood, was discovered

---

22 Compare H. O'Sullivan, 'The Restoration Land Settlement in the Diocese of Armagh, 1660–1684', *Seanchas Ardmhacha: Journal of the Armagh Diocesan Historical Society*, 16 (1994), 1–70; Connolly, *Divided Kingdom*, 134–5.

23 Hugh Montgomery, earl of Mount Alexander to?, 7 February 1663, in R. P. Mahaffy (ed.), *Calendar of the State Papers relating to Ireland Preserved in the Public Record Office* [hereafter *CSPI*], *1662–1665*, ed. R. P. Mahaffy (London: Mackie and Co., 1907), 19.

24 Audley Mervyn, *The Speech of Sir Audley Mervyn Knight … Delivered to His Grace James Duke of Ormond, Lord Lieutenant of Ireland, the 13. Day of February, 1662* (Dublin, 1663), 4.

25 But compare Arnold, *Restoration in County Dublin*, 53 (over 130 nocent, of 829 decisions) and Geraldine Talon (ed.), *Court of Claims: Submissions and Evidence, 1663* (Dublin: Irish Manuscripts Commission, 2006), x–xvi (707 innocent [566 Catholic and 141 Protestant], 113 nocent).

26 James Butler, duke of Ormond, Lord Lieutenant to Secretary Henry Bennet, 7 Mar. 1663, in *CSPI*, *1662–1665*, 34; Ormond to Audley Mervyn, Speaker of the House of Commons, 9 March 1663, in *CSPI*, *1662–1665*, 35. See Dennehy, 'Restoration Parliament', 60.

27 Copy of Bennet to Ormond, *circa* 24 February 1663, in *CSPI* *1662–1665*, 29.

in May. Prevented at the last moment, Blood's Plot would be the last serious attempt to overturn the Restoration regime before 1689. But that was hardly evident at the time. Moreover, even if it failed in its goals – justifying the arrest of Presbyterian leaders in Ulster in the process – Blood's Plot did help shift the balance against the interests of dispossessed Catholics.[28] Already purging an unreliable army, Ormond now considered dissolving parliament to preserve public order. In the end, however, it was the Court of Claims that was shut down, following the contentious restoration of Randal MacDonnell, marquis of Antrim (former president of the Confederate supreme council), in late August 1663.[29] The vast majority of dispossessed claimants would never be heard.

As Ormond was quick to recognise, cleaning up the mess that this series of contradictory pressures and half-measures had created would need another round of legislation. The result was the Act of Explanation, which though drafted in 1663 passed into law only in 1665 after a lengthy sojourn with the English Privy Council – and then only with difficulty, the Irish Commons having thrown out an earlier bill.[30] In belated recognition of Ireland's territorial limits, and in deference to Old Protestant expectations (it was largely the work of Orrery and Arthur Annesley, earl of Anglesey – Ormond's vice-treasurer and among the settlement's biggest winners) the act imposed 'retrenchments' of one-third on Cromwellian adventurers' and soldiers' claims. This was justified in turn by the king's rejection of the 1643 'Doubling Ordinance', by which adventurers had been encouraged to double their claims under the Adventurers' Act of 1642 by paying a fraction of their original subscription.[31] The resulting fund of land was used for reprisals, for satisfying arrears, and for honouring grants made to individual nominees of the king since 1660. Adjudicating this further round of transfers was a second Court of Claims, which sat from January 1666 to January 1669.[32] As this new court was debarred from hearing new claims of innocence – 'for we have plenty of evidence here to swear to the nocency and innocency of the same person at the same time',

28 J. I. McGuire, 'Ormond and Presbyterian Nonconformity, 1660–1663', in Kevin Herlihy (ed.), *The Politics of Irish Dissent, 1650–1800* (Dublin: Four Courts Press [hereafter FCP], 1997), 40–51; Arnold, *Restoration County Dublin*, 71–2.

29 J. Ohlmeyer, *Civil War and Restoration in Three Stuart Kingdoms: The Career of Randal MacDonnell, Marquis of Antrim* (2nd edn., Dublin: FCP, 2001), 258–77.

30 Arnold, *Restoration County Dublin*, 86–96.

31 K. McKenny, 'The Seventeenth-Century Land Settlement in Ireland: Towards a Statistical Interpretation', in Jane Ohlmeyer (ed.), *Ireland from Independence to Occupation 1641–1660* (Cambridge: Cambridge University Press, 1995), 181–200, at 192.

32 Arnold, *Restoration County Dublin*, 97–108.

as Attorney-General Sir William Domvile noted – its greatest significance was that from this point, the losers would remain losers.[33]

Lawsuits dragged on, lobbying continued, and – in moments of resurgent Catholic influence at court, as under the Cabal ministry in the early 1670s and again under James – inquiries would be launched. But in practical terms the legislative phase of the settlement was over. The scale of the transfer it represented has been discussed so frequently and the percentages so often repeated (with slight variations) that further comment seems almost superfluous; any Catholic landowning class, as such, was largely wiped out and Protestant dominance confirmed.[34] Yet the magnitude of the transformation, 'unprecedented in European history', suggests the extent to which Restoration Ireland was built upon revolutionary foundations.[35] That the Old Protestants rather than the New eventually accrued the bulk of the expropriated land meant that most of the great landowning families of the Ascendancy had pre-1641 roots; further, by putting larger estates in fewer hands the land settlement facilitated the emergence of a hybrid service nobility that blended Old and New Protestants and incorporated a handful of favoured or strategically important Catholic aristocrats.[36] If the earlier debate over the Cromwellian transplantation scheme measured different Protestant attitudes, this continuity may have softened the blow to Catholic tenants. But none of this detracts from the radical reduction of Catholic landownership that the Restoration settlement effected, or the similarly radical decline in Irish Catholic political status and institutional power. Given the experience of the 1650s, the implications of this revolution were evident from the outset. What was not yet certain was how long it would last.

The Politics of Religion

Beyond the politics of resentment in Ireland loomed the politics of religion in all three Stuart kingdoms. The original justification for the systematic expropriation underpinning the land settlement was Irish Catholic responsibility for the rising of 1641, and for the massacre of Protestants that had reportedly ensued. But the larger and longer-term problem was the place (specifically,

---

33 William Domvile to Henry Bennet, 19 September 1663, in *CSPI, 1662–1665*, 236–41, at 238.
34 Bottigheimer, 'Restoration Land Settlement', 1, claims that Protestant landownership increased from 41 per cent to 78 per cent; McKenny, 'Restoration Land Settlement', 39, argues for a shift from about 30 per cent to 67 per cent Protestant landownership by 1675.
35 M. Perceval-Maxwell, 'The Irish Land Settlement and its Historians', in Dennehy, *Restoration Ireland*, 19.
36 James, *Lords of the Ascendancy*; Ohlmeyer, *Making Ireland English*, 301–35.

in a Counter-Reformation context, the allegiance) of a Catholic population in a kingdom ruled by an at least nominally Protestant king, under the spiritual jurisdiction of an Anglican establishment, and embedded in an overwhelmingly Protestant multiple monarchy. To argue against the land and religious settlements, Catholics appealed to history, from the Old English role in establishing English rule in Ireland up to the 1649 peace negotiated between the king (represented by Ormond) and the Confederates, which had promised toleration for Catholicism.[37] They pointed also to Protestants' own record of rebellion, regicide, usurpation and sectarian mass violence.[38] Yet the question of Catholic loyalty remained, complicated by the pre-war distinction between Old English and Gaelic Irish and the Confederate-era split between 'Ormondists', Stuart loyalists willing to settle for muted toleration and adherents of the papal nuncio, GianBattista Rinuccini, who sought a public, Counter-Reformation Catholic establishment, whether under the Stuarts or not.[39]

The Restoration of monarchy and of Anglican episcopacy put paid to both possibilities. It did not, however, heal the divisions they reflected. Indeed, parliament's failure to extend the full panoply of English anti-recusant laws to Ireland in 1661–3 preserved space for intra-confessional disputes that a harsher settlement would have suffocated.[40] Thus 'the loyal formulary, or Catholic remonstrance' of 1661, the most important project for Catholic political rehabilitation of Charles II's reign, fell victim not to Protestant opposition or English meddling but to factiousness among the Catholic clergy within and beyond Ireland.[41] Written by Richard Bellings, a diplomat and client of Ormond's, and tirelessly promoted by the Franciscan Peter Walsh, the Remonstrance proposed a loyalty oath acknowledging the mistakes of the Confederacy, abjuring Catholic justifications of rebellion and regicide, and, crucially, denying the Pope's power to depose kings or absolve subjects of

---

37 Notably John Lynch, *Cambrensis Eversus, seu Potius Historica Fides in Rebus Hibernicis Giraldo Cambrensi Abrogata*, ed. and trans. M. Kelly (2 vols., Dublin: Celtic Society, 1848), i, 29–31, 45. See B. Cunningham, 'Representations of King, Parliament and the Irish People in Geoffrey Keating's *Foras Feasa Ar Eirinn* and John Lynch's *Cambrensis Eversus* (1662)', in J. Ohlmeyer (ed.), *Political Thought in Seventeenth-Century Ireland: Kingdom or Colony* (Cambridge University Press, 2000), 131–54.

38 Lynch, *Cambrensis Eversus*, 17–19.

39 Ohlmeyer, *Civil War and Restoration*, 152–73. See H. O'Sullivan, *John Bellew: A Seventeenth-Century Man of Many Parts, 1605–1679* (Dublin: Irish Academic Press, 2000), 76–7; M. Ó Siochrú, *Confederate Ireland, 1642–1649: A Constitutional and Political Analysis* (Dublin: FCP, 1999).

40 Dennehy, 'Restoration Parliament', 67–8.

41 A. Creighton, 'The Remonstrance', 16–41; J. McHugh, 'Catholic Clerical Responses to the Restoration: The Case of Nicholas French', in Dennehy, *Restoration Ireland*, 99–121.

temporal allegiance.[42] It was a Gallican solution to the plight of Catholics in Stuart Ireland: an effectively nationalised church.[43] From the perspective of the twenty-four clergymen (including one bishop, Oliver Darcy of Dromore) whom Walsh convinced to sign the document in London in early 1662, and from that of the nearly 100 nobles and gentry who subscribed to their own version shortly thereafter, the formulary obviated ideological justifications of sectarian exclusion and diverted government anxiety to more appropriate targets – covenanters, fanatics and remnants of the usurper's regime. In the light of official anxieties about Presbyterians, Cromwellians in the army and plotters in the Commons, such hopes must have seemed plausible.

From the state's perspective, the Remonstrance had other uses, which derived less from its promise of Irish Catholic political rehabilitation than from its function as an index of clerical and *élite* disaffection. (Flushing out opposition may have been Ormond's purpose in convincing Walsh to seek signatures for the document.)[44] As the dominant issue in Irish Catholic politics between 1661 and 1671, both the specific formula of the Remonstrance – attacked by the Catholic primate of all Ireland, Edmund O'Reilly, the Louvain theological faculty and the Pope – and its larger project of reconciliation augmented pre-existing divisions.[45] For hard-line Protestant critics of the device, the ensuing printed debate merely confirmed suspicions that the bloody ideology of the Counter-Reformation held sway over Catholic clerical leadership, whatever Walsh's pretensions. Although a 1670 General Synod in Dublin produced a revision of the Remonstrance more broadly acceptable to the Irish clergy, the Pope condemned this too and the project was finally dropped. By this time, Ormond had been replaced as lord lieutenant, first in 1669 by the Presbyterian John, second Baron Robartes of Truro and first earl of Radnor, and then the following year by the Catholic sympathiser John, first Baron Berkeley of Stratton, who approved the 1670 formula. The Catholic Church in Ireland, meanwhile, had new leaders in Peter Talbot, archbishop of Dublin from January 1669, and Oliver Plunkett, archbishop of Armagh from July 1669, both enemies of the Remonstrance. Ironically, this momentarily

---

42 *To the King's Most Excellent Majestie the Humble Remonstrance, Acknowledgement, Protestation, and Petition of the Roman Catholick Clergy of Ireland* (London, 1662).

43 Creighton, 'The Remonstrance'.

44 Creighton, 'The Remonstrance', 28.

45 Peter Walsh, *The More Ample Accompt ... Promised in the Advertisement Annexed to the Late Printed Remonstrance, Protestation, &c. Of the Roman Catholick Clergy of Ireland* (London, 1662); Peter Walsh, *The History & Vindication of the Loyal Formulary, or Irish Remonstrance, So Graciously Received by His Majesty Anno 1661. Against All Calumnies and Censures* (London, 1673); Creighton, 'The Remonstrance', 33–4.

pro-Catholic political atmosphere, by strengthening the hand of the clerical hierarchy, doomed Walsh's project for an essentially secular mechanism
of Catholic inclusion.[46] Against a backdrop of resurgent French influence
at the English court (the 1670 Treaty of Dover, which committed Charles
to toleration and to embracing Catholicism) and the relaxation of Catholic
exclusion from corporations, legal practice and local office in Ireland, clerical
Remonstrants were hounded into obscurity by their own church.[47]

The same shift towards greater *de facto* toleration of Catholicism, which
peaked in England with the 1672 Declaration of Indulgence before being curtailed by the 1673 Test Act, encouraged renewed attacks on the land settlement. Perhaps the sharpest Anglophone critique was the 1668 *Narrative of
the Settlement and Sale of Ireland*, printed at Louvain and often attributed to
Nicholas French, Catholic bishop of Ferns.[48] In Latin and Spanish works,
French had long identified the Irish cause with that of European Catholicism –
seeking international support to give Irish interests greater geopolitical
weight following disappointment with Charles II.[49] The *Narrative* now excoriated the 'cannibal' behaviour of Ireland's 'Protestant Interest', whose machinations in securing narrow qualifications for innocence and then scuppering
the Court of Claims betrayed their goal of 'extirpating' Irish and Old English
alike.[50] Like such Gaelic Irish observers as Daíbhí Ó Bruadair, the *Narrative*
laid special blame on the profiteer and 'turncoat' Ormond, who in 1649 had
commanded the very Irish Royalists the Restoration settlement doomed.[51]
French made similar points in his 1674 *Bleeding Iphigenia*, arguing that the Irish
were persecuted not as rebels – the rebels had been Protestant – but simply
as Catholics.[52]

More immediately effective was a new petition for revision of the settlement, signed by fifty-two Catholic nobles and clergymen and brought to
London in December 1670. Its bearer was Richard Talbot, future earl and

---

46 Creighton, 'The Remonstrance', 37.
47 Walsh, *History & Vindication*, iii.
48 But see McHugh, 'Catholic Clerical Responses', 99–121.
49 McHugh, 'Catholic Clerical Responses'.
50 [Nicholas French?], *A Narrative of the Earl of Clarendon's Settlement and Sale of Ireland*
(Louvain: s.n., 1668). Reprinted in Samuel Henry Bindon (ed.), *The Historical Works of
the Right Rev. Nicholas French, D.D., Bishop of Ferns, &c. &c.*, 2 vols. (Dublin: James Duffy,
1846), vol. 1, 71–126.
51 Daíbhí Ó Bruadair, *O Bruadair: Translations from the Irish*, trans. M. Hartnett
(Dublin: Gallery Press, 1985), 24.
52 Nicholas French, *The Bleeding Iphigenia or An Excellent Preface of a Work Unfinished*
(London?, 1675), reprinted in Samuel Henry Bindon (ed.), *The Historical Works of the
Right Rev. Nicholas French, D.D., Bishop of Ferns, &c. &c.*, 2 vols. (Dublin: James Duffy,
1846), vol. 1, 1–69.

duke of Tyrconnell, and long-time confidant of Henry Bennet, now earl of Arlington. Aware of the Treaty of Dover and likely informed of the duke of York's conversion a few months previously, Talbot successfully pressed his case over Ormond's and Attorney-General Sir Heneage Finch's objections.[53] It was at this time that Blood again attempted an assault on Ormond, apparently sponsored by George Villiers, duke of Buckingham. As a result, transfers of land under the Acts of Settlement and Explanation were suspended, and a committee was formed under Prince Rupert in early February 1671 to review and modify the allocation of estates. Change seemed likely: the earl of Anglesey, shifting with the wind, began to find fault with the settlement that had so benefited him. Much as mutations at the English court had facilitated efforts to revisit the land settlement, however, English parliamentary responses – in the absence of an Irish parliament after 1666 – undid them. Under pressure from the Commons over toleration, the French alliance against the United Provinces, and the seeming advance of popery, the king withdrew Rupert's commission and let the settlement stand – for the time being.[54] In spite of this, its survival would remain a major issue for the remainder of the period.

So too would the wider issue of the confessional balance of power in Ireland and the Three Kingdoms. The appointment of Arthur Capel, earl of Essex as lord lieutenant, lasting from 1672 until Ormond's reinstatement in 1677, began as a sop to English Protestant anxieties about creeping Catholicisation.[55] Yet Essex proved more even-handed in his practical dealings with Catholic transplantees than might have been expected, and the limited degree of political inclusion that Irish Catholics had achieved by the end of the 1660s was maintained.[56] Furthermore, the Catholic 'new interest' grew apace, as private purchases brought the Catholic share of Irish land back up to about 30 per cent by 1675, as against an estimated 22 per cent left them by the settlement acts.[57] Interested commentators like Sir William Petty – architect of the Cromwellian Down Survey on which the settlement rested, and projector of innumerable schemes designed for its salvation in the 1670s and 1680s – knew that their estates depended on a politico-religious climate that was certain to

53 A. Creighton, ' "Grace and Favour": The Cabal Ministry and Irish Catholic Politics, 1667–1673', in Dennehy, *Restoration Ireland*, 141–60, especially 150–7.
54 Creighton, 'Grace and Favour', 157–60.
55 Creighton, 'Grace and Favour', 157.
56 Cunningham, *Conquest and Land*, 134–49.
57 See Chapter 23 by M. Ó Siochrú and D. Brown, this volume. E. Kinsella, ' "Dividing the Bear's Skin Before She Is Taken": Irish Catholics and Land in the Late Stuart Monarchy, 1683–91', in Dennehy, *Restoration Ireland*, 161–78, at 161.

change. For projectors and politicians such as Petty (in proposals directed to Ormond, Essex and Tyrconnell) and Thomas Sheridan (in his 1677 *Discourse on the Rise and Power of Parliaments*), this awareness could lead to a novel pragmatism about confessional politics and an interest in new political arrangements, including Anglo-Irish parliamentary and even demographic union predicated on some combination of religious toleration or comprehension, planned or forced migration and economic improvement.[58] For perhaps the first time, the material incentives and rationality of the general Irish population entered – but fleetingly – into high-level political calculations.

But for many Protestants the threat of a Catholic establishment under either Charles or the future James II and his minions gave new urgency to ancient verities: the treachery of papists, the degeneracy of the Irish and the perpetual risk of English Protestant annihilation. These prejudices came to the fore during Ormond's third viceroyalty (1677–85), in the Popish Plot of 1678 and the ensuing crisis over Exclusion. Titus Oates's revelations initially focused on England. But the political geography of Whig anti-popery and the conspiratorial logic of Oates's own inventions led inexorably to the concoction of an Irish plot, which was exploited to the full by Anthony Ashley-Cooper, earl of Shaftesbury, and his parliamentary following.[59] The result in Ireland – where the sceptical Ormond acquiesced under pressure from Orrery and other enemies at court – was a handful of arrests, most notably of archbishops Talbot of Dublin and Plunkett of Armagh. Talbot died in prison soon after; Plunkett, having been acquitted by an Irish Protestant jury, was hauled to England for re-trial, convicted of treason on suborned testimony, and hanged, drawn and quartered at Tyburn in July 1681.[60] The high tide of the movement for Exclusion having passed by late 1681, no more was heard of the Irish plot.

If the Popish Plot in Ireland was a by-product of English domestic politics, it nevertheless destroyed two Irish Catholic religious leaders. It also reanimated debates over the events of the 1640s in both kingdoms. In particular, Edmund Borlase's virulently anti-Catholic *History of the*

---

58 See T. McCormick, *William Petty and the Ambitions of Political Arithmetic* (OUP, 2009), 168–284; J. Miller, 'Thomas Sheridan (1646–1712) and His "Narrative"', *IHS* 20 (1976): 105–28; V. Geoghegan, 'Thomas Sheridan: Toleration and Royalism', in D. G. Boyce, R. Eccleshall and V. Geoghegan (eds.), *Political Discourse in Seventeenth- and Eighteenth-Century Ireland* (Basingstoke: Palgrave Macmillan, 2001), 32–61.

59 J. Gibney, *Ireland and the Popish Plot* (Basingstoke: Palgrave Macmillan, 2009).

60 J. G. Simms, 'The Restoration, 1660–1685', in T. W. Moody, F. X. Martin and F. J. Byrne (eds.), *A New History of Ireland, iii: Early Modern Ireland, 1534–1691* (3rd impression, OUP, 1991), 420–53, at 432–3.

Execrable Irish Rebellion (1680), appearing on the heels of a reprint of Sir John Temple's incendiary *Irish Rebellion* (1646, reprinted 1679) provoked hostilities between three high-level participants in those events: Ormond, Anglesey and the Catholic James Tuchet, earl of Castlehaven.[61] The latter published memoirs that emphasised Old English loyalism and blamed Old Protestant bigotry for the war; Anglesey, courting Shaftesbury, accused Castlehaven of justifying Irish barbarism and rebellion, an accusation that touched Ormond's dealings with the Confederacy; Ormond condemned Protestant zealots (including, by implication, modern-day Whigs) as well as Catholic rebels.[62] In the end, Ormond rode out the controversy and the wider crisis, while Anglesey lost his position as lord privy seal; Castlehaven's memoirs were revised and republished. More significant than this immediate fallout was the ideological shift revealed by the different interpretations of Irish divisions on offer in the three accounts. While Castlehaven echoed the arguments of earlier Old English writers, and Ormond saw faults on all sides, Anglesey's elision of Protestantism and Englishness, and his monolithic opposition of both to Irishness and Catholicism, would win the day.[63]

Political Structures and Political Cultures

For recent historians, the Popish Plot has illustrated the entanglement of Irish politics with English concerns.[64] Other events of the Restoration testify to Irish political subordination, whether this is framed in colonial, provincial or other terms. From one perspective, Ireland was an amalgam of estates to be gifted and offices to be sold – a resource for Stuart patronage politics

---

61 See Chapter 18 by D. Rankin, this volume. Edmund Borlase, *The History of the Execrable Irish Rebellion Trac'd from Many Preceding Acts, to the Grand Eruption the 23 of October, 1641 and thence Pursued to the Act of Settlement, 1662* (London, 1680); John Temple, *The Irish Rebellion, or, an History of the Beginnings and First Progress of the General Rebellion Raised within the Kingdom of Ireland upon the Three & Twentieth Day of October, in the Year 1641* (London, 1679). See M. Perceval-Maxwell, 'The Anglesey-Ormond-Castlehaven Dispute, 1680–1682: Taking Sides About Ireland in England', in V. P. Carey and U. Lotz-Heumann (eds.), *Taking Sides? Colonial and Confessional Mentalités in Early Modern Ireland: Essays in Honour of Karl S. Bottigheimer* (Dublin: FCP, 2003), 213–30.

62 James Touchet, earl of Castlehaven, *The Memoirs of James, Lord Audley, Earl of Castlehaven, his Engagement and Carriage in the Wars of Ireland from the Year 1642 to the Year 1651 Written by Himself* (London, 1680); Arthur Annesley, earl of Anglesey, *A Letter from a Person of Honour in the Country written to the Earl of Castlehaven* (London, 1681); James Butler, duke of Ormond, *A Letter from His Grace James Duke of Ormond, Lord Lieutenant of Ireland, in Answer to the Right Honourable Arthur Earl of Anglesey Lord Privy-Seal* (London, [1682]).

63 Perceval-Maxwell, 'Anglesey-Ormond-Castlehaven', 230.

64 Gibney, *Ireland and the Popish Plot*, 116–17.

particularly in the first years of the Restoration, when the vagaries of the land settlement were a special temptation to grasping courtiers.[65] From another, it has appeared as the victim of a burgeoning English commercial empire: thus the Cattle Acts of 1663 and 1665, vigorously yet hopelessly opposed by a united front of Old and New Protestant landowners, subjected Irish to metropolitan interests – furnishing a material basis for the crystallisation of a distinctly colonial, or creole, Irish Protestant identity.[66] As mercantilism has been relegated to the status of historiographical myth, alternative bases – rooted in collective memory and popular politics – have been suggested for this identity.[67] Partly in consequence of its role in patronage networks, Ireland was also a theatre for proxy wars between political factions in England. Thus it was Ormond's rival, the duke of Buckingham, who sparked an investigation of Irish finances (leading to then vice-treasurer Anglesey's dismissal in 1667), and who then, with help from Orrery, secured Ormond's recall in 1669 in favour of less-qualified but more pliant men.[68] This picture, in some measure common to proponents of both the 'colonial' reading of Ireland's position and the sometimes Anglo-centric New British History, is the image of an exploited backwater.

The circumstances surrounding Ormond's dismissal and replacements in 1669–1672 point to another constraint on effective government in this period: the weakness of the central administration. This was reflected in the machinations of Old Protestants like Orrery – who wielded influence in and outside parliament as a member of the Boyle family and as lord president of Munster until 1672 – and of well-connected Catholics such as Richard Talbot, who was in close contact with Arlington and York, or the marquis of Antrim, whose connections in Ulster and the Western Isles of Scotland, as well as to the Queen Mother, Henrietta Maria, ensured his political survival despite

---

65 Ohlmeyer, *Making Ireland English*, 334.

66 C. A. Edie, 'The Irish Cattle Bills: A Study in Restoration Politics', *Transactions of the American Philosophical Society*, new series, 60 (1970), 1–66; Dennehy, 'Restoration Parliament', 64.

67 T. C. Barnard, 'Crises of Identity Among Irish Protestants, 1641–1685', *Past & Present* 127 (1990), 39–83; T. C. Barnard, 'The Uses of the 23rd of October 1641 and Irish Protestant celebrations', in T. C. Barnard, *Irish Protestant Ascents and Descents, 1641–1770* (Dublin: FCP, 2004), 111–42; J. Kelly, ' "That Glorious and Immortal Memory": Commemoration and Protestant Identity in Ireland 1660–1800', *Proceedings of the Royal Irish Academy*, 94:C (1994), 25–52; J. Gibney, *The Shadow of a Year: The 1641 Rebellion in Irish History and Memory* (Madison, WI: University of Wisconsin Press, 2013), 20–69. See also T. C. Barnard, 'Athlone, 1685; Limerick, 1710: Religious Riots or Charivaris?' *Studia Hibernica*, 27 (1993), 61–75.

68 J. I. McGuire, 'Why Was Ormond Dismissed in 1669?', *IHS*, 18 (1973), 295–312; Creighton, 'Grace and Favour'.

his dubious record.[69] Such men's ability to mobilise patronage and kinship networks in their own localities and across the Irish Sea meant that Dublin Castle's initiatives were always potentially subject to overt or covert opposition from below and appeals to authorities elsewhere. More generally, this was an era in which the implementation of policy and the enforcement of law, as well as intelligence about the state of the country and threats to its security, heavily depended on the willing participation of local agents.[70] Given limited bureaucratisation, the difficulties of rapid or long-range communication, the relative inaccessibility of western and northern parts of the kingdom, and the perceived unreliability of the standing army (which was only gradually purged of Cromwellian officers), such men, and their connections, were indispensable.[71]

Dublin Castle's weakness was also partly the result of an unstable fiscal situation. Despite the replacement of feudal dues by excise taxes and the introduction in 1662 of a new hearth tax (both mirroring developments in England), as well as income from quit rents associated with the land settlement, Ormond's second lord lieutenancy (1662–1669) was marked by constant budget deficits and appeals to the king for subventions to facilitate the operations of government and to pay the arrears of an army still being purged. Parliamentary subsidies eased these difficulties during the 1660s, and economic growth augmented revenues over the longer term. Yet organisational problems remained. Indeed, throughout the period both the collection of revenues (which was farmed out to private individuals in exchange for annual lump-sum payments) and their administration were political battlegrounds. Buckingham used fiscal issues as the basis for an attack on Ormond in 1667, leading to Anglesey's fall; in 1669, following Ormond's departure, a London consortium took over the revenue farm.[72] Two years after that, Orrery's 'well-connected and unashamedly venal' nephew, Richard Jones, Viscount Ranelagh, secured royal assent to a new scheme giving him control of both revenues and state

---

69 P. Little, *Lord Broghill and the Cromwellian Union with Ireland and Scotland* (Woodbridge: Boydell & Brewer, 2004), 161–89 and 193–208; P. Lenihan, *The Last Cavalier: Richard Talbot, 1631–91* (University College Dublin Press, 2015); Ohlmeyer, *Civil War and Restoration*, 258–89.

70 S. Hindle, *The State and Social Change in Early Modern England, 1550–1640* (Basingstoke: Palgrave, 2002); M. J. Braddick, *State Formation in Early Modern England, c.1550–1700* (Cambridge University Press, 2000); T. C. Barnard, 'Scotland and Ireland in the Later Stewart Monarchy', in S. G. Ellis and S. Barber (eds.), *Conquest and Union: Fashioning a British State, 1485–1725* (London: Longman, 1995), 250–75.

71 Connolly, *Religion, Law and Power*, 25.

72 Simms, 'Restoration, 1660–1685', 438–41.

expenditures – effectively farming out the Irish exchequer itself – for five years.[73] The bane of Essex's viceroyalty, the scheme was a fiasco for all but Louise de Kérouaille, duchess of Portsmouth – a royal mistress and the recipient of secret payments – and Ranelagh himself.[74] After a brief return to the *status quo*, revenues were at last placed in the hands of a royally appointed commission in 1682 – belatedly implementing a provision of the 1662 Customs and Excise Acts.

As all this suggests, the Restoration in Ireland was not a period of particularly aggressive state-building or institutional reform – in contrast to the revolution in landownership and to the dreams of projectors. The lord lieutenant's life may have been made easier in some respects by the absence of parliament after 1666, but it is less clear that his hand was permanently strengthened. To the contrary, it was the Ranelagh scheme that made an Irish parliament seem unnecessary during Essex's term, and the Popish Plot that made one seem dangerous during Ormond's third viceroyalty – spoiling his plans for an act to remedy defective titles and at last finalise the land settlement.[75] The abolition of the Munster and the redundant Connacht presidencies with Essex's appointment in 1672 streamlined the administrative hierarchy, but it did not eliminate the need for local magnates' acquiescence in major initiatives. Nor was it part of any systematic programme of centralisation; rather, it was Charles II's response to Orrery's persecution of Catholics in defiance of the royal preference for leniency.[76] Yet neither was this a period of chaos nor, excepting moments of crisis, of particularly violent repression – at least by the contemporary standards of the other Stuart kingdoms, each of which experienced genuine if localised rebellions, and where religious persecution arguably peaked.[77] Discontent simmered but did not boil over – no serious plot against the government surfaced after the summer of 1663 – and the state rumbled on. The forces making for substantive political change were of another order: on one level, the transgenerational formation of a service nobility; on another, the accumulating resentments and behind-the-scenes networking that would help bring about

---

73 T. C. Barnard, 'Interests in Ireland: The "Fanatic Zeal and Irregular Ambition" of Richard Lawrence', in C. Brady and J. Ohlmeyer (eds.), *British Interventions in Early Modern Ireland* (Cambridge University Press, 2005), 299–314, at 313; Simms, *Jacobite Ireland*, 15; Simms, 'Restoration, 1660–1685', 441–2.

74 Simms, *Jacobite Ireland*, 15.

75 Gibney, *Ireland and the Popish Plot*, 66–98; Kinsella, 'Irish Catholics and Land', 163–4.

76 D. Dickson, *Old World Colony: Cork and South Munster 1630–1830* (Cork University Press, 2005), 54; Little, *Lord Broghill*, 181.

77 T. Harris, *Restoration: Charles II and His Kingdoms, 1660–1685* (London: Penguin, 2006), 379.

a short-lived but radical reaction against the settlement and the order it sustained under James II.[78]

Besides the concerns of institutional and 'New British' approaches, two other aspects of Irish political history have attracted new or renewed attention from scholars. The first of these is the European context. In one sense, continental powers and institutions supplied a matrix that sustained Catholic critics and critiques of English and Protestant activities and policies in Ireland – a role that mirrored their place in Protestant memory and imagination as abettors of Irish rebellion. Excluded for most of Charles II's reign from the institutions of central government and indeed from all but local political office, Catholics relied on patronage networks and court connections to exert influence on policy and its enforcement; to sustain community, refine ideas and sway opinion they could draw on a much greater, more geographically dispersed set of resources. Irish Colleges such as St Anthony's at the University of Louvain, home at different times to Peter Walsh and Nicholas French, provided clerics with platforms – and presses – from which to broadcast their grievances and appeal for support to readers in Ireland as well as to Catholic monarchs and *élites* across Europe.[79] As the fate of the Remonstrance (a project opposed by the Vatican) shows, however, there was equally a European context for internal divisions among Irish Catholics, as different politico-religious agendas found support in different quarters of the church and in different secular courts.[80] Finally, recent research has begun to explore the extent to which the comparative study of other European provinces, such as the Spanish Sicilies or Habsburg Bohemia, can illuminate Ireland's peculiar status within the Stuart multiple monarchy.[81]

A second area of recent interest has been the emergence during the Restoration of new and popular forms of political culture. Given the absence of parliamentary politics between 1666 and 1689, the paucity of voluntary associations before the 1690s, and the circumscribed and comparatively lacklustre efforts of Dublin printers throughout the period, most historians have seen the emergence of a 'public sphere' in the Habermasian sense as

---

78 Ohlmeyer, *Making Ireland English*; Simms, *Jacobite Ireland*; Kinsella, 'Irish Catholics and Land'.
79 J. Casway, 'Gaelic Maccabeanism: The Politics of Reconciliation', in Ohlmeyer (ed.), *Political Thought in Seventeenth-Century Ireland: Kingdom or Colony* (Cambridge University Press, 2000), 176–88. See T. O'Connor (ed.), *The Irish in Europe, 1500–1815* (Dublin: FCP, 2001); T. O'Connor and M. A. Lyons (eds.), *Irish Communities in Early Modern Europe* (Dublin: FCP, 2006); R. Gillespie and R. Ó hUiginn (eds.), *Irish Europe 1600–1650: Writing and Learning* (Dublin: FCP, 2013).
80 Creighton, 'The Remonstrance', 33–4.
81 See Barnard, 'Crises of Identity', 44; Ohlmeyer, *Making Ireland English*, 27.

an eighteenth-century development.[82] Many of the new spaces and forms of association in and through which various publics were constituted – the theatre (in Dublin's Smock Alley, from 1662), the coffeehouse (from 1664) and even the scientific society (the Dublin Philosophical Society, from 1683) – first emerged in Irish cities at this time.[83] Cities themselves expanded, with Dublin leading the way, and with their growth came new possibilities for popular political expression. Regardless of regulation, moreover, the Restoration witnessed explosive growth in the commerce and culture of print. The land settlement, religious differences and Ireland's history over the previous century and more were hashed out in books and pamphlets accessible in Ireland even if printed elsewhere.[84] English plays and poems allegorised ideologies of rule and offered veiled commentaries both on and by the high and mighty; Orrery produced eight plays between 1662 and 1672, while the events of 1678–1681 led Dryden to cast Ormond as the faithful counsellor Barzillai in *Absalom and Achitophel*.[85] Some works, like the plays of Katherine Phillips, circulated or were performed only among *élite* coteries, but others were printed and widely read.[86] While attention naturally focused on those at the very top, even a projector like Petty could find himself publicly satirised; verse broadsides gave vent to still broader confessional and national antipathies.[87] Irish-language poetry from the period was similarly laden with political import and invective, though it was often more lapidary and retrospective in tone and scope – especially as hopes of restoration faded.[88] In more prosaic settings, sermons

82 See Chapter 18 by D. Rankin, this volume. But see P. Coughlan, 'Natural History and Historical Nature: The Project for a Natural History of Ireland', in M. Greengrass, M. Leslie and T. Raylor (eds.), *Samuel Hartlib and the Universal Reformation: Studies in Intellectual Communication* (Cambridge University Press, 1994), 298–317.

83 J. Kelly and M. J. Powell, 'Introduction', and P. Walsh, 'Club Life in late seventeenth- and early eighteenth-century Ireland: In search of an associational world, *c.*1680–1730', both in J. Kelly and M. J. Powell (eds.), *Clubs and Societies in Eighteenth-Century Ireland* (Dublin: FCP, 2010), 17–35 and 36–49 respectively; C. Morash, 'Theatre and Print, 1550–1800', in R. Gillespie and A. Hadfield (eds.), *The Irish Book in English 1550–1800* (OUP, 2006), 319–34; S. C. A. Pincus, ' "Coffee Politicians Does Create": Coffeehouses and Restoration Political Culture', *Journal of Modern History*, 67 (1995), 807–34, at 813; R. Gillespie, *Reading Ireland: Print, Reading, and Social Change in Early Modern Ireland* (Manchester University Press, 2005), 14.

84 R. Gillespie, 'Print Culture, 1550–1700', in Gillespie and Hadfield, *The Irish Book in English*, 17–33, at 23–6.

85 Little, *Lord Broghill*, 180; J. Ohlmeyer and S. Zwicker, 'John Dryden, the House of Ormond, and the Politics of Anglo-Irish Patronage', *Historical Journal*, 49 (2006), 677–706.

86 Gillespie, 'Print Culture', 27–9.

87 A. Carpenter (ed.), *Verse in English from Tudor and Stuart Ireland* (Cork University Press, 2003), 351–489.

88 A. Macinnes, 'Gaelic Culture in the Seventeenth Century: Polarization and Assimilation', in Ellis and Barber, *Conquest and Union*, 162–94. Compare T. J. Dunne, 'The Gaelic Response to Conquest and Colonisation: The Evidence of the Poetry', *Studia Hibernica*,

stoked the memory of rebellion and massacre while commemorative processions in villages and towns straddled the line between communal celebration and sectarian riot.[89] If the period saw any decisive 'modernisation' of Irish political life, it was as much in the discursive and the quotidian as in the realms of high politics and crisis.

Jacobite Ireland

The events of James II's reign in Ireland suggest a condensed, confused reprise of major themes from the preceding quarter-century: contention over land, a violent shift in office holding and parliamentary representation, the exposure of fatal fissures within the Catholic community, royal vacillation between fatally opposed but putatively loyal confessional groups, the frustrated expectation of radical change and the repeated and decisive intrusion of English events and imperatives on Irish political possibilities. The difference, of course, was that the king in question, though English, was Catholic, and that the ultimate re-imposition of a Protestant settlement only followed his defeat and exile by a foreign pretender, William of Orange, through a protracted political struggle – becoming, in Ireland, a bloody war – that brought a new regime to power in all three kingdoms. If the conservative imagery and rhetoric of Restoration concealed a revolutionary transformation of Irish landownership, the Glorious Revolution of 1688–1691 set on firmer foundations the supremacy of an increasingly unified Protestant *élite*. In this sense, it finally closed many of the questions left awkwardly open in 1660.

A revival of Catholic fortunes was apparent not long after the dust of the Exclusion Crisis had settled. The duke of York's return from his brief exile revived Richard Talbot's influence, and while Ormond's long-sought commission for defective titles was finally allowed to proceed, without parliamentary backing, in 1684, it did not long survive the new reign.[90] Ormond's recall had already been determined when news of King Charles's death reached Ireland, but his intended replacement, Laurence Hyde, earl of Rochester, had his commission cancelled before he could set sail. Instead, James's accession raised hopes among Catholics that Talbot, now ennobled as the earl of Tyrconnell, might take charge. The settlement accordingly came under renewed attack, starting with the republication of the *Narrative of... the Settlement and Sale of Ireland* in 1685 and continuing

---

20 (1980), 7–30, with B. Ó Buachalla, 'Review Article: Poetry and Politics in Early Modern Ireland', *Eighteenth-Century Ireland*, 7 (1992), 149–75.

89 Barnard, 'Athlone, 1685'.

90 Arnold, *Restoration in County Dublin*, 131–3; Kinsella, 'Irish Catholics and Land', 166–70.

in 1686 with Richard Nagle's 'Coventry letter', which advised against disappointing Catholics by confirming the settlement. Initially, however, the viceroyalty passed not to Tyrconnell but to the moderate, Anglican Henry Hyde, second earl of Clarendon, who sought as best he could to reassure Protestants, as well as Catholics of the 'new interest', that the settlement would remain in place.[91] Nevertheless, cannier landowners suspected that major changes were brewing, whether in the form of a revocation or a further round of retrenchments.[92] In the mean time, Tyrconnell, having been appointed lieutenant-general, turned his attention to purging the army of Protestant officers.[93]

The pace of change quickened with Clarendon's recall in 1687. Tyrconnell replaced him, taking the lesser title of lord deputy; Nagle, Tyrconnell's client, became attorney-general. The replacement of Protestant army officers with Catholics rapidly proceeded; a parallel conversion of civil offices, from the county level to the Privy Council, accelerated.[94] Fearing Catholic domination of the army and judiciary, and anticipating the reversal of the settlement and perhaps the public establishment of Catholicism, Protestants (including Presbyterians, who ceased to benefit from the *regium donum* or 'royal bounty' instituted by Charles) grew alienated from the Irish *régime* and, ultimately, from the king himself.[95] Some left the country; others, especially in the north, armed themselves.[96] At last, in early 1688, James transmitted two bills to the lord deputy, representing alternative approaches to the land problem: one would have reopened the settlement and re-established a Court of Claims; the other, preferred by Tyrconnell and more representative of the 'new interest' to which he belonged, imposed a blanket retrenchment on disputed lands, with half (minus the value of improvements) to revert to the original owners.[97] But events in England, where William landed in October, soon overtook the king and the lord deputy. By the time the Irish parliament sat, James himself was in Ireland attempting to regain his English throne, and the balance of political power between the interested groups had dramatically altered.

Political crisis thus determined the character of the 'Patriot Parliament', in session from 7 May until cut short on 18 July by the coming of war. The lords

---

91 Simms, *Jacobite Ireland*, 17–32; Kinsella, 'Irish Catholics and Land', 169–73.
92 See Kinsella, 'Irish Catholics and Land', 168.
93 Simms, *Jacobite Ireland*, 17.
94 Simms, *Jacobite Ireland*, 32–6.
95 Simms, *Jacobite Ireland*, 142; R. L. Greaves, *God's Other Children: Protestant Nonconformists and the Emergence of Denominational Churches in Ireland, 1660–1700* (Stanford University Press, 1997), 133–58.
96 Armstrong, 'The War of the Three Kings, 1689–91', 379.
97 Simms, *Jacobite Ireland*, 40–1.

were an unfamiliar amalgam: on the one hand, of the thirty-five temporal lords to sit, only seven were Protestant; on the other hand, the established church not yet having been dismantled, a mere four Church of Ireland bishops were willing to make up the spiritual contingent.[98] Accounting for nearly a quarter of the seats in the upper house, these Protestant lords have been seen as a source of continuity and a moderating influence on subsequent legislation; caught, as Irish Catholics had been hitherto, between divergent loyalties to crown and church, they might also be seen as embodying the inherent instability of the Irish Restoration itself.[99] The lower house, by contrast, was composed almost entirely of Catholics, among whom representatives of the dispossessed outnumbered those of the new interest. Given the desperate state of the Stuart cause, this made the repeal of the settlement inevitable, whatever Tyrconnell's preferences – or the king's. The Act of Repeal curtailed James's already dwindling Protestant support, and the same Parliament also passed over two hundred acts of attainder against Protestants charged with overt or covert allegiance to William.[100] Yet James soon alienated his Irish Catholic supporters, too. While ethnic and religious civil disabilities were removed, the king held fast against the Commons' attempts to undo Poynings' Law; Catholic re-establishment was one thing, Irish independence another.[101] The best that could be got was a Declaratory Act denying the English parliament power to legislate for Ireland (a claim exactly reversed by the Declaratory Act of 1720). Yet although reduced to a foothold in Ireland, James remained, in his own mind, king of England first. Defeated at the Boyne in July 1690, he fled the country. Following the decisive defeat of his forces at Aughrim the following summer, the Treaty of Limerick, signed 3 October 1691, made him no king at all.

The progress of the war and the ensuing history of Irish Jacobitism exceed the scope of this chapter.[102] Once the fighting was over and the revolution established, a new and thoroughly Protestant Irish parliament undid the legislation of 1689, restoring the land settlement and buttressing it with new confiscations and forfeitures. Yet Jacobite Ireland – like the Restoration itself – was no mere 'coda' before the inevitable re-imposition of the Cromwellian settlement.[103] For what emerged in the 1690s, though it resembled in many

---

98 Ohlmeyer, *Making Ireland English*, 356; James, *Lords of the Ascendancy*, 48–50.

99 James, *Lords of the Ascendancy*, 50; A. Carpenter, 'William King and the Threats to the Church of Ireland During the Reign of James II', IHS, 18 (1972), 22–8.

100 Dickson, *Old World Colony*, 56–7.

101 Armstrong, 'War of the Three Kings', 381–2.

102 See chapter 5 by C. I. McGrath. Armstrong, 'War of the Three Kings'; É. Ó Ciardha, *Ireland and the Jacobite Cause, 1685–1766: A Fatal Attachment* (Dublin: FCP, 2004).

103 T. C. Barnard, 'Conclusion', in C. Dennehy (ed.), *Restoration Ireland: Always Settling and Never Settled* (Aldershot: Ashgate, 2008), 179–93, at 184.

ways the Ireland imagined by Protestant framers of earlier settlements, was a harsher, more self-conscious and united colonial regime, based on harder and simpler divisions of the population than had been meaningful or desirable in 1660. Old and New Protestants, divided in the 1660s over the events of the 1640s and the quest for Catholic estates, coalesced into a Protestant Ascendancy; Old English and Gaelic Irish, united, too, in a freshly proscribed Catholicism, were exiled from professions, parliament and civil office. The fitful attempts to balance opposed interests and allegiances that distinguished the political history of the Restoration in Ireland had failed, corroded by internal politics of resentment and then made obsolete by the invasion of foreign armies.

5

Politics, 1692–1730

CHARLES IVAR MCGRATH

Politics in Ireland between 1692 and 1730 was dominated by questions regarding money, religion and security, all of which were engaged with against a backdrop of an ongoing debate about the kingdom of Ireland's constitutional relationship with England and, after 1707, Britain. Several factors rendered the period a new departure for the kingdom of Ireland: the complete and conclusive collapse of Roman Catholic political and economic power; the establishment of a Protestant hegemony in the governance of the country; the advent of regular parliamentary sessions; the adoption and adaptation of new innovations in public finance; and the emergence of Ireland as 'a self-funding garrison for a significant portion of the British standing army'.[1]

The Glorious Revolution of 1688 and the ensuing Irish war of 1689–1691 was a watershed in Irish politics. The bloodless English coup of November 1688 to February 1689 that led to the replacement of the Catholic James II on the thrones of England and Scotland with his Protestant daughter, Mary, and her husband, William, Prince of Orange, also led directly to the outbreak of a bloody war in Ireland as a result of the kingdom remaining loyal to James. The final military victory of the Williamite forces at Limerick in October 1691 brought the kingdom of Ireland back within the early modern European 'multiple monarchies' or 'composite states' model of governance that had previously held sway in the British Isles. However, it was, in certain significant respects, a remodelled model, with the monarchy having its powers slowly eroded by the English parliament at Westminster, which took centre-stage from 1689 onwards in the innovative financial and military developments that would ultimately drive the rapidly expanding British imperial project during the eighteenth century.[2]

---

1 P. Walsh, 'The Fiscal State in Ireland, 1691–1769', *Historical Journal*, 56 (2013), 633.
2 D. W. Hayton and J. Kelly, 'The Irish Parliament in European Context: A Representative Institution in a Composite State' in D. W. Hayton, J. Kelly and J. Bergin (eds.), *The Eighteenth-Century Composite State: Representative Institutions in Ireland and Europe, 1689–1800* (Houndmills: Palgrave Macmillan, 2010), 3–9.

Irish Protestants exiled in London in 1688–1691 watched from the side-lines as the early stages of this process unfolded. Many later returned to Ireland imbued with the rhetoric of change, thereby ensuring that the kingdom of Ireland would become caught up in England's constitutional and financial revolutions of the 1690s and early eighteenth century, and the concomitant emergence of the British fiscal-military state and empire. But, owing to differing interpretations on either side of the Irish Sea of Ireland's constitutional relationship with the monarchy and the English state, it would at times be a torturous political journey.[3]

Irish Roman Catholics, although directly affected in all respects by its outcomes, were for all intents and purposes excluded from this journey. Although a majority of the population, the adherence of Irish Catholics to the cause of James II had finally brought about the complete collapse of their political, economic and social power. The traditional leadership within Catholic Ireland was decimated by the loss of many heads of gentry and noble families during the war, in particular at Aughrim in July 1691 and thereafter by the flight of the 'wild geese' at the end of the war. Although the articles of surrender agreed at Galway and especially at Limerick ostensibly offered some hope for the Catholic political interest, the rump of that traditional leadership grouping that remained in Ireland thereafter proved unable to exercise any significant influence in the corridors of power either in Dublin or London, especially in the face of vehement Irish Protestant hostility to any aspect of the articles of surrender that offered concessions to Irish Catholics.

The Treaty of Limerick and Catholic Ireland

The articles of surrender agreed at Limerick were signed on 3 October 1691. William III's desire to free up his army for participation in the War of the Grand Alliance against France in Europe ensured that the terms agreed were quite favourable to Catholics. The military articles were straightforward, and allowed for any Jacobites who so wished to be transported to France to continue in the service of James II. Ultimately about 12,000 soldiers and dependants did so. The civil articles were much more contentious, however, and quickly became the source of significant discontent within Protestant Ireland. Having won the war, Irish Protestants came to believe they were to lose the peace.

---

3 C. I. McGrath, *Ireland and Empire, 1692–1770* (London: Pickering and Chatto, 2012), 1–12, 37–67.

Article One was the most problematic because it allowed Catholics 'such privileges in the exercise of their religion as are consistent with the laws of Ireland' or as had been allowed under Charles II. William III was also committed by this article to summoning an Irish parliament for the purpose of providing Catholics with 'such farther security in that particular, as may preserve them from any disturbance, upon the account of their religion'. For Catholics, this was a crucial agreement aimed at ensuring that the kind of penal laws that had been introduced in England over the preceding hundred years would never make it to the Irish statute books.

Article Two proved contentious primarily because a clause agreed during negotiations was inadvertently omitted from the final signed copy sent to William III. The omitted clause had extended the protection from forfeiture offered to those in Limerick and other Jacobite garrisons in October 1691 to all those under Jacobite protection in Counties Limerick, Clare, Kerry, Cork and Mayo as well. Although the clause was restored by order of the king, it remained a point of contention because the real issue was to do with the political and economic power bestowed by owning land.[4]

The stipulation in Article Nine that Catholics were only required to take the oath of allegiance also proved problematic. There had been numerous unsuccessful attempts by Irish Catholics throughout the seventeenth century to come up with a new formula of words that would release them from any obligation to take the oath of supremacy, which required them to deny their religious adherence to Rome. Article Nine seemed to provide a solution, given that since February 1689 the oath of allegiance had become a simple *de facto* acknowledgement of William and Mary as the reigning monarchs. From a Protestant perspective, however, refusal to take the oath of supremacy equated to disloyalty. As if confirming that view, within weeks of the Limerick Articles being agreed, the Westminster parliament passed an act for abrogating the oath of supremacy in Ireland and appointing other oaths, which included a new oath of supremacy and a declaration against transubstantiation. Although a saving clause was included for those covered by the articles, the English Oaths Act was the beginning of the end for Article Nine.[5]

Article Twelve committed the king to seeking the Treaty's ratification in the Irish parliament. That pledge, intended as a further guarantee for the implementation of the articles, ultimately proved their undoing. Faced with

---

4 J. G. Simms, *The Treaty of Limerick* (Dundalk: Dundalgan Press, 1965), 3–13, 19–20.
5 E. Kinsella, 'In Pursuit of a Positive Construction: Irish Catholics and the Williamite Articles of Surrender, 1690–1701', *Eighteenth-Century Ireland* [hereafter *ECI*], 24 (2009), 20–1.

vehement opposition from Irish Protestants, the governments in both Dublin and London continually postponed ratification for fear it would undermine other government business. When approval eventually occurred in 1697, it was in a much-mutilated form and only after significant in-roads had already been made by the Irish parliament into undermining the articles, in particular in the first penal laws of 1695. The evidently misnamed 1697 Act for confirming the Articles of Limerick excluded Articles One and Nine completely and left out the omitted clause from Article Two, while none of the remaining articles were confirmed in full. To the government's surprise, a significant minority in the all-Protestant Irish House of Lords, including seven bishops, objected to the act because it did not ratify the treaty in full. The passage of the 1697 Act clearly signalled that the Treaty of Limerick had not managed to achieve the ends for which Catholics had hoped, a fact demonstrated with great regularity in the passage of numerous penal laws against Catholics during the ensuing decades which clearly breached the meaning of the first article in particular and the intended ethos of the Treaty more generally, even when some of those same laws included clauses that protected the individuals and groups specifically covered by the Treaty.

Despite such broken promises, however, the Treaty did significantly reduce the amount of Catholic land confiscated. First, only fifteen of 1,283 claims made by Catholics between 1692 and 1699 under the Articles of Limerick and Galway were unsuccessful. Second, despite failure to ratify the omitted clause from Article Two in 1697, actual confiscation of property previously protected by that clause required government action in the courts, which was not forthcoming. Third, the dispute between William III and the English parliament throughout the 1690s over the disposal of Irish forfeited lands meant that no legislation was enacted for implementing a wholesale confiscation. Instead, the government had to take individual legal proceedings against Jacobite exiles or others not covered by the articles of surrender, a process that hampered confiscations. The English parliament finally resolved the dispute with the 1700 Act of Resumption, which resulted in about forty estates being granted back to Catholic owners via a court of claims that allowed (in whole or part) 1,861 of more than 3,200 submitted claims. Overall, the Williamite confiscation resulted in Catholic landholding dropping from about 22 per cent in 1688 to 14 per cent by 1703. But without the Articles of Limerick, and despite the breaching of them, the final percentage of land in Catholics' hands would have been less.[6]

---

6 See Chapter 23 by M. Ó Siochrú and D. Brown, this volume. J. G. Simms, *The Williamite Confiscation in Ireland 1690–1703* (London: Faber & Faber, 1956), 30–46, 82–120, 136–7, 196.

Ultimately, however, the history of the Limerick Articles demonstrated that the Irish Catholic community had finally lost all meaningful political and economic power. That power now lay firmly in the hands of a minority Protestant ruling *élite*. And the main vehicle through which that power was exercised was the Irish parliament.

The Advent of Regular Parliaments, 1692–1695

Traditionally the Glorious Revolution of 1688 is perceived as heralding the birth of Britain's constitutional monarchy, with the emergence of parliament at the centre of political and economic power. The revolution committed England to massively increased expenditure on an annual basis in order to fund the War of the Grand Alliance, which in turn facilitated the transformation of the Westminster parliament as it began meeting on an annual basis owing to its new-found control over the supply of money to government. Parliament's willingness to engage with new and innovative forms of public financial provision in the 1690s and thereafter, in order to fund ever-increasing government expenditure on war, constituted a financial revolution which facilitated the emergence of the British fiscal-military state and the growth of the empire in the eighteenth century.

While in theory the development of such a role for the Irish parliament was not a necessary contingent part of the Glorious Revolution, from the outset William III proved willing to continue to govern Ireland as before, in particular agreeing to convene the Irish legislature once the 1689–1691 war was concluded. The Limerick Articles also committed William to convening a parliament, which, as a result of the Westminster parliament's 1691 Oaths Act, would be for the first time ever a wholly Protestant assembly. In early 1692, in accordance with Poynings' Law, the Irish government began to consider possible legislation for presentation to parliament. Concerns were expressed at the evident dissatisfaction among Irish Protestants with the Limerick Articles, while allegations of government corruption and financial embezzlement also fuelled discontent. At the same time, however, the ever-increasing awareness in both Dublin and London of a looming financial crisis owing to the collapse of public income during the war focused attention on the need to convene parliament for the purpose of enacting new taxation legislation.[7]

---

7 J. I. McGuire, 'The Irish Parliament of 1692', in T. Bartlett and D. W. Hayton (eds.), *Penal Era and Golden Age: Essays in Irish History, 1690–1800* (Belfast: Ulster Historical Foundation, 1979), 1–31.

Traditionally, parliament voted money for specific requests, often made at times of a particular crisis. On those rare occasions when parliament met, the norm was to provide sufficient additional income to overcome the immediate crisis via subsidies levied directly upon the populace. At all other times the government was expected to live on its own resources. Prior to the Glorious Revolution the Irish government's permanent annual sources of income grew from a low (in 1660) of between £35,000 and £70,000 to a Restoration peak of £286,516 (in 1686). Such growth was facilitated by the creation of a secure tax base by the Irish parliament in 1661–1666, when it voted a financial settlement upon Charles II which included new hereditary revenues made up from quit rents, customs, import and inland excise and a hearth tax. The Restoration parliament's largesse ensured that the government did not need to reconvene parliament thereafter. Irish chief governors during the 1670s and 1680s, however, recognised that if parliament was to be summoned again, it would not repeat the mistake of voting hereditary revenues. The taxation model for future Irish parliaments was to be taken from the innovative practices of the English Restoration parliament in voting short-term additional duties on existing customs and excise rates. To that end, in 1692 the lord lieutenant, Henry, Viscount Sidney, proposed two short-term additional supply bills for raising £70,000 over two years. The first bill was for a one-year additional excise on beer, ale and other liquors, and the second for further duties on grain and other commodities.[8]

The first error the government made in 1692 was to convene parliament without sufficient business to keep MPs busy, given that many of the government's bills were still being considered in London. The second and greater error was that the government took a traditional approach to Poynings' Law and prepared a substantive legislative programme, which did not allow parliament any role in initiating legislation. This was despite parliament's long-standing desire for such a role, which had been expressed as far back as 1613–1615 and pursued with increasing vigour in 1640 1641 and 1661–1666. The third and final error was to present the two supply bills as a *fait accompli*, without any room for input from parliament.[9]

From the earliest days of the 1692 parliament, the House of Commons made it clear that they were intent upon investigating allegations of government

---

8 C. I. McGrath, *The Making of the Eighteenth-Century Irish Constitution: Government, Parliament and the Revenue, 1692–1714* (Dublin: Four Courts Press [hereafter FCP], 2000), 24–38, 49–55, 73–8.

9 C. I. McGrath, 'Government, Parliament and the Constitution: The Reinterpretation of Poynings' Law, 1692–1714', *Irish Historical Studies* [hereafter *IHS*], 35 (2006), 162–6.

corruption and embezzlement. Sidney quickly grew concerned, requesting that London hurry the remaining bills to Ireland in order to occupy MPs. The Commons also began preparing their own legislation by means of 'heads of bills', a process that had been attempted in 1640–1641 and 1661–1666 though with little success.[10]

Matters came to a head following the presentation of the two supply bills. On 27 October the Commons resolved that it was their 'undoubted right … to prepare and resolve the ways and means of raising money' and their 'sole and undoubted right … to prepare heads of bills for raising money'. The one-year excise bill was then proceeded upon because of the government's great financial need, but in order to demonstrate that this was an exceptional circumstance, on the following day the Commons rejected the second supply bill because it had not been initiated by themselves.[11] The 'Sole Right' resolutions and the reasons for rejecting the second supply bill constituted a direct attack on Poynings' Law in relation to supply bills and, more generally, on the crown's prerogative right to initiate legislation. As a result, once the additional excise bill had been enacted, Sidney brought the session to an immediate end by formally recording his protest against the Commons' resolutions. The prorogation also brought the Commons' investigations into government corruption to a premature end, which also suited the purpose of Sidney and other Irish officials.[12]

The actions of the 1692 parliament were motivated by a desire to have a greater say in the running of the country and were inspired by the events of the Glorious Revolution. However, the immediate effect was a political impasse that prevented the reconvening of parliament until 1695. Initially London supported Sidney's stance, but as continuing allegations of government corruption spilled over into the Westminster parliament and pay arrears owing to the army in Ireland continued to escalate, alternatives began to be explored. In July 1693 a new commission of three lords justices was appointed to replace Sidney, and by mid-1694 evidence of a potential compromise solution began to emerge centred around the Whig lord justice, Henry, Baron Capel of Tewkesbury, who promised London a successful session if certain laws were introduced, including penal laws against Catholics, and if parliament was allowed a legislative initiative. In return, Irish politicians promised that the 'Sole Right' claim would be dropped. The deal was sealed when

10 J. Kelly, *Poynings' Law and the Making of Law in Ireland 1660–1800* (Dublin: FCP, 2007), 1–63.
11 *The Journals of the House of Commons of the Kingdom of Ireland* (21 vols., Dublin, 1796–1802) [hereafter *CJI*], ii, 28.
12 McGrath, *Irish Constitution*, 83–8; McGuire, 'Irish Parliament', 18–23.

Capel was made lord deputy and key members of the 1692 opposition were brought into government office, including the Cork Whig, Alan Brodrick, as solicitor-general.[13]

The convening of the second Williamite parliament in 1695 marked the dawning of a new era for the Irish legislature. Capel's opening speech constituted the first ever direct appeal to the Commons for a financial supply, the first acknowledgement of their right to consider the 'ways and means' of raising that supply, the first promise to provide the government's accounts as part of that process, and the first official recognition of the 'heads of bills' procedure as a legitimate means for initiating legislation. In return, the Commons passed a token government supply bill for one year's additional excise on beer, ale and other liquors by way of recognition of the crown's prerogative and Poynings' Law. The Commons then assessed the ways and means for raising the further money required to pay the army and drafted the heads of bills for three further supply acts, each of which was of short duration, with two for imposing additional duties for two and four years respectively and one for a two-year poll tax.[14]

The 1695 parliament also enacted the first two penal laws, for disarming Irish Catholics and for prohibiting foreign education. Both bills took their example from long-standing penal laws against Catholics in England, while at the same time deriving more immediately from continuing Irish Protestant security fears both within Ireland and from the threat of Jacobites in France. Like many later penal laws, the Disarming Act included savings for those covered by the Limerick Articles, in this instance in relation to the ownership of weapons. The saving was included by the English Privy Council on the prompting of two petitions from Irish Catholics against the bill. However, the clauses that prohibited Catholics from owning horses valued at more than £5 because they were deemed to be of a military capacity applied to all Catholics because this issue had not been thought of by those who had negotiated the Limerick Articles. The Foreign Education Act was also deemed a security measure because it was intended to prevent Irish Catholics from coming into contact with exiled Jacobites or falling under

---

13 C. I. McGrath, 'English Ministers, Irish Politicians and the Making of a Parliamentary Settlement in Ireland, 1692–5', *English Historical Review* [hereafter *EHR*], 119 (2004), 585–613.

14 *The Statutes at Large, passed in the Parliaments held in Ireland: from the Third Year of Edward the Second, A.D. 1310, to the First Year of George the Third, A.D. 1761 Inclusive* (8 vols., Dublin, 1765) [hereafter *Stat. Ire.*], iii, 249–50, 289–95, 312–13, 328; C. I. McGrath, 'Parliamentary Additional Supply: The Development and Use of Regular Short-term Taxation in the Irish Parliament, 1692–1716', *Parliamentary History*, 20 (2001), 34–6.

the influence of the regular Catholic clergy who ran the Irish colleges on the continent.[15]

The 1695 compromise established the foundations for a new constitutional understanding in Ireland. The 'heads of bills' procedure quickly became the means for producing the vast majority of legislation in parliament;[16] responsibility for the vast majority of the government's required additional income to pay for the army now lay with the Commons; and, because of the adoption of short-term additional duties as the means of providing that essential extra income, parliament had to meet on a regular basis in the future: it was no longer an occasional event, but rather had become a central part of the machinery of state.

Practical Politics and Constitutional Conflict, 1696–1700

The success of the 1695 compromise was most immediately seen in the improvement of the government's finances. The additional income arising from the 1695 supply acts resulted in a dramatic reduction in pay arrears owed to the army. The government's ongoing annual expenditure, however, continued to increase because of the continuing financial demands of paying and maintaining the enlarged Irish military establishment, a post-Glorious Revolution innovation that was made permanent in 1699 when the English parliament voted that a standing army of 12,000 men be stationed in Ireland and paid for by the Irish treasury. As a result, the Irish parliament had to be convened with regularity in order to meet these increased demands.

In 1697 the second session of the 1695 parliament sat and, in accordance with the compromise agreement, another two short-duration supply acts for a one-year poll tax and further additional duties for between three and four years were drafted by means of the 'heads of bills' procedure. It was not deemed necessary to present a token government supply bill, as the one which had passed in 1695 was considered to be sufficient recognition of the crown's prerogative for the whole lifetime of a parliament. Confusion on this matter arose when the third session of the 1695 parliament convened in

---

15 *Stat. Ire.*, iii, 254–67; C. I. McGrath, 'Securing the Protestant Interest: The Origins and Purpose of the Penal Laws of 1695', *IHS*, 30:117 (1996), 25–46; S. J. Connolly, *Religion, Law and Power: The Making of Protestant Ireland 1660–1760* (Oxford University Press, 1992), 264–8.

16 D. W. Hayton, 'Introduction: The Long Apprenticeship', *Parliamentary History*, 20 (2001), 9–11.

1698–1699, but the politics of the practical won the day and the compromise was upheld again with two more short-duration supply acts for a two-year land tax and further additional duties for four and a half years being produced through the 'heads of bills' procedure.[17]

Of note within the supply acts passed in 1697 and 1698–1699 was the provision of a substantial fund for the commencement of a new and innovative policy for the building of a country-wide network of army barracks to provide permanent residential complexes for Ireland's standing army. Only France, and to a lesser extent Spain, had engaged with the concept of providing permanent army residences before the 1690s, and England would not do so until the end of the eighteenth century because of the association of standing armies with Frenchified Catholic absolutist and tyrannical government. Indeed, the vociferous anti-standing army debate in England following the end of the War of the Grand Alliance in 1697 and the resulting disbandment of William III's army provided added impetus to the Irish barrack-building project because 12,000 men – the single largest part of William's peacetime army – were thereafter stationed in Ireland. For Irish MPs, that army offered a sense of security in the face of a majority Catholic population believed to be inherently disloyal. Irish Protestants also recognised that building residential barracks would alleviate the burden of quartering on public and private houses that brought with it many economic and social problems. The ideological debates in England about standing armies riding roughshod over the liberties, rights and properties of freeborn Englishmen had no place in the considerations of a minority ruling *élite* looking for relief from army billeting and surrounded by an apparently hostile populace. Hence about thirty-five of the initial 102 barracks were small redoubts for internal security – to protect mountain passes, to offer safe passage through sparsely populated areas and to deter Jacobite or privateer activity in remote, inhospitable locations. However, the remaining sixty-seven barracks served primarily as places of residence, organisation and training. It was these latter barracks that quickly became a crucial component in the expansion of the British empire in the eighteenth century. Housing reformed regiments with a higher ratio of officers and non-commissioned officers to private soldiers in peacetime, the barracks became the first port of call for soldiers to fight in far-flung corners of the globe on the numerous occasions when Britain went to war in the eighteenth century.[18]

---

17 *Stat. Ire.*, iii, 353–8, 374–96, 451–70, 471–2; McGrath, *Irish Constitution*, 118–52.
18 McGrath, *Ireland and Empire*, 69–166.

The 1697 and 1698–1699 sessions also enacted new penal laws. Two acts were passed in 1697, for banishing the Catholic ecclesiastical hierarchy and regular clergy and for prohibiting intermarrying between Protestants and Catholics, and one in 1698–1699, for preventing Catholics from being solicitors. The latter law was just the first in a series of measures targeting Catholics in the legal profession, with further acts in 1707, 1728 and 1734, all of which were motivated by the fact that Catholic legal practitioners constituted a powerful and influential grouping within society.[19] However, the most significant of the 1697–1699 penal laws was the 1697 Banishment Act. It originated as 'heads of bills' in 1695, but at that time had been postponed by government owing to pressure from William III's Catholic allies, in particular the Holy Roman Emperor, Leopold I. The bill was reintroduced in 1697 with the government's backing in part as an attempt to counter-balance the negative impact of the pending introduction of the much-delayed bill for ratifying the Limerick Articles. On this occasion the efforts of William's Catholic allies proved futile. The Banishment Act required all Catholic archbishops, bishops and the regular clergy to leave Ireland before 1 May 1698, with any who returned thereafter deemed guilty of high treason. Penalties were included for any new clergy arriving in Ireland and for those who tried to hide them. The act also allowed for the continued dissolution of monasteries and convents, a provision which highlighted the fact that such religious complexes still existed in Ireland almost 160 years after the Henrician dissolution was first embarked upon. Like most other penal laws, the act had a longer history, being based on long-standing English penal laws and various seventeenth-century proclamations.[20]

The theoretical intention of the Banishment Act was that by cutting off the head of the Catholic Church, the remainder would wither away in a generation or so. But in reality there was a security fear evident as well. The Catholic hierarchy and regular clergy were perceived as the primary instigators of all previous rebellions in Ireland, owing to the fact that they exercised a foreign jurisdiction in Ireland because of their spiritual and temporal allegiance to Rome. In reality, however, despite the transportation of somewhere between 400 and 700 clergy in 1698, by the early 1700s the number of Catholic clergy had increased once again and, in the absence of any sort of coordinated or consistent attempts at enforcing the law, continued to do so

19 *Stat. Ire.*, iii, 339–43, 349–53, 512–14; iv, 121–5; v, 287–9; vi, 13–20.
20 J. G. Simms, 'The Bishops' Banishment Act of 1697 (9 Will. III, c. 1)', *IHS*, 17:66 (1970), 185–93; M. Wall, *The Penal Laws, 1691–1760* (Dundalk: Dundalgan Press, 1976), 11–16.

through the eighteenth century. Likewise, Catholic monasteries and convents also continued to exist in Ireland throughout the eighteenth century.[21]

However, the apparent consensus politics behind increased supply and penal legislation in the Irish parliament in the later 1690s belied a growing constitutional conflict centred on the age-old issue of the right of the English parliament to legislate for Ireland. The publication in 1698 by the MP for Trinity College, William Molyneux, of a pamphlet entitled *The Case of Ireland's Being Bound by Acts of Parliament in England, Stated*, was prompted by a lawsuit between the Protestant bishop of Derry, William King, and the Irish Society and by the pending enactment by the Westminster parliament of a law prohibiting the exportation of Irish woollen manufactures and the restriction of the export of raw wool to England only. Previous English legislation had similarly targeted Irish economic activity that was perceived as being too competitive for English equivalents, in particular the Irish cattle industry, while the Navigation Acts (1651, 1660, 1671 and 1681) had placed restrictions on Irish overseas trade. Molyneux's pamphlet rehearsed numerous arguments against the assumed right of the English parliament to legislate for Ireland and borrowed liberally from earlier writers, including the Catholic Patrick Darcy and Protestant Sir Richard Bolton in the 1640s, Molyneux's own father-in-law, Sir William Domville, in the 1660s, and the Protestant bishop of Meath, Anthony Dopping, in 1692. Molyneux however omitted to mention the 1689 Jacobite parliament's Declaratory Act, which had looked to put an end to such English legislative and appellate jurisdiction in Ireland, though his omission was understandable in light of that parliament having been declared null and void by Westminster in 1690 and all its acts destroyed by order of the Irish parliament in 1695. However, the 1689 Declaratory Act and Molyneux's *Case of Ireland* demonstrated that political issues regarding Ireland's constitutional relationship with England could, and often did, transcend religious divisions.[22]

Molyneux's pamphlet caused most trouble in the Westminster parliament, where it was condemned as a danger to the connection between Ireland and England. In Ireland the reaction was less vocal, though the issues at stake came home to roost very quickly, not only with the passage of the English Woollen Act in 1699 which had an obvious detrimental impact upon the Irish woollen industry, but also with the English parliament's Act of Resumption

---

21 Simms, 'Banishment Act', 193–9; Connolly, *Religion, Law and Power*, 149–59.
22 William Molyneux, *The Case of Ireland's being Bound by Acts of Parliament made in England, Stated* (Dublin, 1698), *passim*.

in 1700 which created significant political discontent among Irish Protestants, particularly those who had purchased forfeited lands from William's grantees during the 1690s. That discontent had a galvanising effect upon a significant number of Irish politicians who formed the nucleus of a Whig party in Ireland in the ensuing decades.

Whig and Tory Party Politics, 1700–1714

One impact of the Glorious Revolution in England was the emergence of party politics. The English Whig party evolved out of the political grouping that in 1679–1681 had advocated for the exclusion of James, duke of York, from the royal succession and had, after York succeeded as James II, led the push for his removal in 1687–1688. Advocates of a contractual monarchy, the Whigs believed they would come into their own after 1688 but instead found themselves vying for power with the Tory party, who were named pejoratively after Irish Catholic outlaws known as *Tóraí* (pursuer or hunter) because, as high-churchmen, they believed in the divine right of kings and passive obedience and had defended York's succession right in 1679–1681. The extension of these English party divisions to Ireland occurred slowly during the 1690s, but were never clearly defined during that decade. However, a much more identifiable Irish Whig party emerged out of the discontent caused by the activities in 1700–1703 of the Westminster-appointed Trustees for the forfeitures, who were seen in Ireland as creatures of the English Tory party, and in opposition to the Tory dominance in English politics following the accession of Queen Anne on the death of William III in March 1702.[23]

Led by Alan Brodrick, throughout Anne's reign the Irish Whigs were driven by a desire for annual parliamentary sittings and, more generally, for an increase in the power of the Irish parliament. In the first of Anne's parliaments, in 1703–1704, the Whigs succeeded in getting Brodrick nominated as speaker of the Commons by the Tory-led government of James Butler, second duke of Ormond. To Ormond's surprise and annoyance, Brodrick then proceeded to lead the attempts to restrict the supply acts to only one year's duration, with the aim of ensuring annual parliaments. Although unsuccessful in this endeavour, the Whigs' efforts did result in the additional duties only being voted for two years, which would become the norm from 1715 onwards and would ensure that for much of the eighteenth century Irish parliaments met

---

23 D. W. Hayton, *Ruling Ireland, 1685–1742: Politics, Politicians and Parties* (Woodbridge: Boydell and Brewer, 2004), 35–105.

on a biennial basis.[24] The Whigs were also behind an important address to the queen from the Irish Commons in October 1703, which appeared to advocate for a closer union between the two countries. Traditionally, this address has been interpreted as a request for a parliamentary Union, prompted by the concurrent negotiations for an Anglo-Scottish Union. The simultaneous publication of an anonymously authored pamphlet apparently advocating for an Anglo-Irish Union and the later identification of the pamphlet's author as Henry Maxwell, a stalwart member of the Irish Whig party, would seem to confirm such views, though the complexity of Maxwell's political ideology and independence of thought has only truly been uncovered in recent years.[25] In actual fact, with Maxwell to the fore, the Irish Whigs had manipulated the unionist sentiment of some MPs and used it to turn the address into a forceful demand for a full enjoyment of their constitutional rights, including, in particular, frequent parliaments. They had also made sure to include a hard-hitting list of grievances against the Trustees, government corruption and English interference in Ireland, all of which made the address an embarrassment for the Tory government.[26]

The Whigs continued in opposition in the 1705 session, and again were unsuccessful in trying to restrict the money supply to one year's duration. However, the Whig resurgence in English politics in 1706–1707 saw a shift to a mixed ministry in Ireland in 1707 and the first real success for Brodrick and his allies. In a compromise agreement that Brodrick pedantically claimed was not a change of principles but rather of measures, the party agreed to support a supply of one and three-quarter years in the 1707 session. The continuing swing to the Whigs in England during 1708 resulted in a Whig lord lieutenant, Thomas, first marquis of Wharton, being sent to Ireland in 1709 to oversee a fourth session at which, for the first time ever, the government did not present any legislation and instead all acts began as 'heads of bills'. The session also resulted in the Whigs finally achieving their goal of a one-year duration supply act. It was a short-lived victory, however, as the pendulum of political favour began to swing back to the Tories the following year when a fifth session saw another Whig compromise as the duration of the main supply act

---

24 *Stat. Ire.*, iv, 1–2, 7–10; C. I. McGrath, 'Alan Brodrick and the Speakership of the House of Commons, 1703–4', in J. Kelly, J. McCafferty and C. I. McGrath (eds.), *People, Politics and Power: Essays on Irish History 1660–1850 in Honour of James I. McGuire* (Dublin: UCD Press, 2009), 70–93.

25 D. W. Hayton, *The Anglo-Irish Experience, 1680–1730* (Woodbridge: Boydell and Brewer, 2012), 118–20.

26 C. I. McGrath, 'The "Union" Representation of 1703 in the Irish House of Commons: A Case of Mistaken Identity?', *ECI*, 23 (2008), 11–35.

was extended to one and a half years. By the time parliament convened again in 1711 the pendulum had swung fully back to the Tories, a circumstance most apparent in the return of Ormond as lord lieutenant. Not surprisingly, the sixth and final session of the 1703 parliament returned to voting supply acts of two years duration.[27]

All the party-political wrangling did not however detract attention away from the question of penal legislation. At least one penal law was passed in each of the first four sessions of the 1703 parliament. Of the three acts passed in 1703–1704, the two for preventing clergy coming into Ireland and for registering those already in the country were aimed at building upon the 1697 Banishment Act. However, the third act, to prevent the further growth of popery, was much more far-reaching and was a central pillar of the penal laws. The title itself highlighted the mentality of fear synonymous with the genesis of the penal code, suggesting as it did that Catholicism was increasing in strength despite being outside the law. Irish Catholics mounted a significant campaign against the act, which prompted Speaker Brodrick to allege that substantial sums of Catholic money had been sent to London for bribing English officials. The act itself introduced a wide range of provisions affecting Catholic social, cultural, political and economic activities, including land ownership and inheritance, office-holding, education, guardianship, voting rights and conversion. In 1703 only 14 per cent of land in Ireland remained in Catholics' hands. By prohibiting Catholics from purchasing land, the 1704 act aimed at ensuring that that percentage could not increase. By imposing inheritance by gavelkind, whereby the estate would be sub-divided among all sons or all daughters or all collateral kindred, the act looked to reduce the size and value – and thereby the political, social and economic significance – of Catholic estates. And by prioritising inheritance by primogeniture for any eldest son who converted to the Church of Ireland, the act looked to reduce further the percentage of land in Catholic hands. This last element proved the most successful, in that the decrease in Catholic-owned land in the ensuing decades occurred mainly because of conversion to Protestantism in order to keep estates intact. For its part, the practice of gavelkind seems to have had little impact.[28]

With regard to office-holding, the 1704 act introduced the sacramental test to Ireland. All civil and military office-holders were required to provide

---

27 *Stat. Ire.*, iv, 69–70, 109–12, 187–90, 251–4, 291–3; McGrath, *Irish Constitution*, 181–264.

28 *Stat. Ire.*, iv, 5–6, 12–31, 31–3; J. G. Simms, 'The Making of a Penal Law (2 Anne, c.6), 1703–4', *IHS*, 12:46 (1960), 105–18; L. M. Cullen, 'Catholics under the Penal Laws', *ECI*, 1 (1986), 26–36; Connolly, *Religion, Law and Power*, 308–10.

certified evidence that they had received the sacrament of the lord's supper in accordance with the usage of the Church of Ireland and, upon enrolling that certificate with the courts, to take the oaths of allegiance and new supremacy and subscribe the declaration in accordance with the 1691 Oaths Act. However, the 1704 act required that office-holders also take the newer abjuration oath against the Stuart Pretender and in recognition of the royal succession in the Protestant House of Hanover as legislated for by the English parliament. Initially those Catholics covered by the Limerick Articles were exempted from the new oath, but by 1707 even they were obliged to take it. The sacramental test clearly constituted a part of the practical process of conversion to the Church of Ireland. From a political perspective, however, the inclusion of the test late in the process while the bill was in London stemmed first and foremost from an English Tory agenda targeted at Protestant Dissenters, in particular Presbyterians. The Presbyterian heartland in Ireland was Ulster, and as a grouping that nonconformist community remained politically and economically important. Unsuccessful proposals for repealing the Irish test were mooted between 1707 and 1710 and again in 1715–1716 and 1719, on which latter occasion a very restricted Toleration Act was passed instead.[29]

In the interim, the test had been more fully enshrined as an essential part of the conversion process in the one penal law passed in 1709 which, despite its innocuous title as an Act 'for explaining and amending' the 1704 act, constituted the other central pillar of the penal code. The 1709 act looked to close loopholes that had emerged since 1704 in relation to land purchase and inheritance, education, marriage, conversion, Catholic clergy and many, many other areas of Catholic life. The most notorious element was the introduction of the Protestant 'discoverers' who, in one guise, could get possession of any land illegally purchased by or for Catholics and, in another guise as a 'priest-catcher', would receive £50 for discovery of every archbishop, bishop or other cleric exercising ecclesiastical authority and £20 for each regular priest or unregistered secular priest, as well as £10 for an illegal Catholic schoolmaster. Prior to the 1709 act two other penal laws had been enacted in 1705 and 1707 for amending legislation relating to registering Catholic clergy and excluding Catholics from the legal professions. However, after 1709 the enactment of penal laws became more intermittent and tended to be amendments or additions to existing acts.[30]

---

29 *Stat. Ire.*, iv, 21–3, 121–5, 508–16; Simms, 'Making of a Penal Law', 112–16; Hayton, *Ruling Ireland*, 186–208.

30 *Stat. Ire.*, iv, 71–2, 121–5, 190–216; McGrath, *Ireland and Empire*, 33–5.

Growing uncertainty about the royal succession and a Tory triumph-alism, which caused deep divisions within Irish politics, marked the final years of Anne's reign in Ireland, as in England. The crisis was crystallised by a dispute in the Dublin Corporation over the ongoing refusal of the Privy Council, led by the English arch-Tory, Lord Chancellor Sir Constantine Phipps, to ratify any of the Whig candidates nominated for mayor. The targeting of Whig politicians in lawsuits and the protection from prosecu-tion of Jacobite sympathisers further fuelled tensions. The *dénouement* came in the new parliament convened in November 1713. Expectations of a Tory landslide in the general election proved illusory, a fact reflected in the elec-tion of Brodrick to the speakership ahead of the government's nominee. The ensuing session proved short-lived as the Whigs hijacked the supply process and demanded the immediate removal of Phipps and redress of grievances built up over the preceding four years. Having agreed to pass the government's token supply bill, the Whigs then took control of the committee of public accounts and stalled any progress on heads of further supply bills. With the session in recess over Christmas, the lord lieuten-ant, Charles Talbot, duke of Shrewsbury, tried to negotiate a settlement but instead concluded that parliament could not reconvene as long as the Whigs remained so entrenched in their views. As with the political impasse over the 'Sole Right' in 1692–1693, the government was now in danger of amass-ing large army pay arrears at a time of heightening security concerns as the queen's health faded and fears of a Jacobite invasion increased. However, the queen's death in August 1714 and the succession of the Hanoverian George I actually resolved matters as the Tory party collapsed and the much-hated Phipps was dismissed.[31]

Patriots and Undertakers Revealed, 1714–1730

The demise of the Tory party resulted in Irish politics transforming once again. In the absence of opposition from any other quarter, the Whigs broke up into factions centred around Brodrick, who replaced Phipps as lord chan-cellor and was elevated to the peerage as Viscount Midleton, and William Conolly, who took over as speaker of the Commons. Conolly was the rich-est commoner in Ireland and, as a leading revenue commissioner, a key player in the professionalisation of the revenue service, a process which had been under way since the 1690s and was a central aspect of the evolution of

31 Hayton, *Ruling Ireland*, 159–85; McGrath, *Irish Constitution*, 264–84.

recognisably modern state institutions in Ireland in the eighteenth century. The emergence of these factions also served to illuminate a political process, which had been evolving since the 1690s, but which only became wholly visible from the reign of George I onwards. The 'Undertaker System', whereby leading Irish politicians undertook to manage parliament for the government in return for patronage, position and power, had really commenced when the likes of Brodrick were appointed to office as part of the 1695 compromise. During Anne's reign, however, party politics had obscured such undertakings, but after 1715 the system evolved rapidly, with Conolly emerging as the first great Undertaker and the revenue commission as a core source of patronage and power.[32]

Although the Hanoverian succession passed off peacefully in Ireland, during 1714–1715 there were ongoing concerns over internal security and a possible Jacobite invasion.[33] Government officials expressed regular concerns about Irishmen recruiting for the Jacobite cause and numerous arrests were made. At the same time, Ireland's new-found role as a garrison for the largest part of Britain's standing army came into its own when rebellion broke out in Scotland and the north of England in the autumn of 1715. Not only did Ireland remain at peace during that time, but the government was also able to send twelve regiments to Britain to counter the Jacobite forces.

Such security concerns helped to focus the attention of Irish Protestants in the lead up to the convening of parliament in late 1715. Once again money was top of the agenda. Because it was a newly elected parliament, in keeping with the 1695 compromise a token government money bill of only six months duration was passed and the heads of bills procedure enacted two further supply bills for eighteenth months and two years duration. The most notable innovation in this latter legislation was the introduction of parliament-sanctioned government borrowing and the creation of a National Debt. The threat of a Jacobite invasion at the beginning of 1716 had resulted in parliament passing a vote of credit to the government with a promise to provide for the interest and capital sum of that debt in future supply acts. The purpose of the loan was to raise thirteen regiments to replace those sent to Britain. Although the feared invasion never occurred, the government still borrowed

---

32 Hayton, *Ruling Ireland*, 106–30; P. McNally, *Parties, Patriots and Undertakers: Parliamentary Politics in Early Hanoverian Ireland* (Dublin: FCP, 1997), 118–47; P. Walsh, *The Making of the Irish Protestant Ascendancy: The Life of William Conolly, 1662–1729* (Woodbridge: Boydell and Brewer, 2010), *passim*.

33 See Chapter 1 by V. Morley in Volume 3.

£50,000 – therein the initial principal sum of the Irish National Debt – and raised the regiments.[34]

While the government had borrowed money in the past, this new debt differed in that it was a debt of the nation secured upon the credit of the nation, as represented by parliament. The key innovation was that parliament had undertaken to ensure that money was always provided through future tax legislation to service the interest and principal of the debt, thereby making it a more secure investment for potential creditors. The creation of a National Debt in England had occurred at the outset of the Glorious Revolution, and wider engagement with this form of modern credit and debt financing had developed rapidly thereafter as part of England's Financial Revolution, epitomised by the establishment of the corporate joint-stock Bank of England in 1694 as a key government creditor. Ireland was by circumstance and necessity slower to travel down that route, but by 1716 there were more than enough public creditors ready to invest in government. Parliament fulfilled its part of the bargain by continuing to pass legislation in every session thereafter for servicing the debt. However, it soon became apparent that Ireland was not ready for other aspects of the Financial Revolution, in particular the concept of a corporate joint-stock bank.[35]

Various proposals had been made during the later seventeenth century for establishing some form of a national or countrywide joint-stock bank in Ireland in order to help stimulate the economy. The first to gain any real traction, however, emerged in early 1720 at the height of the rampant speculation throughout the British Isles in the stock of the South Sea Company, which was to result in the first of the great financial bubbles of modern times. Initially, the 1720 bank proposal gained significant support among government and the wider public and a royal charter was prepared pending approval in the Irish parliament. However, by the time parliament met in late 1721, the South Sea Bubble had long since burst and many shareholders, including a significant number from Ireland, had suffered serious financial losses. The resulting loss of confidence in such joint-stock schemes, coupled with a serious economic downturn, did not bode well for the Irish bank scheme.[36] With Ireland's private bankers to the forefront of the assault upon the proposal for fear their

34 *Stat. Ire.*, iv, 315–21, 325–7; C. I. McGrath, 'Securing the Hanoverian Succession in Ireland: Jacobites, Money and Men, 1714–16', *Parliamentary History*, 33 (2014), 140–59.

35 *Stat. Ire.*, iv, 431–8, 504–8; v, 1–5, 75–81, 137–42, 193–8, 201–6, 333–40, 341–63, 483–92; McGrath, *Ireland and Empire*, 181–216.

36 P. Walsh, *The South Sea Bubble and Ireland: Money, Banking and Investment, 1690–1721* (Woodbridge: Boydell and Brewer, 2014); M. Ryder, 'The Bank of Ireland, 1721: Land, Credit and Dependency', *Historical Journal*, 25 (1982), 557–82.

own lucrative enterprises might be undercut, a pamphlet debate took place led by Henry Maxwell for the bank and his uncle, Hercules Rowley, against it. Maxwell was the first to discuss the proposal as being for a National Bank owned by and for the benefit of the public rather than a private corporate lending institution such as the Bank of England.[37] This nascent concept of a truly National Bank was to be developed more fully in the 1730s by Bishop George Berkeley in his famous *Querist*. However, in 1721 the idea of a bank that was ultimately owned by the public could not save the proposal, and it was defeated in two separate votes. The fallout from the defeat of the bank proposal was such that it was another sixty-two years before the Bank of Ireland was finally established, and even then it was as a private corporate lending bank rather than one owned by the public.[38]

Jonathan Swift had been one of the earliest opponents of the bank scheme, taking issue with it in *A Proposal for the Universal Use of Irish Manufacture*, published in May 1720. Swift's main motivation for writing that tract, however, had been the passage in April of the Declaratory Act in the Westminster parliament. The intermittent constitutional conflagration briefly reignited in 1698–1699 by Molyneux and the English Woollen Act had smouldered away thereafter until bursting back into flames in 1717–1719 over the *Sherlock Annesley* case. Primarily because of English factional politics at that time and a short-lived concern about Irish political management, this most recent instalment of the long-running constitutional disagreement resulted in the British parliament finally choosing to legislate on the matter in a manner wholly opposite to the 1689 Jacobite parliament's Declaratory Act. The 1720 act declared that the British parliament 'had, hath, and of right ought to have full power and authority to make laws and statutes of sufficient force and validity to bind the kingdom ... of Ireland' and that the Irish House of Lords had no legal jurisdiction in Irish court cases.[39]

The 1720 Declaratory Act was the final statement in a constitutional debate that had existed for hundreds of years. Irishmen, both Protestant and Catholic, had long contested the matter because they believed that the kingdom of Ireland was a sister realm of equal status with the kingdom of

---

37 Henry Maxwell, *Mr. Maxwell's Second Letter to Mr. Rowley; Wherein the Objections against the Bank are Answer'd* (Dublin, 1721), 10, 22.

38 *CJI*, iii, 249–51, 257–8, 267–8, 289; P. Kelly, 'Berkeley and the idea of a National Bank', *ECI*, 25 (2010), 98, 104–8; F. G. Hall, *The Bank of Ireland 1783–1946* (Dublin: Hodges Figgis, 1949), 34–5.

39 E. Curtis and R. B. McDowell (eds.), *Irish Historical Documents 1172–1922* (London: Methuen, 1943), 186; D. W. Hayton, 'The Stanhope/Sunderland Ministry and the Repudiation of Irish Parliamentary Independence', *EHR*, 113 (1998), 610–36.

England, linked together by the fundamental, inextricable and essential connection of the shared monarch. But Swift's 1720 pamphlet also demonstrated that this long-held sense of a separate identity among Irish Protestants was now being expressed more transparently in relation to a wider range of issues that coalesced around the idea that it was the civic duty of Irish Protestants to advocate for Irish economic and political interests that were being threatened or undermined by the actions of the British government and parliament. This emerging 'patriot politics' was not about separation from Britain but rather about equality within the 'composite monarchies' model. Although antecedents can be seen in the 1690s or earlier, it was only following the collapse of party politics in 1714 that the variegated elements of patriotic politics began to be more readily visible. The catalyst for Irish Protestant political patriotism to emerge onto the public stage in full force was the granting in 1722 of a royal patent for coining copper halfpence and farthings for Ireland to an English ironmonger, William Wood.[40]

In a pre-paper-money world, Ireland had long had a problem with a shortage of coinage. Ostensibly as a means of resolving that issue, the British government issued a patent for minting £100,800 worth of small specie coins – copper halfpence and farthings – to facilitate day-to-day economic activity. The initial recipient of the patent was George I's mistress, Melusine von der Schulenburg, duchess of Kendal, who sold it to Wood for £10,000. When the news reached Ireland it prompted immediate opposition from the government, followed by similar objections among the wider public during 1722–1723. The opposition was two-pronged. On economic grounds it was argued that an English ironmonger would export the profit arising from the coinage out of Ireland, that the real need was for silver and gold coinage, and that the economy would be ruined if flooded with debased copper coinage of little intrinsic value. The political or patriot perspective centred around arguments that the patent should have been issued to an Irish ironmonger, that Ireland should have its own mint, that the profit should stay in Ireland, that Irish economic concerns would always be second to English, and that Ireland was to be treated as a subordinate rather than sister kingdom.

By the time the biennial sitting of parliament occurred in late 1723, the mood across the country was such that a parliamentary address was sent to the king which accused Wood of fraud and deceit and claimed that the patent was highly prejudicial to the public revenue and that it would ruin Irish trade and commerce and endanger landownership. By early 1724 mass resistance

---

40 McNally, *Parties, Patriots and Undertakers*, 174–95; Connolly, *Religion, Law and Power*, 92–3.

was underway through countrywide petitioning and refusal of the coins. While the addled lord lieutenant, Charles Fitzroy, duke of Grafton, prepared to leave the country, Swift jumped on the bandwagon with the publication of the first of his seven anonymous *Drapier's Letters*. However, it was the government reaction to Swift's fourth pamphlet, *A Letter to the Whole People of Ireland*, purposefully published in October 1724 just as the new lord lieutenant, John, Baron Carteret, was arriving in the country, which really caught the public imagination. The ensuing government attempt to prosecute the publisher, John Harding, prompted Swift to pen the anonymous *Seasonable Advice* to the grand jury, which brought matters to a crisis. When the grand jury refused to find against the latter publication and the Dublin mob began to hail Swift as a hero, the government accepted that the situation was untenable. Ultimately, the great fear that the usual financial supplies would not be renewed for a further two years when parliament reconvened in 1725 led to the withdrawal of the patent and the recompensing of Wood with a pension of £3,000 per annum for eight years on the Irish civil establishment.[41]

Despite Wood receiving a handsome pay-off, the successful defeat of the patent was seen as a great patriot victory with Swift garnering most, if not all, of the accolades and being identified as the Hibernian Patriot or Patriot Dean. And, as had been hoped, the 1725–1726 session accordingly renewed the necessary additional supplies for the next two years. The death of George I in 1727 resulted in the dissolution of that parliament before another session convened. The new parliament elected following the accession of George II first met in late 1727 and, like its predecessors, adhered to the 1695 compromise. Following the passage of a token government money bill of three months duration, the Commons produced a further supply act by means of the heads of bill procedure.[42]

The 1727–1728 session was also notable for passing a law for regulating parliamentary elections, which completely removed the franchise from Catholics, and a further penal law against Catholic solicitors. The only other penal measure of that decade, for preventing marriages carried out by degraded clergymen and Catholic priests, had been enacted in 1726. Such relative inactivity was in part caused by the influence of more moderate Protestants and the continuing efforts of Catholic lobbyists in London and on the continent. At

---

41 A. Goodwin, 'Wood's Halfpence', *EHR*, 51 (1936), 647–55; P. McNally, 'Wood's Halfpence, Carteret, and the Government of Ireland, 1723–6', *IHS*, 30:119 (1997), 354–76.
42 *Stat. Ire.*, v, 193–8, 201–6; C. I. McGrath, 'Central Aspects of the Eighteenth-Century Constitutional Framework in Ireland: The Government Supply Bill and Biennial Parliamentary Sessions, 1715–82', *ECI*, 16 (2001), 16–20.

the same time, however, other Irish Protestants still found cause to advocate for further penal laws because of the continuing discord within the Catholic community over the various failed attempts to find an acceptable formula whereby Catholics could declare their loyalty to their Protestant monarch without compromising their confessional allegiance. The controversy in 1727 surrounding a loyal address to the new king signed by Catholic peers and gentry led by Christopher Nugent, Lord Delvin, and the vociferous reaction against it led by the Franciscan friar, Sylvester Lloyd, may well have helped to promote the passage of the two penal measures of 1728.[43]

By the time George II's parliament convened for its second session in late 1729, economic hardship across the country brought on by a series of failed harvests helped to focus minds. In the face of substantial army pay arrears, parliament agreed to expand the principal of the National Debt from £50,000 to £200,000, with the additional £150,000 being used to clear the arrears. Provision for repayment of the new debt was included in a loan act, which was the first in Ireland to appropriate specific duties and create a 'sinking fund' for servicing the National Debt.[44]

The existence of substantial army pay arrears and the willingness and ability of parliament to increase the National Debt in order to pay those arrears highlighted the significant political developments that had occurred since 1692. Through control of the government's purse-strings, parliament had established itself as a central part of the Irish state in the early eighteenth century. The government's increased financial reliance on parliament stemmed from the fact that public expenditure had increased dramatically because of the presence of a 12,000-strong standing army in Ireland from the late 1690s onwards. Parliament for its part was willing to fund that larger army because it offered security against a possible Catholic rebellion or a Jacobite invasion. The financial innovations embraced by government and parliament in order to fund that army brought elements of both the English Financial Revolution and the fiscal-military state paradigms to Ireland. And in practical terms, the building of a countrywide network of residential barracks for housing that

---

43 *Stat. Ire.*, v, 148–50, 224, 287–9; J. G. Simms, 'Irish Catholics and the Parliamentary Franchise, 1692–1728', *IHS*, 12 (1960), 28–37; I. McBride, 'Catholic Politics in the Penal Era: Father Sylvester Lloyd and the Delvin Address of 1727', in J. Bergin, E. Magennis, L. Ní Mhungaile and P. Walsh (eds.), *New Perspectives on the Penal Laws (Eighteenth-Century Ireland*, special issue no. 1, 2011), 115–47; Connolly, *Religion, Law and Power*, 279–89.

44 *Stat. Ire.*, v, 337–40; C. I. McGrath, ' "The Public Wealth is the Sinew, the Life, of every Public Measure": The Creation and Maintenance of a National Debt in Ireland, 1716–45', in D. Carey and C. Finlay (eds.), *The Empire of Credit: The Financial Revolution in the British Atlantic World, 1700–1800* (Dublin: Irish Academic Press, 2011), 178–85.

army ensured that Ireland became the first port of call for soldiers whenever Britain went to war in the eighteenth century. As a result of all of these factors, Ireland became an active partner in the dramatic expansion of the British Empire as the century unfolded. In time, even before repeal of the penal laws started in the 1770s, Irish Catholics would also come to play a significant and active role in the ongoing expansion of that empire.

6

The Emergence of a Protestant Society, 1691–1730

D. W. HAYTON

Ascendancy Re-established

In terms of the transfer of land from Catholic to Protestant hands, the Williamite revolution simply confirmed the work already accomplished by the Cromwellian conquest and confiscations. In this very limited sense William's victory reinforced rather than created a 'Protestant Ascendancy'.[1] The most authoritative estimate of the relative proportions of freehold landownership in the early eighteenth century remains that of the late J. G. Simms, published over sixty years ago. Simms concluded that in 1703, at the close of the process of redistribution following the defeat of James II, Catholics owned 14 per cent of land in Ireland, as against 22 per cent in 1688, figures routinely quoted as authoritative.[2] The fact that Simms was using the mid-century land surveys as his base-line might prompt suspicion of the accuracy of the totals, but such figures are extremely difficult, if not impossible, to calculate precisely and there can be little doubt that the rate of decline in Catholic proprietorship was as he presented it.

Even more important than the amount of land still in Catholic hands was the way in which the outlook of Catholic landowners had changed. The comprehensive defeat of the counter-revolution engineered by Richard Talbot, earl and later duke of Tyrconnell, left the traditional 'Catholic interest' cowed and quiescent. Many of the more substantial Catholic political figures had been killed or exiled for their part in the war against King William. Of the handful of aristocrats to survive, a few, including Richard, fifth Viscount Fitzwilliam or Theobald Burke, sixth Viscount Mayo, conformed to the established church and took an active part in politics in support of the Protestant interest;

---

1 This is the argument presented in S. J. Connolly, *Religion, Law and Power: The Making of Protestant Ireland 1660–1760* (Oxford University Press, 1992), chapter 1.
2 See Chapter 23 by M. Ó Siochrú and D. Brown, this volume. J. G. Simms, *The Williamite Confiscation in Ireland 1690–1703* (London: Faber & Faber 1956).

others were content to remain passive observers of the political scene: this was the case with John Burke, ninth earl of Clanricard, whose outlawry was reversed by an Act of Parliament in 1702, or Alexander MacDonnell, third earl of Antrim, restored to his estates in 1697. Surviving Catholic archives, from families like the Brownes in Galway and Kerry, or the Mansfields in Kildare, demonstrate that their principal, if not sole concern, was the preservation of what estates were left.[3] Of course, not every Irish Catholic took such a defeatist line. Some exhibited strong Jacobite sympathies, but this was a dangerous road to take and few propertied Catholics took it, never enough to give the old Pretender sufficient encouragement to attempt to recover what his father had lost.[4]

Counterpointing the guarded and essentially passive attitude shown by the remnant of the Catholic political class was a reinvigorated assertiveness among Irish Protestants. The events of 1687–1690 had made them more sensitive than ever to their vulnerability to the kind of Catholic resurgence orchestrated by Tyrconnell, which in turn had been made possible by the indulgence shown to Irish Catholics by successive Stuart kings. For the present they could trust the staunchness of William of Orange, their 'great deliverer', but the future was not necessarily certain. It was also a trope of post-revolutionary political discourse in Ireland that the Protestants had themselves accomplished much of their own salvation in 1689, assisted by divine Providence, which was frequently cited in state sermons and the literary effusions of Williamite loyalists, but this too afforded only a limited reassurance. There was no guarantee that they would be in a position to defend themselves successfully again, and Providence was a double-edged sword – God punished vice as well as rewarding virtue, and the possibility of divine judgment was often invoked by preachers and others who lamented the moral failings of late seventeenth-century society.[5]

The Irish parliaments that political and financial exigencies obliged William and his successors to summon were therefore determined to do

---

3 See E. Kinsella, 'The Articles of Surrender and the Williamite Settlement of Ireland: A Case Study of Colonel John Browne (1640–1711)', unpublished PhD thesis, University College Dublin (2011); E. H. Lyons, 'Morristown Lattin: A Case Study of the Lattin and Mansfield families in County Kildare, c.1600–1860', unpublished PhD thesis, University College Dublin (2011).

4 For a more sanguine view of Jacobitism in Ireland, see É. Ó Ciardha, *Ireland and the Jacobite Cause, 1685–1766: A Fatal Attachment* (Dublin: Four Courts Press [hereafter FCP], 2002).

5 T. Bartlett, ' "This famous island set in a Virginian sea": Ireland in the British Empire, 1690–1801', in P. J. Marshall (ed.), *The Oxford History of the British Empire, ii: The Eighteenth Century* (Oxford University Press, 1998), 259–60; D. W. Hayton, *The Anglo-Irish Experience, 1680–1730: Religion, Identity and Patriotism* (Woodbridge: Boydell & Brewer, 2012), 165–7.

whatever they could to prevent another Catholic revival. The requirement already imposed by the English parliament, that Members of Parliament and crown office-holders take the oaths of allegiance and supremacy, effectively excluded Catholics from sitting in either house, assuming that any Catholic possessed the will to do so. Now parliament set about creating a framework of legislation to make it impossible for a latter-day Tyrconnell to carry out a policy of re-Catholicisation. Between 1695 and 1709 a succession of statutes was passed to limit Catholic political and civil rights. Known to contemporaries as 'popery laws', they were later termed 'penal laws', and their enactment has often been taken as a defining characteristic of the period.[6]

While traditional Catholic historical writing, following Edmund Burke and other proponents of Catholic relief in the late eighteenth century, depicted these laws as a 'penal code' designed to destroy the Catholic faith and to render Catholics as second-class citizens, modern 'revisionists' have offered a more nuanced interpretation.[7] They have argued that, rather than forming a comprehensive 'code', these statutes were a collection of separate measures, each the product of a particular set of political circumstances, involving interactions between Irish political interests and English ministers and parties. King William himself, aware from his Dutch experience of the value to the state of a policy of religious toleration, would have preferred a different course;[8] some English ministers were lukewarm; and there was even opposition in Ireland to particular measures. Moreover, there was considerable variation in the way in which the laws were put into effect, partly because of the limited capacity of central and local government to enforce restrictions on Catholic worship, partly because of a limited commitment on the part of some propertied Protestants to persecute their social equals.

---

6 See Chapter 5 by C. I. McGrath, this volume.
7 See in particular, M. Wall, 'The Penal laws, 1691–1760', reprinted in G. O'Brien (ed.), *Catholic Ireland in the Eighteenth Century: Collected Essays of Maureen Wall* (Dublin: Geography Publications, 1989), 1–60; R. E. Burns, 'The Irish Popery Laws: A Study of Eighteenth-century Legislation and Behavior', *Review of Politics*, 24 (1962), 485–508; S. J. Connolly, 'The Penal Laws', in W. A. Maguire (ed.), *Kings in Conflict: The Revolutionary War in Ireland and its Aftermath 1689–1750* (Belfast: Blackstaff Press, 1990), pp 157–72; and J. Kelly, 'Sustaining a Confessional State: the Irish Parliament and Catholicism', in D. W. Hayton, J. Kelly and J. Bergin (eds.), *The Eighteenth-century Composite State: Representative Institutions in Ireland and Europe, 1689–1800* (Houndmills: Palgrave Macmillan, 2010), 44–77. See also J. Kelly, 'The Historiography of the Penal Laws', in J. Bergin, E. Magennis, L. Ní Mhungaile and P. Walsh (eds.), *New Perspectives on the Penal Laws* (*Eighteenth-Century Ireland*, special issue no. 1, 2011), 27–54.
8 W. Troost, 'William III and the Treaty of Limerick (1691–1697): A study of his Irish policy', PhD thesis, University of Leiden (1983).

Nonetheless, taken together the popery laws of 1695–1709 implemented a formidable range of restrictions on the religious, social, economic, professional and political lives of Irish Catholics. Some were specifically concerned with the prospect of a Catholic insurgency: the celebrated Dismounting Act of 1695, for example, which provided that no Catholic could own a horse worth more than £5, and was cited by Burke as a prime example of the pettiness of the 'penal code', was specifically intended to forestall the possibility that a native Catholic cavalry could be raised to support a Jacobite invasion.[9] Laws to prevent Catholics from carrying swords, or from acting as gamekeepers and thus having access to firearms, served a similar purpose. The draconian restrictions imposed on the Catholic clergy – the banning of bishops and religious orders, and the requirement that parish priests be registered and limited in numbers – was intended to minimise the presence of Catholic religious in the country. Had it been fully implemented, and combined with the prohibition on Catholics being educated abroad, it would have resulted in the gradual elimination of all Catholic clergy in Ireland. But again, the purpose of the legislation was political. For one thing, bishops provided leadership; for another, they, and the religious orders, and foreign-educated clergy in general, were likely to be the least amenable to government: bishops were still being appointed by Rome on the recommendation of the exiled Stuart claimant, while the continental education received by Irish priests would be ultramontane.

In a similar way, the limitations imposed on the political and civil rights of Irish Catholics were also directly informed by Protestant memories of Tyrconnell's lord deputyship. The exclusion of Catholics from the judiciary, the Dublin Castle administration and the upper tiers of county government was strengthened in 1703 by the requirement that office-holders also take an oath abjuring the hereditary claim to the crown of 'James III', which meant rejecting the papal recognition of that claim. The same oath was also imposed on voters at parliamentary elections. Catholics were barred from the governing bodies of borough corporations, and from being admitted as freemen, which removed any lingering Catholic presence from the upper reaches of urban government and from the parliamentary electorate in borough constituencies. No repetition would therefore be possible of Tyrconnell's campaign in 1688–1689 to 'pack' an Irish parliament. Longer term security was provided by restrictions on Catholic landownership: the insistence that

---

9 C. I. McGrath, 'Securing the Protestant Interest: The Origins and Purpose of the Penal Laws of 1695', *Irish Historical Studies* [hereafter *IHS*], 30 (1996), 25–46.

inherited property be divided among all children unless a male heir turned Protestant, ensured the division of existing estates, while the prohibition on Catholics acquiring freehold land precluded the appearance of another set of 'new purchasers' similar to the Catholic merchants and professional men who had come to prominence after the Restoration. Disqualifying Catholics from practising the law further supported this strategy in two ways: by closing off an important path to prosperity, and ensuing that Catholic lawsuits over property would have to be pleaded by Protestant barristers.

Protestant Attitudes

While each of these various statutes was the result of a complex process of legislation, they were all informed by the same general outlook, which the vast majority of Irish Protestants shared. Even those who privately questioned the reasonableness of fears of Catholic revanchism were obliged to bow before the public consensus that, despite the crushing defeat of James II's armies, the flight of the 'wild geese', and the confiscation of land, there was still a very real menace to be countered. The machinations of Dublin politicians to bring in popery bills in order to win popularity, raising the 'raw head and bloody bones', as one put it, were founded on a clear understanding of the temper of the political nation.[10] In the generation after the Boyne the common currency of Irish political discourse, at all levels, embodied a belief that 'the established constitution in church and state' remained under threat. Indeed, the title of the most wide-ranging of the anti-popery laws was 'An Act to Prevent the Further Growth of Popery'. This anxiety (which could give way on occasion to real terror), derived from historical fears of Catholic conspiracy and rebellion, in Ireland and further afield, stoked up by recitations in pulpit and press of the dismal record of Protestant sufferings – the Smithfield burnings, the massacre of St Bartholomew's Day, the horrors of the Thirty Years' War – and by the periodic republication of Sir John Temple's history of the Irish rebellion of 1641.[11] But it was also based on a broader appreciation of the European situation, about which Irish Protestants could

10 Edward Southwell to the duke of Ormond, 14 Dec. 1704, in Historical Manuscripts Commission, *Calendar of the Manuscripts of the Marquess of Ormonde*, new series (8 vols., London: HMSO, 1902–1920) viii, 125. The speaker quoted was the solicitor-general, Sir Richard Levinge.

11 T. C. Barnard, 'The Uses of 23 October 1641 and Irish Protestant Celebration', *English Historical Review*, 106 (1991), 889–920; K. M. Noonan, '"Martyrs in flames": Sir John Temple and the Conception of the Irish in English Martyrologies', *Albion*, 36 (2004), 223–55.

read in pamphlets and newspapers sent from England or reprinted in Dublin. Louis XIV was presented as the epitome of the persecuting Catholic monarch, his ill-treatment of Huguenots in France and German Protestants in the Palatinate given a human face by the influx of refugees into Britain and Ireland in the 1690s and 1700s. Even after Louis's death in 1715 newspapers continued to report the grievances of Protestant minorities in Catholic states across Europe, where the reformed religion seemed to be under attack from a resurgent Catholicism.

The emergence in Ireland in the early 1700s of a form of 'party politics' on the English model heightened these tensions. The Irish Protestants who allied with the English Whigs defined themselves by loyalty to the Glorious Revolution, devotion to the memory of its prime mover, William of Orange, and unswerving opposition to 'popery'. Not only were Irish Whigs in general given to displays of alarmist anti-Catholic rhetoric, individuals, including such a seasoned political operator as Alan Brodrick, the speaker of the Irish House of Commons, were gripped by a genuine fear for their lives.[12] The atmosphere across the country during the last winter of Queen Anne's life, when the struggle between the two parties reached its climax, bordered on the hysterical. The maintenance of the Revolution settlement depended on a smooth succession from the ailing queen to Elector George of Hanover, and the Whig opposition in both Ireland and England were deeply suspicious of the Tory ministers; with some justification, since members of the English cabinet were in contact with the Pretender, and the Irish administration was headed, in the absence of the viceroy, by an English Tory, the lord chancellor Sir Constantine Phipps, a man notorious for Jacobite sympathies. The general election in Ireland in the autumn of 1713 saw the appearance of ex-Catholic or crypto-Catholic candidates, and violent crowd scenes at the poll in Dublin city, which left one man dead amid accusations of the involvement of a Catholic mob.[13] One Whig candidate talked of having 'a knife at his throat', while the archbishop of Dublin wrote that the country was in 'a high ferment, higher than ever I saw it except when in actual war'.[14]

---

12 Alan Brodrick to Thomas Brodrick, 24 June 1714, Brodrick Papers, 1248/3/187–8, Surrey History Centre.
13 J. G. Simms, 'Irish Catholics and the Parliamentary Franchise, 1692–1728', *IHS*, 12 (1960), 34–5; D. W. Hayton, *Ruling Ireland, 1685–1742: Politics, Politicians and Parties* (Woodbridge: Boydell & Brewer, 2004), 170–1.
14 Sir Richard Cox to Edward Southwell, 24 Dec. 1713, Southwell Papers, Add. MS 38157, f. 41, British Library [hereafter BL]; Archbishop William King to Francis Annesley, 14 Nov. 1713, King Letterbooks, MS 2532, 222–3, Trinity College Dublin.

The corollary to Whig alarmism was the emergence among some Tories of a different attitude to the Catholic question; not so much a relaxation of anti-Catholic sentiment, as a disparagement of the more extreme sloganising of the Whigs.[15] The response of Tory propagandists to Whig scaremongering was to pooh-pooh their enemies' allegations: one Tory pamphlet was given the title *Hannibal Not at our Gates* ... and took the form of a dialogue between the Whig 'Lord Panic' and a Tory squire, 'George Steady'.[16] In private correspondence a few Tories were beginning to question whether the vulgar anti-popery that suffused parliamentary and public debate was not outmoded. After all, the likelihood of an internal rebellion had receded significantly now that the old Catholic proprietorial class had been drastically reduced in numbers and influence, their 'youth and gentry' being 'destroyed'.[17]

At first this kind of scepticism was confined to a largely silent minority, although we can detect some traces of it in the opposition in the Irish House of Lords to the popery bill of 1709 as unnecessarily punitive. Certainly the collective hyper-ventilation which the Protestant political nation underwent in 1714, before what turned out to be a peaceful transition to Hanoverian rule, demonstrates effectively the continued power of the Catholic bogy. But gradually symptoms of complacency became more visible. Catholic priests were no longer harassed, and it was possible for the Catholic steward to the Protestant O'Briens in County Clare to inform his employers openly that he would be late in starting a journey from Dublin because he intended to hear mass first (in one of the several licensed chapels in the city).[18] Before long a Church of Ireland clergyman, Edward Synge, was publicly recommending a legal toleration for Catholics.[19] By 1730, when Swift published his *Vindication* of the lord lieutenant, John, Lord Carteret, which had great fun ridiculing Whig paranoia about Tories and Jacobites, some Protestants were relaxed enough to argue that the danger from popery was a thing of the past. In that year a young squire was advised by his grandfather that "tis good to have

---

15 In some instances Irish Tories seem to have opposed extensions of the popery laws, but they did so in the relative secrecy of the Privy Council rather than in broad daylight in parliament (George Dodington to [the earl of Sunderland], 1 September 1707, SP 63/ 366, f. 89, The National Archives).

16 *Hannibal Not at our Gates: or, An Enquiry into the Grounds of our Present Fears of Popery and the Pre[ten]der* (London, 1714).

17 'The case of the sacramental test ...', Finch Papers, box 4965, Ire. 9, Leicestershire, Leicester and Rutland Record Office.

18 James Davoren to Mrs Catherine O'Brien, 28 Apr. 1719, Inchiquin Papers, MS 45347/3, National Library of Ireland [hereafter NLI].

19 Edward Synge, *The Case of Toleration Consider'd with Respect both to Religion and Civil Government* ... (Dublin, 1725); I. McBride, *Eighteenth-century Ireland: the Isle of Slaves* (Dublin: Gill & Macmillan, 2009), 207–9.

an estate in England for fear of another Irish revolution', at which one of his friends commented drily, 'he may as well frighten you with the Day of Judgment, and 'twould do you more good'.[20]

Copper Fastening Protestant Ascendancy

Even in the late 1720s and 1730s, however, this kind of insouciance was far from the norm. The legislative record actually shows a resurgence in attempts to tighten up the popery laws in the period 1725–1733. In part this was the product of particular *causes célèbres*. The 'massacre' at Thorn (Toruń) in Catholic Poland in 1724, when Lutheran officials had been executed on government orders following crowd violence against Catholic churches, had revived fears of the bigotry and brutality of Catholic powers in Europe.[21] At home, the 1727 general election in Ireland had given rise to a multiplicity of complaints from defeated candidates about the activities of Catholics, leading to the passage of a statute to disenfranchise Catholics as such. Then the activities of French recruiting agents in Munster in 1730, even though they were operating with government approval, raised atavistic fears of Jacobite insurgency. The French officers were reported to have enlisted men with the promise that they would be fighting in the 'Irish brigades' for the Pretender.[22] Finally, reports in 1735 that the heir to the forfeited earldom of Clancarty was planning legal action against purchasers of his family estates in the Williamite land settlement raised potentially the most vexed question of all.[23] In the background was an ongoing concern with relative demography, and the inescapable fact that Catholics still constituted at least 70 per cent of the population of the island. At the same time, Church of Ireland clergy were agitating over the failure of the church itself, and various voluntary initiatives such as charity schools, to take advantage of the prostration of the Catholic political interest. While there had been high-profile converts to Protestantism, and a flow of propertied Catholics pushed into conformity by statutory disabilities, the opportunity for wholesale proselytisation had not been seized. An inquiry into the state of 'popery' in Ireland in 1731, initiated by bishops and carried

20 Edward Cooke to William Fownes [1730], Fownes Papers, MS 8802/3, NLI.
21 McBride, *Eighteenth-century Ireland*, 206.
22 L. M. Cullen, 'The Blackwater Catholics and County Cork Society and Politics in the Eighteenth Century', in P. Flanagan and C. G. Buttimer (eds.), *Cork: History and Society* (Dublin: Geography Publications, 1993), 540–59; Ó Ciardha, *Ireland and the Jacobite Cause*, 255–60.
23 *Letters of Marmaduke Coghill, 1722–1738*, ed. D. W. Hayton (Dublin: Irish Manuscripts Commission, 2005), 162, 167, 174, 178–9.

out by parish clergy, revealed that the Catholic Church, far from being ham-strung, was in fact flourishing.[24]

The popery bills introduced during this renewed flurry of anti-Catholic anxiety were meant to close loopholes in existing legislation. As well as the parliamentary franchise, they dealt with the ongoing problem of illegal priests, with ensuring Catholic disarmament, and preventing Catholic involve-ment in the legal profession, where Acts passed in 1727 and 1733 reinforced the legal prohibition on Catholics acting as barristers, attorneys or solicitors. It was a sign of the changing times that not all such bills were passed into law. MPs were more concerned with Catholic lawyers than Catholic priests. The other major concern was conversions. Many Protestants, indeed a majority in parliament, were openly sceptical of the sincerity of those who had con-formed to the established church for material reasons, and were particularly suspicious of their involvement in politics. New laws made it impossible for a convert whose wife remained Catholic, or whose children were educated as Catholics, to act as a justice of the peace.

The remorseless process of tightening up existing legislation certainly gave the 'popery laws' the appearance of a systematic code, even if accumulated in a piecemeal fashion. But, contrary to the denunciations of pro-Catholic activ-ists in the eighteenth century and the historians who have echoed their argu-ments, it was not *sui generis*, or even unusual, but typical of the time. Across the British empire it was common practice for governments and representa-tive institutions to insist on the restriction of Catholic political and civil rights. The English parliament had already passed laws to exclude Catholics from government office, from parliament and from borough corporations, and after the Glorious Revolution took anti-Catholic measures further, imposing a double land tax on Catholics and in 1699 introducing a popery bill that pre-figured many aspects of the Irish Popery Act of 1704, including measures to restrict landownership.[25] The clause in the Irish act imposing partible inher-itance was added in the English Privy Council, and used an English model, the Kentish custom of gavelkind.[26] Penal legislation against Catholics was also introduced into England's transatlantic colonies and Caribbean planta-tions. More broadly, it was common practice in the 'confessional states' of eighteenth-century Europe to impose legal discriminations against those who did not give allegiance to the established church, especially to exclude them

24 Wall, 'The Penal Laws, 1691–1760' 35–50; Connolly, *Religion, Law and Power*, 150–1.
25 G. Glickman, *The English Catholic Community 1688–1745: Politics, Culture, and Ideology* (Woodbridge: Boydell & Brewer, 2009), 57.
26 I owe this point to Dr John Bergin.

from participation in government and politics. Just like Irish Catholics, the surviving Protestant communities in eighteenth-century France, Huguenots and Camisards, were subject to a multiplicity of restrictive laws relating to their political rights, to the exercise of their religion and to their economic activities. These were not always implemented in full, and by mid-century a *de facto* toleration obtained in France, but outbursts of local persecution still occurred. Nor was it always a matter of hounding small minorities, as the substantial Calvinist populations in Hungary and Transylvania knew to their cost.

The fact that so few Catholics in Ireland retained freehold property, in a society in which the possession of real estate was understood as the essential qualification for full and active citizenship, meant that Catholics occupied a secondary role not merely in the political system but in public life in general. The extent to which Ireland in the first half of the eighteenth century was a Protestant-dominated society cannot be over-emphasised, and justifies the use of the term 'Protestant Ascendancy', despite its being an anachronism.[27] The institutions of state power were monopolised by Protestants, as were parliament, the law courts and eventually the legal profession. No Catholic was to be found in any borough corporation, or in the trade guilds in Dublin, Cork and other large towns (other than in an inferior and strictly limited capacity), and while some Catholics practised medicine, the organisation which regulated the profession, the Royal College of Physicians in Dublin, was exclusively Protestant. Education was firmly in Protestant hands: the only university, Trinity College, Dublin, was closed to Catholics, as were almost all schools, except for charitable foundations whose explicit aim was to proselytise (and even then few Catholics were actually admitted). Even the many voluntary organisations which sprang up in this period, whether philanthropic or merely sociable, admitted only members of the Protestant ruling *élite*: the boards which ran hospitals or institutions for the poor; the Masonic lodge established in Dublin in 1719; and the Dublin Society, which was founded in 1731 by a group of amateur political economists and progressive landlords with a view to encouraging the economic development of Ireland through exchanging ideas for the advancement of agriculture and manufacture. Occasionally an interested Catholic landowner might communicate to the Dublin Society the result of some experiment on his estate, but he would

27 J. Kelly, 'The Genesis of "Protestant Ascendancy"': The Rightboy Disturbances of the 1780s and their Impact upon Protestant Opinion', in G. O'Brien (ed.), *Parliament, Politics and People: Essays in Eighteenth-century Irish History* (Dublin: Irish Academic Press, 1989), 93–127.

never be invited to join. In fact the society had a pronounced establishment ethos: the original membership included many Church of Ireland clerics, and the lord lieutenant of the day was elected president.[28]

The Social Structure of Protestant Ireland

The propertied class, which thus dominated Irish public life, was little changed in composition from the Restoration period, though the furnace-like experience of a pro-Catholic government in James II's reign had made it more cohesive. While the political and religious changes in Tudor Ireland had resulted in conflict between 'Old' and 'New' English, and the Cromwellian conquest had created further division between 'Old' and 'New Protestants', nothing similar occurred as a consequence of the events of 1689–1691. Confiscated Jacobite estates, having at first been granted in large blocs by King William to trusted courtiers and ministers, eventually found their way through purchase into the hands of existing Protestant landed families. Aside from a small influx of French Huguenot refugees, most of whom had fought in William's armies, the landlord class underwent little change. Individual Englishmen were appointed to office in Ireland, but few settled there, and those who did, mainly clergymen appointed to bishoprics, rapidly merged into the existing *élite*. The most significant sedimentary addition was made up of converting Catholics, and while some undoubtedly converted in name only and for entirely materialistic reasons, others, like the Callaghans (originally O'Callaghans) of Shanbally, County Tipperary, became within a generation among the hottest Protestants in their locality.

It is tempting in individual cases, especially in the age of 'party' conflict in Ireland in Queen Anne's reign, to seek to explain differences in political outlook by examining family origins. Thus Gaelic Irish families like the O'Briens of Dromoland in County Clare, even though they had converted to Protestantism in the distant past, were likely to be Tories (and even Jacobite sympathisers). The same might be true of the old Anglo-Norman dynasties, the Butler dukes of Ormond being the prime example; and indeed James Butler, second duke of Ormond, was widely recognised as the leader of the Tory interest in Ireland between c.1697 and 1715, when, fearing impeachment by the incoming Whig ministry in England, he fled to France. Conversely,

---

28 D. W. Hayton, 'The Church of Ireland Laity in Public Life, c.1660–1740', in R. Gillespie and W. G. Neely (eds.), *The Laity and the Church of Ireland, 1000–2000: All Sorts and Conditions* (Dublin: FCP, 2002), 112–17.

Cromwellian newcomers like the Deanes, Evanses and Tighes were prominent in the ranks of the Whigs. But this kind of analysis will not go very far. Sir Donough O'Brien of Dromoland may have been a Tory, but the head of the family, William O'Brien, third earl of Inchiquin, was, by reason of poverty, much more pragmatic in his politics, and another O'Brien, the seventh earl of Thomond, was a Whig. Similarly, while Ormond remained true to his cavalier past, at least once he had recovered from supporting William of Orange at the Revolution, Robert Fitzgerald, nineteenth earl of Kildare, the head of another great Anglo-Norman magnate family, the Fitzgeralds, was included in the commission of lord justices by the Whig ministers in 1715. And finally, although Swift never tired of reminding his readers of the Cromwellian forbears of men like Richard Tighe, whom he nicknamed 'Dick Fitzbaker' after an ancestor who had supposedly held the bread-contract for the Parliamentarian armies,[29] he said nothing whatsoever about the origins of staunch Tories like Robert Rochfort, whose father, 'Prime-Iron' Rochfort, had been an officer in the New Model Army, or Stephen Ludlow, whose pedigree was even more tainted by republicanism, since he was the nephew of the regicide Edmund Ludlow.

There was, however, some mobility within the landed class, even if not the kind of wholesale change brought about by previous political convulsions. One of the most important results of the Williamite revolution was a sharp acceleration in the decline of the power of the old noble houses and the rise of other powerful landed interests, which in due course took their place in the ranks of the aristocracy. Only the earls of Kildare seem to have been proof against this rule, for reasons that have still to be elucidated. In many cases what happened was a kind of internal collapse, the consequence above all of financial mismanagement, exacerbated by absenteeism. The classic example is the Ormond Butlers, whose territorial empire, centred on Counties Kilkenny and Tipperary, was the largest in Ireland, with an annual rent-roll of £25,000 Irish, an astronomical income in a country in which a few hundred pounds a year was enough to qualify one as a gentleman.[30] The political catastrophe that engulfed the second duke only administered the *coup*

---

29 *The Poems of Jonathan Swift*, ed. H. Williams (2nd edn., 3 vols, Oxford: Clarendon Press, 1958), iii, 782–9, 835; I. Ehrenpreis, *Swift: the Man, his Works, and the Age* (3 vols., London: Methuen, 1962–83), iii, 579–81.

30 D. W. Hayton, 'Dependence, Clientage, and Affinity: The Political Following of the Second Duke of Ormonde', in T.C. Barnard and J. Fenlon (eds.), *The Dukes of Ormonde, 1610–1745* (Woodbridge: Boydell & Brewer, 2000), 211–19; T. C. Barnard, *A New Anatomy of Ireland: The Irish Protestants, 1649–1770* (New Haven & London: Yale University Press, 2003), 51–71.

de grâce to a long-term decline. Ormond's grandfather, the first duke, had begun a disastrous cycle of over-spending, indebtedness, borrowing through mortgages, and thus increasing debt further. His successor blithely carried on to the inevitable deadly reckoning. Private acts of parliament were obtained to enable the sale of entailed property, with the result that the duke's patrimony had shrunk significantly even before his flight in 1715 left the way open for attainder and sequestration. Meanwhile smaller interests in Kilkenny and Tipperary, families like the Flowers and Ponsonbys who had been tenants to some Butler property, and others who had been employed on the estate as agents and receivers, bought up Ormond land and took over as the leading figures in county society and eventually in national politics. By the 1730s Colonel William Flower had become Baron Castle Durrow, a peerage that his son converted in 1751 into a viscountcy. The Ponsonbys did even better: William Ponsonby became Viscount Duncannon in 1723, and his son Brabazon became earl of Bessborough and one of the most important individuals on the Irish political scene.

Even those noble houses that did not suffer confiscation as a consequence of serious political incorrectness, or incur massive debts, but managed to retain their property, could still find themselves losing influence and being supplanted by ambitious local gentry. A key factor was absenteeism. A rentier based permanently in England could not hope to maintain a tight grip over his Irish power-base. English peers like Thomas Thynne, Viscount Weymouth, who had married a Devereux heiress and thus acquired part of the estate of the Elizabethan earl of Essex in County Monaghan, or Thomas Wentworth, earl of Strafford, heir to the Wicklow estates obtained by Lord Deputy Wentworth in the 1630s, had never any intention of coming to Ireland and were thus entirely in the hands of their local agents, who managed the property for them and told them no more than they needed to know.[31] Other great families which in the seventeenth century had been genuinely Anglo-Irish – with property and interests on both sides of the Irish Sea – gradually slipped their moorings in the eighteenth. In the case of the largest planter family, the Boyles in County Cork, what happened was a shift in the centre of gravity from the main line to the cadet branches. The earls of Cork and Burlington, direct descendants of the 'great earl of Cork' who had established the family in Munster in the period leading up to the Civil Wars, settled themselves in England, and left the management

---

31 For Weymouth's correspondence with his agents, see Thynne Papers, 179, Longleat House; for the Wentworths', Wentworth Papers, Add. MS 22,192, BL.

of their estates to local representatives.[32] Other prominent members of the Boyle family did the same, in particular Charles, fourth earl of Orrery, whose unscrupulous land agent held back money and made use of his employer's electoral interest for his own benefit.[33] Eventually control over the political influence deriving from the Boyle territorial empire came into the hands of a distant relation, Colonel Henry Boyle of Castlemartyr, who built up a powerful provincial following in Munster, rose to become speaker of the Irish House of Commons in 1731, and was in due course ennobled in his own right as earl of Shannon.

Upward Mobility

Boyle owed much of his political success, at least in Cork and the surrounding counties, to the fact that he was the man on the spot, who met and talked to squires and freeholders, interceded for them with the government and was in a position to trade jobs for votes. In pursuing a public career he modelled himself on a predecessor in the speaker's chair, William Conolly. During the decade after the Hanoverian succession Conolly had been engaged in a prolonged political struggle with a former colleague in the Whig party, Alan Brodrick, first Viscount Midleton, who, like Boyle, hailed from County Cork. Brodrick, who had been appointed lord chancellor of Ireland in 1714, was an 'Anglo-Irish' figure of the old stamp, in that he had been educated in England, moved in English political circles, and sat in both the Dublin and Westminster parliaments. Conolly, by contrast, made his career entirely in Ireland: he acquired some English and Welsh property, but relatively little, unlike Brodrick, who shuttled between country houses in England and Ireland. Nor did Conolly venture into parliament in England: indeed, he only left Ireland once in his life, preferring to build up a power-base through the acquisition of Irish estates with electoral influence, and through his activities as a commissioner of the revenue, which gave him access to acres of patronage which he could dispose among clients and dependants.[34]

32 T. C. Barnard, 'Land and the Limits of Loyalty: The Second Earl of Cork and the First Earl of Burlington', in T.C. Barnard and J. Clark (eds.), *Lord Burlington: Architecture, Art and Life* (London: Hambledon Press, 1995), 167–99; Barnard, *New Anatomy*, 214–16; R. Wilson, *Elite Women in Ascendancy Ireland, 1690–1745: Imitation and Innovation* (Woodbridge: Boydell & Brewer, 2015), chapter 4.

33 Barnard, *New Anatomy*, 165–8, 213, 218; and Orrery's correspondence with his agent in Orrery Papers, MS 4177, NLI.

34 P. Walsh, *The Making of the Irish Protestant Ascendancy: The Life of William Conolly, 1662–1729* (Woodbridge: Boydell & Brewer, 2010).

In many respects Conolly embodied the class of 'new men' who were coming to dominate Irish public life as the old noble houses went into decline. His own origins were humble; the son of a miller and innkeeper in County Donegal who had been the first in his family to conform to the established church. Unlike his great rival, Brodrick, he was not educated at university and began his career in the law as an attorney, the lowest form of professional life. He made his fortune partly through his own efforts, investing in the bubbling land market created by the Williamite confiscations, and partly by means of a highly advantageous marriage. By the time of his death the extent and value of his landholdings, mainly in north-west Ulster and in the hinterland of Dublin, rivalled the Ormonds' at the peak of their fortunes.[35] He did not receive a peerage title himself – such a precipitous social ascent would have been unheard of, even in England. Nevertheless, he capped his political career by serving several terms as a lord justice, and gave a physical expression to his social eminence by commissioning the construction of a country house, Castletown in County Kildare, designed in the latest Palladian style by the most fashionable architect of his day, Sir Edward Lovett Pearce, who was also responsible, among other buildings, for the new Parliament House in Dublin.

Few of his contemporaries could rival Conolly, either in politics or in conspicuous consumption, but there were nevertheless many who matched his achievements on a lesser scale, 'new men' who had made careers in politics or government service, acquired substantial estates, built new houses and in due course acquired peerages. In parliament Conolly surrounded himself with men of this type, including the young Brabazon Ponsonby. They attended soirees in his Dublin villa and house parties at Castletown. But the type was not confined to Conolly's faction; it was to be found across the political spectrum. The 'constitutional revolution' of 1692–1704, which had turned the Irish parliament from an event into an institution (to adopt the late Conrad Russell's classic description of the seventeenth-century English parliament) and the expansion of the Irish bureaucracy had given new opportunities for the ambitious to make their fortunes in Ireland. In this way the process of state formation helped to transform the nature of the political and social *élite*.

While the inauguration of the new Parliament House in 1731 can be seen as an obvious symbol of the arrival of a new political system in Ireland, it was also emblematic of wider social developments. Despite the boost given to the land market by the Williamite confiscations, and the opportunities for advancement provided by the expansion in

35 Walsh, *Making of the Irish Protestant Ascendancy*, chapters 1, 4.

government and public institutions, the landowning class in Ireland remained relatively small. The 'greater gentry', those who held office in local government and played a part in county politics, were much less numerous than their English equivalents, as well as poorer in terms of rental income. Not even a comparatively large, prosperous and well-planted county like Cork had more than 120 resident squires who could be appointed as justices of the peace, while other, more remote, counties like Mayo had far fewer.[36] The compiler of a list of the gentlemen of Counties Antrim and Down, drawn up in the early 1730s and using as its criterion possession of an estate worth £100 a year, could muster less than 200 for both counties.[37] Moreover, this list included some of those who in England would have been regarded as 'petty gentry' or 'parish gentry', with a more circumscribed round of public duties: members of the grand jury rather than the commission of the peace. In Ireland, by contrast, distinctions among the propertied were far from clear cut. From the rentals of the Brodrick family we can see that many of the smaller landowners were themselves tenants, leasing property from friends and neighbours.[38] The social division between landowners and their agents was much less sharp than in England, while the Irish clergy enjoyed a status much higher than their counterparts across the water, especially in parts of Ireland where gentry households were sparse and the participation of the parson and his family was essential to the maintenance of sociability.[39] Moreover, although it was impossible for a self-made man like William Conolly to aspire to a peerage title in one, or even two, generations, in other respects the barriers to social mobility for the wealthy commercial classes of Dublin, Cork and the few other major cities were strikingly low. Just as in England, successful merchants and financiers in Ireland invested in land, and turned themselves into country gentlemen with the minimum of difficulty.

Of course, Irish Protestant society was composed of more than the gentry class. The 'second eleven' of the Ascendancy, as one historian has called it, comprised the smaller tenants and 'strong farmers' in the countryside, together with shopkeepers, traders and craftsmen in cities and in market towns. Dublin, in particular, and to a lesser extent Cork, boasted large

---

36 List of JPs for County Cork, *temp.* George I, M 2537, 304–6, National Archives of Ireland; commission of the peace for County Mayo, 1714, M 6236/7, National Archives of Ireland. See in general Barnard, *New Anatomy*, 54–5.

37 Antrim and Down Historical Miscellany, MS 24.K.19/1, Royal Irish Academy.

38 Brodrick family rentals, *c*.1728, Brodrick Papers, G145/box 102/4, Surrey History Centre.

39 Barnard, *New Anatomy*, chapter 4; *Considerations upon two Bills sent down from the R[ight] H[onourable] the H[ouse] of L[ords]to the H[onourable] H[ouse]of C[ommons], relating to the Clergy of I[relan]d* (London, 1732).

Protestant populations. These lower-class Protestants were also active in politics and government. The forty-shilling freehold franchise in county elections to parliament was a very low threshold, while in many boroughs the requirements were even less demanding. The majority were corporation boroughs, which only admitted members of the governing body to vote. But there were thirty-six constituencies where the right to vote was in the freemen, a dozen 'potwalloping' boroughs, where five-pound householders could vote, and six 'manor boroughs', where all resident Protestants were polled. Of course, the value of the franchise depended on how often it could be exercised, and until 1768 the only restriction on the duration of an Irish parliament was the life or will of the sovereign. This resulted in only two general elections between 1727 and 1760, but in the preceding period, from 1692 to 1715, there were five. Ordinary Protestants could also take part in municipal politics, though in many towns this too would be dominated by the wealthy. In Dublin the nature of the corporate and guild structure permitted domination by the greater merchants but ordinary freemen and guild members could still have their say, within their guilds and at the quarterly assemblies of the 'commons' in which by-laws were made and municipal elections ratified.[40] In addition, various groups of Dublin tradesmen and manufacturers formed friendly societies under their own direction, which combined social activities with the representation of their interests through petitioning. At a parish level, the constables, sidesmen, churchwardens and the members of the vestry acted as the smallest particle of local government, combining a range of social functions besides the provision of law and order, in a representative institution that involved many poorer Protestants.[41] Indeed, records indicate that some vestrymen in rural parishes were illiterate.[42]

Church and Dissent

Nor was Protestant Ireland uniformly Anglican. The Cromwellian heritage survived in the south, largely in towns, where there were congregations of Presbyterians, Independents and Baptists, and meetings of Quakers. Evidence for the political activities of these various groups is thin, but certainly in

---

40 J. R. Hill, *From Patriots to Unionists: Dublin Civic Politics and Irish Protestant Patriotism, 1660–1840* (Oxford: Clarendon Press, 1997), chapter 2, esp. 42–44.

41 R. Dudley, 'The Dublin Parishes and the Poor: 1660–1740', *Archivium Hibernicum*, 53 (1999), 80–94; R. Dudley, 'The Dublin Parish, 1660–1730', in E. FitzPatrick and R. Gillespie (eds.), *The Parish in Medieval and Early Modern Ireland: Community, Territory and Building* (Dublin: FCP, 2006), 277–96.

42 Hayton, 'Church of Ireland Laity', 123.

Dublin the Dissenting interest was a significant factor in municipal and parliamentary elections, despite the passage in 1704 of a sacramental test specifically designed to exclude non-Anglicans from holding crown or municipal office (and thus from voting in corporation boroughs). Those Presbyterians who belonged to the English tradition were perfectly happy to conform 'occasionally', while borough freemen were in any case not subject to the test. Dissenters supported the Whigs during the party conflict of Queen Anne's reign, and were active again in Dublin elections at the end of the 1720s.[43] They had many other grievances besides the imposition of the test: there was only a limited legal toleration of Dissent, from 1719 onwards, and technically Dissenters were subject to a range of restrictions on the practice of their religion, together with the additional irritation of being obliged to pay tithes to the clergy of the established church as well as a pecuniary support for their own minister. Tithe was systematically enforced, and a grievance to the entire population, not just Dissenters, but the extent to which Dissenters in the south suffered other disabilities seems to have varied considerably.

The real strength of Nonconformity was, however, in Ulster, where hostility between Church and Dissent was most marked.[44] The Presbyterian community in the north remained strongly Scottish in terms of culture and association; indeed, a Presbyterian minister referred to it as a 'Scotch colony'. Ministers were trained in Scotland, Presbyterian merchants in Belfast and Derry kept up strong trading links with Glasgow and other ports in the Scottish south-west, and above all Ulster Presbyterians looked to Scotland for religious leadership. The traditions of Scottish Presbyterianism were very different from those of the Presbyterians in the south of Ireland who had come over from England in the early and mid-seventeenth century. The church in Ulster was tightly organised: sessions were affiliated to presbyteries, and from 1691 the presbyteries were placed under the jurisdiction of a General Synod, modelled on the General Assembly of the Scottish Kirk.

Reinforced by a large-scale migration from the south-west of Scotland in the mid-1690s, Presbyterians in the eighteenth century formed easily the majority of Protestants in some Ulster counties, notably Antrim, and were a very large minority in the rest, with the exception of Fermanagh and Cavan. They were also spreading across the province and beyond, dividing existing congregations and settling others in virgin territory. The community included a handful of

---

43 J. R. Hill, 'Dublin Corporation, Protestant Dissent, and Politics, 1660–1800', in K. Herlihy (ed.), *The Politics of Irish Dissent 1650–1800* (Dublin: FCP, 1997), 32–3.

44 For what follows, see R. Whan, *The Presbyterians of Ulster, 1688–1730* (Woodbridge: Boydell & Brewer, 2013).

landed gentry, and in a few towns like Belfast and Derry Presbyterian merchants dominated commerce, but their centre of gravity lay in the 'middling
sort', shopkeepers, tradesmen and artisans in towns, and tenant farmers in the
countryside. In contrast to Dissenters in the south, they suffered a serious loss
of power and influence as the result of the sacramental test. Presbyterians of
the Scottish stripe were not able to conform occasionally, and so Presbyterian
aldermen and burgesses gave up office, and left their interests to be represented
by sympathetic churchmen. Worse still, in the long run many of the wealthier
elements in Presbyterian society were induced, like landed Catholics, to conform to the established church, depriving the General Synod of direct access
to parliament and government. Organised political campaigns for the repeal of
the test, and the removal of other legal disabilities on Dissenters, faltered and
were eventually abandoned. The focus of Presbyterian political activity was
now the mobilisation of tenants and farmers to vote in parliamentary elections, and in some contests, as in County Antrim in 1715, or County Monaghan
in 1733, they did have an impact, but the infrequency of general elections rendered this weapon only sporadically effective.

The scale of Presbyterian immigration into Ulster in 1694–1697 alarmed
staunch churchmen, both clerical and lay. Individual aspects of Presbyterian
Church structure irked the Anglican clergy – the way in which sessions and
presbyteries disciplined their congregations, for example, seemed to usurp the
functions of the ecclesiastical courts – but it was the very nature of the provincial organisation, which offered the greatest threat. Presbyterians seemed
to have created 'a state within a state'. The re-establishment of Presbyterians
in Scotland in 1689, in a political coup which had seen Episcopalians turned
from the establishment into a persecuted sect, seemed to the more excitable
churchmen to presage a similar revolution in Ireland.

The impact of Presbyterian expansion struck the church at a time when
elements in the episcopate were promoting an agenda of constructive reform,
intended to make the clergy as a whole more effective in attending to the pastoral needs of their flocks, and to advance the cause of the reformed religion
against popish error and superstition.[45] These reformers took a hard line against
Dissent, some publishing pamphlets which denied the validity of Presbyterian
orders and Presbyterian marriages.[46] But they were soon outflanked by more

---

45 S. J. Connolly, 'Reformers and High-flyers: The post-Revolution Church', in A. Ford,
K. Milne and J. I. McGuire (eds.), *As by Law Established: The Church of Ireland since the
Reformation* (Dublin: Lilliput Press, 1995), 153–5.
46 P. O'Regan, *Archbishop William King of Dublin (1650–1729) and the Constitution in Church
and State* (Dublin: FCP, 2000), 74–9; J. C. Beckett, *Protestant Dissent in Ireland 1687–1780*
(London: Faber & Faber, 1948), chapters 3, 11.

extreme figures from the lower clergy, who articulated in an altogether more violent way the concerns of those who had to meet the Presbyterian challenge in the parish. Matters were complicated by the fact that the bishops' reform agenda was making greater demands of the clergy; insisting that they reside, and that they rebuild churches and rectories, but without providing the funds to enable this to be done. The Church of Ireland was seriously under-resourced, and pluralism (the holding of several benefices in one pair of hands), and thus non-residence, was inevitable. Episcopal reform would have seriously depleted the incomes of parsons who already found it hard to collect tithes from recalcitrant parishioners. Moreover, several of the more prominent of the reforming bishops nurtured Whiggish sympathies in politics. The upshot was the appearance in Ireland of a 'High Church' party, which took its inspiration from High Churchmen in England, and saw its cause as an integral element in the struggle of Episcopalians against Dissenters across the British Isles. Unlike the reforming bishops, who were in some respects close in spirit to English Low Churchmen, they saw the answer to the problems of the church in the legal suppression of Nonconformity, resurrecting the kind of authoritarian corporate state that had briefly existed in England during the 1670s.[47] They provided much of the ideological backbone for Irish Toryism in the reign of Queen Anne, and became heavily involved in secular politics, influencing parishioners to cast their votes for Tory candidates.

The 'Improvement' of Ireland

The dependence of the High Church interest on Tory politicians meant that the collapse of Irish Toryism in 1715 spelled the end of the hopes of the High Church clergy. Convocation did not meet in George I's reign, and clerical firebrands like Francis Higgins, the vehemence of whose preaching had troubled the political waters on both sides of the Irish Sea, faded into obscurity. The Hanoverian succession also brought an end to a period in which ecclesiastical issues had been heavily politicised. But it did not mean that the church would return to a peaceful existence. Far from being the corrupt and complacently worldly institution of contemporary caricature, the eighteenth-century Church of Ireland and its clergy is now seen by historians as an organisation seeking to do its best in difficult circumstances. Moreover, the instinct to positive reform surfaced again, in the work of some of the more earnest bishops,

---

47 Connolly, 'Reformers and High-flyers', 155–60; compare Hayton, *Ruling Ireland*, chapter 4.

and in efforts by clergy and by devout laymen to aid pastoral endeavours and to improve opportunities for proselytism through such initiatives as charity schools.[48] Episcopal enthusiasms continued to create tensions with the hard-pressed parish clergy. Again, these spilled over into politics, when the number of English-appointed bishops increased and they became associated with an 'English interest' in politics, supporting the decisions of the English government and the Westminster parliament even when these went directly against Irish economic interests or constitutional pretensions.[49]

There was also an increasing tension between clergy and laity over economic issues. Concern over what seemed to be the backward nature of the Irish economy, highlighted by periods of crisis, when trade collapsed and there was insufficient coinage in circulation to permit tenants to pay their rents, prompted a number of writers to publish analyses of Ireland's economic troubles and prescriptions for their cure. Some, like Swift, blamed the discriminatory legislation passed by the Westminster parliament, especially the Woollen Act of 1699, which had banned the export of woollen manufactures to England and its plantations. His notorious *Proposal for the Universal Use of Irish Manufacture* (1720), recalled the comment of a fellow countryman that 'Ireland would never be happy till a law were made for burning everything that came from England except their people and their coal.' However, other commentators looked for a more positive and practicable response to Ireland's difficulties. Writers like Thomas Prior, Arthur Dobbs and David Bindon saw the potential for the Irish economy to develop without subverting the constitutional relationship with Britain. They gave explicit expression to what was becoming a common outlook among Irish Protestants, that Ireland needed 'improvement'. This was of course a reflection of what had traditionally been accepted as the English mission in Ireland: to civilise Irish society through the introduction of English government, religion and social organisation. But from *c.*1720 onwards, public discussion of the 'improvement' of Ireland increasingly focused on the modernisation of farming techniques and the introduction of new industries such as linen manufacture. This was reflected in parliamentary legislation as well as in economic literature, and in the foundation of the Dublin Society. But 'improvers' soon began to identify the dead hand of the established church as one of the main obstacles

48 Hayton, *Anglo-Irish Experience*, chapter 7.
49 P. McNally, '"Irish and English Interests": National Conflict within the Church of Ireland Episcopate in the Reign of George I', *IHS*, 29 (1995), 295–314.

to 'improvement': the principal issues were the vast tracts of church property rented out by bishops on short leases which discouraged tenants from investing, and the impact of tithe on the rural economy. The culmination was a parliamentary campaign to open up bishops' lands to longer leases and to reform the tithe system, which drew a violent response from clergymen, including Swift.

Varieties of Patriotism

Thus, despite the consolidation of its position, in terms of landownership and political power, the Protestant Ascendancy of the early eighteenth century remained neither united nor comfortable. Party divisions in the form of Whig and Tory may have disappeared in parliament after 1715, but that did not mean that Ireland was politically quiescent. In fact, the disappearance of party politics enabled other, more dangerously divisive, issues to come to the fore, focusing on the economic interests of Ireland and its relations with England. Political debate, inside and outside the Irish parliament, became couched in the language of 'patriotism'. This was of course borrowed from England, where the traditional opposition designation of 'country party' (as representing the true public interest of the country against the corrupt self-interest of 'the court') had been rebranded as 'patriots'. But in Ireland it carried the additional meaning of representing the interests of Ireland in the face of English misrule.

Despite the origins of many of its members in English conquest and settlement, and the essentially colonial nature of viceregal government, the 'Protestant Ascendancy' never saw itself as a colonial class, akin to the planters of Virginia or Barbados. Successive generations of newcomers assumed that Ireland was a historically separate kingdom with its own institutions: the Irish parliament, for example, was not an inferior body but a 'sister' to the Westminster parliament. During the Williamite war Protestants referred to Catholics as 'the Irish' and themselves as 'the English interest'. For a time afterwards, parliamentary addresses and petitions to the monarch spoke on behalf of 'the King's loyal English subjects of Ireland' but at the same time individuals could refer to themselves as 'Irish', usually as a way to distinguish their interests from those of English merchants, manufacturers or politicians, and as time went by they did so more often.

This growing sense among Irish Protestants of their Irishness was one of the defining features of the period. It can be put down in part to the simple passage of time, and the greater sense of security that came with it. It was also in part a response to the emergence in English popular literature of a new stereotype of the 'stage Irishman', ridiculous rather than frightening, and extending to the Protestant squirearchy as well as the Gaelic Irish 'Teague'.[50] It was also promoted by a series of conflicts over the constitutional position of the Irish parliament, and interference from Westminster in Irish affairs. The English Woollen Act of 1699 was one of several provocations at the turn of the century, alongside the assertion by the English House of Lords of an appellate jurisdiction over Irish cases, and the resumption by the English parliament of King William's grants of Irish forfeited estates, which threatened the position of Irish Protestant purchasers. Then in 1717–1720 the issue of the Lords' appellate jurisdiction revived again, culminating in the passage at Westminster of the so-called Declaratory Act, asserting the subordination of the Irish parliament. Shortly afterwards occurred the furore over Wood's Halfpence, when Irish public opinion, mobilised by Swift's *Drapier's Letters*, forced Sir Robert Walpole's ministry to withdraw the patent for Irish copper coinage, which had been purchased by the Birmingham ironmaster William Wood.

It is important not to over-emphasise the element of confrontation in Irish Protestant patriotism. Swift, though popular with the Dublin populace, was regarded by many as a dangerous maverick. A generation ago, it was customary to designate this period as the age of Molyneux and Swift, in reference not only to the *Drapier's Letters* but also to William Molyneux's celebrated pamphlet of 1698, *The Case of Ireland Stated...*, which argued the case for Irish legislative autonomy, and became in retrospect a key text for the Protestant 'patriots' of the late eighteenth century. But at the time of its publication Molyneux's pamphlet was more of an embarrassment than an inspiration to his fellow-countrymen, and while Swift's Anglophobic writings in the 1720s found some echoes among parliamentary back-benchers and stirred up opinion 'out of doors', they by no means represented the majority opinion among the landed *élite*. Resentment at the arrogant interventions of Westminster MPs and English ministers was always tempered by an awareness that in the last resort the maintenance of the Protestant establishment in Ireland depended on British military and financial backing. This did not make the 'Protestant Ascendancy' simply an 'English garrison', but it did encourage a pragmatic approach to political issues, and a form of 'constructive patriotism'

---

50 Hayton, *Anglo-Irish Experience*, 13–17, 34–6.

which aimed at encouraging the improvement of Ireland through practical measures. Men like William Conolly and those around him in the Irish government were aware of the advantages of working with Britain and its emerging global empire rather than engaging in futile flag-waving in pursuit of an unrealisable dream of self-sufficiency.

PART II

★

RELIGION AND WAR

7

Counter Reformation: The Catholic Church, 1550–1641

TADHG Ó hANNRACHÁIN

In terms of the history of European religion, what occurred in Ireland between 1550 and 1641 was distinctly anomalous. For all but five years of this period the monarch on the throne was committed to upholding a church that was not in communion with Rome yet, paradoxically, this was the era in which the mass of the population increasingly came to identify themselves as Catholics in opposition to the church by law established. Moreover, although at the beginning of the period monarchical power over much of the island was tenuous to the point of non-existence, the reach of the state expanded substantially in the course of the long reign of Elizabeth I and by the time of her death in 1603 a full conquest had been accomplished. Even more remarkably, it can be suggested that it was the areas of pronounced medieval English settlement and most open to English influence where rejection of the state church hardened fastest into ideological opposition. Ireland's religious developments thus ran counter to the general pattern of *cuius regio, eius religio* (whose realm, his or her religion), which characterised most of post-Reformation Europe and were particularly anomalous in terms of contemporary Catholicism: nowhere else in Europe during this period did the Church of Rome survive as the majority confession in any polity without state support. It can be noted too that the direction of religious change in the majority Gaelic Irish population differed sharply from among the speakers of other Celtic languages in contemporary Britain. In Gaeliphone Scotland the Reformed Kirk established itself with surprising success, while in both Wales and Cornwall Catholicism lost ground steadily in the course of the Elizabethan and Stuart periods.

Ireland's unusual religious evolution in the era of *cuius regio, eius religio* was the product of two conjoint processes. The first of these involved the limited evangelical and coercive capabilities of the state church, for practically the entire period under review, which fatally coincided with mounting political and economic alienation of the Irish population across the island's ethnic spectrum. But while Catholic success was only made possible by the failure of the Reformation, it was not shaped purely by this. Rather than mere survivalism, what occurred in the island was a dynamic process in which actions and decisions of Irish actors and their aiders and abettors in continental Europe were of key importance.

Religious Change in Late Tudor Ireland

Recent English historiography has portrayed the Marian interlude (1553–8) as a remarkable harbinger of much of what became the classic Counter-Reformation programme in Europe in the wake of the Council of Trent.[1] However, while arguably successful in the short term, ultimately the change of *régime* in 1558 spelled the death knell of English Catholicism as the religion of the majority of the kingdom's inhabitants. Irish historians have also placed a significant emphasis on the Marian period as an important wellspring of a completely contrary movement, namely the confessionalisation of the Irish population within the Church of Rome.[2]

In sharp contrast to England, there was little trace of an indigenous movement of Protestant reform in the early decades of the Tudor Reformation. In Ireland there were to be no Marian burnings because nobody in the island was sufficiently motivated to face the fires on behalf of a church settlement and theology which had essentially been imposed from outside with little evidence of any native support. The most advanced exponents of Edwardian Protestantism, such as John Bale, the bishop of Ossory, were English imports. Despite the avowed efforts of Anthony St Leger, Sir Edward Bellingham and Sir James Croft to impose the first *Book of Common Prayer*, it is probable that relatively little change was effected in traditional religious practice and beliefs even in the English-speaking part of the island. For instance, although William Casey, the bishop of Waterford and Lismore, was an appointment of the Edwardian era, John Bale was repulsed by the communion service that he encountered in the city, which he described as 'used lyke a Popysh masse with the olde apysh toyes of Antichrist, in bowynges and beckynges, knelinges and

1 E. Duffy, *Fires of Faith: Catholic England under Mary Tudor* (New Haven and London: Yale University Press, 2009), *passim*.
2 See for instance J. Murray, *Enforcing the English Reformation in Ireland: Clerical Resistance and Political Conflict in the Diocese of Dublin, 1534–1590* (Cambridge University Press, 2009), 319; U. Lotz-Heumann, 'Confessionalisation in Ireland: Periodisation and Character, 1534–1649', in A. Ford and J. McCafferty (eds.), *The Origins of Sectarianism in Early Modern Ireland* (Cambridge University Press, 2005), 24–53.

knockynges …'.[3] To the north in Dublin, the area of the island most exposed to English influence, Colm Lennon has suggested that at the time of Mary's accession in 1553, other than among 'a small official group and its supporters', the Reformation had made little impact on the city.[4] In the preceding decades preaching to underpin the reconfigured state church was extraordinarily limited in scope, even in the English-speaking part of the island, because the personnel simply did not exist to discharge this function and in Gaelic Ireland it had effectively been non-existent. Moreover, despite the suppression of monasteries in the English-dominated area of the island, the traditional fabric and structures of late medieval Catholicism were not subjected to the same rigour of confiscation and suppression as in England.[5] Chantries, for instance, survived essentially unaffected, even in Dublin.[6]

Bale's brief career as bishop of Ossory offers some limited indications that the task of inculcating reform in Old English Ireland was not impossible. The bishop's account of being rescued and brought to Kilkenny by a large band from the city who sang psalms on the way home, if taken at face value, indicates that his firm commitment to the gospel and the practices of advanced Edwardian Protestantism had struck a chord with at least some of the urban population.[7] But his unhappy time in Ossory provides far more striking evidence concerning the uphill battle that the Reformation would have to fight to gain significant traction. In summing up towards the end of his text, Bale singled out three groups in particular as venomously opposed to his practice of ministry.[8] Tellingly, the first of these was the clergy. Much of the clerical opposition that Bale encountered can probably be related to the simple conservatism of the priests. Lacking as it did a native university culture, Ireland was not a natural breeding ground for advanced evangelical views. But while this was also true of many parts of England, it is interesting that in Ireland the issue of clerical marriage seems to have been of unusual importance. Bale himself was a strong supporter of clerical matrimony on the classical Pauline grounds that it represented a necessary institution to allow men to combat their proclivities to sinful sexual incontinence. But in

---

3 John Bale, *The Vocacyon of John Bale to the Bishoprick of Ossorie in Irelande his Persecucions in the Same and Finall Delyuereaunce*, (Wesel (?), 1553), f. 17v.

4 C. Lennon, *The Lords of Dublin in the Age of Reformation* (Dublin: Irish Academic Press, 1989), 128, 130.

5 B. Bradshaw, *The Dissolution of the Religious Orders in Ireland under Henry VIII* (Cambridge University Press, 1974), 66–205.

6 H. A. Jefferies, *The Irish Church and the Tudor Reformations* (Dublin: Four Courts Press [hereafter FCP], 2010), 101–3.

7 Bale, *Vocacyon of John Bale*, f. 28v.

8 Bale, *Vocacyon of John Bale*, f. 46v.

Ireland the issue of married clergy seems to have created significant tensions.[9] While many reasons can be adduced, it seems possible that in Old English Ireland clerical marriage aroused particular resistance because of the degree to which the identity of the ecclesiastical *élite* was inflected by a strong and often defensive current of anti-Gaelic sentiment. As James Murray has argued, the clerical leadership of the English colony in Ireland consciously evoked their own commitment to the codes of late medieval canon law as part of the process of distinguishing themselves from the perceived barbarity of Gaelic culture.[10] While this reflected a strong belief in the superiority of their own culture, such attitudes became increasingly tinged with defensiveness as creeping Gaelicisation threatened to invade the English colony from the later medieval period. Gaelic laxity with regard to clerical celibacy thus may have come to represent a significant threat to the cultural identity of the Old English colony and this may help to explain why clerical marriage became a particularly charged issue in Ireland, since it offered to eliminate an important distinguishing characteristic between Old English and Gaelic clerical practice.

Aside from the clergy, Bale singled out two other groups for particular criticism, namely the military and lawyers. It seems probable that the hostility of the military classes was largely governed by the attitudes of their employers, the lords of Gaelic and Gaelicised Ireland. That these aristocrats, in contrast with Gaelic Scotland, for instance, largely proved opponents rather than multipliers of the movement of religious reform was undoubtedly highly significant. But that Bale also specifically referred to Irish lawyers is noteworthy. In England, many of the most outspoken opponents of the Reformation had come from the legal profession, but it had also produced significant and important champions of the evangelical movement. In Ireland, by contrast, even as early as the 1550s, lawyers were evidently attracting the hostility of a figure such as Bale. This trope continued throughout the century. In 1564, Bishop Brady of Meath bitterly complained of 'the ungodly lawyers' as 'sworn enemies of the truth' and six years later he insisted that only one single lawyer, Baron Robert Cusack, was well disposed to the state church. In 1588, Lord Deputy Fitzwilliam also adverted to the manner in which lawyers had withdrawn themselves

---

9 Murray, *Enforcing the English Reformation in Ireland*, 247, describes clerical celibacy as 'the litmus test of canonical regularity for the English Irish clerical *élite*'.

10 J. Murray, 'The Diocese of Dublin in the Sixteenth Century: Clerical Opposition and the Failure of the Reformation', in J. Kelly and D. Keogh (eds.), *History of the Catholic Diocese of Dublin* (Dublin: FCP, 2000), 92–111.

from Dublin to avoid attendance at the services to celebrate the failure of the Spanish Armada.[11] This was not insignificant because, as literate laymen formed in a secular educational system, lawyers as a group probably represented the most naturally hospitable environment for evangelical ideas in Anglophone Ireland.[12] That a figure such as Bale essentially treated as irrelevant whether the legal requirements for the imposition of the second *Book of Common Prayer* had been fulfilled, and insisted on being consecrated according to English legal forms, offers a hint perhaps of the origins of the antagonism which he developed towards Irish lawyers but this, arguably, is also emblematic of what became a wider failure of the English administration and its church in the later sixteenth century.[13] At its most simple, the perceived innovative character and increased intrusiveness and destructiveness of the English state in the traditional colony during this period meant that, rather than seeing an Erastian state as the key to the reform of society and its most important aspect, the church, Irish lawyers were more likely to be drawn to associate the new ecclesiastical settlement with a wider programme of economic devastation, exclusion from office and an undermining of the traditional commonwealth.

If Ireland had not produced any semblance of a native culture of evangelical reform in 1550, nevertheless in the previous decade the first Jesuit mission to the island had formed a distinctly negative impression of the long-term prospects of Catholicism. Moreover, the challenges of winning the hearts and minds of unenthusiastic populations were confronted by *régimes* all over early modern Europe during this period and in the main *cuius regio, eius religio* functioned remarkably successfully. Religious change was orchestrated from above by the Habsburgs with often terrifying brutality in Austria and Bohemia and, less thoroughly it is true, through the exercise of much 'softer' power in Hungary. In Norway a Lutheran Reformation was implanted with substantial success, not merely from above but essentially from outside, transmuting identities even if the actual practice of religion often continued to be inflected with the relics of Catholic tradition. And in England, of course, the minority religious *régime*, which took power in 1558, chained and then gradually euthanised the sleeping giant of the kingdom's Catholicism. That something similar could have occurred in

---

11 E. P. Shirley, *Original Letters and Papers of the Church in Ireland under Edward VI, Mary and Elizabeth*, (London: Gilbert and Rivington, 1851), 135; Jefferies, *Tudor Reformations*, 190.

12 In this regard see J. Guy, 'Law, Lawyers and the English Reformation', *History Today* 35 (1985).

13 Bale, *Vocacyon of John Bale*, f. 19r.

Ireland is certainly suggested by the passage of the Reformation legislation in parliament in 1560.[14]

Nevertheless, over the succeeding decades the state was to prove itself incapable of successfully confronting disengagement from and opposition to the new dispensation and this provided the environment in which a movement of Catholic renewal could develop. This broad statement can be taken to hold true for both the Anglophone and Gaelic-speaking areas of the island. James Murray's forensic study of what should have been the nerve centre of reform, the diocese of Dublin, identifies a number of key elements in the failure of the Elizabethan settlement in the Pale. In the first place, he argues that the reconstitution of St Patrick's cathedral during the Marian era was of critical importance. Essentially the same personnel who had been brought together to implement the restoration of Catholicism under Mary remained *in situ* with responsibility for the oversight of the Reformation statutes of Supremacy and Uniformity.[15] In terms of inculcating allegiance to the new settlement, the deleterious effects of this continuity continued to be felt deep into Elizabeth's reign. Why such a situation developed, however, points up a significant difference between the churches in England and Ireland, which the new queen confronted in 1558. In the former, the queen faced massive opposition to the proposed religious settlement. Only one bishop was prepared to take the Oath of Supremacy, while fourteen were ejected from the episcopal bench for refusal. Over half the cathedral prebendaries and office-holders were also deprived, a proportion made even more significant when account is taken of the large mortality among this cohort in the influenza epidemic. The university establishments of Oxford and Cambridge also evinced bitter hostility to the new dispensation.[16]

In Ireland, by contrast, only two bishops suffered deprivation for refusal of the oath and at least two archbishops and five bishops were prepared to swear it, three of whom performed notable service for the *régime* in supporting the new ecclesiastical legislation in parliament.[17] It has been suggested that the greater willingness of Irish ecclesiastical *élites* to support the settlement stemmed from a conscious decision to constitute themselves as a fifth column within the new church but this may be to confuse the role they subsequently played with the reasons governing the original decision.[18] Given the

---

14 H. A. Jefferies, 'The Irish parliament of 1560: The Anglican Reforms Authorised', *Irish Historical Studies*, 26 (1988), 128–41.

15 Murray, *Enforcing the English Reformation in Ireland*, 262.

16 Duffy, *Fires of Faith*, 113, 161.

17 Jefferies, *Tudor Reformations*, 125–7.

18 Murray, *Enforcing the English Reformation in Ireland*, 256–7.

limitations of the Edwardian Reformation in Ireland it may have been that the Irish bishops were less aware than their English counterparts of the full implications of the royal supremacy or that the sops to conservative instincts that were placed in the Irish legislation proved more effective than might have been expected at first glance.[19]

Another vital factor in ensuring that the Irish Elizabethan church would have a more conservative character than its English sister was the more limited degree to which the oath was offered at all. The *régime*'s disinclination to push this point certainly reflected the paucity of alternatives to fill positions that might become vacant for deprivation on this score, but it probably derived even more from the fear of provoking opposition.[20] In England, such recalcitrance had to be confronted because the religious settlement was in itself central to all the political issues of Elizabethan England. This did not obtain in Ireland, where ecclesiastical matters throughout the reign were effectively secondary in importance to the financial, military and constitutional problems of dealing with the Gaelic and Gaelicised hinterland of the island. Not only were many clergy not required to swear the oath, but the laity were often left untroubled. Colm Lennon, for instance, has shown that there is little evidence that the municipal officials of Dublin refused the oath because it does not seem to have been required of them.[21]

Nothing was more symptomatic of this tendency to accord lower priority to religious matters than the failure to establish a Protestant seminary in Ireland until 1592. Without the Protestantisation of Oxbridge, the English Reformation would have limped forward far more slowly but in Ireland there was to be no native pipeline of clergy to staff the established church until 1592, by which point conservative Catholic survivalism was increasingly being overtaken by a more militant brand of post-Tridentine faith. Ironically the survival of the crypto-Catholic power base of St Patrick's cathedral was a major factor in preventing the accumulation of the financial resources necessary for this project in the 1560s, when such an institution would probably have attracted significant numbers of Old English students and could also have laid the basis for a Gaelic-speaking ministry. Some recent scholarship has tended to downplay the significance of this failure. Henry Jefferies, for instance, has argued that Oxford and Cambridge were no more inaccessible to students from Ireland than the continental colleges to which Irish youths

---

19 S. G. Ellis, *Ireland in the Age of the Tudors 1447–1603* (London: Longman, 1998), 225–6.
20 Jefferies, *Tudor Reformations*, 128–30.
21 Lennon, *Lords of Dublin*, 133–4.

flocked in increasing numbers in the later decades of Elizabeth's reign, and that the Irish government seems to have ignored the possibility of providing bursaries for facilitating Irish access to Oxbridge or of providing a more humble seminary.[22] Thus, while not discounting it completely, he has presented the lack of an Irish university as a secondary issue, indeed more of a symptom of the weakness of the state church than a cause of its evangelical failure. Jefferies instead has emphasised the central unwillingness of the Irish population to engage with the established church, which meant that there was no possibility of creating mass conversion by preaching.[23]

Jefferies's work has been of extraordinary value in highlighting the degree of disengagement from the Elizabethan settlement from very early in the reign. He has emphasised the speed with which churches became derelict as communities withdrew their voluntary support for their upkeep and the disappearance of the office of churchwarden, which previously had been a feature of parish life throughout the Pale, in most of the English-speaking areas of the island. The absence of this office then materially impacted on the imposition of fines for failure to attend the services of the established church.[24] His research has also demonstrated a deep hostility towards the settlement from the earliest years of Elizabeth's reign and the persistent lack of educated Protestant clergy. Contesting the common tendency to focus on the poverty of the Elizabethan church, he has argued that there were more adequately resourced benefices in Ireland than suitable ministers to fill them.[25] Even at the end of the century, he has noted that one Irish Protestant witness claimed that there were only twenty-four preachers in Ireland, only a third of whom were Irish born, and furthermore that the majority were actually serving as army chaplains rather than ministering to the Irish population.[26]

Yet the failure to found a university early in the reign was almost certainly of great significance. Given the lack of popular support for the new dispensation, even widespread preaching to adults was unlikely to create genuinely convinced adherents to the Elizabethan church. Indeed, it can be suggested that the function of preaching to adults formed in a different religious context was less to gain their convictions than to assuage their doubts sufficiently to allow their acquiescence in the moulding of their children within a new

---

22 Jefferies, *Tudor Reformations*, 143–5, 170–1, 227–9
23 Jefferies, *Tudor Reformations*, 242, 280.
24 Jefferies, *Tudor Reformations*, 60–1, 141, 171–2; H. A. Jefferies, 'The Role of the Laity in the Parishes of Armagh *inter Anglicos* on the Eve of the Tudor Reformations', *Archivium Hibernicum*, 52, (1988), 77–8.
25 Jefferies, *Tudor Reformations*, 136–42, 282.
26 Jefferies, *Tudor Reformations*, 246.

confessional framework.[27] At a time when relatively limited compulsion could still produce conformity, a university in Dublin would probably have offered the possibility of attracting Irish students who could then have acted as multipliers of the new religion within their local communities. Native clergy offered two substantial advantages: their provenance was undoubtedly an advantage in terms of community receptivity and, almost certainly, it created a wellspring of evangelical enthusiasm within the clergy themselves to minister to what they saw as their own people. In this context, one can note the extraordinary success of Jesuit educational institutions in Poland and Bohemia and the speed with which an originally foreign professoriate was rapidly replaced by natives of both kingdoms, produced within these very schools.[28]

The factors that conspired to delay the foundation of the university till towards the end of the reign provide a telling indication of the difficult environment in which the state church had to function. A fundamental problem was the reluctance of the Elizabethan *régime* to invest significantly in such an enterprise. Indeed, faced with urgent demands on its purse, the state was more likely to cannibalise existing church assets than to provide additional funding. Jeffrey Cox's study of the diocese of Kildare demonstrates, for instance, that the alienation of the episcopal revenues of the see by Alexander Craik in the 1560s, which was to impact severely on the capacity of future bishops to orchestrate religious change, was driven forward by the inflexible requirement of the payment of first fruits which left him little other option. And long into the seventeenth century, benefices assigned for the use of the lord deputy of Ireland were among those most notable in the county for the disrepair of churches and the absence of preaching.[29]

Lack of lay enthusiasm for the new religious dispensation more or less eliminated the possibility of parliament making good the deficit in royal patronage concerning endowment of an Irish university. In that context, only by the conversion of existing assets, particularly St Patrick's cathedral, was there the possibility of creating a viable institution. However, the monies available from such a plan were probably inadequate and it faced substantial opposition even from figures who might have been expected to be natural supporters, such as the archbishop of Dublin, Adam Loftus. Loftus

27 Here my analysis differs from that of Jefferies, *Tudor Reformations*, 242, 288.
28 T. Ó hAnnracháin, *Catholic Europe, 1592–1648: Centre and Peripheries* (Oxford University Press, 2015), chapter 3.
29 J. Cox, 'The Reformation, Catholicism and Religious Change in Kildare, 1560–1640', unpublished PhD thesis, University College Dublin, 2015, especially chapter 1.

may originally have planned to use St Patrick's as part of a wider campaign to win the hearts and minds of the local clerical *élites* towards acceptance of the Elizabethan settlement by demonstrating respect for the sensitivities and traditions of the local church.[30] Any such plans, however, were overtaken by events and in particular the marked resentment of the Pale community towards the perceived innovations of their government. While economic factors relating to the imposition of cess may have created the greatest antagonisms, it seems probable that any processes of ecclesiastical change were also hampered by the fury of the over-burdened local colonial community. Furthermore, Loftus's commitment to the survival of St Patrick's was increasingly influenced by the material advantage that accrued to him personally and to his wider family and network from the assignment of offices and benefices pertaining to it.[31] Genuine divisions within the ecclesiastical and lay administrative *élite* of late Tudor Ireland concerning the best way of advancing the Reformation in Ireland thus inevitably became enmeshed in rivalries founded on personality and interest.

The transformation of the traditional Catholicism of even Old English Ireland was thus beyond the capacity of a state church deprived of resources or any consistent access to the coercive apparatus of the secular arm and which shared by association in the heightening opprobrium engendered by the activities of the growing and ill-disciplined military establishment in Ireland. Throughout the country, Catholic sacraments continued to be ministered both by clergy serving the benefices of the established church who had never even been called on to take the Oath of Supremacy and a network of independently funded priests who were supported by lay generosity. The high level of lay impropriation facilitated this latter development as frequently only miserable portions of the monies accruing to impropriators were made available to support ministers. By the 1590s in Cork, as confessional boundaries hardened, seminary priests returning from the continent evidently found it relatively easy to convince individuals of a traditional bent serving cures in the established church to forsake these to become 'massing priests', not least because there was evidently little if any financial loss involved.[32] It seems certain that such priests educated in continental Europe were critical agents of radicalisation in Irish religion.

In the latter part of Elizabeth's reign, priests trained on the continent were evidently to the fore in seeking to impress on their compatriots the spiritual

---

30 Murray, *Enforcing the Reformation*.
31 Jefferies, *Tudor Reformations*, 229.
32 SP 63/184/27, The National Archives.

dangers that any form of Nicodemism entailed. Simultaneous with this attempt to cause a boycott of the 'devil's service', a hardening of attitudes became more evident on the part of the lay and ecclesiastical officials of the Elizabethan state as their perceptions of the Irish population were increasingly inflected by the burgeoning anti-Catholicism of late Elizabethan England.[33]

The political and economic crisis of late Elizabethan Ireland materially influenced the religious evolution of the island. Not only was the evangelical capacity of the state church damaged by the siphoning of resources to support political and military ends, but the alienation of the local colonial population by ill-disciplined soldiers and the economic costs of supporting the military establishment certainly impeded identification with any type of state-sponsored ecclesiastical innovation. Within Gaelic Ireland, the extraordinary violence and brutality of what became the Tudor conquest, which extended to mass depopulation in Munster during the 1580s and in Ulster at the turn of the century, and which was underpinned by extensive use of martial law, hardly provided a conducive environment for evangelisation, which in any case was accorded little or no priority, particularly when comparison is made with the level of engagement with Welsh culture and literature shown contemporaneously by the Elizabethan church in that principality. In Ireland, the state church effectively produced neither texts nor preachers capable of expression in the native vernacular. The *élites* of the Gaelic and Gaelicised lordships who found themselves locked into confrontation with the state were naturally disposed to frame their resistance in religious terms, not least because this provided a vehicle for seeking assistance from the continental enemies of the Elizabethan *régime*. The dislocation of conquest, particularly for the native learned classes, whose previous roles as poets, historians and genealogists for the Gaelic lords of the island gradually lost currency, in addition facilitated a reorientation of *élite* figures towards the Catholic priesthood. In sharp contrast with Scotland, where the Kirk was able to recruit heavily from the traditional *élites* of the Gaelic order, few were attracted to service in the established church.[34]

The role of such individuals in the island's Catholicism went far beyond mere pastoral activity, for they also played a key role in the elaboration of new identities that insisted on the fundamentally Catholic nature of Gaelic culture. This was achieved by a multi-faceted endeavour of manuscript

---

33 SP 63/184/27, The National Archives.
34 T. Ó hAnnracháin, 'Religious Acculturation and Affiliation in Early Modern Gaelic Scotland, Gaelic Ireland, Wales and Cornwall', in T. Ó hAnnracháin and R. Armstrong (eds.), *Christianities in the Early Modern Celtic World*, (Basingstoke: Palgrave, 2014), 1–13.

collection, hagiographical historical and annalistic compilation, and devotional and catechetical production in both prose and poetry, in which figures from the traditional learned classes, such as Aodh Buidhe Mac an Bhaird, Flaithrí Ó Maolchonaire, Giolla Brighde Ó hEódhasa and Mícheál Ó Cléirigh, played key roles. Of critical importance in this shift was the development of bases of learning in continental Europe, which meant that cultural production became motivated by the twin imperatives of representing Irish experience in a manner intelligible within the intellectual framework of contemporary European Catholicism and of channelling European influences into native Irish culture. The menace that the Anglocentric Church of Ireland was seen to pose to the integrity of Gaelic culture and identity also helped ensure that the lay devotional tradition of the medieval Gaelic world became a tributary stream to processes of Catholic and not Protestant renewal.[35] Roughly 20 per cent of the surviving bardic poems can be classified as devotional in character.[36] The high survival rate of this grouping is an indication of the manner in which their focus on themes such as the cult of the five wounds of Christ, the *arma Christi*, penance and reverence for the Virgin Mary came to be used to underpin the strategies of post-Tridentine reformers.[37]

The Franciscan Order

Significantly, many of the principal figures in these processes of embedding and acculturation were friars. The evolution of Catholicism in early modern Ireland was inextricably entangled with the Franciscan order, which ultimately emerged as a key bastion of the post-Tridentine articulation of the confession. Prior to the Reformation, Ireland had already proved an extraordinarily hospitable environment for the movement of Franciscan Observancy. Indeed, it can be suggested that the trans-ethnic success of the observant reform within the order not only foreshadowed but actively prepared the way for the elaboration of a post-Tridentine Catholic identity which could span the English/Gaelic spectrum within the island. While the prestige of the friars among the Gaelic population was particularly high, the order was also widely cherished by aristocratic colonial dynasties, such as the Flemings of

---

35 M. Caball, 'Religion, Culture and the Bardic Élite', in A. Ford and J. McCafferty (eds.), *The Origins of Sectarianism in Early Modern Ireland* (Cambridge University Press, 2005), 158–82 at 173–80.

36 S. Ryan, 'A Slighted Source: Rehabilitating Irish Bardic Religious Poetry in Historical Discourse', *Cambrian Medieval Celtic Studies*, 48 (2004), 75–99 at 75.

37 T. Finan, 'The Bardic Search for God: Vernacular Theology in Gaelic Ireland, 1200–1400', *Eolas: The Journal of the American Society of Irish Medieval Studies*, 2 (2007), 28–44.

Slane and the Nugents of Delvin, and by the municipal *élites* of the urban Old English. With up to one hundred houses in the island, the Franciscans represented a key challenge to the embedding of the new state church in Ireland, which it signally failed to overcome. Clear hostility to the royal supremacy was evident among the Observants from an early date. The state policy of suppression of the order's houses was conducted in such a way that allowed the friars to adapt with remarkable agility. The first wave of suppressions in the reign of Henry VIII was limited to those regions of the island amenable to English governmental oversight. Even decades after Elizabeth's accession, in Dromahair and Donegal in the north-west, in Moyne in Connacht, and Kilcrea and Timoleague in Munster, the order retained secure bases to act as novitiates.[38] By the time these areas were eventually brought within the ambit of state control, the circumstances proved favourable for the foundation of still more important centres of Irish Franciscan learning on the continent, of which the college of St Anthony's of Louvain took pride of place. Yet more critically, the strength of local attachment to the order meant that, even in localities where houses were officially suppressed, the friars continued to reside under the patronage of local *élites*. The mendicant traditions of the order allowed it to adapt with relative ease to the sequestration of property and, unable to strike a telling blow with this instrument, the state church struggled to locate alternative weapons in its confrontation with the friars. Towards the end of the century, the increasing militarisation of Elizabethan Ireland rendered a number of Franciscans physically vulnerable to capture and execution and at least two dozen members of the order died violent deaths during her reign.[39] Yet this was insufficient to inflict critical damage on the order's organisation or pastoral activity and, by furnishing it with a series of martyrs, such deaths further elevated its prestige and cemented its standing in local devotion.

By the end of the Elizabethan period, the Franciscan order had emerged as a ubiquitous and major obstacle to any attempt of the state church to inculcate popular adherence. Its influence was not confined to Gaelic Ireland, but the order was arguably the single most important conduit in allowing the culture of post-Tridentine Catholicism to permeate the native Irish population. In this regard, the contrast with Gaelic Scotland, where neither the order nor, in particular, the movement towards observant reform in the late medieval

---

38 C. Lennon, 'The Dissolution to the Foundation of St Anthony's College, Louvain, 1534–1607', in E. Bhreathnach, J. MacMahon and J. McCafferty (eds.), *The Irish Franciscans, 1534–1990* (Dublin: FCP, 2009), 14.

39 C. Lennon, 'The Dissolution to the Foundation of St Anthony's College, Louvain', 19.

period enjoyed anything like the same saliency, is particularly noteworthy. While many factors influenced the Scottish Kirk's much greater success in transforming the religious culture of the Scottish *Gàidhealtachd*, the lack of a significant Franciscan challenge was probably of substantial importance.

The Consolidation of Catholicism in Seventeenth-Century Ireland

The state's achievement of military and political control over the entire island by the time of Elizabeth's death in 1603 was therefore paralleled by a more or less complete failure on the part of the established church to cultivate any significant level of adherence. Rather, an increasing attachment to Catholicism was becoming evident in both the Gaelic and Old English population. The four decades down to 1641 saw an intensification of this Catholic confessionalisation from below, which occurred in the absence of any consistent and concerted programme of coercion, such as for instance occurred in contemporary Austria, to punish opposition to the state church.[40] Despite the wishes of Irish administrative and ecclesiastical leaders, the London government in the main acted as a significant restraint on those determined to seek a sustained confrontation with recusancy and this tendency was accentuated from the beginning of the negotiations for the Spanish match towards the end of the second decade of the century.[41] When coercion was employed it was most commonly directed at the poorer socio-economic groups, while *élite* practitioners of Catholicism were either untroubled or could bribe their way out of difficulties.[42] It seems probable that the state's inefficient coercive policy was actually counter-productive. While marked anxieties were created about the future position of Catholics in the island, not least by the consistent support for policies of confiscatory plantation, Catholics, particularly those of Old English origin, maintained control over formidable reservoirs of social and economic power. Moreover by marginalising Catholics from office, which was increasingly monopolised by members of the immigrant New English community, a double instability was created.

Inevitably the *arriviste* New English aspired to match their political and administrative dominance by acquiring the economic underpinnings normal

---

40 R. Pörtner, *The Counter-Reformation in Central Europe: Styria 1580–1630* (Oxford: Clarendon Press, 2001).

41 See Chapter 8 by Colm Lennon, this volume.

42 V. Treadwell (ed.), *The Irish Commission of 1622: An Investigation of the Irish Administration 1615–22 and its Consequences 1623–4* (Dublin: Irish Manuscripts Commission, 2006), 256.

for such eminence in an early modern society, particularly land ownership. Their criticisms of the older colonial community not surprisingly focused on issues of religious disobedience as justification for distrust that naturally created serious worries for Catholic landowners, which were not allayed when two attempts to broker an agreement with the monarch in return for financial contributions collapsed in the 1620s and in 1634. The intermediary role between monarch and Irish *élites*, which the Dublin government assumed, contributed to a situation in which relatively small rewards were made available to native stake-holders for conversion to the confession of the monarch. A significant contrast can be seen in this regard with the Habsburg territories of Central Europe. In both Bohemia and in Hungary, conversion to Catholicism could open a dizzying set of possibilities for the acquisition of wealth and political influence. Critically, Czechs and Hungarians were among the chief beneficiaries of these processes, with native Czech Catholic magnates dominating Bohemian government in the seventeenth century. In Hungary, somewhat more isolated from the centres of Habsburg power, the office of *nádor* or palatine was of key importance. Native Hungarian Catholic magnates held this office and they effectively monopolised the brokering of royal patronage in Hungary and played a key role in incentivising aristocratic conversion. A contrast can certainly be drawn between the remarkable urgency which Catholic converts to Catholicism in Habsburg lands and in Poland demonstrated in facilitating evangelical outreach to the populations under their influence and the relative lack of commitment to conversion of the Irish population exhibited by New English *élites* in seventeenth-century Ireland.[43]

In a similar fashion, it can be suggested that the repressive policies pursued by the state against Catholic clergy were in the long run equally counterproductive. The employment of the coercive apparatus at the Irish government's disposal against clergy was notably uneven. High-profile executions of figures such as the bishop of Down and Connor, Conor O'Devany, and the priest Patrick Loughran did occur. O'Devany's successor in the see, Edmund Dungan, died in custody and other bishops and vicars apostolic were forced to become fugitives because of the attempts of the state to secure their persons. Yet overall, while such policies helped create a profile as martyr for O'Devany, they failed to inflict any critical damage on the organisational or pastoral capacity of the Catholic Church in Ireland. They did, however, promote strong feelings of grievance and probably assisted in heightening the moral standing

---

43 Ó hAnnracháin, *Catholic Europe*, chapter 3.

of the Catholic clergy with the general population. The emotional tenor of Irish Catholicism in the first four decades of the seventeenth century was thus an amalgam of increasing daring and genuine anxiety.

The Gender Dimension of Ireland's Anomalous Development

Ireland's unusual lack of conformity to *cuius regio, eius religio* also had implications for the practice of religion in terms of gender. Patrick Corish has argued that the relative relegation of Catholicism from the public sphere and the inability of the Irish clergy to centre practice on the parish church contributed to a more domestic religion which allowed for greater influence by women.[44] The possibilities that the clandestine status of Catholicism offered to contemporary women in England and the Netherlands have also been noted by a number of scholars.[45] In Ireland, because the state's intermittent efforts to enforce conformity were largely orientated towards male heads of households, women were apparently freer to disengage completely from the established church. Particularly striking female exemplars of commitment to Catholicism included Margaret Ball, whose own conformist son instituted proceedings against her; Anastasia Strong, the mother of Thomas Walsh, later archbishop of Cashel, who provided hospitality for many priests; Mabel Brown, the dowager countess of Kildare, whose house was a major centre for priestly activity; and Joan Roche, the highly devout mother of John Roche, later bishop of Ferns.[46]

Hostile Protestant authors drew attention to the close bond between priests and women by insisting on its sexual dimension. John Bale noted his disgust at the Irish clergy's refusal to marry, which he believed had nothing to do with sexual continence. Following his experiences in late Tudor Ireland, Fynes Moryson believed that the excessive drinking of Irish women allowed their priests a 'luxurious field' in which to triumph.[47] Barnaby Rich bitterly noted that:

---

44 P. Corish, 'Women and Religious Practice', in M. MacCurtain and M. O'Dowd (eds.), *Women in Early Modern Ireland* (Dublin: Wolfhound Press, 1991), 213–4.

45 A. Walsham, 'Translating Trent? English Catholicism and the Counter Reformation', *Historical Research* 78 (2005), 288–310; F. Dolan, 'Gender and the "Lost" Spaces of Catholicism', *Journal of Interdisciplinary History*, 32 (2002), 641–65; J. Spaans, 'Orphans and Students: Recruiting Girls and Boys for the Holland Mission', in B. Kaplan, B. Moore, H. Van Nierop and J. Pollmann (eds.), *Catholic Communities in Protestant States: Britain and the Netherlands c. 1570–1720* (Manchester University Press, 2009), 183–99.

46 Spaans, 'Orphans and Students', 215; Lennon, *Lords of Dublin*, 213–4.

47 *The Irish Sections of Fynes Moryson's Unpublished Itinerary*, ed. G. Kew (Dublin: Irish Manuscripts Commission, 1998), 68.

Our holy holy brood of Iesuites, Seminaries, Fryers and such other, do performe strange thinges, but specially for the increase and propagation of children, not a barren woman in a house where they be lodged.[48]

Parr Lane rhymed sarcastically that Catholic priests 'whom well you fathers call' could make 'more children without wives/than all our married churchmen for their lives'.[49]

The clandestine relationship of woman and priest in the clandestine religious setting of the home was in many ways a logical locus of horror, rich with resonances of Adam's fall, for Protestant reformers and tallied well with a notion of Catholicism as a religion of seduction which operated on human weakness and depravity both at an individual level and in the greater reservoir of human frailty which women represented. But aside from such stereotypical categorisations, observers of this stamp also recognised the problems created by female adherence to the Catholic clergy. Fynes Moryson noted that:

Iesuites and Roman Priests swarmed in all places, filling the houses of lordes, gentlemen, and espetially Cittisens and dominering in them, as they might well doe, for howsoever the men grewe weary of them, they had the wemen on theire sydes.[50]

Rather than being led by their husbands to church, one commentator insisted that 'Romish priests so persuade the women that they declare that they will as soon bring their husbands to the gallows as to our church.'[51] Men who incurred excommunication by the Catholic clergy for conformity apparently risked losing the company of their wives in their beds or at their tables.[52] Men who elected to conform, too, could find themselves isolated in their own households and under particular pressure approaching death as their families:

denyed them relief or rest, keeping meate and all thinges they desyred from them, and the wemen and children continually pinching and disquieting them when they would take rest, that they might thereby force them to turne Papists agayne.[53]

---

48 Barnaby Rich, *A New Description of Ireland* (London, 1610), 47. I am indebted to Clodagh Tait for this reference.

49 Quoted in A. Ford 'Reforming the Holy Isle: Parr Lane and the Conversion of the Irish', in T. C. Barnard, D. Ó Cróinín and K. Simms (eds.), *'A Miracle of Learning': Studies in Manuscripts and Irish Learning. Essays in Honour of William O' Sullivan* (Aldershot: Ashgate, 1998), 144.

50 *The Irish Sections of Fynes Moryson's Itinerary* , 50–1.

51 W. Dennehy, 'Irish Catholics in the Seventeenth Century', *Irish Ecclesiastical Record*, 4th series, 18 (1905), 419.

52 R. Gillespie, *Devoted People: Belief and Religion in Early Modern Ireland* (Manchester University Press, 1997), 30.

53 *The Irish Sections of Fynes Moryson's Itinerary*, 92.

For such men, access to the clergy of the established church was necessarily mediated by their Catholic families, who were often deeply unwilling to facilitate them. In the 1630s, for instance, Edmund Sexton, who was gravely sick, wished to be attended by a Protestant clergyman but his family bitterly opposed any attempt to minister to him. His son, also Edmund Sexton, played a role in this resistance but the other key actors were evidently women, including his daughters and wife.[54]

The extra-legal status of Catholicism in Ireland undoubtedly altered the parameters of practice from those that obtained in Catholic states. To some extent this may have conferred greater agency on women and in Ireland, as in other jurisdictions such as the Netherlands and England where Catholicism was proscribed, the historiographical literature has tended to emphasise the potential benefits to women of this development. In this regard, however, it can be noted that Irish Catholicism produced no equivalent of the *kloppen*, spiritual virgins under a simple vow of chastity, who became such a vital feature of Dutch Catholicism, outnumbering ordained male clergy almost ten to one by the middle of the seventeenth century.[55] In the *Missio Hollandica*, such women acted as sextons and catechists; they collected and distributed alms and ran institutions of teaching and refuge.[56] In Ireland, by contrast, access to such an active apostolate for women was acutely limited outside the confines of the home and family in prescribed roles as wife, mother and daughter. The effect of the Reformation was also probably to restrict the possibility of life as a nun to all but a tiny minority of women from wealthy families, although it probably also reduced the numbers of women who could be forced into such a career by familial pressure.

The Strands of Catholic Identity

The advent of increasing numbers of seminary-trained clergy into all areas of the country was undoubtedly an important driver in terms of consolidating Catholicism in the localities. This aspect of Catholic revival probably occurred earlier and with more marked intensity in the Old English areas of the island than in much of Gaelic Ireland, where the greater poverty of lay *élites* impeded both the process of training and support of continentally educated priests. But Tridentine practice was only one aspect of Catholic identity.

54 SP 63/257/45, ff. 130–5, The National Archives (microfilm p. 2699 in National Library of Ireland).
55 Spaans, 'Recruiting Girls and Boys for the Holland Mission', 191.
56 Ó hAnnracháin, *Catholic Europe*, 71.

Sectarian resentment of a settler community which by 1641 was present in every county of the island, and which had achieved much of its economic success at the expense of the native Irish population, was another important strand and was probably stronger in the Gaelic parts of the island. Anti-settler antagonisms were evidently fuelled by the culture of preaching and mission, not only by Franciscans but also by Jesuits, Capuchins and Dominicans, which created a bonded emotional community of Catholics but which rejected heretics as vectors of pollution.[57] Gaelic Catholicism also drew heavily on traditions of charity and service, of respect for thaumaturgical and sacramental power, on notions of fidelity to Rome as evidenced in the use of the new calendar, and of a consciousness of a heroic past both in terms of the rich traditions of Gaelic sainthood and of war in the Catholic interest against the heretical *régime* of Elizabeth I. Attachment to an ascetic spiritual life posited in opposition to the appetites of the body was a significant theme in the literature of the period. Building from this, in the Catholic invective of the period, Protestantism became linked to notions of corporeal debauchery. Figures such as Eoghan Ó Dubhthaigh and Aodh Mac Cathmhaoil (Mac Aingil) emphasised greed, lust and proclivity to the sins of the body as integral aspects of the lives of Protestant reformers.[58] Such tropes also surfaced in Old English texts such as Robert Rochford's Life of Patrick, Bridget and Colum Cille:

> These delicate reformers, will never challenge a religious, consumed with fasts and weakened by hayre-cloath… as a disciple of their sensual Palencsse, coming of long standing in cold water, a thing never practised by our tender solifidians. Short and broken sleepes taken all alone on a hard flint seeme strange and absurd in the Theology of our libidinous Ministers, who lie immersed in beds of downe, not alone, but embracing their sweet harts with greater devotion, than any Geneva bible.[59]

Of huge importance to the embedding of Catholicism within the population were the multiple bridges that it made to traditional practice in terms of reverence for the Franciscan order, for the sacred landscape of holy wells and sites of pilgrimage, and for the Virgin Mary and traditional saints. As glimpsed in

---

57 I am grateful to my colleague Professor John McCafferty for alerting me to this aspect of early modern preaching in Ireland.

58 M. Mac Craith, 'Collegium S. Antonii Lovanii, quod Collegium est Unicum Remedium ad Conservandam Provinciam', in Bhreathnach, MacMahon and McCafferty (eds.) *The Irish Franciscans*, 233–59, at 248–9.

59 Robert Rochford, *The Life of the Glorious Bishop Saint Patricke Apostle and Primate of Ireland Togeather with the Lives of the Holy Virgin S. Bridgit and of the Glorious Abbot Saint Columbe Patrons of Ireland* (St Omer, 1625), ix.

the literature of the period, the religious *mentalité* of seventeenth-century Gaelic Ireland was evidently deeply informed by notions of providential action that rewarded the just and punished the wicked, and where the super-natural infused the natural world through miracles, wonders and the actions of saints.[60] Nevertheless, if these elements of religion continued to resonate within Gaelic and indeed Old English Catholicism, by the 1640s there is evi-dence of significant educational moulding of the general population towards a Tridentine pattern even in the most remote and isolated Gaelic areas in the island. In 1646, the auditor of the mission of the papal nuncio Rinuccini, Dionysio Massari, was deeply impressed by the attainments of the popula-tion, which he encountered in the area around Kenmare. Even small children were able to recite the Creed, the Our Father and the Hail Mary in Latin and many also evidently knew the Ten Commandments by heart.[61] As Salvador Ryan has noted, this was quantifiable success from a Tridentine educational perspective, which placed a primary emphasis on basic instruction and which would fulfil the requirements to allow the laity to access the salvific economy of the sacraments.[62] Such evidence of religious instruction, however, is less surprising when account is taken of the fact that during the 1630s the diocese of Ardfert appears to have had thirty-one regular clergy who were licensed to preach and another twenty secular priests, including the vicar apostolic, who had studied theology or canon law, presumably on the continent, although six apparently had not taken a degree.[63] This was a telling indication of the capacity of the continental colleges to create a priesthood which could com-pete successfully on the ground with the official seminary of the established church. It seems evident also that the impact of seminary-trained clergy was heightened by the practice of creating vicars forane who supervised the ongoing education of priests of individual deaneries within a diocese.

Continental Colleges

Even from the beginning of Elizabeth's reign a trickle of Irish youths were moving to frequent continental universities, but by the 1580s the num-bers had become significant and gradually generated a movement towards

---

60 B Cunningham, *The Annals of the Four Masters: Irish History, Kingship and Society in the Early Seventeenth Century* (Dublin: FCP, 2010), 228.
61 'Miscell. Varie', 9, 56, Archivio Storico De Propaganda Fide.
62 S. Ryan, 'Continental Catechisms and their Irish Imitators in Spanish Habsburg Lands *c.1550–c.1650*', in R. Gillespie and R. O hUiginn (eds.), *Irish Europe 1600–1650: Writing and Learning* (Dublin: FCP, 2013), 163–82, at 182.
63 'S.O.C.G.', 140, ff. 69r–77r, Archivio Storico De Propaganda Fide.

the creation of specific Irish colleges.[64] Expatriate seminaries such as the *Collegium Germanicum Hungaricum* and the *Collegium Illyricum* in Loreto in Italy and the English College at Douai were a key weapon in the arsenal of the church of Rome in the attempt to create an educated priesthood for European territories such as England, much of the Empire and the Turkish Balkans, which were no longer capable of supporting institutions for that purpose. In the seventeenth century, two hugely important colleges at Cologne and Leuven were founded to underpin the *Missio Hollandica*, which ministered to the second-largest Catholic population outside the jurisdiction of a Catholic state in Western Europe. In the first half of the seventeenth century, too, graduates of the Roman College dominated the leadership of the Polish hierarchy. Of particular relevance to the Irish experience were the Dutch, English and Scottish colleges, which were vital in providing the training of priests that could not be obtained in their native territories. While comparative work on these various national networks is still in its infancy, it would appear that the Irish colleges were ultimately the most successful example of this phenomenon. The return rate from the various English colleges seems on the whole to have been somewhat low, for instance, and of those who did actually make their way to the English mission there seems to have been a net drain of human resources from the areas with significant numbers of Catholics, which actually provided candidates for priestly training, towards the less promising south and east of the country. The formation of priests for the *Missio Hollandica* for its part seems to have been quite tightly supervised by the vicars apostolic, which resulted in a high quality of clergy but relatively small numbers in operation, and a very different model from the English case obtained with communities only being granted the services of priests if they already had the numbers, wealth and influence to maintain and protect them. The *Collegium Illyricum* proved completely inadequate to the task of providing priests for the Catholic communities of the Balkans who suffered a marked decline in the course of the seventeenth century in areas of previous strength, such as Albania.[65] By contrast, the development of the network of Irish colleges, which saw the establishment of roughly twenty foundations in the course of a century, proved a vital instrument in strengthening the position of Irish Catholicism. The individual colleges invariably suffered from financial difficulties and inevitably, despite the

---

64 J. J. Silke, 'The Irish abroad, 1534–1691', in T. W. Moody, F. X. Martin and F. J. Byrne (eds.), *A New History of Ireland* iii: *Early Modern Ireland, 1534–1691* (Oxford University Press, 1976), 617–8.

65 Ó hAnnracháin, *Catholic Europe*, especially chapter 2 and chapter 5.

efforts made to ensure that students committed themselves to returning to minister in Ireland, many of those trained on the continent found the opportunity to remain there. Even Salamanca, the outstanding Irish foundation in Iberia, over the course of one hundred years produced only a rough average of five priests *per annum* for service in the island.[66] But the cumulative effect of the colleges was dramatic.

The Irish colleges were undoubtedly favoured by the political and ecclesiastical context in which they operated. In contrast to England, of course, the vulnerability of their graduates to actual danger was quite low. The size of the Catholic population in Ireland not merely conferred a degree of safety but also meant that the resources existed both to send students to the continent and to support them economically on their return, if not always in the style to which they would have liked to be accustomed. This was in pointed contrast, for instance, with the Balkans, where few native Catholic communities could offer graduate clergy a living in any way commensurate with their level of education. Access to the island was relatively easy from the continent, although the voyage was never entirely without worries.

The Resident Hierarchy

The various colleges also maintained a complex relationship with that other exceptional institutional development of Irish Catholicism, the resident hierarchy. From 1618 Ireland was effectively unique in that area of the world defined in Rome as lying *in partibus infidelium*, namely outside the jurisdiction of a Catholic power, in developing a corpus of bishops, holding title to the historic sees of the island, who actually resided in their dioceses. Contemporaneously, the Habsburg kings of Hungary did appoint bishops to dioceses that had once pertained to the throne of St Stephen but actually lay under Turkish or Transylvanian control, yet these bishops were invariably non-resident. In the Netherlands, vicars apostolic regulated the entire *Missio Hollandica* and even when they received episcopal ordination it was not to one of the traditional Dutch sees. In England also the brief unhappy experience of attempting to institute episcopal authority was confined to the appointment to the titular diocese of Chalcedon.

The fact that Irish Catholic bishops were more likely to become the object of coercive power of the state rather than being able to rely on its support for their regulatory and administrative functions rendered them

66 Silke, 'Irish Abroad', 619.

highly anomalous in contemporary Europe. By continental standards, the bishops were also unique in having access to absolutely no revenues pertaining to their office. Instead, their activities were funded by the generosity of their secular kin and of other lay benefactors, and by taking a share of the voluntary contributions which were made to the priests in their dioceses. Not surprisingly, the bishops, who were invariably the product of continental education, bitterly resented all aspects of this situation. By the 1630s, too, several prelates found their attempts to inculcate reform along Tridentine principles compromised by the willingness of their subordinates to denounce them for the crime of having exercised papal jurisdiction. Yet, in the long run, the inability to rely on anything other than moral sanctions, of which excommunication was the most potent, and the dependence on voluntary support from the lay community, carried advantages in terms of promoting attachment between the ecclesiastical leadership and the mass of the secular population.

The Franciscan order's organisational flexibility, which allowed it to create a religious network independent of the state church, also threatened to allow it to operate in an autonomous fashion from the shadow episcopally governed Catholic Church that began to emerge in Ireland towards the end of the reign of James VI and I. This carried with it a notable potential for tension between Franciscan friars (and members of other orders) and diocesan priests particularly because the secular clergy, deprived by law of any ecclesiastical benefices, were forced to compete with the regulars for voluntary lay support. Certainly tensions between bishops and friars were by no means unknown and occasionally very bitter, especially in the south and east of the island.[67] For a number of reasons, however, the activity of Irish Franciscans proved significantly more compatible with a remodelled diocesan organisation than was the case, for instance, with regard to the Jesuit province of contemporary England. Of importance, in this context, was the willingness of Irish Franciscans (and regulars from other orders) to accept appointment to episcopal positions. Indeed briefly, in 1626, Franciscan incumbents occupied three of the four metropolitan sees within the Irish church. Moreover, Franciscans on the continent often served as witnesses to the Roman curial office, the Datary, concerning candidates for promotion to bishoprics in Ireland. The evidence of Franciscan friars, for instance, was of crucial importance to the decision taken to appoint the secular clerics John O'Cullenan, Hugh O'Reilly

---

67 T. O'Connor, *Irish Jansenists 1600–70: Religion and Politics in Flanders, France, Ireland and Rome* (Dublin: FCP, 2008), 129–48.

and Edmund Dungan to the sees of Raphoe, Kilmore and Down and Connor respectively.[68] Thus when the tensions between regular and secular clergy that had become such a feature of the contemporary English Catholic mission percolated over into Ireland, particularly through the activity of the English priest, Paul Harris, during the 1630s, the epicentre of the conflict actually pitted Harris against the authority of Thomas Fleming, the Franciscan archbishop of Dublin.

Inter-regular disputes were also not uncommon. While the Franciscans evidently outnumbered all other religious orders put together in the first decades of the seventeenth century and were embarking on a period of spectacular growth, the Dominicans, Jesuits and Capuchins also began to exercise increasing influence and expanded their numbers significantly. Rivalry for alms and support between the various orders could occasion very bitter conflicts, most notably in Drogheda where the Franciscans and Dominicans became embroiled in a vicious feud with both the local ordinary and the Jesuits.[69] Much of the impetus for this strife came from the attempt of the Jesuits to recruit for their sodality, which was seen as a threat to the confraternities of the Cord and the Rosary, organised by the Franciscans and Dominicans respectively.[70] The relatively weak regulatory structure of Irish Catholicism made it more difficult to pacify such conflicts. Yet while contemporary clerical observers bemoaned the scandal that was created by such unedifying squabbles over scarce resources, the freedom to engage in such rivalry was in itself proof of the overwhelming vitality of Catholicism within the island. And despite the lack of coercive support from the state, it seems evident that Irish bishops did wield significant authority both over the clergy of their dioceses and among the laity. This became particularly evident in the wake of the rebellion of 1641 when the Irish bishops played a key role in shaping the response of the Catholic population to the crisis. But even during the 1620s and 1630s, despite occasional difficulties, it seems apparent that a unified pattern of Catholic renewal had been established throughout the country.[71]

68 C. Giblin, 'The 'Processus Datariae' and the Appointment of Irish Bishops in the Seventeenth Century', in Franciscan Fathers (eds.), *Father Luke Wadding Commemorative Volume* (Dublin: Clonmore and Reynolds, 1957), 508–616, at 533–8.
69 B. Jackson, 'Sectarianism, Division and Dissent in Irish Catholicism', in A. Ford and J. McCafferty (eds.), *The Origins of Sectarianism in Early Modern Ireland* (Cambridge University Press, 2005), 203–15.
70 B. Mac Cuarta, *Catholic Revival in the North of Ireland* (Dublin: FCP, 1997), 216–26.
71 T. Ó hAnnracháin, *Catholic Reformation in Ireland: The Mission of Rinuccini, 1645–9* (Oxford University Press, 2002), 39–81.

In conclusion, a number of characteristics had begun to distinguish Irish Catholicism by the watershed date of 1641. The mass of both the Old English and the Gaelic populations of the island had increasingly come to identify themselves as adherents of the church of Rome. While the initial impetus towards these confessional positions was undoubtedly influenced by the alienation of these communities from the state and, in the process, from the state church, the internal dynamism of the process was also significant. A persistent resentment of the politically dominant New English *élite* and of the wider settler community which spread throughout the island in the period 1580–1641 ensured that a sharp sense of grievance continued to colour the evolution of Irish Catholicism, but the creation of multiple institutions on the continent for the training of clergy and their return in large numbers to minister in the localities resulted in a significant embedding of the practices and beliefs of Catholic renewal according to the contemporary European understanding of Tridentine reform. The success of this process was undoubtedly facilitated by the insistence of Catholic reformers that they were the maintainers rather than the changers of tradition. This was particularly important in Gaelic Ireland, where the emphasis on its glorious saintly past not only helped cement notions of Catholic identity but helped also to forge common ground with the Old English population of the island whose doubts concerning the Christian civility of the Gaelic world had a long pedigree. Whereas in the pre-Reformation period, notions of religious difference had often served to confirm the cleavage between Gaelic and English in the island, the period under review thus saw significant advances towards the elaboration of the idea of a common Catholic identity, which ultimately found expression in the proto-state of the Confederate Catholics during the 1640s.

8

Protestant Reformations, 1550–1641

COLM LENNON

The sheriff told the bishop's sons that they might use what prayers or what form of burial they pleased; none would interrupt them.[1]

In the midst of rebellion in 1642, this act of generosity towards the family of the recently deceased Church of Ireland bishop of Kilmore, William Bedell, bespoke the respect and honour in which the Catholics of the region held him. An Englishman and Cambridge graduate, Bedell had in many ways gone against the grain of the Protestantism established during the Reformation in Ireland. This 'slightly left-field'[2] figure among the ecclesiastical leaders of the Church of Ireland had learned Irish in order to evangelise native Catholics, believed in an inclusive church, of which all the inhabitants of the island could be members, and rejected the notion that salvation was impossible within the Roman Church. He was uncomfortable with the pragmatic state *régime* of the 1630s that prioritised the management of the church's temporal resources at the expense of its spiritual mission of conversion. Moreover, the gesture of magnanimity on the part of the Irish Catholic rebels (which was in defiance of their own bishop who had banned Bedell's interment in Kilmore churchyard) denoted their religious and military self-confidence. Such a *modus vivendi* may have been quite exceptional, especially in the fraught circumstances of the early 1640s, but it did at the very least attest the fact that Protestants and Catholics co-existed in Ireland one hundred years after the shattering of the integrated Christian faith of the late Middle Ages.[3]

---

1 E. S. Shuckburgh (ed.), *Two Biographies of William Bedell, Bishop of Kilmore* (Cambridge University Press, 1902), 204–5.
2 A. Ford, *James Ussher: Theology, History and Politics in Early Modern Ireland and England* (Oxford University Press, 2007), 162.
3 For a synopsis of Bedell's career, see A. Clarke, 'Bishop William Bedell (1571–1642) and the Irish Reformation', in C. Brady (ed.), *Worsted in the Game: Losers in Irish History* (Dublin: The Lilliput Press, 1989), 61–70.

The ambiguous position of Bishop Bedell within the Church of Ireland reflected issues – pastoral, theological, ecclesiological, political and cultural – that were still unresolved within Protestantism a century after the beginning of the Reformation in Ireland. Many of these have been subjected to critical scholarly attention during the past fifty years of Irish religious history, as indeed has the formation of Protestant and Catholic identities in a confessionally divided country.[4] 'Standing one's ground' in credal territory nowadays not only requires that scholars of either Protestantism or Catholicism examine doctrinal and organisational aspects of the respective ecclesiastical milieux and the history of laities and clergies within their politico-religious contexts, but also note areas of denominational weakness as well as strength. The circularity of thought in the discourse of Reformation failure and Counter-Reformation triumph, which tended to predominate in the field, has been modified to a large extent through a consideration of inter-faith reciprocity as much as contrariety.[5] While the emergence of a movement of Catholic reform in early modern Ireland is the subject of specialised treatment elsewhere in this volume, facets of the Roman revival and response to the Reformation impinge very directly upon this study of the progress of early Protestantism, not least dialectically through Protestant self-definition in the face of an incipient religious majority.

That a community of lay and clerical Protestants even subsisted, let alone flourished, by 1641 is testament to the embedding of the Reformation in Ireland, in spite of structural difficulties and intra- and inter-confessional differences. In order to assess here the character of the early Irish Protestant Reformation, discussion of religious policy and practice revolves around four salient headings in recent historiographical debate. First, the political and constitutional framework for magisterial Protestant reform in Ireland relates to the synchronicity of state and church activity from the 1540s down to the 1630s, raising questions of governmental motive and administrative

---

4 For the formation of Irish Protestant identity, see A. Ford, 'James Ussher and the Creation of an Irish Protestant Identity', in B. Bradshaw and P. Roberts (eds.), *British Consciousness and Identity* (Cambridge University Press, 1998), 185–212; for the Catholic perspective, see C. Lennon, 'Taking Sides: The Emergence of Irish Catholic Ideology', in V. Carey and U. Lotz-Heumann (eds.), *Taking Sides? Colonial and Confessional Mentalities in Early Modern Ireland* (Dublin: Four Courts Press [hereafter FCP], 2003), 78–93.

5 Historiographical trends are discussed in A. Ford, *The Protestant Reformation in Ireland, 1590–1641* (Dublin: FCP, 1997), 7–20; J. Murray, *Enforcing the English Reformation in Ireland: Clerical Resistance and Political Conflict in the Diocese of Dublin, 1534–1590* (Cambridge University Press, 2009), 1–19. For a sample of the new approach, see A. Ford and J. McCafferty (eds.), *The Origins of Sectarianism in Early Modern Ireland* (Cambridge University Press, 2005).

capacity for reform. Second, the issue of the enforcement of conformity to the Reformation merits scrutiny in the light of contemporary arguments as to the methods (and their sequencing) for converting men and women to Protestantism. Third, the formulation of credal principles, which codified the beliefs of members of the Church of Ireland, is integral to assessing the evolution of a distinctive Irish Protestant identity. And fourth, the question of the Irish Reformation as a vehicle for Anglicisation has recently been revisited through discussion of those Irish and English Protestants who, like Bedell, favoured evangelisation through the Irish language. A brief *mise-en-scène* for concluding perspectives on the experience of being Protestant in Ireland down to 1641 (insofar as current research allows) attempts to elucidate how these factors of state church, conversion, identity and culture may have effected a separation into two worshipping communities of the population of later sixteenth- and early seventeenth-century Ireland.

State and Church

Protestantism was first introduced into Ireland in 1547 not through any ferment of religious ideas at home or direct spiritual influences from abroad, but rather by decree of King Edward VI, whose spiritual preferences (in consultation with the English clergy) were reflected in the reformation of the church. The religious reforms were framed constitutionally and politically by acts of the Irish parliament: those for royal supremacy and management of a Church of Ireland in 1536–7, and that for kingly title in 1541, which raised Ireland to the status of kingdom under the English monarchy. Even before Protestantism, a template for the establishment of a national church was adumbrated by the lord deputy, Sir Anthony St Leger, who worked to affiliate lay and clerical leaders of Gaelic and English origin to Henry VIII's headship of church and state in Ireland. The complexity of such ambitions for an all-island faith was illustrated initially during the Edwardian period under Chief Governors Bellingham and Croft, as well as St Leger, who integrated religious reform into their secular administrations with minimal episcopal support. A Church of Ireland mission was hamstrung at the outset because, while Protestant norms were transmitted by order from England, notably through the *Book of Common Prayer* of 1551 for Ireland (the first text printed in the country), there was no local theological forum for the discussion of curtailing traditional beliefs and devotions, nor was the weakness of the inherited ecclesiastical patrimony addressed. Tension over the ethnicity of any national church was foreshadowed in the clash between Croft's insistence on enlisting

English-born bishops (such as John Bale in Ossory, an arch-critic of Gaelic Ireland) to enforce the religious changes, and St Leger's attempt to adapt the Reformation to the indigenous Gaelic population, through evangelising in the Irish language. And despite the governors' serious engagement with religious policy, their own jurisdictional outreach had yet to expand beyond the towns and territories of the Englishry.[6]

The attempted Protestantisation of Ireland through English political agency down to 1553, and again from 1558 onwards, may have obscured the depth of religious motivation on the part of viceroys from St Leger in the 1540s to Sir John Perrot in the 1580s. The exasperated words of the former during an argument with Archbishop Browne in 1551, 'Go to, go to, your religion will mar all', may undervalue his commitment to reform through persuasion, while the latter had to defend himself from Queen Elizabeth's charge of his being too 'religiously forward' rather than politically discreet in 1585.[7] Of the Elizabethan viceroys, as Brady and Murray have demonstrated, it was Sir Henry Sidney who had both the vision and longevity seriously to attempt to integrate a Protestant national church within his state-building programme for Ireland. Based on a moderately reformed credo of Twelve Articles, formulated and printed for Ireland in 1567 (and not the Thirty-Nine Articles as applied in England), membership of the Church of Ireland, obligatory for all through the Act of Uniformity of 1560, was to be enforced through statute law and secular and ecclesiastical judicial bodies, and all inhabitants of the island were to share the experience of the ecclesiastical liturgy through their own vernacular. A resident preaching ministry was to be trained at a proposed national university as seminary, drawing students from a network of new diocesan grammar schools. And to attract resident clerical graduates, laws were planned for refurbishing church buildings and enhancing benefices through tackling the grave problem of alienation of church lands and revenues by clerical lessors, royal farmers and lay impropriators. Mark Hutchinson has argued that the programme for a Reformation church in Ireland with a functioning preaching ministry, as aspired to by reformed Protestants such as

---

6 D. MacCulloch, *Tudor Church Militant: Edward VI and the Protestant Reformation* (London: The Penguin Press, 1999); Murray, *Enforcing the English Reformation*, 159–203; H. A. Jefferies, *The Irish Church and the Tudor Reformations* (Dublin: FCP, 2010), 88–103; A. Hadfield, 'Translating the Reformation: John Bale's Irish *Vocacyon*', in B. Bradshaw, idem, and W. Maley (eds.), *Representing Ireland: Literature and the Origins of Conflict, 1534–1660* (Cambridge University Press, 1993), 43–59.

7 SP61/4/36(ii), The National Archives; W. M. Brady (ed.), *State papers concerning the Irish church in the time of Queen Elizabeth* (London: Longmans, Green, Reader and Dyer, 1868), 101–2.

Sidney, Christopher Goodman, his chaplain, and Robert Weston, his *protégé*, aimed at creating an integrated godly polity in which 'true obedience' to God would bring about civil obedience to the state magistracy.[8]

This ambitious project, as refined in successive iterations in the 1560s and 1570s, evoked strong opposition from vested interests inside and outside parliament, including senior clergy such as Archbishop Loftus of Dublin, and prominent laypeople among the older English community, fearful of losing their ecclesiastical perquisites and their mediating role as reformers between government and Gaelic Irish.[9] In the discourse of godly reformers, the neglect of provision for Calvinist Protestant preaching denied most of the population of Ireland access to divine grace, through which consciences would have been formed and long-term civil order fostered. Instead they were left susceptible to dissent and rebellion, which were transformed into Catholic recusancy by the 1580s. The subsequent coercive and 'absolutist' *régime* in state and church under Governors Grey and Perrot and Archbishop Loftus and Bishop Thomas Jones, which involved the forcing of consciences, alienated the older English Catholic population from the Church of Ireland.[10] The 'second Reformation', identified by Alan Ford as beginning in the 1590s, which concentrated essentially on the formation of a new preaching ministry from England, was a tacit recognition that the established Protestant church now represented a minority within Ireland, though the claim to inclusiveness of church membership was not formally abandoned. Furthermore, at a time when the entire island came under the effective jurisdiction of the British monarchy for the first time after 1603, despite aspirations to a unitary Erastian polity, the widely held principle in the later Reformation of *cuius regio, eius religio* – whose realm, his or her religion – was inapplicable in Ireland, because the majority of traditional loyalists of the Pale and Old Englishry rejected Protestantism.[11]

8 C. Brady and J. Murray, 'Sir Henry Sidney and the Reformation in Ireland', in E. Boran and C. Gribben (eds.), *Enforcing Reformation in Ireland and Scotland* (Aldershot: Ashgate Publishing Limited, 2006), 13–39; M. Hutchinson, *Calvinism, Reform and the Absolutist State in Elizabethan Ireland* (London: Pickering and Chatto, 2015), 15–37; M. Hutchinson, 'An Irish Perspective on Elizabeth's Religion: Reformation Thought and Sir Henry Sidney's Irish Lord Deputyship, *c.*1560–1580', in B. Kane and V. McGowan-Doyle (eds.), *Elizabeth I and Ireland* (Cambridge University Press, 2014), 142–62.

9 Murray, *Enforcing the English Reformation*, 294–303, 317–21; Brady and Murray, 'Sir Henry Sidney and the Reformation in Ireland', 29–38.

10 Hutchinson, *Calvinism, Reform and the Absolutist State*, 39–62, 92–8; Ford, *Protestant Reformation*, 30; A. Clarke, 'Varieties of Uniformity: The First Century of the Church of Ireland', in W. J. Sheils and D. Wood (eds.), *The Churches, Ireland and the Irish: Studies in Church History, Volume 25* (Oxford: Basil Blackwell, 1989), 118–19.

11 F. Heal, *Reformation in Britain and Ireland* (Oxford: Clarendon Press, 2003), 3–4, 423–4.

Notwithstanding its growing self-confidence in the early Stuart period, the Church of Ireland relied on the secular arm with its now countrywide machinery to implement the many proposals for reform that emanated from royal visitations and commissions under James I and VI and Charles I. But while Irish officials such as Lord Deputy Arthur Chichester and Solicitor General John Davies demonstrated enthusiasm for enforcing conformity, the London government constantly urged caution against attempts to impose national religious uniformity in the context of the European politico-religious imbroglio. Not until 1633 did the perfect conjunction of state and ecclesiastical interests, in the form of Archbishop William Laud of Canterbury, who had direct access to King Charles I, and the domineering lord deputy, Thomas Wentworth, later earl of Strafford, come into being in order to attain a well-resourced and obedient church in a secure and prosperous realm of Ireland. Working in unison for first time since the start of the Reformation, secular and religious authorities in England and Ireland aimed at reconstructing the temporalities of the Church of Ireland in order to attract a resident ministry, which would in turn become the servant of the crown 'in a near hypostatic union'. Significantly, in the context of the assertion of strong royal claims over state and church in all three kingdoms of Charles I, there was to be congruence between the Church of Ireland and its English counterpart, in the application to the smaller island of the Thirty-Nine Articles and the English canons, now adapted for Ireland. Moreover, proposed bills for a reorganisation of parishes, churches and schools to take account of new patterns of settlement and plantation, which would have revived the claim for an island-wide establishment of the Church of Ireland of 1560, fell with the termination of Wentworth's *régime*, though he had postponed the imposition of national uniformity, allowing *de facto* toleration for Catholicism pending the reconstruction of the Church.[12]

Enforcing Conformity

To become firmly established in Ireland, the Protestant Reformation needed parish congregations of conforming laypeople, willing to listen to the preaching of a dedicated clergy. Differences arose among and between state and church authorities as to whether Protestant affiliation should be brought about by outward conformity enforced by penal means, or real conversion

---

12 J. McCafferty, *The Reconstruction of the Church of Ireland: Bishop Bramhall and the Laudian Reforms, 1633–41* (Cambridge University Press, 2007), 32–6, 198–9.

brought about by persuasion, but there was general agreement that without church attendance, even the most inspirational sermons were in vain.[13] After the official restoration of Catholicism in the reign of Queen Mary (1553–1558), careful management of the Irish parliament ensured the passage of the acts governing church authority and liturgical practice in Ireland, those of Supremacy and Uniformity of 1560. The former required all ecclesiastical and public officials to take an oath acknowledging the queen's supreme governorship of the Church of Ireland, while the latter required attendance at divine service and worship according to the *Book of Common Prayer*, on pain of a fine of a shilling for each refusal. No other legislation pertaining to matters of conscience was passed by parliament in the Tudor or early Stuart periods, despite attempts by governors such as Perrot and Chichester to pass new penal laws for religious dissent. There was scope for obfuscation of the changes under Uniformity from the outset with the permitting of a Latin version of the *Book of Common Prayer* in areas where the minister did not speak English, and the allowing of traditional clerical dress and church ornaments in Ireland. After initial campaigns to tender the oath of supremacy to senior clergy and secular officials (which resulted in few deprivations), a circumspect policy of subscription was pursued, particularly in respect of the magistracy of the Pale and towns. Evidence of widespread non-attendance at Church of Ireland services emerged from ecclesiastical visitations of the eastern counties in the earlier 1560s, where members of the influential gentry were notable absentees, while in areas where attendance was enforced, many congregations were found to be inattentive, coming to church 'as to a May game'.[14]

Down to the late 1570s, enforcement of the ecclesiastical laws in the regions of the country under government jurisdiction was sporadic and moderate, the new Ecclesiastical High Commission, for example, first instituted in 1564, being used to issue fines for breaches of the Uniformity law. Lenity of enforcement was replaced, however, with a more rigorous policy of coercion under Loftus and Jones in the 1580s as a response to widespread Catholic dissent, and reports from urban hubs of earlier Protestant evangelism, including Waterford, Cork, Limerick and Galway, indicate that much of the

---

13 For an earlier debate about enforcement and conversion, see B. Bradshaw, 'Sword, Word and Strategy in the Reformation in Ireland', in *Historical Journal*, 21 (1978), 475–502; N. Canny, 'Why the Reformation Failed in Ireland: Une Question Mal Posée', in *Journal of Ecclesiastical History*, 30 (1979), 423–50; K. Bottigheimer, 'The Failure of the Reformation in Ireland: Une Question Bien Posée', *Journal of Ecclesiastical History*, 36 (1985), 196–207.
14 Jefferies, *Irish Church and the Tudor Reformations*, 125–54, 186.

conformity achieved previously was disappearing.[15] While the alienation of most of the Old English from state religious policy and their commitment to recusancy were confirmed by the 1590s, a very small *côterie* of native families completed the transition from conformity to dedicated adherence to Protestantism, indicating perhaps that, given time, enforcement of the Reformation might have been more successful. A forceful approach to recusancy elicited divisions between Irish reformers, such as Sir Nicholas White, the master of the rolls, who urged 'tolerance in matter of oath and religion' and Bishop Jones, who attacked the notion of tolerance, and also between the Dublin administration and the Elizabethan court, where the queen herself was disturbed by stern measures. These included the forced swearing of magistrates and justices to the Act of Supremacy and the draconian use of the Ecclesiastical Commission. During the Nine Years' War, due to the very fraught political situation, the government decided to suspend penal measures against Catholics, much to the displeasure of Loftus, Jones and some native Protestants, including the young James Ussher, who, in a sermon of 1602, railed against the 'toleration of idolatry'.[16]

After 1603, strenuous efforts were made by leading agents of church and state in Ireland to enforce conformity, principally on the Old English gentry and patriciates as social cynosures of town and countryside. Besides imposing the Oath of Supremacy on office-holders and professionals, and mulcting recusancy fines of one shilling (a paltry sum to most of the *élite*), the campaign involved issuing mandates in the towns, which were seen as 'lanterns' to the country round about, summoning leading citizens to church and thus opening them to the possibility of conversion to Protestantism through grace-bearing sermons. Very substantial fines and imprisonment at pleasure were imposed for default, through proceedings in the prerogative Court of Castle Chamber.[17] Proclamations banning Catholic priests, forbidding continental migration for education and restricting severely the unofficial worshipping rights of the Catholic community were also issued. Varying in intensity and consistency during the period, persecution served to deepen recalcitrance on the part of the Catholic community, the most notorious rallying call being the public execution of the Roman Catholic bishop of Down and Connor,

---

15 Jefferies, *Irish Church and the Tudor Reformations*, 155–207; see also Hutchinson, *Calvinism, Reform and the Absolutist State*, 54–6.

16 Ford, *James Ussher*, 30–1; Brady (ed.), *State Papers Concerning the Irish Church in the Time of Queen Elizabeth*, 112–15.

17 C. Lennon, *The Lords of Dublin the Age of Reformation* (Dublin: Irish University Press, 1989), 174–83.

Conor O'Devany, in Dublin in 1612. Conversely, the policy of belated enforcement of the Reformation was a manifestation of a burgeoning Protestant
identity on the part of the principal protagonists of reform. Fuelled by the
theological and ideological certainty that came from university training,
and steeled by entry into controversies with Catholic polemicists in print,
Protestant divines argued for the non-supportability of error and the corruption of the Roman Church as Antichristian in their rejection of toleration. In
this they were strongly backed by secular officials such as Chichester, Davies
and George Brouncker, president of Munster, who supplemented their religious zeal with pragmatic views on the dangers of international Catholic
conspiracy. Proposals for formal toleration, in the form of the 'matters of
grace and bounty', or 'the graces' of 1626, were vehemently opposed in circumstances where the Protestant community represented a minority of the
entire population, facing a Catholic majority organising itself into an alternative church.[18]

In fact, during Wentworth's governorship from 1633, there was *de facto* toleration of Catholicism as he embarked, with episcopal support, on a programme of disciplining of the Church of Ireland, to ensure internal unity and
congruity with the Church of England. Two areas that bore upon the lives of
Protestant clergy and laity were the recovery of much of the temporal estate
of the church to provide livings to attract qualified ministers, and the promulgation of canons for the governing of lay and clerical behaviour. The problems
of the alienation of vast swathes of church land at long leases, and the impropriation of up to half of Irish benefices by the crown and individuals, with
consequent losses to parishes of tithes, advowsons and clerical stipends, were
addressed through the passage in 1634–1635 of acts for preventing the leasing
away of church properties beyond twenty-one years, and for the resumption
of impropriated benefices. Bishop Bramhall subsequently used these acts and
the reconstituted Ecclesiastical High Commission to recover benefices lost to
the church through appropriation by lay and clerical lessors, including Richard
Boyle, first earl of Cork, and Lewis Jones, the bishop of Killaloe. Before the fall
of the *régime* in 1640, the state–church nexus had greatly enhanced the value
of hundreds of diocesan and parochial livings, at least on paper. The reform

---

18 A. Ford, ' "Force and fear of punishment" ', Protestants and religious coercion in Ireland,
    1603–33', in Boran and Gribben, (eds.), *Enforcing Reformation in Ireland and Scotland*, 91–
    130; E. Boran, 'Printing in Early Seventeenth-Century Dublin: Combatting Heresy in
    Serpentine Times', in Boran and Gribben (eds.), *Enforcing Reformation in Ireland and
    Scotland*, 40–65.

of church order and discipline involved the adoption of a first set of canons for the Church of Ireland and of a new charter for Trinity College. The Irish canons emerged after intensive debate by the Convocation of the clergy in 1634 as a reduced number by comparison with the English set, due to merging and omission, and there were a significant number that related specifically to the Irish social and religious milieu. A third issue broached by gubernatorial action was the incidence of Presbyterianism introduced by Scottish settlers in the north of Ireland. In 1639 the so-called 'black oath' was administered to the Presbyterians, whereby they abjured the resistance to the *Book of Common Prayer* in Scotland and swore to obey King Charles I.[19]

Faith and Identity

By the time Protestantism arrived in Ireland, the influence of the second generation of reformers was being strongly felt in Britain, and, mainly through transmission thence, the Irish Reformation in succeeding decades remained highly receptive to the ideas of Swiss reformers, and John Calvin in particular. During the Elizabethan period, distance from the metropolis ensured that the western island was a haven for those who were less than at ease in the established Church of England, including radical preachers such as Christopher Goodman, who championed conscientious resistance to tyrannical rule, and Thomas Cartwright, an advocate of Presbyterianism. Doctrinal and liturgical fluidity in Ireland was facilitated by the adoption in 1567 of a printed set of Twelve Articles of Faith, instead of the Thirty-Nine Articles of the Church of England. While culled from an earlier English formulation and cautiously framed on basic Reformation principles, including royal supremacy, rejection of papal authority and the canonicity of the *Prayer Book*, the Articles did not preclude the possibility of further debate and controversy, especially in areas of church ritual and order, which were of particular concern to those of a Puritanical disposition.[20] Puritan influences weighed heavily in the public career of Archbishop Adam Loftus, as evidenced, for example, by his vociferous objection in 1565 to the removal from office in England of clergy who, when celebrating communion, refused to wear traditional surplices, or 'popish

---

19 McCafferty, *Reconstruction of the Church of Ireland*, chapters 2, 3 and 5; P. Adair, *A True Narrative of the Rise and Progress of the Presbyterian Church in Ireland* (Belfast: C. Aitchison, 1866), 59–62.
20 *A Brefe Declaration of Certain Principall Articles of Religion* (Dublin, 1566); the Articles were translated and printed in Irish in *Aibidil Gaoidheilge [agus] Caiticiosma* (Dublin, 1571), the first book to be printed in an Irish language type-face.

rags', as he termed them. A Puritan ethos was carried over into the foundation of the new university, Trinity College, in 1592, of which Loftus became
first provost, followed by four successive provosts who were sympathetic to
Puritan ideas.[21]

While native theological debate in Ireland may have been lacking in the
early Reformation years, Protestant religious thought there gradually developed in response to the practical experience of local evangelism on the part of
commentators and divines. A Christian humanist strain of reform, premised
on the human intellect's willingly accepting proffered divine grace, underpinned older English educational schemes in the early Elizabethan period,
and chimed with reformed Protestant proposals, though the latter rejected
the efficacy of human volition. Such a consensus broke down, however, in the
pessimism engendered by widespread rebellion, which raised doubts on the
part of reformed Protestants about the reformability of the Irish, as evident
in their rejection of the grace-filled opportunities offered by the preaching of
godly ministers (such as were present). In his continuation of the history of
Ireland in Holinshed's *Chronicles* in 1586, John Hooker, an English Protestant
servitor, placed recent events within an apocalyptic framework, drawing
upon the struggle of Christ and Antichrist in the New Testament to interpret the Desmond rebellions of the 1570s and 1580s. In this conceptualisation,
the forces of the Catholic Church were represented as Anti-Christian, and in
accordance with biblical prophecy would be triumphed over by the forces of
Christ, in the form of his Protestant followers. First introduced into the discourse of godly reform by John Bale in his *Vocacyon* in respect of good and
evil in Ireland, the apocalyptic strand was a powerful force in the theology of
Protestants in early modern Ireland as they sought to highlight their providential role. Meanwhile, formal controversialist debate began to focus minds
on theological issues as graduates of the new Trinity College entered the
lists with members of the Society of Jesus in face-to-face encounters and in
printed polemics.[22]

With the adoption of its confession of 104 Articles of Faith in 1615, the
Church of Ireland was asserting itself as an independent church with its own
distinctive theological position. The summoning of a national Convocation of
the clergy for the first time in conjunction with the parliament of 1613–1615, in

---

21 H. Robinson-Hammerstein, 'Archbishop Adam Loftus, the First Provost of Trinity
College, Dublin', in H. Robinson-Hammerstein (ed.), *European Universities in the Age of
Reformation and Counter-Reformation* (Dublin: FCP, 1998), 34–52.
22 Hutchinson, *Calvinism, Reform and the Absolutist State*, 34–7, 139–43; A. Ford, 'James
Ussher and the Creation of an Irish Protestant Identity', pp. 189–90.

itself a statement of clerical self-confidence, was the occasion for the drafting of the Articles. The Thirty-Nine Articles were no more than a starting-point, as the Irish set omitted, added and changed a great deal to take account of the theological sensitivities of early seventeenth-century Irish Protestantism. For example, English Articles 35 and 36, referring to homilies, and the consecration of bishops and priests respectively, were dropped, in the first case because of Puritan objections to reading sermons written by others, and in the second due to nonconformist doubts about the episcopacy among some Protestants in Ireland. A Puritan mentality was also attested in the articles in respect of church organisation, biblical authority and the sacredness of the Sabbath. Above all, the 104 Articles were notable for their anti-Roman thrust. Article 80 holds that the pope was 'that man of sin, foretold in the Holy Scriptures'. And there was a much greater emphasis, spread over seven articles, on the Calvinist tenet of predestination: God's eternal decree of salvation for certain numbers of the just (which was the limit of the English Articles' profession) was balanced by that of reprobation of fixed numbers of the damned, or double predestination. The Irish Articles were a reflection of how the Church had fared in the decades since its establishment and an answer to new challenges thrown up by a half-century of theological debate. The Church of Ireland emerged as a small community of the predestined, elect among the damned, beset by signs of Antichrist, and shaped by Calvinistic and Puritan influences.[23]

Allied to its new theological certitude, there developed within the Church of Ireland in the seventeenth century a consciousness of its roots in Irish antiquity. Although Englishmen such as Meredith Hanmer and John Rider made the earliest contributions to an Irish Protestant historiography, the most crucial role in establishing an origin myth for Irish Protestantism was that of the Dublin-born James Ussher, who helped in the drafting of the 104 Articles. A renowned theologian and scholar, Ussher, who became archbishop of Armagh in 1625, used his formidable intellectual powers to defend the position of his church against both external threat from Roman Catholicism and internal forces such as Arminianism, or a revisionist approach to Calvinist orthodoxy. It was in the context of a scholarly war for the origins of Irish Christianity, waged against Catholic historians, that Ussher wrote what became *A discourse of the religion anciently professed by the Irish and the Brittish* (1631), in which he showed how the early Irish church was pure in its

23 Ford, *James Ussher*, chapter 4; P. Kilroy, *Protestant Dissent and Controversy in Ireland* (Cork University Press, 1994), 2–4.

beliefs, sanctity and leaning until corrupted by Roman influences in the eleventh century. Thus he could claim that St Patrick was a forerunner of Irish Protestantism, despite the saint's having had contacts with Rome. Besides his assertion of the Irishness of Protestantism, Ussher was also anxious to demonstrate the independence of the Irish church from the British one. In his magnum opus as historian, *Britannicarum ecclesiarum antiquitates* (1639), he traced the origins of Christianity in Britain and Ireland, using a vast range of sources, including many Irish-language manuscripts. By drawing upon a network of fellow Irish scholars, Catholic as well as Protestant, Ussher gained access to Gaelic learning, which he enlisted in the study of early Irish history.[24]

English and Protestantism

While Ussher's study of Irish sources may have been influential in later Protestant scholarship, the mission of the Church of Ireland from its inception had been carried out principally through the medium of English language and culture. Although it predated Protestantism, the 1537 Act for English order, habit and language, which provided for a system of parochial primary schools, came to exert significant influence on evangelism during the Reformation. The act envisaged an anglophone clergy setting up schools in their parishes for teaching English, and for promoting 'the profession and knowledge of Christ's religion'. While primary schooling was slow to develop in many parts of Ireland, the symbiosis of Anglicising and evangelising was adhered to as a principle of state policy in religion. For example, in 1594, at the start of a new reform movement in the Church of Ireland, it was claimed that the failure to enforce the statute of 1537 had been the cause of 'great frowardness, perverseness, and dangerous diversity amongst our people in Ireland, and especially in the clergy'. In 1634, Bishop Bedell's argument for divine service to be conducted in Irish was rebuffed on the basis that it would contravene the terms of the 1537 Act for English order, habit and language. A second state educational initiative – an Act for free diocesan grammar schools in 1570 – aimed explicitly at inculcating English civility and 'due and humble obedience to [the] prince' through 'good discipline', but implicit was the purpose of preparing students for a university training for the ministry of the Church of Ireland. That the scheme got off to a very uncertain start was due to a complex division of responsibility for funding,

---

24 Ford, 'James Ussher and the Creation of an Irish Protestant Identity', 185–212; Ford, *James Ussher*, chapters 6 and 9.

buildings and appointments between secular and ecclesiastical authorities. Meanwhile, a number of municipal and private schools in Kilkenny, Limerick and Waterford, for example, were run by Catholic schoolmasters, many of whose students began to travel to the continent for further education.[25]

One of the purposes of the native university, founded as Trinity College in 1592 after a long-drawn out campaign, was to stem the flow of migration of Irish students abroad where they could be 'infected with popery'. Instead the new institution in Dublin was to be 'the seed and fry of the holy ministry throughout the realm'. Established as it was at the beginning of the 'second Reformation', however, when the trend towards the Anglicisation of the Church of Ireland was becoming more pronounced, the academy shaped its mission around a godly English ethos. Earlier university proposals, mostly centred on the site and buildings of St Patrick's cathedral, Dublin, and all envisaging a core curriculum of theology and divinity studies, had fallen foul of one vested interest or another. Proposed legislation for a national university in 1569–1570, for example, came to grief because of disagreement between its moderate church papist supporters on one side and godly reformers on the other. Pending the resolution of the issues of a site and identity for an Irish university, some native Irish scholars were attracted to Oxford or Cambridge on bursaries arranged under Protestant patronage, and these returned to take up positions in the Irish church. Meanwhile, plans for Catholic colleges for Irish students abroad, in default of institutions at home, were gathering pace and the first foundation was at Salamanca, also in 1592. Thus, in a confessionally divided educational milieu, Trinity was, on its foundation, strictly Protestant, being modelled on the predominantly Puritan Emmanuel College, Cambridge. Despite its professed aim of preventing Irish youths from migrating to the continent for education, it was not particularly hospitable to native students of moderate religious affiliation, nor did it prioritise the evangelising of the Gaelic Irish population.[26]

The printing press, introduced under Protestant aegis in Ireland for the *Book of Common Prayer* in 1551, evoked ambiguous responses from state and church officials when viewed as a medium of communication in the Irish language. Making available a Latin translation of the *Prayer Book* in areas

25 C. Lennon, 'Education and Religious Identity in Early Modern Ireland', in *Pedagogica Historica, supplementary series*, 5 (1999), 57–75.

26 J. Murray, 'St Patrick's Cathedral and the University Question in Ireland c.1547–1585', in Robinson-Hammerstein (ed.), *European Universities*, 1–33; H. Robinson-Hammerstein, 'Aspects of the Continental Education of Irish Students in the Reign of Elizabeth I', in *Historical Studies*, 8 (1971), 137–54; Ford, *Protestant Reformation*, 77–80, 88–97.

where English was not the vernacular of clergy or laity was a short-term expedient in evangelising the native Irish, due to the difficulties of printing an Irish version, and the paucity of readers of the language.[27] Queen Elizabeth sponsored a venture for the casting of a font of Irish letters in the 1560s, designed to facilitate a Gaelic Irish version of the New Testament, and modelled on John Carswell's classical Gaelic translation of the Calvinist *Book of Common Order*, printed in Edinburgh in 1567. While the major project did not materialise until after 1600, Seán Ó Cearnaigh's (John Kearney) translation, *Aibidil Gaoidheilge agus Caiticiosma* became the first Irish-language book, when printed in 1571 under the patronage of Alderman John Ussher, a Protestant native of Dublin. Ó Cearnaigh, who was a Cambridge-educated Protestant cleric from a Gaelic family, included linguistic guidance for the neophyte, as well as an Irish catechism based on a 1559 version of the *Prayer Book*, prayers translated from the *Scots Gaelic Prayer Book* and the translated Twelve Articles issued by Sir Henry Sidney. In his address to the reader, Ó Cearnaigh, while exhibiting sensitivity to the bardic tradition, reveals his innovatory purpose as allowing access through the printed Irish language to the means of divine redemption in tandem with secular reform under civil law and authority. The *Aibidil*, as well as a contemporaneous broadsheet of a devotional poem by the bard, Pilib Bocht Ó hUiginn, possibly a trial-piece, adumbrated a Protestant outreach to Gaelic people through print culture for the first time.[28]

When a Gaelic New Testament was eventually published in Dublin in 1602 under the patronage of Sir William Ussher, there was continuity from the work of Ó Cearnaigh and his collaborator, Nicholas Walsh, but the main editorial voice was that of Uilliam Ó Domhnuill (William Daniel), another Gaelic cleric and graduate of Cambridge, who was a fellow of Trinity College, Dublin. He collated the work of a small *côterie* of Gaelic scholars who had been associated with an Irish-language printing press in the university, and produced a text dedicated to King James VI and I. Ó Domhnuill also produced an Irish translation of the *Book of Common Prayer* at John Franckton's Dublin press in 1608. In the context of expressions of firm Protestantism and virulent anti-papalism, Ó Domhnuill aspired in his prefaces to his biblical and liturgical translations to bring to his Gaelic readers the grace of true religious reform, which would in turn be productive of political allegiance to the

---

27 *The Statutes at Large passed in the Parliaments held in Ireland* (2 vols, Dublin, 1786–1801), i, 275–90 (2 Eliz., c. 2).
28 M. Caball, 'Print, Protestantism and Cultural Authority in Elizabethan Ireland', in Kane and McGowan-Doyle (eds.), *Elizabeth I and Ireland*, 286–308.

monarchy. Notwithstanding the lively interest in Gaelic sources for antiquarian studies on the part of Protestant scholars such as Ussher and Sir James Ware, attempts to evangelise the Irish through the medium of print were not followed up assiduously in the succeeding half-century, there being no Irish version of the Old Testament in print, for example, until 1685 when William Bedell's translation was published.[29]

Separation of Confessions

To what extent is the discussion hitherto of early Protestant Reformation policy and practice in Ireland susceptible to interpretation as 'confessionalisation', that is, the process whereby the institutions of church and state combined to forge a single national faith and to mould an obedient laity through social disciplining? In applying the conceptual framework to the Irish Reformation, Ute Lotz-Heumann has propounded the notion of 'dual confessionalisation', which counterpoints Protestant confessionalisation 'from above' with Catholic confessionalisation 'from below'.

As has been discussed, the state's aim to form a homogeneous island-wide faith community was circumscribed by political and cultural limitations for some or all of the period under review. In terms of its forging of a uniform and identifiable Protestant community among the minority of older and newer English, discernible efforts fell short of the criteria posited for strict confessionalisation. Only in Sidney's early attempt to attain a national church, and in Wentworth's later campaign to reconstruct the Church of Ireland, was there a real integration of ecclesiastical and state policy. Even within this dynamic, and certainly in its absence, a credo for a latitudinarian Protestant church clashed with Erastian pressures for doctrinal orthodoxy; the agents of enforcement of conformity were rarely in full harmony across authorities of church and state, and in Dublin and London; dissemination of printed religious material, even in English, was erratic and limited; educational institutions developed slowly and, even then, in the case of Trinity, there was misdirection of mission; the reforms demanded by commissions and visitations were constantly ignored; and areas of ritual were subject to contention between high church and Puritan reformers. Although the terminology has not found universal acceptance

---

29 M. Caball, 'Gaelic and Protestant: a Case-Study in Early Modern Self-Fashioning, 1567–1608', *Proceedings of the Royal Irish Academy*, C:110 (2010), 191–215; M. Empey, 'Protestants and Gaelic Culture in Seventeenth-Century Ireland' (Maynooth University Library eprints, no. 5606).

in Irish Reformation historiography, the notion of duality speaks usefully to the divided religious milieu, though Alan Ford prefers the use of the term 'sectarianism', both in its technical and pejorative forms, as more suitable for the mutually hostile yet co-existing communities in early modern Ireland.[30]

For the Protestant community on the ground, living in symbiosis with its confessional nemesis helped to sharpen self-awareness of religious belief and difference. Catholicism came to claim a substantial majority of the population of Ireland, but could never in this period aspire to become the national religion. Nor could toleration be formally granted to this majority of dissenters from state Protestantism before 1641, as to do so would undermine the notion of a Protestant state, though the enforcement of penal measures could be suspended from time to time. Thus, a popular 'confession-building' process was at work in Catholicism, rather than centralised confessionalisation. If church papistry marked a transitional phase of nominal conformity, it was short-lived, as many were galvanised into taking the Catholic side by the witness of the iconic Archbishop Richard Creagh, a long-standing prisoner of conscience, for example, and the Baltinglass rebels, who died on the scaffold in defiance of Protestantism. More promising as a bridge to Protestantism was the commonwealth humanism of Old English politicians such as James Stanyhurst, Rowland White and Nicholas White, but this tendency died out in the coercive politico-religious atmosphere of the late 1580s. Recusancy became the mode of dissent for those who rallied to the cause of traditional corporate liberties in parliament and outside, as well as to the defence of the Catholic practice of the Mass and other ceremonies. Martyrologies written by Catholic exiles, venerating those who died for reasons of conscience, such as Archbishop Dermot O'Hurley and Creagh, served to consolidate Catholic self-identification. The diaspora also fostered Catholic education through the colleges founded in the Spanish Netherlands, the Iberian peninsula, France and elsewhere. This first generation of migrants produced the university-trained clerics and bishops who returned to Ireland to catechise the norms of the Council of Trent and Catholic renewal. A Protestant community was faced with

---

30 U. Lotz-Heumann, 'Confessionalisation', in D.M. Whitford (ed.), *Reformation and Early Modern Europe: A Guide to Research* (Kirksville, MS: Truman State University Press, 2008), 136–60; U. Lotz-Heumann, 'Confessionalisation in Ireland: Periodisation and Character, 1534–1649', in Ford and McCafferty (eds.), *Origins of Sectarianism in Early Modern Ireland*, 24–53; A. Ford, 'Sectarianism in Early Modern Ireland', in Ford and McCafferty (eds.), *Origins of Sectarianism in Early Modern Ireland*, 6–17.

direct competition from a renewed and organised Catholic Church under its resident, dynamic bishops.[31]

Protestant Community in Ireland

Central to the formation of this Protestant community in Ireland after 1550 was an adequate ministry, comprising pastors who were educated to expound true divinity as professed by their church. Pending the availability of such preachers, who would ideally be graduates of the long-sought native university, the burden of service in the parishes fell upon the existing clergy who were mostly conservative in outlook and commonly Irish speaking. These clerics availed themselves fully of the concession whereby the celebration of the liturgy through Latin was allowed, thus preserving an aura of familiarity about the new order of service. In general, although they were excoriated as 'ignorant papists' by Archbishop Loftus and many other Protestant reformers for their lack of learning and piety, the native ministry helped to mediate the changes, while preserving pastoral and sacramental service to their parishioners. Several Gaelic clerics, particularly in areas of the west of the country, were attracted to the reformed church, perhaps through the possibility of valid clerical marriage, and some even availed themselves of bursaries to study at Oxford or Cambridge under Protestant patronage. But these Irish bishops and clergy found it almost impossible to reconcile their religious convictions with their membership of an overwhelmingly Catholic Gaelic society, and so their influence waned in the Church of Ireland of the 'second Reformation'. In the 1590s, Loftus made extensive use of the Ecclesiastical High Commission and the Court of Faculties (a body dealing with the licensing of clergy) to deprive contumacious clerics, and to replace them with newcomers, if necessary from England. A small number of English recruits to preaching ministries in the Irish church had already come through appointment to the chapter of St Patrick's cathedral, Dublin, under Loftus's patronage. By the end of the century most of the older reading ministers were either dying out or had transferred to the renewed Catholic pastorate, and a drive began to recruit British-born preachers for the task of Protestant evangelism.[32]

31 C. Lennon, 'Mass in the Manor-House: The Counter-Reformation in Dublin, 1560–1630', in J. Kelly and D. Keogh (eds.), *History of the Catholic Archdiocese of Dublin* (Dublin: FCP, 2000), 112–26; Lennon, 'Taking sides'; T. Ó hAnnracháin, *Catholic Counter-Reformation in Ireland: the Mission of Rinuccini, 1645–1649* (Oxford University Press, 2002), 39–81.

32 Ford, *Protestant Reformation*, 31–47; C. Lennon and C. Diamond, 'The Ministry of the Church of Ireland, 1536–1636', in T. C. Barnard and W. G. Neely (eds.), *The Clergy of the Church of Ireland, 1000–2000* (Dublin: FCP, 2006), 44–58.

The bishops as a corporate entity played a major leadership role in embedding a Church of Ireland community throughout the country after 1600. Few of the episcopal bench inherited by the Stuart *régime* had been active as reformers down to 1603, the majority being traditional conservatives of Irish birth, such as the notorious pluralist, Miler Magrath of Cashel. The Jacobean bishops, who filled the many vacancies, were expected to be preachers and pastors, charged with visitation and oversight of their dioceses, as well as state officials. Notwithstanding the high number of dioceses, a full complement of bishops, overwhelmingly British, was now maintained. Members of the new episcopate were fully committed to pastoral improvement in parishes across the regions, from the settled Pale and former Englishry, through the Gaelic territories in the west, to the newly planted areas of Ulster and Munster, as brief case studies of each may show. As bishop of Ferns and Leighlin (1605–1634), Thomas Ram, who had been chaplain to Lord Deputy Mountjoy, presided over a scheme of rebuilding of churches, attracted preachers to benefices where incomes were slowly recovering, and placed reading ministers in Irish-speaking curacies, pending the return of benefice-holders whom he had sent to Trinity College to train as preaching ministers in the vernacular. The Englishman and Trinity Fellow, Bishop Edward King of Elphin (1611–1639), appointed mostly English-preaching ministers to revalued benefices, restored much alienated property to the diocese, and rebuilt his cathedral and town at Elphin, which was transformed into a 'handsome English village'. And, in Ulster, Bishop Andrew Knox of Raphoe (1611–1633), a Scotsman, brought to bear his coercive approach as sometime bishop of the Isles towards Gaelic Catholic dissent, along with a pastoral zeal for preaching and rebuilding. He appointed many Scottish clergy to serve the immigrant planters, but also promoted some native clergy and a schoolmaster to begin the work of converting the Irish population.[33]

High expectations were entertained of ministers appointed under a supportive episcopate in early seventeenth-century Ireland. Required by the imperative of the 1537 act to speak and promote English in their evangelism, the newly professionalised clergy were almost all university-trained preachers who brought families with them, or set up such units in their parishes.

33 J. McCafferty, 'Protestant Prelates or Godly Pastors? The Dilemma of the Early Stuart Episcopate', in Ford and McCafferty (eds.), *Origins of Sectarianism in Early Modern Ireland*, 54–72; Ford, *Protestant Reformation*, 140–3; R. Bagwell, rev. A. Ford, 'Ram, Thomas', in *Oxford Dictionary of National Biography* (Oxford University Press, 2004), www.oxforddnb.com/view/article/23065 (accessed 13 June 2017); C. Diamond, 'King, Edward (c.1576–1639)', in *Oxford Dictionary of National Biography* (Oxford University Press, 2004), www.oxforddnb.com/view/article/67220 (accessed 13 June 2015).

The majority were of English or Scottish birth, and even though half of the preachers appointed in the old Pale area were graduates of Trinity College by 1634, most of these were of newly arrived English origin. As migrants to a new environment without a native support network, ministers normally overcame the challenge of straitened incomes in most dioceses by resorting to holding two or more benefices to make a sufficient living, though thereby creating problems of non-residence and thin pastoral coverage. Naturally drawn to the clusters of Protestant worshippers in the larger cities or the newly planted areas, the graduate preachers tended to reside in the more lucrative of their benefices, perhaps consigning the less wealthy ones to poorly paid curates. In the newly settled areas of Munster and Ulster, provision was made by estate owners for the building of new churches, and the endowment of vicarages, for example, though glebe houses were rare until the eighteenth century. In their parishes, besides being expected to preach and teach, the clergy had to maintain the church building through the collection of tithes, and they also had to act as officials of central government by keeping parish registers of births, marriages and deaths. In addition, many of them provided hospitality, poor relief and education.[34]

Although Ireland did attract some less reputable clergy from Britain who were fleeing a chequered past, for the most part the new ministers were sober family men who took their duties as pastors seriously. Raymond Gillespie has depicted them as belonging to a distinctive social order, which, though containing clergymen of differing theological views and varying incomes, drew coherence from common ordination in the Church and an *esprit de corps* as evangelists on the frontier of the Reformation. The canons of 1634 showed that the elevated position of the minister as guardian of the *Book of Common Prayer* in the Irish church elicited reciprocating expectations of the clergy in respect of professional demeanour and dress. Many ministers experienced cultural and social isolation as *émigré* missioners of, in the eyes of Catholics, an alien church. While the institution of clerical marriage brought comfort and stability, ministers' wives sometimes faced an uncertain response from Catholic society, unused to valid clerical matrimonial unions. Others such as Leah Mawe, wife of Bishop Bedell, were widely admired as helpers of their husbands, and were used by religious writers as models of godly womanhood. By contrast, the phenomenon of Catholic wives and children

---

34 Á. Hensey, 'A Comparative Study of the Lives of Church of Ireland and Roman Catholic Clergy in the South-Eastern Dioceses of Ireland from 1550–1650', unpublished PhD thesis, Maynooth University (2012), 180–210; Ford, *Protestant Reformation*, chapters 4–7.

of ministers and bishops caused great disapproval and mistrust among the wider Protestant community in Ireland. Many ministers had to supplement their clerical incomes by taking up additional occupations including farming and moneylending. Some grew comparatively wealthy and the records of depredations done to clerical homes in the uprising of 1641 indicate moderate levels of accumulation of property and other possessions, including books.[35]

A lay Protestant community of several thousand, clustered mainly in the towns, north-east and west Ulster, and east Munster, and scattered throughout the Pale, the midlands and south-east, is testimony to the foothold gained by the Reformation in Ireland by 1640.[36] Most lay Protestants were recent migrants, but a *côterie* of older-established Church of Ireland families, including the Usshers, exercised considerable influence in social and religious life. While conformity to Protestantism in cities such as Kilkenny, Limerick and Galway did not endure, it was in Dublin that a core group of native urbanites emerged as dedicated to the advancement of the Reformation in city and country. Besides branches of the Ussher family, at least half a dozen other patrician clans, including those of Ball, Challoner, Money and Forster were notable as supporters of evangelical initiatives such as the founding of the municipal school and Trinity College. It was at the house of John Ussher that the Irish-language Protestant catechism was printed, and William, his son, likewise facilitated a Gaelic printing – of the *Tiomna Nuadh*. While maintaining generally harmonious relations with their Catholic fellow patricians, members of this *côterie* demonstrated their Protestant sympathies in their choice of marital partners, choosing them predominantly from among their fellow Dublin Protestants and the newly arrived English families. Among the clergy of this Dublin Protestant milieu were Henry Ussher, archbishop of Armagh (1595–1613), his son, Robert, bishop of Kildare (1635–1642), his nephew, James, a successor in Armagh (1625–1656), and Lucas Challoner, a founding fellow of Trinity College. A sampling of Dublin Protestant endogamy reveals that Challoner's own daughter, Phoebe, from his marriage to a daughter of Alderman Walter Ball, a staunch reformer, wedded James Ussher.[37]

Old English Protestants in the earlier seventeenth century contributed greatly to maintaining stability in civic and parochial life through their role as intermediaries between their fellow citizens in the Catholic majority and the centralising state. In the interests of continuity in municipal politics,

---

35 R. Gillespie, 'The Church of Ireland Clergy, *c*.1640' in Barnard and Neely (eds.), *Clergy of the Church of Ireland*, 59–77.

36 See N. Canny, *Making Ireland British, 1580–1650* (Oxford University Press, 2001), 301–401.

37 Lennon, *Lords of Dublin*, 134–8.

Protestant councillors, including Robert Ball in Dublin and Edmund Sexton in Limerick, for example, undertook the mayoralty in years when their Catholic brethren were being forced to take the oath of supremacy, and notable Church of Ireland members took office as masters of trade guilds when their charters were being questioned by central government. Despite their confessional differences, Protestants and Catholics cooperated in the management of old urban religious fraternities, which had not been dissolved during the Irish Reformation, leasing their properties and sharing in their sociability. The wealthiest of the surviving Catholic fraternities, that of St Anne in St Audoen's parish in Dublin, continued to contribute to the upkeep of the parish church, a place of Protestant worship, throughout the seventeenth century. In that parish, as well as others, Catholics were not excluded from Church of Ireland vestries, serving as cessors and sidesmen, and even churchwardens, before the Oath of Supremacy was enforced on holders in the later seventeenth century. The sacred space of the parish graveyard continued to be shared as the resting place of Protestants and Catholics. Protestant civic families took the lead in preserving the parochial system of welfare and poor relief in the face of government attempts to abolish old institutions and impose more disciplinarian and confessional modes of charity. Older English Protestant families tended to favour extending poor relief through schemes that privileged urban brotherhood and sisterhood above confessional allegiance, and their participation in the running of civic hospitals, almshouses and outdoor poor relief was disproportionate to their numbers.[38]

In the plantation estates and towns, such as those of the earl of Cork in east Munster, which contained comparatively heavy settlements of Protestants, a disciplinary and confessionalised system of poor relief was more easily integrated within a reformed Protestant civic milieu. Here, under the patronage and protection of the estate owners, the practice of Protestantism was less fraught, as laymen and women interacted with a ministry drawn mainly from the same background as themselves. While the building of new churches and the restoration of older ones was funded by the beneficence of wealthy Protestants such as Cork, the tithes of members of congregations contributed to the quotidian maintenance of parish buildings

---

38 C. Lennon, 'The Shaping of a Lay Community in the Church of Ireland, 1558–1640', in R. Gillespie and W. G. Neely (eds.), *The Laity and the Church of Ireland, 1000–2000* (Dublin: FCP, 2002), 49–69; R. Gillespie, 'Urban Parishes in Early Seventeenth-Century Ireland: The Case of Dublin', in E. Fitzpatrick and R. Gillespie (eds.), *The Parish in Medieval and Early Modern Ireland* (Dublin: FCP, 2006), 228–41; R. Gillespie, 'Godly Order: Enforcing Peace in the Irish Reformation', in Boran and Gribben (eds.), *Enforcing Reformation in Ireland and Scotland*, 184–210.

and clergy, though attempts to implement a country-wide reform of the complex and varied system of payment and collection were unsuccessful. As to the tenor of Protestant spirituality and worship, Raymond Gillespie has pointed to the importance of the reading and hearing of the books of the Bible and *Common Prayer* in the formation of Church of Ireland community. Ownership of a copy of the Bible became common among members of the Church, possibly as the only book in their possession, to be used at worship or for private reading and reflection. By contrast with the scriptures, which symbolised affiliation to the wider world of Protestantism, the *Book of Common Prayer* was synonymous with the rituals of the church. Not only were the prayers the bedrock of uniformity for all liturgical occasions, with any deviations by ministers giving rise to criticism from parishioners, but the *Book* was also frequently used in a domestic setting for family prayer or individual meditation. Literacy among Protestant men and women was fostered through familiarity with the key texts, as well as popular devotional works such as Lewis Bayly's *The practice of piety*.[39]

One such bibliophile was Edmund Sexton (1569–1639), a dedicated Protestant patrician in Limerick, who was for many years the only one of his persuasion among the aldermanic class. The grandson of an urbanised man of Gaelic background, who had received many grants of former monastic properties from Henry VIII, Edmund had a large collection of works of piety and divinity in his library of 131 books. Sexton had struggled earnestly to maintain a Protestant presence in a largely Catholic city, of which he served as mayor on four occasions in the interests of civic solidarity. He had developed a network of marriage and gossipred with Protestants throughout Munster to protect his faith and that of his large family. Yet Sexton's isolation was evident when Catholic relatives, including his wife and some of his children, caused a fracas while trying to convert him on his deathbed and preventing access by Protestant ministers to him. Another example of riotous behaviour on the death of a Protestant was that of female relatives of Luke Plunkett, Lord Killeen, Catholic husband of the Protestant, Susanna Brabazon, when she was being buried in 1622 in accordance with the rites of the *Book of Common Prayer*. The breakdown of harmony on occasions such as funerals or even baptisms attests the fragility of the social cohesion that normally prevailed despite confessional differences.[40]

39 R. Gillespie, 'Lay Spirituality and Worship, 1558–1750: Holy Books and Godly Readers', in Gillespie and Neely (eds.), *The Laity and the Church of Ireland* (Dublin: FCP, 2002), 133–51.

40 Lennon, 'Shaping of a Lay Community', 64–9; C. Tait, *Death, Burial and Commemoration in Ireland, 1550–1650* (Basingstoke: Palgrave MacMillan, 2002), 55–6.

Conclusion

Such isolated confrontations were a foretaste of the widespread clashes in 1641, when tensions under the surface of inter-communal relations exploded. The damage done to the process of getting along with neighbours across the confessional divide was almost irreparable. The grim evidence of the 1641 Depositions reveals the extent of the onslaughts on Protestant clergy, laymen and women throughout the country. In this dark period, the respectful treatment afforded to the body of William Bedell shines out as a beacon, as do some other examples of goodness. Yet any limited progress made by the work of the irenic Bedell in his mission to the Catholic Irish proved to be no more durable than that achieved by more coercive reformers who eschewed his persuasive methods. The conflict of the 1640s was also a severe test of Protestantism in Ireland, and the fact that it survived into the later century, albeit in divided form, is testimony to its rootedness, particularly in communities where the self-awareness of Protestants was sharpened by close interplay with their confessional counterparts and perhaps even by resistance to the centralising state.

9

Establishing a Confessional Ireland, 1641–1691

ROBERT ARMSTRONG

Ireland in the second half of the seventeenth century sustained three capacious communities of faith: Catholic, established-church Protestant and Presbyterian. All three faced comparable problems. All adhered to an ideal where membership of church duplicated that of nation, and where the institutions of the civil kingdom supported, and were sustained by, those of the true church. None attained it. All faced the difficulty of securing adequate resources to fulfil their calling, both the human resources of sufficient numbers of morally, spiritually and educationally adequate pastors, and the material resources which would embed that ministry into integrated, bounded local faith communities. All needed to make the most of intangible resources to address those shortcomings. Goats as well as sheep merited access to the channels of grace, the questing souls seeking depths of devotion, the more occasionally or conventionally devout, or even those on the fringes of a communal religion, more interested in its social than its spiritual benefits. Theological argument and reassurance, shaped internationally was translated (sometimes literally) and transmitted in rural as well as urban settings, in small printed texts for private prayer, in catechism lessons or in sermons. All managed to root their religious practices, in varying manner cultivating a sense of place and of the past, ancient or recent. All attempted to use the 'regal office' of the church to ensure that their practice was 'at once edifying, expedient and true'.[1] All, and indeed a range of smaller sects and movements, were forced to adapt to conditions where state favour was never wholehearted enough to assure to them the triumph of their ambitions, but state hostility never so extreme as to ensure their destruction. Each community faced significant internal division – indeed arguably the Presbyterian/Episcopalian divide never quite lost its character as a rift within

---

1 The phrase is Newman's: J. H. Newman, *The* Via Media *of the Anglican Church*, ed. H. D. Weidner (Oxford University Press, 1990), 26.

a shared Protestant tradition, at least in Presbyterian eyes – sometimes prin-cipled, perhaps more often the crabbed fruit of all-too-human ambition, contentiousness or self-will.

The 1640s

For Catholic churchmen the violence and disorder unleashed by the 1641 rebellion also meant the removal of constraints imposed on the church by the need to operate within a Protestant kingdom, and gave place to a new political order, one which leading clerics helped to shape, and in which they were guaranteed an entrenched position. It meant a greater prospect of ful-filment for an agenda patiently and persistently pursued for the past sev-eral decades, one to which the label 'Tridentine' (from the sixteenth-century Council of Trent) may be applied. What was envisaged, and in part accom-plished, was a church order centred around resident and active bishops and functioning parishes. What was intended was above all to secure greater participation in a regular sacramental life, greater instruction of the faithful through basic catechesis and clear moral instruction, and greater regulation to produce a more disciplined and effective clergy and a more upright as well as devoted flock.[2]

A national synod, gathered at Kilkenny in May 1642, which declared 'that war openly Catholic to be lawful and just', pressed for a 'bond of union' backed with an organisational framework for this time of present danger. The Catholic Confederate government, which emerged by the autumn, was one in which the Catholic bishops took their place, as a clerical estate within the General Assembly, and with individual bishops seated on succes-sive Supreme Councils. An oath pledging loyalty to the king and the laws of Ireland, and obedience to the Confederate Supreme Council, and binding its takers to 'defend, uphold and maintain … the free exercise of the Roman Catholic faith and religion throughout this land' was mandated to 'be taken solemnly, after Confession and receiving the sacrament in the parish churches throughout the kingdom'. It was a mobilisation of conscience, an enlistment in a cause considered at once patriotic, constitutional and religious, which was such a defining feature of the decade across the three Stuart kingdoms, from the signing of the National Covenant in Scotland in 1638. The first of the Confederates' General Assemblies pledged that 'the Roman Catholic

2 T. Ó hAnnracháin, *Catholic Reformation in Ireland: the Mission of Rinuccini, 1645–1649* (Oxford University Press, 2002) chapter two, for these developments to 1642.

church in Ireland shall and may have and enjoy the privileges and immunities' accorded it in the thirteenth century, under Magna Carta.[3]

But the emergence of a Catholic polity, in effective control of most of the island, sharpened, rather than easing, the long-standing dilemma of how to reconcile Catholic priorities with continued claims of allegiance to a Protestant monarch, and this not least because Ireland now faced the kinds of tensions between spiritual and temporal power prevalent throughout Catholic Europe, and brought more clearly to light in Ireland with the arrival of papal emissaries, above all, in 1645, of a nuncio, GianBattista Rinuccini. The inclusion in peace negotiations with the crown's representatives of clerical demands for full and free exercise of an ecclesiastical jurisdiction derived from Rome, and for secure possession of church buildings and property, held before the wars by the established Protestant Church, was immensely damaging both to the unity of the Catholic leadership, and to their chances of securing a lasting settlement. They were demands which the Protestant monarchy would not concede, and many in Catholic ranks were reluctant to press. But for churchmen, they went to the heart of what was needed to fully, and lastingly, accomplish the church's goals. Both demands had arisen out of the conditions of the pre-war years, where such absences clearly impeded the Tridentine mission.[4] The financial resources unlocked could allow for a universal parish ministry, but one, crucially, less dependent on voluntary lay support, even as the possession of churches provided a nationwide infrastructure for shared, sacramental participation and, given the ages-old continuity in the location of church buildings, a visible indication of a Catholic nation long rooted in Irish soil. The exercise of jurisdiction enhanced the ability of the church both to regulate and direct the actions of its clergy, and to facilitate the governing of the consciences as well as the outward actions of its members.

For the nuncio, Rinuccini, this was in some ways but the beginning of his stated obligation to 'restore and establish the public exercise of the Catholic religion in the island of Ireland'. For him this meant challenging the lack of enthusiasm for 'the splendour and grandeur of Religion', which he detected among the 'old bishops'.[5] Historians have drawn attention to his criticisms of an Irish readiness to 'content themselves with a Mass in their cabins', a homeliness of religious practice which offended his sensibilities, but which has been reckoned to have perhaps better secured the long-term viability of Catholic

---

3 J. T. Gilbert (ed.), *History of the Irish Confederation and the War in Ireland* (7 vols., Dublin, 1882–91), ii, 35–6, 74, 85–6; here and elsewhere spelling has been modernised.

4 Ó hAnnracháin, *Catholic Reformation*, 45, 50.

5 Translated, and quoted in Ó hAnnracháin, *Catholic Reformation*, 232, 248.

practice in Ireland.[6] But his perspective is important to remember. If public spectacle and *splendore* allowed for a form of worship more worthy of the divine, it also had the potential to engage a population whom he believed susceptible to the outward workings of religion, true or false – public Protestant rites must be blocked 'because heresy comes easily to the nature and facility of uneducated people'. His experiences, particularly in such urban settings as Kilkenny, Limerick and, perhaps above all, Galway, demonstrated the readiness of the population at large to respond with enthusiasm to processions and public devotions.[7] There seems little reason to doubt that, as elsewhere in Europe, 'Baroque' Catholicism would have had considerable potential to win popular engagement, emphasising what was distinctly Catholic in a divided society, utilising the resources of music or art to do so, and above all by enacting participation in a communal religion. And, of course, the promotion of Italian-style devotions was paralleled by efforts to restore indigenous cults: John Burke, archbishop of Tuam, had the ruined oratory of St Jarlath rebuilt, and the shrine with the saint's relics restored to it.[8]

Rinuccini could excuse 'laxity'; what he could not condone was 'a beginning ... to all those excesses ... approaching to the introduction of heresy, or at least apostasy' which could be detected in 'acts against the Holy See and ecclesiastical immunity'. It has been convincingly argued that what he was detecting in a sequence of actions by the Confederate authorities to preserve the crumbling prospects of a settlement with the king, and to curtail clerical assertiveness, was a fundamental threat to the Tridentine project. Across Catholic Europe this was predicated upon close cooperation, but also some compromise, between Catholic *régimes* and Rome. What Rinuccini thought he detected was an intrusion upon the freedoms essential to the church if it was truly to discharge its spiritual duty to direct a Christian society and, indeed, a readiness to surrender the ambition of bringing into being a truly Catholic kingdom and nation through pandering to a Protestant monarchy.[9] He was confronted with a very different understanding of the respective responsibilities of church and civil power, one predicated upon upholding 'the law of the

---

6 See, e.g., P. J. Corish, *The Catholic Community in the Seventeenth and Eighteenth Centuries* (Dublin: Helicon, 1981), 42; such comments echo J. Bossy, 'The Counter-Reformation and the People of Catholic Ireland, 1596–1641', in T. D. Williams (ed.), *Historical Studies VIII* (Dublin: Gill and Macmillan, 1971), 169.

7 Ó hAnnracháin, *Catholic Reformation*, 248–52 (quoted at 248).

8 T. Connors, 'Religion and the Laity in Early Modern Galway', in Gerard Moran ed., *Galway: History and Society* (Dublin: Geography Publications, 1996), 141.

9 The interpretation in this paragraph is reliant on Ó hAnnracháin, *Catholic Reformation*, 214–29, where the quotations from Rinuccini may be found.

land, as in Catholic time it was practiced'. Taking the Confederate *régime* to be the inheritor of royal prerogatives, it could be asserted that 'our holy mother the catholic church ... teacheth... that all subjects both laics and ecclesiastics... are bound under mortal sin and eternal damnation to obey all orders of the civil magistrate'.[10] Civil loyalty was a religious duty, especially given Catholic assumptions that Protestantism was the path to social and civil disorder as well as spiritual ruin, and that temporal kingdoms, too, had their divine calling.

The pre-war established, Protestant, church had entered upon two decades of defeat with the rising of 1641. The obstinate determination of its champion, the king's lord lieutenant, James Butler, marquis of Ormond, to press upon the Confederates the case for Protestant repossession of churches (taken into Catholic hands over most of Ireland) and sole exercise of ecclesiastical juris-diction may appear at once grasping and at least as obstructive of a settlement as the demands of the Catholic bishops. But he and his own episcopal backers could hardly do less, if they were to satisfy their claim to be 'that part of the Catholic church that is established by law within this kingdom'. Assembled bishops insisted they could not 'with a good conscience forego the power of the keys which Christ hath committed unto us'. Ormond believed he had made, if reluctantly, the concessions needed to allow freedom of Catholic religious practice. But neither he nor his royal master could countenance a definition of 'penal laws' which extended to medieval legislation intended to safeguard royal power in matters ecclesiastical – what George Synge, bishop of Cloyne, termed 'all the laws made to repress the popish invasion upon the state ecclesiastical, made long before ... Henry the Eighth' – even though such legislation had been used to harry Catholic clergy before the wars. The heroic labours of James Ussher in the 1620s and 1630s had produced a schol-arly, and enduring, Protestant interpretation of history which cast the ancient Irish church of St Patrick and his heirs as a precursor of their own, in doctrine and order.[11] With less sophistication, but much determination, Protestant churchmen and their supporters now defended their church as heir to Magna Carta, its spiritual responsibilities and privileges entrenched by law within an Irish kingdom itself framed through English common law.[12]

---

10 *Queries Concerning the Lawfulnesse of the Present Cessation* ([Kilkenny, 1648]), 47–8; T. O'Connor, *Irish Jansenists, 1600–70: Religion and Politics in Flanders, France, Ireland and Rome* (Dublin: Four Courts Press [hereafter FCP], 2008), 282–6.

11 A. Ford, *James Ussher: Theology, History and Politics in Early Modern Ireland and England* (Oxford University Press, 2007), chapter 6.

12 For documents quoted in this, and the next paragraph, see R. Armstrong, 'Protestant Churchmen and the Confederate Wars' in C. Brady and J. Ohlmeyer (eds.), *British Interventions in Early Modern Ireland* (Cambridge University Press, 2005), 230–51.

For all that the Church of Ireland was modelled on that of England, in its articles of faith, its governance and its liturgy, it would be defended against the attempt of any authority, civil or ecclesiastical, in England – or Scotland – to impose new rulings upon the 'free' Irish church; to bow to such changes would be 'submitting to the same Tyranny over the Conscience, and blind obedience, which we have justly condemned the papacy for'. Civil war divisions in England had seen the Westminster parliament align itself with the Covenanting *régime* in Scotland, adopting a Solemn League and Covenant widely interpreted as pledging a 'reformation of religion' on Presbyterian lines in all three kingdoms, and by 1644 support for the Covenant was spreading in Protestant Ireland. By 1646 a cluster of eleven Protestant bishops could thank their protector, Ormond, for ensuring, in Dublin and its environs, 'the free and full exercise of the true reformed religion according to the liturgy and canons so many years received in the Church', but feared this was 'more than we know to be in any part of the three Dominions'. A year later and worship according to the *Book of Common Prayer* was prohibited even in Dublin, following the handover of the city to English parliamentary control. The protests of leading city clergymen as to the right of 'the free national Church of Ireland' to determine its own liturgy were unavailing.

For some Catholic clerics Episcopal Protestants were somewhat less in error, and somewhat less destructive of order than 'Parliamentarie Protestants' or 'Puritans', having at least upheld the historical structures of the church and maintained claims to its historic possessions.[13] In this light Presbyterianism could only be a destructive force. The first meeting of in Ireland of a 'Presbytery' – a body of ministers and representative elders exercising authority over local congregations or parishes – was held at Carrickfergus in June 1642, and comprised chaplains and officers of the Scottish army sent to Ulster to combat the rising. By 1644 the agreement of the Scottish general, Robert Monro, was secured to enforce obedience from all the inhabitants in the counties of Antrim and Down to the Presbytery, which had now incorporated locally based ministers and congregations.[14] But Presbyterianism was driven forward by its own dynamic within Ulster society, and the Presbytery would show itself as determined as its competitors to pursue its transforming vision unshackled by civil or military power.

---

13 T. Ó hAnnracháin, '"In imitation of that holy patron of prelates the blessed St Charles": Episcopal Activity in Ireland and the Formation of a Confessional Identity, 1618–1653', in A. Ford and J. McCafferty (eds.), *The Origins of Sectarianism in Early Modern Ireland* (Cambridge University Press, 2005), 89–90.

14 R. Armstrong, 'Ireland's Puritan Revolution? The Emergence of Ulster Presbyterianism Reconsidered', *English Historical Review*, 121 (2006), 1048–74, especially p. 1062.

From the 1610s, and more especially the 1620s, increasing numbers of Scots clergymen had taken up postings within the established church in Ulster. They did not establish a fully Presbyterian order, but some pursued Presbyterian priorities, not least a sacramental ministry shorn of what they considered superstitious usages, and the cultivation of an active disciplinary framework, overseen by elders, within their parishes. Meetings for large-scale worship across parish boundaries carried a revivalist flavour, and opportunity was taken for consultation among like-minded brethren.[15] All had been shut down with a greater drive for conformity within the Church of Ireland of the 1630s, though later accounts testified to the persistence of gospel ministry in small, private meetings. Here, again, the collapse of order in 1641 offered opportunity. A sequence of petitions from individual Ulster parishes or in the name of wider communities called for the restoration of godly ministers who had once served among them but had been swept away by the dastardly actions of bishops ('prelates'), or their replacement from the ranks of the Scottish church. Exiled or established Scottish ministers tended to visit for short-term preaching tours only, though the effects should not be underestimated: one of the most eminent, John Livingstone, reported prodigious travels with daily sermons, two on the Sabbath, for the 'hunger of the people' for ministry had become 'very great'.[16] If some of those who swore the Covenant in Ulster did so with an eye on the military and political relief it might bring them, the atmosphere of religious revival which the ministers reported should not be discounted, swearing ceremonies being blended with Presbyterian preaching and communion. The Covenant was used to provide justification for the Presbyterian campaign of 'reformation', though no legislation had enacted the Presbyterian order in Ireland, and the battered shield offered by the Scottish army never extended to all the areas that Presbyterian religion would reach.

The Presbyterian advance won ground steadily but securely. Parishes were stirred to seek ministry, but also to find ways to sustain a minister, and to secure for themselves a body of elders drawn from the local community. Scottish 'expectants', graduates as yet unplaced in parishes, from the mid-1640s took up the challenge of ordination and long-term service, sometimes sinking decades in one particular Ulster parish. By contrast, existing Protestant clergy could be uprooted by the Presbytery, or rebuffed: one, Thomas Vesey (father of a future archbishop), claimed to have been faced with a demand to commit

---

15 A. Ford, 'The Origins of Irish Dissent', in K. Herlihy (ed.), *The Religion of Irish Dissent, 1650–1800* (Dublin: FCP, 1996), 9–30.
16 Quoted in Armstrong, 'Ireland's Puritan Revolution', 1067.

himself to Presbyterianism by divine right 'as it is exercised in the Church of Scotland (where I was never in my life)'.[17] Records for Templepatrick in County Antrim show fourteen local elders acting in rotation in monthly meetings of the Presbytery at Carrickfergus, and together with their minister imposing moral discipline locally, over Sabbath-breakers, fornicators, drunkards and slanderers. Political authority in wartime Ulster was broken or distant; the Presbyterian system stitched together communities across the eastern, and, more patchily, the north-western, counties. By 1649 the Presbytery openly took a stand for covenanted reformation across the three kingdoms, mobilising regional opposition to both resurgent Royalism within Ireland and an encroaching English Republic not minded to preserve 'Presbyterian government (the hedge and bulwark of religion)'.[18] The Republic's triumph would mean the Presbyterians' – temporary – eclipse.

The 1650s

The religious ambitions of the English Commonwealth or Republic, and indeed the Protectorate *régime* which succeeded it from 1653, were to purge false religion from within and without the national church; to promote a Puritan Protestantism and a preaching ministry; to protect those whose consciences jibbed at conformity so long as they would 'profess faith in Jesus Christ', avoid 'popery or prelacy' and not create disturbance. Its means were the direct enforcement of English legislation, past and future, in Ireland. But Ireland was not England, where the vast majority of the population were retained within a functioning parish-based Protestant Church.[19] The new *régime* was determined that England's harsher anti-Catholic laws be enforced in Ireland. As the war ground on, Catholic clergy captured after battle or the fall of Confederate towns or fortresses were killed. In January 1652 it was affirmed that Catholic clergy would be excluded from all surrender articles, and a year later their banishment ordered, on pain of the capital penalties imposed by English law.[20] But the other side of the refusal of the 'least

---

17 Armstrong, 'Ireland's Puritan Revolution', 1065.
18 R. Armstrong, 'Viscount Ards and the Presbytery: Politics and Religion among the Scots of Ulster in the 1640s', in W. P. Kelly and J. R. Young (eds.), *Scotland and the Ulster Plantations* (Dublin: FCP, 2009), 18–40 (quoting the presbytery's *Necessary Representation*).
19 A. Hughes, '"The public profession of these nations": The National Church in Interregnum England', in C. Durston and J. Maltby (eds.), *Religion in Revolutionary England* (Manchester University Press, 2006), 93–114.
20 B. Millett, 'Survival and Reorganization 1650–1695', in P. J. Corish (ed.) *History of Irish Catholicism*, iii, fasc. 7 (Dublin: Gill and Son, 1968), 4–5.

Toleration' was, for the moment at least, an expressed intention 'not to compel any the Recusants in this nation to their worship or divine service contrary to their consciences'.[21] The Catholic majority, for the moment, would be left in a religious no-man's-land, denied the exercise of their faith while not coerced towards that of the state.

Plans for a legislative overhaul of the established Church of Ireland stalled, but the military and political agents of the new *régime*, and those from the local *élite* who could be co-opted to join them, moved to sweep away the old order in worship and church governance, and to appoint 'persons of pious life and conversation ... qualified with gifts for preaching'.[22] Timothy Taylor of Carrickfergus, one of the prominent new appointees, did not reckon as incompatible his conception of the church as comprising only 'visible Saints or such as in Ground of charity had positive holiness', not a mixed body determined by geography, bolstered by an Independent ecclesiology which saw each local congregation, so constituted, as autonomous and self-governing, and his holding of a salaried post within a national religious order, which imposed no higher ecclesiastic authority, but a duty to preach the gospel to all comers.[23] But it was a departure, all the same, from mainstream English Puritan understanding of a church offering its services to all in return for their conformity and financial contribution, while recognising that not all would respond to the call of the gospel in conversion. The radical John Rogers could maintain a salaried preaching post in Christ Church cathedral, Dublin, alongside leadership of a gathered church, later publishing the conversion narratives required of prospective members to testify to the reality of their individual spiritual experience.[24] But for others the logic of a 'gathered' church took them outside a national structure altogether, and it was such 'separatist' groups that the English Republic, and more especially its army, were determined to protect. Few pastors promoting believer's baptism as a distinguishing feature of a truly constituted church accepted state-salaried positions, but

---

21 R. Dunlop (ed.), *Ireland under the Commonwealth* (2 vols., Manchester, 1913), i, 200, 203; J. Cunningham, 'Lay Catholicism and Religious Policy in Cromwellian Ireland', *Journal of Ecclesiastical History* 64 (2013), 773–4.

22 Dunlop (ed.), *Ireland under the Commonwealth*, i, 2, 5; T. C. Barnard, *Cromwellian Ireland* (2nd edn., Oxford: Clarendon Press, 2000), 95, 97, 144.

23 Patrick Adair and Andrew Stewart, *Presbyterian History in Ireland: Two Seventeenth-Century Narratives*, ed. R. Armstrong, A. R. Holmes, R. S. Spurlock and P. Walsh (Belfast: Ulster Historical Foundation, 2016), 199; Barnard, *Cromwellian Ireland*, 136–7.

24 For Rogers, see C. Gribben, *God's Irishmen: Theological Debates in Cromwellian Ireland* (Oxford University Press, 2007), chapter 2. Salaries were preferred as untying dependence from an unregenerate flock. The state diverted income from confiscated church lands and tithes to support ministers, though by 1658 over half the cost of preachers' salaries needed to be made good from general revenue: Barnard, *Cromwellian Ireland*, 156.

Baptist congregations were promoted in key Irish urban centres, not least by military governors. Restriction of church membership to converted and baptised believers threatened the demise of a national church, and even state-sponsored ministers moved to denounce the divisiveness of Baptist principles within Protestant ranks. Membership of the close-knit Baptist network was believed to offer political advantage; as it came to be seen to shelter opposition to the new Protectorate, so its influence rapidly waned.[25]

As in England the *régime* change in 1653 gave renewed impetus to many of the intended measures of reform of the national church, but greater voice to those who wished to define it in more conservative terms. Mechanisms for the appointment and removal of ministers became more formalised. Numbers grew. The 110 or so official preachers of 1655 had more than doubled in number by 1658, to around 250, though that was only about half the number of Church of Ireland clergy by the late 1660s, or indeed before the wars. They were, though, better paid, not least as a result of a readiness to undertake a rationalisation of clerical provision. Some, though not too many, pre-war Church of Ireland clergymen found places as state-sponsored ministers; others continued to minister outside the national church, using the *Book of Common Prayer*. Clerical appointments moved closer to the kind of minister found in English parishes, committed to an ordained ministry serving an integrated parish community within a unified national church.[26] They faced new threats. From the mid-1650s, Quakers could be found challenging all forms of outward ministry, particularly in the urban south. One early convert, Barbara Blaugdone, was one of those reckoned 'extremely troublesome' by the Limerick minister, Claudius Gilbert, for whom Quakers 'disturbed both the worshipers of God, and the public Peace ... ensnared many of our soldiers, infected divers of our Citizens, gathered many disciples in the Garrisons and Country, and railed most vilely at the Magistrates and Ministers of Christ'. In Cork, Barbara found 'those that were my former Acquaintance, with whom I had formerly been very conversant ... now were afraid of me, ... and some said, I was a Witch'.[27]

Elsewhere there was reconciliation. In 1649–1650 items from the London press denounced 'the piteous slavery they lie under, where a Presbytery is

---

25 Barnard, *Cromwellian Ireland*, 100–9; Gribben, *God's Irishmen*, chapter 3.

26 Barnard, *Cromwellian Ireland*, 94, 140, 146, 161–6; Gribben, *God's Irishmen*, 39. Barnard reckons at least 67 (or 17 per cent of) salaried ministers had previously been beneficed in the Church of Ireland.

27 *An Account of the Travels, Sufferings & Persecution of Barbara Blaugdone* (London, published 1691), 27–8; Claudius Gilbert, *The Libertine School'd* ... (London, 1656), 52, 57.

established'.[28] With Presbyterian ministers in Ulster shunning the regicide *régime*, their numbers plummeted as they faced arrest and deportation to Scotland. Yet by 1654 the Dublin authorities pondered whether they might not be 'persons of the Scots nation ... godly, of peaceable, not of turbulent dispositions' who might qualify as preaching ministers. No longer pressed to recognition of the 'usurping power', half a dozen Ulster Presbyterians are known to have been salaried that year, and thereafter the rise in numbers was precipitous: by 1659–1660 closer to eighty Presbyterian ministers openly served congregations in Ulster, most within the state system. Though included as individuals, they operated what was in effect a church-within-a-church, not only reviving but expanding the structures operational a decade earlier to a total of five 'meetings' or Presbyteries, which addressed questions of moral discipline, oversaw the appointment of elders, assessed applications by parishes for ministers, and tested, approved and ordained candidates.[29]

The Presbyterians benefited most from the conservative drift of the Protectorate; Catholics suffered most. Legislation from the parliament of 1656–1657 included a new act directed against 'popish recusants', which imposed a doctrinally specific oath of abjuration of Catholic doctrine, threatening the full penalties of recusancy on those who refused it, including loss of property, as well as imposing fines and imprisonment for attendance at mass. An act for observance of the Lord's Day, principally directed at profanation of the Sabbath, also clarified that non-attendance at church could only be for those present instead at some other meeting-place of Christians, 'not differing in matters of faith from the public profession of the nation'. Applied to Ireland, this gave much scope for tightening the screw, and convincing evidence has been assembled as to the imposition of abjuration, despite the reservations of some of those in power in Ireland.[30] One Cork minister claimed to echo the lord deputy himself in his calls for civic authorities to uphold the Sabbath and to 'make use of provided and proscribed means for the conversion of the Popish *Irish*', by 'bringing of the Natives to Public Worship. *Compel them to come in ...*'.[31]

As the Commonwealth *régime* spluttered towards collapse, a parliamentary Convention, broadly representative of Protestant opinion, which assembled

---

28 *News from Ireland* (London, 1650), sig. A2.
29 R. Armstrong, 'The Scots of Ireland and the English Republic, 1649–60', in D. Edwards (ed.), *The Scots in Early Stuart Ireland* (Manchester University Press, 2016), 251–78.
30 Cunningham, 'Lay Catholicism and Religious Policy in Cromwellian Ireland', *Journal of Ecclesiastical History* 64 (2013), 769–86, at 783–5.
31 'Epistle dedicatory' to the magistrates and people of Cork, dated 7 September 1658, in Joseph Eyres, *The Church-Sleeper Awakened* (London, 1659).

in Dublin in March 1660, called for a parish-based, tithe-supported, 'Learned and Orthodox Preaching Ministry' and renounced 'anabaptistical and other fanatic spirits'.[32] The Reformation of the 1650s was the most statist, and the most English, of those attempted in the mid-seventeenth century; it also failed the most resoundingly. The Catholic Church would take decades to recover its position, but even in 1658 it had proven possible to hold a Catholic synod in the western province of Tuam. Concerns expressed over mixed marriages, and marriages and baptisms conducted by Protestant clergy, reflected the fallout from recent turbulence, but also a rallying which would result in mass reconciliations of temporarily conforming Catholics in the years ahead.[33] For all the harsh measures against Catholic clergy, the Irish majority were not subjected to either the mass coercion or the imaginative conversion drives which successfully re-Catholicised parts of central Europe. The national church was not permanently re-modelled on Puritan lines, nor was space guaranteed for the conscientious godly. The Presbyterians incubated their church order within the state system and tightened their hold on the Scottish population of Ireland. The spiritual creativity of the decade spurred Protestant Ireland back towards an integrated, parish-based model with a settled ministry, one that could translate with relative ease into a restored church of prayer book and bishop.

The Restoration and the Protestant Churches

The swiftness and thoroughness with which the established religion was restored in 1660–1661 is striking: one of the first deeds of the parliament which assembled in May 1661 was to draft and despatch a declaration affirming that all subjects must 'conform to Church Government by Episcopacy, and to the Liturgy, as it is established by Law'.[34] It was a parliament graced with a full representation of bishops, the eight survivors complemented by new appointees, many of them (two archbishops and ten diocesans) consecrated together in St Patrick's cathedral, Dublin, on 27 January, most of them with steady past careers in the Irish church, usually back to the 1630s, as well as a more recent record of commitment to prayer book and episcopacy.[35] The filling up of the

---

32 A. Clarke, *Prelude to Restoration in Ireland* (Cambridge University Press, 1999), 250.
33 A. Forrestal, *Catholic Synods in Ireland, 1600–1690* (Dublin: FCP, 1998), 105–6; Corish, *Catholic Community*, 49–50.
34 *Journals of the House of Lords of the Kingdom of Ireland* (8 vols., Dublin, 1779–1800), i, 234–6.
35 J. McGuire, 'Policy and Patronage: The Appointment of Bishops 1660–61', in A. Ford, J. McGuire and K. Milne (eds.), *As by Law established: The Church of Ireland since the Reformation* (Dublin: The Lilliput Press, 1995), 112–19.

clerical body, not least at parish level, could mean the restoration of clergy-men displaced by Catholic control or ousted by Presbyterians during the war years. In other parishes it might mean reconciliation of ministers who had served in the church of the 1650s, in yet others it could mean recruitment of younger men, some of whom had already secured an underground episcopal ordination.[36] This last would be an unconditional requirement even for those who believed they had secured ordination already, perhaps by Presbyterian means. In Ulster that meant the displacement of around sixty ministers who had held parishes in the 1650s.[37] In the eyes of the new parliament and old church, pre-1641 legislation simply regained its effective force.

The need to uphold a true, public profession in the sight of God and before the world meant that, though their fortunes would vary in the decades ahead, for Catholics and nonconforming Protestants religious practice must, on the one hand, be moved as far as possible from the public gaze and, on the other, must not intrude the exercise of 'jurisdiction' in conflict with the tight nexus of state and canonical law. The legalised geography of the established church mandated a clerical presence in every corner of the island, though the Protestant population was clustered in some areas, almost absent in others, and disproportionately present in urban settings. A legal basis was created for a rationalisation of parishes, and Primate Bramhall was depicted drawing up a map of the Armagh diocese including possible locations for churches 'with more advantage to the Minister and People' not least in the light of the consequences of a 'long and destructive war'.[38] Of course the infrastructure problems were much deeper and older than that – for Bishop Taylor 'this very poor Church, ... groans under the Calamities and permanent effects of a War acted by Intervals about 400 years'[39] – and reform on this scale was not effected. But churches were rebuilt – seven in Dublin in the 1660s to 1680s – even if much less was done before the very end of the century towards the building of residences for parish clergy, despite an awareness that this lack contributed to clerical absence.[40] Plain within, for the most part, perhaps with painted wall texts, the tendency towards railed-in altars appears to have been

36 R. Armstrong, 'The Bishops of Ireland and the Beasts at Ephesus: Reconstruction, Conformity and the Presbyterian Knot 1660–2', in N. H. Keeble (ed.), 'Settling the peace of the church': 1662 Revisited (Oxford University Press, 2014), 114–43.

37 W. T. Latimer, A History of the Irish Presbyterians (2nd edn., Belfast: James Cleeland, 1902), 128–32.

38 F. R. Bolton, The Caroline Tradition of the Church of Ireland (London: SPCK, 1958), 206.

39 Jeremy Taylor, A Discourse of Confirmation ... (Dublin, 1663), epistle dedicatory.

40 W. Roulston, 'Accommodating Clergymen: Church of Ireland Ministers and their Houses in the North of Ireland, c.1600–1870', in T. C. Barnard and W. G. Neely (eds.), The Clergy of the Church of Ireland 1000–2000 (Dublin: FCP, 2006), 108.

becoming more apparent within the Restoration church, perhaps reflective of a growing frequency in the celebration of communion (monthly at least in some Dublin parishes) and growing numbers communicating. Sermons had not lost their importance. Edward Wetenhall (a future bishop of Cork) was of the view that it was possible 'to get people to Church twice in the day, and keep them there too, and have full congregations, if we so often preach diligently to them'. But he had decided views on what acceptable preaching involved, or did not involve, not least when practised by dissenters over-given to sermons which left them 'moved and wrought upon' but not necessarily well-instructed.[41] Wetenhall was committed to instruction through catechism, not least in terms of basic instruction for children, and published and distributed, free, a text with such an end in view. The rather more complex catechetical texts used by Presbyterians would lead to charges that they made too much use of 'hard works, ... and abstruse notions' neither necessary nor intelligible to ordinary believers, let alone their children.[42]

As for the instruction of established Church clergy, this was now, overwhelmingly, being undertaken at Trinity College, Dublin, undergoing a 'renaissance' from the 1660s, the eventual products including some of the energetic, reforming bishops active in the 1690s, the generation of William King and Nathaniel Foy.[43] The English-born provost, Narcissus Marsh (later archbishop of Dublin) not only sought to encourage an Irish-speaking ministry but worked with the polymath Robert Boyle to ensure publication of an Irish-language Bible, though the results on both fronts proved disappointing and for Marsh, in the longer term, disillusioning.[44] The Church of Ireland was clearly and increasingly an Irish church, for all that its adherents spoke of its religion as the faith of the 'Church of England' and for all the failure to engage with the majority Irish-speaking population.

But its monopoly on Protestantism in Ireland was gone for good. Outside Ulster, Protestant dissent was disparate, scattered and prone to leakage into the wider Protestant community gathered into the established church.

---

41 Bolton, *The Caroline Tradition*, 155, 173–5, 233–4; R. Gillespie, *Devoted People: Belief and Religion in Early Modern Ireland* (Manchester University Press, 1997), 93, 97–8; R. Gillespie, 'The Reformed Preacher: Irish Protestant Preaching, 1660–1700', in A. J. Fletcher and R. Gillespie (eds.), *Irish Preaching, 700–1700* (Dublin: FCP, 2001), 139.

42 I. Green, '"The necessary knowledge of the principles of religion": Catechisms and Catechizing in Ireland, c.1560–1700', in Ford *et al.* (eds.), *As by Law Established*, 77–9; William King, *A Discourse Concerning the Inventions of Men in the Worship of God* (Dublin, 1694), 83.

43 T. C. Barnard, '"Almoners of providence": The Clergy, 1647 to c.1780', in Barnard and Neely (eds.), *Clergy of the Church of Ireland*, 89.

44 T. C. Barnard, 'Protestants and the Irish Language, c. 1675–1725', *Journal of Ecclesiastical History*, 44 (1993), 243–72.

Baptists remained exclusive in their membership, a safeguard given that powers of decision-making rested with the membership of a congregation as a whole. But in practice distinctions could be blurred between Independents and Presbyterians who, outside Ulster, were both mostly of English origin. Cooperation could extend to shared or alternating ministers, joint worship or eventual merger. Even the more robust Ulster Presbyterian organisation expressed openness to working with both Presbyterians and Congregationalists scattered in urban congregations in Munster and Leinster.[45] Such openness was not extended to Quakers. From an unconstrained movement in the 1650s, by the later decades of the century they had generated a tightly knit organisation. Their spread and numbers are more readily known: with perhaps 3,000 members by century's end, the number of meetings had grown from around thirty in 1660 to over fifty, with a particular concentration in Leinster. With no formal ministry, local meetings provided a base from which delegates were sent to provincial and, twice a year, national meetings. Separate, parallel, meetings of delegates were held for men and for women; if the former held overall authority, including over forms of worship or standards of behaviour, the women's meetings also monitored the standards, behaviour and sometimes the decisions of members, notably over marriage. Quakers were determined to maintain their distinctive testimony to truth, and in many ways their repudiation of the ways of the wider society, whether in trading practices or a disavowal of 'gay apparel'.[46]

Presbyterian ministers in Ulster had consulted together as they pondered their position in 1660–1661, had sought means to retain their parishes while avoiding the taint of prayer-book worship or re-ordination, and departed, almost to a man, with a ready-made means to sustain a separate organisation and a broad potential support among the Scottish Protestant population. Even so, the 1660s were a bruising decade. The records of Templepatrick congregation record the celebration of communion in June 1670 after a break of ten years on account of 'the p[er]section of the prelates'. But by the following decade the five regional Presbyteries were again operational, and the decision to pursue the writing of a 'history of the church of Ireland' drawn from their own records is a telling indication of a community confident not only in its past but in its future. If the most significant outcome of the initiative was the 'True narrative' written by Patrick Adair, a detailed and influential

45 R. L. Greaves, *God's Other Children: Protestant Nonconformists and the Emergence of Denominational Churches in Ireland, 1660–1700* (Stanford, CA: Stanford University Press, 1997) 161–2, 171, 201–4, 260.

46 Greaves, *God's Other Children*, 270, 288–9, 294–5, 318–24.

account of Presbyterian fortunes from the 1620s, one other unpublished history, by Andrew Stewart of Donaghadee, attempted to claim Presbyterian roots in Ireland back to the church of St Patrick.[47] Presbyteries were clear, by the 1670s, that church discipline, whether exercised within the local congregation or by wider church bodies, needed to be re-introduced as a public measure, but caution needed to be exercised, perhaps with regard to flocks grown unaccustomed to such approaches, certainly with regard to civil and established church authorities. Structures mattered to Presbyterians. It was not just that they provided mechanisms to allow the church to endure and expand, though they did: Presbyterians continued to respect a parish-bounded system, but lacked the resources to operate one universally; instead they stitched new parishes into a patchwork, as Presbyteries responded to local requests. They mattered, too, as vehicles for spiritual formation. It was in the 'exercise' at Presbytery meetings that recruits to the ministry were put through their paces, and where seasoned ministers, too, monitored one another's sermons, and one another's conduct. This sociable spirituality, Patrick Adair claimed, had endured even when formal arrangements could not be maintained, in private encouragement, edification and advice. It was a pattern believed to be biblical in origin and spiritually effective in practice, for 'a society of godly ministers may expect more assistance and light than a single person'.[48]

Presbyterian practice was not, as with other dissenting Protestants, to restrict narrowly membership, and participation could be extensive, not least at the communion season, when several parishes could flock together for several days of preaching and prayer culminating in a celebration of the Lord's Supper. But this sat alongside a commitment to a Calvinist theology of election and conversionist spirituality – preaching, the sacraments, even church discipline, were considered 'converting ordinances'. None should make their outward religious practices a plea for salvation. If 'the work of conversion is ordinarily of persons within the visible church' yet religious practice, public and private, was but 'a groundless assurance that all is well and will be well' without a work of grace, a 'renewing of your mind' and a 'converting of the heart'.[49] One Armagh Presbyterian who

---

47 Both texts are published in Adair and Stewart, *Presbyterian History in Ireland: Two Seventeenth-Century Narratives*.
48 R. Armstrong, 'The Irish Alternative: Scottish and English Presbyterianism in Ireland', in R. Armstrong and T. Ó hAnnracháin (eds.), *Insular Christianity: Alternative Models of the Church in Britain and Ireland, 1570–1700* (Manchester University Press, 2013), 216, 217–18, 219, 221.
49 Armstrong, 'The Irish Alternative', 220–2; James Alexander Sermon Book (unpaginated), sermons dated August–September 1685, Presbyterian Historical Society, Belfast.

wrote her own 'account of the Lord's dealing with me' recorded a very personal response on the 'day never to be forgotten' when 'my heart did warm' and 'I embraced Jesus Christ for my Saviour upon his own terms, to be my king, priest and prophet. I gave myself away to him to be his for ever' after prolonged torment of soul and a direct encounter with scripture promises. Yet inner testimony was matched with outer profession.[50] James Alexander's Donegal flock were warned, in a December sermon, against observing saints' days, and above all Christmas: 'an old heathenish day, and an old popish day; but an old Christian day it is not'. They 'should eat your meat and work your work as on other days; but I tell you, your complying in these things will bring the vengeance of God upon you'. So doing, of course, set them clearly apart from the established church as well as the Catholic population. And, indeed, Presbyterian discourse presented themselves as the true Protestants, free from the dangers attending the establishment – for 'your prelacy is the way of Rome', and the 'service book is but the mass book a little purged'.[51]

The Restoration and the Catholic Church

The significance of the relatively long reign of Charles II and the relative space offered for Catholic religious life, during most of its duration, can too easily be overlooked. The process of rebuilding a functioning Catholic Church was slow and painful, but possible. If there was no legislative relief for Catholics, nor were there new penal laws, and proposals raised in the Dublin Commons to enact for Ireland as the fiercer English penal legislation ran aground.[52] Repression could be severe, but was intermittent. Clampdowns often followed the contours of court politics, or English politics more widely. From 1673 the principal targets of government proclamations tended to be regular clergy (members of religious orders) and, more especially, any clergy exercising jurisdiction, from bishops downwards, a pattern which would receive legislative force in 1697. Even that most notorious instance, the judicial killing of Oliver Plunkett, archbishop of Armagh in 1681, was principally determined by the course of the English 'popish' plot, and was preceded by a failed trial

---

50 W. K. Tweedie (ed.), *Select Biographies* (2 vols., Edinburgh: Wodrow Society, 1845–7), ii, 483–4. The author of this testimony did not record her name, only that of her husband, John Goodale.

51 James Alexander Sermon Book, sermons dated December 1685 and January 1686, Presbyterian Historical Society, Belfast.

52 R. P. Mahaffy (ed.), *Calendar of the State Papers relating to Ireland, 1663–1665* (London: HMSO, 1907), 65–6.

in Dundalk; the plot produced no executions in Ireland.[53] More constant were the lack of resources, human and material, which dogged Catholic efforts, and were at least partly responsible for a persistent undercurrent of internal dispute.

Indeed the institutional church can seem wracked with tensions. In the early 1660s a prolonged and bitter dispute surrounded a 'Remonstrance' intended to address the vexed question of Catholic loyalties by pledging obedience to the king 'notwithstanding any pretension of the pope' and rejecting the right of any external power to 'free, discharge or absolve' Catholics from their allegiance. Rome frowned on it, clerics wrestled with it, but for the most part rejected it, and Ormond, now returned to the office of lord lieutenant, saw in it an opportunity for division in Catholic ranks.[54] Meanwhile, reports to the internuncio in Flanders, or to Rome, admittedly of their nature likely to draw attention to problems, highlighted less high-minded faction and dispute within dioceses, fuelling accusations of incapacity, immorality and injustice directed against priests and more especially those in positions of authority.[55] Such conflict was real, and damaging. But the remonstrance only ever gained limited traction among clerics, and though no alternative formulation proved more acceptable, nor was there an enduring polarisation within clerical ranks.[56] Thereafter successive synods could pledge parish prayers for the king, and indeed for his ministers or the viceroy, and Archbishop Plunkett insisted on his detachment from 'political or temporal matters'[57] in circumstances where the civil power proved less intrusive in the inner working of the church than would be the case where it professed Catholicism.

Many of the troubles on the ground were the long-drawn-out consequences of the collapse of the 1650s. Rome had proven ready to appoint a slate of vicars apostolic as early as 1657, but it was only in the years between 1669 and 1671 that a new generation of bishops was provided. The Restoration-era episcopate has not been subjected to the same analysis as its pre-war counterpart, but it is telling that only four bishops out

---

53 S. J. Connolly, *Religion, Law and Power: The Making of Protestant Ireland 1660–1760* (Oxford: Clarendon Press, 1992), 22–4, 30–1, 268–70. Plunkett's rival Peter Talbot, archbishop of Dublin, perished in prison in November 1680.

54 A. Creighton, 'The Remonstrance of December 1661 and Catholic politics in Restoration Ireland', *Irish Historical Studies* 34 (2004), 16–41 (quoted at 29).

55 For examples, see J. Kelly, 'The Catholic Church in the Diocese of Ardagh, 1650–1870', in R. Gillespie and G. Moran (eds.), *Longford: Essays in County History* (Dublin: The Lilliput Press, 1991), 68–71; J. Kelly, 'The Formation of the Modern Catholic Church in the Diocese of Kilmore, 1580–1880', in R. Gillespie (ed.), *Cavan: Essays on the History of an Irish County* (Blackrock, Co. Dublin: Irish Academic Press, 1995), 120–3.

56 Creighton, 'Remonstrance', 40 reckons that by 1670 only four or five clerical subscribers remained in Ireland, under pressure from the hierarchy.

57 Forrestal, *Catholic Synods in Ireland*, 100–3 (quoted at 103).

of fourteen were regular clergy, and that only three are known to have had previously exercised pastoral care in Ireland.[58] They encountered conditions where lines of authority had necessarily become blurred, perhaps for decades; even the determined Oliver Plunkett would have to seek advice as to what constituted legally correct authority in conditions where chapters had collapsed or shrunk to one survivor.[59] They faced a crisis in resources for the support of clergy, which would lead some bishops to call for fewer, rather than more, priests. Prioritising settled pastors so as to ensure some coverage of ministry to the flock at large probably determined the greater readiness to reduce the role of regular clergy within the parish system, and rein in their activities under greater episcopal oversight, which has been reckoned a feature of synods held after 1658, as opposed to those earlier in the century.[60] Of course the state remained tender towards any exercise of 'jurisdiction'. In Waterford, Bishop John Brenan did not hold a court; he 'adjudicates on the disputes of his people ... but privately'.[61] Peter Talbot, archbishop of Dublin, fell foul of accusations that he had pressed matters all the way to the excommunication of a Dominican friar, John Byrne. He was reckoned to have done so because of Byrne's 'indiscretion', adding that, 'not content to travel up and down the country in his monastic habit, [he] ceases not to blow his horn to assemble the people to his chapel ... to mass and sermons'.[62]

A parish-centred approach offered the prospect of regularity – regular reception of sacraments, regularity of instruction, regulation of pastoral clergy – and thereby the opportunity to serve the spiritual wellbeing not only of individuals but of each individual community. If the intention to secure a fixed place for parochial mass was only translated into a built 'mass-house' in parts of Ireland,[63] the Catholic parish should be reckoned more than merely a church-with-hinterland; burial sites or holy wells, or the intangible bonds around patron saints, pilgrimage occasions or holy days, were alternative means of enabling a communal faith. Where numbers of priests were too few to serve all of the older parishes, mergers in some instances combined, rather

---

58 Millett, *Survival and Reorganization*, 13, 22–3, 43.
59 *The Letters of Saint Oliver Plunkett*, ed. John Hanly (Dublin: Dolmen Press, 1979), 98, 150, 189–90, 218–19.
60 Forrestal, *Catholic Synods in Ireland*, 94–8.
61 *A Bishop of the Penal Times: being Letters and Reports of John Brenan, Bishop of Waterford (1671–93) and Archbishop of Cashel (1677–93)*, ed. P. Power (Cork University Press, 1932) 65 (1678).
62 W. P. Burke (ed.), *The Irish Priests in the Penal Times* (Waterford: N. Harvey & Co., 1914), 33 (1672).
63 Corish, *Catholic Community*, 58, 96; Forrestal, *Catholic Synods*, 114–15, 177–9.

than redrew, older units.[64] Indeed it can be helpful to think of co-existing 'sub-cultures' even within parish-level Catholicism, some harking back to traditional rites fixed to sacred sites, others infused with the 'reformed' Catholicism of printed literature or the group solidarity of sodalities or confraternities, but which could be bound together as sacramental community.[65] Even in impoverished northern dioceses most priests had possession of silver chalices and 'decent vestments' with which to celebrate the Eucharist.[66]

Bishop Brenan of Waterford and Lismore, in 1678, reported positively on a 'tenacious' flock and a diligent parish priesthood, only one among thirty-two of whom had not been educated abroad. Under the supervision of rural deans, they met in monthly conferences to discuss 'cases of conscience' and allow 'younger priests give a short exhortation for their own training and exercise' and make 'spiritual exercises before entering on the care of souls'.[67] Practised clergy could better instruct the laity. Catechesis could encompass instruction of children, but could also include varying forms of oral instruction offered to the congregation gathered for mass. Printed catechisms, which priests could draw upon, circulated, in Latin, English and Irish. Irish-language catechisms produced in the early seventeenth century are better known than their successors, but the attraction of Anthony Gearnon's *Parrthas an Anma* ('Paradise of the soul'), printed at Louvain in 1645, doubtless lay in its combination of a lengthy question-and-answer catechism with a collection of translated prayers, both presented with admirable clarity, with the latter part being repeatedly copied into manuscript into the nineteenth century. Bishop Wadding of Ferns distributed dozens of small devotional and instructional works, written in, or translated into, English, to 'relations, friends, benefactors, poor gentry and widows, children etc.' across several decades. His own inclination towards French Jesuit and Salesian spirituality has been detected, and indeed Francis de Sales's *Introduction to the devout life* was one of the continental spiritual works translated into Irish, probably in the 1670s. Perhaps the most telling production in Irish, though, was the *Lucerna fidelium / Lóchrann na gCreidmheach* (1676) of Froinsias Ó Maolmhuaidh (Francis O'Molloy), printed in Rome, and sent back to Ireland as Propaganda with returning missioners. Where

---

64 P. J. Duffy, 'The Shape of the Parish', in E. FitzPatrick and R. Gillespie (eds.), *The Parish in Medieval and Early Modern Ireland* (Dublin: FCP, 2006), 37–9.

65 R. Gillespie, 'Catholic Religious Cultures in the Diocese of Dublin, 1614–97', in J. Kelly and D. Keogh (eds.), *History of the Catholic Diocese of Dublin* (Dublin: FCP, 2000), 127–43.

66 Forrestal, *Catholic Synods*, 179.

67 *A bishop of the Penal Times*, ed. Power, 62–4; compare Forrestal, *Catholic Synods*, 89.

its catechetical section recycled Gearnon, its two dialogue sections, challenging Protestant teaching, drew upon French luminaries Jacques-Bénigne Bossuet and François Véron.[68]

It was crucial, especially in disordered times, that Irish Catholicism provided multiple means for the inclusion of the faithful within the sacred bounds of the church, and combined local resources with those of the church international. Not least was this the case with the paths pursued by the regular orders. For the exiled abbess of the Poor Clares of Galway, the Franciscan rule 'which Christ dictated to Saint Francis' and from which her own order's derived, was 'so perfect ... that those who observe it find a sure place in heaven'. She could only lament that, for all the 'holy people' in the convents of the Spain to which she fled in 1653, 'none of these convents keep to the strict observance of fasting, silence and poverty, and such other austerities as are practised in the convents of Ireland'.[69] When the two orders of Dominicans and Franciscans clashed over their rights to collect alms across much of Ulster, the latter were able to mobilise parish-level support, with agents nominated at 'public mass' to lay the Franciscan case before the primate, claiming that Dominican demands left 'the poor commonalty ... not able to maintain themselves or their usual, always and accustomed clergy, both secular, and Franciscan friars' causing 'incessant troubles, confusions and dangers amongst themselves and also misrespects before the British nation'.[70] The Jesuit Richard Archdekin spent most of his life in the Spanish Netherlands. His *Treatise of miracles* considered a world where scripture was prone 'to innumerable false interpretations' and the fathers or councils 'abused', but where 'that party which is approved by a true miracle is approved by a testimony which proceedeth from God alone'. The miracles he recounted were not those of a saint of primitive times, but of St Francis Xavier, canonised in 1622. If his particular focus were on the healings that surrounded the 'parcel of the right arm' in the Jesuit church at Mechlin, he blended these with news of cures wrought in Dublin and Waterford, and reported from Kilkenny and New Ross.[71]

---

68 Green, ' "The necessary knowledge of the principles of religion" ', 70–1, 82; C. Giblin, 'The Contribution of Irish Franciscans on the Continent in the Seventeenth Century', in M. Maher (ed.), *Irish Spirituality* (Dublin: Veritas Publications, 1981), 96–9; Corish, *Catholic Community*, 63–4.
69 *Recollections of an Irish Poor Clare in the Seventeenth Century: Mother Mary Bonaventure, Third Abbess of Galway, 1647–1650*, ed. C. O'Brien O.F.M. (Galway: Poor Clares, 1993), 17–18.
70 P. J. Campbell, 'The Franciscan Petition Lists: Diocese of Armagh, 1670–1', *Seanchas Ardmhacha*, 15 (1992–1993), 192.
71 Richard Archdekin, *A Treatise of Miracles* (Louvain, 1667), 'Preface' and 9, 90–3, 105–6.

Reign of James II

The short reign of the new Catholic king, James II, had some of the characteristics of an accelerated re-run of 1640s, ending with war on a comparable scale, if mercifully briefer. As Catholics regained some position within the military, and civil administration, so Catholic worship became more open, Catholic clergy more visible, with moves afoot to build or purchase churches or religious houses even in Dublin by 1686. In 1687 the English Declaration of Indulgence was reissued in Ireland, formalising a greater freedom of religious practice for Protestant dissenters as well as Catholics. Catholic bishops received royal pensions, and were reported as determined to 'openly own and exercise their Episcopal Ecclesiastical Jurisdiction'. Catholic worship was now entrenched at the heart of governance, the chapel of Dublin Castle.[72] The established church was not overturned, any more than in James's other kingdoms, though anxieties mounted as key vacancies remained unfilled and their revenue accrued to the crown – thus indirectly supporting Catholic clergy – and not least when the conversion of the Dean of Derry, Peter Manby, did not prevent his retaining his post, and its income. Not the least important result of that incident was the response in print from that up-and-coming clergyman, William King, his defence of the authority and freedom of a national church, from the claims of Rome, crown or Canterbury, or indeed nonconformists who had spurned their 'lawful governors', signalling the emergence of the doughtiest champion of church interests of the post-war decades.[73]

In the autumn of 1688, James was toppled from his two British thrones; the following spring would see him in Ireland, presiding over a predominantly Catholic parliament in Dublin. A pamphlet would later purport to print an 'Address or Memorial' from Catholic bishops and provincials, headed by Patrick Russell, archbishop of Dublin, which urged on the king not only a repeal of 'penal laws' but also that all levels of Catholic clergy 'be restored to their livings, churches and full exercise of their ecclesiastical jurisdiction', a replication of the position adopted in the 1640s.[74] A bill to this effect appears to have been introduced into the Commons. But royal sponsorship, partly with an eye to reactions in the other kingdoms, and partly it would seem

---

72 T. Harris, *Revolution: The Great Crisis of the British Monarchy, 1685–1720* (London: Allen Lane, 2006), 119; Greaves, *God's Other Children*, 138–9.
73 P. O'Regan, *Archbishop William King of Dublin (1650–1729) and the Constitution in Church and State* (Dublin: FCP, 2000), 16–18.
74 *An Address given in to the Late king James by the Titular Archbishop of Dublin … now Publish'd with Reflections …*(London, 1690).

grounded in James's own conviction, ensured the enactment instead of a remarkable piece of legislation not only removing all penalties imposed on the basis of religion, but permitting all Christian churches to worship according to their own rites.[75] Further legislation provided that individuals pay their tithes to clergy of their own profession. Still the established church remained established. Its bishops had been summoned to James's parliament, though only four attended. Its property remained secure, including the revenues of its bishops, though one contemporary Jacobite historian, whilst regarding this outcome as 'irreligious' reckoned it temporary, only intended 'to afford a decent livelihood to heretical prelates during their life'. On that reading a long game would see Catholicism restored without a frontal assault on the Protestant establishment, which would fade into an ever-more ghostly existence. Its spokesmen claimed that in the meantime churches were seized or vandalised, after 1690 in open disregard of a royal proclamation. Not that James had not given some countenance to such activities, even if he did not authorise them, when he attended mass in Christ Church cathedral in Dublin, newly restored for Catholic worship.[76]

Yet Christ Church would prove a Trojan Horse. For all that he was a Catholic, James was also a Stuart, and half a Bourbon. It was reported that his unhappiness with the proposed legislation for a more far-reaching establishment of the Catholic religion was partly due to the threat it posed to his own prerogative powers. The act awarding tithes to Catholic clergy indicated that those would be deemed 'Catholic' bishops or deans who were so recognised by the king. In 1685 James had been conceded the right to nomination of Catholic bishops by Innocent XI. Now, in Dublin, some senior Catholic churchmen detected a determination to intrude the crown into the process of appointment more widely, perhaps emulating the wider powers exercised by the French king, Louis XIV. The chapter at Christ Church was reported to be enduring a 'subtle schism' around the question of royal or papal appointment. The charge appears in a letter recounting conditions by 1690, likely written by Michael Moore, vicar-general of Dublin, and nominee as provost of Trinity College, which lamented 'the wounds which this church has received during the short time in which his majesty has been in this country'.[77]

---

75 J. Bergin and A. Lyall (eds.), *The Acts of James II's Irish Parliament of 1689* (Dublin: Irish Manuscripts Commission, 2016), 19–21; Harris, *Revolution*, 441.
76 J. T. Gilbert (ed.), *A Jacobite Narrative of the War in Ireland* (Dublin: J. Dollard, 1892), 69; J. G. Simms, *Jacobite Ireland 1685–91* (London Routledge and Kegan Paul, 1969), 88–9.
77 L. Chambers, *Michael Moore c.1639–1726* (Dublin: FCP, 2005), 53–8; Simms, *Jacobite Ireland*, 89; Harris, *Revolution*, 441; *A Bishop of Penal Times*, ed. Power, 97–8.

By then open war had engulfed Ireland. Over half of Presbyterian ministers were reckoned to have departed for Scotland, where they made some attempt to retain their own distinct organisation; of those who remained, several clustered into the besieged city of Derry, where worship in the cathedral was shared with conformists in a short-lived gesture of Protestant solidarity. Presbyterian consciences squirmed less than those of at least some conformists at the prospect of resisting James, or transferring allegiance to the newly proclaimed monarchs, William III and Mary. Approaches had been made before the end of 1688, and in the spring of 1689 Presbyterian ministers joined in rallying military resistance in Ulster to James's *régime*. A Presbyterian delegation hastened to the newly-landed William in Carrickfergus in June 1690, this time winning from him a promise to restore and increase the *regium donum*, a royal grant promised ministers by Charles II in 1672, but hardly ever paid; after some delays, William proved himself a more generous and more consistent benefactor.[78]

The short reign of James II demonstrated – once again – the Catholic Church's capacity to step from the shadows towards 'the splendour of the true religion' which it was believed James was ready to promote.[79] In its aftermath, a more formidable battery of anti-Catholic legislation would be imposed by a newly-empowered Dublin parliament, though in the longer term directed more at the exclusion of Catholics from economic and political power, than at the destruction of Catholic religious practice. It witnessed, again, the tensions which public religion brought between Catholic spiritual and temporal power, even more so than in the Confederate era, with an interventionist Catholic king intruding into church questions left to the purview of local or distant Roman interests for decades, and with his own particular agenda for Catholic revival, which cut across pleas for greater rapidity in consolidating a Catholic order in Ireland which emanated from churchmen as well as lawyers or politicians. An again-beleaguered Protestant establishment weathered this storm, too, with some renewed energy for reform and much determination against a resurgent Presbyterianism. Again, the time of troubles seemed to have bolstered that community most, though it did not secure the legal toleration accorded to

---

78 K. Middleton, 'Religious Revolution and Social Crisis in Southwest Scotland and Ulster, 1687–1714', unpublished PhD dissertation, Trinity College Dublin (2010), 30–1, 39; Greaves, *God's Other Children*, 141–3, 146–7.
79 *A Bishop of penal times*, ed. Power, 88.

English nonconformists in 1689, let alone the establishment status gained by their co-religionists in Scotland in 1690. Its numbers and geographical reach would expand significantly with mass Scottish migration in the 1690s. Its memory of the war years bolstered its self-understanding as not merely part of a wider Protestant tradition in Ireland, but its most truly Protestant part, in its principles of civil liberty as well as in a religion staunch against superstition and tyranny.

Conclusion

The five decades between 1641 and 1691 had seen repeated contests over the provision of a 'public profession' of religion for Ireland. All the principal religious groups in Ireland insisted that close cooperation with civil authority was their desired goal, but that the freedom to attend to the spiritual obligations imposed on their own consciences came first. Yet all could only hope to attain the fullness of their ambitions in favourable political settings. The Tridentine agenda required a self-regulating church, which could encapsulate moral and theological authority and a universal network of parish-level sacramental ministry; it could achieve them only by escaping the confines imposed by a Protestant state. Confederate politicians, and later James II and his circle, as well as supportive churchmen, saw the need for a church that could recognise how it was entwined with the laws and institutions of a temporal kingdom which was also a vehicle of the divine work in the world, and one where a politic space for Protestants might win their reintegration to a Catholic order in due course.[80] Protestant Episcopalians twice fell back upon the crown, and more especially upon amenable political changes in London, to restore their position as the church by law established. But they had resources of their own. One was a closely reasoned and adaptable case for themselves as the embodiment of the church universal ('Catholic') in Ireland. Another was the sustenance of integrated parish communities of the worshipping faithful, not universally present, perhaps, but embedded in their local settings. Presbyterians had fallen furthest short of their hope to transform

---

80 Compare I. W. S. Campbell, 'John Lynch and Renaissance Humanism in Stuart Ireland: Catholic Intellectuals, Protestant Noblemen, and the Irish *Respublica*', *Éire-Ireland*, 45 (2010), 27–40; M. R. F. Williams, 'Between King, Faith and Reason: Father Peter Talbot (SJ) and Catholic Royalist Thought in Exile', *English Historical Review*, 127 (2012), 1063–99.

the church of St Patrick back to an apostolic purity in their own image. They were quicker to recognise, and adapt to, the fact that they relied on the allegiance of the 'meaner' or at best middling people and upon those of Scottish origin. But their numbers and their organisation ensured that they, too, would prove a lasting feature of the Irish religious landscape.

10

Wars of Religion, 1641–1691

JOHN JEREMIAH CRONIN AND PÁDRAIG LENIHAN

This chapter will track four themes across the Confederate and Cromwellian Wars (1641–1653) on the one hand and the Williamite Wars (1689–1691) on the other. Three of these concern 'native', 'settler' and 'English' armies. The final theme will contrast the impact of the two wars on the civilian population. The Confederate and Cromwellian Wars were exceptionally complex because they were at once part of 'an interlocking set of conflicts' engulfing three kingdoms while at the same time Ireland occupied an 'anomalous position' within the Stuart composite state, being 'part kingdom, part colony'.[1] The Williamite Wars, too, were both civil wars and ethnic conflicts in which religion supplied the main marker of national difference. The wars therefore demand a skeletal narrative framework on which to hang those four themes.

The rising that began in October 1641 was a stillborn coup that triggered civil war between Charles I and most members of the English parliament (later joined by Scottish Covenanters) who claimed to suspect him of complicity in the rising. While Britain was torn apart by civil war, the Confederate Catholics were able to hold about two-thirds of Ireland and fight a war characterised by few battles, many sieges and much cavalry-led pillaging and raiding, in the manner of a late-medieval *chevauchée*. After the founding of the Confederate Catholics in late summer 1642 military actions were fought in and around four Protestant zones of 'control' and 'disruption'.[2] Moving from north to south, these were east Ulster (the main actions were at Charlemont in August 1644 and Benburb on 5 June 1646) and west Ulster–north Connacht (Clones on 13 June 1643, Sligo in July 1645 and on 31 October 1645 respectively and Roscommon from 29 June to 8 July 1646).

---

1 J. Ohlmeyer, 'The Wars of the Three Kingdoms', *History Today* 48 (1998), 16. T. Bartlett, *The Academy of Warre: Military Affairs in Ireland 1600 to 1800: The O'Donnell Lecture 2002* (Dublin: National University of Ireland, 2002), 23.
2 R. Armstrong, *Protestant War: The 'British' of Ireland and the Wars of the Three Kingdoms* (Manchester University Press, 2005), 35.

The third pocket comprised Dublin and its satellite garrisons spread across the medieval Pale (Rathconnell on 7 February 1643, Thomas Preston's and Owen Roe O'Neill's siege of Dublin in November 1646 and Dungan's Hill on 4 August 1647). Here the royalist writ of James Butler, twelfth earl and later marquis of Ormond, ran until he surrendered his command to the English parliament in 1647. The fourth enclave was a tongue of territory in Munster that encompassed the zone of heaviest Protestant settlement.[3] The base of the tongue ran along the coastline from Bandon to Youghal, while its northern tip almost touched County Limerick (Liscarroll on 3 September 1642, Cloghlea on 4 June 1643, Youghal from June–August 1645, Cashel on 14 September 1647 and Knocknanuss on 13 November 1647). A few operations took place outside those zones, like the battle of Ross County Wexford (18 March 1643), the siege of Duncannon in Waterford harbour (January–March 1645) and the siege of Bunratty (April–July 1646), near the Shannon estuary, which were dictated, directly or indirectly, by the naval operations of the English parliament.

The Confederate Catholics had been set up to counter immediate military threats and negotiate a settlement with Charles I. By January 1649 they had signed a definitive peace with the royalists, won significant concessions and voluntarily disbanded. But to argue that the Confederates were thereby successful would be to ignore the catastrophe that followed. Capitalising on the stupefied reaction to the execution of Charles I, Ormond cobbled together a royalist coalition of Catholics and disaffected parliamentarians and covenanters. Ormond was more skilled in diplomacy and political intrigue than military command and his siege camp at Rathmines, near Dublin, was overrun on 2 August 1649 in 'the most important battle of the Cromwellian conquest'.[4] Less than a fortnight later Oliver Cromwell, the future lord protector, had a secure port in which to disembark. By the time Cromwell returned to England in May 1650, leaving his son in-law Henry Ireton in charge, a series of sieges, most notoriously at Drogheda, had apparently secured the south Leinster and east Munster heartlands of the Confederate Catholics together with the abutting Protestant enclaves in Munster and the Pale.

Later in 1650 Charles II repudiated his alliance with Irish Catholics in return for Scottish support, Ormond fled Ireland and other Protestant royalists, who had not already done so, changed sides. According to a contemporary

---

3 N Canny, *Making Ireland British, 1580–1650* (Oxford University Press, 2001), 336–7.
4 J. Scott Wheeler, *Cromwell in Ireland* (Dublin: Gill and Macmillan, 1999), 79.

observer, the war 'will end where it did begin, betwixt the English Protestant and the Irish Papist'.[5] The climax of that war came in the summer and autumn of 1651 when Henry Ireton sat before Limerick. An attempt to break the siege was held off at Knockbrack on 26 July of that summer in north-west County Cork, one of only two battles in the Cromwellian conquest (the other was at Scariffhollis near Letterkenny, County Donegal, on 21 June 1650).[6] The war would drag on until 1653, when the last scattered pockets of resistance were mopped up.

In contrast to 1641, when an attempted Irish coup provoked a war in England, the Williamite War (1689–1691) in Ireland began after a coup in England. This war was shorter than the Confederate and Cromwellian Wars but more intense. The Irish Catholic *élite* owned much less land than a generation before and so enjoyed less of that wealth and seigneurial status so helpful for recruiting, mobilising and leading their subalterns. Yet they enjoyed some clear advantages. Louis XIV of France supported them with money, specialist officers, provisions, munitions and even troops. Whereas the Confederate Catholics had been riven by debates over how far to trust the Stuarts, now the Jacobites were all fighting for the *rí ceart* (true king) and their quarrels were no more than the recriminations one would expect in any losing cause.[7]

The 'Glorious Revolution' of 1688, as the English *coup d'état* was known, was a pre-emptive strike by William the stadholder of the United Provinces to depose James II lest he side with Louis XIV in the looming War of the Grand Alliance. Anxious to foment a diversionary war, Louis sent James to Ireland in March 1689 where Richard Talbot, earl of Tyrconnell, had managed to hold three of Ireland's four provinces for his king.[8] Regional militias, known as Protestant Associations, controlled the fourth, Ulster. Initially, the war was fought in north Connacht and Ulster where the Jacobites under Count Von Rosen and Richard Hamilton routed the Associations' forces, driving them behind the walls of Derry and into a pocket around Enniskillen in County Fermanagh. The Irish could not capture Derry, which was relieved on 28 July 1689, and three days later the Enniskillen men annihilated a Jacobite army at Newtownbutler in County Fermanagh. Frederick Herman, first duke of Schomberg – until recently a marshal of France – was sent in August 1689 with a large army to

---

5 Cited in P. Lenihan, *Consolidating Conquest: Ireland 1603–1727* (Harlow: Pearson Longman, 2008), 131.

6 Wheeler, *Cromwell in Ireland*, 217.

7 B. Ó Buachalla, *Dánta Aodhagáin Uí Rathaille: Reassessments* (Dublin: Irish Texts Society, 2004), 33.

8 H. Murtagh, 'The Williamite War 1689–91', *History Ireland*, 1 (1993), 39–41.

strike a knockout blow to the tottering Jacobite regime.[9] He penetrated no further south than Dundalk before withdrawing into winter quarters in Ulster.[10]

William III came to Ireland to take personal command of a reinforced army, marched south and successfully forced battle on James at the Boyne (1 July 1690), thereby winning Leinster and east Munster. But he failed to cross the Shannon at Limerick, while another Williamite force under James Douglas stalled before Athlone (July–August 1690). William then departed for the main cockpit of the war in the Spanish Netherlands, leaving his army under the command of Godard van Reede van Ginkel. The Jacobites had ensured that war would drag on but this success was tempered by the loss of Cork and Kinsale in September 1690.[11] In the last campaigning season, that of 1691, Ginkel took Athlone, breaking the Shannon line (30 June), and twelve days later decisively defeated the Irish field army at Aughrim (12 July 1691). The surviving Jacobite garrisons of Sligo and Limerick finally capitulated in September.[12]

Neither war had a foregone conclusion. Lacking a 'grand strategy', the Confederate Catholics did not conquer all Ireland, or even the Munster enclave and the Pale, in the mid-1640s while the English parliament was still preoccupied with fighting Charles I. This might just have made any eventual parliamentary re-conquest so costly as to force a mediated post-war settlement.[13] Or what if James had taken Derry? He would have used Ireland as a base whence to invade Scotland and the war would have shifted there, with incalculable consequences for William's still fragile and unpopular administration.

Actual as opposed to 'what if' outcomes have political as well as military explanations, but we argue that specifically military shortcomings and advantages help explain the ultimate failure or success of native, settler and English armies. One must therefore weigh military capability, contingency and consequence.

Native Armies

Of course the categories of native, settler and English are not watertight. For example, many of the rank and file in 'native' armies were Gaelic Scots

9 M. Glozier, *Marshal Schomberg 1615–1690: 'The Ablest Soldier of his Age'* (Brighton: Sussex Academic Press, 2005), vii.

10 J. G. Simms, *Jacobite Ireland* (new edn., Dublin: Fourt Courts Press [hereafter FCP], 2000), 56–122.

11 D. Ó Murchadha, 'The Siege of Cork in 1690', *Journal of the Cork Historical and Archaeological Society*, 95 (1990), 12.

12 J. Childs, *The Williamite Wars in Ireland* (London: Hambledon Press, 2007), 342, 362–3, 383–5.

13 J. Ohlmeyer, 'A Failed Revolution? The Irish Confederate War in Its European Context', *History Ireland*, 3 (1995), 25–6.

(Dungan's Hill and Knocknanuss), English (Drogheda) or French and German (the Boyne). Nor does the 1649 siege of Derry, which brought Protestant royalists and Protestant Parliamentarians into conflict, fit such categories.[14] That said, 'native' or 'Irish' is an admissible category for present purposes. How, and how well, did Irish armies wage war?

For over half a century it has been impossible to write about early modern warfare without using the 'military revolution' paradigm. According to Michael Roberts, the dramatic increase in the size of European armies in the century 1560–1660 was ultimately driven by new linear formations that made more effective use of available firepower. Geoffrey Parker thought that the spread of bastioned fortifications demanded bigger armies and found much evidence of this military revolution in Ireland after 1641 brought by an estimated 1,000 Irish officers and soldiers returning from France, Spain, the Holy Roman Empire and the Spanish Netherlands. Four of these, John Bourke, Owen Roe O'Neill, Thomas Preston and Garrett Barry, took command of the Confederate Catholic provincial armies of Connacht, Ulster, Leinster and Munster respectively.[15] In contrast, the Jacobites had relatively fewer continental veterans or indeed veterans of any sort, having squandered one-third of the army's regulars on the eve of war by sending them to England in a doomed bid to prop up James. They had just a thin leavening of veteran lieutenant colonels in the regiments of foot to support the amateur colonels who were commissioned for their wealth rather than their military skill.[16]

Critics have assailed the 'military revolution' thesis as expounded by Roberts and Parker. Jeremy Black, for example, points out that cited figures often include militiamen who were usually mobilised only episodically and locally.[17] Estimates of the size of Confederate Catholic armies are subject to comparable uncertainty.[18] Moreover, John A. Lynn claims that the 'staggering' jump in the size of European armies came in the half-century after 1660, the terminal date of the Roberts/Parker revolution. This jump was a

---

14 W. P. Kelly, 'The Forgotten Siege of Derry, March–August 1649', in W. P. Kelly (ed.), *The Sieges of Derry* (Dublin: FCP, 2001), 31–52.

15 R. Loeber and G. Parker, 'The Military Revolution in Seventeenth-Century Ireland', in J. Ohlmeyer (ed.), *Ireland from Independence to Occupation, 1641–1660* (Cambridge University Press, 1995) 68–72.

16 J. Childs, 'The Williamite War, 1689–91,' in T. Bartlett and K. Jeffery (eds.), *A Military History of Ireland* (Cambridge University Press, 1996), 189; P. Lenihan, *The Last Cavalier. Richard Talbot (1631–91)* (University College Dublin Press, 2015), 122.

17 J. Black, *A Military Revolution? Military Change and European Society 1550–1800* (London: Macmillan, 1991), 6.

18 J. Scott Wheeler, 'Four Armies in Ireland', in Ohlmeyer, (ed.), *Ireland from Independence to Occupation*, 51.

consequence of Louis XIV's diplomatic isolation and overweening ambitions, not of bastioned fortifications.[19]

At first glance native armies appear to have shared in the pattern of huge growth in the latter decades of the seventeenth century described by Lynn. At Knocknanuss, the biggest battle of the Confederate Wars, Theobald, Viscount Taaffe, led about 8,000 men. At the Boyne, the Jacobites had between 23,000 and 25,000. But this impression of an almost threefold increase is misleading because of the different way that Confederate and Jacobite forces were organised. The Confederate Catholics maintained provincial armies to fight in different theatres because they faced enemies or potential enemies in all four provinces, though the fighting in Connacht was an overspill from west Ulster.[20] The Williamite War was characterised, in contrast, by a shifting military frontier behind which each side controlled large and contiguous blocks of territory. In those circumstances there was no enemy to fight in, for example, Munster in 1689, so regiments from there could be gathered into the large army mobilised near Dundalk. The single Jacobite field army typically peaked at about the same total in any one year; varying from between 18,000 and 20,000 near Dundalk in 1689, to 23,000 at the Boyne to about 17,000 at Aughrim (1691).[21] In the summer of 1646, however, the Confederate Catholics were able to wage war in three provinces simultaneously. Preston captured Roscommon Castle, Taaffe captured Bunratty Castle (County Clare) and Owen Roe O'Neill was victorious at Benburb. Their armies cumulatively numbered at least 20,000 men. The following year the three armies comprised between 22,000 and 25,000 mobilised troops.[22] In other words, there was no appreciable difference in the troop numbers put into the field by native armies in the 1640s and in 1689–1691.

The construction of a constellation of star-shaped, artillery-resistant and European-inspired *trace italienne* fortifications across the country by the mid-century provides tangible evidence of military revolution. Galway's stout landward ramparts and their three massive bastions were impregnable and Sir Charles Coote junior was obliged to wait for nine months from July 1651

---

19 J. A. Lynn, 'The Trace Italienne and the Growth of Armies: The French Case', *The Journal of Military History*, 55 (1991), 649–77; J. A. Lynn, *Giant of the Grand Siècle: The French Army 1610–1715* (Cambridge University Press, 1997), 55–62.

20 K. McKenny, *The Laggan Army in Ireland, 1640–1685* (Dublin: FCP, 2005), 71, 77, 81–2.

21 D. Murtagh and H. Murtagh, 'The Irish Jacobite Army, 1689–91', *The Irish Sword*, 18 (1990), 32–3. M. McNally, *The Battle of Aughrim 1691* (Stroud: History Press, 2008), 172; P. Lenihan, 'Unhappy Campers: Dundalk (1689) and After', *Journal of Conflict Archaeology*, 3 (2007), 199. Simms, *Jacobite Ireland*, 70–1.

22 George Leyburn, *Memoirs* (London, 1722), 10–11.

to April 1652 before the city surrendered.[23] The cumulative military experience of the veterans of Spanish Flanders had been overwhelmingly of siege and defence and this expertise is reflected in Preston's capture of Duncannon Fort, a technically sophisticated operation that saw ample powder expended in accurate gunnery against enemy ships and fortifications together with extensive sapping and what was probably the earliest use of mortars in Ireland.[24] However the insurgents and, to a lesser extent, Confederate Catholics suffered a lack of artillery and gunpowder: at the 1642 siege of Drogheda (December 1641–March 1642) the defenders taunted their Irish attackers 'offering to throw them a bag if they would but fetch it'.[25]

Thanks to Louis XIV the Jacobites had more military supplies, but what aptitude they showed in siege warfare was due to French advisors: the siege of Derry was a loose blockade rather than a conventional 'siege in form' that would have involved digging trenches and dragging big guns close enough to batter a breach. But the defenders had more guns and better gunners. Twice the Irish, led by Lieutenant General Richard Hamilton, tried to take Windmill Hill just outside the walls and so constrict the defenders and twice they bungled the attack. The Irish did rather better defending walls than attacking them and it is no wonder that Limerick (1690) should be so prominent in Irish historical memory. Led by a French governor, the marquis de Boisseleau, the Jacobites defended a secondary and temporary defensive work, 'a work resolved to be disputed inch by inch', behind the breach in the Irishtown's ramparts.[26] Despite the heroism of Athlone's defenders in holding the bridge over the Shannon, the town fell in June 1691 when Ginkel gambled on a last river crossing through shallows beside the bridge. He succeeded because his opposite number, the marquis de Saint Ruth, left just two raw regiments within the town ruins and left the western ramparts standing so that the main body of the army could not launch an immediate counter-attack to drive out the assailants.

According to some accounts, cavalry generally declined in relative numbers, effectiveness and importance during the military revolution. Yet, this consequence of the revolution seems irrelevant to the native experience with cavalry in Ireland. Confederate Catholic armies were usually beaten in

---

23 E. P. Duffy, 'The Siege and Surrender of Galway 1651–1652', *Journal of the Galway Archaeological and Historical Society*, 39 (1983), 115.

24 P. Lenihan, *Confederate Catholics at War, 1642 – 1649* (Cork University Press, 2001), 178–89.

25 Cited in Bartlett, *Academy of Warre*, 19.

26 Anon., *The New Method of Fortification as practiced by Monsieur de Vauban…* (London, 1691), 18.

open-field battle by Protestant forces and in these defeats (Ross, Rathconnell, Knocknanuss and Dungan's Hill to take four of the many cases in point) the cavalry fled and abandoned their infantry comrades. At Ross and Dungan's Hill, Preston deprived his cavalry of room to manoeuvre by posting them in narrow boreens.[27] The Confederate Catholics did raise a fairly small number of well-mounted troops from the Pale who scored victories at Cloughlea and Roscommon, but weakness in cavalry limited Irish ability to penetrate hostile territory and fight, for instance, within the Pale's frontiers of mountain and bog.[28] Feebleness in cavalry may be down to the relative lack of tillage, and consequently of horse-breeding stock outside the Pale. However, this does not explain why the Irish cavalry were so much more formidable in the Williamite Wars.

Consider how quickly Patrick Sarsfield recaptured Sligo in autumn 1689 and re-established the Shannon line. While advancing from Athlone towards Sligo he sent fast moving cavalry detachments ahead to threaten Williamite outposts at Jamestown and Boyle, and succeeded in pushing Thomas Lloyd's Enniskillen regiment back to Ballysadare. He then sent 300 foot, 100 dragoons and 70 cavalry under Henry Luttrell (the same man who would be accused of treachery at Aughrim) on an enveloping manoeuvre to fall on the rear of the Enniskillen men holding that town. Luttrell's dragoons and infantry fell behind, yet his handful of horsemen were still able to overcome an enemy column marching from Sligo and then threaten the rear of the Williamite troops at Ballysadare soon after Sarsfield had engaged them from the front. Fast-moving and aggressive, Jacobite cavalry kept the Enniskillen men, themselves daring raiders, off balance and forced them to abandon the outer defences of Sligo.

At the Boyne repeated and costly cavalry charges against Williamite infantry as they waded over at Oldbridge slowed William's advance. The Dutch Guards beat off the offensive but the Huguenots and English were thrown into confusion, while the Danes huddled behind *chevaux-de-frise*; a dramatic name for what was little more than a set of portable wooden spikes. What might have been achieved if the cavalry had charged just a little sooner? Later, a body of dragoons led by Richard Hamilton provided cover for the retreating

---

27 A. Miller, 'The Relief of Athlone and the Battle of Rathconnell', *Ríocht na Midhe*, 5 (1972), 84; A. Miller, 'The Battle of Ross: A Controversial Military Event', *The Irish Sword*, 10 (1971), 141–58; B. O'Brien, 'The Battle of Knocknanuss', *An Cosantóir*, 28 (1968), 83. Lenihan, *Confederate Catholics at War*, 200–1.

28 N. Brunicardi, 'The Battle of Manning Ford, 4 June 1643', *The Irish Sword*, 22 (2000–2001), 3–14. A. Duignan, 'All Confused in Opposition to Each Other: Politics and War in Connacht, 1641–9', unpublished PhD thesis, University College Dublin (2006), 198.

Jacobite army by mounting a dogged and effective rearguard action at Donore Churchyard against Dutch, Huguenot, Danish and Irish Protestant horsemen.

Parker's variant of the 'military revolution' remain relevant to understanding the strengths *and* limitations of Irish armies in the 1640s. The experiences of Preston, Barry and O'Neill in that crucible of military revolution, the Spanish Netherlands, did not really fit them for battlefield command in Ireland. Preston's incompetence and dithering caused a well-equipped and experienced army to be annihilated at Dungan's Hill. Barry, a military theorist who pedantically explained the arithmetic necessary for elaborate battle squares of pike and shot in *A Discourse of Military Discipline* was not up to the demands of command on the battlefield at Liscarroll (3 September 1642). O'Neill at least won one battle at Benburb in County Tyrone when his army of 5,000 men 'by push of like' destroyed a somewhat bigger Covenanter force, but his overall record is quite mixed. Unfortunately for the Irish, their amateur leaders were hardly better. Like Preston at Dungan's Hill, Theobald Viscount Taaffe, commander of the Catholic army at Knocknanuss, contrived to deploy so clumsily as to block the component parts of his army from helping each other. Defeat at Scarriffhollis can be blamed on Bishop Heber Mac Mahon, who took over the Ulster army after O'Neill's death. By ignoring his council of war and abandoning a strong defensive position, he allowed Sir Charles Coote to destroy his army.[29]

The elderly and, literally, shortsighted Justin MacCarthy, Viscount Mountcashel, was the nearest the Jacobites came to a veteran of continental warfare like Preston or Barry. In 1689 Mountcashel commanded an army that was beaten from a strong position overlooking a narrow causeway over a bog by a smaller army of Enniskillen men. This is usually blamed on his 'raw and undisciplined' men, but Mountcashel must shoulder some of the blame for the *débâcle*.[30] In contrast, the Jacobites possessed in Sarsfield and Hamilton generals who were superlative field commanders if clumsy and rash in siege warfare.

Settler Armies

In his preliminary musings in an otherwise superlative history of the Williamite Wars, Childs lauded the locally raised Enniskillen and Derry regiments as 'hard,

---

29 J. T. Gilbert (ed.), *A Contemporary History of Affairs in Ireland from 1641 to 1652* (3 vols., Dublin: Irish Archaeological and Celtic Society, 1879–1880), ii, 84–6. R. Bagwell, *Ireland under the Stuarts and during the interregnum* (3 vols., London, 1909–1916), ii, 229–30. Scott Wheeler, *Cromwell in Ireland*, 170–2.
30 Simms, *Jacobite Ireland*, 119.

tough, resourceful, aggressive, fierce men' used to rough riding and skirmishing who thrashed larger Irish armies who served with 'insufficient resolution' under 'inept' leaders.[31] Is this opinion based on an uncritical reading of Williamite sources, which regularly reported plucky Protestants routing a cowardly papist rabble, or is there a kernel of truth to it? If true, furthermore, does it hold for both wars under study? To answer these questions we shall, in the first place, compare the effectiveness of the various settler armies in Ireland during these wars, placing particular emphasis on the Laggan army of the 1640s and the Derry / Enniskillen troops in 1689.

Why emphasise these in particular given the 'sheer scale' of Protestant incorporation into locally raised units everywhere?[32] Three regiments were recruited in Dublin from the refugees who flooded into the capital in the early months of the 1641 rebellion.[33] The long-awaited reinforcements from England began to disembark in Dublin and Cork from late spring 1642. Most settler units were merged with these newly-imported troops and became indistinguishable from the new arrivals. That being said, settlers did supply a disproportionately large part of those very mounted troops who frequently broke Irish pike formations.[34] In 1642 Scottish Covenanters, anxious both to protect their Ulster compatriots and to extend their influence into Ireland, initially sent 10,000 troops under Robert Munro to Carrickfergus. They soon overshadowed the locally raised 'British' forces in east Ulster. The Laggan army remains the best example of a wholly settler and large army. In 1646 it still stood at about 4,500 men as distinct from the forces of Sir Charles Coote junior, Parliamentary Lord President of Connacht, who had another 3,000 men in the north of that province.[35]

The Laggan may be defined as the north-eastern half of County Donegal, with the exception of the Inishowen and Fanad peninsulas, and from the start of the rising the Protestant inhabitants of the Laggan reacted much more aggressively than their counterparts elsewhere in Ulster, who tended to be paralysed by shock and indecision. Until about May 1642, the Laggan army repulsed attacks on its core area and even kept tenuous contact with

31 Childs, *The Williamite Wars in Ireland*, 47.

32 Armstrong, *Protestant War*, 37.

33 H. Murtagh, *Athlone: History and Settlement to 1800* (Athlone: Old Athlone Society, 2000), 98. 'Deposition of Thomas Syson', MS 817, f. 73r, Trinity College Dublin.

34 D. O'Carroll, 'Change and Continuity in Weapons and Tactics, 1594–1691', in P. Lenihan (ed.), *Conquest and Resistance: War in Seventeenth Century Ireland* (Leiden, Brill, 2001), 244.

35 R. P. Mahaffy (ed.), *Calendar of State Papers Relating to Ireland of the Reign of Charles I, 1633–47* [hereafter *CSPI*] (London: HMSO, 1901), 433–4. *A Remonstrance of Sir Frederick Hammilton* ([London, 1643]); K. Forkan, 'Army List of the Ulster British Forces, 1642–1646', *Archivium Hibernicum*, 59 (2005), 51–65.

further-flung outposts at Donegal, Ballyshannon, Enniskillen, Manorhamilton and Omagh. It probably helped that the settler population was unusually dense, though hardly more so than Clandeboy in east Ulster where the settlers needed to be rescued by Monro's army.[36] Another reason for the success of the Laggan forces must be the leadership of men like Sir Robert and Sir William Stewart and Sir William Cole of Enniskillen, who were all army veterans.

Seven months into the rising the Laggan army ventured further afield. The Protestant forces in County Derry had suffered reverses at Garvagh (December 1641), Portna (January 1642) and Bendooragh (February 1642), and were now crowded into Coleraine. The Laggan army broke through in May 1642 by capturing Dungiven Castle and brushing aside a large O'Cahan army. Later Sir Phelim O'Neill and Alastiar Mac Colla MacDonnell invaded the Laggan until stopped at Glenmaquin, County Donegal, on 16 June 1642. Here, musketeers positioned behind hastily erected breastworks raked the attacking Irish whose usual furious charge spent itself. The Laggan forces then counter-attacked and broke the Irish, chasing them for two miles. The sequel to the battle was the final raising of the blockade of Coleraine.[37] For the next few years Sir William Stewart's strategic reach extended far. In 1643 he routed Owen Roe O'Neill at Clones, County Monaghan, as the latter's army and creaghts fled the province.[38] The next year Stewart joined Monro at Charlemont, County Armagh, and in 1645 helped in capturing Sligo and in the subsequent penetration of Connacht.[39]

What, then, of the later war? The Protestant Association militias of 1689 seem far less formidable to judge from Richard Hamilton's 'break' [rout] at Dromore of eastern Ulster's settler forces.[40] Later, a settler army failed to stop Jacobite crossings of the river Finn at Clady Bridge and Lifford in the so-called battle of the Fords and fled in panic back to Derry.[41] The settlers themselves blamed the governor of Derry, a regular officer named Robert Lundy, and insisted that the troops needed 'more care and resolution in their Leader than Courage in themselves'.[42]

---

36 R. J. Hunter, 'Plantation in Donegal', in W. Nolan, L. Ronayne and M. Dunlevy (eds.), *Donegal History and Society* (Dublin: Geography Publications, 1995), 295–6, 303, 313

37 P. McCarthy, 'Preserving Donegal: The Battle of Glenmaquin, 16 June 1642', *The Irish Sword* 23 (2003), 361–82.

38 P. Ó Mórdha, 'The Battle of Clones, 1643', *Clogher Record: Journal of the Clogher Historical Society*, 4 (1962), 148–54.

39 McKenny, *The Laggan Army in Ireland*, 77–82.

40 Childs, *The Williamite Wars in Ireland*, 40.

41 Simms, *Jacobite Ireland*, 57, 97; R. Doherty, *The Williamite War in Ireland* (Dublin: FCP, 1998), 48–9.

42 J. Mackenzie, *A Narrative of the Siege of London-Derry* (London, 1690), 24.

The Derry/Enniskillen troops proved their mettle during and after the siege of Derry, being greatly helped by the appointment of experienced and capable officers to command them. Specifically, two officers rose to prominence. The first was Colonel William Wolseley, an English officer who commanded the settlers at Newtownbutler.[43] The second was Thomas Lloyd. Once again, as during the 1640s, when competent leadership presented itself, the settler forces of western Ulster proved effective. By 1690 the irregulars had been formally incorporated into the Williamite army, contributing nine regiments (six foot, two dragoon and one horse) or roughly between 6,000 and 7,000 troops.

English Armies

The best way to evaluate the English war effort in Ireland is to compare its biggest operations in 1649–1653 and 1689–1691 respectively. The map 'Cromwellian and Williamite Conquests Compared' (Map 3) helps us to assess progress after eighteen months. Both conquests had by then taken in the biggest and most populous part of Ireland, namely that part lying east of a line Carrickfergus–Limerick–Cork. But they achieved this by different means.

This is the appropriate point to take up the biggest contrast between William III and Oliver Cromwell, namely the latter's ill repute in Irish historical memory. The debate over Cromwell is linked to two interconnected questions. The first is whether his men were justified in massacring the royalist garrison during and after the storm of Drogheda. The second concerns the extent to which civilians were also slaughtered in this massacre.[44] Dealing with the second question first, the words 'and many inhabitants' conclude a list of the slain at Drogheda appended to Cromwell's letter of 27 September.[45] Answering the first question requires a more nuanced grasp of that siege's specific moral context. Insofar as the opposing royalist commander, Ormond, had a plan it was to reassure – generally insincerely – beleaguered governors and townspeople that he would relieve them while trusting to 'Colonel Hunger and Major Sickness' to gnaw away at Cromwell as he sat down before

---

43 Simms, *Jacobite Ireland*, 114–16.

44 M. Ó Siochru, *God's Executioner: Oliver Cromwell and the Conquest of Ireland* (London: Faber & Faber, 2008), 82–7.

45 J. Morrill, 'The Drogheda Massacre in Cromwellian Context' and M. Ó Siochru, 'Propaganda, Rumour and Myth: Oliver Cromwell and the Massacre at Drogheda', in D. Edwards, P. Lenihan and C. Tait (eds.), *Age of Atrocity: Violence and Political Conflict in Early Modern Ireland* (Dublin: FCP, 2007), 254, 266–82. T. Reilly, *Cromwell was Framed: Ireland 1649* (London: Chronos, 2014), 68, 78, 84, 87, 158.

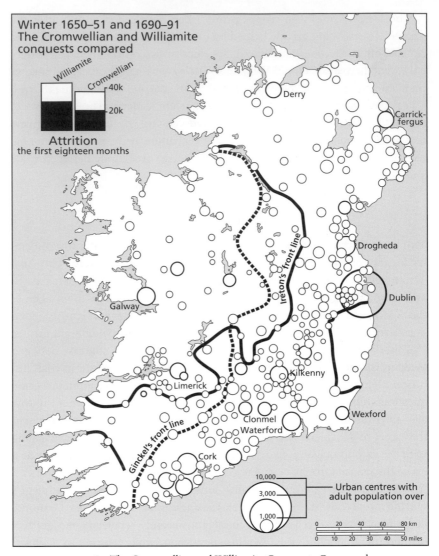

MAP 3. The Cromwellian and Williamite Conquests Compared.

one town after another.[46] Cromwell knew or guessed this and summoned the governor of Drogheda to surrender, advising him that 'if this be refused you will have no cause to blame me'. When refused, he had to show that his threat was no empty one.

46 J.G. Simms, 'Cromwell at Drogheda 1649', in D. Hayton and G. O'Brien (eds.), *War and Politics in Ireland 1649–1730* (London: Hambledon Press, 1986), 4.

A code softened by Christian values was starting to mitigate this cold expediency and insist that even if were not a 'breach of faith' to slaughter prisoners and civilians during a storm, it would be 'cruel inhumanity.'[47] Ormond, for example, spared the lives of parliamentary troops taken in the storm of Rathfarnham castle on 28 July 1649, during his siege of Dublin.

If Drogheda stands out 'for its combination of ruthlessness and calculation...', the calculation that it would encourage other towns to surrender was skewed and, despite the terrible example of Drogheda, all but two (Wexford and Ross) of the larger urban targets offered significant resistance.[48] Such resistance often resulted in heavy losses for the besiegers. These might be suffered in storming the town or fort, such as happened in 1650 at Clonmel (up to 2,500 casualties in April–May that year) or Charlemont (at least 500 casualties in the following July).[49] More were usually lost indirectly through sickness, as Ormond had expected, while encamped without the walls.

Cromwell 'like a lightning passed through the land', recalled Bishop French of Ferns. The phrase, then, gives a misleading impression of speed and decisiveness and by 'lightning', French may well have been trying to evoke the flash and crack of cannon fire in what was a siege war.[50] In fact Cromwell and Ireton progressed slowly, if steadily, over the first eighteen months. In contrast, the Williamite conquest got off to a false start when Schomberg disembarked at Belfast Lough in August 1689. Delaying because he was 'tired, over-cautious and pedestrian', Schomberg at last marched towards Dublin but stopped half-way at Dundalk and pitched camp for ten weeks for fear of a hastily assembled Jacobite army to the south.[51] By the time he slunk back north into winter quarters, he was well on the way to losing half of his troops after epidemic dysentery and typhus swept his sodden tents and bothies.[52]

Reluctantly, William came in person the next year. James tempted decisive defeat by deploying a significantly smaller army overlooking the banks of the Boyne when he should have stood further north covering the Moyry Pass and

---

47 James Turner, *Pallas Armata* (London, 1683), 336.

48 Morrill, 'The Drogheda Massacre', 264–5.

49 Ó Siochrú, *God's Executioner*, 124, 139. Scott Wheeler, *Cromwell in Ireland*, 136.

50 P. Corish, 'The Cromwellian Conquest, 1649–53', in T. W. Moody, F. X. Martin and F. J. Byrne (eds.), *A New History of Ireland iii: Early Modern Ireland, 1534–1691* (Oxford University Press, 1976), 336, 339.

51 Childs, *The Williamite Wars*, 173. Lenihan, 'Unhappy Campers: Dundalk (1689) and After', 197–216.

52 George Story, *A True and Impartial History of the Most Material Occurrences during the last Two Years. With the Present State of both armies* (London, 1693), 41.

thereby, at the very least, forced William's army onto a slow detour inland.[53] Tactically, a riverside deployment invited William to cross upstream and envelop James who, obligingly, had placed his army in a box defined by the Boyne to his northern front, the Irish sea to his right, a ravine to his left and the Nanny Water across his rear.

William narrowly escaped death from artillery shot while on a provocatively reckless reconnaissance and had he been killed 'it would have been of fatal consequence to the Army at the time'.[54] William's subsequent attack developed more as a crude frontal assault, which simply pushed the Irish back, than as a deft envelopment to cut off their retreat. The Irish field army remained in being. Despite this William believed his own propaganda and promised pardon only to the 'meaner sort' while threatening to make the propertied Irish, the army officers, 'sensible of their errors'.[55]

His optimism must have seemed justified because the capital fell without a fight after the Boyne and so too did all those Leinster towns that had cost Cromwell so much. Yet William's progress jarred to a halt at Limerick. Here he showed himself to be as clumsy and precipitate as Cromwell had been in siege warfare. His 27 August assault on Limerick's Irishtown replicated Cromwell's at Clonmel forty years earlier. In their haste, both commanders squeezed their men through an unfeasibly narrow breach in the walls into a prepared killing ground, a funnel constricted by improvised ramparts and swept by artillery. Both times the consequences were predictably dire, with William's storm troops suffering over 2,000 casualties that afternoon.

Another parallel between both conquests was their extensive use of shipping to carry heavy siege guns, munitions, reinforcements and such provisions as could not be obtained in Ireland. The Cromwellian conquest had depended on sea power. Similarly, the Williamite descent on Cork in autumn 1690 was a good example of power projection by sea.

A final parallel is worth noting. Both William and Oliver departed Ireland after a few months, leaving the work to underlings. The position of Henry Ireton, who replaced Cromwell, was less secure than that of Ginkel, who succeeded when William left in September 1690. Ireton's line was fluid and

---

53 Childs, *The Williamite Wars*, 207. B. Ó Buachalla, 'Briseadh na Bóinne', *Éigse*, 23, (1989), 84, 91, 100–3; H. Murtagh, 'The War in Ireland, 1689–1691', in W. A. Maguire (ed.), *Kings in Conflict: The Revolutionary War in Ireland and its Aftermath, 1689–1750* (Belfast: Blackstaff Press, 1990), 80.

54 Story, *A True and Impartial History*, 76.

55 J. G. Simms, 'Williamite Peace Tactics, 1690–1', in D. Hayton and G. O'Brien (eds.), *War and Politics in Ireland 1649–1730* (London: Hambledon Press, 1986), 183–4.

permeable, especially in the winter of 1650–1.[56] Moreover, he had left behind his ill-defined front lines a large block of mountain country whence 'skulking Tories' could range widely and even capture a walled town like Ross. Despite the opprobrious term 'tory', which denoted a common bandit, these were in fact large portions of the royalist armies: Hugh Mac Phelim O'Byrne and Thomas Scurlock could reportedly gather some 3,000 foot and 300 horse in Wicklow and Wexford.[57] To combat this threat, Ireton would resort to depopulation and relocation in order to starve out the guerrillas.[58] In contrast, Ginkel's line was more stable throughout the winter of 1690–1691 and raids by Irish irregulars (now called rapparees) were less pervasive and damaging.[59]

Casualties had been heavy in both cases, even if desertion had been light. The annual attrition rate among raw soldiers in the Thirty Years' War usually ran at between 20 and 30 per cent.[60] Cromwell and William had lost 46 and 52 per cent, respectively, of their cumulative troop strengths in the eighteen month periods under review. Cromwell took 12,000 troops to Ireland in August 1649, absorbed another 11,000 troops already there and, by December 1649, had got another 14,000 recruits, making a cumulative total of 37,000.[61] Ireton had about 20,000 men under his command at the end of 1650. That implies attrition during the eighteen months between August 1649 and January 1651 of 17,000 men or 46 per cent of the cumulative troop strength.[62]

---

56 In October, Ireton's troops lost outposts at Ferbane, Kilcolgan and near Birr but took another at Meelick, which they later abandoned. William Basill, *A letter from William Basill … Concerning a Great Victory Obtained by the Parliaments Forces against the Rebels in Meleek Island* (London, 1650); John Hewson, *A letter from Colonel Hewson from Finagh in Ireland* (London, 1651); *A Perfect Diurnall*, no. 73 (28 April to 5 May 1650), 998–1001; Edmund Ludlow, *Memoirs*, (3 vols., Vevay, 1698–1699) ii, 337; Bulstrode Whitelocke, *Memorials of the English Affairs* (London, 1682), 463.

57 Samuel Pecke (ed.), *A Perfect Diurnall of some Passages and Proceedings of, and in Relation to, the Armies in England and Ireland*, no. 44 (7th–14th October 1650), 479.

58 J. Cunningham, *Conquest and Land in Ireland: The Transplantation to Connacht, 1649–1680* (Woodbridge: Boydell and Brewer), 16.

59 SPD 8/8/69, the National Archives. Story, *A true and Impartial History*, 46, 59–60, 63, 65–7, 69, 73–5, 78, 83.

60 G. Parker, 'The Universal Soldier', in G. Parker (ed.), *The Thirty Years War* (London: Routledge and Kegan Paul, 1987) 182. P. H. Wilson, *Europe's Tragedy: A History of the Thirty Years War*, (London: Allen Lane, 2009) 483.

61 Scott Wheeler, *Cromwell in Ireland*, 192–4, 201. D. Murphy, *Cromwell in Ireland: A History of Cromwell's Irish Campaign*, (Dublin: M. H. Gill and Son, 1883), 373–5; SPD 25/94/507, the National Archives.

62 There were nearly 35,000 English soldiers under arms by the start of the campaigning season in May 1651. Between January and May 1651 some 15,000 troops were raised, one-third being volunteers enlisted by regimental recruiting officers and two-thirds being militiamen pressed into overseas service. SPD 18/19/25, 18/19/133, 18/20/163, 25/101/87, 25/101/93, 25/101/103, 25/101/117, 25/101/131, 25/101/135, 25/101/147, 25/101/161, 25/101/153, 25/101/155, 25/65/145, 25/65/215, 25/65/217, 25/96/143, 25/96/163, 25/96/191, 25/96/145, 25/101/249, 25/119/100, 46/102/145, 46/102/157, the National Archives.

Taking into account the Enniskillen force, the survivors of the Derry garrison, and the troops sent to the latter city's relief, Schomberg started with some 22,850 regular troops under his command.[63] This figure was augmented in spring 1690 by some 16,000 new troops in fresh units, mostly Danish and Dutch, together with 5,360 recruits for English regiments already in Ireland.[64] So, about 44,000 troops had been fed into the Irish wars by the winter of 1690–1691 and about 20,000 were left.[65] This implies that during the eighteen months between August 1689 and January 1691 attrition accounted for 25,000 men or, rounded up, 57 per cent of the cumulative strength to date.[66]

In the circumstances such heavy attrition is credible. Cromwell's army suffered from his decision to campaign into winter and lost an estimated 1,000 men through sickness in November and December 1650.[67] Ireton's army must have lost about 15 per cent of its strength in the bubonic plague outbreak of 1650. The following summer, a plague-free season, the parliamentary commissioners complained of 'what vast numbers' of their soldiers died of hardship and disease including one-third of that season's draft of recruits, many of whom had been 'lame, blind, children, aged and fitter for a hospital than an army'.[68] That the Williamite army had lost over half its strength is also believable when one considers how heavily it had been smitten by epidemic disease at Dundalk.

Looking forward from the eighteen-month mark, the two conquests diverge, with the Williamite War being wound up in a year and the Cromwellian conquest dragging on for three years. William's war ended because he was at last persuaded to forgo a punitive peace and wholesale land confiscations and Ginkel announced these more attractive peace terms at the opening of what would prove to be the last campaigning season. This peace offer, as much as defeat at Aughrim, would bring the Irish to capitulate at Limerick. In its original meaning a capitulation was a contract containing various articles or 'heads' of agreement. The Limerick treaty in which the Jacobite negotiators presumed to

---

63 J. Childs, *General Percy Kirke and the Later Stuart Army* (London: Bloomsbury, 2014), 137, 151. Childs, *The Williamite Wars*, 134, 148.

64 K. Ferguson, 'The Organisation of King William's Army in Ireland, 1689–91', *The Irish Sword*, 70 (1990), 69–71, 77–9. George Story, *A Continuation of the Impartial History of the Wars of Ireland* (London, 1693), 14. Childs, *The Williamite Wars*, 195; SPD 8/8/62, The National Archives. Story, *A True and Impartial History*, 97; Childs, *The Williamite Wars*, 268.

65 Taking the seven battalions to number, by a generous estimate, 500 men each gives up to 3,000 men, including the cavalry.

66 The figure for losses is double that computed by Story, *Continuation*, 317. SPI 63/353/6, The National Archives; SPI 63/353/12, the National Archives; W. H. Hardy (ed.), *Calendar of State Papers Domestic: William and Mary, 1690–1* (London, HMSO 1898), 318.

67 J. Scott Wheeler, 'Logistics and Supply in Cromwell's Conquest of Ireland', in M. Fissel (ed.), *War and Government in Britain, 1598–1650* (Manchester University Press, 1991), 43.

68 R. Dunlop (ed.), *Ireland Under the Commonwealth*, (2 vols., Manchester University Press, 1913), i, 50.

treat for a whole nation implicitly recognised that the losers still had bargaining chips. They had kept a united front and Limerick's massively upgraded defences stood as yet unbroken. As late as the evening of 23 September 1691, the very day when the Jacobites asked for a parley to discuss, Ginkel had glumly concluded that an outright attack would be 'impracticable'.[69] More important still, Louis XIV now professed he was 'resolved to support Ireland as much as possible' and belatedly started shipping enough money, provisions, weapons and munitions to keep the war alive.[70] More than ever, William needed to close down the war and would promise Irish Catholics whatever it took, notably that they should 'enjoy such privileges in the exercise of their Religion, as are consistent with the Laws of Ireland'.[71] While the war lasted and William was beholden to Catholic allies, no anti-Catholic laws were passed, other than ones forbidding them from carrying arms and owning good horses.

The contrast with the external context of the Commonwealth's reconquest could not be starker. The Commonwealth's armies had been over-stretched on the Scottish and Irish fronts in summer 1651. So long as the bulk of the English army sat at Limerick, fragments of the royalist provincial armies frequently coalesced to attack English garrisons. The forts covering the Shannon fords of Rachra (Shannonbridge) and Meelick were surprised and even Dublin was on the front line. Tories swooped on Baggotrath (modern-day Baggot Street), stole horses and lured pursuers into an ambush.[72] But Cromwell's defeat of the Covenanter invasion of England at the Worcester campaign in September 1651 knocked an enemy's enemy out of the war.

Nor were patrons to be found further afield. For France and Spain the Thirty Years' War was not over and they would vie for an alliance with Cromwell's Protectorate. The Pope was wary of any further involvement after the collapse of his papal nuncio's mission. The scramble to secure even a relatively minor figure like Charles, duke of Lorraine as a protector tells us much about the diplomatic isolation of the Irish.[73]

Tory raids went on and Galway held out, but Parliamentary commanders Edmund Ludlow and Charles Fleetwood would not 'capitulate [negotiate] with those who ought to submit'.[74] In the end the Irish did submit and the vast land

---

69 Historical Manuscripts Commission, *Fourth Report* (London: HMSO, 1874), 323.
70 S. Mulloy (ed.), *Franco-Irish Correspondence* (3 vols., Dublin: Irish Manuscripts Commission, 1983–1984), 85. T. Ó hAnnracháin, 'The Strategic Involvement of Continental Powers in Ireland, 1596–1691', in Lenihan (ed.), *Conquest and Resistance*, 47.
71 *A Diary of the Siege and Surrender of Lymerick* (Dublin, 1692), 19.
72 Dunlop (ed.), *Ireland under the Commonwealth*, i, 27, 33, 38, 48–50, 63, 69, 71, 74.
73 Ó Siochrú, *God's Executioner*, 174–5.
74 Scott Wheeler, *Cromwell in Ireland*, 222.

confiscations envisaged by the 1652 Act of Settlement went ahead.[75] The Commonwealth's demand for unconditional surrender dragged out a war into that most destructive end-phase that marks out the Cromwellian from the Williamite conquest.[76]

The Human Cost

Long-run economic trends confirm that Ireland bounced back much more quickly from the Williamite than from the Cromwellian reconquest and its destructiveness was 'in no way comparable'.[77] But considering the brevity of the Williamite War, the destruction was nonetheless serious. Alan Smyth has used quantitative sources such as post- and pre-war hearth tax returns to convey the regional impact county by county. This particular index is reproduced in 'War Damage in the Williamite War' (Map 4) and the worst hit counties (those shaded in this map) correspond to what one would expect from qualitative sources, with the exception of County Clare. The unshaded counties experienced either no fall in hearth tax or falls of less than 50 per cent.

Derry endured a three-month siege and the besieger's retreat to Dundalk left a trail of burnt homes, desecrated churches, crops destroyed and livestock rustled.[78] The following winter a swathe of south Ulster and County Louth formed a no-man's land between forward Williamite garrisons like Newry in County Down and Jacobite outposts like Ardee in County Louth. This was protected by neither side and plundered by both. The no-man's land in the midlands during the winter of 1690–1691 was even more extensive and the luckless inhabitants were harassed and molested by all sides. Connacht/Clare was burdened by heavy demands from the Jacobite army during that winter and the subsistence crisis had grown so acute by the spring of 1691 that nearly all the soldiers holding the Shannon crossings had deserted their posts in order to scavenge.

75 Cunningham, *Conquest and Land in Ireland*, 31, 46. Lenihan, *Consolidating Conquest*, 146. See Chapter 23 by M. Ó Siochrú and D. Brown, this volume.
76 Dunlop (ed.), *Ireland under the Commonwealth*, i, cxxix, 147, 150–1, 155–7.
77 R. Gillespie, *The Transformation of the Irish Economy 1550–1700* (Dundalk: Dundalgan Press, 1991), 59; L. M. Cullen, 'Economic Trends 1660–9', in Moody, *et al.* (eds.), *A New History of* Ireland, iii, 407 and L. M. Cullen, 'Economic Developments 1691–1750', in T. W. Moody and W. E. Vaughan (eds.), *A New History of Ireland* iv: *Eighteenth Century Ireland, 1691–1800* (Oxford University Press, 1986), 132. A. J. Smyth, 'The Social and Economic Impact of the Williamite War on Ireland, 1688–91', unpublished PhD thesis, Trinity College Dublin (2013).
78 Smyth, 'Social and Economic Impact of the Williamite War', 32–3, 63, 113–14, 162–4, 179.

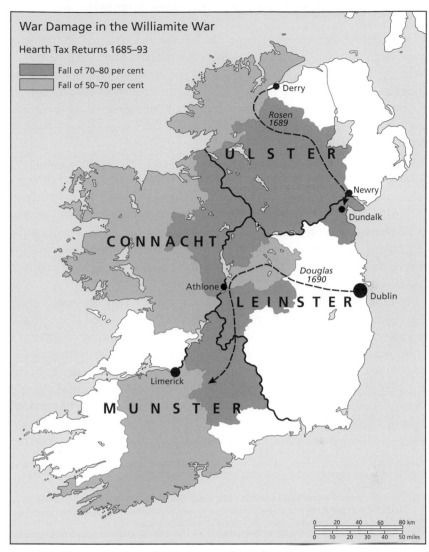

War Damage in the Williamite War

Hearth Tax Returns 1685–93

▨ Fall of 70–80 per cent
▨ Fall of 50–70 per cent

Derry

Rosen 1689

U L S T E R

Newry

Dundalk

C O N N A C H T

Douglas 1690

Athlone

L E I N S T E R

Dublin

Limerick

M U N S T E R

0   20   40   60   80 km
0   10   20   30   40   50 miles

MAP 4. War Damage in the Williamite War.

Though massacres of Protestant civilians during the winter of 1641–1642 were inflated into a black legend of papist perfidy, the fact remains that native insurgents often massacred captives in prison (at Sligo, for instance) or while being conveyed (Shrule, County Mayo and Portadown, County Armagh, for instance) to a safe haven.[79] Far greater numbers of settlers died

79 E. Darcy, *The Irish Rebellion of 1641 and the Wars of the Three Kingdoms* (Woodbridge: Boydell and Brewer, 2013), 105, 133, 169.

265

in besieged towns and forts: some 220 (of the 800 crowded within) succumbed to 'flux' in King John's Castle of Limerick in May and June 1642.[80] When reinforced English forces regained the initiative later that summer they frequently massacred native civilians in their forays as at Rathcoole in County Kildare, for instance. Massacres would not recur to anything like the same extent after 1642, but civilians would fall victim to war's indirect but far deadlier death toll.[81]

A wave of bubonic plague swept across three of the country's four provinces (Ulster escaped) in the summer of 1650.[82] Galway Corporation's chronicler recorded that a 'contagious infection of the plague' broke out in the city in July 1649 and that it persisted until late March 1650. 'Most' of the townspeople would have died if they had not fled to the countryside. Given the extensive landholdings of Galway's wealthier merchants right across Connacht, this was doubtless sufficient to begin to spread the plague through the province and beyond.[83]

To capture the dimensions of this catastrophe, one must set aside incredible claims such as William Petty's assertion that Dubliners died of the plague at a rate of 1,300 a week throughout that summer or the *Weekly Intelligencer's* claim that 17,000 Dubliners (Dublin's population was hardly more than 20–25,000) died of the plague that summer.[84] These are exaggerations. The burial registers of St John's Parish, Dublin, hint at the true dimensions of the epidemic.[85] The death toll for July 1650 spiked at well over four times the previous peak of October 1649, which had reflected the footprint of autumnal disease where soldiers sick with dysentery or 'bloody flux' and typhoid were billeted

80 K. Wiggins, *Anatomy of a Siege: King John's Castle, Limerick, 1642*, (Woodbridge: Boydell Press, 2001), 176–7.

81 M. Clinton, L. Fibiger and D. Shiels, 'The Carrickmines Mass Grave and the Siege of March 1642' and K. W. Nicholls, 'The Other Massacre: English Killings of Irish, 1641–2', in Edwards, Lenihan and Tait (eds.), *Age of Atrocity*, 183–6, 200–3.

82 P. F. Moran (ed.), *Spicilegium Ossoriense: Being a Collection of Original Letters and Papers Illustrative of the History of the Irish Church from the Reformation to the Year 1800* (3 vols., Dublin: W.B. Kelly, 1874–84), i, 337, 369.

83 Galway Corporation Statute Book, Liber A, f. 205, James Hardiman Library, NUI Galway, http://archives.library.nuigalway.ie/LiberA/html/LiberA.html (accessed 30 January 2016).

84 Edmund Borlase, *The History of the Execrable Irish Rebellion* (London, 1680), 282. Richard Collings (ed.), *The Weekly Intelligencer of the Commonwealth* (8–15 October 1650), 20. William Petty, *The Political Anatomy of Ireland*, (London, 1691), 19. Richard O'Ferrall and Robert O'Connell, *Commentarius Rinuccinianus de Sedisapostolicae legatione ad Foederatos Hiberniae Catholicos per annos 1645–1649* (6 vols., Dublin: Irish Manuscripts Commission, 1932–49), v, 80; L. A. Clarkson, *Death, Disease and Famine in Pre-Industrial England* (Dublin: Gill and Macmillan, 1975), 60–2.

85 J. Mills (ed.), *Registers of the Parish of St John the Evangelist, Dublin, 1619–1699* (Dublin: Parish Register Society of Dublin, 1906). Our thanks to John Cunningham for pointing out this source.

on civilians.[86] The register reveals that no remotely comparable epidemic to that of 1650 hit St John's parish afterwards, despite scattered reports of subsequent outbreaks of 'sickness' and even of 'pestilence' in Dublin until 1655.[87] The parish taxed 239 households in a 1643 cess of 'parishioners and inhabitants'. Employing a multiplier of five yields a parish population estimate of 1,195 for that year. Working with this population figure, and studying the parish burial registers, reveals that between June and August 1650 the death rate for St John's exceeded the average for the same months in the years before and after 1649 by some 260 parishioners.[88] Two hundred and sixty plague deaths represents just over a fifth of the parish's population.

This is a relatively low toll when compared to plague mortality in, for example, some Italian cities in the 1650s.[89] Plague mortality outside Dublin probably ran much higher in some places: we are told by a credible local informant that plague swept away 'the greater part' of the people of Galway city and county while a somewhat less reliable informant reported that the people of Wexford were 'almost all dead of the plague'.[90] The mayor of Waterford declared on 2 July 1650 that 400 of his besieged citizens were dying of the plague every week.[91] Allowing for no plague in Ulster and exceptionally heavy plague mortality across Connacht and in places like Waterford, the figure of one-fifth may be typical of countrywide plague mortality.

But can one characterise the plague dead as victims of war? It was commonplace to yoke war, famine and pestilence together. On 30 July 1650, Ireton bemoaned how God had caused the plague to spread 'of late' to 'His own people' [the English] after He had smitten the Irish with 'the Sword and Pestilence with somewhat of Famine also in many places', which consumed 'whole Towns and Cities, and lay waste almost whole Countries'.[92] Troop movements during the

---

86 R. Gillespie, 'War and the Irish Town: The Early Modern Experience', in Lenihan (ed.), *Conquest and Resistance*, 302–7; M. Lindemann, *Medicine and Society in Early Modern Europe* (Cambridge University Press, 1999), 51.

87 Dunlop (ed.), *Ireland under the Commonwealth*, i, 10, 241, 263. Whitelocke, *Memorials*, 453, 456, 459. Samuel Pecke (ed.), *A Perfect Diurnall*, no. 74 (5–12 May 1651), 1018.

88 MS P328/5/1, 229–37, 245–7, 260–5, Representative Church Body Library Dublin. For the multiplier cf L. A. Clarkson 'Irish Population Revisited, 1687–1821', in J. M. Goldstrom and L.A. Clarkson (eds.), *Irish Population, Economy and Society* (Oxford: Clarendon Press, 1981), 25–6.

89 Lindemann, *Medicine and Society*, 67.

90 Moran (ed.), *Spicilegium Ossoriense*, 355. Whitelocke, *Memorials*, 453.

91 John Lyvett, mayor of Waterford to Ormond, 2 July 1650, Carte MS 30, f. 112r-v, Bodleian Library. Our thanks to John Cunningham for this source. J. G. Simms, 'The Restoration 1660–85', in Moody *et al.* (eds.), *A New History of Ireland*, iii, 452; *Spicilegium Ossoriensie*, i, 364.

92 Henry Ireton, *A Declaration and Proclamation of the Deputy-General of Ireland Concerning the Present Hand of God in the Visitation of the Plague* (Cork, 1650), 4.

Thirty Years' War hastened the spread of the 1632–1637 plague epidemic and doubtless troop movements in Ireland did likewise. Moreover other epidemic diseases such as dysentery and typhus broke out wherever the uprooted, hungry, demoralised, cold and unwashed huddled together, and so such diseases were more directly connected to refugee movements.[93]

Counter-insurgency and hunger were connected as is plain from Colonel George Cooke, who boasted of a sweep he led across north County Wexford in March 1652: 'In searching the woods and bogs, we found great store of corn, which we burnt, also all the houses and cabins we could find: in all which we found great plenty of corn. We continued burning and destroying for four days.'[94] North and mid-Wexford lay within what the Commonwealth decreed to be one of the tracts of tory-dominated countryside where crops were to be destroyed, habitations burned, stock driven off and peasants killed if they did not move to English-controlled country and cluster in villages of at least thirty inhabitants.[95]

Large regions were thus left depopulated. Apart from the 'small habitation' of Tulsk, the two parishes of Kilcooley and Ogulla in the heart of the fertile Maghery of north Roscommon lay 'altogether waste and uninhabited'. The extensive Herbert estates in County Kerry had 'no house or inhabitant thereon', Kilcormick parish in north County Wexford had 'no house or church upon it' and only forty of the 1,300 plough lands of County Clare were reportedly inhabited in June 1653.[96] One might argue that these reports simply reflected temporary depopulation, but that would be to disregard the fact that uprooted peasants were exceptionally vulnerable to famine fevers.

Reports of localised famine conditions began as early as autumn 1649 and in June 1650 the Catholic archbishop of Dublin (whose see encompassed Counties Dublin and Wicklow) was appalled that his flock was 'for the most

93 J. Walter and R. Schofield, 'Famine, Disease and Crisis Mortality in Early Modern Society', in J. Walter and R. Schofield (eds.), *Famine, Disease and the Social Order in Early Modern Society* (Cambridge University Press, 1989), 18; Q. Outram, 'The Socio-Economic Relations of Warfare and the Military Mortality Crises of the Thirty Years' War', *Medical History*, 45 (2001), 167–70, 175.

94 H. Cary (ed.), *Memorials of the Great Civil War in England from 1646 to 1652* (2 vols., London, 1842) ii, 419–20.

95 R. Steele (ed.), *Tudor and Stuart Proclamations, 1485–1714* (2 vols., Oxford: Clarendon Press, 1910) ii, 63, nos. 503–11.

96 C. W. Russell and J. P. Prendergast (eds.), *Carte Manuscripts in the Bodleian Library* (London: HMSO, 1871), 85. W. J. Smith (ed.), *Herbert Correspondence* (Cardiff: University of Wales Press, 1963), 141. William Petty, 'Parish Maps of County Wexford', 'The Down Survey of Ireland', http://downsurvey.tcd.ie/ 'Parrish of Killcormacke' (accessed 30 January 2016); J. P. Prendergast, *The Cromwellian Settlement of Ireland* (New York: P. M. Haverty, 1868), 121.

part wiped out by war and famine, even though the pestilence has barely broken out here yet'.[97] Reports of widespread famine persisted and in June 1653 a news book claimed that famine was then 'so sore' in Connacht and in County Cork that 'the living [are] eating the dead'.[98]

The price of wheat doubled or trebled in different regions, especially from the summer of 1651, and a significant correlation between Irish cereal prices and mortality certainly existed at the time.[99] A sharper but shorter spike in French cereal prices in 1693 was associated with a famine that, quite apart from epidemic diseases, carried off 10 per cent of the French population.[100] A Thirty Years' War analogue for the Irish experience is the five years of especially intense warfare, involving armies of between 30,000 and 40,000 on each side, punctuated by an outbreak of plague, across the Habsburg crown lands of Bohemia, Moravia and Silesia. This caused a population loss of one-third.[101]

To sum up, scholars have pitched estimates of population loss during the Cromwellian conquest at anything from one-tenth to one-quarter.[102] We endorse an even higher estimate. A plague outbreak of 1650 carried off some 20 per cent of the population. As to the remaining 10 per cent, famine, and its attendant epidemic diseases, preceded, accompanied and followed the plague. Add to this the exodus of between 30,000 and 40,000 Irish soldiers to Spain and France, trailed by camp followers, and the mass transportation to the West Indies of about 12,000 prisoners-of-war and the homeless youths and girls described as 'idle and vagrant persons'.[103] Taking the qualitative and quantitative evidence as a whole, some 30 per cent of Ireland's population may have perished during the Cromwellian conquest.

97 Moran (ed.), *SpicilegiumOssoriense*, i, 329, 331, 341.
98 John Hall, *Mercurius Politicus* (9–16 June 1653).
99 Mahaffy (ed.), *CSPI, 1633–47*, 597. Petty, *Political Anatomy*, 314–15; J. Ainsworth and E. Mac Lysaght, 'The Arthur Manuscript', *North Munster Antiquarian Journal* (1953), 172; Dunlop (ed.) *Ireland under the Commonwealth*, i, 113, 131.
100 A. B. Appleby, 'Grain Prices and Subsistence Crises in England and France, 1590–1740', *The Journal of Economic History*, 39 (1979), 865, 867, 871. Our thanks to Niall Ó Ciosáin for help with these references.
101 C. W. Ingrao, *The Habsburg Monarchy, 1618–1815* (Cambridge University Press, 2000), 49; Outram, 'Mortality Crises of the Thirty Years' War', 166, 169; J. R. Ruff, *Violence in Early Modern Europe 1500–1800* (Cambridge University Press, 2001), 61.
102 J. Ohlmeyer, 'The Wars of Religion, 1603–60', in *A Military History of Ireland*, ed. Thomas Bartlett and Keith Jeffery (Cambridge University Press, 1996), 185. D. Dickson, *Old World Colony Cork and South Munster 1630–1830* (Cork University Press, 2005), 4; Cullen 'Economic Trends 1660–9' in Moody, *et al.* (eds.) 389; P. Lenihan, 'War and Population 1649–52', *Irish Economic and Social History*, 24 (1997), 1–21.
103 S. O'Callaghan, *To Hell or Barbados* (Dingle: Brandon Books, 2001), 78–9, 81, 104; R. A. Stradling, *The Spanish Monarchy and Irish Mercenaries 1618–68* (Dublin: Irish Academic Press, 1994), 139.

Conclusion

The Confederate and Cromwellian Wars 'cost vast expense of English Blood and Treasure', perhaps three times as much of the latter as the Williamite Wars.[104] The English Commonwealth was grimly prepared to absorb these costs and to entirely disregard the horrendous civilian end-phase death toll in single-minded pursuit of total victory and could do so without fear of serious external intervention. We have seen that in a comparable eighteen-month period both Schomberg/William and Cromwell/Ireton sustained heavy loss of life but William was far less committed to total victory regardless of cost and heedless of diplomatic complications.

Consequently, the Irish would have needed to mount an especially formidable resistance in the 1641–1653 wars. They did not, for reasons that have little to do with the military revolution, but all to do with an enduring weakness in cavalry and chronically poor battlefield leadership. Conversely, the Laggan army and Enniskillen army scored well on both those counts. If such 'great man' explanations appear old-fashioned and facile it must be remembered that, while a general could do little enough once action was joined his preliminary deployments mattered a great deal, as did the confidence, or distrust, an officer like Lundy inspired. While in no way discounting the specifically military or tactical explanations for win/lose outcomes, the edge enjoyed by English armies in Ireland was financial, logistical, diplomatic and political.

104 Borlase, *The History of the Execrable Irish Rebellion*, 62, 176; R. Gillespie, 'The End of an Era: Ulster and the Outbreak of the 1641 Rising', in C. Brady and R. Gillespie, (eds.), *Natives and Newcomers: Essays on the Making of Irish Colonial Society, 1534–1641* (Dublin: Irish Academic Press, 1986), 191.

PART III

★

SOCIETY

11

Society, 1550–1700

CLODAGH TAIT

Several of the early modern funerary monuments that stand in Kilkenny graveyards remind viewers that all are equal in death. 'Neither ancient lineage, nor honest material wealth, nor eloquent tongue escapes the power of death' proclaims the tomb of Elias Shee and Margaret Archer (*c*.1613). However, few neglect to mention the earthly status of the deceased, either in words or via heraldry. John Brenan who died in 1646 was a carpenter; Patrick Murphy (d. 1648) was a burgess, alderman, and former mayor; Lord Richard Butler had 'sprung forth from the most ancient families of the chief nobility in Ireland'; and Mrs Mary Stoughton was the wife of Anthony Stoughton, 'Gent[leman]' and daughter of 'the right worshipfull Henry Maynwaringe ... Esq[uire]', a master of the Court of Chancery. But the stories behind some of these tombs also reveal contemporary anxieties about the attribution of status. The Stoughton family, for example, were fooled into permitting the marriage of Mary and Anthony's daughter and a conman, John Heyden, who appeared in Kilkenny in the 1640s pretending eminent connections, 'to hir utter ruin and overthrow'.[1] Given such potential pitfalls, how was social standing presented, defended and augmented? More importantly, what did designations like 'gentleman' and 'burgess' actually mean to those who claimed them, and to their communities, at a time of huge social and cultural change?

For the Gaelic Irish, ancient lineage, land and military prowess were markers of high status. Philip O'Sullivan Beare characterised the Irish nobles as 'great soldiers but allso warriors', and traced their origins to his country of exile: 'all the titularyes and knightes of the auncient Irish doe descende from

---

1 J. Graves and J. G. A. Prim, *The History, Architecture and Antiquities of the Cathedral Church of St Canice Kilkenny* (Dublin: Hodges, Smith & Co., 1857); P. Cockerham, 'My Body to be Buried in my own Monument: The Social and Political Context of County Kilkenny Funeral Monuments, 1600–1700', *Proceedings of the Royal Irish Academy*, 109:C (2009), 239–365; P. Cockerham and A. Harris, 'Kilkenny Funeral Monuments 1500–1600: A Statistical and Analytical Account', *Proceedings of the Royal Irish Academy*, 101:C (2001), 135–88.

the Kings of Spayne and Ireland, and are of auncient bloud royall'.[2] Sir John Davies, writing in 1612, commented that in Ireland 'every man being born to land, as well bastard as legitimate, they all hold themselves to be gentlemen'.[3] At the other end of the scale were those pitiable beings dismissed by Conall Mageoghagan in 1627 as 'mere churls and labouring men, [not] one of whom knows his own great-grandfather'.[4] Geoffrey Keating, the Old English chronicler of Gaelic Ireland, divided the Irish population into 'uachtarán and iochtarán', the upper and lower orders, adding other choice epithets for the latter – 'inferior people', 'rabble', and 'wretched petty underlings'. Such individuals were below the notice of works of history, since their activities would merely cast nations in a bad light.[5]

While historians have been slow to discard this indifference to the experiences of the lower orders, a much more nuanced picture of social structures and interpersonal relationships is beginning to emerge.[6] As Mary O'Dowd and Kenneth Nicholls have pointed out, in reality even Gaelic society was not 'rigidly and simply divided between two classes'. O'Dowd describes 'wide social diversity' among the tenants of Irish lords, a diversity only tangentially visible in the records.[7] The fiants and patent rolls afford glimpses of social stratification in Gaelic and anglicised Ireland. Gaelic military men are usually assigned according to their specific role – horseman, kern, horseboy/ groom, gallowglass, arquebusier/shot – rather than just as 'soldier', and other individuals are identified by patronyms and townlands of residence. We can assume that similar care was taken when it came to classifying overall status. Thus when individuals are categorised as gentleman, yeoman, farmer, freeholder, husbandman, cott[i]er and labourer, these labels seem to reflect real economic and social differences. For example, the 1603 pardon of Donough O'Connor Sligo and hundreds of inhabitants of his territory provides a rough snapshot of the social profile of the lordship from gentlemen,

---

2 W. J. Battersby (ed.), 'A briefe relation of Ireland', www.ucc.ie/celt/published/T100077/index.html (accessed 3 January 2015).

3 H. Morgan, 'Lawes of Ireland (1609)', *The Irish Jurist*, 31 (1995–1996), 307–12.

4 K. Nicholls, *Gaelic and Gaelicised Ireland in the Middle Ages* (Dublin: Gill and Macmillan, 1972), 8–10.

5 B. Cunningham, *The World of Geoffrey Keating* (Dublin: Four Courts Press [hereafter FCP], 2004), 152–3.

6 For example, M. Ní Mhurchadha, *Fingal, 1603–60: Contending Neighbours in North Dublin* (Dublin: FCP, 2005).

7 M. O'Dowd, 'Gaelic Economy and Society', in C. Brady and R. Gillespie (eds.), *Natives and Newcomers: Essays on the Making of Irish Colonial Society* (Dublin: Irish Academic Press, 1986), 128–30; M. O'Dowd, *Power, Politics and Land: Early Modern Sligo 1568–1688* (Belfast: Institute of Irish Studies, 1991), 83–4; K. Nicholls, *Land, Law and Society in Sixteenth-Century Ireland* (Dublin: National University of Ireland, 1976), 10.

to professionals like bards and 'rhymers', to craftsmen, down to labourers.[8] In Anglicised areas, similar social diversity prevailed. The 1558 pardon of Donell Kelle, Teige O'Brien and Piers Walsh for the murder by Walsh of Patrick Kelle of Sigenston, County Kildare, did not indicate how or why Patrick was killed, but it did distinguish the social status of Kelle and O'Brien (cottiers), from that of Walsh, a yeoman.[9] Status indicators became even more regularly used in the seventeenth century. The 1642 deposition of John Radcliffe of Cahercow, Aghabulloge, County Cork, listing debts owed him by both English and Irishmen, identified them by patronyms and residence, and carefully distinguished between gentlemen, yeomen and husbandmen, as well as between different craft occupations.[10]

The seventeenth century also saw greater use in Ireland of what Keith Wrightson calls 'the language of sorts', a rather vaguer (and therefore more flexible) twofold or threefold delineation of society into the 'meaner', 'poorer' or 'vulgar', the 'middling', and the 'better' or 'greater' sorts, terms that indicated groups with common interests and broadly similar economic situations.[11] When the English of Armagh town were expelled in 1641, they 'were gathered together at three severall times, those of the meanest sort being first sent away, those of the middle sort next, and the chiefest reserved for last'.[12]

Social status meant something in peoples' lives and shaped their interactions with others. However, it can be difficult to make out what particular labels implied about levels of wealth and standing. The problems of aligning the status attributed by individuals to themselves with the assessments of others or with actual financial standing are familiar to historians. Personal ambition regularly meant that an individual's self-description might not accord with how he was labelled by others. When the tory (highwayman) Redmond O'Hanlon and his associates were called 'yeomen' in a proclamation seeking their capture of 1674, they likely would have cavilled at the description and instead claimed gentry status for themselves. Their ostensible economic means would have meanwhile placed them far lower.[13] Thus

8 O'Dowd, *Sligo*, 63; Irish Record Commission, *Irish Patent Rolls of James I* (Dublin: Stationery Office, 1966), 20–4.

9 'Calendar of the Fiants of Philip and Mary', in *The Ninth Report of the Deputy Keeper of the Public Records in Ireland* (Dublin: Alexander Thom, 1877), no. 195.

10 Ms 824, f.42r–42v, Trinity College Dublin.

11 K. Wrightson, '"Sorts of People" in Tudor and Stuart England', in J. Barry and C. Brooks (eds.), *The Middling Sort of People* (London: Palgrave Macmillan, 1994), 28–51; K. Wrightson, *English Society, 1580–1680* (London: Hutchinson, 1982).

12 E. Darcy, 'The Social Order of the 1641 Rebellion', in E. Darcy, A. Margey and E. Murphy (eds.), *The 1641 Depositions and the Irish Rebellion* (London: Pickering and Chatto, 2012), 109.

13 *By the Lord Deputy and Council Whereas Redmond O'Hanlon ...* (Dublin, 1674).

far from being an immutable system that exactly represented economic and social capital, social status was a matter of contestation and was negotiated in everyday life by means of status signifiers such as material culture (clothing, houses, horses, funerary monuments), forms of address and gesture (before whom did one sit, stand, kneel, bow, or 'uncover' – take off one's hat?). Social mobility was far more common in the sixteenth and seventeenth centuries than might be expected, and was regularly more precipitous in Ireland than elsewhere.

The 'Chiefest' Sorts

Many of the nobility and wealthier gentry of Ireland are well known to us from surviving sources. But even they posed difficulties for contemporaries who endeavoured to map the human landscape of diverse communities. The author of the 1598 *Description of Ireland*, which listed the heads of prominent families in each county, clearly faced problems in adequately representing these men's relative standing. Using terms like 'Gentlemen of the better and meaner sort', 'Men of name', 'Principall Gentlemen' and 'Chief Men' he highlighted the difficulty of drawing a clear line between nobles and other gentlemen when Gaelic society in particular understood the idea of nobility to extend beyond the small group of titled peers and their immediate families. He also encountered the more common problem of distinguishing between 'better' and 'meaner' gentry, and between them and 'men of name' who were not technically gentlemen.[14]

In sixteenth-century Ireland, it was in the Anglicised east and south that the nobility most resembled that of England. There, the nobles held their titles from the king, practiced primogeniture, sat in the Irish parliament and had similar rights and privileges to their English counterparts. In Gaelic Ireland the heads of the myriad of lordships and their extended families understood themselves to be of noble birth. Rather than receiving power through direct linear inheritance, the chief of the sept, clan or 'name' – the *rí* or *ceannfine* – was selected from amongst the *derbfine* (descendants of a common great-grandfather). This core privileged group had preferential access to land (not all land within a *tuath* belonged to the ruling sept, and customs by which it was divided differed in different areas). They were also expected to assist in war and raiding, though often pursuit of their own

---

14 E. Hogan (ed.), *The Description of Ireland and the State thereof as it is at Present in Anno 1598* (Dublin: M. H. Gill and Son, 1878).

interests clashed with such responsibilities. In the sixteenth century, surrender and regrant policies offered – or imposed on – Irish lords hereditary titles along English lines or knighthoods in return for their cooperation in pacifying their localities and converting landholding systems in their lordships to mirror English custom. Significant portions of this volume chronicle other crown initiatives to curb the lords' considerable powers of autonomous action.[15]

Meanwhile, Catholic Old English aristocrats who resisted Tudor bureaucratic centralisation found their protestations of loyalty increasingly coming under suspicion.[16] As also discussed elsewhere, the reigns of James I and Charles I, particularly the 1620s, saw a rapid expansion of the number of peers, mostly New English in background, as a result of the so-called 'inflation of honours' as well as plantation and land redistribution. Overall, as Jane Ohlmeyer has shown, the effect was the creation of an increasingly Anglicised and Protestantised nobility. Some peers were absentees; others looked to Britain for cultural influences, education and spouses for their children.[17] The rise of Richard Boyle, a Kent native who could just about claim gentry origins is often cited. By the 1620s he was earl of Cork and one of the richest men in the Irish and British Isles. He, like others of his rank, deployed material culture to demonstrate his standing and the marriages of his children to consolidate his position.[18] In a world where the character of the nobility was changing so greatly, meanwhile, surviving Gaelic and Old English peers like the earls of Thomond and Clanricard fashioned themselves and defended their rights just as energetically, using other tools at their disposal – such as ancient lineage and long connections to Irish land and its inhabitants – 'to adapt to change, reconfiguring both older and more recent concepts of honour and nobility'.[19]

---

15 For two examples, see B. Cunningham, *Clanricard and Thomond, 1540–1640* (Dublin: FCP, 2012).

16 M. O'Dowd, 'Land and Lordship in Sixteenth- and Early Seventeenth-Century Ireland', in R. Mitchison and P. Roebuck (eds.), *Economy and Society in Scotland and Ireland 1500–1939* (Edinburgh: John Donald, 1988), 17–26; G. Power, 'Hidden in Plain Sight: The Nobility of Tudor Ireland', *History Ireland* 20 (2012), 16; C. Maginn, 'The Gaelic Peers, the Tudor Sovereigns, and English Multiple Monarchy', *Journal of British Studies*, 50 (2011), 566–86; V. McGowan Doyle, *The Book of Howth: Elizabethan Conquest and the Old English* (Cork University Press, 2011).

17 J. Ohlmeyer, *Making Ireland English: The Irish Aristocracy in the Seventeenth Century* (London and New Haven: Yale University Press, 2012).

18 N. Canny, *The Upstart Earl: A Study of the Social and Mental World of Richard Boyle, first Earl of Cork* (Cambridge University Press, 1982); D. Edwards and C. Rynne (eds.), *The Colonial World of Richard Boyle, First Earl of Cork* (Dublin: FCP, 2017).

19 B. Kane, *The Politics and Culture of Honour in Britain and Ireland, 1541–1641* (Cambridge University Press, 2010).

The Irish gentry are less well studied than the nobility. This is not least a result of their wide social and financial diversity. They ranged from military men knighted for their service to the crown but of varying levels of wealth, to individuals of comfortable means who could point to very ancient origins, to prosperous urban merchants with recently acquired estates. In the Anglicised areas of Ireland, the gentry wielded considerable influence in the politics and religious life of their localities in the sixteenth and early seventeenth centuries. Many further benefited from the redistribution of ecclesiastical property following the dissolution of the monasteries. They were widely intermarried and interconnected. The expansion of the Dublin bureaucracy in the sixteenth century offered opportunities to some and Ireland, like England, seems to have witnessed something of a 'rise of the gentry' – many Leinster gentry families in particular gained from involvement in local and national governance during this period.[20]

Given the burgeoning role of gentry and aristocratic families in patronising the resurgent Catholic church and in challenging the financial burden placed on communities by cess and other exactions, by the end of Elizabeth's reign Catholics within the Dublin administration were increasingly viewed with suspicion. Plantation, alongside the fact that crown servants were often rewarded with land, meant that by the early seventeenth century the gentry group, like the aristocracy, was becoming infiltrated and augmented by Protestant settlers. However, certain of the Catholic gentry and aspirant gentry from among the wealthier sections of urban society also saw opportunities for expansion locally and further afield in Connacht and Ulster. For example, from 1585 the townsmen of Galway were acquiring land in Connacht. Not all settler gentry were Protestant – numerous English Catholics also made up the 'New English'.[21] In the meantime, many members of Gaelic septs who had maintained access to land also made both practical and symbolic efforts to consolidate their position. One area in which this is seen is in the expansion of the activities of the Irish Office of Arms (from 1552) and its heralds. Since only those of the rank of gentleman and above had the right to display coats of arms, the heralds inquired into the heraldry used by families and

---

20 F. Heal and C. Holmes, *The Gentry in England and Wales 1500–1700* (London: Macmillan, 1994); D. Jackson, *Intermarriage in Ireland 1550–1650* (Montreal: Cultural and Educational Productions, 1970). There are numerous studies of individual families, but few of gentry networks.

21 See Introduction by Ohlmeyer, this volume. D. Edwards, 'A Haven of Popery: English Catholic Migration to Ireland in the Age of Plantations', in A. Ford and J. Mc Cafferty (eds.), *The Origins of Sectarianism in Early Modern Ireland* (Cambridge University Press, 2005), 95–126.

decided on entitlement to new grants of arms. They also claimed the right to supervise the arrangement of the often conspicuously elaborate funerals of members of such families, or at least to record their deaths, along with details of family connections. It has been noted that the numbers of enrolments of 'funeral certificates' expanded greatly in the 1620s and 1630s, as individuals from Gaelic, as well as Old and New English, families took advantage of the opportunity formally to validate their claims to gentility.[22]

Catholic gentlemen began to encounter severe financial difficulties as they endeavoured to live on reduced estates, and as aspects of the economic and social world familiar to their predecessors were transformed in the seventeenth century. Finding themselves obliged to keep up traditions of hospitality and liberality and increasingly enmeshed in a growing market economy that was fuelled by extensive credit networks, many were increasingly burdened by debt.[23] The 'Anglicisation and Protestantisation' of local government further eroded their influence and opportunities. It is therefore no surprise that a large proportion of Catholic gentlemen were unable to avoid becoming involved in the 1641 rebellion and other conflicts, with many losing land subsequently. Geographers have noted the effects of later seventeenth-century changes in landholding on wider communities and landscapes, with numerous old settlements based on gentry houses declining or disappearing. However, some families did hold onto estates and even where they failed to, significant numbers continued in their areas of origin, sometimes leasing from the new owners. In the east and south-east, the decayed Catholic gentry retained considerable local influence and 'held on to powerful hinge or middleman positions in the urban and rural hierarchies and ensured that the relative success of the new landlord-inspired economy would both be based on and in part mediated/ negotiated by them'. Kevin Whelan calls their eighteenth-century descendants an 'underground gentry'. The parallel increase in the influence of the Protestant gentry is charted elsewhere in this volume.[24]

22 C. Tait, *Death, Burial and Commemoration in Ireland 1550–1650* (Basingstoke: Palgrave Macmillan, 2002); T. F. McCarthy, 'Ulster Office, 1552–1800', unpublished MA thesis, Queen's University Belfast (1983); B. Cunningham, 'Colonized Catholics: Perceptions of Honour and History in Michael Kearney's Reading of *Foras Feasa ar Éirinn*', in V. P. Carey and U. Lotz-Heumann (eds.), *Taking Sides: Colonial and Confessional Mentalités in Early Modern Ireland* (Dublin: FCP, 2003), 154–5.

23 N. Canny, *Making Ireland British* (Oxford University Press, 2001).

24 See Chapters 5 and 6 by C. I. McGrath and D. W. Hayton, this volume. T. Barnard, *A New Anatomy of Ireland* (London and New Haven: Yale University Press, 2003); W. J. Smyth, *Map-making, Landscapes and Memory: A Geography of Colonial and Early Modern Ireland, c.1530–c.1750* (Cork University Press, 2006), chapters 7–9, quote at 303; D. Dickson, 'Middlemen', in T. Bartlett and D. W. Hayton (eds.), *Penal Era and Golden Age: Essays in*

The Middle Sort

On the fringes of the gentry were small groups of professional men whose standing was rising in the sixteenth and seventeenth centuries. For the professional middling sort – lawyers, administrators and the clergy (especially those representing the Church of Ireland) – education, talent and luck might combine with inherited wealth, crown service and social connections to consolidate social status. In the larger towns and cities whose charters guaranteed them extensive powers of self-government, merchants and wealthier trades- and craftsmen played a significant role, acting as a sort of gentry and seeing themselves as superior in dignity and ancestry to their fellow burgesses. They controlled the trade and craft guilds, which regulated economic activities, and dominated the aldermanic bench and officeholding in corporations. The town *élites* tended to be from Old English backgrounds and generally intermarried within a core group of citizens of similar status or influence, or with the gentry of the surrounding counties. The wealthier townsmen (incomes of several hundred pounds a year were usual among Dublin's aldermen) often facilitated the lifestyles of the gentry and aristocracy by providing loans and consumer goods. Towns were also administrative, legal and business centres. All of this aided their inhabitants in setting up useful connections.[25]

If the town *élites* were upwardly mobile, so too were those below them, and some men of Gaelic origin, like the Carrolls of Dublin and the Sextons of Limerick, even managed to infiltrate their ranks and to advance their children by education and marriage. A few urban families were early converts to Protestantism, such as the Sextons, and branches of the Usshers and Balls in Dublin, a fact that helped them thrive in the mid-seventeenth century when the fortunes of their Catholic brethren faltered. By the 1650s, most town corporations were almost wholly Protestant in composition.[26]

    Irish History, 1690–1800 (Belfast: Ulster Historical Foundation, 1979), 162–85; K. Whelan, 'An Underground Gentry: Catholic Middlemen in the 18th Century', in J. S. Donnelly and K. Millar (eds.), *Irish Popular Culture 1650–1850* (Dublin: Irish Academic Press, 1998), 118–72.

25 C. Lennon, *The Lords of Dublin in the Age of Reformation* (Dublin: Irish Academic Press, 1989); C. Lennon, *The Urban Patriciates of Early Modern Ireland: a Case-Study of Limerick* (Dublin: National University of Ireland, 1999); B. McGrath, 'The Communities of Clonmel, 1608–49', in R. Armstrong and T. Ó Hannracháin (eds.), *Community in Early Modern Ireland* (Dublin: FCP, 2006), 103–19; A. Sheehan, 'Irish Towns in a Period of Change', in Brady and Gillespie (eds.), *Natives and Newcomers*, 93–119; J. Ohlmeyer and É. Ó Ciardha (eds.), *The Irish Statute Staple Books, 1596–1687* (Dublin: FCP, 1998); M. Clark and R. Refaussé, *Directory of Historic Dublin Guilds* (Dublin: Dublin Public Libraries, 1993).

26 Lennon, *Lords of Dublin*; C. Lennon, 'Religious and Social Change in Early Modern Limerick: The Testimony of the Sexton Family Papers', in L. Irwin and G. Ó Tuathaigh (eds.), *Limerick: History and Society* (Dublin: Geography Publications, 2009), 113–28.

Hilary French's ordering of English townspeople according to the earning potential of particular occupations and their perceived respectability is also pertinent to Ireland. At the top came 'the "clean" retail trades (innkeepers, and large-scale shop-merchants)' and professionals such as apothecaries, notaries and makers of luxury goods. 'Prosperous "dirty" manual occupations (tanners, butchers, or skilled metal and wood workers)' may be distinguished from 'the poorly capitalized manual crafts (weavers, tailors, shoemakers or petty retailers)', and from the building trades. At the bottom of French's hierarchy are the 'labouring poor', subsisting on day labour or in more menial occupations.[27] Further divisions existed between those who were 'free' of a city or town (burgesses or freemen) and those who were not. Burgesses were permitted to trade within the walls of the town, to vote in council elections and to hold municipal office. Freedom was conferred by birth, marriage to the daughter of a freeman, or the successful completion of an apprenticeship, and was something that people took pride in, as indicated by the fact that they often recorded this status alongside their trade on their tombstones.[28]

Ireland was under-industrialised by comparison to England well into the seventeenth century. However, especially in the towns and on plantation estates, though increasingly elsewhere as well, skilled artisans formed a crucial part of local economies. In rural areas, these individuals often leased gardens or small amounts of land to supplement incomes. Wages for craftsmen are sometimes recorded in proclamations, accounts and corporation records, such as those of the Irishtown of Kilkenny where in 1605 the rates for the building trades 'without meat and drink' were 12 pence sterling for a master carpenter or mason 8 pence for a carpenter or mason, and 6 pence for apprentices. Prices for various foodstuffs and commodities such as cloth, candles and shoes, were also set out. However, economic fluctuations could affect both wages and prices: in Irishtown, wages halved after the peak in the first decade of the seventeenth century. The Irishtown records also indicate the importance to craftsmen of trade guilds or companies, which offered support, sociability and other benefits to their members and lobbied on their behalf. In 1609 the 'masters of the seaven treades' were named – the trades were shoemakers, tailors, carpenters, smiths, cotners (cottoners, involved in finishing fabrics), glovers and weavers. Several of the masters appear in

27 H. R. French, 'The Search for the "middle sort of people" in England, 1600–1800', *Historical Journal*, 43 (2000), 283–4.
28 Lennon, *Lords of Dublin*; Sheehan, 'Irish Towns'; Tait, *Death*, 121–2.

other minor positions in the corporation, indicating the public roles middling-sort craftsmen might play in local communities.[29]

Ireland's rural middling sort are more difficult to track and categorise than their English counterparts. Though English terminology was used to designate groups like yeomen and husbandmen, we cannot be certain that such labels meant the same thing in both contexts. Nicholas Canny points out that those using such terms in the depositions were usually 'specialist agriculturists'. However, inventories indicate that some yeomen (and gentlemen) carried on other businesses alongside farming, such as tanning and malting. Toby Barnard speculates that 'yeoman' in particular was regularly used as a courtesy label and that as a result, 'many were advanced in official documents beyond the value which they enjoyed in their immediate neighbourhoods'.[30] This is seen in the Ulster gaol delivery records of the mid-1610s, where almost all defendants were accorded yeoman status, while jurors were designated 'esquire', a title originally signifying someone in the higher ranks of the gentry or an officeholder but which was used increasingly imprecisely.[31] Imprecision was inherent in the concept of the yeoman, a descriptor which connoted a level of social and moral as well as economic worth. For William Harrison a yeoman was a married man, with 'a certain pre-eminence and more estimation than labourers and artificiers'. The yeoman was thus a mature man of local standing and economic substance who could not (yet) aspire to being recognised as a gentleman: 'a gentleman in ore', as Thomas Fuller put it, 'whom the next age may see refined'.[32] There are hints of this idea in an Irish context. For example, in a 1563 indenture, Patrick Forstall, yeoman, was granted 3½ townlands for three years at £41 13s 4d, with the proviso that 'he shall to the uttermost of his power cause his children to be brought up in civility and in some honest knowledge'.[33] The term 'yeoman' was increasingly used in Ireland subsequently. The 1641 Depositions can be used to give a rough picture of the economic situation of those identifying as yeomen. Often the level of wealth in goods, projected profits and debts owing was in the low hundreds of pounds. John Latchford of Killmagh, County

29 J. Ainsworth, 'Corporation Book of the Irishtown of Kilkenny, 1537–1628', *Analecta Hibernica*, 28 (1978), 3–78.

30 Canny, *Making Ireland British*, 339–46; Barnard, *New Anatomy*, 7–9, 243–4; Smyth, *Map-making*, 264–5.

31 J. F. Ferguson, 'The Ulster Roll of Gaol Delivery', *Ulster Journal of Archaeology*, fifth series, 1 (1853), 260–70; 2 (1854), 25–9.

32 A. J. Schmidt, *The Yeoman in Tudor and Stuart England* (Washington: Folger Shakespeare Library, 1961).

33 E. Curtis (ed.), *Calendar of Ormond Deeds* v, *1547–1584* (Dublin: Stationery Office, 1941), 132–3.

Cork, valued his estate as £269 in 'goods and chattles', and he was owed £23. However, most of his wealth was tied in stock and crops in the ground and he owned only £10 in 'household goods', giving us a picture of a comfortably off household, but one where there was little extravagant material display.[34]

As well as referring to yeomen, the fiants used the labels 'freeholder' and 'farmer' (someone with some access to freehold or 'fee farm' land, granted in perpetuity). In Connacht and Ulster 'freeholder' is also applied to Irish lords and some of their former chief tenants (who might lay claim to gentry status), who had been granted sections of former family lands. In the Ulster plantation it was also used for the recipients of new fee farm grants, which were 'viewed as a means of introducing substantial tenants to an estate who would form the backbone of society'. Ulster plantation freeholders usually held between 60 and 120 acres, though over 200 acres was possible. However, some, such as the freeholders of Tullyhunco, County Cavan, complained in 1622 that they were too poor 'to do service at assizes and sessions'.[35] Here was another role of 'people of any worth': they formed the backbone of local administration and office holding, particularly as jurors. In 1617 a Jesuit writer described the trouble caused in several towns over refusals by officeholders to take oaths of supremacy and by juries to 'present recusants'. He complained that new juries were impanelled 'from the dregs of the people, butchers, craftsmen, the ushers of the pseudo-bishops, common soldiers, strangers and renegades, all Protestants to a man', thereby implicitly indicating the standing ordinarily expected of jurors.[36]

Those called husbandmen were 'petty farmers', and were of similar status to less well-off artisans or craftsmen, and small traders – some combined farming and craft occupations. George Owen's 1594 description of Welsh husbandmen emphasised self-sufficiency: 'The poorest husbandman liveth on his own travail, having corn, butter, cheese, beef, mutton, poultry and the like of his own sufficient to maintain his house. He maketh the apparel of him and his family of his own wool, and seldom useth any money'.[37] Their tenure of land was often more insecure than those above them – Gillespie notes that on the earl of Antrim's estate in

---

34 Ms 822, f. 4r, Trinity College Dublin.
35 R. A. Houston, *Peasant Petitions: Social Relations and Economic Life on Landed Estates, 1600–1850* (Basingstoke: Palgrave Macmillan, 2014), 104; G. Hill, *An Historical Account of the Plantation of Ulster* (Belfast: McCaw, Stevenson and Orr, 1877).
36 J. Mockler, 'A Letter Sent in 1617, from the East Munster (Ormond) "Residence" of the Jesuits', *Journal of the Waterford and South East of Ireland Archaeological Society* (hereafter *JWSEIAS*), 6 (1900), 113.
37 B. Howells, 'The Lower Orders of Society', in J. G. Jones, *Class, Community and Culture in Tudor Wales* (Cardiff: University of Wales Press, 1989), 237–59.

1638 'all but one of the husbandmen were sub-tenants', and as a result paid relatively high rents.[38] Incidental information in the 1641 Depositions of those describing themselves as husbandmen can shed light on their activities and finances. For example, Charles Hart of Kilgobinet, County Waterford, lost heifers and hogs, 'corne in the house', garden fruits, and household goods and clothing worth a total of £9 5s, while Martin Bosten of the same parish reported losses totalling £118 10s. Andrew Grimes of Lismore parish lost £30 of property, including household goods to the value of £1.[39]

Many better-off rural tenants were obliged by their leases to take up roles within their communities. On both sixteenth-century and plantation estates, manor tenants were expected to attend at the manor court that arbitrated in matters at issue between inhabitants and to serve as jurors if required. One court of this kind, that of the manor of Esker in Dublin, dealt with interpersonal disputes, assault and affray, land and boundary disputes, debt, nuisance livestock, and use of communal resources such as access to water, grazing and fuel.[40]

The Meanest Sort

Below the yeomen and husbandmen in rural hierarchies throughout the islands were cotters/cottiers/cottagers, and 'living-out labourers'. They rented modest dwellings, often paying their rents in part through labour services, and getting by otherwise by means of work for wages, and other by-employments. Many labourers had skills that were in demand seasonally such as ploughing, shearing, reaping and threshing, and they might also avail themselves of common and marginal land for grazing and gathering fuel. The work of women, such as delivering and wet-nursing children, brewing, laying out the dead, as well as agricultural labour, would also have contributed significantly to household economies – women were paid 4 pence per day to weed Richard Boyle's gardens in Lismore and Youghal in the 1620s.[41]

---

38 R. Gillespie, *Colonial Ulster: The Settlement of East Ulster, 1600–1641* (Cork University Press, 1985), 116–17.

39 Ms 820, ff. 121, 131, 147, Trinity College Dublin.

40 E. Curtis, 'The Court Book of Esker and Crumlin, 1592–1600', *Journal of the Royal Society of Antiquaries of Ireland*, 19 (1929), 128–48; 20 (1930), 38–55; 20 (1930) 137–49; J. Lyttleton and T. O'Keeffe (eds.), *The Manor in Medieval and Early Modern Ireland* (Dublin: FCP, 2005); R. Gillespie, 'A Manor Court in Seventeenth Century Ireland', *Irish Economic and Social History*, 25 (1998), 81–7.

41 L. M. Cullen, T. C. Smout and A. Gibson, 'Wages and Comparative Development in Ireland and Scotland, 1565–1780', in Mitchison and Roebuck (eds.), *Economy and Society*,

Wages for unskilled labour seem to have been relatively higher in Ireland than Scotland by the early seventeenth century, and prices lower. However, given that wages for day labourers in about 1610 varied from 4 pence per day in Irishtown (only 2 pence during the winter months) and 6 pence in Dublin, it is easy to imagine that labourers and cottiers shaded in and out of poverty, and were especially vulnerable to inflation, demographic changes, harvest crises, disease, warfare and billeting of troops. Though in general the Irish lived in relatively humble circumstances, cottiers and labourers were most likely to live in less durable single-roomed buildings, of the kind called 'cabbins' or 'creaghts' in contemporary documents. For example, the sixteenth/seventeenth-century cottier settlement near the Sedgrave family's Killegland Castle, County Meath, excavated by Bill Frazer, comprised a group of humble stone-footed and mud-walled buildings. Their occupants had limited material goods: 'even household crockery is scarce'. Despite this, concern with security is evidenced by the number of keys for doors and trunks found on the site. Repeated changes in the ownership of the land on which they lived in the seventeenth century eventually seem to have forced the abandonment of the village. However, its inhabitants should not merely be seen as the passive victims of historical forces beyond their control. Frazer argues for the recovery of the agency of peasant populations, suggesting that though in Killegland decisions about the alteration of farming methods and the adoption of new crops such as potatoes were made by cottiers partly in response to troubled times, their decision-making was 'pragmatic, adaptable and tactically improvisational'.[42] We see such characteristics of lower-sort populations at other times as well. For example, from many parts of Gaelic Ireland in the sixteenth century come indications that tenants and labourers regularly moved in search of better conditions. Low population densities made people more valuable than land, but their mobility proved a disincentive to agricultural improvement and led to charges of idleness.[43] A similar situation seems to be implied by the periodic disappearance of cottiers from certain Ulster plantation lands: on Sir James Craig's estate the number of those described as 'cottagers' dropped from twenty-one in 1619 to three in 1622. Even later, in 1665, a Donegal agent described how poor

105–16; M. O'Dowd, 'Women and Paid Work in Rural Ireland, *c.* 1500–1800', in B. Whelan (ed.), *Women and Paid Work in Ireland, 1500–1930* (Dublin: FCP, 2000), 13–29.

42 W. O. Frazer, 'Field of Fire: Evidence for Wartime Conflict in a 17th-century Cottier Settlement in County Meath, Ireland', in T. Pollard and I. Banks (eds.), *Scorched Earth: Studies in the Archaeology of Conflict* (Leiden: Brill, 2008), 173–96.

43 Nicholls, *Land, Law and Society*, 10; O'Dowd, 'Gaelic Economy and Society', 129.

tenants 'snail-like, carry their houses on their heads, and will easily abscond themselves'.[44]

Nor should their humble dwellings fool us into lumping all labourers and cottiers together as one mass. Within the Cavan plantation in the 1610s, the acreage leased by 'cottagers' varied widely, from a few to as many as 30 acres. A survey of forfeited lands in Meath, Louth and Cavan of about 1700 gives detailed descriptions of each townland: the conditions of many inhabitants would have been similar to fifty years before. The compilers distinguished carefully between building types, from the 'good' farmhouses of yeomen and lesser gentry, through 'ordinary' farmhouses, often mud-walled and thatched, to 'cabbins', classified variously as large, tolerable, small and very bad. Most cabins had a garden associated with them, as in the case of Brownstown, County Meath, where 'sixteen small cabins & as many gardens' were occupied by 'poor labourers' on the 700-acre estate of Captain Edmund Stafford. Some paid significant money rents, while others paid in kind. There are even examples of sharecropping: in Drakestown, tenants of twenty poor cabins were allocated land by the landlord, who received 'ye Moiety [half] of there harvest'. In Ratoath, the properties associated with cabins ranged in value from 7– 24 shillings *per annum*: their values varying according to the size and quality of the garden. The survey also detailed other available resources, such as access to common land for grazing, water and bogs and other sources of fuel. Though people are hardly mentioned at all, in such sketches of their varied living conditions we get a sense of the potential variety of the experiences of the lowest sections of society.[45]

While the lower sorts were allowed limited participation in local and national affairs, they were not without political influence and could be articulate and proactive in local politics, finding a variety of ways by which to lobby governors and officeholders and to attempt to manipulate their decisions. It is increasingly clear that throughout the Irish and British Isles, people of all social backgrounds knew a lot about the law and current affairs. As well as discussing issues and grievances amongst themselves, they might also seek to influence those in authority for personal, communal and political gain, and to resist changes and policies that they perceived to be disadvantageous to them.[46]

---

44 W. Roulston, 'The Scots in Plantation Cavan, 1610–42', in B. Scott (ed.), *Culture and Society in Early Modern Breifne/Cavan* (Dublin: FCP, 2009), 136; Barnard, *New Anatomy*, 289.

45 Roulston, 'Scots in Plantation Cavan', 136; A. Horner and R. Loeber, 'Landscape in Transition: Descriptions of Forfeited Properties in Counties Meath, Louth and Cavan in 1700', *Analecta Hibernica*, 42 (2011), 59–179.

46 M. J. Braddick and J. Walter (eds.), *Negotiating Power in Early Modern Society* (Cambridge University Press, 2001); J. Walter, *Crowds and Popular Politics in Early Modern England* (Manchester University Press, 2006).

Petitioning provided one avenue for those – of any status – who perceived their interests to be under threat. As was the case in paternalistic societies elsewhere, it was expected that in return for obedience and deference, the greater sorts would reward the meaner with appropriate respect and concern. A fairly standard petition from the community of fishermen at Sillypoint in Rincurren near Kinsale in County Cork to Lord Deputy Wentworth, illustrates this point. The petitioners complained of the 'greivous molestacions and accions' of the sovereign of Kinsale, David Roche, who insisted on his rights to purchase their catch 'at his own price', even though the fishing community fell outside the jurisdiction of Kinsale, and though they were extremely poor, living in Irish cabins with less than 3 acres apiece. Roche had imprisoned protestors and seized their rudders and sails, 'to the utter ruine of your poore Petecioners, their wives and many small children'. Thomas Wentworth, earl of Strafford, was requested to authorise the local justices of the peace to adjudicate, and within a month an agreement had been reached where fixed prices were set out for the catch. This may seem like a relatively trivial matter, but the ease with which the fishermen gained a hearing and the rapid resolution of their problem indicate that all sections of society theoretically had some voice in matters that affected them. The way the petition was couched – its elaborately humble language, its claim to the moral high ground, and its appeal to the duties of the great to assist the poor, especially poor women and children – also indicates a tactical awareness of how to influence those in power.[47]

The meaner sorts, along with other seemingly politically powerless groups like women, young men and 'common' soldiers, also participated in the politics of rumour and riot. The few accounts of riot that come down to us from sixteenth- and seventeenth-century Ireland, most from urban areas, indicate that, as in Britain, all sections of society might become involved in protesting about dearth, taxes, exactions such as cess, and religious matters. As in the case of petitioning, those involved regularly showed a sophisticated awareness of how far they could go in making their grievances known without bringing any retribution on themselves.[48]

47 R. C[aulfield], 'Petition of the Poor Fishermen of Silly-point, near Kinsale', *Notes and Queries* second series, 12 (1861), 65–6; Houston, *Peasant Petitions*; R. W. Hoyle, 'Petitioning as Popular Politics in Early Sixteenth-Century England', *Historical Research*, 75 (2002), 365–87; M. L. Coolahan, *Women, Writing, and Language in Early Modern Ireland* (Oxford University Press, 2010), 102–39.

48 C. Tait, 'Rioting in Limerick in 1599', in Irwin and Ó Tuathaigh (eds.), *Limerick*, 91–111; C. Tait, 'Catholics and Protest in Ireland, 1570–1640', in R. Armstrong and T. Ó hAnnracháin (eds.), *Insular Christianity: Alternative Models of the Church in Britain and Ireland*,

Servants and Apprentices

At any one time, large numbers of the population of early modern Britain and Ireland were apprentices or servants, a word that applied both to household and administrative staff and 'servants in husbandry' working in farming occupations. For example, 54 per cent of the adult population (nearly 500 people in total) living in the baronies of Uppercross and Newcastle in south County Dublin in 1650–1652 were in service, and the majority of households employed one or more servants. Such a high proportion of servants may have reflected economic circumstances: since generally they were partially paid in kind (food, clothes and lodgings), when food costs were low it was cheaper to employ servants than to pay monetary wages to labourers. Most servants and apprentices were young, unmarried people, as was the case in Dublin in about 1652 – David Dickson, looking at the transplantation certificates for Dublin city, found that those women described as maids and servants had a mean age of twenty-six (compared with 33.7 for wives), and made up 24 per cent of the population. Only 23 per cent of women aged twenty were married, climbing to 79 per cent of those aged thirty: many of the unmarried cohort in their teens and twenties would have been servants. For many, service was a stage in the life cycle and was seen as a means of training young people for their later roles as householders and employers. Servants cannot be seen as a uniform group. Many servants and apprentices were the sons and daughters of husbandmen, yeomen and even gentry, and did not forfeit this status even when working for others. Their parental status, ethnicity and age, as well as levels of experience, fed into internal 'family' hierarchies (a chambermaid outranked a kitchen maid, and was likely to be from a different social background). In Newcastle and Uppercross, surname analysis suggests that most servants were from the locality or north Wicklow, but that those working in the households of the middling sort were more likely to have migrated there over longer distances, even from England and Wales.[49]

Service could lead to lifelong connections between individuals. Though Richard Boyle paid scant attention to most of those who attended his family, we get glimpses in his papers of some of the family's personal servants. His wife

c.1570–c.1700 (Manchester University Press, 2013), 67–87; W. Sheehan and M. Cronin (eds.), *Riotous Assemblies: Rebels, Riots and Revolts in Ireland* (Cork: Mercier Press, 2011); S. Carroll, 'Reform Government and the Politics of Protest in Early Seventeenth-Century Ireland', unpublished PhD thesis, Trinty College Dublin (2013).

49 Smyth, *Map-making*, 165–7; D. Dickson, 'No Scythians Here: Women and Marriage in Seventeenth-Century Ireland', in M. MacCurtain and M. O'Dowd (eds.), *Women in Early Modern Ireland* (Dublin: Wolfhound Press, 1991), 223–35. See R. C. Richardson, *Household*

employed at least one chambermaid and a 'gentlewoman', and there were wet-nurses (usually married women), footmen, secretaries and other functionaries, coming from New English, Old English and Gaelic backgrounds. Some senior servants remained in Boyle's employ after they were married. Several long-time or 'honest' servants became officeholders in Youghal and Tallow, and favourable leases were given to those who knew his secrets. He regularly gave charity to 'old' servants, recorded their deaths, and attended their funerals. He supported entrepreneurial servants, for example lending Valentine Waynman £20 in 1636 'to put him in a stock of Tobako'. He arranged marriages for others – in November 1642 he noted on Lyon Beecher's wedding to Thomas Williams' widow that 'I procured him that ritch wyffe and gave him her in marriage'.[50]

Of course, many servants experienced worse treatment, though given the limitations especially of legal records we can recover little of this. There are some glimpses of relationships with other members of the households in which they worked. In 1616, Margery Cook sought Catherine Boyle's advice about a former maid pregnant by her husband, but there is no information on whether the woman had experienced coercion. Some servants faced violence from their employers – in the infamous case when Christopher St Lawrence, seventh baron of Howth, beat his daughter to death and severely injured his wife, a servant who went to help them was also attacked. At times of crisis young servants could find themselves in considerable difficulty. The 1641 Depositions suggest that their social standing and weak ties to their employers' families and local communities meant that English female servants in particular could be vulnerable to assault and murder: for example, in four cases from County Cork female servants were reported to have been killed by rebels while out doing errands such as collecting water and delivering messages.[51]

The relatively small size of Ireland's urban centres naturally restricted the opportunities of those who wished to break into their trading and craft *élites*. Most apprentices were men, with occasional mentions of female apprentices especially in cloth-working trades – several women were made free of Dublin

Servants in Early Modern England (Manchester University Press, 2010); A. Kussmaul, *Servants in Husbandry in Early Modern England* (Cambridge University Press, 1981).

50 A. B. Grosart (ed.), *The Lismore Papers* (10 vols., London, 1886–1888), first series, 4, 214; 5, 117.

51 C. Tait, 'Good Ladies and Ill Wives: Women on Boyle's Estates', in Edwards and Rynne (eds.), *World of Richard Boyle*, 205–22; McGowan-Doyle, *Book of Howth*, 28–33; Ms 825, f. 240r, Trinity College Dublin; Ms 826, ff. 68r, 71r, 248r, Trinity College Dublin.

'having served apprenticeship' in the 1570s and 1580s.[52] The few formal apprenticeship indentures that survive, such as those replicated in the Galway corporation records, indicate that in Ireland as in Britain, apprentices were expected to be of good behaviour, and that there was some effort on the part of civic officials and trade guilds to oversee the terms of such indentures.[53] Corporations also periodically tried to curb troublesome antics by young men such as drunkenness, 'fornication', and the adopting of unseemly and expensive fashions. As was the case elsewhere, apprentices might seek to influence local politics: in Dublin in 1671 they were involved in riots about a new bridge. The surviving corporation books record the enrolment of apprentices as freemen of towns, and something of their careers. Newly minted freemen occasionally faced difficulties in setting up as independent traders. For example, Dublin corporation in 1605 intervened on behalf of 'certaine poore young men, being Artisans' who on completing their apprenticeships were being obliged to pay £4 to the relevant guild or 'give a great dinner'. The charge was reduced to 20 shillings.[54]

The Poor

In both rural and urban areas, individuals described as 'poor' are visible. Many of the cottiers and labourers mentioned above, some husbandmen, as well as sections of the urban population, and vulnerable groups like orphans, were intermittently at risk of destitution. Those who got by reasonably well when their earnings were augmented by those of a partner, when they were young or fit enough to labour, or when they could find adequate employment, might easily find themselves in penury when personal circumstances or underlying economic trends changed. John Aylmer, yeoman, of Dollardstown, had presumably fallen on hard times when in 1554 he received a grant of a 'place of one of the poor' (allowing him accommodation and a stipend) at St Patrick's cathedral.[55]

---

52 J. T. Gilbert and R. Gilbert (eds.), *Calendar of the Ancient Records of Dublin* (19 vols., Dublin: Dollard, 1889–1944), ii, 110, 137, 139, 149, 169, 178, 182.

53 J. T. Gilbert (ed.), 'Archives of the Town of Galway', in Historical Manuscripts Commission, *Tenth Report*, appendix, part 5 (London: Stationery Office, 1885), 437–8; 441–2; 444–8; 452.

54 Gilbert and Gilbert (eds.), *Dublin*, ii, 450, 459–60; Barnard, *New Anatomy*, 306–16.

55 'Fiants Philip and Mary', *Ninth Report of the Deputy Keeper of the Public Records in Ireland* (Dublin: Alexander Thom, 1877), no. 40. The main account of early modern poverty is P. Fitzgerald, 'Poverty and Vagrancy in Early Modern Ireland', unpublished PhD thesis, Queen's University Belfast (1994).

Little is known about giving to the poor in late medieval Gaelic Ireland. Records of the monasteries, traditionally understood as places where the needy were relieved, are scant. Gaelic lords were bound by custom to provide hospitality to all comers, but it is far clearer how this worked in relation to the *élites*, clergy, poets and travellers than in the case of the poor, though it seems that relieving the poor was one role embraced by Gaelic noblewomen.[56] There is more evidence of provision for the urban poor: Colm Lennon has found that hospitals run by religious orders and set up as part of chantry foundations, as well as religious guilds, were important channels of benefactions even after the Reformation.[57]

The question of what was to be done about the indigent became a live issue in sixteenth- and seventeenth-century Europe, with changes to the provision of relief resulting from religious change, humanist ideas, and the effects of economic and social shifts.[58] Though a category of 'labouring poor' was recognised by the later sixteenth century, methods of dealing with poverty were often premised on the opinion that a proportion of poor people were 'idle' and 'undeserving', improvident and lazy rather than indigent. Such perceptions of the poor placed a burden on the 'deserving' to display in their actions and demeanour adequate humility, sobriety, honesty, godliness and gratitude, and to tell convincing stories about the causes of their destitution.[59]

Little trace is left of the many poor people assisted privately, though it is clear that considerable *ad hoc* charitable giving went on. For Catholics, belief that works of charity were necessary for salvation and the expectation that the prayers of beneficiaries would help speed the donor's soul through Purgatory mean that surviving wills can provide a good snapshot of debt forgiveness and charitable provision. Thus in 1585, Nicholas Ley left two shillings and a frieze mantle or gown to every leper in the leper house in Kilkenny. He also bequeathed gowns to twelve 'decayed old men' and mantles to twelve women of Waterford, £30 to poor widows, £5 to the poor of Kilkenny, and provided for three bushels of corn to be made into bread and distributed among them every Good Friday.[60]

---

56 C. M. O'Sullivan, *Hospitality in Medieval Ireland 900–1500* (Dublin: FCP, 2004), pp. 197–210.

57 C. Lennon, 'Dives and Lazarus in Sixteenth-Century Ireland', in C. Lennon and J. Hill (eds.), *Luxury and Austerity: Historical Studies XXI* (University College Dublin Press, 1999), 46–61.

58 R. Jutte, *Poverty and Deviance in Early Modern Europe* (Cambridge University Press, 1994).

59 S. Hindle, 'Civility, Honesty and the Identification of the Deserving Poor in Seventeenth-Century England', in H. French and J. Barry (eds.), *Identity and Agency in England, 1500–1800* (London: Palgrave Macmillan, 2004), 38–59.

60 W. Carrigan, 'Old Waterford Wills III', *JWSEIAS*, 9 (1906), 210–14.

Private or semi-private funding of hospitals and almshouses was another way the poor could be helped while benefactors achieved religious and social aims. Some medieval hospitals were taken over by urban corporations following the dissolution of the monasteries, often continuing to combine charitable and religious purposes by sheltering Catholic priests as well as the ill and indigent. New almshouses were being founded in the Irish towns by corporations and by both Protestant and Catholic patrons from the early sixteenth century, like those created by Richard Shee in Kilkenny and by Richard Boyle in Youghal: a second almshouse in Youghal was run by the corporation. Accommodation in such institutions usually remained in the gift of the family of the founder or the community, allowing the restriction of aid to the dutiful and well-connected.[61]

In urban areas a variety of taxation strategies were implemented to pay for poor relief, such as the levy on turf put in place in Clonmel. For corporations, poor relief was perceived as a matter of civic duty as well as a practical necessity. In 1628, Galway corporation justified a grant of £10 *per annum* to poor widows, as well as other statutes to deal with beggars and the needy, as an investment that 'may increase our comings in and thereby enable us to doe worke tending to God's glorie and the good of the commonwealth'. A tendency to restrict charity to the local poor is evident: the widows assisted in Galway were to be 'of the birth and bloode of the towne', and the Clonmel deerhundred decided admittance to its hospital. Increasingly in the seventeenth century those who still needed to beg were given licences or badges to distinguish for benefactors the deserving and undeserving, or special times might be set aside when the solicitation of alms was permitted. In 1620s Galway, for example, there was concern about 'multitudes' of 'foreign beggars and pretended scholars', and a resolution was passed that 'such poore and needie men borne in the towne as shalbe allowed of to begg shal have a lead[en] token or marcke fastened to his capp'.[62]

Innovative charitable initiatives focussing on fostering self-reliance among the poor increasingly appear in the records. In 1633 Henry Lynch set up a foundation in Galway to provide poor women with dowries that would allow them to marry and set up solvent households. Benefactors might finance apprenticeships for poor children, or donate seed capital for new businesses. Richard Boyle recorded paying for a young woman to be apprenticed to a

---

61 Fitzgerald, 'Poverty and Vagrancy'; Lennon, '*Dives* and Lazarus'.
62 Gilbert (ed.), 'Archives of Galway', 473–5; McGrath, 'Clonmel', 114–16. See S. Hindle, 'Dependency, Shame and Belonging: Badging the Deserving Poor, *c*.1550–1750', *Cultural and Social History*, 1 (2004), 6–35.

bonelace maker, and gave money to widows 'on condicon they should buy some wool therwith, & fall to worck & beg no more'.[63]

Despite the absence of legislation setting in place a parish-based poor law regime along English lines, in many parishes provision for the poor was unofficially delegated to Anglican officials. When in 1664 Vertue Lastley 'a very poor man' petitioned the corporation of Old Ross in County Wexford for payment of the half-crown due to him weekly for the upkeep of three orphaned children of Ezekiel Harsnet he was referred to the churchwardens and overseers of the poor. By the end of the century the Church of Ireland parish vestries were directing the licensing of the deserving poor in many locations, and raising funds for relief via collections, pew-sales, fines and bequests. Moral behaviour was enjoined on recipients of poor relief, and they seem to have been expected to attend church, though David Dickson suggests that the Dublin poor lists were multi-denominational. Given that few vestry records survive, however, it is difficult to gauge either the extent or the effectiveness of what were essentially ad hoc measures, based on English and Scots models but lacking a legislative basis. The Church of Ireland's minority status also inhibited the vestries' effectiveness.[64]

The wandering poor were increasingly a focus of concern.[65] Vagrants in Britain were often young, and up to a quarter of them were female, but it is difficult to ascertain the social profile of their Irish counterparts. Numbers of women beggars increased in times of crisis: in 1653 large numbers of female and child vagrants were 'wandering up and down the country that perish daily in ditches for want of relief'.[66] Paul Slack talks of the periodic English acts against vagrants and beggars as 'a matter of social hygiene': the cleansing of the commonwealth of vagabonds contributed to cleansing it of sin and vice.[67] Galway's 1628 statutes on begging included provisions to control 'blinde' alehouses which relieved 'idlers and malefactors whoe ... doe disturb the quiet and peace of this towne', and caused dearth of corn through 'brewing and

63 RC 5/4, ff. 4/7–90, National Archives of Ireland; C. Tait, 'The Wills of the Irish Catholic Community, *c*.1550–*c*.1660', in Armstrong and Ó hAnnracháin (eds.), *Community in Early Modern Ireland*, 191–6; Tait, 'Good Ladies'.

64 P. D. Vigors, 'Extracts from the Books of the Old Corporation of Ross, County Wexford', *Journal of the Royal Society of Antiquaries of Ireland*, 2 (1892), 175; Lennon, '*Dives* and *Lazarus*'; Fitzgerald, 'Poverty and Vagrancy'; R. Dudley, 'The Dublin Parishes and the Poor, 1660–1740', *Archivium Hibernicum*, 53 (1999), 80–94; D. Dickson, 'In Search of the Old Irish Poor Law' in Mitchison and Roebuck (eds.), *Economy and Society*, 149–59.

65 T. K. Moylan, 'Vagabonds and Sturdy Beggars', *Dublin Historical Record*, 1 (1938), 11–18, 40–9.

66 R. Steele (ed.), *Tudor and Stuart Proclamations 1485–1714* (2 vols., Oxford: Clarendon Press, 1910), ii, 65.

67 P. Slack, *Poverty and Policy in Tudor and Stuart England* (London: Longman, 1988).

selling of beere, ale and aqua vite'. Officials and administrators also expressed concerns that vagabonds and alehouses facilitated the spread of seditious talk and criminal and immoral behaviour, especially prostitution.[68]

As was the case in Britain and Europe, there are signs in Ireland of a move towards the criminalisation and confinement of the undeserving poor. From the later sixteenth century, provost marshals increasingly took charge of dealing with masterless vagrants – sometimes by summary execution.[69] There were calls from 1602 for the setting up of institutions to reform sturdy beggars. In 1625, for example, Lord Deputy Falkland ordered the building of houses of correction, and that 'beggars, chapmen, common-rymers or bards, without licence from two Justices' should be arrested, whipped and returned to their parishes, while 'dangerous rogues' should be banished overseas. Such definitions were wide enough to comprehend other peripatetic groups such as Catholic clerics, allowing anti-vagrancy measures to be employed for purposes other than reforming the poor.[70] It is difficult to make out the degree to which these measures were implemented. In 1631 Richard Boyle claimed that as lord justice he had set up houses of correction 'in which the beggarly youth are taught trades', and similar institutions were created in some of his Munster towns.[71] Given such initiatives, and widespread dearth in the late 1620s and early 1630s, increasing numbers of Irish beggars made their way to England: complaints came from Somerset and the south west about the 'great oppression, annoyance and evil example' they presented. In the 1640s numerous destitute Protestant refugees from Ireland also sought relief in English and Scots parishes.[72] By the 1650s, vagrants like the misfortunate women and children mentioned above were being transported to the Caribbean.

Contesting Social Status

Though looking at different status groups allows us to construct some sort of picture of life-experiences in early modern Ireland, it is important to remember that status was not immutable. Movement up and down in the world was

68 Gilbert, 'Archives of Galway', 474.
69 D. Edwards, 'Two Fools and a Martial Law Commissioner: Cultural Conflict at the Limerick Assize of 1606', in D. Edwards (ed.), *Regions and Rulers in Ireland, 1100–1650* (Dublin: FCP, 2004), 237–65.
70 Steele (ed.), *Proclamations*, ii, 29; also 20, 31–2, 34.
71 R. P. Mahaffy (ed.), *Calendar of State Papers Relating to Ireland, 1625–1632* (London: HMSO, 1900), 611; Fitzgerald, 'Poverty and Vagrancy'.
72 P. Fitzgerald, 'Like Crickets to the Crevice of Brew House: Poor Irish Migrants in England, 1560–1640', in P. O'Sullivan (ed.), *The Irish World Wide*, i, *Patterns of Migration* (Leicester University Press, 1992), 13–35; *A Proclamation for the Speedy Sending away of*

as endemic in Ireland as elsewhere. Opportunities for social mobility varied according to wider social and political circumstances. For some, mobility was cyclical, and short-lived: a householder might achieve status and wealth during the prime of his life, but slip back into more reduced circumstances in old age. Fathers seeking to do their best for all their children often endeavoured in their wills to spread their resources in some way evenly, but younger sons might find it difficult to recreate the status of the household of their birth. For example, the 1557 pardon of Maurice of Moile of Offaly and his three sons calls them 'gentlemen and yeomen': Maurice may have been a gentleman, but his sons did not automatically share that status.[73] Rory Rapple talks about younger sons as 'casualties of primogeniture', pointing out that most military captains in Ireland were second or third sons of gentry families.[74] Raymond Gillespie notes the threat posed by younger sons to the consolidation of what estates had been salvaged by branches the O'Farrell family of Longford during the 'social revolution' of the seventeenth century, and the importance of careers in the church and continental armies as outlets for them.[75]

Women were particularly socially mobile. On the one hand, their status in large part depended on that of the men with whom they were associated and they were dragged up and down with them. Work and marriage might facilitate self-advancement, but widowhood, large numbers of children, or age and incapacity could lead back to poverty. On the other hand, there are examples like Jenet Sarsfield who married six times, aggressively pursuing the financial interests due to her from her deceased husbands' estates. Her highest-status husband was the third, Lord Dunsany, and Sarsfield continued to use her title as the dowager Lady Dunsany ever after, being commemorated by that style on her grave in County Meath.[76]

As this volume demonstrates, extensive land redistribution, as well as expanding credit networks, provided unprecedented opportunities to build fortunes and status. The Old English and new settlers tended towards the view that though respectable ancestry was important, sufficient property

---

the *Irish Beggars* (London, 1629, 1633, 1634); J. R. Young, 'Escaping Massacre: Refugees in Scotland in the Aftermath of the 1641 Ulster Rebellion', in D. Edwards, P. Lenihan and C. Tait (eds.), *Age of Atrocity: Violence and Political Conflict in Early Modern Ireland* (Dublin: FCP, 2007), 219–41.

73 'Fiants Philip and Mary', no. 152.

74 R. Rapple, *Martial Power and Elizabethan Political Culture* (Cambridge University Press, 2009), 55–9.

75 R. Gillespie and G. Moran, 'Land, Politics and Religion in Longford since 1600', in R. Gillespie and G. Moran (eds.), *Longford: Essays in County History* (Dublin: Lilliput Press, 1991), 24–5.

76 B. Scott, 'Career Wives and Wicked Stepmothers', *History Ireland*, 17 (2009), 14–17.

and wealth, as well as honourable service to the state, could also raise one in society. Some, such as Richard Boyle, actively celebrated penurious backgrounds. He wrote of arriving in Ireland with just a few pounds in his pocket and gave an (edited) account of his rise to the earldom of Cork.[77] Despite Boyle's bravado, however, his manner of spinning social mobility was strongly contested. For Irish nobles, both the lower orders within their territories and upstart English settlers (both labelled as 'churls') were contemptible people. No wonder then that on plantation estates difficulties arose in 'assigning a man to his place in the social order' and status 'was in the gift of the leasing policy of the landlord'. Despite their claims to gentry status, existing occupants might find themselves moving down the social scale as land was leased to new settlers above their heads, forcing them to become subtenants, or pushing them out totally.[78] Meanwhile, the pretensions of many of the 'new' gentry, some of whom had come from relatively humble backgrounds, were frequently questioned. In their poetry, Geoffrey Keating and Brian Mac Giolla Phádraig argued that emulating English fashion and language and brandishing genealogies did not make lowly people respectable.[79] To a greater degree than elsewhere, competing definitions of what made one noble or worthy meant that claims to status were insecure or contested.

As a result, we regularly see the deployment of insults to ancestry and other symbolic and even violent acts of 'social lowering' as a means of undermining enemies. In 1617, during a series of verbal and physical attacks by William and Nicholas Walsh of Galtowne, County Wicklow, on John Wolverston, justice of the peace and 'esquier', William referred to Wolverston's inferior 'bloud and byrth'. When Wolverston called Nicholas a 'churle', Nicholas retorted that 'the Walshes were better than the Woulverstons and that the said Woulverston was noe gent but by the mother syde'.[80] Anthony Nixon's 1600 poem, 'England's Hope against Irish Hate', excoriates Irish rebel leaders as a 'vile ribble rabble up-start crew'.[81] During the 1640s, the Irish referred to Protestants as 'English doggs' and 'churls', they refused burials appropriate to peoples' status, and in stripping them of their possessions and clothing they also removed the visual signs of standing and ethnicity.[82]

77 Canny, *Upstart Earl*.
78 Gillespie, *Colonial Ulster*, 113–20.
79 Cunningham, *World of Geoffrey Keating*, 156–7.
80 J. G. Crawford, *A Star Chamber Court in Ireland* (Dublin: FCP, 2005), 533–5.
81 A. Carpenter (ed.), *Verse in English from Tudor and Stuart Ireland* (Cork University Press, 2003), 98–107.
82 Tait, *Death, Burial and Commemoration*, 81–3, 94–5, 137–8.

Much work remains to be done on the subject of social relations in early modern Ireland. What is clear, however, is that social status was as important an issue there as anywhere in Europe, shaping peoples' life experiences and their interactions with others. Changes to land ownership and society made the task of accurately describing an individual's social location especially contentious and might necessitate adaptations to the way individuals spoke about status: Richard Archdeacon 'alias MacOtho' (McCody) of Bawnmore, County Kilkenny, was described in a 1616 memorial in Thomastown both in the English style as 'armiger' (esquire or gentleman) and in the Irish as *sui nominum capetaneus*, chief of his name.[83] The fraught political context might also provoke denials of the claims of others to standing as well as to honour, with potentially catastrophic results.

83 Cockerham, 'My Body', 262.

12

Men, Women, Children and the Family, 1550–1730

MARY O'DOWD

In January 1700, Thomas Moriarty sent a petition to John Hawkins, the vicar general of the ecclesiastical court in the diocese of Killaloe. Moriarty, a single man, admitted having had sexual intercourse with Margaret MacNamara who was also single. He, however, pleaded with Hawkins not to 'expose him' to the scandal of having to perform a public penance for his sin. Instead, Moriarty asked that his punishment be commuted to a fine. Hawkins granted the request and ordered Moriarty to pay the sum of £1 to the court. A month later, however, McNamara petitioned Hawkins and alleged that Moriarty had not told the full story of their relationship. She described how Moriarty had sworn on the Bible 'at several times' to marry her. About a year previously, she had given birth to their son and, although Moriarty had given her money for the child, he was obviously unwilling to fulfil his promise of marriage. McNamara's petition obviously impressed the vicar general. He gave her permission to sue Moriarty for breach of a marriage contract and instructed court officials not to issue Moriarty with a license to marry anyone else until McNamara's case was heard.[1] We do not know the outcome of the case but if McNamara had persuaded the court of the veracity of her claim, the vicar general could have compelled Moriarty to marry her in a public ceremony.

Despite the incomplete nature of the documentation, the chance survival of petitions presented to the officials in the ecclesiastical court at Killaloe provides a tantalising glimpse of the richness of the records of the Irish ecclesiastical courts which were lost in the burning of the Public Record Office in 1922. They tell stories of sex outside marriage, slander, disputes over wills, single mothers struggling to care for their children and young men trying to avoid the consequences of their sexual encounters. The *clientele* of the ecclesiastical courts was not, as is sometimes assumed, confined to members of the Church of Ireland. All denominations were obliged to use the courts for the

---

1 Add Ms 31821, ff. 51, 85, British Library.

probate of wills and for any disputes that arose in relation to them. It is clear from the surviving documentation that Catholic men and women regularly attended the 'bishop's court'. The absence of consistory court manuscripts (along with a similar loss of civic court records), has had, therefore, a profound impact on the way in which Irish social history has been written or, until recently, not been written. It is no longer possible to document the regular engagement of men and women from all social and religious backgrounds with the local ecclesiastical court or to analyse the wider implications for our understanding of Irish society of that engagement.

It is difficult to conceive of English social history without ecclesiastical court records. Since the 1980s the exploitation of the extensive archive of diocesan records has been at the core of the historiography on early modern England. Through an examination of consistory court records, historians have examined the rituals and practices associated with births, marriages and deaths.[2] They have analysed marital relations and domestic violence and traced the existence and strength of support networks between neighbours.[3] Most recently, Alexandra Shepard has used court records to refine our understanding of masculinity and to compound our perceptions of social status and hierarchy.[4]

The loss of an equivalent Irish archive means that the writing of Irish social history will always have its limitations. In recent years, however, scholars have begun to focus on the positive and to identify the potential of the sources that have survived. Scattered in archives throughout Ireland and Britain are original records of the early modern Irish administration, transcripts of wills and other testamentary documentation, fragments of court records such as those of the Killaloe court, supporting legal documentation and family correspondence. This chapter makes use of this dispersed archive to explore rituals and customs linked to the loves and lives of men, women and children in early modern Ireland. It looks, in particular, at changes in legal, religious and social structures and how these impacted on people's lives. A central argument is that the process of change was not a straightforward one of the replacement of

---

2 See, for example, M. Ingram, *Church Courts, Sex and Marriage in England, 1570–1640* (Cambridge University Press, 1987); D. Cressy, *Birth, Marriage and Death. Ritual, Religion and the Life-Cycle in Tudor and Stuart England* (Oxford University Press, 1997).

3 See, for example, K. Wrightson, *English Society, 1580–1680* (London: Routledge, 1982); E. Foyster, *Marital Violence: An English Family History, 1660–1857* (Cambridge University Press, 2005).

4 A. Shepard, *Meanings of Manhood in Early Modern England* (Oxford University Press, 2003); A. Shepard, *Accounting for Oneself. Worth, Status, and the Social Order in Early Modern England* (Oxford University Press, 2015).

Gaelic customary law with English practices based on common law. Men and women in Gaelic society exploited English legal structures to maintain traditional family practices. At the same time, new English and Scottish settlers introduced new customs and rituals to regulate family and community relations. The interaction of Gaelic and English law; the disappearance of some customs and the retention and introduction of others shaped the context for the regulation of the family life of men, women and children in early modern Ireland.

Marriage

Of all aspects of family life, marriage was the site of most contention as the legal, religious and political establishments struggled to define what constituted a valid union while men and women defied regulatory restrictions to marry in a form that best suited their personal circumstances. In medieval European society, marriage was a verbal contract between a man and a woman. The marriage was legally perceived to have existed when the couple made a promise to marry either in the present or in the future. Sexual consummation was not necessary; nor was the presence of a priest or witnesses required to make the marriage valid. In the course of the late Middle Ages, the church authorities attempted to exert greater control over the marriage contract by insisting on witnesses, the presence of a priest and evidence of the willing consent of both partners and their parents. The marriage service, church guidelines also asserted, should be publicised through the proclamation of church banns to allow for the presentation of possible reasons why the marriage should not proceed.[5]

Failure to adhere to these practices did not, however, make the marriage invalid, only 'clandestine' or 'irregular'. In 1563, the Council of Trent, through its *Tametsi* decree, continued the efforts of the church to impose uniformity on marriage regulations and to eliminate regional practices and customs. In Ireland, however, it had the opposite effect. The decree was only valid when it had been published or promulgated in a parish, a process that took a long time in Ireland. By the end of the seventeenth century, *Tametsi* had not been published in most dioceses in Munster or in Leinster where, consequently, the older, more private form of marriage was still considered valid by the

---

5 P. L. Reynolds, 'Marrying and its Documentation in Pre-Modern Europe: Consent, Celebration and Property', in P. L. Reynolds and J. Witte Jr (eds.), *To Have and to Hold. Marrying and its Documentation in Western Christendom, 400–1600* (Cambridge University Press, 2007), 1–42.

Catholic Church.[6] Even in parishes where *Tametsi* was proclaimed there were difficulties in enforcing it.[7]

The impact of *Tametsi* was, therefore, to create considerable confusion within the Irish Catholic Church as to what constituted a valid marriage. The strict regulations outlined in the Tridentine decree were at best selectively implemented and in many parts of the country ignored. Marriages were routinely held in private houses and, sometimes, without the presence of a clergyman. In 1585, John Shearman, an English school teacher claimed that in Waterford City, 'there is not one couple among twenty maryed according to Her Majesty's injunctions, but handfasted only, or else married at home with a masse'.[8]

In addition to ecclesiastically sanctioned marriages, historians have identified the survival into the sixteenth century of a 'Celtic' form of secular marriage.[9] The distinction between a pre-Tridentine private vow of marriage and a Gaelic style customary marriage was, however, a blurred one. Marriages solemnised without the presence of a minister occurred within Old English as well as Gaelic communities. Even in the latter, there was often a concern, as Art Cosgrove noted, to 'clothe Gaelic practices in canonical respectability'.[10] When, for example, Cale McFerrall O'Reilly agreed to marry Margaret O'Reilly in the late sixteenth century, he took her and her dowry of animal stock 'home to his house ... promising faithfully before many gentlemen to marry her in open church within twelve months'.[11] The arrangements for the marriage may have recalled an earlier form of Gaelic secular marriage but the report of it also reveals an awareness of the desirability of having a customary practice sanctioned by the ecclesiastical authorities.

Three months after he had taken Margaret O'Reilly and her dowry to his house, Cale McFerrall O'Reilly sent her home to her father. No reason is recorded for the failure of the union, but O'Reilly was taking advantage of one aspect of Gaelic customary law that survived into the sixteenth

---

6 P. J. Corish, *The Irish Catholic Experience. A Historical Survey* (Dublin: Gill and Macmillan, 1985), 106–7.

7 A. Forrestal, *Catholic Synods in Ireland, 1600–1690* (Dublin: Four Courts Press [hereafter FCP], 1998) documents the largely unsuccessful attempts of the Irish hierarchy to implement *Tametsi*.

8 John Shearman to John Long, Archbishop of Armagh, SP 63/118/29, The National Archives; Forrestal, *Catholic Synods*, 19–20; Corish, *The Irish Catholic Experience*, 88–9.

9 K. Nicholls, *Gaelic and Gaelicised Ireland in the Middle Ages* (Dublin: Gill and Macmillan, 1972), 73–7.

10 A. Cosgrove, 'Marriage in Medieval Ireland', in Art Cosgrove (ed.), *Marriage in Ireland* (Dublin: College Press, 1985), 33.

11 CP, F/2, National Archives of Ireland (hereafter NAI).

century: divorce and remarriage. Canon law permitted divorce in very limited circumstances and did not allow remarriage unless the marriage had
been deemed invalid and, therefore, null and void. Gaelic aristocratic families
retained the more traditional form of divorce because it was politically expedient. A marital union was often included in the terms of a political alliance
and could be dissolved if the agreement was abandoned. By the sixteenth century, Gaelic men were, however, also concerned to explain and defend marriage separations, if they could, in terms of canon law. Marriage among Gaelic
aristocratic families was frequently, as in the O'Reilly case, with someone
of the same surname and it was not difficult to prove that they contravened
church rules on consanguinity or affinity. Callaghan O'Callaghan secured a
divorce from his wife of eleven years claiming not to have known that she had
been married to his dead brother (and thus broke the church rule on affinity)
although his father had arranged the marriages of his two sons to the same
woman.[12] In 1574, Hugh O'Neill, second earl of Tyrone, was careful to get
his separation from his first wife, Siobhán O'Donnell, authorised by church
authorities on grounds of consanguinity.[13] He kept the documentation on his
divorce safe and produced it seventeen years later when the validity of his third
marriage to Mabel Bagenal was queried.[14] It is also clear that cooperative clergymen issued Gaelic lords with canonically valid dispensations to permit marriages within the prohibited degrees and, subsequently, conceded to requests
for divorce based on the contravention of the same church laws.[15]

The newly established Protestant Church of Ireland retained the regulations of the medieval church on the public nature of marriage. The Anglican
Church made, however, two important revisions to canon law. First, it reduced
the prohibited degrees of consanguinity and affinity to the second degree, a
change which Catholic clerics claimed encouraged converts to Protestantism.
A couple that was refused permission to marry by a Catholic priest now had
the option of asking a Protestant minister to perform the service.[16] Second,
the Protestant Church reduced the number of sacraments to two: baptism
and communion. Although this development removed the sacramental status

---

12 Undated CP, I/222, NAI.
13 N. Canny, 'O'Neill, Hugh (c.1550–1616)', in H. C. G. Matthew and B. Harrison (ed.),
   Oxford Dictionary of National Biography (60 vols., Oxford University Press, 2004).
14 See pp. 343–6.
15 See B. Mac Cuarta, *Catholic Revival in the North of Ireland, 1603–41* (Dublin: FCP, 2007),
   109–13.
16 M. Harding, 'The Curious Incident of the Marriage Act (No 2) 1537 and the Irish Statute
   Book', *Legal Studies*, 32 (2012), 78–108. For Catholic clerical concern see *The Letters of
   Saint Oliver Plunkett*, ed. J. Hanly (Dublin: Dolmen Press, 1979), 215.

of marriage, it reinforced the concept of marriage as a promise between two human beings that did not require divine intervention to make it valid. This was a view that was also endorsed by most of the dissenting sects that emerged in the seventeenth century. As Belfast Presbyterian minister John McBride pointed out, marriage was the first 'Divine Institution', a covenant made by God between Adam and Eve:

> Nor do we look on the Presence and Prayer of a Minister, as absolutely necessary to the being of this Relation; for the first was good, tho no Priest present, God himself joyning them, and so not to be put asunder.[17]

While McBride advised that a public marriage ceremony was desirable, the minutes of kirk sessions indicate that private promises of marriage followed by sexual consummation were a common feature in some Irish Presbyterian communities in the late seventeenth and eighteenth centuries. In May 1706, for example, Jean Cargill voluntarily appeared before the sessions in Aghadowey, County Londonderry, and claimed that there 'has been not only solemn vow … but a marriag' between herself and William McAulay with whom she had been living since the previous June.[18] The Cargill and McAulay case was unusual in that there appeared to be no proof that a formal marriage had taken place, but they were not unusual in having had sex before a church-approved ceremony. The majority of those who were accused at the kirk session in Aghadowey between 1702 and 1729, of the offence of fornication (i.e. pre-nuptial sexual intercourse), subsequently married their partners.[19] An admission of pre-marital sex was considered an offence by the elders but its seriousness was mitigated if the couple subsequently had their marriages sanctioned by a Presbyterian minister. It is likely that, as in the case of Cargill and McAulay, many of the couples who engaged in pre-marital sex had exchanged promises of marriage to one another. Session book records indicate that such private commitments continued to be made in Presbyterian communities in Ulster throughout the eighteenth century.[20]

The refusal of the state to recognise Presbyterian marriages compounded the difficulties involved in defining a legally valid marriage. The penal legislation prohibited marriages performed by a Catholic priest between a Catholic

---

17 John McBride, *A Vindication of Marriage as Solemnized by Presbyterians, in the North of Ireland* (Belfast, 1702), 22. See also 8–9.
18 Entry dated 21 May 1706, Session Minutes of Aghadowey, 27b, Presbyterian Historical Society, Belfast.
19 Entry dated 21 May 1706, Session Minutes of Aghadowey, 27b, Presbyterian Historical Society, Belfast.
20 M. Luddy and M. O'Dowd, *A History of Marriage in Ireland, 1660–1925* (forthcoming, 2018).

and a Protestant but it did not outlaw the marriage of two Catholics by a Catholic priest. To the dismay of the Presbyterian community, marriages celebrated by Presbyterian ministers were not recognised as legitimate until 1737 and then only in a grudging fashion.[21] Presbyterians planning to marry had, therefore, to decide which marriage service, if any, they would select. They could choose to be married by a Presbyterian minister or a Catholic priest but their marriage would not be legally valid and their children would not be recognised as their legitimate heirs. Alternatively, a couple could determine to solemnise the marriage with an Anglican minister and subsequently seek forgiveness from their minister and elders in their local kirk session. It is not clear how many couples opted for the latter solution but kirk session books regularly rebuked and ultimately forgave couples who had had 'irregular marriages', which had not been formalised in the presence of a Presbyterian minister.[22]

Courtship

Regardless of religious or ethnic background, wealthy parents shared similar goals in choosing marriage partners for their children. Fathers such as Garret Fitzgerald, eighth earl of Kildare, Shane O'Neill, Lord of Tir Eoghain, Hugh O'Neill, second earl of Tyrone, and Richard Boyle, first earl of Cork, arranged the marriages of their offspring in a similar fashion and with a common aim: to maximise the political and social connections of the extended family. Each man carefully planned the marriages of his children to ally with politically influential families in Ireland, England and Scotland.[23]

Endogamy and communal solidarity were also strong motivating factors behind the choice of a marriage partner. Colm Lennon has graphically illustrated the inter-connections and inter-marriage of Old English families as they endeavoured to maintain their communal bonds and distinct identity.[24] The marriage pattern of New English and Scottish settlers suggests a similar tendency towards endogamy, which was, as in the Old English community,

21 J. C. Beckett, *Protestant Dissent in Ireland, 1687–1780* (London: Faber, 1948), 116–23.

22 See, for example, Session Book of Aghadowey, Presbyterian Historical Society, Belfast.

23 N. Canny, *The Upstart Earl: A Study of the Social and Mental World of Richard Boyle, First Earl of Cork, 1566–1643* (Cambridge University Press, 1982), 77–123; P. Little, 'The Geraldine Ambitions of the First Earl of Cork', *Irish Historical Studies*, 33 (2002), 151–68; J. Ohlmeyer, *Making Ireland English. The Irish Aristocracy in the Seventeenth Century* (London and New Haven: Yale University Press, 2012), 169–207; M. O'Dowd, *A History of Women in Early Modern Ireland, 1500–1800* (Harlow: Pearson Education, 2005), 9–42.

24 C. Lennon, *The Lords of Dublin in the Age of Reformation* (Dublin: Irish Academic Press, 1989), 72–81.

reinforced by religious affiliation.[25] Among poorer, Irish families a spouse was chosen from within the local community. This meant that many people married within the canonically prohibited degrees, but it was a practice that also fostered loyalty to the kin group and strong inter-connecting family bonds.

The choice of spouse was, therefore, regulated by family considerations and was normally directed by parents. The latter (and particularly fathers) could threaten financial or other penalties if their choice was rejected. In 1622, for example, Thomas Netterville told the Dublin Chancery Court that when his daughter Anne married Laurence Tallon he reduced her marriage portion from £250 to £100. He justified his actions because he said that 'of all the men in the world', Lawrence was not the husband that he would have chosen for his daughter. Anne and Lawrence, however, 'bearing mutual affection' to one another, married without Thomas's approval.[26]

The danger of a young couple privately committing themselves to an undissolvable promise must also have been a cause of concern for parents. As the petition of Margaret McNamara indicates, the vicar general in the ecclesiastical court in Killaloe in the late seventeenth and early eighteenth century received pleas from single mothers who claimed that the fathers of their children had promised to marry them prior to having had sexual intercourse with them. Thomas Moriarty was not unusual in confessing to the sin of fornication but refusing to acknowledge that he had made a marital pledge. He also shared with other men a desire to have his public penance commuted to a more discrete payment of a fine.[27] Another young man found guilty of fornication, Florence McNamara, told the vicar general that the performance of his penance in public would be 'a very great barr to his future'. His father had already expressed disapproval of his son's conduct and had thrown him out of the house.[28] The father was possibly aware that McNamara, like Moriarty, had fathered a child out of wedlock.

As these petitions make clear, parents often faced a dilemma in accepting the courtship practices of their children. According to canon law, parents or guardians could not force a son or daughter to marry against their wishes. They had to observe a fine balance between coercion and encouragement. The majority were probably not indifferent to the desirability of an emotional bond between couples. Robert Dillon, for example, countenanced the

25 See, for example, D. Jackson, *Intermarriage in Ireland, 1550–1650* (Cultural and Educational Promotions: Montreal, 1970).
26 CP, BB/148, NAI.
27 See note 1 above.
28 Add Ms 31821, ff. 51, 83, 85, 98, 111, 114, 134, British Library.

wooing of his sister, Sisly, by George Strong, even though he was a yeoman of a 'bare estate' because Sisly had a 'good liking' of him.[29] Mathew Haye broke off his negotiations with Hammon Stafford for the marriage of his daughter saying 'I perceive you love not my daughter and therefore I will sicke [seek] no more after you.'[30] Young men and women were also prepared to risk their parents' disapproval to marry out of 'passion' or 'love'. In 1521, when the father of John McCan opposed his son's choice of wife, John said that 'he would not deny it were his father to cut off his head'.[31] Mary Boyle also described how Charles Rich 'did insensibly steal away my heart' so that she could 'not with any patience endure to hear' about the suitors recommended by her father.[32]

The rituals of courtship, when a suitable potential candidate had been identified, are only fleetingly glimpsed in the surviving records. For children in wealthy families, such as those of the earl of Cork, whose marriages were arranged in childhood, courtship involved living in the homes of their future in-laws for many years prior to the marriage taking place.[33] In politically arranged marriages among Gaelic families, courtship rituals may also have been minimal. Hugh O'Neill, second earl of Tyrone, seems to have organised the marriages of his daughters with little concern for courtship etiquette. Sir Ross McMahon married one of Tyrone's daughters, but in 1579 her father threatened that he would take her away and marry her to another Ulster lord if McMahon did not behave as he instructed.[34] Rose, another daughter of Tyrone, married Hugh Roe O'Donnell as part of the political network created by her father in Ulster. They subsequently separated and Rose was married to another of Tyrone's vassals, Domhnall Ballach O'Cahan, who had previously been married to a sister of O'Donnell. In the early seventeenth-century Ulster O'Cahan allied with the English administration against his father-in-law and, as a consequence, he separated from Rose and sent her home to her father.[35]

Although Hugh O'Neill moved his daughters crudely from one marriage to another, his courtship of his third wife, Mabel Bagenal, demonstrated his

---

29 CP, BB/240, NAI.

30 CP, BB/221, NAI.

31 L. P. Murray (ed.), 'Archbishop Cromer's Register', *County Louth Archaeological Society Journal*, 8 (1935), 271–2.

32 *Autobiography of Mary Countess of Warwick*, ed. T. Crofton Croker (London: The Percy Society, 1848), 7.

33 Canny, *The Upstart Earl*, 77–123.

34 P. Walsh, 'The Will and Family of Hugh O'Neill', *The Irish Ecclesiastical Record*, fifth series, 13 (1919), 33–6.

35 J. Casway, 'The Decline and Fate of Dónal Ballagh O'Cahan and his Family', in M. Ó Siochrú (ed.), *Kingdoms in Crisis. Ireland in the 1640s. Essays in Honour of Dónal Cregan* (Dublin: FCP, 2001), 45–6; C. P. Meehan, *The Fate and Fortunes of Hugh O'Neill, Earl of Tyrone, and Rory O'Donel, Earl of Tyrconnell* (Dublin: James Duffy, 1879), 194–5.

awareness of the ritual expected in Old and New English society. Following the death of his second wife, Tyrone allegedly developed a 'wondrefull affection' for the youngest daughter of Englishman, Sir Nicholas Bagenal, who had settled in Newry in the 1550s. Mabel Bagenal was about twenty years of age when her father died in February 1591. In the absence of her father, Tyrone approached Mabel's brother, Henry, for permission to marry his sister. Bagenal prevaricated and refused to approve the marriage until he had consulted with the London authorities. Tyrone claimed that he approached Bagenal 'at least six several times for his consent' and also asked friends and family to act on his behalf. Frustrated by Bagenal's reluctance to agree to the marriage and impatient with his 'vehement affection of love', Tyrone seized an opportunity to approach Mabel directly while she was residing at her sister's home in County Louth. He accepted an invitation from Mabel's brother-in-law, Sir Patrick Barnewall, to stay the night in the course of which the couple were 'trothed together' and, as a token of their promise to marry, Tyrone gave Mabel a gift of a gold chain. In the following weeks, the couple exchanged messages 'which confirmed our love'. They also agreed a plan in which Mabel would elope from her sister's house to be married to Tyrone. The union was solemnised in a private house by Thomas Jones, bishop of Meath. In his account of the marriage, Tyrone was anxious to emphasise that he had behaved honourably towards Mabel and that he did 'not once touch hir' until the marriage service was performed.[36] The earlier betrothal may, however, have involved sexual consummation. Mabel, according to the bishop of Meath, urged him to 'perfecte the mariage betweene us, the sooner the better for my creditts sake'. The bishop defended his actions in solemnising the marriage because the couple had already been betrothed. It was, therefore, essential for Mabel's reputation that the marriage be formalised. According to the bishop:

> I resolved chieflie in regarde of the daunger wherein the gentlewomans creditt and chastitie stoode, to perfecte that knott wch themselves before had knytte, and did accordinglie ... celebrate that marriage.[37]

Tyrone's wooing of Mabel Bagenal suggests that he could, as in other aspects of his life, move easily between Gaelic and English modes of behaviour and

---

36 H. C. Hamilton (ed.), *Calendar of State Papers, Ireland, 1588–1592* (London: HMSO, 1885), 436.
37 D. Mac Carthy, ' "Of the Takeing Awaie of a Gentlewoman, the Youngest Daughter of Sir Nicholas Bagenall, Late Marshall of Her Majestie's Armie, by the Erle of Tirowen"; As Revealed by the Documents Preserved in Her Majesty's State Paper Office', *Journal of the Kilkenny and South-East of Ireland Archaeological Society*, new series, 1 (1857), 298–311.

fulfil the requirements of a courting gentleman. He requested formal permission from Mabel's male guardian; he enlisted friends and family to act as intermediaries; he visited the house of his potential bride and when she agreed, they became formally betrothed. Like other courtiers, Tyrone presented Mabel with a gift and exchanged love letters with her. The elopement of the couple, while unusual, was not exceptional. Mabel may in fact have been twenty-one by the time she married and was, therefore, free to marry whom she chose without the approval of her brother. Nor was mutual affection and attraction missing from the marriage. Although, Henry Bagenal presented the marriage as a cynical move on Tyrone's part to humiliate him, contemporary accounts stressed the strong feelings that Tyrone had for Mabel. The bishop of Meath describes Tyrone as 'wholly possessed with the love of the gentlewoman', while Tyrone himself referred to his 'earnest affection' and 'love' for Mabel.[38] For her part, Mabel was clearly attracted to Tyrone and assured the bishop of Meath that she left her sister's house of her own free will.

The only ritual absent from the Bagenal/Tyrone courtship was the financial negotiation that Tyrone claimed that he had offered to agree with Henry Bagenal on a number of occasions.[39] The economic terms of a marriage were normally determined by fathers or, as in the Bagenal case, with a male guardian. A bride's dowry could be in kind or in cash and property. Among wealthy Gaelic families, marriage portions were usually in the form of animal stock and farm and household goods. The similarity of dowries in kind listed in surviving chancery pleadings suggests that there was an accepted custom as to their content. The typical dowry consisted of a specified number of cows, a team of plough horses, a certain number of sheep and riding horses, a brass pan and a griddle iron. Some, but not all, also included pigs and a horse cart.[40] The number of animals varied, but in all cases the stock and goods would have been sufficient for the couple to establish a farm of their own. In his will of 1612, Cormac O'Hara acknowledged the right of his wife, Oonagh Gallagher, according to Gaelic customary law, to receive as a widow the stock and goods that she had brought to the marriage. O'Hara's bequest to Oonagh indicated the contribution that her dowry had made to the family farm. He bequeathed to her 'in consideration of her portion' almost all of his cows

---

38 Mac Carthy, '"Of the Takeing Awaie of a Gentlewoman"', 305; Hamilton (ed.), *Calendar of State Papers, 1588–1592*, 435.

39 H. C. Hamilton (ed.), *Calendar of State Papers Ireland, 1592–1596* (London: HMSO, 1890), 170–2.

40 See, for example, CP B/40, G/1, G/303, I/146, J/166, NAI.

(thirty out of thirty-four), bulls and heifers (twenty out of twenty-seven) and a quantity of corn and a jewelled cross.[41]

Dowries in kind were gradually replaced by cash sums. In the 1570s and 1580s, dowries of between £200 and £400 were common although some fathers were more generous. Nicholas Bagenal, for example, bequeathed £1,000 for his daughter Mabel's marriage.[42] By the 1630s, marriage portions of between £300 and £500 were the norm in families at gentry level, while the largest landowners were by that time leaving portions of between £1,000 and £3,000 to their daughters and, again, occasionally more.[43] Jane Ohlmeyer has estimated that in the 1650s, the average marriage portion among Irish aristocratic families was £3,000. In merchant families, a cash sum could be augmented by offering the groom a share in the family business or accommodation in the family home.[44]

In his account of the elopement of Mabel Bagenal, the bishop of Meath noted that he had spoken with her apart from Tyrone to confirm that she had not left her sister's house under coercion. The question was likely to have been provoked by awareness that the violent abduction of young wealthy women was not uncommon in sixteenth-century Ireland.[45] In one of the most well-publicised cases in seventeenth-century Ireland, Mary Ware, the granddaughter of the author, James Ware, was taken from her home by James Shirley in 1668. Shirley had gone through a more regular form of courtship in visiting the Ware home and asking her father's permission to marry. When his request was rejected, he colluded with a maid servant to seize Mary from her home and attempted to rape her. Mary escaped and sued Shirley for the assault. The publicity that the case received may have been partly to emphasise that no sexual intercourse had taken place. Mary married not long after her abduction, which might not have been possible if she had had sex with Shirley.[46]

Patriarchy and Family Relations

The marriage patterns of all social and ethnic groups in sixteenth-century Ireland testify to the importance of the extended family unit. Across ethnic

---

41 Will and inventory of goods of Cormac O'Hara als O'Hara Boy, 18 August 1612, O'Hara Papers, National Library of Ireland.
42 Hamilton (ed.), *Calendar of State Papers Ireland, 1592–1596*, 170–2.
43 O'Dowd, *A History of Women in Ireland*, 77–9.
44 Ohlmeyer, *Making Ireland English*, 414.
45 J. G. Crawford, *A Star Chamber Court in Ireland. The Court of Castle Chamber 1571–1641* (Dublin: FCP, 2005), 364–5, 475.
46 Dudley Loftus, *The Case of Ware and Sherley As It Was Set Forth in Matter of Fact and Argued in Several Points of Law in the Consistory of Dublin, in Michaelmas Term 1668* (Dublin, 1669).

divisions, the patriarchal head of extended kin groups retained an important social, financial and, sometimes, political role. In 1593 Sir Morogh ne Doe O'Flaherty outlined in his last will and testament the 'reverence and dewe obedience' the 'name, kindred, and countrye' should give to the head or lord of the extended kin group. This form of Gaelic patriarchy was only slowly eroded in the course of the seventeenth century. In 1626, Sir Morogh ne Doe's successor as head of the O'Flahertys, Morogh ne Moyre, directed that his territory be divided in a fashion that prioritised the nuclear family over the wider kin unit. Rather than upholding the system of Gaelic partible inherit-ance as his predecessors had done, O'Flaherty allotted a part of his estate to be held 'absolutely' or permanently by each of his three younger sons while bequeathing most of his estate 'absolutely' to his eldest son. This effectively broke up the wider family unit for future generations and reinforced the principle of primogeniture. Morogh ne Moyre also provided for his widow according to English rather than Gaelic law.[47]

Although his will recognised the importance of the nuclear family, Morogh na Moyre O'Flaherty also bolstered the patriarchal role of his eldest son, Morogh na Marte, within the extended family. His younger sons were to pay an annual rent to their older brother 'for ever' and 'be obedient' to him. If any of them died without heirs male, the land was to be remaindered to Morogh na Marte. In addition, Morogh ne Moyre instructed his principal heir to con-tribute towards the marriage portions of his granddaughters whose father had died, a request that also recognised Morogh na Marte's patriarchal role within the wider kin group.[48]

The extended family was also the mechanism through which some English men developed their power bases in Ireland. Nicholas Canny has analysed the nature of the patriarchal control exercised by Richard Boyle, first earl of Cork who 'respected neither the theory nor the reality of the nuclear family'. He insisted that his married daughters continue to recognise him as 'head of a kinship group', sometimes at the expense of the obedi-ence due to their husbands.[49] Adam Loftus, first Viscount Ely, a member of another family network developed by his uncle, Archbishop Adam Loftus, was also dismissive of the concept of the nuclear family when he attemped

47 *A Chorographical Description of West or H-Iar Connaught: Written A.D. 1684 by Roderic O'Flaherty; Edited From a Ms. in the Library of Trinity College, Dublin, With Notes and Illustrations by James Hardiman*, ed. J.Hardiman (Dublin: Irish Archaeological Society, 1846), 399, 404–5.

48 *A Chorographical Description of West or H-Iar Connaught*, 404–5.

49 N. Canny, *The Upstart Earl: A Study of the Social and Mental World of Richard Boyle, First Earl of Cork, 1566–1643*, (Cambridge University Press, 1982), 120.

to disinherit his eldest son, Robert, due to their disagreement about Robert's marriage settlement.[50]

Historians have suggested that the central position of the nuclear family in early modern England weakened connections with extended kin networks. In times of crisis, men and women were more likely to turn to friends and neighbours than they were to summon members of their extended family for support.[51] When English (and Scottish) people come to Ireland, however, reliance on extended kin members assumed an importance that it did not have in their home environments. Administrators, soldiers and settlers encouraged members of their wider family to join them in Ireland. In the Tudor administration and in the army, brothers, uncles, nephews and cousins served side by side. Similarly, civilian settlers appreciated their kin connections as they set up home in isolated parts of Ireland. When Susan Montgomery, the wife of George Montgomery, bishop of Derry, Raphoe and Clogher, arrived in Derry in 1605, she was very pleased to discover a daughter of a distant cousin living in the city. Montgomery's husband encouraged other members of their extended family to settle near them in the north of Ireland, suggesting to his brother-in-law that he would find in Ireland a 'new colony of your own kindred in all the four branches and families your children are nearest unto: of Steynings, Willoughbyes, Culms and Freyes'.[52]

Extant wills provide evidence of the ways in which men asserted their authority in their immediate family, while also recognising the claims of the wider kin group. Edward Ball, an alderman and mayor of Dublin, manifested in his will of 1621 a typical mixture of benign care for his wife and daughter and a determination to maintain male authority and control. He provided generously for his wife, leaving her a house and other property and did not limit her possession to widowhood, as many husbands did. Ball also named his daughter, Anne, as his executor and gave her an annual allowance until she married. At the same time, however, Ball took measures to deprive Anne of her inheritance as his only child. He nominated his brother as his main heir and remaindered the property to his nephews and another brother.[53]

50 B. Kane, *The Politics and Culture of Honour in Britain and Ireland, 1541–1641* (Cambridge University Press, 2010), 245–60. For the Loftus family network, see Jackson, *Intermarriage in Ireland, 1550–1650*. See also Ohlmeyer, *Making Ireland English*, 420–5.

51 For the discussion on the role of kinship in early modern England see D. Cressy, 'Kinship and Kin Interaction in Early Modern England', *Past & Present*, 113 (1986), 38–69.

52 W. C. Trevelyan and C. E. Trevelyan (eds.), *Trevelyan Papers Part III* (Camden Society: London, 1872), 149–50. For Susan Montgomery's letter, see 100.

53 W. B. Wright, *Ball Family Records. Genealogical Memoirs of Some Ball Families of Great Britain, Ireland and America* (York: Yorkshire Printing County Ltd: 1908), xcxiii–xxiv.

The extended kin group existed, therefore, in an uneasy relationship with the nuclear family unit. English equity and common law gave priority to the claims of the latter but this was often resisted by Gaelic families. The Dublin courts frequently became the location for a clash of two different concepts of the Irish family. The legal rights of women under English law were a particular source of contention. The Chancery Court upheld the right of women to inherit their father's property if he had no sons. Men from Gaelic society, however, pleaded with the chancellor to consider the equity of maintaining customary inheritance practices which prohibited female inheritance.[54]

Despite the different practices in relation to female inheritance, early modern Gaelic and English society shared a common belief in the superior role of a husband in marriage. There was general agreement that a husband could chastise his wife physically but there was ambiguity around the level of violence that was appropriate. The behaviour of Lord Howth who beat his wife and daughter so badly that the latter died and the former lay sick in bed for several days was considered intolerable.[55] When, however, the earl of Tyrone drew a sword on his fourth wife, Catherine Magennis, and ordered her to accompany him to the continent in 1607, his actions would probably have been considered by many contemporaries as within the realm of acceptable treatment of a disobedient wife.[56]

A husband who was perceived to be dominated by his wife was mocked in both Gaelic and English popular culture.[57] English officials in Ireland were intrigued by the power exercised by Gráinne O'Malley. Lord Deputy Sir Henry Sidney described how O'Malley who controlled three manned galleys, 'was by sea as by land more than Mrs Mate' with her husband, Richard an Iarainn Burke.[58] In early modern England, communal skimmingtons or ridings publicly humiliated husbands who found themselves in the same position as Richard an Iarainn by, among other customs, leading them on a horse through the locality. In 1638, inhabitants of Christ

---

54 M. O'Dowd, 'Women and the Irish Chancery Court in the Late Sixteenth and Early Seventeenth Centuries', *Irish Historical Studies*, 31 (1999), 484–6; K. W. Nicholls, 'Some Documents on Irish Law and Custom in the Sixteenth Century', *Analecta Hibernica*, 6 (1970), 105–29.

55 Crawford, *A Star Chamber Court in Ireland*, 223–5, 443–5.

56 C. W. Russell and J. P. Prendergast (eds.), *Calendar of State Papers Ireland, 1606–8* (London: Longmans, 1874), pp 270–4.

57 H. Roodenburg and P. Spierenburg (eds.), *Social Control in Europe*, i, *1500–1800* (Columbus, OH: Ohio State University Press, 2004); C. Marstrander, 'Bídh Crínna', *Eriú*, 5 (1911), 126–43.

58 M. O'Dowd, 'O'Malley, Gráinne (fl. 1577–1597)', in Matthew and Harrison (eds.), *Oxford Dictionary of National Biography*.

Church Yard in Dublin described what seems to have been a communal effort to shame a man who was regularly beaten by his wife. A horse was placed in front of his house in the Yard. The wife had defended her action by claiming that it was a 'good meanes' to keep her husband in order. Tobias Norris, a shopkeeper in the Yard, argued, however, that the wife's behaviour 'tendeth to the discredit of the rest of the inhabitants' and that the riding was intended to reassure her neighbours who might become 'dishartened if men [were] to loose there authoritie if woman [were] to assume the like'. The riding came to an abrupt end when the intended victim came out of his house swinging a sword. He killed the horse and injured a young girl who was standing nearby. Witnesses of the event defended the ritual as part of 'the ancient custom of England' and, according to some, it was also, 'the former practise' of Christ Church Yard.[59] English artisans and craftsmen who had settled in the neighbourhood of the Dublin cathedral in the seventeenth century appear to have attempted to introduce or revive a custom, which would have been a more familiar sight in English villages and towns.[60]

Childbirth and Children

English commentators expressed surprise at the apparent ease with which Irish women gave birth, a phenomenon that they attributed to their physical 'hardiness'.[61] The differences between the childbirth practices of Irish and English women were, however, cultural rather than physical. Although we know little about the childbirth rituals of Gaelic Ireland, the long lying-in period common among middle and upper sections of English society seems not to have been an Irish custom.

Despite the perception that Irish women had no need for assistance in childbirth, the medical profession in medieval and early modern Ireland was familiar with European writings on gynaecology and childbirth. Medieval scribes translated the 'Trotula' and other medieval texts on women's medicine

---

59 M2448, 365–7, NAI. See also 362–4, 370–1, 377. For a description of the seventeenth-century community in Christ Church Yard, see R. Stalley, 'The Architecture of the Cathedral and Priory Buildings, 1250–1530', in K. Milne (ed.), *Christ Church Cathedral, Dublin. A History* (Dublin: FCP, 2000), 128.

60 For the introduction of folk drama to Ireland by Scottish settlers, see A. Gailey, *Irish Folk Drama* (Cork: Mercier Press, 1969), 8–12, 49–50.

61 See, for example, James Wolveridge, *Speculum Matricis, Or, The Irish Midwives Handmaid Catechistically Composed by James Wolveridge, M.D.; With a Copious Alphabetical Index* (London, 1670), preface.

into Irish.[62] Later, in the seventeenth century, Cork-based doctor, James Wolveridge, drew on the latest medical research for his *Speculum Matricis Hybernicum, or, The Irish Midwives Handmaid*. The volume, which was 'one of the earliest books on midwifery in English', was intended as a practical guide for the 'Matrons of England and Ireland'.[63] Illustrated with a twenty-page index, *Speculum Matricis Hybernicum* provided helpful information on a wide range of topics from how to deal with a breach birth to the best diet for a pregnant woman.

Wolveridge shared the view of clergymen of all denominations that a woman should, if she could, nurse her own infants. Throughout the period, however, the use of wet nurses was widespread. In Gaelic society, the presentation of an infant to a nursing foster mother was common. The child might remain in the home of the foster parents for a number of years, forming a political bond between the two families.[64] Wolveridge, recognising that his advice on breastfeeding was likely to be ignored, included a chapter in *Speculum Matricis Hybernicum* on how to select a nurse. It mixed practical advice on ensuring that the nurse maintained high standards of hygiene with more traditional warnings that the temperament of a nurse might be passed on to the child through her milk. Wolveridge also recommended that it was advisable to choose a nurse who had given birth to a boy because her milk was likely to make male and female infants more 'spritely' while there was a risk that the milk of a mother of a girl would make a male child 'effeminate'.[65]

As in early modern England, the most dangerous time for an infant was the first years of life. Clodagh Tait's pioneering work on parish records suggests that the mortality rate of one- to two-year-old children was not, however, higher, and may have been lower, than in seventeenth-century England. Older children remained, of course, vulnerable to a range of diseases. Tait, for example, points to the rise in child deaths in Killaloe in 1685, which she attributes to a smallpox epidemic.[66] Mothers were usually responsible for administering herbal medicines to their children and the women in wealthy

---

62 W. Wulff (ed.), *A Mediaeval Handbook of Gynaecology and Midwifery* ... (London: Sheed and Ward, 1934); 'Medical Texts of Ireland, 1350–1650', www.ucc.ie/celt/medical.html (accessed 1 August 2015).

63 A. Carpenter (ed.), *Verse in English from Tudor and Stuart Ireland* (Cork University Press, 2003), 418; Wolveridge, 'The Author to the Reader', *Speculum Matricis*.

64 F. Fitzsimons, 'Fosterage and Gossipred in Late Medieval Ireland: Some New Evidence', in P. Duffy, D. Edwards and E. Fitzpatrick (eds.), *Gaelic Ireland. c.1250–1650. Land, Lordship and Settlement* (Dublin: FCP, 2001), 138–52.

65 Wolveridge, *Speculum Matricis*, 145.

66 C. Tait, 'Some Sources for the Study of Infant and Maternal Mortality in Later Seventeenth-Century Ireland', in Elaine Farrell (ed.), *'She Said She Was in the Family*

families such as the O'Briens kept collections of medical recipes, which were valued as heirlooms and passed from one generation to the next.[67]

In sixteenth-century Gaelic Ireland, at the age of nine or ten, boys began to be taught military skills. Serving initially as horse boys, they were prepared for admission as soldiers into the retinue of the local lord when they were about sixteen. English captains in the Irish Tudor army adopted this custom and employed Irish horse boys in local garrisons, training them in the use of modern military tactics.[68]

The transformation of the Irish boy was also central to the Tudor reform programme in Ireland. Selected sons of Gaelic chiefs were removed from their homes and brought to live in the house of a trusted English or Old English official. Although this practice might seem like a blunt instrument of a colonial *régime*, the sending of children away from home for an extended period of time was a common custom in both Gaelic and English society. In England, children were apprenticed for seven or eight years from the age of eleven or twelve, while in wealthier families young boys and girls frequently spent time living in the household of a godparent or a friend or ally of their parents. English families like the Boyles brought this custom to Ireland where it merged with fosterage customs in Gaelic society.[69]

The success of the reform programme in Anglicising the youth of Ireland was minimal and by the seventeenth century, the parents of Catholic boys opted out of the Irish educational system by taking their sons to the continent for an education. Protestant aristocratic families preferred an Irish education for their children, although after 1700 they too sent their children away to be educated in English public schools.[70]

The late teens were an important stage in the transition from boyhood to manhood. At the age of sixteen, all males were expected to serve in the local musters and this was also the time when horse boys joined a Gaelic lord's army as fully-fledged soldiers. Not surprisingly, therefore, many Gaelic lords performed their first recorded military actions in their later teenage

Way'. *Pregnancy and Infancy in Modern Ireland* (London: Institute of Historical Research, 2012), 69–72.

67 M. Shanahan, *Manuscript Recipe Books as Archaeological Objects: Text and Food in the Early Modern World* (London: Lexington Books, 2015); R. Wilson, *Elite Women in Ascendancy Ireland,1690–1745. Imitation and Innovation* (Boydell Press: Woodbridge, Suffolk, 2015), 41–4; Ohlmeyer, *Making Ireland English*, 428–33

68 M. O'Dowd, 'Early Modern Ireland and the History of the Child', in M. Luddy and J. M. Smith (eds.), *Children, Childhood and Irish Society* (Dublin: FCP, 2014), 29–45.

69 O'Dowd, 'Early Modern Ireland and the History of the Child', 29–45.

70 Ohlmeyer, *Making Ireland English*, 433–42; Wilson, *Elite Women in Ascendancy Ireland*, 50–5.

years. The first recorded military action of Shane O'Neill, for example, was in 1548 when he was about eighteen years of age. Fiach Mac Hugh O'Byrne was about nineteen when he first appears in the historical record and Owny McRory O'More was of a similar age when he 'made his mark' with an attack on an English settler family in Laois in 1596.[71] By the late teens, Irish youths were also eligible to join Catholic armies on the continent, which many did in the seventeenth century.

Alexandra Shepard has identified the dominant form of masculinity in early modern England as centred on the household and the validation of a man's reputation through his credit worthiness, economic independence and the trust that others placed in him. English boys were trained in such values in their apprenticeship years.[72] In the predominantly rural society of sixteenth- and seventeenth-century Ireland, the rhetoric of valuing a man by his credit worthiness is less in evidence and used mainly by Englishmen trading in Ireland.[73]

Militarism was clearly a central tenet of early modern Irish masculinity. Despite the elimination of the private retinues of Gaelic lords, young men continued to value martial skills and military prowess. The wars in Ireland and on the continent in the seventeenth century reinforced the manifestation of manhood through armed combat. There are, however, other aspects to the construction of Irish manhood that remain to be teased out. It could be argued, for example, that masculinity in early modern Ireland was centred on the family rather than on the individual household. Men esteemed loyalty to family and the kin group, a trait that was considered essential in times of war. In the 1640s, military commanders had difficulties persuading men to serve in regiments not led by a man from a local chieftain family.[74] In the civic context of the Dublin courtroom and in their wills, men, across the ethnic divide, demonstrated their belief that one of their main responsibilities was the care of their family, a view reinforced by Protestant theologians such as James Ussher who listed among the duties of parents the provision for children and the preservation of the family property and wealth.[75] By the end of the seventeenth century, the contrasting education of Catholic

71 O'Dowd, 'Early Modern Ireland and the History of the Child', 34.
72 A. Shepard, *Meanings of Manhood in Early Modern England, 1560–1640* (Oxford University Press, 2003).
73 See, for example, M2448, 321, 401, NAI.
74 See, for example, M. O'Dowd, *Power, Politics and Land: Early Modern Sligo, 1568–1688* (Belfast: Institute of Irish Studies, 1991), 128.
75 James Ussher, *A Body of Divinitie, Or the Summe and Substance of Christian Religion* (London, 1657), 261–2.

and Protestant boys may also have resulted in their valuing different forms of manhood. Catholic literature, for example, presented priests as heroic figures who risked their lives to defend their faith while Protestant boys educated in England were more likely to have been taught a concept of masculinity that valued individual credit worthiness and trust.[76] It may, therefore, be more useful to reflect on the plurality of masculinities that existed in seventeenth-century Ireland rather than attempting to identify a dominant or hegemonic form.[77]

Irish girls were of less concern to the early modern state than boys and, consequently, there is not as much documentation on their childhood. Among wealthy families, mothers and private tutors educated girls throughout the period at home.[78] It was not until the end of the seventeenth century that formal education for girls became available and then it was primarily directed at training poor girls in the Protestant religion and in employment skills such as needlework, spinning and housework. The first conduct book addressed to young women to be published in Ireland was Lord George Halifax's *The Lady's New-Years Gift: Or, Advice to a Daughter*, the sixth edition of which was printed in Dublin in 1699. Halifax explained that the volume was written to prepare his twelve-year-old daughter for her life as a wife and mother. While advising that she cultivate the traditional virtues of chastity, modesty and mildness of temperament, Halifax also indicated his awareness of the 'inequality' in marital relations. 'Obey', he acknowledged was an ungenteel word. Halifax suggested ways in which his daughter might navigate around the 'unfairness' of rules that permitted men to commit adultery while condemning the same act in women.[79]

Halifax's denunciation of boorish husbands was slightly tongue in cheek but other advice to women also acknowledged the difficulties of being an obedient wife. Lady Frances Keightley, who was separated from her husband, recommended that her daughter think carefully about whether she wanted to get married or enter a convent. If she did marry, Keightley

---

76 On the heroic image of Catholic priests, see E. Hogan, *Distinguished Irishmen of the Sixteenth Century: First Series* (London: Burns and Oates, 1894).

77 A. Shepard, 'From Anxious Patriarchs to Refined Gentlemen? Manhood in Britain, circa 1500–1700', *Journal of British Studies*, 44 (2005), 292–5. See also Shepard, *Meanings of Manhood*.

78 M. MacCurtain, 'Women, Education and Learning in Early Modern Ireland', in M. MacCurtain and M. O'Dowd (eds.), *Women In Early Modern Ireland* (Edinburgh University Press, 1991), 160–78; Ohlmeyer, *Making Ireland English*, 434–5; Wilson, *Elite Women in Ascendancy Ireland*, 45–50.

79 George Savile, Marquis of Halifax, *The Lady's New-Years Gift: Or, Advice to a Daughter* … (6th edn., Dublin, 1699), 24–68.

recommended that her daughter occupy her time by reading as much as possible.[80] By the late seventeenth century, fathers occasionally bequeathed property or a cash sum to their daughters with specific instructions that it was for her sole use. In 1718 Mathias Smith, a Cork merchant, left his daughter, Ann, an annuity of £30 for her 'sole separate use'. Smith's instruction for Ann's receipt of the money suggests an awareness of the importance of a wife having some economic independence. He directed that the annuity should be 'exclusive always of Anthony Goss her now husband and every other husband she shall have hereafter marry' and that she was to hold it 'as if she was sole and unmarried'.[81] The legal validity of such bequests is less important than the fact that fathers acknowledged the separate economic identity of their daughters.

Old Age

Gaelic Ireland was no country for old men or women. In the military world of Gaelic lordship, the corporeal strength of youth prevailed over the perceived weakness of old age. Chieftains who had ruled for a long period of time might be pressurised into yielding control to a younger man. Manus O'Donnell was about sixty years of age when, in 1555, his position as lord of Tyrconnell was usurped by his son who imprisoned his father until his death in 1563.[82] Turlough Luineach O'Neill was about the same age when he was forced in 1593 to give way as lord of Tyrone to the younger Hugh O'Neill.[83]

The Dublin administration was also ruled for much of the sixteenth century by young men. The earl of Sussex was thirty when he was appointed head of the Irish administration in 1556, while Sir Henry Sidney was lord justice at twenty-eight and Sir William Fitzwilliam also began his Irish service at the same age. When Sir William Skeffington was appointed lord lieutenant at the age of sixty-three, contemporaries attributed his failure to curb the rebellion of the earl of Kildare partly to his advanced age and age-related illness.[84]

80 G. M. Ashford, ' "Advice to a daughter": Lady Frances Keightley to her Daughter Catherine, September 1681', *Analecta Hibernica*, 43 (2012), 41–5. See also P. Little (ed.), 'Providence and Posterity: A Letter from Lord Mountnorris to His Daughter, 1642', *Irish Historical Studies*, 32 (2001), 556–66.
81 23/515/14264, Registry of Deeds, Dublin.
82 D. McGettigan, 'O'Donnell, Manus', in J. McGuire and J. Quinn (eds.), *Dictionary of Irish Biography* (9 vols., Cambridge University Press, 2009).
83 C. Brady, 'O'Neill, Turlough Luineach', in McGuire and Quinn (eds.), *Dictionary of Irish Biography*.
84 M. A. Lyons, 'Skeffington, Sir William (d. 1535)', in Matthew and Harrison (eds.), *Oxford Dictionary of National Biography*.

In the aftermath of war in the seventeenth century, experience and loyalty were preferred over youthful ambition for appointment to official posts. The duke of Ormond, for example, was sixty-six when he began his last term as lord lieutenant in 1677.[85]

The public provision for older people was minimal. As Clodagh Tait notes elsewere in this volume, small, often privately funded almshouses identified widows with children as the social group most in need of assistance and provided some relief in the larger towns.[86] State funding for the elderly was mainly directed at provision for former soldiers. This was formalised in 1684 with the opening of the Royal Hospital of King Charles II, which provided accommodation for 400 'antient and maimed' soldiers.[87] Efforts, however, to establish a network of publicly funded institutions for care of the 'deserving' poor, which included the elderly, were consistently stymied in the Irish parliament whose members were reluctant to fund it.[88]

Most older people had to rely on their families to maintain them but this was a process that was often fraught with difficulties. By the seventeenth century, the Gaelic system of returning to a widow the dowry that she brought to her marriage was replaced by the English custom of dower or jointure. Some husbands also instructed in their wills that their wives should remain in the family home during their widowhood. In 1682, for example, Robert Cary of Whitecastle, County Down, directed that his widow should have an annual allowance of £30, the 'best chamber' in the house and that their eldest son was to provide food for his mother and her maid.[89] Many of the petitions to the Dublin Chancery Court were, however, from widows whose sons 'unnaturally' refused to carry out their fathers' wishes.[90]

In poorer households, older people depended on the good will of their relatives but may also have arranged for relief outside of their family networks. In England, historians have documented the financial agreements that older

---

85 T. Barnard, 'Butler, James, first duke of Ormond (1610–1688)', in Matthew and Harrison (eds.), *Oxford Dictionary of National Biography*.

86 See Chapter 11 by Tait, this volume. See also P. D. Fitzgerald, 'Poverty and Vagrancy in Early Modern Ireland, 1540–1770', Unpublished PhD thesis, Queen's University Belfast, 1994, 3–64.

87 *Abstract of the by-laws, rules and orders, made by the governors of the Royal Hospital of King Charles II near Dublin* (Dublin: George Faulkner, 1752).

88 Fitzgerald, 'Poverty and Vagrancy in Early Modern Ireland, 1540–1770', 3–64, 230–68.

89 D3045/4/1/14, Public Record Office of Northern Ireland.

90 O'Dowd, 'Women and the Irish Chancery Court', 476–82.

people, particularly men, made with kin and non-kin to accommodate them through old age.[91] There are occasional references in legal petitions to similar arrangements being made in seventeenth-century Ireland. In 1638 Paul Leslie from Killmaddan, County Dublin, explained to the Court of Castle Chamber that he had made an agreement with his son, Donough, that he could come to live on his father's property in return for maintaining him 'in his old age, in sufficient meat and drink and lodging during his life'. The problems arose, Leslie later alleged, when his son leased out some of the land without consulting him. In the same year, William Owen Byrne from Newrath in County Wicklow, who was over eighty years of age and described himself as a poor yeoman, told the court that his sons had refused to give him any relief. 'Wanting means to maintain life in himself', he had rented out half of his property.[92] Family resistance or inability to provide for elderly relatives must have meant that older people were among the many beggars who crowded into Irish towns throughout the early modern period.[93]

Conclusion

There is no tidy chronology in the transformation of family life for men, women and children in early modern Ireland. Despite the predominance of English common law in Ireland by 1730, the rituals and customs adopted by men and women in Irish society made it a very different place to live from England. The continuing disagreement over what constituted a legally valid marriage meant that couples in Ireland had more options and could marry more privately and quicker than their English counterparts. Gaelic forms of lordship and partriarchy may have declined in importance but in the 1690s the descendant of Sir Morogh Ne Doe O'Flaherty was still referred to as 'the most considerable man in this territorye... the chiefe of the clan or family'.[94] The arrival of a large emigrant British community also strengthened bonds between kin in ways that were less evident in England. In addition, the new settlers introduced new customs for regulating family life that merged or overlapped with Irish practices.

91 B.A. Hanawalt, *The Ties that Bound: Peasant Families in Medieval England* (Oxford University Press, 1986), 229–37.
92 M2448,82 and M2448, 26, NAI.
93 Fitzgerald, 'Poverty and Vagrancy in Early Modern Ireland, 1540–1770' is the only detailed study on this topic.
94 John Dunton, *Teague Land: or, a Merry Ramble to the Wild Irish (1698)*, ed. A. Carpenter (Dublin: FCP, 2003), 57.

13

Domestic Materiality in Ireland, 1550–1730

SUSAN FLAVIN

Over the past four decades, there has been a proliferation in historical studies of material culture. These include explorations of changing attitudes towards acquisition and ownership as well as the ways in which consumer goods were interpreted. This work was originally stimulated in the 1980s, when Neil McKendrick provocatively proclaimed a 'consumer revolution' in eighteenth-century Britain, leading to a surge in quantitative studies attempting to chart its development.[1] In more recent years, however, the trend has been towards studies that move beyond the enumeration of goods to explore the meaning attached to objects and practices. There are problems inherent in both approaches. On the one hand, broad quantitative studies de-contextualise things and shed little light on the creative potential of belongings. On the other, micro-historical, semiotic studies can present an atypical and rarefied view of the cultural meaning of things. Such issues aside, however, there is little doubt that the intensive interest in consumption and its materiality, rooted in the use of previously neglected sources, and in the development of multi-disciplinary approaches, has transformed our understanding of early modern society.

In Ireland, the study of material culture has been slow to interest historians. Until recently, work in this area was limited almost entirely to attempts to chart the development of specific expressions of Irish culture, focussing, in the 'traditional' historiographical manner, on production, rather than consumption, and providing little cultural context of the 'meaning of things' beyond their utility. There are a number of reasons for this lack of engagement with the post-production life of objects.

First, the dearth of appropriate source material, particularly for the earlier part of this period, is a significant issue. The poor survival, recovery and

---

1 N. McKendrick, J. Brewer and J. H. Plumb (eds.), *The Birth of a Consumer Society: The Commercialization of Eighteenth-Century England* (London: Europa, 1982).

recording of the physical evidence, along with the shortage of documentary material, means that the scope for engagement is limited. That said, however, such sources as exist have not been fully exploited by historians. While, for instance, there may not be a sufficient number of surviving probate inventories or wills to generate macro-analytical studies of consumption patterns and the changing use of objects in Ireland, micro-analytical approaches are certainly possible, and have proven useful elsewhere. In an English context, for example, Elizabeth Salter analysed a small sample of early modern wills to investigate the social and cultural significance of 'gifting strategies' with regards to material culture, an approach with potential in Ireland.[2] There has also been interesting work, by historical archaeologists, on the linguistic components of inventories, to examine 'past systems of meaning' with regards to material culture.[3] This methodology can be applied to other sources such as account books, sales catalogues or indeed any source that records objects, and may yield interesting results in an Irish context. The 1641 Depositions, for instance, while generally approached from a political or economic perspective, list and sometimes describe in detail, the contents of the household, shedding light on the significance of everyday goods in a contested and volatile environment. Source problems, therefore, while an obvious barrier to engagement, can be somewhat ameliorated by engagement with emerging methodologies.

Perhaps more difficult to address are the ideological obstacles to this field of study. There is a tendency in Ireland, as elsewhere, to see certain areas of life rather than others as being 'serious, significant, worthy of attention'.[4] These are the areas defined as public and male: politics, industry and science. The devalued areas, the private and female, are seen as less worthy of attention. Objects, particularly consumer goods, enter the private realm once they are produced. As Carrier put it, 'They enter stores. People shop for them. People take them to what may be the most private and female realm there is, home.'[5] This ideological resistance is compounded in an Irish context. As T. C. Barnard noted, in a society where many died of famine, the materials of life, often not sufficing for subsistence, are assumed to be unworthy or too

---

2 E. Salter, 'Re-worked Material: Discourses of Clothing Culture in Sixteenth-Century Greenwich', in C. Richardson (ed.), *Clothing Culture 1350–1650* (Hampshire: Ashgate, 2004), 179–91.
3 M. Beudry, 'Words for Things: Linguistic Analysis of Probate Inventories', in M. Beudry (ed.), *Documentary Archaeology in the New World* (Cambridge University Press, 1988), 43–51.
4 J. G. Carrier, *Gifts and Commodities: Exchange and Western Capitalism since 1700* (London: Routledge, 195), 1.
5 Carrier, *Gifts and Commodities*, 1.

sparse to warrant investigation.[6] Related to this issue is the persistent over-emphasis on Irish economic underdevelopment and cultural isolation, particularly earlier in this period; along with a tendency to view any evidence for development as a function of colonisation.[7] These assumptions mean that when it is considered at all, Irish material culture tends to be presented as monolithic, reactive or emulative, with tastes and preferences imposed upon society, rather than developing organically, or in relation to wider European and global influences. Likewise, while some studies are certainly sensitive to the complexities of identity formation in relation to material culture, there is a tendency in general to present a dichotomised picture of consumption and material culture, with 'traditional' Irish native habits on the one hand, opposing or becoming 'modernised' by English habits and tastes, on the other.

The result is that the issues, questions and approaches generating interest elsewhere, tend to be sidelined in an Irish context. Nonetheless, work currently underway in a number of areas of Irish material culture shows significant development and engagement with broader historiographical trends. Recent studies, for example, have begun to widen the chronological approach of material culture studies beyond the traditional eighteenth-century focus, which has generated a clearer picture of the complexity and sophistication of material culture in Ireland in the pre-plantation period.[8] There has also been an effort to develop new methodological approaches to the history of objects through the integration of quantitative and qualitative approaches to establish a contextualised framework for changes in consumption.[9] The use of previously overlooked sources has also facilitated the development of studies. Madeline Shanahan's work on early modern recipe books at the National Library of Ireland, in particular, has placed Irish culinary and material developments in a broader context, and has added significantly to our understanding of the relationship between women and material culture.[10] Likewise, there has been an effort to expand the study of objects to include not only the *élite*, rare and expensive, but also the stuff of 'everyday life' which has opened a valuable

6 T. Barnard, *A Guide to the Sources for the History of Material Culture in Ireland, 1500–2000* (Dublin: Four Courts Press [hereafter FCP], 2005), 17.

7 J. Thirsk, *Economic Policy and Projects: The Development of a Consumer Society in Early Modern England* (Oxford: Clarendon Press, 1978), 125, n. 47.

8 S. Flavin, *Consumption and Culture in Sixteenth-Century Ireland, Saffron, Stockings and Silk* (Woodbridge: Boydell & Brewer, 2014).

9 Flavin, *Consumption and Culture*.

10 M. Shanahan, *Recipe Writing in the Early Modern World: An Historical Archaeology of Domestic Manuscripts from Restoration and Georgian Ireland* (London: Lexington, 2014).

window on domestic life; an area attracting much attention in English and American historiography of late.[11] Most important, however, is the development of interdisciplinary studies in the field, facilitated by the collaboration of post-medieval archaeologists and historians. A recent interdisciplinary conference, 'Becoming and Belonging in Ireland 1200–1600', for example, aimed to 'provide a space for archaeologists and historians to consider how peoples on the island … constructed and transformed self and group identities in this key period, and how their senses of belonging were made manifest through their cultural practices'.[12] Together these emergent approaches have affected a sea change in the study of material culture in Ireland and this has become a fruitful, collaborative field with significant potential for further development.

This chapter explores the 'meaning of things' in early modern Ireland by focussing on one key representative area: the material culture of food. It considers what food-related 'objects', in the broadest sense, can tell us about the changing nature of domestic life. Analysing new archival evidence for material culture in household accounts, port books, recipe books, wills and inventories, the chapter adopts a thematic approach, examining the use of utensils, vessels, furniture, ephemera, manuscript books, food, and domestic space, in relation to early modern concepts of civility, kinship and authority. It explores the Irish evidence comparatively, using current micro-historical methodologies, and places Irish historical developments and historiography within the context of broader social issues and historiographical debates.

Civility and Manners

During the early modern period the physical and symbolic experience of eating underwent profound changes across Europe. These were linked to globalisation and commercialisation, which led to an ever-increasing range of domestic objects and dining paraphernalia, but also to the so-called 'civilising process', which influenced how people interacted with these objects, with their food and with each other. The nature of this process remains contested, but a number of food-related 'civilising' trends, linked to wider political and social processes, have been identified from the mid-sixteenth

---

11 E. Fitzpatrick and J. Kelly (eds.), *Domestic Life in Ireland* (Dublin: Royal Irish Academy, 2011).
12 See https://becomingandbelonginginireland.wordpress.com. See also, E. Campbell, E. Fitzpatrick and A. Horning (eds.), *Becoming and Belonging in Ireland 1200–1600 AD: Essays on Identity and Cultural Practice* (Cork University Press, forthcoming 2018). The Irish Post-Medieval Archaeology Group, which was established in order to raise the profile of post-medieval material culture, has had a significant impact on this field.

century, including the rise of 'individualism'; a growing preoccupation with self-regulation and bodily propriety; and an increased emphasis on domestic 'privacy'.

Although little attention has been paid to Irish developments in this context, it is clear that here, as elsewhere, table manners became more formalised and codified from the sixteenth century. Contemporary manners books became increasingly available, and affordable, indicating a growing concern with corporeal propriety, self-regulation and education. 'Small books for children', most likely referring to the popular late medieval *The Little Children's Little Book*, and Francis Seager's *The School of Virtue* were imported from at least 1576; the pre-plantation date, raising questions about the relative significance of Anglicisation on the 'civilising process' in Ireland.[13] Both books contained advice to children regarding manners and food hygiene, including detailed instructions on hand washing before and after eating. Etiquette books were accompanied by other material signifiers of 'civility' in the sixteenth century. Fine napery and hand towels occur in sixteenth- and seventeenth-century wills and inventories, accompanied sometimes by the descriptors 'old' or 'Irish', a reminder that manners, even if evolving, were not new, and not necessarily imported.[14] Other items suggest the extent to which behaviour at the table was influenced by emerging fashions. Children's bibs and scented washing balls, 'luxuries' imported for the first time in the late sixteenth century, certainly indicate an early element of conspicuous consumption in relation to table manners.[15]

The dearth of sources and work in this area means that it is difficult to trace the elaboration of manners in Ireland, or to establish the pace at which behaviour became standardised below *élite* society. If sixteenth-century etiquette books, however, indicate the growing codification and formalisation of behaviour in Ireland, then the menu plans of the eighteenth century show a peak in this movement. Table settings and menu plans appear in women's recipe manuscripts from the mid-seventeenth century, illustrating the extent to which the physical experience of *élite* dining had developed.[16] As Shanahan

---

13 'The Little book for Little Children', Harleian MS 541 f. 210 and Egerton MS 1995, British Library. See also, R. Gillespie, 'The Book Trade in Southern Ireland, 1590–1640', in G. Long (ed.), *Books Beyond the Pale: Aspects of the Provincial Book Trade in Ireland Before 1850* (Dublin: Rare Books Group of the Library Association of Ireland, 1996) and Flavin, *Consumption and Culture*, 191–3.

14 For example, Caulfield Will Transcripts, U226, 32, Cork City and County Archives (hereafter CCCA); Flavin, *Consumption and Culture*, 192–3.

15 Flavin, *Consumption and Culture*, 134.

16 A. Fitzgerald, 'Taste in High Life: Dining in the Dublin Town House', in C. Casey (ed.), *The Eighteenth-Century Dublin Town House: Form, Function and Finance* (Dublin: FCP, 2010), 120–7; M. Shanahan, *Recipe Writing*, 58–60; 104–5.

notes, menu plans, which were influenced by contemporary printed advice books in Britain and Europe, provide a graphic description of the layout of the late early modern table, showing how meals were served and arranged and how diners physically related to each other and to the materiality of food. These plans show the extreme formalisation of dining by this period relating to the 'increasing control and restraint of modern society'.[17] People were acutely aware of the 'correct' way to eat. The basic behavioural advice laid out in earlier prescriptive literature, such as not spitting, farting or belching at the table, had been fully internalised. Standardisation of behaviour at this level of society was now such that people were literally told how to 'correctly' lay the table, what to eat, how to serve it and when to eat it.[18]

These changing sensibilities had a direct impact on the material culture of eating in this period. In broad terms, from the sixteenth century, food consumption throughout Europe evolved from a communal, to an individualised event. By the seventeenth century, in *élite* homes, shared messes had been replaced with individual plates and cups; long tables and benches with individual chairs; and fingers with a bewildering range of cutlery, which served to further separate the diner from the 'brutish' process of eating. Again, the pace of such broad developments is very difficult to track, but occasional documentary evidence presents a glimpse of a world in transition. A will made by Andrew Roche Fitz Michael in Cork in 1618 shows that he possessed a mix of furniture associated with 'traditional' and 'modern' modes of dining. Fitz Michael bequeathed his son table boards, and forms, or backless benches, clearly still high-status items since they were engraved with the donor's name. On the one hand, the presence of these items suggests that the family dined in a formal and probably 'communal' manner, seated on display along one side of the long board. On the other, Fitz Michael also owned some individual chairs, an item used to display high social status in the medieval period, but becoming part of standardised practice in the seventeenth century. Chairs accompanied modern tables, which were lighter, smaller and more mobile and allowed the family to dine intimately, seated individually, as 'civil' behaviour required.[19] An inventory of the goods of Roger Boyle, earl of Orrery, taken in Castlemartyr in 1677, suggests the full progression to individualised

17 Shanahan, *Recipe Writing*, 105.
18 Shanahan, *Recipe Writing*, 105.
19 R. Caulfield (ed.), 'Wills and inventories, Cork, temp, Elizabeth and James I', *The Gentlemen's Magazine*, April 1862, 441. For a useful discussion of the meaning of goods, see M. Overton, *Production and Consumption in English Households 1600–1750* (London: Routledge 2004), 94.

dining in certain homes by that date. The goods listed in the dining room include, for example, '24 chairs of Turkey work' and '1 oval table'.[20]

It is generally assumed that the evolution of eating habits was slow, spanning the entire period, and only applicable to the upper echelons of society. Irish evidence, intriguingly, both agrees with and contradicts this analysis. Quantitative evidence, for instance, suggests that the spread of new modes of eating could be surprisingly rapid and widely diffused. Import records show that the humble wooden trencher became an item of mass consumption in the south of the country by the 1590s, with almost 22,000 common trenchers imported by various merchants in that year.[21] The massive increase in the use of this non-*élite* item of tableware may well have been stimulated by the arrival of settlers with the Munster plantation, but the fact that such large numbers were imported, and continued to be imported after the collapse of the enterprise, suggests that demand for this particular type of wooden dish developed quickly in Ireland. The reasons are unclear. The trend may have been stimulated by economic reasons; the wooden trencher replaced the bread trencher, which made it a particularly practical item in times of grain shortage. It may also be that the item was adopted for emulative or coercive reasons; its use representing the civilisation of eating habits. Whatever the reasons, its acceptance suggests a swift shift in non-*élite* modes of dining and the growing individuality and standardisation of eating practices in parts of Ireland, which certainly deserves further attention.

While change might not always have been slow, it was most likely restricted by social and regional factors. As anecdotal evidence suggests, certain signifiers of 'civilised' dining, for instance the fork, remained limited to fashionable circles until at least the early eighteenth century.[22] Reverend Caesar Otway, for example, described dining with a knife only and drinking from a wooden noggin rather than a cup in 1698.[23] For the poor, especially in more rural areas, it is likely that little changed in their experience of eating, with few objects involved in meal times at all.[24] Detailed studies of consumer behaviour in Britain however, should serve as a warning against the acceptance of simple dichotomies in consumption such as urban/rural, upper/lower class

20 *Calendar of the Orrery Papers*, ed. Edward MacLysaght (Dublin: Irish Manuscripts Commission, 1941), 168–79.
21 Flavin, *Consumption and Culture*, 196.
22 M. Shanahan, 'An Historical Archaeology of Recipe Manuscripts from Early Modern Ireland (circa 1660 to 1830)', unpublished PhD thesis, University College Dublin (2012), 25.
23 Shanahan, 'Historical Archaeology of Recipe Manuscripts', 25.
24 Shanahan, 'Historical Archaeology of Recipe Manuscripts', 25.

or indeed Irish/English, which are too simplistic and mask the complexities of consumer culture.[25]

The evolution of manners related not only to the use of material goods but also to changes in the design and function of domestic space. Between the late sixteenth and eighteenth centuries, communal, multifunctional spaces in houses declined and there was a rise in specialised rooms for activities such as cooking, eating and sleeping. Over time, the domestic environment became more complicated, with increasing possibilities for arranging rooms and the objects within them.[26] In Ireland, recent efforts to examine the domestic environment have shown similar trends. Focussing on the development of the Gaelic tower-house in the sixteenth and seventeenth centuries, Sherlock, for example, noted, that while there was considerable diversity in practice at regional and social levels, the open hall was in decline in favour of more specialised spaces.[27] The development of Bunratty castle exemplifies these changes. An inventory of the castle in 1639 values the furnishings of the great hall at just £2, a 'paltry sum' when compared to the valuation of over £52 in the new dining room, added by Donough O'Brien, fourth earl of Thomond.[28] Jane Fenlon has also explored changes in great house design and room usage in this period. Again, in line with continental and English developments, the homes of the *élite* were found to have become less communal, more hierarchical and increasingly commodified, with a profusion of lavish furnishings and new luxury goods serving to differentiate the status of rooms.[29]

Yet, while a considerable amount is known about the fabric and structure of early modern buildings, at least at *élite* level, there is little agreement about what the 'civilising' of domestic space meant in social and cultural terms. For many years, the standard narrative of developments in the built environment was that they represented the gradual and generalised retreat of families to less accessible spaces in search of privacy. This is a contested and profoundly important issue, since the increasing desire for privacy has been linked not only to the changing use of domestic space, but to broader social trends such

25 L. Weatherill, *Consumer Behaviour and Material Culture in Britain* (2nd edn., London: Routledge, 1996).

26 Overton, *Production and Consumption*, 121–36.

27 R. Sherlock, 'The Evolution of the Irish Tower-House as a Domestic Space', in Fitzpatrick and Kelly (eds.), *Domestic Life*, 116–40.

28 Sherlock, 'The Evolution of the Irish Tower-House', 33; J. Fenlon, 'Moving towards the Formal House: Room Usage in Early Modern Ireland', in Fitzpatrick and Kelly (eds.), *Domestic Life*, 153.

29 Fenlon, 'Moving towards the Formal House', 115–66.

as the decline of open hospitality, and the segregation of activities and members of the household, particularly in terms of social class and gender.[30]

In Ireland, as elsewhere, an increasing desire for privacy has been linked to material changes.[31] Where evidence can be found for the actual use of space, however, the picture is more nuanced. Household accounts kept at Dublin castle in the mid-1570s and 1590s, in particular, present a vivid, if atypical, view of the negotiation of domestic space in the earlier part of this period. As the seat of English power in Ireland, Dublin castle was still, in many ways, a typical medieval structure, retaining its great hall and serving a very public function in the provision of hospitality. Nonetheless, as has been argued in an English context, while such spaces might have been more open and inclusive than their successors, they nevertheless had distinct separatist agencies. The purchase of items such as 'black buckram screens', curtains and canopies at Dublin castle indicate how 'privacy' could be attained without any architectural change.[32] Likewise, a seventeenth-century inventory of the goods of Katherine Villiers, duchess of Buckingham, taken at Dunluce castle, County Antrim, contains a large number of curtains and screens including two 'large folding screens' valued at a substantial £13 and three 'red folding screens', valued at £4 10s.[33]

Similarly, architectural change cannot always be taken as evidence of absolute change in practice. In the late sixteenth century, significant building work at Dublin castle saw the interior much improved, and a new house built for the lord deputy. The new layout provided ample 'private' dining opportunities for the chief governor and his wife, yet the daily accounts show that meals, for the most part, continued to be eaten formally and in public, with the lord and lady seated at a long board in the dining chamber.[34] Further, it should not be assumed that architectural and material changes in this period led progressively towards either privacy or 'civility'. While newer houses had many more rooms and 'intimate' spaces, they also had many more areas designed for public consumption. Ornate staircases, plaster ceilings, carved doors, mantelpieces, wainscoting and turkey carpets were all showpieces, and it is difficult to assess which items were intended for private enjoyment and which were for public display.[35] Likewise, some

---

30 Overton, *Production and Consumption*, 121–36; See also L. C. Orlin, *Locating Privacy in Tudor London* (Oxford University Press, 2010).

31 Fenlon, 'Moving towards the Formal House', 142.

32 Fitzwilliam Manuscripts (Irish), 31, Northamptonshire Record Office (hereafter NRO).

33 H. MacDonnell, 'A Seventeenth Century Inventory from Dunluce Castle, County Antrim', *Journal of the Royal Society of Antiquaries of Ireland*, 122 (1992), 109–27.

34 Fitzwilliam Manuscripts (Irish), 51, NRO.

35 Orlin, *Locating Privacy*, 109; Overton, *Production and Consumption*, 135.

'innovations' in this period may actually have reduced privacy and indeed civility. The manufacture of a 'close stool' for Lord Deputy Fitzwilliam, in 1575, is a crude but thought-provoking example.[36] Changing design features in the early modern period led to the abandonment of the private garde-robe (or latrine) and the adoption, in wealthy homes, of the early modern close stool; a covered chamber pot enclosed in a wooden frame.[37] This was a less hygienic, and far less 'private' alternative, since it was not always situated in the seclusion of the bedroom, and had, of course, to be emptied by servants.[38]

Social hierarchies had always been carefully maintained with regards to the rituals of dining. Certain foods were restricted to the *élite* palate: objects and furnishings, such as the great salt or an elaborately carved chair, served to reinforce the status of the host in relation to his guests; architectural features such as an elevated dais or a decorative canopy distinguished the *élite* family in the great hall. Nonetheless, there is little doubt that early modern developments greatly facilitated the reinforcement of social hierarchies, in particular, through the physical segregation of individuals. At Dublin castle, for example, while the great hall continued in use in the late sixteenth century, its status had already been downgraded to that of a mess hall. While the gentlemen ate at the long board in the presence chamber, square boards were set up in great hall, for the officers and stewards, who never ate in their presence.[39] A century later, an inventory of the castle, taken in 1678, shows the evolution of the dining space which had by now become a fully specialised 'dining room' for *élite* guests, containing 24 'turkey work' chairs along with a range of other luxurious furnishings.[40] Likewise, an inventory of Kilkenny castle from 1639, also shows a separate 'dining room' in this case richly decorated with '5 pieces of Imagery hanging 10 foot deep' and valued at a staggering £55.[41] In contrast, nine years previously, in 1630, the 'Great Chamber' at Kilkenny castle was seemingly furnished with only an 'old moth-eaten green carpet'.[42]

---

36 Fitzwilliam Manuscripts (Irish), 51, NRO.
37 N. Cooper, *Houses of the Gentry 1480–1680* (New Haven and London: Yale University Press, 1999), 297–8; Orlin, *Locating Privacy*, 108.
38 Orlin, *Locating Privacy*, 108.
39 Fitzwilliam Manuscripts (Irish), 51, NRO.
40 MS 2554, National Library of Ireland (hereafter NLI); J. Fenlon (ed.), *Goods and Chattels: A Survey of Early Modern Inventories in Ireland* (Dublin: Stationery Office, 2003), 100.
41 MS 2552 verso ff. 19–20, NLI (possibly Dunmore House or Ormond castle); Fenlon (ed.), *Goods and Chattels*, 30.
42 MS 2552, NLI; Fenlon (ed.), *Goods and Chattels*, p. 26.

There are also some intriguing hints in the archival material at the gendered use of space in this period, another issue that has not yet been explored in an Irish context. At Dublin castle, in the late sixteenth century, when Lady Anne Fitzwilliam chose to 'keep to her chamber', her gentlewomen ate apart from the gentlemen at a square board in the dining chamber.[43] This was presumably a more 'proper' arrangement for unaccompanied women that, as the prevailing civil code demanded, kept them removed from the male public gaze. There are other suggestions too, of the segregation of women within this particular space. Lady Anne and her daughter, for example, kept individual closets, often located in seemingly deeply secluded and inaccessible places. Lady Anne's had multiple locks, as did the chamber where it was probably contained, and also her chests, trunks, cupboards and desk. Yet there is little evidence to suggest the use of space to subordinate women. Indeed, of late, the so-called 'separate spheres' theory, just like that of privacy, has come under considerable scrutiny, with historians showing the nuanced and complex ways in which people experienced space in this period.[44] Certainly, there are hints, even within this single source, of the complex negotiation of space in gendered terms. While there were certain spaces where the gentlewomen did not dine, for example the newly built council chamber, there were also a number of occasions when the women's dining requirements superseded the men's, and where the ladies actively appropriated the main dining space. In 1574, for example, Lady Anne hosted a number of private 'drinkings' for her gentlewomen; events that took place in the main dining chamber, replacing the usual supper meal and seemingly displacing the men.[45] Likewise, rather than remaining 'becomingly within' as prescribed by contemporary patriarchal ideology, when the lord deputy was away, his wife and her ladies dined out, and were hosted by both men and women.[46] Women could control domestic space in more subtle ways too. It is significant, for example, that in a castle comprising all male kitchen staff, Marie, a lady's maid, was solely responsible for the spices, the most expensive consumables in use, indicating that social class was more significant than gender with regards to domestic authority in this period.[47]

---

43 Fitzwilliam Manuscripts (Irish), 51, NRO.
44 A. Flather, *Gender and Space in Early Modern England* (Woodbridge: Boydell and Brewer, 2007).
45 Fitzwilliam Manuscripts (Irish), 51, NRO.
46 Thomas Becon, *The Workes of Thomas Becon*, Vol. 1 (London, 1564), 545; 667–8; Fitzwilliam Manuscripts (Irish), 51, NRO.
47 Fitzwilliam Manuscripts (Irish), 27, NRO.

Kinship and Consumption

As a political and social concept, civility encompassed ideals beyond polite manners and physical decorum. It was a code of civic conduct intrinsic to the maintenance of social order, most vitally preserved at the level of the patriarchal household. At this most basic collective unit of society, objects and their ritual use served to reinforce the 'corporate identity' of the family.[48] In Ireland, as in England, family status 'rose and fell as a result of the efforts of each generation to increase the standing and honour of the lineage'.[49] Family consumption was a reciprocal and collective process spanning generations. To satisfy the 'cult of family status', objects needed particular qualities. They had to be able to withstand many generations of ownership and they had to be able to assume 'patina', or the 'mysterious ability to grow more valuable as they became more ancient and decrepit'.[50] New objects might show wealth and standing, but 'patina' symbolically reassured the observer that the family were well-bred and not newcomers to their status.

Certain objects were particularly favoured in this regard. These were generally expensive items that held a strong ritual association.[51] Wills from Cork show that merchants and the civic *élite* particularly prized silver standing cups and salts; items of high symbolic value which contributed to the rituals and ceremony of luxury dining.[52] The standing salt, for example, held a prominent and specific position on the *élite* dining table, to the right of the host, visually and physically indicating his prosperity and status. The seating placement of other guests in relation to the salt served to identify their social status in relation to their host. The transmission and continued use of such items reaffirmed paternal authority within the household, preserved the social hierarchy of the family in relation to outsiders and, crucially, served as a reminder of the heir's responsibility in maintaining the honour of the family and the memory of the deceased.

An object's 'patina' in this period was not merely assumed through the bumps and scrapes of age. Engraving, in particular, served to prove the

48 G. McCracken, *Culture and Consumption* (Bloomington, IN; Indiana University Press, 1988), 12–6; 31–40.
49 L. Stone, *The Crisis of the Aristocracy 1558–1641* (Oxford: Clarendon Press, 1965); M. E. James, *Family, Lineage and Civil Society* (Oxford: Clarendon Press, 1974).
50 McCracken, *Culture and Consumption*, 13.
51 For the ritual significance of domestic objects, see M. Douglas and B. Isherwood, *The World of Goods: Towards an Anthropology of Consumption* (new edn., London: Routledge, 1996), 56–69.
52 Flavin, *Consumption and Culture*, 194–201.

provenance of *élite* objects and increase their prestige.[53] Domestic plate, jewellery and furniture were frequently emblazoned with the family crest or with a personal name. Maurice Roche Fitz Edmond, for example, in 1582, bequeathed his heir his 'yellow bell piece cup double gilt and graven descended to me from my father'.[54] Likewise, David Tirry left his son his 'principal cup', while Andrew Roche Fitz Michael left his son 'two formes' or benches, 'with my one name' along with a goblet and salt engraved with the family arms.[55] Testators took particular precautions to ensure that such items remained within the family. In 1582, Edmond White bequeathed pewter dishes, candlesticks and an exotic coconut cup to his brother, Sir Perceval, to be held during his lifetime, stipulating that they must be passed on to White's own son and heir on Perceval's death.[56] Keeping the silver within the family was also on Andrew Galway's mind, when he bequeathed 'three silver spoons' to his third son Richard, with the stipulation that he was not to inherit them should he 'enter in religion or become a priest'.[57] Similarly, Richard Boyle, first earl of Cork, made specific changes to his will after the death of his son Lewis, Viscount Kinalmeaky, to ensure that his silver vessels and white plate 'engraven and marked' with his 'arms', a 'crescent' and a 'Viscount coronet' should pass to one of his remaining sons, Roger.[58]

While objects played a key role in ordering masculine relationships within the patriarchal household, they were also central to the development of female identity and the negotiation of gendered relationships. It has been argued that in patriarchal society, household goods, like domestic space, 'enclosed and subordinated' women.[59] On the one hand, cooking, largely the province of women, 'generated little esteem' and cooking pots were not 'objects to which power accrued'.[60] On the other, recent analyses have begun to expand the view of women's agency in 'creating and modifying the cultural framework within which they lived' through their engagement with domestic objects and food

---

53 T. Barnard, *Making the Grand Figure, Lives and Possessions in Ireland, 1641–1770* (New Haven, CT: Yale University Press, 2004), 135.

54 Caulfield Will Transcripts, U226, 27, CCCA.

55 Caulfield (ed.), 'Wills and inventories', 441.

56 Caulfield Will Transcripts, U226, 22, CCCA.

57 Caulfield Will Transcripts, U226, 38, CCCA.

58 D. Townshend, *Life and Letters of the Great Earl of Cork* (London: Duckworth, 1904), appendix III, 471.

59 See S. Pennell, 'The Material Culture of Food in Early Modern England *c.*1650–1750', in S. Tarlow and S. West (eds.), *Familiar Pasts? Archaeologies of Later Historical Britain 1550–1860* (London: Routledge, 1999), 35–50.

60 A. E. Yentsch, 'The Symbolic Divisions of Pottery: Sex-Related Attributes of English and Anglo-American Household Pots', in R. H. McGuire and R. Paynter (eds.), *The Archaeology of Inequality* (Oxford: Blackwell, 1991), 192–230.

stuffs.[61] Objects were used to negotiate kinship and community bonds, show-case female expertise, as well as demonstrate the 'civility' of the early modern household. Material culture is thus seen as central to the concept of female identity, having complex meanings and a key role in ordering society.

In Ireland, there is no doubt that 'mundane' objects were invested with personal significance beyond their utility. Cooking utensils, hearth goods, and table ware, along with clothing, were part of the 'paraphernalia' legally allowed as limited property to married women and were common bequests between female kin and friends. Ellyne ny Connyly, in 1581, bequeathed her granddaughter two 'brassen panns' and a pipe of barley, while leaving her table cloths, to Catherine Tirry.[62] Tablecloths, just like ceremonial vessels, were items invested with ritual and symbolic significance and the use of the possessive descriptor 'my' in relation to the bequest, indicates the personal value attached to the item.[63] Gennett Creaghe, in 1582, carefully itemised her durable household things, including all her pewter, 'greatest' brass pans and a brass 'sarvyse' and divided these between her female relatives. The more valuable domestic items, including a silver cup, were left to the unmarried women, who had yet to set up home, while her married daughters were bequeathed mainly clothing. John Creaghe, her nephew, was left unspecified 'timbre household stuff', while a further male relative, possibly a stepson, received a 'brass pan that lackett one leg', perhaps indicating a less than per-fect relationship.[64] The recipient intended such objects for practical use, but their 'heritable potential' also communicated 'physical and moral solidity, the recognisable and the durable retained amongst the ephemeral'.[65] These were personal items and treasured family possessions, and just like *élite* goods, were often inscribed with decorative details, a monogram, date or even a moralis-ing verse. Their bequest was not only a means of practically assisting the liv-ing, but reaffirming maternal lineage through time.

The relegation of domestic objects and utensils to the 'female sphere', however, should not be overemphasised. While it is interesting to question

61 W. Wall, *Staging Domesticity: Household Work and English Identity in Early Modern Drama* (Cambridge University Press, 2002); S. Pennell, 'Mundane Materiality, or should Small Things still be Forgotten? Material Culture, Microhistories and the Problem of Scale', in K. Harvey (ed.), *History and Material Culture: a Student's Guide to Approaching Alternative Sources* (London: Routledge, 2009), 173–91.
62 Caulfield Will Transcripts, U226, 15, CCCA.
63 Flavin, *Consumption and Culture*, 193; M. Visser, *The Rituals of Dinner* (London: Viking, 1992), 156.
64 Caulfield Will Transcripts, U226, 35, CCCA.
65 S. Pennell ' "Pots and Pans History": The Material Culture of the Kitchen in Early Modern England', *Journal of Design History*, 11 (1998), 211.

the extent to which women were 'subordinated' by domesticity, feminising such objects, even in a positive way, simplifies the role of everyday things in negotiating kinship relations. Fathers, too, bequeathed their daughters domestic objects. Henry Verdon, in 1572, left brass services to both his daughters on their marriages, a gift both reinforcing and supporting their domestic role.[66] Also, while there was a tendency for men to leave their sons items that assumed 'patina', rather than 'everyday' goods, this was by no means absolute. Andrew Roche, in 1618, left his son a brass pan owned by his grandfather, suggesting that 'ordinary' cooking equipment could traverse gendered lines and had a status value to men beyond its monetary worth.[67] Roche also bequeathed his son a 'jug that his mother had'.[68] Indeed, all of the carefully itemised domestic items in Roche's will were left to his son while his current wife merely retained the 'use of a brandiron' if 'it was idle and she had occasion to use it'.[69] Roche's gifting strategy was designed to honour his first wife, with whom he and his children were to buried, while placing his current wife in a position of obligation to his heir. There are other, less cynical, examples of men using gifting strategies to negotiate and reaffirm gendered relationships. Edmund White, in 1582, used his gifts to honour a female friendship, leaving his maid, Anastas, 'the chest that was my wife's and a little brass pan and the brandiron'.[70]

Conversely, women might sometimes own and bequeath objects traditionally associated with masculinity and paternal authority. Francis Aungier, baron of Longford, for example, in 1628, bequeathed his wife Margaret 'a silver tankard she brought with her' and a cup given by Lord Grandison on their marriage'.[71] Likewise, Elizabeth Boyle, Viscountess Shannon, owned silver cups engraved with her mark 'E.S', along with 'a clock that goes a month'. Her ownership of the latter raises interesting questions about the gendered control of timekeeping in the early modern home.[72]

For both men and women, then, in the earlier part of this period, the durable, the solid and the antique, be they high status or more everyday items, were highly prized and central to the maintenance of kinship bonds. This, however, was changing. By the late sixteenth century in England,

66 Caulfield Will Transcripts, 35–6, CCCA.
67 Caulfield 'Wills and inventories', 441.
68 Caulfield 'Wills and inventories', 441.
69 Caulfield 'Wills and inventories', 441.
70 Caulfield Will Transcripts, 23, CCCA.
71 Will of Francis Aungier, PROB 11/163/252, The National Archives.
72 Will of Elizabeth Boyle, PROB 5/2596, The National Archives; See Pennell, 'Pots and Pans History', 265.

writers such as William Harrison were already lamenting the investment of family money in the ephemeral; in objects such as glass and earthenware that 'all go one way, that is to shards at the last ... their pieces do turn onto no profit'.[73] This fascination with the flimsy, rare and exotic had led to a 'loathing' of traditional gold and silver vessels among the well-off, who now spent their money on delicate luxuries, with no thought to future generations.[74]

The extent to which Irish consumption evolved in this context is uncertain. Novelty may indeed have become an 'irrepressible drug' in the latter part of the period, but the affluent were slow to throw over objects that could assume 'patina' for those that could not.[75] Historians examining the consumption of silverware in the seventeenth and eighteenth centuries have noted its feverish accumulation by the upper classes, in contrast to contemporary tastes in England.[76] This may relate to economic factors. Banking was slow to develop in Ireland and coin remained scarce, meaning that silver continued to be valued as a currency.[77] It could also be read as symptomatic of the instability of Irish society, where visual reminders of status and lineage remained vitally important. In the 1736 the Kildares, for example, 'trumpeted' their re-entry to Irish Protestant society with commissions of ostentatious silver services to the extent that it was remarked that Lord Kildare 'makes a much greater show of his plate than of his virtues'.[78] Certainly, there is also evidence that silver continued to be bequeathed along traditional family lines.[79] The pace, however, at which it changed hands and followed fashion suggests a relative change in its perceived value.[80] Barnard, for example, notes a lack of sentiment with regards to the treatment of bequests in the seventeenth and eighteenth centuries. In the 1680s, the widow of Roger, first earl of Orrery, unsentimentally disposed of 3,700 ounces of silver bequeathed her by her husband.[81] Likewise, in 1748, on the death of Lord Barrymore, the family silver was removed from the ancestral seat at Castlelyons, in 'defiance of the expectation that it would be "left as an heirloom" '.[82]

---

73 W. Harrison, *The Description of England*, ed. G. Edelen (New York: The Folger Shakespeare Library and Dover Publications, 1994), 128.
74 Harrison, *The Description of England*, 128.
75 McCracken, *Culture and Consumption*, 40.
76 Barnard, *Making the Grand Figure*, 140.
77 Barnard, *Making the Grand Figure*, 138; Flavin, *Consumption and Culture*, 209–10.
78 Barnard, *Making the Grand Figure*, 139.
79 Barnard, *Making the Grand Figure*, 141.
80 For silverware see FitzGerald, 'Taste in High Life'.
81 Barnard, *Making the Grand Figure*, 142.
82 Barnard, *Making the Grand Figure*, 142.

Yet, despite the continued popularity of silver, there is little doubt that the relative value attached to objects was changing in Ireland, in line with trends noted elsewhere. The newer objects appearing on the market in the early modern period, being semi-durable, fragile and often without a significant second-hand value, are difficult to trace in contemporary records. Likewise, as already noted, archaeological evidence is sparse.[83] What evidence does exist, however, suggests that even by the late sixteenth century, Irish families too were investing their wealth in items that 'went to shards'.[84] Highly decorated Iberian earthenware, attractive for its fineness and thinness was already widely prized; while such delicate exotica as Ming china had penetrated *élite* Gaelic society.[85] These trends gained pace. As the European luxury ceramics and the Irish delftware markets developed in the late seventeenth century, those aspiring to gentility on a budget could now acquire fashionable and high-quality copies of luxury items like Chinese porcelain. Indeed, between 1692 and 1695, 280,000 pieces of earthenware and glass were imported to Ireland, the quantity suggesting that desire for novelty had spread well beyond the *upper classes*. As the trappings of noble status became easier to counterfeit, gentile consumption became ever more extravagant, defined as much by quantity and novelty as by quality. An inventory of the Inchiquin O'Brien china from the mid-eighteenth century shows the range of goods now required by the assertively 'civilised' and 'polite' family. Serving china alone included significant quantities of round plates, square plates, lobster, soup and scallop shell bowls, japanned bowls and candle cups along with a suite of items required for the serving of new beverages, tea, coffee and chocolate, commodities that were themselves indicators of status.[86]

But, what did early modern commodification 'mean' with regards to family identity? To what extent, for example, was 'fashionable' spending directed towards the immediate needs of status competition, rather than the long-term needs of the family?[87] The evidence is intriguing and conflicting. Undoubtedly, certain rare and expensive items of porcelain tableware were still purchased with an eye to preserving the families' reputation through time, and just as with silver, were often emblazoned with the family crest and

---

83 C. McCutcheon and R. Meenan, 'Pots on the Hearth: Domestic Pottery in Historic Ireland', in Fitzpatrick and Kelly (eds.), *Domestic Life*, 102.

84 Harrison, *The Description of England*, 128.

85 McCutcheon and Meenan, 'Pots on the Hearth', p. 104; C. Breen, 'The Maritime Cultural Landscape in Medieval Gaelic Ireland', in P. J. Duffy, D. Edwards and E. Fitzpatrick (eds.), *Gaelic Ireland c. 1250–1650: Land, Lordship and Settlement* (Dublin: FCP, 2001), 427–8.

86 Ms 14,786, NLI.

87 McCracken, *Culture and Consumption*, 16.

coats of arms.[88] Despite their fragility, novelty items were mended when they were broken and, like plate, remained within family collections over generations, as a visual and symbolic reminder of their social and kinship connections. The O'Brien's, for example, listed 'one very small blue and white pot with a silver spout, this belonged to [the] Queen'.[89] Tellingly, however, no other items in the inventory have a recorded provenance, and the descriptors for the most part are concerned with distinguishing the old from the new, rather than the lineage of the item.[90] This preoccupation with the new is also evident in the archaeological evidence. The important recent discovery of a 'hoard' of discarded domestic goods at Rathfarnham castle, including glass, pottery and porcelain, suggests that as in England, commodification had led to distinct elements of 'conspicuous' family consumption even by the mid-seventeenth century.[91]

This is not to say, however, that use of domestic objects had become devoid of social meaning. As consumption practices evolved, new domestic rituals emerged, which served to reinforce the 'civility' of the family and regulate kinship relations. Perhaps the best example of this is the tea drinking ritual, which developed from the early eighteenth century. Tea was a domestic event; a 'training ground' for adult behaviour and polite manners; and a symbol of 'respectable' family life.[92] It was not a ritual from which men were excluded, but nonetheless, its symbolic power undoubtedly lay within the female 'sphere'. It was women, for example, who generally presided over general decorum and conversation in the tea room; making, pouring and distributing tea, and acting out the role of 'civiliser' and domestic executive in the early modern household.[93] Certainly there are strong hints at the gendered nature of the ritual in an Irish context. An inventory of goods in the O'Brien recipe manuscript, for example, compiled most likely by Mary O'Brien, lists all the tea-making equipment under the category 'China in my Closett', suggesting the gendered nature of tea-related consumption and space. If, as Douglas claims, 'the more costly the ritual trappings, the stronger we can assume the intention to fix meanings to be', then the tea meal was by far the most important symbolic domestic ceremony in this period.[94] The necessary

---

88 Barnard, *Making the Grand Figure*, 127.
89 Ms 14,786, f. 122, NLI.
90 Ms 14,786, f. 122, NLI.
91 This might be usefully compared to an English case study considered by M. Johnson, *The Archaeology of Capitalism* (Oxford:Blackwell, 1995), 182–3.
92 W. D. Smith, *Consumption and the Making of Respectability, 1600–1800* (London: Routledge, 2002), 171–5.
93 Smith, *Consumption and the Making of Respectability*, 174.
94 Douglas and Isherwood, *World of Goods*, 65.

list of equipment and accoutrements was extensive, and costly.[95] Those who could afford to, spent their money on spoons, cups and saucers, canisters, tea tables, slop bowls, teapots, kettles and lamps; not to mention the tea itself.[96] The less well-off invested over time and worked their way towards owning all of the necessary items.[97] That tea was significant, more for its symbolic value than for private enjoyment or indeed taste, is suggested by the fact that in the absence of the real thing, consumers were willing to resort to artificial substitutes. Jane Burton's manuscript recipe book, for example, features a recipe for 'artificial tea' comprised of 'new hay, black and white thorn and honeysuckle', a concoction presumably served with all the expected ritual formality.[98]

Authority and Expertise

In addition to the exchange of objects and the performance of domestic rituals, women used domestic artefacts to construct and transmit authority in other ways. Traditionally, domesticity has been viewed by historians as trivial and trivialising, a particularly anachronistic assumption given the post-Reformation glorification of the household.[99] Recent scholarship, however, has done much to rescue early modern domesticity from this perception. Work on didactic literature has explored the cultural significance of domesticity, and the dynamic nature of female expertise.[100] Likewise, an analysis of manuscript recipe books has shed light not only on the material culture of food and the kitchen, but on the role of domestic expertise in the manifestation of female authority and identity. Rather than a 'dull and routinized' sphere, the kitchen, in historiographical terms, has become a creative space; a 'laboratory' where women constructed themselves as authorities on matters relating to cooking, domestic life and health.[101]

Irish historians have been slow to engage in this area. Recent work in the field of historical archaeology, however, based on the extensive collection of recipe manuscripts at the National Library of Ireland, has opened a new window on material culture in this period, and highlighted the potential for

95 Barnard, *Making the Grand Figure*, 129
96 Barnard, *Making the Grand Figure*, 129, 146.
97 Barnard, *Making the Grand Figure*, 130.
98 Ms 19,729, NLI. See Shanahan, *Recipe Writing*, 102.
99 Wall, *Staging Domesticity*, 9.
100 W. Wall, 'Distillation, Transformations in and out of the Kitchen', in J. Fitzpatrick (ed.), *Renaissance Food from Rabelais to Shakespeare* (Farnham: Ashgate, 2010), 89–106.
101 Pennell, "Pots and Pans", 202.

interdisciplinary engagement.[102] As Shanahan argues, recipe books are a vital source *for* material culture; recording the objects and foodstuffs in actual, or aspirational, use in the early modern kitchen. In addition, though, they are also cultural artefacts in their own right; objects that held symbolic significance, and can facilitate our understanding of the flow and dissemination of domestic expertise, which 'served to animate and maintain relationships across and between social, geographic and intellectual space'.[103]

In Ireland, as elsewhere, recipe books were shared documents, frequently annotated with the names of donors, thus providing a unique map of the social connections of the compiler, both within and without their own kinship and status groups. Recipes in the Irish collection show that domestic expertise could traverse gender, social and intergenerational divisions. Mothers, grandmothers, sisters, aunts and female in-laws frequently donated recipes, along with doctors, clergymen, lay women, servants and cooks, raising further questions about the issue of gendered and social spheres in relation to the diffusion, and authority, of knowledge. In this space, individual expertise could be immortalised. A note under a recipe for Mrs French's currant wine, in the Inchiquin O'Brien book, for example, notes that 'the late Mrs Synge told me the very best white wine she ever tasted was made of white currants entirely, and sweet sugar'.[104] Likewise, as objects, recipe manuscripts were highly valued female heirlooms. The O'Brien manuscript, for instance, started in the late seventeenth century, was added to by four generations of women in the family; its elaborate title page and careful curation evidence of its high estimation in the eye of its inheritors.[105]

While knowledge could traverse social divisions, many recipes in these collections are from women of similar *élite* social standing. In the O'Brien example, donors include the duchess of Buckingham, Lady Powerscourt and Lady Blessington; the book clearly representing a 'social register' of the family's connections.[106] Recipes, in a similar manner to domestic objects, showcased the wealth, sophistication and lineage of the household. A recipe for 'Lady Hewitt's water', for example, contains a list of eighty exotic items, including gold leaf, saffron, besoar and China root and is annotated with a note reading, 'this is my Lady Hewitt's original receipt given by my Lady Wiseman

102 Shanahan, 'Historical Archaeology of Recipe Manuscripts'.
103 S. Pennell, 'Perfecting practice? Women, Manuscript Recipes and Knowledge in Early Modern England', in V. E. Burke and J. Gibson (eds.), *Early Modern Women's Manuscript Writing* (Aldershot: Ashgate, 2004), 250.
104 Ms 14,786 NLI.
105 Ms 14,786, NLI; Shanahan, *Recipe Writing*, 134–5.
106 Shanahan, *Recipe Writing*, 138.

to our family'.[107] The distinct lack of wear on some of these books indicates that rather than being functional objects designed for use in a busy kitchen, they were 'artefacts of display and social prestige' – symbolic items that reinforced the *élite* identity of the owner, by emphasising the illustrious status of her friends and family.[108]

The role of such items in the formation of social and gender identity is, of course, particularly significant in the context of early modern Ireland, where food culture was highly politicised and where the expertise of the housewife was used as a yardstick with which to measure 'civility' in an ethnic context.[109] The Inchiquin O'Brien's, for example, were of noble Gaelic origin but the recipe manuscripts were compiled by aristocratic English women marrying into the family, thereby raising the interesting question of the role of food culture in 'making Ireland English'.[110] Certainly, the spread of 'English' modes of 'genteel' food writing implies, and may have facilitated, the Anglicisation of Irish food ways and domestic practice, but it is important to remember that cultural exchange was a two-way process of acculturation. A recipe 'To make Usquebagh the best sort' in the O'Brien manuscript is in fact a Gaelic Irish recipe, made with raisins and liquorice but 'modernised' and 'Anglicised' by the addition of refined brown sugar.[111]

Beyond their symbolic function, recipe manuscripts shed a great deal of light on the development of female expertise in practical terms. In this period new scientific methods, informed by empiricism, with the emphasis on experimentation and observation, had a major influence on female practice and on the scope of the female role. Recipe books show how women attained and organised knowledge and how they tested and proved it, in effect, becoming scientists in their own distilling rooms, sickrooms and kitchens. The recording of recipes requiring a 'limbeck' (distillation vessel), for example, shows that *élite* Irish women had, by the seventeenth century, embraced the distillation craze sweeping England and the continent, and were experimenting with complex recipes in their still rooms. Annotations

---

107 Ms 14,786, NLI.
108 Shanahan, *Recipe Writing*, 138.
109 See, for example, Fynes Moryson, 'The Itinerary of Fynes Moryson', in C. L. Falkiner (ed.), *Illustrations of Irish Topography Mainly of the Seventeenth Century* (London: Longmans, 1904), 225–30.
110 J. Ohlmeyer, *Making Ireland English: The Irish Aristocracy in the Seventeenth Century* (New Haven and London: Yale University Press, 2012), 170; Shanahan, *Recipe Writing*, 86.
111 Fynes Moryson, 'An Itinerary', in J. Myers (ed.) *Elizabethan Ireland: A Selection of Writings by Elizabethan Writers on Ireland* (Hamden, CT: Archon Books, 1983), 187; Luke Gernon, 'Discourse of Ireland Anno 1620', in Falkiner (ed.), *Illustrations of Irish Topography*, 361; Flavin, *Consumption and Culture*, 155–6.

and marginalia show which recipes women self-tested, and those that did not make the grade. In the O'Brien manuscript, a recipe for dying yellow hair brown has an annotation reading 'as tried', signifying its approval and trustworthiness.[112] In contrast, a recipe for spitting of blood, given by Mr Annesley is crossed out, while an ointment purportedly 'good for any breaking out' is also crossed out with an annotation deeming it 'unsafe'.[113] The word 'approved' is frequently found in recipes, often added to the marginalia of older manuscripts by later hands, signifying that the new owner had reproduced and improved upon a recipe or cure and taken ownership of it.[114] It is also clear from the recipes that domestic expertise was often remarkably 'up to date' in scientific terms. A 'poultice for the worms', for example, originating with a lower-class woman, Mrs Berney, prescribes the use of ground earthworms to treat infantile intestinal worms, suggesting engagement with controversial Paracelsian theory which, in contrast to traditional Galenism, argued that 'like cured like'.[115] Similarly, there is evidence that women had knowledge of treatments for conditions before they became authorised and formalised by professional medicine. Irish women, for example, were recommending citrus fruit for the treatment of scurvy well before the publication of Lind's findings in 1753.[116]

The arrangement and organisation of women's recipe books also sheds light on female domestic practice. These manuscripts were living artefacts, evolving to reflect wider social and technological change. With regard to measurements, for example, analysis shows the overlap of a traditional organic system of quantification relying on know-how and experience, with more precise and standardised instructions, shaped by empirical science.[117] This was also a trend with the organisation of knowledge itself. Women restructured and organised messy books begun by earlier hands.[118] Indeed by the end of this period, the personal and chaotic arrangement of these manuscripts was being replaced by a more structured approach: alphabetised and tabulated, suggesting, as Shanahan argues, that Irish women were engaging with printed cookery books from England and the continent, which had started to adopt a new level of organisation.[119]

112 Ms 14,786, NLI.
113 Ms 14,786, NLI.
114 Shanahan, *Recipe Writing*, 129.
115 Ms 14,786, NLI.
116 Ms 14,786, NLI.
117 Shanahan, *Recipe Writing*, 72
118 Shanahan, *Recipe Writing*, 130.
119 Shanahan, *Recipe Writing*, 129–30, 41.

Finally, domestic expertise and material culture in this period facilitated more overt forms of female authority. Nowhere is this clearer than in the practice of domestic medicine. In Ireland, as elsewhere, the early modern home was the primary location for medical care and the centre for female authority in medical matters.[120] In line with prevailing humoral theory, manipulating the diet was the key to maintaining health, and medical and culinary skills placed the housewife in a profoundly authoritative position. Cures might require household members to submit to regimens that induced sweating, vomiting and fasting or procedures including the application of hot poultices, bloodletting or the lancing of boils. The preparation of remedies required killing, plucking, dismembering, grinding or distilling the essences of a range of domestic and wild animals, indicating a level of licensed brutality often overlooked and intriguingly at odds with both modern and contemporary depictions of the idealised subservient housewife.[121]

Recipes required the procurement and handling of such items as mouse ears, earthworms, ground crab's eye, fresh adder tongues, pigeons and dog grease. The use of such ephemera, entirely ignored in the historiography of Irish material culture, can reveal many aspects of the domestic experience. In the Irish kitchen, something as transient and fragile as a feather could affect submission to female authority and cause considerable discomfort and even humiliation. A treatment for 'convulsions or anything in the head', for example, required de-feathering a pigeon and clapping the 'vent' of the (hopefully) dead bird to the anus of the sufferer, 'letting it lye till it parts extreamly; & so aplye fresh one after another till you find relief by them'.[122] The same object could also be used to facilitate female creativity in the culinary arts. The creation of marchpane tarts, for example, required the use of a feather to delicately apply a 'good icing', which would make them 'very pretty'.[123] A feather could also express and demonstrate female agency. Elizabeth Hughes, most likely, deployed her quill to experiment with the 'invisible ink' recipe she recorded in her manuscript, along with other directions such as 'how to hide a letter in an egg'.[124] Such ephemera raise intriguing questions about the paradoxes of early modern society as expressed through material culture. It is difficult, for example, to reconcile the medicinal and cosmetic use of dog grease, which in

120 C. Field, '"Many hands hands": Writing the Self in Early Modern Women's Recipe Books', in Michelle M. Dowd and Julie A. Eckerle (eds.), *Genre and Women's Life Writing in Early Modern England* (Aldershot: Ashgate, 2007), 52.

121 Wall, *Staging Domesticity*, 21.

122 Ms 14,786, NLI.

123 Ms 14,786, NLI.

124 Ms 41,603/2 (1), NLI; Shanahan, *Recipe Writing*, 17.

some cases involved the boiling alive of dogs, with extravagant expenditure on the accoutrements of pet ownership, including such luxuries as silver dog collars and lavish portraits.[125]

Conclusion

In early modern Ireland, as elsewhere, domestic objects were invested with value beyond their utility. In a changing society, domestic goods served to reinforce social status and civility; negotiate kinship and gendered relationships and demonstrate female agency, authority and expertise. Examining evidence for the material expression of civility and manners in an Irish context has indicated trends similar to those noted elsewhere: the increasing codification of manners; the commodification of dining rituals; and the standardisation of eating practices. It has also shown, however, the dangers inherent in broad and overarching explanations of such changes, suggesting nuanced and complex attitudes to issues of privacy and gendered spaces and spheres. Likewise, evidence for the role of material goods in the maintenance of kinship bonds sheds interesting light on the overlapping values attached by men and women to everyday goods and the significant value of extending the scope of analysis in Ireland, to include consideration of 'mundane' materiality. Finally, engagement with the issues of expertise and authority, as expressed broadly through the use of domestic objects, perishables and ephemera, opens a new window on the generally forgotten items of daily life, and highlights the scope of the domestic role for female agency, creativity and cooperation.

Work in the field of Irish material culture is still in its infancy. Since Barnard's groundbreaking work, just over a decade ago, few have taken up the challenge to engage with the study of objects as a discipline, and far fewer have ventured into the world of 'everyday' materiality. This however seems likely to change with emerging Irish studies showing innovative approaches, methodologies and the use of previously untapped sources. There, is however, much work to be done. While multidisciplinary collaborations exist, there is room for significant development and the stimulation of dialogue, between not just historians and archaeologists, but also art historians, curators, anthropologists and sociologists, all of whom can contribute significantly to the expansion of the field. There is also an urgent need for training in this area of history. One of the most significant barriers to the use of non-textual evidence by historians is the inability to 'read' and integrate objects. In

---

125 On dog collars see Barnard, *Making the Grand Figure*, 149, 184.

Ireland, there has as yet been no significant debate about the methodological issues inherent in the study of objects, either in quantitative or qualitative terms, an issue that should be addressed before progress is made in the field. Finally, and most importantly, as this chapter shows, there is great value in expanding the focus of Irish studies of material culture beyond the issues of colonisation and Anglicisation. People consumed goods for many reasons, and the historiographical focus on oversimplified and dichotomised expressions of identity retards progress in this field and masks the complexities of material culture in early modern society.

14

Irish Art and Architecture, 1550–1730

JANE FENLON

Despite the recurring disruptions caused by turbulent upheavals and the impact of plantation schemes during the early modern period, all groupings in Irish society continued to build or adapt towers, houses and church buildings. An outstanding example of this activity would be Archbishop Adam Loftus's new building at Rathfarnham that serves as a bellicose statement of intent to prevail. It personifies the socio-political climate of that time. Here was a New English churchman who, having recently acquired huge tracts of lands, had an impressive fortress\house based on Italianate designs constructed on the borderlands of the Pale. This building stands as a symbol of the ambition and determination of Loftus and other New English arrivistes to mark out their territories and was probably regarded as an affront by their Gaelic landowning neighbours, in this case the O Byrnes and O Tooles of Wicklow. Such a strong architectural statement as that made by the building at Rathfarnham may be understood to convey a broad range of information that announces a new cultural hegemony in Ireland (Illustration 1).

Students of the early modern period may be surprised to find that Irish art and architecture received such scant coverage in volume 3 of the *New History of Ireland*.[1] Yet in the 1970s the subject of Irish Art History was not taught widely in universities and colleges. Few publications on the architecture of the early modern period were available, with archaeologists claiming the sixteenth century and Georgian enthusiasts looking to the eighteenth century, leaving the seventeenth century to historians in the main. Meanwhile the subject of Irish painting had to await the publication of Anne Crookshank's own work in *Painters of Ireland*, co-written with Desmond FitzGerald, the Knight of Glin, in 1978. In sharp contrast to this, during the early twenty-first century a new generation

---

1 T. W. Moody, F. X. Martin and F. J. Byrne, (eds.), *A New History of Ireland*, iii, *Early Modern Ireland, 1534–1691* (Oxford University Press, 1976).

1. Rathfarnham Castle, County Dublin, viewed from northeast. © National Monuments Service Photographic Unit, Dublin.

of scholars have explored in depth art, architecture and archaeology. It now seems almost unimaginable, particularly from an art historian's viewpoint, that the buildings and paintings of early modern Ireland elicited so little interest in the not so distant past.[2]

As well as being an era of tumultuous change in Ireland, the early modern period was a time when Renaissance ideas spread throughout Europe. Italian and French publications on architecture were being translated and referred to in buildings that were being erected in these islands. The role of architects and artificers in the planning and execution of buildings was commanding growing respect from those who commissioned them. This broad area of study where the physical and mental worlds of the early modern period meshed is being explored and analysed in ever increasing numbers of publications. From these studies a more complete picture of these important components in the genesis of modern Ireland is emerging. This chapter is primarily concerned with the art history of the period, the buildings, paintings, interiors and their decoration, as gleaned from the meagre stock of standing structures, artefacts and relevant documents that remain.

2 A. Carpenter, (General ed.), *Art and Architecture of Ireland* (5 vols., Dublin, London and New Haven: Royal Irish Academy and Yale University Press, 2014).

Of course much has been lost. The dissolution of the monasteries during the mid-sixteenth century resulted in the re-distribution of church lands
and the transfer of wealth from religious hands to secular purses. In turn,
some of these financial gains would allow for the construction, purchase or
refurbishment of fine buildings. In relation to religious artefacts we may only
imagine how great was the loss in ecclesiastical plate, metalwork, altarpieces,
paintings, illuminated manuscripts, richly embroidered vestments and statuary, including tomb sculpture, that were confiscated or destroyed during the
suppression of the religious houses and particularly during the later upheavals of the 1640s.[3] The landed classes and the clergy would have commissioned
such objects along with wealthy merchants and their wives who presented
religious accoutrements and made monetary contributions towards building and repairs of churches.[4] By the early seventeenth century, in cemeteries
and within churches, funerary monuments of increasing size with elaborate
Renaissance-influenced decoration would become a common feature. These
new-style monuments indicated a significant shift in the devotional emphasis
of such memorials and demonstrate the impact of New English settlers on
the artistic and cultural development of this country. Some of these edifices
would be imported from England while others were designed and executed
by sculptors resident in Ireland.[5]

Prior to the plantations of the mid-sixteenth century, tower houses were
the most numerous type of large, stone, high-status, defensive residences
constructed during the early modern period.[6] These were of varying size,
mainly rectangular, often with detached halls and set within a walled bawn.
People of all cultural backgrounds living on the island built such towers.
Bunratty, County Clare, is a massive example built on an earlier structure by
the Mac Conmaras; later it became an O'Brien stronghold. A more complete
picture of this type of building is provided by the tower at Pallas, County
Galway, erected for the Burkes, still standing within its well-preserved bawn

---

3 C. Ó Clabaigh, 'Vestments', in R. Moss, (ed.) *Art and Architecture of Ireland*, i, *Medieval,
c.400–c.1600*, 401–5.

4 R. Moss, 'Continuity and Change: The Material Setting of Public Worship in the
Sixteenth-Century Pale', in M. Potterton and T. Herron (eds.), *Dublin and the Pale in the
Renaissance c. 1540–1660* (Dublin: Four Courts Press [hereafter FCP], 2011),182–206.

5 R. Moss, 'Tombs and Sarcophagi', in Moss (ed.) *Art and Architecture of Ireland*, i, 466–74.
P. Cockerham, '"To mak a Tombe for the Earell of Ormon and to set it up in Iarland":
Renaissance Ideals in Irish Funeral Monuments', in T. Herron and M. Potterton (eds.),
Ireland in the Renaissance c.1540–1660, (Dublin: FCP, 2007), 195–230.

6 R. Sherlock, 'Cross-Cultural Occurrences of Mutations in Tower House
Architecture: Evidence for Cultural Homogeneity in Late Medieval Ireland', *The Journal
of Irish Archaeology*, 15 (2006), 73–92 and R. Sherlock 'The Evolution of the Irish Tower-
House as a Domestic Space', *Proceedings of the Royal Irish Academy*, 111:C (2011), 115–40.

2. Pallas, County Galway, © National Monuments Service Photographic Unit, Dublin.

(Illustration 2). Towers also featured in the urban landscapes in places as far apart as Dalkey, County Dublin, Ardee, County Louth and Youghal in County Cork. Descendants of Norman-Irish lords would continue to inhabit larger, more complex castles, such as Kilkenny, seat of the Butlers of Ormond and Askeaton, one of the many Desmond castles.

With a few notable exceptions, such as the fortified houses at Rathfarnham and Mallow, the question of measurable influences or changes is irrelevant for much of the sixteenth century.[7] Most of the newcomers who had settled on lands during the Marian plantation of Laois-Offaly (1556) simply moved into tower houses vacated by their previous owners. Thirty years later, during the early years of the plantation of Munster, a similar pattern emerged when many of the principal undertakers to that venture occupied buildings that had belonged to the earl of Desmond.

In order to provide protection for the incoming settlers to the new planta-tions, forts and fortifications were constructed in many areas.[8] Several military engineers who had experienced European warfare, particularly in the Low

---

7 R. Loeber, 'The Early Seventeenth-Century Ulster and Midland Plantations, Part I: Pre-Plantation Architecture and Building Regulations and Part II: The New Architecture', in O. Horsfall Turner (ed.), *'The Mirror of Great Britain': National Identity in Seventeenth-Century British Architecture* (Reading, Spire Books, 2012), 73–138.

8 Margey, Chapter 22, this publication.

Countries, such as Josias Bodley (*c.* 1550–1617), Paul Ives (*c.* 1584–1604) and Samuel Molyneux (*c.* 1584–1625) came to Ireland to lend their expertise in the building of these defensive structures. The construction of Fort Protector at Phillipstown, in County Offaly, and Fort Governor at Maryborough, County Laois, had marked a new phase in the building of permanent forts as part of strategy for the Tudor re-conquest. Later, they served to protect the new plantations of counties Laois and Offaly (Illustration 28).[9]

The Conversion of Towers, Castles and Religious Properties

New settlers were granted many of the standing towers, ruinous castles and religious properties along with their attached lands. Their priority was to fortify and convert such buildings into defensive dwellings. A documented example of the problems faced by settlers in making their newly acquired properties habitable was the ruinous Desmond Castle of Newcastle West, County Limerick, granted in 1583 to Sir William Courtenay (1553–1630) from Powderham in Devon, in his position as 'an English Undertaker'. At that time the castle was a collection of ruinous buildings within an enclosed space, while outside there were gardens and orchards. Some forty years later, in 1622, that castle was still under repair. Then it was described as 'a large fair castle which hath been somewhat ruinous, but it is now much repaired and is in contin-ual reparation'.[10] Religious houses were occupied in a similar fashion. When Anthony Colclough purchased the lease of Tintern Abbey, County Wexford, in 1566 he was instructed 'to fortify within three years the site of the abbey' (Illustration 3).[11] Similarly, Sir Edward Denny converted Tralee Friary, County Kerry, into a dwelling house during the 1580s.[12]

An early example of building additions to the towers was the sophisticated arrangement at Carrick House, now called Ormond Castle, Carrick on Suir, County Tipperary. Here, a U-shaped, largely symmetrical, two-storey with attic building abutting two earlier towers, was constructed as a new north range. The work was carried out for Thomas Butler, tenth earl of Ormond, during the 1560s. Prior to these new additions, Carrick had been a rambling

---

9 P. Kerrigan, *Castles and Fortifications in Ireland* (Cork: The Collins Press, 1995), 17–56.

10 R. Dunlop, 'An Unpublished Survey of the Plantation of Munster in 1622', *Journal of the Royal Society of Antiquaries of Ireland*, 54 (1924), 129–46.

11 A. Lynch, *Tintern Abbey, County Wexford: Cistercians and Colcloughs. Excavations 1982–2007* (Dublin: The Stationary Office, 2010), 6.

12 R. Moss, 'Continuity and Change: the Material Setting of Public Worship in the Sixteenth-Century Pale', 182–206.

3. Tintern Abbey, showing Colclough House integrated in structure. © National
Monuments Service Photographic Unit, Dublin.

collection of buildings mainly dating from the end of the fifteenth century.
Externally, creamy lime-render on the walls served to unite the disparate
structural elements. Ormond's architectural interventions created an orderly
courtyard house that was described by William Brereton in 1635 when he
wrote admiringly 'My Lord of Ormond's house, daintily seated on the river-
bank … this court is paved. There are also two other courts, the one a quad-
rangle'.[13] Gardens and orchards surrounded the house and ranges of service
buildings within an extensive parkland setting (Illustration 4).

During the seventeenth century, landowners, both native and newcomers
alike, began to add symmetrical houses with horizontal floor plans to their
existing towers in order to meet contemporary requirements for defence,
comfort and status. New English undertakers were adapting and adding to
earlier buildings. At Ross Castle, County Kerry, for instance, the Browns, in
what would become common practice among settlers, enlarged and glazed
the windows of the tower, breaking through walls to provide doorways for
access to new adjoining buildings and installing wooden panelling in some of
the rooms. Ross Castle was important because it was a large tower that had
been a stronghold of the local Gaelic chiefs, the O'Donoghues, and as such

13 'Travels of Sir William Brereton in Ireland 1635', in C. Litton Falkiner (ed.), *Illustrations
of Irish History and Topography Mainly of the Seventeenth Century* (London: Longmans,
1904), 402.

4. Carrick House, now renamed Ormond Castle, Carrick on Suir, County Tipperary, view from north-east. © National Monuments Service Photographic Unit, Dublin.

would have conveyed some of that status upon the new inhabitant. It was also close to Killarney town where, as an undertaker of the Munster plantation, Browne had settled his English tenants. By 1622, that town had forty 'good English-like houses' (Illustration 5).[14] At Lemenagh House in County Clare, Conor O'Brien (d.1651) added a symmetrical fortified house consisting of three storeys with an attic, to part of a sectional-constructed existing tower.[15] Members of the Old English Dowdall family had a large gabled

14 D. Fenlon and J. Fenlon, 'Ross Castle', in J. Larner (ed.), *Killarney History & Heritage* (Cork, The Collins Press, 2005), 63–73.
15 Sherlock, 'Cross-Cultural Occurrences of Mutations in Tower House Architecture', 78.

5. Ross Castle, Killarney, County Kerry. © National Monuments Service
Photographic Unit, Dublin.

house of three storeys attached to their existing tower at Athlumney castle,
County Meath.

Fortified Houses

Rathfarnham, County Dublin, as already mentioned, was the outstanding
example of a new form of building, the fortified house, built for Archbishop
Adam Loftus (1533/4–1605). Constructed between 1583 and 1585 Rathfarnham
incorporated Renaissance ideas of defensive structures in the angle bastion-
shaped corner towers, combined with comfortable living accommodation.
Of compact design, with three storeys over a semi-basement with a massive
central spine wall, the building was innovative in concept, in the symmetry of
elevation (the curved bay on the east side was an eighteenth-century addition),
and the regular, more horizontal layout of the floor plan. The principal
entrance was centrally placed and a yett or iron grid protected the basement-
level, side-entrance. Rathfarnham was probably built by a military engineer

on a plan derived from a type used in the books of the Italian architect Sebastiano Serlio (1475–c.1554).[16] Some narrow, stone two-light mullioned windows and several gun-loops are also still in evidence on the facade. Other New English administrators constructed defensive houses, situated close to Dublin, during the 1630s. Archbishop Lancelot Bulkeley had an H plan, two-storey house with attic, built on a moated site at Oldbawn in south County Dublin (c.1635, demolished). Of a similar type and date, Brazeel House in north County Dublin, was built for Sir Richard Bolton, lord chancellor of Ireland (1630s, demolished); it featured elaborate, arcaded brick chimneys, and was located within a defensive fosse.[17]

Several other fortified houses were built on plans that were also symmetrical, although there was a great deal of variety in ground plan, leading to them being described as L-, U- and T- shaped structures. Staircases were sometimes housed in projections to the rear of buildings, while others had rectangular or round towers at the corners. Rooflines were often 'busy' with tall chimneystacks and ornate gables. Some of these houses were constructed for new settlers, an example being that of the 'goodly, strong and sumptuous house' at Mallow (c.1598) built for Sir Thomas Norris. Others were built for local landowners, like Coppinger's Court, County Cork (1601), with its massive machicolations and three projecting square towers constructed for the Cork merchant family of the same name, and nearby Ightermurragh (1641) built on a cross plan, for Edmund Supple. Fortified houses usually sat within walled enclosures that had small defensive towers incorporated in them (Illustration 6).[18]

A further architectural development in this type of house was the new semi-fortified Portumna House, County Galway, completed before 1617, built on a 'full developed compact plan', of three storeys over a semi-basement with attic, with four corner towers for Richard, fourth earl of Clanricard

---

16 *Sebastiano Serlio on Architecture: Books VI and VII of 'Tutte L'Opere D'Architettura et Prospetiva'*, ed. and trans. V. Hart and P. Hicks (2 vols., New Haven and London: Yale University Press, 2001), ii, 58–9.

17 H. G. Leask, 'Early Seventeenth-Century Houses in Ireland', in E. M. Jope (ed.), *Studies in Building History* (London: Odhams Press, 1961), 243–50; P. Melvin and Lord Longford, 'Letters of Lord Longford and others on Irish Affairs 1689–1702', *Analecta Hibernica*, 32 (1985), 58.

18 Dunlop, 'An Unpublished Survey', 143; T. O'Keefe, and S. Quirke, 'A House at the Birth of Modernity: Ightermurragh Castle in Context', in J. Lyttleton and C. Rynne (eds.), *Plantation Ireland: Settlement and Material Culture, c.1550–1700* (Dublin, FCP, 2009), 86–112; S. Weadick, 'How Popular were Fortified Houses in Irish Castle Building History? A Look at their Numbers in the Archaeological Record and Distribution Patterns', in Lyttleton and Rynne (eds.), *Plantation Ireland*, 61–85. D. Sweetman, *The Medieval Castles of Ireland* (Collins Press, Cork, 2005) 175–98.

6. Coppingers Court, County Cork. © National Monuments Service
Photographic Unit, Dublin.

(1572–1635).[19] It had a ground plan of two parallel ranges and a central corridor, and could be described as a triple-pile house. Massive chimney-stacks, curvilinear gables with pargetting and stone-carved gablets enlivened the roofline. Decoration of the principal doorway with strapwork, c-scrolls, small obelisks and other motifs derived from Serlio added height to that entrance, which was defended by an iron grid or yett. Portumna House was as innovative a building for its time, as Rathfarnham had been in the previous half-century (Illustration 7). A number of smaller, less confidently designed symmetrical houses of regular plan with corner towers were built for other patrons such as the McCarthys at Kanturk. That house had some awkwardly executed classical elements incorporated in the carved stone door-case of the principal entrance. Mountlong (1631) and Monkstown (1636), both in County Cork and Glinsk in County Galway (1643), which has a truly impressive appearance, are all examples of the fortified house and could be described as the most uniquely Irish type of

19 A. Gomme and A. Maguire, *Design and Plan in the Country House from Castle Donjon to Palladian Boxes* (New Haven and London: Yale University Press, 2008), chapter 6.

7. Portumna House, County Galway, © National Monuments Service
Photographic Unit, Dublin.

building of the period. The interior of Mountlong had fragments of plasterwork frieze decoration with small female figures and swags that suggest
the interiors were more decorative than their austere exteriors would lead
one to expect. Rathfarnham, Portumna and Old Bawn all had gardens surrounding the house with axial approach that led to the principal entrance
through courts or bawns.[20]

Unique amongst all of the buildings of the 1630s was Jigginstown, County
Kildare, built for Thomas Wentworth, earl of Strafford, lord deputy of
Ireland. It was constructed in layers of locally made brick, colour washed and
with skilfully cut and rubbed moulded brickwork details.[21] It had an enormously long frontage of 115.9 metres and in Wentworth's own words he had
built a house 'fit for a king'. This comment explains the internal planning
of the house, where the large-scale rooms and a second kitchen pavilion
were located to the west end. Wentworth possibly devised the outline plan

20 J. Fenlon, 'Portumna: A Great Many Windowed and Gabled House', in J. Fenlon
   (ed.), *Clanricard's Castle: Portumna House, County Galway* (Dublin, FCP, 2012), 49–82.
   M. Girouard 'Introduction', in Fenlon (ed.), *Clanricard's Castle*, 1–7.
21 A. Dolan, 'Case Study: Jigginstown House, 1635–37, Naas County Kildare, Republic of
   Ireland', the Principal Architect's Perspective', in G. Lynch (ed.), *The History of Gauged
   Brickwork* (Oxford, Butterworth-Heinemann, 2007), 99–110.

as he regarded himself as 'a very pretty architect' to be compared with the renowned practitioner Inigo Jones. He seems to have drawn on information or advice either directly from his old friend and possible architectural mentor, Sir Henry Wooton, or from Wooton's publication *The Elements of Architecture* (1624).

Jigginstown could be considered impressive in its ambition and scale but ultimately it was no more than an over-extended house with mundane detailing in the artist-mannerist style then current in England.[22] Wentworth's nemesis, the adventurer Richard Boyle, later earl of Cork, was another ambitious and enthusiastic builder. Unlike many of his contemporaries, Cork did not accommodate himself to ruined buildings for very long. Instead, both he and his close associate Laurence Parsons of Birr set to work at their newly acquired properties, immediately renovating, improving and extending the buildings. During the 1620s, Parsons recorded in great detail the work being carried out on 'my English House'.[23] The list of Cork's Irish properties and those of his family is impressive, although most of his building projects could be classed as architecturally utilitarian rather than innovative because they involved the remodelling of and additions to older, often ruined, structures.[24] Later he would concern himself with building for his sons, and for those he would commission new builds at Askeaton Castle, County Limerick, and Castlemartyr, County Cork. From a design viewpoint the most interesting of Cork's own building projects was the small hunting lodge, Castle Dollard or Dodard, located in the Knockmealdown mountains in County Waterford. Small buildings like hunting lodges afforded patrons the opportunity for imaginative designs. An example of this may be seen in sketchy architectural drawings by an unknown hand, found in the Perceval papers. There, amongst various rough scribbles, a triangular ground plan close to that used at Castle Dollard and also a possible elevation of Ballyclough, County Tipperary, a Perceval property, are identifiable.[25] The lodge at Castle Dollard, now much altered, was built on a

---

22 J. Fenlon, '"They say I build up to the sky": Thomas Wentworth, Jigginstown House and Dublin Castle', in Potterton and Herron (eds.), *Dublin and the Pale*, 207–22.

23 J. Fenlon, 'Some Early Seventeenth-Century Building Accounts in Ireland', *Irish Architectural and Decorative Studies, The Journal of the Irish Georgian Society*, 1 (1998), 96.

24 J. Lyttleton, '"A godly resolucon to rebwilde": Richard Boyle's patronage of elite architecture', in C. Rynne and D. Edwards (eds.), *The World of Richard Boyle, 1st Earl of Cork*, forthcoming (Dublin: FCP, 2017).

25 R. Loeber, 'Early Irish Architectural Sketches from the Perceval/Egmont Collection', in A. Bernelle (ed.), *Decantations: A Tribute to Maurice Craig* (Dublin: Lilliput Press, 1992), 110–20.

triangular plan with circular towers on each corner. The design was perhaps prompted by the similar ground plan of Longford Castle, in Wiltshire (1591), which Cork could have seen during his travels in England (Illustration 8). His rival Wentworth had also had a lodge built in his park at Cosha, County Wicklow, which he claimed to have designed while using a deck of cards to model it over Christmas-tide.[26]

Towns

Existing towns had been built, mainly, though not exclusively, in the colonised areas of the country and most of these were located on major rivers or sea inlets. By the early sixteenth century many towns still retained their walls, which often had towers and gateways incorporated into their structures. Apart from their defensive use, such gateways also facilitated the collection of taxes and tolls from those who brought goods to trade at town markets. In Dublin, according to Casey 'the seventeenth-century extensions to the city were determined by the location and extent of the former monastic estates'.[27] On John Speed's map of 1610, these extensions are clearly shown, with rows of houses depicted straggling outwards from the monastic cores of St Thomas's Abbey and the various suppressed mendicant houses in the town (Illustration 9).[28] Dame Street is shown leading eastwards from the medieval centre to the college situated on lands that had belonged to All Hallows Priory, where the university of Dublin, Trinity College, was founded in 1592. On the north bank of the River Liffey, across the single bridge, more houses and development are depicted on lands previously owned by St Mary's Abbey and brick buildings were replacing the older, mainly wooden structures. Civic buildings of various types, particularly tholsels and market houses were being constructed or refurbished in towns all over the country, including a custom-house built in Dublin in 1621.

Older urban areas expanded while new planned towns were built. Several of these were laid out in organised patterns, sometimes on a grid; others

---

26 Gomme and Maguire, *Design and Plan*, 116. Fenlon, 'They say I build up to the sky', in Potterton and Herron (eds.), *Dublin and the Pale*, 220, R. Loeber, 'Settlers' Utilisation of the Natural Resources', in K. Hannigan and W. Nolan (eds.), *Wicklow: History & Society* (Dublin: Geography Publications, 1994), 271–3.
27 C. Casey, *The Buildings of Ireland: Dublin* (New Haven and London: Yale University Press, 2005), 23.
28 R. Moss, 'Reduce, Reuse, Recycle: Irish Monastic Architecture c.1540–1640', in R. Stalley (ed.), *Irish Gothic Architecture: Construction, Decay and Reinvention* (Dublin: Wordwell, 2012), 115–59.

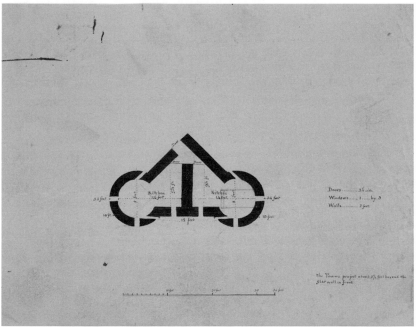

8. Castle Dollard, County Waterford, Hunting Lodge. National Library of Ireland.

359

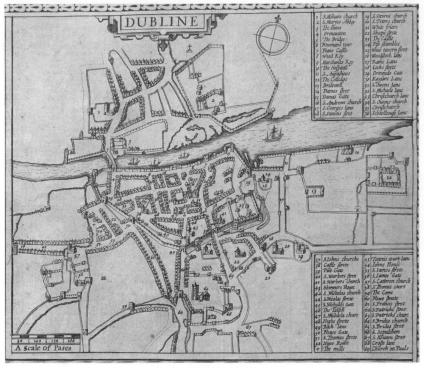

9. John Speed's Map of Dublin.

were built around a triangular or diamond green. An early example was the new walled town of Bandon, County Cork, built during the 1620s on a grid pattern on both sides of the River Bandon for the first earl of Cork. In 1622 it contained some 250 houses, 'all very convenient and many very fair', which probably meant stone-built houses with slated roofs, although clusters of small cabins housing the Gaelic Irish inhabitants would have been in evidence on the fringes of the town.[29] In Ulster, where settler numbers were at their highest, particularly in urban areas, several small towns were built with formidable defensive features. Coleraine, built c.1610–12, was enclosed within earthen ramparts and Derry, dating from 1613 to 1619, within stone walls some 6 metres high. In general, houses in provincial towns around the

---

29 Dunlop, 'An Unpublished Survey', 141. P. O'Flanagan, 'Three Hundred Years of Urban Life: Villages and Towns in County Cork c.1600 to 1901', in P. O'Flanagan and C. G, Buttimer (eds.), *Cork: History & Society* (Geography Publications: Dublin 1993), 392–410.

country remained largely unfortified because they were afforded the protection of town walls. Large merchant houses constructed in both stone and wooden cage-construction had been located in towns since medieval times. Later, fabric from some of these stone houses would be integrated into early modern, urban structures, such as those built in Kilkenny, Kilmallock, Galway and Drogheda. In Kilkenny city, Rothe House, a stone-built courtyard house, was begun in 1594 for the wealthy merchant John Rothe, and situated on a long narrow burgage plot. This type of courtyard building was common enough in Kilkenny city at that time. In leases of the period these houses were usually referred to as being built of stone, with slated, stone back-houses to the rear.[30] In 1620 a description of the houses in Kilkenny, where 'the houses are of grey marble fayrely builte, the fronts of theyr houses are supported (most of them) with pillars or arches under which there is an open pavement to walk on', conjures up an image of arcaded walkways along the street, similar to those that exist in Italian cities such as Padua and Bologna.[31] Prior to 1641, the Rothes and Shees and other Kilkenny merchant families had accumulated a level of wealth that also allowed them to build or acquire fine houses and estates, such as Uppercourt and Bonnetstown, out in the countryside.[32]

Interiors

Many of the new urban houses had richly textured interiors. Household inventories of the period inform us that interiors of grand houses, including those owned by wealthy merchants, were furnished with tapestries, canvas hangings and wood panelling or wainscot, and decorated with plasterwork friezes and overmantels. When the Kilkenny merchant, John FitzPiers Rothe (d. 1620) wrote in his will that he wished the wainscot, and other items of wooden furniture be reserved to his heir for the duration of his life, this was surely an indicator of the continuing importance of this item.[33] Most wooden furniture of the period was plain and made from oak, although beds, as important and expensive pieces of furniture, were often heavily carved.

30 Ormonde Papers, Ms 7864, National Library of Ireland.
31 J. Fenlon, 'Kilkenny', in R. Loeber, H. Campbell, l. Hurley, J. Montague and E. Rowley (eds.), *Art and Architecture of Ireland*, iv, *Architecture, 1600–2000*, (Dublin, London and New Haven: Royal Irish Academy and Yale University Press, 2015), 464–6.
32 J. Ainsworth and E. MacLysaght, 'Power O'Shee Papers', *Analecta Hibernica*, 20, (1958), 226.
33 W. Healy, *History and Antiquities of Kilkenny* (Kilkenny: P. M. Egan, 1893), 381–97.

Few of the roofless and ruined sixteenth- and seventeenth-century buildings located in the countryside today have retained any trace of their interior
finishes or room divisions. In those few that are still roofed, most of the interiors have been altered beyond recognition. It was usual for dwelling houses
of the period to have interior divisions made of friable lathe and plaster. For
some solid evidence on room decoration for this period we must return to
Carrick House/Ormond Castle, County Tipperary, which had been occupied almost continuously up to the twentieth century.[34] During the renova-
tion of existing buildings on the site, Thomas Butler, tenth earl of Ormond,
had the interiors of earlier important spaces re-decorated in a manner that
would integrate them with those of the new north range. This was achieved,
mainly by the insertion of impressive stone fireplaces, wainscot, some of it
imported from Antwerp, and Flemish influenced plasterwork decoration that
utilised the same motifs as those in the new north range. The long gallery at
Carrick remains the earliest surviving example of this room type in Ireland
(Illustration 10).[35] In 1580/1, Ormond would also build a fashionable long
gallery at Kilkenny Castle, the principal family seat, where it was situated
on the second floor of an earlier building. Usually the longest room in the
house, galleries were commonly used for indoor exercise and, when located
on upper floors, provided views over the surrounding gardens. Collections
of portraits would become a feature of these rooms where images of roy-
alty, powerful patrons, family members and noble ancestors were displayed
to impress visitors.[36] The renovations and additions made to Carrick were
not merely decorative, for they enabled circulation within the house and
facilitated a processional route through the extended building. According to
Girouard, writing on the English experience; 'to have a great chamber, withdrawing chamber, best bedchamber and gallery *en suite* on the first floor was
the commonest Elizabethan and Jacobean recipe for magnificence'.[37] In the
overall design of the house Italianate, Flemish and French influenced ideas
were manifest in the symmetry of the exterior, the architectural planning
and the decorative elements of the interiors. Although the exterior of the

---

34 J. Fenlon, 'The Decorative Plasterwork at Ormond Castle', *Architectural History: Journal
of the Society of Architectural Historians of Great Britain*, 41 (1998), 67–81 and J. Fenlon,
Kilkenny Castle: Visitor's Guide (Dublin: Office of Public Works, 2007).

35 R. Coope, 'The Gallery in England and its Relationship to the Principal Rooms (1520–1600)',
in J. Guillame (ed.), *Architecture et Vie Sociale à la Renaissance* (Paris: Picard, 1994), 245–55.

36 J. Fenlon, *Goods and Chattels: A Survey of Early Household Inventories in Ireland*
(Dublin: Stationery Office, 2003), 19.

37 M. Girouard, *Life in the English Country House* (New Haven and London: Yale University
Press, 1984), 102.

10. Carrick House, detail of a plasterwork frieze in long gallery, showing bust portrait of Queen Elizabeth in roundel. © National Monuments Service Photographic Unit, Dublin.

north range at Carrick was plain and modest in scale, its appearance was commonplace in gentry houses in the south-west of England. Within the walls, however, the interior decoration and fittings combined to display the magnificence of Thomas, earl of Ormond, and his family. Bunratty Castle in County Clare is another early example of extensive remodelling that incorporated high-quality decorative plasterwork with Renaissance motifs. It was carried out during the renovations and re-building there by Donough O'Brien, fourth earl of Thomond in *c.* 1597 (Illustration 11).

Painting

Church reforms, introduced post-1540, limited painting within cathedrals and parish churches to reproductions of the royal arms and quotations from the scriptures, resulting in a drop in demand for painted altar pieces and other religious works. To an extent this trend was counter-balanced by the growth in demand for individual portraits influenced by humanist ideas; the image of man had moved centre stage, no longer was he to be side-lined in the donor position on altar pieces, now it was bold representations of the individual signalling their status in society. Based on the evidence of existing works from the 1530s, mainly surviving portraits of members of the Ormond and

11. Bunratty Castle, County Clare. © National Monuments Service
Photographic Unit, Dublin.

FitzGerald families, it would seem that these were all painted while the sitters were at court in London and may be attributed to the German artist Hans Holbein the younger (*c*.1497–1543), and followers.[38] Throughout the sixteenth century, portraits of Irish sitters continued to be painted abroad or by visiting foreign artists, similar to the situation then current in England. Dating from the 1560s, portraits of *Elizabeth FitzGerald, 'The Fair Geraldine', later Countess of Lincoln*, attributed to the British School, and that of *Thomas, tenth earl of Ormond*, attributed to Stevan van der Meulen (1543–1564), were painted while they were at court in England (Illustration 12). Slightly later, and possibly painted in Ireland, are two small portraits identified as *Donogh O'Brien of Lemaneh* and *Slaney O'Brien*, dated 1574. However, the existence of several examples of wall paintings in towers such as Ardmullivan in County Galway and in churches dating from the early modern period suggests that there were a number of skilled painters working in Ireland at that time. Perhaps Gaelic Irish patrons had yet to adopt the 'foreign' habit of having their portraits painted and instead they continued to employ talented local artists to decorate the interiors of their towers, castles and churches (Illustration 13).[39]

38 A. Crookshank and the Knight of Glin, *Ireland's Painters 1600–1940* (London and New Haven: Yale University Press 2002), 1–10.
39 K. Morton, 'A Spectacular Revelation: Medieval Wall Paintings at Ardamullivan', *Irish Arts Review Yearbook*, 18 (2002), 104–13.

12. Thomas Butler, tenth earl of Ormond, oil on panel, attributed to
Stevan van der Meulen. National Gallery of Ireland.

Portraiture and works by foreign painters continued to predominate during the opening decades of the seventeenth century. Several portraits dating from the 1630s that are examples of provincial interpretations after works by skilled painters from the Low Countries have survived. A full-length portrait of *Elizabeth Preston, Countess of Ormond with her son Lord Ossory*, is an example of the provincial Van Dyckian type, with the countess depicted wearing fashionable dress, in the style of Queen Henrietta Maria. Another full-length portrait from the same period is dated 1634 and painted by the same hand; it depicts *Helena (nee Poyntz), Lady Thurles*, Ormond's mother, in widow's dress. The pose used in the Thurles portrait has nothing of Van Dyck about it, but is typical of the more static style of earlier artists (Illustration 14). From the same decade, and also painted in sub-Flemish style, possibly by the same hand as the two described above, is a portrait of *George FitzGerald, earl of Kildare*, dated 1633. This painting has suffered extensive damage to its paint surface and has been cut down in size. Attribution and identification of portraits from this period have often proved difficult, if not impossible.

13. Ardmullivan (Tower House), Gort, County Galway, interior detail with fragment of wall painting. © National Monuments Service Photographic Unit, Dublin.

14. Elizabeth Poyntz, Lady Thurles, oil on canvas, unknown artist, inscribed Lady Thurles, 1634. Private Collection, Ireland.

After the Restoration in 1660, portraits continued to be the most common form of painting produced in Ireland and there was a sharp increase in demand for these artefacts. By comparison to previous decades, scores of mid- to late seventeenth-century portraits of Irish sitters have survived and stylistically most of these derived mainly from works by two artists who dominated the field of portraiture in England: Peter Lely (1618–1680) and Godfrey Kneller (1646–1723). Although foreigners, these artists had studios in London where they employed large numbers of assistants. Their influence was widespread, particularly later in the century when mezzotints and engravings of their portraits became more freely available.[40] Among the dozens of artists who came to Dublin from London and elsewhere, some to settle, others as transients, was Thomas Carleton senior (*fl.*1662–d.1687), whose full-length portrait of *Sir Audley Mervyn* (*c.*1662), is the earliest confirmed attribution to an artist who worked in Ireland. Although we cannot be sure whether this particular portrait was painted in London or Dublin, it is a typical example of a provincial interpretation derived from portraits by Flemish artists. Carleton was a member of the Painter-Stainers Company in London and a founder of Guild of St Luke the Evangelist, also known as The Cutlers, Painter Stainers and Stationers Company of Dublin, when it received a royal charter in 1670. Carleton settled in the city, where both he and his son, also named Thomas (d.1730), continued to practise. English-born Thomas Pooley (1646–1723) had trained in London before coming to Dublin in 1676, where he enjoyed a successful career as a portrait painter. His early work includes several portraits of members of the Perceval family and their relatives the Southwells. Probably the finest of his portraits are three fresh, stylish images of the Perceval boys, painted while they were in London. Later in life he painted several institutional portraits in the style of both Lely and Kneller for Dublin corporation, the College of Physicians and the Royal Hospital, Kilmainham (Illustration 15). Garret Morphey (*c.*1650–1715), an artist of Irish origin who worked in England and Ireland, enjoyed the patronage of Catholic gentry in both countries. Morphey, a Catholic, was born in Yorkshire to an Irish father and an English mother and could be described as the first Irish artist in the early modern period. In addition to his Irish ancestry, he spent the later part of his career working in Ireland and eventually settled there with his wife. Although Morphey was a self-confessed admirer of Van

---

40 J. Fenlon, 'Portraiture in Ireland', in N. Figgis (ed.), *Art and Architecture of Ireland*, ii, *Painting, 1600–1900* (Dublin, London and New Haven: Royal Irish Academy and Yale University Press, 2015), 63–7.

15. Prince George of Denmark, royal consort, oil on canvas, artist Thomas Pooley.
Office of Public Works, Royal Hospital, Kilmainham.

Dyck, his portraits, which are often charming, if vacuous, would tend to belie
this statement. Pooley and Morphey could be termed 'Gentlemen Painters' in
that they married well, had successful careers as painters where they earned
a good income, and left substantial wealth when they died.[41] Pooley owned
extensive property in Dublin city, having married a Crowe heiress. Morphey,
in an unusual arrangement, had an agreement to pay his annual rent in paintings to his landlord, Richard Parsons, first Viscount Rosse (d. 1703), for his
leased property in County Dublin (Illustration 16).[42] It was more usual for
Irish artists to paint sitters at gentry level in society and to carry out institutional commissions, while Irish grandees continued to visit London where

41 J. Fenlon, 'Garret Morphy and his Circle', *Irish Arts Review Yearbook*, 8 (1991–1992), 135–
48 and J. Fenlon, 'A good painter may get good bread', Thomas Pooley and Garret
Morphey, Two Gentlemen Painters', in R. Gillespie and R. F. Foster (eds.), *Irish Provincial
Cultures in the Long Eighteenth-Century* (Dublin: FCP, 2012), 220–30; J. Fenlon, 'Portraiture
in Ireland' and 'Visiting Painters in Ireland', in Figgis, (ed.), *Art and Architecture of
Ireland*, ii, 63–7, 130–4.
42 40/170/248829, 1720, Registry of Deeds, Dublin.

16. Elizabeth Hamilton, Countess of Rosse, oil on canvas, artist Garret Morphy. Birr
Scientific and Heritage Foundation, courtesy of the Earl of Ross.

they had themselves painted by Lely and Kneller. Later, the Swedish artist Michael Dahl, another London-based court painter, and his pupil Hans
Hysing (1678–1752/3), would become popular with visiting Irish patrons such
as the O'Briens of Dromoland Castle, County Clare.

A number of Catholic artists, including John Michael Wright (1617–94), fled
from London to the comparative safety of Dublin at the time of the 'Popish
Plot'. During his stay the artist painted Catholic members of the Ormond
family, including the duke of Ormond's sister *Lady Clancarty* and a posthu-
mous portrait of his mother, *Elizabeth Poyntz, Lady Thurles*, as well as the
charming French-influenced image of the daughters of Richard Talbot, earl
of Tyrconnell. Wright is also famous for one of the most iconic Irish images
of the seventeenth century; a portrait of *Sir Neil O Neill dressed in Irish garb,*
c. 1680 (Illustration 17).

With the advent of the eighteenth century came a new generation of Irish-
born painters: Charles Jervas (1675–1739), Hugh Howard (1675–1738) and
Francis Bindon (1690–1765). Unlike their predecessors, we know from whom

17. Sir Neil O Neill, oil on canvas, artist John Michael Wright. Dunrobin Castle, Scotland, courtesy of Lord Strathnaver.

these painters received their artistic tuition. Jervas and Bindon attended Kneller's academy in London and then travelled in Europe, presumably to further their education. Howard also had links with Kneller and had travelled to Italy, where he had been a pupil of Carlo Maratta(i) in Rome at an earlier date. Bindon was the only one of the three artists to make his career in Ireland when he settled in Dublin. He painted portraits but was also engaged in architectural collaboration with Richard Castle. Howard and Jervas set up studios in London where they both practised their art. Jervas enjoyed the patronage of Sir Horace Walpole, who was influential in his appointment to the post of principal painter to the king following the death of his old master Kneller.

In the early 1720s, another young Irish artist, James Latham (1696–1747), emerged as talented portrait painter. His earliest known works are portraits commissioned by the Catholic Butlers of Kilcash, County Tipperary, *Thomas Butler of Kilcash* and his brother *Christopher Butler, Archbishop of Cashel*.[43] It is

---

43 As these portraits always belonged to the Kilcash branch of the Butlers, it is safe to assume that it was they who commissioned them. J. Fenlon, *The Ormonde Picture Collection* (Gandon Editions: Kinsale, 2001).

not known who instructed Latham in his art but his painterly and sophisticated later works mark him out as the finest Irish portrait painter of the first
half of the eighteenth century.

Pastels, Drawings and Prints

Small portraits executed in pastel began to appear in collections in Ireland *c.*
1680. Some, like the portrait of *James, first duke of Ormond*, by Edmund Ashfield
(*fl.* 1660–1690), were drawn in England and then, apparently copied in Ireland
by the pastellist, Simon Digby (d. 1720) (Illustration 18). Thomas Dingley, a
visiting antiquarian, Francis Place, a topographical artist and Thomas Phillips
(1635–1693), a military engineer, all came to Ireland during the 1680s and 1690s
and their legacy of architectural drawings has proved invaluable for those
interested in the architecture of the period. Particularly important are drawings by Dingley of various buildings around the country as well as Place's
drawings of the cities of Dublin, Kilkenny, Waterford and other towns.

18. James Butler, first duke of Ormond, pastel on paper, artist Simon Digby. Private
Collection, Ireland.

19. Kilkenny Castle and City from Wind Gap Hill, pen and ink on paper, artist Francis Place. National Gallery of Ireland.

Phillips also painted some very fine views of cities and coastal defences (Illustration 19).

Prints and engravings began to appear in fashionable interiors, sometimes replacing oil paintings as decorative elements in a room. The earliest recorded evidence for this practice occurs in 1705, during the viceroyalty of James, second duke of Ormond, when forty-nine prints of works by famous continental artists were bought in Dublin for the drawing room of Dublin Castle.

Architecture Post 1660

The Restoration also marked a period when architects names began to emerge from anonymity as their position in society was further advanced. The most prominent among them were the architects/engineers such as Captain James Archer (c.1632–1680) and Captain John Morton (fl.1662–1668), employed by Ormond on various domestic building projects at Carrick-on-Suir, Clonmel, Dunmore House and at their principal seat, Kilkenny Castle. Later William Robinson (c. 1643–1712), appointed surveyor general in 1671, would become the architect of choice for the Ormonds, while Archer, described by the earl of Orrery as 'an Irishman and a Papist – but a brilliant engineer', would be involved in the design and works carried out at Charlesfort, Kinsale, County Cork (Illustration 20).[44] William Molyneux (1656–1696) took up the post of

---

44 Ormonde Ms, 72, f. 389, National Library of Ireland.

joint surveyor general in 1684, shortly before Robinson departed for England. Although Molyneux has few architectural projects attributed to him, he is of interest because it appears that he was sent to Europe specifically to study fortifications and he was the owner of an extensive library of architectural books of Italian and French origin.[45]

In Dublin, a surge in population resulted in extensive development schemes being carried out at several locations in the city. Among the earliest and most impressive of these was the Aungier estate, a planned development laid out on lands inherited by Francis, first earl of Longford (*c.*1632–1700), from his uncle Gerald, second Baron Aungier. The estate was located on lands previously owned by the White Friars (Carmelites). In 1663, to the east of Aungier's lands, Dublin corporation carried out a survey on an area that would become St Stephen's Green. It was perhaps hoping to emulate developments that were taking place in London, where new town squares were being built. This public development was matched by another on the north side of the city at Smithfield, where a large paved market place was laid out. Around Hoggen, later College Green, grand town dwellings, like the gabled house of Lord Clancarty, were built. Several houses with gables to the street were built there, and this type was often known as a 'Dutch Billy' and was particularly suited to narrow urban plots. Other lesser developments followed on both sides of the River Liffey. Quays were constructed to enclose the spreading River Liffey along part of its length; Ormond quay was added during the early 1680s. Soon there would be three bridges across the Liffey. Present day Capel Street and Jervis Street were also being developed as part of the Jervis estate and brick was now the material of choice for the terraces of houses. Westwards, the city had grown on both banks of the river. On the southside it extended out to Kilmainham, where the Royal Hospital designed by Robinson was his major architectural contribution to Dublin as the first truly classical building introduced into the country. As an institution to house old soldiers, it owes a debt to Les Invalides in Paris, though not in terms of its architecture. One expert describes it as 'an example of brick-dressed, dormer-windowed, alms house classicism' (Illustration 21).[46]

As a consequence of the inflow of newcomers, several craft guilds were set up during the post-Restoration period and soon buildings would

---

45 R. Loeber, *A Biographical Dictionary of Architects in Ireland* (London: John Murray, 1981), 73–5.
46 E. Mc Parland, 'Royal hospital Kilmainham', *Country Life*, 176 (9 and 16 May 1985) nos. 4577 and 4578.

20. Charlesfort, Kinsale, County Cork.

be required for their meetings and other activities. The surviving Tailors' Hall in Back Lane, built 1703, is a much-altered example. The burgeoning economy in Dublin would also require more and larger public and commercial buildings. An earlier Tholsel building that stood in Skinner's Row was modernised during the 1670s, when it was refaced with a symmetrical facade, embellished with classical elements. On the upper floor there were niches containing statues executed by the sculptor William de Keyser (*fl.c.* 1683). Nearby, Dublin Castle, the principal seat of administration, was also in need of urgent rebuilding. The castle had been badly damaged in a disastrous fire on the site in the early 1670s, followed by an even greater conflagration resulting from an explosion in the powder tower in 1684. When compared with the original designs drawn up by William Robinson, the new ranges of buildings erected at the castle by William Molyneux were modest in execution.[47]

---

47 E. Mc Parland, *Public Architecture in Ireland 1680–1760* (London and New Haven: Yale University Press, 2001), 91–8; see also T. Barnard, *Making the Grand Figure: Lives and Possessions in Ireland, 1641–1770* (New Haven and London: Yale University Press, 2004), chapter 9.

Towns Post 1660

Provincial towns expanded also and there was a demand for new or refurbished civic buildings. In Kilkenny city, new aldermen, mostly ex-Cromwellian soldiers, had replaced the Catholic Old English merchant oligarchy. The return of the duke of Ormond meant that the town would prosper with the major refurbishment that was being carried out at the castle, where an army of tradesmen was employed. Works included the laying out of a new mall (the parade) leading up to the classical gateway of the castle erected during the 1680s. Architects such as William Robinson were employed on the project, whilst advice was sought from prominent English practitioners Hugh May (1621–1684) and Christopher Wren (1632–1723). Robinson was also engaged to oversee the construction of a fine Court House (the main guard) on a prominent site in Clonmel, County Tipperary, the centre of Ormond's palatinate (Illustration 22). New market houses and exchanges were erected to handle the increased commerce.[48] In Limerick, the local civic authority paid for a fine exchange building (1673) and in the city of Derry an even more impressive example (1690s) was designed by Captain Richard Neville.[49] More planned towns and villages were built to house tenants and service the nearby great houses and demesnes. In 1680 Dingley, a visiting antiquarian, captured in a drawing the layout around a triangular green of the village of Staplestown, County Carlow. Other towns were based on industrial development, such as the settlements at Ballitore – based on an *émigré* population of *c.*1707 – and Castle Matrix, County Limerick (*c.* 1709).

The Big House

Out in the countryside there was something of a scramble to build fine new houses as the later generations of settlers bedded in. The time of the massively built fortified house had passed and would be replaced by lighter, more compact dwellings similar in type to those made popular in England by architects such as Roger Pratt (1620–84), who designed Coleshill in Berkshire and Clarendon House in London. These houses were often double-pile, symmetrical, with large windows at first-floor level and centrally placed front doors. In the grander houses the internal arrangements were now influenced by the French practice of dividing spaces into *apartements* and this would set the

---

48 M. Craig, *The Architecture of Ireland*, (London: Batsford, 1982), 200–7.
49 McParland, *Public Architecture in Ireland*, 29.

21. Royal Hospital, Kilmainham, Dublin. © National Monuments Service Photographic Unit, Dublin.

template for most of the larger houses that were constructed in the second half of the century. Later, following practices introduced by Hugh May in England, a more Dutch-influenced aspect was applied to houses. The use of architectural elements derived from the classical vocabulary had also progressed by mid-century. No longer was piecemeal application of decorative motifs on buildings the common practice. Instead, classical elements were now being incorporated into the structure of buildings.

Houses began to have a more uniform appearance and, as already mentioned, were similar to those being built in England. Before the end of the century, classical elements such as porticos would be added to the facades of houses, windows would change from stone mullion and transom examples to sash windows, and dormers were often inserted in attics. Roger Boyle, earl of Orrery, was among the first out of the starting blocks when he began building his vast house

22. Main Guard, previously Palatinate Court House, Clonmel, Co. Tipperary.
© National Monuments Service Photographic Unit, Dublin.

at Charleville, County Cork, in 1662. The house was demolished and no plans exist but we know that by 1680 it had sixty-five hearths.[50] Eyrecourt, County Galway, built before 1677, although ruined, provides some information about the smaller, new-build, compact, symmetrical and horizontally planned house of the time. It was a house of two storeys over basement with attic dormers (Illustration 23). Unusually, it was constructed with a lining of red brick inside an outer layer of rubble masonry. The height and applied decorative details on Eyrecourt's main doorway, which also had an inset oval window, were unusual – if not unique – in Ireland. On the hipped roof at Eyrecourt there was a viewing platform, a feature that was common enough in these islands. The wide-eaves of the roof were supported on heavy carved wooden consoles (brackets). A similar arrangement of brackets was used at Kilkenny Castle during the remodelling of that building in the 1670s and apparently also used at Valentine Browne, Viscount Kenmare's

---

50 T. Barnard, 'The Political, Material and Mental Culture of the Cork Settlers', in O'Flanagan and Buttimer (eds.), *Cork: History & Society*, 322.

23. Eyrecourt, County Galway. Irish Architectural Archive.

new-built 'Capital Seat' at Ross Castle, completed in 1688.[51] The ground plan of Eyrecourt House was probably similar to that used at Burton House, County Cork, designed by the architect William Kenn (c.1653–1671) for Sir John Perceval in the mid-1660s.[52] A plan of the setting of Burton House, 1671, shows it to have had several enclosures with defensive features as well as pleasure gardens to the rear of the house. Dunmore in County Kilkenny, Lady Ormond's own house, was, as befitted Ireland's only duchess, constructed on a much larger scale than the previously named examples. Nothing remains of this house but documentary evidence indicates that it was remodelled and added to by Captain John Morton during the early 1660s. It was laid out in two suites of grand rooms on two floors and each suite contained a bed 'alcove' behind balustrades in the latest French fashion. Rooms within the house continued to be arranged in a formal series, usually with all doorways on an axis (*en enfilade*).[53] Both Dunmore House and Kilkenny Castle were set within elaborately laid out gardens. A drawing of *Kilkenny City and Castle* by Francis Place (1647–1728), shows that serried

51 Fenlon and Fenlon, 'Ross Castle', 70.
52 R. Loeber and J. O'Connell, 'Eyrecourt Castle, County Galway', in *Irish Arts Review Yearbook*, i (1988), 40–8.
53 J. Fenlon, 'The Duchess of Ormonde's House at Dunmore, County Kilkenny', in J. Kirwan (ed.), *Kilkenny, Studies in Honour of Margaret M. Phelan* (Kilkenny: Kilkenny Archaeological Society, 1997), 79–87.

24. Tapestry, *Marcus Valerius consecrates Decius Mus*, linen and wool, Dutch. Kilkenny Castle, Historic Properties, Office of Public Works.

ranks of trees were planted outside the old castle walls. Within the encircling walls of the castle, pleasure gardens with fountains and a banqueting house with a classical peristyle that doubled as a water house in its lower level was located to the south-east. For the privy garden at Kilkenny the Ormonds stipulated that the statuary carved by John Bonnier should be the same as in the kings privy garden at Whitehall.[54]

Detailed descriptions of post-Restoration houses contained in inventories inform us of the importance of textiles use for the furnishing of these interiors. Tapestries remained popular as wall coverings, but were being gradually replaced by silk and velvet hangings made with fabrics imported from France and Italy (Illustration 24). Wooden panelling, often elaborately carved with flowers, lined the walls of some rooms (Illustration 25). Staircases were usually made of wood, often massive with intricate carving like that at Eyrecourt. Fireplaces were tall, usually made of carved stone, sometimes with painted 'marbling'. Chairs had become ever more ornate, with carved and gilded wooden

54 J. Fenlon, *Kilkenny Castle: Visitor's Guide*, 30.

25. Detail of seventeenth-century carved wooden panelling, with ribands and pomegranate motif from Kilkenny Castle. Kilkenny Castle, Historic Properties, Office of Public Works, Dublin.

frames covered in silk brocades with rich gold or silver fringing, often matching the fabrics used on elaborate beds. Day beds, sofas and fashionable reclining chairs were listed among the furniture.[55] In terms of art collections in Ireland, none could come near that of the dukes of Ormond. There were hundreds of paintings in the Ormond picture collection; these were housed in their various residences in Ireland and England. The majority of these art works consisted of Landscapes, Still Life paintings and History paintings (this was the classification given to biblical or classical subjects at that time) of Dutch, English, French and Italian origin. Only a handful of these pictures would have been painted in Ireland. Just one early reference to a local landscape painted in oils has been located; *A View of Kilkenny* is recorded in 1684 in the ducal collection in Kilkenny Castle.[56] In the castle, paintings were mainly displayed in a series of rooms that made up the formal route of procession through the house and gallery. Dutch paintings were most

---

55 P. Thornton, *Seventeenth-Century Interior Decoration in England France & Holland* (New Haven and London: Yale University Press, 1984), 231; Fenlon, *Goods and Chattels*, 110.
56 Ormonde papers, Ms, 2554, National Library of Ireland.

frequently framed in plain black wood, whilst history paintings and important portraits were displayed in intricately carved, gilded and silvered frames.

Emergent Anglo-Ireland

Construction of the architecture of emergent Anglo-Ireland began quietly enough in the early decades of the eighteenth century. The administrative infrastructure for the new order took shape in the many barracks, civic buildings and churches being built all around the country and in the number of hospitals, schools and poor houses that were being constructed, especially in Dublin. Following on from the upheavals and land seizures of the Williamite wars, this period would see huge public expenditure on military buildings. Plans were drawn up for elaborate forts and citadels to be built in Dublin, but these came to nothing. Such militaristic ambitions may be appreciated in the upsurge in military buildings that had begun *c.* 1696, when dozens of new barracks would be erected throughout the country. It has been estimated that over ninety had been built by 1704, in order 'to secure the safety of the king's Protestant subjects'.[57] In Dublin, the extensive royal barracks (occupied 1708), with a frontage measuring 1,000 feet, designed by Thomas Burgh (1670–1730), was built on the north bank of the River Liffey.[58] Originally of two storeys over an open arcade, the upper storeys were a later addition. Further developments in Dublin city are best appreciated by consulting Brooking's map of 1728, where the rapid growth of the city outside the walls is clearly indicated. The map includes illustrations of several of the key buildings of the period, including a number of new, large-scale churches required for the expanding city, although these should be viewed with caution as certain details on some of the buildings are depicted incorrectly. Notable is William Robinson's St Mary's – situated in Mary Street – after a design by Christopher Wren, which has a striking east window with baroque features. Taking up the baton from Robinson, his successor, Thomas Burgh (surveyor general), was responsible for St Werburgh's Church, Werburgh Street (1715–1719), and St Anne's Church, Dawson Street (1720), whose facades have been described as 'examples of canonical Italianate classicism' and Roman Catholic in design.[59] Burgh was also responsible for the new workhouse, which had an entrance door after a design by Michaelangelo, a

57 Kerrigan, *Castles and Fortifications in Ireland*, 130–1.
58 Mc Parland, *Public Architecture*, 124, 132.
59 Mc Parland, *Public Architecture*, 44–5.

new custom-house at Essex Bridge in 1707 and the linen hall of the 1720s at the top of Bolton Street, all in Dublin.[60] Burgh's most important work was the old library building at Trinity College Dublin (foundation laid in 1712), now regarded as the culmination of his classicism. Dr Steeven's hospital, begun 1719, also by Burgh, was built around a courtyard with an arcade like its near neighbour the Royal Hospital. It will be noted that in his designs Burgh reused, with some variations, the prototype that had been established by Robinson in the courtyard of the Royal Hospital.

Undoubtedly, the influx of new settlers – of English, Scottish and continental origin – who moved to Ireland throughout the sixteenth and in increasing numbers during the seventeenth century, was influential in accelerating trends towards new ideas about the role of art and architecture in society that had already begun to appear, if tentatively, during the early years of the sixteenth century. The houses that had been built during the seventeenth century displayed influences derived from French, Italian, Dutch and Scottish sources, although these were often through an English filter. Later, in common with several other European countries – among the gentry and newly ennobled of the period – the acquisition of affluence based on extensive and often recently acquired land ownership allowed them to commission impressive buildings and other art works. Disparate architectural influences such as those brought to Ulster by Scottish settlers were not widely disseminated beyond that province. Tower houses and fortified houses could be regarded as the most definably Irish type of building. Houses in the English style were frequently built and in particular for townspeople; this would later become the most acceptable form. Builders of country houses, particularly those deriving from the post-Restoration era, also conformed more closely to English norms, in their use of compact plans, symmetrical exteriors and parkland settings.[61]

At the dawn of the eighteenth century, several new towns had been planned and built, and urban living had become more generally acceptable to native and newcomer alike. With regard to country-house building, by the eighteenth century, advances in architectural skills and ambition that had accrued within that emergent Anglo-Irish society manifested a bravura display of Italianate ideas in the building of the grand palace of Castletown, County Kildare, for William Conolly (Illustration 26). In painting circles, stylistic

---

60 For instance, the doorway of the workhouse and the roofline of Dr Steeven's Hospital; see also Mc Parland, *Public Architecture*, 76, figure 92.
61 Also see Chapter 27 in Volume 3. Barnard, *Making the Grand Figure*, chapter 6.

26. Castletown House, Celbridge, County Kildare © National Monuments Service Photographic Unit, Dublin.

27. Self-portrait, oil on canvas, artist James Latham, National Gallery of Ireland.

advances would occur slightly later and may be appreciated in the portraits of the emerging Irish artist James Latham (1696–1747) (Illustration 27). In both of these examples, European concepts would be amalgamated with what was deemed fashionable in English society circles of the period although, in addition, there would be a discernable 'Irish' dimension to them.

15

Ireland in the Atlantic World: Migration and Cultural Transfer

WILLIAM O'REILLY

In Mexico City in 1641, a befreckled, redheaded Irishman hatched a plan to make himself king of New Spain and free the land from tyrannical rule. William Lamport, born thirty years earlier in Wexford, had reinvented himself as the Spanish nobleman Don Guillén de Lombardo, a soldier of fortune, ambitious adventurer and at times crazed visionary, who would, in 1659, be burned at the stake after the failure of his brooding attempts to establish himself as the legitimate heir to Philip III. The Irishman's attempts to install himself as a monarch to rule a kingdom in which, he proclaimed, African slaves, *castas*, mulattos and Native Americans would be free and granted the same liberties as whites, and where commerce and trade with Spain's old enemies would be opened up, is representative of the scale of opportunities open to Irish immigrants in the early modern Atlantic world. Like many economic, social, religious, political refugees and migrants from Ireland, Lamport, together with his sister and two brothers, left Ireland and travelled first to the European continent: his sister Catherine found a new life as a nun, his older sibling John became a Franciscan friar and Gerald, his younger brother, a mercenary. William travelled from Ireland to France, where he connected with long-established Irish trade networks, and further to Spain, where again he relied on the support of the large and well-respected Irish community. Lamport joined the other *españoles del norte* and attended the Irish College at Santiago de Compostela, before moving on to Lorenzo College at the Escorial. He crossed the Alps and fought in the army of Philip IV at Nördlingen in July 1634, and appeared again, together with his brother Gerald, as a soldier in the Basque country in 1638. Embroiled in a scandal when he refused to marry the well-born woman with whom he formed a household, 'Don Guillén' left Spain in 1640, crossing the Atlantic for New Spain, possibly under the patronage of the Count-Duke Olivares. In Mexico, the adventurer and opportunist grew in confidence, building on his many experiences.[1] Claiming to be the half brother of Philip IV of Spain, Lamport's ultimate fate – denounced as a magician, an astrologer and a Protestant, spending seventeen years in an Inquisition gaol was that he was paraded through the thronged streets of Mexico City on the way to an *auto de fé*, burned alive for heresy and sedition.[2]

It is likely that William Lamport knew all too well of his real ancestry and knew, too, that in the long-established tradition of ousting kings, claiming royal blood bestowed on the pretender at very least a veneer of legitimacy. And Lamport knew, too, that only with the popular support of the majority – in this case, of slaves, *castas* and mulattos – would he stand any chance of success. And perhaps the Irishman could have succeeded; that he did not is only less impressive than that he felt he might. Lamport had spent his life avoiding monarchical rule in Ireland, serving another sovereign abroad, before rejecting that rule, too, in favour of a self-serving utopianism built of his experiences in Ireland, France, Germany, Spain and New Spain. His story is exceptional, of course, yet it goes some way to show the range of possibilities open to pre-nineteenth-century Irish migrants in the Atlantic world.

For much of its history, the Irish in the Atlantic world, or even the notion of an 'Irish Atlantic' in the period before the age of steam, has been portrayed as little more than the trade in indentured servants, with Irish emigration to continental Europe represented as a distinct historiography and a distinctive feature of life-in-exile for a Catholic middling sort who found service and opportunities at court and in academic, administrative, mercantile, military and religious service in Madrid, Paris, Vienna, Prague and satellite cities in Catholic Europe. Irish migration into the Atlantic sea, and resettlement throughout the Americas, has been seen as a secondary result of the primary necessity to leave Ireland, largely for reasons of religious persecution and dispossession. Undoubtedly, a large number of Irish people were forcibly removed from the country in the mid-seventeenth century, and still more were subject to a punitive colonising economic system which strong-armed the able into accepting there was little chance of improvement at home, and thus created an outflow of literate and skilled men, and some women, in search of a better life. Yet it would be both misleading and simply wrong

---

1 S. Kline, 'William Lamport/Guillén de Lombardo (1611–1659)', in Karen Racine and Beatriz G. Mamigonian (eds.), *The Human Tradition in the Atlantic World, 1500–1850* (Plymouth: Rowman & Littlefield, 2010), 43–56.

2 R. D. Crewe, 'Brave New Spain: An Irishman's Independence Plot in Seventeenth Century Mexico', *Past & Present*, 207 (2010), 53–87.

to represent the Irish in the Atlantic as a diasporic community. This was no classic uprooted migration narrative, certainly not before the nineteenth century, and cultural life and religious practice continued unabated, whatever the challenges.[3] Rather, Irish involvement in the Atlantic world was an activated option for the majority involved: men and women joined an international labour market – in commerce, in social and religious care, in education, in soldiering, in manual labour – which saw them fare well in some contexts, thrive and excel in others, and which saw most serve, and a few claim to be, kings. Irish identity in the pre-famine Atlantic world was built more on contemporary aspirations for betterment and improvement than it was on exile and persecution, watchwords of a later cultural-political nationalism which placed emphasis, *post-hoc*, on the overarching feature of commonality shared by the majority, their confessional identity. This is not to say that dreams of a different Ireland did not exist: powerful poetry provides evidence of that; albeit, the greater part of that corpus seeks to displace one foreign king for another. Yet 'no collective identity… is static' and any sense of identity in the pre-modern period was both 'place-specific and time specific'.[4] Jack Greene identifies four parts of a collective self-image in this age before mass print and media: the sense of place, the identification of goals, the insistence on standards and the sense of history.[5] On these terms, and considering the Irish in the Atlantic world, there were no shared goals and standards whatever about a shared place of origin and a shared history – albeit in Ireland that history was, at one and the same time, being repressed, repackaged and rewritten. There was no 'Irish' press in the Atlantic world beyond Ireland, and certainly not in the Irish language; this absence may have held up the process of identity formation, as it did in other parts of the Atlantic.[6] Attempts to position Ireland as an island polity ancient and true continued, but these efforts were roundly attacked and squarely upended by an English-language community retailing a different antiquarian political genealogy.[7] In 1625, the Irish historian Philip

---

3 O. Handlin, *The Uprooted. The Epic Story of the Great Migrations that made the American People* (Philadelphia: The University of Pennsylvania Press, 2002), 2nd edn.

4 'An analysis of its changing content reveals, perhaps as well as can the study of any other single phenomenon, the character of a given colony's responses to the successive social, economic, cultural, and political transformations it underwent' N. Canny and A. Pagden (eds.), *Colonial Identity in the Atlantic World, 1500–1800* (Princeton: Princeton University Press, 1987), 8.

5 Canny and Pagden (eds.), *Colonial Identity in the Atlantic World*, 9.

6 As in, for example, Brazil; Canny and Pagden (eds.), *Colonial Identity in the Atlantic World*, 12.

7 C. O'Halloran, *Golden Ages and Barbarous Nations. Antiquarian Debate and Cultural Politics in Ireland, c.1750–1800* (Cork University Press, 2004), especially 'Phoenicians and Goths', 41–70 and 'Irish Custom, Law and Lawlessness', 127–40.

O'Sullivan Beare concentrated entirely upon countering Cambrensis and all those who were relying on him for their views of the country: 'Ireland is not deserted, without roads, and boggy, as Cambrensis would have it, but is heaped with glory under many headings.'[8] Yet while Cambrensis's writings were widely circulated in the sixteenth century, with the antiquarian William Camden publishing a further edition in 1602, O'Sullivan Beare's refutation was not published in his own lifetime; the circulated views of Ireland were not necessarily those captured with Irish eyes. The cultural *élite* of an emerging Anglo-Irish community grew to denigrate the contemporary Gaelic nation as barbaric and benighted.[9] The unequal power relations which silenced the perspective of the majority disallowed a canonical reading of Irish identity, at home as abroad.[10] In the Atlantic world, the Irish were more like the Scots, perhaps the Dutch, than the Sephardic Jewish diaspora or the Huguenots. This was an Irish international, not an Irish diaspora.

Ireland in the Atlantic sea

Long before Irish settlement in the Americas, magical and invisible things were known to inhabit the Celtic world of the Atlantic coast of Europe. The Irish, as in the *Leabhar Gabhála*, knew of three routes which brought people to their island: in the east, from the European continent and across St George's Channel; in the south, from the near Atlantic and Hispania; and in the north, from Scandinavia and the Baltic.[11] No mention was made of a route from the west, where Hy Brasil, and Tír na nÓg and eternal youth were to be found. Nor did the Irish refer to the 'Atlantic', but rather to 'Talamh an Éisc' and later 'Newland' and 'New England'.[12] Irish and English activities in the near Atlantic changed, in the fifteenth century, when the rising Hanseatic League began to exclude foreigners from the profitable market in the Baltic;

---

8 Philip O'Sullivan Beare, *Vindiciae Hibernicae contra Giraldum Cambrensem et alios vel Zoilomastigis* (Cork University Press, 2009), Book One, 267.

9 C. Kidd, *British Identities before Nationalism: Ethnicity and Nationhood in the Atlantic World, 1600–1800* (Cambridge University Press, 1999), 181.

10 A. Horning, 'Challenging Colonial Equations? The Gaelic Experience in Early Modern Ireland', in N. Ferris, R. Harrison and M. V. Wilcox (eds.), *Rethinking Colonial Pasts through Archaeology* (Oxford University Press, 2014), 297.

11 R. Sainero, *The Celts and Historical and Cultural Origins of Atlantic Europe* (Palo Alto, CA: Academica Press, 2013), 131.

12 Aogán Ó Rathaille, 'Tairngreacht Dhoinn Firínne' used 'Newlan'; in 'Carraig Seac', writing: 'Chuaigh scéal ar an mbualadh thar na tonnta taosach/go Talamh an Éisc agus go Sasana Nua'. *Aogán Ó Rathaille*, ed. B. Ó Buachalla (Baile Átha Cliath: Field Day Publications, 2007), 33; D. Ó hÓgáin, *Dunaire Osraíoch* (Baile Átha Cliath: An Clóchomhar, 1980), 42.

fishermen were driven to look elsewhere for fish stocks, and the place they chose was Iceland.[13] Knowledge of the routes between Ireland and the North Atlantic increased, as a result, and with them claims to ownership of territories 'discovered'. Accounts of the early Christian missionary Brendan of Ardfert and Clonfert (c.484–580), 'the Navigator', in the *Navigatio sancti Brendani Abbatis*, tell of the monk's journeys over the sea towards the west, sailing for seven years before eventually finding 'the Promised Land, which God will give to those who come after us at the end of time'. Some writers reached antiquarian heights in efforts to have Brendan visit Mexican shores so that he became the Aztec Quetzalcoatl; the white-skinned and bearded figure who promised to return was Brendan.[14] Wherever he may have sailed, if at all, his account was used in the later sixteenth century by the Tudor apologist John Dee as evidence for Elizabeth I's claim to northern lands and the New World. Whether Brendan reached Newfoundland in c.550 or not, the actions of the ancients in Ireland granted, by precedent, Dee's new 'British empire' jurisdiction over all that lay to Ireland's west.

In the fifteenth and sixteenth centuries, Irish activity in the Atlantic ocean was largely a west-of-Ireland venture, with vessels setting sail near-exclusively from the port of Galway. Fishing and whaling were well established off the Irish coast and even Ottoman maps of the early sixteenth century describe the activity; by the early eighteenth century, whale and shark oil lit lamps from Donegal to Galway.[15] Domestic cartography, shipbuilding and exploration was certainly underdeveloped when compared with continental European neighbours, and much Irish Atlantic activity resembled littoral hop-scotch, skimming from port to port; from Iberia to southern England to southern and western Ireland. Trade with northern Spain thrived in the fifteenth century; much of it was in the hands of Basque shippers who, working from Santander, Bilbao and other smaller ports in the region, traded northward to Ireland.[16] And Irish goods and people went in the opposite direction, too. Penitents frequently made the journey to Santiago de Compostella, venerating the shrine of St James. For pilgrims from Ireland all the major ports – from Dublin in the east to Galway in the west – provided ships, as did the ships of

---

13 B. Cunliffe, *Facing the Ocean: The Atlantic and its People, 8000 BC–AD 1500* (Oxford University Press, 2001), 539.
14 G. A. Little, *Brendan the Navigator: An Interpretation* (Dublin: Gill, 1945).
15 See A. Afetinan, *Life and Works of Piri Reis: The Oldest Map of America* (2nd edn., Ankara: Turkish Historical Society 1987); A. E. J. Went and S Ó Súilleabháin, 'Fishing for the Sun-Fish or Basking Shark in Irish Waters', *Proceedings of the Royal Irish Academy*, 65:C (1966–1967), 91–115.
16 Cunliffe, *Facing the Ocean*, 534–5.

Bristol, sometimes stopping at Plymouth *en route*, and carrying as many as a hundred pilgrims at a time.[17] Irish engagement with Spain and Portugal continued throughout the fifteenth and sixteenth centuries, and substantial Irish confraternities existed in Seville and elsewhere.[18] Irish mariners manned ships for Spain and Portugal, and served aboard vessels sailing in and out of the Mediterranean; Irish corsairs were active in privateering and piracy outfits in the near Atlantic. The great pirate queen Gráinne O'Malley journeyed from Clew Bay in 1593 to meet Elizabeth I. As shown by the strength of evidence from France and Spain of large confraternities, Irish mercantile families were scattered around the Atlantic and beyond, benefiting from their position on the western-most coast of Europe and on the tightrope of Dee's emerging empire.

Undoubtedly, distinct cultural institutions and geographical location worked to the advantage of the Irish in the Atlantic and these factors were exploited. Like the Scots in their Atlantic activities, the Irish grew in ingenious ways in this Atlantic world, learning to overcome the later mercantilist system within the seventeenth- and eighteenth-century Navigation Acts. Ireland would become a centre for a provision trade based in Cork which exported supplies and victualled slave plantations and coastal American ports; for a burgeoning linen trade centred in Belfast which exported to all parts of the Atlantic world and for a west-coast trade in butter, salt fish and migrants. A native landed gentry may have been missing in rural Ireland, especially from the start of the seventeenth century, but this did not stop the growth of Dublin as the commercial centre for the island, or the rise of Irish networks throughout the Atlantic and beyond. Not unlike the Dutch, the Irish in the Atlantic world were connected by the ocean, and not divided by it.

Ireland and Latin America

As already described, by the sixteenth century Ireland's contacts with the Iberian peninsula were well established and flourishing. Trade and communication were frequent and, perhaps most signal in this regard, trade between the Canary islands and the Iberian peninsula brought the merchant Christopher Columbus to Galway in 1477; one William Eris, or Ayres, a native of the city, is remembered as a member of the voyage of 1492, one of the

---

17 Cunliffe, *Facing the Ocean*, 534–5.
18 K. Schüller, *Die Beziehungen zwischen Spanien und Irland im 16. und 17. Jahrhundert: Diplomatie, Handel und die Soziale Integration Katholischer Exulanten* (Münster: Aschendorff, 1999).

forty volunteers remaining behind on Hispaniola in December that year. Another three Galway sailors sailed with Ferdinand Magellan on his circumnavigation in 1519–1522.

What did change in the course of the sixteenth century, however, was as a consequence of growing English involvement in the political life of Ireland and of confessional conflict. Members of Ireland's Old English families began to withdraw their sons from the universities of Oxford and Cambridge, choosing instead to send them to Catholic universities in continental Europe. Influenced by the zealous spirit of Counter-Reformation Catholicism, they were involved in the establishment of a number of Irish Colleges, notably in Alcalá de Henares, Santiago de Compostela, Seville, Madrid, Paris, Lisbon and Salamanca. The opening of the *Real Colegió de San Patricio de Nobles Irlandeses* in Salamanca in 1592 gave Irish students their largest base on the continent; a royal annuity and a *viaticum* of £10 for each student who finished his course and returned to Ireland meant that students were secure in their studies and could go on to play important roles in religious, military and administrative life in Spanish service in the Americas.[19] With Salamanca in particular, Irish and Old English families had a base for émigré religious, military and commercial migrants, even before Kinsale (1601). Contacts with Portugal and Spain certainly precede Salamanca and the *confraternidades* in Seville and Cádiz, but they attained quasi-plenipotentiary rights in the form of the Salamanca College which appeared, to many, as having the status of an extra-territorial mission.

It was through their contacts with Catholic Europe, and most especially Spain, that Irish men and women began to cross the Atlantic, working as soldiers, missionaries and labourers. Franciscans and Jesuits, from Ireland and of Irish heritage, served in Spanish and Portuguese stations and were seen to have an advantage over their Iberian coreligionists; as missionaries they could speak English and therefore counter the work of Dutch and English colonisers whom they might encounter abroad. Juan and Tomás Farel (Farrell) were in the 1536 expedition of Pedro de Mendoza to the River Plate, and they went on to found and settle Buenos Aires. One early missionary active in Latin America was Limerick-born Thomas Field (1547–1626) who, three years after joining the Society of Jesus in Rome, arrived in Spanish Brazil in 1577. After spending three years in Piratininga (São Paulo), he continued to Paraguay and proselytised among the Guaraní people. Field is most likely the first Irish-born cleric to have engaged in a mission in the Americas. He died in Asunción, at the centre

---

19 M. Henchy, 'The Irish College at Salamanca', *Studies* 70 (1981), 220–27.

of the 'Giant Province of the Indies' (*Provincia Gigante de Indias*) in 1626. As with Field, many of the early Irish migrants in the Atlantic served as proxy agents of European imperial ventures: as missionaries, as soldiers, as merchants, planters and colonists in French, Spanish and Portuguese service. Others, as is evident from the records of the Dutch West and East Indies Companies, worked in the service of the United Provinces, in short-lived German ventures to the Caribbean in the early seventeenth century and, of course, in English service. In 1612 for example, James and Philip Purcell negotiated with the Portuguese crown and helped establish a colony at Tauregue named 'Purcell's Creek', at the mouth of the Amazon River; they lived there together with Dutch, English and French settlers. Eight years later they were joined by a dozen settlers from County Clare, led by Bernardo O'Brien, and they built a fortress on the north bank of the Amazon near Macapa, trading in dyes, hardwood and tobacco and having outposts from Cabo do Norte (Amapá) to the equator. The settlers – with family names de Courcy, Moore and Mulryan amongst them – established good terms with the local Tupí Indians and they proved a useful ally for the natives against the Portuguese. O'Brien became expert in navigating the tributaries at the mouth of the Amazon and he was conversant in the local Arruan language; his linguistic and navigational skills helped him make a considerable profit and led to many further migrants from Ireland following in his wake. This Irish colony on the Amazon may be the earliest example of an independent Irish colonial project in the Americas; serving first for the Dutch West India Company, the Irish settlers later petitioned the Spanish crown for a licence to settle the Amazon. Only the restoration of the Portuguese monarchy in 1640 and changing foreign policy interests of the English and others ended this colonial venture.[20]

Early Irish migrants to Latin America were compliant members of the imperial system; only in the later eighteenth century did their descendants become French-inspired republicans and emerge as proxy revolutionaries for their new homelands. Whether in the Portuguese Amazon, in Spanish Mexico, on French Caribbean islands, in Dutch service or working in partnerships based in Bristol or Ireland itself, the Irish in the Atlantic were adroit in forging Atlantic networks not always dependent on English, or indeed other, patrons. Yet while the terms 'Irish', 'Irish nation' and 'Irish Catholics' appear in both English and Spanish archives for this period, in matters of commerce it was felt that wherever the Irish went, they brought in the English.[21] And it

20 J. Lorimer, *English and Irish Settlement on the River Amazon, 1550–1646* (London: Hakluyt Society, 1989).
21 Lorimer (ed.), *English and Irish Settlement on the River Amazon*, 401–6.

was in English service and in English territories that the Irish in the Atlantic were most active.

Ireland and the 'Commercialising of Colonisation'

Ireland was one of only two European countries, together with the Netherlands, which in the early modern period was both a country of immigration as well as emigration. As Nicholas Canny has argued, when it came to the colonisation of its Atlantic colonies both England and the Netherlands relied to a large extent on foreigners. In the first century of English activity in the Americas, more English settlers migrated to Ireland than they did to the Chesapeake. England's experience of Atlantic colonisation relied for, a large part, on Irish and Scots who could, in large numbers, be used to colonise the British West Indies and Chesapeake.

The transatlantic colonial economy also served to expand opportunities for emigration, thereby creating multinational British colonies later in the early modern period.[22] Colonial migration created avenues of mobility for the Irish and others, denied them within the domestic framework. English state interests were also served through the migration of these cultural groups to the colonies, which enabled the containment of Irish autonomy within the project of British imperialism.[23] The prospect of colonial settlement provided the opportunity to erase internal divisions, or in the words of Shakespeare's Henry IV, to 'busy giddy minds / With foreign quarrels' (2 Henry IV, 4.5.213–14). Colonial expansion ultimately served to reinforce inequalities between core and peripheral regions, as expanding resources of capital became increasingly centralised in London, a process that marginalised not only Ireland, but also emerging commercial centres like Dublin and Bristol.[24]

Without question, contact with, and experience in, Ireland affected English attitudes towards the Irish in the Atlantic world. The establishment of numerous 'non-trading' Atlantic ventures from the start of the seventeenth century increased the importance of colonial ventures in the portfolios of investors in London and elsewhere. Colonial connections between England and

---

22 B. Bailyn and P. D. Morgan, 'Introduction', in B. Bailyn and P. D. Morgan (eds.), *Strangers within the Realm: Cultural Margins of the First British Empire* (Chapel Hill, NC: University of North Carolina Press, 1991), 1–31.

23 M. Netzloff, 'Writing Britain from the Margins: Scottish, Irish, and Welsh Projects for American Colonization', *Prose Studies: History, Theory, Criticism*, 25 (2002), 3.

24 D. Harris Sacks. *The Widening Gate: Bristol and the Atlantic Economy, 1450–1700* (Berkeley, CA: University of California Press, 1991).

the Americas were stronger by 1613 than at any other point, thanks to the recent growth of the Virginia and Irish Companies, both of which attracted a lot of interest from East India Company (EIC) members. The year 1613 was also the busiest period for the EIC in terms of its own colonial activities; the Company developed three villages in Dundaniel, County Cork, to take advantage of commodity extraction from Ireland, linking Irish trade and commerce at this early stage, albeit in a minor way, to the Indian, and not just Atlantic, ocean.[25] Attempting to convince settlers to follow him to Ireland, Robert Payne argued that the peacefully inclined Irish were avid readers of Las Casas's tales of Spanish cruelty in the Americas and so were especially keen to accept English rule rather than throw their lot in with the Catholic Iberian empire.[26] English colonial texts progressively replaced an older chivalric model of adventure with a more commercially minded framework of economic 'ventures', in what has been termed 'the commercialising of colonisation'. This is best demonstrated by the dominance of London-based companies in plantation efforts in Ulster, Virginia and the Caribbean in the first decades of the seventeenth century.[27]

Yet there was an English anxiety concerning the levels of cultural contamination which might take place, were Irish migrants to gain access to English settlements; this can be seen in Spenser's *A View of the Present State of Ireland* (*c.*1596) and other texts when describing Englishmen who had become assimilated within Irish culture.[28] Like Spenser, Henry Cary, Viscount Falkland, associated the threatening possibility of English cultural 'degeneration' with Irish women, prompting him to stipulate that all female immigrants to English colonies should be English, a specification not extended to male colonists: 'then it is noe great matter of wha[t] nation the men bee soe the women bee English'.[29]

25 P. O'Sullivan, 'The English East India Company at Dundaniel', *Bandon Historical Journal*, 4 (1988), 3–15; E. Smith, 'Naval Violence and Trading Privileges in Early Seventeenth-Century Asia', *International Journal of Maritime History*, 25 (2013), 147–58.

26 Robert Payne, *A Briefe Description of Ireland: Made in this yeere, 1589*, ed. A. Smith (Dublin: Irish Archaeological Society, 1841); A. Hadfield, 'British Colonial Expansion Westwards: Ireland and America', in S. Castillo and I. Schweitzer (eds.), *A Companion to the Literatures of Colonial America* (Oxford: Blackwell Publishing, 2005),196.

27 M. Nerlich, *Ideology of Adventure: Studies in Modern Consciousness, 1100–1750*, trans. R. Crowley (2 vols., Minneapolis, MN: University of Minnesota Press, 1987), i, 164; C. Shammas, 'English Commercial Development and American Colonization, 1560–1620', in K. R. Andrews (ed.), *The Westward Enterprise: English Activities in Ireland, The Atlantic, and America, 1480–1650* (Detroit, MI: Wayne State University Press, 1979), 151–74.

28 N. Canny, *Making Ireland British, 1580–1650* (Oxford University Press, 2001).

29 Falkland, 'To the Well Affected Planters in New Fownde Lande', in G.T. Cell (ed.), *Newfoundland Discovered: English Attempts at Colonisation, 1610–1630* (London: Hakluyt Society, 1982), 244–5 (quote at 245).

Falkland's early seventeenth-century receptiveness to the immigration of Irish men into the English Atlantic world, including Catholics, even while he strictly enforced the religious and national origin of female migrants, might attempt to conceal an effort for forced conversion, a possible hope that male Irish Catholic migrants into the Atlantic colonies would, by default, marry the only (Protestant) women in the colonies, and thereby accept Protestantism. By so doing, Falkland intended to place Protestant English women in the same position of authority over acculturation that Spenser and others had found so threatening when assumed by Irish women.[30] Falkland's kinsman, Thomas Cary, penned the sole example of a text promoting colonisation, *A Short Discourse of the New-found-land* (1623), published in Dublin in the early modern period.[31] In *New-found-land* he argued that Irish settlement overseas would produce a degree of economic self-sufficiency for Ireland, encouraging Irish manufacture and creating an outlet for Irish goods in the Americas, yet at the same time acknowledging that the ultimate beneficiary of Irish prosperity would be England.[32] Only later, at the end of the eighteenth century, was Newfoundland a prime site of Irish immigration.

Following Falkland, William Petty continued with this commodification of Irish labour – everything's value could be reduced to the amount of labour it took to produce.[33] Petty discussed how deaths due to rebellion and unrest in Ireland could be offset by an increase in population in the American plantations. 'Besides it is hoped that New England, where few or no Women are Barren, and most have many Children, and where People live long, and healthfully, hath produced an increase of as many People, as were destroyed in the late Tumults in Ireland.'[34]

Ireland, Africa and the Americas

Most studies of Ireland and the country's contacts with Atlantic Africa, especially southern Africa, begin their story in 1795.[35] The history is a much older one, however, and it certainly possesses a lengthy chapter on Irish involvement

30 Netzloff, 'Writing Britain from the Margins', 12.
31 Netzloff, 'Writing Britain from the Margins', 12.
32 Netzloff, 'Writing Britain from the Margins', 12.
33 William Petty, 'Treatise of Taxes', in *The Economic Writings of Sir William Petty*, ed. C. H. Hull (2 vols., Cambridge University Press, 1899), i, 43.
34 William Petty, 'Political Arithmetick', in *Economic Writings of Sir William Petty*, ed. Hull, i, 303.
35 D. McCracken (ed.), *The Irish in southern Africa, 1795–1910* (Durban: Ireland and Southern Africa Project, 1991).

in the Atlantic slave trade. While the Atlantic crossing from Ireland may have been unpleasant, the rigours of the voyage were hardly comparable to those involved in crossing 'that frightful ocean' in a state of slavery.[36] The transatlantic voyage was, for Irish migrants, 'the decisive divide of their lives', yet it cannot be compared with the experience of cultural, linguistic and individual isolation that befell the millions of enslaved Africans robbed of freedom.[37]

Irish merchants' exclusion from membership of the slave-trading Royal Africa Company (1660–1752) meant that Ireland was banned from participation in the infamous triangular trade for most of the eighteenth century. Ireland underwrote the slave trade in other ways, however. Goods, including barrelled butter and salt beef for slaves, and spiced salmon and pickled tongue for masters, were exported from Cork to the West Indian plantations. 'Caribbean butter' made the dairy farmers who produced it and the Cork merchants who sold it, some of the wealthiest in the country. And merchants like Henry Blake of Galway amassed a small fortune and lands in Ireland from sugar produced by African slaves. In 1729 alone, the majority of the 5,855 slaves on the Caribbean island of Montserrat were owned by Irish families, including the Farrills (Farrells), Husseys, Lynches, Roaches and others. About one in eight of all sailors (some 12 per cent) aboard slaving ships working out of the port of Liverpool (which accounted for one-third of Europe's trade in enslaved Africans in the eighteenth century) were Irish men – the highest non-English group involved in the trade. Included in this slaving group were the Irish Catholic David Tuohy and the Ulsterman-turned-Antiguan planter Samuel Martin; the latter turned away from slaving only later in life. South from Ireland on the French coast, men of Irish heritage such as Antoine Walsh (1703–1763) were infamous as slave traders; Walsh's ventures made him famous in Nantes and St Malo and he became one of the wealthiest of the many Irish merchants in the French Atlantic slave trade. These Irish merchants, in France, England and the Americas, were directly connected to the Company of Merchants Trading to Africa, the successor to the old Royal African Company: the first governor of the Province of Senegambia appointed in 1756 was one Charles O'Hara, illegitimate son of James, Baron Kilmaine. O'Hara was followed in post by Matthew MacNamara and he by John Clarke; Britain's first formal colony in west Africa was run predominately by Irishmen.[38]

36 Canny and Pagden (eds.), *Colonial Identity in the Atlantic world*, 4.
37 Canny and Pagden (eds.), *Colonial Identity in the Atlantic world*, 7.
38 J. D. Newton, 'Naval Power and the Province of Senegambia, 1758–1779', *Journal for Maritime Research*, 15:2 (2013), 129–47.

While African slavery and slaves were rare in Ireland, there is evidence of slaving ships operating out of Dublin. Despite having failed twice at establishing slaving companies later in the eighteenth century (at Limerick in 1784 and Belfast in 1786), Irish merchants were very active in supplying slave plantations in the Caribbean. Newspapers in Cork and Dublin very occasionally carried advertisements of slaves for sale and notices of runaways, and one Samuel Burke, a South Carolinian 'Irish-speaking negro', was identified as a resident of Cork.[39] How much of the wealth made in the slave trade made its way into Ireland? It is difficult to know; just as difficult, perhaps, as to ascertain how 'Irish' the merchants involved in the trade in Antigua, Liverpool or St Malo felt, or what level of unease – if at all – they felt in dispossessing and degrading other peoples while themselves dispossessed. When the Slave Compensation Commission began recompensing slave holders for their 'lost property' in 1834, it was an Irishman, James Blair of Newry, who collected the largest single sum in the British Empire, owing over 1,500 slaves. At best, many Irish slavers and slave owners were creole Irish; at worst, they learned lessons from their neighbours, gaining advantage from the slave trade. In this way, perhaps, they belonged to that class already seen in late sixteenth-century Ireland by Laoiseach Mac an Bhaird when he wrote, '*A fhir ghlacas an ghalldacht*' ('O man who follows English ways').[40]

Ireland and the Caribbean

Arriving, disappearing and re-emerging in different forms, the Irish have been a changing but constant presence in the history of the Caribbean. Of all the areas of Irish settlement in the early modern Atlantic, the preferred destination for the Irish was the island of St Christopher, whose founder and governor, Sir Thomas Warner, was himself an adventurer from an earlier settlement in Guyana. From 'St Kitts', the Irish made their way to nearby islands including Antigua, Montserrat and Nevis. Montserrat, a 'noble plantation of Irish Catholiques' (1634) was in 1668 described as 'almost an Irish colony' that had been created by Catholic Irishmen who had fled Virginia because 'the Virginians would not suffer to live with them'.[41] By 1639 there were some 3,000 Irish Catholics living on the Leeward islands.

39 1762 and 1768, respectively. N. Rodgers, *Ireland, Slavery and Anti-Slavery: 1612–1865* (London: Palgrave Macmillan, 2007), 33.

40 D. Greene and F. Kelly (eds.), *Irish Bardic Poetry: Texts and Translations, Together with an Introductory Lecture by Osborn Bergin* (Dublin Institute for Advanced Studies, 1970, repr. 1984), 49–50, 231–2.

41 K. Block and J. Shaw, 'Subjects without an Empire: The Irish in the Early Modern Caribbean', *Past & Present*, 210 (2011), 35, n. 7.

An Irish presence was not limited to these islands. The soldier of fortune John Murphy Fitzgerald Burke, 'Don Morfo Geraldino y Burco', who described himself as a noble from Galway, established a real presence on Hispaniola. Using his Irishness as a passport to Spanish employment and deserting the French and English buccaneers of Tortuga, he led a Spanish raid on the island and later, in 1655, Don Murfo successfully led the Spanish forces from Hispaniola against Cromwell's Western Design.[42]

In French service in the western Atlantic, the Irish played a crucial role in gaining Montserrat and parts of St Christopher from England and for France in 1666. Although in later negotiations the islands were returned to England and the Irish Protestant governor of Montserrat, Anthony Briskett, was relieved of his position, he was replaced by an Irish Catholic governor, William Stapleton, because it was felt he would 'understand how to govern his countrymen'. By the 1670s, Stapleton had amassed governorships of all the English Leeward islands.[43] From an Old English Tipperary family, Stapleton was both a soldier and crown loyalist – a Catholic who built two parish churches on the island while also securing the services of the first resident Anglican clergyman – and the husband of a well-established English heiress to the largest English estate on the island of Nevis. Stapleton never took the required oaths of allegiance and supremacy, although he enthusiastically reaffirmed his loyalty to the crown and took every opportunity to underscore his unwavering record of support for Charles II. Urging fellow Irish men on Montserrat to do likewise, under Stapleton's tenure Irish Catholics on Montserrat rose to positions as elected assemblymen and came to hold numerous positions of importance.[44] Under his instruction an island census was taken in 1678 and it unusually recorded 'nationality': 69 per cent of whites were recorded as 'Irish'. Yet Montserrat was no Irish colony: English planters like John Wyke always dominated, albeit only with the support of Protestant Irish families like Parsons (Laois/Offaly) and Frye (Limerick). Irish Catholics who did well, from Connacht and Munster, formed a middling-class of traders and planters, whose position on the social ladder was elevated predominately because they stood on the backs of African slaves.

By 1690 in the Caribbean, Governor Christopher Codrington feared that Irish Catholics would follow the example set by those on St Christopher and

42 N. Rodgers, 'A Changing Presence. The Irish in the Caribbean in the Seventeenth and Eighteenth Centuries', in A. Donnell, M. McGarrity and E. O'Callaghan (eds.), *Caribbean Irish Connections: Interdisciplinary Perspectives* (Kingston, Jamaica: The University of the West Indies Press, 2015), 20.
43 A. Burns, *History of the British West Indies* (New York: Barnes and Noble, 1965), 342.
44 Rodgers, 'A Changing Presence', 20.

would declare for King James, or worse would arm the slaves and rise up with them, as was rumoured to have happened on Barbados.[45] Even after authority was restored, Codrington feared the Irish would cross the colour line, or at least make it less diametric. At times, Irish settlers in the Caribbean may have seemed less white than their English overlords, but they were never subject to the same levels of colour prejudice that damned labourers of African heritage.[46]

Irish servants who remained on Barbados mixed with English people of similar social status, lost their distinctive Irish language, accent and Catholicism, and became 'poor whites'. Once the servant class disappeared, the largest number of Irish-speakers was to be found among the sailors; only on Montserrat did a few words of Irish make their way into the quotidian English patois used by all. As long as slavery lasted they enjoyed certain privileges as 'military tenants', supplied with small plots of land to enable them to man the militia. As time moved on, they seem to have been ever less aware of their Irish roots, and almost certainly held no developed sense of an Irish identity before the late eighteenth century, at earliest. The many descendants of white Irish-slave relationships were certainly unaware of any sense of belonging to the Irish nation.

Ireland, North America and Emigration

Migration from Ireland into the Atlantic world before the mid-eighteenth century can be distinguished by magnitude and destination associated with two consecutive episodes: the first, from small-scale emigration in the sixteenth and early seventeenth centuries, which was not always directly from Ireland, down to the end of the 1670s; and the second, from the establishment of Pennsylvania until the later eighteenth century. In the very early 1600s, Irish emigration to North America was negligible and consisted primarily of unmarried, Catholic males, but by the end of the 1600s, some 100,000 Irish emigrants had made their way to North American and Caribbean colonies. On the American mainland, the first documentary record of Irish inhabitants of Newfoundland comes from 1622; four decades later in 1663, Irish inhabitants are recorded in New France. In the entire first phase of migration, perhaps as many as 400,000 people were transported to the British

---

45 H. McD. Beckles, "A 'Riotous and Unruly Lot'": Irish Indentured Servants and Freeman in the English West Indies, 1644–1713', *William and Mary Quarterly* 47 (1990), 503.
46 M. Lamotte, 'Colour Prejudice in the Early Modern French Empire, *c.*1635–1767', unpublished PhD dissertation, University of Cambridge (2015).

American colonies, amongst them many Irish migrants. Chartered companies recruited labourers for plantation settlements where cash crops including
cotton, sugar and tobacco were cultivated for market. Of the total number
who crossed the Atlantic from Ireland and Britain before 1680, over one-half
went to the Caribbean islands, 120,000 to the Chesapeake and another 20,000
went to New England. More than 75 per cent of the total were indentured
servants, most were under the age of twenty-five and most were from the
lowest socio-economic sector of society. Migrants into English and British
colonies were typically unskilled, semi-skilled or servant women.[47] Migrants
commonly travelled with relatives and many emigrants retained kinship
connections and communitarian practices in the New World. Unmarried
men, who made up the bulk of all European migrants in the pre-eighteenth-
century period, had the greatest opportunity. Because women had traditionally
left home only to marry or to carry out service in prearranged locations, in
this period few women – other than servants – moved alone to the Atlantic
colonies. Very few Irish migrants could afford their own passage or could
establish themselves as planters or merchants. On arrival, Irish migrants like
all others faced a hostile disease environment (especially in the Chesapeake
and the Caribbean), and mortality rates were as high as 40 per cent in the
years immediately after arrival.[48] Population growth was impeded in these
first decades by the disproportionate sex ratio; by the 1660s, men outnumbered women by three to one in the Chesapeake.[49] By the late 1670s, more
Irish and Scots migrants moved to the Chesapeake and Caribbean colonies –
and more African slaves were transported – as it grew more difficult to attract
English migrants because of the harsh environment.

The Caribbean islands were the most favoured destination in the pre-1660
period; at this time 40 per cent of all colonists in the English American colonies lived in the Caribbean. In the 1650s, emigrants from Ireland rounded
up after the Cromwellian campaigns in Drogheda and Dundalk added to the
number. Barbados and Jamaica continued to attract large numbers of settlers
and the Irish presence became significant on several islands; the change from

---

47 J. Horn, 'Tobacco Colonies: The Shaping of English Society in the Seventeenth-century
   Chesapeake', in N. Canny (ed.), *The Oxford History of the British Empire, i: The Origins
   of Empire: British Overseas Expansion to the Close of the Seventeenth Century* (Oxford
   University Press, 1998), 176–7.
48 J. Horn, *Adapting to a New World: English Society in the Seventeenth-Century Chesapeake*
   (Chapel Hill, NC: The University of North Carolina Press, 1994), 23–6; R. S. Dunn,
   Sugar and Slaves: The Rise of the Planter Class in the English West Indies, 1624–1713 (Chapel
   Hill, NC: The University of North Carolina Press, 1972).
49 Horn, 'Tobacco Colonies', 182–4.

cotton and tobacco to sugar in the later seventeenth century, and from indentured labour to slave society over the course of two generations, meant that by 1700 the islands no longer proved as attractive to Irish labourers. Sugar cultivation altered the demographics of the Caribbean, and Irish migrants, like their English and Scottish counterparts, were more attracted to mainland, than to island, colonies.

In the second phase of emigration from Ireland, after 1680 and before the 1770s, the most evident change from the preceding period was the staggering increase in the number of Irish migrants, both Catholic and Protestant, crossing the Atlantic. The number of English and Welsh migrants declined, dropping from 350,000 in the seventeenth century to 80,000 in the eighteenth.[50] At the same time, ten times more Scots and Scots-Irish immigrated to the Americas in the eighteenth than in the seventeenth century and at least three times more Irish migrants made the crossing in the pre-revolutionary period.[51] Convicts, too, were transported.[52] More migrants arrived to populate Pennsylvania and the middle colonies, and moved southwards along the valleys of the Appalachian mountains. Eighteenth-century migrants were more likely than their seventeenth-century predecessors to travel in family or community groups, and were usually more skilled or better informed on how to establish a household once their indentures had expired. By the time emigration from Ireland to the Americas resumed after the Seven Years War, ships from Ireland and England were carrying more non-English migrants than English colonists, and Irish migrants were swelling the numbers. The English American colonies were demographically, culturally and linguistically less English than they had ever previously been.

It is difficult to ascertain exact numbers of migrants from Ireland in this period, but records of exceptional individual success, and ship records and reports of departures, offer a representative sample of forms and types of emigration to the Americas. Already in 1621, Daniel Gookin, a merchant from Carrigaline, Cork, led a party of Irish settlers to Newport News, Virginia, on board the *Flying Harte*. Gookin's non-conformist son, Daniel the Younger, would go on to be a member of the governor's council of Massachusetts, representing Cambridge, and superintendent of Indian affairs. In the 1630s,

---

50 J. Horn, 'British Diaspora: Emigration from Britain, 1680–1815', in P. J. Marshall (ed.), *The Oxford History of the British Empire*, ii: *The Eighteenth Century* (Oxford University Press, 1998), 30–2.

51 Horn, 'British Diaspora', 30–2.

52 A. R. Ekirch, *Bound for America: The Transportation of British Convicts to the Colonies, 1718–1775* (Oxford University Press, 1987), 112–15.

religious tolerance in Maryland encouraged a number of Irish Catholics to emigrate to the commonwealth, joining the significant English Catholic community. After the Test Acts of the 1670s and the subsequent fall of the Stuarts however, Catholic Irish migration was both discouraged and unwanted; occasional conformity favoured Presbyterians and Quakers from Ireland, if any non-Anglicans were at all to be permitted. In 1682, Thomas Dongan (1634–1715) became the first Irish Catholic governor of New York. Remembered most for the 'Charter of Libertyes and Privileges' ('Dongan's Charter'), Dongan convened the first representative assembly of New York Province on 4 October 1683, defining the form of government for the colony and recognising basic political and personal rights. Dongan was active in the same years as Charles Carroll, member of one of the most prosperous Irish families in North America at this time. Carroll became attorney general of Maryland in 1688; his grandson, Charles Carroll of Carrollton, was the only Catholic signatory to the Declaration of Independence. Maryland would not always remain so tolerant of Catholics; in 1704, laws were enacted to discourage the immigration and importation of Catholics.

Protestant Irish emigrants made up the greatest number of emigrants from Ireland by the early 1700s; by 1717, large-scale emigration from Ulster was in full flow and by 1775, as many as a quarter of a million Ulster-Scots had left Ireland for North America. From the early 1680s, outbreaks of disease and violence in Ulster and a severe winter in 1683–1684 threatened the pastoral economic base of the north of the country. Some Presbyterian dissenters, in County Tyrone, in early 1684 (prompted by the introduction of official measures against Presbyterian worship), were brought to conform, but 'others threaten to go to Carolina. Thither, I believe, some may go, but the noise of it is chiefly raised by such as think to make their landlords more indulgent to them from the apprehension of having their lands laid waste. We have had a very hard winter.'[53] In the same year a number of ministers from the suppressed Laggan Presbytery announced their intention to emigrate, citing not only 'persecutions' and the lack of access to their ministry but also the 'general poverty abounding in these parts'.[54] In 1703 a proposal was made to transport a colony of 500 'inhabitants about Belfast, many of

---

53 Historical Manuscripts Commission, *Calendar of the Manuscripts of the Marquess of Ormonde* (new series, 8 vols., London: HMSO, 1902–1920), vii, 181; after G. Kirkham, 'Ulster Emigration to North America, 1680–1720', in H. T. Blethen and C. W. Wood Jr (eds.), *Ulster and North America. Transatlantic Perspectives on the Scotch-Irish* (Tuscaloosa and London, The University of Alabama Press, 1997), 77

54 A. G. Lecky, *The Laggan and its Presbyterianism* (Belfast: Davidson and McCormack, 1905), reprinted as *Roots of Presbyterianism in Donegal* (Omagh: Graham and Sons, 1978), 18.

them farmers of some substance' to Virginia or Maryland; the colonies were known because of ties with previous migrants to the region.[55]

Ulster ports continued to trade across the Atlantic throughout the War of Spanish Succession (1701–1714) and customs records show exports to the 'plantations' in every year from Belfast and Derry, as well as occasional ventures from other northern ports, including Donaghadee, Dundalk (including Newry), Killybegs (including Ballyshannon) and Sligo.[56] There are few references to shipping arrivals from Ireland in the American press during the war, and it seems likely that much of this trade was with the West Indies or to the Chesapeake, for which newspaper coverage of maritime activity was poor and so shipping ventures continued largely unabated. There were few Irish migrants in this time: a small number of Quakers arrived in Philadelphia and a group of Donegal Presbyterians settled at Newcastle on the Delaware in 1706; another small migration took place to New England. The risks of travel in wartime and relatively good harvests in the first decade of the eighteenth century dissuaded greater migration; Britain effectively withdrew from the war in 1711 and the number of emigrant voyages once again picked up.

In the period 1713–1726, ten voyages to Virginia and Maryland from Irish ports outside Ulster are recorded, with four recording their cargo as servants and passengers; other Irish emigrants made their way to Virginia from Liverpool and other English ports.[57] Even more migrants left in these years for the Caribbean and 1717 witnessed the great surge in emigration from Ireland. 'Last year some thousands of families are gone to the West Indies', wrote Archbishop King in early 1718 and although he likely exaggerated the size of the movement, and erroneously recorded the destination of the migrants (most, in fact, went to mainland American colonies), numbers did increase. In 1717 alone, twelve ships left Irish ports for America. One, the *Friends Goodwill* arrived in Boston in September 1717 direct from Dublin (although it may have briefly dropped anchor at Larne); the vessel had endured a horrifically long crossing of some eighteen weeks and the fifty-two crew, passengers and servants aboard were close to their end when they reached New England.[58]

Of the 'Scots-Irish' Ulster migrants, most came from Antrim, Derry, Donegal and Tyrone at this time, but not just: others came from Down,

55 C. Hedlam (ed.), *Calendar of State Papers, Colonial Series: America and the West Indies, Dec. 1, 1702–1703* (London: HMSO, 1913), 263, 269–70.
56 'Ledgers of Imports and Exports of Ireland', CUST 15, The National Archives; Kirkham, 'Ulster Emigration to North America', 76–97, 79.
57 Kirkham, 'Ulster Emigration to North America', 76–97, 80.
58 Dickinson to John Askew, 24 October 1717, Letterbook of Jonathan Dickinson, Library Company of Philadelphia (held at the Historical Society of Pennsylvania).

Fermanagh, Monaghan and from neighbouring Sligo, too. 'Nor do only Dissenters leave us, but proportionally of all sorts, except Papists', King wrote in June 1719. Driven out by increased rents: 'one reason they give for their going is the raising of the rent of the land to such a high rate that they cannot support their families thereon with the greatest industry'.[59] Tithes, too, played a part in encouraging emigration.

In 1716, legislation enacted by the South Carolina assembly to encourage the immigration of white indentured servants and to promote settlement on the frontier was publicised in Ireland. It included a package of measures, including 300 acres of land for each male settler of military age.[60] In New England, too, moves to entice settlers to the undeveloped lands of various proprietors and to defend the frontier grew from c.1714.[61] Advertisements for passage from Dublin to Boston appeared in Dublin newspapers throughout this period. After 1720, and primarily because of its increasing trade with Ulster and its religious tolerance, Pennsylvania became the primary destination of Irish Protestant immigrants. Gradually moving from the southwest further westward towards the frontier, they reached the backcountry in the south with Georgia. The growing influence of Irish Presbyterians in Philadelphia and Boston was well noted, as was the growing number of poor and destitute Irish arriving in these ports. On St Patrick's Day 1737, in Boston, twenty-six Irishmen founded the Charitable Irish Society, the oldest Irish society in North America, to address the growing crisis faced by the city in dealing with impoverished migrants arriving in the months from March to October every year. Irish men and women became a significant body of labourers in the North American colonies, most spending a period of time in indenture, and many running away from it as many advertisements in colonial broadsheets bear witness:

> RUN away on the 27th of April past, at Night, from Samuel Butt of Plumsted Township, Bucks County, an Irish Servant Man, named William Cough [Cuugh], short of Stature, bow legged, flat footed, of a dark Complexion, round and full fac'd, much mark'd with the Small Pox, is watry eyed, and wears a Cap or light colour'd Wig: Had a good Felt Hat, a blue Duroy Coat lin'd with Silk Crape, a pretty good white Dimmity Jacket, and new Breeches of the same, a new fine Shirt and two new

---

59 Joseph Marriott, August 12, 1718, quoted in R. J. Dickson, *Ulster Emigration to Colonial America, 1718–1775* (New York: Humanities Press, 1966), 29.

60 R. L. Meriweather, *The Expansion of South Carolina, 1729–1765* (Kingsport, TN: Southern Publishers, 1940; repr. Philadelphia: Porcupine Press, 1974), 17.

61 R. H. Akagi, *The Town Proprietors of the New England Colonies* (Philadelphia: University of Pennsylvania Press, 1924; repr. Gloucester, MA: Peter Smith, 1963), 256–62.

homepsun ones, two new Muslin Stocks, white Cotton Stockings and a pair of grey yarn ones, old round toe'd Shoes with strings in them. He has taken his own and another Man's Indentures with him. Whoever takes up and secures the said Servant, so that his Master may have him again, shall have Forty Shillings Reward, and reasonable Charges, paid by SAMUEL BUTT.[62]

Religious Confessionalism, *Patria* and Nation

Ireland, home to a predominantly Catholic population and a succession of Protestant colonisation schemes, was but one of the many vigorously contested territories in the Atlantic world between Catholic and Protestant interests.[63] When in the late eighteenth century, Edmund Burke deplored the assimilation of Protestants in general into a 'master caste', monopolising 'every franchise, every honour, every trust, every place down to the very lowest and least confidential', he signalled that religion had assumed central importance: no longer merely one badge of privilege.[64] Confessional identity made a difference, without question, when deciding where one might settle and where one could gain refuge, but sectarianism was less blunt in the Atlantic colonies than it regularly was in Ireland at this time. Irish migrants lived and worked in Catholic and Protestant territories and, while not always by choice, Catholic Irish did not flee to a Catholic colony at first chance.

In Ireland, on the one hand, the 'Old English' discarded a sense of ethnic kinship with England in the course of the seventeenth century and its Catholic community assimilated to an indigenous Irish identity. New English settlers, on the other hand, remained a colonial nation with a stronger sense of *nación* and a correspondingly weaker sense of Irish *patria*. This near-creole identity, intellectually justified in the writings of James Ussher, amongst others, sought to establish an indigenous pedigree for Irish Protestantism, removing it from the tainted legacy of English colonialism.[65] Irish Catholic migrants had a greater sense of coming from and belonging to a *patria* than possessing a sense of *nación*. Only after this period would these relative investments slip and be inverted.

62 *Pennsylvania Gazette*, 11 May 1738.
63 J. Ohlmeyer, 'A Laboratory for Empire: Early Modern Ireland and English Imperialism', in K. Kenny (ed.), *Ireland and the British Empire* (Oxford University Press, 2006), 26–60.
64 Edmund Burke, 'A letter to Sir Hercules Langrishe' (1792) in *The Works of the Right Honourable Edmund Burke* (12 vols., London: John C. Nimmo, 1887), iv, 252.
65 Kidd, *British Identities before Nationalism*, 180–1.

Diversity and interconnectedness of Protestantism around the Atlantic also produced conflicts within denominations, and in the case of migrants from Ireland, especially in the relations between Anglicans, Presbyterians and Quakers. From the 1730s, religious revivals, collectively labelled as the 'Great Awakening', crossed the sea, with historians uncovering evidence of inter-related sets of revivals in Ireland, Britain, the Americas and elsewhere, revealing deep disagreements about what it meant to be a Protestant and, in some contexts, what it meant to be Irish.[66]

In the Spanish Caribbean and on mainland Spanish colonies, Catholic practice eased entry into the highest branches of office. Alexander O'Reilly, for example, born in Baltrasna, County Meath, in 1722, helped to build fortresses in Havana and Puerto Rico and went on to be governor of Louisiana and Cuba. Like clerics, soldiers of Irish birth and ancestry were found throughout the Atlantic world. Not all remained loyal to Rome and success in the Caribbean turned many Irish Catholics into Protestants. Edmond Kelly, of Lisaduff, County Galway, became attorney general of Jamaica in the 1720s and in the 1740s Denis Kelly – 'Jamaica Kelly' – was appointed chief justice. The family owned an estate that ran from the north to the south of the island. Kelly's daughter and heiress, Elizabeth, married into the once-Catholic, now Protestant, Browne family of Westport, County Mayo, in 1752 and with Elizabeth's wealth, the Brownes became Ireland's premier absentee plantation owners in the British Caribbean.[67]

Other Irish families traded on, and with, the Dutch and Danish islands of St Eustatius and Saint Croix. The sugar trade filled the coffers of Montserratian families including the Bodkins, Blakes and Brownes, the Kirwans, Skerrets and Ryans, making it seem like a tribes-of-Galway commercial venture. The Montserrat-born Nicholas Tuite (1705–1772), 'an English planter' for London eyes, was an Irishman for the Danes when the king of Denmark bestowed Danish citizenship on him in 1760. Irish identity, based on shared faith and historical experience, had evolved into a West Indian colonial identity.[68] In England, and especially amongst English Catholics, they were particularly well received and in London and Bath they were hosted and feted. Irish Catholics married into English Catholic families, and while their Irish identity was forgotten, their Catholicism was maintained.

The Irish appeared early in the Caribbean, but their failure to found a colony meant that their history was rarely considered part of the official

---

66 S. O'Brien, 'A Transatlantic Community of Saints: The Great Awakening and the First Evangelical Network, 1735–1755', *American Historical Review*, 91 (1986), 811–32.

67 N. Rodgers, 'A Changing Presence', 24.

68 N. Rodgers, 'A Changing Presence', 26.

account. Working within others' empires, they left behind no distinctive state structure, language or architectural style, as other Europeans did. They were largely shut out by the Spanish, used by the French as allies when convenient, and treated as second-class subjects by the British; assimilation into these dominant groups increasingly became the only strategic possibility. They did, however, play an important part in turning the Leewards and Barbados into tobacco colonies, helped to prevent the Cromwellian conquest of Hispaniola, and applied their expertise to the development of Jamaica as a sugar island. In all these ventures, the Irish could be found in every social group, from indentured servant to slave and plantation owner.

A 'Green' Atlantic?

Ireland and the Atlantic world before the mid-eighteenth century was a very different iteration of the green Atlantic of the nineteenth century and thereafter. The ethno-religious identity of Irish migrants in the Atlantic world after 1845 must be reassessed against the preceding Irish Atlantic.

Historians of the Huguenot diaspora have recognised a wider, trans-Atlantic context of trade networks and familial links; a 'Protestant International' of trade, familial and scholarly networks superimposed over the Atlantic by the larger Protestant diaspora, of which the Huguenot migrations were a part. It was 'family relationships that formed the heart of the Protestant International'.[69] Ireland and the Atlantic world pre-1750 is also of this model: networks enabled the maintenance of links of commonality with Irish communities around the Atlantic and in Europe. To substitute the word 'Irish' for 'Huguenot' in a line from Louis Cullen, demonstrates that these networks were 'not simply an offshoot of persecution, but a vital and ongoing part of the ... activities of [the Irish overseas]'.[70] At least in the first generations in the Atlantic world, Irish emigrants were more like *peninsulares* (Spanish colonists) or the *criollos* of Cuba, spearheading and playing roles in others' colonial projects. Just as the *criollos*, over time, came to distance themselves from new Spanish colonists and a 'Spanish' identity, the Irish in the Atlantic world transformed, developing a worldview at odds with the majority population

69 For a discussion of this 'Protestant International', see J. F. Boscher, 'Huguenot Merchants and the Protestant International in the Seventeenth Century', *William and Mary Quarterly*, third series, 52 (1995) 77–102.

70 L. Cullen 'The Huguenots from the Perspective of the Merchant Networks of Western Europe 1680–1890: The Example of the Brandy Trade', in C. E. J. Caldicott, H. Gough and J. P. Pittion (eds.), *The Huguenots in Ireland: Anatomy of an Emigration* (Dun Laoghaire: Glendale, 1987), 129–49.

around them. Underpinning that social framework were men who bore Irish surnames and were imbued with ambition, foot soldiers of empire in diverse projects of empire building. In the vanguard came cash-strapped members of a landed gentry from Ireland –perhaps not self-identifying as Irish *per se*, but from the island – vying for colonial governorships to pay off debts and support their lifestyles. And the majority were the poor sort, men and women from Ireland who moved, or were removed, out of need and persecution and who sought a new, improved, life overseas.

In the contentious matter of 'Irishness' in this period, for the vast majority of Irish people in the Atlantic world, Irish identity was protean, unlike the fixed, confessionalised, status of identity that limited the Irish in Ireland. The community of Irish Catholic planters of Montserrat, the island frequently presented as a model for how the Irish might (just) have run an Atlantic empire, was, to paraphrase Voltaire, neither Holy, nor Roman, nor an empire: they held slaves, did not suffer the same economic disabilities as Catholics in Ireland, and if theirs was an empire, it was a British, not an Irish, one, turning as they did to London to acquire houses and marry off their children and have them accepted into the metropolitan world. Amidst the ebb and flow of Irish migrants around the Atlantic flow, it is sure only that the pre-eighteenth century 'Irish International' in the Atlantic world helped to enable the mass emigration of the nineteenth century.

PART IV

★

CULTURE

16

Language, Print and Literature in Irish, 1550–1630

MARC CABALL

Gaelic society and culture in Ireland from 1550 to 1630 were characterised paradoxically by intersecting processes of political retrenchment and cultural regeneration. As Gaelic and gaelicised Old English lords increasingly faltered under the pressure of the consolidation of Tudor and Stuart dominion, an extended process of cultural diversification was concurrently facilitated and developed by praise poets, traditional custodians of high Gaelic culture. This professional *élite* was largely supplanted in the first decades of the seventeenth century by gentlemen poets influenced by an amalgam of Gaelic tradition and Renaissance scholarship. Both the Reformation and Counter-Reformation underpinned a nascent Gaelic print culture during these years. This chapter seeks to examine critical developments in Gaelic culture during this seminal period, while also suggesting that a short-lived engagement with print ultimately vitiated external perception of the authority of Irish literature and scholarship notwithstanding its vibrancy. Drawing on an interpretative framework, which has defined the pre-Reformation English church in terms of concurrent vitality and vulnerability, it is proposed that late sixteenth- and early seventeenth-century Gaelic culture was informed by a high level of creativity which masked an emergent structural weakness.[1]

A capacity for cultural recalibration within a context of retrenchment was remarkable given that the bardic institution was linked to the Gaelic and gaelicised lords whose eclipse during the later decades of the sixteenth century and the early decades of the seventeenth century also obviated the dynastic rationale for bardic validation. Indeed, praise poets were key agents in the initial predication of an Irish identity centred on both of the island's historic ethnicities, which was subsequently refined within a Counter-Reformation milieu by Gaelic *literati*, often clerics, in continental exile and

---

1 G. W. Bernard, *The Late Medieval English Church: Vitality and Vulnerability before the Break with Rome* (New Haven and London: Yale University Press, 2012).

which culminates domestically with the completion of Geoffrey Keating's monumental history of Ireland in 1634. Moreover, the Cambridge formation of a cohort of Gaelic Protestant clergymen committed to a programme of evangelical publications further emphasises the transnational dimension to Gaelic culture in the early modern period. The arrival of significant numbers of newcomers from Britain in Ireland engendered a multiplicity of encounters, which are evidenced in Gaelic literature. If this period witnessed the decline of the bardic apparatus, it is more accurate to speak of cultural transformation than termination in so far as much of the thematic stock in trade of the old institution was incorporated within the work of a new cohort of gentlemen and amateur poets and writers.

Tradition and Innovation: Praise Poetry

Late medieval and early modern Gaelic Ireland was dominated politically by a mosaic of lordships of varying degrees of size, military capacity and dynastic influence. Indeed, it was estimated in 1515 that Ireland was characterised by around sixty Gaelic and thirty gaelicised Anglo-Norman lordships, which were all notionally autonomous though in reality vulnerable to the exercise of superior military force.[2] The inhabitants of these territories were subject to a lord from a specific lineage who claimed descent from a common ancestor and where, theoretically, succession to the lordship was confined to those descended within four generations from a ruling or previous lord. Given the level of control claimed by lords over lands and peoples within their territories, it is arguable that Gaelic patterns of landowning were developing along feudal lines in the sixteenth century.[3] The role of the lord was largely centred on the provision of military leadership and the patronage of the learned *élites* dedicated to poetry, law, history and genealogy, and medicine.[4] While politically fragmented, late medieval Gaelic Ireland accessed a common literary patrimony and a vernacular devotional culture centred on a network of Observant Franciscan friaries. The success of the Observant reform movement in Gaelic areas in the fifteenth century resulted in the creation of a shared religious and cultural sphere, which extended across Irish-speaking

---

2 P. J. Duffy, D. Edwards and E. Fitzpatrick (eds.), *Gaelic Ireland c.1250–c.1650: Land, Lordship and Settlement* (Dublin: Four Courts Press [hereafter FCP], 2001), 39.

3 K. W. Nicholls, *Land, Law and Society in Sixteenth-Century Ireland* (Dublin: National University of Ireland, 1976), 4.

4 S. J. Connolly, *Contested Island: Ireland 1460–1630* (Oxford University Press, 2007), 14.

territories.⁵ Therefore, although the Gaelic *élites* lacked a centralised political framework, their cultural idiom was far from regional or local in scope. On the contrary, a highly developed sense of ethnicity and cultural integrity was enshrined in a prescriptive literary canon.⁶ The emergence of a bardic apparatus characterised by a standard language based on a normative grammar and a syllabic metrical system has been dated to the late twelfth and early thirteenth centuries.⁷ The use of a literary language down to the seventeenth century, which was codified in a series of linguistic tracts, suggests that poets undertook an act of cultural creation during the late twelfth century.⁸ The latter period also witnessed the emergence of hereditary professional literary families who effectively dominated the profession subsequently.⁹ Moreover, the literacy of poets exposed them to different influences from the period of their elusive institutional genesis, and by the sixteenth century it is evident that the impact of the Renaissance and print culture informed their outlook in ways which countered intellectual reification.¹⁰

Poets and Patrons

The relationship between a poet and his patron was articulated within codified parameters of mutual engagement and defined by a normative set of behaviours and expectations. Poets provided the *élite* with a template of sanctioned lordship whose thematic currency was valid across the Gaelic sphere. Giolla Brighde Mac Con Midhe, who was active during the second half of the thirteenth century, encapsulated the essence of bardic validation when he opposed a purported ban on praise poetry emanating from the Church in Rome. Mac Con Midhe argued that if poetry were suppressed, the social

---

5 C. N. Ó Clabaigh, *The Franciscans in Ireland, 1400–1534: from Reform to Reformation* (Dublin: FCP, 2002).

6 K. Simms, *From Kings to Warlords: the Changing Political Structure of Gaelic Ireland in the Later Middle Ages* (Woodbridge: Boydell Press, 2000), 4–5.

7 P. Ó Macháin, 'The Early Modern Irish Prosodic Tracts and the Editing of "Bardic Verse"', in H. L. C. Tristram (ed.), *Metrik und Medienwechsel: Metrics and Media* (Tübingen: Gunter Narr Verlag, 1991), 273–87, 273.

8 D. McManus, 'The Bardic Poet as Teacher, Student and Critic: A Context for the Grammatical Tracts', in C. G. Ó Háinle and D. E. Meek (eds.), *Léann na Tríonóide. Trinity Irish Studies* (Dublin: School of Irish, Trinity College, 2004), 97–123.

9 P. Mac Cana, 'The Rise of the Later Schools of *Filidheacht*', *Ériu*, 25 (1974), 126–46.

10 K. Simms, 'Literacy and the Irish Bards', in H. Pryce (ed.), *Literacy in Medieval Celtic Societies* (Cambridge University Press, 1998), 238–58, at 239; M. Mac Craith, 'Gaelic Ireland and the Renaissance', in G. Williams and R. O. Jones (eds.), *The Celts and the Renaissance: Tradition and Innovation* (Cardiff: University of Wales Press, 1989), 57–89; T. Ó Dúshláine, *An Eoraip agus Litríocht na Gaeilge 1600–1650* (Dublin: An Clóchomhar, 1987).

consequences would be inimical to a hierarchical society. In the absence of ready access to genealogy, history and poetry, social and cultural memory would be defined within the limits of one generation.[11] The implications of such a deliberate process of amnesia would leave the nobles ignorant of distinguished ancestors and Gaelic lineages. In a situation where the descent of noble families and the deeds of aristocrats were forgotten and uncelebrated, the consequences for the *élite* could only be disastrous in terms of prestige and status.[12] Mac Con Midhe concluded that if the men of Ireland decided to banish praise poets then every nobleman would be accounted a churl. As purveyors of dynastic sanction, poets enjoyed intimate access to the ranks of the *élite* and in some cases poets must have wielded considerable influence. Eochaidh Ó hEódhusa, in a composition for Hugh Maguire, lord of Fermanagh (d. 1600), was specific in his emphasis on the semi-diplomatic function of a lord's poet. In the poem beginning 'Mór an t-ainm ollamh flatha' ('Great is the title chief's poet'), Ó hEódhusa is assertive in his vindication of the status and emoluments of a poet of the highest rank. Among bardic privileges, he alluded to a poet's right of 'primacy in counsel', which surely positioned poets centrally in terms of political debate.[13] The composition of poems of counsel in the manner of the *speculum principis* genre by Tadhg Mac Bruaideadha for Donough O'Brien, fourth earl of Thomond (1581–1624), illustrates bardic self-fashioning within a nexus of authority.[14] The assumption by poets of a political role as functionary is evidenced in remarks made by the Munster nobleman Florence MacCarthy Reagh (d. *c.*1641) in a letter addressed to Sir Robert Cecil in 1602. MacCarthy emphasised that two cohorts in particular in Ireland enjoyed a high degree of status and influence: poets and priests. While priests were confirmed in their hostility to the crown, he suggested that some poets were amenable to overtures from the state and even in such cases, their primary loyalty rested with their patrons.[15] References from

11 *The Poems of Giolla Brighde Mac Con Midhe*, ed. N. J. A. Williams (London: Irish Texts Society (hereafter ITS), 1980), no. XVIII, 208, quatrain 21.
12 *Poems of Mac Con Midhe*, 210, quatrain 23.
13 S. H. O'Grady and R. Flower (eds.), *Catalogue of Irish Manuscripts in the British Library [formerly British Museum]* (3 vols, London: The British Museum, 1926–1953; repr. Dublin: Dublin Institute of Advanced Studies (hereafter DIAS), 1992), i, 474–76; P. A. Breatnach, 'The Chief's Poet', *Proceedings of the Royal Irish Academy*, 83:C (1983), 37–79, at 56.
14 E. Nic Cárthaigh (ed.), 'Mo Cheithre Rainn Duit, a Dhonnchaidh: Advice to a Prince by Tadhg (mac Dáire) Mac Bruaideadha', in E. Purcell, P. MacCotter, J. Nyhan and J. Sheehan (eds.), *Clerics, Kings and Vikings: Essays on Medieval Ireland in Honour of Donnchadh Ó Corráin* (Dublin: FCP, 2015), 490–517.
15 D. MacCarthy (ed.), *The Life and Letters of Florence MacCarthy Reagh* (London: Longmans, 1867), 362.

the sixteenth century suggest that poets often served their patrons as functionaries more broadly. In a 1539 agreement between Manus O'Donnell and Tadhg O'Connor in which the latter undertook to hold Sligo castle subject to Manus's terms, the prospect of bardic sanction was invoked. In the event that O'Connor breached the terms of the agreement, it was stipulated that he suffer excommunication from the church and that three named poets would satirise him as demanded by O'Donnell.[16] Likewise, in an agreement dated 1580 between Cú Chonnacht Maguire, lord of Fermanagh, and Cathal Maguire, abbot of the Augustinian monastery of Lisgoole, in which the latter agreed to surrender the disused monastery and a portion of lands for use by Franciscan friars, bardic sanction was also adduced in the case of failure to implement the agreed terms. In this instance, it was stipulated that any such persons who discommoded the friars would be vilified by poets from three named families, including the Ó hEódhusa family.[17]

A poem composed by Eochaidh Ó hEódhusa for Cú Chonnacht Maguire subtly illustrates aspects of the etiquette, which informed a poet's relationship with his patron. The family of Ó hEódhusa seems to have achieved a degree of prominence by the beginning of the fourteenth century. By the end of the sixteenth century, they had apparently supplanted the Ó Fialáin and Mac Rithbheartaigh families who previously provided poets for the Maguires.[18] The poem beginning 'Anois molfam Mág Uidhir' ('I will praise Maguire now') is preserved in the *duanaire* or poem-book of Cú Chonnacht, who was lord of the Maguires from 1566 until his death in 1589.[19] Generally, such poembooks were repositories of material composed for patrons and other family members and as such contain compositions of a dynastic nature.[20] In what was apparently his first composition for Maguire, Eochaidh described how his delay in presenting a poem to the lord of Fermanagh was occasioned by his desire to undertake a comprehensive bardic formation to prepare for his inaugural composition. In typical bardic fashion, Ó hEódhusa recounted an *exemplum* by way of historical precedent for his course of action.[21] In this case, a young poet called Brian Ruadh Mac Con Midhe had refrained from

---

16 M. Carney (ed.), 'Select documents III. Agreement between Ó Domhnaill and Tadhg Ó Conchobhair concerning Sligo Castle (23 June 1539)', *Irish Historical Studies*, 3 (1942–1043), 282–95.

17 K. W. Nicholls (ed.), 'The Lisgoole Agreement of 1580', *Clogher Record*, 7 (1969), 27–33.

18 C. McGrath, 'Í Eódhosa', *Clogher Record*, 2 (1957), 1–19, at 6.

19 David Greene (ed.), *Duanaire Mhéig Uidhir* (Dublin: DIAS, 1972), no. XXIII, 216–25.

20 B. Ó Cuív, *The Irish Bardic Duanaire or 'Poem-Book'* (Dublin: National Library of Ireland Society, 1973).

21 L. P. Ó Caithnia, *Apalóga na bhFili 1200–1650* (Dublin: An Clóchomhar, 1984).

composing a poem for Éinrí O'Neill (d. 1489) until he had perfected his craft.[22] By way of explanation of his tardiness, Ó hEódhusa explained that he too had been seeking to excel in bardic composition before approaching Maguire with a poem. Accordingly, he sought out the best teachers available with a view to preparing for his vocation. Maguire is addressed in stereotypical bardic terms of endorsement. The lord of Fermanagh is depicted by his supposedly neophyte poet as a warrior who commands obeisance from the Irish. The dominion of Maguire results in fertility and abundance and such is his fame and wealth that other poets are also drawn to him. The communal perspective, which is central to eulogy, is further developed in the poet's allusion to Cú Chonnacht's son and heir, Hugh Maguire (d. 1600). Intended either as an enduring token of friendship or by way of a shrewd strategic gesture, Eochaidh stated that he had promised Hugh a quatrain in every poem he composed.[23] Moving to Maguire's wife, Mairghréag, daughter of Shane O'Neill, Ó hEódhusa proceeded over the course of three quatrains to assert her eminence among the women of Ulster, stressing her beauty and superlative piety in an all-Ireland context, while her resemblance to the mythical Emer endowed her with significance in a western European context.[24] Although poets typically focused their eulogistic work on patrons whose influence was localised, their use of a thematic repertoire whose valency was generic afforded them a relatively high degree of mobility, along with other cohorts such as jurists and physicians.[25]

In a poem composed for Cú Chonnacht Maguire by Maoilín Ó an Cháinte beginning 'Leis féin moltar Mág Uidhir' ('Maguire is praised by himself'), the juxtaposition of the local and pan-insular is woven within the fabric of the composition.[26] In what is essentially a classic example of bardic encomium, Maguire is immediately situated in an all-island context when in the opening quatrain he is presented as the preeminent *Gaoidheal* of Ireland whose own praise is best generated by himself. In the second quatrain, the emphasis shifts to the local when Maguire is portrayed as a valiant lord of the Erne who disdains tribute and as such he serves as his own panegyrist.[27] Indeed, Maguire's fame rests not on his own vaunting nor on the extensive praise bestowed on him by poets of all ranks; rather, his noble deeds more than suffice to

---

22 Ó Caithnia, *Apalóga*, 120.

23 J. Carney, *The Irish Bardic Poet* (Dublin: Dolmen Press, 1967; repr. Dublin: DIAS, 1985), 14.

24 Greene, *Duanaire*, 225, line 2909.

25 K. W. Nicholls, *Gaelic and Gaelicised Ireland in the Middle Ages* (Dublin: Gill and Macmillan, 1972), 79–84.

26 Greene, *Duanaire*, no. XXII, 204–15.

27 Greene, *Duanaire*, 204, line 2623.

underwrite his reputation. In the estimation of the poet, Maguire manifests an ideal notion of masculinity: a heroic demeanour leavened by humility. Furthermore, the lord of Fermanagh, deemed a worthy mate of Ireland by virtue of the antique trope which depicted the island in the guise of a feminine embodiment of sovereignty, exemplifies the 'true fame of honour' in terms of his martial agility, his gentleness among the weak, his support for equity and just dominion, his patronage of poets, and stalwart defence of his territories and people. Guided by tradition, Cú Chonnacht was familiar with the gnomic text *Tecosca Cormaic* in which the bountiful hero Cormac advised his son Cairbre Lifechair on matters of kingship. Maguire, deemed worthy of the kingship of Ireland, was comparable to the Greek leader and military hero Alexander. Accordingly, an exemplum was adduced to present Maguire in a highly favourable light. Such was the fame of Alexander in his day that he had no princely equivalent anywhere in Europe. Notwithstanding the glory that accrued to him, Alexander supposedly issued an ordinance to the effect that he was not to be praised by others on the basis that his deeds provided sufficient testimony in their own right. However, Alexander's fame endured after his death as the poets of Greece had recorded his deeds in writing in spite of their overwhelming grief. By way of rhetorical flourish, the poet proceeds to place Maguire in the same company as Alexander when he claims that the virtues of the lord of Fermanagh, likewise, were sufficient to underwrite his fame. Although Alexander and Maguire had little in common in terms of the disparate nature of their respective wealth, the lord of Fermanagh resembled the Macedonian warrior in that his fame alone also generated respect. In fact, Maguire had no need to have his fame further proclaimed, such was the self-sustaining quality of his reputation. This poem constitutes an accomplished example of the use of encomium to legitimate a lord's status within the parameters of Gaelic lordship.

Bardic Responses to Change: Continuity and Recalibration

The expansion of Tudor imperium in Ireland cumulatively negated the rationale for the predication of Gaelic seigneurial virtue, such was the impact of the crown's policy of surrender and regrant in terms especially of the primacy of primogeniture. Another poem in Maguire's *duanaire* provides an affective illustration of the turbulence that increasingly required praise poets to adapt to changing circumstances. In a poem addressed to Maguire beginning 'Gabh m'égnach, a Chú Chonnacht' ('Receive my complaint, Cú

Chonnacht'), Conchubhar Ó Dálaigh laments his exile from Munster and explains why he has been forced to travel north to Ulster to seek patronage from the lord of Fermanagh.[28] The violent deaths of three previous patrons in close succession had obliged him to quit the southern province for the north. These high-ranking individuals were James Fitzmaurice (d. 1579), Gerald Fitzgerald, earl of Desmond (d. 1583), and his brother John (d. 1582). It is indicative of the acculturation of many leading Anglo-Norman families within Gaelic rituals of sociability that Ó Dálaigh's Munster patrons were descended from medieval colonial dynasties. In despair, the poet now turns to Maguire invoking the metaphorical intimacy of a patron's relationship with a poet. He requests the lord of Fermanagh to take him as his lover and he insists that he has not trysted since the demise of his quondam patronal lovers.[29] Crucially, Ó Dálaigh presents Maguire as both a regional potentate and as a figure of pan-insular significance. More specifically, the poet asks that Maguire appoint him as his chief poet, thereby becoming his fourth spouse and not merely to engage with him as a peripatetic poet.[30] Having presented his case for preferment, the poet concludes by lauding Maguire's wife Mairghréag in conventional terms of emphasis on her elegance and generosity to visiting poets.

Given that Gerald, earl of Desmond, was killed in rebellion in November 1583, it is possible that Ó Dálaigh travelled northwards at some stage in 1584. In fact, Ó Dálaigh was closely associated with Desmond and was among a small band of loyal retainers accompanying Gerald at the time of his murder.[31] The Ó Dálaigh family had a long association with the Fitzgeralds of Desmond and held lands from them in east Kerry.[32] The inclusion of Ó Dálaigh's name and his description as the late earl of Desmond's poet on a list of Gaelic *literati* compiled by the authorities in Cork in late 1584 indicates that such was his reputation, he was considered a dissident.[33] Already in the same year, Ó Dálaigh's name had figured during an inquisition held at Dingle, where his lands were confiscated. Although pardoned in 1584, he was named in a 1586 act of attainder of the late earl of Desmond and his followers.[34] Unsuccessful

---

28 Greene, *Duanaire*, no. XIX, 170–9.
29 Greene, *Duanaire*, no. XIX, 172, line 2184.
30 Greene, *Duanaire*, no. XIX, 176, line 2245.
31 D. O'Daly,*The Rise, Increase, and Exit of the Geraldines, Earls of Desmond*, trans. C. P. Meehan, (2nd edn., Dublin: James Duffy, 1878), 119–20.
32 M. Caball, 'Notes on an Elizabethan Kerry Bardic Family', *Ériu*, 43 (1992), 32–42, at 33.
33 R. Ó Muireadhaigh (ed.), 'Aos Dána na Mumhan, 1584', *Irisleabhar Muighe Nuadhat*, (1960), 81–4, at 83.
34 *The Statutes at Large Passed in the Parliaments of Ireland* (18 vols., Dublin: George Grierson, 1765–1799), i, 423; *The Irish Fiants of the Tudor Sovereigns* (4 vols., Dublin: Éamonn de Búrca, 1994), ii, no.4555.

in his ambition to become Maguire's chief poet, who seems to have favoured the younger Eochaidh Ó hEódhusa, Ó Dálaigh returned to Munster where his attempt in 1592 to recover his confiscated lands was unsuccessful.[35] Ironically, Conchubhar's brother, Cú Chonnacht Ó Dálaigh, also a praise poet, likewise migrated to Ulster in search of patronage, where he composed an extraordinarily politically acute poem for 'Red' Hugh O'Donnell (d. 1602) in the final years of the sixteenth century.[36] Moreover, in another indication of bardic mobility during the turbulent last two decades of the sixteenth century, Cú Chonnacht is also known to have composed a poem for Feilim O'Byrne (d. 1631), of Gabhal Raghnuill in Wicklow, before returning to Kerry where he was granted a pardon by the authorities in 1601.[37] The example of the Ó Dálaigh brothers illustrates the disruption of patterns of cultural expression, which poets attempted to negotiate by means of tradition and innovation.[38]

In fact, Henry VIII's inaugural efforts at the consolidation of Tudor authority in Ireland had provoked an acerbic commentary from an anonymous poet and such bardic political engagement expanded and deepened in succeeding decades as the impact of conquest and Reformation was intensified. In the poem beginning 'Fúbún fúibh, a shluagh Gaoidheal' ('Shame on you, Gaelic host'), the author castigates a number of leading Gaelic families, such as the McCarthys of Munster and the O'Neills and O'Donnells of Ulster, for what he considered their overly emollient disposition in the face of English political and religious expansionism.[39] While extant praise poems vividly and often lavishly chronicle traditional notions of Gaelic lordship and civility, occasional voices in the 1570s and 1580s hint at inchoate rupture and dislocation. For instance, the unprecedented execution in 1572 of a number of poets by Conor O'Brien, earl of Thomond (d. 1581), elicited a bitterly outraged response from one of their colleagues, Uilliam Óg Mac an Bhaird. It is not known why O'Brien, who was largely loyal to Elizabeth I during his tenure as head of the O'Brien family, had the poets put to death as there is no evidence

---

35 H. F. Hore, 'The Munster Bards', *Ulster Journal of Archaeology*, 7 (1859), 93–115, at 107.

36 P. A. Breatnach (ed.), 'Cú Chonnacht Ó Dálaigh's Poem before Leaving Aodh Ruadh', in D. Ó Corráin, L. Breatnach and K. McCone (eds.), *Sages, Saints and Storytellers: Celtic Studies in Honour of Professor James Carney* (Maynooth: An Sagart, 1989), 32–42.

37 T. F. O'Rahilly, 'Irish Poets, Historians, and Judges in English Documents, 1538–1615', *Proceedings of the Royal Irish Academy*, 36:C (1922), 86–120, at 112; S. Mac Airt (ed.), *Leabhar Branach* (Dublin: DIAS, 1944), no. 51, 184–8.

38 M. Caball, *Poets and Politics: Continuity and Reaction in Irish Poetry, 1558–1625* (Cork University Press and Field Day, 1998).

39 B. Ó Cuív (ed.), 'A Sixteenth-Century Political Poem', *Éigse*, 15 (1973–1974), 261–76. For a different view of the poem's date see Nicholas Canny, *Making Ireland British 1580–1650* (Oxford University Press, 2001), 421.

to suggest that he refrained from Gaelic cultural patronage.[40] The author of an anonymous poem possibly composed during the period 1565 to 1579 during a time of upheaval in the west Munster Geraldine territories bemoans apparently unprecedented levels of chaos in an environment where sanctuary was no longer available in castles, monasteries or among poets.[41] Now that papal authority counted for little, it was hardly surprising that an onslaught against the population unfolded in conjunction with the devastation of the church. Such was the gravity of the situation that clerics were obliged to flee. Indeed, these circumstances also augured poorly for the prospects of those armed bands of Gaelic soldiers known as kerne. Notwithstanding the esteem in which they were previously held, friars were now forced to hide their habits, such was their fear of violence. However, the poet claims that the greed, deceit and dishonesty of some churchmen seriously vitiated their standing. Since the poet describes these discredited clergymen as members of the Church ('eaglais'), it seems that his observations relate to dissension within the local Catholic Church as opposed to tensions generated by the intrusion of evangelical divines. A sense of internal societal discord is also evidenced in his demand to local lords that they exchange places with poets in order to experience at first hand the depredations visited on the latter. The author complains that the bardic cohort is often robbed with little prospect of restitution and by way of further insult to poets, half of what is taken from them is bestowed on the lords by way of custom. Directly confronting the seigneurial *élite* on the basis of their presumed nobility, he asks them if what was reported of them was not a source of shame. More bluntly still, the poet proclaims to his aristocratic audience that those of them who dishonour the *literati* should meet with like disregard from God. In fact, if robbery, violence and ambush are the distinguishing traits of the lordly *élite*, then nobility itself is scarcely to be encountered among the men of west Munster.[42] Whatever the precise nature of the poem's compositional rationale and milieu, it strongly hints at dissension within the seigneurial and ecclesiastical ranks of the southwest on the eve of the Munster plantation.

A similar complexity and nuance of interchange between poets and the *élite* is evident in a poem composed by Tadhg Dall Ó hUiginn for the Ulster lord Turlough Luineach O'Neill, who secured the leadership of his family in 1567. Tadhg Dall was born around the year 1550, possibly in modern County

40 B. Ó Cuív (ed.), 'The Earl of Thomond and the Poets, A.D. 1572', *Celtica*, 12 (1977), 125–45, at 127.

41 R. A. Breatnach (ed.), 'Anarchy in West Munster', *Éigse*, 23 (1989), 57–66, quatrain 4 at 58.

42 Breatnach, 'Anarchy', 58–60, quatrains 5–15.

Sligo. Descended from a bardic lineage which traced its descent to Tadhg Óg Ó hUiginn (d. 1448), Tadhg Dall seems to have been fostered among the O'Donnells of Tír Chonaill and may have studied at a bardic school in modern County Galway. A reference in a manuscript written in the Low Countries by Fearghal Ó Gadhra of Sligo during the years 1655–59 claims that Tadhg Dall's brother was Maolmhuire Ó hUiginn. The latter was consecrated archbishop of Tuam in 1586 and apparently passed away in Antwerp *circa* 1590 on his return trip to Ireland. Although Tadhg Dall's poems evince a shrewd appraisal of contemporary politics and ethnic antagonisms, his service as a juror for various inquisitions held in Sligo in 1584 and in 1590 demonstrates his status locally and a capacity for quotidian accommodation shared by other contemporary poets.[43] Significantly, Tadhg Dall, who suffered a violent death in 1591, was succeeded by his son Tadhg Óg (b. 1582) who in a 1603 pardon was described as a 'rymer' and who replicated his father's social and intellectual agility in equal if not greater measure.[44] Adept in his manipulation of the complex political environment of early seventeenth-century Sligo, Tadhg Óg was ranked among the largest native landowners in the county by the 1630s and his appointment as sheriff of Sligo in 1634 and selection in the 1640s as a delegate to the Confederate assembly in Kilkenny attest to the capacity of some Gaelic professional families to manage dislocation within a context of a relatively assured transition to a new political dispensation.[45]

In the poem beginning 'Nodlaig do-chuamair don Chraoibh' ('At Christmas we went to the Creeve'), Tadhg Dall celebrates a seasonal banquet for the poets of Ireland hosted by Turlough Luineach O'Neill. It has been suggested that An Chraobh was a *crannóg* owned by O'Neill near Stewartstown.[46] This work seems consciously to echo a fourteenth-century poem composed by Gofraidh Fionn Ó Dálaigh to mark the hosting of a Christmas feast for the poets and scholars of Ireland in 1351 by William O'Kelly. In the poem for O'Neill, which may possibly have been composed around 1577, Tadhg Dall describes a scenario where a retinue of poets, including himself, approached O'Neill's residence expectantly and experienced a mounting sense of awe

---

43 *The bardic poems of Tadhg Dall Ó hUiginn (1550–1591)*, ed. Eleanor Knott (2 vols., London: ITS, 1922–1926), i, xiv–xxxii; M. Caball, 'Culture, Politics and Identity in Sixteenth-Century Ireland: The Testimony of Tadhg Dall Ó hUiginn (c.1550–1591)', in P. Riggs (ed.), *Tadhg Dall Ó hUiginn: his Historical and Literary Context* (London: ITS, 2010), 1–21.

44 *Poems of Tadhg Dall Ó hUiginn*, i, xxxii.

45 M. O'Dowd, *Power, Politics and Land: Early Modern Sligo 1568–1688* (Belfast: Institute of Irish Studies, Queen's University Belfast, 1991), 58–9, 78.

46 D. Ó Doibhlin, 'Tyrone's Gaelic Literary Legacy', in C. Dillon and H. A. Jefferies (eds.), *Tyrone: History & Society* (Dublin: Geography Publications, 2000), 403–32, at 427.

and anticipation as they were treated to a lavish banquet within an exquisitely decorated hall. Although the poets enjoyed sumptuous hospitality on the first night of their sojourn, O'Neill himself had not yet deigned to appear in person to receive his guests. However, he dispatched his servant the following morning to inquire of the visitors if they had composed poems in celebration of his exploits. They replied that they had not composed such martial eulogies but instead had elected to concentrate on poems establishing the genealogical ramifications of O'Neill and his sept and his territorial entitlements. On this information being relayed to him by his minion, O'Neill declared haughtily that such work was merely generic and that while he would pay for the poems, he would refrain from hearing them recited. Next the crestfallen poets were confronted in person by a reproachful O'Neill whose sulking demeanour thoroughly intimidated the assembled cohort. Unsuccessful in a collective attempt to assuage Turlough Luineach's anger, Tadhg Dall steps forward from among his coevals and in the first person singular assumes the role of O'Neill's interlocutor. By way of deflection of his annoyance, Ó hUiginn assures O'Neill that both his lineage is revered and that his authority is recognised across Ireland. While admitting that the poets had not celebrated his military prowess in the form of a *caithréim* or listing of his victories, this was simply because of the overwhelming extent of O'Neill's achievements in battle. Indeed, so numerous were O'Neill's exploits that he would be waiting until Doomsday for verse accounts which chronicled his acts of valour. In locating his narrative within a communal sphere of castle and banqueting hall, Tadhg Dall illustrates both the privileged role of the poet as communal interlocutor before a powerful lord within semantic and thematic parameters informed by tradition.[47]

In a poem addressed to Brian na Múrtha O'Rourke of west Bréifne, Ó hUiginn manifests a strategic awareness of broader political developments and he argues for the efficacy of total war as an instrument of resistance. The composition beginning 'D'fhior chogaidh comhailtear síothcháin' ('Towards the warlike man peace is observed') was possibly composed around 1588 at a time when O'Rourke had incurred the enmity of Sir Richard Bingham, lord president of Connacht, for having assisted survivors from armada wrecks off the north-west coast, and, later, for permitting an effigy of Queen Elizabeth to be publicly reviled.[48] In 1590, O'Rourke was forced to flee his lordship and

---

47 *Poems of Tadhg Dall Ó hUiginn*, i, no. 8, 50–6.
48 S. E. McKibben, *Endangered Masculinities in Irish Poetry 1540–1780* (Dublin: UCD Press, 2010), 21–2.

in the following year, he crossed the North Channel to Scotland. However, James VI immediately handed him over to the English authorities and he was subsequently hanged at Tyburn in 1591. The poem is remarkable for its incisive assertion of the need to meet English expansion with a coherent and forceful military response from O'Rourke and the Gaelic Irish generally. The poet's central premise in this poetic *tour de force* is that a leader of warlike disposition more readily deters potential aggressors. In this regard, Ó hUiginn argues that the Gaelic Irish will not secure an enduring peace from the English on the basis of eirenic civility. In fact, the gravity of the situation was such that the Gaelic Irish were already being pushed to the margins of the island, while the English occupied its heartlands.[49] Moreover, the poets of Ireland are obliged to incite the Irish to wage war against the English and in this respect, O'Rourke was ideally qualified to lead his people in battle against the foreign interlopers. Ireland will unite militarily under O'Rourke's direction and lords and their heirs across the island will join his ranks as the fire of resistance spreads metaphorically from house to house.[50]

As soon as the men of Ireland become aware that O'Rourke has begun a campaign of war, no part of the island will be free from destruction.[51] Implacable in making the case for war, Ó hUiginn warns O'Rourke not to be duped by the honeyed words of the English. By way of illustration of his case, he recounts an *exemplum*, which ultimately derived from *Aesop's Fables*.[52] A wily lion invited various animals to visit his abode. Throngs of animals accepted the lion's invitation. However, the head of the foxes stayed away until an appropriate opportunity presented itself. The foxes approached the lion's cave in single file and the lead fox, noticing the solely inward direction of previous tracks, immediately ordered their retreat. Translated to the contemporary political context, Ó hUiginn identifies the lion's cave as the 'court of the foreign battalions', while the slain animals are representative of the Irish.[53] Accordingly, O'Rourke is advised to place no trust in the English. Supported by the men of Connacht and Ulster, he will advance on Dublin leaving a trail of devastation in his wake. Ferocious warfare will ensue and although many of the Gaelic Irish will perish, the foreigners will be vanquished. From the moment of battle's proclamation, only Irishmen will exercise authority in Ireland.[54] While Tadhg Dall emphasises that victory will be achieved only

---

49 *Poems of Tadhg Dall Ó hUiginn*, i, no. 16, 108–19, quatrain 6 at 109.
50 *Poems of Tadhg Dall Ó hUiginn*, i, no. 16, quatrains 14–15 at 110.
51 *Poems of Tadhg Dall Ó hUiginn*, i, no. 16, quatrain 16 at 110.
52 Ó Caithnia, *Apalóga*, 196–97.
53 *Poems of Tadhg Dall Ó hUiginn*, i, no. 16, quatrain 42 at 114.
54 *Poems of Tadhg Dall Ó hUiginn*, i, no. 16, quatrain 68 at 118.

at significant human and material cost, his depiction of Dublin, seat of the Tudor administration in Ireland, conquered by a Gaelic army was a highly potent allusion to contemporary issues of ethnic conflict within a pan-insular context.[55]

The flux consequent on the failure of the Desmond rebellion, the subsequent plantation of large swathes of land across Munster with English settlers and the severe dislocation and disruption unleashed by the Nine Years War (1594–1603) cumulatively challenged the rationale and cogency of bardic praxis. With the diminution of the autonomy exercised by Gaelic and gaelicised Anglo-Norman lords and the decline of their financial fortunes in many cases, poets were obliged to negotiate alternate but in some respects complementary strands of tradition and innovation. A piece by an obscure west Munster poet called Ó Cuill, composed against an extended backdrop of the impact of the fall of the house of Desmond and the Nine Years War, chronicles a supposed collapse in bardic patronage and, affectingly, he enumerates the names of dead patrons among the west-Munster *élite*. Emblematic of a broader waning of aristocratic sociability, the poet in a reference to the deceased Thomas Fitzmaurice, lord of Kerry and baron of Lixnaw (d. 1590), laments how his passing has essentially terminated the purchase of wine and horses, along with praise poetry.[56] While such a declaration was in some measure rhetorical, nonetheless, it illustrates how the social and cultural conventions of Gaelic lordship were destabilised within a period of relatively accelerated change. However, bardic responses to change were variegated and not uniformly articulated within a discourse circumscribed by an apparently static tradition. In eschewing the notion of an absolutist bardic appraisal of transformation, it is necessary to acknowledge contemporary capacity for negotiation as individual poets responded in both personal and institutional terms to particular circumstances and constraints. A similar accommodation of tradition was also undertaken textually by members of another Gaelic learned cohort. Indeed, it is possible that, in contrast to their hostility to praise poets, the English authorities were more benign in their view of other Gaelic professions such as those of jurists and chroniclers.[57] More specifically, it has been argued that the north Leinster O'Doran family of jurists responded strategically to English accusations of Irish lawlessness in the 1560s and 1570s.

---

55 *Poems of Tadhg Dall Ó hUiginn*, i, no. 16, quatrain 56 at 116.
56 P. A. Breatnach (ed.), 'A Poem on the End of Patronage', *Éigse*, 31 (1999), 79–88, quatrain 10 at 86.
57 J. Fraser, P. Grosjean and J. G. O'Keeffe (eds.), *Irish Texts* (fascs. 1–5, London: Sheed and Ward, 1931–1934), iv, 27–29.

Contemporary recensions of the 'pseudo-historical prologue' to the compilation of traditional Irish law known as the *Senchus már* were deployed to legitimate capital punishment for homicide instead of customary recourse to *éraic* or wergeld by way of accommodation to English law.[58]

An amalgam of tradition and thematic reconfiguration is evident, for instance, in poems composed to mark the journey of Red Hugh O'Donnell to Spain and, shortly afterwards, his death there in 1602. Following the defeat of the Irish forces at Kinsale in December 1601, O'Donnell had sailed to Spain on a mission to persuade Philip III to send reinforcements to enable a resumption of a campaign of war. However, Red Hugh passed away in Simancas in September 1602 before he had accomplished his objective. While a poem by the distinguished northern poet Fearghal Óg Mac an Bhaird commemorates the death of O'Donnell, a composition by another prominent northern poet, Eoghan Ruadh Mac an Bhaird, was apparently conceived as a poetic *bon voyage* for the Ulster lord. Although both works were composed by Ulster poets for a northern magnate, they are inflected with a pronounced pan-insular perspective. Eoghan Ruadh's 'Rob soruidh t'eachtra, a Aodh Ruaidh' ('Godspeed, Hugh Roe') and Fearghal Óg's 'Teasda Éire san Easpáinn' ('Ireland has expired in Spain') are attentive to the all-Ireland implications of Red Hugh's diplomacy and demise. At the outset, Eoghan Ruadh's poem is conventional in its extension of best wishes to O'Donnell for a safe journey and successful mission. However, he moves beyond such formal sentiment when he stresses the wider import of Red Hugh's demarche for the well-being of Gaelic Ireland. The island's inhabitants, nobility, *literati* and commoners, anxiously await the outcome of a venture predicated on the relief of the Gaelic Irish. Critically, the ship which sailed to Spain contained Ireland's hopes and its political sovereignty.[59] In a similar vein, Fearghal Óg bitterly laments O'Donnell's passing with an emphasis on its pan-insular significance. He presents the deceased Ulster lord as the symbolic embodiment of Ireland and as such the country itself has metaphorically perished in Spain. Accordingly, the honour of the island's five traditional provinces has expired along with Red Hugh, and across the land foreigners impose themselves. Now, the island is adrift and bereft of leadership given that Hugh Roe was not spared to secure Ireland's sovereignty. Quite simply, the Gaelic Irish

---

58 N. Patterson, 'Gaelic Law and the Tudor Conquest of Ireland: The Social Background of the Sixteenth-Century Recensions of the Pseudo-Historical Prologue to the *Senchas Már*', *Irish Historical Studies*, 27 (1991), 193–215.

59 D. Greene and F. Kelly (eds.), *Irish Bardic Poetry: Texts and Translations, Together with an Introductory Lecture by Osborn Bergin* (Dublin: DIAS, 1970), no. 3, 31–4, quatrain 24 at 34.

are no longer in possession of Ireland.[60] The presentation of Red Hugh as a guarantor of the island's territorial integrity was not simply the product of elegiac hyperbole. As far back as 1590 when the teenage Red Hugh was incarcerated in Dublin castle, the poet Maolmhuire Mac an Bhaird cast him in the guise of a leader whose remit was pan-insular.[61] If Fearghal Óg Mac an Bhaird confronted the loss of a dynamic Gaelic leader with a sense of bleak despondency, this is not to say that on other occasions he and fellow poets interpreted events in a fashion which emphasised strategic accommodation.

Responses to Transformation: New Vistas

The accession of James VI of Scotland to the English throne following the death of Elizabeth I on 24 March 1603 provided the *literati* with a new rhetorical perspective from which to envisage and articulate beneficial Gaelic interaction with a monarch whose realms now encompassed England, Scotland and Ireland. The putative ancient Gaelic lineage of the Stuarts enabled poets seamlessly to incorporate James and his descendants within Irish literary and historical discourse down to the eighteenth century.[62] A poem by Fearghal Óg Mac an Bhaird which celebrates the Scottish sovereign's entitlement to the three kingdoms was possibly influenced by a visit he paid to Scotland in the early 1580s. Although it is recorded that in 1581 Mac an Bhaird received official payment for poetry he composed for James VI, the evidence of a poem he seems to have composed at the period indicates the unsettling impression made on him by the progress of the Reformation in Scotland.[63] In fact, the success of Calvinism in Gaelic Scotland, and the entrenchment of Counter-Reformation Catholicism in Ireland from the 1590s, progressively vitiated a common Gaelic cultural legacy.[64] In his poem on James VI and I, beginning 'Trí coróna i gcairt Shéamais' ('The three crowns in James's charter'), which apparently dates to around 1603, Mac an Bhaird places Ireland firmly within a three kingdoms'

---

60 P. A. Breatnach (ed.), 'Marbhna Aodha Ruaidh Uí Dhomhnaill (†1602)', *Éigse*, 15 (1973–1974), 31–50.

61 P. A. Breatnach (ed.), 'Select documents XL: An Address to Aodh Ruadh Ó Domhnaill in Captivity, 1590', *Irish Historical Studies*, 25 (1986), 198–213.

62 B. Ó Buachalla, *Aisling Ghéar: na Stíobhartaigh agus an t-Aos Léinn 1603–1788* (Dublin: An Clóchomhar, 1996).

63 M. Caball, 'Politics and Religion in the Poetry of Fearghal Óg Mac an Bhaird and Eoghan Ruadh Mac an Bhaird', in P. Ó Riain (ed.), *Beatha Aodha Ruaidh: The Life of Red Hugh O'Donnell. Historical and Literary Contexts* (London: ITS, 2002), 74–97, at 81.

64 W. McLeod, *Divided Gaels: Gaelic Cultural Identities in Scotland and Ireland c.1200–1650* (Oxford University Press, 2004).

context.[65] Moreover, while he adduces a genealogical basis for James's claim to the Scottish and English thrones, his entitlement to Ireland derives from the island's possession by the English crown and as such the western island falls to him by default. However, English dominion had been resented and the ascent of the Scottish king to the English throne suggests the inauguration of a more beneficent era for Ireland. Dramatically, he advises James directly that he is *Éire's* prophesied spouse.[66] Eochaidh Ó hEódhusa also hailed James Stuart's accession to the English throne by suggesting in 'Mór theasda dh'obair Óivid' ('Ovid's work is greatly lacking') that such a development would have merited the attention of Ovid in his *Metamorphoses* verse chronicle of epic transformations. Moreover, Ó hEódhusa claims that the new dynastic dispensation heralds the advent of an era of good fortune, while liberty of discourse had been restored to the oppressed and concomitantly the voice of injustice had been suppressed. In fact, the Irish could now bid farewell to past distress such were the transformative implications of James's accession.[67]

However, the experiences of these and other poets illustrate the complex political and social circumstances which confronted the bardic cohort at this critical juncture of transition and which no doubt resulted in a diversity of responses ranging from accommodation to exile. In the case of Ó hEódhusa, he was included in a general pardon of the denizens of Fermanagh in 1607 and he secured plantation land grants in 1610–1611. A manuscript obituary in Irish records that he passed away in 1612 and that he was held in high record both by the Irish and English. Clearly, Ó hEódhusa, and other Gaelic intellectuals, enjoyed a level of social status and professional accomplishment which enabled them to negotiate challenges inherent to a new order.[68] In contrast, Eoghan Ruadh Mac an Bhaird travelled to the continent, where he served in the retinues of the earls of Tyrconnell and Tyrone and was in receipt of a pension from the Spanish crown from 1608.[69] Fearghal Óg Mac an Bhaird journeyed to Leuven in the Spanish Netherlands, possibly around 1618, where he addressed at least two poems to Florence Conry, archbishop of Tuam.[70] Of course, an amalgam of political, legal and financial factors consequent

65 L. McKenna (ed.), *Aithdioghluim Dána* (2 vols., Dublin: ITS, 1939–1940), i, no. 44, 177–80.
66 McKenna, *Aithdioghluim Dána*, i, no. 44, quatrains 22–3 at 179.
67 P. A. Breatnach (ed.), 'Metamorphosis 1603: Dán le hEochaidh Ó hEódhasa', *Éigse*, 17 (1977–1979), 169–80, quatrains 4–6 at 172; quatrain 13 at 174.
68 M. Caball, 'Responses to Transformation: Gaelic Poets and the Plantation of Ulster', in É. Ó Ciardha and M. Ó Siochrú (eds.), *The Plantation of Ulster: Ideology and Practice* (Manchester University Press, 2012), 176–97, at 180, 185.
69 B. Ó Buachalla, 'Cúlra is Tábhacht an Dáin *A leabhráin ainmnighthear d'Aodh*', *Celtica*, 21 (1990), 402–16, at 407.
70 Caball, 'Politics and Religion', 81–2.

to the consolidation of the crown's writ in Ireland had combined to attenuate the professional rationale of bardic composition. What was effectively a corporate *caesura* inevitably truncated long-established hereditary patterns of practice. For example, Dominic O'Daly, son of Conchubhar Ó Dálaigh, who is remembered today for his history of the earls of Desmond published in Lisbon in 1655, achieved distinction as a Dominican priest, scholar and diplomat in Portugal. Ordained a priest at Mechelen in 1609, Giolla Brighde Ó hEódhusa had abandoned a bardic career and left his native Ulster to study theology at Douai and Leuven.[71] Others, such as Maoilín Óg Mac Bruaideadha, who assisted in the evangelical translation of the Gaelic New Testament in the 1590s, availed themselves of new opportunities at a time of flux.[72]

Intersecting strands of innovation and tradition broadly characterise Gaelic literary production, in both prose and poetry, during this period. The impact of Reformation and Counter-Reformation further inflected new writing.[73] In a context where Irish was spoken by the greater part of the population, the language was inevitably the medium of cultural expression across a thematic spectrum ranging from demotic to learned. As elsewhere in early modern Europe, the spoken word, essentially evanescent, enshrined a protean oral culture. Significantly, English was increasingly perceived as a means to social and financial advancement from the late sixteenth century.[74] In this regard, Conall Mac Eochagáin's 1627 English version of the 'Annals of Clonmacnoise' is indicative of both the enhancement of the profile of non-professional Gaelic *literati* and their awareness of a need for interchange with English intellectuals.[75] Building on trends discernible in the late sixteenth century, the early decades of the ensuing century witnessed a remarkable diversity in genre, theme and geographical perspective. In spite of institutional attrition, poets continued to compose material which was thematically and stylistically conceived within the parameters of tradition. Not surprisingly, a strongly elegiac timbre inflects several important poems dating from the first two decades of the

---

71 M. Caball, 'Articulating Irish Identity in Early Seventeenth-Century Europe: The case of Giolla Brighde Ó hEódhusa (*c*.1570–1614)', *Archivium Hibernicum*, 62 (2009), 271–93.

72 N. Williams, *I bPrionta i Leabhar: na Protastúin agus Prós na Gaeilge 1567–1724* (Dublin: An Clóchomhar, 1986), 29.

73 A. Dooley, 'Literature and Society in Early Seventeenth-Century Ireland: The Evaluation of Change', in C. J. Byrne, M. Harry and P. Ó Siadhail (eds.), *Celtic Languages and Celtic Peoples: Proceedings of the Second North American Congress of Celtic Studies* (Halifax: Saint Mary's University, 1992), 513–34, at 515.

74 B. Cunningham, 'Loss and Gain: Attitudes towards the English Language in Early Modern Ireland', in Brian Mac Cuarta (ed.), *Reshaping Ireland 1550–1700: Colonization and its Consequences* (Dublin: FCP, 2011), 163–86.

75 D. Casey, 'Irish Pseudohistory in Conall Mag Eochagáin's *Annals of Clonmacnoise*', *Proceedings of the Harvard Celtic Colloquium*, 32 (2012), 74–94.

seventeenth century. Lochlainn Ó Dalaigh, for example, in a poem beginning 'Cáit ar ghabhadar Gaoidhil?' ('Where have the Gaels gone?'), laments the replacement of Ireland's Gaelic *élite* and their aristocratic milieu by socially inferior arrivistes from England and Scotland.[76] The poet, like other Gaelic intellectuals at this time of profound upheaval, discerned a providentialist causation in the predicament of the Gaelic Irish and in urging repentance to assuage divine wrath, he compared his compatriots to the Israelites during their Egyptian bondage.[77] In a similar vein, Fear Flatha Ó Gnímh lamented the demise of the O'Neills against an apocalyptic scenario which signalled the dramatic end of an era across Ireland.[78] An awareness of dispossession and exile permeates such material. Eoghan Ruadh Mac an Bhaird depicted Nuala O'Donnell as a lone mourner at the tomb of her kinsmen in Rome, obliged to maintain a lonely vigil bereft of the elaborate communal rituals of grieving which would have accompanied such an occasion in Ireland.[79] Likewise, in a poem composed in honour of Nuala's sisters, Mary and Margaret, Fearghal Óg Mac an Bhaird lamented the plight of the women whose four brothers, including Red Hugh and Rory, now lay dead, while Nuala was in continental exile. If the fate of the O'Donnells was undoubtedly tragic, the tragedy which had enveloped Ireland occasioned profound anguish.[80] Acknowledgement of trauma and displacement, however, did not preclude strategic negotiation of prevailing circumstances. Tadhg Ó Dálaigh addressed a poem around 1618 to Sir George Carew, a high-ranking English military official and sometime lord president of Munster, seeking his patronage on the basis of Carew's ancestor, Robert, who owned lands in west Cork during the thirteenth century and who had supposedly granted a holding at Muntervary to the bardic family of Ó Dálaigh. Tadhg now approached Sir George, possibly in London, on the assumption of mutually binding ties of poet and patron. It is not known how Carew responded, although a copy of the poem was preserved among his historical papers.[81] Likewise, in the case of Martha Stafford, wife of Sir Henry O'Neill of Clandeboye, an English lineage proved no hindrance to her deft incorporation within a bardic eulogistic framework.[82] No more than matters of ethnicity, diversity of political affiliation proved no less amenable to bardic

---

76 W. Gillies (ed.), 'A Poem on the Downfall of the Gaoidhil', *Éigse*, 13 (1969–70), 203–10.
77 Gillies, 'A Poem on the Downfall', quatrains 19–24, at 208–9.
78 B. Ó Cuív (ed.), 'A Poem on the Í Néill', *Celtica*, 2 (1954), 245–51.
79 E. Knott (ed.), 'Mac an Bhaird's Elegy on the Ulster Lords', *Celtica*, 5 (1960), 161–71.
80 Greene and Kelly (eds.), *Irish Bardic Poetry*, no. 8, 46–8.
81 A. O'Sullivan (ed.), 'Tadhg O'Daly and Sir George Carew', *Éigse*, 14 (1971–1972), 27–38.
82 T. Ó Donnchadha (ed.), *Leabhar Cloinne Aodha Buidhe* (Dublin: Irish Manuscripts Commission, 1931), 203–17.

validation. Strikingly, the loyalty and service of Donough O'Brien, fourth earl of Thomond, to the crown, were hailed in an elegy following his death in 1624.[83] An elegy composed by Domhnall Ó Dálaigh in memory of Domhnall O'Sullivan Beare, who famously led his followers' retreat from Glengarriff to O'Rourke's country in 1602, following his murder in exile in 1618, is a superb example of bardic continuity of tradition. Having failed to secure the restoration of his lands from James I and VI, O'Sullivan went to Spain where he was granted a pension and created count of Bearehaven by Philip III. Nonetheless, the poet highlights the implications of his loss for Gaelic Ireland, which now lies fully subject to crown dominion.[84] Indeed, the invocation of tradition no doubt also served as an intellectual bulwark from which to articulate a case for the integrity and primacy of *élite* Gaelic culture. The apparently apolitical antiquarian poetic debate about the relative historic merits of the ancient northern and southern divisions of Ireland initiated by Tadhg Mac Bruaideadha around 1616 was surely a collective bardic assertion of integrity in the face of desuetude.[85]

Increasingly, the voice of non-professional poets was heard. Ironically, institutional stasis permitted and possibly enabled a process of cultural innovation and creativity. The extant poems of William Nugent, scion of an aristocratic Westmeath Anglo-Irish family, which seem to date from his time as a student at Oxford in the early 1570s, are emblematic of an Irish patriotism transcending traditional ethnic divisions.[86] A hybrid cultural and linguistic identity is evident in the poetry of the Kerry Anglo-Irish poet Muiris Mac Gearailt who flourished during the first two decades of the seventeenth century.[87] The poetry of Geoffrey Keating, who studied at universities in France before returning to Ireland in 1613 to serve as a priest in the diocese of Waterford and Lismore, is also indicative of an inclusive sense of national identity centring on Gaelic cultural values and Counter-Reformation Catholicism.[88] Occasional tantalising references to women

---

83 B. Ó Cuív (ed.), 'An Elegy on Donnchadh Ó Briain, Fourth Earl of Thomond', *Celtica*, 16 (1984), 87–105.

84 R. B. Breatnach (ed.), 'Elegy on Donal O'Sullivan Beare (†1618)', *Éigse*, 7 (1954), 162–81.

85 J. Leerssen, *The Contention of the Bards (Iomarbhágh na bhFileadh) and its Place in Irish Political and Literary History* (London: ITS, 1994).

86 G. Murphy (ed.), 'Poems of Exile by Uilliam Nuinseann Mac Barúin Dealbhna', *Éigse*, 6 (1949), 8–15.

87 *Dánta Mhuiris Mhic Dháibhí Dhuibh Mhic Gearailt*, ed. N. Williams (Dublin: An Clóchomhar, 1979).

88 M. Caball, 'Patriotism, Culture and Identity: The Poetry of Geoffrey Keating', in P. Ó Riain (ed.), *Geoffrey Keating's Foras Feasa ar Éirinn: Reassessments* (London: ITS, 2008), 19–38.

poets caution against an assumption of the exclusive cultural authority of men.[89] Fionnghuala Ní Bhriain's lament for her husband Uaithne Mór Ó Lochlainn, who died around 1617, is suggestive of women's central role in communal mourning so graphically documented in the eighteenth and nineteenth centuries.[90] The elusive early seventeenth-century Thomond poetess known only as Caitilín Dubh composed elegies, which were included in a collection of poems addressed to the O'Briens of Thomond.[91] A stray survival such as a companion's decidedly biting lament for an individual called Eoghan Mac Criostail hints at a vibrant popular culture which is essentially undocumented in the extant archive.[92] The survival of a corpus of love poetry, however, reflects the ludic preoccupations of both an intellectual and social *élite*.[93]

The cultivation of prose material during this period was also diverse and likewise subject to new intellectual currents and the cosmopolitan continental experiences of many Irish intellectuals. Romantic tales and stories inspired by the Fionn cycle (characterised by remarkable and wondrous episodes) were evidently popular in sixteenth- and seventeenth-century scribal milieus and, it seems, by implication, among Gaelic readers and, more frequently, audiences.[94] Tellingly, in view of the continental exile of many Gaelic intellectuals, a large collection of such material known as *fiannaigheacht* was compiled in Flanders between 1626 and 1627 at the behest of Somhairle Mac Domhnaill, an officer in the Irish regiment of the Spanish army.[95] However, the cultivation of such prose was far from static in creative terms. It has been demonstrated that redactions of romantic tales in the later sixteenth century were responsive to contemporary political considerations.[96] Gaelic medical texts, deriving from continental exemplars, continued to be copied in the sixteenth century.[97] In the field of history, scribes continued to record

89 H. F. Hore, 'Irish Bardism in 1561', *Ulster Journal of Archaeology*, 6 (1858), 165–67, 202–12, at 167; Ó Muireadhaigh, 'Aos Dána', 83.

90 L. P. Ó Murchú (ed.), 'Caoineadh ar Uaithne Mór Ó Lochlainn, 1617', *Éigse*, 27 (1993), 67 79).

91 L. P. Ó Murchú, 'Caitilín Dubh', in B. Lalor (ed.), *The Encyclopaedia of Ireland* (Dublin: Gill and Macmillan, 2003), 149.

92 P. Ó Ciardha (ed.), 'The Lament for Eoghan Mac Criostail', *The Irish Sword*, 13 (1977–1979), 378–81.

93 M. Mac Craith, *Lorg na hIasachta ar na Dánta Grádha* (Dublin: An Clóchomhar, 1989).

94 G. Murphy, *The Ossianic Lore and Romantic Tales of Medieval Ireland* (Dublin: Cultural Relations Committee, 1961).

95 R. Ó hUiginn, 'Duanaire Finn: Patron and Text', in J. Carey (ed.), *Duanaire Finn: Reassessments* (London: ITS, 2003), 79–106.

96 C. Breatnach (ed.), *Patronage, Politics and Prose* (Maynooth: An Sagart, 1996).

97 E. Ní Ghallchobhair (ed.), *Anathomia Gydo* (London: ITS, 2014), 4–6; C. Dillon, 'Medical Practice and Gaelic Ireland', in J. Kelly and F. Clark (eds.), *Ireland and Medicine in the Seventeenth and Eighteenth Centuries* (Farnham: Ashgate, 2010), 39–52.

events in the traditional annalistic format as evidenced in the Annals of Loch Cé, compiled between 1588 and 1589 in their extant version, or the now lost annals of Maoilín Óg Mac Bruaideadha.[98] The somewhat more expansive character of Lughaidh Ó Cléirigh's prose account of Hugh O'Donnell, possibly composed between 1616 and 1636, is essentially traditional in timbre but with a Renaissance inflection.[99] The first version of the anonymous prose satire *Pairlement Chloinne Tomáis*, possibly composed by Muiris Mac Gearailt around 1608–1611, mocks the social pretensions of a parvenu cohort of Gaelic upstarts.[100] Tadhg Ó Cianáin's narrative of the departure of Hugh O'Neill and his retinue to the continent in 1607, and their subsequent experiences prior to reaching Rome, uniquely reflects the predicament of the Ulster *élite*.[101] A marked Counter-Reformation influence in Gaelic prose was evident as far back as 1593, when Flaithrí Ó Maolconaire translated a Spanish catechism into Irish which he apparently sent to Ireland in 1598.[102] Later, Geoffrey Keating's devotional prose works, a defence of the mass (*c*.1619) and a meditation on death and penance composed in the late 1620s and early 1630s, circulated in manuscript format.[103]

Print in Irish: A Partial Debut

Ironically, however, at a time of diversification and recalibration, Gaelic literature and scholarship were essentially bypassed by the advent of print, which was transformative in its impact across Europe. Unable to access large urban centres of trade, commerce and learning, the incorporation of Gaelic culture within the ecology of print was sporadic and tenuous. Moreover, early modern Irish print culture was essentially a sectarian phenomenon embodying alternately a Protestant or Counter-Reformation Catholic agenda. The publication of Gaelic evangelical liturgical and catechetical works in Edinburgh and Dublin in 1567 and 1571 respectively

---

98 B. Cunningham, *The Annals of the Four Masters: Irish History, Kingship and Society in the Early Seventeenth Century* (Dublin: FCP, 2010), 51–4; 62–3.

99 G. Mac Niocaill, *The Medieval Irish Annals* (Dublin: Dublin Historical Association, 1975), 37; M. Mac Craith, 'The *Beatha* in the Context of the Literature of the Renaissance', in Ó Riain, *Beatha*, 36–53.

100 M. Caball, 'Pairlement Chloinne Tomáis I: a Reassessment', *Éigse*, 27 (1993), 47–57.

101 F. Ó Fearghail (ed.), *Tadhg Ó Cianáin: An Irish Scholar in Rome* (Dublin: Mater Dei, 2011).

102 B. Ó Cuív (ed.), 'Flaithrí Ó Maolchonaire's Catechism of Christian Doctrine', *Celtica*, 1 (1950), 161–206.

103 B. Kane, 'Domesticating the Counter-Reformation: Bridging the Bardic and Catholic Traditions in Geoffrey Keating's *The three Shafts of Death*', *The Sixteenth Century Journal*, 40 (2009), 1029–44.

are suggestive of an indigenous commitment to Reformation attentive to Gaelic cultural integrity.[104] The relatively late appearance of a Gaelic New Testament in 1602/3 and the publication of the Gaelic translation of the *Book of Common Prayer* in 1608 under the auspices of a state-endorsed process of translation are indicative of the cleavage increasingly separating Protestantism and Gaelic culture in Ireland. William Daniel dedicated his translation of the *Book of Common Prayer* to Lord Deputy Sir Arthur Chichester and the survival of the latter's presentation copy in pristine condition is evocative of the frustrated ambitions of a cohort of Gaelic evangelicals.[105] A counter-programme of Catholic devotional publications was initiated at the Irish Franciscan College of St Anthony in Leuven, founded in 1607 to train Franciscans for the home missions, where in 1614/15 Giolla Brighde Ó hEódhusa reprinted a Christian doctrine in Irish first published by his order at Antwerp in 1611. Other devotional works issued from the printing press at St Anthony's College and they no doubt further strengthened a highly influential alignment of Catholicism, Gaelic culture and Irish national identity. If a handful of Gaelic intellectuals, such as Dermot O'Meara and Nial O'Glacan, engaged with print generally, a vibrant corpus of Gaelic scholarship continued to circulate in manuscript format. However, in an age where epistemological authority and prestige were mediated via print, Gaelic learning was destined to remain immured within a sphere increasingly marginal in terms of status and external perception. The compilation in Ostend in 1631 of the manuscript known as the 'Book of the O'Conor Don', a critically important collection of bardic poems composed between the thirteenth and seventeenth centuries, is emblematic of the extrusion of *élite* Gaelic scholarship from Ireland and its continued, but ultimately problematic, reliance on manuscript dissemination.[106]

---

104 M. Caball, 'Gaelic and Protestant: A Case Study in Early Modern Self-Fashioning, 1567–1608', *Proceedings of the Royal Irish Academy*, 110:C (2010), 191–215; M. Caball, 'The Bible in Early Modern Gaelic Ireland: Tradition, Collaboration, and Alienation', in K. Killeen, H. Smith and R. Willie (eds.), *The Oxford Handbook of the Bible in Early Modern England, c.1530–1700* (Oxford University Press, 2015), 332–49.

105 *Leabhar na nUrnaightheadh gComhchoidchiond agus Mheinisdraldachda na Sacrameinteadh* (Dublin, 1608), (PML 22709), Pierpont Morgan Library, New York.

106 R. Ó hUiginn, 'Irish Literature in Spanish Flanders', in T. O'Connor and M. A. Lyons (eds.), *The Ulster Earls and Baroque Europe: Refashioning Irish Identities, 1600–1800* (Dublin: FCP, 2010), 349–61.

17

Language, Literature and Print in Irish, 1630–1730

BERNADETTE CUNNINGHAM

In his *Irish Historical Library* published in 1724, Bishop William Nicolson real-ised that he had omitted some important Irish language material in his survey of historical sources. He rectified this in an appendix, not finding a way inte-grate it into his main narrative. In one sense little has changed since then: the two closely interlinked language cultures of early modern Ireland and their literatures are rarely studied together. The two-strand approach has the effect of emphasising differences rather than commonalities. And yet, as the Irish language sources reveal, cultural frontiers in early modern Ireland were more permeable than contemporaries were prepared openly to concede.[1]

Language, 1630–1660

Irish was still the language of everyday conversation in many parts of Ireland in 1630, but English was preferred in some contexts. While cultural legislation aimed at curtailing the use of Irish had been abandoned by government by 1615,[2] the increased use of English was a matter of comment among contem-poraries. English was no longer just the language of the administrative *élite*, it was the language of urban commerce and was one of the languages of the literate. Knowledge of more than one language could serve as an indicator of social status in a context where education was the mark of a gentleman. This, coupled with the functional value of English in dealings with the state, contributed to making English fashionable among the Irish by the mid-seven-teenth century. Writing in the late 1620s, the antiquarian Conall Mageoghegan was acerbic in his comments about a lack of respect for the Irish manuscript heritage even among the descendants of the learned class:

---

1 J. Kelly and C. Mac Murchaidh (eds.), *Irish and English: Essays on the Irish Linguistic and Cultural Frontier, 1600–1900* (Dublin: Four Courts Press [hereafter FCP], 2012).
2 E. G. Atkinson (ed.), *Acts of the Privy Council of England, 1615–1616* (London: HMSO, 1925), 80.

because they cannot enjoy that respect & gaine by their said profession as heretofore ... they set naught by the s[ai]d knowledge, neglect their Bookes, and choose rather to put their children to learn eng[lish] than their own native Language, in soe much that some of them suffer Taylors to cut the leaves of the said Books (which their auncestors held in great accoumpt, & sliece them in long peeces to make their measures off) that the posterities are like to fall into meer Ignorance of any things happened before theire tyme.[3]

In a similar vein, in the mid-1630s, the translator Michael Kearney, writing in County Tipperary, observed that English was 'now the more respected language among us'.[4] Kearney defended the status of the Irish language relative to English, insisting that 'for antiquity, propriety of character (being the archetype of their letters) and copiosity of phrase, without little or no beholdingness to any other tongue, is unto their language nothing inferior'.[5] This belief in the high status of Irish lasted well into the eighteenth century. At the same time, the range of imported books in English and Latin in circulation increased through the seventeenth century; the commercialisation of the economy helped to ensure their wider distribution.[6] Other circumstances favouring the pragmatic acquisition of English included the arrival of a new English-speaking landed class and the implementation of the common law. More limited was the impact of the foundation of Trinity College, Dublin in 1592 and the presence of predominantly English-speaking clergy within the Church of Ireland. The slow pace of language change through the seventeenth and eighteenth centuries reflects the reality that primary language learning took place within familial/domestic settings, where the first language of mothers and nurses was the first language learned by the children in their care, irrespective of social or economic status or ethnic background.

Many early modern newcomers to Ireland learned some Irish. In the early seventeenth century one of the most successful English settlers in Munster, Richard Boyle, earl of Cork, arranged for his children to learn Irish.[7] The 1641 Depositions, which record claims for losses in the rebellion, document some settlers reporting on conversations in Irish that they overheard.[8] Robin, the fictional English pedlar of tobacco depicted in *Pairlement Chloinne Tomáis* I (c.1615–1630), was more competent in Irish than his customers were

3 D. Murphy (ed.), *The Annals of Clonmacnoise* (Dublin: Dublin University Press, 1896), 8.
4 MS 24 G 16, f. 34r, Royal Irish Academy [hereafter RIA].
5 MS 24 G 16, f. 34r, RIA.
6 R. Gillespie, *Reading Ireland: Print, Reading and Social Change in Early Modern Ireland* (Manchester University Press, 2005).
7 M. MacCarthy-Morrogh, *The Munster Plantation* (Oxford University Press, 1986), 275.
8 N. Canny, *Making Ireland British, 1580–1650* (Oxford University Press, 2001), 450–5.

in English. In the 1660s continuation of that text, the fictional 'Domhall an Deannuigh' character learned his English doing business in the big houses of Leinster and Meath.[9] Existing side by side, some knowledge of the second language simplified routine daily interactions. Throughout the century, many Protestant landowners who might be expected to be monoglot English speakers had contact with the Irish language in their routine interactions with Irish servants, nurses and tenants.[10]

Yet, in *Pairlement Chloinne Tomáis* II (*c*.1660–1663), the author satirised the pragmatism of those who created social bonds with their new landlords: '*D'órduigheadur mar an gcéadna dalta uileamhna & dedarbhchara láidir Shagsanuig do bheith ag gach n-aon díobh, & bairille & buidéal & ól tuatha & baile mhóir do thabhairt dó, go ndéanadh cosnamh dhóibh ar aghaidh éagcóra & anfhórluinn na ndaoine uaisle*' ('Likewise they ordered that every of them should have a foster-son and a powerful bosom friend of an Englishman, and barrel and bottle and country and town ale be given him, so that he might protect them against the injustices and oppression of the nobility').[11] Similarly, the preface to Richard Plunkett's Latin–Irish dictionary, compiled in County Meath *c*.1662, criticised those who neglected the Irish language but, like *Pairlement Chloinne Tomáis II*, the dictionary's many borrowings from English reveal the depth of language contact in north Leinster. While these texts were ostensibly concerned to preserve an older social and linguistic environment, their authors were not immune from the linguistic pressures of their own bilingual world.[12]

Discussing the Irish language in his *Cambrensis Eversus* (1662) John Lynch, a Galway-born priest, asserted '*ea per omnes Hiberniae regiones sic hodie diffusa est ut ubique ferme fit vernacula*' ('it is at this day so generally diffused through Ireland, that it is strictly our vernacular tongue'), and again '*omnes Hibernice loquamur, et Anglice plerique legamus et scribamus*' ('we all speak Irish, and many of us can read and write English').[13] This suggests that while Irish was the

---

9 N. Williams (ed. and trans.), *Pairlement Chloinne Tomáis* (Dublin Institute for Advanced Studies, 1981), lines 1241–89; 1549–51.

10 T. Barnard, 'Protestants and the Irish Language, *c*.1675–1725', in T. Barnard, *Protestant Ascents and Descents, 1641–1770* (Dublin: FCP, 2004), 182.

11 Translation adapted from Williams (ed. and trans.), *Pairlement Chloinne Tomáis*, lines 1883–8.

12 Plunkett's unpublished dictionary, 'Vocabularium Latinum et Hibernum', now Marsh's Library MS Z4.2.5. M. Ní Mhurchú and D. Breathnach, *1560–1781: Beatháisnéis* (Dublin: An Clóchomhar, 2001), 175; A. Harrison, *The Dean's Friend: Anthony Raymond 1676–1726, Jonathan Swift and the Irish Language* (Dublin: Éamonn de Búrca, 1999), 40.

13 J. Lynch, *Cambrensis Eversus*, ed. and trans. M. Kelly (3 vols, Dublin: Celtic Society, 1848–1852), i, 192–3.

primary language of everyday conversation, literate people probably knew English and perhaps Latin. However, not all Irish speakers who were literate in English also achieved literacy in Irish. For the upwardly mobile that was an unnecessary step. Literacy in English was advantageous for those engaging in commerce, or with the common law, or with local or central government. Literacy in Irish was a luxury few could afford, although Lynch observed that some older people were drawn by the attractiveness of their native language to read and write Irish. He insisted that knowledge of multiple languages was never a burden and was always valued.[14]

Recognising the linguistic pragmatism of his contemporaries, Lynch noted that self-interest rather than the enforcement of legislation had prompted conquered nations to adopt the language of the coloniser, it being particularly advantageous in legal contexts. He rejected Giraldus Cambrensis's assertions that the Irish people had been conquered in medieval times, insisting they had not adopted English law, language and manners until recently. Yet, Lynch conceded that the era of profound knowledge of the Irish language had ended because of the loss of hereditary patronage for the professional learned class.[15]

Language, 1660–1700

Lynch's work as a translator reveals his belief that certain texts were best disseminated in Latin. He produced a Latin version of Geoffrey Keating's history of Ireland because, he said, the histories of other nations were in Latin.[16] While his translation widened access to authentic Gaelic sources on early Irish history, demand continued for the same text in Irish and English. Manuscript copies of Keating's *Foras feasa ar Éirinn* circulated in three languages – Irish, Latin and English – by the mid-seventeenth century. The Cromwellian soldier Thomas Harte, the Welsh antiquary Edward Lhuyd and the lord chancellor, Sir Richard Cox (1650–1733), were among those who read Keating's history in English decades before any version became available in print.[17] Access to such texts was not confined to one linguistic or political community. In multilingual contexts, where demand existed, translators were always available. The genealogist Dubhaltach Mac Fhirbhisigh (c.1600–1671) could produce works as diverse as a translation into Irish of the Rule of St Clare for Poor

---

14 Lynch, *Cambrensis Eversus*, i, 190–1; 180–1.
15 Lynch, *Cambrensis Eversus*, i, 280–1; 190–1.
16 Translator's preface, Latin translation of *Foras Feasa*, MS 24 I 5, 2, RIA.
17 B. Cunningham, *The World of Geoffrey Keating* (Dublin: FCP, 2000), 201–11.

Clare nuns in Galway in 1647 and a translation into English of late medieval Irish annals for Sir James Ware in the 1660s.[18]

A market developed for English translations of Irish language manuscript sources that were recognised as a storehouse of early history. By the late seventeenth century, second- and third-generation Ulster settler families were keen to learn about their adopted country and their place in it. 'More curious than ordinary' was Arthur Brownlow (1645–1710) in Lurgan, County Armagh, who assembled a collection of Irish manuscripts. Brownlow's English grand-father had received land in the Ulster plantation.[19] Significant Anglicisation had occurred in Brownlow's neighbourhood, and in 1682 the Reverend William Brook of Drumcree observed that 'those few Irish we have amongst us are very much reclaimed of their barbarous customs, the most of them speaking English and for agriculture they are little inferior to the English themselves'.[20] Brownlow could read the Irish manuscripts he acquired, and his antiquar-ian interests suggest contact across cultural frontiers within Ulster plantation society. Perhaps his mixed ancestry – his paternal grandmother was Elinor O'Doherty from Derry – helps explains the ease with which he straddled two cultural worlds. However, his ability to interact with the custodians of Irish manuscripts and with those from whom he learned Irish may not be explained by genealogy alone.

Even partially bilingual people made choices daily about the languages they spoke, influenced by social context. Movement between language zones – such as movement to an urban centre from a rural area – was probably a significant influence. Attempts to map language zones in Ireland c.1700 have been made by Diarmait Mac Giolla Chríost and adopted by others.[21] In this cartographic simplification of a complex social and cultural reality the cities and hinterlands of Dublin, Limerick, Wexford and Belfast were predomin-antly English speaking, with most of the remainder of eastern Ireland being bilingual. The rural south-west, west and north-west still mostly comprised near-monoglot Irish-speakers in 1700. Yet, Tadhg Ó Rodaighe (d.1706) could report to William Molyneux regarding County Leitrim c.1683 that 'both sexes

---

18 MS D i 2, p. [161]v (Rule of St Clare), RIA; 'The Annals of Ireland from the Year 1441 to 1468, Translated from the Irish by Dudley Firbisse', *Miscellany of the Irish Archaeological Society*, 1 (Dublin: Irish Archaeological Society, 1846), 198–302.

19 B. Cunningham and R. Gillespie, 'An Ulster Settler and his Irish Manuscripts', *Éigse*, 21 (1986), 27–36.

20 R. M. Young (ed.), 'An account of the barony of O'Neiland', *Ulster Journal of Archaeology*, 2nd series, 4 (1898), 241.

21 D. Mac Giolla Chríost, *The Irish Language in Ireland* (London: Routledge, 2005), cited in A. Doyle, *A History of the Irish Language* (Oxford University Press, 2015), 66.

speak reasonable proper English generally', possibly a consequence of the 1620 plantation.[22] Ó Rodaighe himself was competent in three languages.

Nor should the extent of bilingualism in towns be underestimated. Urban society facilitated increased contact across social and cultural boundaries. In 1657 the Dublin city assembly observed that 'there is Irish commonly and usually spoken, and the Irish habit worn not only in the streets, but by such as live in the country and come to this city on market days, but also by and in several families in this city'.[23] Cities and towns were not unitary social entities and Irish-speaking communities could find a home in each of the larger Irish towns and their hinterlands, including Dublin.[24] The movement of population into Dublin probably led to an increase in the Irish-speaking population in the city in the early eighteenth century. Those who moved to urban areas may have acquired some English, but their new social circumstances did not require that they cease to use Irish in domestic settings, nor would the acquisition of functional English have obliterated cultural understandings of the value of Irish in other contexts.

The ready availability in Ireland of books in English or Latin by the late seventeenth century was such that it became accepted that English and Latin were the languages of print. The Connacht antiquary Roderick O'Flaherty chose Latin as the language of his history of Ireland, *Ogygia: seu, Rerum Hibernicarum Chronologia*, and London as its place of publication in 1685. Known for his knowledge of Irish manuscript sources, his history revealed him to be a sophisticated reader of print. Peter Walsh's *A Prospect of the State of Ireland from the Year of the World 1576 to the Year of Christ 1652* (London, 1682), incorporated a brief digest of Keating's history in English. Later, the English adaptation of Keating's history, published in Dublin and London in 1723, was a commercial success.[25] It is a good example of English being chosen as the language of print for a work available in Irish through scribal publication. In the late 1680s even the Catholic literature on sale in Dublin was 'overwhelmingly in English and frequently by English authors', and contemporaries understood the implications.[26] As Francis Walsh, OFM, observed in the

---

22 J. Logan, 'Tadhg O Roddy and two Surveys of Co. Leitrim', *Breifne*, 4 (1971), 333.

23 J. T. Gilbert and R. Gilbert (eds.), *Calendar of the Ancient Records of Dublin* (19 vols., Dublin: Dollard, 1889–1944), iv, 118.

24 D. Dickson, *Dublin: The Making of a Capital City* (London: Profile, 2014), 75–6.

25 *The General History of Ireland … Collected by the Learned Jeoffry Keating … Faithfully Translated from the Irish by Dermo'd O'Connor* (London and Dublin, 1723; other edns. London, 1726, 1732).

26 T. Barnard, 'The Impact of Print in Ireland, 1680–1800: Problems and Perils', in J. MacElligott and E. Patten (eds.), *The Perils of Print Culture* (Basinstoke: Palgrave, 2014), 108.

preface to his unpublished *Grammatica Anglo-Hibernica* (1713), 'Since the time printing has been introduced not only the study, but also the publick use and practise of the Irish language has either been laid aside, or utterly discouraged in this our Catholic nation of Ireland.'[27]

Language, 1700–1730

By the early eighteenth century an English-speaking *élite* was politically secure and, in time, the antiquarian value of the Irish language, even for settlers, came to be appreciated. Edward Lhuyd's work on Celtic languages, published in 1707 as part of his *Archaeologia Britannica*, a study of 'the Language, Histories, and Customs of the Original Inhabitants of Great Britain', was influential. Across Europe, the study of comparative linguistics led to an interest in Irish, perceived by Gottfried Wilhelm Leibniz (1646–1716) to be a very early language form amongst European languages.[28] Gradually, an understanding developed of the cultural value of individual vernaculars within the development of European civilisation. Lhuyd's work on the Irish language impacted on the work of later lexicographers, and in this way some of Richard Plunkett's lexicographical work (and even Lhuyd's misreading of Plunkett) filtered through into modern dictionaries.[29]

The first English–Irish dictionary was published at Paris in 1732. The work of Conchubhar Ó Beaglaoich (Conor Begley) and Aodh Buí Mac Cruitín, it was modelled on Nathan Bailey's *An Universal Etymological Dictionary* (London, 1721) and Abel Boyer's *The Royal Dictionary* (London, 1699). These were followed so closely that some of the entries were irrelevant in an Irish cultural context. Significantly, Irish lexicography was pursued in a dual-language context utilising either Latin or English in the scholarly interpretation of Irish, indicating that those with a scholarly interest in Irish after 1700 could normally be expected to be literate in Latin or English also.

Literature in Irish, 1630–1660

Little writing of a secular nature found its way into print in Irish in the early modern period, but much has survived in manuscript form. More manuscript

---

27 Cited in Harrison, *The Dean's Friend*, 38.
28 E. Poppe, 'Leibniz and Eckhart on the Irish Language', *Eighteenth-Century Ireland*, 1 (1986), 69–72.
29 T. de Bhaldraithe, 'Irish Dictionaries', in *Corpas na Gaeilge, 1660–1882: Foclóir na Nua-Ghaeilge: The Irish Language Corpus* (Dublin: Royal Irish Academy, 2004), 77.

material in Irish survives from the years between 1630 and 1730 than for any preceding century. Paper had become more readily available and an antiquarian mentality had taken root, leading to the preservation of older poetry and prose in new manuscript compilations. Commentaries on contemporary circumstances, in both poetry and prose, have also survived, together with some substantial works on early Irish history. Well before 1730, prose satire became a popular genre in Irish as well as in English, even if few could hope to match the mighty pen of Jonathan Swift.

In the early seventeenth century, patronage of Irish literature was shifting to continental Europe and one of the most remarkable manuscript compilations of Irish poetry ever assembled was produced in the Low Countries in 1631. The *Book of the O'Conor Don* was written by Aodh Ó Dochartaigh for Somhairle Mac Domhnaill, mostly at Ostend in Flanders.[30] It preserves 352 bardic poems, ranging in date from the late twelfth to the early seventeenth century; eighty-eight of them are unique to this manuscript.[31] The compilation reveals the riches of the Gaelic poetic tradition and the interest in continuing that tradition into the seventeenth century. Material was arranged systematically, opening with poems on the poetic and musical professions, followed by satirical compositions and love poems along with devotional and didactic poems. Poems relating to specific lordly families then follow, beginning with O'Neill, then O'Donnell, Maguire, Maguinness, O'Rourke, O'Brien, O'Conor, Burke, MacCarthy, Kelly, Fitzgerald, MacSwiney, MacDermott and O'Hara. The volume concludes with general themes, many of a political nature, including work by exiled poets. It was the kind of organised collection of Gaelic literature that might have been printed in the 1630s if financial resources and anticipated readership had made such an enterprise viable.

In the same decade that the *Book of the O'Conor Don* was compiled at Ostend, two substantial prose histories were compiled in Ireland. These general histories were indicative of the desire to present Ireland in a favourable light in Europe and to rethink Irish identity. The *Annals of the Four Masters*, an Irish-language history of Ireland from earliest times down to 1616, was the work of a group of professional historians and scribes led by Mícheál Ó

---

30 In private ownership [Clonalis House, County Roscommon]. Digital edition at www. isos.dias.ie.

31 P. Ní Mhurchú, 'The Book of O'Conor Don: Catalogue Raisonné', unpublished MPhil thesis, University College Dublin (1995), appendix 2, cited in P. A. Breatnach, 'The Book of the O'Conor Don and the Manuscripts of St Anthony's College, Louvain', in P. Ó Macháin (ed.), *The Book of the O'Conor Don* (Dublin Institute for Advanced Studies, 2010), 120 n.

Cléirigh, OFM, and written in Donegal between 1632 and 1636.[32] These annals combined national origin legends with stories of kings, saints and secular heroes within a long chronological framework, offering a new version of Irish history acceptable to seventeenth-century Catholics.[33]

While work progressed on the *Annals of the Four Masters*, Geoffrey Keating (Seathrún Céitinn), an Old English Catholic priest educated in French seminaries, completed his narrative history of Ireland from earliest times to the twelfth century. An accomplished storyteller, Keating recounted stories of past kings and heroes that were already familiar to his readers. Trained in the art of rhetoric, thoroughly immersed in the literature of medieval Ireland, and well versed in the Irish language, Keating had all the skills needed to write a history of the origins of the Irish people. His *Foras Feasa ar Éirinn* ('Compendium of knowledge about Ireland') quickly became a 'best-seller' in manuscript. Both these works catered for the demand among an Irish Catholic readership for a retelling of Irish history. They reflected a new confidence in the kingdom of Ireland, a confidence undermined less than a decade later following the outbreak of rebellion.

Keating's reaction to the 1641 rebellion and its aftermath can be gleaned from a poem in which he expressed his sorrow at the state of Ireland. *Mo thruaighe mar tá Éire* ('My sorrow at the state of Ireland'), in the syllabic metre of traditional bardic poetry, blamed foreigners for Ireland's decline and depicted Ireland as bereft of friend or lover, a condition worsened by the enforced exile of many. The poet cited dissension among the Irish as an explanation for the triumph of foreigners. He created an image of Ireland abandoned like an orphan by those of her own people who should have nurtured her.[34] The divisive nature of Irish Catholic politics in the 1640s would have disappointed Keating, whose historical writings had linked language and religion as the basis of Irish Catholic identity.

The interconnections between Roman Catholicism and Irishness also informed the political poetry of Pádraigín Haicéad (*c*.1610–1654), an Irish Dominican from County Tipperary educated in Louvain and in France. Following the split in the Confederation in 1646, Haicéad was vocal in his support of the papal nuncio, GianBattista Rinuccini, and he satirised those

---

32 John O'Donovan (ed. and trans.), *Annála Ríoghachta Éireann: Annals of the Kingdom of Ireland by the Four Masters* (7 vols., Dublin: Hodges and Smith, 1848–1851).

33 B. Cunningham, *The Annals of the Four Masters: Irish History, Kingship and Society in the Early Seventeenth Century* (Dublin: FCP, 2010), 301–4.

34 M. Caball, 'Patriotism, Culture and Identity: The Poetry of Geoffrey Keating', in P. Ó Riain (ed.), *Geoffrey Keating's Foras Feasa ar Éirinn: Reassessments*. Irish Texts Society, subsidiary series, 19 (London: Irish Texts Society, 2008), 19–38.

in the opposite faction. His best-known poem, *Múscail do mhisneach a Bhanba* ('Rouse up your courage, my Ireland'), dated to 1646, was an assertion of the entitlements of Irish Catholics, and illustrated the complexities of political divisions in that decade.

> *Músgail do mhisneach, a Bhanbha;*
> *Breatnaigh feasda forlann t'uilc;*
> *in bhur bhgaill ar feadh an fhillse*
> *ná caill seadh, a linnse Luirc.*
> *Do himreadh ort feall go fiadhnach,*
> *Má do gealladh ar fonn fós;*
> *Gearradh mín ar mheall do bhrághad*
> *Do shin tar fheall námhad nós.*
> *Móide is gránna grain a ngníomha*
> *Gaoidhil féin ar fearaibh Fáil*
> *D'imirt an fhill ghoimhigh ghránna*
> *Cinn oiris is chána cháigh.*

('Rouse up your country, my Ireland! / Now confront your evil fate; / do not lose heart, my country, / at your treacherously neglected state. / Betrayal was practised as surely / as ever a land was betrayed; / the finesse of the slash at your windpipe / surpassing the enemies' usual ways. / And all the more ugly the horror / done by the Irish on Irish men: / the chieftains to whom all paid taxes / using treachery on their own.')[35]

The impact of the poet's continental education cannot be disregarded in evaluating his political outlook. One of his exile poems *Cuirim séad suirghe chum seise* ('I send a love token to my beloved'), highlighted the literary and military achievements of the Irish but also alluded to the predicament of oppressed clergy. The persistence of these themes is evident in the work of later authors: pride in the excellence of Irish literature, language, and tradition is juxtaposed with lament at political or religious oppression. One of the features of the age was that fidelity to Roman Catholicism proved stronger than fidelity to the language and traditions of the Gaelic world. Catholicism demanded clear-cut allegiance; languages offered choice and accommodated dual loyalties.

A political activist and poet, Piaras Feiritéar (*c.*1600–1653) is often regarded as one of the finest seventeenth-century Irish-language poets. Also fluent in English, though no poems in English by him survive, his personal poetry has

---

35 M. Ní Cheallacháin (ed.), *Filíocht Phádraigín Haicéad* (Dublin: An Clóchomhar, 1962), 38; translation from M. Hartnett, *Haicéad* (Oldcastle: Gallery Press, 1993), 61.

been compared with the work of contemporary English poets Thomas Carew (*c*.1595–1639) and Robert Herrick (1591–1674).[36] As elsewhere, the era of the gentleman poet, not writing for a paymaster, had arrived. Feiritéar's work includes some accomplished love poems. *An bhean do b'annsa liom fán ngréin* ('The woman dearest to me under the sun') is a poem of unrequited love, while *Ní truagh galar acht grádh folaigh* ('Illness is no misfortune compared to secret love'), reveals his previously secret love for Meg Russell.[37] The extent to which these poems were known or recognised by contemporaries outside the immediate local context in which they were composed is unclear. Curiously, even in his native Kerry, it is not his poetry but a mis-remembered romantic version of his life as a dashing political activist that survived in popular lore into modern times.[38] That oral tradition may have been initiated by the reference to him in *Tuireamh na hÉireann* ('Ireland's lament'), probably the most renowned poem to survive from the mid-seventeenth century.

Seán Ó Conaill's *Tuireamh na hÉireann* was composed *c*.1657 and emphasised the suffering endured by the Catholic Irish in the political upheavals of the mid-century.[39] It was anti-English, but also self-reliant, blaming the Irish predicament on the Irish themselves. Replete with classical allusions as well as legal terminology in English, it provided a masterly overview of Irish history while its linguistic code-mixing gave it subversive appeal. It was particularly popular with later scribes. In an era when neither print nor manuscript was a cheap and affordable option, only the affluent could afford their own copy of Keating's *History of Ireland*, and only the literate could read it for themselves. A poem of 496 lines was more accessible and *Tuireamh na hÉireann* probably reached a wide audience through the eighteenth century.[40] It also circulated in various English translations, the best known of which opened with the line 'Irish heroes when I remind', though the earliest copies of this may belong to the late eighteenth century.[41]

The predicament of Irish Catholics in the Cromwellian era was discussed in several long political poems. *Aiste Dháibhí Cúndún* ('Dáibhí Cúndún's composition') directly addressed the politics of the 1650s.

---

36 M. Mac Craith, *Lorg na hIasachta ar na Dánta Grá* (Dublin: An Clóchomhar, 1989), 177–84.

37 A. Ó Beoláin, *Merriman agus Filí eile* (Dublin: An Clóchomhar, 1985), 38–49; P. Ua Duinnín (ed.), *Dánta Phiarais Feiritéir* (Dublin: Connradh na Gaedhilge, 1903).

38 M. Caball, 'Feiritéar, Piaras', in J. McGuire and J. Quinn (eds.), *Dictionary of Irish Biography* (9 vols., Cambridge University Press, 2009).

39 C. O'Rahilly (ed.), *Five Seventeenth-Century Political Poems* (Dublin Institute for Advanced Studies, 1952), 50–82.

40 V. Morley, *Ó Chéitinn go Raifteataí: mar a Cumadh Stair na hÉireann* (Dublin: Coiscéim, 2011), 63–100.

41 The copies in MS 23 I 18, RIA and MS 3 B 46, RIA date from the 1790s.

Referencing both classical and Gaelic historical events, the poet was troubled by his inability to find any appropriate historical precedent for the Cromwellian era. He blamed the misfortunes of the Irish on their own shortcomings.[42] In *Créacht do dháil mé* ('A faithful wound hath made of me') written by the mid-1650s, Dáibhí Ó Bruadair (1625–1698) attributed Irish Catholic suffering in the Cromwellian era to punishment by God, a consequence of disunity and deception: ignorant boors have taken possession of the castles and learning is disregarded; many Irish seek favour with the new *régime* by pretending to be of English descent; the poet calls for a change of heart.[43]

Éamonn an Dúna's mid-1650s political poem, *Mo lá leoin go deo go néagad* ('My day of ruin forever till I die') was an expression of the consequences of war, famine, plague and the Cromwellian confiscations which had impacted on his own region of west Munster. The harsh treatment of Catholic priests and teachers, the desecration of churches, the falseness of court procedures, the ruthless transportation of people to the West Indies and the American colonies, were all drawn into the poem. Despite the suffering experienced under the Cromwellian *régime*, the explanation offered by the poet echoed that of Ó Bruadair: the failings of the Irish had prompted divine retribution. The poet concluded by looking to the future, anticipating the return of the duke of York and the restoration of the leadership of the rightful king, Charles II.[44]

The linguistic code-mixing employed in some of these mid-seventeenth-century political poems, including that of Éamonn an Dúna, expressed alienation from government institutions. The play on languages drew attention to the contradictions and inequalities inherent within Irish society. It was an empowering mechanism for asserting difference, even while absorbing elements of another culture; a refusal to conform ideologically while pragmatically obeying the law. In eighteenth-century Munster, a new 'warrant' genre further developed this literary subversion in a mixture of poetry and prose that parodied legal warrants, with linguistic code-mixing as a defining feature.[45]

---

42 O'Rahilly (ed.), *Five Seventeenth-Century Political Poems*, 33–49.

43 J. Mac Erlean (ed. and trans.), *Duanaire Dháibhidh Uí Bhruadair* (3 vols., London: Irish Texts Society, 1910–1917), i, 26–51.

44 O'Rahilly (ed.), *Five Seventeenth-Century Political Poems*, 82–100.

45 L. Mac Mathúna, *Béarla sa Ghaeilge: Cabhair Choigríche: an Códmheascadh Gaeilge/Béarla i Litríocht na Gaeilge, 1600–1900* (Dublin: An Clóchomhar, 2007), 116–27; P. Ó Fiannachta, *An Barántas I: Réamhrá, Téacs, Malairtí* (Maynooth: An Sagart, 1978).

Literature in Irish, 1660–1700

For some, the years of adjustment after the Restoration provided the opportunity for families in various parts of Ireland to compile their own histories, generally for private circulation in manuscript. In south Ulster in the 1670s, a genealogical history of the O'Reillys asserted the status of one of the remaining Catholic landed families.[46] Further north a more traditional family book, *Leabhar Cloinne Aodha Buí* ('Book of the O'Neills of Clandeboy'), was compiled in 1680 by Ruairí Ó hUiginn for Colonel Cormac O'Neill of Clandeboy (d.1707).[47] The families for whom such works were compiled were those that had survived the turmoil of mid-century and had the potential to emerge as a new Catholic middle class. A little later, Hugh O'Donnell of Larkfield, County Leitrim, who sponsored an impressive O'Donnell poem-book in 1727,[48] and Brian O'Loghlen of Ennis, County Clare, recipient of the Book of O'Loghlen,[49] exemplified these new patrons.

Large tenant farmers, middlemen, doctors, clergy, teachers and poets were among the audience for the Irish language literary output of the late seventeenth and early eighteenth centuries. Some of this middling group could claim descent from a displaced Gaelic *élite* and felt entitled to be resentful of social upstarts. They were certainly the intended audience for *Pairlement Chloinne Tomáis II*, a social satire in the European tradition. Set in a fictitious parliament in Mullingar in north Leinster, it lampooned the social ambitions of manual labourers. The disloyalty of the upstart 'Clan Thomas' towards their own people and their inability to agree amongst themselves were recurrent themes. The unidentified author, who may have suffered personal losses in the Cromwellian land confiscations, modelled his satire on an earlier work set in Kerry, although this later author was less familiar with Irish literary tradition than was the author of *Pairlement Chloinne Tomáis I*.

A similar satirical text, *Lucht na Simléirí* ('The chimney people'), reveals the extent to which English was being adopted before the end of the seventeenth century. The story depicts the occupant of a big house in conversation with a beggar at the door. Not only did the big house owner speak English, the beggar had some English also.[50] Also set in a bilingual context, *Comhairle Mhic*

---

46 J. Carney (ed.), *Genealogical History of the O'Reillys* (Cavan: Cumann Sheanchuis Bhreifne, 1959).
47 T. Ó Donnchadha (ed.), *Leabhar Cloinne Aodha Buidhe* (Dublin: Oifig an tSoláthair, 1931).
48 MS G 167, National Library of Ireland (hereafter NLI).
49 MS E iv 3, RIA.
50 A. Harrison (ed.), 'Lucht na Simléirí', *Éigse*, 15 (1973–4), 189–202; Mac Mathúna, *Bearla sa Ghaeilge*, 143–7.

Clamha ó Achadh na Muilleann ('The advice of Mac Clave from Aughnamullen', c.1680) was an entertaining satire on uneducated Catholic clergy and laity who were frowned on by their continentally educated colleagues. Believed to be the work of a Tyrone priest, Eoghan Ó Donnghaile (1649–c.1724), the satire was not directed at those outside the Catholic Irish-speaking community and did not look to the past; it was introspective and present-centred.[51] Such satires are evidence of social distinctions within the Catholic community sufficiently obvious for the satire to have entertainment value. They drew inspiration from the linguistic complexity and social diversity of a partially bilingual society.

Far more hostile were English language texts such as *The Irish Hudibras: or Fingallian Prince*, a parody of Irish speakers in north County Dublin. Loosely modelled on Virgil's *Aeneid VI*, its publication in 1689, two decades after the texts it emulated were composed, reveals the cultural antagonism of the Williamite war era.[52] Language was still a signifier of difference in times of conflict and people's poor command of English was an easy target for the satirist. Contact across cultures could serve to reinforce negative stereotypes at times of crisis.

The prolific poet Dáibhí Ó Bruadair was outspoken in his hostility to the English language and all it represented. Having experienced the Cromwellian trauma in his youth, he was confronted late in life by the finality of defeat by the Williamite forces. He conveyed the impact of political events on Irish Catholics by highlighting his own decline in social status. In *An Longbhriseadh* ('The shipwreck') Ó Bruadair portrayed the 1690s in terms of unprecedented social breakdown that the Irish brought on themselves. As in the 1650s, a lack of discipline and lack of respect for the law were used to explain the social dislocation that accompanied defeat. Yet, neither Irish nor Catholic inferiority was conceded.[53] He was not alone in his despair and it has been noted that the perspective of this poem is precisely in accord with that of the anonymous author of *A Light to the Blind*, written in the years after 1691.[54]

---

51 S. Ó Dufaigh and B. E. Rainey, (ed. and trans.), *Comhairle Mhic Clamha ó Achadh na Muileann: The Advice of Mac Clave from Aughnamullen* (Presses Universitaires de Lille, 1981).

52 A. Carpenter, 'Literature in print, 1550–1800', in R. Gillespie and A. Hadfield (eds.), *The Oxford History of the Irish Book, III: The Irish Book in English* (Oxford University Press, 2006), 300–18 at 311.

53 Mac Erlean (ed. and trans.), *Duanaire Dháibhidh Uí Bhruadair*, iii, 164–81 at 180–1.

54 B. Ó Buachalla, *Aisling Ghéar* (Dublin: An Clóchomhar, 1996), 185; J. T. Gilbert (ed.), *A Jacobite Narrative of the War in Ireland, 1688–91* (Dublin: J. Dollard, 1892).

Literature in Irish, 1700–1730

The west Munster poet Aogán Ó Rathaille (*c*.1670–1729) struggled to contend with societal change that had undermined the profession of poetry. His *Eachtra Thaidhg Dhuibh Uí Chróinín* ('Adventure of Tadhg Dubh Cronin'), *c*. 1713, a late example of burlesque satire in Irish, is set in an Irish parliament of impolite characters who have benefited from the dispossession of other Irishmen. It ridicules a local tax collector and those who benefited from the confiscation of the Kenmare estate in County Kerry.[55] It has been observed, however, that Ó Rathaille's own ancestors may never have enjoyed the patronage of the MacCarthys or Brownes, and this aspect of Ó Rathaille's worldview was probably a fabrication.[56]

A particularly powerful lament, *Cabhair ní ghoirfead go gcuirtear me i gcruinn-chomhrainn* ('I will not cry for help till I am put into a narrow coffin'), reputedly written by Ó Rathaille on his deathbed, ranged far beyond his personal predicament to express grief at the losses suffered by his country and hereditary rulers in the Williamite wars.[57] The editors of his collected poetry commented that 'never were a nation's woes depicted with such vivid anguish and such passionate outbursts of grief' as in the work of Ó Rathaille. His literature 'ever appealing to the glories of the past, ever stinging with keen sarcasm those who attempted to supplant the rightful heirs of Irish soil, ever taunting the oppressor with his cruelty and treachery, kept alive in the Irish heart, to use the words of [Edmund] Burke, "even in servitude itself, the spirit of an exalted freedom"'.[58] As has been observed in a later context, 'the old victim culture … was also, in its way, a culture of superiority'.[59] An ardent supporter of the Stuarts as the rightful kings of Ireland, Ó Rathaille, together with fellow Munster poet Seán Clárach Mac Dónaill (1691–1754), practised the *aisling* genre of poetry in the early eighteenth century.[60] His poem on the prophecy of Donn Fírinne envisaged better times in the reign of James III:

> *Beidh Éire go súgach 's a dúnta go haerach,*
> *is Gaeilge dá scrúdadh 'na múraibh ag éigsibh,*

---

55 P. S. Dinneen and T. O'Donoghue (eds. and trans.), *Dánta Aodhagáin Uí Rathaille* (2nd edn., London: Irish Texts Society, 1911), 287–98.

56 B. Ó Buachalla (ed.), *Aogán Ó Rathaille* (Dublin: Field Day, 2007), 1 n.

57 Dinneen and O'Donoghue (eds. and trans.), *Dánta Aodhagáin Uí Rathaille*, poem 21.

58 Dinneen and O'Donoghue (eds. and trans.), *Dánta Aodhagáin Uí Rathaille*, xxxiv–xxxvi.

59 R. F. Foster, *The Irish Story* (London: Allen Lane, 2001), xv–xvi.

60 Ó Buachalla, *Aisling Ghéar*, 237–49.

Béarla na mbúr ndubh go cúthail fá néaltaibh,
is Séamas 'na chúirt ghil ag tabhairt cheana Ghaelaibh.[61]

('Erin will be joyful, and her strongholds will be merry; / And the learned
will cultivate Gaelic in their schools; / The language of the black boors will
be humbled and put beneath a cloud, And James in his bright court will show
favour to the Gaels.')

Typical themes of early eighteenth-century Irish political poetry were a sense
of loss of status but with a belief in a better future; a sense of entitlement
denied but about to be reasserted. Hope for a better future was lacking however, in Aogán Ó Rathaille's *Mac an cheannaí* ('The merchant's son'). A lament
for a young maiden (Ireland) whose last hope has gone, with the death of
an influential leader, variously identified as the duke of Berwick or the king
of Spain, it expressed bitterness over his personal circumstances, and despair
over the Jacobite cause. The coded political terminology implied a literary
audience who could understand the allusions.[62] These poems also reveal the
broader political interests of these local poets. Ó Rathaille spent his life in
Counties Cork and Kerry but commented on the death of a Spanish king;
Seán Clárach Mac Dónaill may never have left Counties Limerick and Cork
but was interested in the Austrian War of Succession.

External influences on Irish writing are clearly evident in *Párliament
na mBan*, a didactic prose work by a Catholic priest Domhnall Ó Colmáin
(*c.*1645–*c.*1704), which survives in two versions of 1697 and 1703. Ó Colmáin's
account of the first two sessions is heavily reliant on the 'parliament of
women' in Erasmus's *Colloquia Familaria*. Used for the moral education of
gentlemen, Erasmus's work circulated in Latin and in vernacular translation
throughout Western Europe in the seventeenth century. Ó Colmain's work
is an adaptation, not a faithful translation, and his later sections are more original. Working from Latin, Ó Colmáin may have had his pupil James Cotter
particularly in mind.[63] Multiple manuscript copies survive, the text proving
popular with the Ó Longáin scribes in Munster.

'Courts' of poetry probably existed in Munster from the late seventeenth
century, and were certainly a feature of the eighteenth century. The regular
gathering of poets at Carraig na bhFear in County Cork involved men such as

---

61 Ó Buachalla (ed.), *Aogán Ó Rathaille*, poem 10; translation adapted from Dinneen and
O'Donoghue (eds. and trans.), *Dánta Aodhagáin Uí Rathaille*, poem 28.
62 Ó Buachalla (ed.), *Aogán Ó Rathaille*, 4.
63 J. Stewart, 'Párliament na mBan', *Celtica*, 7 (1966), 135–41; B. Ó Cuív (ed.), *Párliament na
mBan* (Dublin Institute for Advanced Studies, 1952).

Diarmaid Mac Seáin Bhuí Mac Cárthaigh (c.1632–1705), Uilliam Mac Cairteáin an Dúna (c.1668–1724) and Eoghan Ó Caoimh (1656–1726).[64] Aside from the composition and scribal work they may have undertaken individually, their collective activities included gatherings involving performances and competitions. In north Connacht, the literary tradition was sustained by men like Tadhg Ó Rodaighe and Peadar Ó Maoil Chonaire, their area of influence extending over Counties Roscommon, Leitrim, Sligo, Cavan and Monaghan, while in south Ulster Séamas Dall Mac Cuarta (c.1647–1732) and Pádraig Mac a Liondáin (1665–1733) were among the most highly regarded poets in the early eighteenth century.[65]

In addition to these active circles in the provinces, a Dublin scribal circle, centred on Seán Ó Neachtain (c.1640–1729) and later his son Tadhg (c.1671–c.1749), significantly contributed to the transmission of older literary and historical sources. Seán Ó Neachtain's land in south Roscommon had been confiscated under Cromwell. After some years of uncertainty he settled in Dublin and worked as a teacher. His prose writings included *An Gleacaí Géaglonnach* ('The Fierce-limbed Wrestler'),[66] a romantic tale set in the world of a Greek emperor, *Imtheacht an Chúigir* ('The Wanderings of the Five'),[67] a pseudo-Ossianic tale, and works transcribed by Seán Mac Solaidh and other scribes. Seán Ó Neachtain's *Stair Éamuinn Uí Chléirigh* ('The Story of Eamonn O'Clery') was a significant literary achievement almost in the form of a novel. In a parody of the romance tales of the medieval tradition, his bilingual and bicultural puns and wordplay are reminiscent of the humour of Jonathan Swift. The influence of John Bunyan's *The Pilgrim's Progress* (1678) and *The Life and Death of Mr Badman* (1680) has been suggested.[68] In Ó Neachtain's

---

64 B. Ó Conchúir, 'Na Cúirteanna Éigse i gCúige Mumhan', in P. Riggs, B. Ó Conchúir and S. Ó Coileáin (eds.), *Saoi na hÉigse* (Dublin: An Clóchomhar, 2000), 55–81.

65 P. Ó Macháin, 'Tadhg Ó Rodaighe and his School: Aspects of Patronage and Poetic Practice at the Close of the Bardic Era', in S. Duffy (ed.), *Princes, Prelates and Poets in Medieval Ireland* (Dublin: FCP, 2013), 538–51; C. Dillon, 'An Ghaelig Nua: English, Irish and South Ulster Poets and Scribes in the Late Seventeenth and Eighteenth Centuries', in J. Kelly and C. Ó Murchaidh (eds.), *Irish and English: Essays on the Irish Linguistic and Cultural Frontier* (Dublin: FCP, 2012), 141–61.

66 MS G 197, NLI.

67 MS G 62, 177–372, NLI.

68 E. Ó Neachtain (ed.), *Stair Éamuinn Uí Chléire de réir Sheáin Uí Neachtain* (Dublin: Gill, 1918); 'Introduction', in W. Mahon (ed.), *The History of Éamonn O'Clery, Translated and Annotated with an Edition of the Irish Text* (Indreabhán: Cló Iar-Chonnacht, 2000), 3–29; C. Ó Háinle, 'The Novel Frustrated: Developments in 17th- to 19th-century Fiction in Irish', in C. Ó Háinle and D. Meek (eds.), *Unity in Diversity: Studies in Irish and Scottish Gaelic Language, Literature and History* (Dublin: Trinity College, School of Irish, 2004), 125–51; L. Mac Mathúna, 'Getting to Grips with Innovation and Genre Diversification in the Work of the Ó Neachtain Circle in Early Eighteenth-Century Dublin', *Eighteenth-Century Ireland*, 27 (2012), 53–83.

prose allegory, sometimes regarded as semi-autobiographical, the rogue-hero struggles with the demon drink but later recovers and sets up a school. In one episode he encounters a man who speaks unintelligible English. Farcical conversations ensue:

> *'But who is the husband of the woman that uses to be in the house?' ar Éamonn.*
> *'Mandark from two swan', ar eisean.*
> *'Arú, ar Éamonn, what is it in Irish?'*
> *'Feardorcha Ó Dála', ar eisean.*[69]

The phrase 'Mandark from two swan' is nonsense until the reader realises that it is a syllable-by-syllable translation of the name 'Fear-dorcha-Ó-Dá-[ea] la'.[70] For a bilingual audience, the effect is undoubtedly humorous, whether intentionally or not. At another level, however, the satire draws attention to the challenges of mutual comprehension between the two language groups, and the problems surrounding language choice, perhaps particularly for those who migrated to Dublin from rural areas. Those aware of broken English, and offended by it, must have been fluent themselves, and Seán Ó Neachtain and his son Tadhg were fully bilingual. Their bilingualism was a source of creativity, enabling them to experiment with new literary styles and perhaps to become opinion formers within their community.

Tadhg Ó Neachtain taught English, Latin and mathematics at his school in Dublin's Liberties. His research interests included lexicography and grammar. Tadhg also expended a great deal of effort from the late 1720s through to the late 1730s using material from the fourteenth-century Book of Ballymote, then on loan from Trinity College library, to reconstitute the 'Psalter of Tara', a supposed canonical work deemed an authoritative source for early Irish history.[71] Something of the family's wider interests, and presumably the curriculum in their school, is revealed in Ó Neachtain's geographical textbook, *Eolas ar an Domhan*, compiled c. 1721.[72] It drew on English works including Laurence Eachard's *A Most Compleat Compendium of Geography* (London, 1691) and Patrick Gordon's *Geography Anatomised* (London, 1708). It displayed a strong interest in contemporary European affairs. His guide to the buildings of Rome cited authorities such as Richard Lassels, *The Voyage of Italy ...* (Paris, 1670) and Iustus Lipsius, *Opuscula, quae Antiquitates Romanas Spectant,*

---

69 Ó Neachtain (ed.), *Stair Éamuinn Uí Chléire*, 31.

70 Mac Mathúna, *Béarla sa Ghaeilge*, 162–4.

71 His manuscript is MS 1289, Trinity College, Dublin; the Book of Ballymote is MS 23 P 12, RIA.

72 M. Ní Chléirigh (ed.), *Eólas ar an Domhan* (Dublin: Oifig an tSoláthair, 1944).

Selectissima (2 vols, Leiden, 1693), an indication of the range of reading materials available in Dublin.[73] The opening description of Ireland also reflected local Catholic concerns, referencing the religious persecution that had reduced them to *'na sclábhuithe d'éis a gcuid don tsaoghul do challeamh'* ('slaves after losing their worldly possessions').[74]

The Ó Neachtain scholarly circle, which included Risteard Tuibear, Seán Mac Solaidh, Aodh Buí Mac Cruitín, Maurice Newby, Anthony Raymond and perhaps twenty others, facilitated contact between manuscript owners and those who wanted copies. Their network allowed material to circulate beyond local provincial networks in ways not seen in earlier centuries, and often intermingling with the world of print.[75] Aodh Buí Mac Cruitín, a likely source of some of their manuscript exemplars, was a transitional figure from County Clare who spent some years in Dublin. Writing poetry in Irish but choosing English for his published writings, his work was rooted in Irish language sources. Some of his early poems were for O'Brien and O'Loghlen patrons in his native Clare and included elegies for the fourth and fifth Viscounts Clare, who had served as colonels in an Irish military regiment in France. His first printed book, *A Brief Discourse in Vindication of the Antiquity of Ireland* (1717), like his earlier historical poem *A Bhanba is feasach dham do scéala* ('Banba, I know your history'), owed much to Keating's *Foras Feasa* as well as *Tuireamh na hÉireann*, important expressions of the communal memory of Irish speakers.[76] Working as a translator for Dublin patrons, Mac Cruitín offered new audiences access to Irish language sources.

A cultural intermediary who found social acceptability in *élite* circles was Turlough Carolan (1670–1738), from a farming/blacksmithing background. Renowned as a travelling musician throughout west Ulster, north Leinster, Connacht and Clare, his patrons included the Burkes of Clanricarde and Glinsk, the Dillons and the Maguires. Leading Catholic landowners of County Roscommon – the O'Conors and MacDermott Roes – were regular patrons. Some 170 of his tunes for patrons survive.[77] His work reflected the fashion for Italian music in the big houses of Ireland and Antonio Vivaldi and

---

73 MS G 198, NLI; N. Ní Shéaghdha, *Catalogue of Irish Manuscripts in the National Library of Ireland*, V (Dublin Institute for Advanced Studies, 1979), 73.

74 Ní Chléirigh (ed.), *Eólas ar an Domhan*, 9.

75 L. Ní Mhunghaile, 'Scribal Networks and Manuscript Circulation in Meath during the Eighteenth and Early Nineteenth Centuries', *Ríocht na Midhe*, 22 (2011), 131–49.

76 V. Morley, *An Crann os Coill: Aodh Buí Mac Cruitín, c.1680–1755* (Dublin: Coiscéim, 1995), 44–6.

77 J. Trimble, 'Carolan and his Patrons in Fermanagh and Neighbouring Areas', *Clogher Record*, 10 (1979), 26–50.

Archangelo Corelli were leading influences.[78] Carolan is remembered as one whose music and songs brought joy and pleasure, in contrast to the gloom that permeated much of the literary writings of his contemporaries. Because of his connections with *élite* patrons, Carolan's work was in print well before that of contemporary poets who lamented the decline in patronage available to them.[79]

Print in Irish, 1630–1660

Such Catholic printing as was done in the Irish language in the mid-seventeenth century was published on continental Europe. Although printing in Irish was never proscribed, few books in Irish were published in Ireland before the nineteenth century. The Irish Franciscans at Louvain had led the way, printing catechisms and devotional works from 1611 onwards. They acquired a second font of Irish type (Louvain B) before 1641,[80] using it to print the Rule of St Francis, *Riaghuil Threas Uird S. Froinsias dá nGoirthear Ord na hAithrighe*, as translated by Bernard Conny, OFM.[81] Anthony Gearnon's *Parrthas an Anma* ('Paradise of the soul') (1645), used the original Louvain A type, as did John Dowley's *Suim Bhunudhasach an Teaguisg Chriosdaidhe* ('Basic summary of Christian doctrine',1663).[82] These printings were not sufficient to meet demand for catechisms and numerous manuscript copies of printed religious texts were made in the decades and centuries that followed. Gearnon's *Parrthas an Anma*, which served as a prayer book, was particularly popular.[83] Indeed the production of Irish-language prayer books was the stock-in-trade of later Irish scribes. Theological texts that had never been printed, such as Geoffrey Keating's *Trí Bhiorghaoithe an Bháis* ('Three Shafts of Death', c.1631) and *Eochar-Sgiath an Aifrinn* ('Key to the Defence of the Mass', c.1610), circulated in the same way with clergy prominent among the owners of such manuscripts.[84]

---

78 J. Rimmer, 'Patronage, Style and Structure in Music Attributed to Turlough Carolan', *Early Music*, 15 (1987), 164–74.
79 F. Ll. Harrison, 'Music, Poetry and Polity in the Age of Swift', *Eighteenth-Century Ireland*, 1 (1986), 37–63.
80 Undated letter, B. Jennings (ed.), *Louvain Papers, 1606–1827* (Dublin: Irish Manuscripts Commission, 1968), 143–5.
81 P. Ó Súilleabháin (ed.), *Rialachas San Froinsias* (Dublin Institute for Advanced Studies, 1953).
82 D. McGuinne, *Irish Type Design: A History of Printing Types in the Irish Character* (Dublin: Irish Academic Press, 1992), 32–5.
83 Antoin Gearnon, *Parrthas an Anma*, ed. A. Ó Fachtna (Dublin Institute for Advanced Studies, 1953), xvii–xviii.
84 B. Ó Conchúir, *Scríobhaithe Chorcaí, 1700–1850* (Dublin: An Clóchomhar, 1982), 33–6.

Print in Irish, 1660–1700

The locus of Catholic printing in Irish shifted to Rome in the later seventeenth century, but output was very limited. Francis Molloy's *Lochrann na gCreidmheach* (*Lucerna Fidelium*), modelled on earlier Franciscan catechisms, was printed there in 1676. Its Latin title page was token acknowledgement of the Sacred Congregation for the Doctrine of the Faith requirement that foreign works printed on their polyglot press should have a Latin translation.[85] Bonaventure Ó hEodhasa's catechism was reprinted in Rome in 1707 almost 100 years after it was first issued at Louvain, another indication of continuing demand for catechetical texts.

Publishing initiatives in Irish by representatives of the established church included the reprinting of the New Testament in Irish 1681 and the first printing of the Old Testament in Irish in 1685. Both bore London imprints. The linguistic context of these publications was recalled in a preface:

> notwithstanding all the wise statutes and endeavours used to bring this whole nation to a knowledge of the English tongue, experience shows it could not be affected, too many being unable to give such teaching to their children, or get it for themselves. And it is apparent that in Ireland there are many parishes, baronies and whole countries, in which the far greater number of the common people do understand no other language but Irish.[86]

As part of the same proselytising scheme Paul Higgins (*c*.1628–1724), a convert from Catholicism, was employed to teach Irish in Trinity College, Dublin, and to assist in the Old Testament publication project. In the following generation Charles Lynegar (Cathal Ó Luinín, *c*.1678–*c*.1732), a descendant of a hereditary learned family in Fermanagh, taught Irish there from 1708 until perhaps 1730. The provost and fellows hoped the strategy 'might prove a Means, by God's Blessing to convert the Irish Natives and bring them over to the Establish'd Church'.[87]

Print in Irish, 1700–1730

Among the most conscientious proponents of using Irish to advance Protestantism was John Richardson (1668/9–1747), a Trinity graduate

---

85 McGuinne, *Irish Type Design*, 37.
86 *Tiomna Nuadh ár dTighearna agus ár Slanuigheora Iosa Críosd* (London, 1681), Preface 'To the Christian People of Ireland'.
87 Cited in Ní Mhurchú and Breathnach, *1560–1781, Beathaisnéis*, 153.

whose *A Short History of the Attempts … to Convert the Popish Natives of Ireland* was published in 1712. Jonathan Swift complained in 1711, 'I am plagued with one Richardson, an Irish parson, and his project of printing Irish bibles to make you Christians in that country.'[88] Richardson published a book of five sermons in Irish at London in 1711 and in the following year, with the support of the Society for Promoting Christian Knowledge, 6,000 copies of his catechism in Irish were printed, along with a similar quantity of an Irish translation of the 1662 *Book of Common Prayer.* He had the support of William King (1650–1729), archbishop of Dublin, but others equated the language with disloyalty and remained uncomfortable with the concept of Irish-speaking Protestants.

Francis Hutchinson (1660–1739), bishop of Down and Connor, sponsored a bilingual catechism published at Belfast in 1722. Known as the Rathlin catechism, *The Church Catechism in Irish. With the English Placed over Against it in the Same Karakter …* employed the Irish dialect of Rathlin Island. In his bilingual *Irish Almanack* (Dublin, 1724) Hutchinson observed of the Catholic population: 'For my part, I have not the least hope of their losing their Language … If they were but good Christians, good Protestants and good Subjects, their speaking Irish would do no harm to any body.'[89]

While functional religious texts in Irish found their way into print, literary and historical works in Irish continued to circulate among a more restricted audience by means of scribal publication. The industriousness of scribes, combined with the limitations imposed by the low levels of literacy among the Irish-speaking population, may have worked against the commercial viability of printing in Irish. When Irish songs began to be printed for the benefit of readers of English in the 1720s, printers used approximate phonetic renderings of Irish words. Jonathan Swift's translation of the song *Pléaráca na Ruarcach* was given the title 'Plarakanororka' in print in Charles Coffey's ballad opera, *The Female Parson* (1730), having been first published in John and William Neal's *A Collection of the Most Celebrated Irish Tunes* (Dublin, *c*.1724). Turlough Carolan's 'Capten Magan' was similarly printed (anonymously) in the Neals' *Collection*, in the context of a contemporary fashion for ballad operas.

---

88 *Journal to Stella*, 2 April 1711, in Jonathan Swift, *Journal to Stella*, ed. H. Williams (2 vols., Oxford: Clarendon Press, 1948), i, 229.
89 Cited in N. Williams, *I bPrionta i Leabhar* (Dublin: An Clóchomhar: 1986), 126.

Conclusion

The lack of a sufficient market to sustain an Irish language print culture in this period had negative consequences for the status and reputation of Irish literature. Its place in the market was taken by imported works in English and occasionally in other languages. And when Irish speakers sought to reach a wider audience they opted for English or Latin, the economically viable languages of print, for their work. This commercial dimension, coming on top of other influences on language choice, not least the deliberately promoted image of English as the language of power and of Irish as the language of the oppressed – a view voiced most often by Irish speakers – undermined the growth of a viable print culture in the Irish language in the century after 1630.

When the *Memoirs of the Right Honourable Marquis of Clanricarde* was published at London in 1722, incorporating a remarkable preface on the Irish bards and ancient Irish history, it represented a deliberate blurring of the story of the Irish past. Appearing in a book with mainly non-Irish subscribers, the 'Dissertation' which prefaced Clanricarde's *Memoirs* discussed ancient Irish history and literature in the context of classical Greek learning. For the Anglo-Irish whose politics was underpinned by the idea of an ancient constitution, this was a necessary fudging of the question of whose past this was, and one that allowed aspects of Irish language scholarship to be seen in a favourable light. The heraldic plates customised for subscribers of Dermot O'Connor's 'Christian' rather than 'Catholic' translation of Keating's history served a similar purpose.[90] The precise nature of the Irish nation in the past was not scrutinised too closely; its antiquity and their place within it was what mattered to some readers of English in early eighteenth-century Ireland.

But print was not the whole story. Scribal publication continued apace in the century from 1630 to 1730, and was adequate for the circulation needs of many specialist works in Irish such as those customised for particular families or individual patrons. Script and print coexisted in a productive duality in early modern Ireland, each serving specific purposes. The Irish and English languages existed side by side, not in a culturally neutral way, but in a state of creative tension that proved stimulating for the writers and readers of literature in Irish from the seventeenth century onwards. The pragmatism and

---

90 T. Barnard, *Improving Ireland?* (Dublin: FCP, 2008), 103–8; Cunningham, *World of Geoffrey Keating*, 191.

opportunism that informed economic and social ambition ensured that language had ceased to be the predominant cultural identifier of the Catholic Irish before the end of the seventeenth century. The literary possibilities created by the bilingual world were explored by some, though the true extent of the audience that fully appreciated the linguistic nuances of their writings, whether prose social satire or political poem of despondency or hope, is not easily measured.

18

The Emergence of English Print and Literature, 1630–1730

DEANA RANKIN

Let Glad Hibernia Hail the Noble Art
That mends the Mind and cultivates the Heart!
New tune the Harp with permanence secure,
And charm inspiring Muses to thy Lure;
The Rare Machine let all her sons revere,
Nor doubt an Elzever and Stephen here;
While latest Times, Newton, Entire shall boast,
Nor Mourn an Addison, like Livy, lost!

Constantia Grierson's paean to the printer's art was distributed from the horse-drawn press of the Guild of St Luke the Evangelist as its members joined the lord mayor in his extravagant beating of the bounds of Dublin in 1728.[1] The moment offers a sharply focused snapshot of a confident local industry on the threshold of a new era of international expansion. It is well known that Jonathan Swift worked, across the 1720s, with several Dublin-based printers – Edward Waters, John and Sarah Harding, George Faulkner – both to support local production and to give lacerating voice to Irish griev-ances against the English colonial administration. The story of Swift's sub-sequent partnership with the maverick entrepreneur Faulkner: a threat both to the political dominance of the English colonial administration and to the commercial dominance of the London-based printing industry has also been well rehearsed.[2] But as Grierson's festive poem makes clear, and as this chapter will demonstrate, Swift was not the only author in town, and sat-ire was not the only mode in which Irish print operated at the time. The

---

1 Anon., *A Poem of the Art of Printing* [Dublin, 1728]. On attribution, see M. Pollard, *Dictionary of Members of the Dublin Book Trade 1550–1800* (Oxford University Press, 2000), xviii–xx.
2 R. Mahony, *Jonathan Swift: The Irish Identity* (New Haven and London: Yale University Press, 1995); J. MacLaverty, 'George Faulkner and Swift's Collected Works', in P. Bullard and J. MacLaverty (eds.), *Jonathan Swift and the Eighteenth-century Book* (Cambridge University Press, 2013), 154–75.

Swift–Faulkner partnership's monumental Dublin-produced *Works of J. S.*, a project very clearly designed to target both Irish and English markets, began to appear in 1735. But the conditions of possibility for this exceptional collaboration lay in the less well-known but nonetheless vibrant English-language print culture of early modern Ireland in the century or so before 1730.

Prehistories and Afterlives

Dublin's presses had for some time been poised to respond to important events, and Grierson's poem proudly attests to the fact that they already had access to the very latest in printing technologies – Elzevir type (l.6), for instance, later used for Swift's *Works*, first arrived in 1726.[3] Following the death of Sir Isaac Newton in 1727, Irish editions of his work swiftly followed, just as they had in 1719 on the death of Joseph Addison (ll.7–8).[4] All of this supplemented a healthy diet of Livy and the like (l.8): locally produced classical texts aimed principally at the lucrative schools and university market. This was the field in which Constantia and her husband George made themselves adept, with their success confirmed by the granting of the king's patent to the family business in 1732. But it is the foundation and growth of the print industry in Ireland *before* the lord mayor's parade – *before* Swift and *before* the Griersons – that is the principal subject of this chapter. It begins with an overview of the period, first establishing the broad contours of the essentially English colonial regulation which governs the early Irish print industry, then delineating the literary genres which shape the emergence of an English literature in Ireland. This introductory account is followed by three short chronologically ordered case studies, engaging in detail with individual printers and with literary texts. The chapter demonstrates that in spite of a colonial regulatory system designed to discourage expansion and diversity, the print industry in Ireland across this period bore witness to sustained, if slow and unsteady, growth. Crucial to this was harnessing the energies of successive generations of indigenous English-speaking writers and thinkers, intellectuals and artisans.

To trace the roots of the successes of the 1730s is to return to *c.*1618, when the London Stationers' Company first took an interest in the moribund state

---

3 J. W. Phillips, *Printing and Bookselling in Dublin, 1670–1800* (Dublin: Irish Academic Press, 1998), 215–16.

4 James Thomson, *A Poem Sacred to the Memory of Sir Isaac Newton* (Dublin, 1727); *The Chronology of Ancient Kingdoms Amended* (Dublin, 1728); Henry Pemberton, *A View of Sir Isaac Newton's Philosophy* (Dublin, 1728); *The Present State of Ireland* (Dublin, 1729) wryly commemorated Newton's part in the Wood's coinage scandal; Joseph Addison, *The Works of the Right Honourable Joseph Addison* (Dublin, 1722).

of Irish printing under the first official king's printer, John Franckton. If, as Vincent Kinane succinctly put it, '[p]rinting was a late arrival in Ireland', then so too was the establishment of the office of king's printer.[5] In London, in 1506, some thirty years after William Caxton printed the first book in England, Richard Pynson first styled himself 'regius impressor'. In 1540, some thirty years after the first Scottish press was established by Walter Chepman and Androw Myllar under royal charter, Thomas Davidson was appointed the first king's printer in Edinburgh.[6] It was not until 1551 that *The Boke of the Common Praier*, the first book to be printed in Ireland, was published; with it came a claim, articulated by one Humphrey Powell, who had moved from London to Dublin with the financial backing of the privy council, to be 'Printer to the Kynges Maiestie, in his Hyghnesse Realme of Ireland'.[7] The message of this Dublin edition, published just two years after the London original, seems clear: the arrival of print accompanies that of the Edwardian Protestant Reformation in Ireland, and the king's printer is an important cog in the machinery of the nascent English colonial administration. But in fact Powell had no royal charter, and London's support for a broader cultural remit for the Dublin press was lacking: between 1551 and 1567, he published little beyond government declarations, many of which are now lost.[8] The same was true of his successor, William Kearney, who styled himself the queen's printer from 1588 to *c*.1599. Even the establishment of Trinity College in 1592 had no immediate impact on the local printing industry: its scholars sourced the books for their substantial libraries from outside Ireland.[9] English-language writers in Ireland also bypassed the Dublin press: the works which twenty-first-century scholars now interpret as culturally rooted in early modern Ireland – those by Richard Stanihurst, Edmund Spenser, Lodowick Bryskett and Barnaby Rich, amongst others – were originally, carefully, transported to London for publication.

---

5 V. Kinane, *A Brief History of Printing and Publishing in Ireland* (Dublin: National Print Museum, 2002), 7.

6 R. Dickson and J. P. Edmund, *Annals of Scottish Printing* (Cambridge: Macmillan and Bowes, 1890), 1–27.

7 C. Lennon, 'The Print Trade, 1550–1700', in R. Gillespie and A Hadfield (eds.), *The History of the Book in Ireland: Volume iii: The Irish Book in English, 1550–1800* (Oxford University Press, 2006), 61–73.

8 See however Francis Edderman's lost *A Most Pithi and Plesant History Whear in is the Destrouction of Troye Gathered Togethere of all the Chyfeste Autores turned into Englyshe Myttere* (Dublin, *c*.1558), discussed in A. Carpenter (ed.), *Verse in English from Tudor and Stuart Ireland* (Cork University Press, 2003), 48.

9 E. Boran, 'The Libraries of Luke Challoner and James Ussher, 1595–1608', in H. Robinson-Hammerstein (ed.), *European Universities in the Age of Reformation and Counter-Reformation* (Dublin: Four Courts Press [hereafter FCP], 1998), 75–115.

It was not until 1604, some fifty years after Powell's publication of the *Boke of the Common Praier*, that Franckton was granted the first official king's printer patent for Ireland. In England, this patent applied only to government printing, leaving the Company of Stationers, who controlled the presses, free to encourage an expanding, competitive print market. In Ireland, however – as in Scotland – the right to print was vested solely in the king's printer, who was thus, as Franckton's patent makes plain, granted a wide-ranging personal monopoly: 'it shall not bee Lawfull for any to use or exercise that trade of printinge or of Stationers within this Realme during the Liffe of the sayd John, but such as the sayd John shall depute or assigne'.[10] In theory, these restrictions significantly shaped the emerging Irish print industry; the full monopoly held by the king's printer persisted from 1604 to 1732, passing through the hands of just five patentees before Grierson.[11] In practice – as this chapter demonstrates – there had been repeated challenges and disruptions to the official monopoly right across this turbulent century. Grierson's 1732 patent was the first granted in Ireland on the English model: restricted to cover government business only, it signalled the fact that the English authorities had finally, and formally, admitted to the existence of (and indeed sanctioned the demand for) a flourishing publishing industry in early modern Ireland.

Recent scholarship has taught us to identify a number of popular literary genres fuelling the local print market of the 1720s and 1730s: cheap imprints of canonical, popular English authors, some of which inspire a local response; colonial improvement literature; poetry, occasional and collected; historiography, and drama. More surprising, perhaps, is the fact that books in each of these five genres are already being printed in Ireland one hundred years earlier. It is the 1620s and 1630s that mark the first period of commercial experimentation in Irish print. But, as this chapter suggests, significant cultural differences accompany these generic similarities. If the 1720s saw printing dominated by a Protestant Ascendancy, experimenting with colonial nationalism, presses in the 1620s were engaged in the struggle whereby a previous generation of English rulers in Ireland – the Catholic Old English – competed for cultural recognition with their Protestant Old and New English rivals.

Franckton himself did not in fact extend his rights far beyond government printing, but he did begin to expand the import of English books for a growing Irish readership. This captive, potentially lucrative market

10 Carte MS 61, f. 174, Bodleian Library, Oxford, cited in M. Pollard, *Dublin's Trade in Books, 1550–1800* (Oxford: Clarendon Press, 1989), 4.
11 SP 63/392, The National Archives, cited in M. Pollard, *Dictionary of Members of the Dublin Book Trade 1550–1800* (Oxford Clarendon Press, 2000), 255.

attracted the attention of the London Stationers' Company, and in 1618 they took over the king's patent, granted for twenty years.[12] Producing the predictable array of government, legal and ecclesiastical publications, they also followed Franckton's lead, importing London books for Irish sale. Their own crucial innovation was to print, locally, literary works intended for sale both in Ireland and in England. The first of these was the fifth edition of *The Countesse of Pembrokes Arcadia. Written by Sir Philip Sidney Knight* (Dublin, 1621), whose 588 octavo pages made it by far the longest book to be printed to date in Dublin. It included a 'Supplement to a defect in the third book' composed by the Scottish poet William Alexander, earl of Stirling, in response to the Edinburgh *Arcadia* edition of 1599. This Scottish supplement, first printed in Dublin, prompted in turn a specifically Irish sequel. Three years later, Richard Bellings, an Old English writer who would later become secretary to and historian of the Catholic Confederation, published *A sixth booke to the Countesse of Pembrokes Arcadia* (Dublin, 1624), alongside his own poems. Bellings's *A sixth booke* – like Alexander's 'supplement' – was incorporated into all subsequent seventeenth-century editions of the *Arcadia*.[13] If Sidney's *Arcadia* furnishes both Scottish and Irish writers with the means to amplify their own voices in print, it also, clearly, provides colonial publishers with the first ever 'Dublin imprint': a reprint for London export and profit. While the 'Dublin imprint' is a device more associated with eighteenth-century accusations of piracy than with legitimate seventeenth-century stationers' business, Bellings's *A sixth booke* demonstrates the stimulating effect the 'imprint' could have on indigenous literary production. As Swift, wearing his home-spun draper's hat a century later would come to understand, colonial trade controls also had the (unintended) consequence of producing channels for – and voices of – resistance.

If cultural resistance found its way into print in the 1620s, so too did a zeal for quasi-scientific colonial improvement. T. C.' s *A short discourse of the New-found-land* (Dublin, 1623), might take the New World as it subject; it nonetheless speaks to the enthusiasm for colonial 'improvement' literature which appears in – and about – Ireland across the next century. The publication of Gerard and Arnold Boate's *Philosophia naturalis reformata* (Dublin,

---

12 R. J. Hunter, 'John Franckton' in C. Benson and S. Fitzpatrick (eds.), *That Woman!: Studies in Irish Bibliography. A festschrift for Mary 'Paul' Pollard* (Dublin: Lilliput Press, 2005), 1–26.

13 G. Alexander, *Writing after Sidney: The Literary Response to Sir Philip Sidney, 1586–1640* (Oxford University Press, 2006); D. Rankin, *Between Spenser and Swift: English Writing in Seventeenth-century Ireland* (Cambridge University Press, 2005), 191–229.

1641) signals an early Irish printing presence for the extended Hartlib circle.[14] In the mid-1650s, when the Cromwellian policy-maker Richard Lawrence and the long-term settler Vincent Gookin engaged in a pamphlet quarrel about the proposed transplantation of the Irish to Connaught, their war was waged mainly by way of the London presses. But one of the key texts in this quarrel, Lawrence's *The Interest of England in the Irish Transplantation Stated*, was published only in Dublin.[15] Years later, in 1682, when Lawrence, by now himself a long-term settler in Ireland, returned to the terms of the quarrel, his *The Interest of Ireland in its trade and wealth ... Stated* shifts its readers' 'Interest' from that of England to that '*of Ireland*'; Lawrence's new programme for the development of a successful colonial economy is published not in London, but in Dublin, with the city's new entrepreneurial printer, Joseph Ray. In time, Swift would transform such fiercely enthusiastic schemes for improvement into a vicious, satirical art form; his Irish drapers and child-eaters trade on a long publishing tradition.

It was in the 1630s that the first – and highly controversial – English versions of Irish history also began to emerge. Sir James Ware, who had been amassing a considerable manuscript library across the 1620s, presented his *Historie of Ireland* (Dublin, 1633) as an antiquarian collection of three Elizabethan accounts of Ireland. But in truth it was a timely sally in a conflict between historians across Europe. Speaking clearly to the moment of its publication, Ware's book promulgated an Old Protestant colonial version of English intervention in Ireland specifically calculated to counteract – if possible to silence – the accounts by Irish historians circulating in continental Europe. The battle for historiographical dominance, having entered the realm of print, raged across the period as well as across borders and continents.[16] Ware's *Historie* was itself revised and reprinted in 1705 and 1714, by which time it contributed to an animated revisiting of recent Irish history (explored below) conducted both within Ireland and further afield.

By the 1630s, the stationers' presses were also alive to the demand for literary works for the home market; the presence of both university-based and independent scholarship finally began to make its mark on local print

---

14 Gerard Boate, *Irelands Naturall History* (London, 1652); reprinted by Grierson, Dublin, 1726.
15 P. Coughlan, 'Counter-Currents in Colonial Discourse: The Political Thought of Vincent and Daniel Gookin', in J. Ohlmeyer (ed.), *Political Thought in Seventeenth-Century Ireland: Kingdom or Colony* (Cambridge University Press, 2000), 35–55; Rankin, *Between Spenser and Swift*, 61–74.
16 A. Hadfield, 'Historical Writing, 1550–1660' and B. Cunningham, 'Historical Writing, 1660–1750', in Gillespie and Hadfield (eds.), *History of the Irish Book*, 250–63; 264–81.

production, in poetry as well as in history. *Musarum lachrymae* (Dublin, 1630), the first dedicated volume of verse printed in Ireland, was published for Trinity College to mark the death of Catherine, countess of Cork. This substantial collection of elegies in Greek, Hebrew, Latin and English, designed to flatter her (surviving, still thriving) husband, the notoriously successful New English planter, Richard, earl of Cork, inaugurated a succession of commemorative poems, celebrating the lives, deaths and victories of the Protestant aristocracy in Ireland. As Andrew Carpenter's seminal research attests, these developments in print drew on a vibrant culture of private manuscript circulation to produce 'occasional' broadsheets and – increasingly after the Restoration – printed collections of verse.[17] *Poems by Severall Persons* (Dublin, 1663), for example, collects the work of the literary coterie connected to Dublin's Smock Alley theatre, including the celebrated translator and dramatist Katherine Philips.

The last few years of the 1630s witnessed the brief flourishing of dramatic writing and printing in Ireland. In 1637, a group of four London printers – John Crooke, his brother Edmund, Thomas Allot and Richard Sergier – established a bookshop in Dublin, apparently with the permission of those who held the king's patent. Over the next five years, they imported a large volume of books from London and operated a successful business. They were responsive to local markets, as the example of James Shirley, resident playwright at the Werburgh Street theatre, suggests. Although Shirley himself travelled to London to print his plays, the Crooke partnership first imported his London works for sale, then progressed to a 'Dublin imprint'. Copies of Shirley's *The Opportunitie* (Dublin, 1640) announce that they were produced 'In Dublin: Printed for Andrew Crooke, and are to be sold at the Castle gate in Dublin.'[18] This effective model for publishing and bookselling – exploiting the market strengths of both cities – clearly prefigures the joint enterprises which come into their own in the eighteenth century. It also did much to secure John Crooke's own local future: at the Restoration, he was awarded the king's patent for Ireland.

By 1640, then, an expanding Dublin publishing industry had established the collaborative structures necessary both to enforce and exploit the colonial mechanisms of print. It had also recognised the literary and commercial

---

17 A. Carpenter, 'Literature in Print, 1550–1800', in Gillespie and Hadfield (eds.), *History of the Irish Book*, 301–18.

18 A. Stevenson, 'Shirley's Publishers: The Partnership of Crooke and Crooke', *The Library*, 25 (1945), 140–61; R. Gillespie, *Reading Ireland: Print, Reading and Social Change in Early Modern Ireland* (Manchester University Press, 2005), 65–6.

worth of at least five significant genres: prose romance, improvement literature, colonial historiography, occasional verse and drama. These genres feature strongly in the emergence of English literature in an Irish public sphere
increasingly marked by the Protestant Ascendancy as the century progressed.
One should, however, be wary of constructing too triumphalist an account
of the development of an English colonial print industry in Ireland across this
period; for this is also a story about the disruptive, determining, and indeed
transformative effects of war across the three kingdoms.

Printers and Presses at War, 1641–1660

In 1641, the king's patent for Ireland expired. The London Company of
Stationers showed no interest in seeking its renewal; not only had they permitted the establishment of the Crooke partnership in 1637, they had also, in 1639,
sold their Irish stock – along with the rights to government printing – to their
Dublin agent William Bladen.[19] For the next twenty years Bladen styled himself,
without mandate, 'King's Printer'; in fact his allegiances would slip from king to
parliament and back again. This anomaly was the first of a series of disruptions,
occasioned by war or the rumour of war, to the hitherto tightly controlled
colonial print industry. For the first time, multiple printers and presses were
in operation in Ireland.[20] Attempts were made by all sides – Royalists, Catholic
Confederates, Parliamentarians – to use print not only as an index of authority,
but also as a propaganda weapon. The effects of this political plurality on book
production can be glimpsed in the work of two printers who operated the first
presses in Ireland outside Dublin: Thomas Bourke and Peter De Pienne.

In 1642, the Catholic Confederation established itself in Kilkenny as an alter-
native Royalist administration in Ireland; the increasingly Parliamentarian
New English sought to dominate in Dublin while the Old English Protestant,
James Butler, earl of Ormond and leader of his majesty's forces in Ireland,
sought to broker a series of peace treaties with the Confederation.[21] In
Waterford, one Thomas Bourke swiftly declared himself 'printer to the
Confederate Catholicks of Ireland' and operated there from 1643 to 1646,
when the arrival of the papal nuncio, Rinuccinni, shifted Confederate printing
to their capital, Kilkenny. Like Bladen in Dublin, Bourke's primary function

---

19 Pollard, *Dictionary*, 38.
20 W. Sessions, *The First Printers in Waterford, Cork and Kilkenny, pre-1700* (York: Ebor
    Press, 1990).
21 M. Ó Siochrú, *Confederate Ireland, 1642–1649: A Constitutional and Political Analysis*
    (Dublin: FCP, 1999).

was as a government printer. Thus for example, in Dublin, Bladen published Ormond's *Lawes and orders of warre. 1641:* 'printed by the Society of Stationers, printers to ths [*sic*] Kings most Excellent Majestie'; while in Waterford, an alternative version appeared for James Tuchet, earl of Castlehaven: *Lawes and orders of warre, M. DC. XLIII*, its title page announcing that it was 'Printed at Waterford by Thomas Bourke, Printer to the Confederate Catholicks.'

Given the remarkable interest across the three kingdoms in the so-called 'Irish rebellion' of 1641, we might expect Bladen to cash in on current affairs, to print local accounts for export, even to encourage a fledgling local newspaper industry, as others were doing in England. In fact, across the 1640s and 1650s, Dublin printing remained, in entrepreneurial terms, distinctly conservative. While Bladen did occasionally supply Irish news for English printers, on the home front he remained curiously unadventurous, producing very few items that stretched the boundaries of his limited patent.[22] Thomas Bourke had aspirations which went well beyond routine government business: he used his unrestricted access to print to increase the representation of Old English Catholic interests in this emerging, highly-charged public sphere. One of Bourke's earliest publications, *An argument delivered by Patrick Darcy, esquire by the expresse order of the House of Commons in the parliament of Ireland 9 junii 1641* (Waterford, 1643) sets the agenda. In 1641, Darcy's eloquent, stoutly legal, defence of the autonomy of the Irish parliament had articulated the firm alliance of England and Ireland from a Catholic Royalist perspective.[23] Bourke's 1643 printed version of Darcy's speech served both to restate and to legitimise the Royalist credentials of the Confederation, and a year later the publisher took the argument further, with his publication of P[atrick] C[omerford], *The Inquisition of a sermon preached in the cathedral church of the city of Waterford, in February 1617 … by Robert Daborne, Chancellor of the said Cathedral* (Waterford, 1644).

The complex trajectory of this sermon into print deserves some attention. First delivered in Waterford, *c.*1620, it originated as a response to the London publication of Robert Daborne's *A sermon preached in the cathedrall church of the citie of Waterford in Febr. 1617. before the Right Honorable the Lord President of Munster* (1618). Daborne, with both London readers and local congregation in mind, chastised the Waterford authorities for failing to prosecute local practising Catholics. Comerford's counter-blast offered a rigorous, eloquent defence

22 R. Munter, *The History of the Irish Newspaper, 1685–1760* (Cambridge University Press, 1967), 4–5.
23 A. Clarke, 'Patrick Darcy and the Constitutional Relationship between Ireland and England', in Ohlmeyer (ed.), *Political Thought* 35–55.

of the right of loyal Irish subjects to practise Catholicism. In further disseminating this defence, composed as it was by the man who had since become the local Catholic bishop, Bourke was restating a timely case.[24] Where Darcy's *Argument* legitimised the Confederation in legal, secular terms, Comerford's *Sermon* robustly defended its Catholic foundations. Taking up the standard in turn, Bourke articulates, in the remarkable printer's address which prefaces the sermon, his own ambitions for Confederate print. First, he identified the prevailing English restrictions on Irish Catholic learning and publishing:

> it was contrived & plotted, that they should be debarred & hindred, not only from the ways of achiving to learning and literature, but also deprived of all means to publish their learning, which by much toyle and study they acquired in foraine countries.

He then declared his intention to correct these past wrongs: in the battle for hearts and minds, pen and print proved to be valuable weapons in the Confederate arsenal:

> As Soldiers with Swords, Pikes, and Guns doe fight for the restitution, and defence of that onely true Religion, soe it is meet and expedient that the Pen and the Print bestirre themselves also for so worthy a cause.

Although Ireland's presses are dominated by the business of war, they (and Bourke with them) nonetheless make room for the production of original literary writing. All but one of these literary works originated from presses outside Dublin. The noteworthy exception was Henry Burnell's *Landgartha* (Dublin, 1641), a publication which wore its Dublin origins and imprint proudly.[25] Performed just once, on St Patrick's Day, 1640, in Dublin's Werburgh Street theatre, *Landgartha* is the first play by an Irish-born writer to be staged at the first Irish theatre. Published the following year, *Landgartha* survives as a potent piece of allegorical dramatic argument, challenging Charles I to both recognise and value the loyalty of his Irish Catholic subjects. The prefatory material in particular, with its unique Irish example of women's Latin verse, composed by Burnell's daughter, Eleanora, gave voice to a small but engaged Old English literary circle then operating in Dublin. But within the year, by

---

24 A. Ford, '"Firm Catholics" or "Loyal Subjects"?: Religious and Political Allegiance in Early Seventeenth-century Ireland', in D. G. Boyce, R. Eccleshall and V. Geoghegan (eds.), *Political Discourse in Seventeenth- and Eighteenth-century Ireland* (Basingstoke: Palgrave, 2001), 1–32. Bourke also prints Walter Enos, *Alexipharmacon, or A Soveraigne Antidote against a Virulent Cordiall* (Waterford, 1644), a further Catholic response to Protestant attack.

25 Henry Burnell, *Landgartha, a Tragi-comedy*, ed. D. Rankin (Dublin: FCP, 2014).

the time *Landgartha* appeared, the Old English dream of access to power and governance as part of a Dublin administration had disappeared: the publication of this tragi-comic romance is an anomaly among laws and orders of war and reports of rebellion. A Dublin imprint, and a 'first' on several further counts, *Landgartha* was also a remnant of past civility.

The other plays of the 1640s trace the Confederation's movement across Ireland. *Titus; or The palme of Christian courage* (Waterford, 1644), one of Bourke's last publications, anticipates a performance due to take place in the confederate capital: *'to be exhibited by the schollars of the Society of Iesus, at Kilkenny'*. Drawn from the history of the Jesuit mission in Japan, the anonymous fragment of *Titus* reaffirms Bourke's sense of the vital role of religion in Confederate politics and prefigures the imagined effect of the arrival of the papal nuncio, Rinuccini, on the Irish campaigns.[26] One such effect was that, in 1646, the Waterford press fell silent for a time; Confederate printing shifted to Kilkenny, and Bourke – apart from one mention on a Kilkenny broadsheet – disappeared from the printing scene, making way for printers drawn from 'foraine countries'.[27] It is unclear whether Rinuccini brought the Kilkenny press with him from France or requisitioned pre-existing Jesuit machinery. Either way, the Jesuit George Sarrazin, later in charge of the Evora press, in Portugal, operated in Kilkenny until shortly before the nuncio's departure from Ireland in February 1649. Sarrazin produces, anonymously, government business, predominately the fiery toings and froings of testy peace negotiations, including publications around the nuncio's final desperate excommunication of those Confederates who supported the 1646 Ormond peace. Bourke's earlier aspiration to create an Irish Catholic library able to represent the wealth of 'learning and literature' acquired by 'much toyle and study' abroad is eclipsed by the immediate, intensely local demands of war.

Henry Burkhead's *Cola's Furie or Lirenda's Miserie* (Kilkenny, 1646), voices the martial preoccupations of the Confederate's early years.[28] The complexities of family tribal allegiance and ethnic division are here transposed into a morality play: a furious Cola (Sir Charles Coote) leads the Angoleans (English Protestants) in a ruthless campaign to crush the righteous Lirendans (Irish) led by Abner (Thomas Preston). No record survives of any performance of

---

26 J. Kerrigan, *Archipelagic English: Literature, History and Politics, 1603–1707* (Oxford University Press, 2008), 188–94.

27 *By the Supreame Councell of the Confederat Catholicks of Ireland, Printed at Kilkenny by Thomas Bourke … 1648.*

28 P. Coughlan, 'Introduction', in Henry Burkhead, *A Tragedy of Cola's Furie or Lirenda's Miserie*, ed. A. Lynch (Dublin: FCP, 2009), 9–32.

this play. Neither retrospective commemoration, nor prospective anticipation, it is kin to the Parliamentary and Royalist dialogues produced in England: designed to be read aloud as propaganda-entertainment. These texts, however few in number, mark a significant shift in the voice of English literature in print in Ireland: Old English Catholic writing persists in three plays printed in the 1640s but then disappears – or rather retreats into manuscript circulation – with the defeat of the Confederation; and when in the 1650s, a New English Protestant literature begins to emerge in print, it is not a drama, but a historical romance: Roger Boyle's *Parthenissa*, the first volume of which appears in Waterford in 1651, printed (albeit anonymously) by one Peter De Pienne.[29]

If Bourke stands for the printer of intellectual, spiritual and political conviction then De Pienne, his mysterious successor at the Waterford press, is his opposite. All that is known about him is his name, one which suggests that he is an 'outsider', a wandering printer without provenance who somehow ends up in Ireland. His brief Irish printing career nonetheless demonstrates the extraordinary possibilities of that position. Between 1647 and 1651, De Pienne served a series of demanding masters and produced a sparse but remarkably diverse portfolio of Irish print. In 1647, he seemed to be pursuing Bourke's aspirations for the Waterford press, there printing a volume of saints' lives, '*Englished … for the publicque good*' from a recent Latin volume by the Donegal-born, exiled Irish Catholic intellectual, John Colgan.[30] Both De Pienne and the press then moved to Cork, where he became the first printer to operate in that city, publishing, in the wake of Charles I's execution in January 1649, a Cork imprint of John Gauden's international best-seller, *Eikon Basilike*. A publication carefully positioned to support Ormond's intense propaganda campaign to establish Ireland as the last bastion of Royalism within the three kingdoms, it could not avert the coming Cromwellian campaigns.[31] If De Pienne's publication record had, up to this point, been soundly Confederate-Royalist, his next print venture broke the mould. With the ink barely dry on the spiritual reflections of the murdered monarch, De Pienne moved the press

29 C. W. Miller, 'A Bibliographical Study of *Parthenissa* by Roger Boyle Earl of Orrery', *Studies in Bibliography*, 2 (1949–1950), 115–37.

30 John Colgan, *The Lives of the Glorious St David … of Wales … also of Saint Kieran the first-borne saint of Ireland* (Waterford, 1647). Colgan's *Acta Sanctorum … Hiberniae* (Louvain, 1645) was the only one of his projected eight volumes to be published.

31 *Articles of Peace Made, Concluded, Accorded and Agreed Upon, by and between His Excellency Iames Lord Marques of Ormonde, … on the Behalfe of His Most Excellent Majesty* (Cork, 1648); *By the King a Proclamation Declaringe James Marques of Ormond to be… Governour of the Kingdome of Ireland* (Kilkenny, 1649), both printed by William Smith.

back to Waterford, where, in 1651, he published not only (as noted) Boyle's *Parthenissa*, but also a detailed, spirited account of the legality of Charles I's trial and execution, composed by John Cook, leading lawyer for the prosecution and now Cromwell's newly-appointed chief justice of Munster.[32] In 1652, a second Waterford edition of Cook's treatise appears. A commemorative volume following the premature death of Henry Ireton, Cromwell's lord deputy in Ireland, it also evinces metropolitan aspirations. '[T]o be sold at London by Thomas Brewster at the three Bibles in Pauls Church-yard', this version of *Monarchy no Creature* advertises the successes of the Cromwellian campaigns; yet it also reveals, with its mourning for Ireton, their unanticipated dangers.[33]

De Pienne's identity may be a mystery, but his career is instructive. For in a competitive, metropolitan and free-trade print market, the manner in which his work slides across the political spectrum might be unremarkable: a skilled artisan and journeyman, he takes work where it arises. In mid-seventeenth century Ireland, however, his exceptional case proves the rules of the game. While other printers operated within the dominant colonial structures of the Irish industry, De Pienne demonstrates that it is possible to work – for a brief period at least – betwixt and between. Richard Lawrence reportedly confiscated his press after the unauthorised publication of *An Act for the Setling of Ireland* (Waterford, 1652); it then returned to Cork at some point in the 1650s, where it was operated by William Smith, formerly printer for Ormond.[34] Smith's tenure occasioned further redrawing of the boundaries: as John Cook was arrested and sent to London to be tried, and eventually executed, as a regicide, Smith published a commemorative Cork reprint of John Dauncey's *History of His sacred Majesty Charles the II King of England, Scotland, France & Ireland* (Dublin, 1660), first published in London earlier that year. The colonial order of publishing in Ireland was restored.

Restoration and Proliferation, 1661–1700

The Restoration of Charles II also marked the return of the full monopoly of the king's patent for Irish printing and a re-centralisation of print in

---

32 John Cook, *Monarchy no Creature of Gods Making, & c. Wherein is Proved by Scripture and Reason, that Monarchicall Government is Against the Minde of God* (Waterford, 1651). Cook had been admitted to King's Inns, Dublin in 1634.

33 De Pienne probably also published two 1650 accounts of the Cooks' storm-ridden voyage to Kinsale: *A True Relation of Mr. Iohn Cook's Passage* and *Mris: Cooke's Meditations … Composed by Herselfe at her Unexpected Safe Arrival at Corcke*, both 'Printed at Cork, and re-printed at London', then sold by Thomas Brewster.

34 Sessions, *First Printers*, 23.

Dublin. Only the Cork press survived beyond 1660, producing one or two items each decade for the rest of the century, while a second regional press began operating only much later, in 1694, in Belfast.[35] The patent was granted, not to Bladen, but to John Crooke, sole survivor of the bookselling partnership active in Dublin in the late 1630s. His press (re-)opened for business in 1661 with a suitably grand *Panegyrick* celebrating another restoration: the reappointment of Ormond as lord lieutenant of Ireland.[36] The Crooke dynasty kept hold of the king's patent until Grierson's accession in 1732.

It is tempting to see the award of the patent to Crooke as evidence for the eclipse of the Confederate and Republican era: printing restored to its tightly controlled pre-war state. In practice, however, it proved difficult to reverse the printing freedoms of the past twenty years, and the expansion of the industry has as much to do with an increasingly demanding home readership for English print as it does with attempts at centralising control of the means of production. The conditions for competition were such that Bladen could reasonably petition to be reinstated to the patent, deploring Crooke's 'monopolie of printing and booke selling to the destruction of those trades'.[37] Bladen traded successfully until his death in 1663; his son then took over the press and continued to print for a further decade. In 1670 the Guild of St Luke was established in Dublin bringing together a group of disparate trades into one substantial guild: the founding membership of nineteen in 1670 rose to ninety-three by 1700. The Guild served to focus resistance to Crooke's patent; indeed its charter, following the London Stationers' model, explicitly vested the rights of the Dublin book trade in its stationer citizens.[38]

In 1673, Mary Crooke, operating from London, and with the support of the colonial establishment, succeeded in having the Bladen press dismantled; the arrival of Joseph Ray's new press in Dublin in 1680, however, posed a more serious threat to the dynasty. When Crooke complained about the interloper, Ray responded that there were 'of late more Books wanting in this Kingdome than the complainants have bin able to print'.[39] His defiance might have been inspired by recent protests against press monopoly in Scotland; in that case,

35 Glaswegian printers Patrick Neill and James Blow established the press at the mayor's request; see J. Anderson, *Catalogue of Early Belfast Printed Books, 1694–1830* (new edn. with two supplements, Belfast: McCaw, Stevenson and Orr, 1890–1902).

36 F[rancis] S[ynge], *A Panegyricke on the Most Auspicious and Long-Wish'd-For Return of the Great Example of the Greatest Virtue, the Faithful Achates of our Royal Charles, and the Tutelar Angel (as we Justly Hope) of our Church and State, the Most Illustrious James Duke, Marquess, and Earl of Ormond* (Dublin, [1661]).

37 Pollard, *Dublin's Trade*, 5.

38 Pollard, *Dictionary*, ix–xxxiv.

39 Pollard, *Dictionary*, 480.

James, then duke of York, recently appointed king's high commissioner for Scotland, had intervened to restrict the Scottish patent to government printing only.[40] No such public ruling was forthcoming in Ireland, so Ray simply continued to print. That he did so with the Guild's tacit support is evidenced by his being named, in 1681, printer to the city of Dublin. When, in 1685, Ray formally protested against plans to grant the unchanged full monopoly to Mary's son, Andrew, the Guild publicly backed him. However, James II's succession to the throne interrupted the discussions; the possibility of radical change to the terms of the patent was again lost. Eventually granted in 1693, that is to say in the aftermath of the wars of 1689–1691, the new king's patent awarded Andrew Crooke exactly the same exclusive monopoly as Franckton had been granted back in 1604.

On paper, this represented yet another draconian reassertion of English colonial control of the terms of Irish print. In fact, the patent was interpreted to allow a degree of locally flourishing diversity, provided Protestant Ascendancy interests prevailed. Ray continued not only to print but also to expand his book-selling business until his death in 1709. The lapse of the English Licensing Act in 1695, the last obstacle to a free-trade press in Ireland – as elsewhere in the three kingdoms – signalled the need for a re-alignment of the interests of king's printer, city and guild. In 1696, Crooke was admitted to the Guild of St Luke in a silent accommodation of mutual commercial interests. By 1700, at least six printing presses operated in Dublin.

The Crooke dynasty exemplifies the new rules – and renewed possibilities – for the printing of literature written in Ireland across the later decades of the century. In the 1660s John Crooke, inspired by the new Smock Alley theatre, returned to his 1630s experiments, printing Dublin imprints of plays. Now the official king's printer, he collaborated with the local enterprising bookseller, Samuel Dancer. Katherine Philips's *Pompey*, a translation of Pierre Corneille's *La Mort de Pompée*, and the first Restoration tragi-comedy by a woman to be staged in the three kingdoms, was subsequently published in both cities: 'London: printed for John Crooke, at the sign of the Ship in St Paul's Churchyard, 1663; and Dublin, printed by John Crooke… for Samuel Dancer…1663'. This at once theatrical and editorial event gathered together those who had been enemies in the 1640 and 1650s; an impressive coterie of Irish nobility, including Ormond and Orrery, promoted the image of an Irish *élite* united in their eagerness both to assert their loyalty to the monarch, and to represent Dublin's cultural aspirations after a generation of war. The

---

40 James Watson, *The History of the Art of Printing* (Edinburgh, 1713), 14.

Crooke-Dancer partnership was at the heart of this reinvention of post-Restoration Ireland as a worthy, loyal sister-kingdom. Following the publishing success of *Pompey*, the two men further signalled and celebrated Ireland's vibrant cultural life with their 1663 publication of *Poems by Severall Persons* (including the usually reticent Philips): the first commercial collection of poems published in Ireland.

The final decades of the seventeenth century saw the conditions for the proliferation of print in eighteenth-century Ireland firmly established. In retrospect, these conditions privileged Protestant Ascendancy interests to the exclusion of all others. By the century's close Irish Catholics, always marginalised, had been explicitly and actively excluded from the trade: in spite of the securities promised by the 1691 Treaty of Limerick, guild membership – like membership of parliament – required the Oath of Allegiance. But it is important to recognise that this retrenchment of English Protestant power followed the brief period of comparative freedom that Catholic book-traders enjoyed under James II. The career of James Malone, as glimpsed through guild archives and his surviving publications, is illuminating here. An established bookseller, Malone entered the Guild in 1672, 'freed of City by fines and special Grace', the only terms on which Catholics could be members at the time.[41] His business, importing and selling books, fared well; the accession of James II in 1685 and the appointment of former Confederate Richard Talbot, earl of Tyrconnell, as his lord deputy in Ireland opened up exciting new prospects. In 1687, Malone was made an alderman. He served in Talbot's army and, in 1690, shortly after James arrived in Ireland, he was awarded, along with Richard Malone (possibly his son), the patent for king's printer. Having no press of his own, Malone commandeered that of Ray, while Crooke continued to print for the 'other' king, William III.[42] Malone's patent was short-lived: the English Short Title Catalogue nonetheless lists twenty-five publications for 1689–90 'printed for alderman James Malone bookseller in Skinner-Row, and printer to the King's most excellent Majesty'. Most are official proclamations or battle reports, but worthy of further note are two examples of early Irish newspaper publishing: one copy of the *Dublin Gazette* survives from March 1690. One copy also remains of an intriguing broadsheet entitled *The abhorrence, or, Protestant observations in Dublin, upon the principles and practices of the Protestants at London* (Dublin, 1689). Purporting (like the

---

41 Pollard, *Dublin's Trade*, 167.
42 On William III's travelling printer Edward Jones, see W. Sessions, *Further Irish Studies in Early Printing History* (York: Ebor, 1994).

Gazette) to be a weekly newspaper, *The abhorrence* gradually reveals itself to be an elaborate hoax, an anti-Williamite sally on London from Dublin, the last paragraph declaring: 'This Paper shall *Weekly* demonstrate our *Loyalty* to the King, whom you have most barbarously *Abdicated* [...] And we will Now begin, to set ourselves heartily to do *His Majesty Right*, against your Invasion, in order to send the War home to you who so Wickedly began it.' It goes beyond the documentary prose of government business to experiment with a satire which anticipates that of Swift's Irish pamphlets: lest we should fall into its trap, a later reader helpfully added a manuscript warning: 'A popish thing under ye maske of a Church of England man.'

Under the new Williamite rule of 1691, we might expect Malone to be ousted from the Guild in disgrace. In fact no action is taken against him until 1696 when – perhaps spurred by the Jacobite assassination attempt on William – the Guild requests that Malone be disenfranchised, both for his behaviour under James, and because he was 'at this time the principal pro-moter and seller of Popish books'. His demotion certainly did not end his career. Over the next twenty years or so, Malone's name was sporadically linked to publishing scandals in the city: in 1698 he was listed as sales-partner for an unlicensed New Testament printed by the entrepreneur Thomas Somervell, prompting the latter to protest that he 'never Intended nor never will print or Cause to be printed any Popish bookes'; and in 1703 Malone was prosecuted for his seditious imprint of *The Memoirs of King James* (London, 1702). It is clear that, in spite of his role in the 'late troubles', Malone con-tinued to trade as a bookseller, specialising in schoolbooks, until 1718, when he retired and sold his stock.[43] He remains the only Catholic ever to hold the title of king's printer in Ireland.

Malone's example is particular and, by the 1690s, was already distinctly anomalous: Williamite Ireland was a very different place from the Jacobite kingdom. Protestant control of the presses had been further consolidated in a newly competitive print industry and the literary voice of the Irish patriot was being slowly forged. It seems entirely appropriate that at this moment Jonathan Swift publishes – albeit anonymously – his first poem: *Ode. To the KING on his Irish Expedition* (Dublin, 1691). Announcing with pride that it was 'presented to the King on his departure from Ireland', the broadsheet cele-brates William's victory. But it also has a dig at first the Scots, then the English and finally 'The *Giddy Brittish Populace*/The Usurping Robbers of our *Peace*'.

---

43 Luke Dowling, *A Catalogue of a Choice Collection of Books being what Remain'd Unsold in a Late Auction* (Dublin, 1720).

That 'giddy'-ness finds echo in the 'Usurper' himself as he describes James's fate in the closing lines: 'Giddy he grows, and down is hurl'd/... Falls sick in the *Posteriors* of the World.'

The playful, scatological tone of Swift's later Irish literary voice is clearly recognisable here. But to find the hard-hitting, legal and political rhetoric which will come to structure Swift's mature Irish writing in the 1720s, we must look elsewhere. It was being forged not in occasional poetry, but in parliamentary debate. The Irish parliament found itself once again preoccupied with the question of Poynings' Law, the right of England to legislate in Ireland. The new Anglo-Protestant composition of the parliament led to a sustained defence of the right to self-govern; a view compellingly articulated by the Trinity philosopher and friend of John Locke, William Molyneux. Dedicated to William III, his *Case of Ireland's being Bound by Acts of Parliament in England ... Stated* (Dublin, 1698) articulated, by way of Irish legal and historical precedent, the right of Irishmen to be equal to Englishmen. A seminal work, it would structure and inform Irish political thought across the eighteenth century and beyond, with numerous reprints echoing its clarion call: 'That Ireland should be bound by acts of parliament made in England is against reason and the common rights of all mankind.'[44] Molyneux's eloquent fusion of legal discourse with a Lockean notion of government of equals by consent harkens back, in both style and substance, to Patrick Darcy's much earlier *Argument* published by Bourke in Waterford in 1643. Molyneux's constituency, however, was radically different: his idea of equality applied to enfranchised Protestants only.

New Markets, New Voices, 1700–1730

If the development of Irish presses across the seventeenth century had been restricted by colonial legislation and prone to the disruptions of war, then the eighteenth century was set to emerge as a golden age of printing in Ireland. As the century dawned, many of the conditions essential for the next wave of expansion were in place: the king's printer monopoly had been effectively fractured by the proliferation of presses in Dublin and the first regional presses in Belfast and Cork; new freedoms had followed the lapse of the Licensing Act in 1695; successful commercial collaborations were evolving

---

44 P. Kelly, 'Recasting a Tradition: William Molyneux and the Sources of *The Case of Ireland ... Stated* (1698)', in Ohlmeyer (ed.) *Political Thought*, 83–106. Reprints appeared in Dublin, 1706, 1719, 1725, 1749, 1773 and 1782; Belfast, 1776 and London, 1720 and 1770.

between printers and sellers within an increasingly sophisticated trade net-work; moreover the customer base – the educated English-reading middle class – was expanding across the country. Finally, and crucially, Ireland was about to enter a prolonged period of peace and relative political stability; there was, for the first time in decades, opportunity for sustained cultural and political self-reflection.

The first decade of the eighteenth century also witnessed two important changes in legislation which shaped the future of the Irish print industry: the 1707 Act of Union between England and Scotland; and the 1709 Copyright Act which applied only to the union, therefore not to Ireland. The snub occasioned by the Act of Union was keenly felt: it prompted Swift, for instance, to write – but not to publish – *The Story of the Injur'd Lady*, a terse allegory in which loyal Protestant Ireland is figured as the woman jilted at the altar for another, more attractive lover.[45] The Copyright Act offered some consolation: while their English and Scottish counterparts had to pay to protect their authors, all Irish presses were now at liberty to reproduce, sell locally and even export cheap imprints without penalty. The cheap Dublin imprint, pioneered by the London Stationers in their 1621 edition of Sidney's *Arcadia*, would thus become the publishing staple in Dublin. On the negative side, however, the fact that the Copyright Act did not extend to Ireland meant that many Irish writers sought the legal protection which came with a London imprint, rather than publish closer to home. The most popular and successful writers – Swift foremost among them – would work with both English and Irish printers, exploiting both markets to their advantage.[46]

The Act of Union had profound implications for the political and social status of Ireland: the seventeenth-century 'three kingdoms' model, always fraught with colonial anxiety, now seemed obsolete. The conflicts concerning the Hanoverian/Jacobite succession that raged in England, and which Irish readers learned of in a growing number of locally produced newspapers, propelled century-old questions of allegiance into the present. Molyneux was far from alone in retrospectively identifying the mid-seventeenth century wars as the source of an increasingly Whiggish colonial attitude towards England's erstwhile sister-kingdom; his *Case of Ireland … Stated* grew ever more pertinent. Its claims for Irish legislative autonomy became urgent when the English parliament passed the Declaratory Act of 1720, thereby asserting both the

---

45 This was not published until 1746.
46 I. Gadd, 'Leaving the Printer to his Liberty: Swift and the London Book Trade, 1701–1714', in Bullard and MacLaverty (eds.), *Jonathan Swift*, 51–65.

London parliament's right to pass laws for Ireland and that of the House of Lords in Westminster to intervene in Irish court decisions.

The pens of Swift and others sprang to defend the national interest: Molyneux's *Case* was immediately reprinted cheaply, without print provenance, and circulated widely; Swift, anonymous in print though well known in his St Patrick's pulpit, stepped up to engage in a series of pamphlet wars which would, over the next decade, make his Irish reputation. The first of his 'proposals', penned by an array of patriot-personae, appeared in 1720: *A Proposal for the Universal Use of Irish Manufacture in cloathes and furniture of houses & c*. The printer, Edward Waters, refusing to name Swift as author, was summoned before the grand jury, where a sympathetic judge intervened to prevent sentence. But Swift's inventive campaigns continued to put his printers in danger: John Harding, publisher of the *Drapier's Letters* (1724–25), spent time in prison, then died shortly after release. His widow, Sarah, later published the 1728 pamphlets *A Short view of the State of Ireland* and *An Answer to a Paper Called, A Memorial of the poor... of Ireland* at great risk and for little profit. She also takes credit for the publication of *A Modest Proposal* (1729), the first of Swift's Irish tracts to be printed both in Dublin and in London. Indeed this proposal's rough and ready urgency was worn proudly on its title page as a sign of Irish authenticity: 'Dublin: Printed by S. Hardinge: London, Reprinted; and sold by J. Roberts.'

Reprints of influential seventeenth-century publications concerning Ireland's relationship with England such as those of Davies, Ware and Temple continued to appear across the early eighteenth century.[47] More significant still was the publication of two competing versions of Irish history, each of which had been circulating in manuscript for some time: Edward Hyde, earl of Clarendon's *The History of the rebellion and civil wars in Ireland* (1720), and Geoffrey Keating's 'Foras Feasa ar Éirinn', published as *The General History of Ireland* in 1723. As Bernadette Cunningham has expertly demonstrated, Keating's manuscript had exercised a formative influence on Irish history writing of all political persuasions since it emerged in *c*.1634. Its first appearance in print was eagerly anticipated; the subscription list indicates strong support for the project from both disenfranchised Irish Catholics and the

---

47 Sir John Davies, *Historical Relations or A Discovery of the True Causes why Ireland was Never Entirely Subdued*, and Sir James Ware, *The Antiquities and History of Ireland*, both 1704; Sir John Temple, *The Irish Rebellion* 1714, 1716, 1724.

growing number of Protestant patriots with an at once antiquarian and political interest in Ireland's 'Gaelic' past.[48]

Less critical attention has been paid to the earlier publication in both London and Dublin of Clarendon's *History of the ... civil wars in Ireland* (1720). Clarendon's *History of the rebellion and civil wars in England* had been in print since 1702–1704. Edited and published posthumously in Oxford by Clarendon's son, its moderate Royalist account of the past chimed well with contemporary English Tory sensibilities. Regular reprints of the Oxford volumes followed across the next fifteen years and the first Dublin imprint of the English *History*, 'printed for John Hyde and Robert Owen Booksellers', appeared in 1719. It was already well known that Clarendon had written of Ireland; his manuscripts had, for instance, been extensively, if selectively, used by Edmund Borlase in his highly partisan *History of the Execrable Irish Rebellion* (London, 1680).[49] But Clarendon's Irish writings, omitted from the original Oxford edition, remained absent from the *History*'s first Dublin imprint.

Within months, in a flurry of activity between Dublin and London, as if timed to respond to discussions around the Declaratory Act, the *History of the rebellion and civil wars in Ireland* was published in both London ('Printed for H.P. for J. Wilford ... and T. Jauncey') and Dublin ('for Patrick Dugan'). The two versions of this specifically Irish *History* are markedly different. Dugan's Dublin imprint is sparse: it prints only the central Clarendon text. The London version, by contrast, has a richly circumstantial set of prefatory materials, beginning with a lengthy anonymous preface presenting this *History* as a timely correction to: '*Those Things which had been slubber'd over, or spitefully misrepresented* in Borlase's *Account of the Irish Rebellion*' (A7v). This is followed by a full endorsement of Clarendon's defence of his friend and ally, the first duke of Ormond. Amplifying and extending his qualities of '*Honest Loyalty*' further to all 'the Botelers' (Butlers), the London edition also praises other leading figures of the Irish aristocracy, the Boyles in particular. In conclusion, an 'Advertisement' reinforces its credentials: this edition has not only been 'carefully examin'd and compar'd with two Manuscripts in his Grace the Lord Arch-Bishop of *Dublin*'s Library', it also reproduces marginalia made by the archbishop himself in 1686 concerning the authenticity of the Clarendon

---

48 See Chapter 17. Published as *Dr Keting's* [sic] *History of Ireland Translated by Dermod O'Connor* (Dublin, 1723); Bernadette Cunningham, *The World of Geoffrey Keating: History, Myth and Religion in Seventeenth-century Ireland* (Dublin: FCP, 2000).

49 Rankin, *Between Spenser and Swift*, 232–5, 241–3.

manuscripts. By the second London edition, in 1721, the existence of the arch-bishop's notes is proudly displayed on the title page.

The archbishop in question, William King, was well known for his defence of both the Church of Ireland and the new Protestant Ascendancy consensus. He was keenly aware that seventeenth-century animosities still lurked beneath that consensus, and that the Declaratory and Toleration Acts threatened to bring them, again, to the surface.[50] It is all the more striking, then, that the Dublin edition includes none of his material; it ends instead with the tantalising announcement that 'In the Perss [*sic*] and will speedily be published' a supplement to this, the first Dublin printing of Clarendon's specifically Irish *History*.[51] It may be that a deal was struck between the archbishop and the printers: King would supply the 'authentic' text for publication, prefatory materials could be added to the London version, whereas what mattered in Dublin was simply to set the *History* in circulation. But this is speculation; much remains to be discovered about the emergence of these two versions of Clarendon's Irish *History*, which here serve as further incitement to scholars to engage in careful, sustained work on the complex collaborations which were becoming possible between Dublin and London in the early 1720s.

Most of the Dublin imprints discussed in this chapter were published for an engaged Irish readership by printers who specialised in fast, local, low-quality production. But some printers had very different ambitions both for their authors and for their market. George Faulkner's first venture makes a point of collecting and resetting the raw material of the *Drapiers Letters* in a more expensive volume, adorning the work with the resonant title, *Fraud Detected, or The Hibernian Patriot* (Dublin, 1725). In the wake of *A Modest Proposal*'s later success, he published the same volume in London, 1730, as *The Hibernian Patriot: Printed at DUBLIN. LONDON:* Reprinted and sold by A. MOOR in *St Paul's Church-yard*, and the Booksellers of *London* and *Westminster*. The name 'Faulkner' does not appear, but the clue is in the pseudonym – 'A. MOOR' is a name used on fictitious imprints for pirated books. This London imprint does more than make Swift's 'proposal' known

---

50 R. Gillespie, 'Irish Print and Protestant Identity: William King's Pamphlet Wars, 1687–1697', in V. Carey and U. Lotz-Heumann (eds.), *Taking Sides?: Colonial and Confessional Mentalités in Early Modern Ireland* (Dublin: FCP, 2003), 231–50; William King, *The State of the Protestants of Ireland under the Late King James's Government* (London, 1691), reprinted in Dublin, 1713 and 1730.

51 *Lord Clarendon's History of the Grand Rebellion Compleated* appears soon after, 'printed for Dugan and J. Leathley', noting that '[t]hose that have the Folio Edition Printed in *Dublin*, must apply to their own index'.

outside Dublin; it also secures the publisher's rights to his author's work. Even as he traded on Swift's Hibernian credentials, Faulkner marks, with this London publication, a canny ambition: that of registering copyright, and so protecting his own financial interests in one of the most internationally successful authors of his day.

Faulkner's move brings this chapter both full circle and to its conclusion: back to the 1728 *Poem of the art of printing*, the Griersons' publishing partnership, and a Dublin press both confident of its own worth and on the threshold of a new era of international expansion. For if Faulkner recognised and traded on the reputation of Swift as a gifted, innovative and popular literary author beyond the confines of the Dublin *élite*, then the Griersons, perhaps more than any other printers in early eighteenth-century Ireland, worked to provide for – and encourage – the growing local appetite for reading and owning great literature. The list of literary 'Works' produced in the Dublin imprint by their firm is impressive. It includes contemporary writers connected with Swift, such as Alexander Pope, Joseph Addison and Richard Steele; earlier Irish-born writers, such as William Congreve; and writers who were fast attaining the status of English literary icons, such as John Milton. Grierson also published for the first time in Ireland the text that would, across later centuries, come to be the complex marker both of literary excellence and English cultural dominance: *The works of Shakespear. in eight volumes* (Dublin, 1726).

Constantia Grierson was not only a poet, she was also an expert editor who had produced pocket classic editions of Virgil (1724), Terence (1727) and Tacitus (1730); she was working on an edition of Sallust when she died, aged 27, in 1732. If her productive life was short, it also gives a strong sense of the social mobility which the print trade could offer in early eighteenth-century Ireland. Born in County Kilkenny of 'poor illiterate country people', this trainee midwife turned polymath and classical scholar, editor and skilled compositor was admired by Swift, and was a significant member of his literary circle. Her learning was matched by a keen business sense: the publication of her 1730 edition of Tacitus, dedicated to Lord Deputy Carteret, coincides with her husband George Grierson's petition to the Irish House of Commons for the king's patent for printing in Ireland. That petition praised the exemplary Constantia's contribution not only to the particular family business, but also to the general reputation of Ireland. Consciously trading on an understanding of printing as a patriotic endeavour, entwined with the complex political relationship that obtained between Ireland and England, the Griersons' petition argued not only the case of the remarkable Constantia, but also of the sister-kingdom whose newly found cultural worth she so perfectly represents: 'the Art of Printing, through her care and assistance, has been brought to greater perfection than has been hitherto *in this Kingdom*' [*sic*].[52] The case was strong; the Griersons won the patent.

---

52 A. C. Elias, 'A Manuscript Book of Constantia Grierson's', *Swift Studies*, 2 (1987), 33–56, quoted at 40.

19

A World of Honour: Aristocratic *Mentalité*

BRENDAN KANE

Sir George Carew (1555–1629) was obsessed with honour. The markers of his personal honour were manifold: titles (including an earldom); office (lord president of Munster); and military leadership in the Nine Years' War (1594–1603). Above all, he was consumed with matters of blood and lineage, which he saw as central to good governance and the maintenance of order. Though charged with immense responsibility in governing the western realm, Carew made time to draw, in his own hand, the genealogies of Ireland's noble families, Gaelic and English. Hundreds of families were meticulously anatomised, accompanied by biographical and historical commentary, notes and reference to sources. Who ruled, where they came from, the character they and their ancestors displayed, the lands they claimed, what services they performed for the state, which great deeds or great scandals distinguished them: these were fundamental elements to Carew's worldview and political thought. The countless hours this pillar of the *régime* spent researching and scrawling pedigrees, then, was not mere antiquarianism. It was statecraft. For blood and honour were as much the stuff of politics as law and economics.

Early Modern Aristocratic *Mentalité*: A Hidden Ireland?

Later observers have largely overlooked this aspect of early modern Irish history. For instance, Carew's focus on aristocracy and honour was not shared by those Victorian archivist/historians charged with promoting his papers. In the six-volume calendar of his papers there is no mention of the annotated pedigrees Carew himself held so crucial to the definition and practice of governance. Nor was the early modern world of honour explored through the Irish-language archive, the great texts of the age – from bardic poetry to prose works such as Geoffrey Keating's *Foras Feasa ar Éirinn* – being read primarily through nationalist political and/or aesthetic lenses. Moreover, the political climate of the last century did not lend itself to interest in aristocratic mentality, a demotic *zeitgeist* eventually enshrined in Article forty of the Irish Constitution barring the Republic from granting noble titles and blocking its citizens from accepting titles of honour without government approval. To generations of scholars the early modern world of honour constituted a 'hidden Ireland'. This chapter explores that hidden 'world' so as to recapture a defining aspect of early modern political thought and the theory of governance. To understand this period we must confront the reality that high politics were primarily the purview of the nobility, and thus were deeply influenced by that caste's values and behaviours, which is to say by honour.

Recovering the early modern world of honour carries challenges of definition. People at the time argued over what constituted true honour – there was no uniform 'code' – and thus we as observers must be attentive to the semantic range employed by contemporaries, and how it altered over the nearly 200 years this chapter traverses. The 'function' of honour, too, is a matter of debate: contemporaries argued over exactly what role honour played in state and society. So too have modern scholars. Historians have tended to relate it to positive reputation. Social scientists, particularly anthropologists, have delineated subtler distinctions, notably the ways in which honour operates both internally (self-assessment) and externally (assessment by others), and vertically (between social superiors and inferiors) and horizontally (amongst social equals). Nobility also poses a definitional challenge in that it describes both a class of title-bearing *élites* (noun) and the character or qualities commensurate with the pinnacle of human potential (adjective). These usages, as we will see below, were not always coterminous. Indeed, they were frequently in tension and increasingly so across the early modern period.

Shifting and contested definitions raise the question of method: how do we capture multiple moving targets in our pursuit of understanding the 'worlds of honour' and their effects on politics and society? A broad approach is taken here. In surveying the nobility as a social class, this chapter considers both those who held titles from the crown and those of traditional aristocratic families excluded from the noble ranks on account of ethnicity, confession or rebellion. Regarding honour itself, it starts with no set definition but rather follows a lexical approach, exploring how and when the term and its main cognate concepts (glory, fame, reputation and so on) were used and the contexts of that usage. Doing so allows consideration of the pronouncements of the 'honourable' themselves and of the ruminations of theorists and arbiters of honour such as bards, jurists, clerics, heralds and court observers. To most closely approximate how contemporaries experienced and described the world of honour, this chapter tracks chronologically their lives, actions, and *mentalités*.

Ireland's Composite Aristocracy, 1541–1603

Exploration of honour must start with discussion of the nobility themselves, those who embodied the ideals of honour. Ireland in the middle of the sixteenth century lacked a unified aristocracy and two systems of nobility operated: the indigenous Gaelic one, whereby recognition came from being head of a noble lineage, and the English system that designated status by title from the crown. These systems did not overlap: those of Gaelic birth did not hold aristocratic titles, even if they periodically did pledge allegiance to English monarchs; and those of Anglo-Norman stock could not, perforce, find themselves heads of Gaelic families. In terms of practical power the English-Irish nobles dominated. Participants in each system shared common understandings of what made honour, while simultaneously recognising *élites* in the other system as external to their collective identity. Honour in Ireland, unlike in England, was, in terms of structure and organisation, a variegated phenomenon.[1]

Moreover, honour and the mental world of the nobility were multiple in Ireland on account of differences in who was able to define and shape them. When considering aristocratic mentality we must bear in mind that it was not created, or adjudged, solely by aristocrats themselves. Intellectuals and officials played roles in sustaining and defining honour both as system and concept. In England, and thus among the English-Irish, heralds were arbiters of honour: they determined titles, created pedigrees and resolved precedence disputes. At the top of the heraldic hierarchy sat the earl marshal and, ultimately, the monarch, both of whom adjudged matters of relative aristocratic status. Increasingly over the course of the sixteenth century, conduct-book writers were a voice on *élite* comportment. Indeed, Ludowick Bryskett's *Discourse of civill life* (1606) – whose subtitle promised it as 'Fit for the instructing of a Gentleman in the Course of a Vertuous Life' – was supposedly based on a late sixteenth-century conversation in the Pale. Gaelic Ireland had corresponding arbiters, theorists and makers of honour, namely the bards, who performed many of the roles that heralds did in the English system, such as researching and promoting pedigrees, announcing political change, and

---

1 Honour in England was hotly contested, but unlike in Ireland there was no alternate font of honour to the monarch.

presiding over rituals such as inaugurations and deaths.[2] Yet the bards were more than officiators over, and recorders of, the demographics and politics of honour. They were cornerstones of what we might consider the Irish state. Succession did not proceed by primogeniture but through competition among a series of male claimants. Bloodlines, while essential, had to be combined with some claim of virtue and worth. The bard's role was to make and celebrate that claim and thereby legitimate a dynastic contender: no man could be a lord without a chief poet in his court who confirmed his status.[3] The ability to name and confirm a lord was mirrored by the power to satirise him and, in so doing, undermine his legitimacy, perhaps in the interest of supporting a rival claimant. Poems of praise might ennoble a lord, but poems of satire could lead to his fall. Bardic power as kingmakers and deposers was enshrined in Brehon law wherein they carried the same honour price as secular lords. The pinnacle of Irish honour was a binary phenomenon: lords and poets, metaphorical spouses and lovers, were mutually supporting powerbrokers of intimate connection.

These English and Irish honour systems, in spite of incompatibility in how titles were established and recognised, shared common conceptual ground. Genealogy was an obsession on both sides of the cultural divide, and neither system celebrated upstarts. Whatever the circumstances behind their ennoblement – no matter how tawdry the purchase of arms or how treacherous the *pálás* coup – every newly elevated English family or Gaelic cadet claimant-turned-*rí* set to work procuring a pedigree demonstrating their lineal *bona fides*. More broadly, Irish and English alike celebrated a notion of good lordship that shared basic features: military prowess, hospitality, enforcement of justice, fecundity, protection of the weak, patronage of the learned and artistic classes, and a general sense of piety and support of the institutional church ranked as the most important. Unsurprisingly, then, nobles – Gaelic and English-Irish – spoke a mutually comprehensible performative language by which honour was made manifest. Display was crucial, first and foremost by means of the seat of power. And while a Gaelic tower house was no Carrick-on-Suir, the continental-trend-following seat of the Butlers, earls of Ormond, it was built on similar impulses to overawe visitors and entertain the *de rigueur* host of retainers and supplicants. In announcing their personal status, Irish lords made limited use of heralds and armigerous symbols, but

---

2 P. Breatnach, 'The Chief's Poet', *Proceedings of the Royal Irish Academy*, 83:C (1983), 37–79.
3 Generally see K. Simms, *From kings to Warlords: The Changing Political Structure of Gaelic Ireland in the Later Middle Ages* (Woodbridge: Boydell Press, 1987).

even as powerful an indigenous dynasty as the O'Neills adopted some form of heraldic display, the famous red hand of Ulster first appearing emblazoned on a shield in the fifteenth century.[4] Conversely, while the English-Irish may have identified with crown and country east across the Irish Sea, even the mighty earls of Ormond engaged Irish bards to impress upon followers and opponents alike the rightfulness of their power.[5] Noble honour, in concept and display, frequently served as a point of contact in a setting otherwise defined by cultural, social and political difference. It was precisely the connections offered by the *theory* and *practice* of honour that allowed for the previously incompatible *systems* of honour to be integrated in the mid-sixteenth century. While only partly successful, the crown's programme of 'surrender and regrant' sought to incorporate Irish nobles into the honour system based around the monarch.

Surrender and regrant had radical effects on Irish society, culture and politics – some unintended. Perhaps the most surprising of outcomes was that whereas similarities in concepts of honour had allowed the experiment of integrating the nobility, the resulting social amalgamation led in turn to alteration in concepts of honour. Put another way, as the practice of honour amongst the aristocracy became more uniform, the theory of honour became more diverse. In part this was because surrender and regrant, and English state centralisation more generally, pushed a wedge between lord and poet, thus bifurcating Irish honour. To witness poet separating from secular lord is to observe Gaelic Ireland's traditional form of government start to dissolve. This process was detectable as early as 1550 and contained both push and pull dynamics. On the one hand, numerous Irish lords took advantage of aligning with the crown and settling power and succession on their individual line, at the expense of the traditionally wider circle of male claimants.[6] On the other, the English state, realising the defining role bards played in *élite* politics, expended tremendous energy to discredit and suppress them. The resulting bifurcation of Irish sites of political legitimacy produced one of the first profound shifts in the mentality and practice of honour in early modern Ireland, with lords increasingly seeing honour arising from service to the crown and the bards stressing the abstraction of culture as its root. Unsurprisingly, bards

---

4 J. Barry, 'Guide to Records of the Genealogical Office, Dublin, with a Commentary on Heraldry in Ireland and on the History of the Office', *Analecta Hibernica*, 26 (1970), 3–43.
5 J. Carney (ed.), *Poems on the Butlers of Ormond, Cahir and Dunboyne* (Dublin Institute for Advanced Studies, 1945).
6 A classic case study is N. Canny, 'Hugh O'Neill, Earl of Tyrone, and the Changing Face of Gaelic Ulster', *Studia Hibernica*, (1970), 7–35.

complained of Irish lords betraying the precepts of honour and thus forfeiting their right to rule.[7]

Defining honour as service also had a tremendous effect on the character of English power in Ireland. The central state and its representatives were convinced that the English-Irish wallowed in corruption enabled by too much power, or 'liberty'.[8] Honour, seemingly, was not something that existed in a state of nature, but could only appear and thrive in the domesticated setting of state control. That is not to say that the crown wished to crush the English-Irish *élites* – there was much mutual opportunity in cooperation – but it does mean that the definition and performance of service became grounds for honour-based disputes: if service was an honour, exclusion from it was a dishonour. English newcomers had an interest in making resident *élites*, be they regional aristocrats or the lesser nobility of the Pale, appear wanton and ungovernable; English-Irish *élites* responded by tarring their 'New English' competition as over-reaching upstarts, which they did in a broad range of modes and in an increasingly collective voice. The baron of Howth, for instance, constructed a political genealogy of the 'Old English' to demonstrate its members' honour-based claim to participation in high politics.[9] Richard Stanihurst took the fight to the European stage. In his *De rebus in Hibernia gestis*, published on the continent, this Catholic and identitarian polemicist and tutor to the children of the earl of Kildare sought to establish Old English honour through contrast with both the savagery of the Gaelic Irish and the social inferiority and hereticism of Tudor newcomers.[10] In doing so, Stanihurst articulated what was a radical change in aristocratic mentality amongst the old colonial community a change built out of insult at political exclusion, assertion of social status and defence of a confessionalised faith, and whose most explosive result was rebellion by formerly loyal magnates such as the earl of Desmond.

Honour and its assertion should not, however, be exclusively linked with violence. Historians have long seen honour culture as responsible for what they deemed the early modern period's defining disorderliness; the argument being that the need to defend honour guaranteed a setting in which

---

7 M. Caball, *Poets and Politics: Reaction and Continuity in Irish Poetry, 1558–1625* (Cork University Press, 1998).

8 W. Palmer, 'That "Insolent Liberty": Honor, Rites of Power, and Persuasion in Sixteenth-Century Ireland', *Renaissance Quarterly*, 46 (1993), 308–27.

9 V. McGowan-Doyle, *The Book of Howth: Elizabethan conquest and the Old English* (Cork University Press, 2011).

10 Generally, see C. Lennon, *Richard Stanihurst: the Dubliner, 1547–1618* (Dublin: Irish Academic Press, 1981).

interpersonal combat was ever-present.[11] Undoubtedly, the 'touchiness' of honour produced frequent and often significant violence. That said, honour also provided a means to ensure order in an age that had no police force, no standing army, and unreliable access to law courts. Indeed, the aristocratic mentality was obsessed with order, with honour serving as the concept expressing that obsession. In an age suspicious of newness and innovation, lineage, office and hierarchy combined to ensure continuity of social order and political legitimacy; the violence of the defence of honour was to correct and combat transgressions to that order and so restore the proper equilibrium. Consequently, honour provided a language by which *élites* could make plays for authority across the sixteenth century's two great fault lines, faith and nation. For every confessional honour warrior like the earl of Desmond, there was a Butler, earl of Ormond, or a 'Wizard' earl of Kildare, who adopted a *politique* position on religion and argued for their continued inclusion in the state based on lineage, service and personal connection to the monarch.[12]

The multiple threads of honour – structural and conceptual – that ran through Irish society and politics in the latter half of the sixteenth century converged and crystallised during the Nine Years' War (1594–1603). Hugh O'Neill was beneficiary of surrender and regrant and, more broadly, of service and connection in getting himself ennobled as second earl of Tyrone. In spite of that service to the crown, he felt undervalued by the central state as the *régime's* officers impinged upon his local power. If in medieval England the north knew no king but a Percy, so early modern Ireland's north knew no *rí* but an O'Neill. Tyrone may have opportunistically availed himself of an English-style title and used his favoured status with London to further overawe his regional rivals and inferiors, but that arguably overmighty authority was grounded, by his thinking, in his lineage's ancient history of supreme local power and claim to Ireland's high kingship. When his new ally the crown failed in protecting and promoting that authority-by-ancient-right, the Ulster *rí*/earl bristled against the control of his ostensible masters. Chief amongst his concerns was the encroachment of base-born men into his sphere of influence and thus the erosion of his power.[13] With Tyrone's armed protest, Gaelic Ireland threw up its own version of that time-honoured

11 This approach is best exemplified by M. James, *English Politics and the Concept of Honour, 1485–1642* (Oxford: Past & Present Society, 1978).

12 V. Carey, *Surviving the Tudors: the 'Wizard' Earl of Kildare and English Rule in Ireland, 1537–1586* (Dublin: Four Courts Press [hereafter FCP], 2002), 218.

13 'Hugh O'Neill's War Aims' in E. Curtis and R. B. McDowell (eds.), *Irish Historical Documents, 1172–1922* (London and New York: Barnes and Noble, 1943; repr. 1968), 119–20. Digital version at www.ucc.ie/celt/online/E590001-003.html.

aristocratic action against perceived royal disfavour, the 'loyal rebellion'. As with the English-Irish earls of Kildare and Desmond before him, this Gaelic earl understood the exclusion from service to be a dishonour and stood firmly on this principle when rattling the *scian* in pursuit of negotiating his way back into being the queen's unchallenged representative in Ulster. Duly, Elizabeth played her part in this honour ritual by expressing her opinion that Tyrone's humbling was essential for protecting her honour.[14] Even her most famous commander in Ireland, Robert Devereux, second earl of Essex, saw the conflict's resolution in terms of honour: for autonomy in determining strategy, for creating knights in the field, for negotiating with O'Neill, and brokering alliances with indigenous allies like O'Connor Sligo.[15]

Others aside from leaders like O'Neill and Essex viewed the conflict through the lens of honour. Again, the world of honour was partly product of the intellectual classes, and the war years witnessed the rapid development of cultural and confessional definitions of honour: Gaelic poets redoubled their efforts to ground noble honour in defence of culture, and used this 'cultural nationalism' to inspire armed resistance against Anglicisation; clerics worked to refine the traditional marker of honour, defence of the church, to mean defence of the true church.[16] The resulting language of 'faith and fatherland' was no mere discourse but made its way into O'Neill's official pronouncements of war aims. It was no longer a 'loyal' rebellion.[17] Peace negotiations between the crown's representative, Lord Mountjoy, and the Irish leaders resulted in a settlement that sought to harness the ordering cap abilities of honour, with its reinforcing rights and responsibilities: O'Neill was coercively restored to the earldom of Tyrone and O'Donnell compelled to take the title earl of Tyrconnell. Thus, the Nine Years' War's settlement revealed that Irish *élites*, in spite of a maturing 'faith and fatherland' ideology, could pledge loyalty to a foreign prince of differing confession (as O'Neill did before and after the conflict) but not to one that dishonoured them. Perhaps

14 H. Morgan, *Tyrone's rebellion: the outbreak of the Nine Years' War in Tudor Ireland* (Woodbridge: Boydell Press, 1993).

15 B. Kane, *The Politics and Culture of Honour in Britain and Ireland, 1541–1641* (Cambridge University Press, 2010), chapter 3; P. Hammer, ' "Base Rogues" and "Gentlemen of Quality": The Earl of Essex's Irish Knights and Royal Displeasure in 1599', in B. Kane and V. McGowan-Doyle (eds.), *Elizabeth I and Ireland* (Cambridge University Press, 2014), 184–208.

16 See, for instance, H. Morgan, *Tyrone's rebellion: The outbreak of the Nine Years' War in Tudor Ireland* (Woodbridge: Boydell Press, 1993) and M. Carrol, *Poets and Politics: Reaction and Continuity in Irish Poetry, 1558–1625* (Cork University Press, 1998).

17 See for instance his demand that the Church of Ireland be governed by the Pope, in 'Hugh O'Neill's War Aims', 119–20.

ironically, then, the language that had served to make links across lines of ethnic, religious, national and political tension was simultaneously the one least subject to compromise.

Ireland's European Nobilities, 1603–1660

The early Stuart monarchs, to their detriment, misunderstood this truism. Infamously, James VI and I and his son and successor Charles I oversaw an attempted restoration of honour culture in the three kingdoms through the elevation of new peers, the creation of new titles and even a new heraldic category (the baronet), and the revival of the court of chivalry.[18] However, they focused on the 'system' of honour at the expense of the concept. James knew that delegated aristocratic authority was the most plausible way to govern the provinces, that securing those regional grandees' partnership would diminish the chances that his *régime* would face rebellion, 'loyal' or otherwise.[19] But instead of securing the loyalty of traditional regional *élites* through social elevation and inclusion in the growing circle of the court-centred British nobility, James allowed his favourite, George Villiers, duke of Buckingham, to sell made-to-order titles to the highest bidder. The result was merely the patina of a politics of honour. To many it was a mockery. For Buckingham's creations typically had no interest in the responsibilities of local authority, and their counsel to the king was self-interested to a fault.[20] As such, James's politics of honour created scandal across the realms as old nobility, new nobility and a host of commentators hotly debated what defined honour and its relationship to the social and political. Contention over this crucial aspect of legitimacy helped produce the gridlock James experienced when attempting to make his new realm English, manifested in such dramatic events as the Flight of the Earls (1607) and subsequent plantation of Ulster, the precedence disputes that disrupted his only Irish parliamentary session, and the court-centred fight for place pitting his English nobility and those holding Irish and Scottish titles against one another.[21] Inauspiciously, Charles I inherited both Buckingham as favourite and a tense relationship with the aristocracy, whom he believed

---

18 C. R. Mayes, 'The Early Stuarts and the Irish Peerage', *English Historical Review* 73 (1959), 227–51.

19 M. Smuts, 'Organized Violence in the Elizabethan Monarchical Republic', *History*, 99 (2014), 418–43.

20 V. Treadwell, *Buckingham and Ireland, 1616–1628: a Study in Anglo-Irish Politics* (Dublin: FCP, 1998).

21 Kane, *Politics and Honour*, chapter 6.

were key to a right-ordered society but should also be unquestionably loyal to
him as font of honour – which, emphatically, they proved not to be.

One point of contact among these variant voices opining on 'true' honour
was interest to define more narrowly who was honourable. In the wake of
the Nine Years' War, the bards harshly criticised upstarts, New English and
Gaelic, and argued that the Stuart court must include the ancient lineages. In
doing so, they laid claim to the mantle of civility and denounced the Tudors
for abandoning the political bedrock that legitimate government was characterised, in part, by the presence and participation of those of blood and
virtue. In this way Fearghal Óg Mac an Bhaird's celebration of James VI and
I's accession, *'Trí coróna i gcairt Shéamais'* ('Three crowns in James's charter'),
and a contemporary critique of the Elizabethan court such as Eochaidh Ó
hEodhasa's *'Ionmholta malairt bhisigh'* ('A change for the better is laudable')
do not represent mutually exclusive takes on crown rule – one positive, one
negative – but rather are variations, for different audiences, on the common
theme that Irish nobles should by right have a voice in governance of the
realm and the broader state, and both look optimistically to the new Scottish
king.[22] Prose genres were also deployed in the cause of delimiting the ranks
of the honourable. Lughaidh Ó Cléirigh's biographical study of Red Hugh
O'Donnell, *Beatha Aodha Ruaidh Uí Dhomhnaill* ('Life of Red Hugh O'Donnell')
was also an extended essay on true honour and the deleterious effects of its
absence within the governing ranks. Regarding the opposite end of the social
scale, the anonymous prose satire *Pairlement Chloinne Tomáis* ('Parliament
of Clan Thomas') viciously ridiculed Gaelic upstarts who worked the new
'British' dispensation to elevate themselves above their traditional superiors.

Perhaps the most innovative alteration in the discourse of honour was the
equation of honour with confession. Defence of the church and a general
piety were, as noted above, long deemed requirements of the honourable.
By the early seventeenth century, that religious bar was raised significantly to
require not only the defence of a *particular* faith – orthodox Catholicism – but
also personal commitment to it. The mental world of the aristocracy, thus,
became more international in scope, connected as it was to the Reformation.
Tadhg Ó Cianáin's hagiographic chronicle of the 'Flight of the Earls' stressed
the honour of the exiled lords O'Neill and O'Donnell, defined in large part

---

22 B. Ó Buachalla, 'James our True King: The Ideology of Irish Royalism in the Seventeenth
   Century', in D. G. Boyce, R. Eccleshall and V. Geoghegan (eds.), *Political Thought in
   Ireland since the Seventeenth Century* (London: Routledge, 1993), 7–35; P. McQuillan, 'A
   Bardic Critique of Queen and Court: "Ionmholta malairt bhisigh", Eochaidh Ó hEod-
   hasa, 1603', in Kane and McGowan-Doyle (eds.), *Elizabeth I and Ireland*, 60–85.

by their Catholic orthodoxy.[23] Polemical historical works such as Philip O'Sullivan Beare's 'History of Ireland' similarly made the equation of honour, confession and blood on the one hand, and legitimacy of rule on the other. Geoffrey Keating's 'national' history of the island and its waves of settlers – the first such generic undertaking in Irish – was read by some early moderns as defence of the Catholicised 'honour' of the Irish.[24]

There was, of course, a countering discourse of honour that sought to harness traditional definitions in support of Anglicising efforts. Heralds may have been minor figures in Ireland during Elizabeth's reign, the office of Ulster only established in 1552, but by James VI and I's reigns, they were active and powerful agents in determining the rolls of honour. Up jumped the number of 'visitations', by which families' bloodlines and right to bear arms were confirmed or denied, and it was these men who oversaw the confirmation of the new titles created by the early Stuarts, and who planned and prepared the visuals of honour, from printed pedigrees to funerary monuments, from weddings to burial trains.[25] A tried-and-true strategy to make one's new blood old was marriage alliance. Richard Boyle, although he may have bought his title for a tremendous sum, sought to ground purchased status in antiquity by marrying his children into important Irish and English families, such as the Fitzgeralds, earls of Kildare, and the Rich dynasty, earls of Warwick.[26] Others simply traced their pedigrees back into the Irish past, as did Randal MacDonnell, earl of Antrim.[27] Granted, Protestantism was crucial in Cork's and others' claims to true honour, but we should not think that equated to admission of innovation. Quite the contrary, Protestant propagandists, most famously Archbishop James Ussher, viewed Catholicism as the interloping institution and argued that the faith and practice of the Church of Ireland was heir to that celebrated by the ancient Irish. In writing up this argument, Archbishop James Ussher claimed he did so for the 'honour of his country'.[28] This combination of right blood

23 B. Kane, 'Making the Irish European: Gaelic Honor Politics and its Continental Contexts', *Renaissance Quarterly* 61 (2008), 1139–66.
24 B. Cunningham, 'Colonized Catholics: Perceptions of Honour and History: Michael Kearney's Reading of *Foras Feasa ar Éirinn*', in V. Carey and U. Lotz-Heumann (eds.), *Taking Sides? Colonial and Confessional Mentalités in Early Modern Ireland* (Dublin: FCP, 2003), 150–64.
25 Barry, 'Guide to Records'.
26 N. Canny, *The Upstart Earl: A Study of the Social and Mental World of Richard Boyle, First Earl of Cork, 1566–1643* (Cambridge University Press, 1982).
27 J. Ohlmeyer, *Civil War and Restoration in the Three Stuart Kingdoms: The Career of Randal MacDonnell, Marquis of Antrim* (Cambridge University Press, 1993; repr. Dublin: FCP, 2001), 75.
28 James Ussher, 'A Discourse on the Religion Anciently Professed by the Irish and the British' (London, 1631), 128.

and right faith proved central to how honour disputes amongst the Anglicised themselves played out. Failing in health, lacking an heir, and seeing his younger rivals chipping away at his power at home and court, Thomas Butler, tenth earl of Ormond, erstwhile favourite of Elizabeth and hammer of the treasonous, commissioned a Latin Virgilian epic to celebrate his deeds and lineage. Printed in London, the *Ormonius* aimed to impress upon the Stuart political nation the history of Butler orthodoxy in matters of church and state down through the ages and in so doing preserve into the future the family's pre-eminence.[29] Gaelic loyalists likewise sought to wed ancient blood with religious and political conformity. None was more active and creative in this regard than Donough O'Brien, fourth earl of Thomond, who used all means available – the handiwork of heralds, bards, historians, jurists and clerics; state service in the field and in office; and alliance with ascendant nobles like Richard Boyle – to assert himself as the paragon of noble honour in an Anglicised Ireland.[30] Even the socially tone deaf Thomas Wentworth, later earl of Strafford, known for his absolutist style of rule based on the primacy of monarchical privilege, felt keenly the importance of honour in governance and throughout his lord deputyship beseeched Charles I to elevate him to the peerage so that he might enjoy the knee-jerk obeisance of Irish nobles who were proving resistant to his administration.

Ireland, then, for all its local particularities, was participating in a general European trend by which nobility was increasingly a 'juridical entity', the definition of which was influenced by cross-confessional efforts at the reformation of manners.[31] Contests over honour were therefore as much sociological as definitional: traditional traits remained important – blood, prowess, service – but who could lay claim to them was hotly contested. Those who did not fit the 'ideal' of state-sponsored honour were still able to find their way into and amongst the titled nobility of the Stuart multiple monarchy: the Catholic earl of Clanricard, the Gaelic earl of Thomond and even the head of the Magennis dynasty who availed himself of 'surrender and regrant' in 1623. But doing so was increasingly exception, not the rule. Heralds, jurists and court favourites held tremendous power to shape *élite* society and its operative worldview, and a gate-keeping criterion of choice in this bottlenecked world of honour was

---

29 *The Tipperary Hero: Dermot O'Meara's Ormonius (1615)*, ed. and trans. D. Edwards and K. Sidwell (Turnhout: Brepols, 2011).
30 B. Kane, 'Languages of Legitimacy? *An Ghaeilge*, the Earl of Thomond and British Politics in the Renaissance Pale', in T. Herron and M. Potteron (eds.), *Dublin and the Pale in the Renaissance, c.1540–1660* (Dublin: FCP, 2011), 267–79.
31 H. Zmora, *Monarchy, Aristocracy and the State in Europe, 1300–1800* (London and New York: Routledge, 2001).

reputation for virtue. In the late sixteenth century, the baron of Howth experienced no lasting social consequences from repeated charges of horrific domestic abuse.[32] But come the 1610s, Mervyn Tuchet, earl of Castlehaven, was tried and beheaded for sexual irregularities committed in his home, actions deemed crimes against honour for polluting bloodlines.[33] Rightly we should laud developments in punishing gendered and sexual violence, but we should not mistake it for a feminist turn. For the early Stuart executive and juridical moralising of honour had an unmistakably masculine focus that came at the expense of female power. It is difficult to imagine a female dynastic head, such as Grainne Ní Mháille (Grace O'Malley), the so-called 'pirate queen' of the previous century, operating under the early Stuarts. And the political power and erudition for which aristocratic Irish women traditionally garnered bardic encomium dropped out of the honour lexicon of Anglicised Ireland. This is not to say that *élite* women were not figures of immense personal and familial power, or less educated, but simply that such characteristics were evidently deemed less praiseworthy than were sexual propriety and domesticity. The gendered aspects of honour in early modern Ireland, and the honour of women in particular, are topics in dire need of further exploration.[34] A cursory look at the evidence and extant scholarship, however, suggests a moralistic tightening of honour's definition in line with broader trends favouring notions of order dictated by a crown and court obsessed with pious virtue and its role in maintaining social order.

Indeed, aristocratic desire for order helps explain the conduct by Ireland's nobles in the war torn 1640s. The 1641 rising – much like the earlier Nine Years' War – initially bore elements of the honour revolt, or loyal rebellion. The chief conspirators, Sir Phelim O'Neill and Rory O'More, did not take up arms against the crown in an effort to realise an independent, Catholic Irish nation. Rather, they took the opportunity of England's distraction fighting the Scots to mount a protest intended to convince the *régime* to restore them to what they believed was their birthright: social and political pre-eminence, and acknowledgment as the crown's local champions against Parliamentary foes.[35] The subsequent metastasising of *élite* protest into popular rebellion spurred the aristocracy to collective action in a way previously unknown as

---

32 McGowan-Doyle, *The Book of Howth*.
33 C. Herrup, *A House in Gross Disorder: Sex, Law, and the 2nd Earl of Castlehaven* (Oxford University Press, 1999).
34 J. Ohlmeyer, 'The Aristocracy in Seventeenth-Century Ireland: Wider Contexts and Comparisons', *History Compass*, 12 (2014), 33–41.
35 N. Canny, *Making Ireland British: 1580–1650* (Oxford University Press, 2001), chapter 8.

Gaelic and Old English came together in an attempt to bring order to a situation spiralling toward lawlessness and extreme violence. In doing so, these grandees manifested the ancient honour imperatives of martial leadership and the dispensing of justice – and even of service, for much of the decade was taken up negotiating a peace settlement between Catholic and Protestant supporters of Charles, talks which centred largely on the proper relationship between rights and responsibilities linking monarch and noble.[36] Amongst *élites* themselves, even those on opposite sides of the conflict took efforts to protect the property and patrimonies of those to whom they were related; war always has an end, and thus one should be attentive to the *longue durée* of hierarchy and tradition and the order they promised.[37] However, this strategy, and its underlying worldview, did not align well with the more demotic mentality of ethnic and religious demonisation that characterised both the conflict's popular violence and the brutality of Parliamentarian troops. The wanton massacre of Irish and Old English combatants and non-combatants alike at Drogheda and Wexford, for all its horror, was simply the concluding act in a pattern of dehumanising violence levelled by Parliamentary forces convinced that the Irish lay outside the realm of honour and thus the accepted rules of war.[38] Here, the importance of honour to concepts of order becomes painfully apparent and poignant: honour, rather than promoting violence as the historiography tends to suggest, offered a mechanism by which it could be controlled and legitimated. In its absence in rushed the sort of dehumanising violence seen in colonies from Munster to Virginia.

Nevertheless, the language of that violence was still largely conceived of in terms of honour. The importance of trust and the giving of one's word, deemed crucial for the smooth ordering of society in times of peace, became even more central in times of conflict. Accusations of having flouted these basic requirements would dog commanders for the remainder of their lives, and beyond. Cromwell's brutality was deemed a function of overseeing and defending the massacre of civilians, but also for not respecting surrendering soldiers' request for quarter. Swordsmen and non-combatants alike should have had reason to trust their safety would be bound up in the honour of the victorious commander, so went the contemporary analysis, and thus savagery

---

36 M. Ó Siochrú, *Confederate Ireland, 1642–1649: A Constitutional and Political Analysis* (Dublin: FCP, 2008).

37 P. Little, '"Blood and Friendship": The Earl of Essex's Protection of the Earl of Clanricarde's Interests, 1641–6', *English Historical Review*, 112 (1997), 927–41.

38 M. Ó Siochrú, 'Atrocity, Codes of Conduct and the Irish in the British Civil Wars, 1641–1653', *Past & Present*, 195 (2007), 55–86.

and dishonour went hand in hand in anti-Cromwellian propaganda.[39] Similar charges of the foregoing of one's word leading to devastating social and political effect rained down upon the earl of Ormond. As Ireland's premier aristocrat, Ormond enjoyed peerless social prestige, confirmed by his elevation to a dukedom in 1661. But he could not escape public sniping that Ireland's tragic fate was result of his dishonourable decision to look out for self-interest at the expense of the general good. It was not his abandonment of 'Irishness' or of religion that was seen as detrimental, but rather of honour: a nation would stand or fall with the uprightness of those charged to lead it, and Ireland was doomed with the likes of Ormond the 'unkinde deserter' at the helm.[40] Stung by similar charges of dishonourable conduct, the earl of Castlehaven penned his memoirs with the intention of constructing himself as a man of honour and so defending the virtue of his decisions and actions.[41] Particularly vociferous in this debate over conduct in the recent war was the Gaelic intelligentsia, who decried a paucity of *élite* honour and its role in Ireland's subjugation to a foreign power. Circulating widely in manuscript, poetic condemnation targeted both Cromwellian leaders as base-born and crass, and Irish exiles and collaborators as 'traitors' and cowards. True honour was not entirely vanquished from the world, it was simply that those who embodied it had been overrun by barbarous hordes from the east, unleashed by English parliamentary rule.[42] The genealogist Dubhaltach Mac Fhirbhisigh sought to canonise these distinctions when producing his great book of genealogies: the Irish nobility were those descended from the mythical invader *Míl*, whereas the base traced their roots to the *Fir Bholg*, pirates, marauders and other ignoble enemies of good order.[43]

---

39 S. Covington, ' "The odious demon from across the sea". Oliver Cromwell, Memory and the Dislocations of Ireland', in E. Kuijpers, J. Pollmann, J. Muller and J. van der Steen (eds.), *Memory before Modernity: Practices of Memory in Early Modern Europe* (Leiden: Brill, 2013), 149–64.

40 É. Ó Ciardha, 'The Unkinde Deserter and the Bright Duke: The Dukes of Ormond in the Royalist Tradition', in T. Barnard and J. Fenlon (eds.), *The Dukes of Ormonde, 1610–1745* (Woodbridge: Boydell and Brewer, 2000), 177–93.

41 D. Rankin, *Between Spenser and Swift: English Writing in Seventeenth-Century Ireland* (Cambridge University Press, 2007), 260–7.

42 C. Rahilly (ed.), *Five Seventeenth-Century Political Poems* (Dublin Institute for Advanced Studies, 1952); for circulation and reception see V. Morley, *Ó Chéitinn go Raiftearaí: mar a Chumadh Stair na hÉireann* (Dublin: Coiscéim, 2011).

43 On Mac Fhirbhisigh and his work see N. Ó Muraile, *The Celebrated Antiquary: Dubhaltach Mac Fhirbhisigh (c. 1600–71)*, his Lineage, Life and Learning (Maynooth: An Sagart, 1996); for the genealogist's concern for honour, and the honour of the calling, see I. Campbell, *Renaissance Humanism and Ethnicity before Race: the Irish and the English in the Seventeenth Century* (Manchester University Press, 2013), 124–5. Generally on the historical and genealogical efforts of the Irish intellectual classes, see the work of B. Cunningham, e.g.,*The*

Honour-based readings of the mid-century crisis and its consequences played on a European stage. Soon after the war, Richard O'Ferrall undertook a scathing denunciation of Old English members of the Confederate Catholics, the *Commentarius Rinuccinianus*, blaming their willingness to associate with Protestants for the calamitous fall of the budding nation. This Latin treatise was intended for a Continental audience interested to make sense of the loss of a Catholic stronghold in an increasingly Protestant northern Europe. In response, John Lynch, a Catholic intellectual of Old English stock, penned the *Alithinologia* (1664) and the *Supplementum Alithinologia* (1667) wherein he delineated an Irish commonwealth grounded in classical civic theory which held that the healthy polity grew out of individual citizens competing for honour and virtue. Honour, in Lynch's thinking, was taking on a new conceptual importance, integrated as it was with humanist-inflected understandings of political thought localised to fit the Irish context.[44] Simultaneously, it continued to influence the practice of politics, providing a language by which Irish members of the Stuart court in exile manoeuvred for place and prominence. The setting in which these men operated may have been novel, but their guiding understanding of honour as essential to the order of politics and society was not. Duty to the monarch was seen as the foundation for time-honoured hierarchy within which traditional *élites* practiced good lordship over their social inferiors to the benefit of all. Disturbances to this closed system – whether social like the ritualised violence of duelling, or behavioural/moral like Charles II's dissolute living – were met with anxiety that they would usher in chaos capable of collapsing the court and, thus, endangering the re-establishment of the monarchy in the Stuarts' erstwhile three kingdoms.[45]

A Service Nobility and its Critics, 1660–1730

Once restored, the Stuarts enjoyed a more ideologically uniform aristocracy.[46] James VI and I had inherited an Ireland with competing systems of nobility

World of Geoffrey Keating (Dublin: FCP, 2000) and *The Annals of the Four Masters: Irish History, Kingship and Society in the Early Seventeenth Century* (Dublin: FCP, 2010).

44 I. Campbell, 'John Lynch and Renaissance Humanism in Stuart Ireland: Catholic Intellectuals, Protestant Noblemen, and the Irish *Respublica*', *Éire-Ireland* 45 (2010), 27–40 and Campbell, *Renaissance Humanism*, especially chapter 4.

45 M. Williams, *The King's Irishmen: the Irish in the Exiled court of Charles II, 1649–1660* (Woodbridge:Boydell and Brewer, 2014), chapters 6–8.

46 See J. Ohlmeyer, *Making Ireland English: The Irish Aristocracy in the Seventeenth Century* (New Haven and London: Yale University Press, 2012), chapter 3.

and an England eager for social promotion after enduring Elizabeth I's reluctance to create new titles, a situation that largely accounts for the period's lively and controversial traffic in titles. But from the 1640s well into the eighteenth century, expansion of the peerage was slower and more deliberate.[47] Consequently, the worldview of its constituent members was correspondingly more closely circumscribed, aided in part by an emphasis on education as a requirement for taking over the dynastic estate. Cultural convergence continued with the grand tour, increasingly an expectation of those born to rule. In adulthood, nobles tended to have more interpersonal contact with one another than did Irish *élites* in times past. For whereas the man of his 'country', be it in the Englishry or Irishry, in the late medieval period only infrequently saw his peers, the late Stuart Irish noble was in close proximity with his fellows in Dublin, London and other sites of high politics and society – a situation that favoured uniformity over diversity of outlook. Typically excluded by this constriction of the circles of honour were members of the extended family and the local populace. The nuclear family became the centre of aristocratic focus as primogeniture limited succession to a son of the main line, and the open (and frequently open air) hospitality that was so long a plank of good lordship disappeared as *élites* withdrew from such indiscriminate generosity.[48] Tenants and townspeople were thus reduced to spectators of aristocratic power, constrained to see their betters parade their status-identifying finery about town and country, and to admire their increasingly luxurious and elegant estates from afar.

Yet, to say that Ireland's ruling class was more clearly defined by service and crown loyalty is not to say that monarchical and aristocratic notions of honour were wholly correspondent. Consider the duel. Like James VI and I and Charles I before them – and even Cromwell, who believed the practice a courtly vice wanting extinction – the later Stuart monarchs actively sought to quash this extra-legal bit of ceremonial violence. But with limited success. In part the fashion for duelling amongst Irish *élites* was a product of time spent on the continent, where settling disputes with pistols was all the rage; in part it was the result of new patterns of civility in train since the late sixteenth century brought by English and Scottish officers. Those holding military commissions were most likely to duel, and it appears that this ritualised violence offered means to settle disputes between Catholic and Protestant

---

47 T. Barnard, *A New Anatomy of Ireland: the Irish Protestants, 1641–1770* (New Haven and London: Yale University Press, 2003), 23.

48 Ohlmeyer, *Making Ireland English*, 433–47.

commanders and soldiers. The nobility was, after all, a warrior caste and to be shut out of soldiering or to be denied the right to bear arms was a grave dishonour. In the confessionally and politically fluid setting of Restoration Ireland, wherein Catholics and Protestants shared notions of honour and had reasonable hope of securing position in military and governmental upper circles, the duel was a plausible way for touchy nobles and gentlemen to protect and promote their insecure place in state and society. Nevertheless, it remains the case that king and Irish peer occupied mindsets more closely proximate than at any previous point in Irish–English relations. Understanding this, Charles II, while he much preferred that such status combat happened in courtrooms not courtyards, typically looked the other way when informed of his courtiers firing at one another.[49]

Peers and gentlemen courtiers, as noted already, were not the sole claimants to noble honour in Restoration Ireland, nor did they or the crown control the discourse on the subject. Dissenting voices on what constituted true honour came from across confessional, ethnic and even 'class' lines. Perhaps unsurprisingly, the Gaelic intelligentsia continued to decry the disappearance of honour from society and politics, with both natives and newcomers to blame. Daibhi Ó Bruadair (1625–1698) is merely the most famous to skewer Anglicising upstarts and Gaelic 'collaborators' alike as base in blood and boorish in conduct. By contrast, true honour was claimed to live in those of ancient noble lineage who, in spite of having fallen from the ranks of the powerful, remained society's paragons.[50] Thus began the phenomenon, which would prove of tremendous literary traction and popularity through succeeding centuries, of Irish outlaws praised as heroes on grounds of 'genealogical continuity with a dispossessed aristocracy'.[51] Other critics located true honour outside the aristocracy altogether and in the professional and merchant classes. Peers were seen by an increasing number of commentators as parasitic on society, interested only in the rights and privileges of nobility and not in its responsibilities. Absenteeism offered the clearest case of such dishonourable individualism: the mighty were expected to adhere to the time-honoured notions of good lordship and promote the local as well as the national good. Pressure to appear at court, however, was tremendous and peers spent much of their time in Dublin, London and similar haunts of privilege. They spent

---

49 J. Kelly, *'That damn'd thing called honour': Duelling in Ireland, 1570–1860* (Cork University Press, 1995), chapter 2.
50 This is most famously expressed in the poetry of Dáibhidh Ó Bruadair. See *Duanaire Dháibhidh Uí Bhruadair*, ed. J. C. McErlean (3 vols., London: Irish Texts Society; 1910–1917).
51 N. Ó Ciosáin, 'Highwaymen, Tories and Rapparees', *History Ireland,* 1 (1993), 19–21.

much of their wealth there, too, on ostentatious living amongst the increasingly urbanised *élite*. Yet honour as the local peer was not offset by equivalent social prestige in the capitals. For aristocratic wealth was a wildly variant phenomenon, and the fortunes amassed by merchants, professionals and politicos occasionally eclipsed those enjoyed by the armigerous. From such financial convergence it was a short step to attributing 'commoner' wealth to hard work and virtue, and falling noble fortunes to sloth and corruption. The consequent political valence is unsurprising: honour was widely deemed key to the common good, thus those who demonstrated honour – the merchant and professional classes – should be the ones governing.

Arguably the pivot point in Irish honour culture was the Treaty of Limerick and its immediate aftermath. Cessation of hostilities between Williamite and Jacobite forces reflected a cross-confessional understanding that the ranks of honour were effectively blind to matters of religion. Noble supporters of the losing cause were, unlike Drogheda's defenders before Cromwell, not ritualistically dishonoured (let alone slaughtered). Some were allowed to leave the realm in exile, and to take family, retainers and arms with them as they sought comparable places in Catholic Europe. Many of these so-called 'wild geese' would distinguish themselves in the service of continental *régimes*. Those who remained were stripped of office and property, but not of the right to bear arms. Negotiations may have been driven more by William's desire to settle internal conflicts so as to concentrate more fully on troubling the hated Louis XIV than by any respect for Ireland's Catholic *élites*. But whatever the motivation behind them, the treaty's articles show an awareness that the 'honourable' were to be found across lines of national, ethnic and religious difference and that dealings between combatants of status were to be carried out in accordance with mutually legible honour imperatives. In this way, the Treaty of Limerick bears family resemblance to surrender and regrant and to the settlement following the Nine Years' War. Local Protestant reaction to the settlement, however, demonstrated that a cross-realm, *politique* approach to honour had little place in an Ireland that the victors sought to shape in their own image. Piety, as seen above, was a foundational marker of noble honour throughout the medieval and early modern periods. In spite of the divisive nature of post-Reformation religious polemic and the confessionalisation of honour by the likes of Ussher and Keating, aristocrats themselves still frequently adopted a *politique* approach to religion. As Raymond Gillespie writes of Ireland's premier noble in the second half of the century, James Butler, duke of Ormond: 'Institutional religious positions were, for Ormond, a matter of honour and duty. Honour and duty were the responsibilities of men in a religious context, but they were not matters for salvation, that was for God alone to determine.'[52]

The Penal Laws, spotty in passage and in implementation though they may have been, made difficult a position like Ormond's and, thus, seem to have marked an end of era in aristocratic conduct and worldview. The crown's (perceived) leniency on defeated Jacobites was picked away at by means of legislative moves aimed at declawing and dishonouring Catholics. Indeed, it was written in the parliamentary record in 1692 that 'it was for "the honour of the Protestants of Ireland to preserve the records of the Irish barbarity"'.[53] Land ownership was of course fundamentally important to aristocratic status: it was the basis for a noble title, provided the seat and setting for local magnificence, and was the primary source of wealth in the age. Post-1692 legislative efforts from Dublin reduced Catholic land ownership – 14 per cent by 1703, and bottoming out at 5 per cent come 1750 – effectively rendering Irish *élite* society Protestant only. Catholics, who in spite of defeat insisted upon their honour by maintaining arms and seeking military preferment, faced the prospect of humiliating disarmament and corporal punishment at the hands of the Protestant establishment. A case of this is famously memorialised in the verse *'Caoineadh Airt Uí Laoghaire'* ('Lament for Art O'Leary') – a late eighteenth-century example of a man taking a stand on honour against the Penal Laws and finding himself hunted as a result and killed as an outlaw.[54] The laws also sought to bar Catholics from holding office, be it political or judicial. The Test Act (1704), for instance, set an insurmountable bar to membership in the political nation.

Even ascendancy insiders conducted themselves according to standards of honour that would have been alien a century earlier. Landed wealth, for instance, lost some of its stranglehold on definitions of nobility. As noted above, the seventeenth century witnessed progressive blurring between titled peers and the non-titled wealthy: in a world in which material display was increasingly central to honour's projection, winners in the commercial world were frequently better able to preen for the public than were holders of landed estates of uncertain worth. In Barnard's memorable phrase, the landed *élite* were often reduced to pursuing 'shabby stratagems' to boost their rental incomes with state largesse – offices, monopolies, pensions and the like.[55] Unsurprisingly, then, the honour of the merchant class took on a

---

52 R. Gillespie, 'The Religion of the First Duke of Ormond', in Barnard and Fenlon (eds.), *The Dukes of Ormond*, 109.

53 Quoted in R. F. Foster, *Modern Ireland, 1600–1972* (London: Allen Lane, 1988), 159–60.

54 S. Ó Tuama (ed.), *Caoineadh Airt Uí Laoghaire* (Dublin: Clóchomhar, 1963).

55 Barnard, *New Anatomy*, 26

conceptual, even ideological, tenor to match its materiality: it was not simply that these men were wealthier than their armigerous 'betters', but that their success was a sign of superior virtue. Swift was merely the most talented and effective voice within a growing chorus decrying the moral turpitude of the titled. Others celebrated and anatomised the well-compensated virtue of the professional and commercial classes, and a telling shift in the world of honour was marked by demonstrable opinion that localities were better off without a resident peer.[56] So much for the traditions of good lordship when absentee-ism seemed a social good.

The early eighteenth-century estrangement of honour and aristocracy is well illustrated in the person and career of Speaker William Conolly. The son of a miller from Donegal, Conolly was from Gaelic and Catholic stock. He was, however, raised as a Protestant and studied law. Advantageous marriage into a prominent ascendancy family provided the dowry with which he entered the market in confiscated Jacobite land. Successful speculation allowed him to flourish, both on account of rental income and because ownership allowed him to stand for parliament and to control other seats. A dedicated government man, Conolly served as speaker of the Commons and, for shorter spells, as lord justice and chief revenue collector. Position and connections enabled accumulation of one of the greatest fortunes in Ireland, the most spectacular manifestation of this being the Palladian masterpiece, Castletown house. Conolly's rise is reminiscent of Hugh O'Neill's: a native son of limited prospects rose to great heights through crown service and alliance with members of the aristocracy. It also brings to mind the career of Richard Boyle, commoner earl of Cork, which also was grounded on success in post-rebellion land speculation. Like Donough O'Brien, fourth earl of Thomond, Conolly used parliament as a means to cement his power. Aspects of his career even bear some resemblance to that of the great dukes of Ormond in that he, like them, demonstrated the opportunities that came with conversion to the state religion. But compared with all of those earlier paragons of aristocracy and pursuers of honour, Conolly was a creature of state and party nonpareil. There was no honour rebellion in him, loyal or otherwise. When he did push back against the *régime* it was peaceful, but nevertheless of tremendous significance: urged to take his place in the House of Lords he resisted, refusing both a noble title and demotion to the upper parliamentary house. His actions appear less a critique of nobility than a perceptive understanding that real power flowed through the lower house.

56 Barnard, *New Anatomy*, 24–5.

After all, most men with privilege to sit in the Lords demurred and, being frequently in England and at court, satisfied this public duty by appointing proxies. And the Declaratory Act (1720), infamous as a straight jacket on a Commons deemed too stridently independent, was perhaps more effective in neutering the House of Lords as it did away with its right of appellate jurisdiction.[57] Nobles remained important players in the political nation and social landscape. Indeed Conolly's rise was partly facilitated and maintained by the assistance of aristocratic allies, and he mimicked aspects of aristocratic mentality and performance. But behaviours that ostensibly revealed continuity with ones traditional to the Irish nobility on closer inspection betrayed significant differences. For instance, Conolly, like any late medieval or Tudor/early Stuart grandee, understood the importance of building a dynasty. His dynastic ambitions, however, were grounded in politics and office rather than land and lordship, and their goal was a parliamentary dynasty that sprang less from proximity to the king as the fount of honour than from control of party and Commons and the lands that returned parliamentary delegates. Conolly's rejection of a title confirmed that the aristocratic world of honour was no longer coterminous with that of high political power.[58]

The Early Modern World of Honour

Conolly's world, then, was not Sir George Carew's. It seems inconceivable that the speaker would have spent the effort to produce pedigrees of the great families of the age. Why should he have? In Carew's day, the nobility was a patchwork of Gaelic, Old English and New English grandees and aspirants. Sorting them out was a sensible thing for an officer close to the *régime*. Come Conolly's day, there was no such patchwork. Only five peers in the early eighteenth century were of Gaelic origin, and the active peers in the Lords were overwhelmingly of families who had arrived post-1530. Whatever their ethnic or confessional stock, by 1721 it was estimated that no more than eleven of the 119 peers of the realm were Catholic.[59] As one historian succinctly puts it, the 'Irish political *élite* can be identified as a Protestant landed class of New English origin.'[60] Power, consequently, was

---

57 Foster, *Modern Ireland*, 162.
58 Generally see P. Walsh, *The Making of the Irish Protestant Ascendancy: the Life of William Conolly, 1662–1729* (Woodbridge: Boydell and Brewer, 2010).
59 Barnard, *New Anatomy*, 22, 29; S. Connolly, ' "Ag Déanamh Commanding": Elite Responses to Popular Culture', in J. S. Donnelly and K. A. Miller (eds.), *Irish Popular Culture, 1650–1850* (Dublin: Irish Academic Press, 1998), 1–29.
60 Connolly, 'Ag Déanamh', 8.

less in the blood than in education and party, and lineage important on account of its grounding in parliament not the soil. It flowed more from the control of money than of men, and the martial world was increasingly professionalised and decoupled from aristocratic self-definition and justification. Even the duel, so vital to the warrior nobility of Restoration Ireland, largely disappeared from the *élite* martial firmament, casualty of ascendancy uniformity in Ireland's upper society.[61] Out with lineal legitimacy and the martial calling went the concomitant expectations of good lordship in the localities. The titled were increasingly urban, and 'civic activism and moral worth' the new expectations placed on the country honourable, frequently merchants and professionals, Protestant and Catholic alike.[62] If the vertical ties of honour that had bound the great and the commons for centuries were quickly unravelling, so too were the ties binding Irish *élite* and British king. Service remained a defining aspect of honour, but increasingly that meant to party and minister rather than monarch, with parliament not court serving as the main site of power.[63] Perhaps unsurprisingly, nobles started to identify as Irish and to internalise a concern for the honour of the nation. Changed too were the ranks of those arbitrating honour. No longer did the bards sing the praises of, and thus legitimate, those claiming aristocratic power. The Restoration phenomenon of patronising dramatists and other litterateurs to boost the status of an aristocratic lineage followed a similar declension pattern.[64] Even the heralds saw their role diminished – a man like Conolly had no use for them. Far more important as the signifiers of honour were houses, material luxuries, commercial interests, biographies and parliamentary power.

The operative world of honour in Ireland in 1730 was, thus, no longer synonymous with aristocratic mentality. The horizontal bond connecting aristocrats remained one of honour, and honour descriptive of the mental world of the armigerous. But whatever aristocrats' self-definitions, honour was no

---

61 As Kelly argues, it remained a phenomenon in the civil sphere, though it did not increase in frequency until after 1720. Kelly, *Duelling in Ireland*, 35.

62 Quote from Barnard, *New Anatomy*, 38; see also on non-aristocratic honour of Catholic professional classes and, more specifically, on the survival of a Catholic gentry class in Connacht, K. Whelan, 'An Underground Gentry? Catholic Middlemen in Eighteenth-Century Ireland', in Donnelly and Miller (eds.), *Irish Popular Culture*, 118–72.

63 Generally see D. Hayton, *Ruling Ireland, 1685–1742: Politics, Politicians and Parties* (Woodbridge: Boydell Press, 2004), 1, wherein he notes that we still know too little regarding the question of '(H)ow did the members of the Irish propertied *élite* think and act together?'

64 J. Ohlmeyer and S. Zwicker, 'John Dryden, the House of Ormond, and the Politics of Anglo-Irish Patronage', *The Historical Journal*, 49 (2006), 677–706.

longer synonymous with nobility. Noun and adjective had gone their separate ways. Nobles were still juridically determined, but nobility was defined by a far wider and diverse bench of judges – from clerics to literate commoners, from pamphlet writers to satirists. By the end of the century, with the American and French Revolutions and the echoing Irish rebellion of 1798, politics and society had assumed characteristics recognisably modern. By contrast, we might think of the early modern as grounded not in the rights of man, but of men. Very particular men: dynastic aristocrats. It thus comes as little surprise that the nineteenth-century calenderists charged with summarising Sir George Carew's papers failed to register the importance of his catalogue of pedigrees, for it was artefact of an alien world.

20

Irish Political Thought and Intellectual History, 1550–1730

IAN CAMPBELL

In Ireland, as elsewhere in Europe, the transition between the old sciences grounded in the philosophy of Aristotle and the new sciences of the Enlightenment took place in the decades following 1650.[1] Those Aristotelian sciences had dominated the European universities and provided an important, though sometimes contested, resource for Irish political discourse since the twelfth century. The Enlightenment, which was bound up not just with improvements in scientific knowledge but also with the increasing power of European states, offered new ways of speaking about human society. Ireland's seventeenth-century political revolutions thus took place at the same time as this European intellectual revolution. Those living in Ireland resorted to both old and new theories of human society as they attempted to label, categorise and understand the political phenomena surrounding them, to justify their own choices and to convince their contemporaries to undertake particular courses of action. These theories and ways of speaking were thus tools employed by Irish people to achieve certain desired outcomes; but tools themselves habituate their users and leave distinctive marks on their work.

Humanism, Scholasticism and Natural Law

This account of Irish political thought, which emphasises the continuities between medieval scholasticism and Renaissance humanism, complements the approach adopted by Benignus Millett, but differs from that developed by Brendan Bradshaw.[2] By the 1980s, Paul Oskar Kristeller had established a new

---

1 J. Kraye, 'Moral Philosophy', in C. B. Schmitt, Quentin Skinner, Eckhard Kessler, and Jill Kraye (eds.), *The Cambridge History of Renaissance Philosophy* (Cambridge University Press, 1988), 303–86; L. Brockliss, 'Curricula', in H. De Ridder-Symoens (ed.), *A History of the University in Europe, volume ii: Universities in Early Modern Europe (1500–1800)* (Cambridge University Press, 1996), 578–89.
2 B. Bradshaw, *The Irish Constitutional Revolution of the Sixteenth Century* (Cambridge University Press, 1979); B. Bradshaw, 'Transalpine Humanism', in J. H. Burns and M.

506

understanding of humanism as an educational movement, which extended expert knowledge of Latin and Greek from the clerical *élite* to the lay *élite*. Brendan Bradshaw preferred to defend a traditional account of Renaissance humanism as a worldview grounded in the philosophy of Plato, which broke away from university Aristotelianism and medieval intellectual life in general. A widespread reception of Platonic philosophy in early modern Ireland cannot be demonstrated, but it is possible to establish that the political doctrines newly taught in Irish noble households, grammar schools and universities in the late sixteenth and seventeenth centuries were largely the same as those taught in the medieval universities. It was the intense education of the lay *élite* in the classics that was novel.[3] Bradshaw's account of a rupture in Irish political discourse in the sixteenth century has also come under criticism from historians of Irish politics. Bradshaw claimed that talk in the sixteenth-century English Pale of the purpose of all government being the common good was evidence of a new humanist mood. But Christopher Maginn and Steven Ellis have noted that emphasis on the common good was entirely normal in fifteenth-century political correspondence and Irish parliamentary statutes: there was no fundamental change in the discourse.[4] By contrast, Benignus Millett implicitly adopted Kristeller's approach, portraying scholasticism and humanism as complementary cultural movements and emphasising the importance of grammar schools and universities in teaching classical languages and literature.

Millett could not see any evidence of a widespread Irish lay expertise in Latin and Greek before the 1560s, and the 1531 inventory of the library of Maynooth Castle, seat of the earls of Kildare, supports this periodisation.[5] The library of this exceptionally wealthy noble household contained just over one hundred volumes, and included neither Cicero's speeches and

---

Goldie (eds.), *The Cambridge History of Political Thought* (Cambridge University Press, 1991), 95–131; B. Millett, 'Irish Literature in Latin, 1550–1700', in T. W. Moody, F. X. Martin and F. J. Byrne (eds.), *A New History of Ireland*, iii: *Early Modern Ireland 1534–1691* (Oxford University Press, 1976), 561–86.

3 P. O. Kristeller, *Renaissance Thought* (2 vols., New York: Harper & Row, 1961), i, 8–11; B. P. Copenhaver and C. B. Schmitt, *Renaissance Philosophy* (Oxford University Press, 1992), 24–5; A. Rabil (ed.), *Renaissance Humanism: Foundations, Forms and Legacy* (3 vols., Philadelphia: University of Pennsylvania Press, 1988).

4 C. Maginn and S. Ellis, *The Tudor Discovery of Ireland* (Dublin: Four Courts Press [hereafter FCP], 2015), 138–9.

5 A. Byrne, 'The Earls of Kildare and their Books at the End of the Middle Ages', *The Library*, seventh series, 14 (2013), 129–53; compare D. Ó Catháin, 'Some Reflexes of Latin Learning and of the Renaissance in Ireland, c.1450–c.1600', in J. Harris and K. Sidwell (eds.), *Making Ireland Roman: Irish Neo-Latin Writers and the Republic of Letters* (Cork University Press, 2009), 14–37.

moral philosophy, nor Aristotle's more difficult works on ethics and politics. Cicero's *De Officiis* (On Duties), which was fundamental to moral philosophy in the grammar schools and indeed to the education of the young Henry VIII himself, is an especially glaring absence.[6] In fact, it is very likely that the Latin letters taught to the laymen in the castle stopped at Caesar's *Commentaries*, a very basic text. The more sophisticated Latin works in the library, such as Thomas More's *Utopia*, were probably read only by the clergy. Without the establishment of a network of grammar schools and accomplished tutors throughout the island, there could be no true culture of Renaissance human-ism among the Irish gentry and nobility. Such a network did not begin to appear until the mid-sixteenth century.[7]

Nevertheless, the Maynooth library did make a number of scholastic resources for speaking about law, society and politics available to the clergy of the household, which were perhaps then transmitted through conver-sation and sermons to the lay *élite*. The most substantial of these scholas-tic resources was Antoninus Florentinus's *Summa Theologica*.[8] This book compressed Thomas Aquinas's theological system into a form convenient for those preaching, hearing confessions and caring for souls: precisely the duties of the Fitzgeralds' chaplains.[9] Thomist theology had made a number of important borrowings from the philosophy of Aristotle. The Thomists accepted Aristotle's division of all things into essence and accidents, where the essence made a thing what it was and the accidents could be changed without changing the nature of the thing. If one knew the essence of a thing, the Aristotelians thought one would also know what the thing was for, its purpose; this purpose they called the thing's 'final cause'. The essence of a human was his or her rational soul, and the first book of Aristotle's *Politics* argued that the best life for this rational human was political life, because it was in political life that humans used their reason to the utmost and so were most human. The same argument was made in Cicero's ethical works, in a simpler form. The Thomists believed that these pagan arguments were true,

6 A. Pollnitz, *Princely Education in Early Modern Britain* (Cambridge University Press, 2015), 52–5.

7 C. Lennon, 'Education and Religious Identity in Early Modern Ireland', in J. Coolahan, F. Simon and R. Aldritch (eds.), *Faiths and Education: Historical and Comparative Perspectives* (Gent: C.S.H.P., 1999), 57–75.

8 Byrne, 'Earls of Kildare', 143. There were numerous printings of this in the 1470s and 1480s, which lack title pages and can be difficult to distinguish from each other. I have used: Antoninus Florentinus, *Prima Pars Summae theologicae*, (Venice: Nicholas Jenson, 1478) British Library 19734.

9 P. F. Howard, *Aquinas and Antoninus: a Tale of Two Summae in Renaissance Florence*, Etienne Gilson Series 35 (Toronto: Pontifical Institute of Medieval Studies, 2013), 19.

and that one could achieve an excellent life in this, natural, world in this way. Nevertheless, they also believed that the Christian had to look beyond this world to a supernatural final cause: happiness with God.[10]

Antoninus presented his reader with a Christian Aristotelian universe organised around the concept of law. The eternal law was God's reason ordering everything from planets, to seas, to animals, to their purposes in the divine plan. But humans participated in this providential ordering in a special way. Humanity had been made rational in the image of God, and each sane person remained just rational enough, even after the fall, to see that his or her purpose was to love God and love his or her neighbour. Humans were not just directed to a purpose; possessed of free will and responsible for their actions, they directed themselves to that purpose impressed in them by God.[11] From this, one could deduce simple rights and wrongs concerning the person, the family and the political community or commonwealth. This human participation in God's eternal law was natural law: a law naturally evident to all humans in all times and places. All humans knew that theft was against the natural law; the human positive law of cities and princes would prescribe the exact penalty.[12] So for Antoninus classical philosophers like Cicero and Aristotle were right, as far as this world was concerned, when they termed humans political animals who lived best when reasoning, and reasoned best when living together in a commonwealth. Rational humans would best fulfil the purposes impressed in them by God when living together in political society; lying was wrong because it tended towards the dissolution of this society.[13] The purpose of such a society was the common good, rather than the good of any one person or faction.[14] All laws were to look to this common good and should strive to make the members of that society virtuous or excellent (law was not only for providing material safety).[15] Humans were obliged in conscience to obey the commonwealth's laws: it was a sin to break a good law even if no one noticed. Nevertheless, irrational laws and human laws that were contrary to the law of nature did not bind the conscience: one could break those laws without sin.[16] And overall, Antoninus's statements on the organisation of the commonwealth favoured monarchy limited by human

---

10 Bonnie Kent, 'Habits and Virtues (Ia IIae, qq. 49–70)', in S. J. Pope (ed.), *The Ethics of Aquinas* (Washington, DC: Georgetown University Press, 2002), 116–30.

11 Antoninus, *Prima Pars*, title 11, chapter 1, section 4; tit. 12, chap. 1, sec. 2.

12 Antoninus, *Prima Pars*, tit. 13; chap. 1.

13 Antoninus, *Prima Pars*, tit. 13, chap. 2, sec. 3; tit. 14, chap. 4, sec. 12; tit. 17, chap. 1, sec. 2.

14 Antoninus, *Prima Pars*, tit. 11, chap. 2, sec. 1.

15 Antoninus, *Prima Pars*, tit. 17, chap. 1, sec. 2.

16 Antoninus, *Prima Pars*, tit. 18, chap. 1, sec. 2.

law rather than absolute monarchy free from human law. He explained the traditional distinction between monarchy, aristocracy and democracy (rule by the one, the few and the many), and argued that the best commonwealth was a harmonious mixture of all three.[17] This Thomist, Aristotelian natural law theory was commonplace among both Irish Catholics and those Protestants less inclined towards Calvinism up to the 1650s and beyond.

From the 1560s Catholic grammar schools, which taught the basics of Ciceronian moral philosophy in the final forms, began to appear in Kilkenny, Waterford, Limerick, Drogheda, Dundalk and Galway; they were well established by the turn of the century.[18] Protestant grammar schools were supposed to function in each diocese (though in cities like Dublin these took in Catholic pupils also), but were supplemented by the endowments of Protestant noblemen.[19] Six grammar schools were planned as part of the Ulster Plantation, and most of these had come into existence by the 1620s.[20] Trinity College Dublin began to receive undergraduates in 1594, and taught a thoroughly Ciceronian and Aristotelian curriculum in moral philosophy; but universities outside Ireland were at least as important to Irish intellectual life.[21] The Irish Protestant episcopate of 1641 had all been educated in universities in Ireland, England and Scotland. One-fifth of the Irish temporal peerage in the seventeenth century attended universities in Ireland, England, Scotland, France, the Spanish Low Countries and the Dutch Republic. By the 1640s, the entire Irish Catholic episcopate had been educated at universities in the Spanish Low Countries, France, Spain, Portugal, Italy and Bohemia. All of these universities drilled their bachelors of arts in Aristotelian philosophy as a preparation for higher degrees in medicine, theology and law.[22]

By the middle of the seventeenth century, noble libraries in Ireland were much bigger than they had been a century earlier, and contained much more classical philosophy. The library assembled by Edward, Viscount Conway and Killultagh, at Lisnagarvey (Lisburn) before 1641 contained more than 8,000 volumes.[23] The catalogue of this library, compiled by Conway's chaplain

17 Antoninus, *Prima Pars*, tit. 18, chap. 1. sec. 1.
18 Millett, 'Irish literature in Latin', 563–5 ; B. Mac Cuarta, *Catholic Revival in the North of Ireland, 1603–41* (Dublin: FCP, 2007), 217–18.
19 Lennon, 'Education and Religious Identity'; A. Ford, *The Protestant Reformation in Ireland, 1590–1641* (Frankfurt am Main: Peter Lang, 1987), 101–2, 130–1, 168, 170–1, 289.
20 P. Robinson, *The Plantation of Ulster* (2nd edn., Belfast: Ulster Historical Association, 1994), 82–3, 148–9.
21 I. Campbell, 'Calvinist Absolutism: Archbishop James Ussher and Royal Power', *Journal of British Studies*, 53 (2014), 594–5.
22 I. Campbell, *Renaissance Humanism and Ethnicity before Race: The Irish and the English in the Seventeenth Century* (Manchester University Press, 2013), 25–6.
23 D. Starza Smith, *John Donne and the Conway Papers* (Oxford University Press, 2014), 118.

and a local schoolmaster, listed multiple editions of Aristotle's *Nichomachean Ethics* and *Politics* in a variety of sizes, as well as editions of Cicero's works, including *De Officiis*.[24] By the end of the century, as the Irish *élite* began to turn away from Aristotle to more modern theorisations of human life, an English-language literary culture had begun to spread beyond the nobility and gentry to the 'middling sort' of merchants, artisans and prosperous farmers.[25]

Natural law, as inherited from the Middle Ages and taught in the early modern universities, provided both a theory of history and an ideology of empire, and it was a doctrine directly relevant to the transformation of the lordship of Ireland into the kingdom of Ireland in 1541. The law of nature was valid across time: humans applied the same reason to similar political problems in the twelfth century and in the sixteenth, so that the Kildare library's chronicles and annals in Latin, French and English of Ireland, England, France and the Holy Land carried perennially relevant political examples and messages. Giraldus Cambrensis's *Expugnatio Hibernica* in English and Irish translations not only told the earls of Kildare how their ancestors had come to Ireland in the twelfth century, including the papal grant of the island to the kings of England, but also emphasised the triumph of what Giraldus called English virtue over Irish barbarism.[26] The law of nature was also valid across space: as there was one human reason, so there was one right way to live, and the English inevitably interpreted this to mean that their way of life was superior to that of the Irish. In 1541, the Irish parliament declared that since Henry VIII and his predecessors had truly enjoyed all the powers of kings in Ireland, he and his successors should henceforth be known as kings, rather than lords, of Ireland. The implication of this was that the island would no longer be divided between fragmented political communities (the king's English subjects and the king's Irish enemies), but that the new Irish kingdom was a complete or 'perfect' political community, capable of providing self-sufficiently for the common good of all its inhabitants.[27] This self-sufficiency was somewhat undermined in the Irish case by Poynings' Law of 1494, which provided that the Irish viceroy could not summon a parliament in Ireland without royal approval, and that the bills to be made law in that parliament should also be

24 MS KH II 39, ff. 186r–197r, 198r, Armagh Public Library.
25 R. Gillespie, 'Print Culture, 1550–1700', in R. Gillespie and A. Hadfield (eds.), *The Oxford History of the Irish Book, iii, The Irish Book in English 1550–1700* (Oxford University Press, 2006), 17–33.
26 A. Byrne, 'Family, Locality, and Nationality: Vernacular Adaptations of the *Expugnatio Hibernica* in Late Medieval Ireland', *Medium Aevum*, 82 (2013), 101–18.
27 Bradshaw, *Irish Constitutional Revolution*, 231–8; C. G. Kossel, 'Natural Law and Human Law (Ia IIae, qq. 90–97)', in Pope (ed.), *Ethics of Aquinas*, 170.

approved by the king and his Privy Council.[28] Despite the occasional use of Poynings' Law by the king's subjects in Ireland to limit the viceroys' freedom of action, the interaction between these two acts established a constitutional paradox – a kingdom implicitly self-sufficient but practically subordinate – important to Irish politics up to the Act of Union in 1800. But the argument of the Kingship Act itself was more limited: it emphasised the justice and rightfulness of the king's jurisdiction, and the treachery of those in Ireland who impugned it, whether English or Irish.

Humanist Political Theory: Civility and Barbarism

Humanist political theory was the promulgation among the lay *élite* of ideas long established in scholastic political theology. The English had condemned the Irish as barbarians since the time of Gerald of Wales; the more intense education of the lay *élite* in the classics from the later sixteenth century sharpened this condemnatory vocabulary. Ireland's greatest humanist was Richard Stanihurst. He had been educated at an excellent grammar school in Kilkenny, at University College, Oxford, and at the Inns of Court in London. In the late 1570s he served in the household of Gerald FitzGerald, the eleventh earl of Kildare.[29] Stanihurst's political works – an English description of Ireland printed in 1577, and a Latin history of the twelfth-century English conquest of Ireland, printed in 1584 – were chiefly concerned with the distinction between civility and barbarism.[30] Civility was the true political life achieved by rational humans, and barbarism was a failure to achieve that virtuous condition. All humanists and scholastics insisted on the importance of eloquence to human life because they considered reason and speech effectively synonymous: good reason was impossible without good speech.[31] A central part of Stanihurst's attack on Gaelic Ireland was his insistence that the Irish language was inferior to English: one could not reason well in Irish, and consequently one could

28 R. D. Edwards and T. W. Moody, 'The history of Poynings' Law, Pt. 1: 1494–1615', *Irish Historical Studies* 2 (1941), 415–24; A. Clarke, 'The History of Poynings' Law, 1615–41', *Irish Historical Studies*, 18 (1972), 207–22; J. Kelly, *Poynings' Law and the Making of Law in Ireland, 1660–1800* (Dublin: FCP, 2007).

29 C. Lennon, *Richard Stanihurst the Dubliner, 1547–1618* (Dublin: Irish Academic Press, 1981); Richard Stanihurst, *Great Deeds in Ireland: Richard Stanihurst's De Rebus in Hibernia Gestis*, ed. J. Barry and H. Morgan (Cork University Press, 2013), 1–72.

30 *Holinshed's Irish Chronicle*, ed. L. Miller and E. Power (Dublin: Dolmen Press, 1979); Richard Stanihurst, *De Rebus in Hibernia Gestis* (Antwerp, 1584); Stanihurst, *Great Deeds in Ireland*.

31 Aristotle, *Politics*, book I, trans. by Harris Rackham (London: William Heinemann, 1932); H. H. Gray, 'Renaissance Humanism: The Pursuit of Eloquence', *Journal of the History of Ideas*, 24 (1963), 497–514.

not be truly political or civil in Irish.[32] Stanihurst held that Gaelic society was composed of warrior factions and tyrants who looked only to their own benefit, rather than to the common good. Because the factionalised Gaelic Irish did not look to the common good, they had no commonwealth.[33] Stanihurst explained that Henry II was granted lordship of Ireland under the terms of Pope Adrian IV's bull *Laudabiliter* on condition that he establish (*constituere*) an Irish commonwealth, putting an end to (*delere*) the barbarism of the people, and planting (*conserere*) laws congruent with the Catholic faith.[34]

Stanihurst had one eye on some English and Italian writers who ascribed an extreme barbarism to the Irish. All barbarians were thought irrational, but Aristotle had tended to conflate barbarians with natural slaves, persons so stupid that they could own neither themselves nor any property. Some historians and geographers had described the Gaelic Irish in terms that seemed to hint at natural slavery. Stanihurst thought these allegations absurd, and insisted that the Gaelic Irish were rational humans who might be brought to a true (and English) political life primarily through education.[35] Nevertheless, Stanihurst's most complete description of this civilising process was his history of the twelfth-century conquest of the island in the *De Rebus in Hibernia Gestis*: a just war which incorporated acts of shocking violence. Even for Ciceronian humanists like Stanihurst, force was an inevitable part of all human government, and the distinction between civility and barbarism served as an efficient ideology of ethnic domination. Classical ideologies of civility and barbarism like this were staples of Old and New English writing on government well into the seventeenth century.[36]

Humanism and Ireland's Ancient Constitution

There is some evidence that the more accomplished Irish parliamentarians made use of basic scholastic and humanist concepts when speaking in the House of Commons. Richard Stanihurst's father James served as speaker of the Commons in the parliament of 1569–1571. Addressing Lord Deputy Sir Henry Sidney in December 1570, he praised Sidney's employment both of 'sword and wisdome' in Ireland, celebrated the dispatch of young members of the *élite* to England to study law and attend school and university, and

---

32 Miller and Power (eds.), *Holinshed's Irish Chronicle*, 15–20.
33 Stanihurst, *Great Deeds*, 110–11, 115.
34 Stanihurst, *Great Deeds*, 270–1.
35 Stanihurst, *Great Deeds*, 111; Miller and Power (eds.), *Holinshed's Irish Chronicle*, 113–14.
36 Campbell, *Renaissance Humanism and Ethnicity before Race*, 53–82.

then called for the establishment of grammar schools in every diocese, where schoolmasters would accustom children to 'a pure English tongue, habite, fashion, discipline' which would induce them to abandon barbarous practices, before lamenting the failure of Sidney's plan to establish an Irish university.[37] The speaker of the Irish Commons in the parliament of 1585–1586 was the Old English Protestant Sir Nicholas Walsh; he addressed the Commons in May 1586. Dealing with a lord deputy determined both to extract more taxation from the Pale to support the military establishment, and to import English measures against Old English recusants, Walsh wished to remind his auditors of the fundamental nature and aims of government.[38] As humans were distinguished from other animals by speech and reason, Walsh began, so they were framed by nature for society. He continued with a touch of Christian pessimism, explaining that human wickedness meant that this natural inclination to society was not enough for good order, and so laws and magistrates were necessary.[39] Of the three kinds of government, Walsh thought monarchy the best; but Queen Elizabeth's government in Ireland was a mixed monarchy that 'draweth thereunto the best parts of the other two, in a most happy harmony, to the universal comfort of all estates'.[40] That word harmony was important: the three estates were expected to collaborate rationally and virtuously for the common good. The idea that a government might be established in which factional struggle could be harnessed to strengthen rather than weaken the state was not widely adopted in the Atlantic world until the eighteenth century.[41] And so in parliament the Commons, 'called to this society as interested for the multitude', and the peers were both annexed to the sovereignty of the prince. Moreover, Walsh argued that this relationship between the one, few and many was found throughout the Irish commonwealth. In courts of law, the queen was the one, the judges (taken as a body) the few and the jury represented the many. Cities and corporate towns also followed this pattern.[42] Walsh strongly implied that the lord deputy was obliged to respect these eminently rational constitutional arrangements. Scholastic political theory, in digestible humanist form, thus helped Walsh to analyse the world around him: the late sixteenth-century Irish and English

37 Sir James Ware (ed.), *The Historie of Ireland* (Dublin, 1633), 131–3.
38 M. A. Hutchinson, 'Nicholas Walsh's Oration to the Irish House of Commons, May 1586', *Analecta Hibernica*, 45 (2014), 35–52.
39 Hutchinson, 'Nicholas Walsh's Oration', 43.
40 Hutchinson, 'Nicholas Walsh's Oration', 44–5.
41 P. A. Rahe, *Republics Ancient and Modern*, (3 vols., Chapel Hill, NC: University of North Carolina Press, 1994), iii, 31–74.
42 Rahe, *Republics Ancient and Modern*, 45.

kingdoms were indeed mixed rather than absolute monarchies. These 'thin' states were very limited in their capacity for coercion and profoundly dependent on the participation of local office-holders of all kinds from justices of the peace in County Dublin to stewards of manorial courts in County Kilkenny.[43]

The common law itself provided rich resources for speaking about political life, resources not antipathetic to the scholastic and humanist theories described above. To support his argument that Ireland was a mixed monarchy, Walsh had cited Sir John Fortescue's fourteenth-century *De Laudibus Legum Angliae*.[44] This was a dialogue between an English prince and a lord chancellor, which advanced the argument that England was a mixed monarchy, limited by human law, rather than an absolute one in which the king was free of human law. Fortescue was keen to align his arguments with university learning, and cited both Aristotle and Aquinas in support of his mixed monarchy doctrine.[45] English statutes were made not just by the king, but by the assent of the whole realm, which meant, for example, that the king could not tax his subjects, alter their laws or make new laws, 'without the expresse consente and agreement of his whole royalme in his Parliament'.[46] Fortescue identified the common law as a customary law in concord with the law of nature, and so far neither better nor worse than the laws of other peoples. What made the English common law especially refined was its great antiquity: England had been ruled by the same customs since the time of the ancient Britons. Had these laws not been good, rational Englishmen would have changed them. English laws were the most rational and thus the best; their antiquity confirmed their quality.[47]

Historians have labelled this conjunction of ideas about law, reason and time the Ancient Constitution, and there are grounds to believe that it constituted a powerful ideology among the Irish common lawyers from the 1570s to the 1640s.[48] Many Irish lawyers were educated in London at the Inns of Court where the ideology was prominent, and Sir John Davies, Archbishop

---

43 M. Goldie, 'The Unacknowledged Republic: Officeholding in Early Modern England', in T. Harris (ed.), *The Politics of the Excluded, c.1500–1850* (Basingstoke: Palgrave, 2001), 153–94; C. Brady, *The Chief Governors: The Rise and Fall of Reform Government in Tudor Ireland 1536–1588* (Cambridge University Press, 1994), 209–44.

44 Sir John Fortescue, *A Learned Commendation of the Politique Lawes of England*, trans. Richard Mulcaster (London, 1599).

45 C. W. Brooks, *Law, Politics and Society in Early Modern England* (Cambridge University Press, 2008), 23–5.

46 Fortescue, *A Learned Commendation*, f. 84v.

47 Ibid., f. 38r–38v.

48 J. Greenberg, *The Radical Face of the Ancient Constitution: St Edward's 'Laws' in Early Modern Political Thought* (Cambridge University Press, 2001).

James Ussher and Thomas Wentworth, later earl of Strafford, all identified it as a defence adopted by Old English recusants.[49] The Galway lawyer Patrick Darcy, who attended the Middle Temple from 1617 to about 1622, was the most accomplished defender of the Irish Ancient Constitution. Addressing the Irish House of Lords on 9 June 1641, Darcy insisted that the English common law as it operated in Ireland was 'the best human law'. Darcy drew on Fortescue to argue that English government was the best in the world, and a mixed rather than absolute monarchy, so that no English king had ever altered the laws or taxed his subjects without the consent of parliament.[50] Darcy also put very great emphasis on the Irish Magna Carta of 1216, which he believed limited royal power over the lives and property of subjects.[51] Despite insisting on the Englishness of the law of the Irish kingdom, Darcy held that statutes had force in Ireland only when received and enacted by the king and his Irish lords and commons. The English parliament had no power to make law for Ireland as Ireland was 'annexed to the crown of England', not to the English parliament.[52] That latter point became vital to the Confederate Catholics of Ireland after the English parliament's passing of the Adventurer's Act of 1642, and explains both the printing of the *Argument* at a Confederate press in 1643, and the point's further elaboration in other Confederate treatises in succeeding years.[53]

Alternatives to Aristotelianism: Reason of State and Absolutism

This political discourse among the English of Ireland, a compound of scholastic, humanist and common law concepts, came under attack in the 1590s from New English ideologues employing 'reason of state' theory. Dismayed by the rebellion of Hugh O'Neill, earl of Tyrone, against Queen Elizabeth I, some New English emphasised the value and fragility of political order, and recommended undertaking actions which might be judged illegal under natural and positive law in order to preserve that order; it was the latter position

---

49 B. McGrath, 'Ireland and the Third University: Attendance at the Inns of Court, 1603–1650', in D. Edwards (ed.), *Regions and Rulers in Ireland 1100–1650* (Dublin: FCP, 2004), 217–36.

50 Patrick Darcy, 'An Argument', ed. C. E. J. Caldicott, *Camden Miscellany*, 31 (1992), 191–320, at 271, 280.

51 Darcy, 'An Argument', 235, 278, 281, 285–6, 290, 303–6.

52 Darcy, 'An Argument', 270, 274, 294, 294–96; A. Clarke, 'Patrick Darcy and the Constitutional Relationship between Ireland and Britain', in J. H. Ohlmeyer (ed.), *Political Thought in Seventeenth-Century Ireland* (Cambridge University Press, 2000), 43.

53 Clarke, 'Patrick Darcy', 48.

that seemed irreligious to many contemporaries.[54] Richard Beacon's *Solon his Follie* was printed in 1594, probably in support of Sir William Russell's lord deputyship, and sought solutions to Irish problems in Niccolò Machiavelli's *Discourses on Livy*. Beacon advised English governors in Ireland to lie, to encourage the plebs and nobility to pursue their own private interests rather than the common good, and to pursue glory through aggressive wars, whether just or unjust.[55] Still more radical was Edmund Spenser's *View of the Present State of Ireland*. Completed in 1596 and circulated in at least twenty-one manuscript copies before its printing in 1633, this dialogue urged the elevation of martial law over common law and the killing of nearly all the Gaelic Irish *élite*.[56] Spenser was very hostile to the Old English gentry and nobility of Ireland, their parliament and their common law, and he also mocked the traditional ethical vocabulary of the scholastics and humanists. Spenser argued that one's only criterion in law making should be the material safety of the commonwealth – not wider questions of right and wrong.[57] Although scholars generally take Spenser to have been a conventional Protestant conformist, he nonetheless appears to have had a reputation among his peers not only for learning (especially in Greek philosophy) but also for unorthodox religious opinions.[58] Whatever about Spenser's own beliefs, the number of surviving manuscripts of the *View* suggests that contemporaries were interested by his radical arguments. Nevertheless, the importance of these arguments should not be overestimated. Reason of state theory was not included in the curricula of grammar schools or universities, nor bound into the learning of powerful professions, and its denial of natural law placed it at odds with the wider Christian culture.

Absolutist political theory was far more useful to early seventeenth-century Protestants who wished to undermine the position of the Old English *élite*. The first Englishman to articulate an absolutist vision of the Irish constitution was Sir John Davies, attorney general for Ireland from 1606 to 1619. His

---

54 Rahe, *Republics Ancient and Modern*, i, 32–7.
55 Richard Beacon, *Solon his Follie*, ed. C. Carroll and V. Carey (Binghamton, NY: Centre for Medieval and Early Renaissance Studies, 1996).
56 Edmund Spenser, 'A View of the Present State of Ireland', in *Spenser's Prose Works*, ed. Rudolf Gottfried (Baltimore, MD: Johns Hopkins Press, 1949), 158, 177–8, 209, 216, 219; P. Beal, *Index of English Literary Manuscripts, Volume 1, 1450–1625, Part 2 Douglas-Wyatt* (London: Mansell, 1980), 530–1; D. Edwards, 'Ideology and Experience: Spenser's View and Martial Law in Ireland', in H. Morgan (ed.), *Political Ideology in Ireland, 1541–1641* (Dublin: FCP, 1999), 127–57.
57 Spenser, 'A View', 65–6.
58 Lodowick Bryskett, *A Discourse of Civill Life: Containing the Ethicke part of Morall Philosophie* (London, 1606), 26–8, 271–6, 278.

Discovery of the True Causes of 1612 attempted to resolve the ideologically unhelpful medieval history of Ireland – with its papal grants, jurisdictional complexity and powerful representative institutions – more efficiently than the Kingship Act of 1541.[59] Davies's book borrowed heavily from Jean Bodin's *Six livres de la république*.[60] Bodin, generally hostile to traditional scholasticism, thought mixed government merely a destructive fantasy that had contributed to the civil wars in France. In reality, the jurist argued, the most important thing about a political community was the location of sovereignty (the power of command without appeal) within it. It had to be held by monarch, or nobles, or people, and it could not be shared or divided without dissolving the state.[61] The location of sovereignty thus determined whether the community in question was a monarchy, aristocracy or democracy.[62] And because aristocracy and democracy involved the sharing of sovereignty they were imperfect. Absolute monarchy was thus not just the best form of government; it was the only real government, the only real alternative to anarchy.[63]

The *Discovery of the True Causes* argued that conquest meant the achievement of sovereignty. But Davies wrote that during the Middle Ages the English government in Ireland had certainly not been able to exercise sovereignty over the whole island. Therefore there had been no true conquest of Ireland in the twelfth century.[64] The Gaelic kings had been independent princes paying tribute to the English crown, rather than subjects of the English crown.[65] The Kingship Act of 1541 was no more than a trivial name-change, which did nothing to alter the facts.[66] The first true conquest of Ireland, and the English crown's first true achievement of sovereignty on the island, came with the conclusion of the Nine Years' War in 1603.[67] The medieval Irish parliament was thus not the common council of the whole community aiming at the common good, but a trivial colonial assembly concerned with factional benefit, which openly excluded the Gaelic Irish from English law.[68] Davies joined

---

59 Sir John Davies, *A Discovery of the True Causes why Ireland Was Never Entirely Subdued [and] Brought under Obedience of the Crown of England until the Beginning of His Majesty's Happy Reign*, ed. J. P. Myers (Washington, DC: Catholic University of America, 1988).

60 I. Campbell, 'Aristotelian Ancient Constitution and anti-Aristotelian Sovereignty in Stuart Ireland', *Historical Journal*, 53 (2010), 586.

61 Jean Bodin, *Les Six Livres de la République* (Paris, 1583; facsimile reprint, Darmstadt: Scientia Verlag Aalen, 1977), Bk 1, chapter 10, 213.

62 Bodin, *Les Six Livres*, Bk 2, chapter 1, 251–2, 266–7.

63 Bodin, *Les Six Livres*, Bk 6, chapter 4, 961, 971.

64 Davies, *Discovery*, 71–2, 76.

65 Davies, *Discovery*, 75–6.

66 Davies, *Discovery*, 204.

67 Davies, *Discovery*, 211.

68 Davies, *Discovery*, 171–4, 187–90.

to this the most detailed portrayal of the barbarity of Gaelic law yet undertaken, as well as a thorough account of how the imposition of English law would reform Gaelic society, concluding with a glowing account of the Ulster Plantation (the practical administration of which was one of his central concerns).[69] Davies reinforced these arguments in the preface to his law reports of 1615, when he aggressively justified the elevation of the decisions of his judges over the statute law of the Irish parliament. Hans Pawlisch has argued convincingly that this use of judicial resolutions, rather than statute law, to complete the unfinished Tudor conquest was in fact the English government's primary governmental strategy in the first two decades of the seventeenth century in Ireland.[70] All this amounted to a breathtaking attack on Old English political culture as it had developed since the Middle Ages.

Archbishop James Ussher of Armagh was also a convinced advocate of absolutism, which provided a basis both for excluding the Catholic *élite* from government and also for neutralising the threat of resistance from Protestants more radically alienated by Charles I's religious policies than the archbishop himself.[71] Whether he came to Bodin through Davies or independently, Ussher made heavy use of the Frenchman's doctrine of sovereignty. Speaking at the opening of Lord Deputy Thomas Wentworth's first Irish parliament in 1634, Ussher explained that while the presence of the knights and burgesses representing the commons might make the kingdom appear to incorporate an element of democracy, and the presence of the nobles might make it appear to include a degree of aristocracy, nevertheless the government of Ireland was not 'a mixt government, but an absolute monarchye'. Sovereignty lay with the king, who assembled or dissolved the two houses, and allowed or disallowed their acts, at his pleasure. Whether in the Irish case or with any other governments – Ussher instanced Biblical Israel, Sparta, Switzerland and Venice – the only real constitutional choice was between absolute monarchy and a de-centralised drift towards anarchy.[72]

But unlike Davies, Ussher placed divine power at the centre of human political life. In reaction to increasing tension over church government within

---

69 Davies, *Discovery*, 221–3.

70 Sir John Davies, *Le Primer Report des Cases in les Courts del Roy* (Dublin, 1615), sig. *2r-v; H. Pawlisch, *Sir John Davies and the Conquest of Ireland: A Study in Legal Imperialism* (Cambridge University Press, 1985), 34–51.

71 A. Ford, *James Ussher: Theology, History, and Politics in Early Modern Ireland and England* (Oxford University Press, 2007), 225–6, 261, 270; A. Ford, 'James Ussher and the Godly Prince in Early Seventeenth-Century Ireland', in Morgan (ed.), *Political Ideology*, 203–28; I. Campbell, 'Calvinist Absolutism', 588–610.

72 MS Rawlinson D 1290, ff. 76v–77r, Bodleian Library, Oxford.

British and Irish Protestantism from the 1590s into the early seventeenth century, theologians who wished to defend the monarch against what they saw as Puritan or Presbyterian insubordination began to argue that political power came to the king not by delegation from the community, but directly from God.[73] By 1640, and in the face of Scottish resistance to Stuart ecclesiastical innovation, Ussher was preaching a highly polished form of that doctrine – and that same year he expanded these sermons into a substantial treatise on royal power, which was printed only after his death.[74] Ussher argued that because the monarch received his power directly from God, resisting his command was not just a crime but a sin. St Paul's instruction to obey the powers that be (Romans 13) meant that even the most evil king might only be resisted passively, by a withdrawal of cooperation.[75]

During the 1630s, Lord Deputy Thomas Wentworth and John Bramhall, bishop of Derry, sought to rid the Church of Ireland of its Calvinist tendencies in line with Archbishop William Laud of Canterbury's attempted reforms throughout the Stuart kingdoms, and Ussher did indeed attempt to withdraw into private life. The practical absolutism of Wentworth's government was manifested in its disregard for the common law, enhancement of the power of senior prerogative courts and aggressive practices of parliamentary management.[76] Wentworth and his more important servants were nevertheless careful to avoid losing touch with Ussher. As part of the preparations for the 1640 parliament the lord deputy's secretary, Sir George Radcliffe, sent Ussher a short manuscript treatise on government. Radcliffe's treatise covered much of the same ground mentioned above: political power had been granted to kings directly by God, and it had never lain in the people. But Radcliffe expanded on the difference between this absolutist theory of government and that advanced both by medieval scholastics and contemporary Catholic theologians. These Catholics portrayed political power as a natural thing rather than a supernatural thing, Radcliffe argued, only because they wanted to elevate the supernatural monarchy of the Pope over the natural monarchy of kings and emperors.[77] Radcliffe and Ussher were at one on the

73 P. Lake, *Anglicans and Puritans? Presbyterianism and English Conformist Thought from Whitgift to Hooker* (London: Unwin, 1988).

74 James Ussher, *The Power Communicated by God to the Prince and the Obedience Required of the Subject*, ed. Robert Sanderson (London, 1661).

75 Ussher, *The Power Communicated by God*, 1–3, 145–6, 150.

76 H. Kearney, *Strafford In Ireland, 1633–41* (Cambridge University Press, 1989).

77 Ian Campbell, 'Select Document: Sir George Radcliffe's "Originall of Government" (1639) and Absolutist Political Theory in Stuart Ireland', *Irish Historical Studies*, 39 (2014), 308–22.

supernatural character of royal power. It was in reaction to this absolutist discourse at Wentworth's court that Patrick Darcy had advanced his fundamentally traditional account of political power in the Irish kingdom.

Irish Catholic Scholasticism and Revolution

Patrick Darcy and the vast majority of his Catholic contemporaries accepted the fundamental legitimacy of Stuart power in Ireland, but differed with Wentworth's court on the origins of that power, and the purposes to which it was to be applied. But a small number of predominantly Gaelic Irish Catholics insisted that Stuart power was wholly illegitimate, and they employed scholastic political theology to make that case. This anti-Stuart political tradition arose among those exiled to the Spanish Habsburg territories at the conclusion of the Nine Years' War and carried on into the 1660s; it disintegrated permanently with the accession of the Catholic James II to the throne in 1685. Irish Catholic Stuart loyalists, as well as Protestants like Archbishop Ussher, feared that the exiles intended not just the destruction of the Stuart *régime* in Ireland, but also a social revolution resulting from the restoration of former ecclesiastical property to the Catholic Church and the return of planted lands to their previous owners.[78] Pioneered by Archbishop Peter Lombard of Armagh in a manuscript treatise composed about 1600, the first major printed statement of this anti-Stuart ideology came in 1621 with Philip O'Sullivan Beare's *Historiae Catholicae Iberniae Compendium* (Summary of the Catholic History of Ireland).[79] O'Sullivan Beare's history complemented the letters and treatises that Archbishop Florence Conry of Tuam circulated in Ireland and Spain during the 1610s and 1620s.[80] Conor O'Mahony's *Disputatio Apologetica* of 1645 cited O'Sullivan Beare extensively and was far more open in its attacks on Stuart power.[81] Several Gaelic Irish anti-Stuart extremists resided in the household of GianBattista Rinuccini, papal nuncio to the Confederate Catholics of Ireland between 1645 and 1649. One of those extremists, Richard O'Ferrall, later advanced these

---

78 T. Ó hAnnracháin, *Catholic Reformation in Ireland: The Mission of Rinuccini, 1645–1649* (Oxford University Press, 2002), 26–32.

79 T. O'Connor, 'A Justification for Foreign Intervention in Early Modern Ireland: Peter Lombard's *Commentarius*', in T. O'Connor and M. A. Lyons (eds.), *Irish Migrants in Europe after Kinsale, 1602–1820* (Dublin: FCP, 2003), 14–31; Philip O'Sullivan Beare, *Historiae Catholicae Iberniae Compendium* (Lisbon, 1621).

80 B. Hazard, *Faith and Patronage: The Political Career of Flaithrí Ó Maolchonaire, c. 1560–1629* (Dublin: Irish Academic Press, 2010).

81 Conor O'Mahony, *An Argument Defending the Right of the Kingdom of Ireland*, trans. John Minahane (Aubane Historical Society, 2010).

anti-Stuart positions in Rome and Florence in the 1650s and 1660s, resulting in the monumental anti-Stuart and anti-Protestant history of Ireland, the *Commentarius Rinuccinianus*.[82]

Certain fundamental assumptions, grounded in Thomist political theology, underlay all these works. All assumed that the Irish kingdom was a 'perfect' political community possessing a right of self-defence, that the purpose of government was the good of the community as a whole, and that since the twelfth century the English monarchy had governed Ireland in the interest of a narrow faction of colonists alone in a manner flatly contradicting natural law. All implied that the Irish kingdom was thus obliged to choose a new monarch, and Conry and O'Mahony made this argument overtly. Conry openly admitted, and none of the rest would have denied, that the Pope possessed the right to excommunicate evil princes thus absolving subjects of their allegiance, as Pope Pius V had attempted to depose Elizabeth I in 1570.[83] But as no seventeenth-century Pope had any intention of excommunicating the Stuarts by name or attempting their deposition, the papal deposing power was not much use to these anti-Stuart revolutionaries. Moreover, no member of this mainstream anti-Stuart tradition claimed that it was the Protestantism of the Stuart monarchs that invalidated their rule in Ireland. This claim would have implied that sinners could not exercise political authority, a heresy condemned at the Council of Constance (1414–1418). Only John Punch, a highly accomplished Franciscan theologian teaching at Rome in the 1630s and 1640s, argued that what he saw as the Irish war against the Stuarts was justified by their Protestantism alone.[84] Punch's advocacy of holy war was very uncommon among the Irish Catholic *élite*; the majority of the Catholic revolutionaries grounded their arguments in nature rather than supernature.

While the papal deposing power was of little use to Ireland's anti-Stuart revolutionaries, it was a constant, draining liability for Catholics loyal to the Stuarts up to the defeat of James II, and indeed for Catholics seeking to establish a relationship with the new *régime* into the eighteenth century.

---

82 N. Tjoelker and I. Campbell, 'Transcription and Translation of the London Version of Richard O'Ferrall's Report to Propaganda Fide (1658)', *Archivium Hibernicum*, 61 (2008), 7–61; Richard O'Ferrall and Robert O'Connell, *Commentarius Rinuccinianus, de Sedis Apostolicae Legatione ad Foederatos Hiberniae Catholicos per Annos 1645–9*, ed. Stanislaus Kavanagh (6 vols., Dublin: Irish Manuscripts Commission, 1932–1949).

83 M. Mac Craith, 'The Political and Religious Thought of Florence Conry and Hugh McCaughwell', in A. Ford and J. McCafferty (eds.), *The Origins of Sectarianism in Early Modern Ireland* (Cambridge University Press, 2005), 183–202.

84 John Punch, *Integer Theologiae Cursus ad Mentem Scoti* (Paris, 1652), 404–5.

When a high commission investigating recusancy in Cork in 1600 asked the recorder and three aldermen of the city whether Pius V might lawfully discharge the queen's subjects from their oath of loyalty, two aldermen claimed not to be learned enough to answer the question, another replied that he would obey the queen (which was an answer to a different question), and the recorder himself said that he was ignorant and that anyway the extent of the Pope's authority was disputed among the theologians.[85] The problem of the deposing power became if anything more awkward for Catholics loyal to the Stuarts over the course of the century, not least in 1648 when the papal nuncio Rinuccini, using a power delegated to him by the Pope, excommunicated the Catholic government to which he had been accredited. The papacy's reluctant confirmation of the excommunication engendered a burning sense of injustice among a small number of mainly Old English Catholic clergy, who up to the 1680s experimented with forms of oaths and declarations that deprecated papal power. The talented but erratic Franciscan Peter Walsh was especially prominent in this movement in the 1660s and 1670s: his *History & Vindication* was shot through with disgust at the papacy's 'uncanonical and tyrannical' encroachment on civil jurisdictions.[86] Walsh's brand of Catholicism looked too much like schism to most of his peers. A very much milder critique of the excesses of papal power, as well as an unrestrained endorsement of Stuart monarchy, was to be found in the Latin works of John Lynch, Catholic archdeacon of Tuam.[87] During the course of his polemics against extremists like O'Ferrall, Lynch also insisted that members of both Ireland's Catholic and Protestant *élites* should be regarded as equal citizens of the Irish political community.[88] Lynch, who had served as chaplain to the Old English lawyer and speaker of the Confederate general assembly, Sir Richard Blake, in the 1630s and 1640s, took great pains to defend the common law from radicals like O'Ferrall.[89]

85 A. J. Sheehan (ed.), 'Attitudes to Religious and Temporal Authority in Cork in 1600: A Document from Laud MS 612', *Analecta Hibernica*, 31 (1984), 67.

86 A. Creighton, 'The Remonstrance of December 1661 and Catholic Politics in Restoration Ireland', *Irish Historical Studies*, 34 (2004), 16–41; Peter Walsh, *The History and Vindication of the Loyal Formulary, or Irish Remonstrance* ([London], 1674), second part of first treatise, 759.

87 [John Lynch], *Cambrensis Eversus* (St Malo, 1662).

88 [John Lynch], *Alithinologia* ([St Malo], 1664), 18; John Lynch, *Supplementum alithinologiae* ([St Malo], 1667), 58–9.

89 Lynch, *Supplementum*, 51–5.

Early Enlightenment, the New Natural Law and the State

By the 1650s the criticisms that the new scientists had been making of the old Aristotelian learning since the turn of the century were finally resulting in serious curriculum change in the progressive universities of Scotland and the Dutch Republic. Contrary to the impression given in some popular accounts, the Enlightenment was not a spontaneous outbreak of kindness, moderation and common-sense among Europeans; rather it was at heart a radical revision of the scope and ability of human reason. Aristotelian scholastics and Enlightened *philosophes* were both deeply preoccupied by human reason; but each group used the term 'reason' to mean something quite different. Early Enlightenment science either flatly denied that human reason could perceive essences and final causes, or redefined the older terms in revolutionary ways.[90] These innovations contributed to new ways of speaking about politics that emphasised material advantage and disadvantage alone, without consideration for the purposes of things locked into chains of cause and effect by God's Providence.[91] Thomas Hobbes, who pioneered this new politics among Anglophones, argued that natural law was merely the recognition of one's true material interest, which was physical safety; natural law was certainly not the recognition of final causes impressed in humans by God. There was no real connection between reason and language for Hobbes, so that language was merely the arbitrary application of words to things, which made it hard even for good humans to keep contracts with one another. Safety could thus only be achieved when all members of a commonwealth alienated all their powers to an absolute sovereign. Positive law was no more than the will of that sovereign; there could be no appeal from that sovereign, and nothing could invalidate the sovereign's positive law.[92] Bishop Bramhall, attempting to defend a conventional scholastic account of natural law against Hobbes in Paris in the 1640s, realised that Hobbes wished to establish a truly secular space in which politics might be conducted, one entirely drained of the divine. The only measures of right and wrong for Hobbes, as the horrified

---

90 J. Israel, *Radical Enlightenment: Philosophy and the Making of Modernity 1650–1750* (Oxford University Press, 2001); J. Robertson, *The Case for the Enlightenment: Scotland and Naples 1680–1760* (Cambridge University Press, 2005).

91 R. Tuck, 'The "Modern" Theory of Natural Law', in Anthony Pagden (ed.), *The Languages of Political Theory in Early Modern Europe* (Cambridge University Press, 1987), 99–119.

92 Thomas Hobbes, *Leviathan* (London, 1651), part 1, chapter 5; chapter 14; chapter 4; part 2, chapters 17–18.

Bramhall recognised, were 'the arbitrary edicts of a mortal law giver, who may command us to turn Turks or Pagans tomorrow'.[93] Hobbes had one important Irish follower. Sir William Petty had served Hobbes as an amanuensis in Paris in the 1640s.[94] Petty did not follow Hobbes in his absolutism, but developed Hobbesian principles into a practical science for serving any state. Human reason, for Petty, was quantitative rather than qualitative: it was a power capable of identifying number, weight and measure but not essences or final causes.[95] Petty applied this quantitative reason to the government of Ireland with his surveys of the country for the Parliamentarian *régime* in the 1650s; his theoretical reflections on what would become the modern science of statistics were printed posthumously as *Political Arithmetick* in 1690.

The political theory of John Locke, which he developed in the 1680s in order to justify rebellion against James II, shared a number of fundamental assumptions with that of Hobbes and Petty. Locke's major work on knowledge, the *Essay concerning Human Understanding*, admitted that essences might exist, but denied that human reason could perceive them.[96] But Locke's *Two Treatises of Government*, eventually printed in 1689, developed this materialist foundation into a theory of limited rather than absolute monarchy. The aim of humans entering into society was the preservation of their lives and property (the latter necessary to the former) under a law common to all. But these humans logically had to distribute the power of punishing criminals and the power of making laws to two different branches of government, because if those two powers were united in one person, that person would no longer be subject to the law. Subjecting oneself to a monarch not bound by the law would be contrary to the reason for entering into society in the first place, and in fact the moment that a monarch took both the executive and legislative powers into his own hands, that monarch had placed himself outside the political community. The community would now be free to establish another executive power in his place.[97]

Locke, too, had an important Irish follower: William Molyneux. As an undergraduate at Trinity College Dublin in the 1670s, Molyneux had ignored the still-Aristotelian curriculum, soaking himself instead in the new science

---

93 John Bramhall, *Castigations of Mr Hobbes* (London, 1658), 201–2.
94 T. McCormick, *William Petty and the Ambitions of Political Arithmetic* (Oxford University Press, 2009), 36–8, 95–103.
95 Sir William Petty, *Political Arithmetick* (London, 1690), preface.
96 John Locke, *An Essay concerning Human Understanding*, ed. P. H. Nidditch (Oxford University Press, 1975), 417–18.
97 John Locke, *Two Treatises of Government*, ed. P. Laslett, (3rd edn., Cambridge University Press, 1988), treatise 2, sections 4–13, 26–30, 87–94.

of Francis Bacon, René Descartes and possibly also Hobbes. Molyneux certainly recommended Hobbes's books in print, and he played a central role in the foundation of the Dublin Philosophical Society, which was devoted to the promulgation of the new learning in Ireland, in 1683.[98]

Molyneux's major political work was *The Case of Ireland's being bound by Acts of Parliament in England, Stated* of 1698, which was composed in reaction to the English parliament's attempted regulation of Irish woollen exports, and claimed that Ireland was subject to the English crown, rather than the English parliament. This was not an original argument even among Irish Protestants: his father-in-law, William Domville, had argued the same at the Restoration in 1660.[99] The string of multiple redundant arguments that Molyneux constructed around conquest were not especially original either. Molyneux argued that Ireland had not been conquered by Henry II; that even if Ireland had been conquered in a just war, that would have provided the crown only with rights over the lives and property of the directly conquered, not over their descendants; and that even if ancient conquest provided the crown with unlimited rights over the descendants of the conquered, most of the Irish population of Molyneux's day were descendants of the English conquerors and so unaffected. The central thought was that in any war there was a just side and an unjust one, and that in the event of victory the just side had the right to remake the polity of the unjust side so that they would not undertake unjust wars in the future. Molyneux openly borrowed this argument from Locke, but it was also commonplace among the scholastics and common lawyers.[100]

Molyneux's originality, and the main point on which he differed from Darcy, Domville and many of his Anglican contemporaries, was that he based his arguments on the origin of human society in a common desire for material safety and prosperity.[101] Because government was legitimate only in so far as it provided for that safety and prosperity, laws that endangered those basic qualities were void, and so England should not legislate for Ireland to its own advantage. Locke had developed his largely secular account of limited

---

98 J. G. Simms, *William Molyneux of Dublin, 1656–1776* (Dublin: Irish Academic Press, 1982), 18–20.

99 A. Clarke, 'Colonial Constitutional Attitudes in Ireland, 1640–1660', *Proceedings of the Royal Irish Academy*, 90:C (1990), 363–4.

100 Locke, *Two Treatises*, treatise 2, sections 175–96; John Punch, *Commentarii Theologici*, 4 vols. in 6 parts (Paris, 1661), iv 4, 327–8; Sir Edward Coke, *The Reports of Sir Edward Coke* (London, 1658), 601–2.

101 P. Kelly, 'William Molyneux and the Spirit of Liberty in Eighteenth-Century Ireland', *Eighteenth-Century Ireland*, 3 (1988), 133–48.

monarchy in reaction to theories of Stuart kingship similar to those advanced by Archbishop Ussher.[102] Locke's approach was useful to Molyneux because it allowed the Irishman to evade the argument that England had conquered Ireland by God's Providence, and so had a continuing duty to intervene in its government. This argument was well known to Irish Protestants: the idea of a providential conquest animated Sir John Temple's frequently reprinted history of the 1641 rebellion, and was important to Bishop William King of Derry's more sober *State of the Protestants of Ireland under the Late King James's Government* of 1691 and the sermons which King delivered in defence of the rebellion against James II.[103]

Jonathan Swift, educated at Trinity College Dublin in the 1680s and appointed dean of St Patrick's Cathedral in 1713, agreed with Molyneux that the kingdoms of Ireland and England were independently attached to the same monarch. Despite the British parliament's assertion of its right to legislate for Ireland in the Declaratory Act of 1720, the dean continued to assert Ireland's legislative independence in the seven Drapier's letters published in the 1720s and 1730s.[104] Swift also followed Locke and Molyneux in endorsing a theory of human society based in the pursuit of rational, material self-interest.[105] Preoccupied as Swift was by the wickedness of those Protestants who dissented from the Established Church, the sermon on the martyrdom of Charles I that he preached at St Patrick's Cathedral in 1726 emphasised the unlawfulness of the killing rather than its sacrilegious character.[106] The fact that Swift always rejected absolute monarchy and the divine origin of political power, and his subscription to a materialistic account of human society which placed commerce at the heart of the common good, should make it easy to place him securely in the Irish Enlightenment. But there were many aspects of Britain and Ireland's Enlightened modernity that Swift sincerely hated, including proposals for the toleration of dissenters, and the existence

---

102 William Molyneux, *The Case of Ireland's being bound by Acts of Parliament in England, Stated* (Dublin, 1698).

103 Sir John Temple, *The Irish Rebellion* (London, 1646); S. Connolly, 'The Glorious Revolution in Irish Protestant Political Thinking', in S. Connolly (ed.), *Political Ideas in Eighteenth-Century Ireland* (Dublin: FCP, 2000), 27–63.

104 Jonathan Swift, *The Drapier's Letters to the People of Ireland*, ed. H. Davis (2nd edn., Oxford University Press, 1965).

105 I. Ehrenpreis, 'Swift on Liberty', in A. Norman Jeffries (ed.), *Swift: Modern Judgements* (London: Macmillan, 1968), 59–73.

106 S. Connolly, 'Swift and Protestant Ireland: Images and Realities', in Aileen Douglas, Patrick Kelly, and Ian Campbell Ross (eds.), *Locating Swift* (Dublin: FCP, 1998), 28–46; S. Connolly, 'The Church of Ireland and the Royal Martyr: Regicide and Revolution in Anglican political thought *c.*1660–*c.*1745', *Journal of Ecclesiastical History*, 54 (2003), 484–506.

of political parties.[107] Swift's *Tale of a Tub* of 1704 even-handedly satirised both Aristotelian essentialism and Enlightened empiricism.[108] Especially sharp was Swift's parody of the new natural law theory, entitled 'A Digression on the Nature, Usefulness, and Necessity of Wars and Quarrels', which suggested that if a state of war were natural to all creatures, and if each human had a 'natural right to take from them all that he thinks due to himself', then there was effectively a natural right to theft.[109] This was directed chiefly at Hobbes, but might have discomforted Lockeans also. Swift was a highly sensitive analyst of his own culture who defies categorisation.

There can be no doubt about Swift's Protestant orthodoxy, which was a world away from the efforts of radicals like John Toland (born in Donegal in 1670) to subordinate Christianity entirely to the new Enlightened reason.[110]* But Petty, Molyneux, Swift and others like them had begun to argue over politics in ways which did not refer to the chains of final causes by which God might still have ordered the world. In this way, they began to create a truly secular sphere. The Aristotelians like Antoninus, Stanihurst, O'Sullivan Beare or Bramhall, had all admitted that there was more to Christian life than obedience to God's direct command. They had recognised the existence of a natural sphere, where humans made rational by God were left free to pursue ends implanted in them by God. And so, although God might not intervene directly in this natural sphere, it was still pervaded by God's power. By contrast, the secular sphere was one drained of the divine. This was the Enlightenment's great innovation, and it began to appear in Ireland during the 1690s.

107 Ehrenpreis, 'Swift on Liberty', 61, 65–6.
108 Jonathan Swift, *A Tale of a Tub and Other Works*, ed. A. Ross and D. Woolley (Oxford University Press, 1986), 83–4, 117.
109 Swift, *Tale of a Tub and Other Works*, 144–5.
110 [John Toland], *Christianity not Mysterious* (London, 1696).

* I am indebted to Jane Ohlmeyer, Peter Crooks, and Sean Connolly for their generous advice on this chapter.

PART V

★

ECONOMY AND ENVIRONMENT

21

Economic Life, 1550–1730

RAYMOND GILLESPIE

Discussion of the Irish economy in the sixteenth and seventeenth centuries emerged from the rise of economic history as a university subject in the late nineteenth century. Ada Longfield's *Anglo-Irish trade in the sixteenth century* (London, 1929) resulted from a University of London MA thesis and George O'Brien's *The economic history of Ireland in the seventeenth century* (Dublin and London, 1919) was an outgrowth from his work on the eighteenth century that developed from his University College Dublin MA thesis. O'Brien, later Professor of Political Economy in UCD, wrote in a tradition that linked economic and political difficulties, seeing the seventeenth century as a period of 'economic development [that] was periodically impeded by political cataclysms'.[1] That tradition dominated writing about Irish economic life until the transformative work of L. M. Cullen in the late 1960s and 1970s. His chapter on late seventeenth-century Ireland, together with that of Aidan Clarke on the early seventeenth century, in the third volume of the *New history of Ireland* (Oxford, 1976), served to shape ways of thinking about economic life focused on economic realities rather than political rhetoric.

While the seventeenth century has found historians of economic life the sixteenth century is less well served. The social assumptions of large parts of Ireland in the sixteenth century were not amenable to the economic logic applied in the seventeenth century. No one in sixteenth-century Ireland thought about 'the economy', the sixteenth-century word 'economy' meaning household management.[2] Residents of Gaelic Ireland, dominated by lordships rather than estates and gifts rather than sales, did not generate or preserve the sort of sources that economic historians utilised. However, the work of, in particular, K. W. Nicholls and Katharine Simms, makes it possible

---

1 G. O'Brien, *The Economic History of Ireland in the Seventeenth Century* (Dublin and London: Maunsel, 1919), 7.
2 For example see K. Wrightson, *Earthly Necessities: Economic Lives in Early Modern Britain* (New Haven and London: Yale University Press, 2000).

to frame the questions that surviving sources might answer, demonstrating the importance of F. J. Fisher's dictum that 'the darkness of the sixteenth and seventeenth centuries depends upon the angle from which they are approached and upon the questions that are asked about them'.[3] Considering the economy as socially embedded relationships, rather than mechanistic markets for exchange, we can bridge cultural worlds and use economic life as an organising principle for describing early modern Ireland. Economic life, therefore, is concerned both with the world of money and with the spheres of politics and religion that were continually affected by finance.

These approaches resulted in reassessments of the evidence. Projectors and economic commentators, such as William Petty, have been to some degree dethroned as witnesses to economic life, though they remain important for economic thought and perception. Trade data, in port books and more aggregated forms, are of greater importance, as are the surveys of land confiscation from the middle of the seventeenth century. Even deploying this evidence, we cannot penetrate many of the economic arrangements that made life workable. Little is recoverable, for example, about the most fundamental building block of economic activity, the household. There may be alternative approaches to this problem and the study of material culture, for instance, has revealed much about economic life.

Economic Life, c.1550

Ireland c.1550 might be divided into three broad types of social formation, each with its embedded economic networks. These boundaries are blurred and transient but they provide a way of thinking about this world. In the east and south of the country lay a land where the bulk of the Irish population was concentrated, and in which the primary form of lordship exercised by the *élite* was over land. This society was based on great and lesser estates established in a common law tradition following the Anglo-Norman settlement. Here tenants were bound to their lords by written leases or customary copyholds. Archaeological evidence suggests this region had a well-developed material culture with goods traded in a network of local markets, often linked to larger towns, including Cork, Dublin, Wexford or Waterford, that engaged in overseas trade. Markets for land and labour also existed. Most households had

---

3 F. J. Fisher, 'The Sixteenth and Seventeenth Centuries: The Dark Ages in English Economic History?', in N. B. Harte (ed.), *The Study of Economic History* (London: Cass, 1971), 200.

only a limited engagement with markets, supplying their food from their own mixed agriculture farms. Limited transactions were usually in cash, which facilitated the exchange of agricultural surplus for material goods, and was needed to pay rent, though this was sometimes rendered in kind where custom dictated.[4] These regions were subject to the financial shocks that affected a commercialised world. Before its dissolution in the middle of the sixteenth century the Irish mint operated only erratically and coin was in short supply, governments needing new silver supplies to augment the Irish coinage. The introduction of German miners into Clonmines in Wexford in 1552, for instance, was part of a quest for silver to maintain the Irish coinage. Coinage shortages, exacerbated by a series of harvest failures in the early 1550s, led to an economic downturn and contributed to a debasement of the Irish coinage in those years. For most in this world their aim was survival rather than enrichment. Economics was subject to morality and one's economic guideline in, for example, setting prices, leasing land or lending money, was still the good of the community, a view reflected in the political language of 'commonwealth' adopted by the Anglo-Irish gentry of the Pale.

In the north of Ireland and in parts of the midlands there was a different construction of social order. Here population was low and the primary form of lordship was over men. Land was not organised into estates but into smaller holdings owned by lineages (real or fictive) and evidence of ownership was provided not by written deeds but by genealogy, usually maintained orally for malleability. Such lands were not specialised farms but units self-sufficient in food and other needs. Lords also held some land within the lordship by virtue of their office, and many claimed the right to occupy unworked land within their area of influence. Greater lords competed not for land but for followers from among the lesser families, which meant that the boundaries of lordships were in constant flux as families shifted allegiance. Within the lordship, in return for traditionally sanctioned payments (the '*ceart*' or '*cíos*'), greater lords provided services to lesser landholding families, such as military protection and arbitration in disputes. Status was not determined by wealth or contract but controlled by genealogy, by the ability to command lesser families and by the accumulation of cultural capital, usually through literary patronage. Thus the commissioning of bardic poetry or the collecting of prestige manuscripts, for example, were investments in status. In this

---

4 For the system in the Dublin region see M. Murphy and M. Potterton, *The Dublin Region in the Middle Ages: Settlement, Land Use and Economy* (Dublin: Four Courts Press [hereafter FCP], 2010).

economic arrangement the principal form of exchange was not market-led but a series of renders or 'gifts', usually of cattle or other agricultural produce, from follower to lord that was often given the spurious sanction of antiquity. Lords wished to maximise the social product of their lordship, rather than its income, by increasing the number of people under their jurisdiction. Increases in numbers of followers allowed lords to demonstrate their power and to maximise food rent that could be translated into status through cultural and military display. Such agricultural 'gifts' were recirculated in the form of feasts given by lords at which followers were present, thus binding lords and followers together in a network of reciprocal gift giving. Thus most of the local agricultural surplus remained within the lordship and urban centres with market functions were unusual, though localised places of exchange may have existed in the houses clustered around lordly tower houses. Coin was rare, though not unknown, since there was some external commercial activity involving the lordships, often with Pale merchants or traders from Europe who provided necessities such as wine or salt. The town of Cavan, where a local coinage also circulated, was a significant exception, though Longford town also had commercial features. Links to the Anglo-Irish Pale, with its networks of markets, may help to explain these exceptions in lordships close to Anglo-Norman settlement.

A third structure was that of mixed lordship, comprising the remnants of the Anglo-Norman settlement in Munster and Connacht, where both lordship over men and over land co-existed, albeit uneasily at times. A tract of c.1570 from the Mayo lordship of MacWilliam Burke, the 'Seanchas Búrcach', described the rights of the Burkes, in an apparently traditional document, and listed the 'gifts' due from those MacWilliam claimed were his traditional followers. Yet it also stated that 'it is on the land [soil] that MacWilliam's rent [cíos] is charged and it is not reported that this claim was ever challenged'.[5] This melding of two traditions, of lordship over men and lordship over land, is also implied by the number of written land deeds that survive from the MacWilliam lordship. Such survivals suggest a blending of common law, with its emphasis on written deeds and native Irish custom, relying on oral traditions.[6] Again in the Clanricard lordship in Galway, there are indications that the fourth earl took advantage of these two traditions and tried to alter

---

5 T. Ó Raghallaigh (ed.), 'Seanchus Búrcach', *Journal of the Galway Archaeological and Historical Society*, 13 (1922–1928), 53.

6 See the discussion in B. Cunningham and R Gillespie, 'Manuscript Cultures in Early Modern Mayo', in G. Moran and N. Ó Muraíle (eds.), *Mayo: History and Society* (Dublin: Geography Publications, 2014), 199–201.

relations with the freeholders of the traditional families, thus transforming himself into a landlord in the common law tradition.[7] In economic terms such melding allowed a market and a gift economy to co-exist, explaining the survival of mercantile communities in sixteenth-century Galway and Sligo in the middle of what should have been a 'gift'-based economy. Elsewhere in the Desmond lordship in Munster the 1585 Peyton survey reveals two systems co-existing.[8] A manorial structure, with freeholds from which cash payments were made, existed with 'chargeable lands' from which customary payments of 'shragh' and 'mart' were payable in kind to the lord. The cash element was strong enough to allow trading ports, including Dingle, to exist, as well as towns – such as Tralee and Killarney – with burgage tenure. This type of lordship transformed a physical space into a social space that was identified and structured through the families who occupied it so that land and people were woven together and status was realised by control over both land and people.

Developments in the Sixteenth-Century Economy

Reconstructing the later sixteenth-century economy presents considerable difficulties. Measuring developments in different economic systems is problematic and this is compounded by fragmentary and intractable sources. Customs data are fragmentary and of limited value because of the exemptions given to port towns and individuals. English port books are more useful, but not free from problems. The port books of Chester, the main destination for trade from eastern Ireland, begin late and the exemptions for the palatinate make them difficult to interpret. One substitute here may be the sheriffs' books, which record ships entering the port of Chester, name the master and list the cargo.[9] These confirm the dominance of Irish frieze, tallow, hides and pipe-staves in the trade. However, such trade data are far from being a reliable measure of economic activity. Irish grain, for example, rarely appears in English port books but this is more a reflection of penal customs duties rather than low levels of Irish grain production. The need to feed a significant urban population in the Pale would indicate local grain production in Ireland. Outside the Pale, at least some traditional renders from households to lords were in grain. Given the lack of interregional trade, most lordships would have produced

---

7 The fourth earl of Thomond in Clare was engaged in the same exercise, see
  B. Cunningham, *Clanricard and Thomond, 1540–1640: Provincial Politics and Society Transformed* (Dublin: FCP, 2012), 30–3, 36–7, 44–56.
8 MS M2759, 5037–9, National Archives of Ireland.
9 Especially SB/10–15, Chester City Archives.

grain.[10] Perhaps the most problematic aspect of the Chester data is that there are no records of exports to Ireland. However, the Bristol port books for the late sixteenth century provide both export and import figures for trading with Munster.[11] These data on imports into Ireland reveal that domestic demand after 1550 was growing rapidly, both by expansion of markets in traditional goods and a dramatic diversification of trade from luxury cloth to personal items such as books or tobacco pipes. In the first half of the sixteenth century the value of imports may have doubled, suggesting that even without colonisation Munster was being drawn into a world of English imports while still maintaining a favourable balance of trade to support higher levels of consumption. Paradoxically, after mid-century, while the range of imports increased, their value collapsed, just as the Munster plantation was initiated. The Bristol evidence plays down the significance of plantation and colonisation in economic change in sixteenth-century Ireland and emphasises the importance of indigenous factors causing shifts towards traded goods.[12]

It is difficult to explain this contradiction, but an answer may lie in changing patterns of Irish trade with continental Europe not recorded in the Bristol port books. The scale of this continental trade is uncertain. French trade with Ireland was modest but sustained through the sixteenth century, reflecting the 'fundamentally complementary character of the Irish and French markets', Ireland exporting fish, timber, grain and cattle products and receiving wine, iron and salt in return. Spanish trade with Ireland, mainly in wine, salt and fish, by contrast, grew with the Basque, Austurian and Galician ports receiving about 40 per cent of the growing Irish trade with Spain in the sixteenth century.[13] By the end of the sixteenth century this trade was concentrated in the southern part of Ireland south of a line from Drogheda to Galway. The evidence of sixteenth-century pottery from archaeological excavations helps to place this

---

10 For example K. W. Nicholls (ed.), *The O'Doyne (Ó Duinn) Manuscript* (Dublin: Irish Manuscripts Commission, 1983), 3–6.

11 For the raw data see S. Flavin and E. T. Jones (eds.), *Bristol's Trade with Ireland and the Continent, 1503–1601* (Dublin: FCP, 2009).

12 S. Flavin, *Consumption and Culture in Sixteenth-Century Ireland* (Woodbridge: Boydell, 2014), especially 23–42. Also see Chapter 13 by Flavin in this volume.

13 M. A. Lyons, 'Maritime Relations between France and Ireland, c.1480–c.1630', *Irish Economic and Social History*, 27 (2000), 23; K. Schüller, 'Special Conditions of the Irish–Iberian Trade during the Spanish–English War', in Enrique García Hernán, Miguel Ángel de Bunes, Óscar Recio Morales and Bernardo J. García García (eds.), *Irlanda y la Monarquía Hispánica: Kinsale 1601–2001* (Madrid: Consejo Superior de Investigaciones Científicas, 2002), 447–68; J. J. Puig, 'El Comércio Maritimo en Galicia 1525–1640', unpublished PhD thesis, University of Santiago (2012), 563–8. I am grateful to Professor Thomas O'Connor for this last reference.

trade in context. In Galway excavations the dominant foreign pottery source was Iberia, a confirmation of more impressionistic sources that list the town as the main trading port for Spain, followed by Germany and then France. In Cork, German wares predominated, followed by French and Iberian ones. However, elsewhere in County Cork there are more local concentrations of Spanish pottery from excavations, as at Dunboy castle. It is important not to exaggerate the scale of this continental trade. Reconstructions of minimum numbers of pottery vessels from the Galway excavations suggest that the Iberian vessels comprised just over 6 per cent of all vessels while the English trade accounted for some 82 per cent of vessels. Such data can only be suggestive since merchants rarely traded with only one port and re-exports were common. One group of notarial records from early seventeenth-century Amsterdam puts the Irish trade in context. In 1601, for instance, one Dutch ship left Amsterdam for Norway and then sailed to Ireland, Spain, Portugal, the Canaries and finally to England before returning to Amsterdam.[14] Thus Ireland was knit into a complex pattern of European trading that is difficult to untangle.

Outside the world of settler Ireland evidence for economic change is weaker. Since little is known about the household and its landholdings, horizontal economic relations within Gaelic lordships are vague. Households and families were in continual flux. Partible inheritance, usually described as 'gavelkind', in many lordships meant that family holdings were continually partitioned, and hence fragmented, leading to the impoverishment of one family and the consequent rise of others. More revealing of economic change in Gaelic and Gaelicised Ireland are the vertical relations between lords and followers. The most significant feature of Gaelic Ireland in the late sixteenth century was the militarisation that followed attempts by the Dublin administration to extend its authority outside the Pale either by colonisation or negotiation. The numbers of Scottish mercenaries employed by O'Neill and O'Donnell in Ulster grew from the 1560s. Such gallowglasses needed to be paid and the resources of Gaelic lords were restricted, being confined to what they could raise from their own lordships or from cattle raiding. Lordships were not intended to be engines of economic growth, so the basis for any increased taxation was limited. There was little regional specialisation or diversification and the low population provided little incentive to diversify. For instance, while Gaelic Ireland produced linen yarn, traded through 'grey merchants' into the Pale and thence to England, no one showed much

---

14 I am grateful to Professor Rolf Loeber for a copy of his list of this collection.

interest in working that yarn into cloth, thus increasing its value. That was done by weavers in Lancashire. This was due to the conservatism of economic life that was shaped by householder utility and adversity to risk rather than the demands of the market, also reflected in the limited specialisation in the economy. A second explanation is that Gaelic Ireland seems to have suffered a skills shortage. Craftspeople were regarded as lowly figures in a society dominated by landholders. Weavers, for example, were regarded as low status and few were attracted to the craft. In the pardons for some 990 followers of O'Connor Sligo at the end of the Nine Years' War, only twenty-six described themselves as craftsmen.[15] The gift-exchange economy of a lordship was organised around consumption, whereas what was now required was capital investment and income to fund militarisation.

The alternative to developing new income streams was to exploit existing sources more ruthlessly. O'Donnell, for instance, levied taxes on Spanish fishermen wishing to fish off the shores of his lordship. Indeed the income from fishing probably played a large part in funding the building projects in western Ireland in the sixteenth century, particularly the Franciscan friaries sponsored by Irish lords. A second source of lordly income were the families within the lordship and it is likely that lords increased levies on these families to pay for mercenaries and satisfy their own demands for luxury goods, such as wine. This gave rise to complaints by English administrators that Irish lords imposed arbitrary exactions on their followers, reducing them to slaves. This process is clear in the case of Hugh O'Neill, earl of Tyrone, who, in the late sixteenth century, introduced a series of innovations partly driven by the exigencies of war.[16] O'Neill attempted to transform himself from an Irish lord to an English style landlord with increased control over tenants. Part of that transformation was an economic modernisation of the lordship with the establishment of a market structure based on exchange rather than consumption. In 1587, for instance, he was granted a patent for a market in his area of influence at Dungannon and also at Armagh and Omagh.[17] It is clear that O'Neill was not alone in making such changes. From the early sixteenth century some Irish magnates, such as the O'Briens in Clare and the Burkes in east Galway, had seen the potential offered by the processes of composition and

---

15 Irish Record Commission, *Irish Patent Rolls of James I* (Dublin: Stationery Office, 1966), 20–4.

16 N. Canny, 'Hugh O'Neill and the Changing Face of Gaelic Ulster', *Studia Hibernica*, 10 (1970), 7–35.

17 J. Morrin (ed.), *Calendar of Patent and Close Rolls of Chancery in Ireland Elizabeth, 19th Year to End of Reign* (Dublin: Thom, 1862), 123.

surrender and regrant to enhance their power and increase their wealth. The scale of the resulting economic change is difficult to measure, but in at least some cases the economy of Gaelic and Gaelicised Ireland in the late sixteenth century had the capacity to develop and was already moving in the direction that it would take in the early seventeenth century.

Plantation, Colonisation and Economic Growth

Insofar as political changes serve as a marker for shifts in economic life, the end of the Nine Years' War in 1603 was pivotal. The breaking of the great Gaelic lordships drew Ireland into an economic world underpinned by a common law framework of property rights. Transfers of property from native Irish owners to Old English and New English followed. There were various mechanisms for this. Indebted native Irish lords, who had dabbled ineffectively in the market economy and fallen into debt in the late sixteenth century, sold lands to Old English merchants and to settlers. Colonisation schemes in the Irish midlands and in Wexford created new landowners with relatively few obligations to develop their estates, but in Ulster a sophisticated plantation scheme dealt with the redistribution of land in the wake of the flight of the earls and promoted a unique vision for social and economic engineering. These developments created three dynamics for economic change: a rapid growth in population (and hence the labour supply), a redistribution of resources and a dramatic commercialisation of the economy.

The evidence for the size of the Irish population in the early seventeenth century is thin and estimates are tentative but the broad trends are clear. Between 1600 and 1641 the Irish population grew from about 1.4 million to about 2.1 million, mainly as a result of immigration linked to both colonisation and plantation.[18] Crude measures of population growth do not reflect the full demographic impact of these changes. Inflows from Scotland and Ireland were offset by outflows of people to continental Europe and to England in the wake of the Nine Years' War, particularly soldiers serving in Irish regiments abroad. Therefore the composition of the population changed to a much greater extent than aggregate population figures suggest.

The economic implications of population growth from a low base are clear. Increase in labour supply was the main factor in economic change, most settlers in Ireland having little capital. Moreover, given the low levels

---

18 L. M. Cullen, 'Population Trends in Seventeenth-Century Ireland', *Economic and Social Review*, 6 (1974–5), 149–65.

of population in the late sixteenth century, which were probably further depressed by the Nine Years' War, the marginal gains to agricultural productivity from any increase in labour supply were high. Growth in output more than outstripped population change, leading to economic growth per capita. Migrants were attracted to areas in which sixteenth-century population appears to have been particularly low. Sixteenth-century population densities seem to have been highest in the Pale and in the northern part of Munster. Ulster, the Midlands and the south-west of Ireland as well as Connacht had lower population densities and it was to these areas that plantation projects, as well as more informal colonisation, directed settlers.

This increase in labour supply had another implication. Shortage of capital and limited technological resources meant that while output increased, the basic structure of the early seventeenth-century economy remained much as it was in the late sixteenth century. Settlers simply expanded output and in some cases, such as that of ploughing by tail, adopted native technical solutions to local challenges. The mainstay of the economy, measured using trade data and comments of contemporaries, was live cattle. Although they had not featured in the sixteenth-century trade, cattle were important within Ireland for dairying rather than beef and were also a measure of wealth, liable to be raided by rival lords. This dominance of livestock in seventeenth-century trade is unsurprising. Increasing demand for meat across Europe saw a surge in cattle prices. In England between the 1590s and the 1630s live cattle prices rose by over 50 per cent, whereas grain prices increased by 34 per cent and dairy and beef prices rose by 22 per cent. Trade data suggest that grain was a regionally substantial, though declining, part of the seventeenth-century Irish economy. Exports of oats from Ulster to Scotland, for instance, were so great that they were banned by the Scottish parliament in 1619. The other mainstays of seventeenth-century trade had all been present in the sixteenth century: wool, tallow and fish. A new element that flourished in the early seventeenth-century economy was timber, generated by asset stripping of estates by early settlers. Such clearance brought low productivity woodland into much higher productivity agricultural use. This did not last long and timber's share in Irish trade fell so that by 1641 Ireland was a net importer of timber. Only one industrial product appeared, again with a short life, in Irish trade: iron. Like timber, this was the result of asset stripping of estates in the early stages of colonisation. The early seventeenth-century economy concentrated on the production of raw material rather than manufacturing, a consequence of expanding a workforce in a world of abundant land but limited capital and skills.

If the sources for population growth are uncertain, evidence for the redistribution of resources, especially land, is more abundant. This was achieved by formal plantation and, more importantly, informal colonisation and the emergence of a land market. Estimates of land ownership by religious groups are crude measures of this change, since not all settlers were Protestants and transfers of land were often effected by sale or mortgage, in which confessional stance mattered little. However, measurement by confessional grouping offers one way of quantifying shifts in land ownership. In 1641, Catholics probably held about 60 per cent of the land of Ireland and by 1688 this had fallen to 27 per cent. By 1703 it had declined to 15 per cent. More important than these estimates is the way in which land was held.[19] After 1603, Gaelic lordships were replaced with estates held by grants from the king and the relationship between landlord and tenant was regulated by a contract, the lease. This created a market in land within a common law framework that had not existed previously, with property changing hands for money, or being used as security for borrowing money. This saw the creation of a standard form of landholding across the island and brought about rules for trading, whether in land or other goods, that were enforceable in royal courts. The new allocation of resources created a more precise definition of private property, whether by mapping in large state surveys, such as the Down Survey in the 1650s, or more local private estate surveys, or legally by means of the body of land law passed by the Irish parliament, especially in the 1630s. Redefinitions of property rights created opportunities for some. In Gowran, County Kilkenny, for instance, the customary exactions paid to the earl of Ormond came under scrutiny in the light of enhanced market and common law realities, giving rise to conflicts between custom and commercial norms. A similar process seems to have been under way elsewhere in Kilkenny, but its extent is unclear.[20]

The final dynamic for change was rapid commercialisation. The spread of royal authority undermined the Gaelic lordships with their arrangements for recirculating goods within a gift-exchange economy. Over the seventeenth century there was a shift, only partly effected by colonisation, from a concern with the use value of products to the exchange value of goods. Formal marketing structures spread quickly with some 500 grants of the right to hold local markets made between 1600 and 1649, though many of these may have

---

19 See Chapter 23 by Ó Siochrú and Brown in this volume.
20 A. Empey, *Gowran, Co. Kilkenny, 1190–1610: Custom and Conflict in a Baronial Town* (Dublin: FCP, 2015), 39–51.

been speculative. Larger port towns, such as Cork and Youghal, probably doubled their populations in the early seventeenth century on the back of a trade boom. The dominance of Dublin became clear, with a growing proportion of the Irish customs being generated from its trade: a third by 1630 and almost one half by 1662–1663. The city boomed, using its new-found wealth to build and rebuild. One visitor, the well-travelled James Howell, noted in 1639 that 'traffic increaseth here wonderfully with all kinds of bravery and buildings'.[21] The spread of commercial activity resulted in a greater proportion of goods moving through markets. This, combined with the expansion in output as a result of an increased labour supply, generated a trade boom. Trade in specific commodities over time provides evidence of this. In the late 1580s, between twenty-five and sixty dickers (bales of ten) of hides were landed at Chester from Ireland each year whereas by 1639 this had increased to 1,289 dickers. Similarly, between eleven and seventy packs of yarn were sent annually to Chester in the 1580s, which had grown to 113 packs by 1639. Tallow exports also increased, from fifty cwt in 1592–1593 to 619 cwt in 1639. Wool exports to Chester exploded, from between 100 and 200 stone in the late 1580s to 6,666 stone in 1639. However the success story was the expansion in the live cattle trade at Chester, which grew from nothing in the late 1500s to 15,000 beasts a year in the late 1630s.

This commercialisation of the economy acted as a social solvent. Both the native Irish and the Old English of the Pale benefited from the economic growth of the early seventeenth century. Gaelic Ireland produced a literature of protest, complaining about these *nouveaux riches* who benefited from the market. Perhaps the most vitriolic of these works was *'Pairlement Chloinne Tomáis I'*, probably written in the early 1630s in Kerry. The text ruthlessly satirised those who benefited from the commercial order and flaunted their new status by wearing fashionable clothes, educating their children and marrying above their station so that they became prominent figures in local society. Particular venom was reserved for those who had achieved this by buying and selling, a skill that required the use of English as well as the capacity to use money to obtain the latest consumer product such as tobacco.[22] That this was complained of in an unplanted area of Kerry and in a text in which British settlers never feature suggests that commercialisation and social mobility were not obviously linked to British settlement, but that some form of indigenous

---

21 James Howell, *Epistolas Ho-Eliana* (London, 1655), 281.
22 N. Williams (ed. and trans.), *Pairlement Chloinne Tomáis* (Dublin Institute for Advanced Studies, 1981), 40, 97; 22–3, 83.

change was taking place. Kerry was not the only area from which complaints about the consequences of commercialisation in undermining social order came. In Tipperary, again outside plantations, the poet and priest Geoffrey Keating criticised this new sort of people and in Ossory the poet Brian mac Giolla Phádraig engaged in similar polemics.

The effect of these interlocking changes was to create expansionary impulses in the Irish economy. The yield of the Irish customs grew almost continuously over the early seventeenth century, even allowing for the changes in books of rates over that period. However, it is more difficult than it first appears to isolate the beneficiaries of this prosperity. Some men certainly received a considerable fixed capital asset in land through plantation schemes (though some were inclined to attribute it to the providence of God), but few of these had the resources to develop it. Those who benefited from plantation schemes, royal favourites, younger sons or those who hoped to reverse decaying fortunes by an Irish adventure, had little capital. Such handicaps were worsened by the malfunctioning of a rudimentary financial system coupled with high interest rates, driven up by the risky nature of lending in a colonial environment. Surveys of the Ulster Plantation scheme, for instance, noted the failure of the grantees to build or to improve their lands. There was little sign of investment in, for example, iron working and while in Munster Richard Boyle, earl of Cork, did invest in this enterprise, he made little profit and used the trade as a money transmission system. Attempts to establish cloth working in Munster failed due to lack of domestic demand and it was left to the state under Lord Deputy Wentworth to set up an unsuccessful cloth-making factory near Dublin. Landlords, trying to raise capital to consolidate estates, were forced to make long leases with low rents and high entry fines that mortgaged future income for present gain. Some became mired in debt from which they could not escape and many went bankrupt in the 1640s.[23]

Those best placed to take advantage of this land market were the Old English, some of whom had mercantile roots and hence benefited from the trade boom. By 1641 the Old English, whose sixteenth-century landholding was largely in the east of the country, held almost half the profitable land in County Mayo and almost 20 per cent in Kerry and Sligo. By 1641 some fifty Old English merchants from Galway had 18 per cent of the profitable land in County Galway, 11 per cent in Mayo and 14 per cent in Sligo. The burden

---

23 For example see P. Roebuck, 'Landlord Indebtedness in Ulster in the Seventeenth and Eighteenth Centuries', in J. M. Goldstrom and L. A. Clarkson (eds.), *Irish Population, Economy and Society* (Oxford University Press, 1981), 135–55.

of taxation and the harvest crises of the 1620s adversely affected native land-owners in Connacht, leaving them as easy pickings for Galway merchants who acquired land through mortgages. Around Cork and Kilkenny a similar process operated. The difficulty for early seventeenth-century governments was how to align this newly acquired economic power wielded by Catholics with the demands of the confessional state that there should be no official recognition of such potential political influence. The result was a series of political conflicts, of which the most dramatic was 'the Graces' controversy in the late 1620s. Ultimately the failure to solve that problem alienated the economic *élite* from government and posed future problems.

The Economy at War

What characterised the Irish economy before the mid-1630s was a prolonged period of growth fuelled by an increased labour supply and dramatic com-mercialisation. That growth was, admittedly, uneven with harvest crises in the early 1620s and again in 1629–1632, but the trend was increasing output and growth in trade. In 1637 that growth was again interrupted by a harvest crisis. Successive harvest crises between 1637 and 1640 depressed trade and customs revenue probably fell by more than a third. Since Ireland had no mint, it depended on a favourable trade balance to provide enough coin to ensure that, in the absence of paper money, the money supply was sufficient to sustain economic activity. The shift of the trade balance to deficit for a pro-longed period meant that money supply became insufficient for even normal transactions. In the more commercialised parts of the country the harvest crisis of the late 1630s escalated into a financial crisis, the economy contracted as markets ground to a halt and rents and the royal subsidy remained unpaid. In other areas, mainly in the north-west and south-west, in which the market was less well developed, there were fewer signs of distress. The outbreak of war in late 1641 in Ulster escalated the crisis into a full-blown recession. Over the next two years government grappled not just with war but also with trade collapse and financial chaos in which food prices soared. By the end of 1642 there are signs that the economy was stabilising, but at a much lower level than pre-war conditions, and the harvest of that year was good. The Irish governor, James Butler, earl of Ormond, tried to ease the situation by strik-ing a coinage using surrendered silver plate, but the impact was small. By 1643 the situation worsened again with the outbreak of civil war in England. Imports of Irish wool into the ports of south-west England engaged in the Munster trade fell from 10,356 cwt in the 1630s to 506 cwt in 1646–1647 and barrelled beef imports were halved between 1639 and 1646–1647. Tallow shipments from Ireland had fallen to a third of their former level. Despite this, two rival armies, the government's and the Kilkenny Confederation's, had to be maintained. Even a cessation of hostilities in September 1643 had little impact on the economy, with rent receipts on the Boyle estates in Cork barely affected. As a result the Confederation looked to Europe to maintain their establishment since they had no access to ports, and hence customs, to fund their activities. Others in Ireland, deprived of the income from the exchequer, looked to king or parliament for support. The opening of English markets following the end of the first civil war in 1647 provided some relief and Ormond's surrender of Dublin to parliament lifted the naval blockade of the port. The degeneration in political conditions in 1648 undermined any confidence that was established by these events as rent payments spiralled downwards and trade collapsed.

The legacy of the 1640s was one of considerable destruction, partly due to military action but, more importantly, the general dislocation that accompanied war. Military action is clear from the Civil Survey of 1654. In Kildare the value of buildings fell from almost £126,000 in 1641 to £4,350 in 1654. In Armagh and Down the value of tithes between 1641 and 1657, as recorded in the Cromwellian surveys of church property, fell by 30 and 32 per cent respectively, while in Antrim they fell by 25 per cent. Rental incomes, too, collapsed and did not recover quickly. In 1677 on the Perceval estate in Cork rents were between 10 and 20 per cent below their 1641 level and on the Brownlow estate in Armagh, rents fell from £782 per annum in 1635 to £488 in 1659. The greatest impact of the war was felt in towns. The Civil Survey recorded large numbers of waste tenements in the towns of Munster, probably due to the Cromwellian campaign of reconquest, but more general destruction was caused by quartered armies that tore down buildings for firewood and looted properties to make up for their lack of pay.[24]

The 1650s did not start well in economic terms. Bubonic plague arrived in Galway in 1649; by 1650 it had spread to Munster and Dublin, ravaging a population already depleted by war and emigration. The impact can only be guessed at but a decline of 10 per cent in Dublin, where William Petty estimated the plague killed 1,300 a week at its height, and 20 per cent in Connacht and Munster seems plausible. By 1652, Petty guessed that the Irish

---

24 R. Gillespie, 'War and the Irish Town: The Early Modern Experience', in P. Lenihan (ed.), *Conquest and Resistance: War in Seventeenth-Century Ireland* (Leiden: Brill, 2001), 295–315.

population had fallen to some 40 per cent of its pre-war level.[25] There were further unsettling events to come. Plans for a Cromwellian land settlement, with threats of disrupting the labour supply by transplantation, evolved through the 1650s creating considerable instability in the land market, from which some profited. Irish exchequer income fell far short of needs and it was rumoured that in 1659 the subvention from England would cease, imposing new burdens on the economy. Despite this inauspicious start, the 1650s were not the economic disaster that some feared. The shock of war in the 1640s and crippling taxation in the 1650s broke the last remnants of the customary world of the sixteenth century and forced many in the 1650s to reconsider their economic options by focusing on markets. A case in point is the livestock trade. William Petty reckoned that livestock in Ireland were worth more than £4 million in 1641 but by 1652 that value had fallen to £0.5 million. The prohibition on the export of hides, beef, pork, tallow and cattle in the early 1650s served to conserve some stock but rebuilding the agricultural economy forced producers to think about how they could maximise return with reduced resources. That meant paying even closer attention to price signals.

Others began experimenting. Ideas about 'improvement', underpinned by early science, led to some landlords experimenting with 'projects' to develop their lands, inspired by the prospect of reduced costs and higher yields. Much of this was small scale: planting fruit trees, draining bogs, making potash, introducing new crops and making soap. By themselves, these projects produced little income but landowners' willingness to explore and engage with new ideas, on the assumption that the landscape as well as those in it could be reformed, created a foundation for economic prosperity. By the late 1650s there were signs of a resurgence in Irish trade. Good harvests in 1657 and 1658 improved matters and by 1659 the number of Irish ships entering Bristol was almost 70 per cent of the pre-war peak. Property values also began to rise, with the state increasing rents charged on confiscated Catholic property in towns by almost a quarter between 1654 and 1657. In the Munster towns, where Catholic merchants had been expelled, the state had most problems in finding tenants whereas in Dublin, unaffected by the expulsion of Catholic merchants, trade recovered rapidly providing a solid base for the city's dramatic growth in the late seventeenth century.

25 P. Lenihan, 'War and Population, 1649–52', *Irish Economic and Social History*, 24 (1997), 1–21.

The Coming of Prosperity

In the years after the Restoration the full logic of the early seventeenth-century economic changes became clearer. The spread of the market, for example, undermined traditional tenurial arrangements not only in Gaelic Ireland but in the Pale also. A survey of the archbishop of Dublin's estate in 1660, for instance, noted the conversion of copyholds to freeholds, a process that had taken place in Ulster at the plantation. The Restoration land settlement generated standard land patents, eliminating local customs present in earlier grants. Elements of the world of lordships, described by the Civil Survey as 'chieferies' and poorly defined boundaries, were clarified and standardised in line with market demands. Such standardisation is also clear in weights and measures that had begun to attain some measure of uniformity, necessary for trading, by the end of the century.

This expansion of the market, together with the reduction of the powers of many landlords as a result of war, meant that people became increasingly responsive to market signals when making economic decisions. Those price signals were clear. The English prices for live cattle, that had dominated the early seventeenth-century trade, fell by almost 10 per cent between the 1650s and the 1680s. Beef prices fared rather better, remaining fairly stable over the period and butter and cheese prices also stabilised. Since the English market was the main destination for Irish agricultural exports, price signals indicated a shift towards processed goods. Price signals from other markets reinforced this. In Utrecht, for example, butter and beef prices were rising, as opposed to stagnating in England, and this explains why Irish merchants developed a trade in beef and dairy products with the Low Countries and France in the late seventeenth century. While the Cattle Acts of 1663 and 1667 may have helped speed up the transition from livestock to barrelled beef and dairy, they did not initiate it. Already by 1665 barrel beef exports were twice what they had been in 1641, while live cattle exports had only increased by a quarter. Finally, the opening of new colonial markets offered Irish merchants the opportunity to expand their interests in the provisions trade. By the 1680s Galway and Cork, convenient for the trans-Atlantic trade, emerged as the main centres for trade in barrelled beef while Belfast, Youghal and Limerick, all ports with strong European connections, were key ports for the butter trade.

This implied the emergence of a more regionally specialised agricultural economy in the late seventeenth century. With the rise of a separate butter and provisions trade, divisions emerged between breeding and fattening areas for cattle, the latter requiring better land than the former. East Connacht and the midlands became established as fattening country while more marginal lands in Counties Clare, Leitrim, Roscommon, Limerick and Westmeath were given over to sheep. Tipperary became the dairying centre par excellence, followed by north Cork and the Lagan Valley in Ulster. Dairying was labour intensive and hence these were areas of high population density. It also required capital investment in dairies and equipment for butter and cheese making, so these areas saw additional investment with, presumably, commensurate returns in output. Distinct agricultural regions forced the emergence of inter-regional trade, underpinned by livestock fairs, of which there were some 503 operating by 1685. It also marked the rise of the inland market town. Whereas coastal ports had benefited from the trade boom of the early seventeenth century, with the emergence of regional economies, the inland towns that served as marketing centres, through which specialist goods were funnelled to the ports, prospered. Mullingar, Kildare, Charleville and Lisburn, for instance, all grew because of their links with nearby large ports.

The second consequence of a regionally specialised agriculture linked through a network of markets and fairs was that landlords and merchants began to explore the potential of an enlarged market to produce other types of goods. The most obvious area for growth was in textiles. The duke of Ormond, for instance, encouraged weaving at Clonmel, bringing in French weavers. He was also behind the establishment of linen production at Chapelizod. In the 1690s on the Abercorn estate in Tyrone, the landlord promoted spinning and weaving competitions to boost the linen trade and at Lurgan, in County Armagh, the local landlord, Arthur Brownlow, controlled a market in linen by buying up all the webs offered for sale. He sold on some of the finer linens using Quaker merchants, with their international connections, who had settled on his estates, a good example of the initiative of landlords and merchants working together.

These changes conspired to ensure that Restoration Ireland became prosperous after 1660. Dublin expanded dramatically. In the early part of the century Dublin had been unfavourably compared with the provincial town of Bristol, yet in 1685 William Petty likened it favourably to Paris, London, Amsterdam, Venice and Rome. In 1600 it had a population of about 5,000, yet by 1706 it had almost 62,000 souls. It was the fastest-growing city in the British Isles and the largest after London. Evidence of prosperity was not only to be found in Dublin. In Munster the ports of Youghal and Cork also grew rapidly as did Belfast and Derry in Ulster. The consumption of luxury goods increased, suggesting some people could afford a lavish lifestyle.

Tobacco consumption rose sharply and continuously from the 1660s to the 1680s, with a doubling of imports. By 1700 it had increased by a further 50 per cent. Wine imports grew and silver vessels from which it could be drunk became more common, the quantity of silver plate assayed in Dublin in the late 1630s being only 5 per cent of what would be assayed in 1700 alone. All this was funded from the profits of land – William Petty reckoned rentals had risen from £0.9 million in 1672 to £1.2 million in 1687 – and the profits of trade.

The prosperity apparent after 1660 was far from assured. The Dutch wars, for instance, posed problems for an Irish trade that was only recovering from the depression of the 1650s. Thus between 1660 and 1670 customs revenues remained stagnant, or perhaps fell slightly. There were also domestic threats to rising prosperity. The most important of these was government itself. In the early part of the century direct taxation had been limited to occasional subsidies. New taxes had been introduced to support the war of the 1640s and the army in the 1650s. In the 1660s another tax, the hearth tax, was introduced, requiring regular cash payments to be made by Irish householders. This additional tax was introduced as agricultural prices were falling and the population was rising. Landlord incomes, almost entirely dependent on rent receipts, relied increasingly on the sale of produce and demands for additional taxation might have an impact on markets. The state also involved itself in another potentially damaging way: the passage in 1663 and 1665 of legislation restricting the import of live Irish cattle into England. Falling cattle prices caused discontent among English breeders, who felt their trade was being undermined by Irish and Scottish livestock, and they lobbied for this legislation, against the wishes of the government in the case of the second act. Again the passage of the Navigation Acts of 1660 and 1671 and the Staple Act of 1663 had the potential to destabilise the Irish colonial trade by forcing merchants to land goods in England first, thus increasing the cost of colonial imports in Ireland.

While taxation and legislation were both potentially destabilising in the longer term, their impact was much less than was feared at the time. A greater danger, less commented on by contemporaries, was the growth in population that threatened to absorb the growth in national output, causing a fall in per capita wealth. In 1641, the Irish population stood at about 2.1 million. The effects of war and the plague of the 1650s were still being felt in the 1680s when William Petty estimated the Irish population to be 1.3 million, but there are good reasons to adjust this upwards to about 1.9 million. The hearth tax suggests that there were regional variations in growth rates. The fastest growth was experienced in Ulster, while that in Munster was more restricted. Emigration from England, which went mainly to Munster, was discouraged after 1660 since contemporaries felt that the English population would decrease. As a result Munster relied more on natural increase for its population growth. The demographic behaviour of Irish Quakers in the late seventeenth century suggests that this was not as perilous as it might have been. Irish Quakers had lower marriage ages than their English counterparts and the average size of completed Irish Quaker families was larger than in England – 5.4 persons as opposed to 4. Lower infant mortality meant that more children survived and in general Irish Quakers might live two years longer than their English counterparts. All this pointed to a faster than expected natural growth rate.[26] In Ulster the engine of population change was immigration, mainly from Scotland, fed by the discontent generated by the Covenanter disturbances. The population of Ulster may have increased by 50 per cent between 1660 and 1685. These additional people had to be accommodated within an increasingly rigid tenurial grid. Finding an income for these migrants, and a way for them to engage in the market economy, was a problem that some tried to solve after 1660.

While the evidence is slight, there was some cause for concern. In Dublin, for instance, real wages fell sharply in the 1680s after almost twenty years of growth, suggesting a fall in living standards.[27] Since Ireland lacked any official poor relief scheme, this was done informally at local level by Church of Ireland parishes and by landlords. It was in the rapidly growing areas of Ulster's Lagan valley that the earliest evidence of parish schemes, which issued badges to their poor, appeared, soon followed by similar schemes in Dublin. Some landlord innovations, such as linen manufacture, may have been initiatives designed to allow poorer tenants to generate cash for rent. Others who engaged with the problem of poverty, such as the contemporary Irish novelist and dramatist Richard Head, turned to print to complain about social mobility and resulting pressures as the commercial world, particularly in towns, triumphed over an older, more structured society.[28]

---

26 D. C. Eversley, 'The Demography of the Irish Quakers, 1650–1850', in Goldstrom and Clarkson (eds.), *Irish Population, Economy and Society*, 57–88.

27 L. M. Culllen, T. C. Smout and A. Gibson, 'Wages and Comparative Development in Ireland and Scotland, 1565–1780', in R. Mitchison and P. Roebuck (eds.), *Economy and Society in Scotland and Ireland, 1500–1939* (Edinburgh: John Donald, 1988), 109.

28 R. Gillespie, 'Richard Head's *The Miss display'd* and Irish Restoration Society', in *Irish University Review*, 34 (2004), 213–28.

War and Reconstruction

In the late 1680s the prosperity that characterised the years after 1670 came to a shuddering halt. The immediate cause, as in the 1630s, was a harvest crisis. The harvests of 1686 and 1687 were exceptionally good and exports increased significantly, pushing agricultural prices down. Growth in trade was achieved by an expansion of volume in an age of declining prices across Europe and hence a reversal in output growth had serious financial consequences. In 1688 the customs yield was less than half what it had been in 1687. The impact of the harvest crisis was different to that of the late 1630s. One reason was that the social basis of taxation had changed over the seventeenth century. In the 1620s about a quarter of Irish revenue came from customs and excise, while another half originated in rents and compositions. By 1685, rents only accounted for about a fifth of gross revenue while the customs now generated about a third of income. Thus most taxes came from highly mobile mercantile capital rather than fixed assets such as land. In addition about 10 per cent of income in 1685 came from the hearth tax, which fell on the mass of the population and was vulnerable to political discontent. The harvest crisis of 1688 translated into a crisis for economic activity, and for the exchequer, as merchants fled Ireland.

This formed the backdrop to the breakdown of law and order in 1688 and 1689. Conditions were exacerbated by the quartering of the army, now largely Catholic, on the localities, where it was sent in an attempt to maintain law and order. Scaremongering and rumours of a general massacre, as in 1641, all fed into sectarian tensions and instability. The resulting wars of 1689–91 undoubtedly had a short-term economic impact, but in comparison with the 1640s they were more muted. The relatively short military campaign during the Williamite wars focused on a series of high-profile battles and sieges rather than a long war of attrition, as in the 1640s. The evidence of war could be seen in the fabric of the towns of Derry and Newry at the beginning of the eighteenth century, but already by 1700 rent levels had recovered their 1685 levels and in some cases surpassed them. Trade, too, was restored to pre-war levels by 1697. Some external forces favoured economic recovery in the 1690s. The 1690s was a poor harvest decade across Europe and food prices increased. In England, Ireland's main market, livestock product prices rose by 13 per cent in the 1690s and grain prices grew by 20 per cent. Ireland saw relatively good harvests in the 1690s and the share of grain in exports from Ireland increased. The benign economic environment in the 1690s, together with a shortage of tenants because of the migration back to England and Scotland during the crisis of 1688–91, prompted a significant influx of people into Ireland that brought an increased capital inflow which, in turn, funded the high level of imports needed to rebuild the economy after 1691.

Regionally the effects of this were diverse. Ulster benefited most, with the severe harvest crises in Scotland in the 1690s prompting immigration. This altered the ethnic and religious composition of the province. One contemporary noted that before the 1690s, notwithstanding the plantation, most Ulster tenants were Catholics, but after the war 'Scottish men came over into the north with their families and effects and settled there so that they are now at this present the greater proportion of the inhabitants of Ulster.'[29] The geography of this growth can be mapped by the expansion of Presbyterian congregations along the Foyle valley and into south and west Ulster, areas that were previously little developed. In this migration lay the roots of the political problems that the dominance of Presbyterian dissenters in Ulster would generate in the eighteenth century. The effect of migration was much more muted in Munster, but here, by 1700, the population was back to its 1680s peak and it would continue to grow by natural increase over the next two decades.

The exceptional conditions of the 1690s did not last. After 1710 the Irish economy went into a prolonged recession. Population growth slowed and in some places ceased. In Ulster, parishes such as Derry began to show a surplus of burials over baptisms and by the 1730s, the population was also falling in Munster. The immigration that had characterised the seventeenth century was replaced by emigration in some parts of the country. This was underpinned by a severe economic recession that contemporaries explained in political language. They traced their economic woes to the Woollen Act of 1699, which restricted the import of Irish wool into England. The export of new draperies from Ireland in 1698 was double what it had been a decade earlier and this gave rise to worries among English merchants that trade might be damaged by Irish competition. The reaction to this economic event was political, the crystallisation of the diffuse Anglo-Irish sense of Ireland as a kingdom, expressed in the work of William Molyneux. Such criticism extended into the early eighteenth century. Jonathan Swift in the 1720s railed against political corruption over the issue of Wood's Halfpence and the debate on a national bank was conditioned more by political than economic considerations. In reality the causes of the early eighteenth-century difficulties lay

29 J. T. Gilbert (ed.), *A Jacobite Narrative of the War in Ireland* (Dublin: J. Dollard, 1892), 55–6.

elsewhere. At home, a series of harvest crises wrecked havoc on the domestic economy. Abroad, European wars disrupted the patterns of continental trade that Irish merchants had carefully constructed in the late seventeenth century and this created commercial problems that exacerbated natural ones. The outbreak of the European war in 1702 interrupted trade and slowed Irish markets, but some respite was provided by a series of bad harvests and cattle disease in France in 1710 that generated demand for Irish imports. Matters should have improved after the peace of Utrecht in 1713, but a series of financial crises in Ireland's largest market, England, together with domestic harvest problems, delayed the recovery of the Irish economy until the middle of the eighteenth century.

Conclusion

The changes that engulfed early modern Ireland were a series of interlinked revolutions operating at a variety of levels. Law moved from a set of traditional arrangements, determined mainly by custom, to an English common law tradition, previously only effective in the Pale. Political arrangements were transformed from a network of local lordships, organised on extended lineage systems, to a national settler-dominated government. Underpinning this was a shift in the ownership of land and the introduction of settlers, through formal plantation schemes and informal colonisation, into the previously thinly settled north, west and south-west of Ireland. Land, organised in both estates and family properties in the later Middle Ages, was shaped into an estate system that created a framework for economic development through exploiting natural resources and building marketing structures. In architectural terms, the *élite* abandoned their fifteenth-century fortified tower houses to live in greater comfort in the undefended mansions that spoke of improvement in the early eighteenth century. All of this was reflected in shifting settlement patterns and a landscape organised in a more complex way to suit commercialised agriculture. Perhaps most dramatic was the shift in redistribution of economic surpluses from local lineages, in which continuously circulating gifts were exchanged between lords and followers (the size of which 'gifts' was determined by custom and modified by force), to the market as the main means of economic interaction. As a result a materially impoverished world was flooded with imported commercial goods, in both settled and non-settled areas, that transformed the lives of the inhabitants of early modern Ireland. None of this was inevitable. There was no clear link, for example, between colonisation and commercialisation, the two processes apparently working with their own dynamic and at their own pace. In the short term harvest crises, which had the potential to trigger commercial crises, shaped patterns of activity, while in the medium term developments in an increasingly internationalised economy had the capacity to retard and encourage change. The nature and pace of change varied from place to place and in some of the more marginal economies of northern and western Ireland commercialisation, experienced by much of Ireland in the early seventeenth century, had little impact before the early eighteenth century. Such realities reveal the complexity of regional patterns of economic life and the variegated ways in which that diversity had evolved.

22

Plantations, 1550–1641

ANNALEIGH MARGEY

The early modern period is synonymous with the mass movement of people across the world. In particular, Europeans were on the move. Spanish and Portuguese conquistadores; the Dutch joint-stock companies; and French pioneers explored, and later colonised, lands throughout the Asian and Atlantic worlds. England joined these pursuits from the 1550s, with their earliest settlements taking place in Ireland. Settlement began in the counties of Laois and Offaly, before later expanding into Munster, Ulster and the remainder of the Midlands. These Irish settlements became exemplars of future British imperial expansion. The influence of Ireland on Britain's imperial policy has long been alluded to by historians, who argue that Ireland was the first step in the westward expansion of England and, as a result, became 'a laboratory for empire'. This 'westward expansion' saw Ireland become the home of new settlers from across England, Scotland and Wales, who participated in the political, social and cultural transformation of the country.[1]

Yet, settlement by the English in Ireland was not new in the sixteenth century. Englishmen and their descendants had lived in Ireland since the eleventh century. By the sixteenth century, however, administrators were re-evaluating English policy in Ireland. So, what had changed? During the reign of Henry VIII, the traditional English power base was under threat. Incursions into the Pale by raiding Gaelic lords; a lack of English control across vast swathes of Ireland; an increasingly Gaelicised Anglo-Irish population; and a fear of invasion caused significant problems for English administrators. These threats to English control in Ireland coincided with the aforementioned attempts by England to expand her empire. English administrators proposed plans for a final resolution to the Irish problem that would see Ireland become a central component of England's, and later, Britain's early modern empire. While

---

1 See Introduction and Chapter 15 by Ohlmeyer and O'Reilly, this volume.

military subjugation was considered a necessity, many administrators proposed the idea of the settlement of Ireland by loyal, English-born men. In the first instance, they suggested settlements for locations of strategic importance, such as the Pale borders and the Irish coastline. As the sixteenth century progressed, however, further proposals emerged for plantation schemes across parts of Ireland that had recently been in rebellion. In many of the schemes, planners carved out a place for the Gaelic Irish, bringing about a situation where native Irish, English and later, British settlers, lived side-by-side. By the seventeenth century, plantation had become the foremost British policy in Ireland.

This chapter seeks to trace the evolution of these plantations in Ireland from genesis to completion. It begins with an appraisal of the field of Irish plantation studies and explores some of the theories put forward by Englishmen on how best to subdue Ireland in the aftermath of successive rebellions across the country. The central focus is on the development of individual plantation schemes between 1550 and 1641: the major government-directed schemes of plantation in Leix-Offaly, Munster, Ulster and Londonderry, alongside the smaller, seventeenth-century schemes in Wexford, Longford, Leitrim, King's County, Queen's County and Westmeath; and the 'private' plantation schemes in late sixteenth-century Ulster. The chapter also discusses how these schemes, often referred to as 'social engineering' projects, transformed the Irish landscape and had wide ramifications for politics, society and culture.

Historians and the Irish Plantations

In recent decades, the study of early modern Irish history has undergone something of a renaissance, and with it, so have studies of the Irish plantations. Prior to the 1950s and 1960s, the plantations had attracted little scholarly attention. Such was the dearth of work that of the 421 works identified in *The Bibliography of British and Irish History* pertaining to the Irish plantations, a mere thirty-one appeared before 1950. Robert Dunlop emerged as a prolific, early scholar of the subject, producing four separate studies of various plantations in Ireland between the 1880s and the 1920s. His work remains a strong starting point for historians, as it showcases the array of primary sources for the subject. While the Ulster plantation received some attention thereafter, the next major study of any Irish plantation did not emerge until T. W. Moody's seminal work on the Londonderry Plantation in the 1930s. Moody exposed the staggering range of London source materials for the subject, including the records of individual Livery Companies and the Irish Society.[2] Surprisingly, it took until the early 2000s for studies of all the individual plantations to be completed.[3]

From the mid-twentieth century more specialised works appeared. Individual county studies for Donegal and Armagh, for example, highlighted the impact of plantation on a local level in Ulster, while the results of some of the first excavations of post-medieval Ireland unveiled what could be learned from the physical remains of plantation houses, castles and bawns.[4] More thematic studies included the pioneering work of R. J. Hunter on plantation towns.[5] Studies of individuals, who directed plantation policy or, became settlers in their own right, also emerged.[6] Comparative work with other colonial sites became a dominant theme, as historians looked for synergies within

2 'The Bibliography of British and Irish History' (http://cpps.brepolis.net.jproxy.dkit.ie/bbih/search.cfm) (accessed 15 July 2015); R. Dunlop, 'The Plantation of Munster, 1584–1589', *English Historical Review*, 3 (1888), 240–69; R. Dunlop, 'The Plantation of Leix and Offaly, 1556–1622', *English Historical Review*, 6 (1891), 61–96; R. Dunlop, 'Ireland from the Plantation of Ulster to the Cromwellian Settlement (1611–1659)', in A. W. Ward, G. W. Prothero and S. Leathes (eds.), *Cambridge Modern History*, iv: The Thirty Years' War (Cambridge University Press, 1906), 513–38; 'Sixteenth-Century Schemes for the Plantation of Ulster', *Scottish Historical Reviews*, 22 (1925), 199–212; T. W. Moody, *The Londonderry Plantation, 1609–41: The City of London and the Plantation in Ulster* (Belfast: W. Mullan and Son, 1939).

3 D. B. Quinn, 'Sir Thomas Smith (1513–1577) and the Beginnings of English Colonial Theory', *Proceedings of the American Philosophical Society*, 89 (1945), 543–60; D. G. White, 'The Tudor Plantations in Ireland before 1571', unpublished PhD thesis, Trinity College Dublin (1968); P. S. Robinson, *The Plantation of Ulster: British Settlement in an Irish landscape, 1600–70* (Dublin: Gill and MacMillan, 1984); M. McCarthy-Morrogh, *The Munster Plantation: English Migration to Southern Ireland, 1583–1641* (Oxford: Clarendon Press, 1986); B. Mac Cuarta, 'The Plantation of Leitrim, 1620–41', *Irish Historical Studies*, 32 (2001), 297–320.

4 V. W. Treadwell, 'The Plantation of Donegal: A Survey', *Donegal Annual*, 2 (1954), 511–17; T. G. F. Paterson, 'County Armagh in 1622: A Plantation Survey', *Seanchas Ardmhacha*, 4 (1961), 103–40; E. M. Jope, 'Moyry, Charlemont, Castleraw and Richhill: Fortification to Architecture in the North of Ireland, 1570–1700', *Ulster Journal of Archaeology*, 23 (1960), 97–123.

5 R. J. Hunter, 'Towns in the Ulster Plantation', *Studia Hibernica*, 11 (1971), 40–79. See also R. Gillespie, 'The Origins and Development of an Ulster Urban Network, 1600–1641', *Irish Historical Studies*, 24 (1984), 15–29; A. Sheehan, 'Irish Towns in a Period of Change, 1588–1625', in C. Brady and R. Gillespie (eds.), *Natives and Newcomers: Essays on the Making of Irish Colonial Society, 1534–1641* (Dublin: Irish Academic Press, 1986), 93–119.

6 T. O. Ranger, 'Richard Boyle and the Making of an Irish Fortune, 1588–1614', *Irish Historical Studies*, 10 (1956–1957), 257–97; N. P. Canny, *The Upstart Earl: A Study of the Social and Mental World of Richard Boyle, First Earl of Cork, 1566–1643* (Cambridge University Press, 1982). For later studies see: R. Loeber, 'Civilisation Through Plantation: The Projects of Mathew de Renzi', in H. Murtagh (ed.), *Irish Midland Studies: Essays in Commemoration of N. W. English* (Athlone: Old Athlone Society, 1980).

the Atlantic world.[7] Plantation also retained a central place in histories of Ireland, with *The New History of Ireland* incorporating the theme across several chapters.[8]

Since the 1980s plantation studies have become more dynamic. This has been brought about by the increasing interest of literary scholars, archaeologists and geographers in the field. Many historians, for example, adopted what could be described as a more 'literary turn', incorporating the contemporary 'reform' literature into their work.[9] Historical geographers addressed the transformation of the Irish landscape under plantation.[10] Historians of cartography explored the role of maps in visualising how plantation would, and did, transform the landscape of Ireland.[11] Similarly, an upsurge in archaeology developed further our understanding of the changing cultural landscape.[12] The social and economic history of the plantations also attracted interest; for example, historians have studied the importance of gender and particular ethnic groups, such as the Scots, within the plantations.[13] Increasingly, the 1641

---

7 D. B. Quinn, *Ireland and America: their Early Associations, 1500–1640* (Liverpool University Press, 1991); N. P. Canny, *Kingdom and Colony: Ireland in the Atlantic World, 1560–1800* (London: Johns Hopkins University Press, 1988).

8 T. W. Moody, F. X. Martin and F. J. Byrne (eds.), *A New History of Ireland, iii: Early Modern Ireland, 1534–1691* (Oxford University Press, 1976).

9 See: N. P. Canny, *Making Ireland British* (Oxford University Press, 2001); C. Brady, 'Spenser's Irish Crisis: Humanism and Experience in the 1590s', *Past & Present*, 111 (1986), 17–49; J. R. Brink, 'Sir John Davies: Lawyer and Poet', in T. Herron and M. Potterton (eds.), *Ireland in the Renaissance, c.1540–1660* (Dublin: Four Courts Press [hereafter FCP], 2007), 88–104; J. H. Ohlmeyer, ' "Civilizinge those rude partes": Colonisation within Britain and Ireland, 1580s–1640s', in N. P. Canny (ed.), *The Origins of Empire: British Overseas Enterprise to the Close of the Seventeenth Century* (Oxford University Press, 1998), 124–47; J. McLaughlin, 'Select Documents XLVII: Richard Hadsor's "Discourse" on the Irish State, 1604', *Irish Historical Studies*, 30 (1997), 337–53.

10 W. J. Smyth, *Map-Making, Landscapes and Memory: A Geography of Colonial and Early Modern Ireland, c.1530–1750* (Cork University Press, 2006).

11 See, for example, J. H. Andrews, 'Colonial Cartography in a European Setting: The Case of Tudor Ireland', in D. Woodward (ed.), *History of Cartography, Vol. 3: Cartography in the European Renaissance* (Chicago University Press, 2007), 1670–83; A. Margey, 'Representing Plantation Landscapes: The Mapping of Ulster, c.1560–1640', in J. Lyttleton and C. Rynne (eds.), *Plantation Ireland: Settlement and Material Culture, c.1550–1700* (Dublin: FCP, 2009), 140–64.

12 See: The Northern Ireland Sites and Monuments Record, http://apps.ehsni.gov.uk/ambit/Default.aspx; A. Horning, , R. Ó Baoill, C. Donnelly and P. Logue (eds.), *The Post-Medieval Archaeology of Ireland, 1550–1850* (Bray: Wordwell, 2007); E. Klingelhofer, *Castles and Colonists: An Archaeology of Elizabethan Ireland* (Manchester University Press, 2010); J. Lyttleton, *The Jacobean Plantations in Seventeenth-Century Offaly: an Archaeology of a Changing World* (Dublin: FCP, 2013).

13 M. MacCurtain and M. O'Dowd (eds.), *Women in Early Modern Ireland* (Edinburgh University Press, 1991); R. Gillespie, *The Transformation of the Irish Economy, 1550–1700* (Dundalk: Dundalgan Press for the Economic and Social History of Ireland, 1991); M. Perceval-Maxwell, *The Scottish Migration to Ulster in the Reign of James I* (London: Routledge and Kegan Paul, 1973).

Depositions have been analysed as sources that can offer a window onto the settler society in Ireland before the rebellion.[14]

So what remains to be done? Well, despite the continued increase in scholarship, many aspects of the plantations are still under-studied. The private schemes of Ulster have to date only been studied in a small number of journal articles, while the concept of corporatism within these schemes has only recently been addressed. As a group, the English and natives in the Ulster Plantation have had little attention to date. The plantations of the 1610s and 1620s remain under-studied, while further research could be undertaken on Munster and Leix-Offaly. What is obvious is that this is a field of study that keeps on giving. Previously inaccessible, unknown or little-used sources, as well as new approaches to its study, continue to add value to the field.[15]

Theorising Plantation

The practicalities of English, and British, settlement in Ireland developed in the midst of a culture of writing by theorists, who sought to debate the 'defects' of Gaelic Ireland and how to subdue and reform the country. Many early modern writers took their cues from Giraldus Cambrensis. Giraldus's *Topographia Hibernica* and *Expugnatio Hibernica*, in the twelfth century, inculcated a common trope of the native Irish as barbarous people, referring to their 'primitive habits' and how they lived 'themselves like beasts'.[16] Giraldus's opinions underpinned early modern English opinion of Ireland, as a backward and savage country in need of reform. The nature of these reforms became the building blocks of tracts in the sixteenth and seventeenth centuries. These tracts emanated from men who had been classically educated, steeped in humanist traditions. Their work, as a result, often invoked classical precedents for settlement in Ireland, including the concepts, drawn from the Roman Empire of hierarchy, colonisation and military subjugation. Among these theorists were men from Ireland's political, administrative and settler networks including Edmund Spenser, Sir Thomas Smith and Sir John Davies. It is to their writings that scholars often return, when seeking to uncover

---

14 N. P. Canny, 'The 1641 Depositions as a Source for the Writing of Social History: Cork as a Case Study', in P. O'Flanagan and C. Buttimer (eds.), *Cork: History and Society* (Dublin: Geography Publications, 1993), 249–308.
15 P. Withington, 'Plantation and Civil Society', in É. Ó Ciardha and M. Ó Siochrú (eds.), *The Plantation of Ulster: Ideology and Practice* (Manchester University Press, 2012), 55–77.
16 Ohlmeyer, ' "Civilizinge of those rude partes" ', 131.

some of the ideological frameworks that pervaded the thinking of those who played an active role in shaping the Irish plantations.

Perhaps the most famous of these writers was Edmund Spenser, who wrote *A View of the Present State of Ireland* in 1596. This work, first published in 1633 by Sir James Ware, has long been *feted* as one of the most controversial works on Ireland, due to its sharp observations and prescription for reform. It discussed issues relating to 'ethnography, genealogy, degeneracy and cultural formation'.[17] While controversial, the text is often considered a strong 'synthesis of New English opinion' at the end of the sixteenth century, offering an insight into perceived Irish abuses and deficiencies, while suggesting some remedies.[18] Using the form of a dialogue, Spenser introduced readers to the problems of Ireland through a conversation/debate between two central characters: Eudoxus and Irenius. Eudoxus represented a senior official in England, with an interest in Irish affairs, while Irenius embodied an Englishman 'who had practical experience in Irish affairs'.[19] Amongst the deficiencies identified by the debate were the very basis of law and order and England's attempts to settle the country in the past. Their suggested remedies included military subjugation and extensive powers that even included the killing of civilians.[20] While some of Spenser's more controversial remedies shock the modern reader, many of his more moderate suggestions, such as military intervention and re-settlement, were in fact elements of many plantation schemes.

By the seventeenth century, the tone of English discourse relating to Ireland had not changed significantly. As administrators proposed plantation for Ulster, several new writers joined the debates on the nature of the Irish and how they might be reformed. Fynes Moryson, for example, in his *Itinerary*, reserved particular criticism for the Irish, describing them as 'mere Irish' and 'barbarous'.[21] Further criticism came from Barnaby Rich, who pronounced the Irish as 'very cruell in their executions, and no lesse bloudy in their disposition'. He suggested, however, that their cruelty was not their own fault, but came from 'the malice and hatred they bear to the English government'.

---

17 Edmund Spenser, *A View of the Present State of Ireland*, ed. A. Hadfield and W. Maley (Oxford: Blackwell, 2000), xvi.
18 Arguments of Nicholas Canny discussed in C. Brady, 'Spenser's Irish Crisis', 22.
19 N. Canny, 'Reviewing *A View of the Present State of Ireland*', *Irish University Review*, 26 (1986), 255.
20 Canny, 'Reviewing *A View*', 262–4.
21 Fynes Moryson, *An Itinerary VVritten by Fynes Moryson Gent. Containing his Ten Yeeres Travel throvgh the Twelve Domjnions of Germany, Bohmerland, Sweitzerland, Netherland, Denmarke, Poland, Italy, Turky, France, England, Scotland and Ireland* (London, 1617), 162 (Part III, Book 3) and 299 (Part II, Book 3).

Plantation in Ulster would, he proffered, offer an opportunity to reform the Irish people and society, as it would provide 'a patterne of good example, as well of Godly as Ciuill Government'.[22]

Sir John Davies, the Irish attorney general, continued to hold the view that the Irish were barbarous. Yet he acknowledged that the defects of government in Ireland came from both the Irish and English sides. He argued

> That ever since our Nation had any footing in this Land, the State of England did earnestly desire … to perfect the Conquest of this Kingdom, but that in every page there were found such impediments and defects in both Realms, as caused almost an impossibility.[23]

He suggested that English policies in Ireland had inherent problems, chief amongst them 'that the Crown of England did not from the beginning give laws to the Irishry' and that early land grants in Ireland had been far too large.[24] Unsurprisingly, given his successive appointments by James VI and I, he argued that in James's reign 'there hath been more done in the work and reformation of this Kingdom, than in the 440 years which are past since the Conquest was first attempted'.[25] For Davies, an effective final solution was one that included both native Irish and British settlers, and he singled out the Ulster Plantation as an exemplar for future schemes.[26] In sum, for Davies, a strong, ordered and structured settlement, including British and 'loyal' Irish, could bring about radical changes to Britain's interaction with Ireland.

The Leix-Offaly Plantation

While these writers theorised about the best solutions to the 'Irish problem', the English government began their practical interventions in the settlement of Ireland from the late 1540s. By the end of Henry VIII's reign, problems had begun to mount on the borders of the Pale in present-day Counties Laois and Offaly, where successive rebellions from the 1520s caused grave concern. Throughout the period of rebellion, the English authorities considered establishing a settlement of loyal Englishmen, who would ensure the permanent subjugation of the region. The use of plantation, as a means of conquest

---

22 Barnaby Rich, *A New Description of Ireland, Wherin is Described the Disposition of the Irish whervnto they are Inclined* (London, 1610), An Epistle, n.p., and chapter 5, p. 17.

23 John Davies, *A Discovery of the True Causes why Ireland was Never Intirely Subdued* (3rd edn., Dublin, 1666), 4.

24 Davies, *A Discovery*, 89.

25 Brink, 'Sir John Davies', 100; Davies, *A Discovery*, 231.

26 Davies, *A discovery*, 249–51.

in Leix-Offaly, however, only evolved on a practical level from the reign of Edward VI. The development of the Leix-Offaly plantation is fundamental to understanding the evolution of plantation policy as a whole, as English authorities tried, tested and adapted policies from what they learned. It is, therefore, not surprising that similarities exist between all schemes in Ireland. Following the suppression of rebellions, the government identified lands for settlement, and commissioned surveyors to assess. This, in turn, laid the foundations for the land grants. Quite often, lands were assigned for urban development. Finally, government officials monitored the plantation's development, often adapting policies in response to perceived failures. The plantation of Leix-Offaly progressed through all of these stages.

Before the formal plantation scheme emerged, English intervention had gained momentum from 1548 when Lord Deputy Edward Bellingham began a campaign to subdue the territories and built two fortresses, Fort Protector and Fort Governor. These initial steps were followed by the formal pardons of the lords of Leix and Offaly, before authorities undertook cess assessments for the building and fortifying of the counties. Bellingham's successor, Anthony St Leger, took the lead on formalising the plantation. On his arrival, he visited both Fort Governor and Fort Protector, possibly signalling an intention to grant some of these lands to undertakers. In November 1550 Walter Cowley undertook a survey of Leix-Offaly. The distinguishing of the plantation lands formed an important part of his work, as the plantation did not cover the entirety of the two counties. The survey began in Offaly, which White suggests was more of a 'terra incognita' to the English than Laois. Both counties were surveyed by 10 December 1550. Unusually for a plantation surveyor, Cowley became involved in the plans for the division and actual granting of the estates to undertakers. In Offaly, for example, he suggested that the tenants whose estates lacked timber should 'have free license in all the great woods of Offaly next to their farms ... to cut and carry with them at their pleasure to build'.[27]

Following the survey, government officials drew up the plantation conditions. Similar to later schemes, they placed restrictions on the re-assignment of lands and the introduction of natives, particularly those from the O'Connor and O'More families. Grantees had to ensure that all settlers were armed and resided on their estates. The first wave of letters patent followed, with twenty-nine grants in Laois and eleven in Offaly. The settlers included

27 M. MacCurtain, *Tudor and Stuart Ireland* (Dublin: Gill and MacMillan 1972), 54; White, 'The Tudor Plantations', 245–8.

a variety of groups: Englishmen and Welshmen, drawn from soldiers and administrators; others of Anglo-Irish (later Old English) provenance; members of the native Irish community; and a small number of Scottish galloglass. Grantees received leases for twenty-one years and soldiers were stationed at garrisons across the new plantations.[28] There appeared to be significant continuity in leases between the tenure of St Leger and Sir James Croft as lord deputy, although Croft sought to eliminate the Irish and the galloglass settlers. In its infancy, the plantation's authorities dealt with numerous issues. By the reign of Mary I, many elements of the scheme had not been determined, including the exact rent, the framework of administration and even the terms of tenure. Such was the general upheaval that by December 1556, Mary issued her own set of instructions for the plantation, effectively changing some of the terms and conditions of the scheme. Significantly, she suggested a curb on Irish involvement, restricting the size of their grants to two ploughlands or 240 acres.[29] In 1557, Mary formally incorporated Fort Protector and Fort Governor, as Maryborough and Philipstown respectively, and enacted the legal foundation of Queen's County (Laois) and King's County (Offaly).[30] In the same year, however, the first stage of the plantation effectively ended due to Irish incursions.

The Leix-Offaly plantation re-emerged under the new monarch, Queen Elizabeth I. In 1562, she requested a fresh survey and, from 1564, issued new grants, which resulted in another wave of migration. In fact, such was the growth in numbers that Rolf Loeber notes twice as many settlers came to the Midlands in the second wave, as the first wave, with fifty-one in Offaly and thirty-seven in Laois. This wave also saw about half of the land grants given to soldiers, the majority of whom were Catholic. Under the terms of their grants, the settlers had to provide military strength to the plantation; adhere to English laws and customs; and reside on their estates. Further restrictions were placed on their interactions with Irish natives. Elizabeth formally incorporated the two plantation towns – Maryborough and Philipstown – in January 1567. A sketch of Maryborough (Illustration 28) in the 1570s by John Tomkins depicted a walled settlement, with a square-shaped fort at the

---

28 White, 'The Tudor plantations', vol. 1, 253. R. Loeber, *The Geography and Practice of English Colonisation in Ireland from 1534 to 1609* (Athlone: The Group for the study of Irish Historic Settlement, 1991), 17.

29 White, 'The Tudor Plantations', vol. 1, 262, 351; H. C. Hamilton (ed.), *Calendar of State Papers Ireland, 1509–1573* (London: Longman, Green, Longman & Roberts, 1860), 134 (hereafter *CSPI*).

30 H. C. Hamilton, *Calendar of the State Papers relating to Ireland of the reigns of Henry VIIII, Edward VI, Mary and Elizabeth, 1509-1573* (London: HMSO, 1860), 324.

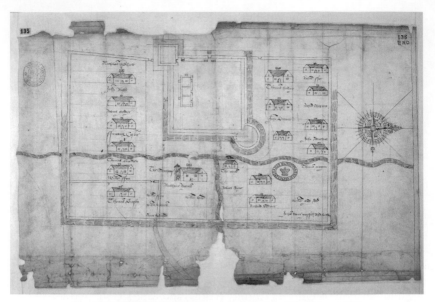

28. TNA MPF1/277, Maryborough Fort, John Tomkins, *c.*1571.

centre. A garrison building, in plan, is evident within the fort. The growth of the town is most obvious in the settlement outside the fort of houses and cabins. In all, twenty-two settler names are inscribed on the map.[31]

Shortly after this depiction, however, the settlement was in turmoil, as it faced renewed attacks by Rory Óg O'More and his followers. By 1576, a slight lull in activities enabled a short return to normality on the plantation estates. However, renewed rebellion in the late 1570s received a significant boost from contemporaneous risings in Munster. By the 1580s, 'the plantation was in a languishing condition', to the extent that many settlers actively sought to offload their estates. Rebellion raged on throughout the 1580s and 1590s, leaving much destruction in its wake, but some settlers maintained and retained their lands. At the turn of the seventeenth century, there was some hope for a re-strengthening of the settlement, following the battle of Kinsale (1601). Evidence of both this retention, and the industry of the settlers, comes to light in the reports of the 1622 Commission, where the commissioners reported:

---

31 Loeber, *The Geography and Practice*, 26; White, 'The Tudor Plantations', vol. 2, 40–1; Maryborough Fort, John Tomkins, *c.*1571, MPF1/277, the National Archives (hereafter TNA).

that this plantation in the King's and Queen's Counties as it was well begun so it hath prosperously continued, and is for the most part well built and peopled by the English and a great strength in the country.[32]

Private Plantations in Ulster

By the 1570s the idea of privately financed settlement gained momentum due to the financial constraints facing Queen Elizabeth's government. Traditionally historians have referred to these schemes as the 'private plantations', but more recent scholarship has stressed that these schemes were more akin to corporate associations. These reflected the concept of civil organisation, where people paid into the enterprise and established themselves in settlements that brought civility to uncivil lands.[33] While first implemented in Ireland, it was envisaged that these schemes might well take the lead in settlement in America. Men such as Sir Richard Grenville and Humphrey Gilbert, for example, with interests in proposing schemes for Ireland, later transferred their attentions to America.[34]

Several examples of these 'private' schemes emerged in Ulster, but perhaps the most significant of these were those by Sir Thomas Smith in the Ards and Walter Devereux, first earl of Essex, in Antrim. Before his entry into the Irish arena, Sir Thomas Smith had written several tracts on how best to govern and advance the English nation. As a member of the Privy Council, he actively commented on, and took a firm interest in, settlement in Ireland. Writing in 1572, and taking inspiration from his classical education, he considered the importance of a strong, hierarchical structure within his plantation. He argued that 'adventurers' in the scheme should be 'colonels', as 'they had responsibility to lead forth *colonias* to people the country with civil men brought up in the law of England'. Central to this structure would be an urban site that Smith, in deference to the queen, proposed to call 'Elizabetha', and which would become a 'centre for defence, then of civilisation and trade'. Such was the strength of Smith's reform zeal that D. B. Quinn argued he viewed the English in Ireland as 'the modern Romans, bringing to a savage land, law, peace and civilisation'.[35]

---

32 Dunlop, 'The Plantation of Leix and Offaly', 85; V. Treadwell, *The Irish Commission of 1622: an Investigation of the Irish Administration 1615–22 and it Consequences 1623–24* (Dublin: Irish Manuscripts Commission, 2006), 461.

33 Withington, 'Plantation and Civil Society', 55–7.

34 Quinn, 'Sir Thomas Smith', 545.

35 Canny, *Making Ireland British*, 121; Quinn, 'Sir Thomas Smith', 546.

In practice, however, Smith's plan did not materialise. Historians have commented on its 'inadequacies of practice', arguing that while Smith envisaged his scheme as a means of strengthening England's position in Ireland, he also expected, as all adventurers did, to ensure 'the enrichment of himself and his son'. By November 1571, his 'Enterprise for Ulster' had helped him to secure a grant of 'all possessions in the Great Arde, Little Arde and Clandeboye'. The grant stipulated that the settlement had to be completed by 28 March 1579. From the beginning, Smith faced an uphill battle. He felt the instant wrath of the existing lord deputy, William Fitzwilliam, who was aggrieved that he had not been consulted about the scheme, particularly due to the burden of having to defend it against attack. He also faced opposition from the Gaelic Irish, led by Sir Brian McPhelim O'Neill, who continued to assert rights to lands in south Antrim and north Down.[36]

Initially Smith was undeterred. He recruited adventurers to participate in his scheme using promotional literature, the first time that this tactic was used for an Irish plantation. He intended to make the participants members of a body akin to the joint-stock companies that settled the Atlantic world in the sixteenth and seventeenth centuries. By spring 1572 his son, Thomas Smith, had amassed 800 potential settlers who arrived in Liverpool, enthusiastic to cross to the Ards. Their passage, however, faced delays and by the time Smith finally arrived on 31 August 1572, only 100 men remained. This left the new settlers entirely open to attack by avenging Irish armies. Their initial base was at Comber, County Down, where they intended to use existing stone buildings for shelter, before expanding their settlement. The native Irish, however, recognised this intention and laid waste to the landscape. By March 1573 Sir Thomas sent reinforcements to the settlement, but they never reached Ireland. Later that year, despite the arrival of Essex to head up a colony to the north of Smith's, the settlement was attacked by Gaelic Irish, who killed Thomas Smith junior. Later attempts to revitalise the settlement continued to fail. A renewed effort in August 1574, fell foul of the native Irish, led by Niall Faghertach O'Neill, with many of the men driven out of the settlement and into hiding in the lower Ards. Despite the continued problems, Sir Thomas's nephew, William Smith, who had inherited his lands, attempted a third settlement as late as June 1579, with forty men. Once again, the effort failed.[37]

---

36 H. Morgan, 'The Colonial Venture of Sir Thomas Smith in Ulster, 1571–75', *The Historical Journal*, 28 (1985), 261, 263; Quinn, 'Sir Thomas Smith', 545–6, 553; C. Lennon, *Sixteenth-Century Ireland: the Incomplete Conquest* (Dublin: Gill and Macmillan, 1994), 277–8.
37 Quinn, 'Sir Thomas Smith', 548–50.

While the Smiths laboured in the Ards, Robert Devereux, second earl of Essex, attempted his own settlement. Late in 1573 he received a grant to the lands of Clandeboy in County Down, along with the Route and the Glynns in County Antrim. For his part Essex agreed to establish a new corporate town near Belfast, surrounded by a fortified wall, with a storehouse for provisions. By January 1574 he had already drawn up articles of agreement with adventurers, envisaging a form of corporate association to include both gentlemen and soldiers. The soldiers would be a ready-made force to protect his settlement. The queen agreed to match his proposal of 200 horse and 400 footmen in order that he could raise the confidence of potential investors in the scheme and ensure their protection. Like Smith, Essex faced opposition from the Gaelic Irish. Throughout late 1574 and early 1575 Essex fought back. The queen appointed him governor of Ulster and he actively pursued the Gaelic leaders, Turlough Luineach and Sir Brian McPhelim O'Neill. He used particularly heavy-handed tactics including slaughtering Sir Brian McPhelim O'Neill, his wife and many of his followers. Despite the savagery, he made little progress in the plantation, only successfully settling around Carrickfergus.[38] The spectacular failure of these schemes provided lessons for future plantation plans, especially the importance of having the full military and financial backing of the crown and the Dublin government.

The Munster Plantation

Elizabethan settlement in Ireland is most synonymous with plantation in Munster. While formal plantation took place in the mid-1580s, plans began to emerge as early as the 1560s. A small private settlement at Kerrycurrihy, County Cork, headed by Sir Warham St Leger, was the first tangible evidence of New English settlement in the province. The possibility of further colonisation became possible when, from the 1560s, many of the Old English families went into open rebellion. Gerald fitz James Fitzgerald, fifteenth earl of Desmond, led the final stage of this rebellion in the late 1570s. When he was captured and beheaded in November 1583, the crown confiscated his lands and those of his supporters.

Debate surrounded the form of plantation that should be implemented, while the experience gained in Leix-Offaly and Ulster also influenced

---

38 Lennon, *Sixteenth Century Ireland*, 277–9; C. Hamilton (ed.), *Calendar of State Papers Ireland, 1574–1585* (London: Longman, Green, Longman & Roberts, 1867); G. A. Hayes-McCoy, 'The Completion of the Tudor Conquest and the Advance of the Counter-Reformation, 1571–1603', in Moody, Martin and Byrne (eds.), *A New History of Ireland*, iii, 97.

decisions. Even during the earl's rebellion, the queen's advisors suggested the need 'to eradicate all rebels and to erect a completely new society in place of the defective commonwealth that had previously prevailed'. After the earl's demise, the first step in the process was the completion of a comprehensive survey 'to determine the limits and values of the respective property'. Both local jurors and a commission of Englishmen conducted the survey, known as 'The Peyton Survey'. It provided details on the extent, ownership, value and topography of the lands. The survey began on 1 September 1584 and the commissioners conducted an estimated eighteen inquisitions while they were in Munster. Their survey methods, however, were questionable. The inquisition-style approach did little to provide an accurate report of the extent and quality of forfeited lands. What they did successfully, however, was to inform the queen that the lands of Munster were indeed valuable, worth almost £10,000.[39] This proved sufficient for her to proceed with the formal attainder of the earl and his followers.

When the official confiscation occurred, it became obvious that the lands were scattered across several counties, including Kerry, Limerick, Cork, Tipperary and Waterford. On 27 June 1586 the government issued the plantation conditions (instructions). The proposed scheme differed greatly from Leix-Offaly. First, the estate or seignory sizes were much larger at 12,000, 8,000, 6,000 and 4,000 acres. Each seignory was to be settled by an 'undertaker', who undertook to bring ninety-one Englishmen to the estate within seven years. The completion date was set as Christmas 1594. The commission proposed rents at differing rates across the province, depending on the estate size. The overall style of settlement also changed with the introduction of English systems such as a manor, court leet and militia. The Irish tenants were to be excluded from estates for at least seven years. The plantation authorities, therefore, envisaged a very ordered plantation that would bring civility to the province. This goal is also obvious in a seignory plan that survives in the State Papers (Illustration 29). The plan espoused order and civility. A Protestant church stood at the centre of the estate, reflecting the religion of the plantation. The undertaker's home was at the corner, while the plan broke the rest of the estate into ninety-one ordered and hierarchical holdings, as per the plantation conditions.[40]

39 N. Canny, *From Reformation to Restoration: Ireland, 1534–1660* (Dublin: Helicon, 1987), 100; McCarthy Morrogh, *The Munster Plantation*, 4–6, 16.
40 McCarthy-Morrogh, *The Munster Plantation*, 30–32, 61; 'The Plotte for a Parishe in Ireland', 1586, MPF1/305, TNA.

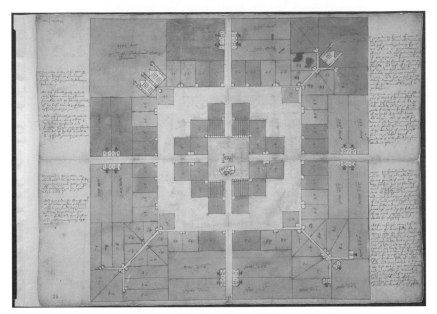

29. TNA MPF1/305, 'The Plotte for a Parishe in Ireland', 1586.

The 'undertakers' were to be 'men of substance', with preference given to settlers from the west of England. Justices of the Peace advertised the scheme, attracting suitable candidates, many of who were English knights or their sons. They undertook to invest a substantial £2,577. Many of the undertakers actively recruited settlers from their home counties. Almost from the beginning, however, the plantation faced problems. Once the conditions had been set down, a new survey began. This became the first to employ two trained surveyors – Arthur Robbins and Francis Jobson – who became responsible for dividing Munster into seignories, containing lands of good quality. They faced an uphill struggle, however, to divide the lands in time for the undertakers' arrival. By the end of 1586, only two estates, those of Sir Christopher Hatton and Sir Walter Raleigh, had in fact been measured. Such was the task ahead of the surveyors that they were still surveying the province in 1589.[41]

It is, therefore, not surprising that numerous problems faced the new landowners on their arrival in Munster. Many undertakers received a vague

41 Canny, *From Reformation to Restoration*, 121; T. Ó hAnnracháin, 'Plantation, 1580–1641', in A. Jackson (ed.), *The Oxford History of Modern Irish History* (Oxford University Press, 2014), 297; McCarthy-Morrogh, *The Munster Plantation*, 61.

indication of their estate's boundaries, with some complaining that their estate's acreage was either grossly above, or below, the prescribed size. On arrival, they faced constant battles to maintain legal ownership of their lands, as the Gaelic Irish asserted ownership. The level of claims became so high that the plantation authorities established a new commission in 1588 to investigate titles. Furthermore, many native Irish were not fully removed from the lands. Many left Munster temporarily, gradually moving back, reoccupying lands, and continuing their preferred pastoral agriculture practices.[42] Surveyors also uncovered concealed lands, which led to a common complaint from settlers that these were being granted to government officials.

Further surveys in the early 1590s attempted to ascertain whether progress had been made on the estates. By 1590, almost 3,000 English settlers had arrived in Munster, yet Gaelic Irish and Old English still vastly outnumbered them. The English settlers did, however, lay the foundations of a settlement, espousing English practices. While many settlers used existing tower houses and monastic foundations as a basis for their homes, others introduced English architecture, such as Spenser's Kilcolman Castle. Settlers also encouraged English agricultural practices, bringing English ploughs, cows and bulls for breeding. Furthermore, industry developed. Raleigh's estate along the Blackwater River emerged as the centre of a strong timber industry, exporting products back to England (Illustration 30). The outbreak of rebellion in 1598, however, interrupted progress as the Gaelic Irish attacked estates and many settlers fled home to England.[43]

The plantation re-emerged after 1603, but with significant changes in land ownership. From 1598 to 1611, thirteen seignories secured new owners, including Raleigh's estate, purchased by Richard Boyle, the future earl of Cork. Boyle emerged as Munster's foremost landowner in the aftermath of the rebellion, acquiring seven plantation seignories and Bandonbridge, which became the strongest plantation town in the province. Bandonbridge's growth owed much to Boyle, who invested heavily in building a fortified town that straddled both sides of the Bandon River. By 1622, it had an estimated 250 houses. The plantation surveys in 1611 and 1622 indicate the extent of change in the province. While the initial plantation plan had been very prescriptive about estate sizes, after the rebellion, landlords, in general, consolidated their holdings. By 1622, one-third of the whole province was actually in the hands

---

42 Quinn, 'The Munster Plantation: Problems and Opportunities', *Journal of Cork Historical and Archaeological Society*, 71 (1966), 28.
43 Quinn, 'The Munster Plantation, 30, 32. Also see Chapter 14 by J. Fenlon, this volume.

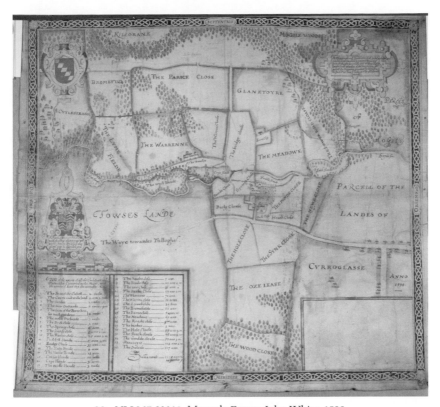

30. NLI MS 20028, Mogeely Estate, John White, 1598.

of Boyle and George Courtney. Furthermore, the English population continued to rise, with an estimated 20,000 settlers in the province by 1641.[44]

The Ulster Plantation

The undoubted pinnacle of the Irish plantations was the Jacobean plantation of Ulster. It can be argued that this plantation went further than any other as a scheme of social engineering, radically transforming the social, economic and cultural landscape of the province. Its success owed much to the lessons learned by government officials from the failures of previous schemes. The problems that had emerged included issues with estate sizes and with establishing title to lands, as well as the relative ease with which natives attacked

44 Quinn, 'The Munster Plantation', 37–9; Ó hAnnracháin, 'Plantation, 1540–1641', 298.

plantation settlements in Leix-Offaly and Munster. All became key considerations of officials, as they determined their scheme for Ulster. By the time
officials rolled out plantation, Ulster had proved problematic to the English
for decades. The rebellion of Shane O'Neill, the failure of early private plantation schemes and the emergence of Scottish settlements in north Antrim
had all hampered England's early relations with the province. By the late sixteenth century, Gaelic politics and culture in Ulster had already overcome
attempts to shire the province and had united several of the Ulster chieftains
against the crown in the Nine Years' War.[45]

The tide turned in favour of the English, however, with Gaelic defeat at
the battle of Kinsale and Hugh O'Neill's submission at Mellifont in 1603.
Thereafter, the power and prestige of the Ulster lords quickly waned. Their
inability to reconcile to the new power balance in the province, and their hope
that they might receive foreign aid to overthrow the English, led to the Flight
of the Earls from Rathmullan, County Donegal, in September 1607. This, and
the subsequent rebellion of Sir Cahir O'Doherty, lord of Inishowen in 1608,
set in the train the confiscation of their lands and the formulation of plans
for a plantation in six Ulster counties – Donegal, Coleraine, Tyrone, Armagh,
Fermanagh and Cavan. In fact, prior to both the Flight and the O'Doherty
rebellion, James VI and I's courtiers had already discussed plans for a plantation. Lord Deputy Arthur Chichester proposed plans including the establishment of freeholders in Ulster to break the bond between the lords and their
followers, as well as schemes giving lands to servitors, who had served in a
military or administrative capacity in Ireland.[46]

In 1608, the king commissioned a survey of the forfeited lands. The commissioners conducted the survey by inquisition, examining the ownership
of the land, investigating the right of the king to the title, and determining
the extent of lands and the value of the property. They also elucidated the
extent of ecclesiastical lands, the potential value of fisheries in the province
and the best locations for urban sites. Their evidence enticed the king to
move towards a formal settlement in the province. In 1609, as officials finalised the plantation scheme, a second survey began. Sir William Parsons, the
surveyor general, led the survey, but it is better known as 'Bodley's Survey'
after the mapmaker who drew over forty maps of Ulster's baronies. In these
maps, Bodley very carefully delineated the land boundaries of the plantation

---

45 See Chapter 1 by C. Brady, this volume.
46 R. Gillespie, 'Success and Failure in the Ulster Plantation', in Ó Ciardha and Ó Siochrú
    (ed.), *The Plantation of Ulster*, 101.

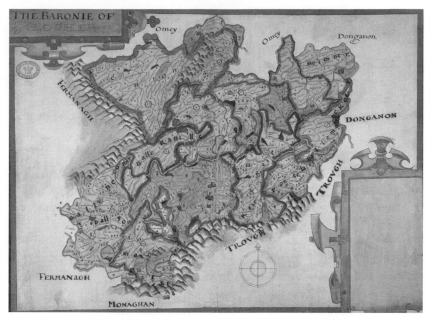

31. TNA MPF1/51, 'The Baronie of Clogher', Josias Bodley, 1609.

(Illustration 31). Each barony became the footprint for the plantation 'precinct', while the townlands of Ulster became the 'proportions' of roughly 60 acres. Bodley gave the plantation authorities their first insight into the quality of the lands that had fallen into their hands. He distinguished river systems, mountains, bogs and forests – all of which dictated the extent and potential economic value of estates. Furthermore, Bodley included details of Gaelic buildings, such as castles, churches and forts that could be adapted by settlers for their own use. He completed the maps by early 1610 and provided strong visual aids to the development, and assigning, of estates.[47]

By 1610, the formal plantation conditions had been finalised. The plans embedded a strong realisation of the past failures of plantation in Ireland. In the first instance, they set down smaller, more manageable estate sizes of 2,000, 1,500 and 1,000 acres. They also included three groups of grantees – English and Scottish undertakers, servitors and 'deserving' natives. The incorporation of the Scots into the plantation was a nod to James VI and I's

---

47 C. McNeill (ed.), 'MS. Rawlinson A. 237, The Bodleian Library, Oxford', *Analecta Hibernica*, 3 (1931), 151–218; J. H. Andrews, 'The Maps of the Escheated Counties of Ulster, 1609–10', *Proceedings of the Royal Irish Academy*, 74:C (1974), 133–70; Bodley barony maps, Josias Bodley, 1609–10, MPF1/38–64, TNA.

Scottish heritage and signalled this plantation as the first 'British' settlement in Ireland. The inclusion of servitors, unlike in Munster, meant that ready forces of trained soldiers were available to help maintain law and order. The granting of lands to 'deserving' natives potentially lessened the chances of reprisals from disgruntled Gaelic Irish. Under the conditions, groups were assigned to particular baronies, dispersing the natives amongst the English and Scottish settlers to immerse them in an exemplar of civility.[48]

Depending on estate sizes, the undertakers had to fulfil certain building requirements. On a 2,000 acre estate, for example, they had to build a stone house and bawn, while on a 1,000 acre estate, they had to build a bawn. The undertaker was expected to settle twenty-four English or Scottish men above eighteen years of age on every 1,000 acres. These men and their families were required to live in a clustered pattern near the main house, to ensure their security. Again, this clause was informed by experience in Munster, where the dispersed nature of settlement had contributed to how easily it was overrun in 1598. The conditions also included the storage of arms, so that the settlers would have some means of defence. Settlers held the lands in free and common socage (i.e. a form of land tenure whereby 'the tenant's chief obligation was to pay rent', with less emphasis on the payment of feudal dues such as military service or relief), at an annual rent of £5 6s 8d per 1,000 acres, with natives charged the higher rate of £10 3s 4d. To ensure that the plantation had the strongest possibility of survival, the main grantee had to be resident in Ulster for at least the first five years. The grantees and their settlers were also expected to take the Oath of Supremacy. Reflecting the prestige of the scheme, the Scottish and English undertakers in Ulster were relatively well off and even included two of the king's Scottish cousins, the duke of Lennox and Lord Aubigny.[49]

The scheme also carved out land for Trinity College Dublin, the Church of Ireland, corporate towns and schools. Furthermore, the king offered a land grant to the city of London in return for investment. The city, in turn, applied to the twelve great livery companies – the Mercers, Grocers, Drapers, Fishmongers, Goldsmiths, Skinners, Merchant Taylors, Haberdashers, Salters, Ironmongers, Vintners and Clothworkers – for money to undertake the scheme. These companies held great wealth and had, in the previous few years, invested in the settlement in Virginia. A scheme was proposed whereby

---

48 Canny, *Making Ireland British, 202–204;* Ó hAnnracháin, 'Plantation, 1540–1641', 299–300.
49 Robinson, *The Plantation of Ulster,* 63–5; S. G. Ellis, *Tudor Ireland: Crown, Community and the conflict of cultures, 1470–1603* (London: Longman Publishing Group, 1985), 321; Perceval-Maxwell, *Scottish Migration to Ulster,* 92.

the then County Coleraine and part of north Tyrone would be granted to the city, as the new County Londonderry, which would be divided into twelve proportions, one for each livery company. The city was also expected to develop two towns – Londonderry and Coleraine. Londonderry was to be developed at the site of Sir Henry Docwra's early fort on the mouth of the River Foyle, while Coleraine would be expanded at the existing settlement on the River Bann. The intention was that these towns would become the commercial hubs of the settlement, offering direct waterway access to, and from, London for trade.

In the early stages of the settlement, London's common council attempted to levy £15,000 on the companies, but by 1616, over £60,000 had been secured. Unsurprisingly the companies initially proved reluctant to participate. They were, however, enticed to take part by an early visit to the site, led by Sir Thomas Phillips, who had settled in, and developed, the area around Coleraine. Phillips proved an enthusiastic salesman, showcasing the vast forests of Loughlinsholin and wide waterways of Ulster. In order to manage the overall scheme, the city established the Honourable Irish Society, which received its charter in March 1613. The Irish Society became a *de facto* joint-stock company, similar to others that settled the Atlantic world and Asia. It took on responsibility for overseeing the development of the two towns, while liaising with the companies to ensure the smooth development of the plantation. The society began the task of allocating lands to the companies by lot. The companies, in turn, then developed their proportions under similar guidelines to those observed by the planters in the main scheme.[50]

The urban development embodied in the grant to the Irish Society and the livery companies became another feature of the wider plantation scheme, as land was set aside for twenty-five new corporate towns across the six counties. These areas were to become an integral part of the civilising force of the plantation, ensuring a certain level of economic and social regulation similar to Britain. The towns would form corporations, with aldermen and burgesses; they would hold markets and fairs; they would be the centres of law and order with sessions houses and gaols; and they would be the forgers of early industrial development. In all, 459,110 acres were to be distributed: 162,500 to the English and Scottish undertakers; 45,520 to the London companies; 74,852

---

50 I. W. Archer, 'The City of London and the Ulster Plantation', in Ó Ciardha and Ó Siochrú (eds.), *The Plantation of Ulster*, 83; Moody, *The Londonderry Plantation*, 72–4, 81–2, 121–42.

to the church; 54,632 to the servitors; 27,593 to Trinity College Dublin, forts, towns and schools, and finally, 94,013 to natives.[51]

Given the problems experienced by earlier plantations, the authorities closely monitored developments in Ulster. They commissioned surveys in 1611, 1614, 1618 and 1622 and scrutinised every plantation proportion at regular intervals, enabling a thorough analysis of the performance of the undertakers. For historians, these surveys provide an opportunity to view just how Ulster's landscape evolved and was reshaped under the plantation scheme. In the first instance, the retention of undertakers in the scheme can be adjudged. By the late 1610s, only twenty-nine of the original fifty-one English allotments remained in the hands of the original grantees, while thirty-three of the fifty-nine Scottish estates had changed hands. Furthermore, the reports suggested that the numbers of English settlers enticed to Ulster by the grantees fell well below expectations. As a result, the evidence points to large numbers of settlers retaining native Irish tenants to cultivate their estates. The reports, however, also acknowledge the extent of progress made by some undertakers in the development and settlement of their estates. While some of the stone houses and bawns built in Ulster during the plantation are still visible, none of the individual houses of either British or Irish tenants have survived in their hinterland. Contemporary evidence of what these settlements possibly looked like is available, however, in maps that survive from the 1622 Commission report. These maps show the settlements of the London companies. At Bellaghy, for example, the Vintners' Company tenant, Sir Baptist Jones, developed a strong stone house and bawn, part of which stands at the top of Castle Street today (Illustration 32). The cartographer, Thomas Raven, displayed a very ordered English settlement around the main house. The exoskeleton wood frames, the chief markers of British architecture from the period, are obvious. In contrast, the thatched cabins of the Irish tenants are visible in the foreground.[52]

While the king continued to be disappointed with the development of plantations in Ireland, evidence suggests that Ulster thrived, with the muster rolls from 1630 confirming strong clusters of British (i.e. English and Scottish) settlement in the province. These included mid-Ulster, particularly to the south and west of Lough Neagh; north Armagh; east Tyrone; Clogher Valley and the Foyle Basin. Further evidence of strong settlement in mid-Cavan,

---

51 Ó hAnnracháin, 'Plantation, 1540–1641', 300
52 Robinson, *The Plantation of Ulster*, 79–80; 'The Vintners Bvildinges at Balle Aghe', Thomas Raven, 1622, MS +793, Drapers' Hall, London.

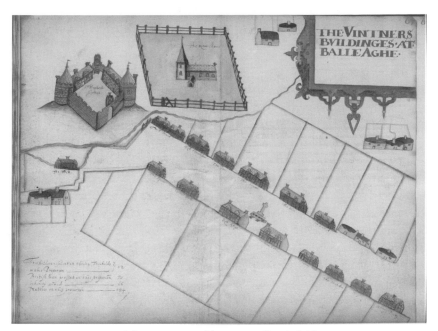

32. DH MS +793, 'The Vintners Bvildinges at Balleaghe', Thomas Raven, 1622.

the Erne Basin, the lower Bann Valley and north-east County Derry has also been distinguished by historians. These clusters were bolstered by the already strong presence of Scots in east Ulster, particularly in Antrim and Down, from the sixteenth century. In 1622, Ulster's population had reached about 6,902 adult men, giving a population of about 12,079 in the six counties. Despite, this evident success, however, the king remained fundamentally unimpressed by the settlement of the London companies. Much of his annoyance was fuelled by Sir Thomas Phillips who, in order to ensure the grant to the Companies, had been dispossessed of his lands at Coleraine and moved to the Limavady area. Thereafter, he kept a watchful eye on the progress of the plantation, and kept the king informed. He carefully built up a strong portfolio of evidence that led the city of London to the Star Chamber in 1635, where they were prosecuted for their failure to meet plantation requirements and lost their charters.[53] Little wonder, then, that when civil war broke out a few years later the city opted to support his parliamentary opponents, rather than the king.

53 Robinson, *The Plantation of Ulster*, 94–5; Canny, *Making Ireland British*, 211.

Other Seventeenth-Century Plantations

While the Ulster plantation took root, Jacobean settlement schemes emerged for other parts of Ireland. These plantations in Wexford, Longford, Leitrim, King's County, Laois and Westmeath, took place in the 1610s and 1620s, affecting 110,000 acres. They became the final instalment in the push to expand England's control across the Midlands into Connacht and south to Munster. They differed greatly from the formal settlement of Ulster, with historians acknowledging that they 'they were nothing but a new, predatory form of surrender and regrant directed towards the enrichment of the New English'.[54] Lord Deputy Chichester was the chief proponent of schemes for plantation in Wexford, Longford and Leitrim. As early as February 1611, he wrote to Salisbury, the secretary of state, asking to be 'authorised to deal with the Irish countries of Wexford and the county of Longford'.[55] He proposed to settle the counties, before moving attention to O'Carroll's country in King's County and also to Leitrim. Chichester promoted these schemes for two reasons: to compensate servitors, who had lost out on lands in Ulster, and to curb native power.[56]

The first settlement took place in Wexford, where much of the land had already fallen into crown hands by the seventeenth century. Authorities attempted to implement four separate plantation schemes between 1612 and 1618, each with differing degrees of success due to the strong opposition of Old English and Gaelic Irish inhabitants. The last scheme led to the confiscation of 84,900 acres. Eighteen undertakers, mainly English settlers, received 28,000 acres, in estates of between 1,000 and 3,100 acres. The scheme also granted 3,100 acres to seven servitors, who received estates of between 300 and 800 acres. The remaining lands were granted to existing landowners in the county, including Old English and New English families and the Gaelic Kavanagh family. The scheme proposed that any Irish or Old English landowners with estates over 100 acres would retain their lands. The four schemes took some cues from Ulster, establishing the towns of Enniscorthy and Gorey as corporate towns, in 1613 and 1618 respectively. Unsurprisingly, given the significant transformation of landholding that the plantation entailed, opposition

---

54 Ó hAnnracháin, 'Plantation, 1540–1641', 304; Mac Cuarta, 'The Plantation of Leitrim', 299; A. Clarke, 'Pacification, plantation, and the catholic question, 1603-23', in Moody, Martin and Byrne (eds.), *A New History of Ireland, iii* (Oxford University Press, 2009), 222.

55 J. P. Prendergast and C.W. Russell (eds.), *Calendar of State Papers Ireland, 1611–1614* (London: Longman & Co., 1877), 16.

56 Ó hAnnracháin, 'Plantation, 1540–1641', 304.

came from the Old English and the Gaelic Irish, delaying the implementation of the schemes across the 1610s.[57]

The Wexford Plantation became the template for other Jacobean settlements. The Longford Plantation was one such scheme. The O'Farrell family, Longford's most prominent Gaelic Irish family, were brought to submission by surrender and regrant in the 1570s. The location of their territory, on the edge of Ulster and within a short distance of the Pale, made the area an attractive prospect for English authorities. Chichester first mooted a plantation for the county in 1611, before proposing a scheme in 1615. He advised the king to grant the lands to the Gaelic Irish, who had agreements under surrender and regrant for their letters patent. He argued that breaking these agreements would break their trust, while dispossessing the natives might add to their general discontentment following the widespread forfeitures in Ulster. By 1619, however, a scheme had been developed that sought to both restructure landholdings in the territories and implement a small settlement of British undertakers. The scheme required native landowners to surrender their lands, in return for a regrant of three-quarters of it. New undertakers would receive the remaining quarter. The scheme established towns, such as St Johnstown (Ballinalee), Granard and Longford, with patents for markets and fairs. Authorities extended the Longford scheme to the territory of Ely O'Carroll in King's County. This was just one of several contemporary initiatives in the Midlands that also included settlements in King's County and Westmeath. Many of these had been proposed by the English settlers themselves. From 1610, for example, Patrick Crosby and Sir Matthew de Renzy both petitioned for plantations in Ely O'Carroll and MacCoghlan's lands, King's County, respectively.[58]

From 1615, inquisitions took place to establish the king's title in Leitrim. The Dublin authorities cleared the way for plantation by bringing the O'Rourke heir to England to complete his education, before imprisoning him in London. With no heir apparent, and little leadership, the remaining Gaelic lords submitted to the crown. Two plantations took place in 1619 and

---

57 H. Goff, 'English Conquest of an Irish Barony: The Changing Patterns of Land Ownership in the Barony of Scarawalsh, 1540–1640', in K. Whelan and W. Nolan (eds.), *Wexford History and Society* (Dublin: Geography Publications, 1992), 138–9.

58 Prendergast and Russell, (eds.), *Calendar of State Papers Ireland, 1611–1614*, 14, 49–51, 81; C. W. Russell and J. P. Prendergast, *Calendar of State Papers Ireland, 1615–1625* (London: HMSO, 1880), 108, 263; Canny, *Making Ireland British*, 176; see also: Mac Cuarta, 'The Plantation of Leitrim', 299–306; J. McCavitt, *Sir Arthur Chichester, Lord Deputy of Ireland, 1605–1616* (Belfast: Institute of Irish Studies), 161.

1620, and about half of the conditions proposed for the Longford plantation were transferred to the Leitrim scheme. The treatment of natives, however, was quite different. Instead of being granted their lands, Brian and Hugh O'Rourke, the Gaelic chieftains, received pensions, resulting in their influence dwindling. The natives who received lands under the scheme, did so on the proviso that they would lose their lands if they rebelled, while those at the bottom of the native order were to be reduced to tenants. They became the primary tenants, as few British tenants were introduced.[59]

The plantation authorities planned to grant much of Leitrim to servitors. The largest grant, however, went to George Villiers, duke of Buckingham, who set aside the central portion of the O'Rourke lands for himself. The remaining undertakers received particularly large grants of lands, in contrast to the other Midland plantations. Similar to Longford, the Leitrim undertakers were dispersed among the natives and lands were allocated to a school, an incorporated town and the established church. While these schemes aimed to bring civility to the Midlands, Nicholas Canny suggests that 'English Protestant settlers were the principal beneficiaries of the scheme'. He noted the damning 1622 report of Francis Blundell, which claimed 'that the arrangements recently made in Longford and Ely O'Carroll, did not deserve to be called a plantation but a show of something where nothing is done'. Blundell identified absenteeism amongst the grantees and a concern only with rental income as particular problems. Despite this, however, Blundell acknowledged that the plantations were very much in their infancy in 1622 and would potentially develop as strong settlements in the future.[60]

With the expansion into the Midlands complete, it is not surprising that contemporary plans also emerged for a settlement in Connacht. The plantation of Connacht would have brought newcomers to a region that had as yet seen no significant English settlement in the early modern period, and would also have lessened strategic concerns. However, one of the primary reasons for the proposed plantation was financial gain, as commissioners felt that the Composition of Connacht, which accrued £3,000 to the crown each year, could have been increased. The 1620s saw a hiatus in the planning as, in 1623, commissioners recommended no further plantations in Ireland. At the same time, Charles I struggled to reach agreement with the Old English over the Graces. The idea gained traction again in the 1630s, particularly, after Sir

---

59 Mac Cuarta, 'The Plantation of Leitrim', 300–1.
60 Mac Cuarta, 'The Plantation of Leitrim', 301–4; Canny, *Making Ireland British*, 178–9.

Thomas Wentworth, earl of Stafford, was appointed lord deputy in 1631. In 1634, he wrote to the king proposing a potential plantation for Ormond and Connacht and by April 1635, he was taking steps to establish the king's title to lands. He faced strong opposition from the Old English, particularly, Richard Burke, earl of Clanricard, who protested that his continued loyalty to the crown made any scheme unjust. Agents were sent to England to relay the opposition of the Old English, but their effectiveness was undermined by Clanricard's untimely death in November 1635.[61]

In April 1636, Wentworth was still promoting the scheme, estimating the value of the plantation at £20,000. In the same month, surveyors began to assess Mayo, Sligo and Roscommon. The opposition from Galway remained strong, but the need for money to pay his father's debts drove the new earl of Clanricard, Ulick Burke, to persuade the other landowners of Galway to submit. By March 1637, surveyors were active in Galway and by August 1637, landowners in Clare were also admitting the king's title to their lands. Following the forfeiture of lands to the crown, Wentworth proposed a plantation of half the forfeited land in Galway and a potential one-quarter to one-third of lands in the other counties. The plan also included the granting of lands to existing landowners. Just as the plans seemed to be gaining momentum, however, persistent rumours of war filtered back to Ireland. With the return to England and subsequent trial of Wentworth, any further plantation plans were scuppered.[62]

Conclusion

The sixteenth and seventeenth centuries marked a distinct watershed in the history of Ireland, as the arrival of British settlers through the various schemes of plantation transformed the country. By 1641 these were widespread across Ireland. The 1641 Depositions show that settlement went beyond the confines of the traditional plantation areas, with English, Scottish and Welsh settlers, some of whom identified themselves as British, testifying to their losses in all of Ireland's thirty-two counties. It appears that once in Ireland, many of the new settlers moved beyond the confines of plantation areas, purchasing and leasing estates across the country. The Depositions point to a significant process of Anglicisation, with strong settler communities interacting with, and enveloping, many of the traditional Gaelic landscapes of Ireland. These

61 H. Kearney, *Strafford in Ireland, 1633–41: A Study in Absolutism* (2nd edn., Cambridge University Press, 1989), 85–93.
62 Kearney, *Strafford in Ireland*, 94–102.

communities signalled widespread political, social, economic and cultural change by the mid-seventeenth century.

On a political level, Ireland had been transformed. The boundaries of traditional Gaelic lordships of Ireland had been swept aside by the introduction of an English-style county system. These counties cut across traditional Gaelic boundaries, engulfing lands in political units that had hitherto been quite disparate. On a smaller level, this new political geography introduced baronies to Ireland, which, in turn, became the footprint of plantation grants to new settlers. In local areas, these political transformations also gave rise to the introduction of systems of governance that included aldermen, burgesses, sessions houses and jails, for example. This political change also impacted heavily on traditional society in Ireland. The society based around the Gaelic chieftains was gone forever, with many Gaelic Irish subsumed into the land grants of the plantations or reduced to tenants on the estates of the new settlers. By including the Gaelic Irish in these plantation schemes, the authorities hoped to bring civility to a wild and barbarous people. The intermittent reports from the plantations suggest that many of the Gaelic Irish lived peacefully amongst the new settlers, engaging in agriculture, industrial development and leasing of lands to their new neighbours.

The plantations also brought significant economic change to Ireland. At the forefront of this change was the staggering increase in commercial and industrial development. Chief amongst these industries was timber, a resource that Ireland had in abundance in the early years of plantation. By the seventeenth century, the large swathes of forest were slowly being depleted, as new settlements in Ireland and industrial development in Britain called for more intensive cutting of trees. Moreover, the commercial links developed by the plantation to London, integrated Ireland more widely into the London economy. The burgeoning English Empire on both sides of the Atlantic also meant more widespread access to new products and markets for those living in Ireland. In terms of agriculture, the plantations also gave rise to wider diversification, moving away from a pastoral economy to more mixed farming. Culturally, Ireland also changed as a result of interactions with English and Scottish colonists. Not only did these settlers bring new languages, but they also brought new styles of clothing, architecture and societal norms to the lands of Ireland.[63]

---

63 See Chapter 21 by Gillespie, and Chapter 24 by Ludlow and Crampsie, this volume.

Yet, the outbreak of rebellion in 1641 indicated that much of this transformation was not deeply rooted. The peace of plantation society in Ireland was shattered, and with it the assumption that plantation had succeeded in Anglicising Ireland. The attacks by mainly Gaelic settlers, quite often on their English neighbours, indicated some deep-seated problems with the plantations. In the first instance, while many schemes included Gaelic grantees, they also alienated many more, who continued to feel aggrieved at their loss of lands. While this process of Anglicisation had also sought to introduce the Protestant religion across the plantation lands, the recusancy of many rebels, and the prevalence of Catholic friars and priests amongst their numbers, also indicated its failings. The willingness of many of the Old English lords of the Pale to side with the rebels suggests their complete alienation from English government in Ireland. The elevation of some newcomers to the ranks of the aristocracy, the more favourable terms of land grants to newcomers and the lessening political influence of the Old English, were just some of the factors that led to their actions. The rebellion's impact cannot be underestimated. The settler communities in Ireland were undermined, as many fled back to England. Rebels destroyed their homes, their agriculture, their livestock and the communal bonds and wiped out much of the footprint of these early plantations. While some settlers eventually returned to their lands, the subsequent plantations under Cromwell, the Restoration and the Williamite era, re-structured many of these early settler communities, making them more difficult to distinguish in the Irish landscape.

23

The Down Survey and the Cromwellian Land Settlement

MICHEÁL Ó SIOCHRÚ AND DAVID BROWN

Rubb and a good Cast is the gamster's creed;
You'le say he winnes that winnes at Last indeed
Behould the ffloods are ebd, our Land appears,
And Catholickes defy the Presbyters.[1]

(Anonymous tract, *c*.1662)

In May 1660, Charles II returned from a prolonged exile and entered London in triumph amid scenes of wild celebration. Oliver Cromwell was dead and the experiment in republican government at an end. In Ireland, the restoration of the monarchy threatened to undermine the entire post-war settlement, which had resulted in one of the largest transfers of land anywhere in early modern Europe. Catholic ownership of land had collapsed from over 50 per cent of the total in 1641 to just 14 per cent by the late 1650s, concentrated exclusively in the western province of Connacht. With James Butler, marquis and later duke of Ormond, firmly established, however, as one of the king's closest advisors, Catholics hoped to revive the treaty he had signed with the Confederates at Kilkenny in 1649, which included a number of significant concessions on land. Moreover, many leading Irish Catholics had joined their monarch on the continent, sharing his hardships, and they expected (as expressed in the tract above) to be suitably rewarded for their loyalty by recovering forfeited estates. Protestants in Ireland watched these developments with growing alarm. Few of them, of whatever political persuasion, had not collaborated with the Cromwellian *régime* to some degree. They were anxious for a return to traditional monarchical government, but terrified of losing their newly acquired lands in the process. Similarly, the Cromwellian

---

1 'On the Act of Settlement', in A. Carpenter (ed.), *Verse in English from Tudor and Stuart Ireland* (Cork University Press, 2003), 359–60.

adventurers and soldiers urgently needed to develop strategies to help secure their estates in the event of a *régime* change. Ireland's future was at stake and in these tumultuous times nothing could be taken for granted.

Historians have long understood the centrality of the land issue in Irish life and Anglo-Irish relations, from the colonial settlements of the thirteenth century, through subsequent divisions between the 'land of peace' and the 'land of war', to the plantations of the Tudor and Stuart periods.[2] This struggle over land continually reshaped the island for 500 years. The Cromwellian settlement of the 1650s, however, proved to be the concluding act in the replacement of a long-established native Irish and Old English Catholic *élite* with a new class of English Protestant planters, who dominated the political, economic and social order until the great land reforms of the late nineteenth century. William Smyth, in his magisterial study of early modern Ireland, describes the Cromwellian settlement as 'the most epic and monumental transformation of Irish life, property and landscape that the island has ever known'.[3] In the Irish public mind at least, Oliver Cromwell continues to enjoy the status of super villain, guilty of a litany of crimes. The outcomes of his conquest, and more specifically the extensive land settlement, are well attested but the processes by which they happened remain little understood, even in academic circles.

Understandably, recent works focus for the most part on the military conflict from 1641 to 1653, perhaps the bloodiest and most tragic period in Irish history.[4] In contrast, the post-war era, from the establishment of the Cromwellian Protectorate in 1653 to the restoration of Charles II in 1660, has attracted comparatively scant scholarly attention.[5] In the nineteenth century, J. P. Prendergast responded to attempts by Thomas Carlyle and others to rehabilitate Cromwell's reputation by highlighting the sufferings of the Catholic Irish in the 1650s, utilising sources subsequently destroyed in the early

---

2 For the development of the colonial settlements in medieval times, see R. Frame, *Colonial Ireland, 1169–1369* (2nd edn., Dublin: Four Courts Press [hereafter FCP], 2012), 94–100. Also see Chapter 22 by A. Margey, this volume.

3 W. J. Smyth, *Map-Making, Landscapes and Memory: A Geography of Colonial and Early Modern Ireland, c.1530–1750* (Cork University Press, 2006), 196.

4 For recent studies of the military conquest, see M. Ó Siochrú, *God's Executioner: Oliver Cromwell and the Conquest of Ireland* (London: Faber & Faber, 2008) and J. S. Wheeler, *Cromwell in Ireland* (Dublin: Gill and Macmillan, 1999).

5 In a recent chapter on the land and the people in Ireland from 1600, the events of the 1650s warrant only a few lines of text. See T. Dooley, 'Land and the People', in A. Jackson (ed.), *The Oxford Handbook of Modern Irish History* (Oxford University Press, 2014), 107–25. In fairness to Dooley, he clearly wished to focus his chapter on the land reforms of the nineteenth century, but these were predicated on overturning the Cromwellian settlement, which surely required more detailed explanation.

twentieth century.[6] Possibly as a result of these archival losses, further signifi-cant publications did not appear until the 1970s. Patrick Corish's survey chap-ter in the *New History of Ireland* series, alongside the works of Toby Barnard and Karl Bottigheimer, provided the key building blocks for future research.[7] Barnard's *Cromwellian Ireland* concentrated on the mechanics of Cromwellian government in Ireland, in fields such as finance, trade, the law and educa-tion, while Bottigheimer's *English Money and Irish Land* examined the legis-lation concerning the land settlement within the broader context of English plantations in Ireland.[8] Aidan Clarke's definitive book, *Prelude to Restoration in Ireland*, reconstructed political developments in 1659–60 but did not con-cern itself with the minutiae of the redistribution of land.[9] More recently, John Cunningham produced a long overdue and impressively comprehensive study of the transplantation process, while the launch in 2013 of the Down Survey website (www.downsurvey.tcd.ie) by a Trinity College Dublin-led pro-ject provided public access for the first time to the cartographic and related material from the 1650s.[10] This chapter will focus on the processes underpin-ning England's most ambitious attempt at social engineering in Ireland.

The Cromwellian Land Settlement

Details of the causes and course of the 1641 rebellion are dealt with elsewhere in this volume but it is important to stress from the outset that the redistri-bution of Irish land to English settlers had already emerged as a central tenet of royal policy in Ireland from the mid-sixteenth century.[11] This began with the dissolution of the monasteries in the 1530s and 1540s, when a number of New English Protestant settlers established themselves on former monastic lands. During the 1550s, the colonial authorities in Dublin transplanted the principal native Irish families in the Midlands to the west of the kingdom, in order to clear a problem region and prepare the ground for plantation by

---

6 J. P. Prendergast, *The Cromwellian Settlement of Ireland* (London: Longman, Roberts and Green, 1865; repr. London: Constable, 1996).

7 P. Corish, 'The Cromwellian *Régime*, 1650–1660', in T. W. Moody, F. X. Martin and F. J. Byrne (eds.), *A New History of Ireland*, iii, *Early Modern Ireland, 1534–1691* (Oxford University Press, 1976; third impression 1991), 353–86.

8 T. Barnard, *Cromwellian Ireland: English Government and Reform in Ireland, 1649–1660* (Oxford University Press, 1975); K. Bottigheimer, *English Money and Irish Land: The 'Adventurers' in the Cromwellian Settlement of Ireland* (Oxford: Clarendon Press, 1971).

9 A. Clarke, *Prelude to Restoration in Ireland: The End of the Commonwealth, 1659–1660* (Cambridge University Press, 1999).

10 J. Cunningham, *Conquest and Land in Ireland: The Transplantation to Connacht, 1649–1660* (Woodbridge: Boydell and Brewer, 2011).

11 See Chapter 17 by J. Cunningham, this volume.

military servitors. Thirty years later, the destruction of the Desmond lordship in Munster facilitated a further round of land seizures and settlement. In the early decades of the seventeenth century, the government of James VI and I forced thousands of natives off their lands in Ulster, replacing them with mainly Protestant migrants from both Scotland and England, while also moving the so-called 'deserving Irish' from their homes to elsewhere in the province. The 1620s and 1630s witnessed further plantation schemes across the island, from Leitrim in the north-west to Wexford in the south-east, particularly during the tenure of office of Lord Deputy Thomas Wentworth. The drastic upheavals of the mid-seventeenth century, therefore, cannot be viewed in isolation.

On 22 October 1641, native Irish insurgents in Ulster began a series of attacks on government strongholds across the province, triggering a nationwide uprising. Less than six months later, the Adventurers Act, passed by the English parliament on 14 March 1642 and subsequently ratified by King Charles I, established the legal basis for the Cromwellian land settlement of the 1650s. Land owned by Irish rebels would provide security for a proposed loan of £1 million from English merchants and MPs to crush the insurgency in Ireland.[12] The act assumed that the rebellion was a general one, implicating all Irish Catholics, and as a consequence military defeat would automatically result in the total forfeiture of their estates.[13] The English parliament estimated the amount of land available at 2.5 million acres and produced simple valuations for the redistribution process; land in Ulster was valued at 4 shillings per acre, while in Connaught, Munster and Leinster the rates were 6, 10 and 12 shillings respectively. This forfeited land represented potentially the single largest seizure of Irish land in history and introduced from the outset a winner-takes-all aspect to the conflict in Ireland. There could be no negotiated settlement, only total, unconditional victory.

Seventeenth-century landowners in Ireland were, in modern terms, tenants of the crown with indeterminate leases and special covenants that determined whether or not a lease would be re-granted when it expired. These covenants proved particularly important in the case of plantation grants, which contained explicit conditions concerning tenancies and land

---

12 J. Raithby (ed.), *Statutes of the Realm: volume 5, 1628–80* (London: Great Britain Record Commission, 1819), 168–72.

13 Prendergast, *Cromwellian Settlement*, 72–9. On the adventurers, in addition to Bottigheimer, see R. P. Mahaffy, (ed.), *Calendar of State Papers Relating to Ireland Preserved in the Public Record Office: Adventurers for Land, 1642–59* (London: HMSO, 1903); J. R. McCormack, 'The Adventurers and the Civil War', *Irish Historical Studies*, 10 (1956), 45–67; K. Lindley, 'Irish Adventurers and Godly Militants in the 1640s', *Irish Historical Studies*, 29 (1994), 1–12.

improvements.[14] The century prior to 1641 witnessed a gradual introduction of land registration according to the English legal system. Raymond Gillespie summarised this process in his study of County Cavan:

> In the sixteenth century a Cavan family held their lands by virtue of their genealogy. Greater lords had no claim on the lands of their freeholders but held their own mensal land by virtue of the chieftainship of their family. By the seventeenth century a man's landholding and social position was determined not by his family or his background but by the contracts and leases into which he entered.[15]

The challenge for those proposing the new land settlement, in addition to determining the extent of each landholding, and the identity of its owner, was to establish a uniform title, making future conveyancing and, more importantly, taxation of land comparatively straightforward.

By the summer of 1652, defeated and defenceless after ten years of relentless warfare, the Catholic Irish faced an uncertain future at the hands of an unforgiving and rapacious *régime* in England. The basic outline of the post-war settlement in the event of a parliamentary victory had not been in doubt since the Adventurers Act. The only question mark lay over the extent of the confiscations, and how best to divide the spoils among the victors. The length of the war had greatly expanded the cost of the conquest, thus increasing the pressure for a large-scale redistribution of property. The expropriation and transplantation of all Catholic landowners guaranteed the maximum return of land. The imposition of such harsh conditions, however, leaving Catholics with little alternative but to fight to the bitter end, threatened to prolong the conflict indefinitely. Conversely, too lenient a settlement, allowing large numbers to retain their estates, risked disappointing and alienating those adventurers and others seeking the repayment of long-standing debts. Since the early 1650s, this latter group included over 30,000 English soldiers serving in Ireland, who could not be easily ignored. As the war drew to a close, the military began to exert increasing pressure on parliament to make arrangements for the redistribution of confiscated lands.

As far back as April 1651, the English House of Commons considered proposals from Henry Ireton, Cromwell's deputy in Ireland, for the exclusion of certain key groups and individuals from any future settlement. MPs quickly

---

14 Many of these lease covenants are reproduced in V. Treadwell (ed.), *The Irish Commission of 1622*, (Dublin: Irish Manuscripts Commission, 2006).
15 R. Gillespie, *Cavan, Essays on the History of an Irish County*, (Dublin: Irish Academic Press, 1995), 110.

agreed to target anybody involved in the first year of the rebellion, or who subsequently served on the Supreme Council of the Catholic Confederate Association. They also requested that the English Council of State identify specific individuals to be excluded from pardon.[16] The council's tardiness in this matter reflected growing tensions between the military and the civil government on a range of issues. Many MPs feared the growing power of the army, and supported moves towards a gradual demobilisation in England. Regarding Ireland, however, all sides agreed on the need to complete the conquest, although they differed on the best tactics to achieve this goal. Leading army officers, many of them religious radicals, advocated harsh measures against the entire Catholic population, based on the principle of collective guilt. This argument dovetailed neatly with the desire to secure the maximum return of confiscated land for English soldiers in lieu of pay. The English parliamentary commissioners in Dublin, no friends of the Catholic Irish, nonetheless adopted a more conciliatory position, in the hope of bringing the war to a speedy conclusion.

In a conversation with Edmund Ludlow, Cromwell allegedly described Ireland 'as a clean paper', which following the victory of the New Model Army could be remodelled in the interests of England.[17] The Act of Settlement, passed in August 1652, finally outlined in detail the fate of the country and its inhabitants.[18] The preamble reassured the general population that the parliamentary *régime* did not intend 'to extirpate the whole nation', offering instead to extend mercy and pardon 'to all husbandmen, plowmen, labourers, artificers and others of the inferior sort', as long as they lived 'peaceably and obediently' under the colonial government. In contrast to the commoners, the Catholic *élite*, meaning those with estates valued at more than £10 annually, would be judged 'according to the respective demerits and considerations under which they fall'. The act contained a number of clauses, specifically excluding certain groups and named individuals from the general pardon. The first clause focused on those guilty of the massacre of Protestant settlers in the first year of the rebellion. The parliamentarians defined 'involvement' in the broadest possible sense to include not only those actively 'bearing arms', but also any person who contributed 'men, arms, horse, plate, money, victual, or other furniture or habiliments of war' to the rebels during the first

---

16 *Journals of the House of Commons: Volume 6, 1648–1651* (London: HMSO, 1802), 566–7, 607, 609, 621.

17 Edmund Ludlow, *Memoirs of Edmund Ludlow Esq.*, (2 vols., Vivay, 1698), i, 319.

18 *An Act for the Setling of Ireland* (London, 1652).

twelve months of the rebellion. Technically at least, this encompassed vast numbers of the Catholic population.

The second clause targeted Catholic clergy, while the next listed over 100 named individuals, mainly confederate political and military leaders, as the parliamentarians sought to ensure that few major Catholic landowners escaped proscription. Moreover, all those living in Ireland who had not manifested 'their constant and good affection to the interest of the Commonwealth of England' throughout the war would forfeit one-third of their estates, with the remaining two-thirds to be assigned elsewhere in the country. As the English parliament controlled little of Ireland for much of the 1640s, few Catholics could possibly avoid the confiscation of at least part of their lands. The act concluded with a guarantee that parliament would adhere to all articles of surrender already signed, although the authorities in Dublin reserved the right to move any individual to another part of the country if deemed necessary for reasons of 'public safety'. The Act of Settlement, therefore, potentially condemned thousands to death for their involvement in the insurgency, while all Catholic landowners would be subject to full or partial confiscation of their estates. It soon became clear, however, that land not blood was the primary goal of this legislative assault.

Retribution, Transportation and Transplantation

Individual trials did indeed take place from late 1652, following the establishment of a High Courts of Justice, 'to hear and determine all murders and massacres of any Protestants, English or other person or persons whatsoever', since October 1641.[19] These courts sentenced hundreds to death, but most of the insurgents were either already dead or in exile and the legal retribution was relatively contained compared to the widespread, indiscriminate bloodletting that had preceded it.[20] As for the common soldiers, they provided a lucrative source of revenue to military entrepreneurs and merchants with shipping at their disposal. The authorities in Dublin, anxious to rid the country of hostile soldiers, licensed military entrepreneurs to transport large numbers of Catholics into Spanish and French service. Between 1651 and 1654, as many as 40,000 Catholic Irishmen sailed for the continent, often on English merchant ships. While the government encouraged enemy soldiers to leave

---

19 'Establishment of the High Court in Kilkenny', Ms Z2.1.7, f. 51, Marsh's Library, Dublin.
20 J. Wells (ed.), 'Proceedings at the High Court of Justice at Dublin and Cork', *Archivium Hibernicum*, 66 (2013), 63–260 and, 67, (2014), 76–274; M. McCartan, 'The Cromwellian High Courts of Justice in Ulster, 1653', *Seanchas Ard Mhacha*, 23 (2010), 91–161.

for the continent, a different fate awaited those civilians unsuitable for military service. From the beginning of the seventeenth century, England had acquired colonies in the Caribbean, and developed lucrative sugar plantations from the mid-1640s.[21] African slaves provided most of the field labour, but a demand existed for indentured servants of European stock, who worked for a fixed period of time, 'under a yoke harsher then that of the Turks', before theoretically at least obtaining their freedom.[22] The first shipment from Ireland occurred in late 1649, when Oliver Cromwell ordered the few surviving members of the Drogheda garrison to be sent to Barbados.[23] Over the next ten years, unscrupulous merchants shipped thousands of Catholic women and children, many of them destitute and homeless as a result of the wars, across the Atlantic.[24] The authorities in Dublin, concerned by the 'great multitudes of poor swarming in all parts of this nation' welcomed this trade in human cargo as a means of clearing the country of vagrants.[25]

As for the Catholic landowners, the Act of Settlement condemned thousands to lose their entire estates, but failed to specify the fate of those who only forfeited part of their holdings. Would they continue to reside in their own homes or, as the act suggested, be transported to lands elsewhere in the country? The ongoing power struggle between the military and civil government in England prevented the parliamentary commissioners in Dublin from making any significant progress in the redistribution of land. In April 1653, serious disagreements on Ireland, particularly whether the adventurers should get priority over army claimants, contributed to Cromwell's decision to dissolve the Rump Parliament and establish effective military rule in the three former Stuart kingdoms.[26] Shortly afterwards, on 2 July, the Council of State in London ordered all Catholic landowners in Ireland who had borne arms against the Commonwealth to transport themselves west of the River Shannon, into Connacht and Clare. These orders, confirmed by an act of the

---

21 R. R. Menard, *Sweet Negotiations: Sugar, Slavery and Plantation Agriculture in Early Barbados* (Charlottesville: University Press of Virginia, 2006). Many of these plantation owners were also adventurers in Irish land.

22 Richard O'Ferrall and Robert O'Connell, *Commentarius Rinuccinianus, de Sedis Apostolicae Legatione ad Foederatos Hiberniae Catholicos per Annos 1645–9* (6 vols., Dublin: Irish Manuscripts Commission, 1932–1949), v, 174–7.

23 *The Writings and Speeches of Oliver Cromwell*, ed. W. C. Abbott (4 vols., Cambridge, MA: Harvard University Press, 1937–1947), ii, 125–8.

24 Corish, 'Cromwellian *Régime*', 364 and H. Beckles, 'A "riotous and unruly lot": Irish Indentured Servants and Freemen in the English West Indies, 1644–1713', *The William and Mary Quarterly*, 57 (1990), 502–22.

25 Prendergast, *Cromwellian Settlement*, 149.

26 S. Barber, 'Irish Undercurrents to the Politics of April 1653', *Historical Research*, 65 (1992), 315–35.

so-called 'Barebones' parliament on 26 September, instructed landowners to present themselves to commissioners at the town of Loughrea in County Galway, to receive lands equal to one-third of the value of their estates in Leinster, Munster and Ulster. Landowners in Clare and Connaught were also to be displaced to smaller holdings within the province to make way for the influx from elsewhere in the country.

The transplantation scheme remains one of the most contentious aspects of the Cromwellian land settlement, as it involved not only the seizure of property but also the removal of a people on the basis of their religion.[27] Opinion differed in government circles as to whether all Catholics should be removed from the lands to be settled or merely the existing landowners and their dependants. After a robust debate, the authorities opted for the latter policy, primarily for pragmatic reasons: the new landlords required tenants to work the land.[28] Moreover, despite the draconian intent of the legislation, implementation proved problematic. Pádraig Lenihan reveals that in the barony of Bantry in County Wexford, for example, only 72 out of 256 landowners registered their property in order to obtain a certificate from the Transplantation Commissioners. Of that seventy-two, only sixty-four actually received certificates, and out of these only eight are listed as landowners in Connacht in the Books of Survey and Distribution for 1670. This leaves 248 out of 256 landowners unaccounted for, although many may have died or fled into exile.[29] The fragmented nature of the surviving sources makes it difficult to draw definitive conclusions. Thousands almost certainly crossed the Shannon but it appears as if the majority of Catholics either remained in their homes or returned from Connacht to become tenants of the new patentees, with or without formal tenancy agreements.[30]

27 For the process and mechanics of the transplantation, see R. C. Simington (ed.), *The Transplantation to Connaught 1654–58* (Shannon: Irish Manuscripts Commission, 1970) and J. Cunningham, *Conquest and Land in Ireland: The Transplantation to Connacht, 1649–1660* (Woodbridge Boydell and Brewer), 74–99. Proposals to transplant Ulster Scots Protestants to Munster came to nothing.

28 This debate was famously played out in print between the Protestant settler, Vincent Gookin and the English army officer, Richard Lawrence. See [Vincent Gookin] *The Great Case of Transplantation in Ireland Discussed* (London, 1655); Richard Lawrence, *The Interest of England in the Irish Transplantation Stated* (London, 1655).

29 P. Lenihan, *Consolidating Conquest: Ireland 1603–1727* (Harlow: Pearson Longman, 2007), 201.

30 See S. Pender (ed.), *A census of Ireland circa 1659* (Dublin: Irish Manuscripts Commission, 1939; repr. 2002). The impact of the transplantation is discussed in detail in Cunningham, *Conquest and Land in Ireland*, chapter 4 and Smyth, *Map-making, Landscapes and Memory*, chapter 5.

Land Redistribution

With tens of thousands of Catholics displaced through the upheavals of war, transportation or transplantation, the process of land redistribution could finally begin. On 1 June 1653, a month before the order to transplant to Connacht, the Council of State established a new Committee for Claims for Lands in Ireland to oversee the redistribution process, headed by William Webster and Elias Roberts. They were both London merchants but also close business associates of leading adventurers, including Maurice Thompson, Robert Thompson and William Pennoyer, who continued to exert influence on the Irish land settlement despite their dissatisfaction with the dissolution of the Rump Parliament.[31] Maurice Thompson and William Pennoyer had been heavily involved in supplying the English armies in Ireland since the outbreak of the 1641 rebellion and Thompson also financed Cromwell's successful military campaign to Ireland in 1649.[32] By late summer 1653, the adventurers appear to have been reconciled with the new *régime* and they held their first lottery in August. This determined the county in which they would receive their allocations, while a second round in January 1654 assigned them to a particular barony within that county.[33] Before any redistribution could happen, however, all forfeited lands in Ireland would have to be extensively surveyed and mapped.

In order to control the process of measuring and allocating lands, Maurice Thompson and his allies managed to secure the appointment of Benjamin Worsley as surveyor general of Ireland.[34] Worsley had recently worked with several of the adventurers on the Navigation Act of 1651 and had also produced a list of landowners for the Virginia colony.[35] On 26 September 1653 the 'Act for Satisfaction of Soldiers and Adventurers' commissioned the 'Gross and Brief Survey', which

31 'Certificate of the Committee of Claims for Lands in Ireland', SP 63/301, f. 153, the National Archives (hereafter TNA); R. Dunlop (ed.), *Ireland under the Commonwealth* (2 vols., Manchester, 1913), ii, 465; C. H. Firth (ed.), *The Clarke Papers* (4 vols., London: Camden Society, 1891–1901), iii, 6.
32 For the career of Maurice Thompson see R. Brenner, *Merchants and Revolution: Commercial Change, Political Conflict, and London's Overseas Traders, 1550–1653* (Cambridge University Press, 1993). See 'Digest of the expenses of troops to Ireland, with warrants for payment, 7 March 1649–18 February 1650', SP 25/118, TNA, for Thompson's financial accounts for Cromwell's campaign in Ireland.
33 'List of those who drew land ...', SP 63/300, ff. 137–71, TNA. The hierarchy of land division was as follows – county, barony, parish, townland.
34 J. E. Farnell, 'The Navigation Act of 1651, the First Dutch War, and the London Merchant Community', *Economic History Review*, 2nd series, 16 (1961–1962), 441.
35 For a biography of Benjamin Worsley, see T. Leng, *Benjamin Worsley (1618–1677): Trade, Interest and the Spirit in Revolutionary England*, (Woodbridge: Boydell and Brewer, 2008).

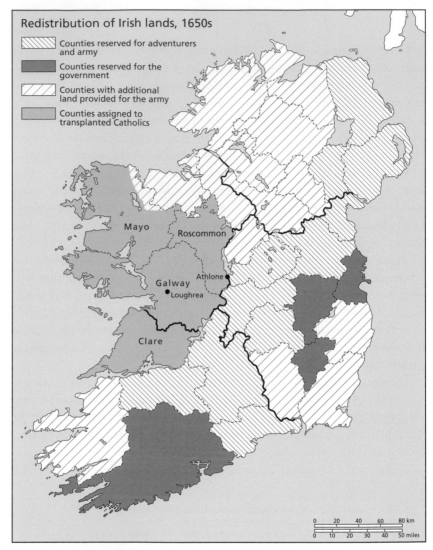

MAP 5. Redistribution of Irish Lands, 1650s.[36]

surveyed forfeited lands in counties Limerick, Tipperary and Waterford in Munster; Laois, Offaly, Meath and Westmeath in Leinster and finally Down, Antrim and Armagh in Ulster.[37] County Louth would also be included if the

36 Thanks to Matthew Stout for preparing the original map.
37 C. H. Firth and R. S. Rait (eds.), *Acts and Ordinances of the Interregnum, 1642–1660* (3 vols., London: HMSO, 1911), i, 722–53.

available land proved insufficient to meet the number of claims. The primary purpose of the Gross Survey was to provide a rough estimate of the area of forfeited land available in each barony (hence the name 'Gross Survey') and to determine the ownership of each estate. The revenue commissioners for each of the fifteen administrative districts established in post-war Ireland oversaw operations and reported directly to Worsley. Little of the Gross Survey survives apart from a fragment for the town of Mullingar, in County Westmeath, is dated 3 October 1653.[38] This implies that preparatory work had already been done in advance of the legislation, possibly by the adventurers who, months earlier, had commissioned their own surveys.[39]

The land identified by the Gross Survey did indeed prove insufficient to satisfy all claims, so a commission to undertake a second, more ambitious, survey was awarded to Worsley on 14 April 1654, not by the army but by the civil authorities in Dublin, hence the name 'Civil Survey'.[40] Whereas the Gross survey focused on ten counties (plus Louth), the Civil Survey eventually covered much of the country, to provide for additional claims, principally from thousands of army officers and soldiers, but also from government officials and anybody else seeking compensation from the state. The so-called Strafford Survey from the 1630s, undertaken at the behest of Lord Deputy Wentworth, who later obtained the title earl of Strafford, was used for the province of Connacht.[41] According to William O'Sullivan, the main purpose of the Strafford Survey had been to determine royal title to the land, but the remit of this new survey extended much further.[42] Worsley provided detailed instructions to his assistants on how to perform the various tasks, using the methodology of previous surveys of crown lands in England.[43] Surveyors

38 A copy of the Gross Survey for Mullingar, County Westmeath, is in MS 2477, National Archives of Ireland (hereafter NAI). The Gross Survey was destroyed in the Four Courts fire of 1922 and the most recent descriptions of it are by nineteenth-century historians. See W. H. Hardinge, 'On manuscript Mapped and Other Townland Surveys in Ireland of a Public Character, Embracing the Gross, Civil and Down Surveys, from 1640 to 1688', *Transactions of the Royal Irish Academy*, 24 (1873), 3–118.

39 George Rawdon to Col. Edward Conway, 5 September 1653, SP 63/284, f. 40, TNA.

40 R. C. Simington (ed.), *The Civil Survey A.D. 1654–1656, County of Tipperary*, (Dublin: Irish Manuscripts Commission, 1931), viii.

41 There is no explicit mention of the Strafford Survey in the text of the Civil Survey, but this link can be established by comparing the Survey and Distribution data with the surviving Strafford Survey material. See R. C. Simington (ed.), *Books of Survey and Distribution, Galway: being Abstracts of Various Surveys and Instruments of Title, 1636–1703* (Dublin: Irish Manuscripts Commission, 1962), xxxiii–xxxviii.

42 W. O'Sullivan (ed.), *Strafford's Inquisition of Mayo* (Dublin: Irish Manuscripts Commission, 1958).

43 Land formerly in the possession of Charles I was sold off following his execution in 1649. For an overview of the English land forfeitures, see S. J. Madge, *The Domesday of Crown Lands* (London: G. Routledge and Sons, 1938).

established the ownership of every townland, identified the lands to be forfeited and estimated (but did not measure) the extent and value of each estate. The scope of the Civil Survey indicates that its primary purpose was to determine the greatest amount of possible forfeitures, with the lands to be redistributed categorised as follows: Catholic-owned land, forfeited according to various acts of the English parliament; land owned by the Anglican Church; land owned by Protestant Royalists in Ireland; land owned by the king; and finally land owned by English Royalists, whose estates in England had already been confiscated by parliament and, by extension, their estates in Ireland and the colonies as well. In the end, the redistribution of Catholic estates alone, which comprised over half of the land in Ireland, proved sufficient.

With the Civil Survey underway, Oliver Cromwell, Lord Protector of the Commonwealth of England, Scotland and Ireland since December 1653, appointed a new Committee of Adventurers on 1 August 1654 to oversee the allocation of individual parcels of land. The adventurers had already extracted major concessions from Cromwell, including a complete remission of taxes on land for two years, the creation of a free trade zone between England and Ireland and a guarantee that they would not have to offer soldiers free quarter on their lands.[44] The new committee, which comprised the giants of state finance during the 1650s, wielded considerable influence. The adventurers William Pennoyer and Maurice Thompson appeared on the list of members, as did Sir David Watkins, former secretary to the parliament's Committee for Irish Affairs, and Thomas Andrews, the original treasurer for the Adventure for Irish Land and many additional parliamentary finance committees. Other members included Michael Herring, former treasurer of the Committee for Compounding; Thomas Vincent, former secretary of the main treasury at Goldsmiths Hall; Samuel Avery, Governor of the Merchant Adventurers of England; Richard Waring, former treasurer at Goldsmith's Hall; Thomas Foot, former excise commissioner and finally Sir John Clotworthy, a major Ulster landowner who had consistently championed the re-conquest of Ireland since the outbreak of the rebellion in 1641.[45]

The adventurers' lottery in September 1654 proved to be far from a random process. As when financing an overseas trade expedition, the adventurers organised themselves into consortia, with an agent nominated to draw lots for each group. The gatherings for the lottery at Grocers Hall in London were remarkably robust affairs. The ranks of the adventurers now comprised

44 Firth and Rait (eds), *Acts and Ordinances*, i, 924–9.
45 'Copy of Award of certain Commissioners who are empowered to make Regulations in regard to allotments in different Baronies In Ireland', SP 66/B, f. 26, TNA.

England's most powerful merchants, operating on a global scale, alongside parliamentary veterans of the bloodiest battles of the civil wars. The agents appointed by the adventurers collected together all claims on behalf of their clients and reassigned them into the particular baronies from which the individual allocations would be determined.[46] One of the original adventurers, George Almery, recorded each allocation at his office in Old Jewry, in the heart of the city of London. The surviving documents only record those registrations and not the results of the lottery.[47]

To counter the adventurers' domination of the surveying process, the army lobbied in late 1654 for the appointment of William Petty, an army surgeon and personal physician to Oliver Cromwell's son, Henry, to be the surveyor of forfeited lands.[48] The army did not accept the estimates provided by the Civil Survey, believing them to be widely inaccurate, and Petty embarked on a defamatory campaign against Worsley, describing his rival as a con-man who had moved to Ireland to 'repair himself upon a less knowing and more credulous people'.[49] It proved essential to undermine the adventurers' man in order to replace him with an army nominee, who would actually measure the land and adjudicate on claims to the satisfaction of the soldiers. On 8 September 1654, therefore, only three months after work on the Civil Survey had begun, the authorities in Dublin appointed a Committee of Surveys, chaired by Colonel Hardress Waller and dominated by army supporters. The committee reported that the methods adopted by the Civil Survey would lead to many disputes and made the case for a more exact survey, by measurement. Petty claimed he could produce such a survey within one year, but Worsley made every effort to block the appointment of his rival.[50] On 10 October, Colonel John Reynolds and Charles Coote joined Waller on the new committee.[51] As commissary-general, Reynolds sought to protect the interests of the adventurers, while Coote was a member of one of the leading Protestant families in Ireland. In this way, the three groups most concerned with the

---

46 'Edward Turner: Case, etc., concerning lands in Ireland: 1655–1658', Egerton MS 2651: Barrington Papers, vol. 8, f. 229, British Library (hereafter BL).
47 'List of receipts from adventurers', SP 46/130, ffs. 64–66, TNA.
48 The classic text on the Down Survey is based on Petty's own diaries. See T. Larcom (ed.), *The History of the Survey of Ireland Commonly Called the Down Survey*, (Dublin: Irish Archaeological Society, 1851). For the toponymy of the Down Survey, see Y. M. Goblet, *A Topographical Index of the Parishes and Townlands of Ireland* (Dublin: Irish Manuscripts Commission, 1932) and for Petty's surveying techniques see J. H. Andrews, *Plantation Acres: An Historical Study of the Irish Land Surveyor and his techniques*, (Belfast: Ulster Historical Foundation, 1985), 63–72.
49 E. G. Fitzmaurice, *Life of William Petty* (London: John Murray, 1895), 29.
50 Larcom, *The History of the Survey of Ireland*, 3–6.
51 Dunlop (ed.), *Ireland under the Commonwealth*, ii, 452.

land settlement – adventurers, English soldiers and Irish Protestants – came to be represented in the land redistribution process. By December, despite Worsley's objections, Petty received a contract for a new survey, which unlike the Civil Survey would not only accurately measure all forfeited land but also provide accompanying maps. For the moment, both surveys would continue in parallel, forcing Worsley and Petty to cooperate, albeit with bad grace. Petty, however, gained 'free access to all documents & records' he required, enabling him to make use of Worsley's work to date.[52] Tensions between the two men continued to fester and the Civil Survey was finally abandoned in 1656. Worsley left office the following year, leaving Petty in sole control of the surveying process and the subsequent redistribution of land.[53]

Sir William Petty and the Down Survey

Petty's survey, later called the Down Survey, because 'a chain was laid down and a scale made', was the third and final survey of the land allocation process.[54] According to John Andrews, the 1650s was probably the last decade in which 'anyone calling himself a natural philosopher could hope to pass muster with a survey by chain and circumferentor', but the results are extraordinary.[55] Using the Civil Survey as a guide, teams of soldier-surveyors, working parish by parish, set out to measure every townland to be redistributed to soldiers and adventurers. The resulting cadastral maps, made at a scale of forty Irish perches to one inch (the modern equivalent of 1:10,000), are unique for the time. Nothing as systematic or on such a large scale exists anywhere else in the world during the early modern period. The primary purpose of these maps was to record the boundaries of each townland and to calculate their areas with great precision but they are also rich in other detail, showing churches, roads, rivers, castles, houses and fortifications in addition to all the principal topographical features. The survey was restricted to forfeited land in Ulster, Leinster and most of Munster, relying on the Strafford Survey for coverage of Connacht, Clare and north Tipperary. Petty's assistant and subsequent rival, Thomas Taylor, later claimed that Petty had been given

52 Dunlop (ed.), *Ireland under the Commonwealth*, ii, 465.
53 The surviving volumes of the Civil Survey, for counties Derry, Donegal and Tyrone in Ulster, Dublin, Kildare, Meath and Wexford in Leinster, and Limerick, Tipperary and Waterford in Munster were published by the Irish Manuscripts Commission in ten volumes from 1931 to 1961.
54 Quit Rent Box 2A.12.51, NAI.
55 J. H. Andrews, *Shapes of Ireland: Maps and their makers, 1564–1839* (Dublin: Geography Publications, 1997), 135.

33. Down Survey Map – Billy Parish, Cary Barony, County Antrim.[56]

the Strafford maps, but instead of acknowledging them he 'left out here and there a line to disguise the work ... and Patrick Raggett the surveyor did it, as I remember, and never surveyed the land and yet was paid for it'.[57] Similarly, Petty failed to acknowledge Worsley's work on the Civil Survey. Nonetheless, the forfeited lands measured by Petty, alongside all other available material, made up roughly half the surface area of Ireland. Many Protestant estates were not surveyed and as Andrews shrewdly observed, albeit in a slightly different context, the Down Survey was essentially a survey of Catholic Ireland, not of the entire island.[58]

Petty's main contribution to the survey was that of manager and he imposed a clear hierarchical structure to ensure that the project finished on time. Working on the project was both physically demanding and highly dangerous, as the Catholic inhabitants fully understood its purpose and likely outcome. In addition to producing accurate measurements of profitable land, the surveyors also had to identify unprofitable land to be assigned for

56 Copies of Down Survey maps by William Molesworth (1911), Bittie (Billy) Parish, D/ 597/1/1, f. 12, Public Record Office of Northern Ireland. Image courtesy of PRONI.
57 Andrews, *Shapes of Ireland*, 137.
58 Andrews, *Shapes of Ireland*, 147.

free alongside the profitable allocations. Grantees could clearly benefit from under-measurements of the profitable land, while unprofitable land did not attract the Quit Rent, the land tax designed to secure the future revenue of the country. Both these factors had the potential to corrupt the surveying process, but despite such distortions the Down Survey remains the monumental achievement of early modern cartography, not only in terms of its ambition, scale and speed of execution but also the accuracy of the results. An analysis of sample townlands in the survey, where a direct comparison can be made with modern measurements, shows an average deficiency of just over 11.5 per cent, a truly remarkable figure given the primitive nature of the surveying tools and the difficult conditions faced by the surveyors.[59]

In May 1656, with their man now firmly in control of the surveying process and producing acceptable land measurements, the Council of Officers in Ireland finally formed their own board of trustees for settling soldiers' claims, the equivalent of the Committee for Adventurers. The trustees consisted of senior army figures, such as Waller, Colonel Daniel Abbott, Colonel Thomas Sadlier and Major Anthony Morgan, as well as the Munster landowner Vincent Gookin, senior army surgeon William Petty and Myles Symner, a mathematician from Trinity College Dublin, with Petty and Symner undertaking most of the work.[60] Soldiers' claims were taken away from Worsley's surveyor-general's office and placed in the hands of a separate committee, which reported to the army's board of trustees, using Petty's survey for its deliberations. This committee devised its own lottery system for allocating lands in those baronies set aside for the soldiers. Whoever drew the first number had first choice of the lands within each barony, while the second had second choice from the remaining lands, and so on.[61] In this way, the committee redistributed vast swathes of the land of Ireland.

Petty's organisational genius can leave the impression that all this proceeded in a transparent and orderly manner but the reality proved very different, due in part to the deficiencies in the surveys outlined above but also

---

59 Andrews, *Plantation Acres*, 72–3.
60 The minutes of this committee are in 'Original day-book of Proceedings of the Trustees', appointed 14 May, 1656, 'for satisfying of the armyes arrears due for service in Ireland since the 6th of June, 1649, as also English arrears satisfyable in Ireland by Act of Parliament', ADD MS 35102, BL. The correspondence is preserved in the 'Day Book of the Trustees for the Satisfaction of claims in Ireland', MS 11D, Oireachtas Library and Research Service.
61 ADD MS 35102, f. 28, BL.

because of what Aidan Clarke describes as 'the untidiness of human behaviour'.[62] It quickly became apparent that the government intended to give away a huge amount of land in Ireland to anyone who could make a plausible case for compensation. Indeed, the Act of Satisfaction in 1653 included a provision that any forfeited land not required for soldiers and adventurers could be used to settle public debt. The Committee of Adventurers, sitting in London and working completely independently of the Committee of Surveys in Dublin, freely exchanged debts due to army officers for service in England in return for forfeited land in Ireland.[63] The Council of State in London also received numerous petitions seeking Irish land in compensation for damages relating to the English civil wars. Sir Robert Pye, for example, whose father had lost a salaried post granted by Charles I, sought an Irish estate worth £500 per year.[64] Corruption also featured at the top levels of the colonial administration, with individuals acquiring substantial estates of their own, such as Edward Roberts, a treasury official, who received 2,000 acres in counties Dublin, Galway, Meath and Tyrone.[65] Widows of fallen soldiers and pensioners of the state besieged Petty with claims for redress in the form of Irish land.[66] Senior army officers and existing Protestant landowners sought to maximise their own holdings by purchasing the entitlements of rank and file soldiers for a fraction of their value. The constant exchange of land on the basis of scraps of paper and receipts of increasingly dubious legal validity led to a serious decline in property values. In July 1657, for example, a financially straitened Lord Broghill sold an estate in Cork worth £10,000 in normal circumstances for a mere £1,450 to Admiral Sir William Penn.[67] Such was the untidy reality of the Cromwellian land settlement.

Upon its completion in 1659 the Down Survey was housed in Dublin, along with the Strafford Survey, in the care of Worsley's successor as surveyor-general, Vincent Gookin.[68] The maps and accompanying terriers (textual descriptions) were bound into volumes and made available for public consultation until the destruction of a large amount of the material in an accidental fire in the surveyor-general's office in Dublin in 1711. The Down

---

62 A. Clarke, *Prelude to Restoration in Ireland: The End of the Commonwealth, 1659–1660* (Cambridge University Press, 1999), 7.
63 SP 63/301, f. 119, TNA.
64 SP 18/71, f. 87, TNA.
65 'A thin folio of parchment containing a survey of lands in Ireland by Tho. Taylor in 1659'. Harley MS 4784, BL.
66 ADD MSS 35102, fos. 17–29, BL.
67 P. Little, *Lord Broghill and the Cromwellian Union with Ireland and Scotland* (Woodbridge: Boydell and Brewer, 2004), 10–12.
68 See Leng, *Benjamin Worsley*, 89.

Survey survived in its entirety for ten counties – Derry, Donegal, Tyrone (Ulster); Carlow, Dublin, Westmeath, Wexford and Wicklow (Leinster); Leitrim (Connacht); Waterford (Munster) – while the volumes for Clare and Kerry (Munster); and Galway and Roscommon (Connacht) were completely destroyed. Partial papers survived for the rest. All the extant original maps were finally destroyed in 1922, when Free State forces bombarded the Four Courts. Numerous copies, however, were made between 1711 and 1922. In 1786 Daniel O'Brien copied those maps bound in books that had survived the fire in reasonably good order and this collection was purchased in two lots in 1965 by the National Library of Ireland and the Public Record Office of Northern Ireland. These manuscripts form the bulk of the parish maps and terriers now available to the public on the Down Survey website.

The Later Land Settlements

The death of Oliver Cromwell and the subsequent collapse of the English Republic threatened to destroy the foundations of the land settlement. In early 1660, therefore, a convention in Dublin, consisting of the Protestants of Ireland, soldiers and civilians, worked together to preserve their respective interests, regardless of past differences, and presented Charles II with a powerful, united front he simply could not ignore. The public expressions of joy at the Restoration in May of that year masked the king's political weakness, and his reliance on many stalwarts of the Cromwellian *régime*, particularly leading figures in the army. They agreed to support his return from exile only after receiving assurances that it would not result in widespread acts of recrimination. Charles II, painfully aware of the hostility felt by the majority of Englishmen towards Irish Catholics, inevitably sided with his Protestant subjects. An Act of Pardon and Indemnity in August 1660 specifically excluded from pardon those involved 'in the plotting, contriving, or designing the great and heinous rebellion of Ireland', or who had subsequently assisted the rebels in any way.[69] The king retained the right, however, to pardon individual Catholics, regardless of their actions during the 1640s, for loyal service to the crown, especially during his years of exile.

At the end of November 1660, Charles II published a 'Gracious Declaration', outlining in detail his plans for Ireland. The king acknowledged the 'many difficulties, in the providing for, and complying with the several interests and

---

69 *An Act of Free and General Pardon, Indemnity and Oblivion* (London, 1660), 6.

pretences there', but highlighted the debt he owed to Protestant leaders for facilitating the restoration of the monarchy. Charles accepted the validity of the peace treaty signed by the marquis of Ormond with the Confederates in 1649, but the declaration confirmed all the adventurers and soldiers in their estates, with the exception of those identified in the Act of Pardon, as having taken part in the trial and execution of Charles I.[70]

Ormond recovered his entire estate, as did all Protestant Royalists. Jane Ohlmeyer's definitive study of the Irish aristocracy in the seventeenth century, however, also demonstrates how the Catholic nobility featured prominently among the lists of those she terms 'winners' and 'survivors'.[71] The declaration identified thirty-six individuals, mostly Catholic nobles such as the earl of Clanricard (recently deceased), the earl of Clancarthy (formerly Viscount Muskerry) and Viscount Taaffe, who would be fully restored to their former estates 'without being put to any further proof', while the king deemed 200 Catholic officers who had served overseas to be worthy of royal grace and favour.[72] Charles clearly distinguished between supporters who followed him into exile, and those who accepted lands as part of the transplantation scheme. He restored the former to their original estates, but insisted that the transplanted landowners be bound by the terms of the Cromwellian settlement, in effect penalising them for not abandoning their families. Only after settling the 'jarring interests' relating to land did the king intend to pass a general act of pardon in Ireland, except of course for those 'notorious murderers' involved in the initial rebellion.[73]

The king's 'Gracious Declaration', therefore, established the year 1660, not 1641, as the benchmark for all future land claims, consolidating the Cromwellian settlement in the process, and dashing the hopes of Irish Catholics. Thousands of families never recovered their estates. The Irish parliament, now an exclusively Protestant assembly apart from a handful of Catholic nobles in the House of Lords, subsequently passed the Act of Settlement (1662) and the Act of Explanation (1665).[74] The Act of Settlement confirmed the value of lands allocated to the holders of adventurer's certificates and soldiers, but not their location. This would only happen with the

---

70 *His Majesties Gracious Declaration for the Settlement of his Kingdom of Ireland* (London, 1660), 1–8.

71 J. Ohlmeyer, *Making Ireland English: The Irish aristocracy in the seventeenth century* (New Haven and London: Yale University Press, 2012), 310–35.

72 *His Majesties Gracious Declaration*, 21.

73 *His Majesties Gracious Declaration*, 27, 32.

74 The *Statutes passed in the Parliaments held in Ireland* (20 vols., Dublin, 1765–1801), i, 338–64, and ii, 1–137. Also see Chapter 4 by T. McCormick, this volume.

issuing of letters patent following the Act of Explanation in 1665. In effect, the legislation sacrificed Catholic Ireland to the demands of the adventurers and soldiers. This is hardly surprising. Among the adventurers, men like Maurice Thompson had risen to become the wealthiest men in England, upon whom Charles II now depended to finance his realm, while the soldiers underpinned the security of the restored monarchy.

A significant aspect of both Restoration land acts is that they did not impose any plantation conditions, such as an obligation to introduce English Protestant settlers. Similarly, individual certificates, confirming each owner's lands by letters patent, contained no specific covenants. The Restoration thus marks the end of the plantation period in Ireland and the emergence of a new type of colony, one based purely on economic exploitation. The removal of any requirement on the part of the landowner to live on his newly awarded lands provided the impetus for absentee landlordism. Irish land became an investment to be managed remotely in much the same way as a sugar plantation in Bermuda or a tobacco plantation in Virginia. A significant landowning aristocracy, both Protestant and Catholic, continued to reside in Ireland but, writing in the 1670s, Petty believed that the owners of some 25 per cent of the real estate of Ireland now lived in England. He estimated that as much as £100,000 per year of profits from Irish estates, in addition to the £90,000 remitted directly to the king for taxes on land, flowed from Ireland to England. As money remained in short supply in Ireland during this time, with as little as £400,000 in circulation, this constituted a major drain on the country's wealth.[75]

The experience of navigating the Acts of Settlement and Explanation through parliament drew together the main factions with an interest in Irish land, and they now began to work together in developing England's wider colonial ambitions. The Society for the Propagation of the Gospel in New England, formed in 1662, included Ormond, Arthur Annesley, earl of Anglesey and leading adventurers such as Erasmus Smith, William Thompson, Nicholas Crisp and William Pennoyer among its members.[76] Some families, such as the Barringtons, were awarded lands in the course of the Cromwellian settlements and simultaneously expanded their holdings in the Caribbean.[77] Many of the adventurers already had such interests, but increasingly close ties with the colonies in the Americas enabled Ireland to become a leading player in trans-Atlantic trade. The adventurers

---

75 William Petty, *The Political Anatomy of Ireland*, (London, 1673), 61–3. For information on the resident peerage, see Ohlmeyer, *Making Ireland English*, 575–607.

76 'Contemporary office copy of the Charter for Incorporation', CLC/540 New England Company, MS07909, London Metropolitan Archives.

77 Egerton MS 2648, Barrington Papers, vol. 5, f. 263, BL.

J.G. Simms:

1641: Catholics 59% Protestants 41%

1688: Catholics 22% Protestants 78%

TCD Down Survey Project:

1641: Catholics 54% Protestants 46%

1670: Catholics 23% Protestants 77%

Figure 3. Transfer of land in Seventeenth-Century Ireland.

had also taken control of the East India Company in 1657, so by the Restoration these colonial networks, many of them forged in Ireland, spanned the globe.

Not surprisingly, years of litigation followed the Restoration land acts, as Catholics desperately sought to regain lost estates and Cromwellian proprietors for the most part refused to relinquish any part of their holdings. The Act of Settlement did establish a Court of Claims, which sat from 20 September 1662 to 21 August 1663 to hear the cases of landowners who believed they had been wrongfully dispossessed. This court awarded 829 decrees, with 115 claimants declared guilty and the rest, including 140 Protestants, innocent. According to contemporary estimates, 8,000 claims remained unheard when the court closed, almost all of them from Catholic landowners.[78] According to J. G. Simms, the Protestants emerged as the clear victors from this process, with Catholics left in possession of only one-fifth of the land total, a huge reduction from the 60 per cent they owned prior to the 1641 rebellion.[79] Historians since Simms have accepted his figures uncritically and few have engaged with the voluminous surviving documentation relating to the land settlements, such as the Books of Survey and Distribution, an amalgam of material outlining changes in land ownership from 1640 to the early eighteenth century. The Trinity College Dublin Down Survey project, however, has brought the tabular and cartographic evidence together for the first time in three hundred years and is in the process of re-examining the issue. The interim results are fascinating, but years of research are still required before any definitive conclusions can be reached.

The revised figures for 1641, however, show a significant discrepancy in relation to Catholic landownership: 59 per cent in Simms as against 54 per cent in the TCD project. The latter results suggest that during the early decades of the seventeenth century, the Catholic *élite* faced far greater competition

---

78 For a survey of the deliberations of this court, see L. J. Arnold, 'The Irish Court of Claims of 1663', *Irish Historical Studies*, 24 (1985), 417–30; G. Tallon (ed.), *Court of Claims: Submissions and Evidence, 1663* (Dublin: Irish Manuscripts Commission, 2006).

79 J. G. Simms, 'The Restoration, 1660–85', in Moody, Martin and Byrne (eds.), *New History of Ireland*, iii, 428.

for land than hitherto understood. This may help explain why large numbers committed themselves to the 1641 insurgency at such an early stage. Already excluded from government office, they faced the very real prospect of being eclipsed as the major landowners in Ireland, with the attendant loss of social and economic control that such a development would entail. For many, the writing was on the wall unless they took immediate action to preserve what they had against further encroachments from the New English.

For the latter part of the seventeenth century, however, the figures produced by the Down Survey project and by Simms for the proportion of land owned by Catholics, in 1670 and 1688 respectively, are almost identical. These figures illustrate the dual effects of the Court of Claims during the reign of Charles II and the Commission of Grace under James VII and II. The combination of both facilitated the partial recovery of Irish Catholics from the low point of the late 1650s. Nonetheless, this still represents the single largest shift in land ownership anywhere in Europe (and possibly beyond) during the early modern period and proved to be Cromwell's lasting legacy in Ireland. That legacy was briefly threatened by the accession of a Catholic monarch, James VII and II, in 1685. Driven from England by his son-in-law, William of Orange, James fled to Ireland via France, and in 1689 presided over a parliament in Dublin. This Jacobite assembly, composed almost entirely of Catholics, many of them direct descendants of the Confederates, seized the opportunity to overthrow the Cromwellian land settlement, and proscribed thousands of Protestant landowners in the process. The subsequent military defeat of the Jacobites, however, put paid to any prospect of a Catholic recovery. In fact, the position of Catholic landowners deteriorated further following the subsequent Williamite confiscations.[80] As with the Cromwellian forfeitures, the land had to be mapped and measured using techniques very similar to those employed by Petty and his immediate predecessors.[81] The original maps of the Williamite land forfeitures, the Trustees Survey (so called because the land was vested in trustees prior to sale), no longer survive, although tracings made in the nineteenth century are preserved in the National Archives of Ireland. Unlike the Cromwellian forfeitures and distribution lotteries, once the land had been identified and measured it was sold in a series of auctions held at Chichester House in Dublin, the building used for sittings of the Irish parliament. Half of the land was sold locally to existing landowners seeking to consolidate their estates or to merchants who

---

80 For further reading on this topic, see J. G. Simms, *The Williamite Confiscation in Ireland, 1690–1703*, (London: Faber & Faber, 1956).

81 See DS series, NAI, with some additional copies from certain counties in ADD MSS 13956, 14405 and 41159, BL.

wanted to ascend into the ranks of the minor gentry. By the end of this process Catholic land ownership had shrunk to just 15 per cent of the total and this percentage continued to decline thereafter.[82]

The Protestant ascendancy class which emerged triumphant from the upheavals of the seventeenth century dominated the political, economic and social life of the country until Catholic emancipation and major land reforms transformed the landscape of nineteenth-century Ireland. None of this could have happened without the work of William Petty and his team of surveyors. The Down Survey was a stunning technical achievement for its time, undertaken by the English in a largely hostile country, devastated by twelve years of almost continuous warfare. Petty's project was unique in many ways but Michael Clanchy, writing about Domesday Book in England, argues that the purpose of that survey 'was to bring order out of the inevitable chaos caused by the Norman Conquest'. The same could be said of the Down Survey in the wake of the Cromwellian conquest. Clanchy concludes that Domesday Book entitled the Normans to rule, 'literally in the sense that it recorded the titles to their lands and symbolically in the sense that it demonstrated their capacity to organize'.[83] Again this applies to the Down Survey, which effectively redistributed Irish land in a systematic, quasi-scientific manner and in the process, according to Ted McCormick, provided an excellent example of how colonisation and commercialisation went hand in hand.[84] The language of economic exploitation eclipsed the rhetoric of improvement and reform. Much as Domesday Book refashioned eleventh-century England, a new Ireland emerged from the wreckage of the Cromwellian conquest, shaped by the vision of its creator, William Petty. As Andrews has observed, there were no more Down Surveys until the Ordnance Survey of the 1830s, 'and no more Pettys ever'.[85]

---

82 J. G. Simms, 'Land Owned by Catholics in Ireland in 1688', *Irish Historical Studies*, 7 (1951), 180–90.

83 M. Clanchy, *England and its Rulers, 1066–1307* (4th edn., Oxford: Wiley-Blackwell, 2014), 44–5. Thanks to Mark Hennessy for this reference.

84 T. McCormick, *William Petty and the Ambitions of Political Arithmetic* (Oxford University Press, 2009), 117.

85 Andrews, *Shapes of Ireland*, 149.

24

Environmental History of Ireland, 1550–1730

FRANCIS LUDLOW AND ARLENE CRAMPSIE

Environmental history addresses three interrelated themes: first, the influence of the environment on human societies; second, changes to the environment wrought by humans; and third, human attitudes towards and perception of the environment.[1] Now a thriving discipline internationally, its study in Ireland has only recently begun in a concerted manner, but can draw from the abundant work already undertaken by social, economic and political historians, historical geographers, anthropologists, industrial and environmental archaeologists and palaeoecologists.[2] Ireland's rich history, moreover, with deep and varied historical and natural archives, makes it an ideal location to study environmental history. This chapter presents an overview of several existing research themes relevant to Irish environmental history for the transformative period between 1550 and 1730, supplementing this with information drawn from documentary sources and natural environmental archives such as ice cores and tree-rings. In doing so, this chapter seeks to help situate the studies by other contributors to this volume in their broader environmental context and to explore a hitherto little-examined aspect of Irish historiography. It also provides an overview of the environmental and landscape impact of the dramatic political and social developments of the period, including the introduction of new agricultural practices, the emergence of new settlement types and impacts from the greater integration of the Irish economy into that of Europe and the Atlantic World.

Internationally the period 1550 to 1730 was one of major political, economic and social upheaval and reorganisation. In recent years the role of the environment in these changes has received increasing academic attention,[3] partly

---

1 J. D. Hughes, *What is Environmental History?* (Cambridge: Polity, 2006), 3.
2 J. Adelman and F. Ludlow, 'The Past, Present and Future of Irish Environmental History', *Proceedings of the Royal Irish Academy*, 114:C (2014), 359–91.
3 S. White, *The Climate of Rebellion in the Early Modern Ottoman Empire* (Cambridge University Press, 2011); G. Parker, *Global Crisis: War, Climate Change and Catastrophe in the Seventeenth Century* (New Haven and London: Yale University Press, 2013).

enabled by a rapid growth in palaeoclimatic reconstructions based upon an array of natural and written archives. The seventeenth and early eighteenth centuries constitute in many reconstructions the coldest sustained period of the broader Little Ice Age (*c.*1350–*c.*1850), a period of climatic instability likely to have been driven or enhanced by marked oscillations in solar activity and a notable series of major volcanic eruptions known for their capability to disrupt the global climate. Such events contributed not only to prolonged changes in background average temperature and precipitation patterns, but also to an increased frequency and severity of extreme weather events. This chapter will review the climate history of the period, assess the contribution of climate to Irish history in this era, and provide two case studies of the potential role of abrupt climatic changes and extreme weather in major political, social and economic events of the seventeenth century.

Human Influences on the Irish Environment

The period from 1550 to 1730 was one of multifaceted and interlinked transformation, and while continuities can be identified with earlier centuries, change reached practically all levels of society and culture, and refashioned the Irish environment. From a predominantly rural landscape with comparatively small urban centres of Viking and Anglo-Norman origin that favoured coastal or riverine locations, the influence of urban Ireland reached effectively the entire island by the mid-eighteenth century. By the start of the sixteenth century, land ownership beyond the Pale had largely returned to the control of Gaelic Irish chieftains, being mainly administered according to Gaelic laws and customs, with enduring Anglo-Norman (later, Old English) areas exhibiting varying degrees of hybridity. However, with the onset of plantation schemes, the Acts of Settlement and the influence of the penal laws, came changes in land ownership and management, agricultural practices, settlement types and structures, significantly altering the Irish environment, against a background of religious and political upheaval, war, disease and pronounced climatic variability.

Sixteenth-century Ireland was marked by warfare, rebellion and general unrest. The consequent agricultural and landscape burden of sustained military campaigns featuring large armies and the proliferation of 'scorched earth' tactics on all sides inflicted significant environmental damage, and subjected local populations to starvation and disease, bringing further environmental impacts. Information on these tactics and the ensuing human and environmental devastation survive in fine annual detail in the Irish Annals. Describing events in 1600 which occurred at the height of the Nine

Years' War, 1594 to 1603, the *Annals of the Four Masters* (henceforth, *Four Masters*) reveal the scale of the environmental destruction and its tactical goal, relating how, O'Neill

> remained in the territory [of the lordship of Barry More, Co. Cork, loyal to the crown] until he traversed, plundered, and burned it, from one extremity to the other, both plain and wood, both level and rugged, so that no one hoped or expected that it could be inhabited for a long time afterwards.[4]

These tactics were not confined to Gaelic forces. During the Nine Years' War, crown forces employed the same techniques after provisioning their troops from the land.[5] Raymond Gillespie also notes at least eight harvest failures between 1550 and 1600.[6] All combined, the outcome was frequently disastrous for local populations, and transformative of the environment. In his presumed eyewitness account, Edmund Spenser, secretary to Lord Deputy Arthur Grey, depicted the extremities to which people were driven in Munster towards the end of the sixteenth century, when 'a most populous and plentiful country [was] suddenly left void of man or beast'. Spenser hints at the impacts on flora and fauna arising from famine subsistence and human population displacements, noting how 'Out of every corner of the woods and glens they came creeping forth ...', resorting to eating '... dead carrion ... and one another soon after ... and if they found a plot of water-cresses or shamrocks, there they flocked as to a feast.'[7]

The landscape transformations that emerged in the immediate aftermath of the Nine Years' War were, however, more significant and far reaching than those wrought by the foregoing destruction. In this new century 'the axes and engines of the civil and military organisers' of the crown surmounted the 'natural frontiers of mountain, bog and forest [that had] enclosed many [Gaelic] communities... [and had] reinforced cultural distinctiveness'.[8] Sheila Cavanagh notes that the writings of Elizabethan-era English commentators on Ireland 'work to perpetuate an image of the Irish as sufficiently removed from the English in manners, customs, and values to warrant severe and protracted

4 J. O'Donovan (ed.), *Annála Ríoghachta Éireann: Annals of the Kingdom of Ireland by the Four Masters, from the Earliest Period to the Year 1616* (7 vols., Dublin: Hodges & Smith, 1848–1851), vi, 2151.
5 R. Gillespie, 'Harvest Crises in Early Seventeenth-Century Ireland', *Irish Economic and Social History*, 11 (1984), 8.
6 Gillespie, 'Harvest Crises', 8.
7 Edmund Spenser, *A View of the State of Ireland – From the First Printed Edition (1633)*, ed. A. Hadfield and W. Maley (Oxford: Blackwell, 1997), 102.
8 C. Lennon, *Sixteenth-Century Ireland: The Incomplete Conquest* (Dublin: Gill and Macmillan, 1994), 3.

attempts at "reformation"'.[9] Contrasting environmental perceptions were a key part of the differing cultural norms alluded to by Cavanagh. In the crucible of social, economic, religious, demographic and climatic pressures transforming England in the sixteenth and seventeenth centuries, these tracts cultivated the perception of an underexploited Irish environment, something that was seen not only as lamentable, but immoral.[10] While plantations of the sixteenth century had achieved only limited success, they established the blueprint that would remake the Irish landscape, most successfully in Ulster from 1609.

As part of this, it was envisioned that the new British settlers would not only introduce a civilised husbandry of the land, but would assist in incorporating Ireland into a growing global market. At the centre of this was the development of the Irish urban network and the introduction of around four hundred new 'plantation towns'. These, it was hoped, would offer a focus for the recently arrived settler community, encourage infrastructural developments and further promote economic activity.[11] These towns were also intended as new religious centres for the established church. Across the Irish landscape, once vibrant medieval villages based around the pre-Reformation church and the tower houses of the ruling Gaelic and Old English families fell into disrepair and decay. In his 1620 treatise, Luke Gernon, magistrate for Munster, remarked upon the patchwork nature of these older villages in the east Limerick area, being 'distant from each other [by] about two miles. In every village is a castle and a church, but both in ruins'.[12] As time passed, however, these old village centres were frequently reformed as the core of landlord demesnes.

The displacement of population from newly subdued and planted areas increasingly extended human influence into previously less-inhabited landscapes. The redistribution of plantation lands in Ulster ensured that the native population received the least favourable grants, gradually pushing settlement into more upland or other agriculturally marginal and ecologically vulnerable areas. The native population that failed to secure land grants had little option but to withdraw to bogs and woods.[13] For these people,

---

9 S.T. Cavanagh, ' "The fatal destiny of that land": Elizabethan Views of Ireland', in B. Bradshaw, A. Hadfield and W. Maley (eds.), *Representing Ireland: Literature and the Origins of Conflict 1534–1660* (Cambridge University Press, 1993), 116–31.

10 B. Kiernan, *Blood and Soil: A World History of Genocide and Extermination from Sparta to Darfur* (New Haven and London: Yale University Press, 2007), 169.

11 F. Aalen, K. Whelan and M. Stout (eds.), *Atlas of the Irish Rural Landscape* (2nd edn., Cork University Press, 2011), 263. Also see Chapter 22 by Margey, this volume.

12 L. Gernon quoted in Aalen *et al.* (eds.), *Atlas of the Irish Rural Landscape*, 261.

13 A. Clarke, 'Pacification, Plantation and the Catholic Question, 1603–23', in T. W. Moody, A. Clarke and R. Dudley Edwards (eds.), *A New History of Ireland, iii: Early Modern Ireland, 1534–1691* (Oxford University Press, 1976), 204.

subsistence was a daily issue as they were forced to adopt new methods to reclaim and cultivate inhospitable land. Not all previous inhabitants remained in rural areas, however. Colin Breen has argued that the development of 'Irishtowns' outside the walls of larger Munster towns was augmented by displaced and impoverished rural populations, perhaps also often arriving in pulses in times of famine. The swelling of the province's suburban footprint was a process with continuing environmental ramifications for urban hinterlands in pollution, disease and population pressures on natural resources.[14]

While the native populations were displaced from their homelands, necessitating the implementation of new agricultural practices, the new settlers were also encouraged to introduce English farming practices. Yet the introduction of English farming methods fell short in reality, as many settlers abandoned grain growing in areas of Munster and Ulster in which the quality of the agricultural land, combined with Ireland's relatively damp climate, lent a comparative economic advantage to grazing.[15] Indeed, tree-ring-based precipitation data suggest that springs and summers in the years c.1520 to c.1630 were of above-average wetness, compounding difficulties for crop cultivation during the foundational plantations of the period. This was further reinforced by multiple grain shortages and harvest crises in the first half of the seventeenth century (1600–1603, 1607–1608, 1621–1624, 1627–1629, 1630–1633, 1639–1641).[16]

Environmental and climatic conditions thus clearly informed the decision of many settlers to focus on the pre-existing livestock industry, in particular cattle rearing, which would become the dominant form of agricultural activity over large swathes of Ireland in subsequent decades. Sheep farming also developed during this period as the wool industry expanded. Export figures for wool reached 6,666 stone per year by 1639, up from between 100 and 200 in the 1580s.[17] In part, these specialisms were driven by the incorporation of Ireland into the period's burgeoning and globalising economy as exports from Ireland found new markets not just in England but in continental Europe and

---

14 C. Breen, 'Famine and Displacement in Plantation-Period Munster', in J. Lyttleton and C. Rynne (eds.), *Plantation Ireland: Settlement and Material Culture, c.1550–c.1700* (Dublin: Four Courts Press, 2009), 132–39.

15 R. Gillespie, 'Explorers, Exploiters and Entrepreneurs, 1500–1700', in B. J. Graham and L. Proudfoot (eds.), *An Historical Geography of Ireland* (London: Academic Press, 1993), 123–57.

16 Dates from J. Ohlmeyer, 'The Statute Staple in Early Modern Ireland', *History Ireland*, 6 (1998), 36–40; see also R. Gillespie, 'Meal and Money: The Harvest Crisis of 1621–4 and the Irish Economy', in E. M. Crawford (ed.), *Famine: The Irish Experience, 900–1900: Subsistence Crises and Famines in Ireland* (Edinburgh: John Donald, 1989), 75–95. Ohlmeyer cites 1600–1602, while Gillespie cites 1601–1603.

17 Gillespie, 'Explorers, Exploiters and Entrepreneurs', 137–8.

the New World, and thus the Irish environment bore the burden of servicing growing demands beyond the island's shores. When considered alongside the generally low population densities outside the Pale and the attendant potential for agricultural intensification, the economic opportunities for new settlers were clear.

However, the periodic harvest crises, noted above, combined with lingering resentment and other religious, social and political tensions between native and newcomer ensured that, despite the years between 1603 and 1641 being characterised as the 'Early Stuart Peace', unrest and the threat of violence remained a concern that was made manifest in the 1641 rebellion.[18] Accounts contained in the 1641 Depositions are replete with references to the immediate environmental context and consequences of the rebellion. Much loss of life is attributed to exposure to harsh winter weather, while accounts of the burning of houses, churches and towns highlight the landscape impacts of the event.[19]

Indeed, these impacts extended over the duration of the Eleven Years' War (1642 to 1653), resulting in a demographic disaster. The early seventeenth century had witnessed a period of sustained population growth, driven at least in part by new settlers. William Smyth estimates that the island's population had reached between 1.8 and 2.1 million by 1641. But by 1652, as a consequence of wartime atrocities, famine and exposure, outmigration of settlers back to England, Scotland and Wales, and the effects of disease, which ravaged the country between 1649 and 1653, the population had fallen to no more than 1.3 million.[20] The impacts of the plague, reaching Galway from Spain in summer 1649, were likely amplified in a population suffering from wartime deprivation and living in a landscape that had again been wasted, this time by the Cromwellian army. The extent of population loss by 1650 is further reflected in the comment of Cromwell's son-in-law, Henry Ireton, that he had passed through districts *en route* from Waterford to Limerick 'with hardly a house or any living creature to be seen, only ruins and desolation in a plain and pleasant land'.[21] Grain cultivation by the end of the war had almost ceased and, remarkably for an island renowned for its pastures, livestock had to be imported.

18 D. Edwards, 'Out of the Blue? Provincial Unrest in Ireland before 1641', in M. Ó Siochrú and J. Ohlmeyer (eds.), *Ireland, 1641: Contexts and Reactions* (Manchester University Press, 2013), 95–114.

19 A. Margey, '1641 and the Ulster Plantation Towns', in E. Darcy, A. Margey and E. Murphy (eds.), *The 1641 Depositions and the Irish Rebellion* (London: Pickering and Chatto, 2012), 79–96.

20 W. J. Smyth, *Map-making, Landscapes and Memory: A Geography of Colonial and Early Modern Ireland c.1530–1750* (Cork University Press, 2006), 160–1. Also see Chapter 21 by Gillespie, this volume.

21 Smyth, *Map-making, Landscapes and Memory*, 158.

With the defeat of the Irish Confederates and the close of the Eleven Years' War in 1653, the stage was set for the consequent Cromwellian mass land confiscations and transplantations of the incumbent populations. Lessons learned from past plantations ensured that this scheme would proceed on a more scientific and environmentally realistic basis. Forensic attention was paid in the Civil Survey (1654–1656) and the Down Survey (1656–1658), for example, to the apparent agricultural potential of the variable Irish landscape. Characteristic is the description by Thomas Taylor, surveyor of the Barony of Newcastle and Uppercross, County Dublin, who noted that 'the quality of the soil is generally very good arable meadow and pasture with underwood and furz[,] which furz yield as much profit as the arable land'.[22] Although the removal of the disloyal Irish was not achieved to the extent initially planned, a sizeable movement of native populations to less hospitable lands west of the Shannon occurred, while others were transported abroad or emigrated, freeing land for the new wave of settlers.[23]

Timber was perhaps the most significant and sought after commercial export in Ireland in this period and while the extent of Irish woodlands at the start of the sixteenth century is debated, as is the status of these woodlands as ancient or recent-growth forests,[24] it seems likely that one of the most dramatic environmental changes in the period was the ultimate widespread deforestation of the Irish landscape.[25] Occurring for a non-exclusive mix of commercial, military and ideological purposes (with woodland symbolising the uncivilised rebellious Gaelic Irish and indeed providing cover for their activities), its erasure was viewed as vital to further Ireland's submission.[26] The extent and impact of this alteration is suggested in both human and natural archives. The latter include pollen profiles from lake and peat bog sediments,[27] as well as tree-ring records that imply the average age of oak trees used in construction declined rapidly from a peak of almost 130 years

22 R. Simington (ed.), *The Civil Survey, A.D. 1654–1656, Vol. VII: County of Dublin* (Dublin: Irish Manuscripts Commission, 1945), 289. Also see Chapter 23 by M. Ó Siochrú and D. Brown, this volume.

23 For transplantation abroad, see S. O'Callaghan, *To Hell or Barbados: the Ethnic Cleansing of Ireland* (Dingle: Brandon, 2000).

24 Dendrochronology suggests that much Irish oak woodland extant during the sixteenth century had regenerated since the fourteenth-century Black Death; see D. Brown and M. Baillie, 'How Old is that Oak?', in B. Simon (ed.), *A Treasured Landscape. The Heritage of Belvoir Park* (Belfast: The Forest of Belfast, 2005), 85–97; and M. Baillie, *New Light on the Black Death* (Stroud: Tempus, 2006). For palynological evidence of potential landscape abandonment that may be associated with oak wood regeneration, see V. Hall, *The Making of Ireland's Landscape since the Ice Age* (Cork: Collins Press, 2011), 126–7.

25 Adelman and Ludlow, 'The Past, Present and Future of Irish Environmental History'.

26 Smyth, *Map-making, Landscapes and Memory*.

27 For the classic pollen study on landscape clearance and replanting, see G. F. Mitchell, 'Littleton Bog, Tipperary: An Irish Agricultural Record', *The Journal of the Royal Society*

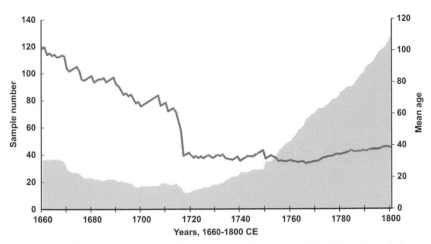

Figure 4. Irish oaks mean age (thick line) and sample numbers (shaded area) underlying the Irish oak tree-ring chronology. Sample numbers *may* mirror broader oak population numbers, reflecting successive human impacts on the landscape via deforestation and the later replanting of young trees on landlord estates.[28]

in the mid-seventeenth century to just thirty-five years by the early years of the eighteenth century (Figure 4). This suggests the removal of the older and larger specimens by the 1660s and an increasing reliance on younger trees, an inference supported by accounts of the general timber trade that described a steady phase of expansion from the 1550s with the best supplies exhausted by the mid-seventeenth century.[29]

Deforestation continued throughout the latter part of the seventeenth century as a return to peacetime conditions (excepting the Williamite Wars, 1689–1691) allowed the population, native and settler, to start rebuilding homes and livelihoods. Agricultural output, exports and population increased, urban Ireland developed via the growth of fairs and markets, and infrastructural improvements opened hitherto less accessible areas to trade and modernisation. The conclusion of the Williamite Wars removed any uncertainty over land and resource ownership, confirming the predominance of the Protestant Ascendancy. Secure in their properties, the settlers embarked on a range of environmental 'improvements' that further altered Irish landscapes and ecologies.

of Antiquaries of Ireland, 95 (1965), 121–32. We thank Ellen O'Carroll and Gill Plunkett for this reference.
28 We thank Edward R. Cook, Michael Baillie and David Brown for access to the oak data.
29 R. Gillespie, 'Explorers, Exploiters and Entrepreneurs', 123–57.

Although some environmental changes of the greatest scale began, or were felt most keenly, in the decades following 1730, the cultural, economic and environmental stage was often set for these during the later seventeenth and early eighteenth centuries. Developments included landlord-driven rural industrialisation, accelerating from the early eighteenth century, a prominent example being flax cultivation and the construction of bleaching works with attendant pollution of watercourses.[30] Other forms of improvement also began early, as the landed classes sought to quickly modernise and increase the profitability of Irish land. Thus, for example, in *Ireland's Natural History* by Gerard Boate (1652), one may find a dedicated section on the 'Draining of the bogs practised by the English in Ireland'.[31]

The new-found confidence of landowners in this period can be read in their alterations of landscapes and built environments. Lands were enclosed to mark not just the wider boundaries of the new estates, but also field boundaries. Though slow initially and geographically dispersed, this enclosure process created patchworks of neatly lined fields that followed the English model so desired by the Dublin government. To a degree, this practice helped reforest the denuded Irish landscape, with hedgerows preferred to earthen banks, though stone walls still remained on the rocky lands of the west coast.

House styles of the gentry ultimately transitioned from the hybrid residential–defensive tower houses of the high and late medieval periods to expansive Georgian mansions embedded in carefully cultivated and manicured demesnes, in the geometric style. The angular, structured, tree-lined avenues (favouring stately lime, elm, chestnut and oak) and vistas associated with these demesnes inscribed the power and control exercised by the new landowners on the Irish landscape. In general, the wealthier the landowner, the more extensive their environmental influence. Together, the planting of trees in field boundaries, their ornamental use in demesne landscapes, and a switch from timber to stone as a more durable building material, contributed to a reversal in the overall decline in Irish tree cover and contributed to the gradual recovery in oak numbers and the sudden drop in sample ages suggested in Figure 4, between 1710 and 1720.

30 See the useful case study by D. Cronin, *A Galway Gentleman in the Age of Improvement: Robert French of Monivea, 1716–76* (Dublin: Irish Academic Press, 1995).
31 Gerard Boate, *Ireland's Natvrall History. Being a True and Ample Defcription of its Situation, Greatnefs, Shape, and Nature...* (London, 1652), 114.

Beyond the family's private realm, the gentry also engaged in developing estate towns. The symbolism inherent in aligning the main streets of these towns to lead from the demesne gate directly to the Protestant church reflected the dominance of the new landowners and their culture in the landscape. For eighteenth-century aristocratic landowners, the environment and landscape was more than a simple physical entity. It was a tool and canvas in an ongoing campaign to civilise and anglicise Ireland.[32]

Environmental Influences on Society

Some of the most exciting advances in Irish environmental history will arise from reconciling documentary evidence with natural archives, including physical (e.g., ice-core) and biological (e.g., tree-ring and pollen) proxies that can reveal a wide array of past environmental conditions and the changes that occurred in these through space and time. Here we review the major trends in Irish climate between 1550 and 1730, taking account of the 'forcing factors' that drove these changes and making use of natural archives that provide information at fine temporal scales, such as 'high resolution' annual tree-ring growth measurements. These archives, becoming increasingly numerous and sophisticated, reflect a broad range of climatic and underlying volcanic and solar forcing influences and enable scholars to integrate climatic influences into economic, social and political histories of Ireland.

Thomas E. Jordan notes, for example, some of the more extreme winters in the sixteenth century, and discusses the likely impact these and other changes in climate during that century may have had on growing seasons and the labour involved in the practice of transhumance or booleying more prevalent in Gaelic areas.[33] References to extreme weather and its impacts on society and the natural world (including the destruction of woodlands, mortality of wild animals, riverine and coastal erosion) can be found in the Gaelic Irish Annals into the sixteenth and early seventeenth centuries.[34] These can be supplemented for the sixteenth to eighteenth centuries by a miscellany of

---

32 Also see Chapter 14 by Fenlon, this volume.
33 T. Jordan, *The Quality of Life in Seventeenth-Century Ireland* (Lewiston: Edwin Mellen, 2008), 25–27.
34 For a full compilation of weather from the Irish Annals, see F. Ludlow, 'The Utility of the Irish Annals as a Source for the Reconstruction of Climate', unpublished PhD thesis, University of Dublin (2010). See also K. Hickey, 'The Historic Record of Cold Spells in Ireland', *Irish Geography*, 44 (2011), 303–21, and F. Ludlow, R. Stine, P. Leahy, E. Murphy, P. A. Mayewski, D. Taylor, J. Killen, M.G.L. Baillie, M. Hennessy and G. Kiely, 'Medieval Irish Chronicles Reveal Persistent Volcanic Forcing of Severe Winter Cold Events, 431–1649 CE', *Environmental Research Letters*, 8 (2013), 024035.

sources such as the *Dublin Chronicle*,[35] weather diaries such as that kept by John Kevan for the duke of Ormond (covering 1682–1683),[36] Thomas Neve's weather diary (covering 1711–1725), kept near Lough Neagh,[37] and incidental references to adverse weather in official documents and personal correspondence. Landlords, for example, paid close attention to weather conditions. As Jane Ohlmeyer notes, 'Their concern for their properties is reflected in the obsessive references in their… correspondence to variations in the weather, the ability of their tenants to pay rents, attempts to secure stock and to sell produce.'[38]

The 'Little Ice Age', one of the most-studied climatic phases of recent millennia, spanned the period *c.*1350–*c.*1850. During this time pronounced drops in Northern Hemisphere summer temperatures occurred (particularly from the latter decades of the sixteenth century), with notable advances of mountain glaciers (particularly in the European Alps from the fourteenth century).[39] Considerable spatial and temporal variation complicates this broad picture and has contributed to debate over whether the Little Ice Age was a global or more regional (e.g., European) phenomenon. Some scholars have questioned the utility of applying a single label to describe such a long period, within which multiple potentially distinct climatic oscillations may be identified (some even towards comparatively milder climate), with different severities, durations and spatial extents.[40] Given the relative lack of published high-resolution natural climatic archives for Ireland, the relevance of major climatic features of the Little Ice Age has often been assumed, based upon natural archives and historical records elsewhere in Europe or further afield. It has been noted, however, that the spatial and temporal complexity of climate, even over nominally short distances as between Ireland and England, can render such inferences less reliable.[41]

---

35 See the heavy rain and flood reported for 1523; see A. Fletcher (ed.), 'The Earliest Extant Recension of the Dublin Chronicle: An Edition, with Commentary, of Dublin, Trinity College, MS 543/2/14', in J. Bradley, A. Fletcher and A. Simms (eds.), *Dublin in the Medieval world: Studies in Honour of Howard B. Clarke* (Dublin: Four Courts Press, 2009), 309–409.

36 K. Rohan, *The Climate of Ireland* (2nd edn., Dublin: Stationery Office, 1986); L. Shields, 'The Beginnings of Scientific Weather Observation in Ireland (1684–1708)', *Weather*, 38 (1983), 304–11.

37 F. Dixon, 'An Irish Weather Diary of 1711–1725', *Quarterly Journal of the Royal Meteorological Society*, 85 (1959), 371–85.

38 J. Ohlmeyer, *Making Ireland English: The Irish Aristocracy in the Seventeenth Century* (New Haven and London: Yale University Press, 2012), 372.

39 For a review, see J. Matthews and K. Briffa, 'The "Little Ice Age": Re-evaluation of an Evolving Concept', *Geografiska Annaler*, 87A (2005), 17–36.

40 A. Ogilvie, 'Historical Climatology, Climatic Change, and Implications for Climate Science in the Twenty-first Century', *Climatic Change*, 100 (2010), 33–47.

41 G. Kiely, P. Leahy, F. Ludlow, B. Stefanini, E. Reilly, M. Monk and J. Harris, *Extreme Weather, Climate and Natural Disasters in Ireland* (Johnstown Castle: Environmental Protection Agency, 2010).

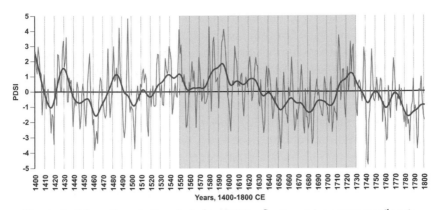

Figure 5. Palmer Drought Severity Index (PDSI) reflecting spring–summer soil moisture, based upon Irish oak tree-ring growth-width measurements, 1400–1800 (1550–1730 is shaded). On the vertical axis, positive values reflect increasing soil moisture, and negative values the opposite (in standardised PDSI units).[42] The thin line shows annual values, with longer-term trends shown in the thick line (representing an 8-point spline smoothing).

In what follows, we draw on natural archives from Ireland, or with known/ potential relevance for Ireland. The scale of changes that occurred in our period is also only apparent when seen in the context of variations over a longer time, and this is reflected in our approach to presenting and reviewing the evidence.

Figure 5 presents a state-of-the-art reconstruction of yearly spring–summer soil moisture for Ireland (1400–1800), known as the Palmer Drought Severity Index (PDSI).[43] As the first such reconstruction using the large numbers of ring-width measurements of precipitation-sensitive Irish oaks compiled in Belfast from the late 1970s onward, the reconstruction is a unique resource for Irish climate history. Relative to the fifteenth century, with its distinct swings between wetter and drier conditions, the reconstruction paints the sixteenth century as one of sustained, if variable, above-average wetness. This subsides by the 1630s from a striking peak in the 1580s and 1590s that prefaces the Nine Years' War. It is thus little surprise that the Irish annals in the 1580s relate how 'Great wind, constant rain … and much tempestuous weather, prevailed successively in these two years' (reported 1582, presumably regarding 1581 and 1582). Similarly in 1585 it was reported that 'There was much rain … so that the greater part of the corn

---

42 Full technical details in E. Cook *et al.*, 'Old World Megadroughts and Pluvials'.
43 Specifically, this is a reconstruction of the self-calibrating PDSI (scPDSI) for Europe, North Africa and the Middle East; see E. Cook *et al.*, 'Old World Megadroughts and Pluvials during the Common Era', *Science Advances*, 1 (2015), e1500561.

of Ireland was destroyed.'[44] In 1586 there was again 'wet weather and unproductive corn', and in 1587 a 'Great mortality amongst the cattle' and a 'great destruction of corn'.[45] For the 1590s Colm Lennon notes 'there can be little doubt that the sequence of appalling summers and autumns … gave rise to mortality on a large scale owing to failure of food supplies'.[46] The onset of a trend toward drier conditions from the 1630s, though punctuated by sporadic reversals, as from 1638 to 1640 in the immediate run up to the 1641 rebellion, is also comparatively sustained, before a return of wetter conditions from 1710 to 1730. Assigning any contributory role for these variations, whether abrupt or longer-term, in the great events and broader historical changes of our period must be undertaken cautiously, but these data provide a means to consider the environmental context against which the history of the period played out.

While no annual resolution temperature reconstruction is available directly using Irish evidence for our period, temperatures tend to vary less in space than precipitation, allowing inferences to be made, with care, from evidence from nearby regions. Figure 6 presents a recent landmark tree-ring-based reconstruction of summer air temperatures that has been specifically tailored to represent broad temperature patterns for the wider European region, including Ireland.[47] After many decades, from the mid-1480s to the mid-1560s, in which summer temperatures varied within a relatively narrow range, they then followed a relentless downward trajectory that reached its nadir during the politically tumultuous 1590s and 1600s. While a rapid recovery occurred thereafter, it was only partial, and the persistence of low average temperatures until the 1720s is a remarkable characteristic of the period, something broadly replicated in many other European temperature reconstructions. Superimposed on this broader trend are individual summers of profound cold, which for the 1550–1730 period include in order of severity: 1601, 1675, 1633, 1608, 1695 and 1596, with 1641, 1606, 1587, 1663 and 1579 comprising the next six most severe (Figure 6).

Of the many contributors to the climatic changes of our period, major explosive volcanic eruptions are perhaps most important. Eruptions primarily impact climate by injecting sulphur dioxide gas (SO_2) into the stratosphere,

44 O'Donovan (ed.), *Annála Ríoghachta Éireann*, v, 1779, 1827.
45 O'Donovan (ed.), *Annála Ríoghachta Éireann*, 1857, and W. Hennessy (ed.), *The Annals of Loch Cé: A Chronicle of Irish Affairs from A.D. 1014 to A.D. 1590* (2 vols., London: Longman, 1871), ii, 479.
46 Colm Lennon, *Sixteenth-Century Ireland*, 8.
47 PAGES 2k Consortium, 'Continental-Scale Temperature Variability during the Past Two Millennia', *Nature Geoscience*, 6 (2013), 339–46.

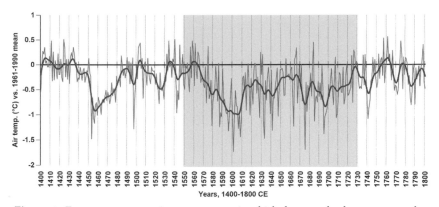

Figure 6. European summer air temperatures, in which the annual values represent the deviation of temperatures from the 1961–1990 average (mean) in °C, for the period 1400–1800 (the 1550–1730 period is shaded), reconstructed by the PAGES 2k Consortium.[48] On the vertical axis, positive values reflect increasing temperature, and negative values the opposite, relative to the 1961–1990 mean. The thin line shows the temperatures at an annual resolution, while longer-term trends are shown in the thick line (representing a 7-point spline smoothing).

where it oxidises to form sulphate aerosol particles that reflect incoming solar (shortwave) radiation to space, cooling the Earth's surface.[49] The observational record of major eruptions does not extend reliably beyond the last 200 years, with eruptions often occurring in locations where written records were infrequently made or have not survived, such as the tropics. In place of written records, work beginning most concertedly in the 1970s has shown elevated concentrations of acids (especially sulphate) in polar ice sheets to be a reliable indicator of explosive volcanism, with modern instrumentation distinguishing even minute changes (parts per billion, ppb) in the sulphate content of the ice. When this content exceeds a certain threshold it may be taken as representing the fallout (deposition) from a major eruption, while the date of this fallout (which may slightly lag behind the eruption date) can be determined by counting the annual layers of snowfall that compress over time into clearly visible bands of ice in locations such as Greenland.

The most recent securely dated record of historic explosive eruptions is presented in Figure 7. The top panel shows sulphate deposition in the NEEM Greenland ice core, 1300 to 1800; here, sudden spikes in annual sulphate levels

---

48 PAGES 2k Consortium, 'Continental-Scale Temperature Variability', 339–46.
49 A. Robock, 'Volcanic Eruptions and Climate', *Reviews of Geophysics* (2000) 38, 191–219; J. Cole-Dai, 'Volcanoes and Climate', *WIREs Climate Change*, 1 (2010), 824–39.

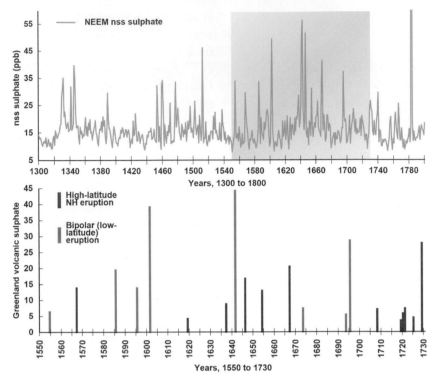

Figure 7. Volcanic Forcing. *Top panel:* annual (non-sea-salt, nss) sulphate values (in parts per billion, ppb) from the NEEM Greenland ice core, 1300–1800, with the 1550–1730 period shaded. Sulphate values for the fissure eruption of Laki (Iceland, starting 1783) are truncated for graphical clarity, as these deposition values are exaggerated by the volcano's proximity to Greenland.

Bottom panel: sulphate values (kg/km²) attributed to explosive eruptions, with background sulphate values removed, 1550–1730, including data from the NEEM and additional Greenland cores.[50]

reveal deposition from explosive eruptions.[51] The figure shows that volcanism is inherently variable in time, and from an historiographical perspective, some periods are more climatically fortunate. In this sense, the 1550 to 1730 period is notably unlucky for the frequency and magnitude of eruptions, having 20 as compared to 14 eruptions in the preceding 181-year period, frequently also of greater magnitude.[52] The bottom panel of Figure 7 presents

50 M. Sigl *et al.*, 'Timing and Climate Forcing of Volcanic Eruptions during the Past 2,500 Years', *Nature*, 523 (2015), 543–9.
51 NEEM stands for North Greenland Eemian Ice Drilling ice core.
52 Excluding Southern Hemisphere mid- to high-latitude eruptions.

a closer look at the years between 1550 and 1730, now solely showing sulphate from major eruptions (i.e., background sulphate deposition not arising from explosive volcanism has been statistically removed). These eruptions are likely to have been primarily responsible for many of the coldest individual summers plotted in Figure 6, with the two largest eruptions depositing considerable volumes of sulphate in 1601 and 1641, dates of obvious significance in Irish history. Explosive eruptions also likely contributed to the broader trend towards colder average summers in the period, with few decades absent of their influence.

Volcanic eruptions can act as historical test-cases of societal response to abrupt climatic shocks, illuminating the character and degree of societal vulnerability in a given era or region. To use these test cases credibly, it is essential to understand the complexities of volcanic climatic impacts. The cooling effect of eruptions on summer temperatures (including late spring/early autumn, generally described as the summer 'half-year' by climatologists) is well known. It may last for several years, and is identifiable for Ireland after modern era eruptions.[53] Their impact on winter (and winter 'half-year') climate is less straightforward, but potentially as significant for more exposed pre-industrial societies. In this, the location (especially latitude) of eruptions has a large bearing on the expected impact. Tropical (low latitude) eruptions have been shown to promote milder and wetter winters over northwest Europe, by promoting a stronger winter westerly airflow and thereby sweeping mild and wet maritime air across northwest Europe.[54] This response is not, however, seen clearly after all tropical eruptions, and the net winter impact may be cooling in some cases, or, if observed for some regions, may be absent for others. It is also possible that the initial winter warming impact from tropical eruptions may give way to cold over the course of several post-eruption winters,[55] or that the cooling impact of sulphate aerosols overwhelms the warming impact of stronger

---

53 S. Galvin, Kieran R. Hickey and Aaron P. Potito, 'Identifying Volcanic Signals in Irish Temperature Observations since AD 1800', *Irish Geography*, 44 (2012), 97–110.
54 Robock, 'Volcanic Eruptions and Climate'; E. Fischer, J. Luterbacher, E. Zorita, S. F. B. Tett, C. Casty and H. Wanner, 'European Climate Response to Tropical Volcanic Eruptions over the Last Half Millennium', *Geophysical Research Letters*, 34 (2007), L05707. A likely mechanism is a differential heating of the stratosphere (caused by sulphate aerosol absorption of outgoing long-wave terrestrial infrared radiation) in the lower latitudes, creating a steepened north–south temperature gradient, that promotes an invigorated westerly airflow.
55 Fischer *et al.*, 'European Climate Response'; for Ireland, see Galvin *et al.*, 'Identifying Volcanic Signals'.

westerly airflows if eruptions release particularly large volumes of sulphur dioxide. High-latitude (e.g., Icelandic) eruptions do not, by contrast, appear to promote a winter warming response, and may be responsible for inducing severe cold in all seasons. The extent to which both tropical and high-latitude eruptions have historically induced cold winters in Ireland is suggested by persistent coincidences between eruptions and cold weather (mainly winter) reported in the Irish Annals.[56] An awareness that the climatic impacts of eruptions are contingent on many factors is thus critical for historians.

The sun provides effectively all energy available to drive the Earth's climate system, with the solar radiation received by the Earth usually described in terms of 'total solar irradiance' (TSI). This is a measure of incoming solar radiation integrated over all wavelengths, including, for example, visible and invisible light (e.g., ultraviolet light at very short wavelengths), and can be expressed in watts received per square metre (w/m²). Only in the later twentieth century, particularly with satellite observations from 1978 onward, was it definitively established that solar irradiance varied continually. Compared to volcanic eruptions, however, it remains less clear whether the character and scale of solar irradiance variations over recent decades, centuries and millennia meaningfully influenced climate. The output of solar radiation progresses through multiple cycles of varying magnitudes, the peaks and troughs of which play out on scales of days, decades and centuries. These are overlain on still longer cycles, the impacts and even existence of which are hard to determine and disentangle, though broad agreement exists on the major variations in our period.

Figure 8 (top panel) shows the famous ~11-year sunspot cycle, as seen in observation of sunspots beginning in 1610 with the advent of telescopic astronomy.[57] Sunspots are solar phenomena consisting of darker and cooler patches on the sun's 'surface'. Despite this, when sunspots are most numerous at the cycle's peak, solar irradiance is also greatest, because the sunspots are more than compensated for by bright patches (*faculae*) that also occur more plentifully toward the cycle's peak.[58] Variations in solar irradiance reaching

---

56 Ludlow *et al.*, 'Medieval Irish Chronicles'.
57 The ~11-year sunspot cycle is also known as the Schwabe Cycle, after German astronomer Samuel Heinrich Schwabe, who in 1843 noted a distinct variation in sunspot frequencies.
58 K. Lang, *The Cambridge Encyclopedia of the Sun* (Cambridge University Press, 2001).

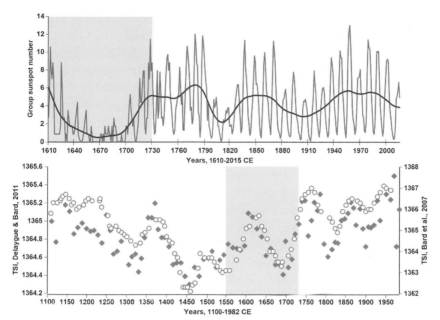

Figure 8. *Top panel:* solar forcing as reflected in yearly counts of the group sunspot number from telescopic observations beginning 1610, showing the ~11-year sunspot cycle (jagged line). The smooth line shows the longer-term trend, using an 8.3-point spline smoothing.[59]

Bottom panel: ice-core-based reconstructions of long-term total solar irradiance (TSI, main text), measured in watts per square metre reaching the Earth's atmosphere. Diamonds correspond to the left hand vertical axis and show the TSI as reconstructed by Delaygue and Bard in 2011, while circles correspond to the right-hand vertical axis and show the Bard *et al.* reconstruction from 2007.[60] Note the different scales on these axes.

the Earth's atmosphere during the ~11-year cycle are, however, small, and so too the direct temperature impact. For example, the TSI increased by only ~0.1% (or ~1 w/m²) from the trough to peak of three recent cycles up

---

59 Group sunspot number (v2.0, 1st July 2015) from the Sunspot Index and Long-term Solar Observations (SILSO) World Data Centre, Royal Observatory of Belgium, Brussels, sidc.be/silso (accessed 13 July 2015). See also: F. Clette, Leif Svalgaard, José M. Vaquero and Edward W. Cliver, 'Revisiting the Sunspot Number. A 400-Year Perspective on the Solar Cycle', *Space Science Reviews*, 186 (2014), 35–103.

60 G. Delaygue and E. Bard, 'An Antarctic view of Beryllium-10 and Solar Activity for the Past Millennium', *Climate Dynamics*, 36 (2011), 2201–2218; E. Bard, G. Raisbeck, G. F. Yiou and J. Jouzel, 'Comment on 'Solar Activity during the Last 1000 yr Inferred from Radionuclide Records', by Muscheler et al. (2007)', *Quaternary Science Reviews*, 26 (2007), 2301–8. Different reconstructions disagree regarding absolute TSI values through time, but generally reproduce a similar trend.

to 2010.[61] Even so, the ~11-year cycle, and more gradual cycles, have been repeatedly linked to notable climate changes, including the Little Ice Age, with work exploring indirect impacts in which 'feedback' processes in the interaction between solar irradiance, the Earth's atmosphere and oceans, may positively reinforce the small initial direct temperature impact.[62] In particular, 'grand solar minima', when the ~11-year cycle weakens for extended periods, may plausibly induce greater direct and indirect impacts, including an increased probability of cold winters in Europe and the northeast Atlantic.[63]

The most famous grand minimum, the 'Maunder Minimum',[64] is traditionally cited as spanning c.1645 to c.1715, a period that witnessed the Cromwellian wars and plantation and the final suppression of the Gaelic Irish. Figure 8 (top panel) shows the marked reduction in observed sunspots associated with this minimum, with the decline arguably setting in from c.1625, perhaps limiting the recovery in temperatures that began c.1610 (Figure 6). The Maunder Minimum was near its deepest in the latter half of the seventeenth century, when an anonymous Dublin author remarked that it was 'not unusual to have frost and deep snows of a fortnight or three weeks continuance; and that twice or thrice, sometimes oftener in a winter'.[65] The Maunder Minimum is one of only 27 grand minima thought to have occurred in the past ~11,000 years and can be placed in a longer-term context beyond the period of telescopic observations using solar irradiance reconstructions based on the levels of cosmogenic isotopes (rare variants of chemical elements) produced in the upper atmosphere in a process influenced by the strength of solar activity.[66] Two well-known reconstructions are shown in Figure 8 (bottom panel) at a resolution too low to resolve the ~11-year cycle, but showing that the

61 J. Lean, 'Cycles and Trends in Solar Irradiance and Climate', WIREs Climate Change, 1 (2010), 111–22.
62 J. Lean, S. Engels and B. van Geel, 'The Effects of Changing Solar Activity on Climate: Contributions from Palaeoclimatological Studies', Journal of Space Weather and Space Climate, 2 (2012), A09.
63 This partly operates by increasing the number of anticyclonic pressure systems with cold northerly or northeasterly winds over the northeast Atlantic and northwest Europe, with clearer skies also allowing greater heat loss to space. M. Lockwood, R. G. Harrison, T. Woollings and S. K. Solanki, 'Are Cold Winters in Europe Associated with Low Solar Activity?', Environmental Research Letters, 5 (2010), 024001.
64 Named after Edward Walter Maunder (1851–1928) who noted reduced sunspots at this time. His wife, Annie Russell Maunder (1868–1947), has only recently had her contribution to this work acknowledged.
65 Anon., 'An Extract of a Letter Written from Dublin to the Publisher, Containing Divers Particulars of a Philosophical Nature …', Philosophical Transactions, 127 (1676), 649.
66 Delaygue and Bard, 'An Antarctic view of Beryllium-10'.

deep Maunder Minimum was closely preceded by the even deeper Spörer Minimum from *c*.1450 to *c*.1550, making these periods key for understanding solar impacts on climate.

The above review reveals the years between 1550 and 1730 as a period of profound climatic volatility and change, and the early modern period is thus particularly relevant for studies of human response, resilience and vulnerability to environmental change. Despite remaining uncertainties, understanding of the character and drivers of these changes is rapidly improving, now increasingly including human-linked drivers such as land-cover changes that alter the *albedo* (reflectivity) of land surfaces, and phases of deforestation/ reforestation in which varying tree populations alter atmospheric concentrations of heat insulating carbon dioxide (CO_2). It has thus been argued that Little Ice Age cooling was part-driven by a large-scale post-Columbian reforestation of the Americas, enabled by massive depopulation from conflict and European-exported diseases.[67] Underlying many of the changes discussed above are particular patterns of atmospheric pressure and circulation, which can also be reconstructed,[68] informing the historian of the changing vigour of the winter westerly winds, for example, and the likelihood of powerful Atlantic cyclones tracking east across Ireland. These were hazardous to maritime trade and communication, and detrimental to settlement in western (often more agriculturally marginal) coastal areas, which bore the full brunt of associated storm surges, salinisation and coastal erosion.[69]

Case Study: The Nine Years' War

Studies that seek to integrate an understanding of past climate (often in terms of the impact of abrupt changes and extreme weather events) into our understanding of human history have a long pedigree, but have proliferated since the 1970s, and particularly during the past decade. Many suggest how the chance intervention of weather has acted to alter the course of major events, often with a focus on military campaigns and the decisions forced upon (or

---

67 W. Ruddiman, *Plows, Plagues and Petroleum: How Humans Took Control of Climate* (Princeton, NJ: Princeton University Press, 2005).

68 P. Ortega, F. Lehner, D. Swingedouw, V. Masson-Delmotte, C. C. Raible, M. Casado and P. Yiou, 'A Model-Tested North Atlantic Oscillation Reconstruction for the Past Millennium', *Nature*, 523 (2015), 71–4.

69 As a model that may prove useful for Ireland, see R. Oram, 'Between a Rock and a Hard Place. Climate, Weather and the Rise of the Lordship of the Isles', in R. Oram (ed.), *The Lordship of the Isles* (Leiden: Brill, 2014), 40–61.

made possible for) participants facing adversarial or facilitative weather conditions. But there are less incidental ways in which climate may be considered to influence history. Abrupt climatic changes, extreme weather and other hazards can be seen as 'revelatory crises' that expose hidden or latent cultural, economic and political fault lines and tensions, revealing them both to contemporaries and, if we are prepared to look, historians.[70] These may be a potent force in catalysing or hastening societal change. Historical studies from many regions have begun to show that violence, conflict, climatic changes and extreme weather have a recurring association;[71] studies of the modern era have also identified associations.[72] The mechanisms underlying any such associations are, however, contested, and are likely to be considerably more complex than acknowledged or allowed for by some studies, often in the absence of input from the humanities and social sciences.[73] There is a need for fine-grained historical analyses that assess the relative contribution of environmental and climatic pressures to any given conflict in its inception, timing, severity and ultimate outcomes, alongside social, political and economic factors.

Although originating in Ulster, the Nine Years' War represented the culmination of growing tensions between the increasingly centralising Protestant state and the Catholic Gaelic Irish and Old English families. Having successfully attracted Spanish assistance, the eventual arrival of Spanish troops in Kinsale, County Cork, in September 1601 at the furthest point from the Gaelic strongholds in Ulster, caused considerable consternation. The English forces under Lord Deputy Mountjoy immediately travelled to Kinsale and laid siege to the Spanish forces, but over the following ten weeks Mountjoy's loss of men as a result of 'cold, sickness, and desertion', as well as lack of food for men and horses, was significant.[74] To relieve the besieged Spanish forces, Hugh O'Neill, second earl of Tyrone, and his O'Donnell allies abandoned their own threatened territories and risked a winter march south. A celebrated moment of that was O'Donnell's escape from Sir George Carew's forces through a frozen pass in the Slieve Felim mountains, County Limerick, in November.

70 J. Solway, 'Drought as a Revelatory Crisis: An Exploration of Shifting Entitlements and Hierarchies in the Kalahari, Botswana', *Development and Change*, 25 (1994), 471–95.
71 See for example, R. Tol and S. Wagner, 'Climate Change and Violent Conflict in Europe over the Last Millennium', *Climatic Change*, 99 (2011), 65–79.
72 S. Hsiang and M. Burke, 'Climate, Conflict, and Social Stability: What Does the Evidence Say?', *Climatic Change*, 123 (2014), 39–55.
73 K. Fan, 'Climatic Change and Dynastic Cycles: A Review Essay', *Climatic Change*, 101 (2010), 565–73.
74 J. McGurk, 'The Kinsale Campaign Siege, Battle and Rout', *Seanchas Ardmhacha: Journal of the Armagh Diocesan Historical Society*, 19:1 (2002), 62.

Mountjoy had sent Carew, lord president of Munster, to intercept O'Donnell, but the onset of a heavy frost allowed O'Donnell's men to traverse the pass, which to that point had been impassable for any army due to recent heavy rains, suggesting that severe cold had already set in.[75] Despite encircling a weakened English army whose supply lines O'Neill and O'Donnell disrupted on their way south, the battle of Kinsale (24 December 1601) ended in defeat for the Irish and Spanish forces, marking the beginning of the end of the Nine Years' War in 1603, setting in train the Flight of the Earls in 1607, and ultimately enabling the Ulster plantation.

The critical winter of 1601/1602 occurred in the immediate climatic aftermath of the great eruption of the Peruvian volcano Huaynaputina (elevation $c.4,850$m) on 19 February 1600, with further eruptive episodes continuing into March.[76] This immense event, reaching point 6 ('Colossal') of 8 on the Volcanic Explosivity Index (VEI),[77] can be identified through sulphate deposited in Greenland as one of the biggest eruptions of the last thousand years. Figure 9 shows the volcanic sulphate measured in the NEEM Greenland ice core for the years 1570 to 1630, in which levels are notably elevated from 1601 to 1602, representing a slight delay between the 1600 eruption date and the transport to Greenland of sulphate from Huaynaputina's tropical location in the southern Peruvian Andes. This eruption is likely responsible for the pronounced drop in European summer temperatures for 1600 (Figure 6, Figure 9). Revealing of the broader geographical significance of this eruption, one tree-ring-density summer temperature reconstruction for the wider Northern Hemisphere registers 1601 as the coldest summer back to the start of this record in 1400.[78] In high-altitude Bristlecone Pine trees from western North America, 1602 also stands out as a notably cold summer with very narrow tree-ring growth,[79] while actual physical damage to tree-rings (i.e., 'frost rings') is found for 1601, indicating exceptionally cold growing season conditions.

75 J. Silke, 'Kinsale Reconsidered', *Studies: An Irish Quarterly Review*, 90 (2001), 415; F. Jones 'The Spaniards and Kinsale, 1601', *Journal of the Galway Archaeological and Historical Society*, 21 (1944), 1–43, 24–8.

76 J.-C. Thouret, 'Reconstruction of the AD 1600 Huaynaputina Eruption Based on the Correlation of Geologic Evidence with Early Spanish Chronicles', *Journal of Volcanology and Geothermal Research*, 115 (2002), 529–70.

77 L. Siebert, T. Simkin and P. Kimberly, *Volcanoes of the World* (3rd edn., Berkeley: University of California Press, 2010).

78 K. Briffa, P. Jones, F. Schweingruber and T. Osborn, 'Influence of Volcanic Eruptions on Northern Hemisphere Summer Temperature over the Past 600 Years', *Nature*, 393 (1998), 450–5.

79 M. Salzer and M. Hughes, 'Bristlecone Pine Tree Rings and Volcanic Eruptions over the Last 5000 Years', *Quaternary Research*, 67 (2007), 57–68.

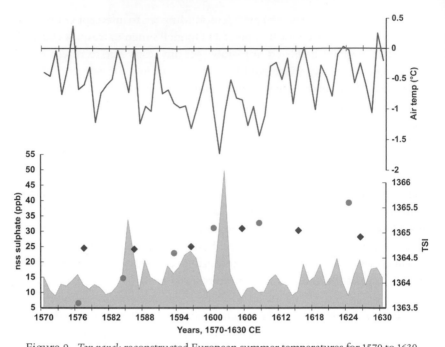

Figure 9. *Top panel:* reconstructed European summer temperatures for 1570 to 1630 relative to 1960 to 1990 mean temperatures (PAGES 2k Consortium data).
Bottom panel: Greenland non-sea-salt sulphate levels from the NEEM ice core in solid shading, and total solar irradiance (TSI) in watts per square metre (diamonds are Bard and Delaygue, 2011 data, and dots are Bard *et al.*, 2007 data).

Climate historians have begun to pay particular attention to instances in which several explosive eruptions occur in close succession, such cases being especially likely to induce marked climatic and societal responses.[80] It is notable therefore that a smaller though substantial eruption of uncertain location (but likely also tropical) closely preceded Huaynaputina, with elevated sulphate deposition spanning the years 1594 to 1597 in Greenland. This earlier eruption also appears to have impacted European temperatures (Figure 9), and both eruptions can in combination be credited with a sizeable contribution to the coldest sustained run of years (*c.*1595 to *c.*1610) in the wider 1550 to 1730 period, with a nadir in the summer of 1600 (Figure 6, Figure 9). Although total solar irradiance was marginally increasing or at least holding

80 C. Kostick and F. Ludlow, 'The Dating of Volcanic Events and their Impacts upon European Climate and Society, 400–800 CE', *European Journal of Post-Classical Archaeologies*, 5 (2015), 7–30.

630

steady across these years, depending upon the reconstruction considered (Figure 9), this did not prevent a protracted period of cold, and it is not until 1611 that temperatures began a partial recovery for any sustained period (Figure 9).

Documentary sources supply crucial evidence on the impact of these eruptions in other seasons, importantly adding to the picture of summer season impacts identifiable in the tree-ring-based evidence above. Sir Josias Bodley, an English soldier and military engineer, recalled conditions at Kinsale 'at Christmas of last year [i.e., of winter 1601/02] when we suffered intolerable cold, dreadful labour, and a want of almost everything…'.[81] In a colourful account of his visit to Lecale, County Down, in 1602/03, he further described conditions in early January 1603 as being 'very cold' and 'exceedingly cold out of doors', also remarking of Newry: 'nor was there any bread, except biscuits, even in the Governor's house'.[82] Thomas Stafford's *Pacata Hibernia* (first published 1633) details key moments of the Nine Years' War from the perspective of crown forces, with plentiful descriptions of weather and its military consequences. A brief sampling includes for 1600 a report of 'continual rain that had lately fallen in great abundance' (at some point before 23 July) that meant that 'the mountain of Sleulogher was impassable for carriages'.[83] In 1601 munitions arrived wet, with later inclement weather from at least 3 October, continuing with instances of 'extreme foulness of weather' and by November a 'great extreme frost', possibly the same that aided O'Donnell's dramatic escape through the Slieve Felim mountains.[84] Lughaidh Ó Cléirigh's *Life of Aodh Ruadh O Domhnaill* (Red Hugh O'Donnell), detailing events from the perspective of the Gaelic Ulster forces, clearly cited interlinked military concerns over cold and hunger in 1601.[85] The *Four Masters* stated that in 1603 'an intolerable famine prevailed all over Ireland', and earlier in their account of this year they note the mortality of 'vast numbers' in the territory of Niall O'Donnell (in northwest Ulster) from 'cold and famine', no doubt

---

81 W. Reeves (ed.), 'A Visit to Lecale, in the County of Down, in the Year 1602–03', *Ulster Journal of Archaeology*, 2 (1854), 73–99, 337 (in hypertext at www.ucc.ie/celt/online/T100074.html, accessed 25 July 2016).
82 Reeves (ed.), 'A Visit to Lecale', 331, 336 and 330.
83 Thomas Stafford, *Pacata Hibernia; or, a History of the Wars in Ireland, During the Reign of Queen Elizabeth* (2 vols., 2nd edn., Dublin: Hibernia-Press Company, 1820), i, 126. The internal chronology of this source is often unclear; our specified dates are not always fully certain.
84 Thomas Stafford, *Pacata Hibernia*, ii, 342, 355, 366, 387.
85 P. Walsh and C. O Lochlainn (eds.), *Life of Aodh Ruadh O Domhnaill* (Dublin: Educational Company of Ireland, 1948), 131, 323, 327, 329.

exacerbated by the theft of 'several thousand heads of cattle' by the followers of Ruairi O'Donnell.[86]

The weather in the final years of the Nine Years' War was, in sum, likely to have been exceptionally severe and worsened by volcanism, affecting all seasons and lasting several years. The occurrence of these conditions and the winding down of the Nine Years' War after the defeat at Kinsale are hardly unrelated. Certainly, the twinned impacts of poor weather and the burden of an ongoing, multi-year conflict diminished the Irish environment's capacity to provision armies and, as Colm Lennon notes, 'closely allied to intemperate weather as a harbinger of death... was disease', with visitations of plague in 1597 and 1602–1604.[87] These weather conditions, and the known links between food scarcity and the spread of disease between large bodies of troops forced into close quarters, were doubtless capitalised upon by the Gaelic chieftains when choking the English supply lines to Kinsale. But such conditions could bite in both directions. Thus, while the hereditary professional historians patronised by the Gaelic nobility were not beyond embellishing accounts of their patrons' military exploits with suitably dramatic weather, their description of O'Donnell's fear 'of the effects of the cold, rough, wintry season on his soldiers ... watching and guarding every night against the English' in the autumn of 1600 was not hyperbole.[88] After Kinsale, the continuance of severe weather likely compounded the scorched earth strategy of Lord Deputy Mountjoy in Ulster as crown forces neutralised the support base of this final substantial Gaelic stronghold, with supporters of O'Neill surrendering to Mountjoy in 1602, and O'Neill's surrender in 1603.

Beyond the case of the Nine Years' War, evidence from other countries and eras suggests that extreme weather may have acted to repeatedly constrain or terminate certain forms of conflict, such as large-scale, organised (e.g., interstate) warfare reliant upon standing armies and requiring considerable natural resources.[89] However, the influence of weather on violence and conflict is context dependent, plausibly varying by the types of weather and violence or conflict under consideration. Studies thus suggest that climatic stressors may trigger (or make more overt) some forms of violence and conflict, including more spontaneous internal unrest and revolt, by promoting

---

86 O'Donovan (ed), *Annála Ríoghachta Éireann*, vi, 2349 and 2347.
87 Lennon, *Sixteenth-Century Ireland*, 8.
88 O'Donovan (ed), *Annála Ríoghachta Éireann*, vi, 2347.
89 F.E. Huggett, *The Land Question and European Society* (London: Thames and Hudson, 1975), 58; U. Büntgen and N. Di Cosmo, 'Climatic and Environmental Aspects of the Mongol Withdrawal from Hungary in 1242 CE', *Scientific Reports*, 6 (2016), 25606.

scarcity and increasing competition for remaining resources.[90] This may be particularly so when societal resilience to extreme weather is diminished, historically including cases in which political, religious or ethnic groups have been marginalised, limiting their capacity to adapt to or mitigate impacts of extreme weather (e.g., by switching to alternative income and food sources).

Case study: The 1641 Rebellion

The reasons underlying the occurrence and timing of this event are contested, but in charting levels of provincial turmoil and unrest in the generation before 1641, David Edwards disputed the notion that the rebellion was a 'bolt from the blue', as is sometimes conceived. He notes the 'near-constant spark and crackle of localised rebellion' in the decades following the end of the Nine Years' War in 1603, particularly in areas bordering newly planted lands, and signalling the ongoing potential for a wider conflagration as began in October 1641.[91] Raymond Gillespie noted the sequence of poor harvests or grain shortages that occurred in the run up to the rebellion, with especially noteworthy events in 1621–1624, 1629–1631 and indeed 1639–1641.[92] He remarked that the latter two of these 'episodes created widespread disruption and were associated with outbreaks of disease, increased pauperisation and emigration both to England and continental Europe', while the difficulties of 1639–1641 'resulted in conditions which, when combined with fears of religious persecution and political instability, formed the background to the rebellion which broke out in late October 1641'.[93]

Many scholars have remarked upon the severity of cold in Europe in the 1640s, with Thomas E. Jordan noting that cold weather from 1641–1643 would have compounded the social disaster wrought by the 1641 rebellion.[94] Natural archives offer the prospect of furthering our understanding of the environmental context of the rebellion, with ice-core data revealing a substantial eruption in the mid to high latitudes of the Northern Hemisphere through elevated Greenland sulphate deposition in 1637 (Figure 10). The climatic impacts of this eruption likely included the cold summer of 1639

90 Hsiang and Burke, 'Climate, Conflict, and Social Stability'.
91 Edwards, 'Out of the blue?', 109.
92 Gillespie, 'Meal and Money'. Also see Chapter 21 by Gillespie, this volume.
93 Gillespie, 'Meal and Money', 76. See also R. Gillespie, 'The End of an Era: Ulster and the Outbreak of the 1641 Rising', in C. Brady and R. Gillespie (eds.), *Natives and Newcomers: Essays on the Making of Irish Colonial Society* (Dublin: Irish Academic Press, 1986), 191–214.
94 Jordan, *The Quality of Life in Seventeenth-Century Ireland*, 12.

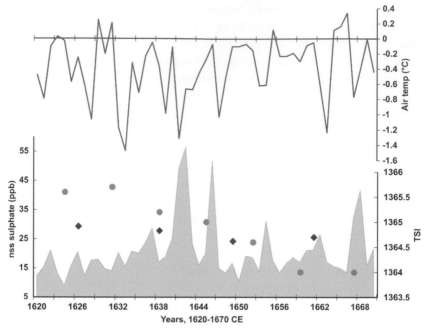

Figure 10. *Top panel:* reconstructed European summer temperatures for 1620 to 1670 relative to the 1960 to 1990 mean (PAGES 2k Consortium data).

Bottom panel: Greenland non-sea-salt sulphate levels from the NEEM ice-core in solid shading, and total solar irradiance (TSI) in watts per square metre (diamonds are Bard and Delaygue, 2011 data, and dots are Bard *et al.*, 2007 data).

seen in the PAGES 2k reconstruction, contributing to the agricultural difficulties experienced from 1639 to 1641, with a further contribution by the much larger eruption that deposited sulphate in Greenland from 1641 to 1642 (Figure 10). Because notable sulphate was also deposited in Antarctica at this time, the source eruption is considered tropical, with one candidate being Parker volcano, Mindanao island, in the Philippines, which erupted violently between December 1640 to January 1641, reaching VEI point 5 ('Paroxysmic'). Hokkaido-Komagatake in Japan may have contributed further to the severe weather of these years, erupting from July to October 1640 and also reaching VEI point 5.[95]

95 See the Global Volcanism Program entry for Parker at volcano.si.edu/volcano.cfm?vn=271011 and for Hokkaido-Komagatake at volcano.si.edu/volcano.cfm?vn=285020. Both eruptions may have contributed to Greenland sulphate at this time, and further contributions are plausible, e.g., from the 1641 Kelut Eruption,

All these eruptions occurred at the onset of the famous Maunder sunspot minimum. Though usually cited as spanning *c*.1645 to *c*.1715, solar activity was already on the wane by the time of the rebellion, having begun a precipitous decline from *c*.1625 (Figure 8), potentially amplifying the climatic impact of these eruptions. The PAGES 2k temperature reconstruction identifies 1641 as experiencing the second coldest European summer in the 50-year period plotted in Figure 10, while the broader geographical impacts of the eruption(s) at this time can be identified in the same natural archives examined above for Huaynaputina in 1600. Thus, in high-altitude Bristlecone Pine trees from western North America, 1641 registers particularly narrow growth,[96] indicating a severely cold growing season. The previously-cited tree-ring-density summer temperature reconstruction for the wider Northern Hemisphere also places 1641 as the third coldest summer since the start of this record in 1400, just superseded by 1601 and the famous 1816 European 'year without a summer' caused by the 1815 eruption of Tambora in Indonesia, an event ranked at point 7 ('Super-Colossal') on the VEI.[97]

Documentary evidence paints a grim picture. A letter (dated September 1642) from John Vaughan and other notables in search of aid for the city of Londonderry noted that 'this city, the only refuge for those parts so grievously afflicted with wants and sickness … is not able to abide that inevitable dissolution which famine and cold will enforce it to before this winter be passed'. He added that 'Since December last have been buried in this little town 800 souls, and it is to be feared without relief 100 more shall perish.'[98] The testimonies contained in the 1641 Depositions also furnish abundant descriptions of weather during winter 1641/42, showing that the cold described above by Vaughan was not run-of-the-mill, with many widows, especially from Ulster and Leinster, commenting on the 'cold snowy weather' and 'the extremity of the winter'.[99] While the question of exaggeration may hang over the evidence of the Depositions, the weather conditions described are consistent with the expected climatic aftermath of significant explosive eruptions in *c*.1641, compounded by the impacts of the closely preceding eruption in *c*.1637.

Indonesia, reaching point 4, 'Cataclysmic', on the VEI (volcano.si.edu/volcano.cfm?vn=263280). All entries were accessed on 2 May 2016.

96 Salzer and Hughes, 'Bristlecone Pine Tree Rings'.

97 Briffa, 'Influence of Volcanic Eruptions'. See also: volcano.si.edu/volcano.cfm?vn=264040 (accessed 02 May 2016).

98 J. Hogan (ed), *Letters and Papers Relating to the Irish Rebellion between 1642–46* (Dublin: Irish Manuscripts Commission, 1936), 120.

99 See Ms 836, fo. 87r and see Ms 831, fo. 77v, Trinity College Dublin. For details of extreme conditions faced by refugees who 'perished by cold and want', see Ms 815, fo.

In sum, natural and written archives confirm a notable environmental context for the 1641 rebellion, in which volcanically induced climatic shocks in an era of low solar activity can be plausibly suggested as a trigger for violence in the context of the great societal transformations in the preceding decades, including the marginalisation of large numbers of the island's population, including former *élites*, and the increasingly precarious subsistence base of many Gaelic Irish. Our argument is not that extreme weather *caused* the rebellion, but that the chance occurrence of very severe weather at a time of profound societal change and tension played a part in the timing and scale of events. In considering David Edwards's question of whether the rebellion was inevitable, had the undermining the Catholic population been less severe, greater resilience may have been afforded against the extreme weather of 1640/41, and the likelihood of a major rebellion consequently lessened. Yet it might also be hypothesised that had the social and economic diminishment of the Catholic population progressed even further before 1640, there might have been insufficient capacity to mount a rebellion on the scale of 1641. Though counterfactual, such thinking can help frame other instances in which weather extremes both did and did not coincide with violence and conflict.

Conclusion

The medieval economic historian Bruce M.S. Campbell has called upon historians to recognise nature as a protagonist in human history,[100] while climate historian Christian Pfister has called for a greater focus upon societal vulnerability to extreme weather,[101] and environmental historian John R. McNeill has emphasised that 'just about anything prior to 1880 is underserved by environmental historians'.[102] For political historians (or history-proper, as often traditionally conceived) nature remains largely absent, with history playing out on a blank, or at least static, canvas. It is not a unique observation to associate this absence of the environment in the great works of nineteenth- and

338r, Trinity College Dublin. All available at 1641.tcd.ie (accessed 28 March 2016). We thank Jane Ohlmeyer for suggesting these references.

100 B. Campbell, 'Nature as Historical Protagonist: Environment and Society in Preindustrial England', *The Economic History Review*, 63 (2010), 281–314.

101 C. Pfister, 'The Vulnerability of Past Societies to Climatic Variation: A New Focus for Historical Climatology in the Twenty-First Century', *Climatic Change*, 100 (2010), 5–31.

102 J. McNeill, 'Future Research Needs in Environmental History: Regions, Eras, Themes', in K. Coulter and C. Mauch (eds.), *The Future of Environmental History: Needs and Opportunities* (Munich: Rachel Carson Center for Environment and Society, 2011), 13.

twentieth-century history with ongoing political apathy over human-driven climate change. As natural scientists develop new palaeoclimatic reconstructions, it is thus little surprise that they have begun to apply their data to questions of the fortunes of past societies, receiving little input from historians, and often simplistically treating agricultural pressures as the lynchpin linking climatic change to social change in a manner that some scholars would label 'neo-environmental determinism'.[103]

Irish climate between 1550 and 1730 experienced some of the most profound changes (often towards colder, and less stable conditions) of the second millennium. It also exhibited a recovery from the deepest trough of the Little Ice Age by the early decades of the eighteenth century, coinciding with a period of economic productivity, the growing fortunes of the Ascendancy and the remodelling of much of the Irish landscape. While caution must be exercised to avoid environmentally deterministic interpretations, situating these events in an appropriate environmental context offers an opportunity to understand better the difficulties and opportunities faced by the new settlers and the dispossessed Irish. For scholars of Irish history to ignore the potential role of these environmental changes – either considering them an irrelevance, or because of a lack of access to or familiarity with natural archives and palaeoclimatic reconstructions – heightens the risk of producing only a partial picture of what drove episodes of major historical change, and diminishes the role of history in informing society of where it is now, and where it may be going.[104]

103 G. Judkins, M., Smith and E. Keys, 'Determinism within Human-Environment Research and the Rediscovery of Environmental Causation', *The Geographical Journal*, 174 (2008), 17–29.
104 Francis Ludlow was supported by a Marie Skłodowska – Curie individual fellowship with additional support from the PAGES Volcanic Impacts on Climate & Society Working Group, and the Centre for Environmental Humanities, TCD.

25

Afterword: Interpreting the History of Early Modern Ireland: From the Sixteenth Century to the Present

NICHOLAS CANNY

The history of early modern Ireland was being written even as the momentous events of that age were unfolding. Authors wrote either to support government efforts to promote the Protestant Reformation in Ireland or to sustain the Irish-born clergy, many of them trained in the Catholic seminaries of Counter-Reformation Europe, in persuading Ireland's population to remain Catholic. Protagonists were adapting to the Irish context confessional histories that had been written to justify religious disputes throughout Europe, but the Irish situation was more complex because the Protestant reform effort was linked to England's assertion of political authority over all parts of Ireland and a reassignment of official positions and landed property to those on whom it could rely. In this context, loyalty to the state became associated with Protestantism when most Protestants were British-born people, or their children, who had settled recently in Ireland.

While we can identify what histories were written on both sides, we know little of the readership of texts. Therefore notions of the 'enduring influence' or 'relative importance' of particular histories were suggested only in the nineteenth century when several early modern compositions were re-edited, or translated into English from Latin or Irish, to lend authority to nineteenth-century arguments.

Conflicting Histories of the Sixteenth Century

The opinions of Richard Stanihurst, a Dublin humanist with an Oxford education, were certainly known to contemporaries, since some of his writings appeared in two successive editions (1577, 1587) of the widely-consulted Holinshed's *Chronicles*.[1] Stanihurst, on the authority of Gerald of Wales, contended that

---

1 The Irish section to the first Holinshed edition is entitled *The Historie of Ireland from the First Inhabitation ...1509, Collected by Raphaell Holinshed, and Continued ... 1547 by Richard*

Ireland had been brought into historical time only with the first English conquest of the twelfth century, and he agreed with Gerald that the Gaelic Irish were then a depraved people, whose principal lords had submitted to King Henry II as the rightful ruler of Ireland. Thereafter, according to Stanihurst, Ireland's history concerned the efforts of the descendants of those original conquerors, including his own family, to uphold the civil conditions that had been introduced to Ireland by King Henry II and to resist the efforts of the barbaric Gaelic Irish to expel them. Stanihurst published a 'Description of Ireland' in Holinshed to demonstrate that the Gaelic population of his generation was still barbaric, and to remind his English audience that the descendants of the conquerors (identified later in the sixteenth century as the Old English) had retained the civility of their forebears more scrupulously than had England's own population, and were therefore best equipped to complete the reform of Ireland.

Stanihurst developed this polemic because several English-born Protestant officials were asserting that only those who had proven their loyalty to the crown by becoming Protestant could promote the reform of Ireland. This was stated more emphatically in 1587 by John Hooker, alias Vowell, an antiquarian of strong Protestant convictions from Exeter who had been previously involved with Ireland, and who edited the Irish section of the second edition of Holinshed's *Chronicle*. What Stanihurst had previously written was reproduced in this edition, but it was now juxtaposed with Hooker's own 'History of Ireland 1546–1586', which challenged Stanihurst's claims concerning the civility of the Old English.

Hooker, like Stanihurst, believed that the purpose of history was to teach by example, but having taken account of what Gerald of Wales, and then Stanihurst, had written of the barbarism of the Gaelic Irish, and having studied Ireland's recent past, he concluded that all one could learn from it was of 'the too great and wondrous works of God, both of his severe judgement against traitors, rebels and disobedient, and of his mercy and loving kindness upon the obedient and dutiful'.[2] He illustrated his difference with Stanihurst by identifying lords of English ancestry as those primarily responsible for Ireland's disorders. Thus, for Hooker, the Kildare rebellion of the 1530s, which Stanihurst had treated as an avoidable accident, was a pre-meditated rejection of the authority of King Henry VIII by a lord of English blood.

Stanyhurst (London, 1577); that to the second edition is entitled *The Second Volume of Chronicles Containing the Description, Conquest, Inhabitation and Troublesome Estate of Ireland first Collected by Raphael Holinshed and … Continued … until this Present Time of Sir John Perrot…by John Hooker, alias Vowell* (London, 1587).

2 *Second Volume*, 103.

Then he emphasised that the rebellion of 1569–70, where his own life had been threatened, had been led by the brothers of the earl of Ormond and the cousin of the earl of Desmond, and when Hooker discussed the even more recent rebellion of Gerald Fitzgerald, sixteenth earl of Desmond and his kindred 'against her scared Majesty' he described the involvement of a family of English descent with foreign intruders to oppose a legitimate English monarch as a 'most unnatural' act. Finally, in detailing the suppression of that rebellion in Munster, Hooker attributed the resultant desolation and depopulation of Munster as 'a heavy but a just judgement of God upon such a Pharoicall and stiffnecked people'.[3]

We can be certain that Stanihurst, who, at this point, had become a voluntary Catholic exile on Continental Europe (where he would later become a priest), would have dissented both from Hooker's linking the lessons to be gleaned from history with Protestant eschatology, and his citing the overthrow of the Fitzgerald house of Desmond – one of the prime Old English lineages – to exemplify the justice of divine punishment. And Stanihurst would have been especially distraught at Hooker's final conclusion that the 'obedient and the dutiful' in Munster (and in Ireland generally) were Protestant in religion and mostly of English birth.

Hooker's contentions were reiterated in many texts (in manuscript and in print) by English authors who considered how Munster, and Ireland more generally, might be reformed. In Edmund Spenser's *A View of the Present State of Ireland* (1596, published 1633), the optimism exuded by Hooker, when a plantation for Munster was being launched, had given way to pessimism because the plantation conditions had not been fulfilled and the settlers left exposed to attack.[4] The predicted onslaught duly came in 1598, when rebels overthrew the plantation. Then, the surviving settlers cried for vengeance upon the perpetrators and identified those killed as Protestant martyrs.[5]

Early Seventeenth-Century Histories of the Early Modern

Protestants in Ireland (mostly of English birth) were thus provided with an interpretation of Ireland's history designed to sustain them into the future.

---

3 *Second Volume*, 458–60.
4 See N. Canny, *Making Ireland British, 1580–1650* (Oxford University Press, 2001), 42–55.
5 See H. Morgan, ' "Tempt not God too long, O Queen": Elizabeth and the Irish Crisis of the 1590s', in B. Kane and V. McGowan-Doyle (eds.), *Elizabeth I and Ireland* (Cambridge University Press, 2014), 209–38.

As the seventeenth century progressed and as the numbers of Protestants in Ireland increased – due both to their being assigned land in plantations, and being appointed to civil, ecclesiastical and military positions – subsequent Protestant authors modified and updated their narrative to take account of changing circumstances. The core message remained that Ireland's history involved a divinely monitored struggle between good and evil.

Educated Catholics were aware of such literature but had scant opportunity to challenge it in print when Ireland was torn by a war that ended only with the death of Queen Elizabeth in 1603 and the surrender of all outstanding government opponents. As the war proceeded, Catholic bishops claimed martyrdom for all Catholics, especially all Catholic clergy, who were killed or executed, and these records were later used by Irish scholars who composed Catholic interpretations of Ireland's ancient and recent history to counter Protestant arguments. For them, as for their Protestant counterparts, defeat was success postponed, and they sought to defend Ireland's Catholic population, in the past as in the present, from the calumnies of their opponents, and to guide them for future actions that would enable them to maintain, or recover, their positions and to practice their faith.

While Catholic historians of Ireland were agreed on objectives, they experienced difficulty in deciding upon a common narrative. They were united in asserting that English Protestant soldiers had recently coarsened life, destroyed property and desecrated revered places and objects, and in identifying these calamities as a divine punishment for their own shortcomings and a spur to amendment. After that, glaring interpretative differences emerged between various authors, determined principally by whether they came from Gaelic or Old English backgrounds. Opinion was especially divided concerning how and when Ireland had become civil, and what obligations Catholic subjects owed Protestant rulers.

Old English authors who attended seminaries in Spanish territories were politically compromised because most of their kin had remained neutral, or had even fought for the English crown, during the recent war in Ireland, which the Spanish monarchy, like the Irish bishops, had deemed a Catholic cause. Moreover, while Old English students attended seminaries on the Continent because the training of priests was prohibited in Ireland, they continued to represent themselves as loyal subjects of the English monarch, not least because their patrons were substantial proprietors in Ireland who were negotiating with England's Protestant monarchs to achieve some religious and political concessions for Catholics.

David Rothe, who would later return to Ireland as Catholic bishop of Ossory, represented this Old English position when, writing from Spain, he endorsed Stanihurst's views on the 'barbarism' of the Gaelic Irish, and on the beneficial impact of England's relationship with Ireland until King Henry VIII had broken with Rome. Notwithstanding the heresy of Henry VIII, Edward and Elizabeth, Rothe insisted that the continued allegiance of the Old English to Catholicism had not compromised a centuries-old political loyalty as was proven during the recent war. He hoped that Catholics in Ireland would be rewarded for this by being granted the same civil rights as English and Scottish subjects and the entitlement to practice their religion privately. To this end he favoured continued peace between the British and Spanish monarchies.[6]

Here, Rothe was at odds with authors of Gaelic background such as Philip O'Sullivan Beare who published from Lisbon in 1621 advocating an abandonment of the peace that had existed between England and Spain since 1604, and recommending that hostilities should commence with an invasion of Ireland. This, he claimed, was justified because those Gaelic lords who had supported the Spanish force that had been sent to assist them in 1601 had been deprived of their patrimonies and forced into exile. Since only change was likely to effect a reversal of fortune for those who had fought for their faith and for Spain, O'Sullivan Beare, and like-minded Gaelic authors, constructed a history of Ireland's past (including its early modern past) that would justify a renewal of conflict in Ireland with military support from Spain. Spain, according to O'Sullivan Beare, was further obliged to assist the Gaelic nobility because as descendants of the *Miles Hispanus*, or Milesians, who had occupied Ireland some thousands of years previously, they belonged to the same stock as Spain's own nobility.

O'Sullivan Beare also drew upon Gaelic sources, and on the lives of Irish saints being compiled by Irish scholars on the Continent, to sustain his assertions, and he rejected the narrative of Ireland's past that associated civility with Englishness, which had been popularised by Gerald of Wales and rehearsed by recent Old English authors, including Stanihurst and Rothe. For O'Sullivan Beare, all association with England had proven pernicious for Ireland and even more so since Protestantism had made the contact malignant. He concluded therefore that the only people in Ireland capable of upholding Catholicism were those of Gaelic ancestry who would require military support from Spain to help them achieve their purpose. In arguing his case,

---

6 On Rothe, see I. Campbell, *Renaissance Humanism and Ethnicity Before Race: The Irish and the English in the Seventeenth Century* (Manchester University Press, 2013). Also see Chapter 20 by Campbell, this volume.

O'Sullivan Beare, and those in his tradition, questioned the religious orthodoxy of the Catholic Old English, while castigating all Protestants whether of
English, Old English or Gaelic lineages. The Old English fell short of being
true Catholics, according to O'Sullivan Beare, both because they had failed
to support the Spanish force sent to assist the Catholic cause in Ireland, and
because they were currently negotiating with a Protestant monarchy without
papal sanction.[7]

The first to attempt bridging the divide between these conflicting Catholic
interpretations of Ireland's past was Geoffrey Keating, a priest-historian whose
Foras Feasa ar Éirinn, written in the Irish language, proved immediately influential. Keating, like Stanihurst and Rothe, was of Old English lineage, and,
like Rothe and O'Sullivan Beare, had been educated on the Continent, albeit
in France rather than Spain. However, as has been documented by Bernadette
Cunningham, Keating did much of his research and writing in Ireland and his
work was circulated extensively in manuscript copies at an early date, and in
an English manuscript translation some decades later. Like O'Sullivan Beare,
he praised the Gaelic archive that had been traduced by authors (Old English
Catholics as well as English Protestants) writing in the tradition of Gerald of
Wales. His essential proposition was that Gaelic sources revealed that indigenous society in Ireland had so approximated Christian living that the pure
Christian religion, brought to Ireland by St Patrick, had taken immediate root
there and flourished until the Protestant Reformers had substituted greed and
disorder for hospitality and tranquillity. As he created a counter-memory and
counter-chronology to that cultivated by critics of Gaelic Ireland, he looked
favourably at the cultural interactions that, he contended, had developed over
time between families of Gaelic and English ancestry, and that, he claimed,
had effected a hybridisation of peoples and cultures that had produced a single Irish Catholic people who had remained steadfast in their faith. Keating's
admiration for the melding of the two traditional populations of Ireland may
be due to his having been pastorally active in Ireland when Catholic leaders
were negotiating with the crown to achieve greater religious and political
liberties.[8]

Keating's admiration for Gaelic culture was matched on the Protestant side
by James Ussher who, like Keating, was of Old English lineage, but from
a Dublin family that had conformed to Protestantism. Ussher was an early

---

7 On O'Sullivan Beare, see Campbell, *Renaissance Humanism.*
8 On Keating see B. Cunningham, *The World of Geoffrey Keating: History, Myth and Religion
in Seventeenth-Century Ireland* (Dublin: Four Courts Press, 2000).

graduate of Trinity College, Dublin, who, after he had become professor of divinity there and begun to reflect on how to convert Irish Catholics to Protestantism, noted the extent to which they had been alienated from the state and its religion by the opinions and actions of Protestant clergy and officials. As he, like Keating, proposed a more accommodating attitude towards his fellow countrymen of Gaelic descent , he reappraised Ireland's ancient past, suggesting that there was nothing in Gaelic culture that rendered it incompatible with Christianity. Rather, he contended, the ancient Irish had embraced the Christian message preached by St Patrick because they were already a civil people, and the church established there by Patrick had been close in form and doctrine to the true religion instituted by Christ and his apostles, and had subsequently produced many holy men who had become evangelists in England and on the Continent after Christianity had been dimmed by barbaric invasion. However, according to Ussher, this Christian church, like all Christian communities throughout Europe, had later been corrupted by the papacy and required the Protestant Reformation to restore it to its original purity.[9]

Transformations after 1641

This generous Protestant interpretation of Ireland's history was perpetuated in the antiquarian writings of Sir James Ware who, as Mark Williams has remarked, had come into contact with Ussher during his student days at Trinity College, Dublin.[10] However, following the Catholic uprising of 22 October 1641, the well-tempered attitudes of Ussher and Keating found little favour in Ireland. Thereafter, the atrocities perpetrated both by the Catholic insurgents of 1641 and by the government forces that took eleven years to restore English authority over Ireland, coloured most of what was subsequently written of Ireland's past.

Those upholding the Protestant interest satisfied themselves with a flood of emotive pamphlets explaining the evils that had befallen them, until, in 1646, a comprehensive account of what had happened, and the circumstances that preceded it, was provided in Sir John Temple *The Irish Rebellion*. Temple was master of the rolls in Dublin when the 1641 insurrection happened, and

---

9 On Ussher, see A. Ford, *James Ussher: Theology, History and Politics* (Oxford University Press, 2007), esp. 123–32.
10 M. Williams, 'History, the Interregnum and the Exiled Irish', in M. Williams and S. P. Forrest (eds.), *Constructing the Past: Writing Irish History, 1600–1800* (Woodbridge: Boydell and Brewer, 2010), 27–48.

he wrote to argue why no terms should be offered to Catholics because of the iniquities they had perpetrated. His work was a 'history' to the extent that he linked his description of the atrocities that he attributed to the Catholic insurgents of 1641 with a general history of Ireland that detailed previous challenges to English authority. This suggested that the eruption of 1641 was an entirely predictable onslaught by barbarians upon a civil people and by malignant papists upon true believers. He, following Hooker's example, cited Gerald of Wales on the barbarism of Ireland's indigenous inhabitants who had resisted the overtures of a succession of English missionaries, until King Henry II undertook 'to conquer Ireland and reduce those beastly men unto the way of truth'. However, according to Temple, all subsequent efforts to introduce civil institutions and colonies to Ireland had been cancelled by the barbarians, so that no semblance of civility existed until Queen Elizabeth finally conquered the country, thus making it possible for British undertakers to establish 'colonies' there. The apparent Irish acquiescence in this was counterfeit, and the Catholics, who had been permitted 'the private exercise of all their religious rites and ceremonies' had been secretly plotting 'the universal destruction of all the British and Protestants there planted'.

While Temple considered priests responsible for the planned massacre, the Irish had been able to launch their attack upon civil living and the Protestant religion because the government had permitted them to live 'promiscuously among the British in all parts'. For Temple, therefore, the lesson of history was that all Catholics should be kept at bay and the authorities should have 'such a wall of separation set up betwixt the Irish and British as it shall not be in their [the Irish] power to rise up (as now and in all former ages they have done) to destroy and root them [the British] out in a moment'. Then, following the example of what had been written of the Munster revolt of 1598 he identified as martyrs all Protestants who had been killed following the 1641 rebellion. To this end, Temple cited liberally from the sworn testimony (now known as the 1641 Depositions) that had been collected from those Protestants who had survived the onslaught.[11]

Pre-existing divisions within the Catholic community became more acute when the initial rebellion was followed by a war that ended only in 1659. Therefore Catholics experienced difficulty in agreeing on a common explanation of the events leading up to 1641. Essentially, wealthier Catholic

---

11 For these and further citations from the Temple text, see N. Canny, '1641 in a Colonial Context', in M. Ó Siochrú and J. Ohlmeyer (eds.), *Ireland 1641* (Manchester University Press, 2013), esp. 59–63.

proprietors, mostly of Old English lineage, denied involvement and continued to seek some accommodation with succeeding English authorities, while those associated with the Gaelic leadership, including Archbishop Rinuccini, the papal nuncio, saw no reason to apologise for their past actions and wished to continue fighting until they attained total victory. In so far as Catholics held any common position, it was that they had been forced to take up arms to defend themselves from an assault that was being planned by officials in the Dublin government supported by anti-Catholic members of England's parliament. Old English authors insisted, however, that it was discontented proprietors in Ulster, many of them in financial difficulty, who had sparked the insurrection of 1641, and that the Old English had become involved with the Catholic Confederacy only when officials in Dublin and officers in the army insisted that all Catholics were equally culpable for what government officials described as a projected massacre of Ireland's Protestants.

Moderate Catholic authors agreed with Temple's description of the harmony and prosperity that had obtained in Ireland in the years preceding the rebellion, but insisted that their contentedness had been genuine rather than simulated. Authors of Gaelic background, whose patrons had suffered from plantation, saw nothing to admire in Ireland's condition before the rebellion, and they attributed the totality of the defeat that, by 1659, had been inflicted on all Catholic armies in Ireland, as a punishment from God because some in the Confederacy (mostly from Old English backgrounds) had been excommunicated from the Catholic fold after negotiating a settlement with Protestant opponents against the express wishes of the papal nuncio. This narrative was entirely consistent with histories of Ireland previously written by Gaelic authors from Continental Europe such as O'Sullivan Beare.

This providential view was first articulated in demotic Gaelic verse by several lesser-known or anonymous poets, some apparently priests, writing in the mid-seventeenth century. Their compositions were intended for oral circulation but manuscript copies were distributed extensively throughout Ireland from the seventeenth until the mid-nineteenth centuries.[12] Together, they offered an interpretation of Ireland's past (including its early modern past) that was the polar opposite to what had been constructed by Temple. Where Temple had denounced the barbarism of Ireland's ancient past, the Gaelic verse historians, following Keating, expounded on its cultural richness that had facilitated the conversion of the population to Christianity and the

---

12 On circulation, see V. Morley, *Ó Chéitinn go Raifteataí: Mar a Cumadh Stair na hÉireann* (Dublin: Coiscéim, 2011), 127–38.

later efflorescence of exemplary religious practice. This had been threatened on several occasions by invasion, but authors contended that Christianity and civility had endured until agents of Luther and Calvin again invaded Ireland in the early modern centuries.

For these oral historians the interlude from the 1530s to the 1650s had been one of unique destruction and humiliation marked by the spoliation of monasteries, the persecution of clergy, the forceful introduction of heresy, the destruction of Ireland's traditional nobility, the confiscation of their land and the ruination of Irish people of all ranks and ethnic origin who, despite their debasement, remained the chosen people of God. They described the English and Scottish Protestants who had profited from the destruction of Ireland's Catholic leaders as greedy, rapacious and uncouth, as opposed to the generous and cultured Irish nobles they had displaced, and their religion was portrayed as the antithesis of Christianity. Their only point of agreement with Temple (who they never cited) was in believing that no compromise was possible between Catholics and Protestants, and where Temple had alerted his audience to be wary of all Catholics, the Gaelic narrators encouraged their audiences to repent for their failings in the expectation that once they were united and had been sufficiently punished, God would enable Catholics to recover what they had lost, probably in the context of an international conflict.[13]

What the poet historians were asserting in popular format was stated more authoritatively in the prose histories written from the Continent by scholars, most of them exiled Irish priests, who, writing in Latin and addressing Continental audiences, offered more reflective accounts and explanations of what had recently befallen what they increasingly represented as a single Irish Catholic community. The tone of interpretation varied and was influenced by several factors such as whether authors were of Gaelic or Old English lineage, or from whence they were writing, or the religious order to which they belonged, or the stance that had been taken by their previous Irish patrons during the political tumults of the mid-century. However, whether one looks at the strident outpourings of Conor O'Mahony in his *Disputatio Apologetica* of 1645 or the account of the overthrow of the Fitzgeralds of Desmond published by Dominic O'Daly in 1655, or at *Cambrensis Eversus* published by John Lynch in 1662, they were agreed on several propositions. They held that in

---

13 For samples of this verse see C. O'Rahilly (ed.), *Five Seventeenth-Century Political Poems* (Dublin Institute for Advanced Studies, 1952). Also see Chapter 3 by Cunningham, this volume.

ancient times the Irish had fostered a society which had been rich culturally and spiritually, and which had been discredited by authors who ignored, or belittled, the literary and architectural archives that bore witness to that civilisation. They were agreed that this golden age had been challenged and dimmed by a sequence of invasions, the most destructive being that which happened after England's rulers began to promote the heresies of Luther and Calvin. Then, as they provided a narrative of the events of the early modern centuries, most authors detailed the closure of Ireland's monasteries and the persecution of Ireland's Catholic clergy; they bewailed the depredations of English soldiers in Ireland; and they chronicled the gradual, but systematic, destruction of Ireland's nobility to make way either for vulgar upstarts from England and Scotland who had secured lands in the plantations, or for heirs to Irish noble houses who had been proselytised to Protestantism from an early age and later matched with Protestant brides.[14]

The old divisions between Catholic authors related now more to the guidance these Continental historians offered for the future than to their interpretation of the recent past, which all represented as an unending sequence of tribulations for Catholics. Authors such as John Lynch, from an Old English mercantile background in Galway, still hoped in 1662 that his former patrons, and also the wider Old English community, would recover some of what had been lost to the Cromwellians. He therefore encouraged his readers to remain loyal to King Charles II in the hope that a grateful monarch would concede some amelioration in their condition. Opposed to this was the view, fostered by those who cherished no hope of benefiting from a Stuart restoration, that Catholics would recover their rightful position only when they secured support from a foreign monarch. Even these latter modified their stance after the Catholic king James II succeeded his brother Charles on the English throne. However, when the support that Irish Catholics had provided King James II in fighting his Protestant son-in-law Prince William of Orange, resulted in a further erosion of the position of Catholics and of Catholicism in Ireland, historians based on the Continent became as fatalistic as the poet/historians resident in Ireland who described what had befallen them as a shipwreck from which, without divine intervention, nothing would be recovered.

Therefore, by the close of the seventeenth century, there were two coherent interpretations – one Catholic and one Protestant – of what had transpired in Ireland during the early modern centuries. The dominant Protestant

---

14 See Campbell, *Renaissance Humanism*; and Williams, 'History, the Interregnum and the Exiled Irish'.

interpretation, re-articulated by Edmund Borlase in 1675, held that every-thing 'good' in Ireland was due to English interventions, and that Ireland's history concerned the conflict between the efforts of a succession of benevo-lent English rulers (notably Henry II, Henry VIII and Elizabeth) to introduce material and constitutional improvements to Ireland and the determination of barbaric Irish lords to reject them. The most recent chapter in that narra-tive, according to Borlase, was part of a papal grand strategy to reverse the achievements of the Protestant Reformation everywhere in Europe.[15]

Borlase's confidence that this conspiracy had been defeated was shat-tered by the events leading to the Williamite/Jacobite conflict, especially the attempt by the Irish supporters of King James to undo the Cromwellian land settlement of Ireland. The experience meant that Irish Protestants remained unconvinced that the Williamite victory in Ireland was sufficient to guaran-tee Protestant security into the future, because some Catholics remained as landed proprietors with associated power over tenants. Many there-fore demanded legislation to prevent 'the further growth of popery'. For these, the definitive history of Ireland remained that of Temple whose *Irish Rebellion*, as John Gibney has detailed, was thereafter reprinted until the early nineteenth century on every occasion that Protestant control over Ireland seemed threatened.[16]

Eighteenth Century Understandings of the Early Modern

Temple's rigid Protestant interpretation was imitated and updated by some eighteenth-century authors, such as Thomas Leland, to take account of more recent threats.[17] What they had to say was mirrored in the interpretation of past events preserved in the Gaelic oral and manuscript tradition that treated of the destruction that had befallen Catholic Ireland during the early modern centuries, which, as we learn from Vincent Morley, were also augmented and updated to take account of fresh humiliations by eighteenth-century poets such as Aodh Buí Mac Cruitín in the mid-century and the blind poet Antaine Raiftearaí at its close.[18] In both instances, those who linked what happened in

---

15 Edmund Borlase, *The Reduction of Ireland to the Crown of England* (London, 1675); A. Ford, 'Past but Still Present', in Brian Mac Cuarta (ed.), *Reshaping Ireland, 1550–1700* (Dublin: Four Courts Press, 2011), 281–99.
16 J. Gibney, *The Shadow of a Year: The 1641 Rebellion in Irish History and Memory* (Madison, WI: University of Winsconsin Press, 2013), 29–34.
17 On Leland, see Gibney, *Shadow*, 93–4.
18 Morley, *Ó Chéitinn*, 139–198. Also see Chapter 1 by V. Morley in volume 3.

the early modern centuries with subsequent threats or injustices were adding to their narrations what Hayden White would describe as 'experientiality', as audiences shared vicariously in the aspirations, fears and suffering of their ancestors which were analogous to what they themselves were experiencing.

Authors on the Protestant side always returned to the Catholic insurrection of 1641 and to the Protestant depositions that bore witness to that event as proof that what the Reformation and the plantations had achieved was constantly under threat. Likewise on the Catholic side as authors dwelt on recent degradations, they traced all their woes to the Protestant Reformation and the plantations. In doing so they identified Luther, Calvin, Cromwell and occasional English monarchs as God's instruments to punish Irish Catholics who, like the Israelites of the Bible, would recover their inheritance only when they repented for past failings and produced a Mosaic leader. This leader was never identified, but it was presumed that any such would have the support of the Irish regiments enlisted in the army of France. For Protestant authors, these same regiments were identified as a greater threat to their security than any possible unaided Catholic insurgency.

These dogmatic accounts of what happened in the two previous centuries were designed by authors who were neither acquainted with their opponents nor interested in debating with them. Rival authors sought rather to achieve solidarity within what were now two rival religious groups. In so far as there was any eighteenth-century reconsideration of what had happened in early modern times, it was prompted by English-language histories composed by authors who were patronised either by liberal-minded Protestants or by individuals associated with what remained of a Catholic merchant, professional and landed *élite* in Ireland. The first Protestant historians in Ireland to abandon the siege mentality encouraged by Temple wrote for some of Ireland's great landed families to laud the achievement of their ancestors in imposing order upon Ireland during the two previous centuries. These histories implied that Ireland's turbulent past was over, which presumption was shared by Catholic authors such as John Curry, Charles O'Conor and Sylvester O'Halloran. These Catholic histories gave close attention to disturbances of the mid-seventeenth century. They argued that none of the ancestors of those Catholic families that still retained property in Ireland had been involved with the 1641 rebellion, and that those Catholics who had joined the Confederate armies had been defending their lives and property from the anti-Catholic animus shared by English Parliamentarians, Dublin Protestant officials and officers in the Cromwellian army. For such authors, the 1641 Depositions that had underpinned Temple's interpretation were unreliable because many reports of atrocity were either fictitious or exaggerated, and because the people who had compiled the Depositions were bent on dispossessing all Catholic proprietors. While discrediting the 1641 Depositions as evidence, these authors drew attention to other official documents bearing witness to massacres of Catholics that had been perpetrated by Protestants.[19]

When Catholic authors described how Catholics as well as Protestants had been victims in the past, they expressed themselves content with the tranquillity and prosperity that obtained in the present, and they pleaded that Ireland's more prosperous Catholics be rewarded for their proven loyalty to the crown by having the more onerous laws against them revoked, thus making them equals with Protestants within the Irish polity. Sylvester O'Halloran, as we learn from Claire Lyons, went further to suggest that Catholics should be permitted to prove their loyalty by enlisting in the royal army.[20]

This case was being addressed to liberal-minded Protestants in both England and Ireland as well as to Catholics, and it contributed to more general arguments for reform that ultimately justified the government in cancelling several of the religious and political disabilities under which Catholics had laboured. All such liberalisation faced stiff opposition from strident Irish Protestants, who harkened back to 1641 and deplored the undoing of the safety mechanisms their ancestors had put in place to prevent Catholic uprisings. Therefore, when another major conflagration erupted in 1798 the doubters asserted that their prognostications had been correct, blithely ignoring that the prime conspirators behind the 1798 rebellion were radical Protestants rather than Catholics. The opportunity to blame all on liberalisation was taken by Sir Richard Musgrave who, in 1801, published his *Memoirs of the Different Rebellions in Ireland* which represented the insurrection led by the United Irishmen in 1798 as the outcome of a conspiracy hatched by the papacy with the purpose of extirpating Protestantism in the same way that the insurgents of 1641 had aimed at the same end. The analogy persisted when Musgrave argued that the Catholic rebels of 1798, together with the allies they had attracted from revolutionary France and those Protestants who had been duped into supporting them, were furthering a greater papist ambition to destroy what Musgrave termed the 'Protestant Empire'. The 1798 rebellion, like that of 1641, had happened because laws designed to keep Catholics in check had been diluted, and Musgrave wrote in the hope that the Act of

---

19 Gibney, *Shadow*, 81–103.
20 C. Lyons, 'An Imperial Harbinger: Sylvester O'Halloran's *General History*', *Irish Historical Studies*, 39 (2015), 357–77.

Union, which had sealed the victory secured by British forces acting in consort with Irish Protestant yeomen in 1798, would not be used to have the Westminster parliament further relax the laws against Catholics in what was now a United Kingdom of Great Britain and Ireland.[21]

The arguments of Musgrave, advising Protestants in Britain and in Ireland to remain vigilant against Catholics, enjoyed considerable support within rigid Protestant circles in Britain as well as in Ireland, while the crisis of 1798, and the associated French revolutionary wars, were fresh in people's minds. To this extent it contributed to the delay in enacting the promised political emancipation of Catholics that was conceded grudgingly in 1829 by the Westminster parliament following the pressure for Catholic Emancipation mobilised by Daniel O'Connell. However, once the Emancipation Act was in place, Musgrave's text became a relic of past times in a more liberal Europe where it was no longer considered reasonable that religious allegiance should determine political and civil rights.

Re-living the Early Modern in the Nineteenth Century

Musgrave's *Memoirs* can be considered the last representative text from a Protestant historiography designed to bolster the dominant position that Protestants had acquired in Ireland following the wars of the seventeenth century. Such Protestant exhortatory history had outlived its usefulness not only because reform was progressing everywhere in Europe but also because, within Ireland, the opposing popular Catholic historiography that had aspired only to see the world upside down in some future time was now publicly identifying practical steps that Catholics might take to reverse past injustices. Breandán Ó Buachalla has explained how Gaelic poets of the early nineteenth century identified O'Connell as the long-desired messianic leader who would challenge the legitimacy of the established order.[22] While articulated in the Irish language, their ambition now also reached an English-reading audience because, as we learn from Vincent Morley's study of 'The Gaelic Society' in early nineteenth-century Dublin, much popular Gaelic verse, from the past as well as the present, was published in English translation and printed both in the *Irish Magazine*, the Society's organ, and in ballad sheets that were

21 Richard Musgrave, *Memoirs of the Different Rebellions in Ireland*, 1801, ed. S. Myers and D. McKnight (Fort Wayne, IA: Round Tower Books, 1995), esp. 1–26.
22 B. Ó Buachalla, *Aisling Ghéar: na Stiobhartaigh agus an t Aos Léinn, 1603–1788* (Dublin: An Clóchomhar, 1996), 650.

retailed extensively at fairs and markets. The circulation of such literature began when memories of the insurrection of 1798, and the assistance the United Irishmen had received from the French Directorate, was fresh in people's minds, and when Gaelic poetry verged on the treasonous by speaking admiringly of Napoleon.[23]

A rendition of Irish Catholic sufferings during the early modern centuries was also broadcast in the English language by Daniel O'Connell who, when promoting Catholic Emancipation, drew upon the store of remembered grievances that had been transmitted and updated in Irish language narratives for two centuries. In doing so he linked past, present and future to advance the political and social as well as the religious rehabilitation of Catholics at the expense of what he depicted as a bigoted Protestant oligarchy that monopolised power in the localities as well as at the centre of government.

Independently of this, the authors of the Young Ireland movement sought, from the 1840s, to create a consciousness of Irish nationhood that would embrace all denominations. This group, comprised of liberal Protestants as well as educated Catholics, strove, as Eric Hobsbawm and Terence Ranger would have it, to invent a tradition by glorifying the achievements of exemplary leaders from Ireland's past. Their emphasis on human agency was in sharp contrast to the providential history of the Gaelic oral tradition that had depicted the Catholic Irish as the collective victims of injustice. While historians of Young Ireland continued to expose what Irish people had suffered from the Reformation and plantations, they showed how some Irish leaders had resisted oppression rather than endorse the fatalism of previous narratives. To this end, as James Quinn has stated, they 'attached a special importance to proving that the Irish were as brave (if not braver) than other nations', and, when evidence failed them, imagined what would have occurred if their heroes had succeeded in uniting a divided population to confront the adversary. Thus the Young Ireland historians constructed a gallery of heroes stretching from Silken Thomas Fitzgerald in the 1530s to Owen Roe O'Neill in the 1640s and to Patrick Sarsfield in the 1690s by merging superficial gleanings from English and Irish documentary sources with fanciful flights of imagination. For John Mitchel, the exemplary hero became Hugh O'Neill, earl of Tyrone (or 'Aodh O'Neill, Prince of Ulster', as Mitchel described him), who had received scant praise either from the Gaelic poets of his own generation or from the Catholic prose and verse historians of later generations.[24]

---

23 Morley, *Ó Chéitinn*, 223–68.
24 J. Quinn, *Young Ireland and the Writing of Irish History* (Dublin: UCD Press, 2015), 4–5.

Mitchel chose Tyrone as his hero over his confederate the dashing Red Hugh O'Donnell who had been accorded unqualified praise by Irish annalists of his generation and who continued to be revered in Catholic histories into the eighteenth century.[25] Perhaps Mitchel considered Tyrone less beholden to Catholic bishops than O'Donnell, and he certainly admired him for bringing previous rivals into a military alliance that, with assistance from Spain, came close to defeating Elizabeth's largest army.

There is no reason to dispute James Quinn's attribution of the biographical interest of the Young Ireland historians to the influence both of Thomas Carlyle and the example of several promoters of nationalist historiographies in continental Europe, but Vincent Morley has shown that some contributors to the *Irish Magazine* had already been praising 'the gallant Tyrone' for resisting the 'oppression' of the crown. The Young Irelands may also have been following the example of the *Irish Magazine* in communicating their interpretation of Ireland's past in English language ballads, which they published in their newspaper, *The Nation*.

The early nineteenth century therefore witnessed the emergence of two bodies of nationalist writing in English that challenged the rigid Protestant interpretation of Ireland's past. One, which was an outgrowth of Gaelic writing of previous centuries, gave attention to the injustices suffered by Irish Catholics in the past and identified the emergent Irish nation with Catholicism. The other imagined a proto-nationalism of the past on which to build an Irish nation of the future that would include Protestants as well as Catholics. Each accorded the early modern centuries a prominent place in historical discourse. The fact that the language of address was English and aimed at mass audiences, whether through O'Connell's speeches, or in broadsheets, or printed ballads, also meant that these compositions elicited responses from all elements of the population – Protestants and Catholics, high and low – that no previous historical writing had done. Special attention was given in each to the early modern centuries, because it was Britain's achievements of those centuries that were being challenged repeatedly in successive political campaigns of the nineteenth century. These concerned the privileged position of the Church of Ireland, political representation at the local and national levels, the management and ownership of land, and the very existence of a Union.

As challenges proceeded, supporters of the establishment responded, and the combatants on both sides invoked history to justify their

---

25 M. Mac Craith, 'Creideamh agus Athartha', in M. Ní Dhonnachdha (ed.), *Nua Léamha* (Dublin: An Clóchomhar, 1996), 7–19.

respective positions. On the establishment – increasingly Protestant – side, history was used to demonstrate how a barbaric country had been improved after Protestants had acquired control of its governance and resources. Then on the Nationalist – increasingly Catholic – side, histories highlighted the injustices (or crimes) of the past, which they aimed to reverse.[26]

All parties recognised that arguments not backed by contemporary evidence were futile, which explains why nineteenth-century scholars invested time in editing and translating texts from the early modern centuries. In this they were matching historians everywhere in Europe, who were being granted access to public evidence through the national archives, libraries and museums then being established, and benefiting from printed calendars and guides to the major documentary sources held in official repositories. And as scholars sought after new evidence, they discredited their opponents by questioning the credibility of their sources. Catholic and Nationalist historians remained uneasy with official sources that had been compiled by people hostile to Irish, and especially Catholic, interests, so they began to garner counter evidence; some gleaned from Catholic archives on Continental Europe and more from surviving Gaelic manuscript sources which scholars began to prepare for print, sometimes with accompanying English translations.

The result was a remarkable output of editions of documents and of histories written in past centuries. If scholars on both sides considered themselves to be countering error, they all proceeded from the Rankean premise that arguments would prevail only when sustained by credible witness. The battle of history books and journals included, besides documentary compilations and multi-volume histories of Ireland through the centuries: the histories (Catholic and Protestant) of individual counties or dioceses; analyses (Catholic and Protestant) of religious developments during the era of Reformation and Counter Reformation; histories of all the principal churches; investigations into particular political episodes or personalities during the early modern centuries; studies, almost invariably by Protestants, of how plantation societies had evolved in particular locations, and counter studies by Catholic and Nationalist authors showing how the property of the indigenous nobility had been seized to make way for plantation; and the compilation of lists of martyrs who had died for their respective faiths.

Many who addressed religious questions were clerics and their feuds extended to disputes over the condition of the church in Ireland on the eve of

---

26 For the pedigree to such arguments, see C. O'Halloran, *Golden Ages and Barbarous Nations* (Cork University Press, 2004).

the Reformation, and to detailed (and carefully documented) arguments over how Reformation legislation came to be enacted by the Irish parliament, and whether a line of episcopal succession had been preserved in the established church from the eve of the Reformation to the close of Elizabeth's reign. Arguments were predictable, but reconciliation proved impossible because the two sets of protagonists cited different sources. Thus, when it came to the contentious issue of identifying martyrs, Catholics relied principally on Vatican sources or archives that had been compiled by religious orders, while Protestants relied on the 1641 Depositions whose admissibility as historical evidence was disputed ever-more vehemently by Nationalists.

Many who supported the establishment enjoyed positions in the Church of Ireland, at Trinity College, Dublin, or in the recently instituted public depositories, while some, notably W. E. H. Lecky and Richard Bagwell, sustained themselves from private resources as did some Presbyterian authors who wrote concerning the achievements of their forebears. Catholic and Nationalist scholars began to compete for a share of public appointments that would enable them to become full-time scholars (here Sir John Gilbert in Dublin City Library is the classic case), while Catholic Church authorities created some sinecure positions for historians in the resurgent Catholic Church of post-Famine Ireland. An extreme example is Father P.F. Moran, nephew to Cardinal Paul Cullen, whose post as vice-rector of the Irish College in Rome enabled him to assemble sources from the Vatican archives that sustained him as a historical scholar during his tenure as bishop of Ossory before becoming cardinal archbishop of Sydney. Some prosperous lay Catholics, including members of the Irish Parliamentary Party, rivalled their Protestant counterparts, by writing histories to complement their political objectives.[27]

Nineteenth-century histories differed from what went before because they attributed change over time to human rather than to divine agency, and authors used history to justify present politics rather than to teach by example. Thus, while Catholic authors continued to emphasise what their ancestors had suffered for their faith, these were now represented as heroes who had fought for Catholicism rather than as helpless victims. To this end Hugh O'Neill, earl of Tyrone, who had been portrayed by John Mitchel as a proto-nationalist, was re-categorised, (together with his O'Donnell confederate) by Father C.P. Meehan – himself initially a Young Ireland historian – as

---

27 For details on all these individuals and their publications see the relevant entries in the J. McGuire and J. Quinn (eds.), *Dictionary of Irish Biography* (9 vols., Cambridge, 2009).

a champion of Catholic Ireland.[28] Therefore the Young Ireland 'National History' that would have included all inhabitants of Ireland in a single grand narrative was being overtaken by a narrative, similar to that favoured by priest historians of the seventeenth century, which made Catholicism a pre-requisite for inclusion within the Irish nation. And in their effort, as Stefan Berger would have it, 'to construct a nation through history', these Catholic historians identified what they termed the 'Penal laws' against Catholics as the gravest of the many injustices of English rule in Ireland.

While history writing may have changed, the issues that divided those con-testing the past remained constant. We have already noted the religious ques-tions being debated, while the crunch issue in the secular sphere remained whether Irish people had the capacity to govern themselves. Those support-ing the *status quo* prepared fresh editions of texts by early modern authors who, in the tradition of Gerald of Wales, had commented disparagingly on Irish people of the sixteenth and seventeenth centuries. Such were countered by scholars usually associated with the Catholic University (later University College, Dublin) who deployed archaeological as well as literary evidence to demonstrate the vibrancy of life and culture in Ancient and Early Christian Ireland. Then, also, Irish language scholars prepared editions, and translations into English, of Irish annals and of the works of Gaelic poets of the medi-eval and early modern centuries which showed how the advanced civilisation of ancient times had flourished until it was destroyed by brute force during the early modern centuries. Even then, while historians – such as Richard Bagwell, who favoured the establishment – chronicled what they believed was the inevitable victory of government forces over irrational opponents, their Nationalist counterparts, following the tradition of the Young Ireland authors, either exulted in the few military victories that Hugh and Owen Roe O'Neill did achieve, or, like Sir John Gilbert, wrote of the Catholic Confederacy when Irish people, still loyal to the English crown, demonstrated that a domestic government could be effective.[29] What was disputed at the national level was fought over within the localities. Thus volumes such as that of the Reverend George Hill expounding on the purpose and achievements of the plantation in Ulster, were countered by those such as *The Great Fraud of Ulster*, where

---

28 C. P. Meehan, *The Fate and Fortunes of Hugh O'Neill … and Rory O'Donnell* (Dublin: J. Duffy, 1868), and see the entry in *Dictionary of Irish Biography* on Meehan, which sees no ten-sion between his support for Young Ireland and his Catholicism.

29 On Gilbert see entry in *Dictionary of Irish Biography*.

T.M. Healy brandished what he knew of Gaelic as well as English law to sustain the arguments pronounced in his title.[30]

While partisan, much of the history published, and the documents edited, brought fresh knowledge to light that sometimes forced combatants to modify their positions, and many editions remain valued today, especially when they drew upon archives that have since been lost. Since current issues being debated in Ireland had serious implications for Britain, it was inevitable that British contestants would be drawn into Ireland's historical battles. In this respect, most attention has been given to exchanges between the Englishman James Anthony Froude, who deplored the failure of successive English governments to compel Ireland's population to pay allegiance to the British government, and the Irish Protestant – but London resident – W.E.H. Lecky, who contended that Ireland's Catholic population had been alienated from the British monarchy because they had been treated harshly and were never trusted. Despite the clamour of their debate, we learn from the studies of Lecky and Froude – conducted respectively by Donal McCartney and Ciaran Brady – that the two were agreed that the history of early modern Ireland had demonstrated that Irish people were incapable of governing themselves. This explains why each concluded that Home Rule had to be opposed because it would be as disastrous for Ireland as it was for the British Empire.[31]

If Froude was a British academic historian whose interest in Ireland's early modern past had been inspired primarily by present politics, Samuel Gardiner and Charles Firth wished to learn how Britain's dealings with Ireland impacted upon British politics of the past, especially during the episode that was then still known as the English Civil War and Interregnum. The standards in empirical scholarship set by these historians were imitated by Robert Dunlop and Philip Wilson, who addressed more purely Irish issues in a nonpartisan fashion. Therefore, if we are to give credit to anybody for releasing the history of early modern Ireland from the partisan debates that had motivated combatants for centuries, it must go to these English scholars of the later nineteenth and early twentieth centuries who, by setting the history of Ireland in a context broader than that of contested national grand narratives, made it possible to advance knowledge about the past in a balanced manner.

---

30 G. Hill, *An Historical Account of the Plantation in Ulster* (Belfast: McCaw, Stevenson and Orr, 1877); T. M. Healy, *The Great Fraud of Ulster* (Dublin: M. H. Gill and Son, 1917).

31 D. McCartney, *W.E.H. Lecky: Historian and Politician, 1838–1903* (Dublin: Lilliput Press, 1994); C. Brady, *James Anthony Froude: an Intellectual Biography of a Victorian Prophet* (Oxford University Press, 2013).

The Early Modern in the Twentieth and Twenty-first Centuries

What was exemplified in the publications of Gardiner and Firth found little favour in twentieth-century Ireland once those involved with constitutional politics were displaced by individuals (Unionist as well as Nationalists) wishing to achieve their ambitions by force. Republicans who favoured the revolutionary path had scant interest in the early modern centuries, besides citing what they believed had happened then as proof of Britain's iniquity. In so far as Nationalists encouraged historical enquiry, it was to learn more of a lost golden age when an ancient Irish nation had both developed admirable legal and constitutional procedures and had became Europe's cultural saviour in the aftermath of barbaric invasions. On the one hand, they accepted that this nation and its accomplishments had been destroyed by invasions from without, the most destructive of which had originated in England, and they were interested in Ireland's subsequent history only to learn of challenges to British rule that might be considered as preludes to the final struggle by a resuscitated Irish nation to achieve independence. On the other, those Irish people who favoured continued union with Britain were interested in the eighteenth century which, for them, was the only era when Ireland had enjoyed a level of peace and prosperity that justified its having been governed by a 'Protestant Nation' under British tutelage. They hoped this would also be the case in Northern Ireland, which became one of the two Irish states to emerge from the conflict of the early twentieth century.

It is unsurprising, therefore, that the historical enquiry encouraged in the universities of Northern Ireland and of the Irish Free State met the expectations of the founders of those entities, and was conducted within a narrow geographic context. Thus the history of Ireland in ancient and early Christian times and of the various bids made to undo the Union of 1801 became the historical subjects of greatest research interest in the universities of Independent Ireland, while the eighteenth century became the prime focus for research in Belfast. The consequence for the sixteenth and seventeenth centuries in both instances was their being considered of but marginal interest. Their relegation became a reality in independent Ireland when T.W. Moody and R. Dudley Edwards took up appointment to history chairs respectively in Trinity College, Dublin, and in University College, Dublin, because each, having been trained in London as an early modernist, began to promote investigations into the nineteenth-century roots of Irish nationalism. Those few individuals, initially G.A. Hayes McCoy and D.B. Quinn, and later J.G. Simms, Hugh Kearney and Aidan Clarke, who persisted with research on the early modern in Irish institutions, seem to have been driven either by curiosity or by the desire to divine an Irish dimension to general historical debates being pursued elsewhere. Thus Quinn, a committed Marxist in his early years, probed into plantations in Ireland and related them to England's global colonisation ventures in the hope of exposing morally questionable roots to British imperialism. Later, Kearney and Clarke, each independently of the other, introduced an Irish dimension to international debates concerning the causes of civil conflict in Britain, and throughout Western Europe, in the mid-seventeenth century. Such endeavours kept academic interest in the early modern alive, while several Irish priest scholars followed in the steps of their predecessors in investigating the Irish Catholic experience abroad, and at home, during the sixteenth and seventeenth centuries.

Academic interest in the early modern quickened during the 1970s when, as the Irish university system expanded, sufficient early modern specialists were appointed to posts in both history and literature to create a community of scholars who promoted the subject through teaching, research, publication, broadcasting and research supervision. It would require a separate chapter to explain how the subject has since developed and it is only possible here to delineate general contours. An initial change in approach was discernable because many appointed to university posts in Ireland from the 1970s forward had had foreign experience, and many of the questions they posed were prompted by ongoing debates concerning developments in Britain, continental Europe and worldwide during the early modern centuries. While historians could not agree on many issues, they all wished to identify what was distinctive about the early modern era that justified its being studied in its own right rather than as a prelude to more 'relevant' happenings in the nineteenth and twentieth centuries. This younger generation was also concerned to break from the rancour and present-mindedness that had characterised much previous writing on the subject, and if publications became less teleological they also became less judgemental as historians sought more to comprehend what motivated people to act as they did in past times rather than to condemn them for their actions. Divining motivations required the investigation of a broader range of sources than had interested previous scholars, and the trawl now extended beyond official documents to include literary sources written in Irish, English and Latin as well as personal correspondence and diaries. Also, as historians brought new material within their purview, they insisted that every documentary collection should be cherished regardless of bias because each provided insights into the past. Thus, even the previously contested 1641 Depositions have now been edited and made available in electronic format.[32]

Because those working on early modern Ireland were locating developments there in ever-widening contexts, more foreign scholars, initially from Britain and North America, and then also from several countries in continental Europe, became involved. Continental scholars have been especially active in exploring archives that hold information on Irish exiles (Protestant as well as Catholic) and how these progressed in various European churches, armies, navies and administrations as well as in several European overseas empires, including that of Britain.

As the interest and perspective of historians has broadened, it has brought them into greater contact with scholars in other disciplines. This has generated friction as well as support. Some scholars of Gaelic literature who consider themselves custodians of the literary archive describing the sufferings of Irish Catholic people in the past, have looked doubtfully at historians who interrogate received wisdom and who, they believe, are pursuing a 'revisionist' agenda designed to deflate Irish nationalism and to defend England's role in Ireland.[33] Many studying Irish literature in English have welcomed the contribution historians have made to elucidating the full extent of English-language dialect and idiom that flourished in early modern times, and some also have welcomed the interest that some historians take in the texts on Ireland composed by 'canonical' authors such as Spenser, Sir John Davies, John Milton and John Dryden. Exponents of post-colonial theory have also welcomed what historians have had to say of English violence in Ireland, but seem disappointed with historians unwilling to join them in recasting Ireland's national grand narrative in post-colonial guise. And yet other scholars –from archaeology, literature

---

32 'The 1641 Depositions', http://1641.tcd.ie (accessed 17 June 2017).
33 See, for example, N. Ó Muraíle, ' "Aimsir an Chogaidh Chreidmhigh". An Dubhaltach Mac Fhirbhisigh a Lucht Aitheantais agus Polaitíocht an Seachtú hAois Déag', in M. Ní Dhonnachdha (ed.), *Nua Léamha*, 89.

and even history – would have historians elide from the record the horror stories associated with England's involvement with Ireland, and to discard from their vocabulary the word 'colonisation', lest the acknowledgment that Ireland was once colonised might be used, as in Algeria, to justify de-colonisation.[34]

These variant responses to recent writing on the history of early modern Ireland are not at all surprising given that the polarities associated with the Nationalist/Unionist historical debates of the late nineteenth century have been revivified by the so-called 'Troubles' of the 1970s and 1980s in Northern Ireland. Thus the more dogmatic exponents of what they term the 'New British History' contend that, for the early modern period, the only valid context within which to consider developments in early modern Ireland is as part of a composite, or proto-composite, British jurisdiction and they challenge the validity of evidence that Irish people were represented, or treated, differently from crown subjects in England and Scotland. And as these look beyond the sixteenth and seventeenth centuries, they visualise a single New British History grand narrative, replete with textbooks, to take the place of the multiple national grand narratives that found favour in the past.[35] At the other extreme is Brendan Bradshaw, an Irish priest historian and distinguished Cambridge scholar, who hankers after a Catholic Nationalist grand narrative for Ireland that would differ from what has gone before in tracing an ideological stemma for Irish republicanism to Christian humanist authors of the sixteenth century rather than to secular republicans of the French Revolution and of 1798. More pragmatically, Bradshaw wishes to bridge the 'credibility gap' that he sees developing between 'academic historians and the general public', and to this end wishes to retrace the 'long march' in 'the development of Irish national consciousness' that commenced in what he describes as 'premodern Ireland'.[36]

There can be no doubting the sincerity of Brendan Bradshaw and also of the advocates for New British History when they appeal to academic historians to join them in composing fresh grand narratives. Moreover, Bradshaw (like TV historians in several countries) is certainly correct in recognising

---

34 See, for example, A. Horning, *Ireland in the Virginian Sea: Colonialism in the British Atlantic* (Chapel Hill, NC: University of North Carolina Press, 2013).

35 For a fine example see S. G. Ellis with C. Maginn, *The Making of the British Isles: the State of Britain and Ireland, 1450–1660* (London: Pearson Longman, 2007).

36 B. Bradshaw, 'And so began the Irish Nation'; *Nationality, National Consciousness and Nationalism in Pre-Modern Ireland* (Farnham: Ashgate, 2015), 33, 57.

that if history is to command and retain the attention of a popular audience, it is best presented in narrative form. However, if the purpose of historical research is to get closer to the truth rather than to confirm people in their prejudices, the future lies with those practitioners who search ceaselessly after fresh knowledge, and employ sophisticated methods and new perspectives that will aid the understanding of how and why people acted as they did in that very turbulent age.

Bibliography

Introduction: Ireland in the Early Modern World

Jane Ohlmeyer

Published Primary Sources

Deposition of William Bailie, 16 July 1645, MS 812, f. 45r-v, Trinity College Dublin.

The 1641 Depositions, http://1641.tcd.ie.

Lynch, John, *Cambrensis Eversus*, trans. Mathew Kelly (3 vols., Dublin: Celtic Society, 1851–2).

Secondary Sources

Akenson, D. H., *If the Irish Ran the World: Montserrat, 1630–1730* (Montreal and Kingston; London: McGill-Queen's University Press, 1997).

Athar Ali, M., *Mughal India. Studies in Polity, Ideas, Society and Culture* (Oxford University Press, 2006).

Bartlett, T., '"This Famous Island Set in a Virginian Sea": Ireland in the British Empire, 1690–1801', in P. J. Marshall (ed.), *The Oxford History of the British Empire*. Vol. II. *The Eighteenth Century* (Oxford University Press, 1998), 253–75.

Bayly, C. A., 'Ireland, India and the Empire: 1780–1914', *Transactions of the Royal Historical Society*, sixth series, 10 (2000), 377–97.

Block, K. and J. Shaw, 'Subjects without an Empire: The Irish in the Early Modern Caribbean', *Past & Present*, 210 (2011), 33–60.

Canny, N., *The Elizabethan Conquest of Ireland: A Pattern Established 1565–1576* (Hassocks: Harvester Press, 1976).

Canny, N. 'Foreword', in K. Kenny (ed.), *Ireland and the British Empire* (Oxford University Press, 2004), ix–xviii.

Canny, N., 'Ireland and Continental Europe', in Alvin Jackson (ed.), *The Oxford Handbook of Modern Irish History* (Oxford University Press, 2014), 333–55.

Canny, N. and P. Morgan (eds.), *The Oxford Handbook of the Atlantic World c.1450–c.1850* (Oxford University Press, 2011).

Cook, S. B., *Imperial Affinities: Nineteenth-Century Analogies and Exchanges Between India and Ireland* (New Delhi: Sage Publications, 1993).

Crosbie, B., *Irish Imperial Networks. Migration, Social Communication and Exchange in Nineteenth-century India* (Cambridge University Press, 2012).

Cullen, L., 'The Irish Diaspora of the Seventeenth and Eighteenth Centuries', in N. Canny (ed.), *Europeans on the Move: Studies on European Migration, 1500–1800* (Oxford University Press, 1994), 113–52.

Cunningham, B. and R. Gillespie, 'The East Ulster Bardic family of Ó Gnímh', *Éigse*, 20 (1984), 106–14.

Dale, S. F., *The Muslim Empires of the Ottomans, Safavids, and Mughals* (Cambridge University Press, 2010).

Elliott, J. H. *Empires of the Atlantic World. Britain and Spain in America 1492-1830* (New Haven: Yale University Press, 2006).

Giacometti, A. and A. MacGowan, *Rathfarnham Castle Excavations, 2014* (Dublin: Archaeology Plan, 2015).

Horning, A., *Ireland in the Virginian Sea* (Chapel Hill, NC: University of North Carolina Press, 2013).

Kenny, K., 'Ireland and the British Empire: An introduction', in K. Kenny (ed.), *Ireland and the British Empire* (Oxford University Press, 2004), 1–15.

Maxwell, C. (ed.), *Irish History from Contemporary Sources (1509–1610)* (London: Allen & Unwin, 1923).

Moody, T. W., F. X. Martin and F. J. Byrne (eds.), *A New History of Ireland* III *Early Modern Ireland 1554-1691* (Oxford University Press, 1976 and reprinted 2001).

Ohlmeyer, J., *Making Ireland English. The Irish Aristocracy in the Seventeenth Century* (New Haven and London: Yale University Press, 2012).

Ohlmeyer, J., 'The Aristocracy in Seventeenth-century Ireland: Wider Contexts and Comparisons', *History Compass* (2014), 33–42.

Ohlmeyer, J., 'Seventeenth-century Ireland and Scotland and their Wider Worlds', in T. O'Connor and M. Lyons (eds.), *Irish Communities in Early Modern Europe* (Dublin: Four Courts Press, 2006), 457–84.

Ohlmeyer, J., 'Conquest, Civilization, Colonization: Ireland, 1540–1660', in R. Bourke and I. MacBride (eds.), *The Princeton Guide to Modern Irish History* (Princeton, NJ: Princeton University Press, 2015), 22–47.

Ohlmeyer, J., 'Eastward Enterprises: Colonial Ireland, Colonial India', *Past & Present* (forthcoming, 2018).

Richards, J. F., 'Fiscal states in Mughal and British India', in B. Yun-Casalilla and P. O'Brien (eds.), *The Rise of Fiscal States: a Global History, 1500–1914* (Cambridge University Press, 2012), 410–41.

Storrs, C., 'Empire and Bureaucracy in the Spanish Monarchy, *c.*1492–1825', a paper delivered at a colloquium on 'Empires and Bureaucracy', Trinity College Dublin, June 2011.

Whelan, K., 'Ireland in the World System 1600–1800', in H.-J. Nitz (ed.), *The Early Modern World-system in Geographical Perspective* (Stuttgart: Franz Steiner, 1993), 204–18.

Withington, P., 'Plantation and Civil Society', in É. Ó Ciardha and M. Ó Siochrú (eds.), *The Plantation of Ulster. Ideology and Practice* (Manchester University Press, 2012), 55–77.

1 Politics, Policy and Power, 1550–1603

Ciaran Brady

Unpublished Primary Sources

The National Archives, Kew

SP 63/31/9, 10
SP 63/112/23
SP 63/124/29, 38, 83, 85
SP 63/125/14
SP 63/139/7
SP 63/164/49
SP 66/1/2

Lambeth Palace Library

Carew Papers, MSS 609, 614

Published Primary Sources

Calendar of Carew Manuscripts, Preserved in the Archiepiscopal Library at Lambeth, 1515–1574, ed. J.S. Brewer and W. Bullen (London: Longmans, Green, Reader & Dyer, 1867).

Davies, John, *A Discovery of the True Causes why Ireland was never Entirely Subdued or brought under Obedience of the Crowne of England untill the Beginninge of His Maiesties Happie Reigne* (London, 1612), reprinted in H. Morley (ed.), *Ireland under Elizabeth and James the First* (London: George Routledge and Sons, 1890).

Heffernan, D. (ed.), *Reform Treatises on Tudor Ireland, 1537–1599* (Dublin, Irish Manuscripts Commission, 2016).

Heffernan, D. (ed.), 'Six Tracts on 'coign and livery', c.1568–78', *Analecta Hibernica*, 45 (2012), 6–45.

The Statutes at Large, Passed in the Parliaments held in Ireland: from the Third Year of Edward the Second, A.D. 1310, to the Twenty-sixth Year of George the Third, A.D. 1786 Inclusive (20 vols., Dublin, 1786–1800).

A Viceroy's Vindication? Sir Henry Sidney's Memoir of service in Ireland, ed. C. Brady (Cork University Press, 2002).

Secondary Sources

Bradshaw, B., *The Irish Constitutional Revolution of the Sixteenth Century* (Cambridge University Press, 1979).

Brady, C., *The Chief Governors: The Rise and Fall of Reform Government in Tudor Ireland, 1536–1588* (Cambridge University Press, 1994).

Brady, C., *Shane O'Neill* (2nd edn., University College Dublin Press, 2015).

Brady, C., 'New English Ideology in Ireland and the two Sir William Herberts', in A. Piesse (ed.), *Sixteenth Century Identities* (Manchester University Press, 2000), 75–111.

Brady, C., 'The attainder of Shane O'Neill, Sir Henry Sidney and the Problems of Tudor State-building in Ireland', in C. Brady and J. Ohlmeyer (eds.), *British Interventions in Early Modern Ireland* (Cambridge University Press, 2005), 28–48.

Brady, C., 'From Policy to Power: the Evolution of Tudor Reform Strategies in Sixteenth-century Ireland', in B. MacCuarta (ed.), *Reshaping Ireland, 1550–1700: Colonization and its Consequences. Essays Presented to Nicholas Canny* (Dublin: Four Courts Press, 2011), 21–42.

Brady, C., 'Viceroys? The Irish Chief Governors, 1541–1641', in P. Gray and O. Purdue (eds.), *The Irish Lord Lieutenancy: c. 1541–1922* (University College Dublin Press, 2012), 15–42.

Canny, N., *The Elizabethan Conquest of Ireland: a Pattern Established, 1565–76* (Hassocks: Harvester Press, 1976).

Canny, N., *Making Ireland British, 1580–1650* (Oxford University Press, 2001).

Canny, N., 'The *Treaty of Mellifont* and the Re-organisation of Ulster, 1603', *Irish Sword*, 9 (1969–70), 249–62.

Carey, V., *Surviving the Tudors: The 'Wizard' Earl of Kildare and English Rule in Ireland, 1537–1586* (Dublin: Four Courts Press, 2002).

Cunningham, B., 'The Composition of Connacht in the Lordships of Clanricard and Thomond, 1577–1641', *Irish Historical Studies*, 24 (1984), 1–14.

Doran, S. M., 'The Political Career of Thomas Radcliffe, 3rd Earl of Sussex', unpublished PhD thesis, University of London (1977).

Edwards, D., *The Ormond Lordship in County Kilkenny, 1515–1642: the Rise and Fall of Butler Feudal Power* (Dublin: Four Courts Press, 2003).

Edwards, D., 'Coyne' in S. Duffy (ed.) *Medieval Ireland: An Encyclopedia* (London: Routledge, 2005), 184–6.

Edwards, D., 'Beyond Reform: Martial Law and the Tudor Reconquest of Ireland', *History Ireland*, 5 (1997), 16–21.

Ellis, S. G., *Reform and Revival: English Government in Ireland, 1470–1534.* (Woodbridge: Boydell Press, 1986).

Ellis, S. G., *Ireland in the Age of the Tudors 1447–1603: English Expansion and the End of Gaelic Rule* (London: Longman, 1999).

Empey, C. A. and K. Simms, 'The Ordinances of the White Earl and the Problem of Coign in the Later Middle Ages', *Proceedings of the Royal Irish Academy*, 75:C (1975), 161–87.

Falkiner, C. L., 'The Counties of Ireland: an Historical Sketch of their Origin, Constitution and Gradual Delimitation', *Proceedings of the Royal Irish Academy*, 24:C (1903), 169–94.

Falls, C., *Elizabeth's Irish Wars* (London: Methuen, 1950).

Hayes McCoy, G., *Scots Mercenary Forces in Ireland* (Dublin and London: Burns, Oates and Washbourne, 1937).

Hill, J. M., *Fire and Sword: Sorley Boy MacDonnell and the Rise of Clan Ian Mor, 1538–1590* (London: Athlone Press, 1993).

Lennon, C., *Sixteenth Century Ireland; the Incomplete Conquest* (2nd edn, Dublin: Gill and Macmillan, 2005).

MacCarthy-Morrogh, M., *The Munster Plantation: English Migration to Southern Ireland, 1585–1641* (Oxford University Press, 1986).

MacCotter, P., *Medieval Ireland: Territorial, Political and Economic Divisions* (Dublin: Four Courts Press, 2014).

McCormack, A. M., *The Earldom of Desmond, 1463–1583: The Decline and Crisis of a Feudal Lordship* (Dublin: Four Courts Press, 2005).

McGettigan, D., *Red Hugh O'Donnell and the Nine Years War* (Dublin: Four Courts Press, 2005).

McGurk, J., *The Elizabethan Conquest of Ireland: The 1590s Crisis* (Manchester University Press, 1997).

Maginn, C., *'Civilizing' Gaelic Leinster: The Extension of Tudor Rule in the O'Byrne and O'Toole Lordships* (Dublin: Four Courts Press, 2005).

Maginn, C., *William Cecil, Ireland, and the Tudor State* (Oxford University Press, 2012).

Maginn, C., '"Surrender and Regrant" in the Historiography of Sixteenth-Century Ireland', *Sixteenth Century Journal*, 38 (2007), 955–74.

Matthew, H. C. G. and B. H. Harrison (eds.), *Oxford Dictionary of National Biography* (60 vols, Oxford University Press, 2004).

Moody, T. W., F. X. Martin and F. J. Byrne (eds), *A New History of Ireland*, viii: *A Chronology of Irish History to 1976. A Companion to Irish History, Part I* (Oxford: Clarendon Press, 1982).

Morgan, H., *Tyrone's Rebellion: The Outbreak of the Nine Years War in Tudor Ireland* (Woodbridge: Boydell Press, 1995).

Morgan, H., 'The Fall of Sir John Perrot', in J. Guy (ed.), *The Reign of Elizabeth I: Court and Culture in the Last Decade* (Cambridge University Press, 1995), 109–25.

Morgan, H., 'The Colonial Venture of Sir Thomas Smith in Ulster, 1571–5', *Historical Journal*, 28 (1985), 261–78.

Nicholls, K. W., *Gaelic and Gaelicised Ireland in the Late Middle Ages*, (2nd edn, Dublin: Lilliput Press, 2003).

O'Neill, J. *The Nine Years' War, 1593–1603: O'Neill, Mountjoy and the Military Revolution* (Dublin: Four Courts Press, 2017).

Quinn, D. B., *The Elizabethans and the Irish* (Ithaca, NY. Cornell University Press, 1966).

Quinn, D. B., 'Renaissance Influences in English Colonisation', *Transactions of the Royal Historical Society*, 26 (1976), 73–93.

Rapple, R., *Martial Power and Elizabethan Political Culture: Military Men in England and Ireland, 1558–1594* (Cambridge University Press, 2012).

Sheehan, A. J., 'Official Reaction to Native Land Claims in the Plantation of Munster', *Irish Historical Studies*, 23 (1983), 297–317.

Sheridan, J., 'The Irish Hydra: English Policy and Plantations in Gaelic Ulster, 1567–79' unpublished PhD thesis, University of Dublin (2015).

Note: The county histories in the 'History and Society' series published by Geography Publications contain a wealth of detailed local histories of later sixteenth-century Ireland, searchable at www.geographypublications.com/index (accessed 31 May 2017).

2 Political Change and Social Transformation, 1603–1641

David Edwards

Unpublished Primary Sources

National Archives of Ireland

Catalogue of Fiants, Vol. ii: James I, no. 1048, Chancery Rolls Office.

Oxfordshire History Centre

Valentia Collection, MS E6/1,7

Published Primary Sources

Barlow, W., *The Summe and Substance of the Conference ... at Hampton Court* (London, 1604).

Historical Manuscripts Commission, *Report on the Manuscripts of Earl Cowper* (3 vols, London 1888–9).

Secondary Sources

Byrne, N. J., 'Jacobean Waterford: Religion and Politics, 1603–25', unpublished PhD thesis, University College Cork (2002).

Caball, M., *Poets and Politics: Reaction and Continuity in Irish Poetry, 1558–1625* (Cork University Press, 1998).

Canny, N., *Making Ireland British, 1580–1650* (Oxford University Press, 2001).

Canny, N., 'The Treaty of Mellifont and the Reorganisation of Ulster, 1603', *Irish Sword*, 9 (1969–70), 380–99.

Clarke, A., *The Old English in Ireland, 1625–42* (London: Macgibbon and Kee, 1966).

Clarke, A., 'Pacification, Plantation, and the Catholic Question, 1603–23', 'Selling Royal Favours, 1624–32', 'The Government of Wentworth, 1632–40', and 'The Breakdown of Authority, 1640–1', in T. W. Moody, F. X. Martin and F. J. Byrne (eds.), *A New History of Ireland, iii: Early Modern Ireland, 1534–1691* (Oxford University Press, 1976), pp 187–232, 233–42, 243–69, and 270–88.

Cooper, J. P., 'Strafford and the Byrnes' Country', *Irish Historical Studies*, 15 (1966), 1–20.

Crawford, J., *A Star Chamber Court in Ireland: The Court of Castle Chamber, 1571–1641* (Dublin: Four Courts Press, 2005).

Curtis, M. P., 'Provincial Government and Administration in Jacobean Munster', unpublished PhD thesis, 2 vols., University College Cork (2006).

Edwards, D., *The Ormond Lordship in County Kilkenny, 1515–1642: The Rise and Fall of Butler Feudal Power* (Dublin: Four Courts Press, 2003).

Edwards, D., 'Legacy of Defeat: The Reduction of Gaelic Ireland after Kinsale', in H. Morgan (ed.), *The Battle of Kinsale* (Bray: Wordwell, 2004), 284–91.

Edwards, D., 'Securing the Jacobean Succession: The Secret Career of James Fullerton of Trinity College, Dublin', in Sean Duffy (ed.), *The World of the Galloglass: Kings, Warlords and Warriors in Ireland and Scotland, 1200–1600* (Dublin: Four Courts Press, 2007), 188–209.

Edwards, D., 'The Plight of the Earls: Tyrone and Tyrconnell's '"Grievances" and Crown Coercion in Ulster, 1603–7', in T. O'Connor and M. A. Lyons (ed.), *The Ulster Earls and Baroque Europe* (Dublin: Four Courts Press, 2010), 53–76.

Edwards, D., 'Out of the Blue? Provincial Unrest in Ireland before 1641', in M. Ó Siochrú & J. Ohlmeyer (eds.), *Ireland 1641: Contexts and Reactions* (Manchester University Press, 2013), 95–114.

Edwards, D., 'Scottish Officials and Secular Government in Early Stuart Ireland', in D. Edwards (ed.), *The Scots in Early Stuart Ireland: Union and Separation in Two Kingdoms* (Manchester University Press, 2016), 29–61.

Edwards, D., 'Lordship and Custom in Gaelic Leinster: Select Documents from Upper Ossory, 1559–1612', *Ossory, Laois & Leinster*, 4 (2010), 27–31.

Finnegan, D., 'Why Did the Earl of Tyrone Join the Flight?', in D. Finnegan, É. Ó Ciardha and M. Peters (ed.), *The Flight of the Earls: Imeacht na nIarlaí* (Derry: Guildhall Press, 2010), 2–12.

Ford, A., '"Force and fear of punishment": Protestants and Religious Coercion in Ireland, 1603–33', in E. Boran and C. Gribben (eds.), *Enforcing Reformation in Ireland and Scotland, 1550–1700* (Aldershot: Routledge, 2006), 91–130.

Gillespie, R., *The Transformation of the Irish Economy, 1550–1700* (Dundalk: Dundalgan Press, 1991).

Gillespie, R., *Seventeenth-Century Ireland: Making Ireland Modern* (Dublin: Gill & Macmillan, 2006).

Heffernan, D., 'Tudor Reform Treatises and Government Policy in Sixteenth-Century Ireland', unpublished PhD thesis, University College Cork (2012).

Henry, G., *The Irish Military Community in Spanish Flanders, 1586–1621* (Dublin: Irish Academic Press, 1992).

Hunter, R. J., *The Ulster Plantation in the Counties of Armagh and Cavan, 1608–1641* (Belfast: Ulster Historical Foundation, 2012).

Kearney, H. F., *Strafford in Ireland: A Study in Absolutism, 1633–1641* (Manchester University Press, 1959).

Kerney Walsh, M., *Destruction by Peace: Hugh O'Neill after Kinsale* (Armagh: Cumann Seanchais Ard Mhacha, 1986).

Lennon, C., *The Lords of Dublin in the Age of Reformation* (Dublin: Irish Academic Press, 1989).

Lynch, M., 'James VI and the "Highland Problem"' in J. Goodare and M. Lynch (ed.), *The Reign of James VI* (East Linton: Tuckwell, 2000), 208–27.

Lyttleton, J., *The Jacobean Plantations in Seventeenth-Century Offaly* (Dublin: Four Courts Press, 2013).

Mac Cuarta, B., 'The Plantation of Leitrim, 1620–41', *Irish Historical Studies*, 32 (2001), 297–320.

MacGregor, M., 'Civilizing Gaelic Scotland: The Scottish Isles and the Stewart Empire', in É. Ó Ciardha and M. Ó Siochrú (eds.), *The Plantation of Ulster: Ideology and Practice* (Manchester University Press, 2012), 33–54.

McCavitt, J., *Sir Arthur Chichester, Lord Deputy of Ireland, 1605–16* (Belfast: Institute of Irish Studies, 1998).

McCavitt, J., *The Flight of the Earls* (Dublin: Gill and Macmillan, 2002).

McLaughlin, J. M., 'The Making of the Irish Leviathan, 1603–25: Statebuilding in Ireland in the Reign of James VI and I', unpublished PhD thesis, 2 vols., National University of Ireland, Galway (1999).

Maguire, J. I. and J. Quinn (eds.), *Dictionary of Irish Biography* (9 vols., Cambridge University Press, 2009).

Maxwell, C., *Irish History from Contemporary Sources, 1509–1610* (London: Allen and Unwin, 1923).

Merritt, J. F., 'The Historical Reputation of Thomas Wentworth', in J. F. Merritt (ed.), *The Political World of Thomas Wentworth, earl of Strafford, 1621–1641* (Cambridge University Press, 1996), 1–23.

Morrill, J., *Stuart Britain: A Very Short Introduction* (Oxford University Press, 2000).

Ohlmeyer, J., *Making Ireland English: The Aristocracy in Seventeenth-Century Ireland* (New Haven, CT: Yale University Press, 2012).

Ohlmeyer, J., '"Scottish Peers" in Seventeenth-century Ireland', in D. Edwards (ed.), *The Scots in Early Stuart Ireland: Union and Separation in Two Kingdoms* (Manchester University Press, 2016), 62–94.

Pawlisch, H. S., *Sir John Davies and the Conquest of Ireland: A Study in Legal Imperialism* (Cambridge University Press,1985).

Perceval-Maxwell, M., *The Outbreak of the Irish Rebellion of 1641* (Montreal and Kingston: McGill-Queen's University Press, 1994).

Ranger, T., 'Strafford in Ireland: A Re-evaluation', in T. Aston (ed.), *Crisis in Europe, 1560–1660* (London: Routledge and Kegan Paul, 1967), 271–93.

Ranger, T., 'Richard Boyle and the Making of an Irish Fortune, 1588–1614', *Irish Historical Studies* 10 (1957), 257–97.

Robinson, P., *The Plantation of Ulster* (Dublin: Gill and Macmillan 1984).

Summerville, J. P. (ed.), *King James VI and I: Political Writings* (Cambridge University Press, 1994).

Treadwell, V., *Buckingham and Ireland, 1616–1628: A Study in Anglo-Irish Relations* (Dublin: Four Courts Press, 1998).

3 Politics, 1641–1660

John Cunningham

Unpublished Primary Sources

[Parsons, William], 'Examen Hiberniae', MS 692, National Library of Ireland.

Published Primary Sources

Acts and Ordinances of the English Interregnum, 1642–1660 ed. C. Firth and R. Rait (London: Stationery Office, 1911), ii, 722–53.

Certain Acts and Declarations made by the Ecclesiasticall Congregation of the Arch-Bishops, Bishops, and other Prelates: met at Clonmacnoise the Fourth Day of December 1649 (London, 1650).

Gookin, V., *The Great Case of Transplantation in Ireland Discussed* (London, 1655).

The Irish Cabinet, or, His Majesties Secret Papers, for Establishing the Papall Clergy in Ireland, with other Matters of High Concernment, taken in the Carriages of the Archbishop of Tuam, who was Slain in the Late Fight at Sliggo in that Kingdom (London, 1645).

Jones, H., *A Remonstrance of Divers Remarkable Passages Concerning the Church and Kingdome of Ireland* (London, 1642).

O'Mahony, C., *Disputatio Apologetica et Manifestativa de Iure Regni Hiberniae pro Catholicis Hibernicis contra Haereticos Anglos* (Lisbon, 1645).

Temple, J., *The Irish Rebellion* (London, 1646).

Secondary Sources

Adamson, J., 'Strafford's Ghost: the British Context of Viscount Lisle's Lieutenancy of Ireland', in J. Ohlmeyer (ed.), *Ireland from Independence to Occupation, 1641–1660* (Cambridge University Press, 1995), 128–59.

Armstrong, R., *Protestant War: the 'British' of Ireland and the Wars of the Three Kingdoms* (Manchester University Press, 2005).

Barnard, T., *Cromwellian Ireland: English Government and Reform in Ireland, 1649–1660* (Oxford University Press, 1975).

Barnard, T., 'Planters and Policies in Cromwellian Ireland', *Past & Present*, 61 (1973), 31–69.

Bottigheimer, K., *English Money and Irish Land: The 'Adventurers' in the Cromwellian Settlement of Ireland* (Oxford: Clarendon Press, 1971).

Canny, N., *Making Ireland British, 1580–1650* (Oxford University Press, 2001).

Clarke, A., *The Old English in Ireland, 1625–1642* (London: Macgibbon and Kee, 1966).

Clarke, A., *Prelude to Restoration in Ireland: The End of the Commonwealth, 1659–1660* (Cambridge University Press, 1999).

Clarke, A., 'The Commission for the Despoiled Subject, 1641–7', in Brian Mac Cuarta (ed.), *Reshaping Ireland, 1550–1700* (Dublin: Four Courts Press, 2011), 241–60.

Corish, P., 'The Rising of 1641 and the Catholic Confederacy, 1641–5', 'Ormond, Rinuccini and the Confederates, 1645–9', and 'The Cromwellian Regime, 1650–1660', in T. W. Moody, F. X. Martin and F. J. Byrne (eds.), *A New History of Ireland, iii: Early Modern Ireland, 1534–1691* (Oxford: Clarendon Press, 1976), 289–335, 353–85.

Cunningham, J., *Conquest and Land in Ireland: The Transplantation to Connacht, 1649–1680* (Woodbridge: Boydell Press, 2011).

Cunningham, J., 'The Gookin-Lawrence Pamphlet Debate and Transplantation in Cromwellian Ireland', in A. McElligott, L. Chambers, C. Breathnach and C. Lawless (eds.), *Power in History*. Historical Studies xxvii (Dublin: Irish Academic Press, 2011), 63–80.

Cunningham, J., 'Lay Catholicism and Religious Policy in Cromwellian Ireland', *Journal of Ecclesiastical History*, 64 (2013), 769–86.

Cunningham, J., 'The Rump Parliament, Cromwell's Army and Ireland', *English Historical Review*, 129 (2014), 830–61.

Darcy, E., *The Irish Rebellion of 1641 and the Wars of the Three Kingdoms* (Woodbridge: Boydell Press, 2013).

Durston, C., '"Let Ireland be Quiet": Opposition in England to the Cromwellian Conquest of Ireland', *History Workshop*, 21 (1986), 105–12.

Forkan, K., 'Ormond's Alternative: The Lord Lieutenant's Secret Contacts with Protestant Ulster, 1645–6', *Historical Research*, 81 (2008), 610–35.

Little, P., *Lord Broghill and the Cromwellian Union with Ireland and Scotland* (Woodbridge: Boydell Press, 2004).

Little, P., 'The Marquess of Ormond and the English Parliament, 1645–1647', in T. Barnard and J. Fenlon (eds.), *The Dukes of Ormonde, 1610–1745* (Woodbridge: Boydell Press, 2000), 83–99.

Little, P., 'The "Irish Independents" and Viscount Lisle's Lieutenancy of Ireland', *Historical Journal*, 44 (2001), 941–61.

Ó hAnnracháin, T., *Catholic Reformation in Ireland: The Mission of Rinuccini, 1645–1649* (Oxford University Press, 2002).

Ó Siochrú, M., *Confederate Ireland, 1642–1649: A Political and Constitutional Analysis* (Dublin: Four Courts Press, 1999).

Ó Siochrú, M., *God's Executioner: Oliver Cromwell and the Conquest of Ireland* (London: Faber & Faber, 2008).

Ohlmeyer, J., *Civil War and Restoration in the Three Stuart Kingdoms: The Political Career of Randal MacDonnell, Marquis of Antrim, 1608–1683* (Cambridge University Press, 1993).

Ohlmeyer, J., 'Ireland Independent: Confederate Foreign Policy and International Relations during the mid-Seventeenth Century', in J. Ohlmeyer (ed.), *Ireland from Independence to Occupation, 1641–1660* (Cambridge University Press, 1995), 89–111.

Perceval-Maxwell, M., *The Outbreak of the Irish Rebellion of 1641* (Montreal and Kingston: McGill-Queen's University Press, 1994).

Robertson, B., *Royalists at War in Scotland and Ireland, 1638–1650* (Farnham: Ashgate, 2014).

Wells, J., 'English Law, Irish Trials and Cromwellian State Building in the 1650s', *Past & Present*, 227 (2015), 77–119.

Wheeler, J., *Cromwell in Ireland* (Dublin: Gill and Macmillian, 1999).

Worden, B., *The Rump Parliament* (Cambridge University Press, 1974).

4 Restoration Politics, 1660–1691

Ted McCormick

Printed Primary Sources

Annesley, Arthur, earl of Anglesey, *A Letter from a Person of Honour in the Countrey written to the Earl of Castlehaven* (London, 1681).

Borlase, Edmund, *The History of the Execrable Irish Rebellion Trac'd from Many Preceding Acts, to the Grand Eruption the 23 of October, 1641 and thence Pursued to the Act of Settlement, 1662* (London, 1680).

Butler, James, duke of Ormond, *A Letter from His Grace James Duke of Ormond, Lord Lieutenant of Ireland, in Answer to the Right Honourable Arthur Earl of Anglesey Lord Privy-Seal* (London, 1682).

Calendar of the State Papers relating to Ireland Preserved in the Public Record Office, 1662–1665, ed. R.P. Mahaffy (London: Mackie and Co., 1907).

Coote, Charles, *The Declaration of Sir Charls Coot, Lord President of Conaught, and the Officers and Soldiers under His Command* (London, 1660).

Eustace, Maurice, *The Speech of the Right Honourable the Lord Chancellor of Ireland made … the 8th. of May 1661* (London, 1661).

His Majesties Gracious Declaration for the Settlement of his Kingdome of Ireland, and Satisfaction of the Severall Interests of Adventurers, Souldiers, and Other His Subjects There (London, 1660).

The Historical Works of the Right Reverend Nicholas French, D. D., Bishop of Ferns, &c., &c., ed. S.H. Bindon (Dublin: James Duffy, 1846).

To the King's Most Excellent Majestie the Humble Remonstrance, Acknowledgement, Protestation, and Petition of the Roman Catholick Clergy of Ireland (London, 1662).

Lynch, John, *Cambrensis Eversus, seu Potius Historica Fides in Rebus Hibernicis Giraldo Cambrensi Abrogata*, ed. and trans. M. Kelly (2 vols., Dublin: Celtic Society, 1848).

Mervyn, Audley, *The Speech of Sir Audley Mervyn Knight … Delivered to His Grace James Duke of Ormond, Lord Lieutenant of Ireland, the 13. Day of February, 1662* (Dublin, 1663).

Ó Bruadair, Daíbhí, *O Bruadair: Translations from the Irish*, trans. M. Hartnett (Dublin: Gallery Press, 1985).

Talon, G. (ed.), *Court of Claims: Submissions and Evidence, 1663* (Dublin: Irish Manuscripts Commission, 2006).

Temple, John, *The Irish Rebellion, or, an History of the Beginnings and First Progress of the General Rebellion Raised within the Kingdom of Ireland upon the Three & Twentieth Day of October, in the Year 1641* (London, 1679).

Touchet, James, earl of Castlehaven, *The Memoirs of James, Lord Audley, Earl of Castlehaven, his Engagement and Carriage in the Wars of Ireland from the Year 1642 to the Year 1651 Written by Himself* (London, 1680).

Walsh, Peter, *The History & Vindication of the Loyal Formulary, or Irish Remonstrance, So Graciously Received by His Majesty Anno 1661. Against All Calumnies and Censures* (London, 1673).

Walsh, Peter, *The More Ample Accompt ... Promised in the Advertisement Annexed to the Late Printed Remonstrance, Protestation, &c. Of the Roman Catholick Clergy of Ireland* (London, 1662).

Waller, Hardress, *The Declaration of Sir Hardress Waller, Major-General of the Parliament's Forces in Ireland, and the Council of Officers There* (Dublin, 1660).

Secondary Sources

Armstrong, R., 'The War of the Three Kings, 1688–91', in A. Jackson (ed.), *The Oxford Handbook of Modern Irish History* (Oxford University Press, 2014), 375–97.

Arnold, L. J., *The Restoration Land Settlement in County Dublin, 1660–1688: A History of the Administration of the Acts of Settlement and Explanation* (Dublin: Irish Academic Press, 1993).

Bagwell, R., *Ireland under the Stuarts and during the Interregnum,* (3 vols., London: Longmans, Green and Co., 1916).

Barnard, T. C., *Cromwellian Ireland: English Government and Reform in Ireland, 1649–1660* (2nd edn., Oxford University Press, 2000).

Barnard, T. C., *Improving Ireland? Projectors, Prophets and Profiteers 1641–1786* (Dublin: Four Courts Press, 2008).

Barnard, T. C., 'Scotland and Ireland in the Later Stewart Monarchy', in S. G. Ellis and S. Barber (eds.), *Conquest and Union: Fashioning a British State, 1485–1725* (London: Longman, 1995), 250–75.

Barnard, T. C., 'The Uses of the 23rd of October 1641 and Irish Protestant celebrations', in T. C. Barnard, *Irish Protestant Ascents and Descents, 1641–1770* (Dublin: Four Courts Press, 2004), 111–42.

Barnard, T. C., 'Interests in Ireland: The "Fanatic Zeal and Irregular Ambition" of Richard Lawrence', in C. Brady and J. Ohlmeyer (eds.), *British Interventions in Early Modern Ireland* (Cambridge University Press, 2005), 299–314.

Barnard, T. C., 'Conclusion', in C. Dennehy (ed.), *Restoration Ireland: Always Settling and Never Settled* (Aldershot: Ashgate, 2008), 179–93.

Barnard, T. C., 'Crises of Identity Among Irish Protestants, 1641–1685', *Past & Present*, 127 (1990), 39–83.

Barnard, T. C., 'Athlone, 1685; Limerick, 1710: Religious Riots or Charivaris?', *Studia Hibernica*, 27 (1993), 61–75.

Bottigheimer, K. S., *English Money and Irish Land: the 'Adventurers' in the Cromwellian Settlement of Ireland* (Oxford University Press, 1971).

Bottigheimer, K. S., 'The Restoration Land Settlement in Ireland: a Structural View', *Irish Historical Studies*, 18 (1972), 1–21

Braddick, M. J., *State Formation in Early Modern England, c.1550–1700* (Cambridge University Press, 2000).

Canny, N., *Making Ireland British, 1580–1650* (Oxford University Press, 2001).

Carpenter, A. (ed.), *Verse in English from Tudor and Stuart Ireland* (Cork University Press, 2003).

Carpenter, A., 'William King and the Threats to the Church of Ireland During the Reign of James II', *Irish Historical Studies*, 18 (1972), 22–8.

Casway, J., 'Gaelic Maccabeanism: The Politics of Reconciliation', in J. Ohlmeyer (ed.), *Political Thought in Seventeenth-Century Ireland: Kingdom or Colony* (Cambridge University Press, 2000), 176–88.

Clarke, A., *Prelude to Restoration in Ireland: the End of the Commonwealth, 1659–1660* (Cambridge University Press, 1999).

Connolly, S. J., *Religion, Law and Power: the Making of Protestant Ireland 1660–1760* (Oxford University Press, 1992).

Connolly, S. J., *Divided Kingdom: Ireland 1630–1800* (Oxford University Press, 2008).

Coughlan, P., 'Natural History and Historical Nature: The Project for a Natural History of Ireland', in M. Greengrass, M. Leslie and T. Raylor (eds.), *Samuel Hartlib and the Universal Reformation: Studies in Intellectual Communication* (Cambridge University Press, 1994), 298–317.

Creighton, A., '"Grace and Favour": The Cabal Ministry and Irish Catholic Politics, 1667–1673', in C. Dennehy (ed.), *Restoration Ireland: Always Settling and Never Settled* (Aldershot: Ashgate, 2008), 141–60.

Creighton, A., 'The Remonstrance of December 1661 and Catholic Politics in Restoration Ireland', *Irish Historical Studies*, 34 (2004), 16–41.

Cunningham, B., 'Representations of King, Parliament and the Irish People in Geoffrey Keating's *Foras Feasa Ar Eirinn* and John Lynch's *Cambrensis Eversus* (1662)', in J. Ohlmeyer (ed.), *Political Thought in Seventeenth-Century Ireland: Kingdom or Colony* (Cambridge University Press, 2000), 131–54.

Cunningham, J., *Conquest and Land in Ireland: the Transplantation into Connacht, 1649–1680* (Woodbridge: Boydell & Brewer, 2011).

Dennehy, C., 'The Restoration Irish Parliament, 1661–6', in C. Dennehy (ed.), *Restoration Ireland: Always Settling and Never Settled* (Aldershot: Ashgate, 2008), 53–68.

Dickson, D., *Old World Colony: Cork and South Munster 1630–1830* (Cork University Press, 2005).

Dunne, T. J., 'The Gaelic Response to Conquest and Colonisation: The Evidence of the Poetry', *Studia Hibernica*, 20 (1980), 7–30.

Edie, C. A., 'The Irish Cattle Bills: A Study in Restoration Politics', *Transactions of the American Philosophical Society*, new series, 60 (1970), 1–66.

Geoghegan, V., 'Thomas Sheridan: Toleration and Royalism', in D. G. Boyce, R. Eccleshall and V. Geoghegan (eds.), *Political Discourse in Seventeenth- and Eighteenth-Century Ireland* (Basingstoke: Palgrave, 2001), 32–61.

Gibney, J., *Ireland and the Popish Plot* (Basingstoke: Palgrave Macmillan, 2009).

Gibney, J., *The Shadow of a Year: The 1641 rebellion in Irish History and Memory* (Madison: University of Wisconsin Press, 2013).

Gillespie, R., *Reading Ireland: Print, Reading, and Social Change in Early Modern Ireland* (Manchester University Press, 2005).

Gillespie, R., and R. Ó hUiginn (eds.), *Irish Europe 1600–1650: Writing and Learning* (Dublin: Four Courts Press, 2013).

Gillespie, R., 'Print Culture, 1550–1700', in R. Gillespie and A. Hadfield (eds.), *The Irish Book in English 1550–1800* (Oxford University Press, 2006), 17–33.

Greaves, R. L., *God's Other Children: Protestant Nonconformists and the Emergence of Denominational Churches in Ireland, 1660–1700* (Stanford University Press, 1997).

Harris, T., *Restoration: Charles II and His Kingdoms, 1660–1685* (London: Penguin, 2006), 379.

Harris, T., 'Restoration Ireland – Themes and Problems', in C. Dennehy (ed.), *Restoration Ireland: Always Settling and Never Settled* (Aldershot: Ashgate, 2008), 1–17.

Hindle, S., *The State and Social Change in Early Modern England, 1550–1640* (Basingstoke: Palgrave, 2002).

James, F., *Lords of the Ascendancy: The Irish House of Lords and Its Members, 1600–1800* (Washington, DC: Catholic University of America Press, 1995).

Kelly, J., '"That Glorious and Immortal Memory": Commemoration and Protestant Identity in Ireland 1660–1800', *Proceedings of the Royal Irish Academy*, 94:C (1994), 25–52.

Kelly, J., and M. J. Powell, 'Introduction', in J. Kelly and M. J. Powell (eds.), *Clubs and Societies in Eighteenth-Century Ireland* (Dublin: Four Courts Press, 2010), 17–35.

Kinsella, E., '"Dividing the Bear's Skin Before She Is Taken": Irish Catholics and Land in the Late Stuart Monarchy, 1683–91', in C. Dennehy (ed.), *Restoration Ireland: Always Settling and Never Settled* (Aldershot: Ashgate, 2008), 161–78.

Lenihan, P., *The Last Cavalier: Richard Talbot, 1631–91* (University College Dublin Press, 2015).

Little, P., *Lord Broghill and the Cromwellian Union with Ireland and Scotland* (Woodbridge: Boydell & Brewer, 2004).

Macinnes, A., 'Gaelic Culture in the Seventeenth Century: Polarization and Assimilation', in S. G. Ellis and S. Barber (eds.), *Conquest and Union: Fashioning a British State, 1485–1725* (London: Longman, 1995), 162–194.

McCormick, T., *William Petty and the Ambitions of Political Arithmetic* (Oxford University Press, 2009).

McGuire, J. I., 'Ormond and Presbyterian Nonconformity, 1660–1663', in Kevin Herlihy (ed.), *The Politics of Irish Dissent, 1650–1800* (Dublin: Four Courts Press, 1997).

McGuire, J. I., 'Why Was Ormond Dismissed in 1669?', *Irish Historical Studies*, 18 (1973), 295–312.

McHugh, J., 'Catholic Clerical Responses to the Restoration: The Case of Nicholas French', in C. Dennehy (ed.), *Restoration Ireland: Always Settling and Never Settled* (Aldershot: Ashgate, 2008), 99–121.

McKenny, K., 'The Seventeenth-Century Land Settlement in Ireland: Towards a Statistical Interpretation', in J. Ohlmeyer (ed.), *Ireland from Independence to Occupation 1641–1660* (Cambridge University Press, 1995), 181–200.

McKenny, K., 'The Restoration Land Settlement in Ireland: A Statistical Interpretation', in C. Dennehy (ed.), *Restoration Ireland: Always Settling and Never Settled* (Aldershot: Ashgate, 2008), 35–52.

Miller, J., 'Thomas Sheridan (1646–1712) and His "Narrative"', *Irish Historical Studies*, 20 (1976): 105–28.

Morash, C., 'Theatre and Print, 1550–1800', in R. Gillespie and A. Hadfield (eds.), *The Irish Book in English 1550–1800* (Oxford University Press, 2006), 319–34.

Ó Buachalla, B., 'Review Article: Poetry and Politics in Early Modern Ireland', *Eighteenth-Century Ireland*, 7 (1992), 149–75.

Ó Ciardha, É., *Ireland and the Jacobite Cause, 1685–1766: A Fatal Attachment* (Dublin: Four Courts Press, 2004).

Ó Siochrú, M., *Confederate Ireland, 1642–1649: A Constitutional and Political Analysis* (Dublin: Four Courts Press, 1999).

O'Connor, T. (ed.), *The Irish in Europe, 1500–1815* (Dublin: Four Courts Press, 2001).

O'Connor, T., and M. A. Lyons (eds.), *Irish Communities in Early Modern Europe* (Dublin: Four Courts Press, 2006).

O'Sullivan, H., *John Bellew: A Seventeenth-Century Man of Many Parts, 1605–1679* (Dublin: Irish Academic Press, 2000), 76–7.

O'Sullivan, H., 'The Restoration Land Settlement in the Diocese of Armagh, 1660–1684', *Seanchas Ardmhacha: Journal of the Armagh Diocesan Historical Society*, 16 (1994), 1–70.

Ohlmeyer, J., *Civil War and Restoration in Three Stuart Kingdoms: The Career of Randal MacDonnell, Marquis of Antrim* (2nd edn., Dublin: Four Courts Press, 2001).

Ohlmeyer, J., *Making Ireland English: the Irish Aristocracy in the Seventeenth Century* (New Haven: Yale University Press, 2012).

Ohlmeyer, J., and S. Zwicker, 'John Dryden, the House of Ormond, and the Politics of Anglo-Irish Patronage', *Historical Journal*, 49 (2006), 677–706.

Perceval-Maxwell, M., 'The Anglesey-Ormond-Castlehaven Dispute, 1680–1682: Taking Sides About Ireland in England', in V. P. Carey and U. Lotz-Heumann (eds.), *Taking Sides? Colonial and Confessional Mentalités in Early Modern Ireland: Essays in Honour of Karl S. Bottigheimer* (Dublin: Four Courts Press, 2003), 213–30.

Perceval-Maxwell, M., 'The Irish Land Settlement and its Historians', in C. Dennehy (ed.), *Restoration Ireland: Always Settling and Never Settled* (Aldershot: Ashgate, 2008), 19–34.

Pincus, S. C. A., '"Coffee Politicians Does Create": Coffeehouses and Restoration Political Culture', *Journal of Modern History*, 67 (1995), 807–34.

Simms, J. G., *Jacobite Ireland, 1685–91* (London: Routledge and Kegan Paul, 1969).

Simms, J. G., 'The Restoration, 1660–1685', in T. W. Moody, F. X. Martin and F. J. Byrne (eds.), *A New History of Ireland, iii: Early Modern Ireland, 1534–1691* (3rd impression, Oxford University Press, 1991), 420–5.

Walsh, P., 'Club Life in late seventeenth- and early eighteenth-century Ireland: In search of an associational world, *c.*1680–1730', in J. Kelly and M. J. Powell (eds.), *Clubs and Societies in Eighteenth-Century Ireland* (Dublin: FCP, 2010), 36–49.

5 Politics, 1692–1730

Charles Ivar McGrath

Printed Primary Sources

The Journals of the House of Commons of the Kingdom of Ireland (21 vols., Dublin, 1796–1802).

Maxwell, Henry, *Mr. Maxwell's Second Letter to Mr. Rowley; Wherein the Objections against the Bank are Answer'd* (Dublin, 1721).

Molyneux, William, *The Case of Ireland's being Bound by Acts of Parliament made in England, Stated* (Dublin, 1698).

The Statutes at Large, passed in the Parliaments held in Ireland: from the Third Year of Edward the Second, A.D. 1310, to the First Year of George the Third, A.D. 1761 Inclusive (8 vols., Dublin, 1765).

Secondary Sources

Connolly, S. J., *Religion, Law and Power: The Making of Protestant Ireland 1660–1760* (Oxford University Press, 1992).

Cullen, L. M., 'Catholics under the Penal Laws', *Eighteenth-Century Ireland*, 1 (1986), 23–36.

Curtis, E. and R. B. McDowell (eds.), *Irish Historical Documents 1172–1922* (London: Methuen, 1943).

Goodwin, A., 'Wood's Halfpence', *English Historical Review*, 51 (1936), 647–74.

Hall, F. G., *The Bank of Ireland 1783–1946* (Dublin: Hodges Figgis, 1949).

Hayton, D. W., *Ruling Ireland, 1685–1742: Politics, Politicians and Parties* (Woodbridge: Boydell and Brewer, 2004).

Hayton, D. W., *The Anglo-Irish Experience, 1680–1730* (Woodbridge: Boydell and Brewer, 2012).

Hayton, D. W. and J. Kelly, 'The Irish Parliament in European Context: A Representative Institution in a Composite State', in D. W. Hayton, J. Kelly and J. Bergin (eds.), *The Eighteenth-Century Composite State: Representative Institutions in Ireland and Europe, 1689–1800* (Houndmills: Palgrave Macmillan, 2010), 3–17.

Hayton, D. W., 'Introduction: The Long Apprenticeship', *Parliamentary History*, 20 (2001), 1–26.

Hayton, D. W., 'The Stanhope/Sunderland Ministry and the Repudiation of Irish Parliamentary Independence', *English Historical Review*, 113 (1998), 610–36.

Kelly, J., *Poynings' Law and the Making of Law in Ireland 1660–1800* (Dublin: Four Courts Press, 2007).

Kelly, P., 'Berkeley and the idea of a National Bank', *Eighteenth-Century Ireland*, 25 (2010), 98–117.

Kinsella, E., 'In Pursuit of a Positive Construction: Irish Catholics and the Williamite Articles of Surrender, 1690–1701', *Eighteenth Century Ireland*, 24 (2009), 11–35.

McBride, I., 'Catholic Politics in the Penal Era: Father Sylvester Lloyd and the Delvin Address of 1727', in J. Bergin, E. Magennis, L. Ní Mhungaile and P. Walsh (eds.), *New Perspectives on the Penal Laws* (*Eighteenth-Century Ireland*, special issue no. 1, 2011), 115–47.

McGrath, C. I., *The Making of the Eighteenth-Century Irish Constitution: Government, Parliament and the Revenue, 1692–1714* (Dublin: Four Courts Press, 2000).

McGrath, C. I., *Ireland and Empire, 1692–1770* (London: Pickering and Chatto, 2012).

McGrath, C. I., 'Alan Brodrick and the Speakership of the House of Commons, 1703–4', in J. Kelly, J. McCafferty and C. I. McGrath (eds.), *People, Politics and Power: Essays on Irish History 1660–1850 in Honour of James I. McGuire* (University College Dublin Press, 2009), 70–93.

McGrath, C. I., '"The Public Wealth is the Sinew, the Life, of every Public Measure": The Creation and Maintenance of a National Debt in Ireland, 1716–45', in D. Carey and C. Finlay (eds.), *The Empire of Credit: The Financial Revolution in the British Atlantic World, 1700–1800* (Dublin: Irish Academic Press, 2011), 171–207.

McGrath, C. I., 'Securing the Protestant Interest: The Origins and Purpose of the Penal Laws of 1695', *Irish Historical Studies*, 30 (1996), 25–46.

McGrath, C. I., 'Parliamentary Additional Supply: The Development and Use of Regular Short-term Taxation in the Irish Parliament, 1692–1716', *Parliamentary History*, 20 (2001), 27–54.

McGrath, C. I., 'Central Aspects of the Eighteenth-Century Constitutional Framework in Ireland: The Government Supply Bill and Biennial Parliamentary Sessions, 1715–82', *Eighteenth-Century Ireland*, 16 (2001), 9–34.

McGrath, C. I., 'English Ministers, Irish Politicians and the Making of a Parliamentary Settlement in Ireland, 1692–5', *English Historical Review*, 119 (2004), 585–613.

McGrath, C. I., 'Government, Parliament and the Constitution: The Reinterpretation of Poynings' Law, 1692–1714', *Irish Historical Studies*, 35 (2006), 160–72.

McGrath, C. I., 'The "Union" Representation of 1703 in the Irish House of Commons: A Case of Mistaken Identity?', *Eighteenth-Century Ireland*, 23 (2008), 11–35.

McGrath, C. I., 'Securing the Hanoverian Succession in Ireland: Jacobites, Money and Men, 1714–16', *Parliamentary History*, 33 (2014), 140–59.

McGuire, J. I., 'The Irish parliament of 1692', in T. Bartlett and D. W. Hayton (eds.), *Penal Era and Golden Age: Essays in Irish History, 1690–1800* (Belfast: Ulster Historical Foundation, 1979), 1–31.

McNally, P., *Parties, Patriots and Undertakers: Parliamentary Politics in Early Hanoverian Ireland* (Dublin: Four Courts Press, 1997).

McNally, P., 'Wood's Halfpence, Carteret, and the Government of Ireland, 1723–6', *IHS*, 30 (1997), 354–76.

Ryder, M., 'The Bank of Ireland, 1721: Land, Credit and Dependency', *Historical Journal*, 25 (1982), 557–82.

Simms, J. G., *The Williamite Confiscation in Ireland 1690–1703* (London: Faber & Faber, 1956).

Simms, J. G., *The Treaty of Limerick* (Dundalk: Dundalgan Press, 1965).

Simms, J. G., 'Irish Catholics and the Parliamentary Franchise, 1692–1728', *Irish Historical Studies*, 12 (1960), 28–37.

Simms, J. G., 'The Making of a Penal Law (2 Anne, c.6), 1703–4', *Irish Historical Studies*, 12 (1960), 105–18.

Simms, J. G., 'The Bishops' Banishment Act of 1697 (9 Will. III, c. 1)', *Irish Historical Studies*, 17 (1970), 185–99.

Wall, M., *The Penal Laws, 1691–1760* (Dundalk: Dundalgan Press, 1976).

Walsh, P., *The Making of the Irish Protestant Ascendancy: The Life of William Conolly, 1662–1729* (Woodbridge: Boydell and Brewer, 2010).

Walsh, P., *The South Sea Bubble and Ireland: Money, Banking and Investment, 1690–1721* (Woodbridge: Boydell and Brewer, 2014).

Walsh, P., 'The Fiscal State in Ireland, 1691–1769', *Historical Journal*, 56 (2013), 629–56.

6 The Emergence of a Protestant Society, 1691–1730

D. W. Hayton

Unpublished Primary Sources

British Library

Southwell Papers, Add. MS 38157
Wentworth Papers, Add. MS 22,192

Leicestershire, Leicester and Rutland Record Office

Finch Papers, box 4965, Ire. 9

Longleat House

Thynne Papers, 179

National Archives of Ireland

M 2537
M 6236/7

The National Archives, Kew

SP 63/366/89

National Library of Ireland

Fownes Papers, MS 8802/3
Inchiquin Papers, MS 45347/3
Orrery Papers, MS 4177

Royal Irish Academy

MS 24.K.19/1

Surrey History Centre

Brodrick Papers, 1248/3/187–8; G145/box 102/4

Trinity College Dublin

Archbishop William King Letterbooks, MS 2532

Published Primary Sources

Considerations upon two Bills sent down from the R[ight]H[onourable] the H[ouse] of L[ords]to the H[onourable] H[ouse]of C[ommons], relating to the Clergy of I[relan]d (London, 1732).
Hannibal Not at our Gates: or, An Enquiry into the Grounds of our Present Fears of Popery and the Pre[ten]der (London, 1714).
Historical Manuscripts Commission, *Calendar of the Manuscripts of the Marquess of Ormonde*, new series (8 vols., London: HMSO, 1902–1920).
Letters of Marmaduke Coghill, 1722–1738, ed. D. W. Hayton (Dublin: Irish Manuscripts Commission, 2005).

The Poems of Jonathan Swift, ed. H. Williams (2nd edn., 3 vols, Oxford: Clarendon Press, 1958).

Synge, Edward, *The Case of Toleration Consider'd with Respect both to Religion and Civil Government* ... (Dublin, 1725).

Secondary Sources

Barnard, T. C., *A New Anatomy of Ireland: The Irish Protestants, 1649–1770* (New Haven & London: Yale University Press, 2003).

Barnard, T. C., *Making the Grand Figure: Lives and possessions in Ireland, 1641–1770* (New Haven & London: Yale University Press, 2004).

Barnard, T. C., 'Land and the Limits of Loyalty: The Second Earl of Cork and the First Earl of Burlington', in T. C. Barnard and J. Clark (eds.), *Lord Burlington: Architecture, Art and Life* (London: Hambledon Press, 1995), 167–99.

Barnard, T. C., 'The Uses of 23 October 1641 and Irish Protestant Celebration', *English Historical Review*, 106 (1991), 889–920.

Bartlett, T., '"This famous island set in a Virginian sea": Ireland in the British Empire, 1690–1801' in P. J. Marshall (ed.), *The Oxford History of the British Empire*, ii: *The Eighteenth Century* (Oxford University Press, 1998), 253–75.

Beckett, J. C., *Protestant Dissent in Ireland 1687–1780* (London: Faber & Faber, 1948).

Burns, R. E., 'The Irish Popery Laws: A Study of Eighteenth-century Legislation and Behavior', in *Review of Politics*, 24 (1962), 485–508.

Connolly, S. J., *Religion, Law and Power: The Making of Protestant Ireland 1660–1760* (Oxford University Press, 1992).

Connolly, S. J., *Divided kingdom: Ireland, 1630–1800* (Oxford University Press, 2008).

Connolly, S. J., 'The Penal Laws', in W. A. Maguire (ed.), *Kings in Conflict: The Revolutionary War in Ireland and its Aftermath 1689–1750* (Belfast: Blackstaff Press, 1990), pp 157–72.

Connolly, S. J., 'Reformers and High-flyers: the post-Revolution Church', in A. Ford, K. Milne and J. I. McGuire (eds.), *As by Law Established: The Church of Ireland since the Reformation* (Dublin: Lilliput Press, 1995), 152–65.

Cullen, L. M., 'The Blackwater Catholics and County Cork Society and Politics in the Eighteenth Century', in P. Flanagan and C. G. Buttimer (eds.), *Cork: History and Society* (Dublin: Geography Publications, 1993), 540–59.

Dudley, R., 'The Dublin Parish, 1660–1730', in E. FitzPatrick and R. Gillespie (eds.), *The Parish in Medieval and Early Modern Ireland: Community, Territory and Building* (Dublin: Four Courts Press, 2006), 277–96.

Dudley, R., 'The Dublin Parishes and the Poor: 1660–1740', *Archivium Hibernicum*, 53 (1999), 80–94.

Ehrenpreis, I., *Swift: the Man, his Works, and the Age* (3 vols., London: Methuen, 1962–83).

Glickman, G., *The English Catholic Community 1688–1745: Politics, Culture, and Ideology* (Woodbridge: Boydell & Brewer, 2009).

Hayton, D. W., *Ruling Ireland, 1685–1742: Politics, Politicians and Parties* (Woodbridge: Boydell & Brewer, 2004).

Hayton, D. W., *The Anglo-Irish Experience, 1680–1730: Religion, Identity and Patriotism* (Woodbridge: Boydell & Brewer, 2012).

Hayton, D. W., 'Dependence, Clientage, and Affinity: the Political Following of the Second Duke of Ormonde', in T. C. Barnard and J. Fenlon (eds.), *The Dukes of Ormonde, 1610–1745* (Woodbridge: Boydell & Brewer, 2000), 211–41.

Hayton, D. W., 'The Church of Ireland Laity in Public Life, *c*.1660–1740', in R. Gillespie and W. G. Neely (eds.), *The Laity and the Church of Ireland, 1000–2000: All Sorts and Conditions* (Dublin: Four Courts Press, 2002), 104–32.

Hill, J. R., *From Patriots to Unionists: Dublin Civic Politics and Irish Protestant Patriotism, 1660–1840* (Oxford: Clarendon Press, 1997).

Hill, J. R., 'Dublin Corporation, Protestant Dissent, and Politics, 1660–1800', in K. Herlihy (ed.), *The Politics of Irish Dissent 1650–1800* (Dublin: Four Courts Press, 1997), 28–39.

Kelly, J., 'The Genesis of "Protestant Ascendancy": The Rightboy Disturbances of the 1780s and their Impact upon Protestant Opinion', in G. O'Brien (ed.), *Parliament, Politics and People: Essays in Eighteenth-century Irish History* (Dublin: Irish Academic Press, 1989), 93–127.

Kelly, J., 'Sustaining a Confessional State: The Irish Parliament and Catholicism', in D. W. Hayton, J. Kelly and J. Bergin (eds.), *The Eighteenth-century Composite State: Representative Institutions in Ireland and Europe, 1689–1800* (Houndmills: Palgrave Macmillan, 2010), 44–77.

Kelly, J., 'The Historiography of the Penal Laws', in J. Bergin, E. Magennis, L. Ní Mhungaile and P. Walsh (eds.), *New Perspectives on the Penal Laws* (*Eighteenth-Century Ireland*, special issue no. 1, 2011), 27–54.

Kinsella, E., 'The Articles of Surrender and the Williamite Settlement of Ireland: A Case Study of Colonel John Browne (1640–1711)', unpublished PhD thesis, University College Dublin (2011).

Lyons, E. H., 'Morristown Lattin: A Case Study of the Lattin and Mansfield families in County Kildare, *c*.1600–1860', unpublished PhD thesis, University College Dublin (2011).

McBride, I., *Eighteenth-century Ireland: The Isle of Slaves* (Dublin: Gill & Macmillan, 2009).

McGrath, C. I., 'Securing the Protestant Interest: The Origins and Purpose of the Penal Laws of 1695', *Irish Historical Studies*, 30 (1996), 25–46.

McNally, P., '"Irish and English Interests": National Conflict within the Church of Ireland Episcopate in the Reign of George I', *Irish Historical Studies*, 29 (1995), 295–314.

Noonan, K. M., '"Martyrs in flames": Sir John Temple and the Conception of the Irish in English Martyrologies', *Albion*, 36 (2004), 223–55.

Ó Ciardha, É., *Ireland and the Jacobite Cause, 1685–1766: A Fatal Attachment* (Dublin: Four Courts Press, 2002).

O'Regan, P., *Archbishop William King of Dublin (1650–1729) and the Constitution in Church and State* (Dublin: Four Courts Press, 2000).

Simms, J. G., *The Williamite Confiscation in Ireland 1690–1703* (London: Faber & Faber 1956).

Simms, J. G., 'Irish Catholics and the Parliamentary Franchise, 1692–1728', *Irish Historical Studies*, 12 (1960), 28–37.

Troost, W., 'William III and the Treaty of Limerick (1691–1697): A study of his Irish policy', PhD thesis, University of Leiden (1983).

Wall, M., 'The Penal laws, 1691–1760', reprinted in G. O'Brien (ed.), *Catholic Ireland in the Eighteenth Century: Collected Essays of Maureen Wall* (Dublin: Geography Publications, 1989), 1–60.

Walsh, P., *The Making of the Irish Protestant Ascendancy: The Life of William Conolly, 1662–1729* (Woodbridge: Boydell & Brewer, 2010).

Whan, R., *The Presbyterians of Ulster, 1688–1730* (Woodbridge: Boydell & Brewer, 2013).

Wilson, R., *Elite Women in Ascendancy Ireland, 1690–1745: Imitation and Innovation* (Woodbridge: Boydell & Brewer, 2015).

7 Counter Reformation: The Catholic Church, 1550–1641

Tadhg Ó hannracháin

Unpublished Primary Sources

Archivio Storico De Propaganda Fide

'Miscell. Varie', 9, p. 56.

'S.O.C.G.', 140, ff. 69r–77r.

The National Archives, Kew

SP 63/184/27.

SP 63/257/45, ff. 130–5 (microfilm p. 2699 in National Library of Ireland).

Published Primary Sources

Bale, John, *The Vocacyon of John Bale to the Bishoprick of Ossorie in Irelande his Persecucions in the Same and Finall Delyuereaunce*, (Wesel (?), 1553).

The Irish Sections of Fynes Moryson's Unpublished Itinerary, ed. G. Kew (Dublin: Irish Manuscripts Commission, 1998).

Rich, Barnaby, *A New Description of Ireland* (London, 1610).

Rochford, Robert, *The Life of the Glorious Bishop Saint Patricke Apostle and Primate of Ireland Togeather with the Lives of the Holy Virgin S. Bridgit and of the Glorious Abbot Saint Columbe Patrons of Ireland* (St Omer, 1625).

Shirley, E. P., *Original Letters and Papers of the Church in Ireland under Edward VI, Mary and Elizabeth*, (London: Gilbert and Rivington, 1851).

Treadwell, V. (ed.), *The Irish Commission of 1622: An Investigation of the Irish Administration 1615–22 and its Consequences 1623–4* (Dublin: Irish Manuscripts Commission, 2006).

Secondary Sources

Bradshaw, B., *The Dissolution of the Religious Orders in Ireland under Henry VIII* (Cambridge University Press, 1974).

Caball, M., 'Religion, Culture and the Bardic Élite', in A. Ford and J. McCafferty (eds.), *The Origins of Sectarianism in Early Modern Ireland* (Cambridge University Press, 2005), 158–82.

Corish, P., 'Women and Religious Practice', in M. MacCurtain and M. O'Dowd (eds.), *Women in Early Modern Ireland* (Dublin: Wolfhound Press, 1991), 212–20.

Cox, J., 'The Reformation, Catholicism and Religious Change in Kildare, 1560–1640', unpublished PhD thesis, University College Dublin, 2015.

Cunningham, B., *The Annals of the Four Masters: Irish History, Kingship and Society in the Early Seventeenth Century* (Dublin: Four Courts Press, 2010).

Dennehy, W., 'Irish Catholics in the Seventeenth Century', *Irish Ecclesiastical Record*, 4th series, 18 (1905), 410–20.

Dolan, F., 'Gender and the "Lost" Spaces of Catholicism', *Journal of Interdisciplinary History*, 32 (2002), 641–65.

Duffy, E., *Fires of Faith: Catholic England under Mary Tudor* (New Haven and London: Yale University Press, 2009).

Ellis, S. G., *Ireland in the Age of the Tudors 1447–1603* (London: Longman, 1998).

Finan, T., 'The Bardic Search for God: Vernacular Theology in Gaelic Ireland, 1200–1400', *Eolas: The Journal of the American Society of Irish Medieval Studies*, 2 (2007), 28–44.

Ford, A., 'Reforming the Holy Isle: Parr Lane and the Conversion of the Irish', in T. C. Barnard, D. Ó Cróinín and K. Simms (eds.), *'A Miracle of Learning': Studies in Manuscripts and Irish Learning. Essays in Honour of William O' Sullivan* (Aldershot: Ashgate, 1998), 137–63.

Giblin, C., 'The "Processus Datariae" and the Appointment of Irish Bishops in the Seventeenth Century', in Franciscan Fathers (eds.), *Father Luke Wadding Commemorative Volume* (Dublin: Clonmore and Reynolds, 1957), 508–616.

Gillespie, R., *Devoted People: Belief and Religion in Early Modern Ireland* (Manchester University Press, 1997).

Guy, J., 'Law, Lawyers and the English Reformation', *History Today* 35 (1985), 16–22.

Jackson, B., 'Sectarianism, Division and Dissent in Irish Catholicism', in A. Ford and J. McCafferty (eds.), *The Origins of Sectarianism in Early Modern Ireland* (Cambridge University Press, 2005), 203–15.

Jefferies, H. A., *The Irish Church and the Tudor Reformations* (Dublin: Four Courts Press, 2010).

Jefferies, H. A., 'The Irish Parliament of 1560: The Anglican Reforms Authorised', *Irish Historical Studies*, 26 (1988), 128–41.

Jefferies, H. A., 'The Role of the Laity in the Parishes of Armagh *inter Anglicos* on the Eve of the Tudor Reformations', *Archivium Hibernicum*, 52, (1988), 73–84.

Lennon, C., *The Lords of Dublin in the Age of Reformation* (Dublin: Irish Academic Press, 1989).

Lennon, C., 'The Dissolution to the Foundation of St Anthony's College, Louvain, 1534–1607', in E. Bhreathnach, J. MacMahon and J. McCafferty (eds.), *The Irish Franciscans, 1534–1990* (Dublin: Four Courts Press, 2009) 5–26.

Lotz-Heumann, U., 'Confessionalisation in Ireland: Periodisation and Character, 1534–1649', in A. Ford and J. McCafferty (eds.), *The Origins of Sectarianism in Early Modern Ireland* (Cambridge University Press, 2005), 24–53.

Mac Craith, M., 'Collegium S. Antonii Lovanii, quod Collegium est Unicum Remedium ad Conservandam Provinciam', in Bhreathnach, MacMahon and McCafferty (eds.) *The Irish Franciscans*, 233–59.

Mac Cuarta, B., *Catholic Revival in the North of Ireland* (Dublin: Four Courts Press, 1997).

Murray, J., *Enforcing the English Reformation in Ireland: Clerical Resistance and Political Conflict in the Diocese of Dublin, 1534–1590* (Cambridge University Press, 2009).

Murray, J., 'The Diocese of Dublin in the Sixteenth Century: Clerical Opposition and the Failure of the Reformation', in J. Kelly and D. Keogh (eds.), *History of the Catholic Diocese of Dublin* (Dublin: Four Courts Press, 2000), 92–111.

Ó hAnnracháin, T., *Catholic Reformation in Ireland: The Mission of Rinuccini, 1645–9* (Oxford University Press, 2002).

Ó hAnnracháin, T., *Catholic Europe, 1592–1648: Centre and Peripheries* (Oxford University Press, 2015).

Ó hAnnracháin, T., 'Religious Acculturation and Affiliation in Early Modern Gaelic Scotland, Gaelic Ireland, Wales and Cornwall', in T. Ó hAnnracháin and R. Armstrong (eds.) *Christianities in the Early Modern Celtic World*, (Basingstoke: Palgrave, 2014), 1–13.

O'Connor, T., *Irish Jansenists 1600–70: Religion and Politics in Flanders, France, Ireland and Rome* (Dublin: Four Courts Press, 2008).

Pörtner, R., *The Counter-Reformation in Central Europe: Styria 1580–1630* (Oxford: Clarendon Press, 2001).

Ryan, S., 'Continental Catechisms and their Irish Imitators in Spanish Habsburg Lands *c.*1550–*c.*1650', in R. Gillespie and R. O hUiginn (eds.), *Irish Europe 1600–1650: Writing and Learning* (Dublin: Four Courts Press, 2013), 163–82.

Ryan, S., *A Slighted Source: Rehabilitating Irish Bardic Religious Poetry in Historical Discourse*, *Cambrian Medieval Celtic Studies*, 48 (2004), 75–99.

Silke, J. J., 'The Irish abroad, 1534–1691', in T. W. Moody, F. X. Martin and F. J. Byrne (eds.), *A New History of Ireland iii: Early Modern Ireland, 1534–1691* (Oxford University Press, 1976), 587–633.

Spaans, J., 'Orphans and Students: Recruiting Girls and Boys for the Holland Mission', in B. Kaplan, B. Moore, H. Van Nierop and J. Pollmann (eds.), *Catholic Communities in Protestant States: Britain and the Netherlands c. 1570–1720* (Manchester University Press, 2009), 183–99.

Walsham, A., 'Translating Trent? English Catholicism and the Counter Reformation', *Historical Research* 78 (2005), 288–310.

8 Protestant Reformations, 1550–1641

Colm Lennon

Unpublished Primary Sources

The National Archives, Kew

SP61/4/36(ii).

Published Primary Sources

Adair, P., *A True Narrative of the Rise and Progress of the Presbyterian Church in Ireland* (Belfast: C. Aitchison, 1866).

Aibidil Gaoidheilge [agus] Caiticiosma (Dublin, 1571).

Brady, W. M. (ed.), *State papers concerning the Irish church in the time of Queen Elizabeth* (London: Longmans, Green, Reader and Dyer, 1868).

A Brefe Declaration of Certain Principall Articles of Religion (Dublin, 1566).

Shuckburgh, E. S. (ed.), *Two Biographies of William Bedell, Bishop of Kilmore* (Cambridge University Press, 1902).

The Statutes at Large passed in the Parliaments held in Ireland (2 vols., Dublin, 1786–1801).

Secondary Sources

Bagwell, R., 'Ram, Thomas (1564–1634)', rev. Alan Ford, *Oxford Dictionary of National Biography* (Oxford University Press, 2004), www.oxforddnb.com/view/article/23065 (accessed 13 June 2017).

Boran, E., 'Printing in Early Seventeenth-Century Dublin: Combatting Heresy in Serpentine Times', in E. Boran and C. Gribben (eds.), *Enforcing Reformation in Ireland and Scotland* (Aldershot: Ashgate Publishing Limited, 2006), 40–65.

Bottigheimer, K., 'The Failure of the Reformation in Ireland: Une Question Bien Posée', *Journal of Ecclesiastical History*, 36 (1985), 196–207.

Bradshaw, B., 'Sword, Word and Strategy in the Reformation in Ireland', *Historical Journal*, 21 (1978), 475–502.

Brady, C. and Murray, J., 'Sir Henry Sidney and the Reformation in Ireland', in E. Boran and C. Gribben (eds.), *Enforcing Reformation in Ireland and Scotland* (Aldershot: Ashgate Publishing Limited, 2006), 13–39.

Caball, M., 'Print, Protestantism and Cultural Authority in Elizabethan Ireland', in B. Kane and V. McGowan-Doyle (eds.), *Elizabeth I and Ireland* (Cambridge University Press, 2014), 286–308.

Caball, M., 'Gaelic and Protestant: A Case-Study in Early Modern Self-Fashioning, 1567–1608', *Proceedings of the Royal Irish Academy*, C:110 (2010), 191–215.

Canny, N., *Making Ireland British, 1580–1650* (Oxford University Press, 2001).

Canny, N., 'Why the Reformation Failed in Ireland: Une Question Mal Posée', *Journal of Ecclesiastical History*, 30 (1979), 423–50.

Clarke, A., 'Bishop William Bedell (1571–1642) and the Irish Reformation', in C. Brady (ed.), *Worsted in the Game: Losers in Irish History* (Dublin: The Lilliput Press, 1989), 61–70.

Clarke, A., 'Varieties of Uniformity: The First Century of the Church of Ireland', in W. J. Sheils and D. Wood (eds.), *The Churches, Ireland and the Irish: Studies in Church History, Volume 25* (Oxford: Basil Blackwell, 1989), 105–22.

Diamond, C., 'King, Edward (c.1576–1639)', *Oxford Dictionary of National Biography* (Oxford University Press, 2004), www.oxforddnb.com/view/article/67220 (accessed 13 June 2017).

Empey, M., 'Protestants and Gaelic Culture in Seventeenth-Century Ireland' (Maynooth University Library e-prints, no. 5606).

Ford, A., *The Protestant Reformation in Ireland, 1590–1641* (Dublin: Four Courts Press, 1997).

Ford, A. '"Force and the fear of punishment": Protestants and Religious Coercion in Ireland, 1603–33', in Elizabethanne Boran and Crawford Gribben, (eds.), *Enforcing Reformation in Ireland and Scotland* (Aldershot: Ashgate Publishing Limited, 2006), 91–130.

Ford, A., *James Ussher: Theology, History and Politics in Early Modern Ireland and England* (Oxford University Press, 2007).

Ford, A., 'James Ussher and the Creation of an Irish Protestant Identity', in B. Bradshaw and P. Roberts (eds.), *British Consciousness and Identity* (Cambridge University Press, 1998), 185–212.

Ford, A., 'Sectarianism in Early Modern Ireland', in A. Ford and J. McCafferty (eds.), *The Origins of Sectarianism in Early Modern Ireland* (Cambridge University Press, 2005), 6–17.

Gillespie, R., 'Lay Spirituality and Worship, 1558–1750: Holy Books and Godly Readers' in R. Gillespie and W. G. Neely (eds.), *The Laity and the Church of Ireland, 1000–2000* (Dublin: Four Courts Press, 2002), 133–51.

Gillespie, R., 'Godly Order: Enforcing Peace in the Irish Reformation', in E. Boran and C. Gribben (eds.), *Enforcing Reformation in Ireland and Scotland* (Aldershot: Ashgate Publishing Limited, 2006), 184–210.

Gillespie, R., 'The Church of Ireland Clergy, c.1640', in T. C. Barnard and W. G. Neely (eds.), *The Clergy of the Church of Ireland, 1000–2000* (Dublin: Four Courts Press, 2006), 59–77.

Gillespie, R., 'Urban Parishes in Early Seventeenth-Century Ireland: the Case of Dublin', in E. Fitzpatrick and R. Gillespie (eds.), *The Parish in Medieval and Early Modern Ireland* (Dublin: Four Courts Press, 2006), 228–41.

Hadfield, A., 'Translating the Reformation: John Bale's Irish *Vocacyon*', in B. Bradshaw and W. Maley (eds.), *Representing Ireland: Literature and the Origins of Conflict, 1534–1660* (Cambridge University Press, 1993), 43–59.

Heal, F., *Reformation in Britain and Ireland* (Oxford: Clarendon Press, 2003).

Hensey, Á., 'A Comparative Study of the Lives of Church of Ireland and Roman Catholic Clergy in the South-Eastern Dioceses of Ireland from 1550–1650', unpublished PhD thesis, Maynooth University, 2012.

Hutchinson, M., *Calvinism, Reform and the Absolutist State in Elizabethan Ireland* (London: Pickering and Chatto, 2015).

Hutchinson, M., 'An Irish Perspective on Elizabeth's Religion: Reformation Thought and Sir Henry Sidney's Irish Lord Deputyship, c.1560–1580', in B. Kane and V. McGowan-Doyle (eds.), *Elizabeth I and Ireland* (Cambridge University Press, 2014), 142–62.

Jefferies, H. A., *The Irish Church and the Tudor Reformations* (Dublin: Four Courts Press, 2010).

Kilroy, P., *Protestant Dissent and Controversy in Ireland* (Cork University Press, 1994).

Lennon, C., *The Lords of Dublin the Age of Reformation* (Dublin: Irish University Press, 1989).

Lennon, C., 'Mass in the Manor-House: The Counter-Reformation in Dublin, 1560–1630', in J. Kelly and D. Keogh (eds.), *History of the Catholic Archdiocese of Dublin* (Dublin: Four Courts Press, 2000), 112–26.

Lennon, C., 'The Shaping of a Lay Community in the Church of Ireland, 1558–1640', in R. Gillespie and W. G. Neely (eds.), *The Laity and the Church of Ireland, 1000–2000* (Dublin: Four Courts Press, 2002), 49–69.

Lennon, C., 'Taking Sides: The Emergence of Irish Catholic Ideology', in V. Carey and U. Lotz-Heumann (eds.), *Taking Sides? Colonial and Confessional Mentalities in Early Modern Ireland* (Dublin: Four Courts Press, 2003), 78–93.

Lennon, C. and C. Diamond, 'The Ministry of the Church of Ireland, 1536–1636', in T. C. Barnard and W. G. Neely (eds.), *The Clergy of the Church of Ireland, 1000–2000* (Dublin: Four Courts Press, 2006), 44–58.

Lennon, C., 'Education and Religious Identity in Early Modern Ireland', *Pedagogica Historica, Supplementary Series*, 5 (1999), 57–75.

Lotz-Heumann, U., 'Confessionalisation in Ireland: Periodisation and Character, 1534–1649', in A. Ford, and J. McCafferty (eds.), *The Origins of Sectarianism in Early Modern Ireland* (Cambridge University Press, 2005), 24–53.

Lotz-Heumann, U., 'Confessionalisation', in D. M. Whitford (ed.), *Reformation and Early Modern Europe: A Guide to Research* (Kirksville, MS.: Truman State University Press, 2008), 136–60.

MacCulloch, D., *Tudor Church Militant: Edward VI and the Protestant Reformation* (London: The Penguin Press, 1999).

Matthew, H. C. G. and B. Harrison (eds.), *Oxford Dictionary of National Biography* (60 vols., Oxford University Press, 2004).

McCafferty, J., *The Reconstruction of the Church of Ireland: Bishop Bramhall and the Laudian Reforms, 1633–41* (Cambridge University Press, 2007).

McCafferty, J., 'Protestant Prelates or Godly Pastors? The Dilemma of the Early Stuart Episcopate', in A. Ford and J. McCafferty (eds.), *The Origins of Sectarianism in Early Modern Ireland* (Cambridge University Press, 2005), 54–72.

Murray, J., *Enforcing the English Reformation in Ireland: Clerical Resistance and Political Conflict in the Diocese of Dublin, 1534–1590* (Cambridge University Press, 2009).

Murray, J., 'St Patrick's Cathedral and the University Question in Ireland c.1547–1585', in H. Robinson-Hammerstein (ed.), *European Universities in the Age of Reformation and Counter-Reformation* (Dublin: Four Courts Press, 1998), 1–33.

Ó hAnnracháin, T., *Catholic Counter-Reformation in Ireland: The Mission of Rinuccini, 1645–1649* (Oxford University Press, 2002).

Robinson-Hammerstein, H., 'Archbishop Adam Loftus, the First Provost of Trinity College, Dublin', in H. Robinson-Hammerstein (ed.), *European Universities in the Age of Reformation and Counter-Reformation* (Dublin: Four Courts Press, 1998), 34–52.

Robinson-Hammerstein, H., 'Aspects of the Continental Education of Irish Students in the Reign of Elizabeth I', in *Historical Studies*, 8 (1971), 137–54.

Tait, C., *Death, Burial and Commemoration in Ireland, 1550–1650* (Basingstoke: Palgrave MacMillan, 2002).

9 Establishing a Confessional Ireland, 1641–1691

Robert Armstrong

Unpublished Primary Sources

Presbyterian Historical Society, Belfast

James Alexander Sermon Book

Published Primary Sources

A Bishop of the Penal Times: being Letters and Reports of John Brenan, Bishop of Waterford (1671–93) and Archbishop of Cashel (1677–93), ed. P. Power (Cork University Press, 1932).

An Account of the Travels, Sufferings & Persecution of Barbara Blaugdone (London, 1691).

Adair, Patrick and Andrew Stewart, *Presbyterian History in Ireland: Two Seventeenth-Century Narratives*, ed. R. Armstrong, A. R. Holmes, R. S. Spurlock and P. Walsh (Belfast: Ulster Historical Foundation, 2016).

An Address given in to the Late king James by the Titular Archbishop of Dublin ... now Publish'd with Reflections...(London, 1690).

Archdekin, Richard, *A Treatise of Miracles* (Louvain, 1667).

Bergin, J., and A. Lyall (eds.), *The Acts of James II's Irish Parliament of 1689* (Dublin: Irish Manuscripts Commission, 2016).

Burke, W. P. (ed.), *The Irish Priests in the Penal Times* (Waterford: N. Harvey & Co., 1914).

Campbell, P. J., 'The Franciscan Petition Lists: Diocese of Armagh, 1670–1', *Seanchas Ardmhacha*, 15 (1992–3), 186–216.

Dunlop, R. (ed.), *Ireland under the Commonwealth* (2 vols., Manchester University Press, 1913).

Eyres, Joseph, *The Church-Sleeper Awakened* (London, 1659).

Gilbert, Claudius, *The Libertine School'd ...* (London, 1656).

Gilbert, J. T. (ed.), *History of the Irish Confederation and the War in Ireland* (7 vols., Dublin: M. H. Gill, 1882–91).

Gilbert, J. T. (ed.), *A Jacobite Narrative of the War in Ireland* (Dublin: J. Dollard, 1892).

Journals of the House of Lords of the Kingdom of Ireland (8 vols., Dublin, 1779–1800).

King, William, *A Discourse Concerning the Inventions of Men in the Worship of God* (Dublin, 1694).

The Letters of Saint Oliver Plunkett, ed. John Hanly (Dublin: Dolmen Press, 1979).

Mahaffy, R. P. (ed.), *Calendar of the State Papers Relating to Ireland, 1663–1665* (London: HMSO, 1907).

Newman, J.H., *The Via Media of the Anglican Church*, ed. H. D. Weidner (Oxford University Press, 1990).

News from Ireland (London, 1650).

Queries Concerning the Lawfulnesse of the Present Cessation ([Kilkenny, 1648]).

Recollections of an Irish Poor Clare in the Seventeenth Century: Mother Mary Bonaventure, Third Abbess of Galway, 1647–1650, ed. C. O'Brien O.F.M. (Galway: Poor Clares, 1993).

Taylor, Jeremy, *A Discourse of Confirmation ...* (Dublin, 1663).

Tweedie, W. K. (ed.), *Select Biographies* (2 vols., Edinburgh: Wodrow Society, 1845–7).

Secondary Sources

Armstrong, R., 'Protestant Churchmen and the Confederate Wars', in C. Brady and J. Ohlmeyer (eds.), *British Interventions in Early Modern Ireland* (Cambridge University Press, 2005), 230–51.

Armstrong, R., 'Viscount Ards and the Presbytery: Politics and Religion among the Scots of Ulster in the 1640s', in W. P. Kelly and J. R. Young (eds.), *Scotland and the Ulster Plantations* (Dublin: Four Courts Press, 2009), 18–40.

Armstrong, R., 'The Irish Alternative: Scottish and English Presbyterianism in Ireland', in R. Armstrong and T. Ó hAnnracháin (eds.), *Insular Christianity: Alternative Models of the Church in Britain and Ireland, 1570–1700* (Manchester University Press, 2013), 207–30.

Armstrong, R., 'The Bishops of Ireland and the Beasts at Ephesus: Reconstruction, Conformity and the Presbyterian Knot 1660–2', in N. H. Keeble (ed.), *'Settling the peace of the church': 1662 Revisited* (Oxford University Press, 2014), 114–43.

Armstrong, R., 'The Scots of Ireland and the English Republic, 1649–60', in D. Edwards (ed.), *The Scots in Early Stuart Ireland* (Manchester University Press, 2016), 251–78.

Armstrong, R., 'Ireland's Puritan Revolution? The Emergence of Ulster Presbyterianism Reconsidered', *English Historical Review*, 121 (2006), 1048–74.

Barnard, T. C., *Cromwellian Ireland* (2nd edn., Oxford University Press, 2000).

Barnard, T. C., '"Almoners of providence": The Clergy, 1647 to *c.*1780', in T. C. Barnard and W. G. Neely (eds.), *The Clergy of the Church of Ireland 1000–2000* (Dublin: Four Courts Press, 2006), 78–105.

Barnard, T. C., 'Protestants and the Irish Language, *c.*1675–1725', *Journal of Ecclesiastical History*, 44 (1993), 243–72.

Bolton, F. R., *The Caroline Tradition of the Church of Ireland* (London: SPCK, 1958).

Bossy, J., 'The Counter-Reformation and the People of Catholic Ireland, 1596–1641', in T. D. Williams (ed.), *Historical Studies VIII* (Dublin: Gill and Macmillan, 1971), 155–69.

Campbell, I. W. S., 'John Lynch and Renaissance Humanism in Stuart Ireland: Catholic Intellectuals, Protestant Noblemen, and the Irish *Respublica*', *Éire-Ireland*, 45 (2010), 27–40.

Chambers, L., *Michael Moore c.1639–1726* (Dublin: Four Courts Press, 2005).

Clarke, A., *Prelude to Restoration in Ireland* (Cambridge University Press, 1999).

Connolly, S. J., *Religion, Law and Power: The Making of Protestant Ireland 1660–1760* (Oxford: Clarendon Press, 1992).

Connors, T., 'Religion and the Laity in Early Modern Galway', in Gerard Moran (ed.), *Galway: History and Society* (Dublin: Geography Publications, 1996), 131–48.

Corish, P. J., *The Catholic Community in the Seventeenth and Eighteenth Centuries* (Dublin: Helicon, 1981).

Creighton, A., 'The Remonstrance of December 1661 and Catholic politics in Restoration Ireland', *Irish Historical Studies*, 34 (2004), 16–41.

Cunningham, J., 'Lay Catholicism and Religious Policy in Cromwellian Ireland', *Journal of Ecclesiastical History*, 64 (2013), 769–86.

Duffy, P. J., 'The Shape of the Parish', in E. FitzPatrick and R. Gillespie (eds.), *The Parish in Medieval and Early Modern Ireland* (Dublin: Four Courts Press, 2006), 33–61.

Ford, A., *James Ussher: Theology, History and Politics in Early Modern Ireland and England* (Oxford University Press, 2007).

Ford, A., 'The Origins of Irish Dissent', in K. Herlihy (ed.), *The Religion of Irish Dissent, 1650–1800* (Dublin: Four Courts Press, 1996), 9–30.

Forrestal, A., *Catholic Synods in Ireland, 1600–1690* (Dublin: Four Courts Press, 1998).

Giblin, C., 'The Contribution of Irish Franciscans on the Continent in the Seventeenth Century', in M. Maher (ed.), *Irish Spirituality* (Dublin: Veritas Publications, 1981), 88–103.

Gillespie, R., *Devoted People: Belief and Religion in Early Modern Ireland* (Manchester University Press, 1997).

Gillespie, R., 'Catholic Religious Cultures in the Diocese of Dublin, 1614–97', in J. Kelly and D. Keogh (eds.), *History of the Catholic Diocese of Dublin* (Dublin: Four Courts Press, 2000), 127–43.

Gillespie, R., 'The Reformed Preacher: Irish Protestant Preaching, 1660–1700', in A. J. Fletcher and R. Gillespie (eds.), *Irish Preaching, 700–1700* (Dublin: Four Courts Press, 2001), 127–43.

Greaves, R. L., *God's Other Children: Protestant Nonconformists and the Emergence of Denominational Churches in Ireland, 1660–1700* (Stanford, CA: Stanford University Press, 1997).

Green, I., '"The necessary knowledge of the principles of religion": Catechisms and Catechizing in Ireland, c.1560–1700', in A. Ford, J. McGuire and K. Milne (eds.), *As by Law established: the Church of Ireland since the Reformation* (Dublin: The Lilliput Press, 1995), 69–88.

Gribben, C., *God's Irishmen: Theological Debates in Cromwellian Ireland* (Oxford University Press, 2007).

Harris, T., *Revolution: The Great Crisis of the British Monarchy, 1685–1720* (London: Allen Lane, 2006).

Hughes, A., '"The public profession of these nations": The National Church in Interregnum England', in C. Durston and J. Maltby (eds.), *Religion in Revolutionary England* (Manchester University Press, 2006), 93–114.

Kelly, J., 'The Catholic Church in the Diocese of Ardagh, 1650–1870', in R. Gillespie and G. Moran (eds.), *Longford: Essays in County History* (Dublin: The Lilliput Press, 1991), 63–91.

Kelly, J., 'The Formation of the Modern Catholic Church in the Diocese of Kilmore, 1580–1880', in R. Gillespie (ed.), *Cavan: Essays on the History of an Irish County* (Blackrock, Co. Dublin: Irish Academic Press, 1995), 115–38.

Latimer, W. T., *A History of the Irish Presbyterians* (2nd edn., Belfast: James Cleeland, 1902).

McGuire, J., 'Policy and Patronage: The Appointment of Bishops 1660–61', in A. Ford, J. McGuire and K. Milne (eds.), *As by Law established: The Church of Ireland since the Reformation* (Dublin: The Lilliput Press, 1995), 112–19.

Middleton, K., 'Religious Revolution and Social Crisis in Southwest Scotland and Ulster, 1687–1714', unpublished PhD dissertation, Trinity College Dublin (2010).

Millett, B., 'Survival and Reorganization 1650–1695', in P. J. Corish (ed.) *History of Irish Catholicism*, iii, fasc. 7 (Dublin: Gill and Son, 1968).

Ó hAnnracháin, T., *Catholic Reformation in Ireland: the Mission of Rinuccini, 1645–1649* (Oxford University Press, 2002).

Ó hAnnracháin, T., '"In imitation of that holy patron of prelates the blessed St Charles": Episcopal Activity in Ireland and the Formation of a Confessional Identity, 1618–1653', in A. Ford and J. McCafferty (eds.), *The Origins of Sectarianism in Early Modern Ireland* (Cambridge University Press, 2005), 73–94.

O'Connor, T., *Irish Jansenists, 1600–70: Religion and Politics in Flanders, France, Ireland and Rome* (Dublin: Four Courts Press, 2008).

O'Regan, P., *Archbishop William King of Dublin (1650–1729) and the Constitution in Church and State* (Dublin: Four Courts Press, 2000).

Roulston, W., 'Accommodating Clergymen: Church of Ireland Ministers and their Houses in the North of Ireland, c.1600–1870', in T. C. Barnard and W. G. Neely (eds.), *The Clergy of the Church of Ireland 1000–2000* (Dublin: Four Courts Press, 2006), 106–27.

Simms, J. G., *Jacobite Ireland 1685–91* (London: Routledge and Kegan Paul, 1969).

Williams, M. R. F., 'Between King, Faith and Reason: Father Peter Talbot (SJ) and Catholic Royalist Thought in Exile', *English Historical Review*, 127 (2012), 1063–99.

10 Wars of Religion, 1641–1691

John Jeremiah Cronin and Pádraig Lenihan

Unpublished Primary Sources
Bodleian Library, Oxford
Carte MS 30

James Hardiman Library, NUI Galway
Galway Corporation Statute Book, Liber A, fo. 205, http://archives.library.nuigalway.ie/
LiberA/html/LiberA.html (accessed 30 January 2016)

The National Archives, UK
SPD 8/8/62, 69

SPD 18/19/25, 133; 18/20/163

SPD 25/65/145, 215, 217; 25/94/507; 25/96/143, 145, 163, 191; 25/101/87, 93, 103, 117, 131,
135, 147, 161, 153, 155, 249; 25/119/100;

SPI 46/102/145, 157

SPI 63/353/6, 12

Representative Church Body Library Dublin
MS P328/5/1

Trinity College Dublin
MS 817

Published Primary Sources

Ainsworth, J. and E. Mac Lysaght, 'The Arthur Manuscript', *North Munster Antiquarian Journal* (1953), 168–82.

Anon., *The New Method of Fortification as practiced by Monsieur de Vauban…* (London, 1691).

Basill, William, *A letter from William Basill … Concerning a Great Victory Obtained by the Parliaments Forces against the Rebels in Meleek Island* (London, 1650).

Barry, Gerat, *A Discourse of Military Discipline* (Brussells, 1634).

Borlase, Edmund, *The History of the Execrable Irish Rebellion* (London, 1680).

Cary, H. (ed.), *Memorials of the Great Civil War in England from 1646 to 1652* (2 vols., London, 1842).

Collings, Richard (ed.), *The Weekly Intelligencer of the Commonwealth* (8–15 October 1650).

A Diary of the Siege and Surrender of Lymerick (Dublin, 1692).

Dunlop, R. (ed.), *Ireland Under the Commonwealth*, (2 vols., Manchester University Press, 1913).

Forkan, K., 'Army List of the Ulster British Forces, 1642–1646', *Archivium Hibernicum*, 59 (2005), 51–65.

Gilbert, J. T. (ed.), *A Contemporary History of Affairs in Ireland from 1641 to 1652* (3 vols., Dublin: Irish Archaeological and Celtic Society, 1879–80).

Hall, John, *Mercurius Politicus* (9–16 June 1653).

Hardy, W. H. (ed.), *Calendar of State Papers Domestic: William and Mary, 1690–1* (London: HMSO 1898).

Hewson, John, *A letter from Colonel Hewson from Finagh in Ireland* (London, 1651).

Historical Manuscripts Commission, *Fourth Report* (London: HMSO, 1874).

Ireton, Henry, *A Declaration and Proclamation of the Deputy-General of Ireland Concerning the Present Hand of God in the Visitation of the Plague* (Cork, 1650).

Leyburn, George, *Memoirs* (London, 1722).

Ludlow, Edmund, *Memoirs*, (3 vols., Vevay, 1698–9).

Mackenzie, J., *A Narrative of the Siege of London-Derry* (London, 1690).

Mahaffy, R. P., (ed.), *Calendar of State Papers Relating to Ireland of the Reign of Charles I, 1633–47* (London: HMSO, 1901).

Mills, J. (ed.), *Registers of the Parish of St John the Evangelist, Dublin, 1619–1699* (Dublin: Parish Register Society of Dublin, 1906).

Moran, P. F. (ed.), *Spicilegium Ossoriense: Being a Collection of Original Letters and Papers Illustrative of the History of the Irish Church from the Reformation to the Year 1800* (3 vols., Dublin: W. B. Kelly, 1874–84).

Mulloy, S. (ed.), *Franco-Irish Correspondence* (3 vols., Dublin: Irish Manuscripts Commission, 1983–4).

O'Ferrall, Richard and Robert O'Connell, *Commentarius Rinuccinianus de Sedis apostolicae legatione ad Foederatos Hiberniae Catholicos per annos 1645–1649* (6 vols., Dublin: Irish Manuscripts Commission, 1932–49).

Pecke, Samuel (ed.), *A Perfect Diurnall of some Passages and Proceedings of, and in Relation to, the Armies in England and Ireland*, no. 44 (7–14 October 1650), no. 73 (28 April–5 May 1650), and no. 74 (5–12 May 1651).

Petty, William, *The Political Anatomy of Ireland*, (London, 1691).

A Remonstrance of Sir Frederick Hammilton ([London, 1643]).

Petty, William, 'The Down Survey of Ireland', http://downsurvey.tcd.ie (accessed 30 Jan. 2016).

Russell, C. W. and J. P. Prendergast (eds.), *Carte Manuscripts in the Bodleian Library* (London: HMSO, 1871).

Smith, W. J. (ed.), *Herbert Correspondence* (Cardiff: University of Wales Press, 1963).

Steele, R. (ed.), *Tudor and Stuart Proclamations, 1485–1714* (2 vols., Oxford: Clarendon Press, 1910).

Story, George, *A Continuation of the Impartial History of the Wars of Ireland* (London, 1693).

Story, George, *A True and Impartial History of the Most Material Occurrences during the last Two Years. With the Present State of both armies* (London, 1693).

Turner, James, *Pallas Armata* (London, 1683).

Whitelocke, Bulstrode, *Memorials of the English Affairs* (London, 1682).

Secondary Sources

Appleby, A. B., 'Grain Prices and Subsistence Crises in England and France, 1590–1740', *The Journal of Economic History*, 39 (1979), 865–87.

Armstrong, R., *Protestant War: The 'British' of Ireland and the Wars of the Three Kingdoms* (Manchester University Press, 2005).

Bagwell, R., *Ireland under the Stuarts and during the interregnum* (3 vols., London, 1909–16).

Bartlett, T., *The Academy of Warre: Military Affairs in Ireland 1600 to 1800: the O'Donnell Lecture 2002* (Dublin: National University of Ireland, 2002).

Black, J., *A Military Revolution? Military Change and European Society 1550–1800* (London: Macmillan, 1991).

Brunicardi, N., 'The Battle of Manning Ford, 4 June 1643', *The Irish Sword*, 22 (2000–1), 3–14.

Canny, N., *Making Ireland British, 1580–1650* (Oxford University Press, 2001).

Childs, J., *The Williamite Wars in Ireland* (London: Hambledon Press, 2007).

Childs, J., *General Percy Kirke and the Later Stuart Army* (London: Bloomsbury, 2014).

Childs, J., 'The Williamite War, 1689–91', in T. Bartlett and K. Jeffery (eds.), *A Military History of Ireland* (Cambridge University Press, 1996), 188–210.

Clarkson, L. A., *Death, Disease and Famine in Pre-Industrial England* (Dublin: Gill and Macmillan, 1975).

Clarkson, L. A., 'Irish Population Revisited, 1687–1821', in J. M. Goldstrom and L. A. Clarkson (eds.), *Irish Population, Economy and Society* (Oxford: Clarendon Press, 1981), 13–35.

Clinton, M., L. Fibiger and D. Shiels, 'The Carrickmines Mass Grave and the Siege of March 1642', in D. Edwards, P. Lenihan and C. Tait (eds.), *Age of Atrocity: Violence and Political Conflict in Early Modern Ireland* (Dublin: Four Courts Press, 2007), 192–203.

Corish, P., 'The Cromwellian Conquest, 1649–53', in T. W. Moody, F. X. Martin and F. J. Byrne (eds.), *A New History of Ireland iii: Early Modern Ireland, 1534–1691* (Oxford University Press, 1976), 336–52.

Cullen, L. M., 'Economic Trends 1660–9', in T. W. Moody, F. X. Martin and F. J. Byrne (eds.), *A New History of Ireland iii: Early Modern Ireland, 1534–1691* (Oxford University Press, 1976), 387–407.

Cullen, L. M., 'Economic Developments 1691–1750', in T. W. Moody and W. E. Vaughan (eds.), *A New History of Ireland iv: Eighteenth Century Ireland, 1691–1800* (Oxford University Press, 1986), 123–40.

Cunningham, J., *Conquest and Land in Ireland: The Transplantation to Connacht, 1649–1680* (Woodbridge: Boydell and Brewer).

Darcy, E., *The Irish Rebellion of 1641 and the Wars of the Three Kingdoms* (Woodbridge: Boydell and Brewer, 2013).

Dickson, D., *Old World Colony Cork and South Munster 1630–1830* (Cork University Press, 2005).

Doherty, R., *The Williamite War in Ireland* (Dublin: Four Courts Press, 1998).

Duffy, E. P., 'The Siege and Surrender of Galway 1651–1652', *Journal of the Galway Archaeological and Historical Society*, 39 (1983), 115–42.

Duignan, A., 'All Confused in Opposition to Each Other': Politics and War in Connacht, 1641–9', unpublished PhD thesis, University College Dublin (2006).

Ferguson, K., 'The Organisation of King William's Army in Ireland, 1689–91' *The Irish Sword*, 70 (1990), 62–79.

Gillespie, R., *The Transformation of the Irish Economy 1550–1700* (Dundalk: Dundalgan Press, 1991).

Gillespie, R., 'The End of an Era: Ulster and the Outbreak of the 1641 Rising', in C. Brady and R. Gillespie, (eds.), *Natives and Newcomers: Essays on the Making of Irish Colonial Society, 1534–1641* (Dublin: Irish Academic Press, 1986), 191–214.

Gillespie, R., 'War and the Irish Town: The Early Modern Experience', in P. Lenihan (ed.), *Conquest and Resistance: War in Seventeenth Century Ireland* (Leiden, Brill, 2001), 293–16.

Glozier, M., *Marshal Schomberg 1615–1690: 'The Ablest Soldier of his Age'* (Brighton: Sussex Academic Press, 2005).

Hunter, R. J., 'Plantation in Donegal', in W. Nolan, L. Ronayne and M. Dunlevy (eds.), *Donegal History and Society* (Dublin: Geography Publications, 1995), 283–324.

Ingrao, C. W., *The Habsburg Monarchy, 1618–1815* (Cambridge University Press, 2000).

Kelly, W. P., 'The Forgotten Siege of Derry, March-August 1649', in W. P. Kelly (ed.), *The Sieges of Derry* (Dublin: Four Courts Press, 2001), 31–52.

Lenihan, P., *Confederate Catholics at War, 1642–1649* (Cork University Press, 2001).

Lenihan, P., *Consolidating Conquest: Ireland 1603–1727* (Harlow: Pearson Longman, 2008).

Lenihan, P., *The Last Cavalier: Richard Talbot (1631–91)* (University College Dublin Press, 2015).

Lenihan, P., 'War and Population 1649–52', *Irish Economic and Social History*, 24 (1997), 1–21.

Lenihan, P., 'Unhappy Campers: Dundalk (1689) and After', *Journal of Conflict Archaeology*, 3 (2007), 197–216.

Lindemann, M., *Medicine and Society in Early Modern Europe* (Cambridge University Press, 1999).

Loeber, R. and G. Parker, 'The Military Revolution in Seventeenth-Century Ireland', in J. Ohlmeyer (ed.), *Ireland from Independence to Occupation, 1641–1660* (Cambridge University Press, 1995) 66–88.

Lynn, J. A., *Giant of the Grand Siècle: The French Army 1610–1715* (Cambridge University Press, 1997).

Lynn, J. A., 'The Trace Italienne and the Growth of Armies: The French Case', *The Journal of Military History*, 55 (1991), 649–677.

McCarthy, P., 'Preserving Donegal: The Battle of Glenmaquin, 16 June 1642', *The Irish Sword* 23 (2003), 361–82.

McKenny, K., *The Laggan Army in Ireland, 1640–1685* (Dublin: Four Courts Press, 2005).

McNally, M., *The Battle of Aughrim 1691* (Stroud: History Press, 2008).

Miller, A., 'The Battle of Ross: A Controversial Military Event', *The Irish Sword*, 10 (1971), 141–58.

Miller, A, 'The Relief of Athlone and the Battle of Rathconnell', *Ríocht na Midhe*, 5 (1972),74–95.

Morrill, J., 'The Drogheda Massacre in Cromwellian Context', in D. Edwards, P. Lenihan and C. Tait (eds.), *Age of Atrocity: Violence and Political Conflict in Early Modern Ireland* (Dublin: Four Courts Press, 2007), 242–65.

Murphy, D., *Cromwell in Ireland: A History of Cromwell's Irish Campaign* (Dublin: M. H. Gill and Son, 1883).

Murtagh, D. and Murtagh, H., 'The Irish Jacobite Army, 1689–91', *The Irish Sword*, 18 (1990), 32–48.

Murtagh, H., *Athlone: History and Settlement to 1800* (Athlone: Old Athlone Society, 2000).

Murtagh, H., 'The War in Ireland, 1689–1691', in W. A. Maguire (ed.), *Kings in Conflict: The Revolutionary War in Ireland and its Aftermath, 1689–1750* (Belfast: Blackstaff Press, 1990), 61–91.

Murtagh, H., 'The Williamite War 1689–91', *History Ireland*, 1(1993), 39–41.

Nicholls, K. W., 'The Other Massacre: English Killings of Irish, 1641–2', in D. Edwards, P. Lenihan and C. Tait (eds.), *Age of Atrocity: Violence and Political Conflict in Early Modern Ireland* (Dublin: Four Courts Press, 2007), 176–91.

Ó Buachalla, B., *Dánta Aodhagáin Uí Rathaille: Reassessments* (Dublin: Irish Texts Society, 2004).

Ó Buachalla, B., 'Briseadh na Bóinne', *Éigse*, 23 (1989), 82–106.

Ó hAnnracháin, T., 'The Strategic Involvement of Continental Powers in Ireland, 1596–1691', in P. Lenihan (ed.), *Conquest and Resistance: War in Seventeenth Century Ireland* (Leiden, Brill, 2001), 25–52.

Ó Mórdha, P., 'The Battle of Clones, 1643', *Clogher Record: Journal of the Clogher Historical Society*, 4 (1962), 148–54.

Ó Murchadha, D., 'The siege of Cork in 1690', *Journal of the Cork Historical and Archaeological Society*, 95 (1990), 1–19.

Ó Siochru, M., *God's Executioner: Oliver Cromwell and the Conquest of Ireland* (London: Faber & Faber, 2008).

Ó Siochru, M., 'Propaganda, Rumour and Myth: Oliver Cromwell and the Massacre at Drogheda', in D. Edwards, P. Lenihan and C. Tait (eds.), *Age of Atrocity: Violence and Political Conflict in Early Modern Ireland* (Dublin: Four Courts Press, 2007), 242–65.

O'Brien, B., 'The Battle of Knocknanuss', *An Cosantóir*, 28 (1968), 80–5.

O'Callaghan, S., *To Hell or Barbados* (Dingle: Brandon Books, 2001).

O'Carroll, D., 'Change and Continuity in Weapons and Tactics, 1594–1691', in P. Lenihan (ed.), *Conquest and Resistance: War in Seventeenth Century Ireland* (Leiden, Brill, 2001), 211–56.

Ohlmeyer, Jane, 'The Wars of Religion,1603-60', in *A Military History of Ireland*, ed. Thomas Bartlett and Keith Jeffery (Cambridge University Press, 1996), 185.

Ohlmeyer, J., 'A Failed Revolution? The Irish Confederate War in Its European Context', *History Ireland*, 3 (1995), 24–8.

Ohlmeyer, J., 'The Wars of the Three Kingdoms', *History Today* 48 (1998), 16–22.

Outram, Q., 'The Socio-Economic Relations of Warfare and the Military Mortality Crises of the Thirty Years' War', *Medical History*, 45 (2001), 151–84.

Parker, G., 'The Universal Soldier', in G. Parker (ed.), *The Thirty Years War* (London: Routledge and Kegan Paul, 1987) 171–86.

Prendergast, J. P., *The Cromwellian Settlement of Ireland* (New York: P.M. Haverty, 1868).

Reilly, T., *Cromwell was Framed: Ireland 1649* (London: Chronos, 2014).

Ruff, J. R., *Violence in Early Modern Europe 1500–1800* (Cambridge University Press, 2001).

Scott Wheeler, J., *Cromwell in Ireland* (Dublin: Gill and Macmillan, 1999).

Scott Wheeler, J., 'Logistics and Supply in Cromwell's Conquest of Ireland', in M. Fissel (ed.), *War and Government in Britain, 1598–1650* (Manchester University Press, 1991), 38–56.

Scott Wheeler, J., 'Four Armies in Ireland', in J. Ohlmeyer (ed.), *Ireland from Independence to Occupation, 1641–1660* (Cambridge University Press, 1995), 43–65.

Simms, J. G., 'Cromwell at Drogheda 1649', in D. Hayton and G. O'Brien (eds.), *War and Politics in Ireland 1649–1730* (London: Hambledon Press, 1986), 1–10.

Simms, J. G., 'Williamite Peace Tactics, 1690–1', in D. Hayton and G. O'Brien (eds.), *War and Politics in Ireland 1649–1730* (London: Hambledon Press, 1986), 181–201.

Simms, J. G., 'The Restoration 1660–85', in T. W. Moody, F. X. Martin and F. J. Byrne (eds.), *A New History of Ireland iii: Early Modern Ireland, 1534–1691* (Oxford University Press, 1976), 420–53.

Simms, J. G., *Jacobite Ireland* (new edn., Dublin: Fourt Courts Press, 2000).

Smyth, A. J., 'The Social and Economic Impact of the Williamite War on Ireland, 1688–91', unpublished PhD thesis, Trinity College Dublin (2013).

Stradling, R. A., *The Spanish Monarchy and Irish Mercenaries 1618–68* (Dublin: Irish Academic Press, 1994).

Walter, J. and R. Schofield, 'Famine, Disease and Crisis Mortality in Early Modern Society', in J. Walter and R. Schofield (eds.), *Famine, Disease and the Social Order in Early Modern Society* (Cambridge University Press, 1989), 1–74

Wiggins, K., *Anatomy of a Siege: King John's Castle, Limerick, 1642*, (Woodbridge: Boydell Press, 2001).

Wilson, P. H., *Europe's Tragedy: A History of the Thirty Years War*, (London: Allen Lane, 2009).

11 Society, 1550–1700

Clodagh Tait

Unpublished Primary Sources

National Archives of Ireland

RC 5/4

Trinity College Dublin

1641 Depositions, MSS 820, 822, 824, 825, 826

Published Primary Sources

Ainsworth, J., 'Corporation Book of the Irishtown of Kilkenny, 1537–1628', *Analecta Hibernica*, 28 (1978), 3–78.

Battersby, W. J. (ed.), 'A briefe relation of Ireland', www.ucc.ie/celt/published/T100077/index.html (accessed 3 January 2015).

By the Lord Deputy and Council Whereas Redmond O'Hanlon … (Dublin, 1674).

Carpenter, A. (ed.), *Verse in English from Tudor and Stuart Ireland* (Cork University Press, 2003).

Carrigan, W., 'Old Waterford Wills III', *Journal of the Waterford and South East of Ireland Archaeological Society*, 9 (1906), 210–14.

C[aulfield], R., 'Petition of the Poor Fishermen of Silly-point, near Kinsale', *Notes and Queries* second series, 12 (1861), 65–6.

Curtis, E. (ed.), *Calendar of Ormond Deeds v, 1547–1584* (Dublin: Stationery Office, 1941).

Curtis, E., 'The Court Book of Esker and Crumlin, 1592–1600', *Journal of the Royal Society of Antiquaries of Ireland*, 19 (1929), 128–48; 20 (1930), 38–55; 20 (1930) 137–49.

Ferguson, J. F., 'The Ulster Roll of Gaol Delivery', *Ulster Journal of Archaeology*, fifth series, 1 (1853), 260–70; 2 (1854), 25–9.

'Fiants-Philip and Mary', *Ninth Report of the Deputy Keeper of the Public Records in Ireland* (Dublin: Alexander Thom, 1877).

Gilbert, J. T. and R Gilbert (eds.), *Calendar of the Ancient Records of Dublin* (19 vols., Dublin: Dollard, 1889–1944).

Gilbert, J. T. (ed.), 'Archives of the Town of Galway', in Historical Manuscripts Commission, *Tenth Report, appendix, part 5* (London: Stationery Office, 1885).

Gillespie, R., 'A Manor Court in Seventeenth Century Ireland', *Irish Economic and Social History*, 25 (1998), 81–7.

Grosart, A. B. (ed.), *The Lismore Papers* (10 vols., London, 1886–8).

Hogan, E. (ed.), *The Description of Ireland and the State thereof as it is at Present in Anno 1598* (Dublin: M. H. Gill and Son, 1878).

Irish Record Commission, *Irish Patent Rolls of James I* (Dublin: Stationery Office, 1966).

Mahaffy, R. P., (ed.), *Calendar of State Papers Relating to Ireland, 1625–1632* (London: HMSO, 1900).

Mockler, J., 'A Letter Sent in 1617, from the East Munster (Ormond) "Residence" of the Jesuits', *Journal of the Waterford and South East of Ireland Archaeological Society*, 6 (1900), 101–22.

Morgan, H., 'Lawes of Ireland (1609)', *The Irish Jurist*, 31 (1995–6), 307–12.

The Ninth Report of the Deputy Keeper of the Public Records in Ireland (Dublin: Alexander Thom, 1877).

Ohlmeyer, J. and É. Ó Ciardha (eds.), *The Irish Statute Staple Books, 1596–1687* (Dublin: Four Courts Press, 1998).

A Proclamation for the Speedy Sending away of the Irish Beggars (London, 1629; 1633, 1634).

Steele, R. (ed.), *Tudor and Stuart Proclamations 1485–1714* (2 vols., Oxford: Clarendon Press, 1910).

Vigors, P. D., 'Extracts from the Books of the Old Corporation of Ross, County Wexford', *Journal of the Royal Society of Antiquaries of Ireland*, 2 (1892), 171–6.

Secondary Sources

Barnard, T., *A New Anatomy of Ireland* (London and New Haven: Yale University Press, 2003).

Braddick, M. J. and J. Walter (eds.), *Negotiating Power in Early Modern Society* (Cambridge University Press, 2001).

Canny, N., *The Upstart Earl: A Study of the Social and Mental World of Richard Boyle, first Earl of Cork* (Cambridge University Press, 1982).

Canny, N., *Making Ireland British* (Oxford University Press, 2001).

Carroll, S., 'Reform Government and the Politics of Protest in Early Seventeenth-Century Ireland', unpublished PhD thesis, Trinity College Dublin (2013).

Clark, M. and R. Refaussé, *Directory of Historic Dublin Guilds* (Dublin: Dublin Public Libraries, 1993).

Cockerham, P. and A. Harris, 'Kilkenny Funeral Monuments 1500–1600: A Statistical and Analytical Account', *Proceedings of the Royal Irish Academy*, 101:C (2001), 135–88.

Cockerham, P., 'My Body to be Buried in my own Monument: The Social and Political Context of County Kilkenny Funeral Monuments, 1600–1700', *Proceedings of the Royal Irish Academy*, 109:C (2009), 239–365.

Coolahan, M. L., *Women, Writing, and Language in Early Modern Ireland* (Oxford University Press, 2010).

Crawford, J. G., *A Star Chamber Court in Ireland* (Dublin: Four Courts Press, 2005).

Cullen, L. M., T. C. Smout and A. Gibson, 'Wages and Comparative Development in Ireland and Scotland, 1565–1780', in R. Mitchison and P. Roebuck (eds.), *Economy and Society in Scotland and Ireland 1500–1939* (Edinburgh: John Donald, 1988), 105–16.

Cunningham, B., *The World of Geoffrey Keating* (Dublin: Four Courts Press, 2004).

Cunningham, B., *Clanricard and Thomond, 1540–1640* (Dublin: Four Courts Press, 2012).

Cunningham, B., 'Colonized Catholics: Perceptions of Honour and History in Michael Kearney's Reading of *Foras Feasa ar Éirinn*', in V. P. Carey and U. Lotz-Heumann (eds.), *Taking Sides: Colonial and Confessional Mentalités in Early Modern Ireland* (Dublin: Four Courts Press, 2003), 150–64.

Darcy, E., 'The Social Order of the 1641 Rebellion', in E. Darcy, A. Margey and E. Murphy (eds.), *The 1641 Depositions and the Irish Rebellion* (London: Pickering and Chatto, 2012), 97–112.

Dickson, D., 'In Search of the Old Irish Poor Law', in Mitchison and Roebuck (eds.), *Economy and Society*, 149–59.

Dickson, D., 'Middlemen', in T. Bartlett and D. W. Hayton (eds.), *Penal Era and Golden Age: Essays in Irish History, 1690–1800* (Belfast: Ulster Historical Foundation, 1979), 162–85.

Dickson, D., 'No Scythians Here: Women and Marriage in Seventeenth-Century Ireland', in M. MacCurtain and M. O'Dowd (eds.), *Women in Early Modern Ireland* (Dublin: Wolfhound Press, 1991), 223–35.

Dudley, R., 'The Dublin Parishes and the Poor, 1660–1740', *Archivium Hibernicum*, 53 (1999), 80–94

Edwards, D. and C. Rynne (eds.), *The Colonial World of Richard Boyle, The First Earl of Cork* (Dublin, Four Courts Press, 2017).

Edwards, D., 'Two Fools and a Martial Law Commissioner: Cultural Conflict at the Limerick Assize of 1606', in D. Edwards (ed.), *Regions and Rulers in Ireland, 1100–1650* (Dublin: Four Courts Press, 2004), 237–65.

Edwards, D., 'A Haven of Popery: English Catholic Migration to Ireland in the Age of Plantations' in A. Ford and J. Mc Cafferty (eds.), *The Origins of Sectarianism in Early Modern Ireland* (Cambridge University Press, 2005), 95–126.

Fitzgerald, P., 'Like Crickets to the Crevice of Brew House: Poor Irish Migrants in England, 1560–1640' in P. O'Sullivan (ed.), *The Irish World Wide, i, Patterns of Migration* (Leicester University Press, 1992), 13–35.

Fitzgerald, P., 'Poverty and Vagrancy in Early Modern Ireland', unpublished PhD thesis, Queen's University Belfast (1994).

Frazer, W. O., 'Field of Fire: Evidence for Wartime Conflict in a 17th-century Cottier Settlement in County Meath, Ireland' in T. Pollard and I. Banks (eds.), *Scorched Earth: Studies in the Archaeology of Conflict* (Leiden: Brill, 2008), 173–96.

French, H. R., 'The Search for the "middle sort of people" in England, 1600–1800', *Historical Journal*, 43 (2000), 277–93.

Gillespie, R., *Colonial Ulster: the Settlement of East Ulster, 1600–1641* (Cork University Press, 1985).

Gillespie, R. and G. Moran, 'Land, Politics and Religion in Longford since 1600', in R. Gillespie and G. Moran (eds.), *Longford: Essays in County History* (Dublin: Lilliput Press, 1991), 24–5.

Graves, J. and J. G. A. Prim, *The History, Architecture and Antiquities of the Cathedral Church of St Canice Kilkenny* (Dublin: Hodges, Smith & Co., 1857).

Heal, F. and C. Holmes, *The Gentry in England and Wales 1500–1700* (London: Macmillan, 1994).

Hill, G., *An Historical Account of the Plantation of Ulster* (Belfast: McCaw, Stevenson and Orr, 1877).

Hindle, S., 'Civility, Honesty and the Identification of the Deserving Poor in Seventeenth-Century England', in H. French and J. Barry (eds.), *Identity and Agency in England, 1500–1800* (London: Palgrave Macmillan, 2004), 38–59.

Hindle, S., 'Dependency, Shame and Belonging: Badging the Deserving Poor, c.1550–1750', *Cultural and Social History*, 1 (2004), 6–35.

Horner, A. and R. Loeber, 'Landscape in Transition: Descriptions of Forfeited Properties in Counties Meath, Louth and Cavan in 1700', *Analecta Hibernica*, 42 (2011), 59–179.

Houston, R. A., *Peasant Petitions: Social Relations and Economic Life on Landed Estates, 1600–1850* (Basingstoke: Palgrave Macmillan, 2014).

Howells, B., 'The Lower Orders of Society', in J. G. Jones, *Class, Community and Culture in Tudor Wales* (Cardiff: University of Wales Press, 1989).

Hoyle, R. W., 'Petitioning as Popular Politics in Early Sixteenth-Century England', *Historical Research*, 75 (2002), 365–87.

Jackson, D., *Intermarriage in Ireland 1550–1650* (Montreal: Cultural and Educational Productions, 1970).

Jutte, R., *Poverty and Deviance in Early Modern Europe* (Cambridge University Press, 1994).

Kane, B., *The Politics and Culture of Honour in Britain and Ireland, 1541–1641* (Cambridge University Press, 2010).

Kussmaul, A., *Servants in Husbandry in Early Modern England* (Cambridge University Press, 1981).

Lennon, C., *The Lords of Dublin in the Age of Reformation* (Dublin: Irish Academic Press, 1989).

Lennon, C., *The Urban Patriciates of Early Modern Ireland: A Case-Study of Limerick* (Dublin: National University of Ireland, 1999).

Lennon, C., '*Dives* and Lazarus in Sixteenth-Century Ireland', in C. Lennon and J. Hill (eds.), *Luxury and Austerity: Historical Studies XXI* (University College Dublin Press, 1999), 46–61.

Lennon, C., 'Religious and Social Change in Early Modern Limerick: The Testimony of the Sexton Family Papers', in L. Irwin and G. Ó Tuathaigh (eds.), *Limerick: History and Society* (Dublin: Geography Publications, 2009), 113–28.

Lyttleton, J. and T. O'Keeffe (eds.), *The Manor in Medieval and Early Modern Ireland* (Dublin: Four Courts Press, 2005).

Maginn, C., 'The Gaelic Peers, the Tudor Sovereigns, and English Multiple Monarchy', *Journal of British Studies* 50 (2011), 566–86.

McCarthy, T. F., 'Ulster Office, 1552–1800', unpublished MA thesis, Queen's University Belfast (1983).

McGowan Doyle, V., *The Book of Howth: Elizabethan Conquest and the Old English* (Cork University Press, 2011).

McGrath, B., 'The Communities of Clonmel, 1608–49', in R. Armstrong and T. Ó Hannracháin (eds.), *Community in Early Modern Ireland* (Dublin: Four Courts Press, 2006), 103–19.

Moylan, T. K., 'Vagabonds and Sturdy Beggars', *Dublin Historical Record*, 1 (1938), 11–18, 40–49.

Ní Mhurchadha, M., *Fingal, 1603–60: Contending Neighbours in North Dublin* (Dublin: Four Courts Press, 2005).

Nicholls, K., *Gaelic and Gaelicised Ireland in the Middle Ages* (Dublin: Gill and Macmillan, 1972).

Nicholls, K., *Land, Law and Society in Sixteenth Century Ireland* (Dublin: National University of Ireland, 1976).

O'Dowd, M., *Power, Politics and Land: Early Modern Sligo 1568–1688* (Belfast: Institute of Irish Studies, 1991).

O'Dowd, M., 'Gaelic Economy and Society', in C. Brady and R. Gillespie (eds.), *Natives and Newcomers: Essays on the Making of Irish Colonial Society* (Dublin: Irish Academic Press, 1986) 128–30.

O'Dowd, M., 'Land and Lordship in Sixteenth and Early Seventeenth-Century Ireland', in R. Mitchison and P. Roebuck (eds.), *Economy and Society in Scotland and Ireland 1500–1939* (Edinburgh: John Donald, 1988), 17–26.

O'Dowd, M., 'Women and Paid Work in Rural Ireland, *c.*1500–1800', in B. Whelan (ed.), *Women and Paid Work in Ireland, 1500–1930* (Dublin: Four Courts Press, 2000), 13–29.

O'Sullivan, C. M., *Hospitality in Medieval Ireland 900–1500* (Dublin: Four Courts Press, 2004).

Ohlmeyer, J., *Making Ireland English: The Irish Aristocracy in the Seventeenth Century* (London and New Haven: Yale University Press, 2012).

Power, G., 'Hidden in Plain Sight: the Nobility of Tudor Ireland', *History Ireland*, 20 (2012), 16–19.

Rapple, R., *Martial Power and Elizabethan Political Culture* (Cambridge University Press, 2009).

Richardson, R. C., *Household Servants in Early Modern England* (Manchester University Press, 2010).

Roulston, W., 'The Scots in Plantation Cavan, 1610–42', in B. Scott (ed.), *Culture and Society in Early Modern Breifne/Cavan* (Dublin: Four Courts Press, 2009), 121–46.

Schmidt, A. J., *The Yeoman in Tudor and Stuart England* (Washington: Folger Shakespeare Library, 1961).

Scott, B., 'Career Wives and Wicked Stepmothers', *History Ireland*, 17 (2009), 14–17.

Sheehan, A., 'Irish Towns in a Period of Change', in C. Brady and R. Gillespie (eds.), *Natives and Newcomers: Essays on the Making of Irish Colonial Society* (Dublin: Irish Academic Press, 1986), 93–119.

Sheehan, W. and M. Cronin (eds.), *Riotous Assemblies: Rebels, Riots and Revolts in Ireland* (Cork: Mercier Press, 2011).

Slack, P., *Poverty and Policy in Tudor and Stuart England* (London: Longman, 1988).

Smyth, W. J., *Map-making, Landscapes and Memory: A Geography of Colonial and Early Modern Ireland, c.1530–c.1750* (Cork University Press, 2006).

Tait, C., *Death, Burial and Commemoration in Ireland 1550–1650* (Basingstoke: Palgrave Macmillan, 2002).

Tait, C., 'The Wills of the Irish Catholic Community, *c.*1550–*c.*1660', in R. Armstrong and T. Ó hAnnracháin (eds.), *Community in Early Modern Ireland* (Dublin: Four Courts Press, 2006), 191–6.

Tait, C., 'Rioting in Limerick in 1599', in L. Irwin and G. Ó Tuathaigh (eds.), *Limerick: History and Society* (Dublin: Geography Publications, 2009), 91–111.

Tait, C., 'Catholics and Protest in Ireland, 1570–1640', in R. Armstrong and T. Ó hAnnracháin (eds.), *Insular Christianity: Alternative Models of the Church in Britain and Ireland, c.1570–c.1700* (Manchester University Press, 2013), 67–87.

Tait, C., 'Good Ladies and Ill Wives: Women on Boyle's Estates', in Edwards and Rynne (eds.), *The Colonial World of Richard Boyle*, 205–22.

Walter, J., *Crowds and Popular Politics in Early Modern England* (Manchester University Press, 2006).

Whelan, K., 'An Underground Gentry: Catholic Middlemen in the 18th Century', in J. S. Donnelly and K. Millar (eds.), *Irish Popular Culture 1650–1850* (Dublin: Irish Academic Press, 1998), 118–72.

Wrightson, K., *English Society, 1580–1680* (London: Hutchinson, 1982).

Wrightson, K., '"Sorts of People" in Tudor and Stuart England', in J. Barry and C. Brooks (eds.), *The Middling Sort of People* (London: Palgrave Macmillan, 1994), 28–51.

Young, J. R., 'Escaping Massacre: Refugees in Scotland in the Aftermath of the 1641 Ulster Rebellion', in D. Edwards, P. Lenihan and C. Tait (eds.), *Age of Atrocity: Violence and Political Conflict in Early Modern Ireland* (Dublin: Four Courts Press, 2007), 219–41.

12 Men, Women, Children and the Family, 1550–1730

Mary O'Dowd

Unpublished Primary Sources
British Library

Add. MS 31821

The National Archives of Ireland

CP, B/40, BB/148, 220, 221, 240, F/2, G/1, 303, I/146, 222, J/166
M2448

The National Archives, UK

SP 63/118/29

National Library of Ireland

Will and inventory of goods of Cormac O'Hara als O'Hara Boy, 18 August 1612, O'Hara Papers

Presbyterian Historical Society, Belfast

Session Minutes of Aghadowey, 1702–1761

Public Record Office of Northern Ireland

D3045/4/1/14

Registry of Deeds, Dublin

23/515/14264

Published Primary Sources

Abstract of the by-laws, rules and orders, made by the governors of the Royal Hospital of King Charles II near Dublin (Dublin: George Faulkner, 1752).

Ashford, G. M., '"Advice to a daughter": Lady Frances Keightley to her Daughter Catherine, September 1681', *Analecta Hibernica*, 43 (2012), 17–46.

Autobiography of Mary Countess of Warwick, ed. T. Crofton Croker (London: The Percy Society, 1848).

Bourke, A., Ní Dhonnchadha, M., MacCurtain, M., Kilfeather, S., Luddy, M., O'Dowd, M., Meaney, G. and Wills, C. (eds.), *Field Day Anthology of Irish Writing Volumes IV & V: Irish Women's Writing and Traditions* (Cork University Press, 2002).

Carpenter, A. (ed.), *Verse in English from Tudor and Stuart Ireland* (Cork University Press, 2003).

A Chorographical Description of West or H-Iar Connaught: Written A.D. 1684 by Roderic O'Flaherty; Edited From a Ms. in the Library of Trinity College, Dublin, With Notes and Illustrations by James Hardiman, ed. J. Hardiman (Dublin: Irish Archaeological Society, 1846).

Dunton, John, *Teague Land: Or, a Merry Ramble to the Wild Irish (1698)*, ed. A. Carpenter (Dublin: Four Courts Press, 2003).

Hamilton, H. C., (ed.), *Calendar of State Papers, Ireland, 1588–1592* (London: HMSO, 1885).

Hamilton, H. C., (ed.), *Calendar of State Papers Ireland, 1592–1596* (London: HMSO, 1890).

The Letters of Saint Oliver Plunkett, ed. J. Hanly (Dublin: Dolmen Press, 1979).

Little, P., (ed.), 'Providence and Posterity: A Letter from Lord Mountnorris to His Daughter, 1642', *Irish Historical Studies*, 32 (2001), 556–66.

Loftus, Dudley, *The Case of Ware and Sherley As It Was Set Forth in Matter of Fact and Argued in Several Points of Law in the Consistory of Dublin, in Michaelmas Term 1668* (Dublin, 1669).

Mac Carthy, D., '"Of the Takeing Awaie of a Gentlewoman, the Youngest Daughter of Sir Nicholas Bagenall, Late Marshall of Her Majestie's Armie, by the Erle of Tirowen"; As Revealed by the Documents Preserved in Her Majesty's State Paper Office', *Journal of the Kilkenny and South-East of Ireland Archaeological Society*, new series, 1 (1857), 298–311.

Marstrander, C., 'Bídh Crínna', *Eriú*, 5 (1911), 126–43.

McBride, John, *A Vindication of Marriage as Solemnized by Presbyterians, in the North of Ireland* (Belfast, 1702).

'Medical Texts of Ireland, 1350–1650', www.ucc.ie/celt/medical.html (accessed 1 August 2015).

Murray, L. P., (ed.), 'Archbishop Cromer's Register', *County Louth Archaeological Society Journal*, 8 (1935), 257–74.

Nicholls, K. W., 'Some Documents on Irish Law and Custom in the Sixteenth Century', *Analecta Hibernica*, 6 (1970), 105–29.

Russell, C. W. and J. P. Prendergast (eds.), *Calendar of State Papers Ireland, 1606–8* (London: Longmans, 1874).

Savile, George, Marquis of Halifax, *The Lady's New-Years Gift: Or, Advice to a Daughter …* (6th edn., Dublin, 1699).

Trevelyan, W. C. and C. E. Trevelyan (eds.), *Trevelyan Papers Part III* (Camden Society: London, 1872).

Ussher, James, *A Body of Divinitie, Or the Summe and Substance of Christian Religion* (London, 1657).

Wolveridge, James, *Speculum Matricis, Or, The Irish Midwives Handmaid Catechistically Composed by James Wolveridge, M.D.; With a Copious Alphabetical Index* (London, 1670).

Wulff, W. (ed.), *A Mediaeval Handbook of Gynaecology and Midwifery …* (London: Sheed and Ward, 1934).

Secondary Sources

Beckett, J. C., *Protestant Dissent in Ireland, 1687–1780* (London: Faber, 1948).

Canny, N., *The Upstart Earl: A Study of the Social and Mental World of Richard Boyle, First Earl of Cork, 1566–1643* (Cambridge University Press, 1982).

Casway, J., 'The Decline and Fate of Dónal Ballagh O'Cahan and his Family', in M. Ó Siochrú (ed.), *Kingdoms in Crisis. Ireland in the 1640s. Essays in Honour of Dónal Cregan* (Dublin: Four Courts, 2001), 44–62.

Corish, P. J., *The Irish Catholic Experience. A Historical Survey* (Dublin: Gill and Macmillan, 1985).

Cosgrove, A., 'Marriage in Medieval Ireland', in Art Cosgrove (ed.), *Marriage in Ireland* (Dublin: College Press, 1985), 25–50.

Crawford, J. G., *A Star Chamber Court in Ireland. The Court of Castle Chamber 1571–1641* (Dublin: Four Courts Press, 2005).

Cressy, D., *Birth, Marriage and Death. Ritual, Religion and the Life-Cycle in Tudor and Stuart England* (Oxford University Press, 1997).

Cressy, D., 'Kinship and Kin Interaction in Early Modern England', *Past & Present*, 113 (1986), 38–69.

Fitzgerald, P. D., 'Poverty and Vagrancy in Early Modern Ireland, 1540–1770', Unpublished PhD thesis, Queen's University Belfast (1994).

Fitzsimons, F., 'Fosterage and Gossipred in Late Medieval Ireland: Some New Evidence', in P. Duffy, D. Edwards and E. Fitzpatrick (eds.), *Gaelic Ireland. c.1250–1650. Land, Lordship and Settlement* (Dublin: Four Courts Press, 2001), 138–52.

Forrestal, A., *Catholic Synods in Ireland, 1600–1690* (Dublin: Four Courts Press, 1998).

Foyster, E., *Marital Violence: An English Family History, 1660–1857* (Cambridge University Press, 2005).

Gailey, A., *Irish Folk Drama* (Cork: Mercier Press, 1969).

Hanawalt, B. A., *The Ties that Bound: Peasant Families in Medieval England* (Oxford University Press, 1986).

Harding, M., 'The Curious Incident of the Marriage Act (No 2) 1537 and the Irish Statute Book', *Legal Studies*, 32 (2012), 78–108.

Hogan, E., *Distinguished Irishmen of the Sixteenth Century: First Series* (London: Burns and Oates, 1894).

Ingram, M., *Church Courts, Sex and Marriage in England, 1570–1640* (Cambridge University Press, 1987)

Jackson, D., *Intermarriage in Ireland, 1550–1650* (Cultural and Educational Promotions: Montreal, 1970).

Kane, B., *The Politics and Culture of Honour in Britain and Ireland, 1541–1641* (Cambridge University Press, 2010).

Lennon, C., *The Lords of Dublin in the Age of Reformation* (Dublin: Irish Academic Press, 1989).

Little, P., 'The Geraldine Ambitions of the First Earl of Cork', *Irish Historical Studies*, 33 (2002), 151–68.

Luddy, M. and M. O'Dowd, *A History of Marriage in Ireland, 1660–1925* (forthcoming, 2018).

Mac Cuarta, B., *Catholic Revival in the North of Ireland, 1603–41* (Dublin: Four Courts Press, 2007).

MacCurtain, M., 'Women, Education and Learning in Early Modern Ireland', in M. MacCurtain and M. O'Dowd (eds.), *Women In Early Modern Ireland* (Edinburgh University Press, 1991), 160–78.

Matthew, H. C. G. and B. Harrison (ed.), *Oxford Dictionary of National Biography* (60 vols., Oxford University Press, 2004).

McGuire, J. and J. Quinn (eds.), *Dictionary of Irish Biography* (9 vols., Cambridge University Press, 2009).

Meehan, C. P., *The Fate and Fortunes of Hugh O'Neill, Earl of Tyrone, and Rory O'Donel, Earl of Tyrconnell* (Dublin: James Duffy, 1879).

Nicholls, K., *Gaelic and Gaelicised Ireland in the Middle Ages* (Dublin: Gill and Macmillan, 1972).

O'Dowd, M., *Power, Politics and Land: Early Modern Sligo, 1568–1688* (Belfast: Institute of Irish Studies, 1991).

O'Dowd, M., *A History of Women in Early Modern Ireland, 1500–1800* (Harlow: Pearson Education, 2005).

O'Dowd, M., 'Early Modern Ireland and the History of the Child', in M. Luddy and J. M. Smith (eds.), *Children, Childhood and Irish Society* (Dublin: Four Courts Press, 2014), 29–45.

O'Dowd, M., 'Women and the Irish Chancery Court in the Late Sixteenth and Early Seventeenth Centuries', *Irish Historical Studies*, 31 (1999), 470–87.

Ohlmeyer, J., *Making Ireland English. The Irish Aristocracy in the Seventeenth Century* (London and New Haven: Yale University Press, 2012).

Reynolds, P. L., 'Marrying and its Documentation in Pre-Modern Europe: Consent, Celebration and Property', in P. L. Reynolds and J. Witte Jr (eds.), *To Have and to Hold. Marrying and its Documentation in Western Christendom, 400–1600* (Cambridge University Press, 2007), 1–42.

Roodenburg, H. and P. Spierenburg (eds.), *Social Control in Europe, i, 1500–1800* (Columbus, OH: Ohio State University Press, 2004).

Shanahan, M., *Manuscript Recipe Books as Archaeological Objects: Text and Food in the Early Modern World* (London: Lexington Books, 2015).

Shepard, A., *Meanings of Manhood in Early Modern England* (Oxford University Press, 2003).

Shepard, A, *Accounting for Oneself. Worth, Status, and the Social Order in Early Modern England* (Oxford University Press, 2015).

Shepard, A., 'From Anxious Patriarchs to Refined Gentlemen? Manhood in Britain, circa 1500–1700', *Journal of British Studies*, 44 (2005), 281–95.

Stalley, R., 'The Architecture of the Cathedral and Priory Buildings, 1250–1530', in K. Milne (ed.), *Christ Church Cathedral, Dublin. A History* (Dublin: Four Courts Press, 2000), 95–129.

Tait, C., 'Some Sources for the Study of Infant and Maternal Mortality in Later Seventeenth-Century Ireland', in Elaine Farrell (ed.), *'She Said She Was in the Family Way'. Pregnancy and Infancy in Modern Ireland* (London: Institute of Historical Research, 2012), 55–73.

Walsh, P., 'The Will and Family of Hugh O'Neill', *The Irish Ecclesiastical Record*, fifth series, 13 (1919), 27–41.

Wilson, R., *Elite Women in Ascendancy Ireland,1690–1745. Imitation and Innovation* (Boydell Press: Woodbridge, Suffolk, 2015).

Wright, W. B., *Ball Family Records. Genealogical Memoirs of Some Ball Families of Great Britain, Ireland and America* (York: Yorkshire Printing County Ltd: 1908).

Wrightson, K., *English Society, 1580–1680* (London: Routledge, 1982).

13 Domestic Materiality in Ireland, 1550–1730

Susan Flavin

Unpublished Primary Sources

British Library

Egerton MS 1995
Harleian MS 541

Cork City and County Archives

Caulfield Will Transcripts, U226

National Library of Ireland

Ms 2552
Ms 2554
Ms 14,786
Ms 19,729
Ms 41,603 / 2 (1)

Northamptonshire Record Office

Fitzwilliam Manuscripts (Irish), nos. 27, 31, 51

The National Archives, UK

Will of Elizabeth Boyle, PROB 5 / 2596
Will of Francis Aungier, PROB 11 / 163 / 252

Published Primary Sources

Becon, Thomas, *The Workes of Thomas Becon, Vol. 1* (London, 1564).

Calendar of the Orrery Papers, ed. Edward MacLysaght (Dublin: Irish Manuscripts Commission, 1941).

Caulfield, R. (ed.), 'Wills and Inventories, Cork, temp, Elizabeth and James I', *The Gentlemen's Magazine*, Apr. 1862, 441.

Fenlon, J. (ed.), *Goods and Chattels: A Survey of Early Modern Inventories in Ireland* (Dublin: Stationery Office, 2003).

Gernon, Luke, 'Discourse of Ireland Anno 1620', in C. L. Falkiner (ed.), *Illustrations of Irish Topography Mainly of the Seventeenth Century* (London: Longmans, 1904), 345–62.

Harrison, W., *The Description of England*, ed. G. Edelen (New York: The Folger Shakespeare Library and Dover Publications, 1994).

MacDonnell, H., 'A Seventeenth Century Inventory from Dunluce Castle, County Antrim', *Journal of the Royal Society of Antiquaries of Ireland*, 122 (1992), 109–27.

Moryson, Fynes, 'An Itinerary', in J. Myers (ed.), *Elizabethan Ireland: A Selection of Writings by Elizabethan Writers on Ireland* (Hamden, CT: Archon Books, 1983), 185–240.

Moryson, Fynes, 'The Itinerary of Fynes Moryson', in C. L. Falkiner (ed.), *Illustrations of Irish Topography Mainly of the Seventeenth Century* (London: Longmans, 1904), 225–30.

Townshend, D., *Life and Letters of the Great Earl of Cork* (London: Duckworth, 1904).

Secondary Sources

Barnard, T., *Making the Grand Figure, Lives and Possessions in Ireland, 1641–1770* (New Haven, CT: Yale University Press, 2004).

Barnard, T., *A Guide to the Sources for the History of Material Culture in Ireland, 1500–2000* (Dublin: Four Courts Press, 2005).

Beudry, M., 'Words for Things: Linguistic Analysis of Probate Inventories', in M. Beudry (ed.), *Documentary Archaeology in the New World* (Cambridge University Press, 1988), 43–51.

Breen, C., 'The Maritime Cultural Landscape in Medieval Gaelic Ireland', in P. J. Duffy, D. Edwards and E. Fitzpatrick (eds.), *Gaelic Ireland c.1250–1650: Land, Lordship and Settlement* (Dublin: Four Courts Press, 2001), 418–35.

Campbell, E., Fitzpatrick, E. and A. Horning (eds.), *Becoming and Belonging in Ireland 1200–1600 AD: Essays on Identity and Cultural Practice* (Cork University Press, forthcoming, 2018).

Carrier, J. G., *Gifts and Commodities: Exchange and Western Capitalism since 1700* (London: Routledge, 1995).

Cooper, N., *Houses of the Gentry 1480–1680* (New Haven and London: Yale University Press, 1999).

Douglas M. and B. Isherwood, *The World of Goods: Towards an Anthropology of Consumption* (new edn., London: Routledge, 1996).

Fenlon, J., 'Moving towards the Formal House: Room Usage in Early Modern Ireland', in . Fitzpatrick and J. Kelly (eds.), *Domestic Life in Ireland* (Dublin: Royal Irish Academy, 2011), 115–66.

Field, C. ' "Many hands hands": Writing the Self in Early Modern Women's Recipe Books', in Michelle M. Dowd and Julie A. Eckerle (eds.), *Genre and Women's Life Writing in Early Modern England* (Aldershot: Ashgate, 2007).

Fitzgerald, A., 'Taste in High Life: Dining in the Dublin Town House', in C. Casey (ed.), *The Eighteenth-Century Dublin Town House: Form, Function and Finance* (Dublin: Four Courts Press, 2010), 120–7.

Fitzpatrick, E. and J. Kelly (eds.), *Domestic Life in Ireland* (Dublin: Royal Irish Academy, 2011).

Flather, A., *Gender and Space in Early Modern England* (Woodbridge: Boydell & Brewer, 2007).

Flavin, S., *Consumption and Culture in Sixteenth-Century Ireland, Saffron, Stockings and Silk* (Woodbridge: Boydell & Brewer, 2014).

Gillespie, R., 'The Book Trade in Southern Ireland, 1590–1640', in G. Long (ed.), *Books Beyond the Pale: Aspects of the Provincial Book Trade in Ireland Before 1850* (Dublin: Rare Books Group of the Library Association of Ireland, 1996).

James, M. E., *Family, Lineage and Civil Society* (Oxford: Clarendon Press, 1974).

Johnson, M., *The Archaeology of Capitalism* (Oxford: Blackwell, 1995).

McCracken, G., *Culture and Consumption* (Bloomington, IN: Indiana University Press, 1988).

McCutcheon, C. and R. Meenan, 'Pots on the Hearth: Domestic Pottery in Historic Ireland', in E. Fitzpatrick and J. Kelly (eds.), *Domestic Life in Ireland* (Dublin: Royal Irish Academy, 2011), 91–113.

McKendrick, N., J. Brewer and J. H. Plumb (eds.), *The Birth of a Consumer Society: The Commercialization of Eighteenth-Century England* (London: Europa, 1982).

Ohlmeyer, J., *Making Ireland English: The Irish Aristocracy in the Seventeenth Century* (New Haven and London: Yale University Press, 2012).

Orlin, L. C., *Locating Privacy in Tudor London* (Oxford University Press, 2010).

Overton, M., *Production and Consumption in English Households 1600–1750* (London: Routledge 2004).

Pennell, S., 'The Material Culture of Food in Early Modern England c. 1650–1750', in S. Tarlow and S. West (eds.), *Familiar Pasts? Archaeologies of Later Historical Britain 1550–1860* (London: Routledge, 1999), 35–50.

Pennell, S., 'Perfecting practice? Women, Manuscript Recipes and Knowledge in Early Modern England', in V. E. Burke and J. Gibson (eds.), *Early Modern Women's Manuscript Writing* (Aldershot: Ashgate, 2004), 237–58.

Pennell, S., 'Mundane Materiality, or should Small Things still be Forgotten? Material Culture, Microhistories and the Problem of Scale', in K. Harvey (ed.), *History and Material Culture: A Student's Guide to Approaching Alternative Sources* (London: Routledge, 2009), 173–91.

Pennell S., '"Pots and Pans History": The Material Culture of the Kitchen in Early Modern England', *Journal of Design History*, 11 (1998), 201–16.

Salter, E., 'Re-worked Material: Discourses of Clothing Culture in Sixteenth-Century Greenwich', in C. Richardson (ed.), *Clothing Culture 1350–1650* (Hampshire: Ashgate, 2004), 179–91.

Shanahan, M., *Recipe Writing in the Early Modern World: An Historical Archaeology of Domestic Manuscripts from Restoration and Georgian Ireland* (London: Lexington, 2014).

Shanahan, M., 'An Historical Archaeology of Recipe Manuscripts from Early Modern Ireland (circa 1660 to 1830)', unpublished PhD thesis, University College Dublin (2012).

Sherlock, R., 'The Evolution of the Irish Tower-House as a Domestic Space', in E. Fitzpatrick and J. Kelly (eds.), *Domestic Life in Ireland* (Dublin: Royal Irish Academy, 2011), 116–40.

Smith, W. D., *Consumption and the Making of Respectability, 1600–1800* (London: Routledge, 2002).

Stone, L., *The Crisis of the Aristocracy 1558–1641* (Oxford: Clarendon Press, 1965).

Thirsk, T., *Economic Policy and Projects: The Development of a Consumer Society in Early Modern England* (Oxford: Clarendon Press, 1978).

Visser, M., *The Rituals of Dinner* (London: Viking, 1992), 156.

Wall, W., *Staging Domesticity: Household Work and English Identity in Early Modern Drama* (Cambridge University Press, 2002).

Wall, W., 'Distillation, Transformations in and out of the Kitchen', in J. Fitzpatrick (ed.), *Renaissance Food from Rabelais to Shakespeare* (Farnham: Ashgate, 2010), 89–106.

Weatherill, L., *Consumer Behaviour and Material Culture in Britain* (2nd edn., London: Routledge, 1996).

Yentsch, A. E., 'The Symbolic Divisions of Pottery: Sex-Related Attributes of English and Anglo-American Household Pots', in R. H. McGuire and R. Paynter (eds.), *The Archaeology of Inequality* (Oxford: Blackwell, 1991), 192–230.

14 Irish Art and Architecture, 1550–1730

Jane Fenlon

Unpublished Primary Sources

National Library of Ireland

Ormonde Papers, Mss 2554, 7864

Ormonde Ms, 72, f 389

Registry of Deeds, Dublin

40/170/248829, 1720

Published Primary Sources

Ainsworth, J. and E. MacLysaght, 'Power O'Shee Papers', *Analecta Hibernica*, 20, (1958), 216–58.

Dunlop, R., 'An Unpublished Survey of the Plantation of Munster in 1622', *Journal of the Royal Society of Antiquaries of Ireland*, 54 (1924), 129–46.

Fenlon, J., *Goods and Chattels: A Survey of Early Household Inventories in Ireland* (Dublin: Stationery Office, 2003).

Fenlon, J., 'Some Early Seventeenth Century Building Accounts in Ireland', *Irish Architectural and Decorative Studies, The Journal of the Irish Georgian Society*, 1 (1998), 84–99.

Loeber, R., 'Early Irish Architectural Sketches from the Perceval/Egmont Collection', in A. Bernelle (ed.), *Decantations: A Tribute to Maurice Craig* (Dublin: Lilliput Press, 1992), 110–20.

Melvin, P. and Lord Longford, 'Letters of Lord Longford and others on Irish Affairs 1689–1702', *Analecta Hibernica*, 32 (1985), 35–124.

Sebastiano Serlio on Architecture: Books VI and VII of 'Tutte L'Opere D'Architettura et Prospetiva' ed. and trans. V. Hart and P. Hicks (2 vols., New Haven and London: Yale University Press, 2001).

'Travels of Sir William Brereton in Ireland 1635', in C. Litton Falkiner (ed.), *Illustrations of Irish History and Topography Mainly of the Seventeenth Century* (London: Longmans, 1904), 365–407.

Wooton, Henry, *The Elements of Architecture* (London, 1624).

Secondary Sources

Barnard, T., *Making the Grand Figure: Lives and Possessions in Ireland, 1641–1770* (New Haven & London: Yale University Press, 2004).

Barnard, T., 'The Political, Material and Mental Culture of the Cork Settlers', in P. O'Flanagan and C. G, Buttimer (eds.), *Cork: History & Society* (Geography Publications: Dublin 1993), 309–65.

Carpenter, A. (General ed.), *Art and Architecture of Ireland* (5 vols., Dublin, London and New Haven: Royal Irish Academy and Yale University Press, 2014).

Casey, C., *The Buildings of Ireland: Dublin* (New Haven and London: Yale University Press, 2005).

Cockerham, P., '"To mak a Tombe for the Earell of Ormon and to set it up in Iarland": Renaissance Ideals in Irish Funeral Monuments', in T. Herron and M. Potterton (eds.), *Ireland in the Renaissance c. 1540–1660*, (Dublin: Four Courts Press [hereafter FCP], 2007), 195–230.

Coope, R., 'The Gallery in England and its Relationship to the Principal Rooms (1520–1600)', in J. Guillame (ed.), *Architecture et Vie Sociale à la Renaissance* (Paris: Picard, 1994), 245–55.

Craig, M., *The Architecture of Ireland*, (London: Batsford, 1982).

Crookshank, A., The Knight of Glin, *Ireland's Painters 1600–1940* (London and New Haven: Yale University Press, 2002).

Dolan, A., 'Case Study: Jigginstown House, 1635–37, Naas County Kildare, Republic of Ireland' the Principal Architect's Perspective', in G. Lynch (ed.), *The History of Gauged Brickwork* (Oxford, Butterworth-Heinemann, 2007), 99–110.

Fenlon, J., *The Ormonde Picture Collection* (Gandon Editions: Kinsale, 2001).

Fenlon, J., *Kilkenny Castle: Visitor's Guide* (Dublin: Office of Public Works, 2007).

Fenlon, J., 'The Duchess of Ormonde's House at Dunmore, County Kilkenny', in J. Kirwan (ed.), *Kilkenny, Studies in Honour of Margaret M. Phelan* (Kilkenny: Kilkenny Archaeological Society, 1997), 79–87.

Fenlon, D. and J. Fenlon, 'Ross Castle', in J. Larner (ed.), *Killarney History & Heritage* (Cork: The Collins Press, 2005), 63–73.

Fenlon, J., '"They say I build up to the sky": Thomas Wentworth, Jigginstown House and Dublin Castle', in M. Potterton and T. Herron (eds.), *Dublin and the Pale in the Renaissance, c.1540–1660* (Dublin: FCP, 2011), 207–23.

Fenlon, J., '"A good painter may get good bread", Thomas Pooley and Garret Morphey, two Gentlemen Painters', in R. Gillespie and R. F. Foster (eds.), *Irish Provincial Cultures in the Long Eighteenth-Century* (Dublin: FCP, 2012), 220–30.

Fenlon, J., 'Portumna: A Great Many Windowed and Gabled House', in J. Fenlon (ed.), *Clanricard's Castle: Portumna House, County Galway* (Dublin: FCP, 2012), 49–82.

Fenlon, J., 'Kilkenny', in R. Loeber, H. Campbell, l. Hurley, J. Montague and E. Rowley (eds.), *Art and Architecture of Ireland, iv, Architecture, 1600–2000*, (Dublin, London and New Haven: Royal Irish Academy and Yale University Press, 2015), 464–66.

Fenlon, J., 'Portraiture in Ireland', in N. Figgis (ed.), *Art and Architecture of Ireland, ii, Painting, 1600–1900* (Dublin, London and New Haven: Royal Irish Academy and Yale University Press, 2015), 63–67.

Fenlon, J., 'Visiting Painters in Ireland', in N. Figgis (ed.), *Art and Architecture of Ireland, ii, Painting, 1600–1900* (Dublin, London and New Haven: Royal Irish Academy and Yale University Press, 2015), 130–34.

Fenlon, J., 'Garret Morphy and his Circle', *Irish Arts Review Yearbook*, 8 (1991–2), 135–48.

Fenlon, J., 'The Decorative Plasterwork at Ormond Castle', *Architectural History: Journal of the Society of Architectural Historians of Great Britain*, 41 (1998), 67–81.

Girouard, M., *Life in the English Country House* (New Haven and London: Yale University Press 1984).

Girouard, M., 'Introduction', in J. Fenlon (ed.), *Clanricard's Castle: Portumna House, County Galway* (Dublin: FCP, 2012), 1–7.

Gomme, A. and A. Maguire, *Design and Plan in the Country House from Castle Donjon to Palladian Boxes* (New Haven and London: Yale University Press, 2008).

Healy, W., *History and Antiquities of Kilkenny* (Kilkenny: P. M. Egan, 1893).

Kerrigan, P., *Castles and Fortifications in Ireland* (Cork: The Collins Press, 1995).

Leask, H. G., 'Early Seventeenth-Century Houses in Ireland', in E. M. Jope (ed.), *Studies in Building History* (London: Odhams Press, 1961), 243–50.

Lyttleton, J., '"A godly resolucon to rebwilde": Richard Boyle's patronage of elite architecture', in C. Rynne and D. Edwards (eds.), *The World of Richard Boyle, 1st Earl of Cork*, (forthcoming Dublin: FCP, 2017).

Loeber, R., *A Biographical Dictionary of Architects in Ireland* (London: John Murray 1981).

Loeber, R., 'Settlers' Utilisation of the Natural Resources', in K. Hannigan and W. Nolan (eds.), *Wicklow: History & Society* (Dublin: Geography Publications, 1994), 267–304.

Loeber, R., 'Part II: the New Architecture', in O. Horsfall Turner (ed.), *'The Mirror of Great Britain': National Identity in Seventeenth-Century British Architecture* (Reading: Spire Books, 2012), 101–39.

Loeber, R., 'The Early Seventeenth-Century Ulster and Midland Plantations, Part I: Pre-Plantation Architecture and Building Regulations', in O. Horsfall Turner (ed.), *'The Mirror of Great Britain': National Identity in Seventeenth-Century British Architecture* (Reading: Spire Books, 2012), 73–99.

Loeber, R. and J. O'Connell, 'Eyrecourt Castle, County Galway', *Irish Arts Review Yearbook*, i (1988), 40–8.

Lynch, A., *Tintern Abbey, County Wexford: Cistercians and Colcloughs. Excavations 1982–2007* (Dublin: The Stationary Office, 2010).

Lyttleton, J., *The Jacobean Plantations in Seventeenth-Century Offaly* (Dublin: FCP, 2013).

Mc Parland, E., *Public Architecture in Ireland 1680–1760* (London and New Haven: Yale University Press, 2001).

Mc Parland, E., 'Royal hospital Kilmainham', *Country Life*, 176 (9 and 16 May 1985) nos. 4577 and 4578.

Moody, T. W., F. X. Martin and F. J. Byrne (eds.), *A New History of Ireland, iii, Early Modern Ireland, 1534–1691* (Oxford University Press, 1976).

Morton, K., 'A Spectacular Revelation: Medieval Wall Paintings at Ardamullivan', *Irish Arts Review Yearbook*, 18 (2002), 104–13.

Moss, R., 'Continuity and Change: The Material Setting of Public Worship in the Sixteenth-Century Pale', in M. Potterton and T. Herron (eds.), *Dublin and the Pale in the Renaissance, c. 1540–1660* (Dublin: FCP, 2011), 182–206.

Moss, R., 'Reduce, Reuse, Recycle: Irish Monastic Architecture *c.*1540–1640', in R. Stalley (ed.), *Irish Gothic Architecture: Construction, Decay and Reinvention* (Dublin: Wordwell, 2012), 115–59.

Moss, R., 'Tombs and Sarcophagi', in R. Moss (ed.), *Art and Architecture of Ireland, i, Medieval, c.400–c.1600* (Dublin, London and New Haven: Royal Irish Academy and Yale University Press, 2014), 466–74.

Ó Clabaigh, C., 'Vestments', in R. Moss, (ed.), *Art and Architecture of Ireland, i, Medieval, c.400–c.1600* (Dublin, London and New Haven: Royal Irish Academy and Yale University Press, 2014), 401–5.

O'Flanagan, P., 'Three Hundred Years of Urban Life: Villages and Towns in County Cork *c.* 1600 to 1901', in P. O'Flanagan and C. G, Buttimer (eds.), *Cork: History & Society* (Geography Publications: Dublin 1993), 392–410.

O'Keefe, T. and S. Quirke, 'A House at the Birth of Modernity: Ightermurragh Castle in Context', in J. Lyttleton and C. Rynne (eds.), *Plantation Ireland: Settlement and Material Culture, c.1550–1700* (Dublin, FCP, 2009), 86–112.

Sherlock, R., 'Cross-Cultural Occurrences of Mutations in Tower House Architecture: Evidence for Cultural Homogeneity in Late Medieval Ireland', *The Journal of Irish Archaeology*, 15 (2006), 73–92.

Sherlock, R., 'The Evolution of the Irish Tower-House as a Domestic Space', *Proceedings of the Royal Irish Academy*, 111:C (2011), 115–40.

Sweetman, D., *The Medieval Castles of Ireland* (Collins Press: Cork, 2005).

Thornton, P., *Seventeenth-Century Interior Decoration in England France & Holland* (New Haven and London: Yale University Press, 1984).

Weadick, S., 'How Popular were Fortified Houses in Irish Castle Building History? A Look at their Numbers in the Archaeological Record and Distribution Patterns', in J. Lyttleton and C. Rynne (eds.), *Plantation Ireland: Settlement and Material Culture, c. 1550–1700* (Dublin, FCP, 2009), 61–85.

15 Ireland in the Atlantic World: Migration and Cultural Transfer

William O'Reilly

Unpublished Primary Sources

Library Company of Philadelphia

Letterbook of Jonathan Dickinson (held at the Historical Society of Pennsylvania)

The National Archives, UK

Ledgers of Imports and Exports of Ireland', CUST 15

Published Primary Sources

Aogán Ó Rathaille, ed. B. Ó Buachalla (Baile Átha Cliath: Field Day Publications, 2007).

Cell, G. T. (ed.), *Newfoundland Discovered: English Attempts at Colonisation, 1610–1630* (London: Hakluyt Society, 1982).

The Economic Writings of Sir William Petty, ed. C.H. Hull (2 vols., Cambridge University Press, 1899).

Greene, D. and F. Kelly (eds.), *Irish Bardic Poetry: Texts and Translations, Together with an Introductory Lecture by Osborn Bergin* (Dublin Institute for Advanced Studies, 1970, repr. 1984).

Hedlam, C. (ed.), *Calendar of State Papers, Colonial Series: America and the West Indies, Dec. 1, 1702–1703* (London: HMSO, 1913).

Historical Manuscripts Commission, *Calendar of the Manuscripts of the Marquess of Ormonde* (new series, 8 vols., London: HMSO, 1902–20).

Lorimer, J., *English and Irish Settlement on the River Amazon, 1550–1646* (London: Hakluyt Society, 1989).

Ó hÓgáin, D., *Dunaire Osraíoch* (Baile Átha Cliath: An Clóchomhar, 1980).

O'Sullivan Beare, Philip, *Vindiciae Hibernicae contra Giraldum Cambrensem et alios vel Zoilomastigis* (Cork University Press, 2009).

Payne, Robert, *A Briefe Description of Ireland: Made in this yeere, 1589*, ed. A. Smith (Dublin: Irish Archaeological Society, 1841).

Pennsylvania Gazette, 11 May 1738.

Wolff, H. (ed.), *America: Early maps of the New World* (Munich: Prestel Verlag, , 1992).

The Works of the Right Honourable Edmund Burke (12 vols., London: John C. Nimmo, 1887).

Secondary Sources

Afetinan, A., *Life and Works of Piri Reis: The Oldest Map of America* (2nd edn., Ankara: Turkish Historical Society, 1987).

Akagi, R. H., *The Town Proprietors of the New England Colonies* (Philadelphia, PA: University of Pennsylvania Press, 1924; repr. Gloucester, MA: Peter Smith, 1963), 256–62.

Bailyn, B. and P. D. Morgan, 'Introduction', in B. Bailyn and P. D. Morgan (eds.), *Strangers within the Realm: Cultural Margins of the First British Empire* (Chapel Hill, NC: University of North Carolina Press, 1991), 1–31.

Beckles, H. McD., 'A "Riotous and Unruly Lot": Irish Indentured Servants and Freeman in the English West Indies, 1644–1713', *William and Mary Quarterly* 47 (1990), 503–22.

Block, K. and J. Shaw, 'Subjects without an Empire: The Irish in the Early Modern Caribbean', *Past & Present*, 210 (2011), 33–60.

Boscher, J. F., 'Huguenot Merchants and the Protestant International in the Seventeenth Century', *William and Mary Quarterly*, third series, 52, (1995) 77–102.

Burns, A., *History of the British West Indies* (New York: Barnes and Noble, 1965).

Canny, N., *Making Ireland British, 1580–1650* (Oxford University Press, 2001).

Canny, N. and A. Pagden (eds.), *Colonial Identity in the Atlantic World, 1500–1800* (Princeton, NJ: Princeton University Press, 1987).

Crewe, R.D., 'Brave New Spain: An Irishman's Independence Plot in Seventeenth Century Mexico', *Past & Present*, 207 (2010), 53–87.

Cullen, L., 'The Huguenots from the Perspective of the Merchant Networks of Western Europe 1680–1890: The Example of the Brandy Trade', in C. E. J. Caldicott, H. Gough and J. P. Pittion (eds.), *The Huguenots in Ireland: Anatomy of an Emigration* (Dun Laoghaire: Glendale, 1987), 129–49.

Cunliffe, B., *Facing the Ocean: The Atlantic and its People, 8000 BC–AD 1500* (Oxford University Press, 2001).

Dickson, R. J., *Ulster Emigration to Colonial America, 1718–1775* (New York: Humanities Press, 1966).

Dunn, R. S., *Sugar and Slaves: The Rise of the Planter Class in the English West Indies, 1624–1713* (Chapel Hill, NC: The University of North Carolina Press, 1972).

Ekirch, A. R., *Bound for America: The Transportation of British Convicts to the Colonies, 1718–1775* (Oxford University Press, 1987).

Hadfield, A., 'British Colonial Expansion Westwards: Ireland and America', in S. Castillo and I. Schweitzer (eds.), *A Companion to the Literatures of Colonial America* (Oxford: Blackwell Publishing, 2005), 195–219.

Handlin, O., *The Uprooted. The Epic Story of the Great Migrations that made the American People* (Philadelphia, PA: The University of Pennsylvania Press, 2002), 2nd edn.

Harris Sacks, D., *The Widening Gate: Bristol and the Atlantic Economy, 1450–1700* (Berkeley, CA: University of California Press, 1991).

Henchy, M., 'The Irish College at Salamanca', *Studies* 70 (1981), 220–27.

Horn, J., *Adapting to a New World: English Society in the Seventeenth-Century Chesapeake* (Chapel Hill, NC: The University of North Carolina Press, 1994).

Horn, J., 'British Diaspora: Emigration from Britain, 1680–1815', in P. J. Marshall (ed.), *The Oxford History of the British Empire, ii: The Eighteenth Century* (Oxford University Press, 1998), 28–52.

Horn, J., 'Tobacco Colonies: The Shaping of English Society in the Seventeenth-century Chesapeake', in N. Canny (ed.), *The Oxford History of the British Empire, i: The Origins of Empire: British Overseas Expansion to the Close of the Seventeenth Century* (Oxford University Press, 1998), 176–7.

Horning, A., 'Challenging Colonial Equations? The Gaelic Experience in Early Modern Ireland', in N. Ferris, R. Harrison and M. V. Wilcox (eds.), *Rethinking Colonial Pasts through Archaeology* (Oxford University Press, 2014), 293–314.

Kidd, C., *British Identities before Nationalism: Ethnicity and Nationhood in the Atlantic World, 1600–1800* (Cambridge University Press, 1999).

Kirkham, G., 'Ulster Emigration to North America, 1680–1720', in H. T. Blethen and C. W. Wood Jr (eds.), *Ulster and North America. Transatlantic Perspectives on the Scotch-Irish* (Tuscaloosa and London, The University of Alabama Press, 1997), 76–97.

Kline, S., 'William Lamport/Guillén de Lombardo (1611–1659)', in K. Racine and B. G. Mamigonian (eds.), *The Human Tradition in the Atlantic World, 1500–1850* (Plymouth: Rowman & Littlefield, 2010), 43–56.

Lamotte, M., 'Colour Prejudice in the Early Modern French Empire, c.1635–1767', unpublished PhD dissertation, University of Cambridge (2015).

Lecky, A. G., *The Laggan and its Presbyterianism* (Belfast: Davidson and McCormack, 1905), reprinted as *Roots of Presbyterianism in Donegal* (Omagh: Graham and Sons, 1978).

Little, G. A., *Brendan the Navigator: An Interpretation* (Dublin: Gill, 1945).

McCracken, D. (ed.), *The Irish in southern Africa, 1795–1910* (Durban: Ireland and Southern Africa Project, 1991).

Meriweather, R. L., *The Expansion of South Carolina, 1729–1765* (Kingsport, TN: Southern Publishers, 1940; repr. Philadelphia: Porcupine Press, 1974), 17.

Nerlich, M., *Ideology of Adventure: Studies in Modern Consciousness, 1100–1750*, trans. R. Crowley (2 vols., Minneapolis, MN: University of Minnesota Press, 1987).

Netzloff, M., 'Writing Britain from the Margins: Scottish, Irish, and Welsh Projects for American Colonization', *Prose Studies: History, Theory, Criticism*, 25 (2002), 3.

Newton, J. D., 'Naval Power and the Province of Senegambia, 1758–1779', *Journal for Maritime Research*, 15 (2013), 129–47.

O'Brien, S., 'A Transatlantic Community of Saints: The Great Awakening and the First Evangelical Network, 1735–1755,' *American Historical Review*, 91 (1986), 811–32.

O'Halloran, C., *Golden Ages and Barbarous Nations. Antiquarian Debate and Cultural Politics in Ireland, c.1750–1800* (Cork University Press, 2004).

O'Sullivan, P., 'The English East India Company at Dundaniel', *Bandon Historical Journal*, 4 (1988), 3–15.

Ohlmeyer, J., 'A Laboratory for Empire: Early Modern Ireland and English Imperialism', in K. Kenny (ed.), *Ireland and the British Empire* (Oxford University Press, 2006), 26–60.

Rodgers, N., *Ireland, Slavery and Anti-Slavery: 1612–1865* (London: Palgrave Macmillan, 2007).

Rodgers, N., 'A Changing Presence. The Irish in the Caribbean in the Seventeenth and Eighteenth Centuries', in A. Donnell, M. McGarrity and E. O'Callaghan (eds.), *Caribbean Irish Connections: Interdisciplinary Perspectives* (Kingston, Jamaica: The University of the West Indies Press, 2015), 17–32.

Sainero, R., *The Celts and Historical and Cultural Origins of Atlantic Europe* (Palo Alto, CA: Academica Press, 2013).

Schüller, K., *Die Beziehungen zwischen Spanien und Irland im 16. und 17. Jahrhundert:Diplomatie, Handel und die Soziale Integration Katholischer Exulanten* (Münster: Aschendorff, 1999).

Shammas, C., 'English Commercial Development and American Colonization, 1560–1620', in K. R. Andrews (ed.), *The Westward Enterprise: English Activities in Ireland, The Atlantic, and America, 1480–1650* (Detroit, MI: Wayne State University Press, 1979), 151–74.

Smith, E., 'Naval Violence and Trading Privileges in Early Seventeenth-Century Asia', *International Journal of Maritime History*, 25 (2013), 147–58.

Went, A. E. J. and S. Ó Súilleabháin, 'Fishing for the Sun-Fish or Basking Shark in Irish Waters', *Proceedings of the Royal Irish Academy*, 65:C (1966–7), 91–115.

16 Language, Print and Literature in Irish, 1550–1630

Marc Caball

Published Primary Sources

The bardic poems of Tadhg Dall Ó hUiginn (1550–1591), ed. Eleanor Knott (2 vols., London: ITS, 1922–1926).

Breatnach, P. A. (ed.), 'Cú Chonnacht Ó Dálaigh's Poem before Leaving Aodh Ruadh', in D. Ó Corráin, L. Breatnach and K. McCone (eds.), *Sages, Saints and Storytellers: Celtic Studies in Honour of Professor James Carney* (Maynooth: An Sagart, 1989), 32–42.

Breatnach, R. B. (ed.), 'Elegy on Donal O'Sullivan Beare (†1618)', *Éigse*, 7 (1954), 162–81.

Breatnach, P. A. (ed.), 'Marbhna Aodha Ruaidh Uí Dhomhnaill (†1602)', *Éigse*, 15 (1973–1974), 31–50.

Breatnach, P. A. (ed.), 'Select documents XL: An Address to Aodh Ruadh Ó Domhnaill in Captivity, 1590', *Irish Historical Studies*, 25 (1986), 198–213.

Breatnach, R. A. (ed.), 'Anarchy in west Munster', *Éigse*, 23 (1989), 57–66.

Breatnach, P. A. (ed.), 'A Poem on the End of Patronage', *Éigse*, 31 (1999), 79–88.

Breatnach, P. A. (ed.), 'Metamorphosis 1603: Dán le hEochaidh Ó hEódhasa', *Éigse*, 17 (1977–1979), 169–80.

Carney, M., (ed.), 'Select documents III. Agreement between Ó Domhnaill and Tadhg Ó Conchobhair concerning Sligo Castle (23 June 1539)', *Irish Historical Studies*, 3 (1942–1943), 282–95.

Dánta Mhuiris Mhic Dháibhí Dhuibh Mhic Gearailt, ed. N. Williams (Dublin: An Clóchomhar, 1979).

Fraser, J., P. Grosjean and J.G. O'Keeffe (eds.), *Irish Texts* (fascs. 1–5, London: Sheed and Ward, 1931–1934).

Gillies, W., (ed.), 'A Poem on the Downfall of the Gaoidhil', *Éigse*, 13 (1969–1970), 203–10.

Greene, D. (ed.), *Duanaire Mhéig Uidhir* (Dublin: DIAS, 1972).

Greene, D. and F. Kelly (eds.), *Irish Bardic Poetry: Texts and Translations, Together with an Introductory Lecture by Osborn Bergin* (Dublin: DIAS, 1970).

The Irish Fiants of the Tudor Sovereigns (4 vols., Dublin: Éamonn de Búrca, 1994).

Knott, E. (ed.), 'Mac an Bhaird's Elegy on the Ulster Lords', *Celtica*, 5 (1960), 161–71.

Leabhar na nUrnaightheadh gComhchoidchiond agus Mheinisdraldachda na Sacrameinteadh (Dublin, 1608), (PML 22709), Pierpont Morgan Library, New York.

Mac Airt, S. (ed.), *Leabhar Branach* (Dublin: DIAS, 1944).

Murphy, G. (ed.), 'Poems of Exile by Uilliam Nuinseann Mac Barúin Dealbhna', *Éigse*, 6 (1949), 8–15.

Ní Ghallchobhair, E. (ed.), *Anathomia Gydo* (London: ITS, 2014).

Nic Cárthaigh, E., (ed.), 'Mo Cheithre Rainn Duit, a Dhonnchaidh: Advice to a Prince by Tadhg (mac Dáire) Mac Bruaideadha', in E. Purcell, P. MacCotter, J. Nyhan and J. Sheehan (eds.), *Clerics, Kings and Vikings: Essays on Medieval Ireland in Honour of Donnchadh Ó Corráin* (Dublin: FCP, 2015), 490–517.

Nicholls, K. W., (ed.), 'The Lisgoole Agreement of 1580', *Clogher Record*, 7 (1969), 27–33.

Ó Ciardha, P. (ed.), 'The Lament for Eoghan Mac Criostail', *The Irish Sword*, 13 (1977–1979), 378–81.

Ó Cuív, B. (ed.), 'Flaithrí Ó Maolchonaire's Catechism of Christian Doctrine', *Celtica*, 1 (1950), 161–206.

Ó Cuív, B. (ed.), 'A Poem on the Í Néill', *Celtica*, 2 (1954), 245–51.

Ó Cuív, B. (ed.), 'A Sixteenth-Century Political Poem', *Éigse*, 15 (1973–1974), 261–76.

Ó Cuív, B. (ed.), 'The Earl of Thomond and the Poets, A.D. 1572', *Celtica*, 12 (1977), 125–45, at 127.

Ó Cuív, B. (ed.), 'An Elegy on Donnchadh Ó Briain, Fourth Earl of Thomond', *Celtica*, 16 (1984), 87–105.

O'Daly, D., *The Rise, Increase, and Exit of the Geraldines, Earls of Desmond*, trans. C. P. Meehan, (2nd edn., Dublin: James Duffy, 1878).

Ó Donnchadha, T. (ed.), *Leabhar Cloinne Aodha Buidhe* (Dublin: Irish Manuscripts Commission, 1931).

Ó Muireadhaigh, R. (ed.), 'Aos Dána na Mumhan, 1584', *Irisleabhar Muighe Nuadhat*, (1960), 81–4.

Ó Murchú, L. P. (ed.), 'Caoineadh ar Uaithne Mór Ó Lochlainn, 1617', *Éigse*, 27 (1993), 67–79.

O'Sullivan, A. (ed.), 'Tadhg O'Daly and Sir George Carew', *Éigse*, 14 (1971–1972), 27–38.

The Poems of Giolla Brighde Mac Con Midhe, ed. N. J. A. Williams (London: ITS, 1980).

The Statutes at Large Passed in the Parliaments of Ireland (18 vols., Dublin: George Grierson, 1765–1799).

Secondary Sources

Bernard, G. W., *The Late Medieval English Church: Vitality and Vulnerability before the Break with Rome* (New Haven and London: Yale University Press, 2012).

Breatnach, C. (ed.), *Patronage, Politics and Prose* (Maynooth: An Sagart, 1996).

Breatnach, P. A., 'The Chief's Poet', *Proceedings of the Royal Irish Academy*, 83:C (1983), 37–79.

Caball, M., *Poets and Politics: Continuity and Reaction in Irish Poetry, 1558–1625* (Cork University Press and Field Day, 1998).

Caball, M., 'Politics and Religion in the Poetry of Fearghal Óg Mac an Bhaird and Eoghan Ruadh Mac an Bhaird', in P. Ó Riain (ed.), *Beatha Aodha Ruaidh: the Life of Red Hugh O'Donnell. Historical and Literary Contexts* (London: ITS, 2002), 74–97.

Caball, M., 'Patriotism, Culture and Identity: The Poetry of Geoffrey Keating', in P. Ó Riain (ed.), *Geoffrey Keating's Foras Feasa ar Éirinn: Reassessments* (London: ITS, 2008), 19–38.

Caball, M., 'Culture, Politics and Identity in Sixteenth-Century Ireland: The Testimony of Tadhg Dall Ó hUiginn (*c.*1550–1591)', in P. Riggs (ed.), *Tadhg Dall Ó hUiginn: his Historical and Literary Context* (London: ITS, 2010), 1–21.

Caball, M., 'Responses to Transformation: Gaelic Poets and the Plantation of Ulster', in É. Ó Ciardha and M. Ó Siochrú (eds.), *The Plantation of Ulster: Ideology and Practice* (Manchester University Press, 2012), 176–97.

Caball, M., 'The Bible in Early Modern Gaelic Ireland: Tradition, Collaboration, and Alienation', in K. Killeen, H. Smith and R. Willie (eds.), *The Oxford Handbook of the Bible in Early Modern England, c.1530–1700* (Oxford University Press, 2015), 332–49.

Caball, M., 'Notes on an Elizabethan Kerry Bardic Family', *Ériu*, 43 (1992), 32–42.

Caball, M., 'Pairlement Chloinne Tomáis I: a Reassessment', *Éigse*, 27 (1993), 47–57.

Caball, M., 'Articulating Irish Identity in Early Seventeenth-Century Europe: The case of Giolla Brighde Ó hEódhusa (c.1570–1614)', *Archivium Hibernicum*, 62 (2009), 271–93.

Caball, M. 'Gaelic and Protestant: A Case Study in Early Modern Self-Fashioning, 1567–1608', *Proceedings of the Royal Irish Academy*, 110:C (2010), 191–215.

Canny, N., *Making Ireland British 1580–1650* (Oxford University Press, 2001).

Carney, J., *The Irish Bardic Poet* (Dublin: Dolmen Press, 1967; repr. Dublin: DIAS, 1985).

Casey, D., 'Irish Pseudohistory in Conall Mag Eochagáin's *Annals of Clonmacnoise*', *Proceedings of the Harvard Celtic Colloquium*, 32 (2012), 74–94.

Connolly, S. J., *Contested Island: Ireland 1460–1630* (Oxford University Press, 2007).

Cunningham, B., *The Annals of the Four Masters: Irish History, Kingship and Society in the Early Seventeenth Century* (Dublin: Four Courts Press, 2010).

Cunningham, B., 'Loss and Gain: Attitudes towards the English Language in Early Modern Ireland', in Brian Mac Cuarta (ed.), *Reshaping Ireland 1550–1700: Colonization and its Consequences* (Dublin: Four Courts Press, 2011), 163–86.

Cunningham, B., 'Catholic intellectual culture in early modern Ireland', in Tadhg Ó hAnnracháin and Robert Armstrong (eds.), *Christianities in the Early Modern Celtic World* (Basingstoke: Palgrave Macmillan, 2014), 151–63.

Dillon, C., 'Medical Practice and Gaelic Ireland', in J. Kelly and F. Clark (eds.), *Ireland and Medicine in the Seventeenth and Eighteenth Centuries* (Farnham: Ashgate, 2010), 39–52.

Dooley, A., 'Literature and Society in Early Seventeenth-Century Ireland: The Evaluation of Change', in C. J. Byrne, M. Harry and P. Ó Siadhail (eds.), *Celtic Languages and Celtic Peoples: Proceedings of the Second North American Congress of Celtic Studies* (Halifax: Saint Mary's University, 1992), 513–34.

Duffy, P. J., D. Edwards and E. Fitzpatrick (eds.), *Gaelic Ireland c.1250–c.1650: Land, Lordship and Settlement* (Dublin: Four Courts Press, 2001).

Hore, H. F., 'Irish Bardism in 1561', *Ulster Journal of Archaeology*, 6 (1858), 165–67, 202–12.

Hore, H. F., 'The Munster Bards', *Ulster Journal of Archaeology*, 7 (1859), 93–115.

Kane, B., 'Domesticating the Counter-Reformation: Bridging the Bardic and Catholic Traditions in Geoffrey Keating's *The three Shafts of Death*', *The Sixteenth Century Journal*, 40 (2009), 1029–44.

Leerssen, J., *The Contention of the Bards (Iomarbhágh na bhFileadh) and its Place in Irish Political and Literary History* (London: ITS, 1994).

Mac Cana, P., 'The Rise of the Later Schools of *Filidheacht*', *Ériu*, 25 (1974), 126–46.

Mac Craith, M., *Lorg na hIasachta ar na Dánta Grádha* (Dublin: An Clóchomhar, 1989).

Mac Craith, M., 'Gaelic Ireland and the Renaissance', in G. Williams and R. O. Jones (eds.), *The Celts and the Renaissance: Tradition and Innovation* (Cardiff: University of Wales Press, 1989), 57–89.

Mac Craith, M., 'The *Beatha* in the Context of the Literature of the Renaissance', in P. Ó Riain (ed.), *Beatha Aodha Ruaidh: the Life of Red Hugh O'Donnell. Historical and Literary Contexts* (London: ITS, 2002), 36–53.

Mac Niocaill, G., *The Medieval Irish Annals* (Dublin: Dublin Historical Association, 1975).

MacCarthy, D., (ed.), *The Life and Letters of Florence MacCarthy Reagh* (London: Longmans, 1867).

McGrath, C., 'Í Eódhosa', *Clogher Record*, 2 (1957), 1–19.

McKenna, L. (ed.), *Aithdioghluim Dána* (2 vols., Dublin: ITS, 1939–1940).

McKibben, S. E., *Endangered Masculinities in Irish Poetry 1540–1780* (Dublin: UCD Press, 2010).

McLeod, W., *Divided Gaels: Gaelic Cultural Identities in Scotland and Ireland c.1200–1650* (Oxford University Press, 2004).

McManus, D., 'The Bardic Poet as Teacher, Student and Critic: a Context for the Grammatical Tracts', in C. G. Ó Háinle and D. E. Meek (eds.), *Léann na Tríonóide. Trinity Irish Studies* (Dublin: School of Irish, Trinity College, 2004), 97–123.

Murphy, G., *The Ossianic Lore and Romantic Tales of Medieval Ireland* (Dublin: Cultural Relations Committee, 1961).

Nicholls, K. W., *Gaelic and Gaelicised Ireland in the Middle Ages* (Dublin: Gill and Macmillan, 1972).

Nicholls, K. W., *Land, Law and Society in Sixteenth-Century Ireland* (Dublin: National University of Ireland, 1976).

Ó Buachalla, B., *Aisling Ghéar: na Stíobhartaigh agus an t-Aos Léinn 1603–1788* (Dublin: An Clóchomhar, 1996).

Ó Buachalla, B., 'Cúlra is Tábhacht an Dáin *A leabhráin ainmnighthear d'Aodh*', *Celtica*, 21 (1990), 402–16.

Ó Caithnia, L. P., *Apalóga na bhFilí 1200–1650* (Dublin: An Clóchomhar, 1984).

Ó Clabaigh, C. N., *The Franciscans in Ireland, 1400–1534: from Reform to Reformation* (Dublin: Four Courts Press, 2002).

Ó Cuív, B., *The Irish Bardic Duanaire or 'Poem-Book'* (Dublin: National Library of Ireland Society, 1973).

Ó Doibhlin, D., 'Tyrone's Gaelic Literary Legacy', in C. Dillon and H. A. Jefferies (eds.), *Tyrone: History & Society* (Dublin: Geography Publications, 2000), 403–32.

O'Dowd, M., *Power, Politics and Land: Early Modern Sligo 1568–1688* (Belfast: Institute of Irish Studies, Queen's University Belfast, 1991).

Ó Dúshláine, T., *An Eoraip agus Litríocht na Gaeilge 1600–1650* (Dublin: An Clóchomhar, 1987).

Ó Fearghail, F. (ed.), *Tadhg Ó Cianáin: An Irish Scholar in Rome* (Dublin: Mater Dei, 2011).

O'Grady, S. H. and R. Flower (eds.), *Catalogue of Irish Manuscripts in the British Library [formerly British Museum]* (3 vols., London: The British Museum, 1926–1953; repr. Dublin: DIAS, 1992).

Ó hUiginn, R., 'Duanaire Finn: Patron and Text', in J. Carey (ed.), *Duanaire Finn: Reassessments* (London: ITS, 2003), 79–106.

Ó hUiginn, R., 'Irish Literature in Spanish Flanders', in T. O'Connor and M. A. Lyons (eds.), *The Ulster Earls and Baroque Europe: Refashioning Irish Identities, 1600–1800* (Dublin: Four Courts Press, 2010), 349–61.

Ó hUiginn, R., 'Fiannaigheacht, Family, Faith and Fatherland', in Sharon J. Arbuthnot and Geraldine Parsons (eds.), *The Gaelic Finn tradition* (Dublin: Four Courts Press, 2012), 151–62.

Ó Macháin, P., 'The Early Modern Irish Prosodic Tracts and the Editing of 'Bardic Verse', in H. L. C. Tristram (ed.), *Metrik und Medienwechsel: Metrics and Media* (Tübingen: Gunter Narr Verlag, 1991), 273–87.

Ó Murchú, L. P., 'Caitilín Dubh', in B. Lalor (ed.), *The Encyclopaedia of Ireland* (Dublin: Gill and Macmillan, 2003), 149.

O'Rahilly, T. F., 'Irish Poets, Historians, and Judges in English Documents, 1538–1615', *Proceedings of the Royal Irish Academy*, 36:C (1922), 86–120.

Patterson, N., 'Gaelic Law and the Tudor Conquest of Ireland: The Social Background of the Sixteenth-Century Recensions of the Pseudo-Historical Prologue to the *Senchas Már*', *Irish Historical Studies*, 27 (1991), 193–215.

Simms, K., *From Kings to Warlords: The Changing Political Structure of Gaelic Ireland in the Later Middle Ages* (Woodbridge: Boydell Press, 2000).

Simms, K., 'Literacy and the Irish Bards', in H. Pryce (ed.), *Literacy in Medieval Celtic Societies* (Cambridge University Press, 1998), 238–58.

Williams, N., *I bPrionta i Leabhar: na Protastúin agus Prós na Gaeilge 1567–1724* (Dublin: An Clóchomhar, 1986).

17 Language, Literature and Print in Irish, 1630–1730

Bernadette Cunningham

Unpublished Primary Sources

Clonalis House, Co. Roscommon
The Book of the O'Conor Don (Digital edition at www.isos.dias.ie)

Marsh's Library, Dublin
MS Z4.2.5 *Vocabularium Latinum et Hibernum*

National Library of Ireland
MS G 62 Poetry and Tales
MS G 167 Poem Book of the O'Donnells
MS G 197 *An Gleacaigh Geuglonnach*
MS G 198 Historical Geography of the World

Royal Irish Academy

MS 3 B 46 Translation of *Tuireamh na hÉireann*
MS 23 I 18 Translation of *Tuireamh na hÉireann*
MS 23 P 12 Book of Ballymote
MS 24 G 16 Michael Kearney's translation of *Foras Feasa ar Éirinn*
MS 24 I 5 John Lynch's Latin translation of *Foras Feasa ar Éirinn*
MS D i 2 Rule of St Clare
MS E iv 3 Book of O'Loghlen

Trinity College Dublin

MS 1289 Tadhg Ó Neachtain's 'Psalter of Tara'

Published Primary Sources

'The Annals of Ireland from the Year 1441 to 1468,' Translated from the Irish by Dudley Firbisse', *Miscellany of the Irish Archaeological Society*, 1 (Dublin: Irish Archaeological Society, 1846), 198–302.

Atkinson, E. G. (ed.), *Acts of the Privy Council of England, 1615–1616* (London: HMSO, 1925).

Carney, J. (ed.), *Genealogical History of the O'Reillys* (Cavan: Cumann Sheanchuis Bhreifne, 1959).

Dinneen, P. S. and T. O'Donoghue (eds. and trans.), *Dánta Aodhagáin Uí Rathaille* (2nd edn., London: Irish Texts Society, 1911).

Gearnon, Antoin, *Parrthas an Anma*, ed. A. Ó Fachtna (Dublin Institute for Advanced Studies, 1953).

The General History of Ireland ... Collected by the Learned Jeoffry Keating ... Faithfully Translated from the Irish by Dermo'd O'Connor (London and Dublin, 1723; other edns. London, 1726, 1732).

Gilbert, J. T. (ed.), *A Jacobite Narrative of the War in Ireland, 1688–91* (Dublin: J. Dollard, 1892).

Gilbert, J. T. and R. Gilbert (eds.), *Calendar of the Ancient Records of Dublin*, (19 vols., Dublin: Dollard, 1889–1944).

Harrison, A. (ed.), 'Lucht na Simléirí', *Éigse*, 15 (1973–4), 189–202.

Hartnett, M., *Haicéad* (Oldcastle: Gallery Press, 1993).

Jennings, B. (ed.), *Louvain Papers, 1606–1827* (Dublin: Irish Manuscripts Commission, 1968).

Lynch, J., *Cambrensis Eversus*, ed. and trans. M. Kelly (3 vols., Dublin: Celtic Society, 1848–52).

Mac Erlean, J. (ed. and trans.), *Duanaire Dháibhidh Uí Bhruadair* (3 vols., London: Irish Texts Society, 1910–17).

Murphy, D. (ed.), *The Annals of Clonmacnoise* (Dublin: The University Press, 1896).

Ní Cheallacháin, M. (ed.), *Filíocht Phádraigín Haicéad* (Dublin: An Clóchomhar, 1962).

Ní Chléirigh, M. (ed.), *Eólas ar an Domhan* (Dublin: Oifig an tSoláthair, 1944).

Ó Buachalla, B. (ed.), *Aogán Ó Rathaille* (Dublin: Field Day, 2007).

Ó Cuív, B. (ed.), *Párliament na mBan* (Dublin Institute for Advanced Studies, 1952).

Ó Doibhlin, B., *Manuail de Litríocht na Gaeilge* [fascicles 3–5] (Dublin: Coiscéim, 2007–9).

Ó Donnchadha, T. (ed.), *Leabhar Cloinne Aodha Buidhe* (Dublin: Oifig an tSoláthair, 1931).

O'Donovan, John (ed. and trans.), *Annála Ríoghachta Éireann: Annals of the Kingdom of Ireland by the Four Masters* (7 vols., Dublin: Hodges and Smith, 1848–51).

Ó Dufaigh, S. and B. E. Rainey, (ed. and trans.), *Comhairle Mhic Clamha ó Achadh na Muileann: The Advice of Mac Clave from Aughnamullen* (Presses Universitaires de Lille, 1981).

Ó Fiannachta, P., *An Barántas I: Réamhrá, Téacs, Malairtí* (Maynooth: An Sagart, 1978).

Ó Neachtain, E. (ed.), *Stair Éamuinn Uí Chléire de réir Sheáin Uí Neachtain* (Dublin: Gill, 1918).

O'Rahilly, C. (ed.), *Five Seventeenth-Century Political Poems* (Dublin Institute for Advanced Studies, 1952).

Ó Súilleabháin, P. (ed.), *Rialachas San Froinsias* (Dublin Institute for Advanced Studies, 1953).

Swift, Jonathan, *Journal to Stella*, ed. H. Williams (2 vols., Oxford: Clarendon Press, 1948).

Tiomna Nuadh ár dTighearna agus ar Slanuigheora Iosa Críosd (London, 1681).

Ua Duinnín, P. (ed.), *Dánta Phiarais Feiritéir* (Dublin: Connradh na Gaedhilge, 1903).

Williams, N. (ed. and trans.), *Pairlement Chloinne Tomáis* (Dublin Institute for Advanced Studies, 1981).

Young, R. M. (ed.), 'An Account of the Barony of O'Neiland', *Ulster Journal of Archaeology*, 2nd series, 4 (1898), 239–41.

Secondary Sources

Barnard, T., *Improving Ireland?* (Dublin: Four Courts Press, 2008).

Barnard, T., 'Protestants and the Irish Language, c.1675–1725', in T. Barnard, *Protestant Ascents and Descents, 1641–1770* (Dublin: Four Courts Press, 2004), 179–207.

Barnard, T., 'The Impact of Print in Ireland, 1680–1800: Problems and Perils', in J. MacElligott and E. Patten (eds.), *The Perils of Print Culture* (Basingstoke: Palgrave, 2014), 95–117.

Breatnach, P. A., 'The Book of the O'Conor Don and the Manuscripts of St Anthony's College, Louvain', in P. Ó Macháin (ed.), *The Book of the O'Conor Don* (Dublin Institute for Advanced Studies, 2010).

Caball, M., 'Patriotism, Culture and Identity: The Poetry of Geoffrey Keating', in P. Ó Riain (ed.), *Geoffrey Keating's Foras Feasa ar Éirinn: Reassessments*. Irish Texts Society, subsidiary series, 19 (London: Irish Texts Society, 2008), 19–38.

Canny, N., *Making Ireland British, 1580–1650* (Oxford University Press, 2001).

Carpenter, A., 'Literature in Print, 1550–1800', in R. Gillespie and A. Hadfield (eds.), *The Oxford History of the Irish Book, III: the Irish Book in English* (Oxford University Press, 2006), 300–18.

Cunningham, B., *The World of Geoffrey Keating* (Dublin: Four Courts Press, 2000).

Cunningham, B., *The Annals of the Four Masters: Irish History, Kingship and Society in the Early Seventeenth Century* (Dublin: Four Courts Press, 2010).

Cunningham, B., 'Loss and Gain: Attitudes to the English Language in Early Modern Ireland', in B. Mac Cuarta (ed.), *Reshaping Ireland, 1500–1700: Colonization and its Consequences* (Dublin: Four Courts Press, 2011), 163–86.

Cunningham, B. and R. Gillespie, 'An Ulster Settler and his Irish Manuscripts', *Éigse*, 21 (1986), 27–36.

de Bhaldraithe, T., 'Irish Dictionaries', in *Corpas na Gaeilge, 1660–1882: Foclóir na Nua-Ghaeilge: The Irish Language Corpus* (Dublin: Royal Irish Academy, 2004).

Dickson, D., *Dublin: the Making of a Capital City* (London: Profile, 2014).

Dillon, C., 'An Ghaelig Nua: English, Irish and South Ulster Poets and Scribes in the Late Seventeenth and Eighteenth Centuries', in J. Kelly and C. Mac Murchaidh (eds.), *Irish and English: Essays on the Irish Linguistic and Cultural Frontier, 1600–1900* (Dublin: Four Courts Press, 2012), 141–61.

Doyle, A., *A History of the Irish Language* (Oxford University Press, 2015).

Foster, R. F., *The Irish Story* (London: Allen Lane, 2001).

Gillespie, R., *Reading Ireland: Print, Reading and Social Change in Early Modern Ireland* (Manchester University Press, 2005).

Gillespie, R., 'The Louvain Franciscans and the Culture of Print', in R. Gillespie and R. Ó hUiginn (eds.), *Irish Europe, 1600–1650: Writing and Learning* (Dublin: Four Courts Press, 2013), 105–20.

Harrison, A., *The Dean's Friend: Anthony Raymond 1676–1726, Jonathan Swift and the Irish Language* (Dublin: Éamonn de Búrca, 1999).

Harrison, F. Ll., 'Music, Poetry and Polity in the Age of Swift', *Eighteenth-Century Ireland*, 1 (1986), 37–63.

Kelly, J., and C. Mac Murchaidh (eds.), *Irish and English: Essays on the Irish Linguistic and Cultural Frontier, 1600–1900* (Dublin: Four Courts Press, 2012).

Logan, J., 'Tadhg O Roddy and Two Surveys of Co. Leitrim', *Breifne*, 4 (1971), 318–34.

Mac Craith, M., *Lorg na hIasachta ar na Dánta Grá* (Dublin: An Clóchomhar, 1989).

Mac Craith, M., 'Literature in Irish, c.1550–1690: From the Elizabethan settlement to the Battle of the Boyne', in M. Kelleher and P. O'Leary (eds.), *The Cambridge History of Irish Literature, Volume 1: to 1890* (Cambridge University Press, 2006), 191–231.

Mac Giolla Chríost, D., *The Irish Language in Ireland* (London: Routledge, 2005).

Mac Mathúna, L., *Béarla sa Ghaeilge: Cabhair Choigríche: an Códmheascadh Gaeilge/Béarla i Litríocht na Gaeilge, 1600–1900* (Dublin: An Clóchomhar, 2007).

Mac Mathúna, L., 'Getting to Grips with Innovation and Genre Diversification in the Work of the Ó Neachtain Circle in Early Eighteenth-Century Dublin', *Eighteenth-Century Ireland*, 27 (2012), 53–83.

MacCarthy-Morrogh, M., *The Munster Plantation* (Oxford University Press, 1986).

McGuinne, D., *Irish Type Design: A History of Printing Types in the Irish Character* (Dublin: Irish Academic Press, 1992), 32–5.

McGuirc, J. and J. Quinn (eds.), *Dictionary of Irish Biography* (9 vols., Cambridge University Press, 2009).

Mahon, W., 'Introduction', in W. Mahon (ed.), *The History of Éamonn O'Clery, Translated and Annotated with an Edition of the Irish text* (Indreabhán: Cló Iar-Chonnacht, 2000), 3–29.

Morley, V., *An Crann os Coill: Aodh Buí Mac Cruitín, c.1680–1755* (Dublin: Coiscéim, 1995).

Morley, V., *Ó Chéitinn go Raiftearaí: mar a Cumadh Stair na hÉireann* (Dublin: Coiscéim, 2011).

Ní Mhunghaile, L., 'Scribal Networks and Manuscript Circulation in Meath during the Eighteenth and Early Nineteenth Centuries', *Ríocht na Mídhe*, 22 (2011), 131–49.

Ní Mhurchú, M. and D. Breathnach, *1560–1781: Beathaisnéis* (Dublin: An Clóchomhar, 2001).

Ní Mhurchú, P., 'The Book of O'Conor Don: Catalogue Raisonné', unpublished MPhil thesis, University College Dublin (1995).

Ní Shéaghdha, N., *Catalogue of Irish Manuscripts in the National Library of Ireland, V* (Dublin Institute for Advanced Studies, 1979).

Ó Beoláin, A., *Merriman agus Filí eile* (Dublin: An Clóchomhar, 1985).

Ó Buachalla, B., *Aisling Ghéar* (Dublin: An Clóchomhar, 1996), 185.

Ó Conchúir, B., *Scríobhaithe Chorcai, 1700–1850* (Dublin: An Clóchomhar, 1982).

Ó Conchúir, B., 'Na Cúirteanna Éigse i gCúige Mumhan', in P. Riggs, B. Ó Conchúir and S. Ó Coileáin (eds.), *Saoi na hÉigse* (Dublin: An Clóchomhar, 2000), 55–81.

Ó Cuív, B., 'The Irish Language in the Early Modern Period', in T. W. Moody, F. X. Martin and F. J. Byrne (eds.), *A New History of Ireland, III, 1534–1691* (Oxford University Press, 1976), 509–45.

Ó Háinle, C., 'The Novel Frustrated: Developments in 17th- to 19th-century Fiction in Irish', in C. Ó Háinle and D. Meek (eds.), *Unity in Diversity: Studies in Irish and Scottish Gaelic Language, Literature and History* (Dublin: Trinity College, School of Irish, 2004), 125–51,

Ó Macháin, P., 'Tadhg Ó Rodaighe and his School: Aspects of Patronage and Poetic Practice at the Close of the Bardic Era', in S. Duffy (ed.), *Princes, Prelates and Poets in Medieval Ireland* (Dublin: Four Courts Press, 2013), 538–51.

Poppe, E., 'Leibniz and Eckhart on the Irish Language', *Eighteenth-Century Ireland*, 1 (1986), 65–84.

Rimmer, J., 'Patronage, Style and Structure in Music Attributed to Turlough Carolan', *Early Music*, 15 (1987), 164–74.

Stewart, J., 'Párliament na mBan', *Celtica*, 7 (1966), 135–41.

Trimble, J., 'Carolan and his Patrons in Fermanagh and Neighbouring Areas', *Clogher Record*, 10 (1979), 26–50.

Williams, N., *I bPrionta i Leabhar* (Dublin: An Clóchomhar: 1986).

18 The Emergence of English Print and Literature, 1630–1730

Deana Rankin

Unpublished Primary Sources

Bodleian Library, Oxford

Carte Ms 61

The National Archives, UK

SP 63/392

Published Primary Sources

Addison, Joseph, *The Works of the Right Honourable Joseph Addison* (Dublin, 1722).

Anon., *A Poem of the Art of Printing* [Dublin, 1728].

Articles of Peace Made, Concluded, Accorded and Agreed Upon, by and between His Excellency Iames Lord Marques of Ormonde, … on the Behalfe of His Most Excellent Majesty (Cork, 1648).

Boate, Gerald, *Irelands Naturall History* (London, 1652).

Burkhead, Henry, *Cola's Furie or Lirenda's Miserie* (Kilkenny, 1646).

Burnell, Henry, *Landgartha, a Tragie-comedy*, ed. D. Rankin (Dublin: Four Courts Press, 2014).

Carpenter, A. (ed.), *Verse in English from Tudor and Stuart Ireland* (Cork University Press, 2003).

Colgan, John, *Acta Sanctorum ... Hiberniae* (Louvain, 1645).

Colgan, John, *The Lives of the Glorious St David ... of Wales ... also of Saint Kieran the first-borne saint of Ireland* (Waterford, 1647).

Cook, Frances, *Mrs. Cooke's Meditations ... Composed by Herselfe at her Unexpected Safe Arrival at Corcke* (Cork and London, 1650).

Cook, John, *A True Relation of Mr. Iohn Cook's Passage* (Cork and London, 1650).

Cook, John, *Monarchy no Creature of Gods Making, & c. Wherein is Proved by Scripture and Reason, that Monarchicall Government is Against the Minde of God* (Waterford, 1651).

Davies, Sir John, *Historical Relations: or, A Discovery of the True Causes why Ireland was Never Entirely Subdued* (Dublin, 1704).

Dowling, Luke, *A Catalogue of a Choice Collection of Books being what Remain'd Unsold in a Late Auction* (Dublin, 1720).

Edderman, Francis, *A Most Pithi and Plesant History Whear in is the Destrouction of Troye Gathered Togethere of all the Chyfeste Autores turned into Englyshe Myttere* (Dublin, c.1558).

Enos, Walter, *Alexipharmacon, or A Soveraigne Antidote against a Virulent Cordiall* (Waterford, 1644).

Hyde, Edward, earl of Clarendon, *Lord Clarendon's History of the Grand Rebellion Compleated* (Dublin, 1720).

Keating, Geoffrey, *Dr Keting's [sic] History of Ireland Translated by Dermod O'Connor* (Dublin, 1723).

By the King a Proclamation Declaringe James Marques of Ormond to be ... Governour of the Kingdome of Ireland (Kilkenny, 1649).

King, William, *The State of the Protestants of Ireland under the Late King James's Government* (London, 1691).

Newton, Isaac, *The Chronology of Ancient Kingdoms Amended* (Dublin, 1728).

Pemberton, Henry, *A View of Sir Isaac Newton's Philosophy* (Dublin, 1728).

The Present State of Ireland (Dublin, 1729).

By the Supreame Councell of the Confederat Catholicks of Ireland, Printed at Kilkenny by Thomas Bourke ... 1648 (Kilkenny, 1648).

Jonathan Swift, *The Works of J.S. D. D.D., D.S.P.D. in four volumes* (Dublin: George Faulkner, 1735).

S[ynge], F[rancis], *A Panegyricke on the Most Auspicious and Long-Wish'd-For Return of the Great Example of the Greatest Virtue, the Faithful Achates of our Royal Charles, and the Tutelar Angel (as we Justly Hope) of our Church and State, the Most Illustrious James Duke, Marquess, and Earl of Ormond* (Dublin, [1661]).

Temple, Sir John, *The Irish Rebellion* (Dublin, 1714).

Thomson, James, *A Poem Sacred to the Memory of Sir Isaac Newton* (Dublin, 1727).

Ware, Sir James, *The Antiquities and History of Ireland* (Dublin, 1704).

Watson, James, *The History of the Art of Printing* (Edinburgh, 1713).

Secondary Sources

Alexander, G., *Writing after Sidney: The Literary Response to Sir Philip Sidney, 1586–1640* (Oxford University Press, 2006).

Anderson, J., *Catalogue of Early Belfast Printed Books, 1694–1830* (new edn., with two supplements, Belfast: McCaw, Stevenson and Orr, 1890–1902).

Boran, E., 'The Libraries of Luke Challoner and James Ussher, 1595–1608', in H. Robinson-Hammerstein (ed.), *European Universities in the Age of Reformation and Counter-Reformation* (Dublin: Four Courts Press, 1998), 75–115.

Carpenter, A., 'Literature in Print, 1550–1800', in R. Gillespie and A Hadfield (eds.), *The History of the Book in Ireland: volume III: The Irish Book in English, 1550–1800* (Oxford University Press, 2006), 301–18.

Clarke, A., 'Patrick Darcy and the Constitutional Relationship between Ireland and England', in J. Ohlmeyer (ed.), *Political Thought in Seventeenth-Century Ireland: Kingdom or Colony* (Cambridge University Press, 2000), 35–55.

Coughlan, P., 'Counter-Currents in Colonial Discourse: the Political Thought of Vincent and Daniel Gookin', in J. Ohlmeyer (ed.), *Political Thought in Seventeenth-Century Ireland: Kingdom or Colony* (Cambridge University Press, 2000), 35–55.

Coughlan, P., 'Introduction', in Henry Burkhead, *A Tragedy of Cola's Furie or Lirenda's Miserie*, ed. A. Lynch (Dublin: Four Courts Press, 2009), 9–32.

Cunningham, B., *The World of Geoffrey Keating: History, Myth and Religion in Seventeenth-century Ireland* (Dublin: Four Courts Press, 2000).

Cunningham, B, 'Historical Writing, 1660–1750', in R. Gillespie and A. Hadfield (eds.), *The History of the Book in Ireland: Volume III: The Irish Book in English, 1550–1800* (Oxford University Press, 2006), 264–81.

Dickson, R., and J. P. Edmund, *Annals of Scottish Printing* (Cambridge: Macmillan and Bowes, 1890).

Dix, E. R. McClintock, *Catalogue of early Dublin-printed books, 1601–1700*. With an historical introduction and bibliographical notes by C.W. Dugan [Dublin, 1898–1912] (New York: Burt Franklin, 1971).

Elias, A. C., 'A Manuscript Book of Constantia Grierson's', *Swift Studies*, 2 (1987), 33–56.

Ford, A., '"Firm Catholics" or "Loyal Subjects"?: Religious and Political Allegiance in Early Seventeenth-century Ireland' in D. G. Boyce, R., Eccleshall and V. Geoghegan (eds.), *Political Discourse in Seventeenth- and Eighteenth-century Ireland* (Basingstoke: Palgrave, 2001), 1–32.

Gadd, Ian, Claude Rawson, Ian Gadd, Ian Higgins, James McLaverty, Valerie Rumbold, Abigail Williams and David Wormersley (eds.), *The Cambridge Edition of the Works of Jonathan Swift* (18 vols., Cambridge University Press, 2008–).

Gadd, I., 'Leaving the Printer to his Liberty: Swift and the London Book Trade, 1701–1714', in P. Bullard and J MacLaverty (eds.), *Jonathan Swift and the Eighteenth-century Book* (Cambridge University Press, 2013), 51–65.

Gillespie, R., *Reading Ireland: Print, Reading and Social Change in Early Modern Ireland* (Manchester University Press, 2005).

Gillespie, R., 'Irish Print and Protestant Identity: Williams King's Pamphlet Wars, 1687–1697', in V. Carey and U. Lotz-Heumann (eds.), *Taking Sides?: Colonial and Confessional Mentalitiés in Early Modern Ireland* (Dublin: Four Courts Press, 2003), 231–50.

Hadfield, A., 'Historical Writing, 1550–1660', in R. Gillespie and A. Hadfield (eds.), *The History of the Book in Ireland: Volume III: The Irish Book in English, 1550–1800* (Oxford University Press, 2006), 250–63.

Hunter, R. J., 'John Franckton' in C. Benson and S. Fitzpatrick (eds.), *That Woman!: Studies in Irish Bibliography. A festschrift for Mary 'Paul' Pollard* (Dublin: Lilliput Press, 2005), 1–26.

Kelly, P., 'Recasting a Tradition: William Molyneux and the Sources of *The Case of Ireland ... Stated* (1698)', in J. Ohlmeyer (ed.), *Political Thought in Seventeenth-Century Ireland: Kingdom or Colony* (Cambridge University Press, 2000), 83–106.

Kerrigan, J., *Archipelagic English: Literature, History and Politics, 1603–1707* (Oxford University Press, 2008).

Kinane, V., *A Brief History of Printing and Publishing in Ireland* (Dublin: National Print Museum, 2002).

Lennon, C., 'The Print Trade, 1550–1700', in R. Gillespie and A. Hadfield (eds.), *The History of the Book in Ireland: Volume III: The Irish Book in English, 1550–1800* (Oxford University Press, 2006), 61–73.

MacLaverty, J., 'George Faulkner and Swift's Collected Works', in P. Bullard and J. MacLaverty (eds.), *Jonathan Swift and the Eighteenth-century Book* (Cambridge University Press, 2013), 154–75.

Mahony, R., *Jonathan Swift: The Irish Identity* (New Haven and London: Yale University Press, 1995).

Miller, C. W., 'A Bibliographical Study of *Parthenissa* by Roger Boyle Earl of Orrery', *Studies in Bibliography*, 2 (1949–1950), 115–37.

Munter, R., *The History of the Irish Newspaper, 1685–1760* (Cambridge University Press, 1967).

Ó Siochrú, M., *Confederate Ireland, 1642–1649: A Constitutional and Political Analysis* (Dublin: Four Courts Press, 1999).

Phillips, J. W., *Printing and Bookselling in Dublin, 1670–1800* (Dublin: Irish Academic Press, 1998).

Pollard, M., *Dublin's Trade in Books, 1550–1800* (Oxford: Clarendon Press, 1989).

Pollard, M., *Dictionary of Members of the Dublin Book Trade 1550–1800* (Oxford University Press, 2000).

Rankin, D., *Between Spenser and Swift: English Writing in Seventeenth-century Ireland* (Cambridge University Press, 2005).

Sessions, W., *The First Printers in Waterford, Cork and Kilkenny, pre-1700* (York: Ebor Press, 1990).

Sessions, W., *Further Irish Studies in Early Printing History* (York: Ebor Press, 1994).

Stevenson, A., 'Shirley's Publishers: the Partnership of Crooke and Crooke', *The Library*, 25 (1945), 140–61.

19 A World of Honour: Aristocratic *Mentalité*

Brendan Kane

Published Primary Sources

Lodwick, *A discovrse of civill life* (London, 1606).

Carney, J. (ed.), *Poems on the Butlers of Ormond, Cahir and Dunboyne* (Dublin Institute for Advanced Studies, 1945).

Curtis, E. and R. B. McDowell (eds.), *Irish Historical Documents, 1172–1922* (London and New York: Barnes and Noble, 1943; repr. 1968).

Duanaire Dháibhidh Uí Bhruadair, ed. J.C. McErlean (3 vols., London: Irish Texts Society; 1910–1917).

Ó Tuama, S. (ed.), *Caoineadh Airt Uí Laoghaire* (Dublin: Clóchomhar, 1963).

Rahilly, C. (ed.), *Five Seventeenth-Century Political Poems* (Dublin Institute for Advanced Studies, 1952).

The Tipperary Hero: Dermot O'Meara's Ormonius (1615), ed. and trans. D. Edwards and K. Sidwell (Turnhout: Brepols, 2011).

Ussher, J., *'A Discourse on the Religion Anciently Professed by the Irish and the British'* (London, 1631), 128.

Secondary Sources

Barnard, T., *A New Anatomy of Ireland: The Irish Protestants, 1641–1770* (New Haven and London: Yale University Press, 2003).

Barry, J., 'Guide to Records of the Genealogical Office, Dublin, with a Commentary on Heraldry in Ireland and on the History of the Office', *Analecta Hibernica*, 26 (1970), 3–43.

Breatnach, P., 'The Chief's Poet', *Proceedings of the Royal Irish Academy*, 83:C (1983), 37–79.

Caball, M., *Poets and Politics: Reaction and Continuity in Irish Poetry, 1558–1625* (Cork University Press, 1998).

Campbell, I., *Renaissance Humanism and Ethnicity before Race: The Irish and the English in the Seventeenth Century* (Manchester University Press, 2013).

Campbell, I., 'John Lynch and Renaissance Humanism in Stuart Ireland: Catholic Intellectuals, Protestant Noblemen, and the Irish *Respublica*', *Éire-Ireland* 45 (2010), 27–40.

Canny, N., *The Upstart Earl: A Study of the Social and Mental World of Richard Boyle, First Earl of Cork, 1566–1643* (Cambridge University Press, 1982).

Canny, N., *Making Ireland British: 1580–1650* (Oxford University Press, 2001).

Canny, N., 'Hugh O'Neill, Earl of Tyrone, and the Changing Face of Gaelic Ulster', *Studia Hibernica*, (1970), 7–35.

Carey, V., *Surviving the Tudors: The 'Wizard' Earl of Kildare and English Rule in Ireland, 1537–1586* (Dublin: Four Courts Press, 2002).

Connolly, S., '"Ag Déanamh Commanding": Elite Responses to Popular Culture', in J. S. Donnelly and K. A. Miller (eds.), *Irish Popular Culture, 1650–1850* (Dublin: Irish Academic Press, 1998), 1–29.

Covington, S., '"The odious demon from across the sea". Oliver Cromwell, Memory and the Dislocations of Ireland', in E. Kuijpers, J. Pollmann, J. Muller and J. van der Steen (eds.), *Memory before Modernity: Practices of Memory in Early Modern Europe* (Leiden: Brill, 2013), 149–64.

Cunningham, B., *The World of Geoffrey Keating* (Dublin: Four Courts Press, 2000).

Cunningham, B., *The Annals of the Four Masters: Irish History, Kingship and Society in the Early Seventeenth Century* (Dublin: Four Courts Press, 2010).

Cunningham, B., 'Colonized Catholics: Perceptions of Honour and History: Michael Kearney's Reading of *Foras Feasa ar Éirinn*', in V. Carey and U. Lotz-Heumann (eds.),

Taking Sides? Colonial and Confessional Mentalités in Early Modern Ireland (Dublin: Four Courts Press, 2003), 150–64.

Foster, R.F., *Modern Ireland, 1600–1972* (London: Allen Lane, 1988).

Gillespie, R., 'The Religion of the First Duke of Ormond', in T. Barnard and J. Fenlon (eds.), *The Dukes of Ormond* (Woodbridge: Boydell Press, 2000), 101–113.

Hammer, P., '"Base Rogues" and "Gentlemen of Quality": the Earl of Essex's Irish Knights and Royal Displeasure in 1599', in B. Kane and V. McGowan-Doyle (eds.), *Elizabeth I and Ireland* (Cambridge University Press, 2014), 184–208.

Hayton, D., *Ruling Ireland, 1685–1742: Politics, Politicians and Parties* (Woodbridge: Boydell Press, 2004).

Herrup, C., *A House in Gross Disorder: Sex, Law, and the 2nd Earl of Castlehaven* (Oxford University Press, 1999).

James, M., *English Politics and the Concept of Honour, 1485–1642* (Oxford: Past & Present Society, 1978).

Kane, B., *The Politics and Culture of Honour in Britain and Ireland, 1541–1641* (Cambridge University Press, 2010).

Kane, B., 'Languages of Legitimacy? *An Ghaeilge*, the Earl of Thomond and British Politics in the Renaissance Pale', in T. Herron and M. Potteron (eds.), *Dublin and the Pale in the Renaissance, c.1540–1660* (Dublin: Four Courts Press, 2011), 267–79.

Kane, B., 'Making the Irish European: Gaelic Honor Politics and its Continental Contexts', *Renaissance Quarterly*, 61 (2008), 1139–66.

Kelly, J., *'That damn'd thing called honour': Duelling in Ireland, 1570–1860* (Cork University Press, 1995).

Lennon, C., *Richard Stanihurst: the Dubliner, 1547–1618* (Dublin: Irish Academic Press, 1981).

Little, P., '"Blood and Friendship": The Earl of Essex's Protection of the Earl of Clanricarde's Interests, 1641–6', *English Historical Review*, 112 (1997), 927–41.

Mayes, C. R., 'The Early Stuarts and the Irish Peerage', *English Historical Review*, 73 (1959), 227–51.

McGowan-Doyle, V., *The Book of Howth: Elizabethan conquest and the Old English* (Cork University Press, 2011).

McQuillan, P., 'A Bardic Critique of Queen and Court: "Ionmholta malairt bhisigh", Eochaidh Ó hEodhasa, 1603', in B. Kane and V. McGowan-Doyle (eds.), *Elizabeth I and Ireland*, 60–85.

Morgan, H., *Tyrone's rebellion: The outbreak of the Nine Years' War in Tudor Ireland* (Woodbridge: Boydell Press, 1993).

Morley, V., *Ó Chéitinn go Raiftearaí: mar a Chumadh Stair na hÉireann* (Dublin: Coiscéim, 2011).

Ó Buachalla, B., 'James our True King: The Ideology of Irish Royalism in the Seventeenth Century', in D. G. Boyce, R. Eccleshall and V. Geoghegan (eds.), *Political Thought in Ireland since the Seventeenth Century* (London: Routledge, 1993), 7–35.

Ó Ciardha, É. 'The Unkinde Deserter and the Bright Duke: The Dukes of Ormond in the Royalist Tradition', in T. Barnard and J. Fenlon (eds.), *The Dukes of Ormonde, 1610–1745* (Woodbridge: Boydell and Brewer, 2000), 177–93.

Ó Ciosáin, N., 'Highwaymen, Tories and Rapparees', *History Ireland* 1 (1993), 19–21.

Ó Muraile, N., *The Celebrated Antiquary: Dubhaltach Mac Fhirbhisigh (c.1600–71), his Lineage, Life and Learning* (Maynooth: An Sagart, 1996).

Ó Siochrú, M., *Confederate Ireland, 1642–1649: a Constitutional and Political Analysis* (Dublin: Four Courts Press, 2008).

Ó Siochrú, M., 'Atrocity, Codes of Conduct and the Irish in the British Civil Wars, 1641–1653', *Past & Present*, 195 (2007), 55–86.

Ohlmeyer, J., *Civil War and Restoration in the Three Stuart Kingdoms: The Career of Randal MacDonnell, Marquis of Antrim* (Cambridge University Press, 1993; repr. Dublin: Four Courts Press, 2001).

Ohlmeyer, J., *Making Ireland English: The Irish Aristocracy in the Seventeenth Century* (New Haven and London: Yale University Press, 2012).

Ohlmeyer, J., 'The Aristocracy in Seventeenth-Century Ireland: Wider Contexts and Comparisons', *History Compass*, 12 (2014), 33–41.

Ohlmeyer, J. and S. Zwicker, 'John Dryden, the House of Ormond, and the Politics of Anglo-Irish Patronage', *The Historical Journal*, 49 (2006), 677–706.

Palmer, W., 'That "Insolent Liberty": Honor, Rites of Power, and Persuasion in Sixteenth-Century Ireland', *Renaissance Quarterly*, 46 (1993), 308–27.

Rankin, D., *Between Spenser and Swift: English Writing in Seventeenth-Century Ireland* (Cambridge University Press, 2007).

Simms, K., *From kings to Warlords: The Changing Political Structure of Gaelic Ireland in the Later Middle Ages* (Woodbridge: Boydell Press, 1987).

Smuts, M., 'Organized Violence in the Elizabethan Monarchical Republic', *History*, 99 (2014), 418–43.

Treadwell, V., *Buckingham and Ireland, 1616–1628: A Study in Anglo-Irish Politics* (Dublin: Four Courts Press, 1998).

Walsh, P., *The Making of the Irish Protestant Ascendancy: The Life of William Conolly, 1662–1729* (Woodbridge: Boydell and Brewer, 2010).

Whelan, K., 'An Underground Gentry? Catholic Middlemen in Eighteenth-Century Ireland', in J. S. Donnelly and K. A. Miller (eds.), *Irish Popular Culture, 1650–1850* (Dublin: Irish Academic Press, 1998), 118–72.

Williams, M., *The King's Irishmen: The Irish in the Exiled court of Charles II, 1649–1660* (Woodbridge: Boydell and Brewer, 2014).

Zmora, H., *Monarchy, Aristocracy and the State in Europe, 1300–1800* (London and New York: Routledge, 2001).

20 Irish Political Thought and Intellectual History, 1550–1730

Ian Campbell

Unpublished Primary Sources

Armagh Public Library

MS KH II 39

Bodleian Library, Oxford

MS Rawlinson D 1290

Published Primary Sources

Aristotle, *The Politics*, trans. by Harris Rackham (London: William Heinemann, 1932).

Beacon, Richard, *Solon his Follie*, ed. C. Carroll and V. Carey (Binghamton, NY: Centre for Medieval and Early Renaissance Studies, 1996).

Bodin, Jean, *Les Six Livres de la République* (Paris, 1583; facsimile reprint, Darmstadt: Scientia Verlag Aalen, 1977).

Bramhall, John, *Castigations of Mr Hobbes* (London, 1658).

Bryskett, Lodowick, *A Discourse of Civill Life: Containing the Ethicke part of Morall Philosophie* (London, 1606).

Campbell, I., 'Select Document: Sir George Radcliffe's "Originall of Government" (1639) and Absolutist Political Theory in Stuart Ireland', *Irish Historical Studies*, 39 (2014), 308–22.

Coke, Sir Edward, *The Reports of Sir Edward Coke* (London, 1658).

Darcy, Patrick, 'An Argument', ed. C. E. J. Caldicott, *Camden Miscellany*, 31 (1992).

Davies, Sir John, *Le Primer Report des Cases in les Courts del Roy* (Dublin, 1615).

Davies, Sir John, *A Discovery of the True Causes why Ireland Was Never Entirely Subdued [and] Brought under Obedience of the Crown of England until the Beginning of His Majesty's Happy Reign*, ed. J. P. Myers (Washington, DC: Catholic University of America, 1988).

Florentinus, Antoninus, *Prima Pars Summae theologicae*, (Venice: Nicholas Jenson, 1478) British Library 19734.

Fortescue, Sir John, *A Learned Commendation of the Politique Lawes of England*, trans. Richard Mulcaster (London, 1599).

Hobbes, Thomas, *Leviathan* (London, 1651).

Holinshed's Irish Chronicle, ed. L. Miller and E. Power (Dublin: Dolmen Press, 1979).

Hutchinson, M. A., 'Nicholas Walsh's Oration to the Irish House of Commons, May 1586', *Analecta Hibernica*, 45 (2014), 35–52.

Locke, John, *An Essay concerning Human Understanding*, ed. P. H. Nidditch (Oxford University Press, 1975).

Locke, John, *Two Treatises of Government*, ed. P. Laslett, (3rd edn., Cambridge University Press, 1988).

Lynch, John, *Cambrensis Eversus* (St Malo, 1662).

Lynch, John, *Alithinologia* (St Malo, 1664).

Lynch, John, *Supplementum alithinologiae* (St Malo, 1667).

Molyneux, William, *The Case of Ireland's being bound by Acts of Parliament in England, Stated* (Dublin, 1698).

O'Ferrall, Richard and Robert O'Connell, *Commentarius Rinuccinianus, de Sedis Apostolicae Legatione ad Foederatos Hiberniae Catholicos per Annos 1645–9*, ed., Stanislaus Kavanagh (6 vols., Dublin: Irish Manuscripts Commission, 1932–49).

O'Mahony, Conor, *An Argument Defending the Right of the Kingdom of Ireland*, trans. John Minahane (Aubane Historical Society, 2010).

O'Sullivan Beare, Philip, *Historiae Catholicae Iberniae Compendium* (Lisbon, 1621).

Petty, Sir William, *Political Arithmetick* (London, 1690).

Punch, John, *Integer Theologiae Cursus ad Mentem Scoti* (Paris, 1652).

Punch, John, *Commentarii Theologici*, 4 vols. in 6 parts (Paris, 1661).

Sheehan, A. J. (ed.), 'Attitudes to Religious and Temporal Authority in Cork in 1600: A Document from Laud MS 612', *Analecta Hibernica*, 31 (1984), 61, 63–68

Spenser, Edmund, 'A View of the Present State of Ireland', in *Spenser's Prose Works*, ed., Rudolf Gottfried (Baltimore, MD: Johns Hopkins Press, 1949), 39–231.

Stanihurst, Richard, *Great Deeds in Ireland: Richard Stanihurst's De Rebus in Hibernia Gestis*, ed., J. Barry and H. Morgan (Cork University Press, 2013).

Stanihurst, Richard, *De Rebus in Hibernia Gestis* (Antwerp, 1584).

Swift, Jonathan, *The Drapier's Letters to the People of Ireland*, ed., H. Davis (2nd edn., Oxford University Press, 1965).

Swift, Jonathan, *A Tale of a Tub and Other Works*, ed., A. Ross and D. Woolley (Oxford University Press, 1986).

Temple, Sir John, *The Irish Rebellion* (London, 1646).

Tjoelker, N. and I. Campbell, 'Transcription and Translation of the London Version of Richard O'Ferrall's Report to Propaganda Fide (1658)', *Archivium Hibernicum*, 61 (2008), 7–61.

Toland, John, *Christianity not Mysterious* (London, 1696).

Ussher, J., *The Power Communicated by God to the Prince and the Obedience Required of the Subject*, ed., Robert Sanderson (London, 1661).

Walsh, Peter, *The History and Vindication of the Loyal Formulary, or Irish Remonstrance* ([London], 1674).

Ware, Sir James, (ed.), *The Historie of Ireland* (Dublin, 1633).

Secondary Sources

Beal, P., *Index of English Literary Manuscripts, Volume 1, 1450–1625, Part 2 Douglas-Wyatt* (London: Mansell, 1980).

Bradshaw, B., *The Irish Constitutional Revolution of the Sixteenth Century* (Cambridge University Press, 1979).

Bradshaw, B., 'Transalpine Humanism', in J. H. Burns and M. Goldie (eds.), *The Cambridge History of Political Thought* (Cambridge University Press, 1991), 95–131.

Brady, C., *The Chief Governors: The Rise and Fall of Reform Government in Tudor Ireland 1536–1588* (Cambridge University Press, 1994).

Brett, A., *Changes of State: Nature and the Limits of the City in Early Modern Natural Law* (Princeton University Press, 2011).

Brockliss, L., 'Curricula', in H. De Ridder-Symoens (ed.), *A History of the University in Europe, volume ii: Universities in Early Modern Europe (1500–1800)* (Cambridge University Press, 1996), 578–89.

Brooks, C. W., *Law, Politics and Society in Early Modern England* (Cambridge University Press, 2008).

Byrne, A., 'The Earls of Kildare and their Books at the End of the Middle Ages', *The Library*, seventh series, 14 (2013), 129–53.

Byrne, A., 'Family, Locality, and Nationality: Vernacular Adaptations of the *Expugnatio Hibernica* in Late Medieval Ireland', *Medium Aevum*, 82 (2013), 101–18.

Campbell, I., *Renaissance Humanism and Ethnicity before Race: The Irish and the English in the Seventeenth Century* (Manchester University Press, 2013).

Campbell, I., 'Aristotelian Ancient Constitution and anti-Aristotelian Sovereignty in Stuart Ireland', *Historical Journal*, 53 (2010), 573–91.

Campbell, I., 'Calvinist Absolutism: Archbishop James Ussher and Royal Power', *Journal of British Studies*, 53 (2014), 588–610.

Clarke, A., 'Patrick Darcy and the Constitutional Relationship between Ireland and Britain', in J. H. Ohlmeyer (ed.), *Political Thought in Seventeenth-Century Ireland* (Cambridge University Press, 2000).

Clarke, A., 'The History of Poynings' Law, 1615–41', *Irish Historical Studies*, 18 (1972), 207–22.

Clarke, A., 'Colonial Constitutional Attitudes in Ireland, 1640–1660', *Proceedings of the Royal Irish Academy*, 90:C (1990), 357–75.

Connolly, S., 'Swift and Protestant Ireland: Images and Realities', in Aileen Douglas, Patrick Kelly and Ian Campbell Ross (eds.), *Locating Swift* (Dublin: Four Courts Press, 1998), 28–46.

Connolly, S., 'The Glorious Revolution in Irish Protestant Political Thinking', in S. Connolly (ed.), *Political Ideas in Eighteenth-Century Ireland* (Dublin: Four Courts Press, 2000), 27–63.

Connolly, S., 'The Church of Ireland and the Royal Martyr: Regicide and Revolution in Anglican Political Thought c.1660–c.1745', *Journal of Ecclesiastical History*, 54 (2003), 484–506.

Copenhaver, B. P. and C. B. Schmitt, *Renaissance Philosophy* (Oxford University Press, 1992).

Creighton, A., 'The Remonstrance of December 1661 and Catholic Politics in Restoration Ireland', *Irish Historical Studies*, 34 (2004), 16–41.

Edwards, D., 'Ideology and Experience: Spenser's View and Martial Law in Ireland', in H. Morgan (ed.), *Political Ideology in Ireland, 1541–1641* (Dublin: Four Courts Press, 1999), 127–57.

Edwards, R. D. and T. W. Moody, 'The History of Poynings' Law, Pt. 1: 1494–1615', *Irish Historical Studies*, 2 (1941), 415–24

Ehrenpreis, I., 'Swift on Liberty', in A. Norman Jeffries (ed.), *Swift: Modern Judgements* (London: Macmillan, 1968), 59–73.

Ford, A., *The Protestant Reformation in Ireland, 1590–1641* (Frankfurt am Main: Peter Lang, 1987).

Ford, A., *James Ussher: Theology, History, and Politics in Early Modern Ireland and England* (Oxford University Press, 2007).

Ford, A., 'James Ussher and the Godly Prince in Early Seventeenth-Century Ireland', in H. Morgan (ed.), *Political Ideology in Ireland, 1541–1641* (Dublin: Four Courts Press, 1999), 203–28.

Gillespie, R., 'Print Culture, 1550–1700', in R. Gillespie and A. Hadfield (eds.), *The Oxford History of the Irish Book, iii, The Irish Book in English 1550–1700* (Oxford University Press, 2006), 17–33.

Goldie, M., 'The Unacknowledged Republic: Officeholding in Early Modern England', in T. Harris (ed.), *The Politics of the Excluded, c.1500–1850* (Basingstoke: Palgrave, 2001), 153–94.

Gray, H. H., 'Renaissance Humanism: The Pursuit of Eloquence', *Journal of the History of Ideas*, 24 (1963), 497–514.

Greenberg, J., *The Radical Face of the Ancient Constitution: St Edward's 'Laws' in Early Modern Political Thought* (Cambridge University Press, 2001).

Hazard, B., *Faith and Patronage: The Political Career of Flaithrí Ó Maolchonaire, c. 1560–1629* (Dublin: Irish Academic Press, 2010).

Howard, P. F., *Aquinas and Antoninus: a Tale of Two Summae in Renaissance Florence*, Etienne Gilson Series 35 (Toronto: Pontifical Institute of Medieval Studies, 2013).

Israel, J., *Radical Enlightenment: Philosophy and the Making of Modernity 1650–1750* (Oxford University Press, 2001).

Kearney, H., *Strafford In Ireland, 1633–41* (Cambridge University Press, 1989).

Kelly, J., *Poynings' Law and the Making of Law in Ireland, 1660–1800* (Dublin: Four Courts Press, 2007).

Kelly, P., 'William Molyneux and the Spirit of Liberty in Eighteenth-Century Ireland', *Eighteenth-Century Ireland*, 3 (1988), 133–48.

Kent, B., 'Habits and Virtues (Ia IIae, qq. 49–70)', in S. J. Pope (ed.), *The Ethics of Aquinas* (Washington, DC: Georgetown University Press, 2002), 116–30.

Kossel, C. G., 'Natural Law and Human Law (Ia IIae, qq. 90–97)', in S. J. Pope (ed.), *The Ethics of Aquinas* (Washington, DC: Georgetown University Press, 2002), 169–93.

Kraye, J., 'Moral Philosophy', in C. B. Schmitt, Quentin Skinner, Eckhard Kessler and Jill Kraye (eds.), *The Cambridge History of Renaissance Philosophy* (Cambridge University Press, 1988), 303–86.

Kristeller, P. O., *Renaissance Thought* (2 vols., New York: Harper & Row, 1961).

Lake, P., *Anglicans and Puritans? Presbyterianism and English Conformist Thought from Whitgift to Hooker* (London: Unwin, 1988).

Lennon, C., *Richard Stanihurst the Dubliner, 1547–1618* (Dublin: Irish Academic Press, 1981).

Lennon, C., 'Education and Religious Identity in Early Modern Ireland', in J. Coolahan, F. Simon and R. Aldritch (eds.), *Faiths and Education: Historical and Comparative Perspectives* (Gent: C.S.H.P., 1999), 57–75.

Mac Craith, M., 'The Political and Religious Thought of Florence Conry and Hugh McCaughwell', in A. Ford and J. McCafferty (eds.), *The Origins of Sectarianism in Early Modern Ireland* (Cambridge University Press, 2005), 183–202.

Mac Cuarta, B., *Catholic Revival in the North of Ireland, 1603–41* (Dublin: Four Courts Press, 2007).

McCormick, T., *William Petty and the Ambitions of Political Arithmetic* (Oxford University Press, 2009).

McGrath, B., 'Ireland and the Third University: Attendance at the Inns of Court, 1603–1650', in D. Edwards (ed.), *Regions and Rulers in Ireland 1100–1650* (Dublin: Four Courts Press, 2004), 217–36.

Maginn, C. and S. Ellis, *The Tudor Discovery of Ireland* (Dublin: Four Courts Press, 2015).

Martin, C., *Subverting Aristotle: Religion, History, and Philosophy in Early Modern Science* (Baltimore, MD: Johns Hopkins University Press, 2014).

Millett, B., 'Irish Literature in Latin, 1550–1700', in T. W. Moody, F. X. Martin and F. J. Byrne (eds.), *A New History of Ireland*, iii: *Early Modern Ireland 1534–1691* (Oxford University Press, 1976), 561–86.

Ó Catháin, D., 'Some Reflexes of Latin Learning and of the Renaissance in Ireland, c.1450–c.1600', in J. Harris and K. Sidwell (eds.), *Making Ireland Roman: Irish Neo-Latin Writers and the Republic of Letters* (Cork University Press, 2009), 14–37.

O'Connor, T., 'A Justification for Foreign Intervention in Early Modern Ireland: Peter Lombard's *Commentarius*', in T. O'Connor and M. A. Lyons (eds.), *Irish Migrants in Europe after Kinsale, 1602–1820* (Dublin: Four Courts Press, 2003), 14–31.

Ó hAnnracháin, T., *Catholic Reformation in Ireland: The Mission of Rinuccini, 1645–1649* (Oxford University Press, 2002).

Pawlisch, H., *Sir John Davies and the Conquest of Ireland: A Study in Legal Imperialism* (Cambridge University Press, 1985).

Pollnitz, A., *Princely Education in Early Modern Britain* (Cambridge University Press, 2015).

Rabil, A. (ed.), *Renaissance Humanism: Foundations, Forms and Legacy* (3 vols., Philadelphia: University of Pennsylvania Press, 1988).

Rahe, P. A., *Republics Ancient and Modern*, (3 vols., Chapel Hill, NC: University of North Carolina Press, 1994).

Robertson, J., *The Case for the Enlightenment: Scotland and Naples 1680–1760* (Cambridge University Press, 2005).

Robinson, P., *The Plantation of Ulster* (2nd edn., Belfast: Ulster Historical Association, 1994).

Simms, J. G., *William Molyneux of Dublin, 1656–1776* (Dublin: Irish Academic Press, 1982).

Starza Smith, D., *John Donne and the Conway Papers* (Oxford University Press, 2014).

Tubbs, J. W., *The Common Law Mind: Medieval and Early Modern Conceptions* (Baltimore, MD: Johns Hopkins University Press, 2000).

Tuck, R., 'The "Modern" Theory of Natural Law', in Anthony Pagden (ed.), *The Languages of Political Theory in Early Modern Europe* (Cambridge University Press, 1987), 99–119.

21 Economic Life, 1550–1730

Raymond Gillespie

Unpublished Primary Sources

Chester City Archives

SB/10–15

National Archives of Ireland

MS M2759

Published Primary Sources

Flavin, S. and E. T. Jones (eds.), *Bristol's Trade with Ireland and the Continent, 1503–1601* (Dublin: Four Courts Press, 2009).

Gilbert, J. T. (ed.), *A Jacobite Narrative of the War in Ireland* (Dublin: J. Dollard, 1892).

Howell, James, *Epistolae Ho-Eliana* (London, 1655).

Irish Record Commission, *Irish Patent Rolls of James I* (Dublin: Stationery Office, 1966).

Morrin, J. (ed.), *Calendar of Patent and Close Rolls of Chancery in Ireland Elizabeth, 19th Year to End of Reign* (Dublin: Thom, 1862).

Nicholls, K. W. (ed.), *The O'Doyne (Ó Duinn) Manuscript* (Dublin: Irish Manuscripts Commission, 1983), 3–6.

Ó Raghallaigh, T. (ed.), 'Seanchus Búrcach', *Journal of the Galway Archaeological and Historical Society*, 13 (1922–1928), 50–60 and 101–37.

Williams, N. (ed. and trans.), *Pairlement Chloinne Tomáis* (Dublin: Institute for Advanced Studies, 1981).

Secondary Sources

Canny, N., *Making Ireland British, 1580–1650* (Oxford University Press, 2001).

Canny, N., 'Hugh O'Neill and the Changing Face of Gaelic Ulster', *Studia Hibernica*, 10 (1970), 7–35.

Culllen, L. M., T. C. Smout and A. Gibson, 'Wages and Comparative Development in Ireland and Scotland, 1565–1780', in R. Mitchison and P. Roebuck (eds.), *Economy and Society in Scotland and Ireland, 1500–1939* (Edinburgh: John Donald, 1988), 105–16.

Cullen, L. M., 'Population Trends in Seventeenth-Century Ireland', *Economic and Social Review*, 6 (1974–1975), 149–65.

Cunningham, B., *Clanricard and Thomond, 1540–1640: Provincial Politics and Society Transformed* (Dublin: Four Courts Press, 2012).

Cunningham, B. and R. Gillespie, 'Manuscript Cultures in Early Modern Mayo', in G. Moran and N. Ó Muraíle (eds.), *Mayo: History and Society* (Dublin: Geography Publications, 2014), 183–205.

Empey, A., *Gowran, Co. Kilkenny, 1190–1610: Custom and Conflict in a Baronial Town* (Dublin: Four Courts Press 2015).

Eversley, D. C., 'The Demography of the Irish Quakers, 1650–1850', in J. M. Goldstrom and L. A. Clarkson (eds.), *Irish Population, Economy and Society* (Oxford University Press, 1981), 57–88.

Fisher, F. J., 'The Sixteenth and Seventeenth Centuries: The Dark Ages in English Economic History?', in N. B. Harte (ed.), *The Study of Economic History* (London: Cass, 1971), 183–200.

Flavin, S., *Consumption and Culture in Sixteenth-Century Ireland* (Woodbridge: Boydell, 2014).

Gillespie, R., *The Transformation of the Irish Economy, 1550–1700* (Dublin: Economic and Social History Society of Ireland, 1998).

Gillespie, R., 'Meal and Money: The Harvest Crisis of 1621–4 and the Irish Economy', in E. M. Crawford (ed.), *Famine: the Irish Experience 900–1900* (Edinburgh: John Donald, 1989), 75–95.

Gillespie, R., 'The Irish Economy at War, 1641–52', in J. Ohlmeyer (ed.), *Ireland from Independence to Occupation, 1641–1660* (Cambridge University Press, 1995), 160–80.

Gillespie, R., 'War and the Irish Town: The Early Modern Experience', in P. Lenihan (ed.), *Conquest and Resistance: War in Seventeenth-Century Ireland* (Leiden: Brill, 2001), 295–315.

Gillespie, R., 'The Changing Structure of Irish Agriculture in the Seventeenth Century', in M. Murphy and M. Stout (eds.), *Agriculture and Settlement in Ireland* (Dublin: Four Courts Press, 2015), 119–38.

Gillespie, R., 'Richard Head's *The Miss display'd* and Irish Restoration Society', *Irish University Review*, 34 (2004), 213–28.

Lenihan, P., 'War and Population, 1649–52', *Irish Economic and Social history*, 24 (1997), 1–21.

Lyons, M. A., 'Maritime Relations between France and Ireland, *c.*1480–*c.*1630', *Irish Economic and Social History*, 27 (2000), 1–24.

Lyttleton, J. and C. Rynne (eds.), *Plantation Ireland: Settlement and Material Culture, c.1550–c.1700* (Dublin: Four Courts Press, 2009).

Murphy, M. and M. Potterton, *The Dublin Region in the Middle Ages: Settlement, Land Use and Economy* (Dublin: Four Courts Press, 2010).

O'Brien, G., *The Economic History of Ireland in the Seventeenth Century* (Dublin and London: Maunsel, 1919).

Puig, J. J., 'El Comércio Maritimo en Galicia 1525–1640', unpublished PhD thesis (University of Santiago, 2012).

Roebuck, P., 'Landlord Indebtedness in Ulster in the Seventeenth and Eighteenth Centuries', in J. M. Goldstrom and L. A. Clarkson (eds.), *Irish Population, Economy and Society* (Oxford University Press, 1981), 135–55.

Schüller, K., 'Special Conditions of the Irish-Iberian Trade during the Spanish-English War', in Enrique García Hernán, Miguel Ángel de Bunes, Óscar Recio Morales and Bernardo J. García García (eds.), *Irlanda y la Monarquía Hispánica: Kinsale 1601–2001* (Madrid: Consejo Superior de Investigaciones Científicas, 2002), 447–68.

Smyth, W. J., *Map-making, Landscapes and Memory: A Geography of Colonial and Early Modern Ireland, c.1530–1750* (Cork University Press, 2006).

Wrightson, K., *Earthly Necessities: Economic Lives in Early Modern Britain* (New Haven and London: Yale University Press, 2000).

22 Plantations, 1550–1641

Annaleigh Margey

Unpublished Primary Sources

Drapers' Hall, London

MS +793

The National Archives, UK

MPF1/38–64, 277, 305

Published Primary Sources

Davies, John, *A Discovery of the True Causes why Ireland was Never Intirely Subdued* (3rd edn., Dublin, 1666).

McLaughlin, J. (ed.), 'Select Documents XLVII: Richard Hadsor's "Discourse" on the Irish State, 1604', *Irish Historical Studies*, 30 (1997), 337–53.

McNeill, C. (ed.), 'MS. Rawlinson A. 237, The Bodleian Library, Oxford', *Analecta Hibernica*, 3 (1931), 151–218.

Moryson, Fynes, *An Itinerary VVritten by Fynes Moryson Gent. Containing his Ten Yeeres Travel throvgh the Twelve Domjnions of Germany, Bohmerland, Sweitzerland, Netherland, Denmarke, Poland, Italy, Turky, France, England, Scotland and Ireland* (London, 1617).

Paterson, T. G. F., 'County Armagh in 1622: A Plantation Survey', *Seanchas Ardmhacha*, 4 (1961), 103–40.

Rich, Barnaby, *A New Description of Ireland, Wherin is Described the Disposition of the Irish whervnto they are Inclined* (London, 1610).

Spenser, Edmund, *A View of the Present State of Ireland*, ed. A. Hadfield and W. Maley (Oxford: Blackwell, 2000).

Treadwell, V., *The Irish Commission of 1622: An Investigation of the Irish Administration 1615–22 and its Consequences 1623–24* (Dublin: Irish Manuscripts Commission, 2006).

Treadwell, V.W., 'The Plantation of Donegal: A Survey', *Donegal Annual*, 2 (1954), 511–17.

Secondary Sources

Andrews, J. H., 'Colonial Cartography in a European Setting: The Case of Tudor Ireland', in D. Woodward (ed.), *History of Cartography, Vol. 3: Cartography in the European Renaissance* (Chicago University Press, 2007), 1670–83.

Andrews, J. H., 'The Maps of the Escheated Counties of Ulster, 1609–10', *Proceedings of the Royal Irish Academy*, 74:C (1974), 133–70.

Archer, I. W., 'The City of London and the Ulster Plantation', in É. Ó Ciardha and M. Ó Siochrú (eds.), *The Plantation of Ulster: Ideology and Practice* (Manchester University Press, 2012), 78–97.

'The Bibliography of British and Irish History' (http://cpps.brepolis.net.jproxy.dkit.ie/bbih/search.cfm) (accessed 15 July 2015).

Brady, C., 'Spenser's Irish Crisis: Humanism and Experience in the 1590s', *Past & Present*, 111 (1986), 17–49.

Brink, J. R., 'Sir John Davies: Lawyer and Poet', in T. Herron and M. Potterton (eds.), *Ireland in the Renaissance, c.1540–1660* (Dublin: Four Courts Press [hereafter FCP], 2007), 88–104.

Canny, N., *From Reformation to Restoration: Ireland, 1534–1660* (Dublin: Helicon, 1987).

Canny, N., 'Reviewing *A View of the Present State of Ireland*', *Irish University Review*, 26 (1986), 252–67.

Canny, N. P., *The Upstart Earl: A Study of the Social and Mental World of Richard Boyle, First Earl of Cork, 1566–1643* (Cambridge University Press, 1982).

Canny, N. P., *Kingdom and Colony: Ireland in the Atlantic World, 1560–1800* (London: Johns Hopkins University Press, 1988).

Canny, N. P., *Making Ireland British* (Oxford University Press, 2001).

Canny, N. P., 'The 1641 Depositions as a Source for the Writing of Social History: Cork as a Case Study', in P. O'Flanagan and C. Buttimer (eds.), *Cork: History and Society* (Dublin: Geography Publications, 1993), 249–308.

Clarke, A., 'Pacification, Plantation and the Catholic Question, 1603–23', in T. W. Moody, F. X. Martin and F. J. Byrne (eds.), *A New History of Ireland, iii: Early Modern Ireland, 1534–1691* (Oxford University Press, 1976), 187–232.

Dunlop, R., 'Ireland from the Plantation of Ulster to the Cromwellian Settlement (1611–1659)', in A.W. Ward, G. W. Prothero and S. Leathes (eds.), *Cambridge Modern History, iv: The Thirty Years' War* (Cambridge University Press, 1906), 513–38.

Dunlop, R., 'The Plantation of Munster, 1584–1589', *English Historical Review*, 3 (1888), 240–69.

Dunlop, R., 'The Plantation of Leix and Offaly, 1556–1622', *English Historical Review*, 6 (1891), 61–96.

Dunlop, R., 'Sixteenth-Century Schemes for the Plantation of Ulster', *Scottish Historical Reviews*, 22 (1925), 199–212.

Gillespie, R., *The Transformation of the Irish Economy, 1550–1700* (Dundalk: Dundalgan Press for the Economic and Social History of Ireland, 1991).

Gillespie, R., 'Success and Failure in the Ulster Plantation', in É. Ó Ciardha and M. Ó Siochrú (eds.), *The Plantation of Ulster: Ideology and Practice* (Manchester University Press, 2012), 98–118.

Gillespie, R., 'The Origins and Development of an Ulster Urban Network, 1600–1641', *Irish Historical Studies*, 24 (1984), 15–29.

Goff, H., 'English Conquest of an Irish Barony: The Changing Patterns of Land Ownership in the Barony of Scarawalsh, 1540–1640', in K. Whelan and W. Nolan (eds.), *Wexford History and Society* (Dublin: Geography Publications, 1992), 122–49.

Hayes-McCoy, G. A., 'The Completion of the Tudor Conquest and the Advance of the Counter-Reformation, 1571–1603', in T. W. Moody, F. X. Martin and F. J. Byrne (eds.), *A New History of Ireland, iii: Early Modern Ireland, 1534–1691* (Oxford University Press, 1976), 94–141.

Horning, A., R. Ó Baoill, C. Donnelly and P. Logue (eds.), *The Post-Medieval Archaeology of Ireland, 1550–1850* (Bray: Wordwell, 2007).

Hunter, R. J., 'Towns in the Ulster Plantation', *Studia Hibernica*, 11 (1971), 40–79.

Jope, E. M., 'Moyry, Charlemont, Castleraw and Richhill: Fortification to Architecture in the North of Ireland, 1570–1700', *Ulster Journal of Archaeology*, 23 (1960), 97–123.

Kearney, H., *Strafford in Ireland, 1633–41: A Study in Absolutism* (2nd edn., Cambridge University Press, 1989).

Klingelhofer, E., *Castles and Colonists: An Archaeology of Elizabethan Ireland* (Manchester University Press, 2010).

Lennon, C., *Sixteenth-Century Ireland: The Incomplete Conquest* (Dublin: Gill and Macmillan, 1994).

Loeber, R., *The Geography and Practice of English Colonisation in Ireland from 1534 to 1609* (Athlone: The Group for the study of Irish Historic Settlement, 1991).

Loeber, R., 'Civilisation Through Plantation: The Projects of Mathew de Renzi', in H. Murtagh (ed.), *Irish Midland Studies: Essays in Commemoration of N. W. English* (Athlone: Old Athlone Society, 1980).

Lyttleton, J., *The Jacobean Plantations in Seventeenth-Century Offaly: An Archaeology of a Changing World* (Dublin: FCP, 2013).

Mac Cuarta, B., 'The Plantation of Leitrim, 1620–41', *Irish Historical Studies*, 32 (2001), 297–320.

MacCurtain, M., *Tudor and Stuart Ireland* (Dublin: Gill and MacMillan 1972).

MacCurtain, M. and M. O'Dowd (eds.), *Women in Early Modern Ireland* (Edinburgh University Press, 1991).

McCarthy-Morrogh, M., *The Munster Plantation: English Migration to Southern Ireland, 1583–1641* (Oxford: Clarendon Press, 1986).

McCavitt, J., *Sir Arthur Chichester, Lord Deputy of Ireland*, 1605–1616 (Belfast: Institute of Irish Studies).

Margey, A., 'Representing Plantation Landscapes: The Mapping of Ulster, *c.*1560–1640', in J. Lyttleton and C. Rynne (eds.), *Plantation Ireland: Settlement and Material Culture, c.1550–1700* (Dublin: FCP, 2009), 140–64.

Moody, T.W., *The Londonderry Plantation, 1609–41: the City of London and the Plantation in Ulster* (Belfast: W. Mullan and Son, 1939).

Moody, T. W., F. X. Martin and F. J. Byrne (eds.), *A New History of Ireland, iii: Early Modern Ireland, 1534–1691* (Oxford University Press, 1976).

Morgan, H., 'The Colonial Venture of Sir Thomas Smith in Ulster, 1571–75', *The Historical Journal*, 28 (1985), 261–78.

'The Northern Ireland Sites and Monuments Record', http://apps.ehsni.gov.uk/ambit/Default.aspx (accessed 15 July 2017).

Ó hAnnracháin, T., 'Plantation, 1580–1641', in A. Jackson (ed.), *The Oxford History of Modern Irish History* (Oxford University Press, 2014), 291–314.

Ohlmeyer, J. H., '"Civilizinge those rude partes": Colonisation within Britin and Ireland, 1580s–1640s', in N. P. Canny (ed.), *The Origins of Empire: British Overseas Enterprise to the Close of the Seventeenth Century* (Oxford University Press, 1998), 124–47.

Perceval-Maxwell, M., *The Scottish Migration to Ulster in the Reign of James I* (London: Routledge and Kegan Paul, 1973).

Quinn, D. B., *Ireland and America: Their Early Associations, 1500–1640* (Liverpool University Press, 1991).

Quinn, D. B., 'Sir Thomas Smith (1513–1577) and the Beginnings of English Colonial Theory', *Proceedings of the American Philosophical Society*, 89 (1945), 543–60.

Quinn, D. B., 'The Munster Plantation: Problems and Opportunities', *Journal of Cork Historical and Archaeological Society*, 71 (1966), 19–40.

Ranger, T.O., 'Richard Boyle and the Making of an Irish Fortune, 1588–1614', *Irish Historical Studies*, 10 (1956–1957), 257–97.

Robinson, P. S., *The Plantation of Ulster: British Settlement in an Irish landscape, 1600–70* (Dublin: Gill and MacMillan, 1984).

Sheehan, A., 'Irish Towns in a Period of Change, 1588–1625', in C. Brady and R. Gillespie (eds.), *Natives and Newcomers: Essays on the Making of Irish Colonial Society, 1534–1641* (Dublin: Irish Academic Press, 1986), 93–119.

Smyth, W. J., *Map-Making, Landscapes and Memory: A Geography of Colonial and Early Modern Ireland, c.1530–1750* (Cork University Press, 2006).

White, D. G., 'The Tudor Plantations in Ireland before 1571', unpublished PhD thesis, Trinity College Dublin (1968).

Withington, P., 'Plantation and Civil Society', in É. Ó Ciardha and M. Ó Siochrú (eds.), *The Plantation of Ulster: Ideology and Practice* (Manchester University Press, 2012), 55–77.

23 The Down Survey and the Cromwellian Land Settlement

Micheál Ó Siochrú and David Brown

Unpublished Primary Sources

British Library

ADD MSS 13956, 14405, 35102, 41159
Egerton MSS 2648, 2651: Barrington Papers
Harley MS 4784

London Metropolitan Archives

CLC/540 New England Company, MS07909

Marsh's Library

MS Z2.1.7

National Archives of Ireland

DS Series
MS 2477
Quit Rent Box 2A.12.51

The National Archives, UK

SP 18/71
SP 25/118
SP 46/130
SP 63/284, 300, 301
SP 66/B

Oireachtas Library and Research Service

11D

Public Record Office of Northern Ireland

D/597/1/1

Published Primary Sources

An Act of Free and General Pardon, Indemnity and Oblivion (London, 1660).
An Act for the Setling of Ireland (London, 1652).
Carpenter, A. (ed.), *Verse in English from Tudor and Stuart Ireland* (Cork University Press, 2003).
Dunlop, R. (ed.), *Ireland under the Commonwealth* (2 vols., Manchester, 1913).
Firth, C. H. (ed.), *The Clarke Papers* (4 vols., London: Camden Society, 1891–1901).
Firth, C. H. and R. S. Rait (eds.), *Acts and Ordinances of the Interregnum, 1642–1660* (3 vols., London: HMSO, 1911).
Goblet, Y. M., *A Topographical Index of the Parishes and Townlands of Ireland* (Dublin: Irish Manuscripts Commission, 1932).

Gookin, Vincent, *The Great Case of Transplantation in Ireland Discussed* (London, 1655).

His Majesties Gracious Declaration for the Settlement of his Kingdom of Ireland (London, 1660).

Journals of the House of Commons: Volume 6, 1648–1651 (London: HMSO, 1802).

Lawrence, Richard, *The Interest of England in the Irish Transplantation Stated* (London, 1655).

Ludlow, Edmund, *Memoirs of Edmund Ludlow Esq.*, (2 vols., Vivay, 1698).

Mahaffy, R. P. (ed.), *Calendar of State Papers Relating to Ireland Preserved in the Public Record Office: Adventurers for Land, 1642–59* (London: HMSO, 1903).

O'Ferrall, Richard and Robert O'Connell, *Commentarius Rinuccinianus, de Sedis Apostolicae Legatione ad Foederatos Hiberniae Catholicos per Annos 1645–9* (6 vols., Dublin: Irish Manuscripts Commission, 1932–49).

O'Sullivan, W. (ed.), *Strafford's Inquisition of Mayo* (Dublin: Irish Manuscripts Commission, 1958).

Pender, S. (ed.), *A Census of Ireland circa 1659* (Dublin: Irish Manuscripts Commission, 1939; repr. 2002).

Petty, William, *The Political Anatomy of Ireland*, (London, 1673).

Raithby, J. (ed.), *Statutes of the Realm: Volume 5, 1628–80* (London: Great Britain Record Commission, 1819).

Simington, R. C. (ed.), *The Civil Survey A.D. 1654–1656, County of Tipperary*, (Dublin: Irish Manuscripts Commission, 1931).

Simington, R. C. (ed.), *Books of Survey and Distribution, Galway: Being Abstracts of Various Surveys and Instruments of Title, 1636–1703* (Dublin: Irish Manuscripts Commission, 1962).

Simington, R. C. (ed.), *The Transplantation to Connaught 1654–58* (Shannon: Irish Manuscripts Commission, 1970).

The Statutes passed in the Parliaments held in Ireland (20 vols., Dublin, 1765–1801).

Tallon, G. (ed.), *Court of Claims: Submissions and Evidence, 1663* (Dublin: Irish Manuscripts Commission, 2006).

Treadwell, V. (ed.), *The Irish Commission of 1622*, (Dublin: Irish Manuscripts Commission, 2006).

Wells, J. (ed.), 'Proceedings at the High Court of Justice at Dublin and Cork', *Archivium Hibernicum*, 66 (2013), 63–260 and, 67, (2014), 76–274.

The Writings and Speeches of Oliver Cromwell, ed. W. C. Abbott (4 vols., Cambridge, MA: Harvard University Press, 1937–47).

Secondary Sources

Andrews, J. H., *Plantation Acres: An Historical Study of the Irish Land Surveyor and His Techniques*, (Belfast: Ulster Historical Foundation, 1985).

Andrews, J. H., *Shapes of Ireland: Maps and their makers, 1564–1839* (Dublin: Geography Publications, 1997).

Arnold, L. J., 'The Irish Court of Claims of 1663', *Irish Historical Studies*, 24 (1985), 417–430.

Barber, S., 'Irish Undercurrents to the Politics of April 1653', *Historical Research*, 65 (1992), 315–35.

Barnard, T., *Cromwellian Ireland: English Government and Reform in Ireland, 1649–1660* (Oxford University Press, 1975).

Beckles, H., 'A "riotous and unruly lot": Irish Indentured Servants and Freemen in the English West Indies, 1644–1713', *The William and Mary Quarterly*, 57 (1990), 502–22.

Bottigheimer, K, *English Money and Irish Land: The 'Adventurers' in the Cromwellian Settlement of Ireland* (Oxford: Clarendon Press, 1971).

Brenner, R., *Merchants and Revolution: Commercial Change, Political Conflict, and London's Overseas Traders, 1550–1653* (Cambridge University Press, 1993).

Clanchy, M., *England and its Rulers, 1066–1307* (4th edn., Oxford: Wiley-Blackwell, 2014).

Clarke, A., *Prelude to Restoration in Ireland: The End of the Commonwealth, 1659–1660* (Cambridge University Press, 1999).

Corish, P., 'The Cromwellian *Régime*, 1650–1660', in T. W. Moody, F. X. Martin and F. J. Byrne (eds.), *A New History of Ireland*, iii, *Early Modern Ireland, 1534–1691* (Oxford University Press, 1976; third impression 1991), 353–86.

Cunningham, J., *Conquest and Land in Ireland: The Transplantation to Connacht, 1649–1660* (Woodbridge: Boydell and Brewer, 2011).

Dooley, T., 'Land and the People', in A. Jackson (ed.), *The Oxford Handbook of Modern Irish History* (Oxford University Press, 2014), 107–25.

Farnell, J. E., 'The Navigation Act of 1651, the First Dutch War, and the London Merchant Community', *Economic History Review*, 2nd series, 16 (1961–1962), 439–54.

Fitzmaurice, E. G., *Life of William Petty* (London: John Murray, 1895).

Frame, R., *Colonial Ireland, 1169–1369* (2nd edn., Dublin: Four Courts Press, 2012).

Gillespie, R., *Cavan, Essays on the History of an Irish County*, (Dublin: Irish Academic Press, 1995).

Hardinge, W. H., 'On manuscript Mapped and Other Townland Surveys in Ireland of a Public Character, Embracing the Gross, Civil and Down Surveys, from 1640 to 1688', *Transactions of the Royal Irish Academy*, 24 (1873), 3–118.

Larcom T. (ed.), *The History of the Survey of Ireland Commonly Called the Down Survey*, (Dublin: Irish Archaeological Society, 1851).

Leng, T., *Benjamin Worsley (1618–1677): Trade, Interest and the Spirit in Revolutionary England*, (Woodbridge: Boydell and Brewer, 2008).

Lenihan, P., *Consolidating Conquest: Ireland 1603–1727* (Harlow: Pearson Longman, 2007).

Lindley, K., 'Irish Adventurers and Godly Militants in the 1640s', *Irish Historical Studies*, 29 (1994), 1–12.

Little, P., *Lord Broghill and the Cromwellian Union with Ireland and Scotland* (Woodbridge: Boydell and Brewer, 2004).

Madge, S. J., *The Domesday of Crown Lands* (London: G. Routledge and Sons, 1938).

McCartan, M., 'The Cromwellian High Courts of Justice in Ulster, 1653', *Seanchas Ard Mhacha*, 23 (2010), 91–161.

McCormack, J.R., 'The Adventurers and the Civil War', *Irish Historical Studies*, 10 (1956), 45–67.

McCormick, T., *William Petty and the Ambitions of Political Arithmetic* (Oxford University Press, 2009).

Menard, R. R., *Sweet Negotiations: Sugar, Slavery and Plantation Agriculture in Early Barbados* (Charlottesville: University Press of Virginia, 2006).

Ó Siochrú, M., *God's Executioner: Oliver Cromwell and the Conquest of Ireland* (London: Faber & Faber, 2008).

Ohlmeyer, J., *Making Ireland English: The Irish Aristocracy in the Seventeenth Century* (New Haven and London: Yale University Press, 2012).

Prendergast, J. P., *The Cromwellian Settlement of Ireland* (London: Longman, Roberts and Green, 1865; repr. London: Constable, 1996).

Simms, J. G., *The Williamite Confiscation in Ireland, 1690–1703*, (London: Faber & Faber, 1956).

Simms, J. G., 'The Restoration, 1660–85', 1660', in T. W. Moody, F. X. Martin and F. J. Byrne (eds.), *A New History of Ireland*, iii, *Early Modern Ireland, 1534–1691* (Oxford University Press, 1976; third impression 1991), 420–53.

Simms, J. G., 'Land Owned by Catholics in Ireland in 1688', *Irish Historical Studies*, 7 (1951), 180–90.

Smyth, W. J., *Map-Making, Landscapes and Memory: A Geography of Colonial and Early Modern Ireland, c.1530–1750* (Cork University Press, 2006).

Wheeler, J. S., *Cromwell in Ireland* (Dublin: Gill and Macmillan, 1999).

24 Environmental History of Ireland, 1550–1730

Francis Ludlow and Arlene Crampsie

Published Primary Sources

'The 1641 Depositions', www.1641.tcd.ie (accessed 28 March 2016).

Anon., 'An Extract of a Letter Written from Dublin to the Publisher, Containing Divers Particulars of a Philosophical Nature …', *Philosophical Transactions*, 127 (1676), 647–53.

Boate, Gerard, *Ireland's Natvrall History. Being a True and Ample Defcription of its Situation, Greatnefs, Shape, and Nature …* (London, 1652).

Fletcher, A. (ed), 'The Earliest Extant Recension of the Dublin Chronicle: An Edition, with Commentary, of Dublin, Trinity College, MS 543/2/14', in J. Bradley, A. Fletcher and A. Simms (eds.), *Dublin in the Medieval world: Studies in Honour of Howard B. Clarke* (Dublin: Four Courts Press, 2009), 309–409.

Hennessy, W. (ed.), *The Annals of Loch Cé: A Chronicle of Irish Affairs from A.D. 1014 to A.D. 1590* (2 vols., London: Longman, 1871).

Hogan, J. (ed), *Letters and Papers Relating to the Irish Rebellion between 1642–46* (Dublin: Irish Manuscripts Commission, 1936).

O'Donovan, J. (ed.), *Annála Ríoghachta Éireann: Annals of the Kingdom of Ireland by the Four Masters, from the Earliest Period to the Year 1616* (7 vols., Dublin: Hodges & Smith), 1848–1851.

Reeves, W. (ed.), 'A Visit to Lecale, in the County of Down, in the Year 1602–03', *Ulster Journal of Archaeology*, 2 (1854) (in hypertext at www.ucc.ie/celt/online/T100074. html, accessed 25 July 2016).

Simington, R. (ed.), *The Civil Survey, A.D. 1654–1656, Vol. VII: County of Dublin* (Dublin: Irish Manuscripts Commission, 1945).

Spenser, Edmund, *A View of the State of Ireland – From the First Printed Edition (1633)*, ed. A. Hadfield and W. Maley (Oxford: Blackwell, 1997).

Stafford, Thomas, *Pacata Hibernia; or, a History of the Wars in Ireland, During the Reign of Queen Elizabeth* (2 vols., 2nd edn., Dublin: Hibernia-Press Company, 1820).

Walsh, P. and C. O Lochlainn (eds.), *Life of Aodh Ruadh O Domhnaill* (Dublin: Educational Company of Ireland, 1948).

Secondary Sources

Aalen, F., Whelan, K., and Stout, M. (eds.), *Atlas of the Irish Rural Landscape* (2nd edn., Cork University Press, 2011).

Adelman. J. and Ludlow, F., 'The Past, Present and Future of Irish Environmental History', *Proceedings of the Royal Irish Academy*, 114:C (2014), 1–33.

Baillie, M., *New Light on the Black Death* (Stroud: Tempus, 2006).

Bard, E., Raisbeck, G. M., Yioue, F., and Jouzel, J., 'Comment on "Solar Activity during the Last 1000 yr Inferred from Radionuclide Records" by Muscheler et al. (2007)', *Quaternary Science Reviews*, 26 (2007), 2301–8.

Breen, C., 'Famine and Displacement in Plantation-Period Munster', in J. Lyttleton and C. Rynne (eds.), *Plantation Ireland: Settlement and Material Culture, c.1550-c.1700* (Dublin: Four Courts Press, 2009), 132–39.

Briffa, K., Jones, P., Schweingruber, F., and Osborn, T., 'Influence of Volcanic Eruptions on Northern Hemisphere Summer Temperature over the Past 600 Years', *Nature, 393* (1998), 450–5.

Brown, D. and Baillie, M., 'How Old is that Oak?', in B. Simon (ed.), *A Treasured Landscape. The Heritage of Belvoir Park* (Belfast: The Forest of Belfast, 2005), 85–97.

Büntgen, U. and Di Cosmo, N., 'Climatic and Environmental Aspects of the Mongol Withdrawal from Hungary in 1242 CE', *Scientific Reports*, 6 (2016), 25606.

Campbell, B., 'Nature as Historical Protagonist: Environment and Society in Preindustrial England', *The Economic History Review*, 63 (2010), 281–314.

Cavanagh, S.T., '"The fatal destiny of that land": Elizabethan Views of Ireland', in B. Bradshaw, A. Hadfield and W. Maley (eds.), *Representing Ireland: Literature and the Origins of Conflict 1534–1660* (Cambridge University Press, 1993), 116–31.

Clarke, A., 'Pacification, Plantation and the Catholic Question, 1603–23', in T. W. Moody, A. Clarke and R. Dudley Edwards (eds.), *A New History of Ireland, iii: Early Modern Ireland, 1534–1691* (Oxford University Press, 1976), 187–232.

Clette, F., Svalgaard, L., Vaquero, J. M., and Cliver, E. W., 'Revisiting the Sunspot Number. A 400-Year Perspective on the Solar Cycle', *Space Science Reviews*, 186 (2014), 35–103.

Cole-Dai, J., 'Volcanoes and Climate', *WIREs Climate Change*, 1 (2010), 824–39.

Cook, W. *et al.*, 'Old World Megadroughts and Pluvials during the Common Era', *Science Advances*, 1 (2015), e1500561.

Cronin, D., *A Galway Gentleman in the Age of Improvement: Robert French of Monivea, 1716–76* (Dublin: Irish Academic Press, 1995).

Delaygue, G. and Bard, E., 'An Antarctic view of Beryllium-10 and Solar Activity for the Past Millennium', *Climate Dynamics*, 36 (2011), 2201–18.

Dixon, F., 'An Irish Weather Diary of 1711–1725', *Quarterly Journal of the Royal Meteorological Society*, 85 (1959), 371–85.

Edwards, D., 'Out of the Blue? Provincial Unrest in Ireland before 1641', in M. Ó Siochrú and J. Ohlmeyer (eds.), *Ireland, 1641: Contexts and Reactions* (Manchester University Press, 2013), 95–114.

Fan, K., 'Climatic Change and Dynastic Cycles: A Review Essay', *Climatic Change*, 101 (2010), 565–73.

Fischer, E., Luterbacher, J., Zorita E., Tett, S. F. B., Casty, C., and Wanner, H., 'European Climate Response to Tropical Volcanic Eruptions over the Last Half Millennium', *Geophysical Research Letters*, 34 (2007), L05707.

Galvin, S., Hickey, K. R. and Potito, A. P., 'Identifying Volcanic Signals in Irish Temperature Observations since AD 1800', *Irish Geography*, 44 (2012), 97–110.

Gillespie, R., 'The End of an Era: Ulster and the Outbreak of the 1641 Rising', in C. Brady and R. Gillespie (eds.), *Natives and Newcomers: Essays on the Making of Irish Colonial Society* (Dublin: Irish Academic Press, 1986), 191–214.

Gillespie, R., 'Meal and Money: The Harvest Crisis of 1621–4 and the Irish Economy', in E.M. Crawford (ed.), *Famine: The Irish Experience, 900–1900: Subsistence Crises and Famines in Ireland* (Edinburgh: John Donald, 1989), 75–95.

Gillespie, R., 'Explorers, Exploiters and Entrepreneurs, 1500–1700', in B. J. Graham and L. Proudfoot (eds.), *An Historical Geography of Ireland* (London: Academic Press, 1993), 123–57.

Gillespie, R., 'Harvest Crises in Early Seventeenth-Century Ireland', *Irish Economic and Social History*, 11 (1984), 5–18.

Global Volcanism Program: Parker, volcano.si.edu/volcano.cfm?vn=271011; Hokkaido-Komagatake, volcano.si.edu/volcano.cfm?vn=285020; Kelut, volcano.si.edu/volcano.cfm?vn=263280; Tambora, volcano.si.edu/volcano.cfm?vn=264040 (accessed 2 May 2016).

Group Sunspot Number (v2.0, 01 July 2015), Sunspot Index and Long-term Solar Observations (SILSO) World Data Centre, Royal Observatory of Belgium, Brussels, sidc.be/silso (accessed 13 July 2015).

Hall, V., *The Making of Ireland's Landscape since the Ice Age* (Cork: Collins Press, 2011).

Hickey, K., 'The Historic Record of Cold Spells in Ireland', *Irish Geography*, 44 (2011), 303–21.

Hsiang, S. and Burke, M., 'Climate, Conflict, and Social Stability: What Does the Evidence Say?', *Climatic Change*, 123 (2014), 39–55.

Huggett, F.E., *The Land Question and European Society* (London: Thames and Hudson, 1975).

Hughes, J. D., *What is Environmental History?* (Cambridge: Polity, 2006).

Jones, F. 'The Spaniards and Kinsale, 1601', *Journal of the Galway Archaeological and Historical Society*, 21 (1944), 1–43, 24–28.

Jordan, T., *The Quality of Life in Seventeenth-Century Ireland* (Lewiston: Edwin Mellen, 2008).

Judkins G., Smith, M., and Keys, E., 'Determinism within Human-Environment Research and the Rediscovery of Environmental Causation', *The Geographical Journal*, 174 (2008), 17–29.

Kiely, G., P. Leahy, P., Ludlow, F., Stefanini, B., Reilly, E., Monk, M. and Harris, J., *Extreme Weather, Climate and Natural Disasters in Ireland* (Johnstown Castle: Environmental Protection Agency, 2010).

Kiernan, B., *Blood and Soil: A World History of Genocide and Extermination from Sparta to Darfur* (New Haven and London: Yale University Press, 2007).

Kostick, C. and Ludlow, F., 'The Dating of Volcanic Events and their Impacts upon European Climate and Society, 400–800 CE', *European Journal of Post-Classical Archaeologies*, 5 (2015), 7–30.

Lang, K., *The Cambridge Encyclopedia of the Sun* (Cambridge University Press, 2001).

Lean, J., 'Cycles and Trends in Solar Irradiance and Climate', *WIREs Climate Change*, 1 (2010), 111–22.

Lean, J., Engels, S. and van Geel, B., 'The Effects of Changing Solar Activity on Climate: Contributions from Palaeoclimatological Studies', *Journal of Space Weather and Space Climate*, 2 (2012), A09.

Lennon, C., *Sixteenth-Century Ireland: The Incomplete Conquest* (Dublin: Gill and Macmillan, 1994).

Lockwood, M., Harrison, R. G., Woollings, T. and Solanki, S. K., 'Are Cold Winters in Europe Associated with Low Solar Activity?', *Environmental Research Letters*, 5 (2010), 024001.

Ludlow, F., Stine, A. R., Leahy, P., Murphy, E., Mayewski, P. A., Taylor, D., Killen, J., Baillie, M. G. L., Hennessy, M. and Kiely, G., 'Medieval Irish Chronicles Reveal Persistent Volcanic Forcing of Severe Winter Cold Events, 431–1649 CE', *Environmental Research Letters*, 8 (2013), 024035.

Ludlow, F., 'The Utility of the Irish Annals as a Source for the Reconstruction of Climate', unpublished PhD thesis, University of Dublin (2010).

Margey, A., '1641 and the Ulster Plantation Towns', in E. Darcy, A. Margey and E. Murphy (eds.), *The 1641 Depositions and the Irish Rebellion* (London: Pickering and Chatto, 2012), 79–96.

Matthews, J. and Briffa, K., 'The 'Little Ice Age': Re-evaluation of an Evolving Concept', *Geografiska Annaler*, 87A (2005), 17–36.

McGurk, J., 'The Kinsale Campaign Siege, Battle and Rout', *Seanchas Ardmhacha: Journal of the Armagh Diocesan Historical Society*, 19 (2002), 59–69.

McNeill, J., 'Future Research Needs in Environmental History: Regions, Eras, Themes', in K. Coulter and C. Mauch (eds.), *The Future of Environmental History: Needs and Opportunities* (Munich: Rachel Carson Center for Environment and Society, 2011), 13.

Mitchell, G. F., 'Littleton Bog, Tipperary: An Irish Agricultural Record', *The Journal of the Royal Society of Antiquaries of Ireland*, 95 (1965), 121–32.

O'Callaghan, S., *To Hell or Barbados: The Ethnic Cleansing of Ireland* (Dingle: Brandon, 2000).

Ogilvie, A., 'Historical Climatology, Climatic Change, and Implications for Climate Science in the Twenty-first Century', *Climatic Change*, 100 (2010), 33–47.

Ohlmeyer, J., *Making Ireland English: The Irish Aristocracy in the Seventeenth Century* (New Haven and London: Yale University Press, 2012).

Ohlmeyer, J., 'The Statute Staple in Early Modern Ireland', *History Ireland*, 6 (1998), 36–40.

Oram, R., 'Between a Rock and a Hard Place. Climate, Weather and the Rise of the Lordship of the Isles', in R. Oram (ed.), *The Lordship of the Isles* (Leiden: Brill, 2014), 40–61.

Ortega, P., Lehner, F., Swingedouw, D., Masson-Delmotte, V., Raible, C. C., Casado, M. and Yiou, P., 'A Model-Tested North Atlantic Oscillation Reconstruction for the Past Millennium', *Nature*, 523 (2015), 71–4.

PAGES 2k Consortium, 'Continental-Scale Temperature Variability during the Past Two Millennia', *Nature Geoscience*, 6 (2013), 339–46.

Parker, G., *Global Crisis: War, Climate Change and Catastrophe in the Seventeenth Century* (New Haven and London: Yale University Press, 2013).

Pfister, C., 'The Vulnerability of Past Societies to Climatic Variation: A New Focus for Historical Climatology in the Twenty-First Century,' *Climatic Change*, 100 (2010) 5–31.

Robock, A., 'Volcanic Eruptions and Climate', *Reviews of Geophysics* (2000) 38, 191–219.

Rohan, K., *The Climate of Ireland* (2nd edn., Dublin: Stationery Office, 1986).

Ruddiman, W., *Plows, Plagues and Petroleum: How Humans Took Control of Climate* (Princeton, NJ: Princeton University Press, 2005).

Salzer, M. and Hughes, M., 'Bristlecone Pine Tree Rings and Volcanic Eruptions over the Last 5000 Years', *Quaternary Research*, 67 (2007), 57–68.

Shields, L., 'The Beginnings of Scientific Weather Observation in Ireland (1684–1708)', *Weather*, 38 (1983), 304–11.

Siebert, L., T. Simkin and Kimberly P., *Volcanoes of the World* (3rd edn., Berkeley: University of California Press, 2010).

Sigl, M. *et al.*, 'Timing and Climate Forcing of Volcanic Eruptions during the Past 2,500 Years', *Nature*, 523 (2015), 543–9.

Silke, J., 'Kinsale Reconsidered', *Studies: An Irish Quarterly Review*, 90 (2001), 412–421.

Smyth, W. J., *Map-making, Landscapes and Memory: A Geography of Colonial and Early Modern Ireland c.1530–1750* (Cork University Press, 2006).

Solway, J., 'Drought as a Revelatory Crisis: An Exploration of Shifting Entitlements and Hierarchies in the Kalahari, Botswana', *Development and Change*, 25 (1994), 471–95.

Thouret, J.-C., 'Reconstruction of the AD 1600 Huaynaputina Eruption Based on the Correlation of Geologic Evidence with Early Spanish Chronicles', *Journal of Volcanology and Geothermal Research*, 115 (2002), 529–70.

Tol, R. and Wagner, S., 'Climate Change and Violent Conflict in Europe over the Last Millennium', *Climatic Change*, 99 (2011), 65–79.

White, S., *The Climate of Rebellion in the Early Modern Ottoman Empire* (Cambridge University Press, 2011).

25 Afterword: Interpreting the History of Early Modern Ireland: From the Sixteenth Century to the Present

Nicholas Canny

Published Primary Sources

'The 1641 Depositions', http://1641.tcd.ie.

Borlase, Edmund, *The Reduction of Ireland to the Crown of England* (London, 1675).

The Historie of Ireland from the First Inhabitation … 1509, Collected by Raphaell Holinshed, and Continued … 1547 by Richard Stanyhurst (London, 1577).

O'Rahilly, C. (ed.), *Five Seventeenth-Century Political Poems* (Dublin Institute for Advanced Studies, 1952).

The Second Volume of Chronicles Containing the Description, Conquest, Inhabitation and Troublesome Estate of Ireland first Collected by Raphael Holinshed and … Continued … until this Present Time of Sir John Perrot…by John Hooker, alias Vowell (London, 1587).

Secondary Sources

Bradshaw, B., *'And so began the Irish Nation'; Nationality, National Consciousness and Nationalism in Pre-Modern Ireland* (Farnham: Ashgate, 2015).

Brady, C., *James Anthony Froude: an Intellectual Biography of a Victorian Prophet* (Oxford University Press, 2013).

Campbell, I., *Renaissance Humanism and Ethnicity Before Race: The Irish and the English in the Seventeenth Century* (Manchester University Press, 2013).

Canny, N., *Making Ireland British, 1580–1650* (Oxford University Press, 2001).

Canny, N., '1641 in a Colonial Context', in M. Ó Siochrú and J. Ohlmeyer (eds.), *Ireland 1641* (Manchester University Press, 2013), esp. 52–70.

Cunningham, B., *The World of Geoffrey Keating: History, Myth and Religion in Seventeenth-Century Ireland* (Dublin: Four Courts Press, 2000).

Ellis, S. G. with C. Maginn, *The Making of the British Isles: the State of Britain and Ireland, 1450–1660* (London: Pearson Longman, 2007).

Empey, M., Ford, A., Moffitt, M. (eds.), *The Church of Ireland and its Past: History, Interpretation and Identity* (Dublin: Four Courts Press, 2017).

Ford, A., *James Ussher: Theology, History and Politics* (Oxford University Press, 2007).

Ford, A., 'Past but Still Present', in Brian Mac Cuarta (ed.), *Reshaping Ireland, 1550–1700* (Dublin: Four Courts Press, 2011), 281–99.

Gibney, J., *The Shadow of a Year: The 1641 Rebellion in Irish History and Memory* (Madison, WI: University of Winsconsin Press, 2013).

Healy, T. M., *The Great Fraud of Ulster* (Dublin: M. H. Gill and Son, 1917).

Hill, G., *An Historical Account of the Plantation in Ulster* (Belfast: McCaw, Stevenson and Orr, 1877).

Horning, A., *Ireland in the Virginian Sea: Colonialism in the British Atlantic* (Chapel Hill, NC: University of North Carolina Press, 2013).

Lyons, C., 'An Imperial Harbinger: Sylvester O'Halloran's *General History*', *Irish Historical Studies*, 39 (2015), 357–77.

Mac Craith, M., 'Creideamh agus Athartha', in M. Ní Dhonnachdha (ed.), *Nua Léamha* (Dublin: An Clóchomhar, 1996), 7–19.

McCartney, D., *W.E.H. Lecky: Historian and Politician, 1838–1903* (Dublin: Lilliput Press, 1994).

McGuire, J. and J. Quinn (eds.), *Dictionary of Irish Biography* (9 vols., Cambridge, 2009).

Meehan, C. P., *The Fate and Fortunes of Hugh O'Neill … and Rory O'Donnell* (Dublin: J. Duffy, 1868).

Morgan, H, '"Tempt not God too long, O Queen": Elizabeth and the Irish Crisis of the 1590s', in B. Kane and V. McGowan-Doyle, (eds.), *Elizabeth I and Ireland* (Cambridge University Press, 2014), 209–38.

Morley, V., *Ó Chéitinn go Raiftearaí: Mar a Cumadh Stair na hÉireann* (Dublin: Coiscéim, 2011).

Morley, V., *The Popular mind in Eighteenth-Century Ireland* (Cork University Press, 2017).

Musgrave, Richard, *Memoirs of the Different Rebellions in Ireland*, 1801, ed. S. Myers and D. McKnight (Fort Wayne, IA: Round Tower Books, 1995).

Ó Buachalla, B., *Aisling Ghéar: na Stíobhartaigh agus an t Aos Léinn, 1603–1788* (Dublin: An Clóchomhar, 1996).

O'Halloran, C., *Golden Ages and Barbarous Nations* (Cork University Press, 2004).

Ó Muraíle, '"Aimsir an Chogaidh Chreidmhigh". An Dubhaltach Mac Fhirbhisigh a Lucht Aitheantais agus Polaitíocht an Seachtú hAois Déag', in M. Ní Dhonnachdha (ed.), *Nua Léamha* (Dublin: An Clóchomhar, 1996), 89–117.

Quinn, J., *Young Ireland and the Writing of Irish History* (Dublin: UCD Press, 2015).

Williams, M., 'History, the Interregnum and the Exiled Irish', in M. Williams and S. P. Forrest (eds.), *Constructing the Past: Writing Irish History, 1600–1800* (Woodbridge: Boydell and Brewer, 2010), 27–48.

Index